T0183201

Lecture Notes in Computer Science   9523

Commenced Publication in 1973
Founding and Former Series Editors:
Gerhard Goos, Juris Hartmanis, and Jan van Leeuwen

More information about this series at http://www.springer.com/series/7407

Sascha Hunold · Alexandru Costan
Domingo Giménez · Alexandru Iosup
Laura Ricci · María Engracia Gómez Requena
Vittorio Scarano · Ana Lucia Varbanescu
Stephen L. Scott · Stefan Lankes
Josef Weidendorfer · Michael Alexander (Eds.)

Euro-Par 2015: Parallel Processing Workshops

Euro-Par 2015 International Workshops
Vienna, Austria, August 24–25, 2015
Revised Selected Papers

 Springer

Editor
Sascha Hunold
Vienna University of Technology
Vienna
Austria

Workshop Editors *see next page*

ISSN 0302-9743   ISSN 1611-3349 (electronic)
Lecture Notes in Computer Science
ISBN 978-3-319-27307-5   ISBN 978-3-319-27308-2 (eBook)
DOI 10.1007/978-3-319-27308-2

Library of Congress Control Number: 2015955875

LNCS Sublibrary: SL1 – Theoretical Computer Science and General Issues

Springer Cham Heidelberg New York Dordrecht London

Printed on acid-free paper

Springer International Publishing AG Switzerland is part of Springer Science+Business Media
(www.springer.com)

Workshop Editors

BigDataCloud
Alexandru Costan
IRISA/INSA Rennes
France
alexandru.costan@inria.fr

Euro-EDUPAR
Domingo Giménez
University of Murcia
Spain
domingo@um.es

HeteroPar
Alexandru Iosup
Delft University of Technology
The Netherlands
A.Iosup@tudelft.nl

LSDVE
Laura Ricci
University of Pisa
Italy
laura.ricci@unipi.it

OMHI
María Engracia Gómez Requena
Universitat Politècnica de València
Spain
megomez@disca.upv.es

PADABS
Vittorio Scarano
Università di Salerno
Italy
vitsca@dia.unisa.it

PELGA
Ana Lucia Varbanescu
University of Amsterdam
The Netherlands
a.l.varbanescu@uva.nl

REPPAR
Sascha Hunold
Vienna University of Technology
Austria
sascha.hunold@tuwien.ac.at

Resilience
Stephen L. Scott
Tennessee Tech University and Oak
Ridge National Laboratory, USA
scottsl@ornl.gov

ROME
Stefan Lankes
RWTH Aachen University
Germany
slankes@eonerc.rwth-aachen.de

UCHPC
Josef Weidendorfer
Technische Universität München
Germany
Josef.Weidendorfer@tum.de

VHPC
Michael Alexander
Vienna University of Technology
Austria
michael.alexander@tuwien.ac.at

Preface

Euro-Par is an annual, international conference on European ground, covering all aspects of parallel and distributed processing, ranging from theory to practice, from small to the largest parallel and distributed systems and infrastructures, from fundamental computational problems to full-fledged applications, from architecture, compiler, language and interface design and implementation to tools, support infrastructures, and application performance aspects. The Euro-Par conference itself is complemented by a workshop program, where workshops dedicated to more specialized themes, to cross-cutting issues, and to upcoming trends and paradigms can be easily and conveniently organized with little administrative overhead.

This year, 17 workshop proposals were submitted, and after a careful revision process, which was led by the workshop co-chairs, 13 workshops were accepted. One workshop had to be canceled later owing to a low number of submissions.

The workshops took place on the two days before the Euro-Par conference and the program included the following 12 workshops:

1. Big Data Management in Clouds (BigDataCloud)
2. Parallel and Distributed Computing Education for Undergraduate Students (Euro-EDUPAR)
3. Algorithms, Models, and Tools for Parallel Computing on Heterogeneous Platforms (HeteroPar)
4. Large-Scale Distributed Virtual Environments (LSDVE)
5. On-Chip Memory Hierarchies and Interconnects: Organization, Management and Implementation (OMHI)
6. Parallel and Distributed Agent-Based Simulations (PADABS)
7. Performance Engineering for Large-Scale Graph Analytics (PELGA)
8. Reproducibility in Parallel Computing (REPPAR)
9. Resiliency in High-Performance Computing with Clouds, Grids, and Clusters (Resilience)
10. Runtime and Operating Systems for the Many-Core Era (ROME)
11. UnConventional High Performance Computing (UCHPC)
12. Virtualization in High-Performance Cloud Computing (VHPC)

All workshops together received a total of 121 submissions from 34 different countries. Each workshop had an independent Program Committee, which was in charge of selecting the papers. The workshop papers received more than three reviews per paper on average (403 reviews in total). Out of the 121 submissions, 67 papers were selected to be presented at the workshops.

The success of the Euro-Par workshops depends on the work of many individuals and organizations. We therefore thank all workshop organizers and reviewers for the time and effort that they invested. The Euro-Par vice-chair Luc Bougé provided guidance and support throughout the whole organizational process of the workshops. We would also like to express our sincere thanks to Springer for their help in publishing the proceedings.

Lastly, we thank all participants, panelists, and keynote speakers of the Euro-Par workshops for contributing to a productive meeting. It was a pleasure to organize and host the Euro-Par workshops 2015 in Vienna.

October 2015   Sascha Hunold

Organization

Euro-Par Steering Committee

Chair

Christian Lengauer   University of Passau, Germany

Vice-Chair

Luc Bougé   ENS Rennes, France

European Representatives

Marco Danelutto   University of Pisa, Italy
Emmanuel Jeannot   LaBRI-Inria, Bordeaux, France
Christos Kaklamanis   Computer Technology Institute, Greece
Paul Kelly   Imperial College, UK
Thomas Ludwig   University of Hamburg, Germany
Emilio Luque   Autonomous University of Barcelona, Spain
Tomàs Margalef   Autonomous University of Barcelona, Spain
Wolfgang Nagel   Dresden University of Technology, Germany
Rizos Sakellariou   University of Manchester, UK
Fernando Silva   University of Porto, Portugal
Henk Sips   Delft University of Technology, The Netherlands
Domenico Talia   University of Calabria, Italy
Felix Wolf   Technische Universität Darmstadt, Germany

Honorary Members

Ron Perrott   Oxford e-Research Centre, UK
Karl Dieter Reinartz   University of Erlangen-Nuremberg, Germany

Observers

Jesper Larsson Träff   Vienna University of Technology, Austria
Denis Trystram   Grenoble Institute of Technology, France

Euro-Par 2015 Organization

Chair

Jesper Larsson Träff   Vienna University of Technology, Austria

Proceedings

Francesco Versaci   Vienna University of Technology, Austria

Workshops

Sascha Hunold   Vienna University of Technology, Austria

Local Organization

Alexandra Carpen-Amarie   Vienna University of Technology, Austria
Christine Kamper   Vienna University of Technology, Austria
Margret Steinbuch   Vienna University of Technology, Austria

Workshop Introduction
and Organization

4th Workshop on Big Data Management in Clouds (BigDataCloud)

Workshop Description

The Workshop on Big Data Management in Clouds was created to provide a platform for the dissemination of recent research efforts that explicitly aim at addressing the challenges related to executing Big Data applications on the cloud. Initially designed for powerful and expensive supercomputers, such applications have seen an increasing adoption on clouds, exploiting their elasticity and economical model. While Map/Reduce covers a large fraction of the development space, there are still many applications that are better served by other models and systems. In such a context, we need to embrace new programming models, scheduling schemes, and hybrid infrastructures and scale out of single datacenters to geographically distributed deployments in order to cope with these new challenges effectively.

Against this backdrop, the BigDataCloud workshop aims to provide a venue for researchers to present and discuss results on all aspects of data management in clouds, new developments, and deployment efforts in running data-intensive computing workloads. In particular, we are interested in how the use of cloud-based technologies can meet the data-intensive scientific challenges of HPC applications that are not well served by the current supercomputers or grids, and are being ported to cloud platforms. The goal of the workshop is to support the assessment of the current state, introduce future directions, and present architectures and services for future clouds supporting data-intensive computing.

BigDataCloud 2015 followed the successful previous editions held in conjunction with EuroPar. Its goal is to aggregate the data management and clouds/grids/P2P communities in order to complement the Big Data handling issues with a comprehensive system/infrastructure perspective. This year's edition was held on August 24 and gathered around 30 enthusiastic researchers from academia and industry. We received six papers, out of which three were selected for presentation. The Big Data theme was strongly reflected in the keynote given this year by Prof. Luc Bougé from École Normale Supérieure Rennes. The talk focused on the challenges of computing in distributed, very-large clouds from the execution and programming models perspective.

We wish to thank all the authors, the keynote speaker, the Program Committee members and the workshop chairs of EuroPar 2015 for their contribution to the success of this edition of BigDataCloud.

Program Chairs

Alexandru Costan   IRISA/INSA Rennes, France
Frédéric Desprez   Inria ENS Lyon, France

Program Committee

Gabriel Antoniu   Inria, France
Luc Bougé   ENS Rennes, France
Shadi Ibrahim   Inria, France
Olivier Nano   Microsoft Research ATLE, Germany
Bogdan Nicolae   IBM Research, Ireland
Maria S. Pérez   Universidad Politecnica de Madrid, Spain
Florin Pop   University Politehnica of Bucharest, Romania
Anna Queralt   Barcelona Supercomputing Center, Spain
Leonardo Querzoni   University of Rome La Sapienza, Italy
Balaji Subramaniam   Virginia Tech, USA
Domenico Talia   University of Calabria, Italy
Osamu Tatebe   University of Tsukuba, Japan
Radu Tudoran   Huawei European Research Center, Germany

First European Workshop on Parallel and Distributed Computing Education for Undergraduate Students (Euro-EDUPAR)

Workshop Description

Today, parallel and distributed computing (PDC) is omnipresent. It is encountered in all computational environments, from mobile devices, laptops, and desktops, to clusters of multicore nodes and supercomputers, usually comprising one or several coprocessors of different types (GPU, MIC, FPGA). This explains why it is vital to educate new generations of scientists and engineers about a range of PDC-related topics as we prepare them to effectively use modern computational systems. In a word, PDC-related topics must appear early and often in modern courses in computational science, computer science, and computer engineering.

In 2010, the IEEE Computer Society Technical Committee on Parallel Processing (TCPP) launched the Curriculum Initiative on Parallel and Distributed Computing, with Core Topics for Undergraduates. This led in 2011 to the EduPar workshop, which is dedicated to parallel and distributed computing education. Given the differences in educational environments in different parts of the world, the Euro-EDUPAR workshop starts with the aim of analyzing PDC education in a European context, i.e., within the structure and organization of European education.

Thus, Euro-EDUPAR is dedicated to analyzing where and how to include topics related to both PDC and HPC (high-performance computing) within the curricula of programs in computer science and engineering and computational science, while emphasizing European undergraduate teaching. The workshop especially seeks papers that report on experiences with incorporating PDC-related topics into undergraduate core courses taken by the majority of students on a degree course. Methods, pedagogical approaches, tools, and techniques that have potential for adoption across the European teaching community are of particular interest.

Topics of interest include: PDC teaching in the European space; pedagogical issues in PDC, educational methods, and learning mechanisms; novel ways of teaching PDC topics, including informal learning environments; curriculum design, models for incorporating PDC topics in core CS/CE curriculum; experience with incorporating PDC topics into core CS/CE courses; experience with incorporating PDC topics in the context of other applications learning; pedagogical tools, programming environments, and languages for PDC; e-Learning, e-Laboratory, Massive Open Online Courses (MOOC), Small Private Online Courses (SPOC); PDC experiences at non-university levels, secondary school, postgraduate, industry, diffusion of PDC.

Program Chairs

Domingo Giménez   University of Murcia, Spain
Sushil K. Prasad   Georgia State University, USA
Arnold L. Rosenberg   Northeastern University, Boston, USA

Program Committee

Marco Aldinucci   University of Turin, Italy
Paolo Bientinesi   RWTH Aachen University, Germany
Florina Ciorba   Technische Universität Dresden, Germany
Pierre-François Dutot   Université Pierre-Mendès Grenoble, France
Anshul Gupta   IBM Research, USA
Emmanuel Jeannot   Inria, France
Eleni Karatza   Aristotle University of Thessaloniki, Greece
Kishore Kothapalli   International Institute of Information Technology,
                           Hyderabad, India
Friedhelm Meyer auf der University of Paderborn, Germany
  Heide
Milan D. Mihajlovic   The University of Manchester, UK
Julio Ortega   University of Granada, Spain
Dana Petcu   West University of Timisoara, Romania
Cynthia Phillips   Sandia National Laboratories, USA
Martin Quinson   University of Lorraine/Inria Nancy, France
Noemi Rodriguez   PUC-Rio, Brazil
Julio Sahuquillo   Technical University of Valencia, Spain
Mitsuhisa Sato   RIKEN Advanced Institute of Computational Science,
                           Japan
Christian Scheideler   Universität Paderborn, Germany
Leonel Sousa   INESC-ID, IST, Universidade de Lisboa, Portugal
Peter Strazdins   Australian National University, Australia
Frédéric Vivien   Inria, France
Roman Wyrzykowski   Czestochowa University of Technology, Poland
Julius Žilinskas   Vilnius University, Lithuania

Additional Reviewers

Javier Cuenca   University of Murcia, Spain
Diego Fabregat-Traver   RWTH Aachen University, Germany
Daniel Ruprecht   University of Leeds, UK

13th International Workshop on Algorithms, Models, and Tools for Parallel Computing on Heterogeneous Platforms (HeteroPar)

Workshop Description

HeteroPar is a forum for researchers working on algorithms, programming languages, tools, and theoretical models aimed at efficiently solving problems on heterogeneous platforms. Heterogeneity is emerging as one of the most profound and challenging characteristics of today's parallel environments. From the macro level, where networks of distributed computers, composed by diverse node architectures, are interconnected with potentially heterogeneous networks, to the micro level, where deeper memory hierarchies and various accelerator architectures are increasingly common, the impact of heterogeneity on all computing tasks is increasing rapidly. Traditional parallel algorithms, programming environments and tools, designed for legacy homogeneous multiprocessors, will at best achieve a small fraction of the efficiency and the potential performance that we should expect from parallel computing in tomorrow's highly diversified and mixed environments. New ideas, innovative algorithms, and specialized programming environments and tools are needed to efficiently use these new and multifarious parallel architectures.

The 13th International Workshop on Algorithms, Models and Tools for Parallel Computing on Heterogeneous Platforms (HeteroPar 2015) was held in Vienna, Austria. For the seventh time, this workshop was organized in conjunction with the Euro-Par 2015 annual series of international conferences. The format of the workshop includes a keynote, followed by technical presentations, and ending with a panel. The workshop was well attended–there was 40 attendees.

This year, we received 26 articles, from 15 countries for review. After a thorough peer-reviewing process, we selected eight articles for presentation at the workshop. The review process focused on innovation and on proven applicability to heterogeneous settings. As a consequence, the quality and the relevance of the selected articles are very high. The acceptance ratio of 31 % is a result of the reviewers' discussion and not of cut-off selection; none of the articles submitted to HeteroPar 2015 was rejected because of the acceptance of other articles. The accepted articles represent an interesting mix of topics, techniques, applications, and scales, exhibiting nicely the diversity and growth of the heterogeneous computing field.

The Panel on Next Generation Heterogeneous Computing was led by, in alphabetical order, Prof. Dr. Henri Bal (VU Amsterdam, The Netherlands), Dr. Guojing Cong (IBM T.J. Watson Research Center, NY, USA), Prof. Dr. Miriam Leeser (Northeastern University in Boston, MA, USA), Dr. Martin Schultz (Lawrence Livermore National Lab, CA, USA), and Christian Iwainsky (TU Darmstadt, Germany).

Last, but certainly not least, I would like to thank the HeteroPar Steering Committee and the HeteroPar 2015 Program Committee, who made the workshop possible. I would also like to thank Euro-Par for hosting our community, and the Euro-Par workshops chair Dr. Sascha Hunold for his timely help.

Steering Committee

Domingo Giménez	University of Murcia, Spain
Alexey Kalinov	Cadence Design Systems, Russia
Alexey Lastovetsky	University College Dublin, Ireland
Yves Robert	Ecole Normale Supérieure de Lyon, France
Leonel Sousa	INESC-ID/IST, TU Lisbon, Portugal
Denis Trystram	LIG, Grenoble, France

Program Chair

Alexandru Iosup	Delft University of Technology, The Netherlands

Program Committee

Rosa M. Badia	Barcelona Supercomputing Center, Spain
Jorge Barbosa	Faculdade de Engenharia do Porto, Portugal
Olivier Beaumont	Inria Futurs Bordeaux, LABRI, France
Cristina Boeres	Universidade Federal Fluminense, Brazil
George Bosilca	ICL, UTK, USA
Louis-Claude Canon	University of Franche-Comte, France
Alexandre Denis	Inria, France
Toshio Endo	Tokyo Institute of Technology, Japan
Jianbin Fang	NUDT, China
Edgar Gabriel	University of Houston, USA
Shuichi Ichikawa	Toyohashi University of Technology, Japan
Emmanuel Jeannot	Inria, France
Helen Karatza	Aristotle University of Thessaloniki, Greece
Hatem Ltaief	KAUST, Saudi Arabia
Pierre Manneback	University of Mons, Belgium
Satoshi Matsuoka	Tokyo Institute of Technology, Japan
Rafael Mayo	Universidad Jaume I, Spain
Wahid Nasri	ESST de Tunis, Tunisia
Nacho Navarro	Barcelona Supercomputing Center, Spain
Dana Petcu	University of Timisoara, Romania
Antonio J. Plaza	University of Extremadura, Spain
Thomas Rauber	University of Bayreuth, Germany
Matei Ripeanu	University of British Columbia, Canada
Vladimir Rychkov	University College Dublin, Ireland
Mitsuhisa Sato	University of Tsukuba, Japan
Erik Saule	University of North Carolina at Charlotte, USA

Tom Scogland	Lawrence Livermore National Laboratory, USA
Henk Sips	Delft University of Technology, The Netherlands
Ana Lucia Varbanescu	University of Amsterdam, The Netherlands
Antonio M. Vidal	Universidad Politecnica de Valencia, Spain
Frederic Vivien	Inria, France
Jon Weissman	University of Minnesota, USA

Third Workshop on Large-Scale Distributed Virtual Environments (LSDVE)

Workshop Description

The focus of the workshop has been the investigation of different aspects of distributed cooperative applications. Several novel applications have emerged in this area in the last few years. These include distributed social networks, distributed social games, collaborative recommender systems, collaborative learning systems, large-scale crowd-based applications, supported collaborative work (CSCW), and massively multi-player games.

The realization of these applications requires affording several challenges, such as the definition of user interfaces, coordination protocols, and proper middleware and architectures supporting distributed cooperation. Collaborative applications may greatly benefit from the support of different kinds of platforms, both cloud and peer to peer and also platforms recently proposed for the Internet of Things (IoT), such as fog computing. The integration of different platforms, for instance, mobile and cloud environments, is currently a challenge.

Some important challenges in the area of large-scale virtual environments are collaborative protocols design, latency reduction/hiding techniques for guaranteeing real-time constraints, large-scale processing of user information, privacy and security issues, state consistency/persistence.

The workshop investigated open challenges in this area, related to the design of new applications and to the definition of proper environments and frameworks for their development. LSDVE 2015 was a venue for researchers to present and discuss important aspects of large-scale collaborative applications and of the platforms supporting them.

The workshop opened with the keynote "Distributed Virtual Environments: From Client Server to Cloud and P2P Architectures: A Tutorial" given by Prof. Laura Ricci, University of Pisa, Italy.

The workshop organizers want to thank the authors of the papers for joining us in Vienna, the Program Committee and all the referees for doing the hard work of reviewing all the submissions, the conference organizers for proving a great support, and the researchers attending the workshop in Vienna.

Program Chairs

Laura Ricci   University of Pisa, Italy
Alexandru Iosup   TU Delft, Delft, The Netherlands
Radu Prodan   University of Innsbruck, Austria

Program Committee

Michele Amoretti   University of Parma, Italy
Emanuele Carlini   ISTI CNR, Pisa, Italy
Massimo Coppola   ISTI CNR, Pisa, Italy
Patrizio Dazzi   ISTI CNR, Pisa, Italy
Juan J. Durillo   University of Innsbruck, Austria
Kalman Graffi   University of Dusseldorf, Germany
Barbara Guidi   University of Pisa, Italy
Alexandru Iosup   TU Delft, The Netherlands
Pedro Garcia Lopez   University Rovira i Virgili, Spain
Pietro Michiardi   EURECOM, France
Dana Petcu   West University of Timisoara, Romania
Radu Prodan   University of Innsbruck, Austria
Laura Ricci   University of Pisa, Pisa, Italy
Alexey Vinel   Tampere University of Technology, Finland

Additional Reviewers

Valerio Arnaboldi   IIT, CNR, Pisa, Italy
Jean Botev   Université du Luxembourg, Luxembourg
Hanna Kavalionak   ISTI, CNR, Pisa, Italy

4th International Workshop on On-Chip Memory Hierarchies and Interconnects (OMHI)

Workshop Description

Current chip multiprocessors (CMPs) include several levels of on-chip caches to avoid the huge latencies of accessing the off-chip DRAM main memory modules. These caches must be efficiently interconnected to avoid performance penalties. On-chip networks are used to interconnect the memory hierarchy inside the processor chip. Latencies can be significantly affected by the devised on-chip memory hierarchy and the interconnect design, whose impact on the overall latency strongly depends on the core count. Consequently, this problem aggravates with the increasing core counts, which is the current commercial trend. By contrast, the main concern in GPUs is on memory bandwidth instead of latencies. Current GPUs are designed to hide memory latencies through fine-grained multithreading. The main goal of on-chip memories in current GPUs is to reduce off-chip memory traffic. In this context, the programmer plays a key role in improving cache access locality. Hence we can conclude that CPUs and GPUs require memory organizations with different characteristics. Thus, as current heterogeneous CPU-GPU systems are proliferating in the market, the memory system must be designed to efficiently support both types of memory organizations: latency-oriented and bandwidth-oriented.

The on-chip memory hierarchy occupies two thirds of the processor area and consumes a significant fraction of the overall system power. To deal with processor scalability issues, new technologies have emerged to implement the on-chip hierarchy. Regarding on-chip memory technologies, current SRAM technologies deployed in on-chip caches present important design challenges in terms of density and leakage currents. Instead, alternative technologies addressing leakage and density, such as eDRAM or MRAM, are being implemented and explored in large CMPs. Also the current electronic technology used in on-chip networks has important performance and power scalability limitations and designs using alternative technologies such as photonics or wireless are being proposed.

To efficiently leverage any on-chip memory hierarchy design, efforts must be focused on the management of shared resources, especially in the context of multicore systems where multiple threads contend while accessing these resources. This management involves, among others, thread allocation policies, cache management strategies, and NoC design. In this context, the synergy between the research on memory organization and management, interconnection networks, as well as novel technologies becomes a key strategy for fostering further developments. With this aim, the International Workshop on On-chip Memory Hierarchy and Interconnects (OMHI) started in 2012 and continued with its fourth edition in 2015, which was held in Vienna, Austria. This workshop is organized in conjunction with the Euro-Par annual series of international conferences dedicated to the promotion and advancement of all aspects of parallel computing.

The goal of the OMHI workshop is to provide a forum for engineers and scientists to address the aforementioned challenges, and to present new ideas for future on-chip memory hierarchies and interconnects focusing on organization, management, and implementation. The specific topics covered by the OMHI workshop have been kept up to date according to technology advances and industrial and academia interests.

The chairs of OMHI were proud to present Prof. Sandro Bartolini as keynote speaker, who gave an interesting talk focusing on the key topics of the workshop entitled "Illuminating Processors: How Photonics Will Help Computing," which together with the paper session resulted in an interesting and very exciting one-day program.

Finally, the chairs would like to thank the members of the Program Committee for their reviews, the Euro-Par organizers, Sandro Bartolini, and all of the attendees. Based on the positive feedback from all of them, we plan to continue the OMHI workshop in conjunction with Euro-Par 2016.

Program Chairs

Julio Sahuquillo   Universitat Politècnica de València, Spain
María Engracia Gómez   Universitat Politècnica de València, Spain
Salvador Petit   Universitat Politècnica de València, Spain

Program Committee

Manuel Acacio   Universidad de Murcia, Spain
Sandro Bartolini   Università di Siena, Italy
João M.P. Cardoso   University of Porto, Portugal
Marcello Coppola   STMicroelectronics, France
Giorgos Dimitrakopoulos   Democritus University of Thrace, Greece
Pierfrancesco Foglia   Università di Pisa, Italy
Holger Fröning   University of Heidelberg, Germany
Crispín Gómez   Universitat Politècnica de València, Spain
Kees Goossens   NXP Semiconductors and Delft University of
                            Technology, The Netherlands
David Kaeli   Northeastern University, USA
Sonia López   Rochester Institute of Technology, USA
Iakovos Mavroidis   Foundation for Research and Technology - Hellas
                            (FORTH), Greece
Pierre Michaud   Inria, France
Tor Skei   Simula Research Laboratory, Norway
Rafael Ubal   Northeastern University, USA

Third Workshop on Parallel and Distributed Agent-Based Simulations (PADABS)

Workshop Description

Agent-based simulation models are an increasingly popular tool for research and management in many fields such as ecology, economics, sociology, etc. In some fields, such as social sciences, these models are seen as a key instrument to the generative approach, essential for understanding complex social phenomena. But also in policy-making, biology, military simulations, control of mobile robots and economics, the relevance and effectiveness of agent-based simulation models has been recently recognized. The computer science community has responded to the need for platforms that can help the development and testing of new models in each specific field by providing tools, libraries, and frameworks that speed up and make massive simulations. The key objective of this workshop is to bring together researchers who are interested in getting more performance from their simulations, by using synchronized, many-core simulations (e.g., GPUs), strongly coupled, parallel simulations (e.g., MPI) and loosely coupled, distributed simulations (distributed heterogeneous setting).

Several frameworks have been recently developed and are active in this field. They range from the GPU-manycore approach, to parallel, to distributed simulation environments. In the first category, you can find FLAME GPU, which also allows non-GPU specialists to harness the GPUs performance for real-time simulation and visualization. For tightly-coupled, large computing clusters and supercomputers a very popular framework is Repast for High-Performance Computing (REPAST-HPC), a C++-based modeling system. On the distributed side, recent work on Distributed Mason, allows non-specialists to use heterogeneous hardware and software in local area networks for enlarging the size and speeding up the simulation of complex agent-based models.

Therefore, our focus and positioning is on the applied side of parallel computing, with a particular emphasis on performance but also on the expressivity of the frameworks, since the field that is the target of our research is multidisciplinary and does not include only "hard-science" scientists.

Program Chairs

Vittorio Scarano (Chair)	Università di Salerno, Italy
Gennaro Cordasco	Seconda Università di Napoli, Italy
Ugo Erra	Università della Basilicata, Italy
Carmine Spagnuolo (Publicity Chair)	Università di Salerno, Italy

Program Committee

Maria Chli	Aston University, UK
Claudio Cioffi-Revilla	George Mason University, USA
Biagio Cosenza	University of Innsbruck, Austria
Nick Collier	Argonne National Laboratory, USA
Rosaria Conte	CNR, Italy
Andrew Evans	University of Leeds, UK
Bernardino Frola	The MathWorks, Cambridge, UK
Joanna Kolodziej	Cracow University of Technology and AGH University of Science and Technology, Cracow, Poland
Nicola Lettieri	Università del Sannio and ISFOL, Italy
Sean Luke	George Mason University, USA
Michael North	Argonne National Laboratory, USA
Mario Paolucci	CNR, Italy
Paul Richmond	The University of Sheffield, UK
Arnold Rosenberg	Northeastern University, USA
Flaminio Squazzoni	Università di Brescia, Italy
Michela Taufer	University of Delaware, USA

Additional Reviewers

Carmine Spagnuolo	Università di Salerno, Italy
Luca Vicidomini	Università di Salerno, Italy

First Workshop on Performance Engineering for Large-Scale Graph Analytics (PELGA)

Workshop Description

The knowledge economy is based on data, of which graphs represent an increasing part, in advanced marketing, in social networking, in life sciences, in health and bioinformatics services, in academic networks, in hiring of professionals, etc. As a consequence, graph analytics is fast becoming a significant consumer of computing resources, due to the ever larger graphs of hundreds of millions up to hundreds of billions of edges, and to the increased complexity of analysis tasks. To enable existing algorithms to fit modern architectures and scale with these new requirements, there is a growing need for performance engineering.

PELGA is a venue that aims to address this need. Its goal is to bring together specialists from both industry and academia to discuss the state of the art of graph processing systems, with a special focus on performance. Hosting PELGA with EuroPar allows the largest community of parallel and distributed systems in Europe and elsewhere to participate in the discussion and acknowledge the new research opportunities that large-scale graph processing presents.

PELGA is a venue that welcomes contributions focusing on graph-centric performance engineering tools and methods, workload characterization, new algorithms and new graph processing systems, and performance modeling. Less conventional workshop topics such as surveys, performance studies, comparative analyses are also encouraged, given the young age of the large-scale graph processing community. We strive to cover the specifics of three large classes of topics.

1. Systems invites contributions focusing on new graph processing systems focused on high-performance analytics, performance studies of existing systems to be used for graph processing, and comparative and/or in-depth analysis of graph processing systems.
2. Algorithms, Applications, and Architectures is the largest topic cluster, including work focusing on new high-performance graph processing algorithms, new performance-aware applications for graph processing algorithms, platform-specific algorithms and their performance optimization (e.g., GPUs, Xeon Phi, heterogeneous platforms) for graph analytics, algorithms and/or architectures for large-scale graph analytics, and partitioning methods for large-scale or otherwise challenging graphs.
3. Characterization, Modeling, and Engineering is the core of the workshop. We encourage novel contributions focusing on graph models for performance tuning and/or prediction of analytics workloads, performance models for prediction or ranking of graph processing platforms, performance analysis and engineering of

existing graph processing algorithms, and tools and benchmarks for graph-centric performance engineering.

In summary, large-scale graph processing is a high-impact field in full development, driven by both data owners and the analytics world. As we recognize the need to adapt traditional performance evaluation, analysis, and modeling to the needs of this dynamic new topic, PELGA is a workshop with a strong community focus, aiming to bring the challenges of large-scale graph processing to the attention of the EuroPar community as an unconventional, yet very relevant topic for parallel and distributed computing.

Program Chairs

Ana Lucia Varbanescu	University of Amsterdam, The Netherlands
Alexandru Iosup	Delft University of Technology, The Netherlands

Program Committee

Arnau Prat-Perez	UPC, Spain
Claudio Martella	VU University Amsterdam, The Netherlands
Hannes Muhleisen	CWI Amsterdam, The Netherlands
Hassan Chafi	Oracle Labs, USA
Sungpack Hong	Oracle Labs, USA
Jan Hidders	Delft University of Technology, The Netherlands
Josep Lluis Larriba Pey	UPC, Spain
Matei Ripeanu	The University of British Columbia, Canada
Mihai Capota	Intel Labs, USA
Ted Willke	Intel Labs, USA

Second International Workshop on Reproducibility in Parallel Computing (REPPAR)

Workshop Description

Conducting sound and reproducible experiments in parallel computing is not easy, as hardware and software architectures of current parallel computers are most often very complex. This high complexity makes it difficult—and often impossible—for computer scientists to model such systems mathematically. For that reason, scientists rely on experiments to study new parallel algorithms, different software solutions (e.g., operating systems), or novel hardware architectures. The situation in parallel computing is made even more difficult than it would be otherwise, as parallel systems are in a constant state of flux, e.g., the total core count is rapidly growing and many programming paradigms for parallel machines have emerged and are actively being used in a hybrid fashion, e.g., MPI, OpenMP, or PGAS.

For these reasons, the workshop is concerned with experimental practices in parallel computing research. We solicit research papers and experience reports on a number of relevant topics, particularly: methods for analysis and visualization of experimental data, best-practice recommendations, results of attempts to replicate previously published experiments, and tools for experimental computational sciences. Some examples of the latter include workflow management systems, experimental testbeds, and systems for archiving and querying large data files.

Program Chairs

Sascha Hunold	Vienna University of Technology, Austria
Arnaud Legrand	CNRS, LIG, Grenoble, France
Lucas Nussbaum	Université de Lorraine, LORIA, France
Mark Stillwell	Imperial College London, UK

Program Committee

Andrew Davison	CNRS, UNIC, Gif-sur-Yvette, France
Georg Hager	University of Erlangen-Nuremberg, Germany
Sascha Hunold	Vienna University of Technology, Austria
Arnaud Legrand	CNRS, LIG, Grenoble, France
Lucas Nussbaum	Université de Lorraine, LORIA, France
Olivier Richard	Université Joseph Fourier, LIG, Grenoble, France
Lucas M. Schnorr	Universidade Federal do Rio Grande do Sul, Porto Alegre, Brazil
Mark Stillwell	Imperial College London, UK
Jesper Larsson Träff	Vienna University of Technology, Austria

8th Workshop on Resiliency in High-Performance Computing in Clusters, Clouds, and Grids (Resilience)

Workshop Description

Clouds, grids, and clusters are three different computational paradigms with the potential to support high-performance computing (HPC) and enterprise IT infrastructure. Currently, they consist of hardware, management, and usage models particular to different computational regimes [e.g., high-performance cluster systems designed to support tightly coupled scientific simulation codes typically utilize high-speed interconnects and commercial cloud systems designed to support software as a service (SAS) typically do not]. However, in order to support HPC, all must at least utilize large numbers of resources and hence effective HPC in any of these paradigms must address the same issue of resiliency at a very large scale.

Recent trends in HPC systems have clearly indicated that future increases in performance, in excess of those resulting from improvements in single-processor performance, will be achieved through corresponding increases in system scale, i.e., using a significantly larger component count. As the raw computational performance of the world's fastest HPC systems increases from today's current multi-petascale to next-generation exascale capability and beyond, their number of computational, networking, and storage components will grow from the ten to one hundred thousand compute nodes of today's systems to several hundreds of thousands of compute nodes in the foreseeable future. This substantial growth in system scale, and the resulting component count, poses a challenge for HPC system and application software with respect to reliability, availability, and serviceability (RAS).

The goal of this workshop is to bring together experts in the area of fault tolerance and resilience for HPC to present the latest achievements and to discuss the challenges ahead. The program of the Resilience 2015 workshop included one keynote and five high-quality papers. The keynote was given by Christian Engelmann from Oak Ridge National Laboratory with the title "Toward A Fault Model and Resilience Design Patterns for Extreme Scale Systems."

Workshop Chairs

Stephen L. Scott   Tennessee Tech University and Oak Ridge National
                                 Laboratory, USA
Chokchai   Louisiana Tech University, USA
  (Box) Leangsuksun

Workshop Program Chairs

Patrick G. Bridges   University of New Mexico, USA
Christian Engelmann   Oak Ridge National Laboratory, USA

Workshop Program Committee

Ferrol Aderholdt   Tennessee Tech University, USA
Vassil Alexandrov   Barcelona Supercomputer Center, Spain
Dorian Arnold   University of New Mexico, USA
Wesley Bland   Intel Corporation, USA
Greg Bronevetsky   Lawrence Livermore National Laboratory, USA
Franck Cappello   Argonne National Laboratory and University of Illinois
                                 at Urbana-Champaign, USA
Zizhong Chen   University of California at Riverside, USA
Andrew A. Chien   University of Chicago and Argonne National
                                 Laboratory, USA
Nathan DeBardeleben   Los Alamos National Laboratory, USA
James Elliott   North Carolina State University, USA
Kurt Ferreira   Sandia National Laboratory, USA
Michael Heroux   Sandia National Laboratories, USA
Larry Kaplan   Cray Inc., USA
Dieter Kranzlmueller   Ludwig Maximilians University of Munich, Germany
Sriram Krishnamoorthy   Pacific Northwest National Laboratory, USA
Ignacio Laguna   Lawrence Livermore National Laboratory, USA
Scott Levy   University of New Mexico, USA
Celso Mendes   University of Illinois at Urbana-Champaign, USA
Kathryn Mohror   Lawrence Livermore National Laboratory, USA
Christine Morin   Inria Rennes, France
Nageswara Rao   Oak Ridge National Laboratory, USA
Alexander Reinefeld   Zuse Institute Berlin, Germany
Rolf Riesen   Intel Corporation, USA
Martin Schulz   Lawrence Livermore National Laboratory, USA
Marc Snir   Argonne National Laboratory, USA
Keita Teranishi   Sandia National Laboratories, USA

Third Workshop on Runtime and Operating Systems for the Many-Core Era (ROME)

Workshop Description

Since the beginning of the multicore era, parallel processing has become prevalent across the board. However, in order to continue a performance increase according to Moore's law, the next step needs to be taken: away from common multicores toward innovative many-core architectures. Such systems, equipped with a significantly higher amount of cores per chip than multicores, pose challenges in both hardware and software design. On the hardware side, complex on-chip networks, scratchpads, hybrid memory cubes, non-volatile memory and stacked memory as well as deep cache hierarchies and novel cache-coherence strategies will enrich the current research areas in the future.

However, the ROME workshop (Runtime and Operating Systems for the Many-Core Era) focuses on the software side because without complying system software, runtime and operating system support, all these new hardware facilities cannot be exploited. Hence, the new challenges in hardware/software co-design are to step beyond traditional approaches and to create new programming models and operating system designs in order to exploit the theoretically available performance of future hardware as effectively and as power-aware as possible.

This focus of the ROME workshop stands in the tradition of a successful series of events originally hosted by the Many-Core Applications Research Community (MARC). Prior MARC symposia took place at ONERA Research Center in Toulouse, at the Hasso Plattner Institute in Potsdam, and at the RWTH Aachen University. Starting in 2013, the organizers continued this series by establishing ROME as one of the co-located workshops of Euro-Par, the prime European conference for parallel and distributed computing.

While the first ROME workshop, which was hosted at Euro-Par 2013 in Aachen, was still a MARC-related follow-up event but for a broader audience, the second ROME workshop, held in conjunction with Euro-Par 2014 in Porto, already expanded its focus to research questions arising from the upcoming generation of heterogeneous and/or massive parallel systems stepping toward a many-core-dominated exascale era.

In 2015, this broader focus was essentially retained for the third ROME workshop, which was held in conjunction with Euro-Par 2015 in Vienna, but the relevance of runtime and operating system aspects was stressed once again as being the primary scope of the ROME workshop series. In this spirit, the organizers were very happy that Dr. Carsten Weinhold from the Operating Systems Group of TU Dresden, Germany, volunteered to give an invited keynote for this third ROME workshop with the title "A Microkernel-Based Operating System for Exascale Computing."

Program Chairs

Stefan Lankes	RWTH Aachen University, Germany
Carsten Clauss	ParTec Cluster Competence Center GmbH

Program Committee

Jens Breitbart	TU München, Germany
André Brinkmann	Johannes Gutenberg-Universität Mainz, Germany
Carsten Clauss	ParTec Cluster Competence Center GmbH
Christos Kartsaklis	Oak Ridge National Laboratory, USA
Stefan Lankes	RWTH Aachen University, Germany
Timothy Mattson	Intel Labs, USA
Jörg Nolte	BTU Cottbus, Germany
Michael Riepen	IAV GmbH, Germany
Bettina Schnor	University of Potsdam, Germany
Christian Terboven	RWTH Aachen University, Germany
Theo Ungerer	Universität Augsburg, Germany
Josef Weidendorfer	TU München, Germany

Additional Reviewers

Steffen Christgau	University of Potsdam, Germany
Sonja Kolen	RWTH Aachen University, Germany
Stefan Petri	University of Potsdam, Germany
Simom Pickartz	RWTH Aachen University, Germany
Lukas Razik	RWTH Aachen University, Germany

8th Workshop on UnConventional High-Performance Computing 2015 (UCHPC)

Workshop Description

Recent issues regarding the power consumption of conventional HPC hardware has resulted both in new interest in accelerator hardware and in usage of mass-market hardware originally not designed for HPC. The most prominent examples are GPUs but FPGAs, DSPs, and embedded designs are also possible candidates to provide higher-power efficiency, as they are used in energy-restricted environments, such as smartphones or tablets. The so-called dark silicon forecast, i.e., not all transistors may be active at the same time, may lead to even more specialized hardware in future mass-market products. Exploiting this hardware for HPC can be a worthwhile challenge.

As the word "UnConventional" in the title suggests, the workshop focuses on usage of hardware or platforms for HPC, which are not (yet) conventionally used today, and may not have been designed for HPC in the first place. Reasons for its use can be raw computing power, good performance per watt, or low cost in general. To address this unconventional hardware, often new programming approaches and paradigms are required to make best use of it. Another focus of the workshop is on innovative, (yet) unconventional, new programming models and algorithms (e.g., Big Data) exploiting unconventional HPC hardware or software.

To this end, UCHPC tries to capture solutions for HPC that are unconventional today but could become conventional and significant tomorrow, and thus provide a glimpse into the future of HPC.

This year was the eigth time the UCHPC workshop took place, and it was the sixth time in a row it was co-located with Euro-Par (each year since 2010). Before that, it was held in conjunction with the International Conference on Computational Science and Its Applications 2008 and with the ACM International Conference on Computing Frontiers 2009. However, UCHPC is a perfect addition to the scientific fields of Euro-Par, and this is confirmed by the continuous interest we see among Euro-Par attendees for this workshop.

While the general focus of the workshop is fixed, the topic is actually a moving target. GPUs were quite unconventional for HPC a few years ago, but today a notable portion of the machines in the Top500 list are making use of them. Currently, the exploitation of mobile processors for HPC – including on-chip GPU and DSPs – is a hot topic. A recent technological breakthrough is mass-market production of 3D stacking technology, which allows us to put memory and logic nearer together. This may result in a revival of the processing-in-memory idea, which is quite unconventional from a programmer's point of view and seems to be a good fit for UCHPC. To this end, we invited Zehra Sura from the IBM T.J. Watson Center to give a keynote about IBM's recent research on "The Active Memory Cube: A Processing-in-Memory System for High-Performance Computing."

These proceedings include the final versions of the papers presented at UCHPC and accepted for publication. They take the feedback from the reviewers and workshop audience into account.

The workshop organizers/program chairs want to thank the authors of the papers for joining us in Vienna, the Program Committee for doing the hard work of reviewing all submissions, the conference organizers for providing such a nice venue, and last but not least the large number of attendees this year.

Program Chairs

Jens Breitbart   Technische Universität München, Germany
Josef Weidendorfer   Technische Universität München, Germany

Program Committee

Michael Bader   Technische Universität München, Germany
Denis Barthou   University of Bordeaux, France
Alex Bartzas   National Technical University of Athens, Greece
Lars Bengtsson   Chalmers University of Technology, Sweden
James Beyer   Cray Inc., USA
Jens Breitbart   Technische Universität München, Germany
Georgios Dimitrakopoulos   Democritus University of Thrace, Greece
Karl Fürlinger   LMU München, Germany
Frank Hannig   University of Erlangen-Nuremberg, Germany
Anders Hast   Uppsala University, Sweden
Paul Keir   University of the West of Scotland, UK
Rainer Keller   Hochschule für Technik Stuttgart, Germany
Gaurav Khanna   University of Massachusetts Dartmouth, USA
Harald Köstler   University of Erlangen-Nuremberg, Germany
Stefan Lankes   RWTH Aachen, Germany
Dimitar Lukarski   Paralution Labs, Germany
Manfred Mücke   Materials Center Leoben, Austria
Yannis Papaefstathiou   Technical University of Crete, Greece
Bertil Schmidt   University of Mainz, Germany
Ioannis Sourdis   Chalmers University of Technology, Sweden
Dylan Stark   Sandia National Laboratories, USA
Robert Strzodka   Universität Heidelberg, Germany
Carsten Trinitis   Technische Universität München, Germany
Josef Weidendorfer   Technische Universität München, Germany
Jan-Philipp Weiss   COMSOL, Sweden
Gerhard Wellein   University of Erlangen-Nuremberg, Germany
Ren Wu   Baidu, China
Peter Zinterhof jun   University of Salzburg, Austria

10th Workshop on Virtualization in High-Performance Cloud Computing (VHPC)

Workshop Description

Virtualization technologies constitute a key enabling factor for flexible resource management in modern data centers, cloud environments, and increasingly in HPC as well. Providers need to dynamically manage complex infrastructures in a seamless fashion for varying workloads and hosted applications, independently of the customers deploying software or users submitting highly dynamic and heterogeneous workloads. Thanks to virtualization, we have the ability to manage vast computing and networking resources dynamically and close to the marginal cost of providing the services, which is unprecedented in the history of scientific and commercial computing.

OS-level virtualization, such as provided by Docker, allows for multiple isolated user-space environments within the same OS kernel. It promises to provide many of the advantages of machine virtualization with high levels of responsiveness and performance; coupled with lightweight OSs it forms a potent architecture with the potential of becoming a mainstream environment for HPC workloads.

Machine virtualization, with its capability to enable consolidation of multiple under-utilized servers with heterogeneous software and operating systems (OSs), and its capability to live-migrate a fully operating virtual machine (VM) with a very short downtime, enables novel and dynamic ways to manage physical servers.

I/O virtualization allows physical network adapters to take traffic from multiple VMs; network virtualization, with its capability to create logical network overlays that are independent of the underlying physical topology and IP addressing, provides the fundamental ground on top of which evolved network services can be realized with an unprecedented level of dynamicity and flexibility. These technologies have to be inter-mixed and integrated in an intelligent way, to support workloads that are increasingly demanding in terms of absolute performance, responsiveness, and interactivity, and have to respect well-specified service-level agreements (SLAs), as needed for industrial-grade provided services.

The Workshop on Virtualization in High-Performance Cloud Computing (VHPC) aims to bring together researchers and industrial practitioners facing the challenges posed by virtualization in order to foster discussion, collaboration, and mutual exchange of knowledge and experience, thereby enabling research to ultimately provide novel solutions for virtualized computing systems of tomorrow.

Program Chairs

Michael Alexander   TU Wien, Austria
Anastassios Nanos   NTUA, Greece
Balazs Gerofi   RIKEN, Japan

Program Committee

Stergios Anastasiadis University of Ioannina, Greece
Costas Bekas   IBM, Switzerland
Jakob Blomer   CERN, Switzerland
Ron Brightwell   Sandia National Laboratories, USA
Roberto Canonico   University of Napoli Federico II, Italy
Julian Chesterfield   OnApp, UK
Piero Castoldi   Sant'Anna School of Advanced Studies, Italy
Patrick Dreher   MIT, USA
William Gardner   University of Guelph, Canada
Kyle Hale   Northwestern University, USA
Marcus Hardt   Karlsruhe Institute of Technology, Germany
Iftekhar Hussain   Infinera, USA
Krishna Kant   Temple University, USA
Eiji Kawai   National Institute of Information and Communications
         Technology, Japan
Romeo Kinzler   IBM, Switzerland
Kornilios Kourtis   ETH, Switzerland
Nectarios Koziris   National Technical University of Athens, Greece
Massimo Lamanna   CERN, Switzerland
Che-Rung Roger Lee National Tsing Hua University, Taiwan
William Magato   University of Cincinnati, USA
Helge Meinhard   CERN, Switzerland
Jean-Marc Menaud   Ecole des Mines de Nantes, France
Christine Morin   Inria, France
Amer Qouneh   University of Florida, USA
Seetharami Seelam   IBM T.J. Watson Research Center, USA
Josh Simons   VMWare, USA
Borja Sotomayor   University of Chicago, USA
Kurt Tutschku   Blekinge Institute of Technology, Sweden
Yasuhiro Watashiba   Osaka University, Japan
Chao-Tung Yang   Tunghai University, Taiwan

Contents

**HeteroPar - Algorithms, Models, and Tools for Parallel Computing
on Heterogeneous Platforms**

REPPAR - Reproducibility in Parallel Computing

Resilience - Resiliency in High Performance Computing with Clouds, Grids, and Clusters

BigDataCloud - Big Data Management in Clouds

Distributed Range-Based Meta-Data Management for an In-Memory Storage

Florian Klein[(⊠)], Kevin Beineke, and Michael Schöttner

Institut für Informatik, Heinrich-Heine-Universität Düsseldorf,
Universitätsstr. 1, 40225 Düsseldorf, Germany
Florian.Klein@uni-duesseldorf.de

Abstract. Large-scale interactive applications and online graph processing require fast data access to billions of small data objects. DXRAM addresses this challenge by keeping all data always in RAM of potentially many nodes aggregated in a data center. Such storage clusters need a space-efficient and fast meta-data management. In this paper we propose a range-based meta-data management allowing fast node lookups while being space efficient by combining data object IDs in ranges. A super-peer overlay network is used to manage these ranges together with backup-node information allowing parallel and fast recovery of meta data and data of failed peers. Furthermore, the same concept can also be used for client-side caching. The measurement results show the benefits of the proposed concepts compared to other meta-data management strategies as well as its very good overall performance evaluated using the social network benchmark BG.

1 Introduction

Large-scale interactive applications and online graph processing must often manage billions of small data objects and require low-latency data access. Facebook for example keeps billions of small data objects in around 1,000 memcached servers to support more than one billion users [11]. Around 70 % of these objects are smaller than 64 byte [10]. The sheer amount of objects and the small data sizes can be found in many other online graph algorithms too. These applications are mostly dominated by read accesses over writes [2]. Whether write accesses are realized as updates or result in a new object version is depending on the system and the type of data.

DXRAM addresses these challenges by keeping all data always in memory. Huge storage capacities can be provided by aggregating many nodes within a data center. A transparent background logging is used to mask node failures and provides persistence even in case of power outages. DXRAM is inspired by many ideas of RAMCloud [12], however instead of larger objects stored in tables we target at managing billions of very small data objects [6]. Furthermore, we do not rely on a single coordinator, but use a super-peer overlay-network for node lookup and recovery coordination of crashed nodes.

© Springer International Publishing Switzerland 2015
S. Hunold et al. (Eds.): Euro-Par 2015 Workshops, LNCS 9523, pp. 3–15, 2015.
DOI: 10.1007/978-3-319-27308-2_1

In a previous publication we have presented a memory management approach, which allows to store up to one billion small data objects on a commodity node [5]. In this paper we focus on the global meta-data management and the mapping of global IDs to single nodes. The sheer amount of objects raise new challenges on these well studied topics. As RAM is expensive a space-efficient meta-data management with a fast lookup is mandatory.

We propose an approach which merges thousands of global IDs into a single ID-range, resulting in a severely reduced amount of mapping entries. The ID ranges are stored using a modified B-tree structure which allows a fast and space-efficient mapping of billions of global IDs to nodes and a client cache optimized for locality-based access-pattern.

The structure of this paper is as follows. In Sect. 2 we give a brief overview of the DXRAM system including the super-peer overlay which is used to realize the proposed meta-data management. The latter is described in Sect. 3 followed by the evaluation in Sect. 4. Related work is discussed in Sect. 5 followed by the conclusions and an outlook on future work in Sect. 6.

2   DXRAM Architecture

The overall architecture of DXRAM is divided into core and extended services. The core services have been designed to support different data models and data consistency strategies as well as extended services (file system, table-based storage, replication, etc.). One of the main objectives in the core services is to keep the functionality and the interface for high layers as compact as possible. Therefore the core service provides essential functionality for the management, storage and transfer of key-value tuples. The minimal interface for the tuples includes `create`, `delete`, `get`, `put` and `lock`.

2.1   Chunks

A key-value tuple in DXRAM is called *chunk*. A chunk consists of a 64 bit globally unique chunk ID (*CID*) and binary data. Chunks have variable sizes defined during their creation and are always stored en bloc. The operations `get` and `put` work always on full chunks.

The CID is split into two parts. The first 16 bit contain the node ID of the chunk creator (NID_C). The creator of a chunk is not necessarily the actual owner of the chunk. The second part contains a 48 bit locally unique value, called *LID*, which is incremented during each local chunk creation ensuring a sequential ID generation scheme for CIDs on every node. This is also the foundation for a efficient local address translation [6] as well as for the later presented range-based B-tree structure. Furthermore, it allows to support locality-based access patterns.

The CID size is configurable, but with the default setting we can address 65,536 nodes each with up to ≈280 trillion chunks. Furthermore, CIDs of deleted chunks are re-used to keep the ID space compact.

The sequential ID generation is not a constraint for applications. When using databases as persistent storage they typically access data through auto-incremented row IDs similar to our LIDs. For all other applications DXRAM provides a naming service allowing user-defined keys. The intention is that not each single object needs a user-defined key but only a subset, e.g. the user-profile record in a social network referring all other data of a user.

Because RAM is expensive the transparent backup logging replicates chunks on multiple *backup nodes* only in flash memory. By default each chunk is replicated on three backup nodes allowing fast recovery of data in case of a node crash similar to RAMCloud [11].

2.2 Super-Peer Overlay

Around 5–10% (configurable) of the available nodes in DXRAM are dedicated super peers. The super peers form a ring, where the node ID (*NID*) defines the position of the super peer on the ring. The resulting ring has similarities with Chord [16]. However, DXRAM does not use a finger table but the super peers know each other, allowing to contact every node of the ring in $\mathcal{O}(1)$. Because of the high-speed network in a data center and the limited number of super peers this is feasible, in contrast to traditional Internet-scale DHTs. Every super peer manages a range of NIDs between the NID of the predecessor super peer and its own NID. A peer is assigned to the super peer which manages its NID.

Every super peer manages the meta data (existing chunks, assigned backup nodes, etc.) for all its peers. In addition, the super peer also monitors its peers and coordinates the recovery of any failed peer it is responsible for.

Obviously, the location of a chunk given its CID needs to be determined before it can be read or written. The NID part of a given CID is sent with a request to the super peer which is responsible for the corresponding NID range. Each super peer sends a list of all running super peers periodically to its associated peers. If the super peer overlay changes, e.g. a super peer joins or fails, it might happen that a node contacts the wrong super peer. In this rare case the contacted super peer searches for the correct super peer and informs the requesting node.

As mentioned before DXRAM allows the migration of hot spots from one node to another for load balancing reasons. We do not expect millions of object migrations, but we have to be able to resolve potential clustering of hot spots on some nodes. For example in a social network it could happen that some famous artists or pop stars (some artists have up to 40 million likes in Facebook [15]) are stored on one DXRAM node but of course overall there will not be millions of famous stars. During a migration three nodes are involved, the source node, the target node and the super peer responsible for the chunk meta data.

After a node fails the recovered data is stored on potentially many nodes which is handled by DXRAM as multiple migrations.

A peer failure is detected through a heart beat protocol between a super peer and its associated peers or by any other node getting a timeout on a request. If a peer failure is detected the super peer contacts all backup nodes of the failed node and coordinates the recovery. An explicit backup update order ensures that the recovery can be executed by the backup nodes themselves. In addition the backup order allows the super peer to recover the meta data in parallel during a running node data recovery. For the super peer the recovery of meta data is the same as bulk migrations.

When a super peer fails the stored meta data is lost and the super-peer overlay is broken. Both is widely researched in the context of Chord [16] and no problem. If all meta data replicas are lost or broken it is still possible to reconstruct the missing meta data from peers.

3   CID-Ranges

Many in-memory systems map global IDs to nodes using hash tables allowing lookups in $\mathcal{O}(1)$, e.g. RAMCloud [14] and Trinity [15]. The problem with hash tables is the necessary collision resolution, which gets expensive with increasing load factors. In the worst case the table size needs to be increased and all entries need to be re-hashed. Collision probability can be reduced by larger tables, which however increases the overhead [1]. Another important overhead aspect is that hash tables also need to store the key with the value in each table entry in order to find the correct key in case of collisions. There is no simple way to group multiple entries or reduce entry sizes without losing important information. Overall hash tables are an excellent data structure but we want to minimize the number of meta-data entries.

Databases and table-based storages in general (both disk based or in-memory based) offer column-indices to be created as needed in order to speed up queries. The implementations include many variants of trees mostly based on B- and T-trees as index structures [8]. Balanced trees have lookup times in $\mathcal{O}(log\ n)$ compared to $\mathcal{O}(1)$ for hash tables and can consume considerable memory for pointers and inner nodes. The advantage of ordered tree-based indices is the possibility to scan keys in sequential order (for range queries) and the use of partially filled blocks for fast insertions and deletions. The DXRAM core does not provide key scanning or a table-based data model. However, fast insertions and deletions are necessary for a flexible meta-data management. The inferior lookup time complexity can be compensated through an intelligent client-side caching (see Sect. 3.3).

As mentioned before storing one mapping entry for each chunk is too expensive. If for example one super peer manages 10 peers, each storing one billion chunks, the super peer would have to manage 10 billion mapping entries. Every entry consists of at least a NID (2 bytes) and if necessary a CID (8 bytes), resulting in an overall memory consumption of 20 to 100 GB. All typical data structures like lists, hash tables and indices require additional memory for empty entries, pointers, overhead for the collision resolution, etc.

The sequential CID generation of DXRAM is the foundation for a more compact representation. Instead of storing one entry for each CID, we store one range containing the start and end CID and the NID where all chunks of the

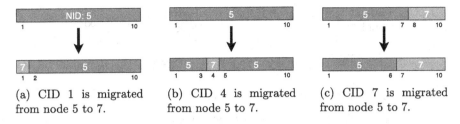

(a) CID 1 is migrated from node 5 to 7.

(b) CID 4 is migrated from node 5 to 7.

(c) CID 7 is migrated from node 5 to 7.

Fig. 1. Effect of chunk migration on CID-ranges.

range reside. In the best case we have to store only one CID range for each node. In the previous example, if there is only one range per node, the memory consumption is reduced by almost 99.99 % to 20 to 100 Byte.

As mentioned before we must support data migrations for load balancing reasons. If a chunk is migrated we have to consider two main scenarios shown in Fig. 1. In both cases the range must be split, resulting in two ranges in (a) and three ranges in (b). In addition a third scenario (c) is shown where two ranges exist and a chunk moves from one range to the another one because of a migration.

We do not expect billions of migrations as there will be only a limited number of hotspots. Thus range splits are rather seldom and are not a space efficiency problem at all. If even 10 million chunks (1 % out of one billion) would be migrated this would result in around 200 million ranges overall, resulting in a memory consumption of 400 to 2000 MB, which is still a space-overhead reduction by over 90 % compared to 20 to 100 GB when using hash tables.

3.1   CID-Tree

Hash- and index-based mappings store one entry for each key, whereas we want to store CID ranges consisting of two keys (the start and end of the range). Such key-key-value (kkv) tuples are rarely researched in the context of in-memory systems and traditional data-structures are not optimized for kkv tuples. We have designed a tree-based data structure for efficiently managing CID ranges, which includes creating, deleting and searching keys in CID ranges.

The CID-Tree approach is based upon a modified B-tree to efficiently manage CID ranges. The start and end LIDs of the ranges are stored inside the inner nodes and the NIDs are the leaves. Figure 2 shows an example of a CID-Tree. A B-tree is divided into ranges in principle. For example, if the tree contains only two entries, there exist three ranges. The first range is between 1 and the first entry, the second range is between the first and second entry and the last range is between the second entry and the maximal value. For every range the tree stores a pointer to a leaf containing the NID of the range.

The migration, deletion and search are executed using (potentially multiple) normal B-tree operations for insert, delete and search and have a complexity of $\mathcal{O}(log\ n)$. During a migration as well as during a deletion it is possible that a key

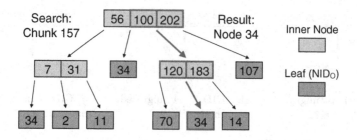

Fig. 2. Searching CID 157 in a CID-Tree returns NID 34

need to be modified, inserted or merged with another key (if a range changes the host node, is split or two ranges need to be merged). A search always requires to follow one path from the root to one leaf of the tree.

The memory consumption of a single entry in the CID-Tree can not be easily calculated, because multiple nodes and pointers have to be considered. The formula below gives a basic approximation:

$$\text{EntrySize} = \frac{2 * \text{Order} * (\Delta\text{Key} + (\Delta\text{Leaf} \lor \Delta\text{ChildRef}))}{\text{EntryCount}}$$

$$\Delta\text{Key} = 6 \text{ byte}, \Delta\text{Leaf} = 2 \text{ byte}, \Delta\text{ChildRef} = 4 \text{ byte}$$

The entry count of a node is at least the order and two times the order maximum, resulting in 8–20 byte memory consumption for a single entry.

3.2   Backup Nodes Integration

As mentioned before, DXRAM uses by default three backup nodes for every chunk to recover failed nodes. In addition to the actual owner of a chunk (NID_O) the three backup nodes have to be stored as well. Like before we do not store backup nodes for each chunk, but only once for each CID range.

To store the backup nodes together with the NID_O we modify the entry size of the CID-Tree. Instead of a short value (2 byte) for the NID we store a long value (8 byte). This increases the size of an entry by additional 6 byte. In the lowest 2 byte of the long value the NID_O for the range is stored. In the other 6 byte the NIDs of the three backup nodes are stored (NID_{B3}, NID_{B2}, NID_{B1}, NID_O). Backups are processed in their order during fault-free execution and a simple shifting to the right repairs the meta data during recovery.

In order to allow a parallel and fast recovery the chunks of a node have to be distributed across many backup nodes [11]. We achieve this by limiting the size of one CID range entry, e.g. 2 million chunks in one CID range.

In the previously used example with 10 billion mapping entries, the integration of the backup nodes results in 5,000 CID ranges (instead of only one) per node, consuming around 32 to 64 KB of memory which is still very space efficient.

3.3 Client-Side Caching

The presented CID-Tree is not only used on super peers, but can also be used without modification on the peers for caching. Super peers answer a node lookup request not only with a single NID, but with the corresponding range (with the NID and the start and end LID), in which the requested CID is located. The requesting peers cache CID ranges in a local CID-Tree and requests to a super peers are only sent in case of a cache miss. Due to space limitations we cannot discuss cache eviction strategies here.

4 Evaluation

In this section we present and discuss the evaluations of the proposed data structures and the client-side caching. We also compare the overall DXRAM performance with MongoDB and Cassandra using the social network benchmark BG.

The data structure evaluation is performed on a single super peer (Intel® Core™ i5-2400 CPU, 4 cores, 3.1 GHz, 32 GB RAM) using Ubuntu 11.04 and the OpenJDK Java Runtime Environment (version 7). The other evaluations are performed on a private cluster using nodes connected by a Gigabit Ethernet network. Each node is equipped with an Intel® Xeon® CPU E3-1220 V2, 4 cores, 3.1 GHz, 16 GB RAM (DDR3) and a 1 TB local disk (HUA722010CLA330). All nodes are running Debian 7.6 and the OpenJDK Java Runtime Environment (version 7). Java is required by the BG Benchmark, DXRAM and Cassandra.

4.1 CID-Tree

The first evaluation compares the proposed CID-Tree with the Java built-in hash table and a cuckoo hash table using primitive data types on a single node.

Every data structure is filled with 1 million, 10 million, 100 million and 1 billion meta-data entries and afterwards 1 %, 5 % and 10 % of the entries are randomly migrated. Afterwards, we measured the memory size of the data structures and the time per migration and per get operation. The throughput of operations is only measured on the localhost to get a better insight of the raw performance of the data structures. The evaluations are repeated at least 10 times with only minimal variation of the results.

Figure 3 shows the results of these measurements. The migration times are very fast for both hash table solutions. The CID-Tree is noticeably slower for 1 million objects but its performance improves for larger object sets, where it is only around 3 to 5 times slower than the hash tables.

The get operations are fast when using Java hash table. The CID-Tree is here slower by a factor of 2. The cuckoo hash table has fast access times for 1 million entries, but gets slower when more entries have to be stored. Although the proposed CID structure has access times in $\mathcal{O}(log\ n)$ compared to $\mathcal{O}(1)$ for the hash tables, the evaluation shows that the access times are only slowly growing and are nearly constant for a very large number of entries.

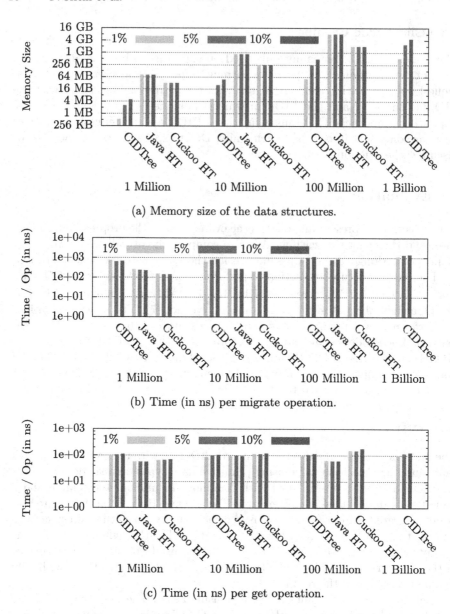

(a) Memory size of the data structures.

(b) Time (in ns) per migrate operation.

(c) Time (in ns) per get operation.

Fig. 3. Comparison of the CID-Tree, the Java hash table and a cuckoo hash table.

It can be observed that the memory size of the CID-Tree is very low. The size of the cuckoo hash table is around 50 times greater and the Java hash table size is even around 150 times greater. The experiment with one billion entries could not be performed for the hash tables because the physical node run out of memory.

The evaluation results show that for managing large-scale object sets the proposed CID-Tree is the best approach. We trade a small amount of speed for a much better space efficiency but still all operations of CID-Trees are much faster than the network request roundtrip times of clients adding only $1\,\mu s$ or less when managing one billion entries.

4.2   Client-Side Caching

In this evaluation DXRAM is set up on three cluster nodes (configuration see above). The first node acts as super peer using a CID-Tree for the meta-data management. The second node is a storage peer managing chunks and requesting migrations of CID ranges (length 1 to 100 CIDs). It is likely that in many cases not single small chunks are migrated but a set of chunks, e.g. the profile of a famous person in a social network together with its friend list, photos, comments etc. (although not all these chunks will be stored within one CID range at least some of them will be, e.g. the friendship list). For the experiments we migrated 1 %, 5 % and 10 % of the chunks on the storage node. The third node emulates a user requesting all CIDs of the chunks created before. This node also runs the client-side cache (if enabled) based on the CID-Tree as well.

The evaluation (with multiple evaluation runs) which can be seen in Fig. 4 shows that the client-side caching works very well and can greatly reduce the access times by up to 98 %.

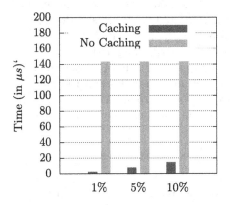
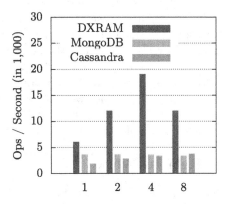

Fig. 4. Time per operation with enabled and disabled client-side caching.

Fig. 5. BG-Benchmark evaluation of DXRAM, MongoDB and Cassandra.

4.3   BG Benchmark

BG is an open-source benchmark to evaluate the performance of data storages for interactive social media networks [3]. It supports a variety of state-of-the-art storage systems like for example MongoDB [13] and Cassandra [7]. BG emulates interactive social networking actions known from Facebook, Twitter and YouTube (more details see [3]).

In the following experiment we compared DXRAM with MongoDB (2.6.4) and Cassandra (3.0.0 snapshot) using BG. We developed a BG client for DXRAM and for MongoDB and Cassandra we used the ones provided with BG. BG was configured to create 10,000 profiles, each with 100 friends and resources resulting in a graph of over 1 million nodes and 2 million edges. The requests are performed with 4 BG nodes executing up to 512 threads (each thread simulating one client). The number of used storage nodes range from 1 to 8 nodes for each system. In the given scenario DXRAM is started with one super peer and MongoDB using sharding, one config server and one query router.

Figure 5 shows the result of the evaluation. MongoDB performs around 3,500 actions per second in every test run limited by the query router, which is the bottleneck of MongoDB. DXRAM scales very well for 1, 2 and 4 storage nodes with results of 6,000, 12,000 and 19,000 actions per second. The performance with 8 storage nodes is lower because the clients could not create enough workload to fully load the storage nodes. For Cassandra we used the default partitioner *Murmur3Partitioner* which distributes rows of tables across storage nodes using consistent hashing for the primary key of a table row. In principle this allows a good load balancing, however for BG we expect a lot of cross-node traffic as this does not support locality of data. For example the friend list entries of a profile might be scattered over several nodes and thus when requesting all friends of a user will cause a lot of network traffic, which explains the lower performance for BG. Nevertheless, we can still see the scalability of Cassandra as throughput increases from 1,800 actions per second to 3,700 when the number of storage nodes is increased as well as the number of clients performing actions.

We also tested DXRAM with up to 500,000 profiles using 4 storage nodes. The resulting graph contains up to more than 50 million nodes and 100 million edges. With 8 BG nodes we achieved a throughput of around 17,000 to 22,000 operations per second. Due to problems with BG we could not perform these tests with MongoDB and Cassandra.

5   Related Work

Meta-data management has been and will be an important research area where much results have been published somehow related to our work. Because of space constraints we can only discuss the most relevant work.

RAMCloud is a distributed in-memory system organizing data in tables [12]. Both memory and backup disks use the same log-structured design. The mapping of 64 bit global IDs to nodes is implemented by a hash table maintained by a central coordinator. The central coordinator is not necessarily a single node, but normally 3 to 7 servers using a consensus protocol [14]. Overall, we are inspired by many ideas from RAMCloud but we aim at supporting many small objects (key-value tuples) whereas RAMCloud does focus on a table-based data model for larger data items.

Trinity Graph Engine is a distributed in-memory graph-database, designed to support algorithms executing on graphs with billions of nodes [15]. It uses a key-value data model implemented in C# on top of a memory cloud. Node lookups use a hash function to first find a memory partition (trunk). The node storing a trunk is found through a globally shared address table. Finally, on this node another hash function is used to get the offset and size of the key-value pair inside the trunk. Because Trinity is not available as open source we could not compare it with our approaches. However, from the evaluations we made, we believe that hashing is less space-efficient than our approach, which allow us to manage even larger graphs in the future.

FaRM utilizes the memory of machines in a cluster as shared address space to implement a distributed computing platform using RDMA for network communication [4]. For low latency network access on remote nodes the operating systems and the NIC device drivers are modified. A hopscotch hashing approach combined with chaining is used for meta-data management allowing a lookup in a small number of RDMA reads. On the contrary DXRAM uses a B-tree structure with only a single network request (instead of multiple RDMA reads) and allows the caching of lookup responses. In Addition the objects stored in FaRM are slightly larger (64 Byte to multiple MB) than in DXRAM.

MongoDB is a NoSQL database and structures its data in documents similar to JSON objects [13]. Documents contain various fields including primitive data types, other documents and array of documents. MongoDB caches as much data as possible in memory and swaps data to disk, if another process needs memory.

Cassandra is a NoSQL database for managing very large amounts of structured data spread out across many commodity servers, while providing highly available service with no single point of failure [7]. Cassandra nodes use a DHT for meta-data management and virtual nodes to evenly distribute keys onto available peers. Obviously, Cassandra as well as MongoDB and other NoSQL databases are designed to run on disks or SSDs providing tables, indices and a SQL-like query language whereas DXRAM is designed to keep all data always in RAM with a focus on very small objects.

BlobSeer is a storage system for large unstructured binary data (blobs) up to 1 TB [9]. The blobs are split into blocks of fixed size (data striping) and distributed among storage providers. Every block is referenced as a range (offset, size) of the blob and the corresponding meta data is managed in a distributed segment tree. On every level of the segment tree the range of the father is halved to the left and right son. In contrast, DXRAM targets many very small objects and CID-ranges contain the meta data of potentially many objects whereas a range in BlobSeer contains a single Block of a large object. The B-tree in DXRAM allows very flexible range sizes contrary to the rigid range size in a segment tree. Finally, tree structures are commonly used in *distributed file systems* for storing locations of file blocks or file block ranges. In contrast DXRAM merges IDs of multiple different objects (not blocks of a single) to ranges.

6   Conclusions

Large-scale interactive applications and online graph analytics often need to process billions of small data objects in short time, which makes fast networks and in-memory storage mandatory. A fast and space-efficient meta-data management is very important for such systems. In this paper we have proposed a range-based meta-data management combined with a super-peer overlay. Each super peer manages tree-based data structures mapping global chunk IDs to peers based on ID ranges. The evaluation shows that the proposed approach has a much better space efficiency than hash tables while at the same time being not much slower ($1\,\mu s$ or less for one billion entries). The overall system performance shows a very good throughput for a social network benchmark, compared to state of the art NoSQL databases. We plan to do more evaluations (including graph algorithms) with more nodes and more data.

References

1. Askitis, N.: Fast and compact hash tables for integer keys. In: Proceedings of the Thirty-Second Australasian Conference on Computer Science, ACSC 2009, Darlinghurst, Australia, vol. 91 (2009)
2. Atikoglu, B., et al.: Workload analysis of a large-scale key-value store. In: Proceedings of the 12th ACM SIGMETRICS/PERFORMANCE Joint International Conference on Measurement and Modeling of Computer Systems, SIGMETRICS 2012, New York, NY, USA (2012)
3. Barahmand, S., Ghandeharizadeh, S.: Bg: a benchmark to evaluate interactive social networking actions. In: CIDR. Citeseer (2013)
4. Dragojević, A., Narayanan, D., Castro, M., Hodson, O.: Farm: fast remote memory. In: 11th USENIX Symposium on Networked Systems Design and Implementation (NSDI 2014), pp. 401–414. USENIX Association, Seattle, April 2014
5. Klein, F., Beineke, K., Schöttner, M.: Memory management for billions of small objects in a distributed in-memory storage. In: IEEE Cluster 2014, September 2014
6. Klein, F., Schöttner, M.: Dxram: a persistent in-memory storage for billions of small objects. In: International Conference on Parallel and Distributed Computing, Applications and Technologies (PDCAT 2013), pp. 103–110, December 2013
7. Lakshman, A., Malik, P.: Cassandra: a decentralized structured storage system. SIGOPS Oper. Syst. Rev. **44**(2), 35–40 (2010)
8. Lu, H., Ng, Y.Y., Tian, Z.: T-tree or b-tree: main memory database index structure revisited. In: 11th Australasian Proceedings of Database Conference, ADC 2000, pp. 65–73 (2000)
9. Nicolae, B., Antoniu, G., Bougé, L.: Enabling high data throughput in desktop grids through decentralized data and metadata management: the blobseer approach. In: Sips, H., Epema, D., Lin, H.-X. (eds.) Euro-Par 2009. LNCS, vol. 5704, pp. 404–416. Springer, Heidelberg (2009)
10. Nishtala, R., et al.: Scaling memcache at facebook. In: Proceedings of the 10th USENIX Symposium on Networked Systems Design and Implementation (NSDI 2013), Lombard, Illinois (2013)
11. Ongaro, D., et al.: Fast crash recovery in ramcloud. In: Proceedings of the Twenty-Third ACM Symposium on Operating Systems Principles, SOSP 2011, New York, NY, USA (2011)

12. Ousterhout, J., et al.: The case for ramclouds: scalable high-performance storage entirely in dram. SIGOPS Oper. Syst. Rev. **43**(4), 92–105 (2010)
13. Plugge, E., Hawkins, T., Membrey, P.: The Definitive Guide to MongoDB: The NoSQL Database for Cloud and Desktop Computing, 1st edn. Apress, Berkely (2010)
14. Rumble, S.M.: Memory and Object Management in RAMCloud. Ph.D. thesis, Stanford University (2014)
15. Shao, B., Wang, H., Li, Y.: Trinity: a distributed graph engine on a memory cloud. In: Proceedings of the 2013 ACM SIGMOD International Conference on Management of Data, SIGMOD 2013, New York, NY, USA (2013)
16. Stoica, I., Morris, R., Karger, D., Kaashoek, M.F., Balakrishnan, H.: Chord: a scalable peer-to-peer lookup service for internet applications. In: Proceedings of the 2001 Conference on Applications, Technologies, Architectures, and Protocols for Computer Communications, SIGCOMM 2001, pp. 149–160. ACM, New York (2001)

Network-Based Data Processing Architecture for Reliable and High-Performance Distributed Storage System

Hiroki Ohtsuji[1,2,3(✉)] and Osamu Tatebe[1,2]

[1] University of Tsukuba, Tsukuba, Ibaraki 305-8573, Japan
ohtsuji@hpcs.cs.tsukuba.ac.jp
[2] JST, CREST, Kawaguchi, Japan
[3] JSPS Research Fellow, Chiyoda, Japan

Abstract. In the era of post peta scale computing, high-performance and reliable storage systems have become much more important. Close cooperation between network and storage is an emerging issue. This paper proposes a network-based data processing architecture to build reliable and high-performance distributed storage system using future programmable network devices. Distributed storage systems use replication or erasure coding for ensuring reliability. However, they require additional data transfer and computing resources. Satisfying both reliability and performance is an important issue for storage systems. Recent studies related to Software Defined Networking (SDN) imply that programmable network switch will become more functional. Currently, SDN intends to provide a flexible routing mechanism. Network switches are starting to have intelligent mechanisms and are expected to have a capability for data processing. In our proposed architecture, storage controller functionality is offloaded to a programmable network switch to eliminate additional data transfer. We conducted experiments to show an advantage of the proposed network-based data processing mechanisms for erasure coding and show an optimized design for distributed storage systems. With the proposed method, the performance gain of a reliable data storage system is 44 % compared with a client compute case.

1 Introduction

1.1 Background

Next generation distributed storage systems have to meet the demands of exascale computing systems. In particular, high-performance and reliable data handling mechanisms are critical problems. In order to add reliability to network storage systems, replication [1] and erasure coding are commonly used. However, when a writer node stores data to a storage system, amount of traffic from the writer node increases by the additional data. This additional data degrades the performance because of the bandwidth limitation of a client node. Figure 1 describes how the parity blocks increase the traffic and cause the performance degradation. In this case, a parity block is added to striped blocks.

© Springer International Publishing Switzerland 2015
S. Hunold et al. (Eds.): Euro-Par 2015 Workshops, LNCS 9523, pp. 16–26, 2015.
DOI: 10.1007/978-3-319-27308-2_2

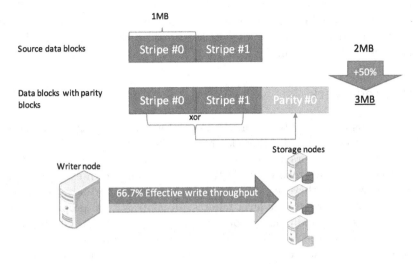

Fig. 1. Parity blocks increase traffic and degrade write throughput.

It causes 50 % traffic increase and 33 % degradation of write throughput. In order to avoid this performance degradation, we need additional mechanisms to eliminate performance bottlenecks.

The target of this paper is optimization of network storage systems which use erasure coding. The optimization utilizes the functions of a programmable network switch.

Existing systems provide reliability through use of the computational power of storage or client nodes. However, as typified by Software Defined Network-ing (SDN), network hardware has started to shift toward programmable devices. This movement suggests the possibility of implementing a data processing mech-anism on the storage network. This study assumes future network devices with programmable functions and proposes a method for utilizing them.

1.2 Our Contribution

This study proposes an architecture design for utilizing data processing mecha-nism on the network in order to improve the performance of reliable distributed storage systems. The architecture off-loads parity generation processes to a net-work switch to eliminate the overhead of reliable storage systems. Our proposal includes a design of network storage system and a methodology for utilizing programmable network switches.

The proposed method achieves zero-overhead with erasure-codes generation whereas existing systems degrade performance because of additional data trans-fer and computing. In preparation for next-generation programmable network devices, this paper shows an efficient way for using them.

Write performance reaches to 5,548 MB/s with redundant data, which is almost same as the network throughput. Performance gain is 14 % to 44 %.

Although we added additional data blocks for reliability, performance does not change. This means that our proposed method realizes the "zero-overhead" reliable network storage system.

2 Related Work

The main focus of our study is a methodology for utilizing programmable network switches to eliminate bottlenecks from reliable network storage systems.

There are existing storage/file systems which use replication and erasure coding in order to improve reliability. RAID [2,3] is a well-known example of reliable storage systems. However, ordinary RAID systems cover only disk failures and cannot recover from node-level failures. In contrast, our proposal intends to provide node-level redundancy for network storage systems. GlusterFS [4], Gfarm [5], Ceph [6], and HDFS [7,8] are network storage/file systems and have a replication mechanism. However, as mentioned before, replication uses twice or more storage space and should be avoided with exa-scale systems. Ceph and HDFS also support Reed-Solomon [9] based erasure coding. HDFS supports erasure coding using the HDFS-RAID [10] module. The most important thing is that all of them does not support "on-the-fly" replication/encoding because of performance issues. Our proposed method generates parity block (erasure code) on an "on-the-fly" basis, hence they are different from our work.

In order to build a zero-overhead reliable storage system, we propose a new architecture which utilizes programmable abilities of a network switch. There are several studies related to this issue that are not only limited to the optimization of storage systems. [11] is a study to optimize MPI collective operations using network switches equipped with FPGA, which utilized NetFPGA [12] and Open-Flow switches and improved the performance of MPI operations. The optimization target is not the same as our work; however, the idea of improving network communication performance using specialized hardware functions is common.

From the perspective of existing network devices, Mellanox provides the function [13] for optimizing MPI communication operations. The target of this hardware is to optimize MPI operations; however, this is only an example of an HPC communication layer accelerated by hardware. Hardware functions that optimize the network of storage systems are in extension of this type of idea. This is the reason we expect that having hardware functions to optimize erasure codes in network storage systems.

In addition, our prototype implementation uses Remote Direct Memory Access (RDMA) to minimize the overhead of network communication by eliminating unnecessary memory copies. Advantages of applying RDMA communication to network storage systems are shown in existing studies. NFS over RDMA [14] is an example of adding RDMA support to NFS [15]. [16] shows performance gain by adding RDMA support to PVFS [17].

3   System Design

3.1   Network-Based Data Processing Architecture

Network-based data processing architecture moves parity generation processes from storage servers to programmable switches. This paper describes a design for data processing architecture for parity generation processes and shows a prototype implementation.

Our target is not a dedicated hardware based large-scale block storage device but a system which consists of multiple storage servers. Conventional network storage systems use computing resources of servers to provide mechanisms for reliability. In that type of system, network only transfers the data between storage servers.

As discussed in Sect. 1.1, bottlenecks come from the reliability issues are owing to the increased amount of data and the limitation of network bandwidth. Utilizing programmable abilities of network switches is a good solution to solve these problems because network switches have enough bandwidth to spread the increased data. At this time, we do not have a network switch (in production and not an FPGA based devices) that has programmable function to implement a mechanism for erasure coding. However, we can propose a method for utilizing the ability of future network switches for reliable storage systems and provide evaluation results with a proof of concept system. The proof of concept system consists of computing nodes with multiple network devices. Following sections describe the proof of concept system of the network-based data processing architecture and the method for reliable storage systems.

3.2   Overview of the System

This study targets network storage systems with parity (erasure coding) data. The aim of this paper is to propose a method to utilize network data processing functions and to show evaluation results of the proof of concept system.

Figure 2 describes the architecture of the target system. A writer node sends the data blocks (Stripes #0 and Stripes #1) to a network switch. This switch has programmable functions and calculates a parity block from Stripe #0 and Stripe #1. The switch sends stripe and parity blocks to storage nodes.

3.3   Data Layout

Figure 3 describes the data layout of the target system. In this figure, the original data blocks are #0 to #5. Two storage nodes store those data blocks and another stores the exclusive OR (XOR) value (parity) of each original data block.

3.4   Switch Architeture

Figure 4 shows how network-based data processing architecture works. The writer node sends data blocks to the switch, which then splits data blocks into striped blocks and calculates their XOR value. Each parity block is sent to storage nodes for striped blocks and a parity node stores the parity blocks.

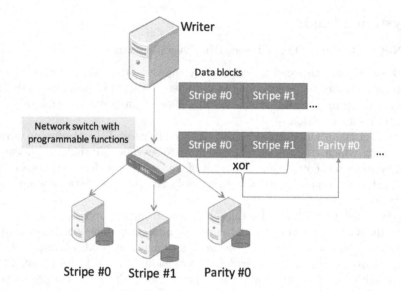

Fig. 2. Target architecture of network storage systems. Our proposal is a method for utilizing a programmable network switch for erasure-coded network storage systems. A writer node sends source data blocks to a programmable switch. The switch generates parity blocks and sends them to storage nodes.

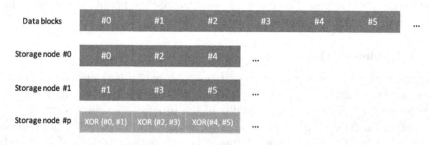

Fig. 3. Data layout of striped blocks and parity block(s). Data blocks are split into striped blocks. Parity blocks are xor value of striped blocks. We can recover missing data blocks by calculating xor value of another block.

3.5   Fallback Mode

Current our experiment environment is only for prototype purpose. However, when we apply the method to a large-scale environment, switch failures become a major trouble.

The system should have a fallback mode in preparation for switch failures. Figure 5 describes the fallback mode of a storage system. If the switch loses programmable functions (left in the figure), the writer node can split the data blocks into striped blocks and calculate the parity blocks. Next, the writer node sends all blocks to storage nodes. In the case of complete network failure (right

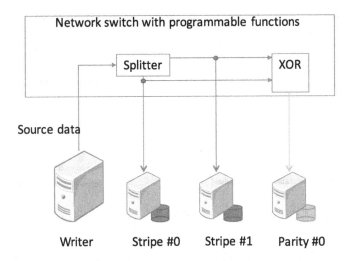

Fig. 4. Architecture of a programmable network switch. A writer sends source data blocks. A switch has a splitter and an XOR calculation module. The splitter splits the source data blocks into striped blocks. The XOR calculation module calculates the XOR value of the striped blocks. Then, the switch sends all data blocks to storage servers.

in the figure), another network mechanism is required. If there is an available network path, the writer can use it to apply the fallback mode.

3.6 Prototype Implementation Overview

Currently, we do not have actual hardware for the programmable network switch; therefore we implemented it with a computer and multiple network cards. Figure 6 describes the connection of each component.

The node has multiple network cards (in this figure, network cards are Infini-Band HCAs). Because of the limitation of the number of PCI Express lanes, we added three InfiniBand HCAs to the node. Figure 7 describes the data transfer mechanism and parity generation process. We utilized the RDMA function of the InfiniBand HCAs to optimize the data transfer processes and save memory space. The data structure and data processing mechanism are described in the next subsection.

3.7 Optimized Data Transfer and Processing with RDMA

Figure 7 describes the zero-copy data structure of the data processing mechanism. Each node has ring buffer(s) to transfer and process the data blocks. In order to use the RDMA data transfer functions, we have to register the memory to the hardware in advance to the actual transfer process. If we use different buffer blocks, each time RDMA transfer occurred, we would have to register it. However, this

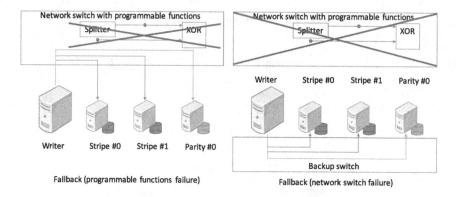

Fig. 5. Two cases of failure of a network switch.

requires considerable time and causes performance degradation [18]. Therefore, we use ring buffer(s) for RDMA communication. Once the ring buffer is registered, we do not require time for memory registration processes. In Fig. 7 the writer nodes send data blocks to the switch. The switch splits the data into two striped blocks and stores them to ring buffers. Then, the switch sends the striped blocks to storage nodes and calculates the XOR value of these two blocks. Finally, the XOR value is sent to the storage node (p).

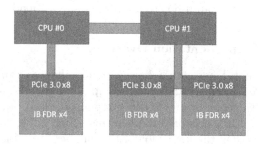

Fig. 6. Components of computer with multiple network devices

4   Evaluation

4.1   Evaluation Target and Conditions

Our proposed method intends to optimize the performance of data write to reliable storage systems.

We conducted an evaluation on the cluster nodes connected with InfiniBand FDR 4x. To implement network-based data processing architecture, we used a node equipped with multiple InfiniBand HCAs. In this evaluation, we installed

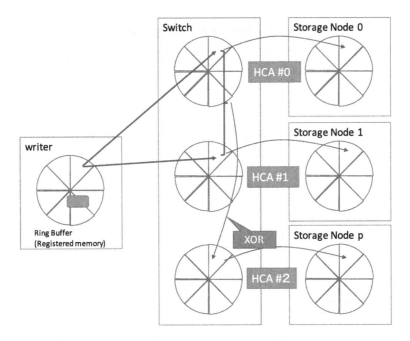

Fig. 7. RDMA data transfer and parity generation. A writer send source data blocks to a programmable switch. The switch splits source data blocks into striped blocks (not described in the figure) and calculates parity blocks. Afterward, the switch sends them to storage nodes using different InfiniBand HCAs. All data blocks are stored in ring buffers and there is no memory copy.

up to three InfiniBand HCAs to a computing node. First, we evaluated the throughput of the multiple InfiniBand HCAs to confirm that the test environment did not have any performance bottlenecks resulting from hardware specifications. Figure 8 shows the results of the total bidirectional bandwidth evaluation. We used perftest tools (ib_write_bw) to evaluate network performance. As can be seen from the graph, the results are in proportion to the number of installed HCAs. We do not see any performance degradation caused by limitation of the PCI Express bus or other interconnect issues.

In addition, we conducted the evaluation without writing to the actual disk because of the limitation of existing storage hardware and the purpose of the evaluation. The aim of the proposed method is optimization of the data transfer mechanism.

All results are average of three measurements.

4.2   Evaluation Results

Figure 9 shows the results of the sequential write throughput evaluation. The X-axis corresponds to stripe size and the Y-axis corresponds to the write throughput from a client node. The blue graph is the result of optimization (using data

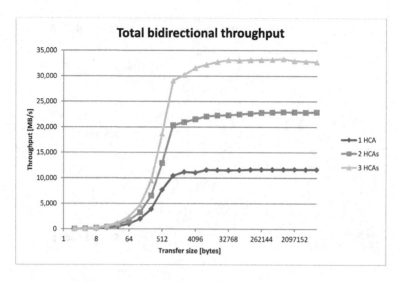

Fig. 8. Bidirectional network (InfiniBand FDR 4x) throughput evaluation with ib_write_bw (perftest tools).

processing architecture of a network switch) and the red graph is the result of naive implementation (the client sends both striped and parity blocks). Performance gain by the optimization was 14 % (8 KB stripe case) to 44 % (64 KB stripe case). With the best case of the optimized implementation, the throughput almost reaches network performance. This means that the proposed method successfully eliminated the bottleneck of the reliable data write. The performance of the fallback mode Sect. 3.5 will be the same as the results of the naive method, provided that the system has the same back up network.

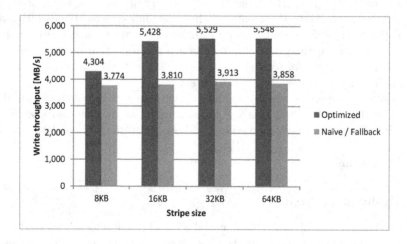

Fig. 9. Write throughput comparison between optimized and naive method

The evaluation results show that the proposed method improves the performance of reliable data write by eliminating the bottleneck. In this evaluation, we implemented the data processing architecture using the node equipped with multiple network devices. However, the method consists of data processing (XOR) pipelines and can be implemented as hardware. This means that immediately after obtaining a network switch with programmable functions, we can implement the proposed method and improve the performance of reliable network storage systems.

5   Conclusion and Future Work

We proposed a methodology for utilizing programmable network switches to eliminate the overhead of reliable network storage systems. Root cause of the performance degradation of reliable network storage system was the increased amount of traffic by additional parity data blocks. Our proposed design moves the parity generation processes to a programmable network switch in order to avoid congestion in a writer node's network. We implemented a prototype system using RDMA transfer operations and conducted evaluations.

The evaluation results showed that the performance gain by the proposed method was 14 % to 44 %.

Currently, we implemented the proposed method using a computer equipped with multiple network devices. However, the method can be implemented as a hardware and can be applied to future programmable network switches.

Applying the method to existing systems and adding support of random/stride write are important issues. In addition, a scalability issue is an important future work when we apply the method to huge systems because this study used a preliminary evaluation environment, which had a single network switch.

The target for the evaluation in this paper was the sequential write to storage systems; however, the results showed good performance in case of 16 KB to 64 KB stripe block size and thus we can expect good performance with real work loads.

Acknowledgemtent. This works is supported by JST CREST "System Software for Post Petascale Data Intensive Science", JST CREST "Extreme Big Data (EBD) Next Generation Big Data Infrastructure Technologies Towards Yottabyte/Year", and JSPS KAKENHI Grant-in-Aid for JSPS Fellows (261967).

References

1. Chervenak, A.L., Foster, I.T., Kesselman, C., Salisbury, C., Tuecke, S.: The data grid: towards an architecture for the distributed management and analysis of large scientific datasets. J. Netw. Comput. Appl. **23**, 187–200 (1999)
2. Patterson, D.A., Gibson, G., Katz, R.H.: A case for redundant arrays of inexpensive disks (RAID). SIGMOD Rec. **17**, 109–116 (1988)
3. Chen, P.M., Lee, E.K., Gibson, G.A., Katz, R.H., Patterson, D.A.: RAID: high-performance, reliable secondary storage. ACM Comput. Surv. **26**, 145–185 (1994)

4. RedHat: Gluster FS. http://www.gluster.org/
5. Tatebe, O., Hiraga, K., Soda, N.: New generation computing. Gfarm Grid File System **28**, 257–275 (2010). Ohmsha Ltd. and Springer
6. Weil, S.A., Brandt, S.A., Miller, E.L., Long, D.D.E., Maltzahn, C.: Ceph: a scalable, high-performance distributed file system. In: Proceedings of the 7th Symposium on Operating Systems Design and Implementation, OSDI 2006, pp. 307–320. USENIX Association, Berkeley (2006)
7. Hadoop. http://hadoop.apache.org/
8. Shvachko, K., Kuang, H., Radia, S., Chansler, R.: The hadoop distributed file system. In: Proceedings of the 2010 IEEE 26th Symposium on Mass Storage Systems and Technologies, MSST 2010, pp. 1–10. IEEE Computer Society, Washington, D.C. (2010)
9. Reed, I.S., Solomon, G.: Polynomial codes over certain finite fields. J. Soc. Ind. Appl. Math. **8**, 300–304 (1960)
10. Fan, B., Tantisiriroj, W., Xiao, L., Gibson, G.: Diskreduce: RAID for data-intensive scalable computing. In: Proceedings of the 4th Annual Workshop on Petascale Data Storage, PDSW 2009, pp. 6–10. ACM, New York (2009)
11. Arap, O., Brown, G., Himebaugh, B., Swany, M.: Software defined multicasting for MPI collective operation offloading with the NetFPGA. In: Silva, F., Dutra, I., Santos Costa, V. (eds.) Euro-Par 2014 Parallel Processing. LNCS, vol. 8632, pp. 632–643. Springer, Heidelberg (2014)
12. Lockwood, J., McKeown, N., Watson, G., Gibb, G., Hartke, P., Naous, J., Raghuraman, R., Luo, J.: NetFPGA-an open platform for gigabit-rate network switching and routing. In: IEEE International Conference on Microelectronic Systems Education, MSE 2007, pp. 160–161 (2007)
13. Mellanox: CORE-Direct The Most Advanced Technology for MPI/SHMEM Collectives Offloads. http://www.mellanox.com/related-docs/whitepapers/TB_CORE-Direct.pdf
14. Callaghan, B., Lingutla-Raj, T., Chiu, A., Staubach, P., Asad, O.: NFS over RDMA. In: Proceedings of the ACM SIGCOMM Workshop on Network-I/O Convergence: Experience, Lessons, Implications, NICELI 2003, pp. 196–208. ACM, New York (2003)
15. Shepler, S., Callaghan, B., Robinson, D., Thurlow, R., Beame, C., Eisler, M., Noveck, D.: Network File System (NFS) version 4 Protocol. RFC 3530 (Proposed Standard) (2003)
16. Wu, J., Wyckoff, P., Panda, D.: PVFS over infiniband: design and performance evaluation (2003)
17. Carns, P.H., Iii, Ross, R.B., Thakur, R.: PVFS: a parallel file system for linux clusters. In: Proceedings of the 4th Annual Linux Showcase and Conference, ALS 2000 (2000)
18. Dalessandro, D., Wyckoff, P.: Memory management strategies for data serving with RDMA. In: 15th Annual IEEE Symposium on High-Performance Interconnects, HOTI 2007, pp. 135–142 (2007)

File-Less Approach to Large Scale Data Management

Bartosz Kryza[✉] and Jacek Kitowski

Department of Computer Science, Faculty of Computer Science,
Electronics and Telecommunications,
AGH University of Science and Technology, Krakow, Poland
bkryza@agh.edu.pl

Abstract. With the continuously increasing amount of online resources and data such use cases as discovery, maintenance and inter-operation become more and more complex. In particular, data management is becoming one of the main issues with respect to both scientific (large scale simulations or data mining applications) as well as consumer use cases (accessing photos or email attachments on mobile devices). We believe that one of the main bottlenecks blocking development of solutions providing truly seamless developer and user experience is the concept of file and filesystem. We present Filess, vision and architecture of file-less information systems where files are not necessary, neither in the application nor operating system layers.

Keywords: File systems · Data management · Hypergraphs

1 Introduction

Files and filesystems have been part of computer systems since the times of punch cards, stored in filing cabinets. Due to the technology used in the early days of computing such as magnetic tapes and until recently magnetic hard drives, files provided efficient way to store data in sequences of blocks which could be read from such media into memory. However, even then several researchers raised various problems related to such data storage [8,18,19]. In our opinion the main problems of modern IT systems related to files and filesystems are the following:

- *Data is unnaturally clustered into files* - once data item is stored in a file it becomes locked in this file, whether or not it is actually a part of a larger data structure or could be accessible on its own (consider for instance an image in a presentation, or a tag in an XML document),
- *Very large unnecessary data redundancy* - file based data management results in very large duplication of data due to the necessity of including data directly inside the file contents instead of referencing it (again images in presentations and rich text documents, attachments in emails, etc.) [7,10]. Existing files and filesystems do not provide means for uniform referencing of other files on a global scale, a feature which is the basis of WWW in the form of hyper links,

© Springer International Publishing Switzerland 2015
S. Hunold et al. (Eds.): Euro-Par 2015 Workshops, LNCS 9523, pp. 27–38, 2015.
DOI: 10.1007/978-3-319-27308-2_3

- *Inflexible hierarchical namespaces* - although it was convenient to store files in tree based directory structures when users had hundreds of files, with tens or hundreds of thousands of files it is impossible to memorize where a given file could be found without global filesystem indexing tools such as Spotlight, Tracker or Search Charm, which however only match queries to files names or using string based search over textual documents contents. No semantic search can be achieved based on relations between elements contained in these files (for instance *Find all images included in this paper*),
- *Barrier for the operating system* - it is impossible to address a specific piece of data inside the file from the level of the operating system (for instance for the use from the command line), thus it is in general impossible to get metadata about an image or music file, an application or specific library has to be executed to extract it, which are specific for each file format,
- *Lack of versioning support* - versioning of data can be achieved only by storing new files under different names (or in some cases storing text or binary differences between version, in application specific ways).

Let's consider for instance a single file such as a text document, presentation or even simple e-mail, which usually contains large amount of information which is lost in the structure of the file and thus not visible for querying by computers or even humans. For example, a corporate document prepared within some organization by several people contains several independent items (tables, charts, diagrams, paragraphs of text) of which each can have distinct author, different authorization policies and can be used in several other documents, while currently all this provenance information is lost once the document is saved as a file. The first problem is that for instance some figure from this document will be duplicated in every copy of this document and also in every new document that will use this figure. Additionally the information provided within the document itself about the picture brings very little information to the reader and no information at all that could be processed by computers. The main hypothesis of this research is that in order to make information actually reusable into knowledge in a world wide distributed setting, information must be stored in a way that it can be freely shared, reused and processed.

We propose to address this issue by introducing an architecture for information systems which departs from the concept of file and filesystem completely. We introduce a flexible and scalable data model based on hypergraphs, where data objects are stored in nodes and all relations are represented through hyperedges (edges which can connect more than 2 nodes). The hypergraph is provided to applications and operating systems via the same abstraction layer, which hides the actual storage system used as well as the fact of data distribution between devices. This paper refines the initial vision and requirements defined in our previous work [12,13].

2   Related Work

Most research in the area of making the existing directory based file systems more flexible can be classified into the area of semantic file systems [8], i.e.

file systems where files have attached meaning. This paper sketches a vision of file systems where files can be annotated in some way, and the basic file system operation such as copy or delete don't take directory paths as arguments but the *semantic* description of the files. The problem with these solutions is that still all the information is either fragmented or clustered into files, and the semantics deal only with meta data attached to these files in the form of some attributes. Nevertheless, these solutions are very important for our work as these approaches address important issues, mainly of how information can be found in file based systems. One of the formal attempts at file system implementation based on set theoretical basis is a file system using Formal Concept Analysis [5], which employs the FCA formal model of classification, neighborhood estimation and Boolean querying. A similar approach, although still bounded by the constraints of regular files, is the Logical File System project [16]. The basic role of this file system is to allow searching for files using first-order logic formulas instead of conventional directory paths. Unfortunately the use of first-order logic inference can seriously impair the scalability of the system in highly distributed settings. Until now, one major industrial attempt at abstracting the file concept from the operating system was the WinFS (Windows File System), which is a research effort from Microsoft [9]. Its basic assumption is to store all information about data in the system, including what would usually be referred to as file in a relational database. Furthermore, on the low level of storage device controllers, there is a trend to move from block device based interfaces (i.e. supporting file oriented systems) towards more flexible solutions such as OSB (Object-based Storage Device) [1], where instead of storing data in fixed size chunks the data can be stored in custom clusters of data along with relevant meta data. Unfortunately, most operating system level approaches still use these devices to store files, even if more efficiently [22,23]. However, with removal of the concept of the file all together, this approach will be a significant factor along with further adoption of SSD storage [17]. In fact Seagate has introduced recently an actual network attached object based device called Kinetic Storage [21], which provides a hardware back end for object based databases without any file system protocol access. Furthermore, certain technology enablers are emerging which provide insight into how the future storage could be improved on the low level. These include for instance various NVRAM (Non-Volatile RAM) solutions in particular memristor [24]. For prototype development an interesting solution is SanDisk's UlltraDIMM SSD [20], which is an SSD storage in the form of DIMM memory units, which can physically replace computers RAM memory. As we can see, there exists already several approaches and basic technologies which can support the proposed research concept. However, none of the existing solutions addresses abandoning the concept of a file as a whole, including all its repercussions on the storage, operating system, application and user interface level.

3   Filess Vision

Since its emergence, Cloud computing has become the leading paradigm in computing. The main reason for this was the fact that users found always-online resources to be much easier and efficient to use. Here resources include computing services, web pages and data. This is also one of the reasons why Cloud storage services such as Dropbox or Google Drive [4] are so popular, i.e. users are mobile and have multiple devices and need access to their content wherever they are. However, all these services have to be built on top of existing operating systems, since none of the mainstream OS has support for such functionality. In fact most operating systems do not have any artifacts for supporting such scenarios as over the network data access, process migration or check-pointing, which would enable developers to provide users with truly seamless experience when using multiple devices, such as working on a single file using multiple applications on different devices simultaneously. Imagine for instance creation of a simple conference presentation. It consists of some slides with text, images, equations sometimes embedded movies. Whenever an image needs to be updated, it has to be done in a separate application, saved into a file and imported into the selected slide in the presentation editor. If the user wants to preview the presentation on her tablet, it needs to be transferred manually there using yet another application. In our vision all these applications would operate on a global data space, managed entirely by the Filess middleware. Thus an image changed in a photo editing application, would make the new image version automatically updated in the presentation and whenever the contents of the presentation had been modified, they would be instantly visible on the presentation preview on users tablet. Then, when the presentation is ready, all the user needs to know in order to present it during the talk is to know the ID of the root node in the graph data model representing the presentation.

Overview of basic assumptions and requirements for this work, as discussed in our previous work [13], is presented below:

- There are no files - neither in the storage, middleware, operating system or user interface layers. Of course, at the prototype stage such approach would be very expensive in order to remove files completely from existing operating systems which use files even for communication with hardware devices,
- Documents, E-mails, images, movies, web pages and all other concepts, which are in practice today synonyms for files, in our architecture are only manifestations/renderings of interconnected groups of objects shown to the user in a context dependent way,
- Data and meta data exist at the same level - for instance there is no difference between the *Image* object and the object describing its author or authorization policy - we do not plan to introduce a meta data mechanism such as Dublin Core or even Semantic Web,
- Data and information replication should be controlled by the middleware - it is not necessary for users to copy and store the information for either security or efficiency reasons. As a consequence data redundancy can be optimized by the middleware,
- The proposed approach inherently supports the ubiquitous computing paradigm i.e., there is no *Load document, Save document* operations. It is possible to work on a laptop, then literally just shut it down and switch to pocket

PC or mobile phone and all the changes will be seamlessly available there, assuming of course network access is omnipresent,
- Security, especially authorization is intertwined within the global information space along with the information itself, i.e. security assertions (and any *annotations* for that matter) are first class objects in the infrastructure.

4   Filess Data Model

The basic assumption of the underlying data model is that all data are stored as objects in the nodes of a hypergraph structure. Hypergraphs provide flexible and scalable data model, where data objects are stored in nodes and all relations are represented through hyperedges (edges which can connect more than 2 nodes). The hypergraph is provided to applications and operating systems via the same abstraction layer, which hides the actual storage system used as well as the fact of data distribution between devices. Hypergraphs enable more natural modeling of n-m relationships and modeling of objects with multiple properties using smaller number of edges. It has been shown, that hypergraphs enable modeling various common data models such as relational model, XML, JSON or even Semantic Web standards such as OWL [11].

4.1   Hypergraphs

Hypergraphs have been studied and applied in various areas of computer science [2,3,6]. Basically a hypergraph is a tuple $H = (V, E)$ where $V = \{v_1, v_2, v_3, \ldots, v_n\}$ is the set of vertices and $E = \{e_1, e_2, e_3, \ldots, e_m\}$ is the set of hyperedges. The main difference and generalization over regular graphs is that a hypergraph edges, called hyperedges, can connect any number of vertices. In case of undirected hypergraphs hyperedges are simple subsets of the power set of V i.e. $E \subset 2^V$. In case of directed hypergraphs, edges are tuples composed

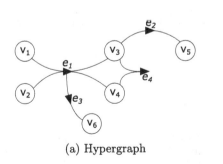

(a) Hypergraph

$$
\begin{array}{c|cccc}
 & e_1 & e_2 & e_3 & e_4 \\
\hline
v_1 & -1 & 0 & 0 & 0 \\
v_2 & -1 & 0 & 0 & 0 \\
v_3 & 1 & -1 & 0 & -1 \\
v_4 & 1 & 0 & 0 & -1 \\
v_5 & 0 & 1 & 0 & 0 \\
v_6 & 0 & 0 & 1 & 0 \\
e_1 & 0 & 0 & -1 & 0 \\
e_2 & 0 & 0 & 0 & 0 \\
e_3 & 0 & 0 & 0 & 0 \\
e_4 & 0 & 0 & 0 & 0 \\
\end{array}
$$

(b) Incidence matrix

Fig. 1. Example of directed hypergraph

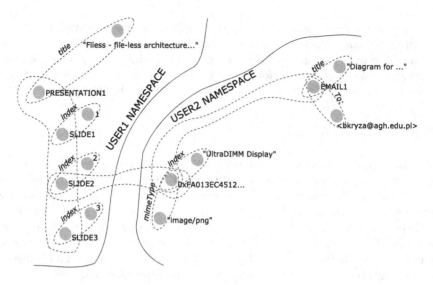

Fig. 2. Filess data model example

of *head* and *tail* sets: $E = (T_E, H_E)$. Hyperedges in general can connect both vertices and other edges. In our model, we assume that edges can appear only in the tail set of the edge (i.e. they can only be used to assign attributes through other edges to vertices). Thus, $T_E \subset V \cup E$ and $H_E \subset V$. We will also define the index sets for vertices and edges of graph H as $I_V(H)$ and $I_E(H)$ respectively. Let's consider an example graph in Fig. 1a and it's incidence matrix Fig. 1b. In the incidence matrix, edges are also as rows in order to model edges which have properties themselves (e.g. e3 on the graph). The example graph can be defined as:

$$H = (\{v_1, v_2, v_3, v_4, v_5, v_6\}, \{e_1 = (\{v_1, v_2\}, \{v_3, v_4\}),$$
$$e_2 = (\{v_3\}, \{v_5\}), e_3 = (\{e_1\}, \{v_6\}), e_4 = (\{v_3, v_4\}, \emptyset)\})$$

The usage of hypergraphs as the underlying formalism for the proposed data model allows us to reuse a large number of theorems and algorithms for their processing and validation.

4.2 Overview

First of all, all data in Filess is stored in data objects which are values assigned to the hypergraph vertices. Edges provide means for creating named relations and attributes between vertices. Leveraging the hypergraph property of allowing multi-vertice edges, it is natural to create n-m relations between data objects. An important aspect of the proposed data model is that of *namespaces*, which provide means for separating the global data object graph into subgraphs, which can intersect, i.e. each data object can belong to multiple namespaces simultaneously. Namespaces are an important part of the model as they provide means for optimizing search and discovery of data in the distributed graph as well as enable basic security. The most important namespace is the user's namespace which is created automatically for each new user after login, which uniquely identifies users objects and relations. Furthermore, namespaces can be assigned to edges in order to provide means for disambiguating their meaning, in a form typical for existing on the web URI. An important notion is that namespaces are flat, i.e. there is no namespace hierarchy as in the case of filesystem directory structure. Namespaces can be considered as system level attributes which can be assigned to any element of the global hypergraph. The uniqueness of namespaces is achieved by using GUID's to define them, while each namespace can have multiple user-friendly names (for instance in various languages). Once a new actor (user or service) joins the global Filess model, the initial node with the actor identity is created in a new namespace. From then on, the data objects can be connected with data objects of other actors through global relations. An overview of this approach is presented in Fig. 2. Each data object can store basic types of values or be a composite object which only contains connections to other data objects:

- *Number* - this is a union data type which allows to store any numeric data type while providing users with a simple API, which handles actual data type identification on the library level,
- *String* - this data object provides means for storing any text in UTF8,
- *List* - most graph data modeling frameworks do not provide lists or arrays, which can be very inefficient when modeling using graph nodes. This data object provides a simple means for compositing a set of data objects into an ordered structure,
- *Binary* - this data object provides means for storing large binary data such as videos, where the actual data is hashed and stored in a separate distributed key-value store,
- *Composite* - composite data objects are objects which do not need to store any actual value in their node, but provide links for other data objects. Any object containing a value can also be a Composite object, in which case the value represents a flattened representation of the objects structure. This situation can occur during decomposition of an object into a graph,
- *Stream* - buffer objects provide abstraction over I/O functionality of the operating system, these objects cannot be transferred between nodes, and are volatile, i.e. their state and value cannot be synchronized and no version information for these objects is maintained, only read or write operations are allowed. These objects enable complete removal of file and filesystem concepts from the applications code.

4.3   Object Composition and Decomposition

The most important operations on data objects from the point of view of the abstract model are composition and decomposition.

Composition. Data object composition provides natural way for creating structure in the data model using hyperedges connecting various data objects, thus enabling data discovery and graph traversal on the middleware level. Any set of data objects can be composed into other composite data objects using these operations without affecting or unnecessarily replicating the referenced data objects. Formally, composition transforms the initial hypergraph $H = (\{v_i\}_{i \in I_V(H)}, \{e_j\}_{j \in I_E(H)})$ as follows:

$$H' = (\{v_i\} \cup \{v'\}, \{e_j\} \cup \{(\{v'\}, \{v_k\}_{k \in I_V(H)})\})$$

i.e. it always extends the vertex set with one element (the new composite data object, v') and adds any number of necessary edges connecting vertices from the initial graph H.

Decomposition. Respectively, each data object can be decomposed into data objects which introduce structure into otherwise flat data object values. For instance consider data object containing a string value "John Smith". This object could be decomposed using 2 edges: (_:firstName, "John") and (_:lastName, "Smith"). However, since the object already existed in the previous form, some applications might rely on its flat representation thus it should remain in the Composite object after decomposition. In the future we are planning to enable adding stored procedures to the data objects which will enable automatic flattening of the composite data objects into various representations (e.g. text, XML, JSON, etc.). Furthermore, a mapping language will be defined for automatic translation of legacy data models such as relational into the hypergraph based data models, similar to our previous work presented in [14]. Formally, decomposition transforms the initial hypergraph $H = (\{v_i\}_{i \in I_V(H)}, \{e_j\}_{j \in I_E(H)})$ as follows:

$$H' = (\{v_i\} \cup \{v_l\}_{l \notin I_V(H)}, \{e_j\} \cup \{(\{v_s\}_{s \notin I_V(H)}, \{v_k\}_{k \in I_V(H)})\})$$

The difference is that composition adds a single vertex grouping a subgraph of objects while decomposition connects existing vertex to new vertices.

5   Representing Existing Data Structures and Formats in Filess

Typical data structures can be represented in hypergraphs in the following ways. Sets can be trivially created by creating a 1-N directed hyperedge. Lists can be created by linking consecutive nodes through a single hyperedge with identical ID such as "_:next", the actual property name is irrevelavant as long as the application wants to interpret a path as a list it is allowed to. However for performance reasons, a special type of node which allows to create order lists has been added. Maps are naturally represented by creating an hyperedge from a head node to any number of tail nodes.

JSON is a text format used to represent key-value pairs, where keys are always strings, and values can be any of the following types: Number, String, Boolean, Array, Object and null. These types map almost naturally into Filess data model. Boolean values can be modelled using Number data object type,

Array's by creating lists and `null` values can be achieved using hyperedges with empty head sets. Object values can be directly represented using Composite data objects. One issue is that of namespaces, as the edges created from the JSON key's must be attached to some namespace in order to disambiguate them from other edges. By default JSON has no concept of namespace, so it is up to the application to provide one.

XML (eXtensible Markup Language) is a W3C recommendation which is a tree based model for representing structure data on the Internet. In contrast to JSON, it provides means for specifying unique namespaces for all elements, ordering of the nodes as well as assigning attributes to nodes (unordered). The mapping of XML data into directed hypergraph can be achieved as follows. All simple tags (containing only values) are converted to simple data objects. All complex tags, which contain children tags are converted to composite data objects. All tag attributes are added to respective data objects using edges.

The representation of relational model using directed hypergraphs can be achieved as follows, assuming that the database is at least in the 3rd normal form. Each relation is composed of a set of value tuples, called rows. Each row is simply mapped to a single composite data object with edges representing the columns and their particular values as target data objects. Each relation (i.e. table) can be represented as a set of data objects representing rows. More interesting is the case of foreign key dependencies. In case of relational model it is impossible to directly create $n{:}m$ relations. Consider the relations *Author* and *Book*, where it is possible that a single book could have many authors as well as a single author could have published several books. In the relational model this requires introduction of intermediate relation (e.g. *BookAuthors*), which assigns authors to books. In case of a hypergraph this relation is not necessary (i.e. it is not necessary to create a new data object), as the relevant property can be modelled directly using hyperedges.

6   Prototype Design and Implementation

Filess provides users with an abstract API enabling basic operations on the data objects such as searching, creating and opening. As mentioned above, each user sees the global data space from their own perspective, which is identical on all devices from which they access the system. Current Filess prototype is implemented as an intermediate layer between user applications and distributed graph database backend (see Fig. 3). The current prototype implementation is created in Java language. *libfiless* library provides methods which can be used directly by users application. The Filess API provides lower level system calls which provide abstraction over currently used data storage backends, so that users applications do not get locked in into particular solution. For the prototype it also keeps the authentication sessions information in memory, however this will be in the future migrated to external database. The Filess layer provides an API with the following groups of operations:

- *Session* - These operation enable the user to login and logout of the system. Each session combines the users key with current machine ID so that the same user can be logged in from multiple devices simultaneously, and see the same state of affairs from these devices,
- *Get* - This category of operations allows for searching and access data objects. Currently the search is limited to node GUI's, as the Filess layer aims to be agnostic of actual graph database backend, an ongoing work is to develop an abstract query language for this purpose,
- *Put* - These operations enable adding new data objects and relating them to other objects,
- *Join* - These operations enable composing existing objects into more complex objects,
- *Split* - These operations enable decomposing existing binary or text objects into graph form,

In order to enable evaluation of the idea, Filess prototype has been developed using available technologies in the area of graph databases. We have evaluated several solutions including [11,15]. Finally we chose OrientDB, which is a multi-document database enabling modeling using document, key-value as well as graph paradigms simultaneously. In order to support legacy applications, an intermediate FUSE filesystem plugin was implemented which allows applications to access the information in the form of files which are composed on demand from the underlying graph when applications try to gain access to the data object. The implementation is based on *fuse-jna* Java Fuse provider, which allowed us to use direct OrientDB Java bindings. Due to very flexible graph model in OrientDB, it was possible to create hypergraph structure by defining custom edge class. Binary, read-only data objects are stored in a separate distributed database called IPFS (Interplanetary File System), which provides efficient hashing and distribution of large binary files between multiple nodes by diving them into blocks and maintaining a tree structure based on the blocks hash values.

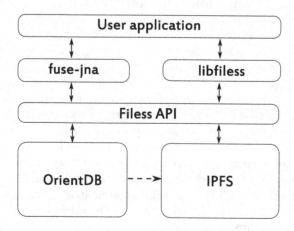

Fig. 3. Architecture of the Filess prototype

7   Conclusions

In this paper we have presented a novel approach to data management and representation in information systems, which departs from the filesystem based designs. Filesystem approach has become already intractable for average users for several reasons such as difficult searching for required files or lack of OS level synchronization of data between devices used to access the system. Presented approach addressing these problems has the potential to enable much more natural access to information, while minimizing the redundancy and data transfer on a global scale, allowing at the same time for highly fine grained access control, not based on files, but on actual data elements, which will enable creation of much more sophisticated and natural computing infrastructures able to handle information processing tasks on a global scale. The presented approach requires both users and application developers to shift the paradigm in which the applications are developed and used. Future work will include design of security layer enabling fine grained control over the operations performed by various users on such global data model, practical evaluation of performance depending on underlying storage solution and development of minimum viable prototype of the truly file-less operating system.

Acknowledgment. This research has been funded by Polish National Science Centre grant *File-less architecture of large scale distributed information systems* number: DEC-2012/05/N/ST6/03463.

References

1. Bandulet, C.: Object-based storage devices (2007). http://developers.sun.com/solaris/articles/osd.html
2. Berge, C.: Hypergraphs: Combinatorics of Finite Sets. North-Holland Mathematical Library, vol. 45. North-Holland, Amsterdam (1989)
3. Boyd, M., Mȼbrien, P.: Comparing and transforming between data models via an intermediate hypergraph data model. In: Spaccapietra, S. (ed.) Journal on Data Semantics IV. LNCS, vol. 3730, pp. 69–109. Springer, Heidelberg (2005)
4. Drago, I., Mellia, M., Munafo, M.M., Sperotto, A., Sadre, R., Pras, A.: Inside dropbox: understanding personal cloud storage services. In: Proceedings of the 2012 ACM Conference on Internet Measurement Conference, IMC 2012, pp. 481–494. ACM, New York (2012)
5. Ferré, S., Ridoux, O.: A file system based on concept analysis. In: Palamidessi, C., Moniz Pereira, L., Lloyd, J.W., Dahl, V., Furbach, U., Kerber, M., Lau, K.-K., Sagiv, Y., Stuckey, P.J. (eds.) CL 2000. LNCS (LNAI), vol. 1861, pp. 1033–1047. Springer, Heidelberg (2000)
6. Gallo, G., Longo, G., Pallottino, S., Nguyen, S.: Directed hypergraphs and applications. Discrete Appl. Math. **42**(2–3), 177–201 (1993)
7. Gantz, J., Reinsel, D.: The Digital Universe in 2020: Big Data, Bigger Digital Shadows, and Biggest Growth in the Far East. International Data Corporation, December 2010. https://www.emc.com/collateral/analyst-reports/idc-digital-universe-united-states.pdf

8. Gifford, D.K., Jouvelot, P., Sheldon, M.A., O'Toole, Jr., J.W.: Semantic file systems. SIGOPS Oper. Syst. Rev. **25**(5), 16–25 (1991)
9. Grimes, R.: Code name WinFS: Revolutionary file storage system lets users search and manage files based on content. MSDN Magazine 19(1) (2004). http://msdn. microsoft.com/msdnmag/issues/04/01/WinFS/
10. IDC iView: The Digital Universe Decade - Are You Ready? International Data Corporation, Framingham, MA, USA (2010). http://www.emc.com/digital_universe
11. Iordanov, B.: HyperGraphDB: a generalized graph database. In: Shen, H.T., Pei, J., Özsu, M.T., Zou, L., Lu, J., Ling, T.-W., Yu, G., Zhuang, Y., Shao, J. (eds.) WAIM 2010. LNCS, vol. 6185, pp. 25–36. Springer, Heidelberg (2010)
12. Kryza, B., Kitowski, J.: Comparison of information representation formalisms for scalable file agnostic information infrastructures. Comput. Inf. **34**, 473–494 (2015)
13. Kryza, B., Kitowski, J.: Filess - file-less architecture for future information systems. In: 2014 IEEE Fourth International Conference on Big Data and Cloud Computing, BDCloud 2014, Sydney, Australia, 3–5 December 2014, pp. 281–282 (2014)
14. Mylka, A., Mylka, A., Kryza, B., Kitowski, J.: Integration of heterogeneous data sources in an ontological knowledge base. Comput. Inf. **31**(1), 189–223 (2012)
15. Orient Technologies: OrientDB project website. http://www.orientechnologies.com
16. Padioleau, Y., Ridoux, O.: A logic file system. In: Proceedings of the General Track: 2003 USENIX Annual Technical Conference, San Antonio, Texas, USA, 9–14 June 2003, pp. 99–112 (2003)
17. Rajimwale, A., Prabhakaran, V., Davis, J.D.: Block management in solid-state devices. In: Proceedings of the 2009 Conference on USENIX Annual Technical Conference, USENIX 2009, pp. 21–21. USENIX Association, Berkeley (2009)
18. Reiser, H.: Futurue vision of reiserfs (2006). https://reiser4.wiki.kernel.org/index. php/Future_Vision
19. Salton, G.: Another look at automatic text-retrieval systems. Commun. ACM **29**(7), 648–656 (1986). http://doi.acm.org/10.1145/6138.6149
20. SanDisk: Ulltradimm product page. http://www.sandisk.com/enterprise/ ulltradimm-ssd/
21. Seagate Technology LLC: The seagate kinetic open storage vision. Seagate Technology LLC (2013). http://www.seagate.com/tech-insights/kinetic-vision-how-seagate-new-developertools-meets-the-needs-of-cloud-storage-platforms-master-ti/
22. Stender, J., Hogqvist, M., Kolbeck, B.: Loosely time-synchronized snapshots in object-based file systems. In: IPCCC, pp. 188–197. IEEE (2010)
23. Wang, F., Brandt, S.A., Miller, E.L., Long, D.D.E.: OBFS: a file system for object-based storage devices. In: Proceedings of the 21st IEEE/12TH NASA Goddard Conference on Mass Storage Systems and Technologies, College Park, MD, pp. 283–300 (2004)
24. Williams, R.: How we found the missing memristor. IEEE Spectr. **45**(12), 28–35 (2008)

Euro-EDUPAR - Parallel and Distributed Computing Education for Undergraduate Students

Parallel Computing vs. Distributed Computing: A Great Confusion? (Position Paper)

Michel Raynal[1,2,3(✉)]

[1] Institut Universitaire de France, Paris, France
[2] IRISA, Université de Rennes, Rennes, France
[3] Department of Computing, Hong Kong Polytechnic University,
Hung Hom, Hong Kong
raynal@irisa.fr

> *"Definierbar ist nur das, was keine Geschichte hat."*
> *"N'est définissable que ce qui n'a pas d'Histoire."*
> *"Only that which has no History can be defined."*
> —Friedrich Nietzsche (1844–1900).

> *"Every sentence I utter must be understood not as an affirmation,*
> *but as a question."*
> —Niels Bohr (1885–1962).

Abstract. This short position paper discusses the fact that, from a *teaching point of view*, parallelism and distributed computing are often confused, while, when looking at their deep nature, they address distinct fundamental issues. Hence, appropriate curricula should be separately designed for each of them. The "everything is in everything (and reciprocally)" attitude does not seem to be a relevant approach to teach students the important concepts which characterize parallelism on the one side, and distributed computing on the other side.

1 A (Very) Quick Look at Parallel Computing

The main aim of parallelism is to produce efficient software. To that end, a lot of research on parallel systems lies at the frontier between programming languages, software engineering, scheduling algorithms, and technology. Moreover, advances in technology cannot be ignored. As noticed by M. Herlihy and V. Luchangco in [16], "Changes in technology can have far-reaching effects on theory. [...] After decades of being respected but not taken seriously, research on multiprocessor algorithms and data structures is going mainstream".

The class of problems which can be parallelized are basically sequential computing problems for which a static decomposition into a task graph, and appropriate scheduling strategies used at run-time, allow us to obtain efficient executions on specific target machines.[1] In a few words, parallelism aims at

---

[1] As explained later, designing a parallel algorithm to solve a given problem does not want to say that there is no sequential algorithm able to solve it (maybe very inefficiently).

© Springer International Publishing Switzerland 2015
S. Hunold et al. (Eds.): Euro-Par 2015 Workshops, LNCS 9523, pp. 41–53, 2015.
DOI: 10.1007/978-3-319-27308-2_4

producing (time-)efficient programs, and its fundamental issue consists in mastering *efficiency* [3, 28][2].

2   What Is Distributed Computing

In a few words, *distributed computing* is about mastering *uncertainty*. Distributed computing arises when one has to solve a problem in terms of distributed entities (usually called processors, nodes, processes, actors, agents, sensors, peers, etc.) such that each entity has only a partial knowledge of the many parameters involved in the problem that has to be solved [32]. Hence, in one way or another, in any distributed computing problem, there are several computing entities, and each of them has to locally take a decision, whose scope is global. The uncertainty is not under the control of the programmer, it is created by the geographical scattering of the computing entities, the asynchrony of their communication, their mobility, the fact that each entity knows only a subset of the whole set of inputs (namely, its own local inputs), etc.

Although distributed algorithms are often made up of a few lines, their behavior can be difficult to understand and their properties hard to state, prove, and implement. Hence, distributed computing is not only a fundamental topic of *Informatics*[3], but also a challenging topic where simplicity, elegance, and beauty are first-class citizens [11, 32].

The Notion of a (Distributed) Task. The basic unit of distributed computing is the notion of a *task*, which was formalized in several papers (e.g., see [18, 19]). A task is made up of n processes p_1, ..., p_n (computing entities), such that each process has its own input (let in_i denote the input of p_i) and must compute its own output (let out_i denote the output of p_i). Let $I = [in_1, \cdots, in_n]$ be an input vector (let us notice that a process knows only its local input, it does not know the whole input vector). Let $O = [out_1, \cdots, out_n]$ be an output vector (similarly, even if a process is required to cooperate with the other processes, it will compute only its local output out_i, and not the whole output vector). A task T is defined by a set $\mathcal{I}$ of input vectors, a set $\mathcal{O}$ of output vectors, and a mapping T from $\mathcal{I}$ to $\mathcal{O}$, such that, given any input vector $I \in \mathcal{I}$, the output vector O (cooperatively computed by processes) is such that $O \in T(I)$. The case $n = 1$ corresponds to sequential computing (see Fig. 1). In this case a task boils down to a function.

---

[2] In a different domain, *real-time* computing is on mastering *on-time* computing [24].

[3] As nicely stated by E.W. Dijkstra (1920–2002): *"Computer science is no more about computers than astronomy is about telescopes"*. Hence, to prevent ambiguities, I use the word *informatics* in place of *computer science*. On a pleasant side, there is no more "computer science" than "washing machine science".

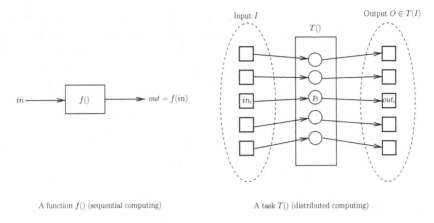

A function $f()$ (sequential computing)   A task $T()$ (distributed computing)

Fig. 1. Function vs. task

3   A Fundamental Difference Between Parallel Computing and Distributed Computing

This difference lies in the fact that a task is distributed by its very definition. This means that the processes, each with its own inputs, are geographically distributed and, due to this imposed distribution, need to communicate to compute their outputs. The geographical *distribution of the computing entities is a not a design choice*, it is an input of the problem which gives its name to *distributed computing*.

Differently, in parallel computing, the inputs are, by essence, centralized. When considering the left part of Fig. 1, a function $f()$, and an input parameter x, parallel computing addresses concepts, methods, and strategies which allow to benefit from parallelism when one has to implement $f(x)$. The input x is given, and (if any) its initial scattering on distinct processors is not a priori imposed, but is a design choice aiming at obtaining efficient implementations of $f()$.

Hence, the *essence* of distributed computing is not on looking for efficiency but on coordination in the presence of "adversaries" such as asynchrony, failures, locality, mobility, heterogeneity, limited bandwidth, etc. From the local point of view of each computing entity, these adversaries create uncertainty generating non-determinism, which (when possible) has to be solved by an appropriate algorithm.

4   On the Computational Side: The *Hardness* of Distributed Computing

From a computability point of view, if the system is reliable, a distributed problem, abstracted as a task T, can be solved in a centralized way. Each process p_i sends its input in_i to a given predetermined process, which computes $T(I)$, and sends back to each process p_j its output out_j.

This is no longer possible if the presence of failures. Let us consider one of the less severe types of failures, namely process crash failures in an asynchronous system. One of the most fundamental impossibility result of distributed computing is the celebrated FLP result due to Fischer, Lynch, and Paterson [12]. This result states that it is impossible to design a deterministic algorithm solving the basic *consensus* problem in an asynchronous distributed system in which even a single process may crash, be the underlying communication medium a message-passing network of a read/write shared memory[4].

Hence, it appears that, in distributed computing, "there are many problems which are not computable, but these limits to computability reflect the difficulty of making decisions in the face of ambiguity, and have little to do with the inherent computational power of individual participants" [18]. As we can see, the essence of distributed computing is far from the efficiency issues motivating parallelism (See also [33]).

5   Parallel vs. Distributed Computing: A Schematic View

Inputs
- Parallel Computing: Inputs are "always" initially centralized. They can be "disseminated" as a design choice to benefit from parallelism. A problem is broken into distinct parts that can be solved concurrently. Parallelism was born from machines to overcome (some) inefficiency of sequential computing.
- Distributed Computing: Inputs are always distributed.

Main concepts
- Parallel Computing is looking for efficiency:
  Array processing, automatic parallelization, load balancing, machine architecture, scheduling [5,6], task graph [34], vector or systolic programming [10], pattern decomposition [27], etc.
- Distributed Computing is about mastering uncertainty:
  Local computation, non-determinism created by the environment, symmetry breaking, agreement, etc.

Outputs
- Parallel Computing: The outputs are a function of the inputs.
- Distributed Computing: The outputs are a function of both the inputs and (possibly) the environment[5].

---

[4] In the consensus problem each process is assumed to propose a value. The problem is defined by the three following properties. If a process do not crash, it has to decide a value (termination). No two processes decide differently (agreement). A decided value is a value that was proposed by a process (validity). As cooperating processes have to agree in one way or another (otherwise the problem is only a control flow problem), a lot of distributed computing problems rely on a solution to the consensus problem, or a variant of it.

[5] A simple example where the output depends on both the inputs and the environment is the *Non-Blocking Atomic Commit* problem (which is defined in Appendix A).

A few paradigmatic problems

- Parallel Computing: simulation, matrix computation, differential equations, etc.
- Distributed Computing: anonymous/oblivious agents (processes), local computing, rendezvous in arbitrary graphs, agreement problems, fault-tolerant cooperation, facing Byzantine failures.

We do not also have to forget that, in both cases (parallel computing or distributed computing), the underlying synchronization is a fundamental issue.

6   An Approach to Teach Distributed Computing

A proven and trusted way to teach the basics of sequential computing consists in teaching its basic components, i.e., *sequential algorithms*. As the algorithms are at the core of *informatics*, their knowledge, and the concepts and techniques they rely on, allow students to understand and master the fundamental concepts of sequential computing.

In a very similar way, I think that teaching basic distributed algorithms constitutes the best way for students to learn the basic elements that allow them to capture, understand, and master the specificity and main features of distributed computing, and discover that distributed computing cannot be reduced to a set processors enriched with a communication medium.

Books have been written on distributed algorithms and distributed computing, e.g., [2,9,20,22,26,35–37]. Differently from a collection of papers, each of these books presents its *view* of the domain, and its way to give a concrete expression to it. Hence, in the same spirit, I present in the following my *personal view* of teaching and introducing students to distributed computing, through distributed algorithms. This view is exposed more deeply in four books I wrote of the topic, each addressing a specific part of it. Of course, being personal, this view may be judged as both partial and questionable.

7   Distributed Algorithms at the Undergraduate Level

At the undergraduate level, I teach distributed algorithms in failure-free systems. The corresponding material is a subset of my book *"Distributed algorithms for message-passing systems"* [32], which is made up of seventeen chapters, structured in six parts:

- Distributed graph algorithms,
- Logical time and global state in distributed systems,
- Mutual exclusion and resource allocation,
- High level communication abstractions,
- Detection of properties of distributed computation,
- Distributed shared memory.

Distributed Graphs Algorithms. A simple way to introduce distributed algorithms to student consists in considering graph problems (such as vertex coloring, or maximal independent set). A processor is associated with each node and processors communicate by sending and receiving messages along channels defined by the edges of the graph. As each node (processor) has only a local view of the whole graph, these distributed graph algorithms lead students to think in distributed way, i.e., a processor can only act locally to solve a *global* problem involving all the nodes.

A Quick Look at Distributed Computability. As in sequential computing, students must be taught the limits of distributed computing from the very beginning. While the FLP result seems too much complicated for undergraduate students, I present in my introductory lectures the impossibility to elect a leader in an anonymous ring network [1]. For students, this is "similar" to the impossibility to design a sequential comparison-based algorithm that sorts an array of n elements in less than $O(n \log n)$ comparisons of elements.

The Nature of Distributed Computing. Then, I address the second part of the book and focus on the nature of distributed executions. This consists in two main presentations. The first one is on the fact that a distributed execution is a partial order on a set of events, and on Chandy-Lamport distributed snapshot algorithm. The second one is the introduction of logical time (mainly Lamport scalar time and vector time) and its use to solve distributed problems. Chandy-Lamport algorithm is particularly important as it allows students to grasp the deep nature of distributed computing: it determines a consistent global state of a distributed computation, but it is impossible to claim that the computation passed through this global state or not. This algorithm exhibits the *relativistic* nature of distributed computing (let us remind that distributed computing is on mastering uncertainty).

Other Topics Addressed in My Lectures. According to time, I then address mainly distributed mutual exclusion, construction of communication abstractions of higher level than send/receive communication (e.g., rendezvous, causal message delivery, total order message delivery), detection of properties of distributed computations, (such as deadlock detection and termination detection), and the construction of a distributed shared memory on top of a distributed asynchronous message-passing system.

I think that, due to their paradigmatic features, distributed algorithms solving the mutual exclusion are important to teach because they are based on distributed principles and techniques that can be used to solve many other problems (examples are given in [32]).

Differently from mutual exclusion, which is not a problem specific to a distributed setting, termination detection is. This problem consists in designing a distributed observation algorithm able to detect if an upper lying distributed application has or not terminated. This is a non-trivial problem[6]. Hence, termination detection introduces students to specific features imposed by distributed settings.

Finally, I use the construction of a distributed read/write shared memory on top of a message-passing system to introduce students to data consistency criteria in a distributed context.

8   Distributed Algorithms at the Graduate Level

At the graduate level (Master 2 and lectures for PhD students) I address distributed computing in the presence of failures. This makes problems much more difficult (or, sometimes, even impossible) to solve. To this end, I wrote three books, one devoted to the case where communication is through a shared memory, and two when it is through an underlying message-passing network (one considers asynchronous systems, while the other one considers synchronous systems). I examine below their contents and my associated lectures.

9   When Communication Is Through a Shared Memory

This book titled "*Concurrent programming: algorithm, principles, and foundations*" [31] is both on synchronization and distributed algorithms where processes communicate through a shared memory. It is composed of seventeen chapters, structured in six parts:

- Lock-based synchronization,
- On the foundations side: the atomicity concept,
- Mutex-free synchronization, and associated progress conditions (the most important being obstruction-freedom [17], lock-freedom –also called "non-blocking"– [21], and wait-freedom [15]),
- The transactional memory approach,
- On the foundations side: from safe bits to atomic registers,
- On the foundations side: the computability power of concurrent objects.

In my lectures, I mainly introduce and develop mutex-free synchronization, and the more theoretical part devoted to the computability power of concurrent objects.

Mutex-Free Synchronization. The design of concurrent objects is a fundamental issue, as those are the objects that allows processes to cooperate in the presence of concurrency. While lock-based algorithms are well-known to implement concurrent objects, they cannot cope with process failures (which can occur in a distributed setting such as a multicore). This is because, if a processor crashes

---

[6] Let us notice that, even if we could observe all processors simultaneously passive, we could not claim that the application terminated. This is because, messages can still be in transit, which will re-activate processors when they will arrive at their destination.

while holding a lock on an object, this object becomes and remains forever inaccessible. Let us remind that in an asynchronous system, it is impossible to distinguish a slow process from a crashed process (the distinction can be done in a synchronous system [30]). Hence, "modern" synchronization [15] (i.e., synchronization in asynchronous systems prone to process crash failures) cannot be solved by a simple patching of traditional synchronization mechanisms as described in [7, 8].

Interestingly, (not all but) many concurrent objects have mutex-free implementations. Those are such that the algorithms implementing the object operations always terminate if the invoking process does not crash, where "always" means "despite the behavior of the other processes" (which can be slow or even crashed). These implementations are not trivial. This come from the fact that it is not possible to prevent several process from accessing simultaneously the internal representation of the concurrent object.

Hence, the aim of this part of the lectures is to make students aware of "modern" synchronization techniques (mainly wait-free computing), so that they are able to cope with the net effect of asynchrony and failures.

The Power of Concurrent Objects. Suppose you have to choose one of the following multicore machines. Both have the same number of processors but, in addition to atomic read/write registers, the hardware of machine A provides a $Test\&Set()$ operation, while the hardware of machine B provides a $Compare\&Swap()$ operation. Which machine do you choose?

In a failure-free context, and from a computability point of view, there is no difference. Actually in such a context, read/write atomic registers are sufficient to allow processes to cooperate. Differently, if processors may crash, machine B is much more powerful than machine A. This is related to the computability power of the operations $Test\&Set()$ and $Compare\&Swap()$, which is measured with the *consensus number* notion, introduced by Herlihy [15]. The consensus number of $Test\&Set()$ is 2, while the one of $Compare\&Swap()$ is $+\infty$. More precisely, this establishes a strict hierarchy on the synchronization power of concurrent objects. (For the interested reader, the consensus number notion is developed in Appendix B.)

The notions of a mutex-free implementation of concurrent objects, and consensus numbers, are fundamental concepts of modern synchronization (where, as aid previously, "modern" means "when we want to cope with the net effect of concurrency and any number of process failures"). They constitute the core of my lectures in systems where communication is through shared memory.

10   When Communication Is by Message-Passing

I addressed distributed computing in the presence of failures in two complementary books, which constitute the base of my teaching concerning failure-prone message-passing distributed systems. The first one is titled *"Communication and agreement abstractions for fault-tolerant asynchronous distributed systems"* [29], and second one is titled "*Fault-tolerant agreement in synchronous distributed systems*" [30].

The first one considers process crash failures in asynchronous systems. It composed of seven chapters, structured in three parts:

– The register abstraction,
– The uniform reliable broadcast abstraction,
– Agreement abstraction.

The second one considers synchronous systems, where processes may fail by crashing, committing omission failures, or behaving arbitrarily (Byzantine processes).

High Level Communication Abstraction. The first lectures are devoted to the construction of a reliable read/write shared memory on top of an asynchronous system prone to process failures. It is shown that this is impossible when half or more processes may crash. I then describe algorithms solving the problem when a majority of processes never crash. This allows students to understand the inherent cost of a shared memory built on top of a crash-prone asynchronous system, and consequently the cost of a strong cooperation object.

Synchrony vs. Asynchrony. A main point of the corresponding lectures is to obtain a deeper understanding of the net effect of asynchrony and failures. As an example, in the part of the lectures devoted to the consensus problem, I show that, while the problem can be solved in a synchronous system where any number of processes may crash, it is impossible to solve if the system is asynchronous, even if a single process may crash, and this is independent of the total number of processes (FLP impossibility). Hence, when considering the synchrony/asynchrony axis, a fundamental question for students is: which is the weakest synchrony assumptions that allows consensus to be solved. This is explored in details during several lectures.

11   Conclusion

While in the Middle Ages, philosophy, scholastic, and logic were considered as a single study domain, they are now considered as distinct domains. It is similar in mathematics, where (as a simple example and since a long time), algebra and calculus are considered as separate domains, each with its own objects, concepts, and tools. As another example, while solving an application may require knowledge in both probability, graph algorithms, and differential equations, those are considered as distinct mathematical areas.

It is the same in *informatics*, where some applications may involve at the same time parallelism and distributed computing. Life is diverse, and so are applications. But, from a teaching point of view, parallelism and distributed computing are distinct scientific areas, and their main concepts should consequently be taught separately to students. Teaching is not an accumulation of facts [23]. It is the exposure of concepts, principles, methodologies, and tools, that (among other targets) non only have to ensure that students will find a job when they finish their studies, but also (and maybe more importantly) ensure that, thanks to their methodological and conceptual background, students will still have a job in twenty-five years!

To conclude, let us remind that this is a position paper, where have been presented a few personal views. As nicely expressed by Niels Bohr:

"*Prediction is very difficult, especially when it is about the future.*"

A   The Non-blocking Atomic Commit Problem

In some applications, each process executes some local computation, at the end of which, it votes *yes* or *no*, according to its local computation. Then, according to their votes, the processes have to collectively commit or abort their local computation. Named non-blocking atomic commit (NBAC), this problem is formalized as follows [4,13,14,29].

Let us consider n asynchronous processes prone to crash failures. Each process proposes a value *yes* or *no*, and has to decide the value COMMIT or the value ABORT. NBAC is defined by the following set of properties[7].

- Validity. A decided value is COMMIT or ABORT. Moreover,
  - Justification. If a process decides COMMIT, all the processes voted *yes*.
  - Obligation. If all processes voted *yes* and there is no crash, no process decides ABORT.
- Integrity. A process decides at most once.
- Agreement. No two processes decide different values.
- Termination. Each non-faulty process decides.

This problem has the same agreement, integrity and termination properties as the consensus problem. It differs from it in the validity property, namely, a decided value is not a proposed value but a value that depends on both the proposed values *and* the failure pattern. Differently, the properties defining the consensus problem do not refer directly to the failure pattern.

B   Remark on the Notion of a Consensus Number of an Object

As previously indicated this notion was introduced by Herlihy [15]. It concerns the computability power of concurrent objects in shared memory systems where any number of processes may experience crash failures (e.g., multicore).

In such a context, a fundamental problem consists in building concurrent objects able to cope with any number of process failures. This is called the *wait-free* model. It is shown that the *consensus* object is *universal* in the sense

---

[7] This means that any algorithm solving the NBAC problem must satisfy all these properties.

that, given read/write registers and consensus objects, it is possible to design algorithms implementing (in the wait-free model) any concurrent object defined by a sequential specification. Such algorithms are called *universal constructions*.

Hence, the key for reliability in the wait-free model is the consensus object. This object can be informally defined as follows. Assuming each process proposes a value, the processes that do not crash have to decide the same value, and this value must be one of the proposed values. This apparently very simple object is impossible to implement in the basic wait-free model where processes communicate by accessing read/write registers only. This is the bad news [12,15,25][8].

But multiprocessor machines are usually endowed with specialized operations to address synchronization issues. Examples of such operations (or objects) are $Test\&Set()$, $Swap()$, $Fetch\&add()$, $Compare\&Swap()$, LL/SC, etc. Hence, the question: "Is the "bad news" still true in a multiprocessor enriched with such an operation?" Herlihy showed in [15] that it is possible to associate an integer with each of these synchronization operations, called *consensus number*, which characterizes its computability power in the wait-free model. More precisely, the consensus number of a synchronization operation is x if it allows to implement a consensus object in a system of x (or less) processes but not in a system of $(x + 1)$ processes. It follows that consensus numbers provide us with a hierarchy measuring the computability power of hardware synchronization operations. The consensus number of read/write is 1. The consensus number of $Test\&Set()$ or $Swap()$ is 2; etc. until operations such as $Compare\&Swap()$ or LL/SC, whose consensus number is $+\infty$.

More developments on consensus objects, universal constructions, and Herlihy's hierarchy can be found in [15,31,33,36].

References

1. Angluin, D.: Local and global properties in networks of processors. In: Proceedings of the 12th ACM Symposium on Theory of Computation (STOC 1981), pp. 82–93, ACM Press (1981)
2. Attiya, H., Welch, J.L.: Distributed Computing: Fundamentals, Simulations and Advanced Topics. Wiley-Interscience, 2nd edn, p. 414. Wiley, New York (2004)
3. Barney, B.: Introduction to parallel computing. https://computing.llnl.gov/tutorials/parallel_comp/#Whatis.UCRL-MI-133316
4. Bernstein, P.A., Hadzilacos, V., Goodman, N.: Concurrency Control and Recovery in Database Systems, p. 370. Addison Wesley, Reading (1987). ISBN 0-201-10715-5
5. Blazewicz, J., Pesch, E., Trystram, D., Zhang, G.: New perspectives in scheduling theory. J. Sched. **18**(4), 333–334 (2015)
6. Bouguerra, M.-M., Kondo, D., Mendonca, F.M., Trystram, D.: Fault-tolerant scheduling on parallel systems with non-memoryless failure distributions. J. Parallel Distrib. Comput. **74**(5), 2411–2422 (2014)

---

[8] Let us recall that, from a computability point of view, read and write operations are sufficient to solve any problem (in a Turing's sense, i.e., computable by Turing's machine) when there are no failures. The "bad news" says that this is no longer true when there are failures.

7. Brinch Hansen, P.: The Architecture of Concurrent Programs, p. 317. Prentice Hall, Englewood Cliffs (1977)
8. Brinch Hansen, P. (ed.): The Origin of Concurrent Programming, p. 534. Springer, New York (2002)
9. Cachin, C., Guerraoui, R., Rodrigues, L.: Introduction to Reliable and Secure Distributed Programming, p. 367. Springer, Heidelberg (2012). ISBN 978-3-642-15259-7
10. Chandy, K.M., Misra, J.: Parallel Program Design, p. 516. Addison Wesley, Reading (1988)
11. Dijkstra, E.W.: Some beautiful arguments using mathematical induction. Algorithmica 13(1), 1–8 (1980)
12. Fischer, M.J., Lynch, N.A., Paterson, M.S.: Impossibility of distributed consensus with one faulty process. J. ACM 32(2), 374–382 (1985)
13. Gray, J.: Notes on Database Operating Systems: and Advanced Course. LNCS, vol. 60, pp. 10–17. Springer, Heildelberg (1978)
14. Hadzilacos, V.: On the relationship between the atomic commitment and consensus problems. In: Simons, B., Spector, A. (eds.) Fault-Tolerant Distributed Computing. LNCS, vol. 448, pp. 201–208. Springer, Heildelberg (1990)
15. Herlihy, M.P.: Wait-free synchronization. Trans. Program. Lang. Syst. 13(1), 124–149 (1991)
16. Herlihy, M.P., Luchangco, V.: Distributed computing and the multicore revolution. ACM SIGACT News 39(1), 62–72 (2008)
17. Herlihy, M.P., Luchangco, V., Moir, M.: Obstruction-free synchronization: double-ended queues as an example. In: Proceedings of 23th International IEEE Conference on Distributed Computing Systems (ICDCS 2003), pp. 522–529. IEEE Press (2003)
18. Herlihy, M.P., Rajsbaum, S., Raynal, M.: Power and limits of distributed computing shared memory models. Theor. Comput. Sci. 509, 3–24 (2013)
19. Herlihy, M., Shavit, N.: The topological structure of asynchronous computability. J. ACM 46(6), 858–923 (1999)
20. Herlihy, M., Shavit, N.: The Art of Multiprocessor Programming, p. 508. Morgan Kaufmann, Burlington (2008). ISBN 978-0-12-370591-4
21. Herlihy, M.P., Wing, J.M.: Linearizability: a correctness condition for concurrent objects. ACM Trans. Program. Lang. Syst. 12(3), 463–492 (1990)
22. Kshemkalyani, A.D., Singhal, M.: Distributed Computing: Principles, p. 736. Algorithms and Systems. Cambridge University Press, Cambridge (2008)
23. Lamport, L.: Teaching concurrency. ACM SIGACT News, Distrib. Comput. Column 40(1), 58–62 (2009)
24. Liu, C.L.: Scheduling algorithms for multiprogramming in a hard-real-time environment. J. ACM 20(1), 46–61 (1973)
25. Loui, M., Abu-Amara, H.: Memory requirements for agreement among unreliable asynchronous processes. In: Advances in Computing Research, vol. 4, pp. 163–183. JAI Press (1987)
26. Lynch, N.A.: Distributed Algorithms, p. 872. Morgan Kaufmann, San Francisco (1996)
27. Matton, T., Sanders, B.A., Massingill, B.: Patterns for Parallel Programming, p. 384. Addison Wesley, Reading (2004). ISBN 978-0-321-22811-6
28. Padua, D. (ed.): Encyclopedia of Parallel Computing, p. 2180. Springer, Heildelberg (2011). ISBN 978-0-387-09765-7

29. Raynal, M.: Communication and Agreement Abstractions for Fault-Tolerant Asynchronous Distributed Systems, p. 251. Morgan & Claypool Pub. (2010). ISBN 978-1-60845-293-4
30. Raynal, M.: Fault-Tolerant Agreement in Synchronous Distributed Systems, p. 167. Morgan & Claypool (2010). ISBN 978-1-608-45525-6
31. Raynal, M.: Concurrent Programming: Algorithms, Principles, and Foundations, p. 530. Springer, Heildelberg (2013). ISBN 978-3-642-32026-2
32. Raynal, M.: Distributed Algorithms for Message-passing Systems, p. 515. Springer, Heilderberg (2013). ISBN 978-3-642-38122-5
33. Raynal, M.: What can be computed in a distributed system? In: Bensalem, S., Lakhneck, Y., Legay, A. (eds.) From Programs to Systems. LNCS, vol. 8415, pp. 209–224. Springer, Heidelberg (2014)
34. Robert, Y.: Task graph scheduling. In: Padua, D. (ed.) Encyclopedia of Parallel Computing, pp. 2013–2025. Springer, Heilderberg (2011)
35. Santoro, N.: Design and Analysis of Distributed Algorithms, p. 589. Wiley, New York (2007)
36. Taubenfeld, G.: Synchronization Algorithms and Concurrent Programming, p. 423. Upper Saddle River, Pearson Education/Prentice Hall (2006). ISBN 0-131-97259-6
37. Tel, G.: Introduction to Distributed Algorithms, p. 596. Cambridge University Press, Cambridge (2000). ISBN 0-521-79483-8

SAUCE: A Web-Based Automated Assessment Tool for Teaching Parallel Programming

Moritz Schlarb[✉], Christian Hundt, and Bertil Schmidt

Institute of Computer Science, Johannes Gutenberg University,
D-55128 Mainz, Germany
{schlarbm,hundt,bertil.schmidt}@uni-mainz.de

Abstract. Many curricula for undergraduate studies in computer science provide a lecture on the fundamentals of parallel programming like multi-threaded computation on shared memory architectures using POSIX threads or OpenMP. The complex structure of parallel programs can be challenging, especially for inexperienced students. Thus, there is a latent need for software supporting the learning process. Subsequent lectures may cover more advanced parallelization techniques such as the Message Passing Interface (MPI) and the Compute Unified Device Architecture (CUDA) languages. Unfortunately, the majority of students cannot easily access MPI clusters or modern hardware accelerators in order to effectively develop parallel programming skills. To overcome this, we present an interactive tool to aid both educators and students in the learning process. This paper describes the "System for AUtomated Code Evaluation" (SAUCE), a web-based open source (available under the AGPL-3.0 license at https://github.com/moschlar/SAUCE) application for programming assignment evaluation and elaborates on its features specifically designed for the teaching of parallel programming. This tool enables educators to provide the required programming environments with a low barrier to entry since it is usable with just a web browser. SAUCE allows for immediate feedback and thus can be used interactively in class room settings.

1 Introduction

The teaching of parallel programming techniques has increasingly gained importance during the last decade due to the ubiquity of multi-core architectures both on portable devices and workstations. Moreover, it is a well-known fact that despite the exponential growth of modern CPUs' compute capabilities their single-threaded performance has barely increased during the recent past. The development of parallel algorithms can be exceedingly difficult for inexperienced students since scaling up the number of cores involves complex restructuring of the program's control flow. As a result, an extensive education of parallelization techniques is becoming increasingly important for every student in computer science.

Besides the theoretical education of parallel algorithms, their practical implementation can be challenging for the students. Race conditions and erroneous

© Springer International Publishing Switzerland 2015
S. Hunold et al. (Eds.): Euro-Par 2015 Workshops, LNCS 9523, pp. 54–65, 2015.
DOI: 10.1007/978-3-319-27308-2_5

synchronization may lead to incorrect results, implicit serialization of concurrent tasks and deadlocks may degrade performance or render the program defective. Hence, practical programming exercises are indispensable to develop the relevant domain knowledge and skills. This process is ideally supervised, such that the student receives immediate feedback after writing the source code. However, due to limited human resources a supervising assistant can often not be provided. A common workflow consists of the following steps:

1. Provide remote logins for a compute cluster or workstation.
2. Submit the student's program to a queuing system and wait for execution.
3. Manually evaluate the program's functionality by verifying its output.

As a result, small programming exercises embedded in lectures are often difficult to realize due to the lack of time. In this paper, we present a unified framework for the automated assessment and evaluation of source code in the field of parallel programming which can be used from any device with just a web browser. The presented "System for AUtomated Code Evaluation" (SAUCE) is free software (AGPL-3.0) and can be downloaded at [12]. A demo instance of SAUCE including the discussed examples using OpenMP, MPI and CUDA can be accessed at our website [13].

The rest of this paper is organized as follows: Sect. 2 discusses related work and compares the presented software solutions regarding the use in teaching environments. Technical aspects of SAUCE including extensibility of the software, teaching-related features and security matters are discussed in Sect. 3. The use case for the computation of a Poisson problem using Jacobi iteration on an MPI cluster is presented in Sect. 4. Further examples include multi-threaded programming with OpenMP and massively parallel programming using CUDA. Section 5 concludes the paper.

2   Related Work

For an educated view on previous work, the functionality offered by SAUCE must be split between offering a modern web-based interface for writing, compiling and running software, which could be considered an Integrated Development Environment (IDE), and the automated assessment of a written piece of software, which is more alike to the principles of Continuous Integration (CI) extended for educational purposes.

While there are some recent projects which provide an IDE in a web browser, like compilr [6] (closed source, paid access only), ideone [9] (closed source, usable anonymously) or Cloud9 [5] (open source), there are far less systems that can be used for programming assessment and to enhance the classical educational feedback loop of practical exercises. There are older approaches to this task for academic environments, like CourseMarker [8] or PC^2 [2], which are both used through Java-based GUI client programs that need to be installed on the student's computer. Current projects that combines a web-based editing interface and an automated assessment of the written sequential programs embedded within a classical university course structure include WebLab (TU Delft) [14], Jack (University of Duisburg-Essen) [7] (both closed source) and Praktomat (KIT) [4] (open source). However, none of the above are explicitly targeted at parallel programming.

3 Technical Aspects

3.1 Python

SAUCE is written in the Python programming language. Python's syntactical and semantical features, along with the vast amount of third-party packages for all purposes, make it a good choice for the development of this state-of-the-art web application. Its widespread use and popularity increase the chance of the project to be further developed and extended in the future.

Python has a clear and readable syntax, which makes the source code comfortably readable, even for people not familiar with the language or with programming at all. A major strength of Python is its extensibility. Moreover, modules can be written in C or C++ with the use of the Python language bindings. This allows developers to combine the power of the interpreted Python language with more efficient and hardware-oriented languages like C or C++ and CUDA.

3.2 SAUCE Web Application

SAUCE is a web application written using the TurboGears 2 rapid web development framework [10], which follows the Model-View-Controller (MVC) pattern (see Fig. 1), which is a common design principle for web applications to achieve separation of concerns. TurboGears 2 provides basic building blocks for controllers and facilitates the coordination between the various components.

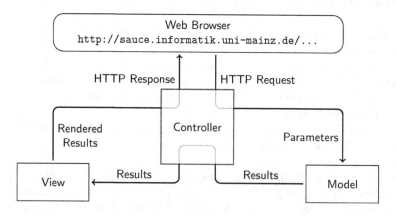

Fig. 1. The control flow within the Model-View-Controller pattern for one request.

Model. The model component defines the structure of the data for the application and the so-called business logic. The model part of SAUCE is realized with the SQLAlchemy object relational mapper (ORM) [3], which allows to use a relational database management system (e.g., SQLite, MySQL, PostgreSQL) like an object database. Hence, the ORM is an abstraction layer between the application and the database that facilitates the usage of object oriented programming paradigms and eliminates many problems regarding security and complexity of classical relational databases.

Controller. The controller is the central part of the application, which is responsible for user interaction. A user might also be another program that accesses the MVC application as a web service. The user requests an action by accessing a specific URL, which triggers a method that handles the input data (i.e., form field values or URL parameters), performs operations on the model data and returns some data to a specific view.

View. Following the paradigm of separation of concerns, the view is only responsible for the presentation of data retrieved from the controller and must not perform any modification on the data. It can also return information in a machine-readable format like XML or JSON. All the templates for SAUCE make use of the Twitter Bootstrap CSS framework, which is a state-of-the-art frontend framework containing styles for basic and advanced HTML5 elements. Bootstrap has been chosen because it features a clean and technical layout with focus on informational and form elements, which both suit the use case of this application.

3.3 Learning Tools Interoperability

SAUCE allows for the usage of its testing functionality from within other teaching platforms like Moodle or Coursera through the Learning Tools Interoperability (LTI) specification [1]. Using this interface makes it possible to provide a seamless experience, since students do not need to log in separately or join a course manually — they simply use the already existing authentication on the calling teaching platform. The testing results will be submitted back to the calling platform for central grading and feedback. As a result, SAUCE can be used as a service in a "headless" mode.

3.4 Security Considerations

Apart from classical security implications of web applications, additional aspects have to be considered since an application like this essentially allows a potential attacker to submit arbitrary code that will be executed within the server operating system.

There are two dangerous classes of users to be considered: Inexperienced programmers that submit faulty programs without intent and programmers who try to intentionally provoke and stress the system or to find ways of gaining unauthorized access to the system. The most common types of attacks in the given context are:

– Intentional and unintentional denial of service attacks like filling the memory or the hard disk with data or endless calculation loops, rendering the system unusable for other users or causing the application to subsequently fail.
– Information leakage by getting credentials to access the system or the database or opening network connections to transfer data in or out of the system.

Explicit security requirements regarding the execution of submitted programs can be summarized as follows:

– Deny read or write access to arbitrary files and directories (white-listing only a temporary directory used for the test run).
– Deny access to arbitrary system resources (e.g., hardware devices).
– Restrict CPU and memory usage and the process runtime.
– Prohibit network access (or at least access to the outside network).

SAUCE uses different techniques to address the aforementioned security requirements.

Traditional Unix Permissions that are based on users, groups and file or directory permissions, are enforced by the operating system with regards to the traditional Unix paradigm that "everything is a file" and thus provide a basic amount of access control on a file system level. Given that the SAUCE application is running under an unprivileged user account, its access to important or sensitive parts of the file system is prohibited.

Sandboxing, which means to separate possibly endangered parts of the application into a container, where their impact is minimized and malicious operations are revertible. It is advisable to use virtualization techniques for this kind of separation, like chroot, LXC or dedicated virtual machines. This also implies using an HTTP reverse proxy which forwards HTTP requests and their responses to and from arbitrary back end "worker" machines where the application itself runs. The distributed execution architecture as outlined in Sect. 3.5 provides implicit sandboxing, regardless of whether individual parts run on physical or virtual machines.

Resource Limits for process groups can be defined on various physical and logical resources and are enforced directly by the operating system kernel. Restrictions can be placed on memory usage, CPU execution time, open file handles, amongst others. By limiting the number of processes, it is possible to prevent a "fork bomb", where a process tries to infinitely spawn new child processes.

Firewall solutions are mandatory for any kind of web application or virtual machine setup. For example, with the Linux firewall tool "iptables", rules can be based on network packet attributes (like source or destination addresses, ports, etc.), but it is also possible to filter based on the Unix user of the application that created the packet. This can be used to allow normal operation of the web server and the application but restrict all network access for the user account that is used for executing the submitted programs.

3.5 Distributed Execution

Especially for programming parallel architectures, the possibility to dispatch steps that require specialized hardware and software, like the compilation and execution of submitted programs to worker nodes depending on their configuration, is important. A dedicated web server, where the SAUCE web application is running will most likely not have direct access to an accelerator card or an MPI cluster. Moreover, it would be inconvenient to set up an instance of the web application on several machines that feature a required piece of hardware. Therefore, we develop a lightweight queuing system for running submission tests on worker nodes instead of the host system (see Fig. 2). A test job is a contiguous unit of work consisting of compilation and repeated execution, once for each defined test case.

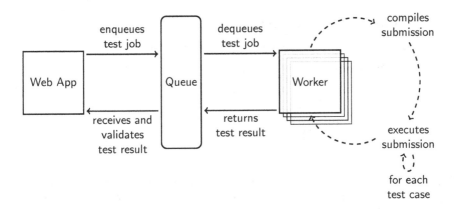

Fig. 2. Schematic overview of the distributed architecture that uses a task queue to dispatch compilation and execution of test jobs to one of many workers.

4 Use Cases

We provide a demo instance[1] of SAUCE featuring three interactive programming exercises for the parallelization techniques MPI, OpenMP and CUDA[2]. The submitted code is compiled and executed on the following platform:

CPU: Intel Xeon X5650 Hex-Core @ 2.67GHz with 96 GB attached RAM
GPU: Nvidia Tesla K40c with 12 GB attached video RAM
Software: GCC 4.8.2, OpenMPI 1.6.5, OpenMP 4.0, NVCC 6.5.12

Note, this instance runs as a freely accessible cloud service and thus the provided resources are limited to one CPU and one GPU. Nevertheless, SAUCE can handle programs on multiple nodes especially during the execution of MPI programs.

---

[1] Visit [13] and log in with username **teacher1** and password **teachpass**.

[2] These assignment examples are also available in the SAUCE repository at [12].

4.1 Solving the Poisson Equation Using MPI

A popular example for the teaching of communication primitives on distributed memory architectures is the iterative computation of the steady-state solution of the Poisson equation $\Delta\phi = f$ over the rectangular domain Ω with Dirichlet boundary condition $\phi(p) = g(p)$ for all $p \in \partial\Omega$. The discretized update rule for unit step size $h = 1$ and a vanishing exterior heat potential $f = 0$ is given by the ordinary average over the four-neighbourhood of a pixel $(i, j) \in \Omega\backslash\partial\Omega$ [11]:

$$\phi[i, j] \leftarrow \frac{\phi[i - 1, j] + \phi[i, j - 1] + \phi[i, j + 1] + \phi[i + 1, j]}{4}.$$

```
double phi[N*M], tmp[N*M]; // input image and temp storage
double error = INFINITY, epsilon = 1E-6;

// update call for entry (i, j) as C++11 lambda
auto update = [&] (const int& i, const int& j) {
    tmp[i*M+j] = 0.25f*(phi[(i-1)*M+j] + phi[i*M+j-1]
                      + phi[(i+1)*M+j] + phi[i*M+j+1]);};

while (error > epsilon) {
    for (int i = 1; i < N-1; i++)
        for (int j = 1; j < M-1; j++)
            update(i, j);
    // determine maximum residue ||phi-tmp||_oo and copy tmp to phi
    error = uniform_norm(phi, tmp, N, M);
    copy_image(tmp, phi, N, M);
    // Note: consider synchronization of processes in your solution
}
```

Fig. 3. Repetitive convolution of an image ϕ of size $N \times M$ by averaging the four-neighborhood of a pixel. Note that the border pixels are not altered by the averaging.

The sequential implementation is similar to a repetitive convolution of an image ϕ with a cross-shaped stencil. Figure 3 depicts the source code for the single-threaded computation of the steady-state solution. A parallelization of the sequential algorithm can be achieved by independently updating each of the $(N - 2) \cdot (M - 2)$ interior points. Note, the implicit barrier at the end of the body of the while-loop. Using MPI, a suitable partitioning of the image ϕ has to be distributed to the individual processes. For the sake of simplicity, we choose a block distribution such that p tiles of size $\frac{(N-2) \cdot M}{p}$ are computed independently on p processes. The communication of the adjacent rows between the p tiles shall be accomplished asynchronously in each iteration of the while-loop (see Fig. 4). Afterwards, a global Allreduce collective determines the maximum error of all tiles and thus enforces synchronization. The educational goal of this task is the teaching of asynchronous communication primitives and the realization of synchronization with global barriers.

The students' task is to write the corresponding source code that handles the communication between the tiles. Figure 5 depicts a code skeleton that has to be completed by the students. This task was embedded as a pair programming exercise during a lecture on High Performance Computing (HPC) at the

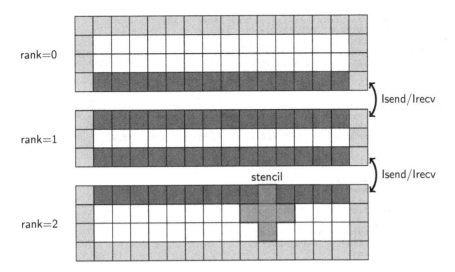

Fig. 4. An example of a block distribution of the image ϕ ($N = 11$ and $M = 16$) into $p = 3$ tiles of height $\frac{N-2}{3} = 3$. Border pixels (gray cells) are not altered during the update step. The adjacent rows (blue cells) have to be communicated between the processes during each iteration. The interior pixels (white cells) can be updated independently while waiting for the asynchronous communication (Color figure online).

Johannes Gutenberg University in the winter term 2014/15. Approximately half of the students could solve it within 15 min. The output verification is presented in textual and visual form: First, a test method determines if the submitted program computes an image ϕ_{par} that agrees with the sequential result ϕ_{seq} within a predefined error threshold (see Fig. 6). Second, SAUCE provides a visual comparison between the expected image and the computed result to the student (see Fig. 7). The additional visual information can be helpful to spot errors in the asynchronous communication calls. Furthermore, it is possible to expose additional information about the program which is not taken into account during the correctness test. As an example, the student can evaluate the program's speedup and efficiency in comparison to sequential code using runtime information.

Further MPI exercises including matrix multiplication using submatrix scattering, traditional matrix vector multiplication and the distributed numeric integration of functions using the trapezoidal rule have been successfully embedded in the tutorials and lectures of the aforementioned HPC course.

4.2 Odd-Even Sort Using OpenMP

SAUCE can also be used to teach parallel programming on shared memory architectures. In this paper, we present a multi-threaded example based on OpenMP. The parallelization of Odd-Even Sort, a modified variant of Bubble Sort that interleaves swaps of odd and even indices, can be used to illustrate the usage of thread pools in OpenMP (see Fig. 8). Furthermore, exercises using POSIX

```
// state sends and receives (upper and lower being the borders of the tile)
/** TO BE COMPLETED BY STUDENTS **
if (rank+1 < size) {
    double * lst_row = phi + (upper-1)*M, * nxt_row = lst_row + M;
    MPI_Isend(lst_row, M, MPI_DOUBLE, rank+1, 0, MPI_COMM_WORLD, req+2);
    MPI_Irecv(nxt_row, M, MPI_DOUBLE, rank+1, 0, MPI_COMM_WORLD, req+3);
}

if (rank > 0) {
    double * prv_row = phi + (lower-1)*M, * fst_row = prv_row + M;
    MPI_Isend(fst_row, M, MPI_DOUBLE, rank-1, 0, MPI_COMM_WORLD, req+0);
    MPI_Irecv(prv_row, M, MPI_DOUBLE, rank-1, 0, MPI_COMM_WORLD, req+1);
}
**/

// update the interior of the tile
for (int i = lower+(rank>0); i < upper-(rank+1<size); i++)
    for (int j = 1; j < M-1; j++)
        update(i, j);

// wait until asynchronous communication done (MPI_Wait)
/** TO BE COMPLETED BY STUDENTS **
if (rank+1 < size)

    MPI_Wait(req+3, sts+3);
if (rank > 0)
    MPI_Wait(req+1, sts+1);
**/

// update halo pixels at the tile borders
if (rank > 0)
    for (int j = 1; j < M-1; j++)
        update(lower, j);
if (rank+1 < size)
    for (int j = 1; j < M-1; j++)
        update(upper-1, j);

// now update error of approximation and copy tmp to phi
error = uniform_error(phi, tmp, N, M, lower, upper, 0, M);
copy_image(phi, tmp, N, M, lower, upper, 0, M);

// make sure all threads have the same error (why is this important?)
MPI_Allreduce(&error, &error, 1, MPI_DOUBLE, MPI_MAX, MPI_COMM_WORLD);
```

Fig. 5. The provided code skeleton of the while-loop body. The students are asked to fill in the blue-colored comments. Furthermore, they have to explain the importance of the Allreduce collective in order to ensure a deadlock-free MPI program (Color figure online).

Threads have also been successfully included in the lecture, e.g., the proper use of atomics, compare and swap loops, condition variables.

4.3 Array Reversal Using CUDA

Massively parallel accelerators can also be used with SAUCE since it effectively supports any programming language that can be compiled and executed on Unix-like operating systems. The demo instance provides a CUDA array reversal algorithm that uses shared memory to ensure coalesced accesses to global memory. The major goal of this task is to train the students' ability to utilize shared memory and the proper usage of the __syncthreads() primitive for

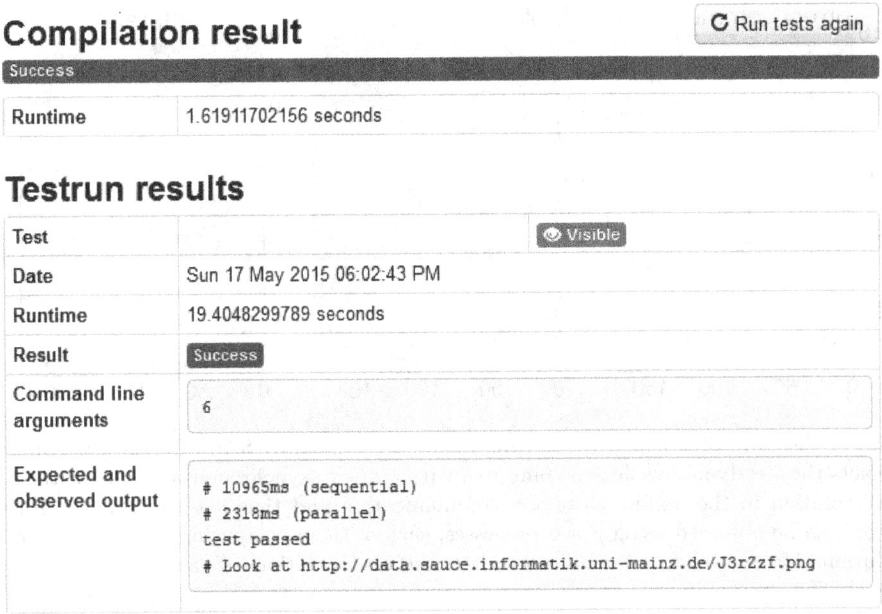

Compilation result

C Run tests again

Success

Runtime	1.61911702156 seconds

Testrun results

Test	⊙ Visible
Date	Sun 17 May 2015 06:02:43 PM
Runtime	19.4048299789 seconds
Result	Success
Command line arguments	6
Expected and observed output	# 10965ms (sequential) # 2318ms (parallel) test passed # Look at http://data.sauce.informatik.uni-mainz.de/J3rZzf.png

Fig. 6. Textual feedback for the correctness of the computed image ϕ provided by SAUCE. The test is passed if the maximum residue between the sequential and the parallel solution $\|\phi_{seq} - \phi_{par}\|_\infty$ is smaller than a predefined threshold. Furthermore, the teacher or student may write comments to the output via a print statement (here lines with leading #) that are not evaluated during the test e.g., the runtime of the program.

the synchronization of CUDA threads within a thread block. Further CUDA examples including matrix multiplication and image convolution have been successfully embedded in the aforementioned HPC course. The possibility to print out execution times allows for a detailed discussion whether the use of shared memory is beneficial in each specific case. Alternatively, a direct comparison of execution times between device and host code is conceivable.

4.4 Grading Features

SAUCE offers several features for the manual correction and grading of submitted source code. First, the teacher can annotate parts of the source code and leave suggestions or an improved version of the program for the students. Second, SAUCE features grading of individual submissions and team submissions of arbitrary size. Third, in rare cases where students submit source code that does not compile correctly, the teacher may clone the submission to his own user account and manipulate it freely. Fourth, it is possible to search the submission database for cases of plagiarism. To achieve this, a similarity score based on the Jaccard index is computed for all pairs of submissions and presented to the

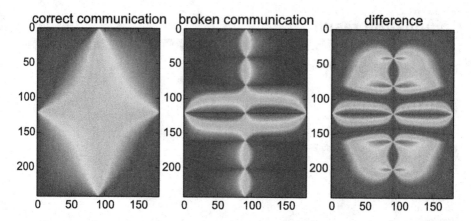

Fig. 7. Visual feedback for the resulting image ϕ provided by SAUCE. The left panel depicts the steady-state solution computed with correct asynchronous communication. The solution in the middle lacks any communication and thus five sharp horizontal edges can be observed using $p = 6$ processes, each of them computing an independent solution. The modulus of the difference between both solutions is plotted in the right panel. The color map (jet) ranges from small values (blue) to high values (red) (Color figure online).

```
void parallel_sort(std::vector<unsigned int>& X) {

    unsigned int i, phase, N = X.size();
    auto swap = [] (unsigned int& x, unsigned int& y)
                   { auto tmp = x; x = y; y = tmp; };
    /** TO BE COMPLETED BY STUDENTS
    #pragma omp parallel private(phase)
    **/
    {
        for (phase = 0; phase < N; phase++)
            if (phase % 2 == 0) {                   //even phase
                /** TO BE COMPLETED BY STUDENTS
                #pragma omp for
                **/
                for (i = 1; i < N; i += 2)
                    if (X[i-1] > X[i])
                        swap(X[i], X[i-1]);
            } else {                                // odd phase
                /** TO BE COMPLETED BY STUDENTS
                #pragma omp for
                **/
                for (i = 1; i < N-1; i += 2)
                    if (X[i] > X[i+1])
                        swap(X[i], X[i+1]);
            }
    }
}
```

Fig. 8. The provided code skeleton for the parallelization of Odd-Even Sort using OpenMP pragma statements. The students are asked to fill in the blue-colored comments. A further task could be the discussion of implicit barriers introduced by the **#pragma omp for** clauses (Color figure online).

teacher in multiple varieties (e.g., a list of the top-k similarity scores or dendrograms). Finally, SAUCE can also be used in programming contest scenarios since it provides dedicated features like hidden test cases as well as a fine-grained definition of time and resource limits.

5 Conclusion

In this paper, we have presented a unified framework for the automated assessment and evaluation of source code in the field of parallel programming which can be used from any device with just a web browser. The presented "System for AUtomated Code Evaluation" (SAUCE) is free and open source software (AGPL-3.0) and can be downloaded at [12]. Moreover, we have discussed its use in interactive programming exercises in the context of parallel programming. Three examples for the major parallelization paradigms MPI, OpenMP and CUDA have been described and provided as SAUCE exercises. A demo instance of SAUCE including the discussed examples can be accessed at our website [13].

References

1. Learning Tools Interoperability. http://www.imsglobal.org/lti/
2. Ashoo, S.E., Boudreau, T., Lane, D.A.: Programming Contest Control System. http://www.ecs.csus.edu/pc2/
3. Bayer, M.: The Python SQL Toolkit and Object Relational Mapper. http://www.sqlalchemy.org/
4. Breitner, J., Hecker, M.: Quality control for programming assignments. https://github.com/KITPraktomatTeam/Praktomat/
5. Cloud9: Online Code Editor. https://c9.io
6. Compilr: Online Editor and Sandbox. https://compilr.com
7. Goedicke, M., Striewe, M., Balz, M.: Computer aided assessments and programming exercises with JACK. Technical report (2008)
8. Higgins, C., Hegazy, T., Symeonidis, P., Tsintsifas, A.: The CourseMarker CBA system: improvements over Ceilidh. Educ. Inf. Technol. 8(3), 287–304 (2003). http://dx.doi.org/10.1023/A:1026364126982
9. Ideone: Online Compiler and Debugging Tool. http://ideone.com
10. Molina, A.: TurboGears: Rapid Web Development Framework. http://turbogears.org
11. Quinn, M.J.: Parallel Programming in C with MPI and OpenMP. McGraw-Hill Education Group, New York (2003)
12. Schlarb, M.: System for AUtomated Code Evaluation on Github. https://github.com/moschlar/SAUCE
13. Schlarb, M., Hundt, C., Schmidt, B.: System for AUtomated Code Evaluation Cloud Service. http://sauce.informatik.uni-mainz.de
14. WebLab: Learning Management System. https://weblab.tudelft.nl/

Teaching Parallel Programming
in Interdisciplinary Studies

Eduardo Cesar, Ana Cortés, Antonio Espinosa, Tomàs Margalef[✉],
Juan Carlos Moure, Anna Sikora, and Remo Suppi

Computer Architecture and Operating Systems Department,
Universitat Autònoma de Barcelona, 08193 Cerdanyola del Vallés, Spain
{eduardo.cesar,ana.cortes,antoniomiguel.espinosa,tomas.margalef,
juancarlos.moure,anna.sikora,remo.suppi}@uab.cat

Abstract. Nowadays many fields of science and engineering are evolving
by the joint contribution of complementary fields. Computer science, and
especially high performance computing, has become a key factor in the
development of many research fields, establishing a new paradigm called
computational science. Researchers and professionals from many different fields require a knowledge of high performance computing, including
parallel programming, to develop a fruitful work in their particular field.
So, at Universitat Autònoma of Barcelona, an interdisciplinary master
on Modeling for science and engineering was started 5 years ago to provide a deep knowledge on the application of modeling and simulation
to graduate students on different fields (Mathematics, Physics, Chemistry, Engineering, Geology, etc.). In this master, Parallel Programming
appears as a compulsory subject, because it is a key topic for them. The
concepts learnt in parallel programming must be applied to real applications. Therefore, a subject on Applied Modelling and Simulation has
also been included. In this paper, the experience on teaching parallel
programming in such interdisciplinary master is shown.

Keywords: Parallel programming · Message passing · Shared memory ·
GPUs · MPI · OpenMP · CUDA

1 Introduction

Many fields of science and engineering are applying the techniques and recent
advances in complementary fields. In this interdisciplinary context, researchers

E. Cesar, A. Cortés, A. Espinosa, T. Margalef, J.C. Moure and A. Sikora—This
work has been partially supported by MICINN-Spain under contract TIN2011-28689-
C02-01, MINECO under contract TIN2014-53234-C2-1-R and GenCat-DIUiE(GRR)
2014-SGR-576.
A. Espinosa and J.C. Moure—We want to thank Nvidia Corporation for the dona-
tion of the GPU systems used in this paper.
R. Suppi—This work has been partially supported by MICINN-Spain under contract TIN2011-24384, MINECO under contract TIN2014-53172-P and GenCat-
DIUiE(GRR) 2014-SGR-1562.

S. Hunold et al. (Eds.): Euro-Par 2015 Workshops, LNCS 9523, pp. 66–77, 2015.
DOI: 10.1007/978-3-319-27308-2_6

and professionals with a wider knowledge are highly demanded by companies and research centres. Universitat Autònoma of Barcelona started a Master degree on Modeling for Science and Engineering to provide such kind of professionals to those companies. The students enroll from different degrees: Mathematics, Physics, Chemistry, Engineering, Computer Science, and others. The master studies has been very successful, attracting students from many countries of origin. Also, companies are actively hiring finishing students and providing internships for students while attending the master.

A key point in the success of the master is the strong collaboration with companies applying such techniques and methods in their everyday business processes, so that the students can realize the significant impact of such techniques and methods and economical savings provided in a specific company.

The master itself involves an interdisciplinary collaboration among professors from different departments; mainly Physics, Mathematics, and Computer Architecture and Operating Systems. Its objective is to provide the students the basic knowledge to be able to model a physical system, to represent it in a mathematical way, to solve it applying different methods such as differential partial equations, optimisation, time series, and related methods. Finally, they program some implementations as high performance computing applications or simulations. The main three pillars of the training of the students are:

- Definition of complex systems.
- Mathematical representation and resolution of such systems.
- High performance computing implementation of designed solutions, typically by means of a software simulation tool.

In this context, we strive for a good training in parallel programming and a successful experience with the efficiency analysis of the implementation of some real small-size applications.

This paper focuses on the description of the training on parallel programming and on applied modelling and simulation that is offered to the students. In Sect. 2 we present the basic concepts on parallel programming shown to the students to establish a common framework. Section 3 describes the parallel programming approaches taught to the students and the lab exercises proposed to them. Then, Sect. 4 presents some examples of real applications that are shown and proposed to the students for their development. Finally, Sect. 5 presents the main conclusions of this teaching experience.

2   Basic Concepts for Interdisciplinary Students

Parallel Programming is a core subject in this interdisciplinary master, but the first challenge is to set a common background for the students. The students of the master typically have some programming knowledge of high level languages such as Java or Python, but usually they have a limited knowledge of C programming language. Since C is at the core of high performance computing, the very first part of the course is devoted to introduce to the students its main concepts and to work on several programming exercises. Usually, students succeed in this initial training part due to their high interest and their previous programming experience. Our previous experiences have showed us that devoting some time for setting this basic C knowledge must become a hard requirement before introducing OpenMP or MPI programming.

Once the students have learned the C programming principles, it is necessary to introduce them to the basic concepts of parallel programming. The first point is the general idea of parallelism itself and how HPC computing platforms are designed. So, a general idea about parallel and distributed systems, multi-core processors, memory hierarchy and GPUs, are presented to the students. These objectives become a challenge because it is necessary to provide the students useful real architecture concepts while avoiding too deep architectural details that are complex to relate to programming issues and may bore them and become a serious problem. For this reason, we provide a gentle introduction with selected further readings for those students particularly interested in these architectural aspects.

The following point in the subject is an introduction to parallel algorithms. Some of the students have some experience in sequential programming or even in object oriented programming, but the computational aspects of parallel algorithm design must be introduced to the students, showing them different current paradigms and related tools.

We provide details on several parallel algorithms for different problems. The first problem considered is matrix multiplication, which most of them know very well and have already programmed in a sequential way. We start by showing them how the problem is inherently parallel. Several matrix multiplication parallel algorithms are shown and analysed considering different aspects such as computational complexity, communication requirements, data size and memory requirements. These different algorithms are analysed considering the previously mentioned architectural aspects, showing the implications of computing capabilities, communication network and memory limitations.

Along the course we identify several important parallel computation patterns [17], which are used in many examples. The *map* pattern is exemplified by the vector addition algorithm (and the outer loops of matrix multiplication). It becomes an appropriate pattern to introduce parallelism as it does not involve any dependence nor communication among threads. The *reduce* pattern is studied in the inner loop of matrix multiplication, we use it to introduce the problem of synchronization and the idea of re-associating arithmetic operations to increase parallelism. The *stencil* pattern is used to simulate the movement of a string, and requires synchronization and to share and communicate boundary data.

Two additional parallel computation patterns are studied by means of exercises proposed to the students. The parallel prefix algorithm (*scan* pattern) and the convex hull problem (*divide and conquer* or *recursive* pattern) are proposed so that students analyse the problem and find out the potential parallelism in the algorithm. The students compare their proposals considering aspects such as algorithm complexity, memory and communication requirements, and so on.

When the students have understood all this basic concepts, it is possible to tackle the parallel programming challenge. This topic is presented in next section.

3 Parallel Programming

Once the basic concepts of programming and parallelism have been presented to the students, it is possible to enter in the core part of Parallel Programming. In this part three paradigms are presented: Shared memory, Message passing and Accelerator-oriented kernel programming (GPUs). The rationale for this organisation is that developing programs with a shared memory model, such as OpenMP, requires a simple modification of a C sequential program by including just some directives. So, the students can parallelise their sequential C programs in just one lab session. After OpenMP, MPI is introduced. In this case, it is necessary to think how to parallelise the algorithm, which processes must be defined, how such processes must communicate, and so on. This implies a larger effort from the students. The last approach introduced is CUDA, as a programming model for GPUs (accelerators), that requires a more detailed understanding of memory hierarchy and the coordinated use of thousands of threads to reach relevant performance gains. The programming sessions are complemented with the introduction of performance analysis tools to understand the benefits of parallel programming and to detect and correct performance bottlenecks. The development of this topics is covered in the following subsections.

3.1 Shared Memory: OpenMP

As mentioned above, once students are familiarized with C and basic concepts about parallel algorithms, the most natural way for introducing parallel applications development is using OpenMP [6].

OpenMP is a portable and flexible directive-based API for shared-memory parallel programming which, for some basic code constructions, allows to express parallelism in an extremely simple way. Given these characteristics, it has become the de-facto standard for multicore share-memory architectures. In addition, current laptops and desktop computers have multicore processors and, consequently, students can test all the examples given in class and develop new ideas in their own computer.

After a few motivating examples, such as the one shown in Listing 1.1, the contents of the OpenMP lecture are structured as follows:

- **Introduction.** Concept of thread, shared and private variables, and need for synchronization.
- **Fork-join model.** The `#pragma omp parallel` clause. Introducing parallel regions.

- **Data parallelism: parallelizing loops.** The #pragma omp for clause. Data management clauses (private, shared, firstprivate).
- **Task parallelism: sections.** The #pragma omp sections and #pragma omp section clauses.
- **OpenMP runtime environment function calls.** Getting the number of threads of a parallel region, getting the thread id, and other functions.
- **Synchronization.** Implicit synchronization, nowait clause. Controlling executing threads, master, single, and barrier clauses. Controlling data dependencies, atomic and reduction clauses.
- **Performance considerations.** Balancing threads' load, schedule clause. Eliminating barriers and critical regions.

Listing 1.1. OpenMP simple example: adding two vectors.

```
#pragma omp parallel for
  for ( i = 0; i < N; i++ )
      c[i] = a[i] + b[i];
```

The concepts introduced in this lecture are reinforced in a lab session, where students must use OpenMP for parallelizing the code for simulating the movement of a string developed in the C labs (see Listing 1.2). In this way, students continue their work and can experience the advantages of using the 4 cores available in each lab equipment.

Listing 1.2. String simulation main computation loop.

```
for (t=1; t<=T; t++) {
    for (x=1; x<X; x++)
        U3[x] = L2*U2[x] + L*(U2[x+1]+U2[x-1]) - U1[x];
    double *TMP =U3;
    // rotate usage of vectors
    U3=U1; U1=U2; U2=TMP;
}
```

Parallelizing this code with OpenMP is straightforward as can be seen in Listing 1.3, its only complexity is that the clause firstprivate(T,U1,U2,U3) must be used to ensure that each thread does the same vector rotation using its private copies. This parallelization is specially designed to be done in a short time, leaving students plenty of opportunities to test the code and analyze its behavior.

Listing 1.3. Parallelized string simulation main computation loop.

```
#pragma omp parallel firstprivate (T,U1,U2,U3)
  for (t=1; t<=T; t++) {
    #pragma omp for
    for (x=1; x<X; x++)
        U3[x] = L2*U2[x] + L*(U2[x+1]+U2[x-1]) - U1[x];
    double *TMP =U3;
```

```
//  rotate  usage  of  vectors
U3=U1;  U1=U2;  U2=TMP;
}
```

3.2 Message Passing: MPI

After explaining parallelism at multi-core level using shared memory, the next step is to introduce cluster parallelism (distribute memory) using message passing. With this objective, the course includes two lectures on Message Passing Interface (MPI) [4] and two lab sessions for developing related exercises.

MPI is by far the most used interface for developing distribute memory parallel programs, mainly because many libraries have been implemented based on the MPI consortium specification (OpenMPI, MPICH, Intel MPI, etc.). MPI includes plenty of features but this course focuses on presenting the basic MPI program structure and the functions for point-to-point as well as collective communication.

The contents of the MPI lectures are structured as follows:

- **Message passing paradigm.** Distributed memory parallel computing, the need for a mechanism for interchanging information. Introducing MPI history.
- **MPI program structure.** Initializing and finalizing the environment `MPI_Init` and `MPI_Finalize`. Communicator's definition (`MPI_COMM_WORLD`), getting the number of processes in the application (`MPI_Comm_size`) and the process rank (`MPI_Comm_rank`). General structure of an MPI call.
- **Point-to-point communication.** Sending and receiving messages (`MPI_Send` and `MPI_Recv`). Sending modes: standard, synchronous, buffered and ready send.
- **Blocking and non-blocking communications.** Waiting for an operation completion (`MPI_Wait` and `MPI_Test`).
- **Collective communication.** Barrier, broadcast, scatter, gather and reduce operations.
- **Performance considerations.** Overlapping communication and computation. Measuring time (`MPI_Time`). Discussion on the communication overhead. Load balancing.

Students work around these concepts in the lab sessions by developing a simple program for computing π approximation using the dartboard approach. This approach simulates throwing darts to a dartboard on a square backing. As each dart is thrown randomly the ratio of darts hitting the board to those landing on the square is equal to the ratio between the two areas, as shown in Fig. 1, which is $\pi/4$.

A parallel implementation of this algorithm can consists of a certain number of processes throwing a fixed number of darts and calculating its own approximation of π, then, one of the processes (the master) receives all approximations and calculates the average value. In this solution workers send their results to the master (process with rank 0) using point-to-point communication.

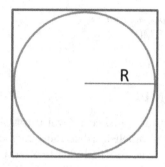

Fig. 1. Dartboard π approximation.

A second approach consists in distributing the total number of throws among all processes, each of them will calculate its number of hits (darts in the circle) and send it to the master process, which will compute π approximation. In this case, the master sends the number of throws that must be done by each process and receives the number of hits using always collective communication functions.

3.3   GPUs: CUDA

CUDA is an extension for massively parallel programming of GPUs (or accelerators). We choose CUDA instead of OpenCL because of the existence of efficient and mature compiling, debugging and profiling tools, and because of the extensive information available. The contents of the CUDA lectures are structured as follows:

- **Introduction.** Hierarchy of threads: warp, CTA (Cooperating Thread Array) and grid. 3-dimensional thread identifiers.
- **Model of an accelerator: host and device.** Moving data among host and device. Allocating memory on the device and synchronizing the execution.
- **Architectural restrictions.** Warp size. Maximum CTA and grid dimensions.
- **Memory space.** Global, local and shared memory.
- **Synchronization.** Warp-level and CTA-level synchronization.
- **Performance considerations.** Excess of threads to tolerate the latencies of data dependencies. Increasing work per thread to improve instruction-level parallelism.

The lecture uses vector addition as an example to introduce the CUDA syntax. Four implementations are provided and evaluated using: (a) one single thread, (b) one CTA, (c) a grid of CTAs where each thread performs a single addition, and (d) a grid of CTAs with more work per thread. We show the performance results (deceiving, for the first implementations) to motivate the different solutions and the need for developing good performance engineering skills.

We present Thrust [11], a high-level parallel algorithms library written in C++, to show the students the benefit of learning object-oriented programming and software engineering concepts. However, due to the limited background of our students and obvious time limitations, it is out of the scope of our course.

Students must use CUDA in a lab session for parallelizing the code that simulates the movement of a string. They explore, step by step, the different obstacles they must save to exploit the full potential of GPUs and increase performance 10x with respect to the multicore CPU code.

3.4   Performance Analysis: Tools

It is not only important to be able to develop applications using the different approaches taught during the course. Parallel programming main goal is to improve applications performance and, consequently, performance analysis should be introduced to students.

During the course labs, students use basic tools, such as nvprof [1], perf Linux command [8], jumpshot [10] and likwid [3] for visualizing and analyzing the behavior of their applications. These tools are enough for the simple applications developed and the small cluster used in this course.

However, our students will likely participate in the development of real parallel applications during their professional life. Consequently, a lecture is used to describe the performance analysis cycle shown in Fig. 2 and introduce the main tools currently available for supporting each of these steps.

For example, Performance API (PAPI) [9] and Dyninst [2] are mentioned as supporting tools for getting execution measurements; Tuning and Analysis Utilities (TAU) [20], Scalasca [21] and Paraver [7] are presented as analysis and visualization tools; and Periscope Tuning Framework (PTF) [18], MATE [19] and Elastic [16] are introduced as automatic analysis and tuning tools.

It is worth mentioning that the Computer Architecture and Operating Systems department of Universitat Autònoma of Barcelona have received support from computation industry leaders for the design and development of computation labs. We have been appointed by Intel as an Academic Partner with the use of Intel Parallel Studio as one of the programming environments for the practical laboratories and we have also been awarded as a GPU Teaching Center by Nvidia Corporation for introducing CUDA and GPU technology into the computer architecture studies. Our materials and systems are well updated to the latest versions released by Nvidia.

4   Applied Modelling and Simulation

The main goal of the Applied Modelling and Simulation subject is to introduce to the students real applications that use modelling and simulation and apply parallel programming. It is very significant to show the need to use high performance computing to make these real applications operational.

So, the proof of concept for this subject are developed by two different parts:

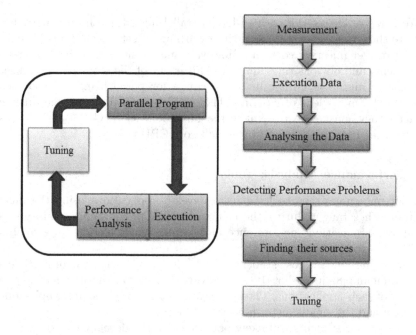

Fig. 2. Performance analysis in the application development cycle.

- simulation model development and its performance analysis,
- analysis of cases of use in collaboration with industry and research laboratories that use modeling and simulation activities every day.

In the first case study, a model of emergency evacuation using Agent Based Modeling is presented to the students [15]. In this model there are different aspects of analysis: the environment and the information (doors and exit signals), policies and procedures for evacuation, and social characteristics of individuals that affect the response during the evacuation. Moreover, the model includes the following hypothesis as a starting point to define it:

- In emergency evacuation situations, people are generally nervous or even in panic, so they tend to perform irrational actions.
- Individuals try to move as quickly as possible (more than normal).
- Individuals try to achieve their objectives and may try to push each other in their attempt to exit through a specific door causing physical injury to other individuals.

Students receive a partial model that includes management of the evacuation of an enclosed area that presents a certain building structure (walls, access, etc.), obstacles, with a particular signaling and the corresponding safe zones and exits. The model also includes individuals who should be evacuated to safe areas. The model has been developed to support different parameters such as: individuals with different ages, total number of people in the area, number of exits, number of chained signals and safe areas, speed of each individual, probability of exchanging information with other individuals. The model is implemented in NetLogo [5] and the Fig. 3 is a representation of its main characteristics.

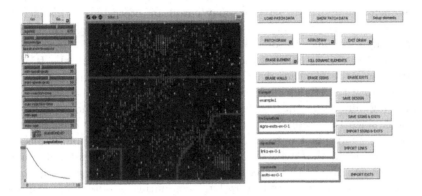

Fig. 3. Agent Based Modeling for emergency evacuations.

The first practical work for the students is to use a single-core architecture to make a performance analysis of the model and then modify it to incorporate a new, not covered, policy: overcrowding in exit zones [14]. With this new model the students must complete a new performance analysis.

Considering the variability of each individual in the model a stability analysis is required. For this the Chebyshov Theorem (also spelled as Tchebysheff) will be used with confidence interval of 95 % and $\alpha = 0.05, m = 6$. The result for this analysis indicates that 720 simulations must be made at least to obtain statistically reliable data. Taking into account the 720 executions on one core processor, the simulation time (average) is 7.34 h for 1000 individuals and 27.44 h for 1,500 individuals per scenario. In order to use this tool as Decision Support System (DSS), the students are instructed of necessary HPC techniques and the embarrassingly parallel computing model is presented to reduce the execution time and the decision-making process time [13]. To perform this task, students must learn how to execute multiple parametric Netlogo model runs in a multi-core system and how to make a performance analysis to evaluate the efficiency and scalability of the proposed method.

The second case presented to the students is the paradigmatic example of meteorological services. Everybody watches the weather forecast on the TV news everyday and can imagine the complexity of the models involved, with huge meshes of points with hundreds of variables estimated for every point, and the computing requirements needed to provide a real prediction. However, in this particular case, it is known that weather prediction models show chaotic behaviour. The way to keep this chaotic behaviour as limited as possible is to execute, not just a single simulation, but a complete set of scenarios (called ensemble) and apply statistical methods to conform the final prediction. This meteorological modelling and prediction part is presented by members of the Servei

Meteorològic de Catalunya (Meteorological Service of Catalonia). Obviously, it is out of the scope of the subject to develop a meteorological model, but the students can use some small specific models such as wind field models (WindNinja [12]) for analysing its execution time, scalability and speedup. In this context, some students (one or two per year) may enroll an internship in this meteorological service developing code for some particular model or applying parallel programming techniques to some of the existing models.

In a similar way, a collaboration has been established with the IC3-BSC (Institut Català de Ciències del Clima - Barcelona Supercomputing Center), but in this case the models and predictions are related to climatological models involving very large time scales. In this case, the real time aspect is not so critical, since the predictions are considered for decades or even centuries. However, the main point is to run hundreds or thousands of simulations with different parameters that make the total amount of computational requirements extremely large. Also in this case, some students carry out a internship in this centre, where they have access to very large computing resources and can make very interesting studies on speedup and scalability.

5 Conclusions

Many fields of science and engineering are evolving by the contribution of complementary fields. This implies that working teams in companies and research centres have significant interdisciplinary components and it is necessary that people from different fields are able to establish a common ground and understand the requirements and problems of all the sides. High performance computing, including parallel and distributed programming, becomes a central factor that is applied to many fields from science and engineering. So, it is necessary that the students from different fields receive a significant training in high performance computing. In this way, they are able to design and develop their own applications and, even more important, they understand the implications of using some particular architecture or programming paradigm. In this way they can establish a common language with computer scientists and work together in the development of more powerful and successful applications. In this interdisciplinary context, the experience of teaching parallel programming in interdisciplinary studies at master level has been presented. The main conclusion is that the experience is very successful and most students enjoy developing parallel programs, analysing their behaviour and trying to improve their performance. After this experience it would be very interesting to introduce similar subjects at the undergraduate level, so that students from different fields are able to apply high performance computing techniques to their computational problems from the very beginning.

References

1. Cuda Visual Profiler. http://docs.nvidia.com/cuda/profiler-users-guide/index.html#visual-profiler. Accessed 18 May 2015

2. Dyninst API. http://www.dyninst.org/. Accessed 18 May 2015
3. Lightweight performance tools. https://code.google.com/p/likwid/. Accessed 18 May 2015
4. Message Passing Interface Forum. http://www.mpi-forum.org/. Accessed 18 May 2015
5. NetLogo. Wilensky, U.: Center for Connected Learning and Computer-Based Modeling. Northwestern University, Evanston, IL (1999). https://ccl.northwestern.edu/netlogo/index.shtml. Accessed 18 May 2015
6. OpenMP. http://openmp.org/. Accessed 18 May 2015
7. Paraver. http://www.bsc.es/computer-sciences/performance-tools/paraver. Accessed 18 May 2015
8. perf: Linux profiling. https://perf.wiki.kernel.org/index.php/Main_Page. Accessed 18 May 2015
9. Performance API. http://icl.cs.utk.edu/papi/. Accessed 18 May 2015
10. Performance Visualization. http://www.mcs.anl.gov/research/projects/perfvis/software/viewers/. Accessed 18 May 2015
11. Bell, N., Hoberock, J.: Thrust: a productivity-oriented library for CUDA. Jade Edition, GPU Computing Gems (2012)
12. Forthofer, J., Shannon, K., Butler, B.W.: Initialization of high resolution surface wind simulations using nws gridded data. In: Proceedings of 3rd Fire Behavior and Fuels Conference, 25–29 October 2010
13. Foster, I.T.: Designing and Building Parallel Programs - Concepts and Tools for Parallel Software Engineering. Addison-Wesley, Reading (1995)
14. Gutierrez-Milla, A., Borges, F., Suppi, R., Luque, E.: Individual-oriented model crowd evacuations distributed simulation. In: Proceedings of the International Conference on Computational Science, ICCS 2014, Cairns, Queensland, Australia, 10–12 June, 2014. pp. 1600–1609 (2014). http://dx.doi.org/10.1016/j.procs.2014.05.145
15. Helbing, D., Buzna, L., Johansson, A., Werner, T.: Self organized pedestrian crowd dynamics: experiments, simulations, and design solutions. Transp. Sci. **39**(1), 1–24 (2005). http://dx.doi.org/10.1287/trsc.1040.0108
16. Martínez, A., Sikora, A., César, E., Sorribes, J.: ELASTIC: a large scale dynamic tuning environment. Sci. Program. **22**(4), 261–271 (2014)
17. McCool, M., Reinders, J., Robison, A.: Structured Parallel Programming: Patterns for Efficient Computation, 1st edn. Morgan Kaufmann Publishers Inc., San Francisco (2012)
18. Miceli, R., Civario, G., Sikora, A., César, E., Gerndt, M., Haitof, H., Navarrete, C., Benkner, S., Sandrieser, M., Morin, L., Bodin, F.: AutoTune: a plugin-driven approach to the automatic tuning of parallel applications. In: Manninen, P., Öster, P. (eds.) PARA. LNCS, vol. 7782, pp. 328–342. Springer, Heidelberg (2013)
19. Morajko, A., Morajko, O., Margalef, T., Luque, E.: MATE: dynamic performance tuning environment. In: Danelutto, M., Vanneschi, M., Laforenza, D. (eds.) Euro-Par 2004. LNCS, vol. 3149, pp. 98–107. Springer, Heidelberg (2004)
20. Shende, S., Malony, A.D.: The Tau parallel performance system. IJHPCA **20**(2), 287–311 (2006)
21. Wolf, F.: Scalasca. In: Encyclopedia of Parallel Computing, pp. 1775–1785 (2011)

On-line Service for Teaching Parallel Programming

Marek Nowicki[1], Maciej Marchwiany[2], Maciej Szpindler[2], and Piotr Bała[2](✉)

[1] Faculty of Mathematics and Computer Science, Nicolaus Copernicus University,
Chopina 12/18, 87-100 Toruń, Poland
`faramir@mat.umk.pl`
[2] Interdisciplinary Centre for Mathematical and Computational Modelling,
University of Warsaw, Pawińskiego 5a, 02-106 Warsaw, Poland
`{memar,m.szpindler,bala}@icm.edu.pl`

Abstract. With the wide adoption of the multicore and multiprocessor systems, parallel programming becomes very important element of the computer science education. However, the number of students exposed to the parallel programming is still limited and it is difficult to increase this number using traditional approach to teaching. The difficulties are caused, amongst others, by the parallel tools, libraries and programming models. The parallel programming using the message passing model is difficult, the shared memory model is easier to learn but writing codes which scales well is not easy. There is quite potential in the PGAS languages but they are not widely popularized. Finally, the teaching of scalable parallel programming requires access to the large computational systems which is not easy to obtain and even then, the operating systems and its specific features like operating and queueing systems provide students with additional challenges. In this paper we present extension of the developed by us *ZawodyWeb* system for on-line validation of the programs sent by the students. The *ZawodyWeb* system has been extended to support parallel programs written in different programming paradigms. With the help of UNICORE middleware, it allows to run students problems on the large scale production facilities. The added value is simple web interface which reduces all peculiarities of the large multiprocessor computers. The developed by us system has been verified during the parallel programming course for the undergraduate students from the computer science program.

Keywords: Parallel computing · Partitioned global address space · PCJ · On-line tools · Java · C

1 Introduction

The number of students exposed to the parallel programming is limited and even not all computer science students are obtaining necessary knowledge and skills. The traditional parallel and distributed programming courses focus often

S. Hunold et al. (Eds.): Euro-Par 2015 Workshops, LNCS 9523, pp. 78–89, 2015.
DOI: 10.1007/978-3-319-27308-2_7

on very basic ideas and problems such as monitors, semaphores etc. and do not address novel high level solutions.

The limited mathematical background of the computer science students makes teaching of the parallel algorithms uneasy task. The difficulties introduced by the programming tools, libraries and job execution with the queueing system makes this task dramatically complex and uneasy. The parallel programming using the message passing model is difficult, the shared memory model is easier to learn but writing codes which scales well is not easy. There is quite potential in the PGAS languages but they are not widely popularized [12]. Development of a scalable parallel programming requires access to the large computational systems located usually in the HPC centers putting additional formal and technical barriers. In order to make teaching of the parallel programming easier, we have to remove as many barriers as possible. The students have to concentrate on the essence of the problem and should not spend time to fight with the not important peculiarities of the parallel computer its operating or queueing system. To make teaching more efficient we should focus on the parallel algorithms and programming paradigms rather then on the teaching programming with the particular library or language. At some point students will have to face technical problems, but they will have much better knowledge, will be better motivated and will be better prepared.

For this purposes, to minimize unnecessary student's and teacher's effort, we have created web solution based on the developed by us *Zawody Web* [9] system for on-line validation of the programs sent by the students. The system has been extended to support parallel programs written in different programming paradigms. With the help of UNICORE middleware, the *Zawody Web* system allows to run students problems on the large scale facilities available in the supercomputer centre. The added value is simple web interface which reduces all complexity of the large multiprocessor computers. The developed by us system has been verified during the parallel programming course for the undergraduate students from the computer science program at University of Warsaw and Cardinal Stefan Wyszyński University in Warsaw.

The paper is organized as follows: Sect. 2 provides motivation and briefly describes available solutions. Next sections provide details on the UNICORE middleware used to access large computational resources (Sect. 4) and on the *Zawody Web* on-line contest system (Sect. 3). Section 6 describes parallel languages and paradigms supported by the *Zawody Web* system with the extended description of the PCJ library for parallel programming in Java. Last two sections present results and conclusions.

2   Motivation

At the beginning of traditional learning loop, a teacher prepares suitable learning material. Then, during the lesson, he/she passes the knowledge to the students. Students can acquire knowledge in full, in part or not at all. Programming is practical activity and teaching should involved number of assignments realized in form of the supervised work in the laboratory or individual work of the student.

All players would like to know whether the knowledge is well acquired. The traditional method to verify this is based on tests and exams. Unfortunately, this solution requires from students to be familiar with the material and checks only their knowledge. The other possibility to measure students' skills is through assignments to be solved at home. Unfortunately, this requires significant effort to check assignments, especially in the computer science, where one task can be solved in many different ways.

Over the years, different kinds of programming contests became very popular. The most popular are: ACM International Collegiate Programming Contest (http://cm2prod.baylor.edu), Imagine Cup (http://imaginecup.com) or Top Coder (http://www.topcoder.com). For that purpose many contests hosting services emerged enabling remote validation of implemented solutions. Some of them are more oriented on algorithms and check if the solutions uses optimal one. Vast majority of the on-line system address validation single threaded problems. In few cases, like Potyczki Algorytmiczne (http://potyczki.mimuw.edu.pl/l/36/), the on-line system has been adopted to the parallel problems but limited to the shared memory programming with the small number of cores. Similar limitations has Mooshak system used for the Spanish Parallel Programming Contests [3]. None of known systems is addressing problem of the execution on the large parallel infrastructures nor provides estimates of scalability of the users solution.

3   ZawodyWeb System

To address problem of automatic validation of the computer programs in the students' education we have developed the *ZawodyWeb* – a web contest system [9]. The main aim of the system is to make teaching of the programming more efficient and extend it to the work performed by the students themselves in the classroom and at home. The *ZawodyWeb* is open source software and is available on GitHub [2].

3.1   Overview

In the *ZawodyWeb* system all teacher and student activities are performed on-line using web browser. A teacher can create problem by entering its name, description, programming languages that can be used to solve the problem, test data (the inputs and outputs) and information about the accessibility. A student has access to the problem description and tries to solve it on the local machine, using the one of the listed programming languages. The student can check solution by himself preparing adequate input data and checking if program he/she wrote generates the same output. Next, the student can submit his solution to the *ZawodyWeb* system, which automatically validates it. Validation is performed through compilation, execution and then checking of the program results on the given input data sets. For the correct solution, the student receives points depends on the difficulty of the task and the correctness of the solution.

When the output of one or more tests differs from those created by the teacher or program execution exceeds the time limit, the student gets that information and can improve his solution. Then he/she can check correctness of the new version. The details of the system can be found elsewhere [9], here we provide brief description.

3.2   Technical Details

The *ZawodyWeb* system is created in the Java language using the Spring Framework and JavaServer Faces libraries (Facelets, Richfaces, Restfaces, etc.). The system is hosted on the Apache/Tomcat web server. The PostgreSQL database is used to store data and Hibernate is used for mapping Java objects to the data The JudgeManager and Judges are written in Java. Architecture of the system is presented in the Fig. 1.

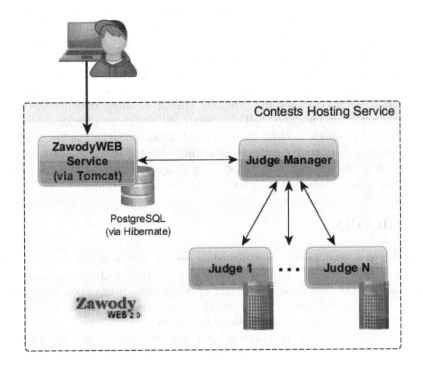

Fig. 1. The architecture of the *ZawodyWeb* system.

3.3   Functionality

Most of the *ZawodyWeb* system functionality is related to the organization of programming contests and to support on-line learning through assignments to be solved in the classroom or at home. System allows to define contests, programming tasks, scores and rankings. It offers different roles for students, teachers (task and contest creators) and administrators. The teacher can use the system for automatic check of the correctness of the solutions. Each student's submission can be viewed on-line by the teacher, so he/she can respond quickly to a variety of problems arising. If the problem description requires advanced texts or drawings, which cannot be done using HTML, it is possible to display the contents of a PDF file attached to the problem. *ZawodyWeb* system allows students to ask the teacher questions related to the problems. Questions are sent to the teacher via e-mail and he/she can answer directly or post comments visible by all students in the proper section of the service. The teacher can block visibility of the student's ranking. There is also possibility to block the ranking for last few minutes, to motivate students to compete and try to solve more problems than their colleagues.

System *ZawodyWeb* allows the teacher to download the students' solutions that are visible in the ranking. This helps to catch solutions that are copied from other sources or dependent. Among useful features there is an ability to block submissions or hide the problems for computers outside defined IP range, e.g. from outside the computer lab. Within the system there is a dedicated class that allows performing operations that are not permitted in programming competitions. Among operations that are not tested are: parsing parameters passed to the program, error codes for the program, custom headers, opening and reading or writing files. The *ZawodyWeb* system has ability to provide additional parameters to compiler. Setting up additional parameters the teacher can force the compiler to check source code compatibility with the selected language standard. There is also an easy way to add new languages and new functionalities by creating a Java class that implements appropriate interface.

4   UNICORE

UNICORE is a grid middleware providing secure and seamless access to the distributed resources. It has been developed since 1997 and is now a software maintained by the dedicated community of developers. It has been successfully used in many scientific projects contributing significantly to the increase of the popularity and applications of distributed computing.

UNICORE middleware [1] builds upon a number of concepts, such as Service Oriented Architecture (SOA) and messaging [10]. The capabilities of a distributed system are organized into well-defined *services*. The UNICORE has typical 3-layer architecture covering target system infrastructure, middleware and user interfaces. For the end user there are different types of interfaces available: UNICORE Rich Client (URC), UNICORE Commandline Client (UCC) and High Level API (HiLA). UCC is a full-featured client for the UNICORE Grid middleware. It provides client commands for all the UNICORE basic services. In particular user can submit and manage jobs and input and output transfers.

UNICORE 7 provides a generic web services hosting environment. Services can be deployed into this environment, in order to benefit from its general features: persistence, security infrastructure, and so on. Since all services are hosted in the same environment, a common web service level security infrastructure is achieved.

The UNICORE security infrastructure [4] offers access control, centralized user and role management and basic transport level security. Communication security uses secure socket layer and transport layer security (SSL and TLS). Users and server components are identified using a X.509 certificate issued by a trusted certification authority.

5 *ZawodyWeb* Support for Parallel Computing

In order to support on-line evaluation of the parallel tasks we had to extend *ZawodyWeb* system with new features. In general, parallel tasks can be divided into two groups: (i) problems that use only one single computer equipped with multiple cores and (ii) problems that run on a clusters containing multiple nodes equipped with multicore processors.

Executing parallel tasks on one single computer (case (i)) is straightforward. A compilation and an execution can be done in the same way as for a serial tasks. For example, adding a `-fopenmp` flag for compiling solution using GCC compiler and running it with proper environmental variable set, is enough for solution using OpenMP. The OpenMP problems can be evaluated on relatively small resources which can be exclusively used by the *ZawodyWeb*.

More difficult case is the second one, i.e. executing parallel tasks on clusters especially production ones. In this case of *ZawodyWeb* system cannot submit jobs directly to the system but has to use queuing system. Because of the administrative restrictions, as well as due to various technical reasons, the *ZawodyWeb* system cannot be installed directly on the submit host of the cluster queueing system. Even if this is possible, the *ZawodyWeb* would be limited to a single cluster and dynamic change of the resources used to verify submitted solutions would not be easy. Therefore we have decided to use UNICORE as a layer between *ZawodyWeb* and queuing systems. With UNICORE, it is possible to run submitted programs on a different clusters, regardless what the underlaying queuing system is. This allows also to install and configure the *ZawodyWeb* only once, and use computing resources available in various UNICORE Sites registered within one registry. Use of the UNICORE simplifies significantly all problems related to the authorization and authentication required to get access to the large computational resources.

From the user's point of view, sending solution for parallel tasks, even through UNICORE and queueing system is the same as for single threaded problems evaluated on the resources dedicated to the *ZawodyWeb*. When user submits problem solution to the *ZawodyWeb*, the web interface informs JudgeManager. It subsequently informs one of the Judges to prepare and submit proper job using UNICORE middleware. The created job contains script to compile and execute submitted solution on the defined test data. Once solution is submitted using UNICORE, the UNICORE job id (called End Point Reference, EPR) is stored in the *ZawodyWeb* database and the solution state is set to *external-check state.*

In order to support new functionality in the *ZawdoyWeb* system, in addition to the *JudgeManager* and *Judges*, the *External-Checker judge* was created. It periodically checks whether there are tasks with *external-check state* set. If so, it checks the UNICORE status of the job. The job with the FAILED status is further examined and a failure reason is stored in the *ZawodyWeb* database, so the user can know the possible cause of failure. In most cases, possible cause of failure is associated with the exceeded memory limit or exceeded time limit. When the job is finished with the SUCCESS status, the output returned by the user's program is compared with the output prepared by the problem's author and user's submission is scored with an appropriate number of points. It can be possibly 0, when the outputs are different.

The integral part of the *ZawodyWeb* system is definition of the tests used to validate solutions submitted by the user. In order to support parallel execution we have added possibility to configure additional parameters both for the problem (i.e. for all tests) and for each test separately. The parameters are passed to the Judge and are used to construct job description submitted using UNICORE. Using this functionality user can define number of nodes used to run test and number of threads/copies started on each node. This allows to run tests with the different number of cores per node used.

The *ZawodyWeb* system has been also extended by the information about the execution time of the particular test. It is displayed together with the result of each test. The time measurement is approximate, especially for Java applications, but it provides information which allows user to estimate scalability of the submitted solution.

6   Supported Languages

The *ZawodyWeb* has been configured to support most popular parallel programming languages such as OpenMP, MPI and selected PGAS languages. In the first two cases students can submit solutions written in C/C++, for the PGAS we have chosen PCJ library which allows to develop parallel applications in Java.

6.1   OpenMP

OpenMP (Open Multi-Processing) is an API that supports multi-platform shared memory multiprocessing programming [5]. It uses a portable, scalable model that gives programmers a simple and flexible interface for developing parallel applications. The runtime environment assigns the number of threads based on environment variables, in particular `OMP_NUM_THREADS`.

6.2   MPI

MPI through years has become a *de facto* standard for communication among processes that model a parallel program running on a distributed memory system. It is a language-independent communications protocol which supports both point-to-point and collective communication. MPI is a message-passing application programmer interface, together with protocol and semantic specifications [7]. The execution of the parallel program is usually realized through mpirun (or mpiexec) command which starts parallel execution on the given set of processors. The detailed number of processors used as well as their configuration is passed through files and parameters to the mpirun command.

6.3   PCJ

The PCJ library is Java library providing parallel programming in the PGAS model. In the PCJ, each task has its own local memory. PCJ stores and access variables only locally. Some variables can be shared between tasks. Shared variables can be accessed, read and modified by other tasks.

Each task can access other tasks variables that are stored in a shared memory. Besides that, shareable variable has to have a special annotation @Shared. The library provides methods to perform basic operations like synchronization of tasks, get and put values in asynchronous one-sided way. Additionally, the library offers methods for creating groups of tasks, broadcasting and monitoring variables. The PCJ library fully complies with Java standards therefore the programmer does not have to use additional libraries, which are not part of the standard Java distribution. In particular, it can use, implemented in Java SE 7, Sockets Direct Protocol (SDP), which can increase network performance over infiniband connections.

In the PCJ one instance of JVM is understood as node. PCJ can run on a single multicore node. One node can hold many tasks – separated instances of PCJ thread that run calculations. This design is aligned with novel computer architectures containing hundreds or thousands of nodes, each of them built of several or even more cores. This forces us to use different communication mechanism for inter- and intranode communication.

In the PCJ there is one node called *Manager*. It is responsible for setting unique identifiers to the tasks, sending messages to other tasks to start calculations, creating groups and synchronizing all tasks in calculations. The *Manager* node has its own tasks and can execute parallel programs.

In the PCJ, there is possibility to assign tasks into groups. Groups can be used for simplify collective operations like *broadcast* or *synchronize* [8].

Each node has its own, unique for whole calculations, identifier. That node is called *physical node id* or *node id* in short. All nodes are connected to each other and that connection is accomplished before starting a calculation. At this stage, nodes are exchanging their *physical node ids*.

The application using PCJ library is run as a Java application using Java Virtual Machine (JVM). In the multinode environment one (or more) JVM has to be started on each node. The PCJ library takes care on this process and allows user to start execution on multiple nodes, running multiple threads on each node. The number of nodes and threads can be easily configured, however the most reasonable choice is to limit on each node number of threads to the number of available cores. Typically, single Java Virtual Machine is run on each physical node.

The communication between different PCJ threads is realized in different manners. If communicating PCJ threads run within the same JVM, the Java concurrency mechanisms can be used to synchronize and exchange information. If data exchange has to be realized between different JVM's the network communication using, for example, sockets is performed.

Tasks can exchange data in asynchronous way. Sending a value to other task storage is performed using the *put* method. The *get* method is used for getting value from other task storage. In these two methods, the other task is nonblocking when process puts or gets message, but the task which initiated exchange process, blocks. There is the *getFutureObject* method that works in fully nonblocking manner – the initializing task can check if the response is received and in meantime do other calculations. There is also the *broadcast* method, which also works in asynchronous way. In the broadcast, all nodes are putting broadcasted value into their storage. The broadcast message is sent using tree structure of nodes.

7   Results

The *ZawodyWeb* system extended with the checking of parallel solutions has been installed at ICM University of Warsaw to support training of the HPC centre users as well as students taking parallel computing course. The web interface allows to verify solutions on the production infrastructure, in particular heterogenous PC cluster *hydra* with Intel and AMD processors. Cluster partition, that consist of nodes with Intel(R) Xeon(R) CPU X5660 (Westmere-EP) processors, is connected with Infiniband QDR and 1 Gb Ethernet. Each board is equipped with 2 processors Intel Xeon 2.8 GHz processors with 6 cores each. Each node is equipped with 24 GB of memory. The cluster has also number of 4-processor nodes with the AMD Opteron (TM) Processors 6272 (Interlagos) (16 cores each) connected with 10 Gb Ethernet. The job submission to the cluster is managed using SLURM queueing system.

Most of the jobs submitted through *ZawodyWeb* system is relatively short and in order to maximize turnover we have created reservation of the resources dedicated to the on-line system. The reservation was possible due to our recent developments which improve access to the infrastructure [6].

The reservation is limited to the 2 nodes (in total 24 cores) which allows for the execution of the tested parallel probems up to 24 cores. The *ZawodyWeb* still allows to submit larger problems to the rest of the system using queues available to all users. The proposed set up can be dynamically changed, and the reservation can be extended in size or limit for the particular period of time if required.

As described in the Sect. 5, the system allows to configure execution of each test or all tests for the particular problem. This is done by the setting up number of environment variables which are passed to the UNICORE job description and than use to modify execution. Example set of variables to modify JVM execution, use of the reservation and executing test on 2 nodes with 12 threads running on each node is presented in the Listing 1.

```
1 UNICORECC_JVMARGS=-Dpcj.redirect.out=0 -Dpcj.redirect.err=0
    -Dpcj.out.node=0
2 UNICORECC_RESERVATION=PCJ
3 UNICORECC_CPU_PER_NODE=12
4 UNICORECC_NODES_COUNT=2
```

Listing 1. Example set of parameters for the test execution.

7.1 Practical Evaluation

The system has been used to support parallel programing course for undergraduate students from the computer science course at University of Warsaw (selected students who finished 2nd year of study) and Cardinal Stefan Wyszyński University in Warsaw (3rd year students). The student registration in the system was performed in the computer lab during lectures together with supervised solution of the training set of problems. Students had no problem with the access and use of the system. Moreover, due to the lack of the ssh access, hidden system specificity and no need to play with the queueing system, they were able to submit solutions and execute them on the system in a short time. The goal was to obtain maximal number of points for two simple projects (printing "Hello world" string from the different parallel threads). Students were able to finish this using no more than 7 attempts. Some of them obtained correct result with single submission, average number was 3.2 submission. The PCJ was used as the parallel programming paradigm.

As the next session students had to implement 3 simple problems: broadcast, reduction, loop parallelization. All examples had been explained during the lectures and code outline using Java with PCJ has been provided to the students. In this case number of attempts was smaller (maximum 4), however half of the students dropped out after first unsuccessful attempt and did not finished the task.

Last, more advanced session was to solve 4 problems: reduction using communication on the ring, finding smallest element in the dataset, evaluation of the dot product and two-dimensional stencil calculations. The first 3 problems has been solved by the students with a couple of attempts (maximum 6). The time between first and last submission was usually a couple of hours, not more than 2 days. Students have been using Java with PCJ to implement solutions, this problem set has been solved only by the students who already solved simple problems.

The two-dimensional stencil problem was not solved, but this was expected since students were provided only short introduction to the parallel computing

(90 min lecture) and solving example problems (60 min) followed by practical introduction to the *Zawody Web* system (30 min).

Taking into account short introduction provided to the students during traditional lectures, the *Zawody Web* system allows student to learn parallel programming in practice. This part of the lecture can be performed on-line, in the time chosen by the student. The observed students' drop-of is characteristic to any on-line activity and has source in the student's self-motivation [11].

8   Conclusions

In this paper we have presented *Zawody Web* – the web solution for on-line validation of the programs sent by the students. The system has been extended to support parallel programs written in different programming paradigms. In result, the *Zawody Web* system allows to run students problems on the large scale facilities available in the supercomputer centre.

The system has been used to support teaching of the computer science students on the undergraduate level. The use of *Zawody Web* allowed us to grant students with the possibility to execute problems on the production systems with the thousands of cores. The same time we were able to hide all complexity of the large multiprocessor computers. The detailed feedback from the students is being gathered and analyzed.

We still have plans to extend system. First of all, we would like to reduce turnaround time, i.e. time required to provide submission evaluation to the student. Currently we observe quite large overhead caused by the both UNICORE and queueing systems.

We also plan to change authorization and authentication mechanism. Currently *Zawody Web* system uses dedicated account to submit jobs. We would like to use student's accounts for these purposes. This scenario is possible now, but user would be able to get access to the directory where input and output files are stored. Therefore user would be able to see tests input as well as correct answer. Currently this is not possible and requires modifications in the UNICORE framework allowing to track where job is submitted from.

Acknowledgements. This work has been performed using the PL-Grid infrastructure. Partial support from the CHIST-ERA consortium (HPDCJ project) and National Centre for Research and Development (OCEAN project) is acknowledged.

References

1. Unicore middleware website (2014). http://unicore.eu
2. ZawodyWeb (2014). https://github.com/faramir/ZawodyWeb
3. Almeida, F., Cuenca, J., Fernández-Pascual, R., Giménez, D., Benito, J.A.P.: The spanish parallel programming contests and its use as an educational resource. In: 2012 IEEE 26th International Parallel and Distributed Processing Symposium Workshops and Ph.D. Forum, pp. 1303–1306. IEEE (2012)

4. Benedyczak, K., Bała, P., van den Berghe, S., Menday, R., Schuller, B.: Key aspects of the unicore 6 security model. Future Generat. Comput. Syst. **27**(2), 195–201 (2011)
5. Dagum, L., Enon, R.: OpenMP: an industry standard API for shared-memory programming. IEEE Comput. Sci. Eng. **5**(1), 46–55 (1998)
6. Kluszczyński, R., Stolarek, M., Marczak, G., Górski, Ł., Nowicki, M., Bała, P.: Development of parallel codes using PL-grid infrastructure (2014)
7. MPI Forum: MPI: A message-passing interface standard. version 2.2, September 2019. http://www.mpi-forum.org
8. Nowicki, M., Bała, P.: Parallel computations in java with PCJ library. In: 2012 International Conference on High Performance Computing and Simulation (HPCS), pp. 381–387. IEEE (2012)
9. Nowicki, M., Mikulski, Ł., Piątkowski, M., Kluszczyński, R., Bała, P.: On-line contests hosting service as a tool to teach computer science students programming (2013)
10. Streit, A., Bala, P., Beck-Ratzka, A., Benedyczak, K., Bergmann, S., Breu, R., Daivandy, J.M., Demuth, B., Eifer, A., Giesler, A., et al.: Unicore 6 recent and future advancements. annales des télécommunications **65**(11–12), 757–762 (2010)
11. Yang, D., Sinha, T., Adamson, D., Rose, C.P.: Turn on, tune in, drop out: anticipating student dropouts in massive open online courses. In: Proceedings of the 2013 NIPS Data-Driven Education Workshop, vol. 11, p. 14 (2013)
12. Yelick, K., Bonachea, D., Chen, W.Y., Colella, P., Datta, K., Duell, J., Graham, S.L., Hargrove, P., Hilfinger, P., Husbands, P., et al.: Productivity and performance using partitioned global address space languages. In: Proceedings of the 2007 International Workshop on Parallel Symbolic Computation, pp. 24–32. ACM (2007)

Challenges of a Systematic Approach to Parallel Computing and Supercomputing Education

Vladimir Voevodin[1]([✉]), Victor Gergel[2], and Nina Popova[1]

[1] Lomonosov Moscow State University, Vorobyevy Gory, Moscow, Russia
voevodin@parallel.ru, popova@cs.msu.su
[2] Lobachevsky State University of Nizhny Novgorod, Nizhny Novgorod, Russia
gergel@unn.ru

Abstract. The scale of changes in the computing world dictates the need to introduce comparably major changes in the education system. Knowledge and skills with a strong foundation in parallelism concepts are becoming key qualities for any modern specialist. The situation cannot be changed by introducing just one training course; progress needs to be achieved in many direction at once, by developing supercomputing education infrastructure. This article is dedicated to presenting work performed in Russia to develop parallel computing, high-performance computing and distributed computing education as well as results which were obtained and lessons we have learnt from the national "Supercomputing Education" project.

Keywords: Parallel computing · Supercomputing · High performance computing · Higher education system · School education · Body of knowledge · Computer technologies

1 Introduction

The computing world is changing. All devices – from mobile phones and personal computers to high-performance supercomputers – are becoming parallel. Computing resources at almost every scale are now available with cloud and distributed computing. The huge capacity of modern supercomputers allows complex problems, previously thought impossible, to be solved. The growth in computing performance is exceptional: with computing speed crossing the Petaflops line in 2008, Exaflops performance is expected by 2020. Supercomputer systems with record-breaking computing performance will be ultra-parallel (up to billions processing cores), containing different types of computing devices within a multi-level hierarchy: distributed computing systems, computing nodes with shared memory, multi-core processors, computing accelerators, SIMD and VLIW functional unites.

The efficient usage of all the opportunities offered by modern computing systems represents a global challenge for the entire range of computer sciences. Tackling the capacity of parallel computing systems, supercomputer technologies

S. Hunold et al. (Eds.): Euro-Par 2015 Workshops, LNCS 9523, pp. 90–101, 2015.
DOI: 10.1007/978-3-319-27308-2_8

and distributed computing requires new knowledge, skills and abilities. The personnel training needed for this must be conducted across the entire range of specialists: from mathematicians and software developers to specialists in the most diverse areas of science, technology, industry and business. Since the number of these specialists is growing all the time, the education system needs to be modified likewise: while parallel computing issues were previously only taught in a master's degree program, they are now included in bachelor degree curriculum. Knowledge and skills with a strong foundation in parallelism concepts are becoming key qualities for any modern specialist.

The importance of education in the area of parallel, distributed and supercomputer technologies is understood by the international education community. A number of large-scale projects can be cited which try to elaborate on and structure this area of education, offering recommendations on preparing teaching materials and providing examples of training courses. These projects include:

– The Russian Supercomputing Education national project [1,2].
– Activities related to developing a computer science curricula (Computer Science 2013) by the ACM and IEEE-CS international communities [3].
– The Curriculum Initiative on Parallel and Distributed Computing project, supported by NSF/IEEE-TCPP [4].

Important recommendations in this area are given as part of the SIAM-EESI project for developing education and research in the area of Computational Science and Engineering [5]. A number of other interesting findings is presented in [6–10].

This article is dedicated to presenting work performed in Russia to develop supercomputing education. It is rather an overview of our activities in this area than a set of concrete technical recipes which can be immediately incorporated into educational courses. Russia's experience can come in handy for Universities from many countries, providing education in supercomputer technologies and high-performance computing, while discussing the results of these works can form grounds for developing extensive international cooperation.

2   Supercomputing Education Infrastructure

The scale of changes in the computing world dictates the need to introduce comparably major changes in the education system. The situation cannot be changed by introducing just one training course; progress needs to be achieved in many direction at once, by developing supercomputing education infrastructure. We have analyzed the global situation with education and identified several key objectives that form the basis for supercomputing education infrastructure in Russia. In this section we will describe the primary infrastructure elements and present specific examples of their practical implementation below.

The central part is a *revision of existing and newly developing educational and methodological materials:* curricula, training courses, textbooks, lab work and workshops. In some cases it is sufficient to mention the possibilities of parallel processing; other courses need a new section, e.g., on the parallel complexity of algorithms. In this regard, curricula need to be reviewed for all university natural sciences departments; many courses related to mathematical modeling and computing technologies must be rewritten from scratch.

The big question for this issue is what should we teach? What should be included in the new curricula? What ideas are fundamental and which ones are only needed to train experts? To find answers to these questions, a *Body of Knowledge* must be developed to help evaluate the scope and completeness of information on parallel computing and supercomputer technologies included in the study curricula.

Supercomputing education infrastructure must *cover all target trainee groups:* from schoolchildren and college students to teachers and staff of various organizations. At the same time, it is necessary to *support various forms of education:* classical university education, employee re-training and advanced training, distant education, internships, etc. It is important to remember that the balance between fundamental notions of parallel computing and the practical skills of working with parallel computing systems needs to be carefully weighed, depending on the target audience. It is vital to *provide trainees with access to powerful supercomputer systems* to conduct individual research projects in a highly parallel environment.

There needs to be *close contact between universities, leading IT companies, research institutes and industry.* This includes access to modern advanced technologies, science and actual industry tasks for teachers and students, as well as building up feedback in the form of a clear understanding of what is currently demanded of specialists in the labor market. These contacts can help in building a *nationwide system of supercomputer conferences and youth schools*, reflecting the interconnection between science, education and industry that is mandatory for the field.

To coordinate activities and ensure prompt interaction, it is important to establish a *tight integration between universities*: this will help to share and disseminate experience, build a single consolidated position and ensure reasonable specialization in the supercomputing education system. A consortium of universities will greatly simplify *interaction with the government, ministries and foundations* which determines the degree of state support and funding for all activities, and ultimately the scale and success of the intended changes.

A mandatory element of the infrastructure is *international cooperation.* It is important to analyze experience accumulated worldwide and adapt it to the national education system. It is equally important to work within the country: the changes are massive, they must be taken positively by the society, and that means *all sorts of PR events to popularize supercomputer technologies* must become a key element of the supercomputing education infrastructure.

A good example illustrating the specific steps taken to create supercomputing education infrastructure in Russia is the *Supercomputing education* national project described below in this paper.

3   Supercomputing Consortium of Russian Universities

One of the first steps in building supercomputing education infrastructure was to establish the Supercomputing Consortium of Russian Universities. This was initiated by four Russian State Universities: Moscow, Nizhny Novgorod, Tomsk and South Ural State, which formed the consortium on December 23rd, 2008. Today, the consortium has 61 permanent or associated members, including 45 leading Russian universities. The consortium is chaired by academician V. A. Sadovnichy, rector of Moscow State University.

The goal of the Consortium is to promote supercomputer technologies throughout the higher education system in Russia, and using the capacity of this system to develop and actively integrate supercomputer technologies into Russian science and industry. Key activities by the Consortium include a review of the current state of supercomputing education in Russian universities, conducting scientific conferences and youth schools on supercomputing-related topics, organizing joint seminars with industry leaders, publishing educational and popular-science literature, among other things. Members of the Supercomputing Consortium of Russian Universities meet once or twice a year to discuss past results and outline future plans.

One of the main and most visible outcomes of the Consortium's efforts in recent years is the implementation of the *Supercomputing education* national project.

4   Supercomputing Education National Project

The idea for this project was proposed to the President of the Russian Federation by V. A. Sadovnichy in 2009. The project was approved and implemented between 2010 and 2012 under the auspices of the President's Committee for the Modernization and Economic Development of Russia. For the first time, the project formulated a program of activities to create an integral system of supercomputing education in Russia. The project involved about 600 people from 63 universities and total financing of about 8 million dollars over three years.

The key to successfully implementing all of the objectives for the *Supercomputing education* project was establishing a national system of Research and Education Centers for Supercomputing Technologies (REC SCT). The system includes 8 centers in 7 Russian federal districts.

The main objective of the Research and Education Centers is to organize work for building supercomputing education system in their respective federal districts. All Centers are based on large universities, members of the Supercomputing Consortium of Russian Universities, which have both experience in research and educational practice in the field of supercomputer technologies. The Central REC, which coordinates the entire system, is at Lomonosov Moscow State University.

Fundamental to developing scientific and methodological support is the Body of Knowledge in the area of parallel computing and supercomputer technologies.

It includes the knowledge and competencies which students must attain to graduate from the respective departments or complete training at various special education forms. The main idea of the Body of Knowledge is to describe the subject area of supercomputers and parallel computing, to get a clear picture of what should be taught and how to organize the study process for each target group of students.

The Body structure was developed following the recommendations of international professional communities such as ACM and IEEE Computer Society, and suggestions made by the NSF/IEEE-TCPP project *Curriculum Initiative on Parallel and Distributed Computing*. The Body of Knowledge consists of five high-level chapters: the mathematical foundations of parallel computing; parallel computing system (computing basics); parallel programming technologies (software engineering basics); parallel algorithms; parallel computing, large tasks and specific subject areas. The chapters are then divided into sections, i.e. individual thematic modules within the subject area. Each section, then, consists of a set of topics representing the lowest level in the hierarchy. Each topic is accompanied by a mandatory/optional mark, complexity level and recommended amount of study time required to learn it. The Body of Knowledge covers more than 400 topics.

For this project, the Body of Knowledge formed the necessary foundation for a number of other tasks: developing a set of training courses, preparing the "Supercomputing education" book series, revising existing educational standards, reviewing curricula for a complete representation of supercomputer technologies, avoiding "blind spots" and the order of materials delivery – all these are easily assessed using the Body of Knowledge.

A unique book series titled "Supercomputing education" has been prepared and published. The series consists of 26 monographs, textbooks and study manuals written by leading Russian and foreign specialists on the main sections of the Body of Knowledge. Some of the books are dedicated to basic issues: computer architecture, programming technologies (MPI, OpenMP), GPU programming, and an introduction to parallel numerical methods and algorithm structure. Other books are dedicated to specific subject areas: supercomputer technologies in climate modeling, computational hydrodynamics, global optimization tasks, and number theory. Up to 50 sets of the "Supercomputing education series have been sent free of charge to 43 universities in Russia – a total of 31,500 books. In 2013, the "Supercomputing education series won the national "Book of the Year" contest in the nomination for "21st Century Textbook". New publications are currently being added to the series.

A lot of work has gone into developing new and expanding existing training courses: materials for 50 courses covering all the key sections in the Body of Knowledge are provided in the public domain. Some of the courses are intended for bachelor's degree studies, but most are targeted towards master's and postgraduate students.

One of the most complex objectives of the project is the actual training of various target groups, which could only be successfully completed thanks to the newly established REC SCT system. Primary emphasis was placed on three areas: basic-level education, training the trainers and specialized education in specific areas through advanced training programs. Basic-level training covered all Russian federal districts, 60 universities in 34 cities, reaching a total of 3,269 attendees. In this case we did not set any strict requirements for the curricula and did not try to make them all the same: each university had the right to decide which supercomputer technologies they preferred. The only requirement was that the curriculum should be at least 72 h.

Unlike the basic-level education, training the trainers and specialized education were conducted on a REC SCT basis. A total of 453 staff from more than 50 Universities were trained during the project. More than 40 groups have been created for training using 15 advanced-level curricula, each at least 72 h (790 specialists in a total).

The national system of supercomputer-related scientific conferences and youth schools had a particularly positive impact. With Russia's huge territory, it is not easy to move from one end to another; now six youth schools are operating on a regular basis from February to December in Arkhangelsk, Saint Petersburg, Moscow, Nizhny Novgorod, and Tomsk. This allows some convenience in choosing the time and place.

The system of conferences and schools is being actively developed. Last year, several conferences decided to merge into one large supercomputer forum "*Russian Supercomputing Days*" (RussianSCDays.org), which combines a scientific conference, exhibition, trainings and workshops, industrial and educational sessions, along with a number of specialized seminars and many other events. The summer school at Moscow State University has also evolved from its original format and was transformed into the Summer Supercomputing Academy. Each year the Academy selects more than 120 students and professors for two weeks of training on six programs. Some of the study programs are traditional (parallel programming technologies such as MPI, OpenMP, CUDA), while some require serious background (e.g., industrial mathematics and computational hydrodynamics). The MSU Summer Supercomputer Academy is increasingly becoming the focal point for all areas of Russia's supercomputing education development: universities, the Russian Academy of Sciences, industry, leading IT companies, and even schools recently. The training at the Academy is free.

The examples above are just some of the outcomes of the *Supercomputing education* project. But even these can provide an idea of the huge amount of work that has been completed to date. Popularizing supercomputer technologies, knowledge quality and testing systems, interaction with foreign universities, institutes and scientists, education as part of an supercomputer technologies Internet-university, suggestions for modifying state standards – all of these activities plus many others are left outside the scope of this article. But all of these together helped lay the foundation for supercomputing education system in Russia. The system certainly needs more development and improvement to become sustainable over the long run. And some elements of this work are already visible today, as we will describe briefly in the next section.

5 Supercomputing Education in Russia's Universities Today

The supercomputing education system in Russia, which has actively been developed in recent years, helped build a firm foundation for implementing various forms of education and study programs on supercomputer technologies at Russia's leading universities. This is the main outcome of the national project, and this can be easily seen from the last overview *Supercomputing Education in Russia* made by the Supercomputing Consortium of Russian Universities. High-performance computing systems that have been installed at many universities throughout the country are of great support for implementing these programs. Besides Moscow and Nizhny Novgorod State Universities, powerful supercomputers are installed at Saint Petersburg Polytechnic University, South Ural and Tomsk State Universities, Moscow Physics and Technical Institute, and many others. Six of the top ten most powerful supercomputers in the CIS Top50 list (top50.supercomputers.ru) are installed at Russian universities.

Every university uses a common approach to organizing training in supercomputer technologies (SCT). Most of the preparation of SCT and high-performance computing specialists for professional work is conducted at faculties for computational mathematics and information science. These faculties implement most of the study programs, organize inter-disciplinary courses and programs, and carry out additional SCT education programs. Another recent trend is the establishment of departments working in supercomputer-related areas. The departments coordinate various areas of research and educational work on SCT and other disciplines at the departmental and university levels.

Traditionally, computational mathematics departments provide high-level training on the fundamentals of mathematics (continuous and discrete) and information science, setting the basis for a fundamental education in mathematical modeling using supercomputers. Examples of this approach in action include Moscow Physics and Technical Institute, Siberian Federal University, South Urals State University, and Saint Petersburg State Polytechnic University.

Bachelor degree programs for SCT specializations include general and special courses that comply with the Body of Knowledge developed as part of the *Supercomputing education* project. The regional specialization of universities is taken into account by including individual modules on SCT topics into general courses and selecting the topics for elective courses. For example, Novosibirsk State University has a "Theory of Parallel Processing" course taught as a basic course, along with specialized courses "Using supercomputers in mathematical modeling," "Parallel computational methods," and "Parallel computing technologies for mathematical modeling."

The leading supercomputer universities are actively offering advanced training courses in SCT for university professors and academic staff. They provide regular training on specific additional education programs. The most common form of education is the 72-h professional advancement course. Examples of such programs include: "Advanced high-performance computing technologies and their application to modern biological and medical tasks" (MIPT), "High-performance computing using GPU" (Perm State National Research University), etc.

Constant coordination of supercomputing activities by universities at joint scientific seminars, curriculum discussion programs, youth schools and conferences allows Russian universities to significantly accelerate the implementation of supercomputer technologies into industry and research.

5.1 Supercomputing Education at Lomonosov Moscow State University

The Faculty of Computational Mathematics and Cybernetics (CMC) at Lomonosov Moscow State University is Russia's leading education center offering training on fundamental research in the areas of applied mathematics, computational technologies and information science. The Faculty trains specialists on issues related to using computers to solve problems in various fields of science, industry and business. About 300 students are enrolled every year.

Studying the theoretical basics and practical applications of high-performance computing and supercomputer technologies is mandatory for all students. The training in this area is based on a one-semester lecture course for bachelor degree students "Supercomputers and Parallel Data Processing." The main objective of the course is to show the close interrelation between parallel computing system architectures, parallel programming technologies and the parallel structure of programs and algorithms. From the second year onwards, students are distributed between departments, where they spend the next two years over specialized training and performing research. Further specialization continues as part of a two-year master's degree program offered by various departments.

An in-depth study of supercomputer technologies is conducted at the Department on Supercomputers and Quantum Informatics of the CMC Faculty. Here students are taught parallel computing methods and facilities, parallel programming technologies, and high-performance cluster-based computations using GPUs. The Department provides the "Supercomputer systems and applications" training as part of a master's degree program. A mandatory element in the Department training is a system of laboratory works offering practical support for supercomputer theory classes. To perform exercises and scientific research, students have an access the "Lomonosov" and Blue Gene/P supercomputers installed at MSU.

The Department cooperates with leading academic institutes and IT companies: institute of RAS, Intel, NVIDIA, T-Platforms, IBM, and others. One of the innovative forms of education introduced by the Department in recent years is the annual Summer Supercomputing Academy, which helps distribute the accumulated experience to higher education institutions throughout Russia.

This concept of education takes into account the growing demands of science and industry for highly skilled staff who are well-versed in modern computing technologies. It supports both general supercomputer training for specialists in mathematical fields, and specialized training for highly skilled specialists to work in new breakthrough areas which utilize high-performance computing systems. Further development of the education system must focus on strengthening the inter-disciplinary aspect of scientific research. For example, in recent years, the Department offers the "Supercomputers and Quantum Informatics" training course for all students of Moscow State University. The course is very popular among students, particularly in the natural sciences.

5.2 Supercomputing Education at the Lobachevsky Nizhny Novgorod State University

One key area of activity for Nizhny Novgorod State University is training and re-training specialists in supercomputer technologies and high-performance computing. NNSU offers bachelor's and master's degrees, post-graduate education, provides career advancement training to teachers from other universities, and organizes scientific and educational schools for young scientists and specialists. More than 300 people take part annually in various training, re-training and advanced training courses in SCT. More than 10 textbooks on parallel programming have been published.

NNSU plays an important role in developing the Body of Knowledge – a systemic foundation for developing SCT education and training programs. The "Fundamental information science and information technologies" course has been chosen as a pilot area in education, and 18 training courses have been expanded to take this change into account. Additional sections included in the updated course curricula are almost entirely compliant with the recommendations of the Body of Knowledge and recommendation made by the NSF/IEEE-TCPP project "Curriculum Initiative on Parallel and Distributed Computing" [4].

To evaluate the knowledge and skills learned, a set of 300 test questions was prepared on the topic of parallel and distributed computing. Students take tests before and after the study program, with the assignment for each student consisting of 28 to 40 questions. In the 2013–2014 academic year, average test scores increased from 23 % to 75 %. Testing helps evaluate the complexity of materials being studied, which can be used to identify the most difficult topics and improve the training courses accordingly. Traditionally, the complex topics for students are around the mathematical basics of supercomputer technologies and methods for assessing the efficiency of parallel computations.

To develop practical skills for applying parallel and distributed computing to specific tasks, students are provided test assignments of low to medium complexity. Assignment topics cover many sections of computational mathematics and computing, including matrix processing, integration, approximation of functions, data sorting, etc. By completing these assignments, students learn (or develop independently) parallel computing methods for various applications, write the necessary parallel codes, and set up computational experiments using supercomputer systems.

To prepare problem-oriented specialists (physicists, chemical engineers, biologists, etc.) who are capable of utilizing the capacity of supercomputer technologies to address tasks in their respective areas, NNSU has developed training modules that are common for all master's degree programs in the physics and mathematics departments.

The principal feature of these modules is a correlation of the volume of studied materials with the applied profile of trained specialists. Sample demonstrations and practical assignments in the study modules have been prepared taking into account the students' areas of specialization. These modules have been tested at NNSU and can be used at other universities.

6 Supercomputer Technologies and School Education

Speaking of establishing a sustainable supercomputing education system, we can't leave out the issue of school education. Computers are everywhere, and parallelism is in every computing device including smartphones and tablet PCs. Even today's schoolchildren, let alone future generations, will have to live in a massively parallel computing world. And, learning the basics should start at school. Moscow State University has been organizing excursions for over 500 schoolchildren to its supercomputer center each year. Kids are always impressed by the supercomputers, revealing a side of the computing world they never knew before. Even after a short explanation, they quickly begin to understand what these giants, occupying at least $1,000 \, m^2$ of floor space and weighing hundred tons, are all about. They understand that every supercomputer today is based on parallelism, which they currently have in their mobile devices. They also see that parallelism is not just here for the long term – it's here to stay.

For the third year in a row, the MSU Summer Supercomputer Academy announced the "Parallel Computing Technologies in School" education program. It targets school teachers, mainly informatics teachers, who feel the promise behind this technology and want to learn the basics of parallel computing so they can include the relevant information in their school classes. There is high demand for this program. Today it isn't just possible – it's mandatory – that elements on parallel computing are included in school curriculum. Perhaps in the form of intuitive understanding, simple examples or visits to supercomputing centers – but kids must get their first understanding of parallelism during their school years – this is the main reason why this program is included in the Academy agenda. If you have more than one surname, please make sure that the Volume Editor knows how you are to be listed in the author index.

7 Conclusion

Comparing the original plans, expectations and intentions with the actual results obtained during the past few years, it is possible to assess how much of the plans were implemented, which lessons have been learned, what was completed and what was not, which steps were right and which objectives still require more work.

A definitely positive step in establishing a supercomputing education system in Russia was the creation of the Supercomputing Consortium of Russian Universities, which took place in 2008, and the national system of Research and Education Centers of Supercomputing Technologies. These structures made it possible to consolidate the academic community, propose and successfully complete the *Supercomputing education* national project, the results of which are currently used in the most natural sciences faculties across Russia. It was definitely the right decision to put special emphasis on training university teachers. Teachers are often busy, and many find it easier to stick with the materials they already have for their courses, rather than learning something new. But changes are extremely necessary in this area. The book series titled "Supercomputing education" became very helpful in organizing the education process: the series started in 2010 and is still evolving.

Developing the Body of Knowledge on Parallel Computing and Supercomputer Technologies had a significant effect, even if it clearly has not been used to its full potential. This is particularly important now, when education in this area is in its initial stages. Study materials must be presented in the right sequence, without omissions, in the right amount and considering the complexity of materials – this is the purpose of the Body of Knowledge. The first versions of the Body have been created, but the work cannot stop there: the area is dynamic, which must be reflected in the Body of Knowledge.

The experience obtained over the past few years clearly shows the importance of making management (from deans and rectors to ministry officials and ministers) aware of the need for such changes. Of course, a lot can be done at the teacher level, but management support takes this activity to a completely new level.

Computing technologies play an exceptionally important role in the modern industry, and engineering education requires drastic changes today. This is the area where the thesis "to out-compete is to out-compute" [11] becomes of paramount importance. That's why it is so important to introduce supercomputer and parallel computing technologies into the engineering curricula. During the first stages, our primary focus was on more fundamental areas, but at the same time more than 40 agreements were signed between business enterprises and universities.

More attention should be paid to academic mobility. There are different scientific schools, different computing facilities, different subject areas and different training systems – to get the necessary knowledge, expand their outlook, and find their calling and a place in life, young people need to be given an opportunity to move between leading schools, universities, institutes, and training centers. We did not think of this before, but it needs to be considered in the future.

So far the capacity for distant education has not been fully realized. In some sense, online courses can cover some specific technological topics. But whether they can be used for large-scale training of really highly qualified specialists – remains to be seen. At the same time, this form of education does have its advantages, particularly in a geographically distributed country such as Russia.

Another serious issue is organizing practical implementation of parallel and supercomputer technologies. A careful selection of questions, examples, exercises, and practical computing tasks plays a very important role in this area. Parallelism and supercomputers must be used only where they are really needed. Why make a program parallel that takes 0.1 s to compute in serial mode? How much would a student understand about parallel computing while performing tasks on a serial machine? Without paying due attention to these questions at the start, you can destroy both the motivation and the training results.

Since recently, issues related to education in parallel computing and supercomputer technologies are being seriously considered by many organizations (IEEE, ACM, SIAM, Informatics Europe, etc.) and projects (PRACE, EESI, etc.). We hope that the experience of developing and implementing the basics of supercomputing education into the higher education system in Russia will be useful when implementing similar changes in other countries.

The results were obtained with the financial support of the Russian Science Foundation (agreement N14-11-00190).

References

1. Supercomputing Education in Russia: Final report on the national project, Supercomputing Education, Supercomputing Consortium of the Russian Universities (2012). http://hpc.msu.ru/files/HPC-Education-in-Russia.pdf
2. Voevodin, V.V., Gergel, V.: Supercomputing education: the third pillar of HPC. Comput. Meth. Softw. Dev. New Comput. Technol. **11**(2), 117–122 (2010). MSU Press, Moscow
3. Computing Curricula Computer Science (2013). http://ai.stanford.edu/users/sahami/CS2013
4. NSF/IEEE-TCPP Curriculum Initiative on Parallel and Distributed Computing. http://www.cs.gsu.edu/~tcpp/curriculum/
5. Future Directions in CSE Education and Research: Report from a Workshop Sponsored by the Society for Industrial and Applied Mathematics (SIAM) and the European Exascale Software Initiative (EESI-2). http://wiki.siam.org/siag-cse/images/siag-cse/f/ff/CSE-report-draft-Mar2015.pdf
6. Computer Science in Parallel (CSinParallel). http://serc.carleton.edu/csinparallel/index.html
7. HPC in Higher Education. http://www.hpcwire.com/2014/10/21/hpc-higher-education
8. A Survey on Training and Education Needs for Petascale Computing. http://www.prace-ri.eu/IMG/pdf/D3-3-1_document_final.pdf
9. Rague, B.: Teaching parallel thinking to the next generation of programmers. J. Educ. Inf. Cybern. **1**(1), 43–48 (2009)
10. Gergel, V., Liniov, A., Meyerov, I., Sysoyev, A.: NSF/IEEE-TCPP curriculum implementation at the State University of Nizhni Novgorod. In: Proceedings of the 2014 IEEE International Parallel and Distributed Processing Symposium Workshops, IPDPSW 2014, pp. 1079–1084. IEEE Computer Society, Washington, D.C. (2014)
11. Council on Competitiveness, U.S. Manufacturing – Global Leadership Through Modeling and Simulation White paper, 4 March 2009. http://www.compete.org/storage/documents/NDEMC_Final_Report_030915.pdf

Teaching Heart Modeling and Simulation on Parallel Computing Systems

Andrey Sozykin[1,2]([✉]), Mikhail Chernoskutov[1,2], Anton Koshelev[1,2],
Vladimir Zverev[1,2], Konstantin Ushenin[1,2], and Olga Solovyova[1,2,3]

[1] Institute of Mathematics and Mechanics UrB RAS, Ekaterinburg, Russia
[2] Ural Federal University, Ekaterinburg, Russia
`Andrej.Sozykin@urfu.ru`
[3] Institute of Immunology and Physiology UrB RAS, Ekaterinburg, Russia

Abstract. High Performance Computing (HPC) is an interdisciplinary field of study, which requires learning a number of topics, including not only parallel programming, but also numerical methods and domain science. Stand-alone parallel computing courses are insufficient for thorough HPC education. We present an interdisciplinary track of coherent courses devoted to modeling and simulation of the heart on parallel computing systems for master students at the Ural Federal University. The track consists of three modules: parallel and distributed computing, heart modeling, and numerical methods. Knowledge of numerical methods and heart modeling provides the students with the ability to acquire profound parallel programming skills by working out on the comprehensive programming assignment and complex heart modeling projects. Interdisciplinary approach also increases students' motivation and involvement.

Keywords: High performance computing · Distributed computing · HPC education · Heart simulation · Living system simulation

1 Introduction

High Performance Computing (HPC) is an interdisciplinary field of study, which requires learning a number of topics. To be able to solve state-of-the-art scientific and engineering problems on parallel computing systems, students have to study not only parallel programming, but also applied mathematics, numerical methods, and domain science. Therefore, stand-alone parallel computing courses are insufficient for thorough HPC education. Instead, the interdisciplinary training programs for various domain sciences are needed.

We present an interdisciplinary track of courses devoted to modeling and simulation of the heart on parallel computing systems. The track consists of the following modules: parallel and distributed computing, heart modeling, and numerical methods. Each module includes both theoretical and hands-on courses.

The course track is primarily aimed at master students in Computer Science, but it is also available for other students. The courses are taught by the Institute of Mathematics and Computer Sciences of the Ural Federal University in

S. Hunold et al. (Eds.): Euro-Par 2015 Workshops, LNCS 9523, pp. 102–113, 2015.
DOI: 10.1007/978-3-319-27308-2_9

cooperation with the Institute of Immunology and Physiology UrB RAS, and the Institute of Mathematics and Mechanics UrB RAS.

The initiative of creating the track was promoted by the scientific laboratory "Modeling of living systems on supercomputers", which carries out research on cardiac modeling [9,14–16]. At present, computer simulations in living systems have become an essential instrument of the medical science and practice, pharmacy, and education. As a part of the global international projects the Physiome [6] and the Virtual Physiological Human [10], the computer models of various systems, organs, and tissues are developed. The HPC is required to tackle biomedical problems due to the complexity of living system models, the enormous amount of input data, and the number of computational operations.

The important goal of the course track is to cultivate student interest in computational modeling and simulation using HPC, and to involve them into research work.

2   Related Work

Nowadays, the interdisciplinary HPC courses, workshops, and educational programs are beginning to emerge. In summer 2011, the City University of New York conducted a three week workshop on cardiac electrophysiology modeling [3]. The workshop combined lectures, hands-on lab experiments, and simulation on the graphics processor units (GPU). Students studied initiation of the spiral waves of electrical activity in the heart and the effect of various parameter values on the dynamics of these reentrant waves. The lecture topics included the current research in cardiac modeling, numerical methods, and tutorial on the compute unified device architecture (CUDA) programming. During the last week of the workshop, the in-depth lectures on GPU implementation of an electrophysiological model of a cardiac cell [5] was presented. The students successfully completed the workshop program and provided positive feedback. Some students continued to work with the researchers who conducted the workshop during the summer.

The interdisciplinary course "Finite Element Methods in Scientific Computing" [18] has been developed at the Texas A&M University. This project-based course covers parallel computing topics (pthreads, MPI), software engineering topics (using compilers, build tools, version control, debugging, *etc.*), and practical applications of the finite element method (FEM). The distinctive feature of the course is the usage of the flipped classroom format. The course authors recorded video lectures and posted them on YouTube [2]; therefore, students were able to watch the lectures outside the class. As a result, the teachers had more time in the class for interaction with students and for providing assistance to them on the projects. The flipped classroom format allows one to balance effectively competitive needs to present new material and to provide feedback to students.

At the University at Buffalo, an interdisciplinary computational and data-enabled science and engineering Ph.D. program has been developed [4]. The program included courses in three areas: applied mathematics and numerical methods, high performance and data intensive computing, and data science. In addition, only students with master degree in any domain science, such as engineering, computer science, and applied mathematics, are eligible for this Ph.D. program. Deep knowledge of the domain science provides the context for training and allows them to quickly apply acquired knowledge for profitable use.

3   The Course Track "Heart Modeling and Simulation on Parallel Computing Systems"

3.1   General Course Track Description

To meet the need for interdisciplinary training in HPC, the course track "Heart Modeling and Simulation on Parallel Computing Systems" has been developed at the Institute of Mathematics and Computer Science of Ural Federal University. The course track brings together researches from a variety of discipline, not only from the Ural Federal University, but also from the Institute of Immunology and Physiology UrB RAS, and the Institute of Mathematics and Mechanics UrB RAS.

The course track includes three modules: parallel and distributed computing, numerical methods, and heart modeling. The complete list of the courses is presented in Table 1.

Table 1. The list of courses in the "Heart Modeling and Simulation on Parallel Computing Systems" track

No	Course name	ECTS credits
1	**Parallel and distributed computing module**	
1.1	Parallel and distributed computing	4
1.2	GPU programming	2
1.3	Xeon Phi programming	2
2	**Numerical methods module**	
2.1	Parallel numerical methods	2
2.2	Science hackathon	4
3	**Heart modeling module**	
3.1	Simulation of living systems	4
3.2	Modeling heart dynamics on parallel computing systems	2
4	**Optional prerequisite courses**	
4.1	Scientific computing in C	2
4.2	Software performance optimization	2

The courses are primarily designed for master students in computer science, but bachelor students and master students with other background are also eligible. Typical class consists of 12–15 students.

Table 2. Recommended sequence of study for master students in computer science

Semester	Course name
1	Parallel and distributed computing
	Simulation of living systems
2	GPU programming
	Modeling heart dynamics on parallel computing systems
	Parallel numerical methods
3	Xeon Phi programming
	Science Hackathon

The recommended sequence of study for Computer Science Master students is presented in Table 2. Most of courses in the track are elective. Students are not required to pass all the courses; they are able to choose ones according to their individual needs and preferences.

3.2 Prerequisite Courses

In addition to three main modules, the course track also includes the optional prerequisite courses: "Scientific computing in C" and "Software performance optimization". The courses are intended for students with non computer science related bachelor degree and limited software development experience. The aim of the module is to provide students with good skills for programming in C language, which are required for parallel computing.

The "Scientific computing in C" is a hands-on course on software development for science. It covers usage of compilers, build tools, mathematical libraries (BLAS, FFTW, MKL, *etc.*), Linux command line, debugging, testing, version control, and teamwork in software development.

The "Software performance optimization" course is devoted to sequential program optimization. The course contributes significantly to the track because parallelization of a poor performing sequential program is often useless and frequently leads to performance degradation instead of improvement. For many real-world applications, it is necessary to achieve maximum speedup for sequential program and only then proceed to parallelization. The course covers contemporary CPU architecture and key factors affecting CPU performance, tools for performance analysis, optimizing compilers, and SIMD vectorization. The course is presented in flipped format. We use the video lectures from the online course "Application optimization using Intel compilers" provided by Intel [1]. During the classroom sessions, students have programming assignments, do hands-on laboratory classes and small team projects.

3.3 Computational Resources

Two parallel computing systems are available for students when working on laboratory classes, doing home programming assignments, and projects. The first system is educational HPC cluster of the Ural Federal University. The cluster has 12 nodes, 144 CPU cores, 12 Intel Xeon Phi 5110P accelerators, and 12 GPU NVIDIA Tesla K20X. The second system is the "URAN" supercomputer of the Institute of Mathematics and Mechanics UrB RAS. The supercomputer consists of 54 nodes with 648 CPU cores and 370 GPU NVIDIA Tesla.

4   Parallel and Distributed Computing Module

4.1   Parallel and Distributed Computing

The "Parallel and Distributed Computing" is the introductory HPC course. It consists of four parts: parallel computing theory, concurrency, parallel programming, and distributed computing using MapReduce. The course includes both lectures and laboratory classes on parallel computing systems. Students are required to hand in six home assignments.

The first part of the course covers architecture of parallel computing systems, theoretical limits to parallelization (Amdahl's and Gustafson's laws), approaches to parallel algorithms design, and popular patterns for parallel programming [12].

The second part of the course is devoted to concurrency. Students study multi-threaded programming for multicore and multiprocessor systems using C++11 concurrency, which now is a part of the standard C++ library. The C++ was used as a programing language for the first time in the spring of 2015. Earlier, the Java was used to study concurrency. During this part of the course, students also examine various pitfalls of concurrent and parallel programming: non-deterministic behavior, race conditions, deadlocks, livelocks, *etc.* Topics of home programming assignments for this part of the course are Dining Philosophers Problem and multi-threaded web crawler.

During the third part of the course, parallel programming using OpenMP and MPI is considered. The C was used as a programming language. Home programming assignments are k-means clustering using OpenMP and Conways Game of life using MPI.

The last part on the distributed computing has been recently added to the course. It is devoted to BigData, which is becoming popular nowadays. Students learn the MapReduce programming model, its implementation in the Apache Hadoop, and various tools from Hadoop ecosystem (Hive, Pig, Mahout, *etc.*). In addition, other popular frameworks for distributed data processing are considered, such as Apache Spark for fast distributed in-memory data processing and Apache Storm for streaming data processing. Home programming assignments for this part of course are analysis of Twitter graph using Hadoop and computing the term frequency-inverse document frequency (TF-IDFs) for Wikipedia articles using Spark.

4.2   GPU Programming

The "GPU Programming" is the advanced HPC course. The GPU offers to its users tremendous computational resources compared to CPU. However, efficient usage of such computational power requires advanced skills from the developers. The course "GPU programming" was developed to meet this problem and to provide students with the basic principles of parallel software development on the CUDA platform.

The course begins with basics of GPU architecture and "hello world" on the CUDA platform. Then, students are introduced to the CUDA memory hierarchy, principles of building grids with blocks of threads. Other topics of specific GPU features and tips for its efficient usage to get maximum performance from underlying hardware are also studied. Another crucial topic within the course is multi-GPU programming using OpenMP and MPI. Students have to understand that even contemporary GPUs have limited memory resources in comparison with CPU RAM. Therefore, they should be able to get profit from using multiple GPUs for solving big real-world computational tasks that require large amount of memory. The course ends with such interesting and complicated topics like performance profiling, optimization, and using various libraries for scientific computing.

The course includes a series of short lectures and a considerable amount of practice with the CUDA software. Participants gain experience in parallel programming by completing GPU programming assignments, which include matrix multiplication, parallel reduction, and multi-GPU sorting.

4.3 Xeon Phi Programming

The second advanced HPC course is devoted to the Intel Xeon Phi programming, which is another popular type of computational accelerators. As well as GPU, the Xeon Phi provides large computational resources, which are difficult to use efficiently. However, Xeon Phi architecture and programming tools differ from GPU ones significantly.

The course covers Xeon Phi architecture, programming models (native, offload, and MPI), and software development tools and techniques. Special attention is paid to Xeon Phi SIMD vectorization capabilities as a crucial tool to achieve the best accelerator performance. Students learn about various approaches to use vectorization: auto-vectorization by compiler, Intel Cilk Plus (array notation and elemental functions), and OpenMP *simd* directive. The techniques for performance profiling, tuning, and optimization for the Xeon Phi are considered. In addition, students explore libraries with the Xeon Phi support, such as Intel MKL and MAGMA [7].

The course is organized in the same way as the "GPU programming" one. It includes 20–30 min lectures, hands-on laboratory classes, and programming assignments. The topics of home programming assignments are matrix multiplication, European option pricing, and molecular dynamics simulation.

5 Numerical Methods Module

5.1 Parallel Numerical Methods

The course "Parallel Numerical Methods" was developed to bridge the gap between courses on various parallel programming technologies (such as Pthreads, OpenMP, and MPI) and high level courses devoted to solving complex real-world scientific problems on parallel computing systems. The course helps students to understand which algorithmic building blocks they should use to build scalable HPC applications. Students should realize that introducing parallelism into some types of algorithms instead of overall performance improvement might lead to its degradation.

The course consists of two parts devoted to using parallel computing for solving compute-intensive and data-intensive tasks. Compute-intensive tasks are bounded by amount of computations and use regular memory access pattern. The examples of such tasks are various physical and mathematical simulations (such as heart simulation). While data-intensive tasks need relatively small number of computational operations and use irregular memory access pattern. Hence, such tasks are bounded by input-output operations. The example of data-intensive task is processing large amount of unstructured data, such as graph of social network.

During the first part of the course, students work on various parallel versions of numerical methods of linear algebra, numerical integration and differentiation, as well as numerical solving of mathematical physics equations. The techniques of effective parallelization of compute-intensive tasks, such as efficient cache usage, data partitioning among the processes, and reducing the communication between the processes are considered.

The second part of the course covers the data-intensive tasks. Special attention is paid to graph algorithms. The main obstacle to efficient parallel processing of large graphs is their irregular structure. Hence, sequential graph algorithms may often outperform their parallel versions. The course provides examples of various parallel graph algorithms, and useful techniques and methods to improve their performance.

The course consist of twelve lectures and three home programming assignments. The programming assignments require not only implementation of the parallel algorithms, but also carrying out the simple researches to investigate their performance and scalability. Such assignments are aimed at providing the students with experience of using various types of parallel algorithms and understanding how to choose the most efficient algorithms for solving real-world scientific challenges.

5.2 Science Hackathon

The "Science Hackaton" is the project-oriented hands-on course on scientific software development focused on HPC. The course is conducted on Saturdays and lasts all the day. During the day, a group of students works on a project under the guidance of a tutor. Usually, the goal of the projects is to produce some usable software. However, some projects may have educational purpose, such as examining the capabilities of particular parallel library or exploring the parallel version of some numerical method.

The objective of the course is to provide students with opportunity to work together with the tutor for a long time. Hackathon participants are able to quickly gain an experience of successfully resolving the real-world scientific problems due to regular guidance from the tutor. Students obtain not only technical knowledge, but also experience in team software development, problem solving skills, and professional confidence.

The topics for Hackathon projects are chosen by students. The course primarily aimed at topics from the heart modeling track, but students are free to suggest other themes for projects. The examples of the spring 2015 projects are working with computational cluster in command line, using auto-vectorization for Xeon Phi, evaluating Intel VML performance on Xeon Phi, and simulating the muscle cube on parallel computing system using FEM and mass-spring method.

6   Heart Modeling Module

6.1   Simulation of Living Systems

The "Simulation of living systems" is the interdisciplinary theoretical course aimed at introducing students to the core concepts of biophysics, biomedical engineering, and biology, which use methods of mathematical modeling and bioinformatics [17]. Students study several classical mathematical models of biological process based on nonlinear theory of dynamic systems. These models represent the characteristic features of biological process and demonstrate the effectiveness of application of mathematical models application to understanding the mechanisms of biological systems.

The course participants become familiar with a number of biological processes (such as transport of substances, chemical kinetics, types of interaction in biological systems), mathematical concepts for describing these processes, a variety of techniques for modeling complex biological systems, and methods of models evaluation. Applications of various numerical schemes to living system simulation are considered.

During the course, the heart modeling is discussed in details. The main function of the heart is to pump blood throughout the body using contractions. Mechanical contraction of the heart is triggered by electrical activation of the myocardium. This process is known as excitation-contraction coupling. In the turn, the mechanical deformation influences the cardiac electrical activity. This process is designated as cardiac mechano-electric feedback. Hereby, the functional heart model consists of three main components: an anatomical model, an electrophysiological model, and a mechanical one. Students study various heart models [13] and the methods of integration of these models into one multiscale model of the heart.

An important advantage of the course is in examining the state-of-the-art heart models developed at the Institute of Immunology and Physiology UrB RAS. Such models include Ekaterinburg-Oxford electromechanical cell model [9,15,16] and mathematical model of the anatomy and fibre orientation field of the left ventricle (LV) of the heart [14].

The course consists of twelve lectures and twelve seminars. The prerequisite courses are applied mathematics and numerical methods. No biology, chemistry, or medicine courses are required.

6.2 Modeling Heart Dynamics on Parallel Computing Systems

The main objective of the course is to provide the students with the hands-on introduction to the contemporary methods of mathematical modeling of complex (multi-level) living systems. As an example of such task, the simulation of electromechanical function of the cardiac LV of the mammal is used during the course.

Application of FEM to multi-level (cell-tissue-organ) modeling of electromechanical contraction of the heart LV is considered. Currently, the FEM is the most widely used method of computer simulation of compound systems with complex geometry.

The course consists of eight lectures, ten workshops, and home programming assignments. During the lectures, the common approaches to the computer modeling of living systems are described. As an example of the heart simulations, the general sequence of computer simulation is demonstrated. Then the structure and physiology of the mammal heart, particularly the LV, are briefly described. Various methods and models of digital representation of the LV by magnetic resonance imaging and ultrasound are considered. The foundation of FEM meshing, meshing quality criteria, and methods of anisotropy vector field construction are presented. After that, FEM simulation of the electrodiffusion and mechanical contraction of the heart LV is examined. Theoretical part of the course ends with discussion of various tools for visualizations of simulation results.

The amount of time allotted for lectures certainly is not enough to present the above-mentioned topics thoroughly, but it is not necessary. The course is aimed at rapid transition from the basic theoretical knowledge to its practical usage.

During the workshops, students build the model of LV using the tetrahedral 3D-network with the help of the "GMsh" library [8]. After that, students utilize FEM implementation from the "FENICS" library [11] to simulate muscle cube on the MPI clusters. Various techniques of optimization by the FEM application on parallel computer systems are examined. To visualize the simulation results, students use the "Paraview" software.

7 Discussion

Our experience demonstrates that teaching HPC in the interdisciplinary education program is very effective. Knowledge of numerical methods and the heart modeling provides the students with the ability to solve nontrivial tasks on parallel computing systems. In turn, comprehensive programming assignments force students to explore the most efficient way of parallel computing technologies usage. For example, the course "Parallel numerical methods" includes two different assignments: numerical integration and single source shortest paths (SSSP) graph problem. To parallelize numerical integration students can use simple "master-slave" or "point-to-point" communication schemes. In both cases, they will achieve good speedup. At that point, many of students may think that parallelization is quite an "easy" research topic: to get performance improvement some MPI_Send and MPI_Recv functions must be inserted in the code to the appropriate places. Situation changes when students encounter the SSSP problem. Firstly students try to use well-known for them "point-to-point" parallelization, but achieve rather small (or even no) speedup due to irregular memory access pattern of the SSSP problem. Efficient solution requires usage of MPI collective communications function MPI_Allgather. Although the MPI_Allgather is heavyweight function and has big overhead, in this particular case of the SSSP problem, the MPI_Allgather allows balancing communications both across the various communication processes within single iteration and across all iterations of the entire SSSP algorithm. Thus, the MPI_Allgather function usage make possible performance speedup and scaling of SSSP graph problem.

Interdisciplinary approach also helps to increase students' motivation. It is very interesting for students to use parallel computing system not only for simple programming assignments, such as π calculation or matrix multiplication, but also for the real-world problems of heart simulation, which are very intensive in computations. Students willingly work on such tasks and try to squeeze last drop of performance from the hardware to speed up the simulation.

8   Conclusion

The interdisciplinary track of coherent courses on using HPC for the heart simulation is presented. The track consists of three modules: parallel computing technologies, heart modeling and simulation, and parallel numerical methods. Now, the track is conducted at the Ural Federal University.

The interdisciplinary approach allows students to gain deep knowledge in HPC by working on nontrivial programming assignments and participation in complex heart simulation projects. In addition, such approach increased students' motivation.

Several students decided to continue working on the heart modeling and obtained research positions at the laboratory "Modeling of living systems on supercomputers". Hence, the goal of involving students in research is achieved.

In the future, we plan to increase application of video lectures and flipped classroom format in hands-on courses. Another important direction of future works is designing interdisciplinary educational tracks for other domains, such as data science.

Acknowledgments. The work is supported by the Programme of Presidium of RAS no. II.4P (PI O.Solovyova). Our study was performed using the "Uran" supercomputer from Institute of Mathematics and Mechanics UrB RAS.

References

1. Anuferenko, A., Idrisov, R., Kasyanov, V., Vladimirovich, N.: Intel academy. Application optimization using intel compilers. http://www.intuit.ru/studies/courses/660/516/info
2. Bangerth, W.: 48 video lectures on computational science (2013). http://www.math.tamu.edu/~bangerth/videos.html
3. Bartocci, E., Singh, R., von Stein, F.B., Amedome, A., Caceres, A.J.J., Castillo, J., Closser, E., Deards, G., Goltsev, A., Ines, R.S., Isbilir, C., Marc, J.K., Moore, D., Pardi, D., Sadhu, S., Sanchez, S., Sharma, P., Singh, A., Rogers, J., Wolinetz, A., Grosso-Applewhite, T., Zhao, K., Filipski, A.B., Gilmour, Jr., R.F., Grosu, R., Glimm, J., Smolka, S.A., Cherry, E.M., Clarke, E.M., Griffeth, N., Fenton, F.H.: Teaching cardiac electrophysiology modeling to undergraduate students: laboratory exercises and gpu programming for the study of arrhythmias and spiral wave dynamics. Adv. Physiol. Educ. **35**(4), 427–437 (2011). http://dx.doi.org/10.1152/advan.00034.2011
4. Bauman, P.T., Chandola, V., Patra, A., Jones, M.: Development of a computational and data-enabled science and engineering Ph.d. program. In: Proceedings of the Workshop on Education for High-Performance Computing, EduHPC 2014, pp. 21–26. IEEE Press, Piscataway (2014). http://dx.doi.org/10.1109/EduHPC.2014.8
5. Bueno-Orovioa, A., Cherryb, E.M., Fenton, F.H.: Minimal model for human ventricular action potentials in tissue. J. Theoret. Biol. **263**(3), 544–560 (2008). http://dx.doi.org/10.1016/j.jtbi.2008.03.029
6. Crampin, E.J., Halstead, M., Hunter, P., Nielsen, P., Noble, D., Smith, N., Tawhai, M.: Computational physiology and the physiome project. Exp. Physiol. **89**(1), 1–26 (2004). http://dx.doi.org/10.1113/expphysiol.2003.026740
7. Dongarra, J., Gates, M., Haidar, A., Jia, Y., Kabir, K., Luszczek, P., Tomov, S.: Portable HPC programming on intel many-integrated-core hardware with MAGMA port to Xeon Phi. In: Wyrzykowski, R., Dongarra, J., Karczewski, K., Waśniewski, J. (eds.) PPAM 2013, Part I. LNCS, vol. 8384, pp. 571–581. Springer, Heidelberg (2014)
8. Geuzaine, C., Remacle, J.F.: GMSH: a 3-d finite element mesh generator with built-in pre- and post-processing facilities. Int. J. Numer. Meth. Eng. **79**(11), 1309–1331 (2009). http://dx.doi.org/10.1002/nme.2579
9. Katsnelson, L.B., Vikulova, N.A., Kursanov, A.G., Solovyova, O.E., Markhasin, V.S.: Electro-mechanical coupling in a one-dimensional model of heart muscle fiber. Russ. J. Numer. Anal. Math. Modell. **29**(5), 275–284 (2014)
10. Kohl, P., Noble, D.: Systems biology and the virtual physiological human. Mol. Syst. Biol. **5**(1), 292 (2009). http://dx.doi.org/10.1038/msb.2009.51
11. Logg, A., Mardal, K.A., Wells, G.N.: Automated Solution of Differential Equations by the Finite Element Method. Lecture Notes in Computational Science and Engineering, vol. 84. Springer, Heidelberg (2012)
12. McCool, M., Reinders, J., Robison, A.: Structured Parallel Programming: Patterns for Efficient Computation. Elsevier, Waltham (2012)

13. Pfeiffer, E.R., Tangney, J.R., Omens, J.H., McCulloch, A.D.: Biomechanics of cardiac electromechanical coupling and mechanoelectric feedback. J. Biomech. Eng. **136**(2), 021007 (2014)
14. Pravdin, S., Berdyshev, V., Panfilov, A., Katsnelson, L., Solovyova, O., Markhasin, V.: Mathematical model of the anatomy and fibre orientation field of the left ventricle of the heart. BioMed. Eng. Online **12**(1), 54 (2013). http://www.biomedical-engineering-online.com/content/12/1/54
15. Pravdin, S.F., Dierckx, H., Katsnelson, L.B., Solovyova, O., Markhasin, V.S., Panfilov, A.V.: Electrical wave propagation in an anisotropic model of the left ventricle based on analytical description of cardiac architecture. PLoS ONE **9**(5), e93617 (2014). http://dx.doi.org/10.1371/journal.pone.0093617
16. Solovyova, O., Katsnelson, L., Konovalov, P., Kursanov, A., Vikulova, N., Kohl, P., Markhasin, V.: The cardiac muscle duplex as a method to study myocardial heterogeneity. Prog. Biophys. Mol. Biol. **115**(23), 115–128 (2014). http://www.sciencedirect.com/science/article/pii/S007961071400073X.   Novel Technologies as Drivers of Progress in Cardiac Biophysics
17. Solovyova, O.E., Markhasin, V.S., Katsnelson, L.B., Sulman, T.B., Vasilyeva, A.D., Kursanov, A.G.: Mathematical Modeling of Living Systems. Urals University Press, Ekaterinburg (2013)
18. Zarestky, J., Bangerth, W.: Teaching high performance computing: Lessons from a flipped classroom, project-based course on finite element methods. In: Proceedings of the Workshop on Education for High-Performance Computing, EduHPC 2014, pp. 34–41. IEEE Press, Piscataway (2014). http://dx.doi.org/10.1109/EduHPC.2014.10

Integration of ICT in Concurrent and Parallel Programming Lectures

Antonio J. Tomeu-Hardasmal[1], Alberto G. Salguero[1]([⊠]),
and Manuel I. Capel[2]

[1] University of Cádiz, Cádiz, Spain
alberto.salguero@uca.es
[2] University of Granada, Granada, Spain

Abstract. An effective teaching and learning in concurrent and parallel programming needs the presentation of short excerpts of code to students in a selected programming language during lectures. This is sometimes necessary to make understandable complicate syntactical constructs. Traditionally, these codes have been presented by the teacher to the students on a blackboard, with slides or by means any projection facilities, together with an oral description of their operation and significance. Teachers try to explain those syntactical constructs with more or less success and students do not usually test program code during lectures, nor can do any modifications to the programs, which are helpful in order to master difficult concepts of parallel programming and Concurrency. In the best possible scenario, students will carry out any tests on the real code of an example presented in lectures during practical lessons at the lab. Nevertheless, without a clear illustration of their actual behavior in a real computer program, any new concepts of concurrent constructs taught in lectures will remain fuzzy and prone to be forgotten. The presented approach consists of changing the traditional teaching and learning model of parallel programming into another where students will be equipped with multicore processors inside their laptops, which in addition to Virtual Campus services will serve to put into practice any programming code that illustrates a programming concept the minute it is presented during any lecture by the teacher to the class.

Keywords: Teaching innovation · Teaching improvement · Virtual campus · ICT integration · Lecturing model · Concurrent programming · Parallel programming · Code · Performance improvement · Interactive theoretical teaching · Students

1 Introduction

Any computer that we purchase nowadays is equipped with a multicore processor that allows the programmer to carry out real concurrent computations or implement "parallelism" in a program if we prefer to call it in this way. Present curricula in Computational Science and Engineering (CSE) have addressed this

© Springer International Publishing Switzerland 2015
S. Hunold et al. (Eds.): Euro-Par 2015 Workshops, LNCS 9523, pp. 114–124, 2015.
DOI: 10.1007/978-3-319-27308-2_10

new reality, and have paid attention to the importance for future graduates of excellence training, which must include mastering well-known Concurrent and Parallel Programming techniques that would enable them to exploit the parallel potential, in terms of speedup, that current multicores are offering nowadays.

In the past, concurrent and parallel programming topics were part of elective courses with a focus on computer architecture or concurrency. Now, they are compulsory subjects to be taken by students in the core CSE curriculum. Nevertheless, this change has not come along with a new way to teach concurrency nor programming, in general [1–10]. In spite of the new teaching models that European Higher Education Space (EHES) promotes, to teach Programming to undergraduate students still needs presenting and discussing pieces of code to the students. This learning model is not likely to be modified in the future. What teachers can modify is the way that students face a concurrent or parallel programming problem.

We propose the students to adopt a protagonist role - instead of the traditional passive role. We present in this paper the results of a teaching innovation project that has been carried out at the University of Cádiz. Thereof, we discuss how to make that didactical change can happen in concurrent and parallel programming courses, and analyze the results obtained from our new teaching model applied to a real study case.

1.1   Environment

The following items describe the conceptual framework within which the experience described here has been developed:

- The mentioned experience has taken place during the past academic year 2013/2014 in a course that has been taught to an audience of 149 enrolled students divided in two classes of 75 students each one for lectures. This course is taken in the first semester of the sophomore year of the CSE degree, to earn 3 credits of lectures and 3 more credits of practical assignments if students are successful.
- This teaching innovation project has been developed and followed by the two tenured teachers assigned to this course, who belong to the same Department but to three different areas of knowledge, Computer Science (CS), Artificial Intelligence (AI) and Software Engineering (SE).
- In order to provide the necessary infrastructure to carry out this new way of giving lectures, a classroom full equipped with laptops (to be used on a deposit–basis) was solicited to the College of Engineering Director, as well as tables with power sockets available to plug in the student owned laptops. The classroom had access to Campus WIFI. A beamer and whiteboard were also available together with a "regular multimedia table" as the ones normally used for traditional teaching.
- The course's lectures run according to the temporal schedule planned by the College beforehand, through a series of theoretical lecture sessions of 2 h each one per week, according to what had been planned by the Vicedean for Academic Affairs.

1.2   Objectives

The objectives to be attained by the experience described here were the following ones:

– Improvement of theoretical content lectures, in particular those on Concurrent and Paralell Programming, and lectures on general programming techniques.
– To mutate the prior passive character of students during lectures into a much more active one.
– To attain the practical integration of Information and communications technology (ICT) in the classical teaching of theoretical contents. We argue that the only use of multimedia, such as the beamer or the whiteboard, do not change the passive nature of students during the presentations carried out by the teacher.
– The work carried out interactively by the class during lectures becomes highly increased.

1.3   Time Schedule

The experience has been developed according to the time schedule shown in Fig. 1, and took place from June 2013 to June 2014. All the semester's theoretical lessons were given according to the methodology which is to be introduced in the following sections. These lectures were given from October 2013 to February 2014.

Previously to carry out the above activities, a preparatory work was necessary in order to:

– Write, debug and test the set of codes that will support the entire experience.
– Configure a virtual platform, fully supported by Moodle, which contains files with the selected set of programming codes, together with the rest of documents that support the course, i.e., readings, slides, examination samples, user manuals, study recommendations, etc.

In the last week of teaching, the final impressions about the new model were collected by using a survey that was previously handed out to the students. Afterwards, the final examinations were taken. Finally, by taking into account the grades that the students obtained in the exams and survey results, we were able to produce the results and conclusions shown in sections three and four of this paper.

2   What Has Been Innovated?

The computers are rarely used as learning tools. Teachers mainly use computers as delivery tools to present instructional content or to captive students by the use of computer-assisted learning applications such as drill and practice, tutorials, and simulations [11]. The teaching of general programming techniques and

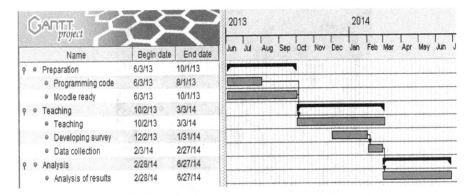

Fig. 1. Project time schedule

```
CONTROL DE Threads: Ejemplo de Cesión de Prioridad  Voluntaria (yield)
public class replaniYield
   extends Thread
{
   private boolean hY;//indicara si el hilo cede prioridad o no.
   private int     v;

   public replaniYield(boolean hacerYield, int vueltas)
   {hY = hacerYield; v = vueltas;}

   public void run()
   {
     for(int i=0; i<v; i++)
       if(i==20&&hY==true){this.yield();}//indica cesion de prioridad.
       else System.out.println("Hilo "+this.getName()+" en iteracion "+i);
   }
   public static void main(String[] args)
   {
     replaniYield h0 = new replaniYield(false, 50);
     replaniYield h1 = new replaniYield(false, 50);
     replaniYield h2 = new replaniYield(true , 50); //cedera prioridad y
     h0.setName("1-NoYield");                        //sera o no considerarda
     h1.setName("2-NoYield"); h2.setName("3-SIYield");
     h0.start(); h1.start(); h2.start();
   }
}
          © Antonio Tomeu                    Creación y Control de Thread en Java 27
```

Fig. 2. Slide case example

particularly Concurrent Programming have been traditionally conducted until
now by discussing pieces of code from computer programs, whether these are
written on the blackboard, or shown with a slide projector (in Fig. 2, a case
example of one slide, similar to the ones that we used to show to the students,
in theoretical lessons, with a beamer before conducting this experience). Usually, teachers explain any relevant concepts and operations on these slides before
going through and... immediately pass on to showing and analyzing the next
slide with another program code. Thereby, students usually ended up with a
partial view of the semantics of every syntactical construction explained in that
way, since they could not immediately test the proposed code by running or
debugging it.

The passive role of the students during a lecture was in the best possible way
only when they could interrupt and ask the teacher to clarify a specific code in
the program being discussed.

Fig. 3. A new model for theoretical teaching

The proposal presented here is a radical rethinking of the student role during a theoretical lesson on Programming. In order to make this new approach feasible, the student must have a laptop or desktop computer with access to "Virtual Campus" (see Fig. 3), as well as one Campus–WIFI driven teaching platform, thoroughly available during the entire session. Within "Virtual Campus", teachers of the different courses have designed material as well as the necessary programs to support the new model. Students can therefore have access to the code on a slide that the Professor is discussing during the lesson, so that they can observe any effects due to download, debug, run and test performed on that code.

In order to support the new teaching model, each "Virtual Campus" block, which correspond to a specific course–subject content, will include a folder with a relevant example of program code, as the one showed in Fig. 4. After downloading that code, the student will start developing the new cycle of his/her assignment as it is proposed during the corresponding theoretical teaching lesson. The sequence of tasks to be done to complete that assignment is shown in Fig. 6. As it can be seen there, the students finally change their behavior from being a "passive information receiver", which is mainly transmitted by their teacher discussing a program code, to become the absolute protagonis of the learning process now. The students have to perform the required empirical analysis of downloaded code from "Virtual Campus", as well as to carry out debugging, execution and analysis of outputs that this code may yield.

On finishing the above stage in the new theoretical teaching process model, if the class has mastered the construct at hand in the code example case, then a series of conceptual reinforcement exercises are proposed, which must be carried out individually. Then, result codes of these exercises are sent to an specific purpose "Virtual Campus" forum. Finally, possible solutions to the exercise are presented to the class and discussed in common to find the best one.

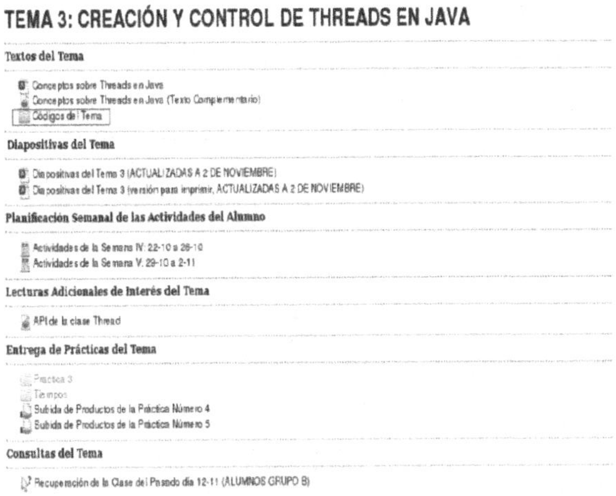

TEMA 3: CREACIÓN Y CONTROL DE THREADS EN JAVA

Textos del Tema

- Conceptos sobre Threads en Java
- Conceptos sobre Threads en Java (Texto Complementario)
- Códigos del Tema

Diapositivas del Tema

- Diapositivas del Tema 3 (ACTUALIZADAS A 2 DE NOVIEMBRE)
- Diapositivas del Tema 3 (versión para imprimir, ACTUALIZADAS A 2 DE NOVIEMBRE)

Planificación Semanal de las Actividades del Alumno

- Actividades de la Semana IV: 22-10 a 26-10
- Actividades de la Semana V: 29-10 a 2-11

Lecturas Adicionales de Interés del Tema

- API de la clase Thread

Entrega de Prácticas del Tema

- Práctica 3
- Tiempos
- Subida de Productos de la Práctica Número 4
- Subida de Productos de la Práctica Número 5

Consultas del Tema

- Recuperación de la Clase del Pasado día 12-11 (ALUMNOS GRUPO B)

Fig. 4. A subject block in "Virtual Campus" platform

2.1 Development Methodology

During the elaboration phase of didactic contents, which are necessary for implementation of the innovation project, the methodological work guideline followed by the course teachers has gone through the following stages:

- For each course's subject block, teachers have developed a set of program codes that illustrate the theoretical concepts which are the selected reinforcement objectives.
- The proposed codes samples, after being cross-checked between the involved teachers, have been available to students the week before teaching them. On a weekly basis, the codes will be available to students inside a specific folder of "Virtual Campus" repository, as we have already mentioned (see Figs. 4 and 5).
  Two versions of each code have been pre-arranged, one is composed of plain text files, and the other one contains a zip file with the set of files for an easier download.
- During the theoretical lesson, and once the teacher has presented the example code case and discussed its functionality, the student is asked to follow the work guideline depicted in the flow diagram in Fig. 6.

3 Results

In order to carry out the experiment's results analysis, it has been chosen a prospective double stage, then a set of analysis relevant actions have been conducted, previously and posteriorly to the curse assessment:

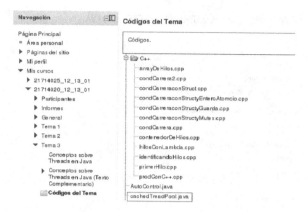

Fig. 5. The "Code" folder

3.1   Pre-assessment

After three complete months of lectures and in order to meet any subjective impression that the new theoretical teaching model was showing among the enrolled students to which it was applied, we also designed a brief survey, aimed at quantitatively measuring the following variables:

– Understanding improvement of concepts presented during theoretical teaching lessons.
– Adjustment of proposed exercises number to reinforce important concepts presented in lessons.
– Adjustment of time devoted to proposed exercises resolution.
– Compliance level with the new model of theoretic teaching.

Each one of the above items could be assessed with a score from one (totally disagree) to 5 (completely agree) and including an additional sixth item to give response to the case in which the student does not want to answer. The following bar charts[1] shows the results. The sampling size was fixed to $n = 78$.

Histogram of Fig. 7 contains the opinion of students regarding the comprehension improvement of the programming concepts, which were introduced, during the theoretical teaching lessons, by using the new model. We see how almost all of the students agree or strongly agree to the benefit that they obtained with the new model compared to the classical passive teaching theoretical scheme.

Histogram of Fig. 8 contains students views regarding the number of exercises proposed during the phase of exercises shown in diagram of Fig. 6. In particular, to know whether the number of exercises is appropriate to reinforce a concept comprehension after its presentation in a lecture. Again, the vast majority of

---

[1] The histogram legend represents absence of response as 0, and classifying the answers according to the already suggested range: 1 for "disagrees" up to 5 for "completely agrees".

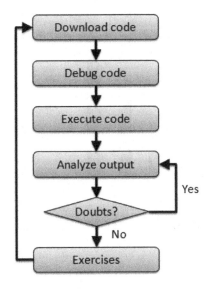

Fig. 6. New model's work cycle

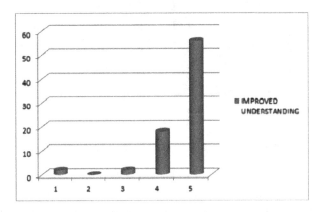

Fig. 7. Understanding amendment

students considered to be so, although this time, we can observe data somewhat more dispersed. A small group of students considered the number of exercises inappropriate, although we can not say if it was by excess or by defect.

Histogram of Fig. 9 shows students opinions about the amount time they were given to solve the proposed exercises. We can appreciate here that approximately one-third of students considered that time to be inappropriate. Again, we do not know whether it was by excess or by defect. We will need to carry out further research on this aspect to take possible actions for attaining an improvement. Histogram of Fig. 10 gathers students opinions regarding their level compliance with respect to the new model of theoretic teaching experienced. Again, the

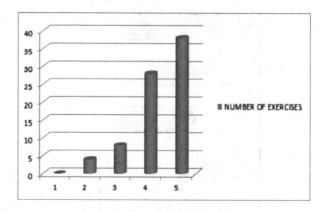

Fig. 8. Exercises number adjustment

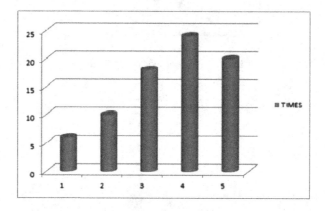

Fig. 9. Exercise resolution time assessment

vast majority of students chose between "agree" or "strongly agree" with it. Additionally, we can notice that with respect to the two items of greatest interest in order to validate the feasibility of the new model(understanding improvement of theoretical contents and agreement level with the new model), the results obtained during the experience were very good in general.

3.2   Post-assessment

In this case, we conducted a comparative analysis of the performance obtained between the academic results of year 2014/2015 and the academic year 2012/13. Thereof, we tackle with an objective measurement of the new model of theoretical teaching goodness degree w.r.t the classical teaching method.

To perform this analysis, we compared the number of students succeeding the course against those who failed. The results of the analysis showed that if during the academic year 2012/2013 only succeeded 35 % of the students, during

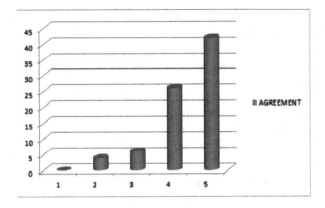

Fig. 10. Agreement level with the model

the academic year 2014/15, by using the proposed methodology in this paper, this percentage showed an improvement of 20.6 % points, then reaching the rate of 55.6 % of students that have succeeded. All these figures refer to the first examination taken by the students.

4 Conclusions and Future Work

After conducting the analysis of the experiment results, which has been carried in Sect. 3.2, and due to the excellent results obtained during the phases of screening and post-assessment, we have come to the conclusion to keep the new model of theoretic teaching in the academic years to come,

- The aimed project objectives have been attained.
- The understanding of programming concepts presented to students in theoretical lectures has been improved.
- We have migrated from a reality where the student behaves passively during theoretical lessons into another in which he or she has to have a more proactive attitude.
- Indirectly, we have achieved a favorable change in students customs, since they now understand the material taught in lectures on a daily basis, thus propitiating a more continuous involvement with the course contents presented in the series of lectures. Since, a good learning cannot be acquired by only attending to listen the teacher's lesson and - eventually - taking some notes. Students need a updated domain of the contents, in order to make an effective use of the new model of theoretical teaching.
- Additionally, in an indirect way, the student becomes more prepared to deal with practical material given during the course; indeed, the new approach has allowed us to increase the workload during practical sessions in labs, as well as increasing the complexity of this material, thus improving the education of students.

– Students are now involved in a more personal and rigorous way with the daily work and course assignments.
– ICT deployment and their effective use have been radically integrated with theoretical teaching of Programming, according to a more effective and less traumatic way of work for the student in order to get success with that course.
– The success rate of students in the course has remarkably improved w.r.t. the previous course, where the traditional model was followed.
– And finally, we should bear it in mind that students tell us that they "like your theoretical lessons as they are given now".

Acknowledgement. We would thank to the Academic Affairs Vicedean of the College of Engineering, who provided us with facilities to put in place the theoretical teaching, which has been the innovation teaching objective in the classroom carried out in this project.

References

1. Area Moreira, M.: Enseñar y aprender con TIC: más allá de las viejas pedagogías. Aprender a educar con tecnología, n2, pp. 4–7, diciembre 2012
2. Area Moreira, M.: Una breve historia de las políticas de incorporación de las tecnologías digitales al sistema escolar en España. Quaderns digitals: Revista de Nuevas Tecnologías y Sociedad, N. 51 (2008). ISSN-e 1575–9393
3. Ben-Ari, M.: A suite of tools for teaching concurrency. In: Proceedings of the 9th Annual SIGCSE Conference on Innovation and Technology in Computer Science Education, ITiCSE 2004, Leeds, UK, 28–30 June 2004
4. Bloom, B.S., et al.: Taxonomy of Educational Objetives: Handbook I, Cognitive Domain. David McKay, New York (1956)
5. Carro, M., Herranz, A., Mario, J.: A model-driven approach to teaching concurrency. ACM Trans. Comput. Educ. **13**(1), 48–67 (2013)
6. Ko, Y., Burgstaller, B. Scholz B.: Parallel from the beginning: the case for multicore programming in the computer science undergraduate curriculum. In: Proceedings of the 44th ACM Technical Symposium on Computer Science Education (2013)
7. Marowka, A., Shenkar, R.: Think parallel: teaching parallel programming today. IEEE Distrib. Syst. Online **9**(8), 1–8 (2008)
8. Paprzycki, M.: Integrating parallel and distributed computing in computer science curricula. IEEE Distrib. Syst. Online **7**(2), 43–49 (2006)
9. Schechter, E.I.: Internet resources for higher education outcomes assessment. JFECS **8**(2), 105–107 (2009)
10. Vilela, A.: Moodle 2 Para Profesores. Ed Rom (2009)
11. Inan, F.A., Lowther, D.L., Ross, S.M., Strahl, D.: Pattern of classroom activities during students' use of computers: relations between instructional strategies and computer applications. Teach. Teach. Educ. **26**(3), 540–546 (2010)

Teamwork Across Disciplines: High-Performance Computing Meets Engineering

Philipp Neumann[1]([✉]), Christoph Kowitz[1], Felix Schranner[2],
and Dmitrii Azarnykh[2]

[1] Department for Informatics, Technische Universität München (TUM),
Boltzmannstr. 3, 85748 Garching, Germany
philipp.neumann@tum.de
[2] Department of Mechanical Engineering, Technische Universität München,
Boltzmannstr. 15, 85748 Garching, Germany

Abstract. We present a general methodology to combine interdisciplinary teamwork experience with classical lecture and lab course concepts, enabling supervised team-based learning among students. The concept is exemplarily applied in a course on high-performance computing (HPC) and computational fluid dynamics (CFD). Evaluation and student feedback suggest that competences on both teamwork as well as on lecture material (CFD and HPC) are acquired.

1 Interdisciplinary Education and Teamwork

1.1 Introduction

There is hardly a field which influences other research disciplines as much as computer science. Cutting-edge innovations in robotics support industrial developments, simulation in science and engineering allows to construct and test virtual bridges, airplanes or cars, or pattern recognition and enhanced search algorithms enable big data evaluations in social sciences (and basically any other field), just to name a few examples.

With various levels of parallelism to be exploited within current processors, this arguing particularly holds for parallel and high-performance computing. Compute- and data-intensive software for both industrial or academic applications needs to support this parallelism. This implies a strong need for interdisciplinary education and teamwork between computer science and the related disciplines ("computer science/HPC + X"). While interdisciplinary study programs—such as computational science and engineering, bioinformatics, or information systems—are widely established, an interdisciplinary education at the course level is rarely realized: single lectures, lab courses or seminars are typically provided and organized by a single department and consequently focus on the perspective of the related discipline, cf. Fig. 1(a). Only few examples at German universities exist which invoke two or more departments for interdisciplinary teaching and education at course level, e.g. courses of the project StiL

© Springer International Publishing Switzerland 2015
S. Hunold et al. (Eds.): Euro-Par 2015 Workshops, LNCS 9523, pp. 125–134, 2015.
DOI: 10.1007/978-3-319-27308-2_11

[6]. Besides, soft skills such as communication, work management, or components of successful, interdisciplinary teamwork are often not encountered in the study programs at all, except for optional pure soft skill courses. The latter courses consider soft skills independent from the current study program—see Fig. 1(b)—which allows to exchange with other disciplines on this topic on the one hand, but hinders from practising/learning interdisciplinary teamwork in a realistic setting on the other hand.

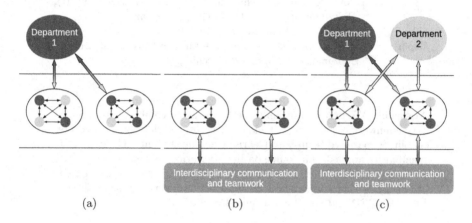

(a)   (b)   (c)

Fig. 1. Different course designs. Filled yellow and blue circles represent students interacting in group work and belonging to department 1 (blue) or department two (yellow). (a) Department 1 teaches students from disciplines 1 and 2; focus of the course is put on discipline 1. (b) Interdisciplinary education. All students are taught interdisciplinary communication and teamwork, abstaining from discipline-specifics. (c) Concept *Teamwork Across Disciplines*. Two departments teach mixed student teams, including soft skill aspects (Color figure online).

(Potentially) Interdisciplinary student projects are more common; examples at German universities comprise the one-year student group project at Univ. Paderborn (8–16 students) [4], or the IDP (interdisciplinary project) at TU München (individual or group projects) [3] as part of the master's programs in computer science. Allowing for individual training and practice of interdisciplinary communication and other soft skills, particular guidance and supervision with respect to the latter is rarely provided.

Only few novel approaches and concepts which differ from Fig. 1(a) and (b) and aim to improve the current state of education in interdisciplinary teamwork have been proposed over the last years. Leiffer, Graff and Gonzalez point out advantages of project teamwork and provide a list of curriculum measures to support the students' teamwork education [1]. Another example is given by the interdisciplinary, team-based, multi-semester teaching approach to games development which is presented in [2] and allows "students to exercise their technical and artistic skills on a multi-semester project while also developing their teamwork, problem-solving, leadership, and communication skills."

1.2   Challenges

The design of a *course on interdisciplinary education and application* has to take into consideration several criteria; we restrict considerations on invoking two disciplines in the following.

The topic of the course needs to be *really interdisciplinary* (C1). A "toy problem" won't do, since no knowledge transfer would be invoked between the disciplines in this case, and the real challenge of understanding each other would not be revealed. Both disciplines need to be involved at the same or similar amount to stimulate bi-directional knowledge transfer, interdisciplinary learning and discussions (C2). This may also hold for the involvement of two departments in the teaching process, cf. Fig. 1(c). The capability to participate in interdisciplinary discussions requires basic understanding of the topic with respect to both disciplines and soft skill education (C3). This requirement either builds a prerequisite for students entering the course, or implies the necessity of a start-up phase in the course which recapitulates the discipline-specific basics. Finally, to stimulate interdisciplinary, open-minded and creative exchange among students, an activating, flexible course setting is required (C4), adapting to the (individual) students' needs.

1.3   Outline

In the following, we provide details on the course concept *Teamwork Across Disciplines* that we exemplarily deployed in our course *Turbulent Flow Simulation on HPC-Systems*. This course brings together students from mechanical engineering and computer science, working in mixed teams to develop a CFD simulation software for compute clusters.

We describe the course design in Sect. 2, and point out how we address the challenges (C1-C4). Based on the teamwork idea, we particularly point out

- how to form interdisciplinary student teams and support the team building process,
- how to assist students at team-based learning and teaching (*supervised teaching*),
- our approach to examine and evaluate teamwork processes.

We detail feedback and outcomes of the course evaluation in Sect. 3 and draw conclusions from this course realization in Sect. 4.

2   Course Curriculum

2.1   Teamwork Across Disciplines: Concept

To allow for "truly interdisciplinary" education, both disciplines D1 and D2 need to be equally involved. Hence, also both respective departments are involved to equal parts in education and teaching. The arising course is embedded into the curricula of both study programs D1 and D2. Though not a strict requirement, we decided to design the course for 12–32 students at master level to make sure that the students potentially have preliminary knowledge of both subjects, and deeper understanding of one of both subjects.

Next, a "problem" P is designed which consists of subproblems related to D1, D2, or both. A strict coupling of D1 and D2 in the problem description is mandatory. In the scope of the course, student teams of 2–4 students shall solve P. Each student team hence needs to have knowledge of both fields D1 and D2 to successfully work on the problem. Besides, students are supported and taught further details to solve P in accompanying lectures throughout the lecture period.

Some of the lectures are dedicated to soft skill components, such as teamwork, communication, or work distribution, cf. (C3). Besides, *supervised team meetings* are introduced once per week. On the one hand, these meetings build a fixed point of contact of the team members. They can have a team meeting, discuss their work progress and solve problems that, e.g., a single team member could not solve himself. On the other hand, the supervised team meetings also build a fixed point of contact of each team with the other teams and the course supervisors (from departments D1, D2). The teams report on their work status, can ask topic-related questions, or discuss teamwork issues with the supervisors. The latter is a challenge for the course supervisors: formulating a teamwork problem properly often comes close to the actual solution—detecting the problem, however, is very difficult. It is thus also the supervisors who need to grasp a look inside the teams, observe the interaction of the team members, analyse strengths and weaknesses of the team, and give respective advice.

2.2   Realization: Turbulent Flow Simulation on HPC-Systems

Prerequisites, Goals and Course Structure. The concept from Sect. 2.1 was realized in the course *Turbulent Flow Simulation on HPC-Systems*. The course is designed for master students from disciplines/departments of computer science (D1:=CS) and mechanical engineering (D2:=ME). It comprises 2×90 min of lectures/supervised team meetings per week. Both study programs ME and CS contain courses in programming or in a minor such as (computational) fluid dynamics, so that a basic knowledge of both ME/CS can be presumed and dictates a sufficient set of course prerequisites.

At the beginning of the course, the students download the C++ code frame NS-EOF for incompressible, laminar, three-dimensional Navier-Stokes-based flow simulations [8]. NS-EOF makes use of most prominent object-oriented software design patterns: data structures, algorithmic and parallelization components are encapsulated and can be exchanged or extended easily. A key component of most incompressible Navier-Stokes solvers is provided by a Poisson solver for the pressure unknowns. In NS-EOF, either a simple SOR-based solver can be employed for this problem, or a more sophisticated implementation based on PETSc [7]. The latter is particularly used in this course.

In the scope of the course, NS-EOF shall be extended by distributed memory parallelism using the message passing interface (MPI) library and by incorporation of at least one turbulence model; the respective components of NS-EOF are thus missing in the code frame. The simulation shall be executed on the mid-sized MAC-cluster [5] administrated by the Leibniz Supercomputing Centre/TUM. The cluster consists of AMD bulldozer, Intel SandyBridge and other partitions and thus builds a perfect "playground" for the students to experiment with different pieces of hardware. Parallelization/turbulence modeling is new to the students from ME/CS. Joint work for successul completion of this problem (P:=extension of code frame by parallelization and turbulence modeling) is hence required.

The course is structured in three phases: *single phase*, *group phase*, and *project phase*. The complete structure for a semester period of twelve weeks is detailed in Table 1 and laid out in the following.

Single Phase. The *single phase* represents the introductory part of the course. Spanning over 2 weeks, the students are introduced to the basics of the (Reynolds averaged) Navier-Stokes equations. Besides, the methodology to numerically solve the Navier-Stokes equations is repeated and illustrated at the given code frame. The latter topic is presented along with a precise introduction to NS-EOF and principles of object-oriented programming. The introductions are designed in form of four plenary lectures; the code introduction is given in form of a mix of lecture and interactive session.

During the single phase, each student is obliged to extend NS-EOF by visualization routines to output VTK-compatible files; these can be read by the free visualization software ParaView. Individually working on this extension, the single phase guarantees that all students become familiar with the concepts of the object-oriented code frame and with the principles of laminar flow simulations (cf. (C3)), visualizing and interpreting results of three benchmark flow problems: lid-driven cavity, free channel flow, and backward-facing step flow. The *lid-driven cavity* problem works on a cubic domain and is a good scenario for qualitative understanding of vortex formation in fluid flow. For *free channel flow*, the analytical solution is known. A quantitative convergence evaluation of the finite-difference solver NS-EOF and the respective pressure Poisson solver is thus possible. Channel flow over a *backward-facing step* yields the formation of vortices on the one hand, but still relies on simple channel-like geometries on the other hand. This allows to study, e.g. turbulence, using relatively simple, yet effective turbulent boundary layer models.

An oral exam is scheduled at the end of the single phase to control the learning outcome.

Group Phase. At the beginning of the *group phase*, the problem P—MPI parallelization and turbulence modeling in NS-EOF—is revealed to the students. A concise task description is provided, including all important steps and subtasks such as domain decomposition, rank-to-coordinate mapping of processes,

Table 1. Structure of course *Turbulent Flow Simulation on HPC-Systems*. Single phase: weeks 1–2. Group phase: weeks 3–8. Project phase: weeks 9–12.

Week	Contents	Learning Outcomes	Format
1A	Reynolds Averaged Navier-Stokes (RANS)	– Comprehension of RANS – Ability to mathematically apply RANS filtering	Lecture
1B	Numerically solving Navier-Stokes	– Knowledge of solving procedure and different algorithmic steps – Ability to derive finite difference expressions for Navier-Stokes and mixed derivatives	Lecture
2A	Introduction to C++-programming	– Ability to implement classes and functions – Comprehension of C++ syntax – Comprehension of principles of object-oriented programming	Lecture
2B	Introduction to NS-EOF	– Comprehension of software design of NS-EOF – Ability to add functionality to NS-EOF	Lecture, Interactive code review
3A	Soft skills: Teamwork	– Knowledge of team structures, roles and processes	Lecture
3B	Team building (for group phase)	– Reflection of personal competences on computational fluid dynamics, turbulence and HPC	Interactive session
4	Parallelization of NS-EOF	– Ability to apply domain decomposition algorithm in NS-EOF – Knowledge of MPI library and usage	Lecture
5A	Supervised team meeting	– Ability to successfully collaborate within team structure – Ability to split work among team members and define/distribute tasks	Group work,interactive session
5B	Turbulence modeling	– Comprehension of principles of turbulence modeling (energy cascade; algebraic, one-, and two-equation models)	Lecture
6A	Supervised team meeting	– see 5A	Group work,interactive session
6B	Soft skills: Communication	– Knowledge of four-sides communication model [10] – Comprehension of potential issues in communication – Knowledge of measures to improve communication (effective listening, feedback)	Lecture, group work

(Continued)

Table 1. (*Continued*)

Week	Contents	Learning Outcomes	Format
7A	Supervised team meeting	– see 5A – Ability to successfully communicate in team discussions	Group work,interactive session
7B	Parallelization: Scaling and Efficiency	– Knowledge of Amdahl's law – Ability to analyze and improve scaling of MPI-parallelized software	Lecture
8A	Supervised team meeting	– see 7A	Group work,interactive session
8B	Turbulence: Error analysis	– Knowledge of boundary layer categorization – Comprehension of turbulent viscosity effects in channel flows – Ability to analyze and validate turbulence simulations	Lecture
9A	Scenario: Backward-facing step	– Knowledge of flow setup – Comprehension of physical effects in (turbulent) backward-facing step flow	Lecture
9B	Presentation of potential project topics	– Knowledge of potential code extensions and model improvements	Lecture
10	Decision on/Choice of project topics		Interactive session
11	Wind tunnel tour	– Knowledge of wind tunnel types and measurement techniques in experimental fluid dynamics	Interactive session
12	Project presentations	– Application of and practising presentation skills	Interactive session

or the evaluation of parallel performance. The problem involves both disciplines: computer scientists are required for the MPI parallelization and software design, mechanical engineers know about turbulence models and respective physical limitations. Moreover, the incorporation of turbulence models also implies modifications in the parallelization process: the global time step reduction required by NS-EOF needs to be adapted and turbulent flow quantities such as the turbulent viscosity need to be communicated between neighbouring processes. The task thus satisfies (C1). Besides, students from both disciplines need to be highly involved in the development of this code extension (C2). After introducing the building blocks of teamwork in a lecture, teams are formed based on individual reflection of personal skills and exchange with the other course participants. Every student can hence search for fellows with orthogonal skills and so become member of an optimal, interdisciplinary team.

Further details on the subtasks are discussed and taught in the following weeks 3–8. In this period, the student teams implement the extensions in NS-EOF, organizing and managing the workload autonomously. Each week, one plenary lecture on parallelization, turbulent flows, or soft skills is held. The other weekly time slot is reserved for the supervised team meetings to allow for exchange with and among the student teams, cf. Sect. 2.1.

The group phase is closed with an individual oral examination and code review to control the contribution of each team member to the team's success. Besides, the knowledge transfer within the team is controlled, e.g. via posing ME/CS questions to CS/ME students.

Project Phase. In the *project phase* (weeks 9–12), students work on an individual project in the scope of turbulent HPC simulations. Potential project topics are presented at the beginning of this phase, amongst others:

– Extension of the MPI-parallelized code NS-EOF by shared memory parallelization: for ME students, this is helpful since shared memory parallelization is typically preferred over message passing for reasons of simplicity and application on Desktop systems. For CS students, this is also a natural extension due to today's heterogeneous and many/multicore hardware devices such as Intel's Xeon Phi accelerator.
– Extension of NS-EOF by checkpointing mechanisms to allow for a restart mechanism and resilience,
– Improvement of parallel I/O routines using, e.g., MPI-IO methods,
– Incorporation of an advanced turbulence model (e.g., the Spalart-Allmaras model [9]),
– Validation of NS-EOF by comparing the simulation results to experimental results.

Students are free to also come up with own project ideas and can hence focus on their individual interests and skills, cf. (C4). Both team- or individual work on the projects is possible. Original teams from the group phase may be dissolved, and new team structures may be formed to allow optimal team constellations in terms of the preferred project topic, previous teamwork experiences etc. To further link the topic of numerical simulation on parallel systems to experimental fluid dynamics, a visit at the TUM wind tunnels and experimental fluid dynamics labs is organized.

The project phase ends with oral examinations for the project groups[1] and a plenary session in which each group presents their project results to the other students.

3   Evaluation

Based on the design described in Sect. 2, the course was conducted in the winter term 2014/15. Fourteen students, split into four groups during the group phase, participated in the course. We evaluated the course concept and design by three means: oral feedback by the students (1), centralized, department-wide mid-term

---

[1] As pointed out, a group may also be an individual student.

course evaluation (2), and a course-internal evaluation round at the end of the course (3).

In (2), students graded various course aspects using an integer system from 1 (positive) to 5 (negative). The course schedule (incl. deliverables) as well as communication of learning outcomes and goals were found to be highly satisfactory (graded 1 ($\sim$50 %), or 2 ($\sim$50 %)). With the clear focus on lab course-like interdisciplinary teamwork, autonomous working phases (graded 1 ($\sim$80 %) and 2 ($\sim$20 %)) and group size/formation (graded 1 ($\sim$85 %) and 2 ($\sim$15 %)) were also evaluated particularly positive. The course-internal evaluation (3) further supports (2): 13 out of 13 students consider the teamwork to be most supportive for their learning process in the course, as well as the support by the course supervisors. For 11 out of 13 students, "learning by doing" in the scope of this course is highly essential for the learning process. Successful learning based on autonomous and supervised working phases is hence enabled by our course concept.

The level and extent of the autonomous work program was considered challenging in (2): on a scale from 1 (much work/high difficulty) to 5 (small amount of work/low difficulty), the course level/work extent were ranked 1.29/1.67 on average. A potential reduction of the workload is currently revised.

In (2), it was also the acquisition of competences that was considered. The students consider themselves capable to work on typical tasks similar to the course contents (avg. grade 1.57 on the same scale 1–5), that is tasks from the fields HPC and CFD. The capability to transfer (scientific) methods to other concrete tasks was rated 2.0. With the evaluation (2) taking place in the middle of the group phase due to the centralized time schedule for department-wide course evaluations, this statement is, however, only of limited value. Oral and individual discussion (1) with the students after the course suggest an even higher level of satisfaction with this respect. We conclude that the supervised team-based learning combined with the lecture blocks allows the transfer of knowledge on turbulence and HPC aspects and respective acquisition of competences.

4 Conclusion

We presented a general methodology to combine interdisciplinary teamwork experience with classical lecture and lab course concepts, enabling supervised team-based learning among students. With both disciplines equally involved with respect to both course contents and student supervision, a "really interdisciplinary" setting could be established. The concept was exemplarily applied in a course on high-performance computing and computational fluid dynamics. Three-fold evaluation/student feedback suggests that the team-based learning experience supports the respective acquisition of competences. The consideration and evaluation of the course concept in other interdisciplinary settings would be of big interest to share experiences on the team-based learning process and to draw respective analogues for best practices.

Acknowledgements. The *Hochschulreferat für Studium und Lehre* of the Tech-ni-sche Uni-ver-si-tät Mün-chen is acknowledged for the financial support to realize the new course concept in the scope of the Ernst-Otto-Fischer teaching price. We thank the Munich Centre of Advanced Computing for providing the MAC-cluster and related computational resources for the student groups of our course. We particularly thank Linda Roppelt and Rudolph Aichner of the TUM-ProLehre team for their continuous advice and support on the course concept and evaluation. P. Neumann acknowledges the financial support by the priority program *1648 Software for Exascale Computing*, funded by the German Research Foundation (DFG).

References

1. Leiffer, P.R., Graff, R.W., Gonzalez, R.V.: Five curriculum Tools to enhance inter-disciplinary teamwork. In: Proceedings of the ASEE Annual Conference & Exposition, pp. 6459–6469 (2005)
2. Kuhl, S.A., Pastel, R., George, R., Meyers, C.M., Freitag, M.L., Lund, J.M., Stefaniak, M.P.: Teaching interdisciplinary teamwork through hands-on game development. In: Proceedings of the ASEE Annual Conference & Exposition (2014)
3. Department of Computer Science, Technische Universität München (2015). http://www.in.tum.de/fuer-studierende/master-studiengaenge/informatik/interdisziplinaeres-projekt/fpo-2007-und-fpso-2012.html
4. Department of Computer Science, University Paderborn (2015). http://www.cs.uni-paderborn.de/en/students/study-components/project-group.html
5. Munich Centre of Advanced Computing (2015). http://www.mac.tum.de
6. StiL, University Leipzig (2015). http://www.stil.uni-leipzig.de, in particular http://www.stil.uni-leipzig.de/wp-content/uploads/2015/06/Poster-Gesellschaft-liche-Strukturen-im-Wandel.pdf
7. Balay, S., Abhyankar, S., Adams, M., Brown, J., Brune, P., Buschelman, K., Eijkhout, V., Gropp, W., Kaushik, D., Knepley, M., Curfman McInnes, L., Rupp, K., Smith, B., Zhang, H.: PETSc Web page (2014). http://www.mcs.anl.gov/petsc
8. Griebel, M., Dornseifer, T., Neunhoeffer, T.: Numerical Simulation in Fluid Dynamics: A Practical Introduction. SIAM, Philadelphia (1997)
9. Spalart, P., Allmaras, S.: A one-equation turbulence model for aerodynamic flows. In: AIAA Paper 92-0439 (1992)
10. Schulz von Thun, F.: Miteinander reden 1: Störungen und Klärungen. Rowohlt Verlag GmbH (2010)

An Educational Module Illustrating How Sparse Matrix-Vector Multiplication on Parallel Processors Connects to Graph Partitioning

M. Ali Rostami[1]([✉]) and H. Martin Bücker[1,2]

[1] Institute for Computer Science, Friedrich Schiller University, 07737 Jena, Germany
`rostamiev@gmail.com`
[2] Michael Stifel Center Jena for Data-Driven and Simulation Science,
07737 Jena, Germany

Abstract. The transition from a curriculum without parallelism topics to a re-designed curriculum that incorporates such issues can be a daunting and time-consuming process. Therefore, it is beneficial to complement this process by gradually integrating elements from parallel computing into existing courses that were previously designed without parallelism in mind. As an example, we propose the multiplication of a sparse matrix by a dense vector on parallel computers with distributed memory. A novel educational module is introduced that illustrates the intimate connection between distributing the data of the sparse matrix-vector multiplication to parallel processes and partitioning a suitably defined graph. This web-based module aims at better involving undergraduate students in the learning process by a high level of interactivity. It can be integrated into any course on data structures with minimal effort by the instructor.

1 Introduction

With the current and noticeable trend toward computer architectures in which multiple processing elements are solving the same problem simultaneously, the need for training future generations of scientists and engineers in parallel computing has become a critical issue. The ubiquity of parallelism is now a fact and is beyond dispute among the experts. However, it is currently not sufficiently recognized in the general academic world. In fact, today, the vast majority of undergraduate curricula in science and engineering, including computer science, does not involve parallelism at all.

For the time being, the absence of parallelism in undergraduate curricula can be accepted for general science and engineering. However, the situation is different for computer science, computer engineering, and computational science. In these disciplines, the importance and relevance of parallelism in all types of computational environments is so high that corresponding undergraduate programs should—if not have to—include topics from parallel and distributed computing. Despite the importance and omnipresence of parallelism in today's computing landscape, its integration into existing degree programs is typically difficult. One

© Springer International Publishing Switzerland 2015
S. Hunold et al. (Eds.): Euro-Par 2015 Workshops, LNCS 9523, pp. 135–146, 2015.
DOI: 10.1007/978-3-319-27308-2_12

of the authors of the present paper was involved in trying to embed a mandatory parallel computing course into the undergraduate programs in computer science at two German universities, RWTH Aachen University in the early 2000 s and Friedrich Schiller University Jena in 2013. Probably the most important lesson learned from these two unsuccessful attempts is that, while it is easy to find arguments to integrate parallel computing, it is extremely difficult to find a common consensus on those contents that will have to be replaced when transforming an existing into a new curriculum. According to the author's experiences at these two German universities, the situation is quite different when degree programs are being developed from scratch. This is witnessed by the successful integration of parallel computing courses into the following new degree programs: computational engineering science (bachelor and master) as well as simulation science (master) both at RWTH Aachen University and computational and data science (master) at Friedrich Schiller University Jena.

The focus of this paper is on the integration of elements from parallel computing into existing undergraduate programs whose mandatory courses do not involve parallelism. One option is to integrate parallel computing into elective courses. This strategy was successfully applied in the undergraduate program in computer science at RWTH Aachen University [2, 4–6] but has the disadvantage that it reaches only a small subset of all enrolled students because the overall teaching load of the department is somehow balanced among competing elective courses in various areas including computer security, database systems, and human computer interaction, to name a few.

Another approach that we advocate in this paper is to integrate a narrow topic from parallel computing into an existing mandatory course. Here, we choose a course in data structures because it is among the core courses in any computing curriculum. We consider the multiplication of a sparse matrix by a dense vector on a parallel computer with distributed memory. We first sketch, in Sect. 2, a simple data structure for a sparse matrix and quote a serial algorithm for the matrix-vector multiplication. In Sect. 3 we briefly summarize the standard issues concerned with finding a suitable data distribution for that operation on a parallel computer and point out the relation to graph partitioning in Sect. 4. The new contribution of this paper is given in Sect. 5 where we introduce an interactive educational module illustrating the connection between finding a data distribution and partitioning a graph. Finally, we point the reader to related work in Sect. 6.

2   A Simple Sparse Matrix Data Structure

Undergraduate students typically think of a matrix as a simple aggregating mechanism that stores some entries in the form of a two-dimensional array. That is, they associate with this term a general dense matrix without any structure. However, in practice, matrices arising from a wide range of different application areas are typically "sparse." According to Wilkinson, a matrix is loosely defined to be sparse *whenever it is possible to take advantage of the number and location of its nonzero entries.* In a course on data structures, sparse matrices offer the opportunity to show students that the range of data structures and operations defined on matrices is much broader than the elementary two-dimensional aggregating mechanism.

Since the focus of this article is not on data structures for sparse matrices, we give only a simple example. Let A denote a sparse $N \times N$ matrix and consider the matrix-vector multiplication

$$\mathbf{y} \leftarrow A\mathbf{x} \tag{1}$$

where the N-dimensional vector $\mathbf{y}$ is the result of applying A to some given N-dimensional vector $\mathbf{x}$. Then, the ith entry of $\mathbf{y}$ is given by

$$y_i = \sum_{j \text{ with } a_{ij} \neq 0} a_{ij} \cdot x_j, \quad i = 1, 2, \ldots, N, \tag{2}$$

where an algorithm that exploits the sparsity of A does not run over all elements of the ith row of A, but only over all elements that are nonzero.

In the compressed row storage (CRS) data structure, the nonzeros of a sparse matrix are stored in three one-dimensional arrays as follows:

```
CRS_matrix = record
    value : array[1 .. nnz] of REAL
    col_ind: array[1 .. nnz] of INTEGER
    row_ptr: array[1 .. N+1] of INTEGER
end_record
```

Here, the number of nonzero elements of A is denoted by nnz. A nonzero element a_{ij} is stored in value(k) if and only if its column index j is stored in col_ind(k) and its row index i satisfies row_ptr$(i) \leq k <$ row_ptr$(i+1)$. Then, assuming row_ptr$(N+1) :=$ nnz $+ 1$, it is well known that the matrix-vector multiplication (1) is computed by the pseudocode

```
for (i = 1; i <= N; ++i)
    y[i] = 0;
    for (j = row_ptr[i]; j < row_ptr[i + 1]; ++j)
        y[i] += value[j] * x[col_ind[j]];
```

The key observation for students is that there is some matrix data structure that stores and operates on the nonzeros only. Further storage schemes for and operations on sparse matrices are described in various books [13, 15, 19–21].

3   Sparse Matrix-Vector Multiplication Goes Parallel

The sparse matrix-vector multiplication is also an illustrating example to introduce parallelism. By inspecting (2) it is obvious that all entries y_i can be computed independently from each other. That is, the matrix-vector multiplication is easily decomposed into tasks that can execute simultaneously. However, it is not obvious to undergraduates how to decompose data required by these tasks. The need for the decomposition of data to parallel processes is lucidly described by introducing a parallel computer as a network that connects multiple serial computers, each with a local memory. This way, an undergraduate course can easily introduce, in a combined way, data structures for sparse matrices that are more advanced than simple two-dimensional arrays as well as parallelism in the form of multiple processes that operate on data accessible via distributed memory.

The following questions then naturally arise: If data representing A, $\mathbf{x}$ and $\mathbf{y}$ are distributed to multiple processes, to what extent does this data distribution have an effect on the computation $\mathbf{y} \leftarrow A\mathbf{x}$? What are the advantages and disadvantages of a given data distribution? What are the criteria for evaluating the quality of a data distribution? How should data be distributed to the processes ideally?

To discuss such questions with undergraduates who are new to parallel computing we suggest to consider the following simple data distribution. The nonzero elements of A are distributed to processes by rows. More precisely, all nonzeros of a row are distributed to the same process. The vectors $\mathbf{x}$ and $\mathbf{y}$ are distributed consistently. That is, if a process stores the nonzeros of row i of A then it also stores the vector entries x_i and y_i. Given a fixed number of processes p, a data distribution may be formally expressed by a mapping called *partition*

$$P : I \rightarrow \{1, 2, \ldots, p\}$$

that decomposes the set of indices $I := \{1, 2, \ldots, N\}$ into p subsets I_1, I_2, $\ldots$, I_p such that

$$I = I_1 \cup I_2 \cup \cdots \cup I_p$$

with $I_i \cap I_j = \emptyset$ for $i \neq j$. That is, if $P(i) = k$ then the nonzeros of row i as well as x_i and y_i are stored on process k.

Since the nonzero a_{ij} is stored on process $P(i)$ and the vector entry x_j is stored on process $P(j)$, one can sort the terms in the sum (2) according to those terms where both operands of the product $a_{ij} \cdot x_j$ are stored on the same process and those where these operands are stored on different processes:

$$y_i = \sum_{\substack{j \text{ with } a_{ij} \neq 0 \\ P(i)=P(j)}} a_{ij} \cdot x_j + \sum_{\substack{j \text{ with } a_{ij} \neq 0 \\ P(i) \neq P(j)}} a_{ij} \cdot x_j, \quad i = 1, 2, \ldots, N. \tag{3}$$

For the sake of simplicity, we assume that the product $a_{ij} \cdot x_j$ is computed by the process $P(i)$ that stores the result y_i to which this product contributes. By (3), the data distribution P has an effect on the amount of data that needs to be communicated between processes. It also determines which processes communicate with each other. Since, on today's computing systems, communication needs significantly more time than computation, it is important to find a data distribution using a goal-oriented approach. A data distribution is desirable that balances the computational load evenly among the processes while, at the same time, minimizes the communication among the processes.

4   An Undirected Graph Model for Data Partitioning

The problem of finding a data distribution is also interesting from another perspective of undergraduate teaching. It offers the opportunity to demonstrate that a theoretical model can serve as a successful abstraction of a practical problem. More precisely, a formal approach using concepts from graph theory is capable of tackling the data distribution problem systematically.

To this end, we now assume that the nonzero pattern of the nonsymmetric matrix A is symmetric. Then, the matrix can be represented by an undirected graph $G = (V, E)$. The set of nodes $V = \{1, 2, \ldots, N\}$ is used to associate a node to every row (or corresponding column) of A. The set of edges

$$E = \{(i, j) \mid i, j \in V \text{ and } a_{ij} \neq 0 \text{ for } i > j\}$$

describes the nonzero entries. Here, the condition $i > j$ indicates that the edge (i, j) is identical to the edge (j, i) and that there is no self-loop in G. The data distribution to p processes is then represented by the partition

$$P : V \to \{1, 2, \ldots, p\}$$

that decomposes the set of nodes V of the graph into p subsets V_1, V_2, $\ldots$, V_p such that

$$V = V_1 \cup V_2 \cup \cdots \cup V_p$$

with $V_i \cap V_j = \emptyset$ for $i \neq j$.

Then, (2) is reformulated in terms of graph terminology by

$$y_i = a_{ii} \cdot x_i + \sum_{\substack{(i,j) \in E \\ P(i) = P(j)}} a_{ij} \cdot x_j + \sum_{\substack{(i,j) \in E \\ P(i) \neq P(j)}} a_{ij} \cdot x_j.$$

Here, the first two terms of the right-hand side can be computed on process $P(i)$ without communication to any other process. The condition $P(i) \neq P(j)$ in the last term shows that the computation of $a_{ij} \cdot x_j$ requires communication between process $P(i)$ which stores a_{ij} and process $P(j)$ which stores x_j. Minimizing interprocess communication then roughly corresponds to minimizing the number of edges connecting nodes in different subsets V_i of the partition P. This number of edges is called the *cut size* and is formally defined by

$$\text{cutsize}(P) = \big| \{(i, j) \in E \mid P(i) \neq P(j)\} \big|. \tag{4}$$

In this graph model, the cut size does not exactly correspond to the number of words communicated between all processes in the computation of $\mathbf{y} \leftarrow A\mathbf{x}$ for a given partition P. However, it gives a reasonable approximation to this amount of communicated data called the *communication volume*; see the corresponding discussion in [17]. The communication volume is exactly described by the cut size if the underlying model is changed from an undirected graph to a hypergraph [11, 12, 22].

Assuming that the number of nonzeros is roughly the same for each row of A, the computation is evenly balanced among the p processes if the partition P is ε-balanced defined as

$$
\max_{1 \leq i \leq p} |V_i| \leq (1 + \varepsilon)\frac{|V|}{p}, \tag{5}
$$

for some given $\varepsilon > 0$. The graph partitioning problem consists of minimizing the cut size of an ε-balanced partition. It is a hard combinatorial problem [14].

5   An Educational Module Illustrating the Connection

To illustrate the connection between computing a sparse matrix-vector multiplication in parallel and partitioning an undirected graph, we propose a novel educational module. This module is part of a growing set of educational modules called EXPLoring Algorithms INteractively (EXPLAIN). This collection of web-based modules is designed to assist in the effectiveness of teachers in the classroom and we plan to make it publicly available in the near future. Figure 1 shows the overall layout of this interactive module for sparse matrix-vector multiplication. The top of this figure visualizes—side by side—the representation of the problem in terms of the graph G as well as in terms of the matrix A and the vector $\mathbf{x}$. Below on the left, there is a panel of colors representing different processes and another panel displaying the order of selecting vertices of the graph. Next, on the right, there is a score diagram recording values characterizing communication and load balancing. At the bottom part, there are input controls used to select a matrix from a predefined set of matrices, to upload a small matrix, and to choose the layout of the graph vertices.

The first figure gives an overall impression of the status of the module after a data distribution is completed. Here, $p = 4$ processes represented by the colors blue, green, red, and yellow get data by interactive actions taken by the student. Figure 2 now shows the status of the module in a phase that is more related to the beginning of that interactive procedure. For a given matrix, the student can distribute the data to the processes by first clicking on a color and then clicking on an arbitrary number of vertices. That is, the distribution of vertices to a single process is determined by first clicking on a color j and then clicking on a certain number of vertices, say $i_1, i_2, \ldots, i_s$ such that $P(i_1) = P(i_2) = \cdots = P(i_s) = j$. Then, by clicking on the next color, this procedure can be repeated until all vertices are interactively colored and, thus, the data distribution P is finally determined.

Figure 2 illustrates the situation after the student distributed vertices 1, 2 and 3 to the blue process and the vertices 7, 8 and 10 to the green process. By interactively assigning a vertex to a process, not only the vertex is colored by the color representing this process, but also the row in the matrix as well as the corresponding vector entry of $\mathbf{x}$ are simultaneously colored with the same color. This way, the data distribution is visualized in the graph and in the matrix

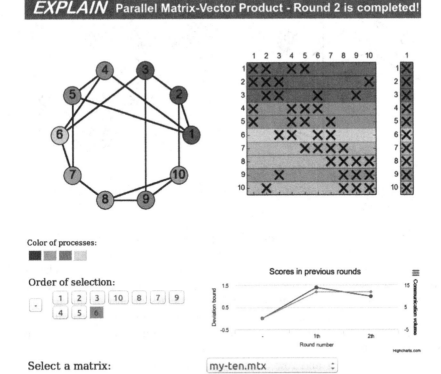

Fig. 1. Overall structure of the sparse matrix-vector multiplication module (Color figure online).

simultaneously which emphasizes the connection between the matrix representation and the graph representation of that problem. The panel labeled "Order of selection" records the order of the vertices that are interactively chosen. By inspection from that panel in Fig. 1, we find out that the status depicted in Fig. 2 is an intermediate step of the interactive session that led to the data distribution in Fig. 1. Any box labeled with the number of the chosen vertex in that panel is also clickable allowing the student to return to any intermediate state and start a rearrangement of the data distribution form that state.

In EXPLAIN, the term "round" refers to the process of solving a single instance of a given problem. In this module, the problem consists of distributing all data needed to compute the matrix-vector product to the processes. Equivalently, the distribution of all vertices of the corresponding graph to the processes is a round. Suppose that round 2 is completed in Fig. 1. Then, the student can explore the data distribution in more detail by clicking on a color in the panel labeled "Color of processes." Suppose that the student chooses the red

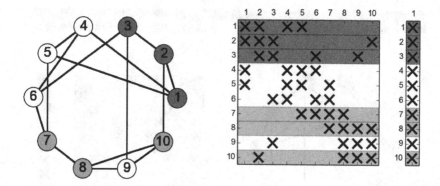

Fig. 2. The intermediate state after the student selected six vertices.

process, then this action will modify the appearance of the vector **x** in the matrix representation to the state given in Fig. 3. Here, all vector entries that need to be communicated to the red process are now also colored red. The background color still represents the process that stores that vector entry. This illustrates, for instance, that the vector entry x_1 is communicated from the blue process to the red process when computing $A\mathbf{x}$ using this particular data distribution. The matrix representation visualizes the reason for this communication. There is at least one row that is colored red and that has a nonzero element in column 1. In this example row 4 and row 5 satisfy this condition. Thus, x_1 is needed to compute y_4 and y_5. Again, EXPLAIN visually illustrates the connection between the linear algebra representation and the graph representation. In the graph representation, all vector entries that need to be communicated to the red process correspond to those non-red vertices that are connected to a red vertex. In this example, this condition is satisfied for vertices 1, 3, 6, 7, 8, 10 which correspond

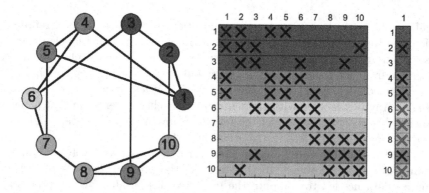

Fig. 3. All vector entries x_i to be communicated to the red process are drawn in red (Color figure online).

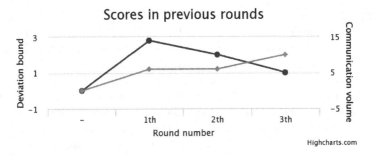

Fig. 4. The communication volume and the deviation bound versus various rounds (Color figure online).

to the vector entries x_1, x_3, x_6, x_7, x_8, x_{10} in the matrix representation that are drawn in red.

When a round is completed it is also instructive to focus on the quality of the data distribution P. Recall that the graph partitioning problem aims at minimizing the cut size of P while balancing the computational load evenly among the processes. To asses these two quantities, the module introduces the score diagram. An example of a score diagram is depicted in Fig. 4. For each round, this diagram shows the cut size defined by (4) using the label "communication volume." As mentioned in the previous section, the cut size in this undirected graph model is not an exact representation of the communication volume. However, it often captures the nature of the communication volume quite well. Therefore, this graph model uses the cut size as a measure of the communication volume. In that score diagram, the student can check his or her attempt to minimize the communication volume over a number of rounds.

The parameter ε introduced in (5) is used to quantify the degree of imbalance allowed in a data distribution. If $\varepsilon = 0$ all processes are assigned exactly $|V|/p$ rows of A, meaning that no imbalance is allowed at all. When increasing ε the load balancing condition (5) is relaxed. The larger ε is chosen, the larger is the allowed imbalance. Thus, in some way, ε quantifies the deviation from a perfect load balance. An equivalent form of (5) is given by

$$\frac{p}{|V|} \max_{1 \leq i \leq p} |V_i| - 1 \leq \varepsilon, \tag{6}$$

which can be interpreted as follows. Suppose that you are not looking for an ε-balanced partition P for a given ε, but rather turn this procedure around and ask: "Given a partition P, how large need ε at least be so that this partition is ε-balanced?" Then the left-hand side of the inequality (6) which we call *deviation bound* gives an answer to that question. The extreme cases for the deviation bound are given by 0 if the distribution is perfectly balanced and $p-1$ if there is one process that gets all the data. The score diagram shows the value of the deviation bound for each round. A low deviation bound indicates a partition that balances the computational load evenly, whereas a large deviation bound represents a large imbalance of the load. The score diagram helps the student to evaluate the quality of a single data distribution and to compare it with distributions obtained in previous rounds. This feedback to the student is designed in the spirit of computer games, where a score has only a low immediate relevance to the current game. However, the idea is to achieve a "high score" and try to motivate the player to beat that score in subsequent rounds, thus offering an extra challenge. For this educational module, a "high score" would consist of a low communication value together with a low deviation bound.

Finally, we mention that EXPLAIN is designed to be extended for problems arising in the general area of combinatorial scientific computing, including but not limited to parallel computing. Previous modules are available on Cholesky factorization [18], nested dissection [7], column compression [9], and bidirectional compression [8].

6 Related Work

The idea to incrementally integrate topics from parallel computing into existing courses is not new. Brown and Schoop [3] introduce a set of flexible teaching modules designed to be used in many potential courses. Our approach is similar in that the syllabus of an existing course requires only minimal changes and that we try to reduce the effort needed by an instructor to deploy the module in a course. A collection of their modules is available at http://csinparallel.org. These modules cover various areas, but have a focus on programming. Like our module, one of the modules of this collection is related to data structures. Another approach is described in [10]. It integrates modules on parallel programming into undergraduate courses in programming languages at the two liberal arts colleges Knox College and Lewis & Clark College. Here, the functional language Haskel is chosen to introduce parallel programming via two class periods of about one hour each. Adams [1] employs the shared-memory parallel programming paradigm OpenMP to introduce parallel design patterns in a data structure course. Also in an existing course on data structures, Grossman and Anderson [16] take a comprehensive approach using fork/join parallelism.

7 Concluding Remarks

The overall idea behind this paper is to integrate elements of parallelism into existing courses that were previously designed with a serial computing paradigm in mind. A natural approach to implement this strategy is to focus on parallel programming. We strongly believe that parallel programming is an important element of any program in computer science, computer engineering, and computational science. However, we also advocate with this article that, in parallel computing, there is more than programming. To this end, we introduce an interactive educational module that can easily be integrated into an existing course on data structures. Though this web-based module can be augmented with parallel programming exercises, its focus is on a higher level of abstraction. It shows to undergraduate students that, when going from serial to parallel computing, it is necessary to consider additional topics of fundamental quality. More precisely, the data distribution needed to balance computational work while minimizing communication is connected to graph partitioning. Thus, a problem like sparse matrix-vector multiplication which is simple on a serial computer leads to a hard combinatorial problem when computed in parallel.

Acknowledgments. This work is partially supported by the German Federal Ministry for the Environment, Nature Conservation, Building and Nuclear Safety (BMUB) and the German Federal Ministry for Economic Affairs and Energy (BMWi) within the project MeProRisk II, contract number 0325389F.

References

1. Adams, J.C.: Injecting parallel computing into CS2. In: Proceedings of the 45th ACM Technical Symposium on Computer Science Education, SIGCSE 2014, pp. 277–282. ACM, New York (2014). http://doi.acm.org/10.1145/2538862.2538883
2. Bischof, C.H., Bücker, H.M., Henrichs, J., Lang, B.: Hands-on training for undergraduates in high-performance computing using Java. In: Sørevik, T., Manne, F., Moe, R., Gebremedhin, A.H. (eds.) PARA 2000. LNCS, vol. 1947, pp. 306–315. Springer, Heidelberg (2001)
3. Brown, R., Shoop, E.: Modules in community: injecting more parallelism into computer science curricula. In: Proceedings of the 42nd ACM Technical Symposium on Computer Science Education, SIGCSE 2011, pp. 447–452. ACM, New York (2011). http://doi.acm.org/10.1145/1953163.1953293
4. Bücker, H.M., Lang, B., Bischof, C.H.: Teaching different parallel programming paradigms using Java. In: Proceedings of the 3rd Annual Workshop on Java for High Performance Computing, Sorrento, Italy, 17 June 2001, pp. 73–81 (2001)
5. Bücker, H.M., Lang, B., Bischof, C.H.: Parallel programming in computational science: an introductory practical training course for computer science undergraduates at Aachen University. Future Gener. Comput. Syst. **19**(8), 1309–1319 (2003)
6. Bücker, H.M., Lang, B., Pflug, H.-J., Vehreschild, A.: Threads in an undergraduate course: a Java example illuminating different multithreading approaches. In: Laganá, A., Gavrilova, M.L., Kumar, V., Mun, Y., Tan, C.J.K., Gervasi, O. (eds.) ICCSA 2004. LNCS, vol. 3044, pp. 882–891. Springer, Heidelberg (2004)
7. Bücker, H.M., Rostami, M.A.: Interactively exploring the connection between nested dissection orderings for parallel Cholesky factorization and vertex separators. In: IEEE 28th International Parallel and Distributed Processing Symposium. IPDPS 2014 Workshops, Phoenix, Arizona, USA, 19–23 May 2014, pp. 1122–1129. IEEE Computer Society, Los Alamitos (2014)
8. Bücker, H.M., Rostami, M.A.: Interactively exploring the connection between bidirectional compression and star bicoloring. In: Koziel, S., Leifsson, L., Lees, M., Krzhizhanovskaya, V.V., Dongarra, J., Sloot, P.M.A. (eds.) International Conference on Computational Science, ICCS 2015 – Computational Science at the Gates of Nature, Reykjavík, Iceland, 1–3 June 2015. Elsevier (2015). Procedia Comput. Sci. **51**, 1917–1926

9. Bücker, H.M., Rostami, M.A., Lülfesmann, M.: An interactive educational module illustrating sparse matrix compression via graph coloring. In: 2013 International Conference on Interactive Collaborative Learning (ICL), Proceedings of the 16th International Conference on Interactive Collaborative Learning, Kazan, Russia, 25–27 September 2013, pp. 330–335. IEEE, Piscataway (2013)
10. Bunde, D.P., Mache, J., Drake, P.: Adding parallel Haskell to the undergraduate programming language course. J. Comput. Sci. Coll. **30**(1), 181–189 (2014). http://dl.acm.org/citation.cfm?id=2667369.2667403
11. Çatalyürek, Ü.V., Aykanat, C.: Hypergraph-partitioning-based decomposition for parallel sparse-matrix vector multiplication. IEEE Trans. Parallel Distrib. Syst. **10**(7), 673–693 (1999)
12. Çatalyürek, Ü.V., Uçar, B., Aykanat, C.: Hypergraph partitioning. In: Padua, D. (ed.) Encyclopedia of Parallel Computing, pp. 871–881. Springer, New York (2011)
13. Duff, I.S., Erisman, A.M., Reid, J.K.: Direct Methods for Sparse Matrices. Clarendon Press, Oxford (1986)
14. Garey, M.R., Johnson, D.S.: Computers and Intractability: A Guide to the Theory of NP-Completeness. Freeman, San Francisco (1979)
15. George, A., Liu, J.W.H.: Computer Solution of Large Sparse Positive Definite Systems. Prentice-Hall, Englewood Cliffs (1981)
16. Grossman, D., Anderson, R.E.: Introducing parallelism and concurrency in the data structures course. In: Proceedings of the 43rd ACM Technical Symposium on Computer Science Education, SIGCSE 2012, pp. 505–510. ACM, New York (2012). http://doi.acm.org/10.1145/2157136.2157285
17. Hendrickson, B., Kolda, T.G.: Graph partitioning models for parallel computing. Parallel Comput. **26**(2), 1519–1534 (2000)
18. Lülfesmann, M., Leßenich, S.R., Bücker, H.M.: Interactively exploring elimination orderings in symbolic sparse Cholesky factorization. In: International Conference on Computational Science, ICCS 2010. Elsevier (2010). Procedia Comput. Sci. **1**(1), 867–874
19. Osterby, O., Zlatev, Z.: Direct Methods for Sparse Matrices. Springer, New York (1983)
20. Pissanetzky, S.: Sparse Matrix Technology. Academic Press, New York (1984)
21. Saad, Y.: Iterative Methods for Sparse Linear Systems, Second edn. SIAM, Philadelphia (2003)
22. Uçar, B., Aykanat, C.: Revisiting hypergraph models for sparse matrix partitioning. SIAM Rev. **49**(4), 595–603 (2007). http://dx.doi.org/10.1137/060662459

FERBJMON Tools - Visualizing Thread Access on Java Objects using Lightweight Runtime Monitoring

Marvin Ferber[✉]

Institute of Computer Science, Technical University Bergakademie Freiberg,
Freiberg, Germany
`marvin.ferber@informatik.tu-freiberg.de`

Abstract. Learning and teaching parallel programming in Java can sometimes be tedious, because the correct behavior of a parallel program can hardly be debugged. A runtime monitoring can help to gather information on the behavior of a parallel program. As Java Bytecode is executed inside a JVM, a runtime monitoring can be applied with almost no changes to the source code. In this paper, FERBJMON tools for monitoring Java objects at runtime are proposed. FERBJMON tools also include a tool for call graph creation and a tool for visualizing chronological accesses of threads on Java objects in a timeline diagram. A lightweight monitoring is necessary to minimize the influence of the monitoring on the program behavior itself. FERBJMON tools address this issue by selecting only one class for the monitoring at the same time and by a fast logging implementation. A producer/consumer program and a program for cooperative task execution are used to demonstrate the applicability and the performance of the logging. FERBJMON tools can be used to understand and optimize thread synchronization in Java programs.

Keywords: Java · Runtime monitoring · Parallel computing · Distributed computing · Education

1 Introduction

The programming language Java is already used in a variety of educational activities such as lectures or practical sessions [7]. Reasons for its popularity include the consistent object-orientation in Java source code, the platform independence, and its large system library, which includes many classes, e. g., for parallel processing. Java has already built-in threading and synchronization mechanisms such as mutual exclusion and signals. Even higher level parallel constructs such as thread pools and complex thread-safe data structures like hash tables are built-in. This makes parallelism easy to use in Java programs.

However, the proper usage of mechanisms for thread synchronization can be difficult when starting to learn parallel programming [4,9]. The chronological

© Springer International Publishing Switzerland 2015
S. Hunold et al. (Eds.): Euro-Par 2015 Workshops, LNCS 9523, pp. 147–159, 2015.
DOI: 10.1007/978-3-319-27308-2_13

order of activities in multiple threads of execution is hard to debug. As a consequence, race conditions may occur or threads may block due to missing signals. A source code analysis may not always detect the causes for such unintended behavior. Runtime monitoring can be used to investigate the behavior of program *in action*. As Java Bytecode is executed in a Java Virtual Machine (JVM), a monitoring can be applied to a JVM at runtime with only minor changes to the source code. This makes it easy to apply for, e. g., multi-threaded programs. Runtime monitoring requires the execution of additional code. It needs to be applied carefully to minimize the influence on the actual program behavior.

In this paper, FERBJMON tools for runtime monitoring of Java programs are proposed. FERBJMON tools can be used to capture runtime information of Java programs in order to create call graphs and timeline diagrams that visualize the chronological accesses of threads on Java objects. FERBJMON tools use Bytecode instrumentation and focus on class instances to monitor access on them. Only parts of the program code are monitored, which allows a lightweight monitoring.

FERBJMON tools can easily be applied in teaching, because only few arguments of the invocation of the Java interpreter and almost no changes to the source code of the program under monitoring are necessary to automatically monitor and visualize the program behavior. Furthermore, the created timeline diagrams provide a different view on execution traces than the widely used UML sequence diagrams, which is better suited to handle fine-grained parallelism in Java. FERBJMON tools are available for Windows and Linux[1].

The article is structured as follows. First, related work on the analysis of multi-threaded programs is discussed. In Sect. 3 the FERBJMON tools, their implementation, and their usage are presented. Example programs and the application of FERBJMON tools in teaching parallel programming are discussed in Sect. 4. Benchmarks investigating the monitoring performance are presented in Sect. 5. Section 6 concludes the paper.

2   Related Work

First steps for successful parallel programming in Java include the usage of programming patterns for parallelism in general [10] and the proper usage of mechanisms and data structures for parallel programming in Java [6]. However, the necessity for tool support for parallel program validation and verification has already been discussed in current literature on parallel programming education [4]. Questions are raised such as "How can I introduce parallelism into my algorithm?" or "How can I measure the benefits of parallelism?" [11]. Different ways exist to capture and analyze the behavior of parallel programs.

A static source code analysis can be applied to detect possible deadlock situations prior to execution. A tool that detects deadlocks in Java libraries using a lock-order graph is proposed in [12]. However, a static analysis may not detect all dependencies in a Java code because of reflection. Such dependencies appear

---

[1] https://github.com/marvinferber/ferbjmon.

at runtime. A runtime analysis can additionally detect the number of concurring threads and the occupancy of data structures. Therefore, tools have been developed to monitor the behavior of concurrent Java programs using program traces. Many early attempts to generate program traces such as JACOT [8] were based on the Java Virtual Machine Debug Interface (JVMDI), which was removed in Java 6. Current attempts such as Javashot [1] and JThreadSpy [9] are therefore based on Bytecode instrumentation to gather runtime information.

Javashot is a tool that generates call graphs from runtime traces of Java programs. JThreadSpy can generate augmented UML sequence diagrams from runtime traces highlighting thread interactions and concurrent access to critical sections in concurrent Java programs. Because UML sequence diagrams are not well prepared for parallel programs, actions of different threads are marked in different color for visualization. JThreadSpy provides a custom visualization software for this purpose. Performance benchmarks on the overhead for logging are not given. FERBJMON tools create a different visualization based on timeline diagrams that visualize the accesses of different threads on each object instance separately, which is better suited for fine-grained access monitoring.

Other tools for runtime monitoring of CPU usage or memory occupation such as the Java Monitoring and Management Console (JConsole) and VisualVM [3] are already shipped with an installation of the Java Development Kit (JDK). All tools named provide different information that can be combined in order to get a comprehensive knowledge on a parallel Java program.

3   Java Runtime Monitoring Using FERBJMON Tools

FERBJMON tools generate traces from program executions using a Bytecode transformation that is executed at runtime in order to inject monitoring code into user-defined classes. FERBJMON tools are applied in three steps:

1. Preparation → mark class of interest and transform Bytecode,
2. Monitoring → run program with transformed Bytecode and generate logs,
3. Visualization → process logs and generate diagrams.

All steps are performed automatically, except the annotation of the class of interest. Only instances of one specific class are monitored at the same time in order to only execute a minimal set of additional code. The class under monitoring must not have public fields because only method invocations can be monitored. Access to public fields is not captured. Getter and setter methods need to be implemented in order to realize a complete monitoring. The monitoring is applied to a class by annotating it using the FERBJMON-specific @Monitored annotation, see Fig. 3 for an illustration. FERBJMON tools require the monitored parts to be encapsulated into one Java class. This sometimes requires to adapt the program code in order to enable the monitoring for the intended behavior. Many data structures such as thread pools or work queues are well encapsulated and can be monitored easily. In contrast, a matrix multiplication may be difficult to monitor unless each matrix update can be encapsulated into a corresponding method.

After a class has been annotated, the monitoring can easily be applied to any Java program by substituting the `java` command-line tool by a FERBJMON-specific wrapper script.

- `java_threadorder` monitors the chronological access of threads on a Java object with the intention to create a timeline diagram.
- `java_callgraph` captures runtime dependencies with the intention to create a call graph.

Both wrapper scripts take exactly the same command-line parameters like the `java` command-line tool. The wrapper scripts additionally apply the Bytecode transformations necessary for monitoring, implement the generation of trace logs while the program is executed, and perform the generation of a default visualization after the execution has finished. Furthermore, the trace logs are also saved to generate user-specific visualizations. FERBJMON tools take optional parameters to influence the logging behavior, which are specified as environmental variables of a Java program. The tools are described in detail in the following subsections.

3.1 Bytecode Instrumentation

Bytecode instrumentation is a mechanism to modify Java Bytecode at runtime. It is applied while a specific Java class is loaded by the classloader. The instrumentation is transparent to the actual program code and can be used to inject additional output messages into the Bytecode. It is helpful to use a Bytecode manipulation library for Bytecode processing. FERBJMON tools use the Javassist Bytecode manipulation library [2]. A filter transformation is used to modify the relevant parts inside a class. Thereby, the syntax tree of the class is traversed and transformations are implemented as callback functions on relevant nodes such as method calls. FERBJMON tools use this technique to inject additional code each time a method is invoked and each time a method returns.

Java has the ability to execute Bytecode instrumentation through a Java agent. The Java agent code is executed before the actual user program starts. Therefore, the method **premain()** needs to be implemented. The agents library can be passed as command-line argument to the `java` command-line tool (e. g., `java -javaagent:PATH/agent.jar -cp CLASSPATH MAINCLASS`). Figure 1 shows the point of execution in a Java program run. The Java agent is executed after the JVM has been initialized and before the **main()** method of the actual program is invoked. Its main purpose is to substitute the default classloader by a custom classloader (modifying loader) that performs the Bytecode modification. Furthermore, the Java agent also registers a global shutdown hook, which is necessary for log file creation after the program has finished.

At runtime, Bytecode instrumentation can only be performed for user classes. System classes are locked and prevented from being substituted once they are loaded. However, it is possible to instrument system classes offline and to load

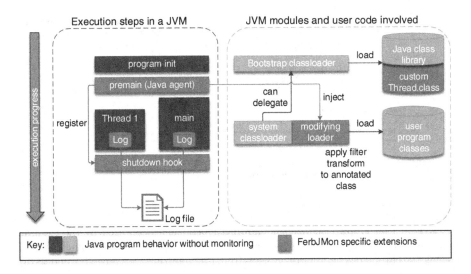

Fig. 1. Overview of the implementation of the runtime monitoring using a JVM. User classes are instrumented based on annotation. Logging is performed by each thread itself using a custom implementation of `java.lang.Thread`. A shutdown hook pulls all log data and writes a common log file (Color figure online).

them during JVM startup. System class loading is performed by the bootstrap classloader even before loading the Java agent. A specific library can be passed to the `java` command-line tool in order to be loaded by the bootstrap classloader, see Fig. 1 for an illustration. So, it is possible to even substitute system classes like `java.lang.Thread`. An exemplary command line would be `java -Xbootclasspath/p:PATH/sys.jar -cp CLASSPATH MAINCLASS`.

FERBJMON tools use a modified version of the system class `java.lang.Thread`, because a custom logging is directly integrated into each thread. So, lock free logging is performed by each thread. This ensures an equally distributed influence of the logging among all threads that access Java objects under monitoring. There are no additional dependencies between threads or threads and common data structures. At the end of a program run, a shutdown hook is executed that actively pulls the logs from each thread and merges them into a single log file.

3.2 FERBJMON Call Graph

A call graph that is captured at runtime can visualize dependencies between those classes that were instantiated in a specific program run. This set of instantiated classes and method invocations is often smaller than the set of all classes of the program, because not all classes may be used in a specific program run. A runtime call graph can be less complex than a call graph captured from a static code analysis. Prior to the actual thread monitoring a call graph analysis can be 'useful to identify classes and threads that access the object under monitoring.

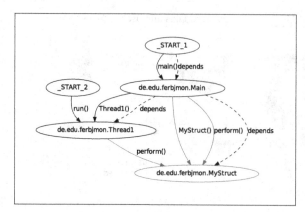
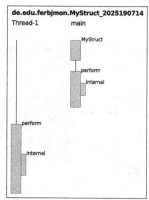

Fig. 2. *Left:* Call graph visualization showing dependencies captured by the runtime monitoring. The monitored class MyStruct is marked red. *Right:* Timeline diagram showing the chronological order of accesses from different threads (Thread-1 and main) on a Java object instance of the class MyStruct.

The tool java_callgraph directly creates a text file as output that contains all captured dependencies in the Graphviz dot language [5]. Graph layout is done by the dot command-line tools. A exemplary graph is shown in Fig. 2 (left). Classes are shown as ellipses containing their fully qualified class name. Call dependencies are visualized as solid directed lines that show the direction of method invocation. Dependencies that arise from non-method invocations, e. g., through parameters in method calls, are visualized as dashed directed lines. The class under monitoring and all ingoing call dependencies of method invocations are marked red. Each thread start (including the main thread) is also visualized by ellipses containing the word _START_. Additionally, there is a dependency from this start ellipse to the corresponding thread class via its startup method. This can be seen in Fig. 2 (left) at the methods main() and run().

The call graph visualization does not contain invocations of methods within a class itself. This would lead to looping dependencies that have the same origin and target. These are not relevant for inter-class dependencies. Invocations on system classes are not visualized, because they can hardly be monitored. Furthermore, the monitoring of system classes can lead to large dependency graphs, because even small programs can involve many system classes in the background.

3.3   FERBJMON Timeline Diagram of Thread Accesses

The chronological order of accesses to a Java class instance can be relevant to validate or optimize the proper usage and implementation of synchronization mechanisms in a parallel Java program. The monitoring is performed by each thread itself, because each thread is extended by a logger implementation for this purpose. The log messages are generated by the instrumented Bytecode of the class under monitoring. Each log entry contains the current system time by means of `System.nanoTime()`, the hash value of the current class object, the method that is considered, the thread that performed an action, and the action itself (enter method or exit method). Using this information, a timeline diagram of thread accesses can be created for each object instance.

As a requirement, logging should not influence the program behavior significantly. If many log entries appear in a short period of time, writing these entries to a file directly can lead to delays in thread execution. This can influence the program behavior. Logging into main memory is limited by the capacity of the RAM but normally much faster. Java provides the class `java.lang.StringBuilder` to collect an unknown amount of strings in main memory. However, writing strings to a preallocated array of characters may provide the best performance. As a drawback, preallocation further limits the available log space, because the size of the array needs to be specified in advance. To suit different logging demands the FERBJMON tool `java_threadorder` implements the following logger:

- `File Logger` a `java.io.BufferedWriter` that writes log entries directly into a file (this is the default logger),
- `StringBuilder Logger` uses `java.lang.StringBuilder` to capture all logs in main memory, and
- `MemArray Logger` creates a fixed size array of characters in main memory and captures all logs in this array.

Data from memory loggers is written to disk during the shutdown hook execution. The selected FERBJMON logger must be specified as global parameter to the JVM invocation (`-Dmyjavamon.logger=<Logger>`). The `MemArray Logger` needs an additional parameter (`-Dmyjavamon.logger.size=<size>`) that specifies the size of the array. Benchmarks on the performance of the different logging implementations in an example application are given in Sect. 5.

A timeline diagram is the default visualization of the log data captured during runtime. It is also created by `java_threadorder`, see Fig. 2 for an illustration. One diagram is created for each object instance that is identified by the fully qualified class name followed by the hash value of the object, see top of Fig. 2 (right). The timeline for each thread and the corresponding thread names are drawn below. Figure 2 (right) shows the `main` thread and `Thread-1`. First, the `main` thread instantiates an object of the class `de.edu.ferbjmon.MyStruct` and calls the constructor. Afterwards, both threads invoke the method `perform()` on this object instance. A nested method call to the public function `internal()` can also be seen. Method calls to private functions are not shown here.

4 Examples

Examples of common problems in parallel programming and their visualization using FERBJMON tools are given in the following.

4.1 Producer and Consumer

The problem of producer and consumer is a common problem in a variety of multi-threaded scenarios. A set of producers offers tasks to a set of threads that execute the work. An application of this problem can be found, e. g., in a Web server. A fixed set of dispatch threads (producer) accept client requests and enqueue them into a queue data structure. A fixed set of worker threads then executes these request in their order of appearance and the results of the requests (a Web document) are returned to the dispatcher thread. This example demonstrates how FERBJMON tools can be used to visualize the usage of a queue.

Java offers different implementations of the interface java.util. concurrent. BlockingQueue. This interface requires the methods put(...) and take() that block the executing thread if the queue is empty or if no space is available (queue full). This data structure can be used to synchronize a producer and consumer scenario. As an example, the data structure MyQueue is implemented as a wrapper class for an java.util.concurrent.ArrayBlockingQueue. MyQueue sets the queue size and realizes the methods enqueue(...) and gather() to insert and remove elements from this queue. The Producer and Consumer thread are derived from the class java.lang.Thread.

- The Producer starts to enqueue three objects immediately with a delay of 5 ms between each.
- The Consumer starts to gather three objects with a delay of 2 ms after an initial delay of 2 ms.

The source code of the classes MyQueue and the timeline diagram of a monitored program run are shown in Fig. 3. First, MyQueue is instantiated by the main thread. The Producer thread enqueues the first item without delay. The second enqueue() action is slightly delayed due to synchronization mechanisms that need to be initialized in this step because a concurring gather() is already waiting for an element to be inserted. The third gather() is largely delayed until the last element is inserted by the Producer thread. A large delay at consumer site may be intended, whereas a large delay on producer site may be caused by an overload. FERBJMON tools can be used to optimize the queue size or the number of Consumer threads.

4.2   Cooperative Task Execution

Some applications require a special communication pattern between threads. As an example, the cooperative incrementation of an integer value using two threads is presented. The integer is encapsulated in the class MyInteger. Two types of threads manipulate the object. The EvenThread is only permitted to increment the value if it is even, the OddThread if it is odd. As a result, a mutual incrementation by both types of threads is realized in the manner of a ping-pong game. The access pattern described is implemented using a synchronized access to the object by both types of threads. Additionally, the object methods wait() and notify() are used to implement the signals that hand over control between the thread instances. The source code of the classes OddThread and the timeline diagram of a monitored program run are shown in Fig. 3. The program ends

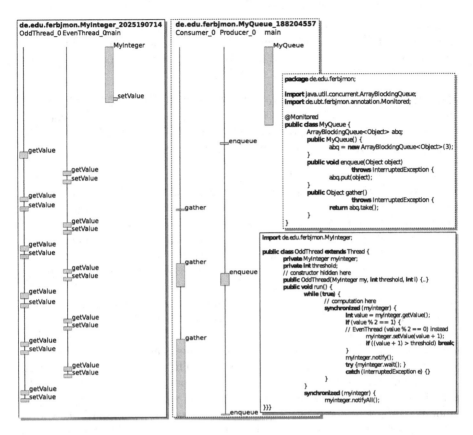

Fig. 3. Timeline diagrams for the monitored Java classes `MyInteger` (Cooperative Task Execution) and `MyQueue` (Producer and Consumer). The Java codes of the classes `MyQueue` and `OddThread` are also given.

after 10 increments. The timeline shows the proper handover between the two threads. By chance, the `OddThread` starts execution first, but it only determines the value and hands over control to the `EvenThread`, which is allowed to increment the value "0". This scenario of cooperative task execution can naively also be solved without an explicit handover between the threads. But using only a `synchronized` access to the object can lead to many unsuccessful incrementation attempts by both threads, which increases the execution time significantly.

5   Performance of FERBJMON Runtime Monitoring

As FERBJMON tools aim at lightweight runtime monitoring, this section presents benchmarks to better understand the capabilities of FERBJMON tools. The runtime monitoring for the construction of the call graph has no influence on the timely relevant behavior of the program, because only dependencies are visualized. Also, the post-processing step of creating the timeline diagram is not relevant for the monitoring. Thus, the runtime monitoring using java_threadorder is benchmarked only. For testing, two different machines are used.

- **DELL 6530 Laptop** Intel Core i7-3720QM (2.60 GHz), 8 GB RAM, SSHD Seagate ST500LX003 (500 GB), Windows 7 and Linux Mint 13 (Kernel 3.2).
- **Megware Workstation** Intel Xeon E5-1680v3 (3.20 GHz), 64 GB RAM, SSD Sandisk SD6SB1M2 (256 GB), Linux Mint 17 (Kernel 3.13).

For all tests, the Oracle Java JDK Version 7 was used. The experiments were conducted using the example program of cooperative task execution, which was presented in Sect. 4.2. Durations of program executions that are presented in the following reflect the average value of 30 test runs with the same configuration. FERBJMON tools provide different logging mechanisms which are benchmarked in this section. Because the tests were performed on Windows and Linux, time measurement was integrated into the example program itself to obtain comparable results. Therefore, a timestamp at the beginning and at the end of the main() function were obtained using the Java method System.currentTimeMillis().

In a first test, the example program for cooperative task execution was executed using a threshold of 10 ($t = 10$) for the incrementation. The execution time measured without monitoring was below 1 ms in most cases. Including the monitoring, the execution times were still below 3 ms. The overall program execution time including Bytecode instrumentation and output creation was measured to approximately 150 ms using the command line tool time in Linux (50 ms for the unmodified program). Such low values can hardly be used for comparison. Therefore, the threshold for cooperative task execution was increased to 100000, which resulted in more meaningful time measurements of approximately 1 s. Although it may not be meaningful to monitor this modified program in real life, it was used to generate comparable results for benchmarking.

The different logging mechanisms were investigated in a second experiment. The results are summarized in Table 1. It can be recognized that the results for Linux and Windows differ significantly especially if the CPU frequency scaling is enabled (SpeedStep, Turbo, and extended C-States enabled). To better understand this effect and to get comparable results, all experiments have also been conducted with CPU frequency scaling disabled (SpeedStep, Turbo, and extended C-States disabled). In this test, 800022 log entries have been captured (about 76 MB log file). The experiment only covers benchmarks of the monitoring and logging. Creating a visualization from this amount of data may take a long time. However, a visualization of the example shown in Fig. 3 ($t = 10$) was created in approximately 500 ms.

The benchmarks revealed that the execution times under monitoring are approximately 3 times higher than in an unmonitored program run. The MemArray Logger showed the best logging performance in 5 of 6 cases. In the experiment using Linux and a fixed CPU frequency on the Dell 6530 the File Logger showed a slightly better performance. In all other tests the File Logger showed the worst performance. This observation may be caused by a side effect

Table 1. Benchmarks of logging implementations and logging overhead (in ms)

	Dell 6530 Laptop				Megware Workst.	
	CPU Freq. variable		CPU Freq. fixed		CPU Freq. variable	CPU Freq. fixed
	Windows	Linux	Windows	Linux	Linux	Linux
Benchmarks of different logging implementations						
No Monitor.	349	997	462	509	706	460
File Logger	1578	3089	1792	1551	1769	1252
StringBuilder	1246	2884	1601	1711	1548	1202
MemArray	1204	2767	1527	1640	1339	1162
Benchmarks of different ratios between synchronization and computation						
No Monitor.[1]	1070	1129	1048	1059	1091	1076
MemArray[1]	1264 18,1%	1491 32,1%	1220 16,4%	1240 17,1%	1273 16,7%	1189 10,5%
No Monitor.[2]	1038	1070	1008	1016	1048	1033
MemArray[2]	1084 4,43%	1218 13,8%	1070 6,15%	1087 6,99%	1130 7,82%	1076 4,16%

1: t=10000 d=0.1 ms   *2*: t=1000 d=1 ms (*t* and *d* are explained in Section 5)

due to the Linux file system cache. However, such effects can thwart reproducibility and stability of the observation and can lead to a distorted monitoring result. The `MemArray Logger` should be preferred, because it provides a good performance and steady behavior. It has also been investigated that the largely extended threshold log files may fit into main memory of current computers easily. The `StringBuilder Logger` is slightly slower than the `MemArray Logger`. If the program behavior is completely unknown the `File Logger` may be used as first try.

In the test program used (t = 100000) most of the code is involved in synchronization. To better investigate the real performance of FERBJMON tools the ratio between computation and synchronization was increased using synthetic computations in each incrementation step, see comment in `OddThread` in Fig. 3. Also, the threshold was reduced. Table 1 shows the execution times using this adapted program for cooperative task execution. The delay *d* that is introduced by the computation in each iteration is limited to 0.1 ms and 1 ms using a time measurement. Only the `MemArray Logger` was used. Table 1 also includes the relative overhead of the execution time compared to the unmonitored program run. The overhead decreases significantly when the computation time per iteration increases. Using 1 ms of computation in each iteration the overhead is only 4–14 % in this experiment. In this test, the overall execution times were less influenced by the operating system and CPU frequency scaling behavior chosen. This can be caused by the increased amount of computations, which may cause all operating system to adjust the CPU frequency to the maximum value.

6 Conclusion

FERBJMON tools can generate call graphs and timeline diagrams of thread accesses on Java objects from runtime traces. The runtime traces are captured using a lightweight monitoring based on Java Bytecode instrumentation. FERB-JMON tools are helpful to understand the chronological order of synchronizations between threads. Examples of a producer/consumer and a cooperative task execution were presented. Benchmarks of the logging mechanisms revealed that the execution time is not increased too much in the examples.

FERBJMON tools have already been used successfully in a course on parallel programming for undergraduate students at the University of Bayreuth, Germany. Students tasks were the detection of race conditions in a multi-threaded program for scalar product computation and the analysis of the lock order on different implementations of read/write locks. Students found it much easier to generate visualizations from their implementations than using *print* statements within the code. Thanks go to Prof. Thomas Rauber for making this possible.

Acknowledgments. The development of FERBJMON tools was improved by many contributors, in particular Sascha Hunold, Thomas Reichel, Björn Krellner, Matthias Korch, and Thomas Rauber are named. Thanks for the discussions and notes.

References

1. Javashot Java Dynamic Call Graph. https://code.google.com/p/javashot/. Accessed 31 May 2015
2. Javassist Java Bytecode Engineering Toolkit. http://jboss-javassist.github.io/javassist/. Accessed 31 May 2015
3. VisualVM. https://visualvm.java.net/. Accessed 31 May 2015
4. Brown, R., Shoop, E., Adams, J., Clifton, C., Gardner, M., Haupt, M., Hinsbeeck, P.: Strategies for preparing computer science students for the multicore world. In: Proceedings of the 2010 ITiCSE Working Group Reports, pp. 97–115. ACM (2010)
5. Ellson, J., Gansner, E.R., Koutsofios, L., North, S.C., Woodhull, G.: Graphviz - open source graph drawing tools. In: Mutzel, P., Jünger, M., Leipert, S. (eds.) GD 2001. LNCS, vol. 2265, p. 483. Springer, Heidelberg (2002)
6. Goetz, B., Peierls, T., Bloch, J., Bowbeer, J., Holmes, D., Lea, D.: Java Concurrency in Practice. Addison-Wesley Professional, Reading (2006)
7. Grossman, D., Anderson, R.E.: introducing parallelism and concurrency in the data structures course. In: Proceedings of the Technical Symposium on Computer Science Education, pp. 505–510. ACM (2012)
8. Leroux, H., Réquilé-Romanczuk, A., Mingins, C.: JACOT: A Tool to dynamically visualise the execution of concurrent Java programs. In: Proceedings of the International Conference on Principles and Practice of Programming in Java, pp. 201–206. Computer Science Press, Inc. (2003)
9. Malnati, G., Cuva, C.M., Barberis, C.: JThreadSpy: teaching multithreading programming by analyzing execution traces. In: Proceedings of the Workshop on Parallel and Distributed Systems: Testing and Debugging, pp. 3–13. ACM (2007)

10. Mattson, T.G., Sanders, B.A., Massingill, B.L.: Patterns for Parallel Programming. Addison Wesley, Reading (2004)
11. Torbert, S., Vishkin, U., Tzur, R., Ellison, D.J.: Is Teaching parallel algorithmic thinking to high school students possible?: one teacher's experience. In: Proceedings of the Technical Symposium on Computer Science Education, pp. 290–294. ACM (2010)
12. Williams, A., Thies, W., Awasthi, P.: Static deadlock detection for Java libraries. In: Gao, X.-X. (ed.) ECOOP 2005. LNCS, vol. 3586, pp. 602–629. Springer, Heidelberg (2005)

Interdisciplinary Practical Course on Parallel Finite Element Method Using HiFlow³

Markus Hoffmann[1][(✉)], Simon Gawlok[2], Eva Treiber[2], Wolfgang Karl[1], and Vincent Heuveline[2]

[1] Institute of Computer Science & Engineering (ITEC),
Chair for Computer Architecture and Parallel Processing (CAPP),
Karlsruhe Institute of Technology (KIT), Kaiserstrasse 12, 76131 Karlsruhe, Germany
markus.hoffmann@kit.edu
[2] Interdisciplinary Center for Scientific Computing (IWR),
Engineering Mathematics and Computing Lab (EMCL), Heidelberg University,
Speyerer Strasse 6, 69115 Heidelberg, Germany

Abstract. In many scientific fields one faces partial differential equations that have to be solved numerically. Applying the widely-used finite element method (FEM) leads to huge systems of equations whose solutions often require parallel computing. The practical course presented in this paper aims at introducing the FEM as well as the concept of parallel computing to students with the help of a FEM library, in this case HiFlow³. To achieve this goal, the students work in interdisciplinary groups on explicit problems originating from different scientific fields. In that way they expand and deepen both their theoretical knowledge concerning numerical mathematics and their practical skills in programming and using HiFlow³.

1 Introduction

In many fields of science as well as in industrial research and development solving problems both fast and accurately is often a tough challenge. While on one hand there is a complex theoretical approach to solve a problem, there are, on the other hand, scientists and engineers who want to tackle their specific problems with the considered methodology. They are often experts in their specific areas of knowledge which differ from the skills needed to approach the problem at hand. Additionally, applying a theory or solution method to a problem does not mean that the resulting software application is in any way automatically optimal with respect to the utilized hardware and therefore also with respect to the appropriate programming paradigms, scalability requirements or models of parallelization.

These three challenges,

- facing the theory,
- applying it to a specific problem and
- developing a parallel application based on the features of the available hardware,

S. Hunold et al. (Eds.): Euro-Par 2015 Workshops, LNCS 9523, pp. 160–171, 2015.
DOI: 10.1007/978-3-319-27308-2_14

are forming the grander challenge of parallel scientific computing as shown in Fig. 1:

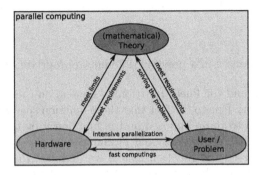

Fig. 1. Challenges of parallel computing

While the compliance with the theoretical requirements of a solution method must be assured throughout the whole process of its application to the specific problem by the user, the choice of a methodology may be limited by the hardware and his' or her's knowledge of programming the hardware platform at hand. Additionally, he or she expects fast results on modern hardware which leads to the need of intense – maybe even hybrid – parallelization which in turn restricts the choice of usable algorithms or even compels a redesign of established solution methods.

This interaction between the given problem, applicable theoretical solution approach, and available hardware, as shown in Fig. 2, challenges the user immensely. Therefore, it is necessary to educate the today's students as early and as extensively as possible to provide them with the knowledge and abilities to face the challenge of parallel computing.

Obviously, it is impossible to teach a single user all the required knowledge about mathematical theory, its application to problems in all fields of science, and all the models, paradigms and requirements of parallel computing on any imaginable combination of hardware. Therefore, an expansion of the challenge of parallel computing to the challenge of parallel computing *within an interdisciplinary team of specialists* is unavoidable. This change in philosophy is particularly demanding for the teaching staff, because, beside the huge amount of knowledge they are required to have in order to teach, they need to find a common base on which a profound education can start.

Fortunately, this common base can be found for many fields of natural sciences in terms of partial differential equations. Partial differential equations (PDE) arise in many fields such as meteorology, biology, or energy research. A well-known and widely used method to numerically solve these equations is the so called finite element method (FEM).

FEM is based on a weak formulation of the PDE: By multiplying the partial differential equation with an arbitrary test-function, integrating the resulting equation by parts, and considering the boundary conditions, one achieves in the case of a linear PDE a variational formulation of the problem with the form:

Find a function u in an appropriate function space such that

$$a(u, v) = l(v) \tag{1}$$

for all test-functions v in a possibly different appropriate function space.

The bilinear form a and the linear functional l depend on the exact problem, as do the function spaces. Due to the fact that these function spaces ease the restrictions on u compared to those imposed on the function u by the original, strong formulation of the PDE, the variational formulation is also called weak formulation. In the next step the function spaces are reduced to finite-dimensional ones to be able to explicitly state a complete basis of the spaces and express u and v as a linear combination of the basis functions. As a result, the above variational formulation yields a finite system of equations that only contains the unknown coefficients of the representation of u. By geometrically dividing the domain of the PDE into small elements and choosing piecewise polynomial functions and basis functions that vanish on almost every element of the mesh, most of the entries of the resulting matrix are zero. This way the task to solve a partial differential equation is converted to the task of solving a linear system of equations with a sparse matrix. Generally, the computation of this matrix is done by calculating the contribution of one element after another and summing them up.

Obviously, the above described construction allows problems with arbitrary many degrees of freedom. Indeed, this is not only a theoretical possibility, but many applications require very fine grids to achieve reasonable results. To solve the huge resulting discrete problems in an acceptable amount of time, parallel computing is unavoidable.

For that reason, students should become familiar with the concepts and methods of parallel computing as early as possible. Furthermore, practical exercises and courses offer a great opportunity to the students to apply their theoretical knowledge in practice, so they can reinforce what they learned in lectures and get deeper insights into the various aspects of being active in the field of numerical mathematics in general, and parallel computing in particular.

A smart introduction into this topic and its handling is offered by different libraries, such as HiFlow[3], for which in particular only a relatively short familiarization period is required. As, additionally, the underlying mathematics can still be seen clearly in the problem-specific part of the code, HiFlow[3] was selected for practical exercises and courses that shall be presented in this paper. Therefore, the next Section aims at introducing HiFlow[3] with its modular approach and provided tools, whereas the ideas and settings of the practical course are centred in Sect. 3. Finally, Sect. 4 offers future prospects regarding this software practical.

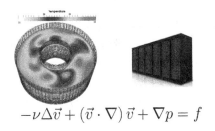

$$-\nu\Delta\vec{v} + (\vec{v}\cdot\nabla)\,\vec{v} + \nabla p = f$$

Fig. 2. Connection of user's perspective, theory and target hardware [6]

2   HiFlow^3

HiFlow^3 [4] is a multi-purpose finite element software developed at EMCL providing powerful tools for the efficient and accurate solution of a wide range of problems modelled by partial differential equations (PDEs). Based on object-oriented concepts and the full capabilities of C++, the HiFlow^3 project follows a modular and generic approach for building efficient parallel numerical solvers. It provides highly capable modules dealing with the mesh setup, finite element spaces, degrees of freedom, linear algebra routines, numerical solvers, and output data for visualization, See Fig. 3. Parallelism — as the basis for high performance simulations on modern computing systems — is introduced on two levels: coarse-grained parallelism by means of distributed grids and distributed data structures, and fine-grained parallelism by means of platform-optimized linear algebra back-ends. The required communication within the distributed grids and distributed data structures is implemented with the aid of the Message-Passing Interface (MPI) standard [10]. Furthermore, the capabilities of different modules can be improved by compiling HiFlow^3 with support for certain third-party libraries, e.g., METIS [8] or Intel Math Kernel Library (MKL) Fig. 2.

The mesh module provides functionality that is needed for dealing with unstructured computational grids in finite element simulations. A mesh may consist of lines, triangles, quads, tetrahedrons, and hexahedrons. Independently, how the initial mesh has been obtained, it can be further refined through different refining strategies to increase the grid's resolution. If the mesh has been constructed or read in sequentially by a single process, the mesh can be partitioned and distributed for coarse-grained distributed memory parallelization. To reduce communication costs during the following computations in the simulation process, a layer of ghost cells is attached to each process' local mesh by a provided helper function Fig. 3.

The finite element method (FEM) and degree of freedom (DoF) modules supply the user with functionalities to construct a finite dimensional function space based on Lagrange finite elements. The user can specify the kind of finite element method, i.e., h or hp version, that is desired for the simulation as well as the degrees of the trial functions of the finite element basis for different solution components, e.g., velocity components and pressure in a computational fluid dynamics (CFD) computation. In the case of hp FEM, the degrees can be

Fig. 3. HiFlow³: Mesh handling, FEM, linear algebra & solvers and applications [6]

specified cell-wise. Furthermore, Gaussian quadrature rules of different orders are provided for all supported element geometries and the user can choose the desired order of accuracy for the assembly process.

HiFlow³ offers assembly strategies for matrices and vectors where the integrals may be defined on elements as well as the boundary of the computational domain. This process can be conducted fully in parallel on the distributed memory parallelization level due to the distributed grids and distributed matrix and vector structures, respectively.

The linear algebra module consists of different implementations of matrices and vectors on a both global, distributed-memory level, and local, per-process level. On the global level, HiFlow³ provides a standard implementation, which takes care of the required communication as well as the correct handling and management of the local matrices and vectors in each process. A wrapper to the PETSc library [1–3] is currently under development. On the local level, HiFlow³ establishes a class hierarchy where different computing devices and implementations on these devices can be configured by the user by simply changing the configuration parameters for the local linear algebra directly in the application code or even in an XML configuration file. This design allows fine-grained parallelism on a shared-memory, i.e., intra-process level. Currently, classical Central Processing Units (CPU) and Graphics Processing Units (GPU) are supported as computing devices. For GPUs, implementations facilitating NVidia CUDA [14] and OpenCL [17] are available. On the CPU side, the following implementations and libraries are supported: a naive, i.e., sequential, and an OpenMP parallelized implementation, as well as wrappers to the BLAS [12], CLAPACK [13] and Intel MKL libraries. Furthermore, the local matrices support a variety of matrix formats, e.g., dense and compressed row (CSR) format. It is important to note that not all matrix formats are available with all implementations.

To solve the arising linear equation systems efficiently, HiFlow³ provides solver classes for the following iterative Krylov subspace methods [15]: conjugate gradient (CG), stabilized bi-conjugate gradient (BiCGSTAB), and (flexible) generalized minimal residual ((F)GMRES). All these solvers are implemented for the use with and without preconditioning techniques, and all solvers are parallelized by means of the parallelized linear algebra, i.e., in the implementation of the solvers no further parallelization needs to be employed. Preconditioning in HiFlow^3 is done block-wise, i.e., the preconditioner only acts locally on the degrees of freedom which are owned by the respective process. This way no communication is done during the preconditioning step. A disadvantage of this methodology is the lacking parallel scalability for very large numbers of parallel processes. Among the local preconditioners are, e.g., Jacobi, Gauß-Seidel, Approximate Inverse, and Incomplete LU (ILU) factorization methods. The capabilities of the linear solver module are extended by wrappers to the MUMPS [11] and ILU++ [9] libraries, respectively.

If the underlying PDE is nonlinear, HiFlow^3 provides an implementation of Newton's method for the solution of the resulting discrete system of equations. Due to the object-oriented approach, any of the above mentioned linear solvers can be used to solve the arising linearized system.

To visualize and rate the results, HiFlow^3 comes with support for visualization output in the (P)VTK [16,18] and XDMF [19] file formats.

Besides these core functionalities for the conduction of finite element simulations, the software package HiFlow^3 offers relevant advantages to the numerical simulation of phenomena occuring in a wide range of research topics, e.g. uncertainty quantification (UQ), computational fluid dynamics (CFD) & meteorology, and elasticity simulations.

The capabilities of HiFlow^3 with respect to performance and scalability on HPC systems have been demonstrated by considering a CFD benchmark problem [5].

The functionalities of HiFlow^3 are documented and demonstrated in several tutorials that are available on the HiFlow^3 homepage [6]. The complexity in terms of mathematics and implementational effort by the user of the tutorials ranges from relatively simple problems like Poisson's equation, which is a prototype of an elliptic linear PDE, to complex problems like solving the incompressible Navier-Stokes equations of fluid motion, or the equations of linear elasticity for soft tissue simulation, for example. All together, there are eleven tutorials available at the moment. Furthermore, HiFlow^3 comes with additional examples of applications which are not documented by a tutorial.

3   Practical Course on Parallel Numerics

Based on HiFlow^3, the Karlsruhe Institute of Technology started a practical course on parallel numerics that aims both at the interdisciplinary cooperation of the students and at teaching methods of parallel computing. At Heidelberg University, this course is embedded in the exercise classes of the lecture "Numerical Methods of Continuum Mechanics" given by the Engineering Mathematics and Computing Lab (EMCL). The course is subdivided into separate projects which are designed to be worked on by small groups of students.

To promote the desired interdisciplinary cooperation, the course is open to students of various departments like mathematics, computer science, physics and many kinds of engineering, which leads to a highly heterogeneous mixture of participants. The schedule itself supports the formation of heterogeneous groups due to the fact that specialized knowledge is required to solve every task of each project suitably. As mentioned in the introduction, this composition of heterogeneous teams is important due to the fact that the amount of needed knowledge is too large to be known by students out of the same field of study. Therefore, each group member has to take on a different role:

– The mathematicians have to face the mathematical theory of the PDE as well as the chosen solution methods in detail and have to make sure that all assumptions are met.
– The computer scientists have to deal with the challenge of parallelization based on both the available hardware and their knowledge about programming paradigms and methods of parallelization.
– The natural scientists have to check the validity of both the used models and the results. Furthermore, they have to instruct the others about the details of the particular problem.

Additionally, all the group members together have to face the tasks, that are beyond their fields of study at large.

Due to the different research interests, skills, and objectives of the individual participants of the course, it is tough to find a basic problem all students can work on with equal effort. The basic problem of choice has to provide a strong focus on practical use and applications for as many kinds of engineering as possible as well as a complex background in theory to challenge the mathematicians. Moreover, the theory has to lead to computationally intensive algorithms, to guide the computer scientists into the field of soft- and hardware-architectures, especially with the focus on parallel computing.

As shown in Sect. 1, the finite element method meets these conditions in an almost optimal way. As a standard approach for solving partial differential equations it is highly relevant for the practical use in most engineering fields. The theoretical background is challenging, particularly in the construction of appropriate solution spaces and integration of boundary conditions, the iterative solvers for the systems of equations and dealing with stability problems, just to name a few examples. Furthermore, solving the huge systems of equations does not only need experts in numerical analysis but also specialists in parallelization techniques like domain decomposition and task scheduling as well as skills in programming with these different parallelization paradigms, e.g., with the Message Passing Interface (MPI) and OpenMP standards. Finally, the FEM is addressing a wide range of problems. Therefore, simple problems that help the students to understand the basic theories can be found as well as very complex problems that challenge the students and to show them the limits in every aspect. For these reasons, the FEM is the basic syllabus in this practical course.

Furthermore, the usage of HiFlow[3] offers an efficient and fast access to the practical use of the FEM. Through the execution of given tasks, students are given the opportunity to see various theoretical results, for instance the different convergence behaviours of h- and hp-method, within practical results achieved by self-performed experiments. With the help of this library it is even easier to access complex problems. The incompressible Navier-Stokes equations for example, which need Taylor-Hood finite elements to be solved certainly, can be equipped with these elements through simple changes to an XML configuration file. Therefore, with the help of Hiflow³, the focus of the curriculum is on discovering the parallel computing and not on the depth of mathematical theory. To be more specific: The students are taught the basics of FEM, i.e., required definitions and basic theorems, such as Lax-Milgram for example. They are also taught parallelization in theory, data reordering strategies or simple domain decomposition methods for example, but because HiFlow³ is hiding a lot of its parallelism, the practical work on parallelization is limited to some simple exercises in the context of OpenMP. Therefore, the focus is on modeling and theoretical debates on parallelism as well as using the provided library and understanding its limitations when it comes to massively parallel computing.

Based on the usage of the FEM and HiFlow³, one can define the learning objectives of this practical course. These objectives can vary for each student due to the interdisciplinarity. Ignoring this specialization-based weighting, the learning objectives can be defined as follows:

- *Working in interdisciplinary teams* as described in this section to get an impression of the advantages and disadvantages of this conception.
- *Understanding the basics of PDEs and the FEM* to avoid mistakes based on the lack of a theoretical background and the limits of the used method.
- *Understanding the needs of parallel computing* such as handling data dependencies or understanding the challenge of scalability.
- *Learning the usage of an example finite element method library*, which is Hiflow³ in our case. Furthermore, it is important to know the advantages and the limits of the library.
- *Application of the FEM to an explicit problem* to learn the usage of the theory on a real problem and to increase the understanding of the method's properties.
- *Application of basic methods of parallel computing* with the focus on rearrangement of the data and simple domain decomposition methods.
- *Evaluation of results* with the help of suitable visualizations.

These objectives in total are giving an overall view of the theory and the challenges of parallel computing as well as working in an interdisciplinary team.

Teaching the students these learning objectives is a challenge we are facing with a strategy of different teaching methods. These methods are chosen in the context of the different backgrounds of the students as well as the fact, that – except for of basic programming skills – no special prerequisites are necessary to visit this practical course, which is a concession to the interdisciplinarity.

First of all, a specific number of classes are marked as theory lectures to provide the opportunity to teach the students the required knowledge within a short time. These lectures are given by way of a presentation with the option to ask questions. Naturally, a compulsory attendance for the students has to be set.

Beside these theory lectures and some other exceptions, all the sessions of this period are practical classes, in which the different groups of students are working on projects independently. During these practical classes they are guided by exercise sheets with tasks leading through the whole project and helping to place the focus on the important items. To teach the students self-studying, some given tasks are including questions, that need very specialized knowledge to be answered. This leads to a mixture of theoretical analysis and practical work within the exercise sheets. This mixture again leads to a smooth transition from learning the theoretical background to applying the theory to a specific problem, all of which helps the students to find their way from theory to practical work.

To describe the single exercise sheets in more detail: A first project can be Poisson's equation on the unit square with Dirichlet boundary conditions. Some tasks on the related exercise sheet can, for example, focus on the derivation of the weak formulation, conditions on the solution u, error computations and different boundary conditions to challenge the mathematicians. One can add tasks like explaining the difference of concepts of MPI and OpenMP, having a look at Amdahl's law, defining terms like speedup and efficiency, starting to work with the library by adding the weak formulation and boundary conditions to an existing code or implement a grid refinement for p-FEM, and explaining why a super-linear speedup can be observed in some cases to involve the computer scientists. Engineers can be included by asking questions with practical relevance like the background of Poisson's equation in physics or the interpretation of the boundary conditions. To bring them all together, one can ask for measurements and result presentation, as well as some literature research, for example.

To give the students the possibility of an open time management, the compulsory attendance is cancelled for the related practical sessions. This supports the interdisciplinary teamwork and it leads to the desired effect, that the students teach each other their specialized knowledge. This method of open time management also gives the students the possibility to determine in which way or speed they learn best.

To support the students during these practical lessons, external access to the needed hard- and software resources is provided. Furthermore, the appointed time of the course can be used by students to ask questions.

Because of the missing compulsory attendance the progress of each group in the context of the learning objectives cannot be checked by observing the groups and their work. For this reason, there is a need for a special lecture with compulsory attendance at the end of each project, in which the students have to present their results and talk about their work. This also includes a short question and answer session, in which the students can be asked questions about their work and results.

The last project in the lecture period is complemented with a special task to give the possibility of an objective grading. The students have to write a report about the theory, their practical work, and the results obtained in their last project. Together with the presentations held at the end of each project, this report is the basis to check in which way the learning objectives are achieved and therefore how to grade the students. Additionally, important skills like proper presentation of scientific results as well as speaking and writing skills are automatically practised in this way.

The time management for the practical course is done by subdividing the lecture period into several sections. The first section is a theory part, in which a general overview of the basics of the FEM is given. This overview includes fundamental knowledge about partial differential equations, the Galerkin Method with focus on variational formulations and weak solutions, discretization based on finite dimensional subspaces, definition of finite elements, grid structures and grid construction, shape functions and degrees of freedom, iterative solvers like CG-method, error estimation, and basics of parallel implementation.

After building interdisciplinary and therefore heterogeneous teams, the second section begins with practical work on a simple problem, the Poisson's equation with different boundary conditions as described for example, guided by exercise sheets. The section ends with the aforementioned presentations of the groups about their work including question and answer sessions.

Because the next practical section requires some more theoretical knowledge, the third section is again a theory part. Here, an overview of some advanced finite element methods is given, including method of lines and Rothe's method for transient problems, solving stability problems, preconditioning methods and basic benchmarks. There is also a focus on parallelism, especially for the preconditioning methods.

The fourth section is filled with a second project which is also guided by exercise sheets. The specific task formulation for this practical section differs for each group depending on their special interests, group composition, or fields of study. The thematic framework includes problems like Convection-Diffusion equations or incompressible Navier-Stokes equations. As in the first project, the students have to face the mathematical theory, investigate stability problems for instance, some practical work like implementing fractional step time-stepping methods, and the challenge of parallelization in terms of load balancing for example. Of course, some of the in project one newly acquired knowledge is also relevant for the second project, such as the usage of the library, or the application of the mathematical theory.

As mentioned before, the course ends with student presentations reviewing the theory and their own work as well as results within their specific problem. Especially for the second project, the students have to write a report to give account of their work and results.

Table 1 shows an exemplary time schedule for the outlined sections of the course based on 14 weeks per lecture period and two 90-minute-classes per week. Based on this schedule and the chosen projects, each student gains 4 ECTS for the practical course on parallel numerics, which means that each student has to achieve about 120 working hours over the lecture period.

The needed human resources are depending on the number of participants of the course. With about 20 participants per semester in our case up to two teaching assistants are needed.

Table 1. Time schedule of the practical course

Number of lecture	Content
01 – 03	Part 1: *parallelization and FEM basics, short introduction to Hiflow[3], team building*
04 – 11	Part 2: *practical work on project 1*
12 – 13	Part 3: *advanced methods*
14 – 23	Part 4: *practical work on project 2*
24 – 28	Part 5: *report writing*

4   Summary and Future Work

The practical course introduced here provides an introduction into the important field of parallel computing. Based on HiFlow[3], a library for solving PDEs with FEM, which incorporates a high level of parallelism, the students gain an impression of techniques and tools of parallel computing while working on projects within an interdisciplinary team.

The teaching contents and the syllabus of this practical course offer a wide spectrum of development. In this paper, we will give an idea of two possible improvements, that are planned for the near future.

First of all, the focus on methods of parallel computing can be intensified by teaching a selection of programming models like MPI, OpenMP, NVidia CUDA, OpenCL, and more. Since we are actually only teaching the theory of some of these paradigms in most cases, this has to be done along with a lot of practical work. Although these extensions on the syllabus can be easily combined with the FEM and HiFlow[3] in terms of additional projects, it is far too much to teach it additionally to the current curriculum within a single semester. Therefore, these improvements will inevitably lead to a syllabus for a two-semester course.

Because most of the lectures don't need a compulsory attendance and most of the work is done outside the lectures, a development towards e-learning methods or blended learning methods, is considered as the second improvement. This includes the installation of simple communication platforms, a forum for example, for questions and answers, and the use of virtual desks such as the ILIAS-platform [7]. It is also conceivable to create small private online courses for special topics, introduction to programming models or background knowledge for the current project for example, or to develop online applications to simplify the access to the content, the PDEs for instance, and to visualize the results comprehensively.

These two approaches for developing the curriculum and the teaching methods will help to move the challenges, techniques and tools of parallel computing into focus more clearly and will support the communication within a single team and across multiple teams to intensify the interdisciplinary cooperation.

References

1. Balay, S., Abhyankar, S., Adams, M.F., Brown, J., Brune, P., Buschelman, K., Eijkhout, V., Gropp, W.D., Kaushik, D., Knepley, M.G., McInnes, L.C., Rupp, K., Smith, B.F., Zhang, H.: PETSc Web page (2014). http://www.mcs.anl.gov/petsc

2. Balay, S., Abhyankars, S., Adams, M.F., Brown, J., Brune, P., Buschelman, K., Eijkhout, V., Gropp, W.D., Kaushik, D., Knepley, M.G., McInnes, L.C., Rupp, K., Smith, B.F., Zhang, H.: PETSc Users Manual. Argonne National Laboratory, ANL-95/11 - Revision 3.5 (2014). http://www.mcs.anl.gov/petsc

3. Balay, S., Gropp, W.D., McInnes, L.C., Smith, B.F.: Efficient management of parallelism in object oriented numerical software libraries. In: Arge, E., Bruaset, A.M., Langtangen, H.P. (eds.) Modern Software Tools in Scientific Computing, pp. 163–202. Birkhäuser Press, Boston (1997)

4. Heuveline, V., et. al.: HiFlow^3: A hardware-aware parallel finite element package. In: Brunst, H., Muller, M.S., Nagel, W.E., Resch, M.M., (eds.) Tools for High Performance Computing 2011, pp. 139–151. Springer, Heidelberg (2012)

5. Heuveline, V., Ketelaer, E., Ronnas, S., Schmidtobreick, M., Wlotzka, M.: Scalability Study of HiFlow^3 based on a Fluid Flow Channel Benchmark. Preprint Series of the Engineering Mathematics and Computing Lab (EMCL) (2012)

6. http://www.hiflow3.org/

7. http://www.ilias.de/

8. Karypis, G., Kumar, V.: A fast and highly quality multilevel scheme for partitioning irregular graphs. SIAM J. Sci. Comput. **20**(1), 359–392 (1999)

9. Mayer, J.: ILU++: A new software package for solving sparse linear systems with iterative methods. PAMM Proc. Appl. Math. Mech. **7**, 2020123–2020124 (2007)

10. http://www.mpi-forum.org/

11. http://mumps-solver.org/

12. http://www.netlib.org/blas/

13. http://www.netlib.org/clapack/

14. Nickolls, J., Buck, I., Garland, M., Skadron, K.: Scalable parallel programming with CUDA. ACM Queue **6**(2), 40–53 (2008)

15. Saad, Y.: Iterative methods for sparse linear systems. 2nd edn. Society for Industrial and Applied Mathematics, Philadelphia (2003)

16. Schroeder, W., et al.: The Visualization Toolkit, 3rd edn. Kitware, Inc. (2003)

17. Stone, J.E., Gohara, D., Shi, G.: OpenCL: a parallel programming standard for heterogeneous computing systems. IEEE Des. Test **12**(3), 66–73 (2010)

18. http://www.vtk.org/

19. http://www.xdmf.org/

HeteroPar - Algorithms, Models, and Tools for Parallel Computing on Heterogeneous Platforms

A Randomized LU-based Solver Using GPU and Intel Xeon Phi Accelerators

Marc Baboulin, Amal Khabou$^{(\boxtimes)}$, and Adrien Rémy

Université Paris-Sud, Orsay, France
{baboulin,amal.khabou,aremy}@lri.fr

Abstract. We present a fast hybrid solver for dense linear systems based on LU factorization. To achieve good performance, we avoid pivoting by using random butterfly transformations for which we developed efficient implementations on heterogeneous architectures. We used both Graphics Processing Units and Intel Xeon Phi as accelerators. The performance results show that the pre-processing due to randomization is negligible and that the solver outperforms the corresponding routines based on partial pivoting.

Keywords: Random Butterfly Transformations (RBT) · LU factorization · Graphics Processing Units (GPU) · Intel Xeon Phi

1 Introduction

The LU factorization with partial pivoting is the most commonly used method to solve general dense linear systems. The pivoting step aims at improving the numerical stability of the method. Even though it does not require extra floating point operations, selecting the pivots involves $\mathcal{O}(n^2)$ comparisons. Moreover swapping the rows of the matrix involves extra data movements. These aspects can deteriorate the performance of the LU factorization due to the cache invalidations they induce.

As a motivation of this work, let us evaluate the overhead of the pivoting step of the LU factorization with partial pivoting using both GPU and Intel Xeon Phi accelerators. To use accelerators in dense linear algebra computations, we base our work on the MAGMA library [4,8,16], which provides LAPACK interface functions, using GPUs or Intel Xeon Phi. Figure 1a shows the results obtained running the corresponding MAGMA routine on an NVIDIA Tesla K20 GPU accelerator. We observe that pivoting takes more than 20% of the total computational time for matrices of size smaller than 10^4. However for larger matrices, the pivoting overhead is reduced and most of the computational time is spent performing the matrix-matrix products (DGEMM) on the GPU. Figure 1b displays the pivoting overhead using an Intel Xeon Phi 7120 coprocessor. Experiments have shown that the Intel Xeon Phi version of the factorization needs a greater amount of data than that of the GPU to be efficient. Indeed, for a matrix size of order 6000, the performance of the LU based solver is around 200 Gflop/s

© Springer International Publishing Switzerland 2015
S. Hunold et al. (Eds.): Euro-Par 2015 Workshops, LNCS 9523, pp. 175–184, 2015.
DOI: 10.1007/978-3-319-27308-2_15

on the Xeon Phi whereas it is around 500 Gflop/s on the GPU. Increasing the size of the problem, the performance of both versions tends towards 800 Gflop/s (for double precision). We note that for small matrices, the pivoting overhead on Xeon Phi is proportionally smaller than on GPU.

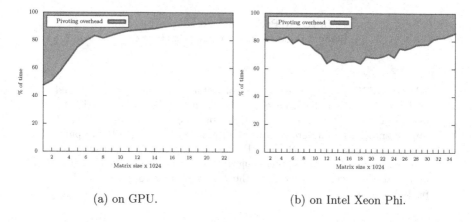

(a) on GPU.   (b) on Intel Xeon Phi.

Fig. 1. Time breakdown for pivoting in the LU factorization.

The previous experiments show that pivoting is a bottleneck in terms of communication cost and parallelism for hybrid CPU/accelerator architectures. To reduce the communication cost of the classical pivoting strategies such as partial pivoting, some alternative pivoting techniques were proposed in the context of the communication-avoiding LU algorithms (CALU then CALU_PRRP) [6,12]. These techniques are based on tournament pivoting, which was shown to be as stable as partial pivoting in practice.

Another approach consists in avoiding pivoting, and therefore improving the performance of the factorization. This approach is based on the use of Random Butterfly Transformations (RBT). It was first described in [14,15], and recently revisited for general systems in [3] and for symmetric indefinite systems in [1,2]. The main difference of the RBT based methods with respect to the classical factorization methods consists in a randomization step, which recursively applies a sequence of butterfly matrices to the input matrix. The main advantage of randomizing is that it allows us to avoid the communication overhead due to pivoting. Tests performed on a collection of matrices [3] show that in practice two recursions are sufficient to obtain a satisfactory accuracy.

The RBT solvers are particularly suitable for accelerators. On one hand, avoiding pivoting on accelerators has an important impact on the performance. On the other hand, the structure of the butterfly matrices can be exploited to perform the randomization at a very low cost. In this work we present the implementation details of a randomized LU-based solver using GPU and Intel Xeon Phi accelerators and discuss its performance on both accelerators.

The remainder of this paper is organized as follows. Section 2 recalls the main principles of the RBT algorithm and how it can be used in a hybrid CPU/accelerator factorization. Sections 3 and 4 describe the implementation and performance of the RBT solver for GPU and Intel Xeon Phi, respectively. Section 5 has concluding remarks.

2   Hybrid RBT Solver

To solve a general linear system $Ax = b$ using a solver based on RBT, we perform the following steps:

- Compute $A_r = U^T A V$ with U, V *random* matrices (recursive butterfly matrices),
- Factorize A_r using Gausian Elimination with No Pivoting (GENP),
- Solve $A_r y = U^T b$, then $x = V y$.

We recall that an n-by-n butterfly matrix B has the following structure,

$$B = \frac{1}{\sqrt{2}} \begin{pmatrix} R & S \\ R & -S \end{pmatrix},$$

where R and S are two random non singular $n/2$-by-$n/2$ diagonal matrices. The matrix B can then be stored in an n elements vector. A recursive butterfly matrix of depth d is defined as

$$W^{<n,d>} = \begin{pmatrix} B_1^{<n/2^{d-1}>} & & 0 \\ & \ddots & \\ 0 & & B_{2^{d-1}}^{<n/2^{d-1}>} \end{pmatrix} \times \cdots \times \begin{pmatrix} B_1^{<n/2>} & 0 \\ 0 & B_2^{<n/2>} \end{pmatrix} \times B^{<n>},$$

$$\tag{1}$$

where all $B_i^{<n>}$ blocks are size n butterfly matrices. When n is not a multiple of 2^d, we "augment" the matrix A with additional 1's on the diagonal.

Note that the GENP algorithm can be unstable due to potentially large growth factor. This is why we systematically perform iterative refinement on the computed solution of the randomized system. In this work, we use two recursion levels for the randomization ($d = 2$). The randomization cost is $8n^2$ flops, due to the block diagonal structure of the butterfly matrices, as demonstrated in [3]. Then the RBT algorithm adapted for hybrid architectures (CPU with an accelerator) performs the following steps:

1. Random generation and packed storage of the butterflies U and V on the host (CPU), while sending A to the device (accelerator) memory (padding is added if the size of the matrix A is not a multiple of 4).
2. The packed U and V are sent from the host memory to the device memory.
3. The randomization of A is performed on the device. It is done in-place (no additional memory needed).

4. The randomized matrix is factorized with GENP: the panel is factored on the host and the update of the trailing submatrix on the device.
5. We compute $U^T b$, and then solve $A_r y = U^T b$ on the device.
6. If necessary, iterative refinement is performed for y, on the device.
7. We compute the solution of $x = V y$ on the device, and then send x to the host memory.

Let us now describe the randomization phase (step 3) using two n-by-n recursive butterfly matrices U and V of depth two. We consider that the input matrix A can be split into 4 blocks of same size, $A = \begin{pmatrix} A_{11} & A_{12} \\ A_{21} & A_{22} \end{pmatrix}$. We consider the matrices $U = U_2 \times U_1$ and $V = V_2 \times V_1$, where U_1, V_1 are two butterfly matrices, and U_2, V_2 are two matrices of the form $\begin{pmatrix} B_1 & 0 \\ 0 & B_2 \end{pmatrix}$. B_1 and B_2 are two $n/2$-by-$n/2$ butterfly matrices as illustrated in Eq. 1. We have $A_r = U^T A V = U_1^T \times U_2^T \times A \times V_2 \times V_1$. Thus we first apply U_2^T and V_2 to A. We note $A_r^1 = U_2^T \times A \times V_2$, the resulting matrix from the first recursion level. Then,

$$A_r^1 = \begin{pmatrix} B_1 & 0 \\ 0 & B_2 \end{pmatrix} \times \begin{pmatrix} A_{11} & A_{12} \\ A_{21} & A_{22} \end{pmatrix} \times \begin{pmatrix} B_1^T & 0 \\ 0 & B_2^T \end{pmatrix} = \begin{pmatrix} B_1 A_{11} B_1^T & B_1 A_{12} B_2^T \\ B_2 A_{21} B_1^T & B_2 A_{22} B_2^T \end{pmatrix}$$

This step consists of four independent products with depth-1 butterfly matrices of size $n/2$-by-$n/2$. We call the kernel used for each product of the form $U^T \times A \times V$ Elementary multiplication. We then compute A_r by applying U_1^T and V_1 to A_r^1. For that we use again the Elementary multiplication kernel. Implementation details of this kernel will be given in the next sections for both GPU and Intel Xeon Phi accelerator.

3   RBT for Graphics Processing Units

Here we present our randomized LU-based solver using GPU. In particular, we give implementation details of the randomization step, which are specific to the targeted accelerator. We note that our RBT solver exists for all precisions used in LAPACK (simple, double, simple complex and double complex) and is part of the MAGMA library since the 1.6.0 version[1].

3.1   Implementation

On hybrid CPU/GPU architectures, the RBT solver is performed as described in Sect. 2. Algorithm 1 describes the randomization steps performed on a given matrix A. It applies the depth-two RBT to the matrix A by processing first each $n/2$-by-$n/2$ quarter block of A (lines 5 . . . 8 in Algorithm 1), and then applying the level one recursion to the whole n-by-n matrix (line 10 in Algorithm 1) as described in Sect. 2. The application of the level two randomization consists in calling a specific GPU kernel, the Elementary Multiplication GPU, on each quarter of the matrix. This is due to the block diagonal structure of the butterfly matrix. Each call to Elementary Multiplication GPU kernel is performed using one GPU thread per element.

---
[1] http://icl.cs.utk.edu/magma/news/news.html?id=351.

Algorithm 1. Two-level randomization on GPU

Require: A a pointer to the matrix A on the GPU.
Require: U a pointer to the matrix U stored as a vector on the GPU.
Require: V a pointer to the matrix V stored as a vector on the GPU.
Require: n the size of the matrix A
Ensure: $A \leftarrow U^T A V$
 1: $block\_height \leftarrow 32$
 2: $block\_width \leftarrow 4$
 3: **Define** a grid of threads per block, size : $(block\_height, block\_width)$
 4: **Define** a grid of blocks, size : $(\frac{n}{4 \times block\_height}, \frac{n}{4 \times block\_width})$
    {Assuming n is divisible by $4 \times block\_height$ and $4 \times block\_width$}
    { All GPU kernels are called with the threads and grid dimensions defined before the call}
 5: **Call** : Elementary Multiplication GPU(A, &$U(n)$, &$V(n)$, $n/2$)
 6: **Call** : Elementary Multiplication GPU(&$A(0, n/2)$, &$U(n)$, &$V(n + n/2)$, $n/2$)
 7: **Call** : Elementary Multiplication GPU(&$A(n/2, 0)$, &$U(n + n/2)$, &$V(n)$, $n/2$)
 8: **Call** : Elementary Multiplication GPU(&$A(n/2, n/2)$, &$U(n + n/2)$, &$V(n + n/2)$, $n/2$)
 9: **Redefine** a grid of blocks, size : $(\frac{n}{2 \times block\_height}, \frac{n}{2 \times block\_width})$
    {Assuming n is divisible by $2 \times block\_height$ and $2 \times block\_width$}
10: **Call** : Elementary Multiplication GPU(A, U, V, n) {Applying level 1 recursion}

The Elementary Multiplication GPU kernel performs $A \leftarrow U^T A V$, where U and V are vectors of size n containing the entries of the depth-one random butterfly matrices. Algorithm 2 shows the implementation details of the Elementary Multiplication GPU kernel. We use shared memory arrays for each block of threads to store the elements of U and V relative to this block and thereby improve the efficiency of the access to these elements.

3.2 Performance Results

In this section, we present performance results of our randomized LU-based solver on GPU. The experiments were carried out on a system composed of a GPU, NVIDIA Kepler K20, with 2496 CUDA cores running at 706 MHz and 4800 MB of memory and a multicore host composed of two Intel Xeon X5680 processors, each with 6 physical cores running at 3.33 GHz, and a Level 3 memory cache of 12 MB. The CPU parts of our code are performed using the multithreaded Intel MKL library [9].

Figure 2a shows that the CUDA [13] implementation of our RBT solver (either with or without iterative refinement) outperforms the classical LU factorization with partial pivoting from MAGMA. For large enough matrices (from size 6000) the obtained performance is about $20 - 30\%$ faster than the solver based on Gaussian elimination with partial pivoting. In our experiments, when we enable iterative refinement, one iteration is generally enough to improve the computed solution giving an accuracy similar to the one obtained using LU factorization with partial pivoting. The iterative refinement is performed on the

---

Algorithm 2. GPU Kernel: Elementary Multiplication GPU(A, U, V, n)

1: **for each** thread block of size $bsize.x \times bsize.y$ of coordinates $b.x$ and $b.y$ **do**
2:   **for each** Thread of coordinates $t.x$ and $t.y$ in the block **do**
3:     $idx \leftarrow b.x \times bsize.x + t.x$
4:     $idy \leftarrow b.y \times bsize.y + t.y$
5:     **if** $idx < n/2$ **and** $idy < n/2$ **then**
6:       Declare 4 shared memory arrays : $U_1[bsize.x]$, $U_2[bsize.x]$, $V_1[bsize.y]$, $V_2[bsize.y]$
7:       $U_1(t.x) \leftarrow U(idx)$
8:       $U_2(t.x) \leftarrow U(idx + n/2)$
9:       $V_1(t.y) \leftarrow V(idy)$
10:      $V_2(t.y) \leftarrow V(idy + n/2)$
11:      **Synchronize** the threads in the block
12:      $a_{00} \leftarrow A(idx, idy)$
13:      $a_{01} \leftarrow A(idx, idy + n/2)$
14:      $a_{10} \leftarrow A(idx + n/2, idy)$
15:      $a_{11} \leftarrow A(idx + n/2, idy + n/2)$
16:      $b_1 \leftarrow a_{00} + a_{01}$
17:      $b_2 \leftarrow a_{10} + a_{11}$
18:      $b_3 \leftarrow a_{00} - a_{01}$
19:      $b_4 \leftarrow a_{10} - a_{11}$
20:      $A(idx, idy) \leftarrow U_1(t.x) \times V_1(t.y) \times (b_1 + b_2)$
21:      $A(idx, idy + n/2) \leftarrow U_1(t.x) \times V_2(t.y) \times (b_3 + b_4)$
22:      $A(idx + n/2, idy) \leftarrow U_2(t.x) \times V_1(t.y) \times (b_1 - b_2)$
23:      $A(idx + n/2, idy + n/2) \leftarrow U_2(t.x) \times V_2(t.y) \times (b_3 - b_4)$
24:    **end if**
25:   **end for**
26: **end for**

GPU and requires $\mathcal{O}(n^2)$ extra floating point operations, which is a low order term in our case and has no significant impact on the performance of our RBT solver.

In Fig. 2b, we can see that the time required to perform the randomization is less than 4% of the computational time for small matrices and becomes less than 2% for larger matrices. This is due to the low computational cost of the randomization ($8n^2$ flops) and to our optimized implementation that use the capabilities of the GPU accelerator.

4   RBT for Intel Xeon Phi

Similarly to the previous section, we present our implementation of the RBT on an Intel Xeon Phi coprocessor and discuss its performance. This solver and all the required routines (randomization, no pivoting LU factorization, iterative refinement) are part of the MAGMA MIC library (version 1.3).

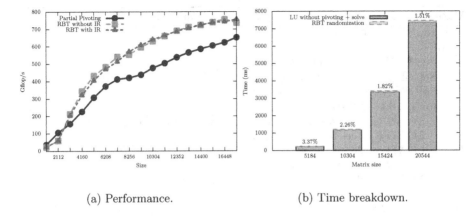

(a) Performance.   (b) Time breakdown.

Fig. 2. Randomized LU-based solver on GPU

4.1 Implementation

Algorithm 3 presents the randomization routine, using depth-two butterfly matrices. It is similar to its GPU counterpart, except that there are no blocks or threads to deal with inside this routine.

Algorithm 3. Two-level randomization on Intel Xeon Phi

Require: A a pointer to the matrix A on the Phi.
Require: U a pointer to the matrix U stored as a vector on the Phi.
Require: V a pointer to the matrix V stored as a vector on the Phi.
Require: n the size of the matrix A
Ensure: $A \leftarrow U^T A V$
1: **Call** : Elementary Multiplication Phi(A, &$U(n)$, &$V(n)$, $n/2$)
2: **Call** : Elementary Multiplication Phi(&$A(0, n/2)$, &$U(n)$, &$V(n + n/2)$, $n/2$)
3: **Call** : Elementary Multiplication Phi(&$A(n/2, 0)$, &$U(n + n/2)$, &$V(n)$, $n/2$)
4: **Call** : Elementary Multiplication Phi(&$A(n/2, n/2)$, &$U(n + n/2)$, &$V(n + n/2)$, $n/2$)
5: **Call** : Elementary Multiplication Phi(A, U, V, n) {Applying level one recursion}

The `Elementary multiplication Phi` kernel, described in Algorithm 4, uses SIMD instructions [5] to improve the performance of each core, and OpenMP to handle thread parallelism between cores. This algorithm is well adapted to the SIMD programming model as the dependencies between the data are separated by a large number of values. In Algorithm 4, we use double precision floating point numbers, each of them using 64 bits. This explains why 8 values are stored in each 512-bits SIMD vector. When using 32 bits reals, 16 values are stored in each vector. For complex numbers, 8 numbers are stored in single precision and 4 in double. We take advantage of the SIMD capabilities of the Intel Xeon Phi coprocessor by using the low level Knight's Corner intrinsics set

---

Algorithm 4. Phi Kernel: Elementary multiplication Phi(A, U, V, n)

1: **OpenMP** parallel for
2: **for** $i = 0$ to $n/2$ **do**
3:     Declare V_1 and V_2 two 512-bit vector registers.
4:     **Set** all values of V_1 with $V(i)$
5:     **Set** all values of V_2 with $V(i + n/2)$
6:     **for** $j = 0$ **to** $n/2$ **step** 8 **do**
7:         Declare a_{00}, a_{01}, a_{10} and a_{11} four 512-bit vector registers.
8:         **LOAD** 8 values from $A(i, j)$ in a_{00}
9:         **LOAD** 8 values from $A(i, j + n/2)$ in a_{01}
10:        **LOAD** 8 values from $A(i + n/2, j)$ in a_{10}
11:        **LOAD** 8 values from $A(i + n/2, j + n/2)$ in a_{11}
12:        Declare b_1, b_2, b_3 and b_4 four 512-bit vector registers.
13:        $b_1 \leftarrow \textbf{ADD}(a_{00}, a_{01})$
14:        $b_2 \leftarrow \textbf{ADD}(a_{10}, a_{11})$
15:        $b_3 \leftarrow \textbf{SUB}(a_{00}, a_{01})$
16:        $b_4 \leftarrow \textbf{SUB}(a_{10}, a_{11})$
17:        Declare U_1 and U_2 two 512-bit vector registers.
18:        **LOAD** 8 values from $U(j)$ in U_1
19:        **LOAD** 8 values from $U(j + n/2)$ in U_2
20:        $a_{00} \leftarrow \textbf{MUL}(U_1, \textbf{MUL}(V_1, \textbf{ADD}(b_1, b_2)))$
21:        $a_{01} \leftarrow \textbf{MUL}(U_1, \textbf{MUL}(V_2, \textbf{ADD}(b_3, b_4)))$
22:        $a_{10} \leftarrow \textbf{MUL}(U_2, \textbf{MUL}(V_1, \textbf{SUB}(b_1, b_2)))$
23:        $a_{11} \leftarrow \textbf{MUL}(U_2, \textbf{MUL}(V_2, \textbf{SUB}(b_3, b_4)))$
24:        **STORE** 8 values from a_{00} at $A(i, j)$
25:        **STORE** 8 values from a_{01} at $A(i, j + n/2)$
26:        **STORE** 8 values from a_{10} at $A(i + n/2, j)$
27:        **STORE** 8 values from a_{11} at $A(i + n/2, j + n/2)$
28:    **end for**
29: **end for**

---

of instructions [10, 11]. The use of the intrinsics allows the use of the assembly SIMD instructions with C style functions.

4.2 Performance Results

Here we present the performance results of our solver. The experiments were carried out using the same multicore host as described in Sect. 3.2 (two Intel Xeon X5680) with an Intel Xeon Phi coprocessor 7120 with 61 cores running at 1.238 GHz, with 16 GB of memory. The cores have 30.5 MB of combined L2 cache memory. We mention that each core can manage 4 threads by using hyper-threading. For the experiments, we use 240 threads in total. Note that we were able to perform tests on larger matrices compared to the GPU version. This is due to the larger size of the Intel Xeon Phi memory.

In Fig. 3a, we notice that the Intel Xeon Phi version is up to 50 % faster than the solver using partial pivoting without iterative refinement, and only 25 % faster with iterative refinement, which is not yet optimized for Intel Xeon Phi.

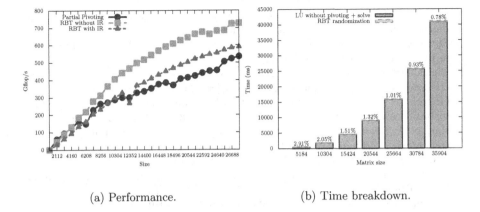

(a) Performance.   (b) Time breakdown.

Fig. 3. Randomized LU-based solver on Intel Xeon Phi

In Fig. 3b, we observe that the randomization requires less than 3 % of the total time and even less than 1 % for larger matrices. We recall that the randomization performed on the Intel Xeon Phi has been optimized using SIMD instructions and OpenMP.

5 Conclusion

In this paper, we have presented two implementations of the RBT solver using accelerators based respectively on GPU and Intel Xeon Phi, resulting in routines that are significantly faster than the reference solver based on the LU factorization with partial pivoting. Thanks to an efficient implementation of the randomization, the overhead for randomizing the original system is negligible compared to the computational cost of the whole solver. Ongoing work include optimizing the iterative refinement on Intel Xeon Phi and solving multiple small systems at the same time using batched solvers [7].

Acknowledgments. The authors would like to thank Stanimire Tomov and Ichitaro Yamasaki from University of Tennessee for the support with the MAGMA library.

References

1. Baboulin, M., Becker, D., Bosilca, G., Danalis, A., Dongarra, J.: An efficient distributed randomized algorithm for solving large dense symmetric indefinite linear systems. Parallel Comput. **40**(7), 213–223 (2014)
2. Baboulin, M., Becker, D., Dongarra, J.: A parallel tiled solver for dense symmetric indefinite systems on multicore architectures. In: 2012 IEEE 26th International Parallel & Distributed Processing Symposium (IPDPS), pp. 14–24. IEEE (2012)
3. Baboulin, M., Dongarra, J., Herrmann, J., Tomov, S.: Accelerating linear system solutions using randomization techniques. ACM Trans. Math. Softw. **39**(2), 1–13 (2013)

4. Baboulin, M., Dongarra, J., Tomov, S.: Some issues in dense linear algebra for multicore and special purpose architectures. In: 9th International Workshop on State-of-the-Art in Scientific and Parallel Computing (PARA'08). Lecture Notes in Computer Science, vol. 6126–6127. Springer-Verlag (2008)
5. Diefendorff, K., Dubey, P.K., Hochsprung, R., Scale, H.: Altivec extension to PowerPC accelerates media processing. IEEE Micro. $20(2)$, 85–95 (2000)
6. Grigori, L., Demmel, J.W., Xiang, H.: CALU: a communication optimal LU factorization algorithm. SIAM J. Matrix Anal. Appl. $32(4)$, 1317–1350 (2011)
7. Haidar, A., Dong, T., Luszczek, P., Tomov, S., Dongarra, J.: Batched matrix computations on hardware accelerators based on GPUs. IJHPCA $29(2)$, 193–208 (2015). http://dx.doi.org/10.1177/1094342014567546
8. Haidar, A., Luszczek, P., Tomov, S., Dongarra, J.: Heterogenous acceleration for linear algebra in multi-coprocessor environments. In: Daydé, M., Marques, O., Nakajima, K. (eds.) VECPAR 2014. LNCS, vol. 8969, pp. 31–42. Springer, Heidelberg (2015)
9. Intel: Math Kernel Library (MKL). http://www.intel.com/software/products/mkl/
10. Intel: Intel Xeon Phi^{TM} Coprocessor System Software Developers Guide (2012). http://software.intel.com/en-us/articles/
11. Jeffers, J., Reinders, J.: Intel Xeon Phi Coprocessor High-Performance Programming. Morgan Kaufmann, Newnes (2013)
12. Khabou, A., Demmel, J.W., Grigori, L., Gu, M.: Lu factorization with panel rank revealing pivoting and its communication avoiding version. SIAM J. Matrix Anal. Appl. $34(3)$, 1401–1429 (2013)
13. Nvidia, C.: Compute Unified Device Architecture programming guide (2007)
14. Parker, D.S.: Random butterfly transformations with applications in computational linear algebra. Technical Report CSD-950023, Computer Science Department, UCLA (1995)
15. Parker, D.S., Pierce, B.: The randomizing FFT: an aternative to pivoting in Gaussian elimination. Technical Report CSD-950037, Computer Science Department, UCLA (1995)
16. Tomov, S., Dongarra, J., Baboulin, M.: Towards dense linear algebra for hybrid GPU accelerated manycore systems. Parallel Comput. $36(5\&6)$, 232–240 (2010)

Identifying Optimization Opportunities Within Kernel Execution in GPU Codes

Robert Lim[⊠], Allen Malony, Boyana Norris, and Nick Chaimov

Performance Research Laboratory, High-Performance Computing Laboratory,
University of Oregon, Eugene, OR, USA
{roblim1,malony,norris,nchaimov}@cs.uoregon.edu
http://tau.uoregon.edu

Abstract. Tuning codes for GPGPU architectures is challenging because few performance tools can pinpoint the exact causes of execution bottlenecks. While profiling applications can reveal execution behavior with a particular architecture, the abundance of collected information can also overwhelm the user. Moreover, performance counters provide cumulative values but does not attribute events to code regions, which makes identifying performance hot spots difficult. This research focuses on characterizing the behavior of GPU application kernels and its performance at the node level by providing a visualization and metrics display that indicates the behavior of the application with respect to the underlying architecture. We demonstrate the effectiveness of our techniques with LAMMPS and LULESH application case studies on a variety of GPU architectures. By sampling instruction mixes for kernel execution runs, we reveal a variety of intrinsic program characteristics relating to computation, memory and control flow.

1 Introduction

Scientific computing has been accelerated in part due to heterogeneous architectures, such as GPUs and integrated manycore devices. Parallelizing applications for heterogeneous architectures can lead to potential speedups, based on dense processor cores, large memories and improved power efficiency. The increasing use of such GPU-accelerated systems has motivated researchers to develop new techniques to analyze the performance of these systems. Characterizing the behavior of kernels executed on the GPU hardware can provide feedback for further code enhancements and support informed decisions for compiler optimizations.

Tuning a workload for a particular architecture requires in-depth knowledge of the characteristics of the application [19]. Workload characterization for general-purpose architectures usually entails profiling benchmarks with hardware performance counters and deriving performance metrics such as instructions per cycle, cache miss rates, and branch misprediction rates. This approach is limited because hardware constraints such as memory sizes and multiprocessor cores are not accounted for and can strongly impact the workload characterization. Moreover, the current profiling methods provide an overview of the

© Springer International Publishing Switzerland 2015
S. Hunold et al. (Eds.): Euro-Par 2015 Workshops, LNCS 9523, pp. 185–196, 2015.
DOI: 10.1007/978-3-319-27308-2_16

behaviors of the application in a summarized manner without exposing sufficient low-level details.

Performance tools that monitor GPU kernel execution are complicated by the limited hardware support of fine-grained kernel measurement and the asynchronous concurrency that exists between the CPU and GPU. With so many GPUs available, identifying which applications will run best on which architectures is not straightforward. Applications that run on GPU accelerators are treated like a black box, where measurements can only be read at the start and stop points of kernel launches. Moreover, the difficulty of tracking and distinguishing which tasks are associated with the CPU versus the GPU makes debugging heterogeneous parallel applications a very complicated task. Thus, analyzing static and dynamic instruction mixes can help identify potential performance bottlenecks in heterogeneous architectures.

1.1 Motivation

Heterogeneous computing presents many challenges in managing the diverse architectures, high-speed networks, interfaces, operating systems, communication protocols and programming environments. For GPUs, more computational units exist over memory, and PCI bus transfers are limited in latency and capacity (fixed GB/sec). Thus, applications that provide parallelism opportunities will benefit most on GPUs. Algorithms with efficient partitioning or mapping strategies are needed to exploit heterogeneity, while syntax directives such as OpenMP and OpenACC facilitate in program productivity. Tools need to be able to measure the individual heterogeneous components to assess the application's performance behavior.

Performance measurements for GPUs are typically collected using the event queue method [14], where an event is injected into the stream immediately before and after the computation kernel. Performance frameworks such as TAU, PAPI, Intel VTune and NVIDIA nvprof provide this capability [1–3,17], where regions of code are annotated with start/stop calls surrounding kernel execution.

Hardware performance counters are often used to monitor application performance, where measurements can be collected through either instrumentation or sampling. Drawbacks of using hardware performance counters include overcounts of results, lack of support across architecture vendors, incompatibilities of events and counters, limited number of hardware counters, and inability to pinpoint transient behavior in program runs [13,18].

In Fig. 1, we show a time series of hardware counters sampled in the GPU, a capability we've added in TAU, and kernels that were executed for the LULESH application. The plot reveals spikes in the hardware samples for the application. However, one cannot correlate those spikes to the dense regions of activities in source code. If timestamps were used to merge GPU events with CPU events for purposes of performance tracing, the times will need to be synchronized between host and device [5], as the GPU device has a different internal clock frequency than the host. Using timestamps to merge profiles may not be sufficient, or even correct. Thus, optimizing and tuning the code would require a best guess effort

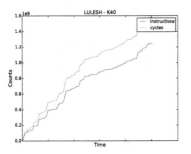 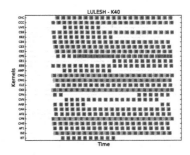

Fig. 1. Sampled hardware counters of instructions executed and active cycles (left) and individual kernel executions (right), both for LULESH (Color figure online).

of where to begin. This motivates our exploration of the use of instruction type mixes in aiding the analysis of potential performance bottlenecks.

1.2   Contributions

In our work, we perform static analysis on CUDA binaries to map source text regions and generate instruction mixes based on the CUDA binaries. We define instruction mix as the types of operation codes in GPU programming [12]. This feature is integrated with TAU to sample region runs on the GPU. We also provide visualization and analysis to identify GPU hotspots and optimization opportunities. This helps the user better understand the application's runtime behavior. In addition, we repeatedly sample instructions as the application executes. To the knowledge of the authors, this work is the first attempt at gaining insight on the behavior of kernel applications on GPUs *in real time*. With our methodology, we can also identify whether an application is compute-bound, memory-bound, or relatively balanced.

2   Background

The TAU Parallel Performance Framework [17] provides scalable profile and trace measurement and analysis for high-performance parallel applications. TAU provides tools for source instrumentation, compiler instrumentation, and library wrapping that allows CPU events to be observed. TAU also offers parallel profiling for GPU-based heterogeneous programs, by providing library wrappings of the CUDA runtime/driver API and preloading of the wrapped library prior to execution. Each call made to a runtime or driver routine is intercepted by TAU for measurement before and after calling the actual CUDA routine.

TAU CUPTI Measurements. TAU collects performance events for CUDA GPU codes asynchronously by tracing an application's CPU and GPU activity [14]. An activity record is created, which logs CPU and GPU activities. Each event kind (e.g. CUpti_ActivityMemcpy) represents a particular activity.

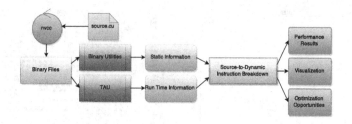

Fig. 2. Overview of our proposed methodology.

CUDA Performance Tool Interface (CUPTI) provides two APIs, the Callback API and the Event API, which enables the creation of profiling and tracing tools that target CUDA applications. The CUPTI Callback API registers a callback in TAU and is invoked whenever an application being profiled calls a CUDA runtime or driver function, or when certain events occur in the CUDA driver. CUPTI fills activity buffers with activity records as corresponding activities occur on the CPU and GPU. The CUPTI Event API allows the tool to query, configure, start, stop, and read the event counters on a CUDA enabled device.

3   Methodology

Our approach to enabling new types of insight into the performance characteristics of GPU kernels includes both static and dynamic measurement and analysis.

3.1   Static Analysis

Each CUDA code is compiled with CUDA 7.0 v.7.0.17, and the "-g -lineinfo" flags, which enables tracking of source code location activity within TAU. Each of the generated code from nvcc is fed into cuobjdump and nvdisasm to statically analyze the code for instruction mixes and source line information. The generated code is then monitored with TAU, which collects performance measurements and dynamically analyzes the code variants.

Binary Utilities. CUDA binaries are disassembled with the binary utilities provided by the NVIDIA SDK. A CUDA binary (cubin) file is an ELF-formatted file, or executable and linkable format, which is a common standard file format for representing executables, object code, shared libraries and core dumps. By default, the CUDA compiler driver nvcc embeds cubin files into the host executable file.

Instruction Breakdown. We start the analysis by categorizing the executed instructions from the disassembled binary output. Figure 3 displays the instruction breakdown for individual kernels in LULESH and LAMMPS applications

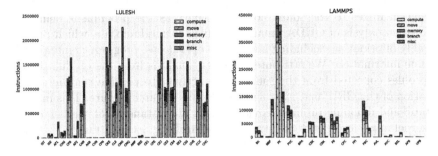

Fig. 3. Instruction breakdown for M2090, K80, and M6000 for individual kernels in LULESH and LAMMPS applications (Color figure online).

for M2090, K80 and M6000 architectures (one per generation). For LAMMPS, the PK kernel shows more computational operations, whereas FII and PBC shows more move operations. For the LULESH kernels CKE, CMG, and CE2 we observe more compute-intensive operations, as well as branches, and moves. One thing to note is that the Maxwell architectures (M6000) in general shows more compute operations for all kernels, when compared with Tesla.

3.2 Dynamic Analysis

The TAU Parallel Performance System monitors various CUDA activities, such as memory transfers and concurrent kernels executed. TAU also tracks source code locator activities, as described below. Hardware counter sampling for CUPTI is also implemented in TAU and is enabled by passing the "ebs" flag to the tau_exec command line [15]. In addition, the environment variable TAU_METRICS is set with events to sample. TAU lists CUPTI events available for a particular GPU with the tau_cupti_avail command. For our experiments, we monitored instructions executed and active cycles, since those events are available across all GPUs.

Source Code Locator Activity. Source code locator information is an activity within the CUPTI runtime environment that makes possible logging of CUPTI activity. Instructions are sampled at a fixed rate of 20 ms. Within each sample, the following events are collected: threads executed, instructions executed, source line information, kernels launched, timestamps, and program counter offsets. Our research utilizes the information collected from the source code locator and instruction execution activities. The activity records are collected as profiles and written out to disk for further analysis.

Runtime Mapping of Instruction Mixes to Source Code Location. Using the source locator activity discussed in Sect. 3.2, we statically collect instruction mixes and source code locations from generated code and map the instruction mixes to the source locator activity as the program is being run. The static analysis of CUDA binaries produce an objdump file, which provides assembly information, including instruction operations, program counter offsets, and line information. We attribute the static analysis from the objdump file to the profiles collected from the source code activity to provide runtime characterization of the GPU as it is being executed on the architecture. This mapping of static and dynamic profiles provides a rich understanding of the behavior of the kernel application with respect to the underlying architecture.

3.3   Instruction Operation Metrics

We define several instruction operation metrics derived from our methodology as follows. These are examples of metrics that can be used to relate the instruction mix of a kernel with a potential performance bottleneck. Let op_j represent the different types of operations as listed in [12], $time_{exec}$ equal the time duration for one kernel execution (ms), and $calls_n$ represent the number of unique kernel launches for that particular kernel.

Efficiency metric describes flops per second, or how well the floating point units are effectively utilized:

$$efficiency = \frac{op_{fp} + op_{int} + op_{simd} + op_{conv}}{time_{exec}} \cdot calls_n \qquad (1)$$

Impact metric describes the performance contribution (operations executed) for a particular kernel j with respect to the overall application:

$$impact = \frac{\sum_{j \in J} op_j}{\sum_{i \in I} \sum_{j \in J} op_{i,j}} \cdot calls_n \qquad (2)$$

Individual metrics for computational intensity, memory intensity and control intensity can be calculated as follows:

$$FLOPS = \frac{op_{fp} + op_{int} + op_{simd} + op_{conv}}{\sum_{j \in J} op_j} \cdot calls_n \qquad (3)$$

$$MemOPS = \frac{op_{ldst} + op_{tex} + op_{surf}}{\sum_{j \in J} op_j} \cdot calls_n \qquad (4)$$

$$CtrlOPS = \frac{op_{ctrl} + op_{move} + op_{pred}}{\sum_{j \in J} op_j} \cdot calls_n \qquad (5)$$

4   Analysis

4.1   Applications

LAMMPS. The Large-scale Atomic/Molecular Massively Parallel Simulator [16] is a molecular dynamics application that integrates Newton's equations of motion for collections of atoms, molecules, and macroscopic particles.

Developed by Sandia National Laboratories, LAMMPS simulates short- or long-range forces with a variety of initial and/or boundary conditions. On parallel machines, LAMMPS uses spatial-decomposition techniques to partition the simulation domain into small 3D sub-domains, where each sub-domain is assigned to a processor. LAMMPS-CUDA offloads neighbor and force computations to GPUs while performing time integration on CPUs. In this work, we focus on the Lennard-Jones (LJ) benchmark, which approximates the interatomic potential between a pair of neutral atoms or molecules.

LULESH. The Livermore Unstructured Lagrange Explicit Shock Hydrodynamics (LULESH) [8] is a highly simplified application that solves a Sedov blast problem, which represents numerical algorithms, data motion, and programming styles typical in scientific applications. Developed by Lawrence Livermore National Laboratory as part of DARPA's Ubiquitous High-Performance Computing Program, LULESH approximates the hydrodynamics equation discretely by partitioning the spatial problem domain into a collection of volumetric elements defined by a mesh. LULESH is built on the concept of an unstructured hex mesh, where a node represents a point where mesh lines intersect. In this paper, we study the LULESH-GPU implementation with TAU.

4.2 Methodology

We profile LULESH and LAMMPS applications on seven different GPUs (listed in [12]) by using the TAU Parallel Performance System. Next, we calculate the performance of the kernel for one pass. Then, we apply the metrics from Sect. 3.3 to identify potentially poorly performing kernels that can be optimized. Note that $calls_n$, which represents the number of times a particular routine is called, can easily be collected with TAU profiling. The overhead associated with running the static analysis of our tool is equivalent to compiling the code and running the objdump results through a parser.

4.3 Results

Figure 5 shows statically analyzed heatmap representations for LAMMPS and LULESH on various architectures. The x-axis represents the kernel name (listed in Appendix of [12]), while the y-axis lists the type of instruction mix. For LAMMPS, overall similarities exist within each architecture generation (Tesla vs. Maxwell), where Maxwell makes greater use of the control and floating-point operations, while Tesla utilizes conversion operations. The GTX980 makes use of predicate instructions, as indicated on the top row of the bottom-middle plot. For LULESH, more use of predicate and conversion operations show up in Fermi and Tesla architectures, versus Maxwell which utilizes SIMD instructions for both AF1 and AF2 kernels. Load/store instructions are particularly heavy in M2090 and the GTX480 for the CKE kernel.

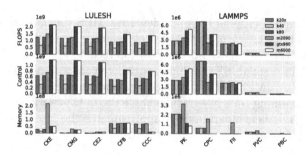

Fig. 4. Metrics for individual kernel execution in LULESH and LAMMPS applications (Color figure online).

Figure 4 displays normalized metrics for FLOPS, control operations and memory operations for the top five poor performing kernels, determined by the *impact* metric (Eq. 2, Fig. 6b). Generally speaking, ideal kernel performance occurs in balanced FLOPS and memory operations, and low branch operations. FLOPS and branches were higher in general for LULESH on the Maxwell architectures, when compared to Tesla. The M2090 architecture showed higher memory operations for the CKE kernel and for all LAMMPS kernels. The M2090 has a smaller global memory compared to Tesla (5 GB vs 11.5 GB), and a smaller L2 cache compared to Maxwell (0.8 MB vs. 3.1 MB), which explains its poor memory performance.

Figure 6a compares divergent branches over total instructions in GPU codes using hardware counters and instruction mix sampling for the top twelve kernels in LULESH, calculated with the *CtrlOPS* metric. The kernels that are closest to the y-axis represent divergent paths that weren't detected with hardware counters (about 33 %), which further affirms the counter's inconsistencies in providing accurate measurements. Our methodology was able to precisely detect divergent branches for kernels that exhibited that behavior.

Figure 7 shows the correlation of computation intensity with memory intensity (normalized) for all seven architectures for the LAMMPS application. For static input size independent analysis (left), differences in code generated are displayed for different architectures. However, the figure in the right shows the instruction mixes for runtime data and reflects that there isn't much of a difference in terms of performance across architectures. The differences between dynamic and static results are primarily due to the lack of control flow information in the static analysis, which will be added in future. While this addition will likely improve the match between the static and dynamic instruction counts, there will always be some discrepancies because not all dynamic behavior can be inferred from the static code for most codes. Nevertheless, by using our static analysis tool, we were able to identify four of the top five time-consuming kernels based only on instruction mix data. The static instruction mixes provide qualitatively comparable information, which can be used to guide optimizations.

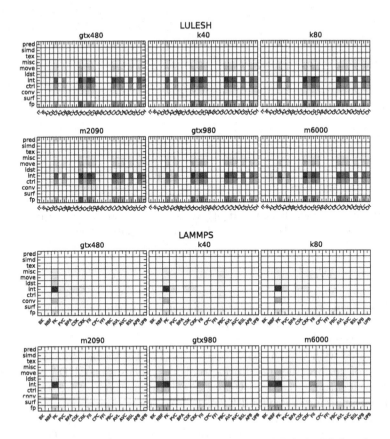

Fig. 5. Heatmap for micro operations for LULESH and LAMMPS benchmarks on various GPU architectures (Color figure online).

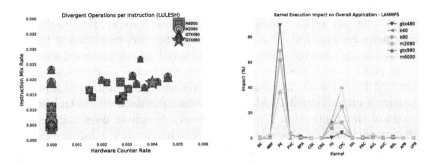

Fig. 6. Two approaches to measuring divergent branches in LULESH: instruction mix sampling, and hardware counters. Kernel impact on overall application in LAMMPS.

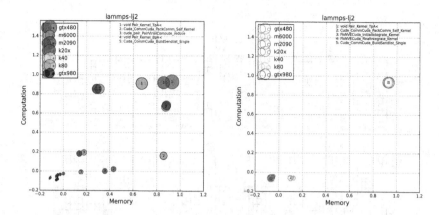

Fig. 7. Static (left) and dynamic (right) analyses for various architectures showing performance of individual kernels in LAMMPS (Color figure online).

5   Related Work

There have been attempts to assess the kernel-level performance of GPUs. However, not much has been done to provide an in-depth analysis of activities that occur inside the GPU.

Distributed with CUDA SDK releases, NVIDIA's Visual Profiler (NVP) [2] has a suite of performance monitoring tools that focuses on CUDA codes. NVP traces the execution of each GPU task, recording method name, start and end times, launch parameters, and GPU hardware counter values, among other information. NVP also makes use of the source code locator activity by displaying source code alongside PTX assembly code. However, NVP doesn't quantify the use of instruction mixes which differs from our work.

G-HPCToolkit [4] characterizes kernel behavior by looking at idleness analysis via blame-shifting and stall analysis for performance degradation. In this work, the authors quantify CPU code regions that execute when a GPU is idle, or GPU tasks that execute when a CPU thread is idle, and accumulate blame to the executing task proportional to the idling task. Vampir [11] also does performance measurements for GPUs. They look at the trace execution at the start and stop times and provide a detailed execution of timing of kernel execution, but do not provide activities that behave inside the kernel. The authors [9] have characterized PTX kernels by creating an internal representation of a program and running it on an emulator, which determines the memory, control flow and parallelism of the application. This work closely resembles ours, but differs in that we perform workload characterization on actual hardware during execution.

Other attempts at modeling performance execution on GPUs can be seen in [7] and [10]. These analytical models provide a tractable solution to calculate GPU performance when given input sizes and hardware constraints. Our work is complementary to those efforts, in that we identify performance execution of kernels using instruction mixes.

6   Conclusion and Future Work

Monitoring performance on accelerators is difficult because of the lack of visibility in GPU execution and the asynchronous behavior between the CPU and GPU. Sampling instruction mixes in real time can help characterize the application behavior with respect to the underlying architecture, as well as identify the best tuning parameters for kernel execution.

In this research, we provide insight on activities that occur as the kernel executes on the GPU. In particular, we characterize the performance of execution at the kernel level based on sampled instruction mixes. In future work, we want to address the divergent branch problem, a known performance bottleneck on accelerators, by building control flow graphs that model execution behavior. In addition, we plan to use the sampled instruction mixes to predict performance parameters and execution time for the Orio code generation framework [6]. The goal is to substantially reduce the number of empirical tests for kernels, which will result in rapid identification of best performance tuning configurations.

Acknowledgements. We would like to thank Duncan Poole and J-C Vasnier of NVIDIA for providing early access to CUDA 7.0 and to the PSG Clusters. We also want to thank the anonymous reviewers in providing constructive feedback. This work is supported by the Department of Energy (Award #DE-SC0005360) for the project "Vancouver 2: Improving Programmability of Contemporary Heterogeneous Architectures."

References

1. Intel VTune Amplifier. https://software.intel.com/en-us/intel-vtune-amplifier-xe
2. NVIDIA Visual Profiler. https://developer.nvidia.com/nvidia-visual-profiler
3. Browne, S., Dongarra, J., Garner, N., Ho, G., Mucci, P.: A portable programming interface for performance evaluation on modern processors. Int. J. High Perform. Comput. Appl. **14**, 189–204 (2000)
4. Chabbi, M., Murthy, K., Fagan, M., Mellor-Crummey, J.: Effective sampling-driven performance tools for GPU-accelerated supercomputers. In: International Conference for High Performance Computing, Networking, Storage and Analysis (SC). IEEE (2013)
5. Dietrich, R., Ilsche, T., Juckeland, G.: Non-intrusive performance analysis of parallel hardware accelerated applications on hybrid architectures. In: First International Workshop on Parallel Software Tools and Tool Infrastructures (PSTI). IEEE Computer Society (2010)
6. Hartono, A., Norris, B., Sadayappan, P.: Annotation-based empirical performance tuning using Orio. In: International Symposium on Parallel & Distributed Processing (IPDPS). IEEE (2009)
7. Hong, S., Kim, H.: An analytical model for a GPU architecture with memory-level and thread-level parallelism awareness. In: ACM SIGARCH Computer Architecture News. ACM (2009)
8. Karlin, I., Bhatele, A., Chamberlain, B., Cohen, J., Devito, Z., Gokhale, M., et al., R.H.: Lulesh programming model and performance ports overview. In: Technical report, Lawrence Livermore National Laboratory (LLNL) Technical Report (2012)

9. Kerr, A., Andrew, G., Yalamanchili, S.: A characterization and analysis of PTX kernels. In: International Symposium on Workload Characterization (IISWC). IEEE (2009)

10. Kim, H., Vuduc, R., Baghsorkhi, S., Choi, J., Hwu, W.: Performance Analysis and Tuning for General Purpose Graphics Processing Units (GPGPU). Morgan & Claypool Publishers (2012)

11. Knpfer, A., Brunst, H., Doleschal, J., Jurenz, M., Lieber, M., Mickler, H., Mller, M., Nagel, W.: The VAMPIR performance analysis tool-set. In: Resch, M., Keller, R., Himmler, V., Krammer, B., Schulz, A. (eds.) Tools for High Performance Computing. Springer, Heidelberg (2008)

12. Lim, R.: Identifying optimization opportunities within kernel launches in GPU architectures, Technical report. University of Oregon, CIS Department (2015)

13. Lim, R., Carrillo-Cisneros, D., Alkowaileet, W., Scherson, I.: Computationally efficient multiplexing of events on hardware counters. In: Linux Symposium (2014)

14. Malony, A., Biersdorff, S., Shende, S., Jagode, H., Tomov, S., Juckeland, G., Dietrich, R., Poole, D., Lamb, C.: Parallel performance measurement of heterogeneous parallel systems with GPUs. In: IEEE International Conference on Parallel Processing (ICPP) (2011)

15. Morris, A., Malony, A., Shende, S., Huck, K.: Design and implementation of a hybrid parallel performance measurement system. In: International Conference on Parallel Processing (ICPP) (2010)

16. Plimpton, S.: Fast parallel algorithms for short-range molecular dynamics. J. Comput. Phys. 117(1), 1–19 (1995)

17. Shende, S., Malony, A.: The TAU parallel performance system. Int. J. High Perform. Comput. Appl. 20(2), 287–311 (2006)

18. Weaver, V., Terpstra, D., Moore, S.: Non-determinism and overcount on modern hardware performance counter implementations. In: International Symposium on Performance Analysis of Systems and Software (ISPASS). IEEE (2013)

19. Shao, Y., Brooks, D.: ISA-independent workload characterization and its implications for specialized architectures. In: IEEE International Symposium Performance Analysis of Systems and Software (ISPASS) (2013)

Modeling Contention and Mapping Effects in Multi-core Clusters

Juan-Antonio Rico-Gallego[1]([✉]), Juan-Carlos Díaz-Martín[1],
and Alexey L. Lastovetsky[2]

[1] University of Extremadura, Avd. Universidad s/n, 10003 Cáceres, Spain
{jarico,juancarl}@unex.es
[2] University College Dublin, Belfield, Dublin 4, Ireland
Alexey.lastovetsky@ucd.ie

Abstract. Modeling and formal analysis of parallel algorithms contribute to optimize their performance. Modern multi-core are complex machines composed of heterogeneous shared communication channels. Parallel Performance Models estimate the cost and capture the behavior of parallel algorithms through a set of parameters, providing valuable information about the behavior of the algorithm in these platforms. LogGP is a representative model using network related parameters to predict the cost of parallel algorithms as a sequence of point-to-point transmissions. Although extensions have been proposed for covering issues derived from modern platforms complexities as contention and channels hierarchy, such specific extensions are not enough to meaningfully and accurately model more than simple algorithms. τ–Lop is an alternative model that takes as a building block for modeling parallel algorithms the concept of concurrent transfers, that helps to capture algorithms behavior and allows to represent and accurately predict their cost in multi-core clusters. This paper shows the analysis capabilities of τ–Lop through two cases of study involving elaborated MPI collective operations.

1 Introduction

Parallel performance models estimate the cost and capture the behavior of parallel algorithms. Message passing defined in the MPI standard [8], is the most used programming model for building scientific applications. MPI is based on independent processes communicating by point-to-point messages and collective operations, whose costs have an important influence in the global performance of applications. The performance of the underlying algorithms implementing MPI collectives vary significantly with the message size, number of involved processes, and the platform characteristics. Modeling and formal analysis of such algorithms is important to gain insights into their performance.

LogGP [1] is a representative message-passing performance model. It was conceived to estimate the cost of a point-to-point message between two processes based on network-related parameters basically representing the latency

© Springer International Publishing Switzerland 2015
S. Hunold et al. (Eds.): Euro-Par 2015 Workshops, LNCS 9523, pp. 197–208, 2015.
DOI: 10.1007/978-3-319-27308-2_17

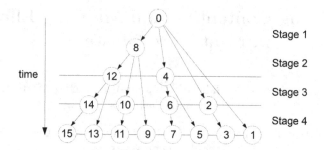

Fig. 1. A *binomial tree* used in MPI_Bcast collective operation.

and bandwidth values. LogGP assumes that collective algorithms are built upon point-to-point message transmissions deployed over a network of mono-processors and models an algorithm as a sequence of stages, each with the cost of a single point-to-point transmission. For instance, a broadcast operation on P processes based on the *binomial tree* algorithm has a cost that equals the height of the tree ($\lceil \log P \rceil$) times the cost of a single transmission between two processes (see Fig. 1). In modern HPC platforms this is an over-simplification that leads to important errors in the cost estimation of an algorithm. In multi-core clusters, processes communicate through different physical channels with very different performance, and usually sharing the available bandwidth. To deal with some of these complexities, extensions of LogGP have appeared, but oriented to specific platforms and topics ([3,7,12]).

More recent $\log_n P$ [2] introduces the concept of *transfer* for describing a point-to-point transmission as a sequence of movements of data between memory entities. Nevertheless, $\log_n P$ is still simplistic and it has not demonstrated its capabilities to model complex algorithms or basic techniques as the segmentation of messages. τ–Lop [10], rooted on $\log_n P$, models algorithms as a sequence of *concurrent transfers* progressing through available communication channels, what allows to capture the effects of the contention in multi-core clusters.

The goal of this paper is to evaluate the capacities of τ–Lop to model the parallel algorithms used regularly in the implementation of MPI collective operations. We present two cases of study in comparison to LogGP. The first case of study shows the influence of the contention on the cost of an algorithm, as well as the capacity of these models to represent it. As a conduit example, two common collective algorithms are modeled in the shared memory communication channel: *binomial tree* and *recursive doubling*, implementing the *MPI_Scatter* and the *MPI_Allgather* operations respectively. The second case of study discusses the *Ring* algorithm when it is used in the *MPI_Allgather* collective. Its cost is predicted for two common mappings under τ–Lop and a LogGP offspring on a multi-core cluster.

Section 2 below briefly reviews some related works in the field of modeling parallel algorithms. Section 3 introduces the models used in this paper, LogGP and τ–Lop. Sections 4 and 5 develop the cases of study. Section 6 gives details on the platforms used for the performance measurements, and Sect. 7 concludes.

2   Related Work

LogGP [1] is a widespread model which characterizes the communication cost according to the five parameters that compose its name: the network latency (L), the overhead or time a processor is engaged in the transmission or reception of a message (o), the time interval between consecutive message transmissions (g), and the time interval between consecutive byte transmissions (G). The cost of a transmission is formulated in terms of these parameters and the size in bytes of the message (m), as $o_S + L + (m-1)G + o_R$, i.e., the overhead in the sender processor, the latency in the network of the first byte, the time of sending the rest ($m-1$ bytes) of the message, and the overhead in the reception processor. For simplicity, it is usually assumed that $o = (o_S + o_R)/2$.

LogGP shows powerful analysis capabilities to guide the development of applications and algorithms. A thorough study of known MPI collective algorithms and its performance under the LogGP model can be found in [9].

Models extending LogGP contribute with specific aspects to model complex communication in modern platforms. *LogGPS* [3] provides the rendezvous protocol cost, *LoGPC* [7] adds contention in meshes with wormhole routing, and *LogGPH* [12] supports representation for hierarchical networks by splitting up the parameters in sets for modeling transmissions over each communication channel.

The *Parametrized* LogP model [4] addresses the performance modeling of parallel algorithms by slightly changing the meaning of some parameters of LogGP and making them (except latency) dependent on the message size. More recent *LMO* model [5] estimates the cost of algorithms in both homogeneous and heterogeneous systems. The per-node parameters separate the cost imputable to the processors and the network in order to gain more accurate results.

The contention modeling issue in Ethernet networks is carried out in [6]. The authors generate an specific model for this type of network based on the study of flow control mechanisms and experimentally deduce *penalty coefficients*, and categorize different types of conflicts. Paper [11] introduces the *contention factor*, represented as a parameter affecting the network performance, which is linearly incremented from the contention-free communication cost.

3   Modeling Parallel Algorithms

LogGP models a parallel algorithm as a sequence of point-to-point transmissions of m bytes between P processes. For instance, the cost of a *Binomial Tree* broadcast algorithm, represented in Fig. 1, is calculated as:

$$T_{Bin}^{LogGP} = \lceil \log P \rceil \times T_{p2p} = \lceil \log P \rceil \times (L + 2o + (m-1)G)$$

τ–Lop considers a message transmission composed of a sequence of *concurrent transfers*. The *Transfer time*, denoted $L(m, \tau)$, is the cost of τ concurrent transfers of a message of size m. The *overhead* (o) is defined as the elapsed time since a message transmission operation is invoked until data begins to be injected in the communication channel, including the communication protocol time. The cost of a transmission is the sum of the costs of its individual transfers plus the overhead. Only contiguous data messages are considered in this paper. For instance, a shared memory transmission could be divided up in two transfers in sequence, from the sender buffer to a pre-allocated intermediate buffer and then to the receiver buffer, with the cost:

$$T_{p2p}(m) = o(m) + 2\, L(m, 1)$$

The number of transfers depends on the channel, but also on the particular implementation of the algorithm and the middleware, a fact ignored by LogGP and derived models.

In respect of collective operations, they are represented in τ–Lop as a sequence of stages, formed in turn of a set of concurrent transmissions. Under a shared communication channel, if the cost of the message transmission between processes 0 and 8 in Fig. 1 is $T_{p2p}(m)$, then the cost between processes 14 and 15 is much higher due to the fact that eight concurrent transmissions share the channel bandwidth. The cost ranges from $T_{p2p}(m)$ for a perfectly parallel channel, to $8 \times T_{p2p}(m)$ for a serial one. The $\parallel$ operator [10] captures this concurrency effect and produces compact and expressive cost equations. For instance, τ–Lop represents the binomial tree algorithm on P processes as:

$$\Theta_{Bin}^{\tau-Lop}(m) = \sum_{i=0}^{\lceil \log_2(P) \rceil - 1} \left(2^i \parallel T_{p2p}(m) \right) = \sum_{i=0}^{\lceil \log_2(P) \rceil - 1} \left(2^i \parallel (o(m) + 2\, L(m, 1)) \right)$$

$$= \sum_{i=0}^{\lceil \log_2(P) \rceil - 1} \left(o(m) + 2\, L(m, 2^i) \right)$$

Note how the $\parallel$ operator affects to the transfers concurrency (τ parameter). The overhead is attributable to the processor, and hence not affected by the operator.

4 Case Study 1: Analyzing the Effect of the Contention in Shared Memory

This section discusses the influence of the communication channel contention in the performance of algorithms through the study of two common algorithms, the *Binomial Tree* and the *Recursive Doubling*, commonly used in the *scatter* and *allgather* collectives respectively.

We use segmentation of messages, a technique commonly used in shared memory. It operates by breaking a message into k smaller chunks of a fixed size S known as *segments*, hence $m = k\, S$. The segments are sent in sequence to

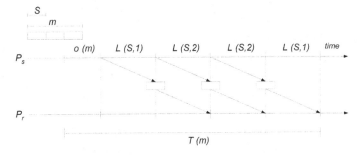

Fig. 2. A segmented point-to-point message transmission in shared memory modeled by τ–Lop. Unlike LogGP, the effect of the intermediate buffers is explicitly represented.

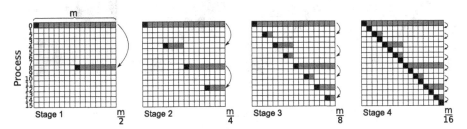

Fig. 3. The scatter binomial tree algorithm for $P = 16$ processes and $\log_2(P) = 4$ stages. An arc represents a point-to-point transmission T. The root has rank 0.

an intermediate shared buffer allowing the overlap with their reception. LogGP models the cost of a point-to-point segmented message as:

$$T_{p2p_S}^{LogGP} = L + 2\,o + (S-1)\,G + (k-1)\,(g + (S-1)\,G)$$
$$\approx L + 2\,o + S\,G + (k-1)\,(g + S\,G)$$

In τ–Lop, a segmented point-to-point message transmission is composed by transfers of the first and last segments proceeding alone, while the intermediate segments are copied concurrently, for a total of $2\,k$ transfers (see Fig. 2). Hence with a cost of:

$$T_{p2p_S}(m) = 2\,L(S,1) + (k-1)\,L(S,2) \approx o(m) + k\,L(S,2)$$

The scatter binomial tree is shown in Fig. 3. In each stage, the root of each subtree receives all the data its descendants expect. The number of concurrent transmissions doubles in each stage, while the size of the message halves.

Under LogGP, the total cost for the scatter is calculated as the cost of the larger path from the root process to a leaf, shown in the Table 1.

For its part, the recursive doubling also completes in $\lceil \log_2 P \rceil$ stages, as shown in Fig. 4. In each stage k, the process with rank p performs an interchange of data with the process with rank $p \oplus 2^k$. The initial size of the message is $m' = m/P$, and it doubles at each stage.

Table 1. The *Binomial Scatter* modeled with LogGP

Stage	Message size	Cost
1	$m/2$	$L + 2o + SG + ((k-1)/2)(g + SG)$
2	$m/4$	$L + 2o + SG + ((k-1)/4)(g + SG)$
3	$m/8$	$L + 2o + SG + ((k-1)/8)(g + SG)$
. .		
$\log_2 P$	$m/2^{\log_2 P}$	$L + 2o + SG + ((k-1)/P)(g + SG)$
Scatter cost		$\log_2 P(L + 2o + SG) + ((P-1)/P)(k-1)(g + SG)$

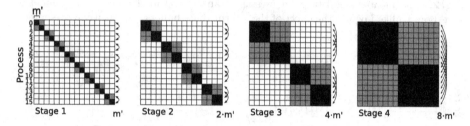

Fig. 4. The allgather recursive doubling algorithm for $P = 16$ processes. An arc represents a *sendrecv* message transmission between two processes.

Table 2. The *Recursive Doubling Allgather* modeled with LogGP

Stage	Message size	Cost
1	m/P	$L + 2o + SG + (1\,(k-1)/P)(g + SG)$
2	$2m/P$	$L + 2o + SG + (2\,(k-1)/P)(g + SG)$
3	$4m/P$	$L + 2o + SG + (4\,(k-1)/P)(g + SG)$
. .		
$\log_2 P$	$2^{\log P - 1}m/P$	$L + 2o + SG + ((k-1)/2)(g + SG)$
Allgather cost		$\log_2 P(L + 2o + SG) + ((P-1)/P)(k-1)(g + SG)$

Table 2 shows the allgather cost modeling in LogGP. Interestingly, both operations have the same cost under LogGP, a definitely inaccurate result. The whole amount of data moved is quite different: $\log_2 P \cdot (m/2)$ bytes in *scatter* versus $(P-1) \cdot m$ bytes in *allgather*, as can be deduced from Figs. 3 and 4.

The binomial scatter algorithm is modeled by τ–Lop as[1]:

$$
\begin{aligned}
\Theta_{Sct_S}(m) &= \sum_{i=0}^{\log P - 1} \left(2^i \parallel T_{p2p_S}\left(\frac{m}{2^{i+1}}\right) \right) = \sum_{i=0}^{\log P - 1} \left(2^i \parallel \left(\frac{k}{2^{i+1}} L(S,2)\right) \right) \\
&= \sum_{i=0}^{\log P - 1} \left(\frac{k}{2^{i+1}} L\left(S, 2^{i+1}\right) \right)
\end{aligned}
\tag{1}
$$

---

[1] The overhead (o(m)) is omitted for clarity in the rest of the paper.

With respect to the recursive doubling algorithm (RDA), Fig. 4 shows that the exchange of messages is done under a pattern of pairs of processes. Each process sends a message to and then receives a message from its partner. The send requires a k segments transfer to the intermediate buffer, and the receive requires an additional k segments transfer from the intermediate buffer. Therefore, the *exchange* operation has a per process cost of $T_{exch_S}(m) = o(m) + 2 k L(S, 1)$. Being P the number of processes involved, the cost of a stage is:

$$P \| T_{exch_S}(m) = P \| [o(m) + 2 k L(S, 1)] = o(m) + 2 k L(S, P) \tag{2}$$

Note that $T_{exch_S} \geq T_{p2p_S}(m)$, because a sequence of $2 k$ transfers perform worse that a sequence of k concurrent pairs, a fact with a key influence on the accuracy of the cost prediction. The RDA cost results in:

$$\Theta_{RDA_S} \left(\frac{m}{P} \right) = \sum_{i=0}^{\log P - 1} \left(P \| T_{exch_S} \left(2^i \frac{m}{P} \right) \right) = \sum_{i=0}^{\log P - 1} \left(P \| \left(\frac{2^{i+1} k}{P} L(S, 1) \right) \right)$$

$$= \sum_{i=0}^{\log P - 1} \left(\frac{2^{i+1} k}{P} L(S, P) \right) \tag{3}$$

We can further expand definitions (1) and (3) as:

$$\Theta_{Sct_S}(m) = \frac{k}{2} L(S, 2) + \frac{k}{4} L(S, 4) + \cdots + \frac{k}{P} L(S, P) \tag{4}$$

$$\Theta_{RDA_S} \left(\frac{m}{P} \right) = \frac{2k}{P} L(S, P) + \frac{4k}{P} L(S, P) + \cdots + \frac{Pk}{P} L(S, P) = 2k \frac{P - 1}{P} L(S, P)$$

Introducing additional contention in (4) in all the stages except in the last one, we get an upper bound for $\Theta_{Sct_S}(m)$:

$$\Theta'_{Sct_S}(m) = \frac{k}{2} L(S, P) + \frac{k}{4} L(S, P) + \cdots + \frac{k}{P} L(S, P) = k \frac{P - 1}{P} L(S, P)$$

So how do RDA and Scatter compare? We have that $\Theta_{RDA_S}(m) = 2 \Theta'_{Sct_S}(m) > 2 \Theta_{Sct_S}(m)$, an expression that shows that the cost of Θ_{RDA_S} exceeds more than twofold that of scatter in Θ_{Sct_S}. Figure 5 shows both the RDA and Scatter costs measured in the *Lusitania* platform (described in Sect. 6) for different P values. The relative mean costs ($\Theta_{RDA_S}/\Theta_{Sct_S}$) for the range of message sizes shown are 2.61 for $P = 32$, 2.83 for $P = 64$ and 3.02 for $P = 128$, increasing with the number of processes because of the difference in the contention between the operations. For any m and P, RDA cost more than doubles that of scatter, what confirms the τ–Lop prediction.

5   Case Sudy 2: Modeling the Mapping Effects on Multi-core Clusters

This section shows the capabilities of the models to capture the mapping effect in the overall cost. The process mapping has a direct influence in the channels

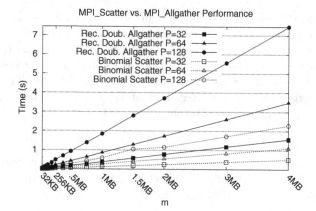

Fig. 5. The MPICH performance of the Binomial Tree Scatter and the Recursive Doubling Allgather with different number of processes P in the Lusitania machine.

used for message transmissions over the multi-core cluster, and indeed in the contention in such channels. As a conduit example, we discuss the *Ring* algorithm when it is used in the *MPI_Allgather*. We consider the *Metropolis* platform (see Sect. 6), with several multi-core nodes connected by Ethernet. Hence, the processes communicate through two channels: shared memory and network. Q is the number of cores per node and M the number of nodes, with $P = Q \times M$. Two common mappings are evaluated: *Sequential* mapping deploys processes on cores in a way that a rank p runs in the node $p \div Q$, and *Round Robin* mapping runs p in the node $p\%M$.

The Ring algorithm is executed in $P - 1$ stages. In each stage, the process p invokes the *MPI_Sendrecv* operation for sending m bytes to the process with number $p+1$, and then receiving from the process with number $p-1$ a message of the same size (with wraparound). Under sequential mapping (left side of Fig. 6), the destination and the source ranks of both point-to-point transmissions could be in the same or different node, therefore, transmissions could progress through shared memory or network. LogGP models the cost of a stage as the cost of the most expensive send-receive, that is, the addition of a shared memory and a network transmissions ($Q \geq 2$). Hence, the cost will be:

$$T_{Ring}^{SEQ} = (P - 1) \times [(L + 2o + (m - 1)G) + (L' + 2o' + (m - 1)G')] \quad (5)$$

where L is the latency of the shared memory channel and L' that of the network, and likely for o and G. This extension to LogGP is proposed in the LogGPH model. The cost for long messages approaches to $(P - 1)m(G + G')$, with the latency and the overhead costs negligible, and considering $G' \gg G$.

Under round robin mapping (see left side of the Fig. 7) all the messages travel through the network. Hence, the cost will be:

$$T_{Ring}^{RR} = (P - 1) \times 2 \times (L' + 2o' + (m - 1)G') \quad (6)$$

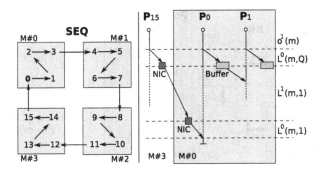

Fig. 6. The Ring algorithm with $P = 16$ processes in $M = 4$ nodes with *sequential* mapping, and a message transmission of P_0 deployed at right side.

The cost for long messages approaches to $(P - 1)\, 2\, m\, G'$, nearly doubling the sequential mapping cost. An important fact is that under LogGP both cost expressions (5) and (6) are independent of the number of processes per node Q, again a non plausible result, in our view.

As LogGP, τ–Lop models the send-receive operation (T_{sr}) as the addition of two point-to-point transmissions. The cost of each individual transmission depends on the channel it progresses (c) and on the contention it suffers, this derived from the process mapping and represented by C^{map}. The *Ring* cost is:

$$\Theta_{Ring}(m) = (P-1) \times [C^{map} \parallel T_{sr}(m)] = (P-1) \times \left[C^{map} \parallel \left(T_{p2p}^c(m) + T_{p2p}^c(m) \right) \right]$$

Under sequential mapping, the contention affects only to shared memory $(c = 0)$, as shown at left side of Fig. 6, with Q concurrent transmissions progressing through shared memory and only one through the network $(c = 1)$. The cost will be:

$$\Theta_{Ring}^{SEQ}(m) = (P - 1) \times \left[C^{SEQ} \parallel \left(T_{p2p}^0(m) + T_{p2p}^1(m) \right) \right]$$
$$= (P - 1) \times \left[Q \parallel T_{p2p}^0(m) + 1 \parallel T_{p2p}^1(m) \right]$$

Besides, τ–Lop allows an alternative lower analysis of the behavior of the Ring operation at transfer level. We consider a transmission through the network composed of three intermediate transfers: first from the sender buffer to the NIC, second from NIC to NIC, and last from the NIC to the receiver buffer. Right side of the Fig. 6 shows the decomposition into transfers of one stage of the Ring under sequential mapping. The first transfer of all processes, either to the NIC or to the intermediate buffer, progresses concurrently through shared memory, hence with the cost $L^0(m, Q)$. Then, a network send transfer of one process per node starts while the rest of processes complete communication through shared memory. These inter- and intra-node transfers progress through different channels, and hence, they do not contend, leading to a cost of $max\{L^0(m, Q - 1), L^1(m, 1)\}$. For instance, with $Q = 8$ in *Metropolis*, $L^1(m, 1) \gg L^0(m, Q - 1)$, leading to the cost:

$$\Theta_{Ring}^{SEQ}(m) = (P - 1) \times \left[L^0(m, Q) + L^1(m, 1) + L^0(m, 1) \right] \tag{7}$$

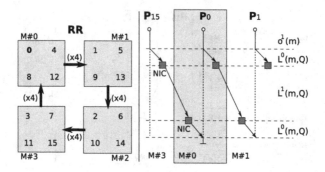

Fig. 7. The Ring algorithm with $P = 16$ processes in $M = 4$ nodes with round *robin* *mapping*, and a message transmission of P_0 deployed at right side.

Note that Q affects only to shared memory transfers.

The cost under round robin mapping comes determined by Q concurrent send and receive network transmissions, with the cost:

$$\Theta_{Ring}^{RR}(m) = (P-1) \times \left[C^{RR} \| T_{sr}(m)\right] = (P-1) \times \left[Q \| \left(T_{p2p}^1(m) + T_{p2p}^1(m)\right)\right]$$

Again, at transfer level, the right side of the Fig. 7 shows the decomposition of the Q concurrent transmissions through the network, leading to:

$$\Theta_{Ring}^{RR}(m) = (P-1) \times \left[L^0(m, Q) + L^1(m, Q) + L^0(m, Q)\right] \qquad (8)$$

The comparison of (7) and (8) shows that the difference is the contention in the channels, determined by the number of processes per node Q, a fact not represented by LogGP. Figure 8 shows the execution cost in terms of the bandwidth of the Ring algorithm, compared to LogGP and τ–Lop former estimations. The left plot (sequential mapping) shows that the influence of the contention on the total cost is relatively small, due to it occurs in the faster shared memory channel. Note the performance increasement effect of the piggybacking mechanism of TCP in small messages, not captured in the models, which provide pessimistic predictions. The right plot shows that round robin mapping saturates links between the nodes with Q concurrent transmissions, making long messages performance to decrease sixfold with only $M = 4$ and $Q = 8$. As LogGP does not model the contention derived cost, its cost estimation is very optimistic.

6   Test Platforms

To model the contention in shared memory (first case of study), we use the *Lusitania* platform. It is a ccNUMA HP Superdome sx2000 machine with 64 Dual-Core Intel Itanium2 Montvale 9140 N processors, with a private $9MB$ L3 cache, that make up a total of 128 cores, split into 16 UMA nodes. *Lusitania* is used as an SMP test platform due to similar intra-UMA and inter-UMA communication channels performance. The operating system is Linux 2.6.16.

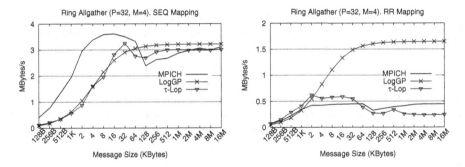

Fig. 8. Estimation of the cost of an Allgather *Ring* with LogGP and τ–Lop models, compared to the real MPICH measured bandwidth. The number of processes is $P = 32$, deployed on $M = 4$ nodes under two mappings, sequential (left) and round robin (right).

To model the mapping effect (second case of study), the platform used, named *Metropolis*, consists of four nodes connected by 10 Gigabit Ethernet through a switch. Each node has two 2.4 GHz Intel Xeon E5620 processors, making a total of eight cores per node, hyperthreading disabled, with a shared 12 MB L3 cache. The operating system is Linux 2.6.32.

IMB (Intel MPI Benchmark) running on MPICH version 1.4.1p1 is used to obtain the execution time in both platforms. The flag turning cache reuse is deactivated to avoid cache effects.

The MPI LogP Benchmark [4] is used for estimating the values of the parameters of the LogGP model. The methodology for measuring the τ–Lop parameters is out of the scope of this paper, and it is described in depth in [10].

7 Conclusions

LogGP is a representative model that estimates the cost of a collective algorithm as the cost of the longest path of the involved point-to-point transmissions. In the other hand, τ–Lop is a new model that uses the *concurrent transfer* concept.

We compare both models through two cases of study. First, we formally evaluate and analyze the influence of the contention in a shared communication channel as shared memory. The bandwidth shrinks in shared channels when several transmissions progress in parallel. τ–Lop is able to represent such concurrent transmissions through a simple but still powerful notation, with the overall result of improving the cost estimation. It has been shown that two algorithms as different as the Scatter Binomial and the Recursive Doubling Allgather are allocated the same cost by LogGP. Second, we model the influence of the process mapping on the cost of an algorithm, derived from the algorithms communication patterns. Such mapping decides the channels used for communicating in the multi-core cluster. Avoiding the representation of the mapping in a model leads to wrong cost predictions. A transfer-based model as τ–Lop offers a higher analysis capacity that provides a good accuracy of the cost prediction.

An additional conclusion of the study is that modern HPC platforms demand better parallel performance models, able of capturing their growing complexity, in particular the increasing number of cores per node and their heterogeneity.

Acknowledgments. This work has been partially supported by the computing facilities of the Extremadura Supercomputing Center (CenitS), by EU under the COST programme Action IC1305, 'Network for Sustainable Ultrascale Computing (NESUS)', and the Extremadura Government through the FEDER Funds.

References

1. Alexandrov, A., Lonescu, M.F., Schauser, K.E., Scheiman, C.: Loggp: incorporating long messages into the logp model - one step closer towards a realistic model for parallel computation. In: Proceedings of the Seventh Annual ACM Symposium on Parallel Algorithms and Architectures, pp. 95–105. SPAA 1995, NY, USA (1995)
2. Cameron, K.W., Ge, R., Sun, X.H.: $\log_m p$ and $\log_3 p$: accurate analytical models of point-to-point communication in distributed systems. IEEE Trans. Comput. **56**(3), 314–327 (2007)
3. Ino, F., Fujimoto, N., Hagihara, K.: Loggps: a parallel computational model for synchronization analysis. SIGPLAN Not. 36, pp. 133–142 (2001). http://doi.acm.org/10.1145/568014.379592
4. Kielmann, T., Bal, H.E., Verstoep, K.: Fast measurement of LogP parameters for message passing platforms. In: Rolim, J.D.P. (ed.) IPDPS-WS 2000. LNCS, vol. 1800, pp. 1176–1183. Springer, Heidelberg (2000)
5. Lastovetsky, A., Rychkov, V.: Accurate and efficient estimation of parameters of heterogeneous communication performance models. Int. J. High Perform. Comput. Appl. **23**(2), 123–139 (2009). http://dx.doi.org/10.1177/1094342009103947
6. Martinasso, M., Méhaut, J.-F.: Prediction of communication latency over complex network behaviors on SMP clusters. In: Bravetti, M., Kloul, L., Zavattaro, G. (eds.) EPEW/WS-EM 2005. LNCS, vol. 3670, pp. 172–186. Springer, Heidelberg (2005)
7. Moritz, C.A., Frank, M.I.: Logpc: modeling network contention in message-passing programs. IEEE Trans. Parallel Distrib. Syst. **12**(4), 404–415 (2001). http://dx.doi.org/10.1109/71.920589
8. MPI Forum: MPI: A message-passing interface standard. Version 3.0 (September 21th 2012). http://www.mpi-forum.org
9. Pješivac-Grbović, J., Angskun, T., Bosilca, G., Fagg, G.E., Gabriel, E., Dongarra, J.J.: Performance analysis of MPI collective operations. Cluster Comput. **10**, 127–143 (2007). http://dl.acm.org/citation.cfm?id=1265235.1265248
10. Rico-Gallego, J.A., Díaz-Martín, J.C.: τ-lop: modeling performance of shared memory MPI. Parallel Comput. **46**, 14–31 (2015)
11. Steffenel, L.: Modeling network contention effects on all-to-all operations. In: 2006 IEEE International Conference on Cluster Computing, pp. 1–10 (2006)
12. Yuan, L., Zhang, Y., Tang, Y., Rao, L., Sun, X.: Loggph: a parallel computational model with hierarchical communication awareness. In: 2010 IEEE 13th International Conference on Computational Science and Engineering (CSE), vol. 2, pp. 268–274 (2010)

Towards Community Detection on Heterogeneous Platforms

Stijn Heldens[1]([⊠]), Ana Lucia Varbanescu[1],
Arnau Prat-Pérez[2], and Josep-Lluis Larriba-Pey[2]

[1] Informatics Institute, University of Amsterdam, Amsterdam, The Netherlands
stijn.heldens@student.uva.nl, a.l.varbanescu@uva.nl
[2] DAMA-UPC, Universitat Politèchnica de Catalunya, Barcelona, Spain
{aprat,larri}@ac.upc.edu

Abstract. Over the last decade, community detection has become an increasingly important topic of research due to its many applications in different fields of research, such as biology and sociology. One example of a modern community detection algorithm is Scalable Community Detection (SCD), which has been shown to produce high-quality results, but its performance remains an issue on large graphs. In this work, we demonstrate how SCD can benefit from the heterogeneity offered by hybrid CPU-GPU platforms by presenting Het-SCD: a heterogeneous version of SCD which combines the larger memory capacity of the CPU with the larger computational power of the GPU. To enable this, we have designed an entirely new version of SCD which efficiently uses the fine-grained parallelism of GPUs. We report performance results on six real-world graphs (up to 1.8 B edges) and six platforms. We observe excellent performance for only the GPU (e.g., 70x speedup over sequential CPU version on graph of 117 M edges) and for combining the CPU and GPU (e.g., 40x speedup for same graph on low-end GPU with insufficient memory to store entire dataset). These results demonstrate that Het-SCD is an excellent solution for large-scale community detection, since it provides high performance while preserving the high quality of the original algorithm.

Keywords: Community detection · Heterogeneous computing · GPU computing · SCD algorithm · WCC metric

1 Introduction

In graph theory, a community is defined as a cluster of densely interconnected vertices which are sparsely connected to the rest of the network (or graph[1]). Community detection, which is the problem of partitioning a network into communities, gives us valuable insight into the structure of complex networks, such as those from biology and sociology [10]. For example, communities can correspond

---

[1] The terms *graph* and *network* are used interchangeably throughout this paper.

© Springer International Publishing Switzerland 2015
S. Hunold et al. (Eds.): Euro-Par 2015 Workshops, LNCS 9523, pp. 209–220, 2015.
DOI: 10.1007/978-3-319-27308-2_18

to proteins having similar functions in protein-protein interaction networks [12], people with the same interests in social networks [15], or researchers working on the same topic in academic collaboration networks [9].

Although much research has gone into understanding the community structure of complex networks and designing community detection algorithms (see [4] for a comprehensive study), no consensus has been reached on how to detect communities and no single algorithm has become universally accepted. Additionally, little effort has been placed on performance, which becomes a problem when the size of these networks grows. Analyzing massive networks consisting of millions, or even billions, of edges can take minutes, or even hours, using state-of-the-art community detection algorithms. Reducing the processing time of these algorithms remains desirable.

Scalable Community Detection (SCD, Sect. 2.2) is an example of a modern algorithm community which has been shown to produce high-quality results. SCD partitions a network into communities by greedily maximizing the *Weighted Community Clustering* (WCC, Sect. 2.1) metric, a novel community quality metric based on triangle counting. SCD has been designed to be highly parallel to run efficiently on modern parallel platforms.

In this work, we show the potential of this algorithm for massively parallel architectures by presenting the first version of SCD specifically designed for GPUs. This version runs the most computationally expensive phase of the algorithm entirely on the GPU. This solution leads to high performance, but requires the entire network to fit into the memory of the device. To tackle this limitation, we have extended this version to *Het-SCD*: a heterogeneous version of SCD which runs on hybrid CPU-GPU platforms. Het-SCD attempts to process as many vertices as possible on one or more GPUs and processes the remaining vertices on the CPU. By doing this, we effectively combine the larger memory capacity of the CPU with the larger computational power of the GPU.

We have evaluated our work on six real-world datasets from the SNAP repository [7], the largest having 1.8 billion edges. The results show that only using the GPU allows Het-SCD to obtain orders of magnitude speedup compared to a sequential CPU implementation. Additionally, our results show that using the GPU is still beneficial for performance even if the size of the network exceeds GPU memory and a fraction of the vertices needs to be processed on the CPU.

2   Background

The *Scalable Community Detection* (SCD) algorithm partitions an undirected unweighted network into communities by maximizing the *Weighted Community Clustering* (WCC) metric. In this section, we briefly introduce WCC and SCD. For more detailed descriptions, we refer to [13,14], respectively.

Fig. 1. The three steps of the SCD algorithm (Sect. 2.2). Het-SCD focuses on the partition refinement (Sect. 3.1).

2.1 The WCC Metric

WCC is a metric that measures the quality of a partitioning of a network into communities. It is based on the intuition that vertices close more triangles with vertices inside the same community than with those outside the community.

Given an undirected unweighted graph $G = (V, E)$, a vertex $x \in V$, and a community $C \subseteq V$, let $t(x, C)$ be the number of triangles that vertex x closes with vertices in C and let $vt(x, C)$ be the number of vertices in C which close at least one triangle with x and a third vertex from C. The cohesion of vertex x to community C is defined as in Eq. 1.

$$WCC(x, C) = \begin{cases} \frac{t(x,C)}{t(x,V)} \cdot \frac{vt(x,V)}{|C\setminus\{x\}|+vt(x,V)-vt(x,C)} & \text{if } t(x,V) \neq 0 \\ 0 & \text{if } t(x,V) = 0 \end{cases} \tag{1}$$

Now, let $\mathcal{P} = \{C_1, \ldots, C_k\}$ be a partition of V, i.e., $C_1 \cup \ldots \cup C_k = V$ and $C_i \cap C_j = \emptyset$ if $i \neq j$. Define C^x as the community to which vertex x belongs. The WCC of $\mathcal{P}$ is defined as in the average $WCC(x, C^x)$ over all vertices x.

2.2 The Scalable Community Detection Algorithm

The SCD algorithm takes a graph $G = (V, E)$, where $n = |V|$ and $m = |E|$, and partitions G into communities by greedily maximizing WCC. Figure 1 shows the three steps of the algorithm: preprocessing, initial partition and partition refinement.

Preprocessing. During preprocessing, the number of triangles closed by each edge is counted. Using this data, the number of triangles closed by each vertex calculated. Edges which do not close any triangles are deleted from the graph since they do not affect the WCC. Vertices which become isolated after this step are also removed: they will be assigned to new singleton communities afterwards. The time complexity of this stage is $\mathcal{O}(m \log n)$ [14], assuming a quasi-linear relation between n and m, i.e., $\mathcal{O}(m) \sim \mathcal{O}(n \log n)$.

Initial Parition. A fast heuristic [14] is used to assign the vertices to initial communities. The vertices are visited in descending order of clustering coefficient[2] (calculated using data from preprocessing) and assigned to newly created

---

[2] The clustering coefficient cc of a vertex x is defined as $cc = 2t/d(d-1)$ where t is the number of triangles x closes and d is the degree of x.

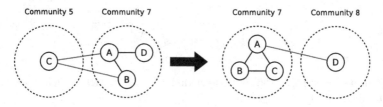

Fig. 2. Results of one refinement iteration: vertices A and B stay in community 7 (action (1)), vertex C is transferred to community 7 (action (2)), and vertex D is placed in a new community (action (3)).

communities. The most expensive operation of this phase is sorting the vertices, which requires $\mathcal{O}(n \log n)$ time.

Partition Refinement. The initial partition serves as input to the refinement phase in which the WCC is iteratively improved. Figure 2 demonstrates one iteration of this phase. In each iteration, all vertices performs the action which leads to the largest increase in WCC. There are three possible types of actions:

(1) **No action**: the vertex stays in its current community.
(2) **Remove**: the vertex is removed from its current community and placed alone in a newly created community.
(3) **Transfer**: the vertex is transferred from its current community to the community of one of its neighbors.

Action (1) does not affect the WCC. Actions (2) and (3) do affect the WCC, but accurately computing the improvement is computationally expensive since it requires recounting many internal triangles in the network. Prat et al. [14] proposed a constant-time approximation model to estimate the impact of these two actions on the WCC. This model allows one to estimate the improvement in WCC when adding/removing a vertex x to/from community C, given the community statistics of C (number of vertices and number of boundary/internal edges), the number of edges from vertex x towards community C and the average clustering coefficient of the entire network.

Note that all vertices select and apply their best action *in parallel*, thus exposing massive parallelism. At the end of each iteration, the WCC of the resulting partition is calculated and the algorithm continues with a new iteration unless the overall increase in WCC is less than a given threshold. Each iteration takes $\mathcal{O}(m \log n)$ time [14]. The number of iterations required to reach convergence depends on the size and the topology of the graph.

3   Design and Implementation

We have designed and implemented Het-SCD: a heterogeneous version of SCD for CPU-GPU platforms. First, we discuss the massively parallel version of SCD which we designed specifically for GPUs. Next, we discuss how we extended this version to support hybrid CPU-GPU platforms. Finally, we discuss how to automatically distribute the vertices of a network over multiple devices.

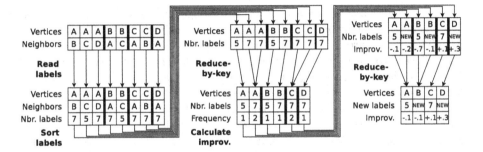

Fig. 3. Procedure used to determine new labels for vertices of graph in Fig. 2.

3.1   The Massively Parallel Version

For our current massively parallel version of SCD, we focused our attention to the partition refinement phase (see Fig. 1) since this is the most expensive phase of the algorithm. After the preprocessing and initial partition phases (performed on the CPU), each vertex is assigned a label corresponding to the identifier of its community. This labeling is transferred to the GPU, together with the graph in *compressed sparse row* format, and the data collected during preprocessing.

Each refinement iteration is performed entirely on the GPU. The three steps of each iteration are: update the labels, collect community statistics, and calculate the WCC.

Update Labels. Updating the vertices of the labels is done by, for each vertex, evaluating all possible actions (Sect. 2.2) and applying the action which leads to the largest increase in WCC. A straight-forward solution to do this using a *vertex-centric* approach, i.e., assigning each vertex to a thread. Each vertex is updated by iterating over its neighbors, keeping track of the frequencies its neighboring labels using an associate array, evaluating the benefit of each possible action, and applying the most beneficial action.

However, a vertex-centric approach is not suitable for massively parallel architectures for a number of reasons. First, it leads to severe **load imbalance**: The work per vertex is determined by its degree and the degree distribution of real-world networks usually follows a *power law* [9], i.e., many low-degree vertices and few high-degree vertices. Second, the amount of **parallelism** is limited: evaluating all possible actions for a single vertex is done sequentially even though it can be parallelized. Third, associative arrays, such as binary trees or hash tables, are often not efficient on massively parallel architectures since they require **dynamic memory allocation** and have poor **memory coalescing**.

To tackle these challenges, we have designed, from the ground up, a new produce to update the vertices using an *action-centric* approach, i.e., all actions for all vertices are evaluated in parallel. Our approach is based on generic global parallel primitives, such as `sort` and `reduce`, to obtain high hardware utilization since many of these primitives have been extensively researched.

Our procedure starts with a sorted directed edge list of the network. For each edge, the label of the incoming endpoint is read, resulting in a list of vertex-label pairs. These pairs are sorted using a global *segmented sort*[3] to place matching pairs adjacent to each other. The frequency of each vertex-label pair (v, C) corresponds to the number of edges between vertex v and community C. A reduce-by-key[4] operation is used to count the frequency of each pair.

For all vertex-label-frequency triples (v, C, f), the improvement in WCC that results from transferring vertex v to community C (action (2)) is calculated using the approximation model (Sect. 2.2). If vertex v is already assigned to community C, the improvement when removing v from C (action (3)) is calculated instead. Finally, another reduce-by-key operation is used select the best action for each vertex. Every vertex adopts the resulting label if the corresponding improvement is positive, other it keeps its current label (action (1)).

For our prototype, we used the reduce-by-key and segemented sort primitives from the Modern GPU library [1].

Collect Community Statistics. Changing the labels of the vertices affects the community statistics (number of vertices and number of internal/boundary edges), so these need to be recalculated. The statistics are updated by processing all vertices and edges in parallel and incrementing counters using atomics.

Calculate WCC. The final step of each iteration is calculating the new WCC to determine whether another iteration is necessary. The only values from Eq. 1 which are not known for each vertex x are $t(x, C^x)$ and $vt(x, C^x)$. The problem of computing these values is similar to the well-studied problem of triangle counting, with the exception that we are only interested in *internal* triangles, i.e., triangles for which all endpoints lie within the same community.

A possible solution to this problem is to intersect the adjacency list of the endpoints of every edge and check, for each triangle found, whether it is internal. However, this method is inefficient since, in practice, only a small fraction of all triangles is internal. Therefore, we prune the graph by first removing all inter-community edges, thus making all triangles internal, and intersect the pruned adjacency lists. This approach exposes a lot of parallelism since both pruning the graph and intersecting adjacency lists can be done in parallel.

Once the WCC of every vertex has been calculated, the average is calculated using a reduction operation and the result is transferred back to the host, which decides whether another iteration is necessary.

3.2   The Heterogeneous Version

The massively parallel version of SCD presented above is able to perform the entire refinement phase on the GPU, but it required the entire network to be

---

[3] Segmented sort takes a list of consecutive non-uniform segments and sorts each one.

[4] Reduce-by-key divides a list of key-value pairs into segments with matching consecutive keys and reduces the values in each segment to a single value.

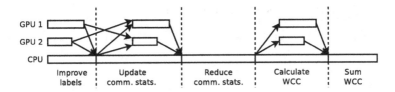

Fig. 4. The steps of refinement phase for our heterogeneous version when using two GPUs.

stored in GPU memory thus limiting the size of the networks that can be processed. To tackle this challenge, we extended this version to *Het-SCD*: a heterogeneous version of SCD which processes as many vertices as possible on one or more GPUs and the remaining vertices on the CPU.

Het-SCD requires each vertex to be assigned to either the CPU or a GPU, resulting in a partitioning of the network into components. Vertices that belong to a component are known as the *core* vertices of the component and adjacent vertices are known as *halo* vertices. Each vertex is thus a core vertex in exactly one component and can duplicated as a halo vertex in several components.

At the start of the refinement phase, subgraphs consisting of core and halo vertices are transferred to the GPUs. Processing the vertices on CPU and GPU in parallel is possible since all steps of the refinement phase are vertex-centric and the vertices of the network are distributed over the available devices. Our GPU implementation is written in CUDA [11] and our CPU implementation was provided by Prat et al. [14] and has been parallelized using OpenMP. The vertices which are processed on GPUs are masked out in the OpenMP implementation.

The CPU and GPUs need to communicate after each step of every refinement iteration as illustrated in Fig. 4. After updating the labels, all devices need to exchange data to update the labels of their halo vertices. After collecting the statistics of the communities in its component, each GPU transfers their statistics to the CPU, the CPU sums the results and transfers the final statistics back to the GPUs. After calculating the average WCC of its vertices, each GPU sends its result to the CPU which computes the overall average WCC.

3.3   Automatic Partitioning

Het-SCD requires, as input, a partitioning of the input network over the available devices without exceeding the memory of any device. This partitioning should have a low cut to minimize the number of halo vertices and thus the storage and communication cost of these vertices. Additionally, the edge density and triangle distribution of all components should be balanced to evenly distribute the work.

We used METIS [6] to automatically partition the network. Each vertex is assigned its degree and number of triangles it closes as weights to evenly distribute the edges and triangles. Experiments show that METIS yields balanced partitionings, but its performance is low. For example, when evenly splitting

Table 1. The platforms used for our experiments.

Platform	GPU name	CUDA	SM count	Clock (Mhz)	Mem (MB)	Bandwidth (GB/s)	Host CPU (Intel Xeon)
A	C2050 (Fermi)	2.0	14	575	2688	144.0	E5620
B	GTX480 (Fermi)	2.0	15	700	1536	177.4	E5620
C	GTX580 (Fermi)	2.0	16	772	3072	193.0	X5650
D	GTX680 (Kepler)	3.0	8	1006	2048	192.3	E5620
E	Tesla K20m (Kepler)	3.5	13	706	5120	208.0	E5-2620
F	GTX-Titan (Kepler)	3.5	14	837	6144	288.0	E5620

Table 2. The networks used for our experiments. **Size** is the size of the graph while **Footprint** includes both the graph and auxiliary data structures in GPU memory.

Name	Type	Vertices (mil.)	Edges (mil.)	Size (MB)	Footprint (MB)
Amazon	Co-purchasing network	0.335	0.926	23.0	54.9
DBLP	Coauthorships network	0.317	1.050	27.2	69.8
YouTube	Social network	1.135	2.988	30.9	92.9
LiveJournal	Social network	3.998	34.681	562.8	1778.6
Orkut	Social network	3.072	117.185	1720.0	5026.6
Friendster	Social network	65.608	1806.067	27812.4	-

LiveJournal (Table 2) into two components, the differences in the number of vertices, edges and triangles are all less than 1 %, but the run-time is 35 s.

4   Evaluation

We have evaluated our solution using six platforms (Table 1) and six networks (Table 2). The networks have been chosen from SNAP [7] since they contain known ground-truth communities, which makes these datasets suitable candidates for a community detection algorithm. The source code and a full report of our results are available online[5]. In this section, we summarize the most important performance results. All our results are averaged over 5 runs. Error bars have been omitted since results were found to be stable. The threshold for WCC improvement was set to 1 % [14].

4.1   The GPU Version

Figure 5 shows the average speedup per iteration of the refinement process for the different GPUs over a serial version of SCD which is based on previous work [14]. This version has also been parallelized for multi-core processors using OpenMP (OMP), and the results for sixteen threads on an Intel E5620 dual-quad-core CPU have been included for comparison.

---

[5] http://github.com/Het-SCD.

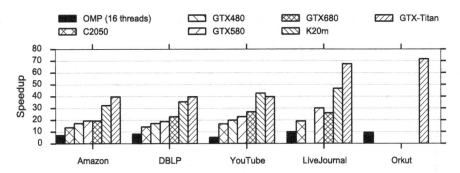

Fig. 5. Average speedup per iteration of the refinement process over serial version on Intel E5620. Missing bars indicate failures due to insufficient memory on the GPU.

The results clearly show that the GPU version is always significantly faster than both the serial and multi-threaded version, regardless of the network or the GPU used. Even the least powerful GPU, the C2050, obtains speedups between 10x and 20x on every graph. The most powerful GPU, the GTX-Titan, obtains speedups from 40x on Amazon up to a massive 70x on Orkut. This is the result of the massive parallelism and increased bandwidth offered by these GPUs.

However, the results also show that the amount of GPU memory is a realistic limitation which cannot be ignored. Friendster has not been included since it does not fit into the memory of any GPU. Orkut is also too large for most of our GPUs and can only be processed by the GTX-Titan. LiveJournal can be processed by most of the GPUs, except the GTX480.

4.2 The Heterogenous Version

The heterogeneous version removes the memory restriction by processing as many vertices as possible on GPUs and the remaining vertices on the CPU.

Figure 6 shows the average time per iteration of the refinement phase for LiveJournal and Orkut when combing CPU and GPU. The results show that Het-SCD can be used to process networks which cannot be processed only by the GPU since they exceed GPU memory. For example, LiveJournal can be processed on the GTX480 by assigning only 20 % of the vertices to the CPU, resulting in a speedup of 3.1x compared to the multi-threaded version and 30.7x compared to the serial version. Orkut can be processed on the K20m by also assigning only 20 % of the vertices to the host, giving a speedup of 4.5x and 41.5x compared to the multi-threaded and serial version, respectively.

The heterogeneous version can also use multiple GPUs simultaneously. Figure 7 shows the speedup for LiveJournal and Orkut when using multiple GTX580 GPUs. For LiveJournal, the speedup is significant up to 4 GPUs. Using more GPUs decreases the speedup due to communication overhead. For Orkut, we have predicted the single GPU performance using information from Fig. 6 since it exceeds the memory of a single GTX580. Using 6 GPUs provides enough memory to process the graph and more GPUs give better performance.

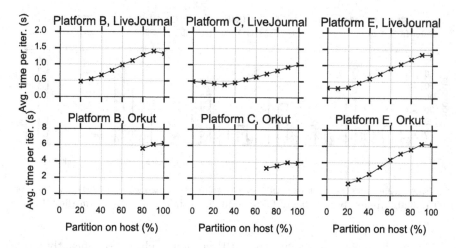

Fig. 6. Average time per iteration of the heterogeneous version for two networks (Live-Journal and Orkut) and three platforms. The number of threads used on the CPU was set to the number of available virtual cores. Missing points indicate failures due to insufficient memory on the GPU.

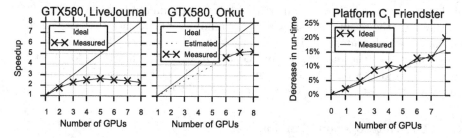

Fig. 7. The speedup when dividing the vertices over multiple GPUs.

Fig. 8. Speedup when combining CPU and GPUs for Friendster.

We also experimented if Friendster, having 1.8 billion edges, can be processed using our solution. Using a back-of-the-envelope calculation, we estimated that 2 % of Friendster can be placed on a single GTX580. We processed this graph by assigning 2 % of the vertices to each GPU and the remaining vertices to the CPU. Figure 8 shows that every added GPU indeed decreases the run-time by roughly additionally 2 %. When using 8 GPUs, the overall run-time is reduced by 20 % (6.1 s per iteration).

4.3 End-to-End Performance

Up to this point, we have only reported the performance of the refinement phase, which is the part we have accelerated. However, the complete Het-SCD application also reads the network from disk, performs preprocessing, creates the initial

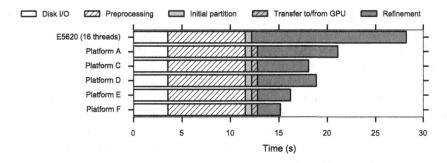

Fig. 9. The end-to-end execution time for LiveJournal.

communities and transfers data between main memory and GPU memory. These steps have not been accelerated by Het-SCD. An example of a complete execution profile for LiveJournal is shown in Fig. 9, the other datasets show a similar result. The figure shows that the refinement phase accounts for more than 55 % of the total execution time when using 16 threads. When using the GPU, this time is reduced by a factor of between 2x and 7x (depending on the chosen GPU), reducing the total execution time by between 25 % and 50 %, which is significant. We propose that parallelizing the preprocessing step and reducing disk I/O should complement Het-SCD, but consider this effort to be out of the scope of this paper.

5 Related Work

Many community detection algorithms have been proposed [4], but only few have been implemented on GPUs. Soman et al. [16] proposed a GPU implementation of an algorithm based on label propagation. Cheong et al. [3] and Staudt et al [17] designed a GPU implementation around the Louvain method [2], an algorithm based on modularity maximization. However, label propagation suffers from "label epidemic" where some labels manage to "plague" the network [8] and modularity maximization suffers from the resolution limit [5]. SCD is a novel algorithm which has been proven to be robust and find meaningful and cohesive communities [14].

Staudt et al [17] also extended their Louvain-based algorithm to support hybrid CPU-GPUs platforms. However, they achieved this by partitioning the graph, running the algorithm on each subgraph, and combining the results. This modification lowers the quality of the original algorithm. We designed Het-SCD to preserve the original algorithm to ensure its high quality, while providing higher performance.

6 Conclusion and Future Work

High-quality community detection in large networks is becoming an important requirement for modern data mining applications. In this work, we target both the performance and scale of the problem: we design the first massively parallel version of SCD, a high-quality community detection algorithm, and an extension of this version to a flexible, large-scale heterogeneous version. Our experimental results demonstrate (1) the superior performance of the GPU version compared to both the sequential and the parallel CPU execution, and (2) the ability of the heterogeneous version to achieve significant performance gains by processing large graphs on the CPU and multiple GPUs in parallel.

There are further steps to be taken to improve Het-SCD. So far, we have only accelerated the refinement phase on the GPU. In the near future, we plan to implement a parallel version of the preprocessing phase and initial partition as well. Finally, the impact of the partitioning on the performance of Het-SCD must be explored. While METIS yields balanced partitions with a low cut size, its performance is low. Designing a custom partition algorithm specifically for Het-SCD might give higher performance.

References

1. Baxter, S.: Modern GPU. http://moderngpu.com/ (2013)
2. Blondel, V.D., Guillaume, J.L., Lambiotte, R., Lefebvre, E.: Fast unfolding of communities in large networks. J. Stat. Mech: Theory Exp. **2008**(10), P10008 (2008)
3. Cheong, C.Y., Huynh, H.P., Lo, D., Goh, R.S.M.: Hierarchical parallel algorithm for modularity-based community detection using GPUs. In: Wolf, F., Mohr, B., an Mey, D. (eds.) Euro-Par 2013. LNCS, vol. 8097, pp. 775–787. Springer, Heidelberg (2013)
4. Fortunato, S.: Community detection in graphs. Phys. Rep. **486**(3), 75–174 (2010)
5. Fortunato, S., Barthélemy, M.: Resolution limit in community detection. Proc. Nat. Acad. Sci. **104**(1), 36–41 (2007)
6. Karypis, G., Kumar, V.: A fast and high quality multilevel scheme for partitioning irregular graphs. SIAM J. Sci. Comput. **20**(1), 359–392 (1998)
7. Leskovec, J., Krevl, A.: SNAP datasets: stanford large network dataset collection (2014). http://snap.stanford.edu/data
8. Leung, I.X., Hui, P., Lio, P., Crowcroft, J.: Towards real-time community detection in large networks. Phys. Rev. E **79**(6), 066107 (2009)
9. Newman, M.E.: The structure and function of complex networks. SIAM Rev. **45**(2), 167–256 (2003)
10. Newman, M.E.: Detecting community structure in networks. Eur. Phys. J. B Condens. Matter Complex Syst. **38**(2), 321–330 (2004)
11. NVIDIA Corporation: NVIDIA CUDA C Programming Guide (2011)
12. Palla, G., Derényi, I., Farkas, I., Vicsek, T.: Uncovering the overlapping community structure of complex networks in nature and society. Nature **435**, 814–818 (2005)
13. Prat-Pérez, A., Dominguez-Sal, D., Brunat, J.M., Larriba-Pey, J.L.: Shaping communities out of triangles. In: CIKM 2012. ACM (2012)
14. Prat-Pérez, A., Dominguez-Sal, D., Larriba-Pey, J.L.: High quality, scalable and parallel community detection for large real graphs. In: WWW 2014 (2014)
15. Scott, J.: Social Network Analysis. Sage, London (2012)
16. Soman, J., Narang, A.: Fast community detection algorithm with GPUs and multicore architectures. In: IPDPS 2011. IEEE (2011)
17. Staudt, C., Meyerhenke, H.: Engineering parallel algorithms for community detection in massive networks. IEEE TPDS **PP**(99), 1 (2015)

A Design Proposal for a Next Generation Scientific Software Framework

Anshu Dubey[(✉)] and Daniel T. Graves

Computational Research Division, Lawrence Berkeley National Laboratory,
University of California, Berkeley, CA 94720, USA
adubey@lbl.gov

Abstract. High performance scientific software has many unique and challenging characteristics. These codes typically consist of many different stages of computation with different algorithms and components with diverse requirements. These heterogeneous algorithms, coupled with platform heterogeneity, create serious performance challenges. To retain performance, portability and maintainability of the software on heterogeneous platforms, more abstractions have to be integrated into the software design. Most of these abstractions are still in the research stage and scientific codes have barely started using them. However, it is urgent that we start considering the abstraction interplay in designing the next generation of software architecture. We propose a software architecture for PDE-based scientific codes that combines three abstractions in a code framework suitable for expected heterogeneity in platforms, while retaining separation of concerns, performance and portability of the software. We support our proposal with an example design for an adaptive mesh refinement based framework.

1 Introduction

Scientific software used for simulation of complex multiphysics phenomena has many characteristics that make it uniquely challenging to architect and maintain. The codes have many different stages of computation, each with different algorithms and components. The components can have diverse requirements from the system hardware and software. Often these requirements conflict with one another, where an optimization for one is a detriment to another. The many moving parts in the application need to interoperate, but often the mechanisms used to achieve interoperability are awkward and inefficient. Furthermore, the codes typically run on high-end high-performance-computing (HPC) platforms which are expected to become increasingly more heterogeneous. The codes are expected to use the platforms effectively because these are extremely expensive and rare resources. It will take a combination of carefully thought out design, hard-nosed trade-offs, and good orchestration capabilities in the framework for a code to meet the demands placed upon it.

The main features of almost all successful frameworks of today are components that encapsulate a functionality, composability of those components, and

© Springer International Publishing Switzerland 2015
S. Hunold et al. (Eds.): Euro-Par 2015 Workshops, LNCS 9523, pp. 221–232, 2015.
DOI: 10.1007/978-3-319-27308-2_19

a separation of concerns. The frameworks are designed so that the sections of the code that pertain to the science of the application can be written and verified as sequential code. These sections are then plugged into the framework with a wrapper. The internals of the framework handle the parallelization and data management. There are several examples of such application codes and frameworks [4,5,15,16,20] that have served their respective scientific communities for a decade or more, and have even branched out to serve other communities.These codes are continuing to serve their communities, but with a change in the hardware paradigm, they are facing a crisis. In addition to heterogeneity in hardware architecture, the codes will have to deal with higher failure rates and deeper and more varied memory hierarchies. Furthermore, they have to do all this with steadily growing solver diversity which is the inevitable result of increasing the model fidelity. The abstractions that may help to tame some of the diversity are still mostly in the research stage. The application code developers have barely begun experimenting with these abstractions. As a result, there is little understanding about what design choices are likely to yield a long-lasting, nimble and portable high performance code that will stand the test of time.

For the forthcoming exascale era, the design space is bigger than ever with more programming abstractions to be incorporated into the software architecture. There has been investment in research on programming models and abstractions that could make it easier to code for the increasingly heterogeneous platforms of the future. There has also been some investment in algorithms that might better deal with new challenges such as decreasing memory per processing unit and the need to minimize data movement. How to architect scientific software with many moving parts into a composable whole, however, remains an open question.

Some consensus is beginning to emerge about which abstractions might prove to be the most useful. Here, we take note of three front runners among programming abstractions; namely, tasking, tiling and embedded domain-specific languages (eDSL). We propose a general software architecture that combines these abstractions in a way that separation of concerns is maintained or even enhanced. The abstraction lifting provided in the proposed architecture applies to a broad class of applications that primarily use partial-differential-equation solvers. We illustrate the applicability of this general purpose architecture with a more specific example of a framework for adaptive mesh refinement (AMR) based codes.

2 Requirements

Many scientific codes that are operating at petascale today have had years of investment in solvers for the physical phenomena they model. Typically, such codes tend to support a large community of researchers which makes code maintainability an important requirement. Even with the relatively uniform fat-node architectures that are still around, there is enough variability in code behavior that performance portability has been an important consideration. Most codes avoid too many platform specific optimizations except in very limited performance critical kernels, where multiple alternative implementations might have existed for different platforms. As the diversity in the platform architecture is increasing this is becoming a bigger challenge. In the past, it was only a matter of performance, now it has also become a matter of being able to use the platform at all. In short, the need for platform-specific code appears to be increasing. Mitigating this challenge would require a framework to support code transformations for different target platforms while allowing the high level code to remain unchanged.

Many long standing obstacles to meeting the above requirements still exist. There has always been a trade-off between modularity and performance. Modularity is necessary for maintainable and reusable code, but it compromises performance. Even today, inter-procedural analysis is unable to deliver the performance across invocations of different functions. Flattening the code by fusing functions manually has proven to increase the execution speed considerably. Similarly, easy adaptability to various different architectures requires a small and nimble code base. This is at odds with the increasing code size from adding more capabilities for higher model fidelity. Some of these conflicting requirements were met in the past through a holistic approach to optimization, where trade-offs were carefully considered and adopted [6]. For example, most composable codes run at a very small fraction (3–8 %) of the peak performance of the machine because they sacrifice performance for multiphysics and composability. In planning of simulation campaigns, the focus is on achieving the overall science objective. Sometimes this means using suboptimal options for individual components. The framework should be able to facilitate such unorthodox approaches and therefore should provide hooks for being able to make these choices.

With the advent of heterogeneity within and across platforms, code and performance portability have become much more critical. At the same time they have become much more difficult to achieve. This is tractable only if coding is done to higher levels of abstraction, with many more tools providing the intermediate levels of support. Normally, it would be more sensible to wait until the current research in abstractions has been hardened into products before considering how to use them to redesign the codes. However, the codes that need to change can be huge and take many person-years to refactor, while the platforms are already becoming more heterogeneous. Therefore, code redesign must begin as soon as possible.

3   Approach

One of the very first choices to make in designing a framework is which abstractions to use, and how to provide footholds for the abstractions in the framework so that they maintain separation of concerns. Every multiphysics high performance computing code has several levels of complexity, each one of which may need a different expertise. While it is true that such interdisciplinary projects demand overlap in the expertise of the participants, it is impossible for any individual to be an expert in everything. Instead, the software design has to be orthogonalized so that various complexities are untangled and experts can focus on what they know best. The complexity of the physical model is typically expressed in terms of parametrized equations. This is the knowledge that the domain scientists provide. The discretization of the equations and the numerical algorithms to solve them are best done by the applied mathematicians. In multicomponent codes, where more than one numerical solver is in use, the issues of data movement and solver interoperability are best managed by the software engineers. The portability and performance of the code on various platforms are best handled by high performance computing experts. A good framework design would allow mostly independent development of these various aspects of the code without significant overlap in expertise.

One way to look at separation of concerns is to abstract the knowledge of the resources from the computation and vice-versa, and differentiate the physical view from the logical view. To illustrate this abstraction with an example, we consider domain decomposition of structured meshes. Here the logical view of the mesh is a self contained collection of discrete points where the "active" points are updated during solution evolution, while the "passive" points are only used in the computations, but are not updated. In rectangular grids the passive points are referred to as "halo" cells surrounding the active grid Here the physical view could be the entire physical domain where the halo points are filled with the values derived from the physical boundaries, or it could be an arbitrarily-sized section of the domain. The section itself could come from one or more physical boundaries or it could come entirely from the interior of the domain. The halo cells of the interior face of the domain section are, in effect, virtual points that hold the same values as the real points in the corresponding neighboring section of the domain, therefore they are also referred to as "ghost" cells in literature. The important point to note here is that the solver concerns itself only with the logical view, while under the hood, the infrastructure can manipulate the physical view to orchestrate the computation to best suit the target platform.

Similarly, it should be possible for a numerical algorithm to be expressed in a way that is essentially oblivious to the underlying micro-architecture of the platform. This means not just the layout of the processing units (cores or accelerators), but also the network, the coherency domains and other aspects of memory hierarchy. This can be achieved by writing solvers without explicit indexing into the data structures, but with the flexibility to operate on arbitrary chunks of provided data. One example of such an approach is stencil-based abstractions for mitigating the hardware dependence of solvers [11,14]. This approach cleanly shields the numerics from the vagaries of the memory hierarchy and data movement. The orchestration of the data to be operated on can be left to the infrastructure.

In the next few sections we describe how we can leverage three of the abstractions that are gaining momentum to design a highly portable, extensible and performant scientific software. These abstractions are embedded domain-specific languages, tiling, and runtime dynamic tasking.

3.1 Embedded Domain-specific-languages

The idea behind eDSL's in our context is to provide abstractions in a high level language that address some domain's repeatedly-used functionality. The abstractions make the job of the compiler easier by constraining the semantics, allowing compilers to generate more optimized code. While it is difficult to persuade a community to switch over to an unproven language, eDSL's provide a way out. They live embedded within high-level languages, and therefore provide an on-ramp. An eDSL can be particularly useful to its target community if it takes care of abstraction lifting for the numerical solvers.

The current generation of computational kernels follow strictly prescriptive semantics. This is true not because of model or algorithmic requirements, but because the available programming models dictate it, the developers understand it, and it was effective on the machines of the time when the codes were developed. In truth, it is often completely unnecessary to be prescriptive in the description of operations, and DSL's such as the tensor-contraction-engine in NWChem, and Nebo-wasatch, an eDSL for updating stencils in Uintah, provide higher level constructs for precisely and concisely specifying the solver algorithm. Another example of successful use of eDSL on heterogeneous platforms is Stella [8]. In all these instances the back-ends transform the human-readable eDSL code into unreadable but highly performant code for the target platform. For each new platform one or more back-ends must be developed, but that is not a concern of the algorithm implementer. This results in a very robust separation of concerns between performance tuning and algorithm development.

3.2 Tiling

Because future machines will be more hierarchical, software design should orient itself to benefit from the hierarchy rather than be challenged by it. This means that the applications must identify the granularities within the models and the algorithms, and match the application granularity with the appropriate level in the machine hierarchy. To some extent, applications are already doing this with the mixed MPI-threading model. As a simple example one can consider a finite difference solver for a partial differential equation on a uniformly discretized mesh. Here the coarse-grain parallelism is achieved by decomposing the domain spatially, where each section of the decomposed domain is mapped to one MPI rank. The most prevalent way to achieve fine-grain parallelism is to exploit the relative independence of operations within loops of the computational kernels evolving the solution by threading the loops. In current multi- or many- core architectures, an MPI rank is typically the node, whereas threads map to different cores within the node. Thus different parallel granularities of the application are cleanly mapped to the two levels of platform architecture hierarchy. This approach is suboptimal because the resulting parallelism is fragile. It can easily break if the loop is modified without exercising sufficient care for it to remain thread-safe. It also violates the separation of concerns between computational kernel and parallelism. Furthermore, this approach also does not address the issue of machine heterogeneity; the code has to change with every different architecture.

A more robust way to expose fine-grained parallelism is to use tiling, especially when one is operating with rectangular domains. A library like TIDA [19] provides hierarchy within tiles and assumes the responsibility of mapping tiles to the most suitable hardware resources. TIDA not only maintains the isolation of kernels from parallelism, but also separates the "within node" parallelism and memory layout handling from macro-parallelism.

3.3 Task Based Runtime Support

The currently dominant bulk-synchronous model is suitable for the distributed memory parallelization model. Enough computation is allotted to each processing unit that the cost of bulk-synchronization is amortized. Scientific codes have been designed for bulk-synchronization not because of any fundamental algorithmic necessity, but because that is a relatively easy way to satisfy dependencies. However, this mode of computation is known to have limitations when different components of the code demand different load distribution or when there is heterogeneity in the performance of individual processing units because of error correction or clock drift. The high performance scientific community is reaching consensus that dynamic runtime task scheduling could be a more desirable model. Dynamic runtimes have been demonstrated to be useful in many situations, such as dense linear algebra [9] and grid workflows [1]. There has been some success in large scientific codes as well, most notably Uintah [12,13] using their own runtime and NAMD [17] using charm++ [10]. However, the majority of codes have either not integrated dynamic runtimes, or are in the early stages of experimentation. Many independent runtime systems and task based execution models are being developed in the community. Gilmanov et al. [7] provide a good summary.

3.4 Proposed Architecture

Fig. 1 provides an overview schematic of scientific code architectures as they exist in many codes now (the left panel), and the modifications to the architecture with abstraction lifting that could help tackle the platform heterogeneity and massive parallelism. Note that in both views different virtual views (effectively programming abstractions) map to different concerns of the code. The boxes in the schematic are color coded to indicate the type of role played by the entity in the box in the overall scheme. Orange boxes represent the base code and its physical view. The pink boxes represent logical or virtual view of the corresponding quantities. The green boxes are for the tools that enable the added abstractions in the code. The blue boxes are for the target optimization. In the figure the top left hand corner box represents the whole application code covering the entire domain, including all the operators that need to be applied to it. Note that we make no assertions about either the discretization or the type of operators. The two branches out of this box represent the spatial and functional decompositions. Again we place no constraints on what the decompositions ought to be for individual applications, each application will find its own granularities and decompose accordingly. The decompositions provide means for employing the logical views of the application in the framework design. Thus the spatial decomposition results in a logical view which allows the numerics to ignore the physical layout of the problem domain in the implementation. With appropriate abstractions in parallelization, for example tiling, and an eDSL for supporting higher level expression of the numerical algorithms, code transformation tools can be employed to optimize the computation and handling or memory hierarchy. The same abstraction also helps in alleviating the challenges posed by platform heterogeneity since code transformation tools can have different processing elements as their targets.

Similar to spatial decomposition, functional decomposition can be done at a granularity best suited for each specific application. In some instances, it would be at the level of one operator. In others, the operator itself may have inherent parallelism capable of finer decomposition. Here two different abstractions can come into play. One is a different class of code transformation techniques that allow operator fusion for memory access and compute optimization. The other is treating each decomposed function object as a task with some dependencies on other tasks. When viewed as tasks, the functions can be assigned to any resource at any time as long as their dependencies have been met. Thus this virtualization makes it possible to optimize for parallelization and scaling if a good dynamic scheduler can be built. In the next section we take these general principles and apply them to a framework for applications that use structured adaptive mesh refinement (SAMR).

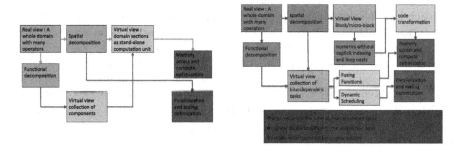

Fig. 1. Schematics of scientific code architecture. The left panel shows the current architecture, while the right panel shows one set of possible modifications to the architecture that could tackle heterogeneity.

4   Example: Structured AMR

Adaptive mesh refinement is a technique applied to logically Cartesian meshes when the target application has many length scales that live in different parts of the domain. Since the length scale dictates the spacing between the consecutive points in the discretized mesh, clearly both memory and computation are saved when fine resolution is used only where the physical conditions of the solution demand it (see [2]).

4.1 Granularities and Decomposition

In any multiphysics AMR code, there are two clear granularities that stand out: a block/patch and the physics operators. A block with its halo of virtual or ghost cells (as they are more generally known) is already used as the logical view of the domain by physics operators in almost all codes that rely on explicit or semi-implicit methods for solving partial differential equations. Thus a block readily maps to the third box on top in Fig. 1. Similarly, most time integration follows operator splitting, which means that operators are applied on the solution data sequentially. Therefore they provide a readily available means of functional decomposition. The current generation code architectures don't view them as such, Uintah being one of the few exceptions. AMR Codes typically iterate over their collection of blocks for one operator, updating the block data as each operator finishes. Often this generates a false dependence, because in most situations the order of application of operators does not matter physically. A simple reformulation where the updates from physics operators are accumulated in a scratch space instead of being applied to the state data in the blocks immediately removes this artificial dependency. Now the application of individual operator on an individual block can be treated as a stand-alone task that can be scheduled when its dependencies are met. This provides us a map into the bottom left box in the schematic of Fig. 1.

Another granularity that is inherent in AMR codes is that of a "level". Recall that each level has all blocks/patches that have same spatial resolution (dx). In most instances, the timestep dt also refines with the same ratio as dx, and is uniform across the level. There is some cross-level interaction. For example, reconciliation of physical quantities such as fluxes at the fine-coarse boundaries, ghost cell filling at those same boundaries and time synchronization of adjacent levels when needed. But levels manage their own meta information and time evolution. We can exploit these characteristics of the levels to enhance the macro-parallelism flexibility. The mapping of boxes in a level to different processing elements can be abstracted from the logical view of all boxes within the level. Once this is done, the processing elements allocated to levels can be adjusted as needed altering the logical view, and therefore bulk of the code.

4.2 Micro-parallelism

So far we have focused on virtualization of the decomposed space and functions along with macro-parallelism. In the many-core and accelerators based heterogeneous world, this is not enough. Finer-grained parallelism potential needs to be exposed in ways that can be harnessed flexibly for different architectures. In AMR, since we already have the abstraction of a "block", in principle it should

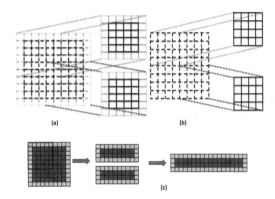

Fig. 2. Exposing micro-parallelism in a parameterizable way

be possible to break a block into smaller blocks and provide arbitrarily fine parallelism. The problem with that approach is that as the block size becomes smaller, the memory used for halo cells begins to dominate. The more common approach of explicit loop threading is not a very desirable solution because that makes the code harder to maintain, and needs to be retuned for every platform. A better approach is to eliminate the in-place update of the state within a block (recall that this is also desirable for functional decomposition). Figure 2 explains how this concept can be exploited to expose greater spatial parallelism through tiling. Here, if we parametrize the index space of the block in order to implement the operators, then the logical view of the tiles within the source block looks like panel (a) in the figure. Note that though the tiles have overlapping cells, they are read only, so they don't present any obstacle to threading. The destination block has similar logical and physical views with no overlap between tiles as shown in panel (b). Because of lack of overlap in the destination tiles there are no spurious dependencies or write conflicts and therefore no obstacle to threading.

Panel (c) shows how this parametrization also allows customization of tile shapes to best match the target processing element. A tile can be arbitrarily small, rectangular or thin, as long as its index space is provided as a parameter, the tiling abstraction can manage it. This is particularly useful when faced with processing elements that prefer to use large vectors or those that have small caches with small cache lines. Depending on the depth of memory hierarchy within the node, it may even be useful to coalesce some of the blocks (similar to Fig. 2(c)) to map them to NUMA/coherence domains.

In our design we use dynamic scheduling within the node. This choice maintains the separation of macro-parallelism from micro-parallelism. Here, the load-balancing generated by regridding of AMR continues to be managed at the macro/distributed memory parallel level. The tasks are generated from the combination of spatial and functional decompositions described earlier. In order for the task based execution model to be useful there should be enough load within the node to amortize the overheads. Confining the dynamic scheduling to within the node limits the size of the dependence graph which can grow non-linearly if done globally. To enable dynamic scheduling very few changes needs to occur in the solver code. One change is that if the solver iterates over blocks explicitly, it has to either let that go completely or make it non-prescriptive (i.e. change from "for" to "while"). The second change is that the solver must articulate any dependencies that cannot be inferred by the framework from the index space information available to it. For example, if order of application of operators matters then the framework has to be informed of it, and the operators have to express it.

4.3 Solvers

AMR codes mostly rely upon explicit or semi-implicit solvers. If need for implicit methods arises, codes typically use dedicated linear algebra libraries which assume control for the duration of the solve. Hence for this discussion we ignore the challenges of implicit solve and focus entirely on explicit and semi-implicit solvers. The chief characteristic of these solvers is that an update of a point in the mesh can be described as a stencil. Stencils can be small or large, but they all collect information from their neighborhood which can be precisely specified geometrically. A stencil update is essentially a weighted sum of specified points in the neighborhood of the point being update. The neighboring points can be specified by shift relative to the target as shown in an example of five point stencil in Fig. 3 (no weights are shown). Stencil computations and their optimization [18] is an active research area with many stencil DSL or eDSL languages under development. Some, such as Stella [8] and the Nebo-Wasatch in Uintah [3] have been successfully deployed in production codes with different back-ends for supporting different hardware. The motivation is the same, they seek to eliminate explicit indexing and dimensioning in expressing the involved arithmetic. Since solvers are the most computation-intensive parts of the code, a good code transformation tool from high level eDSL to optimized code will be critical in achieving performance portability across heterogeneity.

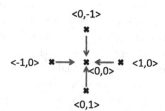

Fig. 3. Example of shifts in a five-point stencil update

5   Conclusions

We propose a software architecture for the next generation of platforms by using a set of programming abstractions that are gaining ground in the community. Our proposed methodology focuses on using these abstractions in ways that function orthogonally to one another, and therefore do not diminish each others' impacts. Additionally, they maintain the separation of concerns which allows a team to map each member's expertise to the most appropriate aspect of code development. We cite efforts where a code has integrated one or two of these abstractions and has had success. We present a way of incorporating these abstractions seamlessly in a framework and we believe we have provided ample reasoning to support that claim. We firmly believe that the scientific codes of today must begin to be refactored to be prepared for future machines, otherwise scientific discovery through simulations will meet with a serious setback.

Acknowledgments. This material is based upon work supported by the U.S. Department of Energy, Office of Science, Office of Advanced Scientific Computer Research.

References

1. Ayyub, S., Abramson, D.: Gridrod: a dynamic runtime scheduler for grid workflows. In: Proceedings of the 21st Annual International Conference on Supercomputing, pp. 43–52. ACM (2007)
2. Berger, M., Oliger, J.: Adaptive mesh refinement for hyperbolic partial differential equations. J. Comput. Phy. **53**, 484–512 (1984)
3. Berzins, M., Luitjens, J., Meng, Q., Harman, T., Wight, C., Peterson, J.: Uintah - a scalable framework for hazard analysis. In: TG 2010: Proceedings of 2010 TeraGrid Conference. ACM, New York (2010)
4. Case, D., Babin, V., Berryman, J., Betz, R., Cai, Q., Cerutti, D., Cheatham Iii, T., Darden, T., Duke, R., Gohlke, H., et al.: Amber 14 (2014)
5. Dubey, A., Antypas, K., Ganapathy, M., Reid, L., Riley, K., Sheeler, D., Siegel, A., Weide, K.: Extensible component-based architecture for FLASH, a massively parallel, multiphysics simulation code. Parallel Comput. **35**(10–11), 512–522 (2009)
6. Dubey, A., Calder, A., Daley, C., Fisher, R., Graziani, C., Jordan, G., Lamb, D., Reid, L., Townsley, D.M., Weide, K.: Pragmatic optimizations for better scientific utilization of large supercomputers. Int. J. High Perform. Comput. Appl. **27**(3), 360–373 (2013)
7. Gilmanov, T., Anderson, M., Brodowicz, M., Sterling, T.: Application characteristics of many-tasking execution models. In: Proceedings of the 2013 International Conference on Parallel and Distributed Processing Techniques and Applications (PDPTA). Citeseer (2013)
8. Gysi, T., Fuhrer, O., Osuna, C., Cumming, B., Schulthess, T.: Stella: a domain-specific embedded language for stencil codes on structured grids. In: EGU General Assembly Conference Abstracts, vol. 16, p. 8464 (2014)
9. Haidar, A., Ltaief, H., YarKhan, A., Dongarra, J.: Analysis of dynamically scheduled tile algorithms for dense linear algebra on multicore architectures. Concurr. Comput.: Pract. Exp. **24**(3), 305–321 (2012)

10. Kale, L.V., Bohm, E., Mendes, C.L., Wilmarth, T., Zheng, G.: Programming petascale applications with Charm++ and AMPI. Petascale Comput.: Algorithms Appl. 1, 421–441 (2007)
11. Maruyama, N., Nomura, T., Sato, K., Matsuoka, S.: Physis: an implicitly parallel programming model for stencil computations on large-scale gpu-accelerated supercomputers. In: 2011 International Conference for High Performance Computing, Networking, Storage and Analysis (SC), pp. 1–12. IEEE (2011)
12. Meng, Q., Luitjens, J., Berzins, M.: Dynamic task scheduling for the uintah framework. In: Proceedings of the 3rd IEEE Workshop on Many-Task Computing on Grids and Supercomputers (MTAGS 2010) (2010). http://www.sci.utah.edu/publications/meng10/Meng_TaskSchedulingUintah2010.pdf
13. Notz, P.K., Pawlowski, R.P., Sutherland, J.C.: Graph-based software design for managing complexity and enabling concurrency in multiphysics PDE software. ACM Trans. Math. Softw. 39(1), 1:1–1:21 (2012)
14. Orchard, D.A., Bolingbroke, M., Mycroft, A.: Ypnos: declarative, parallel structured grid programming. In: Proceedings of the 5th ACM SIGPLAN Workshop on Declarative Aspects Of Multicore Programming, DAMP 2010, pp. 15–24. ACM, New York (2010). http://doi.acm.org/10.1145/1708046.1708053
15. O'Shea, B.W., Bryan, G., Bordner, J., Norman, M.L., Abel, T., Harkness, R., Kritsuk, A.: Introducing Enzo, an AMR cosmology application. In: Plewa, T., Timur, L., Weirs, V. (eds.) Adaptive Mesh Refinement - Theory and Applications. LNCS, vol. 41, pp. 341–349. Springer, Heidelberg (2005)
16. Parker, S.G.: A component-based architecture for parallel multi-physics PDE simulation. Future Gener. Comput. Sys. 22, 204–216 (2006)
17. Phillips, J.C., Braun, R., Wang, W., Gumbart, J., Tajkhorshid, E., Villa, E., Chipot, C., Skeel, R.D., Kale, L., Schulten, K.: Scalable molecular dynamics with namd. J. Comput. Chem. 26(16), 1781–1802 (2005)
18. Stock, K., Kong, M., Grosser, T., Pouchet, L.N., Rastello, F., Ramanujam, J., Sadayappan, P.: A framework for enhancing data reuse via associative reordering. In: Proceedings of the 35th ACM SIGPLAN Conference on Programming Language Design and Implementation, p. 10. ACM (2014)
19. Unat, D., Chan, C., Zhang, W., Bell, J., Shalf, J.: Tiling as a durable abstraction for parallelism and data locality (2013). http://sc13.supercomputing.org/sites/default/files/WorkshopsArchive/pdfs/wp118s1.pdf
20. Valiev, M., Bylaska, E.J., Govind, N., Kowalski, K., Straatsma, T.P., Van Dam, H.J., Wang, D., Nieplocha, J., Apra, E., Windus, T.L., et al.: Nwchem: a comprehensive and scalable open-source solution for large scale molecular simulations. Comput. Phys. Commun. 181(9), 1477–1489 (2010)

Accelerating Direction-Optimized Breadth First Search on Hybrid Architectures

Scott Sallinen[⊠], Abdullah Gharaibeh, and Matei Ripeanu

University of British Columbia, Vancouver, Canada
{scotts,abdullah,matei}@ece.ubc.ca

Abstract. Large scale-free graphs are famously difficult to process efficiently: the skewed vertex degree distribution makes it difficult to obtain balanced partitioning. Our research instead aims to turn this into an advantage by partitioning the workload to match the strength of the individual computing elements in a Hybrid, GPU-accelerated architecture. As a proof of concept we focus on the direction-optimized breadth first search algorithm. We present the key graph partitioning, workload allocation, and communication strategies required for massive concurrency and good overall performance. We show that exploiting specialization enables gains as high as 2.4x in terms of time-to-solution and 2.0x in terms of energy efficiency by adding 2 GPUs to a 2 CPU-only baseline, for synthetic graphs with up to 16 Billion undirected edges as well as for large real-world graphs. We also show that, for a capped energy envelope, it is more efficient to add a GPU than an additional CPU. Finally, our performance would place us at the top of today's [Green]Graph500 challenges for Scale29 graphs.

1 Introduction

Large-scale graph processing plays an important role for a wide range of applications where internal data structures are represented as graphs: from social networks, to protein-protein interactions, to the neuron structure of the human brain. A large class of real-world graphs, the *scale-free graphs*, have a heterogeneous vertex degree distribution: most vertices have a low degree but a few vertices are highly connected [2,10,20].

Breadth First Search (BFS) is the building block for many graph algorithms (e.g., Betweenness Centrality, Connected Components) and it has similar structural properties to other algorithms (e.g., Single Source Shortest Paths - SSSP). BFS also exposes the main challenges in graph processing: data-dependent memory accesses, low compute-to-memory access ratio, and low memory access locality. Additionally, for scale-free graphs, the amount of parallelism exposed is highly heterogeneous and data-dependent. For these reasons the Graph500 [7] and GreenGraph500 [8] graph processing competitions have adopted BFS on scale-free graphs as their main benchmark to compare the efficiency of graph processing platforms in terms of time-to-solution and energy.

© Springer International Publishing Switzerland 2015
S. Hunold et al. (Eds.): Euro-Par 2015 Workshops, LNCS 9523, pp. 233–245, 2015.
DOI: 10.1007/978-3-319-27308-2_20

Recently, Beamer et al. [1] introduced the *direction-optimized* BFS algorithm that takes advantage of the scale-free property (Sect. 2.2). This algorithm combines the classic *top-down* BFS traversal, with inverse *bottom-up* steps and offers a sizable speedup. To date, however, all implementations have focused either on CPU-only platforms [21] or require that the graph fits *entirely* in the accelerator memory [22].

Our past work [5] tests the hypothesis that assembling processing elements with diverse characteristics (i.e., massively-parallel processors optimized for high throughput, and traditional processors optimized for fast sequential processing) is a good match for scale-free graph workloads. While we have proven this hypothesis for a wide set of algorithms (including traditional top-down BFS, Connected Components, SSSP and PageRank), direction-optimized BFS poses new challenges: (i) as it is up to one order of magnitude faster than traditional BFS, it stresses the communication channels between the processing elements of the heterogeneous platform, exposing new bottlenecks; (ii) it requires both pull and push access to vertex state that has to be efficiently exposed by the supporting middleware; (iii) as the processing elements do not share memory, a low-overhead solution must be designed to coordinate them to switch between bottom-up and top-down phases of the algorithm, and finally, (iv) it requires specialized graph partitioning and workload allocation strategies that match the characteristics of the workload to those of the processing elements.

This paper makes the following contributions:

1. It provides further evidence that specialization – i.e., intelligent graph partitioning such that the resulting workload matches a heterogeneous set of processing elements – is key to extracting maximum efficiency when facing a fixed cost or energy constraint. (Sections 3.2, 4.1)
2. It extends TOTEM, our heterogeneous graph processing engine, to support a new class of frontier-based algorithms which require exposing both push and pull access to distributed vertex state. (Section 3)
3. It introduces optimizations key to boost the performance of direction-optimized BFS on a heterogeneous platform: partitioning and workload allocation, communication reduction, and improving access locality. (Sections 3.2, 3.3 and 3.4)

We evaluate these techniques across multiple hardware configurations and multiple large-scale graph workloads. Our evaluation shows an improvement of time-to-solution by up to 2.4x and energy efficiency by up to 2.0x against a CPU-only implementation, and compares favorably against state-of-the-art single node solutions (e.g., GALOIS). (Sections 4.2, 4.3)

2   Challenges and Opportunities

The key difficulty when processing scale-free graphs is a result of the heterogeneous vertex connectivity. (For example, over 70 % of all vertices in the Twitter follower graph [3] have less than 40 in/out edges. The remaining vertices have increasingly large connectivity: the largest having over 3 million edges.)

This property makes obtaining balanced partitions difficult, as generally the memory footprint of a partition is proportional with the number of edges allocated to it, while the processing time is a complex function that depends on the number of vertices and edges allocated to the partition, and the specific properties of the workload (e.g., compute intensity, access locality).

Past work has generally assumed a homogeneous compute platform and has prioritized balancing partitions in terms of size [16]. This leads, however, to unbalanced partitions in terms of processing time due to the high-connectivity nodes. Recent strategies such as 'high degree vertex delegation' [17] continue to assume a homogeneous platform and aim for better load-balancing while dealing with high degree vertices.

2.1 Improving Performance with Hardware Accelerators

A GPU-accelerated system offers the opportunity to benefit from heterogeneity: instead of attempting to balance partitions by evenly distributing the workload based on memory footprint, one can choose to 'embrace' heterogeneity and partition such that the workload generated by a partition matches best the strengths of the processing element the partition is allocated to – e.g., by creating partitions that expose massive parallelism and allocating them to a GPU [4,5].

However, efficiently harnessing a GPU-accelerated setup brings new challenges: First, it is difficult to design partition and allocation strategies that harness the platform efficiently. Second, GPUs tend to have over an order of magnitude less memory than the host and cannot process large partitions. (A key constraint – for example, the edge list of a Scale30 graph, a synthetic graph used in the Graph500 benchmark, occupies 256 GB in the memory-efficient Compressed Sparse Row format, yet a Kepler K40 GPU has only 12 GB of memory).

Note that past projects have explored GPU solutions, but either assume that the graph fits the memory of one [9,22], or multiple GPUs [14]. In both cases, due to the limited memory space available, the scale of the graphs that can be processed is significantly smaller than the large graphs presented in this paper.

In any case, techniques that aim to optimize graph processing on the GPU are complementary to the approach proposed in this work in that they can be applied to the compute kernels to improve the overall performance of the hybrid system. In fact, this work uses the "virtual warp" technique proposed by Hong et al. [9] which aims to reduce divergence among the threads of a warp and hence improve the GPU kernel's performance.

2.2 Improving Performance with Direction-Optimized BFS

Similar to other graph algorithms, level-synchronous Breadth First Search (BFS) exposes the concept of a *frontier*: the set of active vertices, which, for BFS, form the current level. To discover the next level, i.e., the next frontier, the traditional top-down BFS approach explores all edges of the vertices in the current frontier and builds the next frontier as the new vertices that can be reached (i.e., the vertices that have not been visited before). For scale-free graphs, this can cause

high write traffic as many edges out of the current frontier can attempt to add
the same vertex into the next frontier.

Direction-Optimized BFS [1] is based on the key observation that the next
frontier can also be built in a different, *bottom-up* way: by iterating over the
vertices that have never been activated and selecting those that have a neighbour
in the current frontier. Depending on graph topology and the current state of
the algorithm, a bottom-up step can improve performance for two reasons. First,
it can result in exploring fewer edges: once it has been determined that a vertex
has a neighbour in the frontier it is not necessary to visit its other edges, thus
reducing work particularly for high degree vertices. Second, it generates less
contention as the thread that updates a vertex state (i.e., marks it as belonging
to the new frontier) only reads its neighbour's state but does not update it.

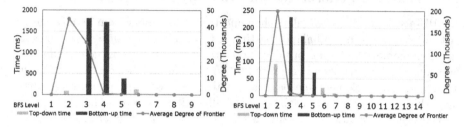

Fig. 1. Processing time per BFS level (left axis) and the average degree of vertices in
the frontier (right axis). Graphs: *Left* Synthetic Scale30. *Right* Twitter [3].

During BFS processing of a scale-free graph, the vertices with high connectivity are quickly reached. Next, with these *few high degree* vertices in the frontier,
the number of vertices in the next frontier will be large. At this point, it becomes
more efficient to employ a bottom-up step: this will reduce the number of edges
explored, and will alleviate write pressure corresponding to the many vertices
that will be added to the frontier. Figure 1 supports this observation: the average degree of the frontier is large immediately after start (i.e., during the initial
top-down steps of direction-optimized BFS). Next, during the bulk of the computation time, the average degree of a processed vertex is lower and continues
to decrease; as a result, bottom-up steps are more efficient, but in effect, the
many low degree vertices may end up being processed unsuccessfully at multiple
BFS levels before they are finally included in the frontier. As the average degree
of the frontier continues to decrease, top-down processing becomes again more
efficient during the last few steps of the algorithm.

3   The Hybrid Algorithm

To harness the opportunities offered by a heterogeneous platform, several issues
need to be addressed: (i) partitioning the graph and allocating partitions to
processing elements to match their strengths and limits (i.e., massive parallelism yet limited accelerator memory); (ii) efficiently communicating between
partitions; and (iii) coordinating the participating processing elements.

Our past work [5] demonstrates that the benefits of using a heterogeneous platform exceed the cost of communication between partitions hosted on different processing elements: the reduction in compute time obtained by adding GPUs is far larger than the added communication time over the PCI bus to synchronize between partitions. However, direction-optimized BFS adds new challenges: first, the bottom-up steps are up to one order of magnitude faster than the equivalent top-down steps thus potentially expose the communication over the PCI bus as the key bottleneck. Second, all processing elements participating in a direction-optimized BFS computation need to coordinate and chose direction at the same time. This coordination can add further communication overheads, as there is no shared state between the processing elements.

3.1   Direction-Optimized BFS for Partitioned Graphs

Our BFS Algorithm 1 is based on the Bulk Synchronous Parallel (BSP) model which supports well a system setup where processing elements that do not share memory, and where the graph needs to be partitioned for processing. Each BFS level of the algorithm contains a communication operation: the top-down steps use a Push-based method; the bottom-up steps a Pull-based method (described in Algorithms 2 and 3). The partitions each have an array of frontiers corresponding to other partitions. In addition, vertices have an associated partition ID, allowing the algorithm to determine whether or not the vertex is remote, and which frontier to use.

Top-down Steps explore the edges of the vertices in the frontier of the local partition: each such vertex activates – mark as belonging to the next frontier – a vertex that is either local or remote (belonging to another partition). During the *push* phase, the remote information is passed to the corresponding partitions, then all partitions wait for synchronization before starting the next round to ensure they all have pushed all necessary information.

Bottom-up Steps start by aggregating, in each partition, the global frontier by *pulling* the required information from all other partitions. Then each partition completes its level by checking its local not-yet-activated vertices against this global frontier. Then partitions synchronize: this ensures that all partitions have completed creating their new local frontier and are ready for the next round.

Optimizations. Key performance gains are achieved due to batch communication and message reduction: the push and pull operations only happen once per BSP round, and only to remote neighbours (i.e., only the data relevant to remote partitions). An additional optimization we apply is specific to the case when the user requires computing the BFS traversal tree as in the Graph500 benchmark (and not only labeling nodes with their 'depth'): To reduce communication overhead, the parent of a vertex is not communicated during the traversal but is collected from the different address spaces in a final aggregation step (only the visited status is updated during traversal).

Algorithm 1. Direction-optimized BFS algorithm for partitioned graphs.

```
1   func BFS_Kernel (Partition PID, StepType STEP)
2     if (STEP == TOP-DOWN) then
3       parallel foreach (Vertex in Frontier[PID]) do
4       | foreach (Nbr in Vertex.Neighbours) do
5       | | if (!Nbr.isVisited) then
6       | |   NextFrontier[Nbr.partition].Add(Nbr)
7       | |   BFSParentTree[Nbr.partition][Nbr] = Vertex
8       | |   Nbr.isVisited = true
9       | | end if
10      | end for
11      end parallel for
12      PushFrontiers(PID)
13    else if (STEP == BOTTOM-UP) then
14      PullFrontiers(PID)
15      parallel foreach (Vertex in Partition[PID]) do
16      | if (!Vertex.isVisited) then
17      |   foreach (Nbr in Vertex.Neighbours) do
18      |   | if (Vertex in Frontier[Nbr.partition]) then
19      |   |   NextFrontier[PID].Add(Vertex)
20      |   |   BFSParentTree[PID][Vertex] = Nbr
21      |   |   Vertex.isVisited = true
22      |   |   break for
23      |   | end if
24      |   end for
25      | end if
26      end parallel for
27    end if
28    Synchronize()
29  end func
```

Algorithm 2. Push Frontiers

```
1  func PushFrontiers (Partition PID)
2   foreach (P in Partitions != PID) do
3   | NextFrontier[P] ==> Frontier[P]
4   |       (local) ==> (remote)
5   end for
6  end func
```

Algorithm 3. Pull Frontiers

```
1  func PullFrontiers (Partition PID)
2   foreach (P in Partitions != PID) do
3   | Frontier[P] <== NextFrontier[P]
4   |     (local) <== (remote)
5   end for
6  end func
```

3.2   Partition Specialization

A performance-critical decision is graph partitioning; in particular, we need to identify the part of the graph that should be placed on the space-constrained GPUs such that overall performance is maximized. We first observe that even though the bottom-up steps can significantly improve performance for some BFS levels (due to the reduction in total edge checks), these bottom-up steps take the longest out of the overall execution (Fig. 1). Thus accelerating these steps is essential for overall processing performance, and our focus.

We partition such that the low-degree vertices are assigned to the GPUs. The intuition behind this decision is threefold: first, processing the many low-degree vertices in parallel fits the GPU compute model (i.e., many small computations with insignificant load imbalance); second, the low-degree vertices occupy a small amount of memory (as they are not attached to many edges), a critical issue to the space constrained GPUs; and third, and most importantly, processing the low-degree vertices during the bottom-up steps is the main bottleneck as we have empirically verified. As we argue in the next section, this partitioning solution adds one additional advantage: it makes it easier to decide when to switch to bottom-up processing without communicating between partitions.

3.3   Switching Processing Direction for a Partitioned Graph

The direction-optimized algorithm requires coordinating all processing elements when the processing switches from top-down to bottom-up (after processing the first few BFS levels) then switching back to top-down processing. These decisions are generally taken based on global information [1, 22] (e.g., the anticipated size of the next frontier) yet obtaining a more precise estimate is costly on a platform that does not offer shared memory.

Top-down to Bottom-up Switch. We estimate the next frontier based on a static percent of the edges out of the current frontier. This worked well in most executions on the scale-free graphs we have experimented with. However, when using this technique on our partitioned setup, it would normally be necessary to synchronize frontier information across each partition. However, as shown in Fig. 1, the frontier is rapidly built by the few high degree vertices, while the low degree vertices have virtually no impact on the decision to switch as they are discovered later. For this reason, the coordinator for switching can be the partition responsible for the high degree vertices: the CPU. This method is less costly than communicating among partitions to precisely anticipate frontier size, while retaining nearly identical accuracy in predicting the optimal switch point.

Bottom-up to top-down switch. The performance gains tends to be low from switching back to top-down processing as the final BFS levels require little time anyways. For this reason, partitions return to top-down after a fixed number of steps, so that all partitions return at the same time without state communicating or voting.

3.4   Optimizations to Improve Access Locality

After partitioning, a vertex is identified by two elements: a global ID which corresponds to its place in the original graph, and a local ID, which corresponds to its place in the partition. This indexing provides flexibility that can be exploited as follows. First, since the partition retains the global ID, permutation of local IDs enables optimizations: we can reorder vertices in memory to improve local partition access locality [18]. Second, the adjacency lists can be ordered in decreasing order of vertex connectivity, so that the highest degree vertex in the adjacency list comes first. This optimization shortens the bottom up-steps as the higher degree vertices are most likely to belong in the frontier, thus scanning the neighbour list has a higher chance to stop earlier (also noted by [21]).

Finally, note that the optimizations discussed in this section are applicable to both CPU-only and GPU-accelerated setups. Indeed, such optimizations makes it even more challenging to show the benefits of a heterogeneous platform as they significantly improve the performance of the CPU-only baseline, and hence they expose the communication and coordination overheads. However, as we show in the next section, our optimizations related to reducing communication overheads successfully eliminate it as a potential bottleneck.

4   Experimental Results

Software Platform. TOTEM [5], the framework we use to support our exploration, hides the complexity of developing graph algorithms from the programmer by providing abstractions for communication, the ability to specify graph partitioning strategies, as well as common optimizations such as bitmap frontier representations and vertex and adjacency list ordering. We implemented the direction-optimized BFS algorithm on top of TOTEM, as well as the optimizations discussed – it is important to note that both the GPU-accelerated and the CPU-only experiments use the same CPU kernel (i.e., they both apply the optimizations discussed in Sect. 3.4).

Hardware Platform. The experiments were executed on a single machine with two Intel Xeon E5-2670v2 processors with 10 cores at 2.5 GHz and 512 GB of shared memory. The machine hosts two NVidia Kepler K40s with 2880 cores at 0.75 GHz and 12 GB of memory each. The peak memory bandwidth of the host is 59.7 GB/s, while on the GPU is 288 GB/s.

Methodology. We employ the experimental methodology defined by Graph500 and GreenGraph500. These require computing the BFS parent of each vertex (as opposed to only its level). While TOTEM uses the CSR format and represents each undirected edge as two directed edges, we do report performance in *undirected traversed edges per second (TEPS)*, as required by Graph500. Reported results are harmonic means over 100 executions. We measure power at the outlet using a WattsUP meter that samples at 1 Hz. To get representative energy consumption, we run each experiment for 10 min (e.g., repeating searches).

Workloads. Unless otherwise mentioned, the synthetic graphs used are Scale30 [1B V, 16B E], built with the Graph500 reference code generator and parameters. The real-world graphs used are undirected versions of Twitter [3] [52M V, 1.9B E], Wikipedia [11] [27M V, 601M E], and LiveJournal [12] [4M V, 69M E].

4.1   The Impact of Specialized Partitioning

Figure 2 (*left*) presents the processing rate for a Scale30 graph for configurations with one or two CPUs, and one or two GPUs. There are two takeaways: first, GPUs provide acceleration in all cases; and, relevantly for budget/energy-limited platforms, it is more efficient to add an additional GPU than an additional CPU.

Second, and most importantly, the plot highlights the benefits of workload specialization: with random partitioning adding GPUs only offers a speedup proportional with memory footprint of the offloaded partition. *The intelligent partitioning scheme we introduce offers a super-linear speedup: despite offloading only 8 % of the graph, 2 GPUs improve performance by 2.4x.*

Figure 2 (*right*) evaluates performance over multiple Graph500 sizes and shows that the GPU-accelerated setup with workload specialization consistently offers large gains. Larger-scale graphs tend to have a smaller TEPS rate due to lower data locality. We note that, despite the ability to allocate a larger part of the smaller graphs to the GPUs the gains level off for scale-free graphs: allocating more low-degree vertices becomes exponentially costly as the vertices have higher connectivity. The largest graph offers more potential for improvement if GPUs had more memory: 'only' 88 % of non-singleton vertices are allocated to the GPUs. This increases to 97 % for Scale29, and 99 % for Scale28; at which point there is not much room for performance gains from GPUs with larger memory.

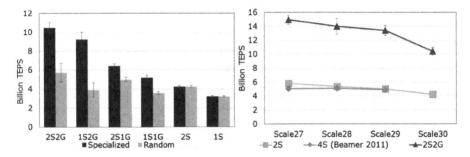

Fig. 2. *Left*: Direction-optimized BFS processing rate for specialized and random partitioning on hardware configurations with variable number of CPU Sockets (S) andGPUs (G) for a Scale30 graph. *Right*: Processing rates for synthetic graphs with size varying over one order of magnitude: Scale27 to Scale30. The curve labeled 4 S presents the performance by Beamer [1] on 4-Socket machine.

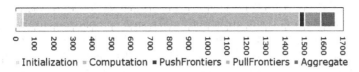

Fig. 3. BFS run time (ms) for a Scale30 graph broken down into components: initializing BFS status data, computation, and push- and pull-communication.

Analyzing the Overheads. Figure 3 highlights that performance is dominated by computation time: initialization, aggregation, and communication (presented separately for push/pull) are only a small fraction of the total runtime.

Figure 4 (*left*) breaks down the total runtime by BFS level for classic top-down BFS and direction-optimized BFS on a traditional (two CPU sockets – labeled 2S) and hybrid (two CPUs and two GPUs – labeled 2S2G) platform. The plot highlights two key points. First, it confirms the benefits of direction-optimization and it shows that these benefits are concentrated on faster processing of bottom-up levels 4 and 5. Second, it highlights the further gains offered by the hybrid platform, and pinpoints the gains to much faster level 4 processing.

As a result of the BSP model, the computation time is determined by the bottleneck processor in each step. Figure 4 (*right*) presents the processing time per-level for each processing element: although occasionally (for levels 5 and beyond) the bottleneck is with the GPUs, the computation time for the initial bottom-up level (level 3) by the CPU dwarfs the rest of the execution time, leaving the other load-balancing inefficiencies nearly irrelevant.

4.2 Comparison with Past Work Using Real-World Graphs

We use real-world graphs to compare performance to that of the state-of-the-art graph processing framework GALOIS, whose direction-optimized BFS implementation compares favorably [15] to that of Ligra [19], PowerGraph [6], and

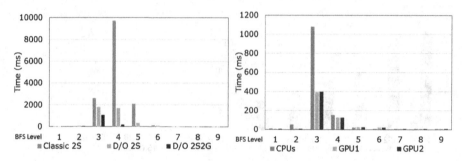

Fig. 4. *Left*: Per-level runtime (ms) for top-down (classic) and direction-optimized (D/O) BFS for a 2 CPU platform (2S), versus 2 CPUs and 2 GPUs (2S2G). *Right*: Per-level execution time for CPUs/GPUs of the 2S2G platform for the direction-optimized execution in the left plot. *Workload*: Scale30 graph.

GraphLab [13]. (We run GALOIS on our experimental machine. We had extensive discussions with GALOIS authors to make sure comparisons are fair.)

Table 1 shows the following: first, as in Fig. 4 (*left*) direction-optimized BFS largely outperforms top-down BFS. Second, our CPU-only versions of top-down and direction-optimized BFS perform largely similar to their GALOIS counterpart: this provides evidence that the baselines we used earlier for comparison to showcase the gains offered by our solution are fair. Furthermore, since in our hybrid algorithm the CPU and GPU kernels are executing concurrently, and the CPU is the bottleneck processor, improving our CPU kernel improves our overall execution rate, thus we have made all efforts to have efficient CPU-only kernels.

The hybrid direction-optimized version provides a performance boost of 2.0x for Twitter compared to the best CPU-only version. The larger diameter and less scale-free nature of the last two graphs reduce the impact of the direction-optimized approach, and expose more of the hybrid implementation overheads. Additionally, these smaller graphs expose less opportunity for the massive parallelism GPUs could harness. Nevertheless the hybrid implementation still offers a 1.3x speedup for LiveJournal and Wikipedia.

The table also highlights that the hybridization and the algorithm-level optimizations are synergetic, and together, they offer a significant boost in performance over generic and even optimized CPU versions. These results suggest that other scale-free real-world graphs will benefit from the techniques we propose.

4.3   The Energy Case

For Scale30 graphs, at 10.86 MTEPS/W, our CPU only implementation respectably ranked #10 in the November 2014 Big Data category of the GreenGraph500 list [8]. The hybrid configuration achieved over 2x better energy efficiency, ranking #6 with 22.36 MTEPS/W. (We note that, our hybrid configuration ranked behind 5 similar submissions by the GraphCrest group [21], that all use more energy-efficient hardware: more and newer CPUs). For Scale29 graphs, on a recently acquired platform (2x Intel E5-2695, DDR4 memory, same GPUs) with

Table 1. TOTEM and GALOIS (v2.2.1) performance in billion TEPS (higher is better), across real-world graphs. TOTEM executions use the same CPU kernel. The Naive kernel shown doesn't apply optimizations discussed in Sect. 3.4.

	Algorithm	Naive-2S	GALOIS-2S	TOTEM-2S	TOTEM-2S2G
Twitter	Top-Down	0.23	0.50	1.39	2.05
	Direction-Optimized		1.96	2.84	**5.78**
Wikipedia	Top-Down	0.84	0.42	1.14	1.29
	Direction-Optimized		1.12	1.49	**2.01**
LiveJournal	Top-Down	0.54	0.99	1.26	1.57
	Direction-Optimized		1.23	1.96	**2.59**

17.3 GTEPS and 30.1 MTEPS/Watt we would rank at the top of today's Graph500 and, respectively, GreenGraph500.

The reason behind the energy gains the hybrid platform offers is that the GPU enables faster race-to-idle for the whole system (including energy expensive RAM), which means that the system draws high power for a significantly shorter period. Moreover, the most important factor that contributes to the energy gains is that the GPU, the processor with the higher Thermal Design Power (TDP), races-to-idle much faster than the CPUs (as shown in Fig. 4). Finally we note that the property we observed for performance holds for energy efficiency: it is always better to add a GPU than a second CPU. For example, if we extrapolate the linear performance improvement from 1 CPU to 2 CPUs as in Fig. 2 to 4 homogeneous CPUs, *and conservatively assume these two new CPUs have no additional energy cost*, a system consisting of 4 of our CPUs would be approximately 16 MTEPS/W, still less efficient than our 2 CPU 2 GPU system.

5   Summary

This work presents the design, implementation and evaluation of a state-of-the-art BFS algorithm (Beamer et al.'s direction-optimized algorithm [1]) on top of a hybrid, GPU-accelerated platform. We present a number of critical optimizations that take advantage of both the characteristics of the hardware platform we target and common properties of many real-world datasets. We show that while the GPU has limited memory space, large-scale graphs can still benefit from GPU acceleration by carefully partitioning the graph such that the GPU is assigned the part of the workload that otherwise critically limits the overall performance. Moreover, we show that by applying simple yet effective optimizations, such gains are achieved even for discrete GPUs connected to the system via high-latency PCI bus. This offers a strong indication that these gains will hold for high-speed GPU platforms, such as AMD Fusion or NVLink.

Making progress on techniques able to harness heterogeneous platforms is essential in the context of current hardware trends: as the cost of energy continues to increase relative to the cost of silicon, future systems will host a wealth of different processing units. In this context, partitioning the workload and assigning the partitions to the processing element where they can be executed most efficiently in terms of power or time becomes a key issue.

Acknowledgement. This work was supported in part by the Institute for Computing, Information and Cognitive Systems (ICICS) at UBC.

References

1. Beamer, S., Patterson, D.A.: Searching for a parent instead of fighting over children: A fast breadth-first search implementation for graph500 (2011)
2. Bullmore, E., Sporns, O.: Complex brain networks: graph theoretical analysis of structural and functional systems. Nat. Rev. Neurosci. **10**(3), 186–198 (2009)
3. Cha, M., Haddadi, H., Benevenuto, F., Gummadi, P.K.: Measuring user influence in twitter: The million follower fallacy. (2010)
4. Cumming, B., Fourestey, G., Fuhrer, O., Gysi, T.: Application centric energy-efficiency study of distributed multi-core and hybrid cpu-gpu systems. In: SC (2014)
5. Gharaibeh, A., Reza, T., Santos-Neto, E., Sallinen, S., Ripeanu, M.: Efficient large-scale graph processing on hybrid cpu and gpu systems. arXiv:1312 (2014)
6. Gonzalez, J.E., Low, Y., Gu, H., Bickson, D., Guestrin, C.: Powergraph: distributed graph-parallel computation on natural graphs. In: OSDI (2012)
7. Graph500. http://www.graph500.org/
8. Green Graph500. http://green.graph500.org/
9. Hong, S., Kim, S.K., Oguntebi, T., Olukotun, K.: Accelerating cuda graph algorithms at maximum warp (2011)
10. Jeong, H., Mason, S.P., Barabási, A.L., Oltvai, Z.N.: Lethality and centrality in protein networks. Nature **411**(6833), 41–42 (2001)
11. Kunegis, J.: The koblenz network collection. In: World Wide Web Companion (2013)
12. Leskovec, J., Krevl, A.: SNAP Datasets: Stanford large network dataset collection, June 2014. http://snap.stanford.edu/data
13. Low, Y., Gonzalez, J.E., Kyrola, A., Bickson, D., Guestrin, C.E., Hellerstein, J.: Graphlab: a new framework for parallel machine learning (2014). arXiv:1408.2041
14. Merrill, D., Garland, M., Grimshaw, A.: Scalable gpu graph traversal. In: ACM SIGPLAN Notices, vol. 47, pp. 117–128. ACM (2012)
15. Nguyen, D., Lenharth, A., Pingali, K.: A lightweight infrastructure for graph analytics. In: SOSP (2013)
16. Pearce, R., Gokhale, M., Amato, N.M.: Scaling techniques for massive scale-free graphs in distributed (external) memory. In: IPDPS (2013)
17. Pearce, R., Gokhale, M., Amato, N.M.: Faster parallel traversal of scale free graphs at extreme scale with vertex delegates. In: SC (2014)
18. Sallinen, S., Borges, D., Gharaibeh, A., Ripeanu, M.: Exploring hybrid hardware and data placement strategies for the graph 500 challenge (2014)
19. Shun, J., Blelloch, G.E.: Ligra: a lightweight graph processing framework for shared memory. In: ACM SIGPLAN Notices, vol. 48, pp. 135–146. ACM (2013)
20. Wang, X.F., Chen, G.: Complex networks: small-world, scale-free and beyond. IEEE Circuits Syst. Mag. **3**(1), 6–20 (2003)

21. Yasui, Y., Fujisawa, K., Sato, Y.: Fast and energy-efficient breadth-first search on a single NUMA system. In: Kunkel, J.M., Ludwig, T., Meuer, H.W. (eds.) ISC 2014. LNCS, vol. 8488, pp. 365–381. Springer, Heidelberg (2014)
22. You, Y., Bader, D., Dehnavi, M.M.: Designing a heuristic cross-architecture combination for breadth-first search. In: ICPP (2014)

FiNS: A Framework for Accelerating Nested Simulations on Heterogeneous Platforms

Joris Cramwinckel[1][✉], Stefan Singor[1,2], and Ana Lucia Varbanescu[3]

[1] Ortec Finance, Rotterdam, The Netherlands
joris.cramwinckel@ortec-finance.com
[2] Delft University of Technology, Delft, The Netherlands
stefan.singor@ortec-finance.com
[3] University of Amsterdam, Amsterdam, The Netherlands
a.l.varbanescu@uva.nl

Abstract. Insurers use advanced risk management models to, among other things, compute required capital for different sources of financial risks. In these models the application of nested simulations becomes increasingly important. To keep computation times within acceptable limits high-performance computing is required. In this work we present a framework designed to significantly improve the performance of nested simulations by using heterogeneous computing. Specifically, we use modern features from CUDA - streams, Hyper-Q, and Multi-Process Service - to take full advantage of the massive parallelism of modern GPUs. We manage to reduce the execution time of such simulations from several hours to tens of minutes.

Keywords: CPU-GPU heterogeneous computing · Asset & Liability Management · Nested simulations · CUDA Streams · CUDA Hyper-Q

1 Introduction

Insurance companies sell products like variable annuities and universal life insurance that include certain rights, such as guarantees and profit sharing. These rights may bring profit to the policy holders but cannot cause a loss. The valuation of these embedded options in insurance contracts is quite challenging, because insurance companies need to value their embedded options for many applications - e.g., Solvency II[1] reporting, monitoring, product pricing and Asset &Liability Management (ALM). For these various applications, one would ideally use the same valuation method in order to maintain consistency, transparency, and ease of interpretation. The preferred valuation method nowadays is risk neutral Monte Carlo simulation [7].

Determining the current ($t = 0$) market value of the embedded option is generally not a problem, since we can gather relevant market data, calibrate risk

---

[1] Solvency II is a new regulatory framework for insurance companies that officially starts as of January 1, 2016.

© Springer International Publishing Switzerland 2015
S. Hunold et al. (Eds.): Euro-Par 2015 Workshops, LNCS 9523, pp. 246–257, 2015.
DOI: 10.1007/978-3-319-27308-2_21

neutral models and perform Monte Carlo valuations to obtain option values. Performing these steps in a scenario simulation context for future time periods ($t > 0$) is more complicated. These so-called nested simulation valuations are, amongst others, required for computing the Solvency Capital Requirement (SCR) based on a 99.5 % Value at Risk (VaR) on a 1-year period[2], the Own Risk and Solvency Assessment, and ALM. Additionally, complementary models for calibration and validation purposes also use nested simulations.

Most nested simulation applications found in financial applications can easily run for days, an obvious bottleneck to their viability. Furthermore, these long-running simulations discourage any research on new models and new methodologies.

Our aim in this work is to significantly improve the performance of nested simulations, making them feasible for both production and more empirically-driven research. Given that Graphical Processing Units (GPUs) are a proven technology in finance for performing Monte Carlo valuation simulations ([1,10]), we aim to make use of these massively parallel architectures to accelerate financial nested simulations. The main challenge here is efficiency, because the multiple layers of parallelism of nested simulations require a tight collaboration of the CPU and the GPU.

Our work introduces a *Financial Nested Simulations* (FiNS) framework, i.e. a CPU-GPU heterogeneous solution for improving the performance of nested simulations in financial applications. FiNS is driven by two important requirements: performance improvement and ease-of-use for financial specialists.

To address performance, FiNS makes extensive use of a set of advanced CUDA abstractions available in the latest NVIDIA architectures (Kepler and newer): CUDA streams [11], Hyper-Q [13], and MPS [14] are all used to efficiently offload simulations to the GPU. To address usability, FiNS is built as a skeleton that can be easily adapted to different applications.

To demonstrate both the performance and usability of FiNS, we build a mock-up model of an existing ALM tool, which emulates the behavior of a full nested simulation. An ALM tool uses many macroeconomic scenarios to provide users insight in future performance of, for example, an insures' or pension funds' balance sheet.

Our results show significant performance improvement over the sequential code, with speed-ups ranging between 26 and 6 for light and heavy cases, respectively. This significant gain is due to our efficient use of both the CPU and the GPU. Although the reference sequential code is by no means optimized, FiNS brings a significant improvement in the way nested simulations can be used in production and research.

Summarizing, the main contribution of this work is threefold:

1. We propose an original way to exploit streams for increasing the efficiency of heterogeneous CPU-GPU platforms in the case of applications with multiple layers of moderate parallelism;

---

[2] This represents the amount of capital the insurer must hold against unforeseen losses during a one-year period.

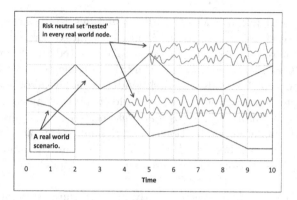

Fig. 1. Risk neutral simulations in a real world simulation. The figure shows two real world scenarios starting at t=0. For each real world scenario, a single nested simulation with two risk neutral scenarios is shown (at $t = 4$ and $t = 5$). In practice, thousands of risk neutral scenarios are used for valuation in each time step of a real world scenario.

2. We design FiNS, a generic framework for using heterogeneous platforms in financial nested simulations;
3. We demonstrate how FiNS can be used to accelerate ALM, a specific case of nested simulation used in risk management for institutional investors like insurance companies or pension funds.

2   Financial Background

For risk management, an insurer wishes to compute all relevant balance sheet components at each time step of a real world scenario. One generally starts with generating real world scenarios (the outer scenarios) for $t \geq 0$. To obtain the value of the embedded options at each time-step of a real world scenario, risk neutral scenarios (the inner scenarios) are required to perform a Monte Carlo valuation [7]. Within a Monte Carlo valuation the discounted pay-off cash flows resulting from the inner scenarios are averaged to obtain the option price. This concept of nested simulations is illustrated in Fig. 1.

While Monte Carlo valuation can easily be used for $t = 0$ applications, it is computationally expensive to apply it in a scenario environment. This problem emerges because Monte Carlo valuations need to be performed in each time step of a real world scenario.

Consider, for example, the case of 2,000 real world scenarios with a horizon of 5 years (annual frequency), then $10,000 + 1$ (including $t = 0$) valuations are required in total. Assuming one valuation takes a few seconds[3], then the total computation time for valuation is ≈ 6 h, which is unacceptable in practice[4]. Therefore, high performance computing is required to reduce the overall computation time.

---

[3] As measured in production using sequential code on a state-of-the-art CPU.

[4] It should be noted that, in practice, multiple valuations are required at each time step for Solvency II and hedging. This results in even higher computation times.

3   GPU Background

GPUs[5] are massively parallel processing units, originally designed for graphics. A GPU has multiple streaming processors (SMs), each grouping tens of simple cores. With hundreds to thousands such cores, the performance to be achieved can easily reach a couple of TFLOPs *for applications with enough concurrency*. Additionally, GPUs have a layered memory system, including private memory per core, shared memory and L1 cache per SM, L2 cache and a global, off-chip memory. Memory bandwidth is typically significantly higher than for CPUs, but it is still the limiting factor for performance in many applications.

GPUs are working as accelerators - i.e., they are not stand-alone processing units, but require a *host* to manage their involvement in computation. Such host is typically a CPU; in such a CPU-GPU platform, the GPU is called a *device*. Note that the host and the device run separate codes: the host code is the main application from which parts are being offloaded for computation by kernels running on the device. Also note that the memory spaces of the CPU and GPU are separated, which means that any application that offloads computation kernels to the GPU might also need to copy data from host to device and/or the other way.

For programming these GPU kernels, the most popular solution is CUDA, a proprietary programming model from NVIDIA. While portable models like OpenCL and higher level models like OpenACC exist and can be successfully used for many applications, they are not suitable for this work because the special features we are using are not yet available in these models. We further describe these features in the paragraphs below.

3.1   CUDA Streams and Hyper-Q

A CUDA stream is an abstraction of a series of tasks run by the GPU. By tasks we mean (1) memory copies, (2) synchronization, and (3) kernels (i.e., computational tasks). The tasks in a single stream are ordered, but they are independent from tasks in different streams.

Using streams can improve the concurrency of an application. For example, within nested simulation we repeat a sequence of tasks for every outer scenario in every period. By embedding this sequence of tasks in a stream, and launching a new stream for each node in the outer simulation (as is displayed in Fig. 1), we have an elegant solution to launch multiple inner simulations that will not interfere with each other.

The most important features of streams necessary for this work are: first, stream launches can be asynchronous, allowing the CPU to compute while the GPU is running. Furthermore, tasks for different hardware engines within streams can run concurrently, i.e. computational tasks (kernels), executed by

---

[5] In this work we focus on NVIDIA GPUs and we make heavy use of CUDA concepts. In theory all other GPUs have the required features, yet programming them remains a challenge which is beyond the scope of this work.

the GPU SMs and memory copies (D2H and H2D), executed by the GPU copy engines. And finally, streams can run concurrently on the device. We further detail the way we exploit these features in the following paragraphs.

CPU-GPU Concurrency. Stream launches are asynchronous by default. To ensure a asynchronous launch, care must be taken that memory copies are initialized with the asynchronous API and that the host memory allocations are pinned [13]. If synchronization between device and host is required, this can be accomplished by either several CUDA synchronize methods or by implicit synchronization. Unintentionally synchronizing the streams on the device is the main difficulty of working with streams.

Compute and Memory Accesses Overlap. Within a stream, it is possible to overlap the memory transfers with computational work by invoking the tasks with the asynchronous API. If this is crucial for the application performance, one needs to chunk the work such that the overlap is optimal. Furthermore, memory copies of a stream can overlap the computations of another stream.

We note that, implicitly, this solution increases application parallelism by decreasing the granularity of the tasks and making use of the engine parallelism in the hardware platform.

Concurrent Kernel Execution. The latest developments in NVIDIA cards increase the concurrency possibilities of the streams within a work queue. This is accomplished by NVIDIAs Hyper-Q feature [13].

Concurrent kernel execution is strictly bound by computational capacity and the device architecture. The latter is at the time of writing a dominant factor. The Kepler (and newer) cards support Hyper-Queuing, which has an important effect on performance.

To illustrate this effect, we present in Figs. 2 and 3 a comparison of the Fermi and Kepler architectures for streams concurrency. The streams contain two kernels: a large `generatePaths` kernel followed by the tiny `priceOptions` kernel. In Fig. 2 we observe a two-way concurrency; because the final (tiny) task of a stream is running concurrently with the first (much larger) task of the subsequent stream. Hardware utilization in this case is low. On the contrary, Fig. 3 displays the benefits of the hyper-Q allowing higher concurrency between streams, resulting in higher hardware utilization.

3.2   Multi Processing Service

Another way to increase the utilization of GPUs is to share the device for kernels from different (local) processes. In order to manage GPU sharing between processes, we used NVIDIA's Multi Processing Service (MPS) [14]. This software layer provides a context manager to handle work launched from different processes. MPS is exclusively available on Linux and is only provided with

 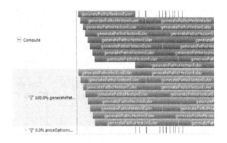

Fig. 2. Stream concurrency on fermi architecture

Fig. 3. Stream concurrency on kepler architecture

NVIDIA Tesla cards with compute capability 5 or higher. Although these restrictions limit applicability, it is a relatively cheap way to explore the concept of kernel offloading from multiple processes to a single GPU. This is an important feature when a single host process cannot generate sufficient work for the GPU, as it allows multiple cores or even multiple machines to collaborate in keeping a single device busy.

We note that previous work on offloading streams in a multi-threaded or multiprocessing environment [20] showed significant GPU utilization in benchmark cases. We implemented the same ideas as [20] for local Python processes. Section 5 provides more detail on how this feature affects our FiNS framework.

4   Framework Architecture

An ideal scenario is for the outer and inner scenarios to run in parallel. In this case, a perfect overlap provides optimal performance. Specifically, this means that within the duration of a real world simulation step (typically tens to hundreds of milliseconds), we must complete a full risk neutral simulation. This requirement demands a heterogeneous solution, which matches CPU + GPU architectures quite well, as seen in Fig. 7. Our work therefor focuses on building a framework that significantly outperforms existing solutions for nested simulations, but is flexible enough to support multiple types of such applications, where the analysis and end-results of the inner and outer simulations can vary in complexity.

The key to efficient heterogeneous programming is in designing the right solution to utilize the available hardware efficiently. In our case, the main challenge is GPU utilization: one inner simulation offloaded to the GPU can not, for most applications, fully utilize a GPU on its own. In order to increase GPU utilization multiple inner simulations will have to run concurrently. Without the concept of streams a custom implementation is needed, and it can become quite complex as one needs to build an aggregated kernel, as an artificial concatenation of kernels, which limits their flexibility in accepting different data sources or data types. When using CUDA streams these kernels can remain independent - thus flexible

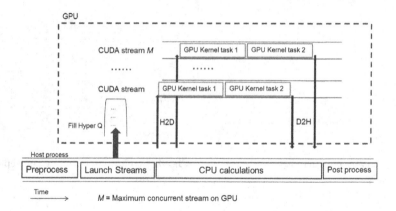

Fig. 4. Using streams in FiNS. The CPU and all GPU streams can run concurrently. The level of concurrency achieved in practice is determined by the actual hardware.

and fully reusable - and the task of concurrently executing them is offloaded to the device itself. From the perspective of flexibility this is an ideal solution for a generic framework, even if it comes with a small performance penalty (below 10 % according to our results [5]).

4.1   The Framework

FiNS is a development framework, that offers a skeleton-like infrastructure for the designers of nested simulation applications. Essentially, we provide a high-concurrency template that needs to be instantiated for a specific application. Using FiNS a developer needs to focus only on the implementation of the outer and inner simulation functionality. The framework will make sure that the mapping of these tasks on the real heterogeneous platform will be optimized for massive parallelism and efficient usage for both the CPU and the GPU.

To achieve this high level of flexibility we make use of CUDA streams, as seen in Fig. 4, displaying the concurrency between host and a number of streams running on the device. The CPU prepares the workload for the GPU and launches the work in streams to the device. The device receives the streams and stacks the work in a Hyper-Q. Note here that the issue order of the streams is not necessarily the order of execution, which clearly requires the computations in streams to be completely independent. If this is not the case, FiNS cannot be used. As mentioned earlier, it is important to have all host memory allocations page-locked or else the CPU-GPU concurrency will break when memory transfers are initialized. Furthermore, the Hyper-Q takes care of optimal hardware utilization by scheduling the streams concurrently. All streams are launched asynchronously, so that the GPU computations can overlap with the CPU tasks. These tasks can consist of, for example, calculating real-world simulation steps, calculating statistics or memory flushes to the hard drive.

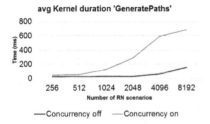

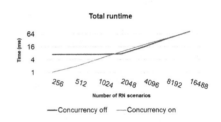

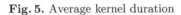

Fig. 5. Average kernel duration   **Fig. 6.** Total runtime

4.2   Streams in Practice

To show the performance behavior of kernel concurrency with streams, we set up a sample workload of 256 streams for the `generatePaths` kernel. We evaluated different sizes of offloaded work, determined by the number of risk neutral scenarios. To understand the performance gain for concurrency, we launched the sample both with and without kernel concurrency. We observe that the average duration of the kernel increases when streams are running concurrently (Fig. 5). However, for a lower number of scenarios (till around $2,000$), the concurrency contributes such that it is faster than the non-concurrent variant (Fig. 6). Moreover, for larger numbers of scenarios there is no performance penalty. This behavior indicates that the CUDA Work Scheduler assigns more resources to single sequential streams than it does to concurrent streams. As a result, kernel concurrency in streams only benefits performance when the offloaded kernels are not large enough to fully utilize the GPU, whereas for larger cases performance remains equal.

5   Nested Simulation for ALM Tooling: A Case Study

Section 2 already described the need for nested simulations in practice. Due to performance reasons the available ALM software is not equipped with the nested simulation features. Instead, we use analytical methodologies, often less accurate. This also means that we have no real reference code to compare against. Therefore, we build a mock-up model of an ALM tool. In this mock-up model outer simulations are emulated by a sleep statement. Since we are interested in the impact on the user-time performance (wall-clock performance) for this application, we assumed three benchmark cases. They differ in the duration of a real world simulation step per scenario per period. We assumed normal distributed duration with means 75, 150 and 300 ms for respectively a light, medium and a heavy case and a 5 ms standard deviation.

5.1   Application Description

Figure 7 displays the concept of offloading risk neutral calculations to the GPU in comparison with a sequential version. With this concept the goal is to perform

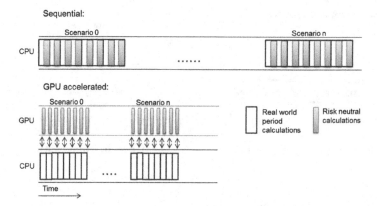

Fig. 7. Overlapping real and nested simulations. Note that all RNs are *different*, yet independent, thus they can be executed concurrently.

all risk neutral tasks within the runtime of a real world period. This is important since ALM models are used in a decision-making process. Any additional runtime on current methodologies is unwanted by its users.

In contrast, with Fig. 7 modern ALM tools perform real world simulations in a multiprocess or multi-threading setting. This makes it more challenging finishing the offloaded risk neutral simulation within the duration of its parent real world simulation step, since the GPU will be receiving tasks from all processes simultaneously.

5.2   Using the Framework

The framework presented in Sect. 4 serves as the greatest common divisor of several FiNS applications. For the ALM applications we extended the framework with multiprocessing support. This way, each host process is launching streams for its risk neutral calculation tasks to a daemon process hosted by the MPS Sect. 3.2. This daemon process manages all GPU requests from its slave processes and queues all received streams in a single hyper-Q. Using a single hyper-Q results in concurrent stream execution over the different processes.

5.3   Evaluation

Consider, again, the case of 2,000 real world scenarios with a horizon of 5 years (annual frequency), which are common dimensions for an insurer's ALM study. In a single process setting, simulations for the benchmark cases take resp. 12.5, 25 and 50 min. Note that we assumed perfect performance scaling for higher numbers processes. We measured that a single inner simulation of 1,000 with a horizon of 100 years and a $\frac{1}{120}$ time steps per year takes 1.875 s on a state-of-the-art CPU. These simulation dimensions are representative for current CPU models. Given that the inner simulations are run $10,000 + 1$ (including $t = 0$)

Table 1. Runtime full nested simulation on GPU framework

Case # Cores	Light	Medium	Heavy
	(in minutes)		
1	12.3	24.9	51.3
2	6.6	12.8	25.3
4	3.7	6.5	12.7
8	3.7	3.9	6.4
16	3.3	3.4	3.9

Table 2. User time speed ups *(maximum theoretical speed up)*

Case # Cores	Light	Medium	Heavy
	(26.0)	*(13.5)*	*(7.25)*
1	26.46	13.53	7.07
2	24.68	13.17	7.16
4	22.03	12.95	7.12
8	11.01	10.83	7.05
16	6.10	6.15	5.76

times for the complete run, the inner simulations represent a workload of over 5 h in a single process setting.

For evaluating the use case on FiNS we used a NVIDIA K20 GPU. Table 1 displays the measured runtime of the mockup model with the heterogeneous framework. We observe that for the lower number of cores the GPU is keeping up with the offloaded work. For a larger number of cores offloading work to the GPU, we observe that tasks stack in the hyper-Q and the CPU has to wait for the GPU results to be finished. Note that the single core results are below the theoretical reference for the Light and Medium case; this is caused by the assumption of normal distributed benchmark timings for the outer simulation.

The maximum speed up of the heterogeneous framework versus the theoretical sequential runtime is bound by the fraction of the tasks to be offloaded. Amdahl's law tell us that maximum achieved speed up is defined by $\frac{1}{B}$ where B represents the fraction of time the models is strictly serial. This results in theoretical maximum speedups of 26.0, 13.5 and 7.25 for all processes in resp. the Light, Medium and Heavy benchmark case. Table 2 displays the speedup of the GPU accelerated model versus the theoretical CPU runtime. The results show that for most of the cases a near to maximum speed up is reached.

The results in Table 1 indicate that, if resources can be scaled (usage of multiple GPUs), the proposed architecture would in theory be able to close in to the theoretical maximum speed up for every case defined in Table 2. Although scalability of the architecture is not implemented yet, we can conclude that the proposed architecture is most promising, since streams are easily distributable over multi GPUs and MPS has multi GPU support. To reveal the importance of NVIDIA MPS we also run the same tests with MPS disabled. We observed that speeds ups as displayed in Table 2 were up to 40 % lower.

6 Related Work

The utility of GPUs in Monte Carlo valuation methods is becoming a proven technology in finance [10]. Such work is focusing strictly on improving the performance of risk neutral simulation. In [1], a CPU-GPU performance comparison is made, achieving up to 10x speedup for both European and American contracts. Additionally, a lot of research has been dedicated to GPU-accelerated solutions for several risk neutral models [4,6,8,18,19]; the observed speedups range between 4 and 150. In our work, we focus on simulation models that require the cooperation of the CPU and the GPUs towards efficient nested simulations.

Financial nested simulations are increasingly important due to new regulations, so their performance becomes a production-level concern. Therefore, [3] describes several numerical methods for reducing the computational intensity of Solvency Capital Requirement (SCR) calculation, making it computationally feasible. Complementary to their study, our work demonstrates that the FiNS framework can render the same simulations feasible by using CPU-GPU heterogeneous computing.

Using heterogeneous computing for large scale simulations is already established as a feasible solution to improve performance for many classes of applications. Systems such as Glinda, Qilin, or Insieme [9,12,16,17] focus on static partitioning of one workload to multiple devices, under the assumption that the GPU is overloaded. Such systems are not suitable for our nested simulations, because in our scenarios the GPU is "underloaded". An alternative is to use a runtime-based system for heterogeneous computing, such as OmpSS or StarPU [2,15]. However, none of these approaches supports sharing devices by multiple kernels, which is an essential performance booster for FiNS.

7 Conclusion and Future Work

Nested simulation applications become increasingly important for insurance companies. Due to the compute-intensive nature of such simulations, CPU-only implementations lack the ability to provide sufficient performance, while GPU-only solutions are unable to efficiently utilize the hardware and lead to disappointing results. In this work we proposed FiNS, a flexible heterogeneous framework which, based on modern technologies such as CUDA Streams, Hyper-Q and NVIDIAs MPS, is able to utilize both the CPU and the GPU to accelerate nested simulations. We demonstrated the use of FiNS for an ALM application, which required multiple CPU processes to offload calculations to the same GPU. To tackle this challenge, we customized the MPS functionality to handle local Python processes and achieved concurrency between streams owned by different local processes. Our results demonstrate that ALM as implemented using FiNS achieves very good parallel efficiency.

We have four main objectives for the future. First, we will focus on running our applications in a multi-GPU environment, to fully overlap the CPU and GPU execution. Second, we expect that the concept of FiNS could be implemented on any many-core architecture, like Intel MIC, but we need to test this. Third, we plan to investigate more applications [5] and the effort needed to implement them in FiNS. Last but not least, we will investigate the possibility of providing an intuitive front-end for this framework together with a computational infrastructure (e.g., in the cloud), enabling financial specialists to use it as a computational service.

References

1. Abbas-Turki, L., Vialle, S., Lapeyre, B., Mercier, P.: Pricing derivatives on graphics processing units using monte carlo simulation. Concurr. Comput.: Pract. Exp. **26**(9), 1679–1697 (2014). http://dx.doi.org/10.1002/cpe.2862
2. Augonnet, C., Thibault, S., Namyst, R., Wacrenier, P.A.: StarPU: a unified platform for task scheduling on heterogeneous multicore architectures. Concurr. Comput.: Pract. Exp. **23**(2), 187–198 (2011)
3. Bauer, D., Reuss, A., Singer, D.: On the calculation of the solvency capital requirement based on nested simulations. Astin Bull. **42**(02), 453–499 (2012)
4. Bernemann, A., Schreyer, R., Spanderen, K.: Accelerating exotic option pricing and model calibration using gpus (2011). http://ssrn.com/abstract=1753596
5. Cramwinckel, J.: GPU Accelerated framework for financial nested simulations. Master's thesis. VU University Amsterdam (2015)
6. Fernández, J., Ferreiro, A., García-Rodríguez, J., Leitao, A., López-Salas, J., Vázquez, C.: Static and dynamic sabr stochastic volatility models: calibration and option pricing using gpus. Math. Comput. Simul. **94**, 55–75 (2013)
7. Glasserman, P.: Monte Carlo Methods in Financial Engineering, vol. 53. Springer, New York (2004)
8. Joshi, M.S.: Graphical asian options. Wilmott J. **2**(2), 97–107 (2010)
9. Kofler, K., Grasso, I., Cosenza, B., Fahringer, T.: An automatic input-sensitive approach for heterogeneous task partitioning. In: ICS 2013 (2013)
10. Lee, A., Yau, C., Giles, M.B., Doucet, A., Holmes, C.C.: On the utility of graphics cards to perform massively parallel simulation of advanced monte carlo methods. J. Comput. Graph. Stat. **19**(4), 769–789 (2010)
11. Luitjens, J.: CUDA streams - best practices and pitfalls, Presentation GTC 2014 (2014)
12. Luk, C.K., Hong, S., Kim, H.: Qilin: exploiting parallelism on heterogeneous multiprocessors with adaptive mapping. In: MICRO 2009 (2009)
13. NVIDIA: Kepler GK110 architecture whitepaper, v1.0 (2012)
14. NVIDIA: Sharing a GPU between MPI processes: Multi-process service (MPS) overview (2013). Technical Brief TB-06737-003
15. Planas, J., Badia, R.M., Ayguadé, E., Labarta, J.: Self-Adaptive ompss tasks in heterogeneous environments. In: IPDPS 2013 (2013)
16. Shen, J., Varbanescu, A.L., Sips, H.: Look before you leap: using the right hardware resources to accelerate applications. In: HPCC (2014)
17. Shen, J., Varbanescu, A.L., Zou, P., Lu, Y., Sips, H.: Improving performance by matching imbalanced workloads with heterogeneous platforms. In: ICS (2014)
18. Tian, Y., Zhu, Z., Klebaner, F.C., Hamza, K.: Option pricing with the sabr model on the gpu. In: 2010 IEEE Workshop on High Performance Computational Finance (WHPCF). IEEE (2010)
19. Tian, Y., Zhu, Z., Klebaner, F.C., Hamza, K.: Pricing barrier and american options under the sabr model on the graphics processing unit. Concurr. Comput.: Pract. Exp. **24**(8), 867–879 (2012)
20. Wende, F., Steinke, T., Cordes, F.: Multi-threaded kernel offloading to gpgpu using hyper-q on kepler architecture. ZIB-Rep. 14–19 June 2014 (2014)

Communication Models Insights
Meet Simulations

Pierre-François Dutot[1,2,3], Millian Poquet[1,2,3]([✉]), and Denis Trystram[1,2,3,4]

[1] Université Grenoble Alpes, LIG, 38000 Grenoble, France
[2] CNRS, LIG, 38000 Grenoble, France
[3] Inria, Grenoble, France
millian.poquet@inria.fr
[4] Institut Universitaire de France, Paris, France

Abstract. It is well-known that taking into account communications while scheduling jobs in large scale parallel computing platforms is a crucial issue. In modern hierarchical platforms, communication times are highly different when occurring inside a cluster or between clusters. Thus, allocating the jobs taking into account locality constraints is a key factor for reaching good performances. However, several theoretical results prove that imposing such constraints reduces the solution space and thus, possibly degrades the performances. In practice, such constraints simplify implementations and most often lead to better results.

Our aim in this work is to bridge theoretical and practical intuitions, and check the differences between constrained and unconstrained schedules (namely with respect to locality and node contiguity) through simulations. We have developed a generic tool, using *SimGrid* as the base simulator, enabling interactions with external batch schedulers to evaluate their scheduling policies. The results confirm that insights gained through theoretical models are ill-suited to current architectures and should be reevaluated.

Keywords: FCFS with backfilling · Simulations · Heterogeneity

1 Introduction

Large scale high performance computing platforms are becoming increasingly more complex. Determining efficient allocation and scheduling strategies that can adapt to their evolutions is a strategic and difficult challenge. We are interested here in the problem of scheduling jobs in hierarchical and heterogeneous large scale platforms. The application developers submit their jobs in a centralized waiting queue. The job management system aims at determining a suitable allocation for the jobs, which all compete against each other for the available computing resources. The performances are measured by some objectives like the maximum completion times or the slowdown. The most common scheduling policy is First Come First Served (FCFS) which takes the jobs one after the other according to their arrival times with backfilling (BF), which is an improvement

© Springer International Publishing Switzerland 2015
S. Hunold et al. (Eds.): Euro-Par 2015 Workshops, LNCS 9523, pp. 258–269, 2015.
DOI: 10.1007/978-3-319-27308-2_22

mechanism that allows to fill idle spaces with smaller jobs while keeping the original order of FCFS.

In practice the job execution times depend on their allocation (due to communication interferences and heterogeneity in both computation and communication), while theoretical models of parallel jobs are usually considering jobs as black boxes with a fixed execution time. Existing communications models do not fully reflect the network complexity and thus, simulations are required to take into account the impact of allocations.

Our goal within this work is to test existing heuristics dealing with allocation constraints, namely contiguity and locality. Contiguity forces jobs to be allotted on resources with a contiguous index (assuming that system administrators numbered their resources by proximity) while locality is a stronger constraint imposing some knowledge of the cluster structure to use allocations restricted to clusters whenever possible.

Contributions. We show in this paper that insights gained while studying theoretical models are sometimes at odd with the practical results due to shortcomings in the models. Moreover, this was done through the development of a framework as a layer above SimGrid. This framework is generic enough to enable a large range of tests and is scheduled for a public release as an open source git project, as soon as the basic documentation is completed.

More precisely, we ran wide range simulations on FCFS/BF focusing on the impact of communications under several scenarios of locality constraints. The main result is to show that taking communications into account matters, but contrary to the intuition given by theoretical models, the most constrained scenarios are the best! In other words, the constrained policies allow greater gains in performances than the overhead due to the cost of the locality constraint. Moreover, this work opens the possibility to study new functionalities in SimGrid with our open access framework (like energy trade-off between speed scaling and shutdown policies or considering release dates).

2   Related Work

Modeling the modern High Performance Computing platforms is a constantly renewed challenge, as the technology evolves and quickly renders obsolete the models developed for the previous generation. While interesting and powerful, the synchronous PRAM model, delay model, LogP model and their variants (such as hierarchical delay, see [2] for a description of these models) are ill-suited to large scale parallelism on hierarchical and heterogeneous platforms.

More recent studies [12] are still refining these models to take into account contentions accurately while remaining tractable enough to provide a useful tool for algorithm design. Even with these models, all but the simplest problems are difficult and polynomial approximations algorithms have mixed results [11].

With millions of processing cores, even polynomial algorithms are impractical when every process and communication have to be individually scheduled. The model of parallel tasks simplifies this problem in a way, by bundling many threads and communications into single boxes, either rigid, rectangular or mal-leable (see [6], Chaps. 25 and 26). However, these models are again ill-adapted to hierarchical and heterogeneous platforms, as the running time depends on more than simply the number of allotted resources. Furthermore, these models hardly match the reality when actual applications are used [3], as some of the basic underlying assumptions on the speed-up functions (such as concavity) are not often valid in practice.

With these limitations in mind, we decided to use simulations to really take into account the communications taking place within the jobs on large scale platforms. While writing a simple simulator is always possible, it appeared more interesting to use a detailed simulator to open our work to a larger set of plat-forms and job characteristics. Among the likely candidates, Simgrid [1] fulfills all our needs. In particular, the communications can be modeled either with a TCP-flow level model as used in this article or at the packet level for a fine grained simulation. While simulation is not always perfect [4], the results we present here are hopefully giving a better insight in the practical behavior of heuristics than the theoretical models.

A complementary approach to ours is to take into account the communi-cations within the jobs themselves by migrating processes depending on their communication affinity [5]. This approach is rooted in the application, while we are positioning ourselves at the resource and job management system level.

Most available open-source and commercial job management systems use an heuristic approach inspired by FCFS with backfilling algorithms [9]. The job priority is determined according to the arrival times of the jobs. Then, BF (the backfilling mechanism) allows a job to run before another job with a highest priority only if it does not delay it. There exist several variants of this algorithm, like conservative backfilling [9] and EASY backfilling [7]. In the former, the job allocation is completely recomputed at each new event (job arrival or job completion) while in the second, the process is purely on-line avoiding costly recomputations. More sophisticated algorithms have been proposed that consider the routing schemes of the data (like topology aware backfilling introduced in [10]). In our article, we consider that the scheduler has a very limited knowledge of the platform, which is insufficient for topology-aware algorithms.

3   Problem Description

Our problem of interest in this paper is the problem of scheduling a set $\mathcal{J}$ of independent and parallel jobs on a computing platform composed by a set M of computational resources (nodes or processors).

Each job $j \in \mathcal{J}$ is characterized by a rigid number $size_j$ of required resources, a walltime w_j (which bounds the execution time: j is killed after w_j seconds), a release date r_j, a computation row matrix c_j where each c_{j_k} represents the amount of computation on the kth resource of job j, a square communication matrix C_j of size $size_j \times size_j$ in which each element $C_j[r, c]$ represents the amount of communication from the rth resource to the cth resource of job j.

Each resource $m \in M$ has a computational power p_m. The resources are connected via a network. The network links have both a bandwidth and a latency. Each resource m has a unique identification number id_m between 0 and $card(M) - 1$.

Since we are interested in the online version of this problem, the scheduler only knows that job j exists once it is released. Two jobs cannot be processed at the same time on the same computational resource. Each job must be computed exactly once. The jobs cannot be preempted. The scheduling algorithms are considered as oblivious about the jobs inner settings c_j and C_j. Furthermore, the algorithms know little about the platform *i.e.* they only know the number of computational resources and their identification numbers.

4 Simulation Framework

As stated in Sect. 2, we turned to simulations to evaluate many batch scheduling algorithms to check if theoretical models match the practical experience. The added benefit over real experiments is that simulation enables reproducibility, and can easily be extended to test a very large number of parameters. The founding principle of our work is to use an existing platform simulation framework and to add a scheduling layer on the top of it. This approach allows us to take advantage of the simulation accuracy and the scalability of recognized software and allows separation of concerns since we are not simulation experts.

The survey [1] compares state-of-the-art simulators that could interest us. We chose to use SimGrid because it allows heterogeneity in both computational power and in network links latency and bandwidth, has a good TCP flow network model, can be used easily (thanks to a good documentation and a lot of examples), is fast, has little chance of becoming unmaintained (still actively developed after 10 years of existence) and comprises features that we may use in the future *e.g.* MPI applications simulation.

One of our main objectives was to be able to use already-developed scheduling algorithms without modifying their programming code a lot and to be able to simply create new algorithms. For this purpose, we base our simulation framework on two separate components: the simulating core and the scheduling module. These two components communicate via an event-based synchronous network protocol. When an event that may imply a scheduling decision occurs in the simulating core, the simulating core tells the scheduling module what happened and waits for its decision. The main events that will interest us in the scope of this paper are when jobs are released and when they complete their execution. In the scope of this paper, scheduling decisions are either to allocate some resources to some jobs or to do nothing.

The simulating core is fully written in C and is based on SimGrid, which is in charge of simulating what happens on the computational resources and on the network. All SimGrid platforms may be used by our simulating core as long as the user specifies which resources are used for the scheduling processes and which ones are used to compute jobs. Since SimGrid allows to create a wide range of simulators, it cannot be used directly to simulate a complex batch system. The purpose of the simulating core is thus to make the use of SimGrid easier in conjunction with event-based batch scheduling algorithms. Our core basically handles the input jobs, asks the scheduling module for decisions, ensures that jobs are simulated by SimGrid according to the topology and produce some output traces and statistics. Since this is a work in progress and not the main point of this paper, it will not be further described in the present paper. It will be published and put at the disposal of the community once mature enough.

The scheduling module can be developed in any programming language that allows network programming via *Unix Domain Sockets*. This component can be seen as an iterative process which consists in waiting an event from the simulating core, updating some data structures then making a scheduling decision. Therefore, existing algorithms which are based on events like job releases or completions can easily be plugged with the simulating core.

5 Evaluation

5.1 Platform and Jobs Description

Since we would like to know how the algorithms presented in [8] behave within realistic simulations, we use the same kind of platforms that the paper described. Our platforms include sets of closely located computational resources called *clusters*. Each cluster c is a tree formed by a switch s_c and a set of computational resources which are all directly connected to it. The cluster switch s_c has an internal bandwidth bw_{s_c} and an internal latency lat_{s_c}. All resources within the cluster c have the same computational power cp_c, the same bandwidth bw_c and latency lat_c between the resource and s_c. The clusters are connected together via a unique switch b whose shared bandwidth is bw_b and whose latency is lat_b. The implementation of the algorithms presented in [8] constrain all the clusters to have the same size. We chose to keep the parameters they used which are 8 clusters of 16 computational resources each, leading to a total of 128 resources per platform.

In the following experiments, each run instance consists of a platform, a workload and a scheduling algorithm. Every generated workload consists of 300 jobs extracted from the cleaned trace (in the SWF format) of the CEA-Curie supercomputer. Our job selection criteria were to remove jobs that cannot fit entirely in one cluster and, in order to obtain interesting workloads, to ensure the resulting schedule makespan is not fixed by the longest job. Tiny jobs fit easily in the backfilling and very big ones are usually in specific queues, we then decided to only keep jobs whose execution time t_j is between two bounds $l_t \leq t_j \leq u_t$. Typical values for the bounds are $l_t = 1$ h and $u_t = 1$ *day*. The method used to select the jobs is to first remove every job that does not fit our criteria then to randomly pick 300 jobs depending on a given random seed.

Since the trace only contains the execution time, without any detail of actual computations or communications patterns, we chose to use basic homogeneous patterns and to create the amounts from the real execution time of the jobs. Let

ret_j be the real execution time of job j in the trace file. Let rw_j be the user-given walltime of job j. Let F_{comp}, F_{comm} and F_w be respectively the computation factor, the communication factor and the walltime factor. For each job j, the computation row matrix c_j is computed via $c_j = R^1_{size_j} \times ret_j \times F_{comp}$ where $R^1_{size_j}$ is a row matrix of $size_j$ columns of 1. For each job j, the communication square matrix C_j is obtained with the following formula $C_j = S^1_{size_j} \times ret_j \times F_{comm}$ where $S^1_{size_j}$ is a square matrix of size $size_j \times size_j$ of 1. For example, $R^1_3 = \begin{pmatrix} 1 & 1 & 1 \end{pmatrix}$ and $S^1_2 = \begin{pmatrix} 1 & 1 \\ 1 & 1 \end{pmatrix}$. For each job j, $size_j$ is read from the trace and w_j is chosen big enough to ensure the job won't be killed via the following formula $w_j = max(rw_j, ret_j \times F_w)$. With small walltimes, the jobs allocations would not matter since jobs would not be allowed to complete and would simply be killed after the same amount of time in any placement. Finally, the release date of each job j is set to 0 to remain in the same experimental setting as in [8], which will allow us to analyse the difference between our results and the previous ones.

5.2   Competing Heuristics

The scheduling algorithms we will compare are variants of the well-known conservative backfilling algorithm [9] targeting the minimization of *makespan* (completion time of the last running job). This algorithm maintains two data structures. The first one is a list of queued jobs and the times at which they are guaranteed to start execution. The other is a profile which stores the expected future processor usage. This profile is usually a list of consecutive time slices which store the resources status for each period. When a new job j_n is submitted, the profile is traversed in order to find a *hole* in the resource usage in which j_n may fit (depending on the job width w_{j_n} and height $size_{j_n}$). Let us suppose the profile traversal is done by ascending date and that this procedure will return different holes in which j_n may fit. When a fitting hole is found, it may either be accepted or rejected. If accepted, the scheduling algorithm must select which resources within the hole will be allocated to j_n. Otherwise, if the hole is rejected, the profile traversal continues and future fitting holes will be found until one is accepted. The algorithms that will be studied in the present paper differ in their last phase, which consists in accepting or rejecting the current hole and selecting which resources are allocated to j_n in case of acceptance. A detailed description of these variants and their pseudo-code is given in [8]. In the remaining of this section, let j_n be the newly submitted job, $H \subseteq M$ the set of available resources in the current hole and $S \subseteq H$ the selection of resources within H on which the job j_n will be executed.

The **basic** variant always accepts the first fitting hole and selects the first resources *i.e.* $S \subseteq H$ such that $card(S) = size_{j_n}$ and $\sum_{s \in S} id_s$ is minimal. The **best effort contiguous** always accepts the first fitting hole and selects a continuous block of resources if possible. In this context, the contiguity of the set of resources S means that there exist resources with contiguous indexes. If there is no contiguous set of resources of size $size_{j_n}$ in H, this variant selects the first resources as the basic variant would do. The **best effort local** variant always accepts the first fitting hole and selects a local set of resources if possible. Otherwise, it returns the first resources as the basic variant would do. In the context of this paper, S is said to be a local set of resources if all the resources in S are located in the same cluster. The **contiguous** variant forces the contiguity constraint on S. Consequently, this variant may reject the first fitting holes if they do not match the constraint. The **local** variant forces the locality constraint on S. Consequently, just as in the case of the contiguous variant, the local variant may reject the first fitting holes if they do not match the locality constraint. Thanks to the authors of the article [8], we were able to directly use their algorithms implementation in conjunction with our simulator which avoided us to reimplement them.

5.3   Homogeneous Platform Experiment

The goal of the first experiment was to compare the behaviour of the different scheduling algorithms when the job amount of communication is increased on the same homogeneous platform. The jobs of this experiment were generated with the following parameters: 20 random seeds were used (0 to 19), leading to 20 different base workloads. We picked $F_{comp} = 10^6$, $F_w = 10^3$, and 40 different values for the F_{comm} parameter have been used which correspond to a linear variation starting from 0 with steps of 10^7. The length bounds to pick the jobs were $l_t = 1\,\mathrm{h}$ and $u_t = 4\,\mathrm{h}$ in order to obtain jobs whose simulated execution time is interesting (*i.e.* the resulting schedule makespan is not only fixed by the biggest job) across the used values of F_{comm}. All the clusters of the platform used in this experiment are the same and defined by the following parameters. $bw_{s_c} = 1.25 \cdot 10^9$, $lat_{s_c} = 0$, $bw_c = 1.25 \cdot 10^6$, $lat_c = 24 \cdot 10^{-9}$. The platform main switch parameters are $bw_b = 1.25 \cdot 10^9$ and $lat_b = 24 \cdot 10^{-9}$. This platform is derived from the existing Grid'5000 Griffon cluster whose platform description was available in the SimGrid examples. The combination of these parameters created 4000 instances (800 per scheduling algorithm variant).

Figure 1 shows the makespan C_{max} of the resulting schedule of every run instance of the first experiment. Additionally, a linear trendline has been computed for a better comparison of the heuristics. The basic algorithm (as defined in the previous section) depicted in the top left is completely without constraints, and has the worst performance of all competing heuristics. Imposing contiguity without any knowledge of the underlying structure gives better performances than basic, while knowledge of locality further improves the results. More surprisingly, the strict heuristics are outperforming the more relaxed heuristics, even though strict heuristics delay some jobs if the constraints cannot be matched. Furthermore, the makespan induced by the forced constraints are much more stable than their best-effort counterparts.

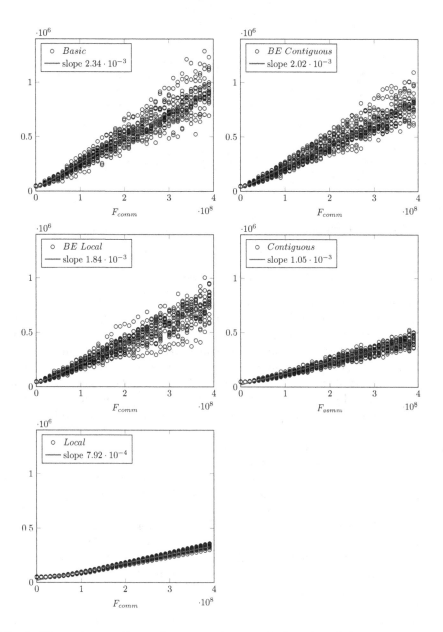

Fig. 1. The makespan C_{max} of every run instance in function of the communication factor F_{comm} for the homogeneous platforms experiment. To each figure corresponds a scheduling algorithm. Each point corresponds to a schedule (800 per scheduling algorithm).

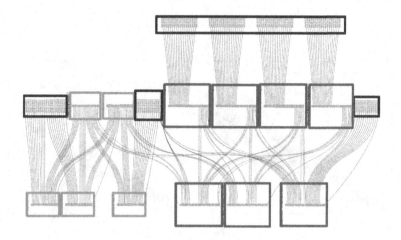

Fig. 2. Grid'5000 cluster architecture in Grenoble (Color figure online).

5.4   Heterogeneous Platform Experiments

The goal of the following two experiments is the same as the homogeneous one: seeing how the different scheduling algorithms behave when the amount of communication within jobs is increased. However, these experiments focus on many heterogeneous platforms instead of one homogeneous platform, to more closely reflect the existing clusters in our computing centers. For example, Fig. 2 gives an idea of the layout of the Grid'5000 cluster in Grenoble[1]. The red rectangles are 40 Gb/s Infiniband switches, orange rectangles are 20 Gb/s Infiniband switches, while the blue rectangles are three different families of computing nodes.

In order to remain realistic in the kind of platform heterogeneity to simulate, we analyzed the network of several Grid'5000 sites and ran a linear algebra benchmarking tool on many machines to have an idea of how much the node computational power may vary within one site. Our results on the Rennes and Grenoble site showed that the network bandwidth might vary between 1 and 4 and that the node computational power may vary between 1 and 3. More precisely, with our benchmark the computational power in the Rennes site were 1, 2.02 and 2.94 times more powerful than the lowest one. On Grenoble we obtained computational powers of 1.24, 1.61 and 1.72 times the lowest one. We then decided to create a set of lowly heterogeneous platforms and a set of highly heterogeneous platforms and see how the different scheduling variants behave on such platforms.

The two heterogeneous experiments use six clusters whose parameters can be found in Table 1. The first heterogeneous experiment uses four platforms formed by 3 clusters c_1, 3 clusters c_2 and 2 clusters c_3. The four platforms differ by the ordering in which the clusters are in the platform. The used orderings are by

---

[1] For more details, a larger version of the figure is available at: https://www.grid5000.fr/mediawiki/index.php/Grenoble:Network.

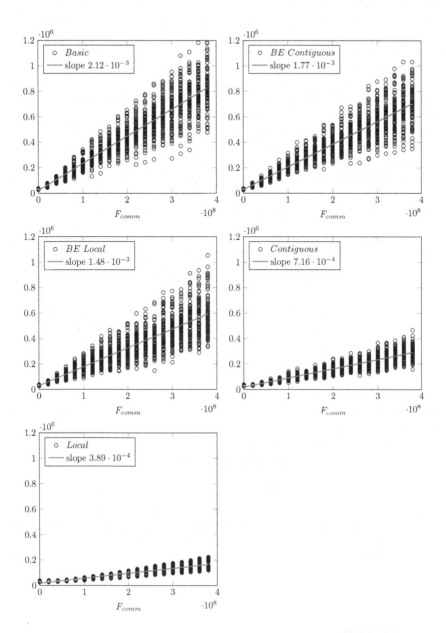

Fig. 3. The makespan C_{max} of every run instance in function of the communication factor F_{comm} for the heterogeneous platforms experiment. To each figure corresponds a scheduling algorithm. Each point corresponds to a schedule (1600 per scheduling algorithm).

ascending computational power $o_1 = (c_1, c_1, c_1, c_2, c_2, c_2, c_3, c_3)$, by descending computational power $o_2 = (c_3, c_3, c_3, c_2, c_2, c_2, c_1, c_1)$ and other orderings $o_3 = (c_1, c_2, c_2, c_3, c_3, c_2, c_1, c_1)$ and $o_4 = (c_3, c_1, c_2, c_3, c_1, c_2, c_1, c_2)$. The workloads of this experiment have been generated with the following parameters: 10 random seeds have been used (0 to 9). We used $F_{comp} = 10^6$, $F_w = 10^3$, and 20 different values for the F_{comm} parameter have been used which correspond to a linear variation starting from 0 with steps of $2 \cdot 10^7$. The length bounds to pick the jobs were $l_t = 1\,\text{h}$ and $u_t = 4\,\text{h}$. The second heterogeneous experiment is exactly the same as the first but its platforms use clusters c_4, c_5, c_6 instead respectively of clusters c_1, c_2 and c_3. We call the first experiment highly heterogeneous because the resource computational power varies from 1 to 3 and the network bandwidth from 1 to 4 within it. We call the second experiment lowly heterogeneous because these amounts doesn't vary as much as in the first experiment. Each experiment consists of 4000 run instances (800 per scheduling algorithm variant).

Table 1. The parameters of the clusters used in heterogeneous experiments. These values are multiplication factors of our base cluster b whose values are $bw_{s_b} = 10\,Gbits \cdot s^{-1}$, $lat_{s_b} = 0\,s$, $cp_b = 286.097 \cdot 10^3\,flop \cdot s^{-1}$, $bw_b = 10\,Gbits \cdot s^{-1}$, $lat_b = 24 \cdot 10^{-9}\,s$.

c	bw_{s_c}	lat_{s_c}	cp_c	bw_c	lat_c
c_1	2	0	1	1	1
c_2	4	0	2.02	1	1
c_3	1	0	2.94	1	1

c	bw_{s_c}	lat_{s_c}	cp_c	bw_c	lat_c
c_4	1	0	1.24	1	1
c_5	2	0	1.61	1	1
c_6	1	0	1.72	1	1

Figure 3 shows the makespan of the different scheduling algorithm variants when the amount of communication is increased in the heterogeneous experiments. These graphs do not differ greatly from the homogeneous case: for the makespan, the forced constraint variants scale better and are more stable than their best-effort counterparts when the amount of communication within jobs is increased. Furthermore, we did not notice any impact of the cluster ordering within one platform on the resulting schedules makespan. We did not notice a great difference between the slightly heterogeneous platforms and the highly heterogeneous ones neither, that is why the results of the two experiments have been plotted together. The most notable result is that in a heterogeneous setting, the locality knowledge is much more important as the gap between the basic heuristic and the locality aware is greatly increased.

6   Conclusion

The purpose of this work was to show through simulations if theoretical models are giving pertinent insight on job scheduling on large scale hierarchical and heterogeneous platforms. The main hypothesis we tested was that enforcing contiguity or locality would not degrade the performance. The results clearly show that the constraints are beneficial to the schedules, by reducing the communication times. More broadly, this shows that models where internal communications are hidden within parallel tasks are very ill-suited to current architectures, and should be reevaluated. The tool we developed is very general and relies on a powerful simulator, which will in the near future enable studies on different network topologies, and assess the impact of scheduling policies on a variety of objectives.

Acknowledgments. The work is partially supported by the ANR project MOEBUS. Experiments presented in this paper were carried out using the Grid'5000 experimental testbed, being developed under the INRIA ALADDIN development action with support from CNRS, RENATER and several Universities as well as other funding bodies (see https://www.grid5000.fr).

References

1. Casanova, H., Giersch, A., Legrand, A., Quinson, M., Suter, F.: Versatile, scalable, and accurate simulation of distributed applications and platforms. J. Parallel Distrib. Comput. **74**(10), 2899–2917 (2014)
2. Giroudeau, R., König, J.C.: Scheduling with communication delay. In: Multiprocessor Scheduling: Theory and Applications, pp. 1–26. ARS Publishing, December 2007
3. Hunold, S.: One step towards bridging the gap between theory and practice in moldable task scheduling with precedence constraints. Concurrency Comput. Pract. Experience **27**(4), 1010–1026 (2015)
4. Hunold, S., Casanova, H., Suter, F.: From simulation to experiment: a case study on multiprocessor task scheduling. In: Proceedings of the 13th Workshop on Advances on Parallel and Distributed Processing Symposium (APDCM) (2011)
5. Jeannot, E., Meneses, E., Mercier, G., Tessier, F., Zheng, G.: Communication and topology-aware load balancing in charm++ with treematch. In: IEEE Cluster 2013. IEEE, Indianapolis, United States, September 2013
6. Leung, J.: Handbook of Scheduling: Algorithms, Models, and Performance Analysis. Chapman and Hall/CRC Computer and Information Science Series. CRC Press, Boca Raton (2004)
7. Lifka, D.A.: The ANL/IBM SP scheduling system. In: Feitelson, D.G., Rudolph, L. (eds.) IPPS-WS 1995 and JSSPP 1995. LNCS, vol. 949. Springer, Heidelberg (1995)
8. Lucarelli, G., Mendonca, F., Trystram, D., Wagner, F.: Contiguity and locality in backfilling scheduling. In: 2015 15th IEEE/ACM International Symposium on Cluster, Cloud and Grid Computing (CCGrid), May 2015
9. Mu'alem, A.W., Feitelson, D.G.: Utilization, predictability, workloads, and user runtime estimates in scheduling the ibm sp2 with backfilling. IEEE Trans. Parallel Distrib. Syst. **12**(6), 529–543 (2001)
10. Pascual, J.A., Navaridas, J., Miguel-Alonso, J.: Effects of topology-aware allocation policies on scheduling performance. In: Frachtenberg, E., Schwiegelshohn, U. (eds.) JSSPP 2009. LNCS, vol. 5798, pp. 138–156. Springer, Heidelberg (2009)
11. Sinnen, O.: Task Scheduling for Parallel Systems. Wiley Series on Parallel and Distributed Computing. Wiley, New York (2007)
12. Sinnen, O., Sousa, L.A., Sandnes, F.E.: Toward a realistic task scheduling model. IEEE Trans. Parallel Distrib. Syst. **17**(3), 263–275 (2006)

LSDVE - Large Scale Distributed Virtual Environments

Community Discovery for Interest Management in DVEs: A Case Study

Emanuele Carlini[1(✉)], Patrizio Dazzi[1], Matteo Mordacchini[2],
Alessandro Lulli[3], and Laura Ricci[3]

[1] ISTI, National Research Council (CNR), Pisa, Italy
{emanuele.Carlini,patrizio.dazzi}@isti.cnr.it
[2] IIT, National Research Council (CNR), Pisa, Italy
matteo.mordacchini@iit.cnr.it
[3] University of Pisa, Pisa, Italy
ricci@di.unipi.it

Abstract. An efficient interest management is a fundamental requirement to support Distributed Virtual Environments (DVEs). As avatars
move across the virtual environment, they often forming *communities*
by gathering around hotspots. Distributed community discovery is a
research area that gained momentum in the last years. In this paper
we propose a case study evaluation on the impact of communities and
community discovery on a distributed gossip-based interest management
architecture for DVEs. Our experimental evaluation shows that communities have a positive impacts on interest management, at the expense of
a small computational and communication overhead.

1 Introduction

Distributed Virtual Environments (DVEs) are geographically distributed applications in which multiple users interact simultaneously in a shared virtual environment. A common trait of DVEs architectures is the distribution of the state
of the virtual environment to the client machines. Many distribution approaches
have been proposed over the years [20], ranging from unstructured solutions
[12,21] to structured ones [3,15]. The fundamental requirement arising from the
distribution of the state is making sure that each client machine has its view of
the virtual environment up-to-date. This requirement is commonly called *Interest
Management* (IM), as the interest of each client is represented by only a specific
portion of the whole virtual environment. A large numbers of approaches have
been proposed to efficiently and effectively support IM (see [23] for a comprehensive list) in a distributed fashion. One of the most commonly used strategies to
support IM is to keep up-to-date only the portion of the virtual environment in
the visual/interaction Area of Interest (AoI) of the participants. AoIs can overlap one each other, especially in presence of hotspot, i.e. popular areas of the
virtual environment. In a sense, when many participants gather together in the
proximity of an hotspot, they form a *virtual community* whose interest is related
to the events happening around the hotspot. In such scenarios, it is interesting

© Springer International Publishing Switzerland 2015
S. Hunold et al. (Eds.): Euro-Par 2015 Workshops, LNCS 9523, pp. 273–285, 2015.
DOI: 10.1007/978-3-319-27308-2_23

to understand if the identification of such communities can be of any support to the management of the IM. In our context, the entities participating to the communities are the virtual agent of the users of the virtual environment (the so called *Avatars*). Due to the distributed nature of the DVEs, we are interested in approaches that perform community discovery in a fully distributed fashion, i.e. by only exploiting the information local to each entity and without the help of any central authority.

The aim of this paper is to evaluate the impact on DVEs of communities and the process of communities discovery. In a previous work [5], we provided preliminary results of an initial attempt to introduce communities in a distributed IM approach. Here, we provide a more organic and structured approach, which aims to provide an answer to the following research questions: (i) can communities identify in a timely manner the hotspots in a virtual environment? (ii) will the inclusion of community leaders in the process of information diffusion benefit to the effectiveness of the IM? (iii) what is the impact in terms of computational and communication overhead of the process of community discovery?

To answer these questions, we considered a solution for the management of IM that employs a set of gossip protocols for the dissemination of the updates in the virtual environment [7]. We integrated this solution with two algorithms for distributed community discovery: (i) GROUP, a gossip-based community discovery approach, and (ii) a gossip-based version of the AffinityPropagation algorithm. We conducted an experimental analysis by means of simulations, which considered two different mobility models. Results showed that the inclusion of communities improves the performance of IM when there is a tendency of avatars to spread in the virtual environment (i.e. to gather less frequently around hotspots), at the expense of an acceptable computational and communication overhead.

2   Related Work

Many DVE architectures and protocols have been proposed over the years [23]. A number of these approaches focused on solving distributed interest management by exploiting structured and unstructured Peer-to-Peer (P2P) solutions.

Approaches based on structured P2P (often based on Distributed Hash Tables) offer a stable and reliable network for the distributed dissemination of the state of the avatars [3,13,15]. However, these solution are often based on a distributed index, which needs to be maintained causing latencies and disruption in the interest management. Compared to structured approaches, unstructured P2P solutions focus on building the overlay according to the spatial proximity of the peers in the virtual environment [12,21]. In order to perform IM, each peer connects with a subset of its neighbours so that peers may warn each other both about their movements and about new peers entering their AoI. These approaches naturally adapt to the rapid evolving scenarios of DVEs and allow for large scalability, but introduce overhead in the complexity of the approach and make strong assumptions on the capability of peers. To combine the advantages of both structured and unstructured P2P solutions, we proposed an hybrid solution based on a combination of a centralized server and a best-effort mechanism providing support for distributed interest management [5]. In this paper we refer to this architecture as the *reference architecture* and it is presented in Sect. 3.

Community discovery is a well studied research problem that has applications to many research fields [17]. In general, a community is defined as a set of entities that share similar interests, which are encoded into a profile, one for each entity. Often associated to the concept of community is the concept of *exemplar* or leader of a community, which is the entity that best represents a community. Some popular solution for distributed community discovery, like CDC from Ramaswamy et al. [19], have the issue that their division of the nodes in clusters is highly dependent on the choice of the starting nodes. Other solutions, like USP2P from Datta et al. [8], assume that interests are uniformly distributed among the peers. However this assumption not necessarily holds in our scenario. For these reasons, for our evaluation we selected two solutions that do not require starting points and perform no strong assumptions, namely AffinityPropagation [10], described in Sect. 4.2, and GROUP [2,9], described in Sect. 4.1.

To the best of our knowledge, there are few gossip-based solutions for hotspot detection in DVE. [22] proposed an approach based on attraction of avatar according to a *mass* criterion. Similarly, [4] developed a gossip-based protocols that exploits a flock model to identifies cluster of avatars and the relative super peers. Both these solutions share many similarities with our approaches, and provide an experimental validation for gossip-based protocols in DVEs. However, we differentiate as we strongly focus on the concept of community, and their ability to approximate hotspots. In addition, the concept of exemplar of a community is slightly different from the concept of super peers. In particular, the latter directly participates to the topology of a network, rather the former represents a community and not necessarily is part of a defined topology.

3   Reference Architecture

The reference architecture considers an IM model where the information is delivered by the combination of an unstructured P2P network and a static server. A detailed presentation of this architecture can be found in [6,7]. Figure 1 presents an overview of the reference architecture. The server works as a regular VE server, i.e. receives information from the clients and in turn periodically informs the client with fresh information about the state of the virtual world. The P2P network is based on multiple layers of gossip protocols. The gossip networks are built and maintained in a purely distributed fashion, without any intervention of the server. The purpose of the P2P network is to give the possibility to increase the period of the server communications with client. In other words, the idea is to reduce the load on the server, and put more load on the set of peers. With a reduction of communication interval, the server can manage more clients in the same region and/or manage a larger region. For the sake of simplicity we consider a single server serving a close region of a generic DVE. Note that our approach applies also to the multi server case, provided that each client knows from which server to communicate with. Clients communicate with the server and among each other to receive update of the content of their AoI.

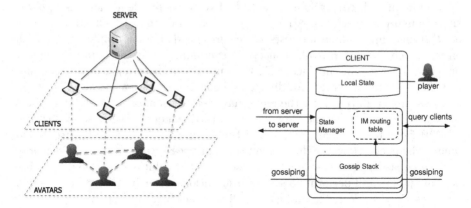

Fig. 1. The general architecture   **Fig. 2.** Components of a client

The component architecture of a client is presented in Fig. 2. The local state contains all the entities that are relevant for the avatar. Players can interact with them by modifying their and other entities' state. The state manager cares to forward these update to the server. Beside that, the other task of the State Manager is to keep the local state up-to-date. To perform this operation it exploits two mechanisms: the periodic feeding from the server and by querying other clients. These two mechanism affect each other, as the more efficient the querying of client is, the lower can be the frequency of the server feeding. However, since the state manager cannot query all the clients, the choice of which client to query must be limited in number and effective.

To provide an effective set of clients to query is indeed the task of the gossip stack component. As its name suggests, this component is composed by a stack of gossiping protocols, each one with a specific purpose. Each protocol feeds with information the protocols above and receive information from the protocols below. In a generic case this information can be whatever; since our ultimate goal is to find an effective set of clients, the information passing through the layers are client descriptors. Beside the connectivity information (such as the IP address), a client descriptor contains the information about the avatar of a particular client, namely: (i) the avatar id, (ii) the avatar's position, and (iii) a time stamp of creation.

By passing peer descriptors across layers is possible to refine the selection of peers. Also, a layered protocol model simplifies the composition of each layer. In our case the upper layers runs the *coverage peer sampling* protocol, which has been initially presented in [6]. We provide more details about the coverage peer sampling in Sect. 3.1. Running CPS alone would result the system to fall into a local minimum solution, and eventually peers may be disconnected from the network. Instead, by exploiting the layered architecture, the bottom layers can provide fresh information that can be used to introduce an amount of wise randomization in the selection of the peer. It is clear that the choice of protocol, especially if community oriented, to execute below CPS have an impact on the capacity of the system to perform interest management. This impact is evaluated experimentally in Sect. 5.

3.1 Coverage Peer Sampling

The goal of the *Coverage Peer Sampling* (CPS) is to provide the best selection of peers that maximise the retrieval of entities in the virtual environment. To clarify its purpose, let us explain the CPS from the point of view of a generic avatar A.

At an arbitrary point in time, A has in its local representation of the virtual environment the replicas of the entities that belong to its AoI. When A travels across the virtual environment, to maintain the content of A's AoI up-to-date, the peer (P) represented by A must discover the new entities belonging to the new AoI. Being in a fully distributed context, P searches for the peers that can efficiently provide such information. The criterion driving the CPS is the area coverage, which is defined as the following. Given a set S of peers and a pivot peer P, the area coverage can be defined as the intersection between the union of the AoIs of the peers in S and the AoI of P. Intuitively, a peer would maintain a view that maximises the coverage of its own AoI, so to have higher chances to obtain relevant information about entities in its proximity.

Therefore, this layer gossips with other clients to obtain a view that maximizes the area coverage defined above. This task is carried out by means of two functions: with *whom* and *what* to gossip. Let us consider a generic peer *P*. If P has some peers in the AoI, it selects the one that maximises the euclidean distance with his position. Conversely, the algorithm selects the peer that minimises the euclidean distance with the current position of P. The rationale behind this behaviour is that by choosing a peer at the borders of its AoI increases the knowledge of a region that could be explored in the close future. Once T has been selected, P evaluates the peer in its AoI with respect to the position of T. The evaluation is an heuristics that partitions the AoI's areas into a set of discrete tiles. and assigns a score to each tile equal to the reciprocal of the number of intersected AoIs. The heuristics then computes the score of a peer as the sum of the scores of each intersected tiles. We covered in full details the effectiveness and the cost of the heuristics in [7].

4 Distributed Community Discovery Protocols

The stack of gossip protocols that feed the CPS have a direct impact on the quality of the interest management. In particular, in terms of the reference architecture, providing proper information to the CPS can improve the area coverage and in turn, reduce the frequency of the communication with the server.

In general, the best information for the CPS are those avatars whose AoIs maximize the area coverage of the client's avatar. In this context, as the avatars gather around in the proximity of the hotspots, they can be seen as communities of avatar. Identifying these communities in real time would improve the results of the CPS, in particular by considering the *exemplar* of the communities. In order to be fully integrated in the reference architecture, the community discovery algorithm must be fully distributed and capable of be implemented as a gossip protocol. To this end, we created an enhanced architecture that improve the reference architecture with a gossip layers of community discovery, which run AffinityPropagation or GROUP.

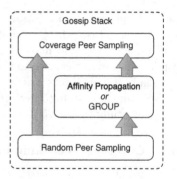

Fig. 3. The gossip protocols stack in the enhanced architecture

Figure 3 shows the stack of the gossip protocol in the enhanced architecture where a new layer for community discovery has been added to the stack. Note that, despite the addition of the community discovery layer, the CPS is still fed by the random peer sampling, for reasons of connectivity and for avoiding to rely only on communities in situations when peers are not gathered into hotspots.

4.1 GROUP

GROUP is a protocol that exploits a gossip-based collaborative process to cooperatively build communities in a P2P network. In GROUP, peers try to identify the nodes that are best suited to represent a community using a distributed voting scheme. Each node expresses a set of votes (i.e. endorsements to potential community representatives) to the most similar peers, among the ones it knows. The number of votes received by each peer represents the consensus achieved by the peer as a community representative. Eventually, the peers that has received the largest amount of votes are elected as representatives and, together with the peers that contributed to their election, form a community. The profile of a representative is used as the community exemplar, and in our case the profile correspond to the position of the avatar in the virtual environment.

The representatives election mechanism is divided in three steps:

1. *Similar Peer Detection*: In this phase each peer selects and votes its k most similar other peers taken from the peer's neighbourhood. This preliminary voting phase will be used in the next step to determine the most central peers in the similarity-based overlay.
2. *Potential Candidates Selection*: After the completion of the previous phase, each peer enters a second phase, in which it exploits the information coming from the previous step. At this point, each peer has to select a potential community representative from its neighbourhood. A peer chooses as a potential representative the neighbour that has received a number of votes higher than a representative threshold θ_r. Then, it "endorses" (i.e., it sends a *potential candidate* vote) the chosen neighbour as a potential representative.

3. *Representative Election Phase*: Finally, in the last phase, a peer p chooses as its representative the peer that has gained the highest number of *"potential candidate"* votes. In case two or more neighbours has received the same number of votes, p chooses the one with the most similar profile to its own. It then uses the profile of the chosen representative as its community identifier.

One remarkable feature of the GROUP protocol is that peers in a community are not required to keep track of their community structure. Peers generally do not have any explicit knowledge about the composition of their own community. The flow of votes during the election mechanism is the only interaction and information required by GROUP.

4.2 Affinity Propagation

AffinityPropagation [10] is an algorithm for clustering data that derives from the belief propagation [14] model. The aim of AffinityPropagation is to discover the best exemplars from a set of data points, namely the points that are more suited for representing a whole set of points. The algorithm is based on a message passing approach, which makes it suitable to be applied in a distributed context.

Starting from its original formulation, we implemented a gossip-based version of the algorithms that has been integrated into our reference architecture. The information needed to discover avatar communities in are organized in three matrix-like data structures: similarity, availability and responsibility. The *similarity* matrix contains the information about the suitability of an avatar j to serve as the exemplar for another avatar i. The similarity between avatars is computed as the negative Euclidean distance between the location of the avatars in the virtual environment. The *availability* matrix counts the messages sent from candidate exemplars to potential members of the community, indicating how appropriate that candidate would be as an exemplar. Finally, the *responsibility* matrix counts the messages sent from community members to candidate exemplars, indicating how well-suited the avatar would be as a member of the candidate exemplar's community.

AffinityPropagation differs from other clustering algorithms such as k means or k-medoids: these algorithms begins with an initial set of randomly selected exemplars, and iteratively refine this set. aiming at reducing the sum of squared errors between the exemplars and the points they represent. Conversely, Affinity Propagation does not require any a-priori knowledge about the number of community to be built and the quality of the result it provides does not depend by the initial selection of potential exemplars.

5   Experimental Evaluation

We conducted our experimental evaluation by using PeerSim [18], considering a virtual environment composed by a squared region with a side of 1200 points. The AoIs of the avatars have a radius of 50 points. The region has 10 circular hotspots, whose radius is 100 points. Each simulation is divided into 1000 steps, and we set to perform a periodic feeding from the server every 10 steps. 1000 avatars move on the map according to the two following mobility models.

- BLUEBANANA, presented by Legtchenko et al. [16], which simulates avatars movement in a commercial MMOG, Second Life [1]. When an avatar reaches a hotspot, it explores the hotspot for some time, and eventually it moves to another hotspot. This mobility model exposes a fair balance between the time spent by avatars in hotspots and outland, and there is no predefined path connects two hotspots;
- Random Way Point (RWP) presented by Hong et al. [11], and initially thought to evaluate the impact of mobility in ad-hoc wireless network. In RWP each avatar moves independently toward a random chosen way point (the hotspots in our case). As soon as an avatar reaches an hotspot it stops there for a random time interval, and afterwards, it chooses another random hotspot.

5.1 Hotspots Approximation

An interesting analysis is to understand how GROUP and AffinityPropagation identify the clusters of players as they gather around the hotspots in the virtual environment. In a sense, an hotspot can be seen like a community of avatars with an interest in a specific area of the DVE. In our setup, community discovery mechanisms can only provide an approximation of the hotspots, mainly for two reasons: (i) in a DVE, not all avatars belong to an hotspot at any given time, while communities usually contain all entities, and (ii) we defined hotposts as circle having fixed radius, while communities can vary in size. To conduct this analysis, we exploited the BB mobility model as in this model the avatars tends to cluster more than with RWP.

The three images in Fig. 4 represent a snapshot of the system, i.e. the position of the avatars at a given point in time. Figure 4a shows the hotspots as circles, while the points represents the avatar. In Fig. 4b and c communities are represented as circles, having the centre with the coordinates of the exemplar avatar, and the radius is equal to the average distance of the avatars participating to the community from the exemplar. From the figures it can be seen that the communities algorithms behave differently, and it can be noted a tendency of GROUP in building larger communities with respect to AP.

In order to study the relationship between communities and hotspot over time, we defined *hotspot approximation* as the percentage of avatars whose closest hotspot is the same than the hotspot associated to the exemplar of the avatar's community. Figure 5 shows the hotspot approximation for GROUP and AffinityPropagation. From the figure, it is evident that AffinityPropagation achieves a better approximation than GROUP. In particular, GROUP has a very stable value of the approximation, indicating that is not reactive enough to sustain the movement of the avatars. By comparison, the communities of AffinityPropagation seem more dynamics, allowing for a better approximation of the moving avatars.

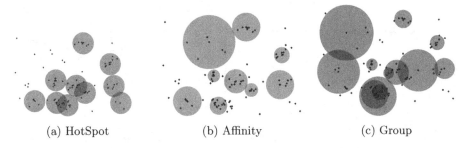

(a) HotSpot	(b) Affinity	(c) Group

Fig. 4. A visual representation of hotspots approximation during a simulation cycle

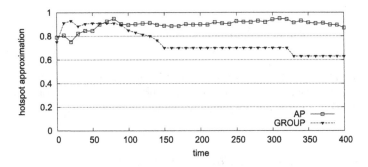

Fig. 5. Approximating hotspots: AffinityPropagation vs GROUP

5.2   Area Coverage

This section compares the impact of GROUP and AffinityPropagation on the interest management. To measure this impact we used the *average area coverage* (AAC). As a baseline, we consider a basic version that just employs a random peer sampling. We computed the AAC by averaging the area coverage of all avatars, computed as defined in Sect. 3.1 and considering the peers in each peer's view.

Figure 6a and b show the AAC with respectively the BLUEBANANA and RWP mobility models. The results of the two models are different, and highlight interesting insight on the impact of communities on the interest management. When considering BLUEBANANA, all the versions behave similarly. The version equipped with just the RPS obtains the best performances, even if the difference is very marginal with the other versions. When considering the RWP instead, the RPS version obtains by far the worst performance, and the AffinityPropagation achieve the best results.

These results suggest a sort of counter-intuitive behaviour when adding community discovery to the reference architecture. When avatars are naturally more clustered (as it happens in BLUEBANANA) communities have a little impacts, rather when avatars are more distributed in the virtual environment (as in RWP) the communities improve the quality of the interest management. In other words, when avatars stay closer to each other, the random peer sampling is enough to

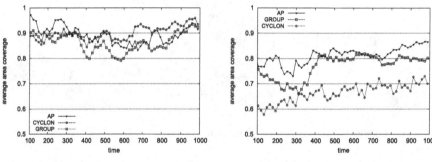

(a) Average Area Coverage with BLUE-BANANA

(b) Average Area Coverage with RWP

Fig. 6. Comparison of average area coverage

discover potential peers that contains useful information for interest management. When avatars are more scattered, a random strategy is not enough and the identification of the communities identifies such peers that contain useful information.

5.3   Message Number and Computational Overhead

In this section we compared how GROUP and AP would impact on the network and the CPU of peers. Specifically the following metrics were used for the analysis: (i) *message number*: the number of message sent by each peer in a step of the simulation; (ii) *computational overhead*: the relative time spent by the coverage peer sampling protocol to merge its view and the views provided by the additional layers and to calculate the AoI coverage.

Table 1 provides an overview of the results, considering BLUEBANANA and RWP. Each value represents the average taken out of 1000 steps, starting from step 100. For the computational overhead is also shown the standard deviation.

In terms of computational overhead we observed that GROUP spent more time in computing the coverage peer sampling. We believe this is a direct consequence of the fact that in GROUP the communities tend to be larger than in AffinityPropagation, as can be observed in the analysis of Fig. 4c. In addition, for the BLUEBANANA mobility model the computational overhead for GROUP is doubled with respect to RWP due to the fact that in BLUEBANANA peers tend to create higher density near hotspots. The analysis of the number of messages shows two interesting insights. First, GROUP requires lesser messages than AP to organize the peer in communities. Second, for AP the number of messages depends neither on the particular mobility models or the specific cycle of the simulation. Conversely, the number of messages of GROUP depends on the mobility models, having less messages when the avatar are more spread thorough the virtual world.

The presented results suggest that there exists a trade off between message number and computational overhead between AP and GROUP. On one side,

Table 1. Comparison of Message number and Computational overhead

		Comp. overhead	Message number
BLUEBANANA	AffinityPropagation	34.56 ± 8.60	32
	GROUP	87.79 ± 23.88	20
RWP	AffinityPropagation	30.09 ± 6.52	32
	GROUP	48.93 ± 10.87	18

GROUP has an higher computational overhead (and an higher standard deviation), however, it uses around 40 % messages less than AP. If analysed together with the results on area coverage discussed in Sect. 5.2 we can conclude that AP would be the protocol of choice, unless the number of messages is a critical parameter of the infrastructure managing the DVE.

6 Conclusion

Whether community discovery can improve the quality of interest management in a DVE is an interesting research question. In this paper we provided an empirical analysis in the effort of answering this question. Even if our experiments are limited to a particular reference architecture, we have found that the introduction of community discovery mechanisms actually can improve interest management especially when there is the tendency of avatars to spread around the virtual environment. Also, this comes with an acceptable computational and communication overhead. To understand if community discovery would have an impact on different scenarios, in the future we plan to investigate further distributed community discovery protocols (e.g. [4,22]). In addition, we plan to evaluate these protocols in combination with other popular solutions that perform IM in DVEs.

References

1. Second life website. http://secondlife.com/, Last Accessed on 6 May 2015
2. Baraglia, R., Dazzi, P., Mordacchini, M., Ricci, L., Alessi, L.: GROUP: a gossip based building community protocol. In: Balandin, S., Koucheryavy, Y., Hu, H. (eds.) NEW2AN 2011 and ruSMART 2011. LNCS, vol. 6869, pp. 496–507. Springer, Heidelberg (2011)
3. Bharambe, A., Douceur, J., Lorch, J., Moscibroda, T., Pang, J., Seshan, S., Zhuang, X.: Donnybrook: enabling large-scale, high-speed, peer-to-peer games. ACM SIGCOMM Comput. Commun. Rev. **38**(4), 389–400 (2008)
4. Botev, J., Rothkugel, S.: Flora: flock-based resource allocation for decentralized distributed virtual environments. In: Proceedings of the 4th International ICST Conference on Simulation Tools and Techniques, pp. 257–264. ICST (Institute for Computer Sciences, Social-Informatics and Telecommunications Engineering) (2011)

5. Carlini, E., Dazzi, P., Mordacchini, M., Ricci, L.: Toward community-driven interest management for distributed virtual environment. In: an Mey, D., Alexander, M., Bientinesi, P., Cannataro, M., Clauss, C., Costan, A., Kecskemeti, G., Morin, C., Ricci, L., Sahuquillo, J., Schulz, M., Scarano, V., Scott, S.L., Weidendorfer, J. (eds.) Euro-Par 2013. LNCS, vol. 8374, pp. 363–373. Springer, Heidelberg (2014)

6. Carlini, E., Ricci, L., Coppola, M.: Reducing server load in MMOG via P2P gossip. In: Proceedings of the 11th Annual Workshop on Network and Systems Support for Games, p. 11. IEEE Press (2012)

7. Carlini, E., Ricci, L., Coppola, M.: Integrating centralized and peer-to-peer architectures to support interest management in massively multiplayer on-line games. Practice and Experience, Concurrency and Computation (2014)

8. Datta, S., Giannella, C., Kargupta, H.: Approximate distributed k-means clustering over a peer-to-peer network. IEEE Trans. Knowl. Data Eng. **21**(10), 1372–1388 (2009)

9. Dazzi, P., Felber, P., Leonini, L., Mordacchini, M., Perego, R., Rajman, M., Rivière, É.: Peer-to-peer clustering of web-browsing users. In: Procedings LSDS-IR, pp. 71–78 (2009)

10. Frey, B.J., Dueck, D.: Clustering by passing messages between data points. Science **315**(5814), 972–976 (2007)

11. Hong, X., Gerla, M., Pei, G., Chiang, C.C.: A group mobility model for Ad hoc wireless networks. In: Proceedings of the 2nd ACM International Workshop on Modeling, Analysis and Simulation of Wireless and Mobile Systems, pp. 53–60. ACM (1999)

12. Hu, S.Y., Chang, S.C., Jiang, J.R.: Voronoi state management for peer-to-peer massively multiplayer online games. In: 5th IEEE Consumer Communications and Networking Conference, 2008, CCNC 2008, pp. 1134–1138. IEEE (2008)

13. Kavalionak, H., Carlini, E., Ricci, L., Montresor, A., Coppola, M.: Integrating peer-to-peer and cloud computing for massively multiuser online games. Peer-to-Peer Networking and Applications, vol. 8(2), pp. 1–19. Springer, New York (2013)

14. Kschischang, F.R., Frey, B.J., Loeliger, H.A.: Factor graphs and the sum-product algorithm. IEEE Trans. Inf. Theor. **47**(2), 498–519 (2006)

15. Kulkarni, S., Douglas, S., Churchill, D.: Badumna: a decentralised network engine for virtual environments. Comput. Netw. **54**(12), 1953–1967 (2010)

16. Legtchenko, S., Monnet, S., Thomas, G.: Blue banana: resilience to avatar mobility in distributed MMOGS. In: 2010 IEEE/IFIP International Conference on Dependable Systems and Networks (DSN), pp. 171–180. IEEE (2010)

17. Malliaros, F.D., Vazirgiannis, M.: Clustering and community detection in directed networks: a survey. Phys. Rep. **533**(4), 95–142 (2013)

18. Montresor, A., Jelasity, M.: PeerSim: a scalable P2P simulator. In: Proceedings of the 9th International Conference on Peer-to-Peer (P2P 2009), pp. 99–100. Seattle, WA, September 2009

19. Ramaswamy, L., Gedik, B., Liu, L.: A distributed approach to node clustering in decentralized peer-to-peer networks. IEEE Trans. Parallel Distrib. Syst. **16**, 814–829 (2005)

20. Ricci, L., Carlini, E.: Distributed virtual environments: from client server to cloud and P2P architectures. In: 2012 International Conference on High Performance Computing and Simulation (HPCS), pp. 8–17. IEEE (2012)

21. Ricci, L., Genovali, L., Carlini, E., Coppola, M.: Aoi-cast in distributed virtual environments: an approach based on delay tolerant reverse compass routing. Practice and Experience, Concurrency and Computation (2012)

22. Scholtes, I., Botev, J., Esch, M., Schloss, H., Sturm, P.: Using epidemic hoarding to minimize load delays in P2P distributed virtual environments. In: Bertino, E., Joshi, J.B.D. (eds.) CollaborateCom 2008. LNICST, vol. 10, pp. 578–593. Springer, Heidelberg (2009)
23. Yahyavi, A., Kemme, B.: Peer-to-peer architectures for massively multiplayer online games: a survey. ACM Comput. Surv. (CSUR) **46**(1), 9 (2013)

Continuation Complexity: A Callback Hell for Distributed Systems

Edgar Zamora-Gómez$^{(\boxtimes)}$, Pedro García-López, and Rubén Mondéjar

Department of Computer Engineering and Mathematics,
Universitat Rovira i Virgili, Tarragona, Spain
{edgar.zamora,pedro.garcia,ruben.mondejar}@urv.cat

Abstract. Designing and validating large-scale distributed systems is still a complex issue. The asynchronous event-based nature of distributed communications makes these systems complex to implement, debug and test. In this article, we introduce the continuation complexity problem, that arises when synchronous invocations must be converted to asynchronous event code. This problem appears in most Actor libraries where communication is mainly asynchronous, and where a synchronous call to other Actor would block the current Actor, precluding the processing of incoming messages.

We propose here a novel parallel invocation abstraction that considerably simplifies the continuation complexity problem for distributed actor systems requiring non-blocking synchronous invocations. Our parallel abstraction extends the message passing concurrency model to support concurrent interleavings of method executions within a single Actor. We present here two candidate solutions for implementing such parallel calls: one based on threads and locking, and other based on green threads and continuations.

We evaluated the simplicity of our solution implementing a well known distributed algorithm like Chord (ring-based structured overlay). We compare our Actor implementation of Chord with three different simulators (PeerSim, PlanetSim, Macedon). This validation demonstrates that our approach is superior in simplicity (less LoC) and complexity (less McAbe complexity), envisaging its great potential for distributed systems scenarios.

Keywords: Actor model · Object actors · Continuation complexity

1 Introduction

Nowadays, modeling, programming, and validating distributed systems is a complex issue requiring advanced skills. On the one hand, multithread programming, locks and concurrency-control can considerably complicate the development of any middleware library. In general, programming event-based systems using callbacks is a challenging task. Callback coordination is complex because different code fragments must manipulate the same data and the order of execution is unpredictable.

© Springer International Publishing Switzerland 2015
S. Hunold et al. (Eds.): Euro-Par 2015 Workshops, LNCS 9523, pp. 286–298, 2015.
DOI: 10.1007/978-3-319-27308-2_24

In literature, the problem of callback management is known as Callback Hell [4]. A recent analysis of Adobe desktop applications revealed that event handling logic caused nearly a half of the bugs reported.

Even if this problem is normally associated to user interface code, the Callback Hell is also very relevant in the development of distributed systems [6,8]. In particular, many distributed systems like Actor libraries, event-based simulators [5,7], and event-based server libraries like node.js impose an asynchronous style of programming.

But the asynchronous event-based nature of distributed protocols implies tangled code using message handlers and callbacks that is difficult to follow and maintain. These problems get even worse when the distributed algorithms rely on Remote Procedure Call (RPC) semantics that require complex state maintenance between messages.

In these cases, a brief and succinct algorithm written with sequential code and RPCs will have to be broken in a number of separated callbacks. Callbacks then become the old *goto* statement revamped for distributed systems.

In this article we first identify and formalize the so called Continuation Complexity problem, which arises when synchronous RPC code must be converted to asynchronous messages and handlers. We also propose a solution to the Continuation Complexity problem for Actor libraries. To this end, we present a novel parallel invocation abstraction that permits blocking synchronous calls to other actors that do not stall the current Actor thread of control. Finally, to validate our approach, we evaluate the simplicity of our solution implementing a well-known distributed algorithm: a ring-based structured overlay (i.e., Chord).

2   Continuation Complexity Problem

The Continuation Complexity Problem arises in distributed systems when synchronous RPC code must be converted to asynchronous messages and handlers. We call this problem Continuation Complexity because it is directly related to the concept of Continuation [9] in programming languages. In distributed settings, the developer is implicitly implementing its own continuation when he must split a synchronous call in different code fragments using messages and handlers (callbacks). Normally, the programming language uses a call stack for storing the variables its functions use. But in this case, the developer must explicitly maintain this information between different messages.

The complexity of programming event-based systems with callbacks is also very relevant in interactive user interface systems. For example, a recent solution to the so-called Callback Hell is the reactive programming paradigm [3].

Another interesting solution in the .NET platform are the powerful *async* and *await* abstractions [1]. They simplify asynchronous programming and improve the clarity of code, and thus reducing the Callback Hell problem. Nevertheless these abstractions are not transparent to the developer and they are not aimed for single-threaded Actor libraries.

In distributed systems, we want to outline two major programming models that can help to cope with asynchronous event programming: distributed state machines and Actor libraries.

Distributed state machines are the classical formal model for the implementation of distributed systems. Macedon [10] is a concise Domain Specific Language (DSL) that aims to cover the entire cycle of distributed systems including design, implementation, experimentation, and evaluation. In any case, we compare our implementation of Chord with Macedon one in Sect. 5.

The *Actor model* [2] has inspired many middleware solutions since it provides an elegant model of concurrent communication, which treats Actors as the universal primitives of concurrent computation.

A recent proposal for distributed Actors is Akka. Akka has an advanced programming model where Futures are integrated with Actor-based receive operations. They provide TypedActors enabling synchronous method invocation over Actors, but they clearly recommend to use asynchronous communications and Futures to avoid blocking the current Actor execution.

This is not an exclusive problem of Actor models, but of the development of event-based system. In this line, event-based simulators [5, 7] require that the algorithms must be converted to asynchronous messages and message handlers.

The Continuation Complexity is a recurrent problem in distributed systems based on RPC semantics like Peer-to-Peer (P2P) algorithms and overlays (e.g., Chord or Kademlia), consensus algorithms (e.g., Paxos or 2PC) and distributed applications (e.g., key-value stores or replication algorithms).

The Continuation Complexity of a function depends directly on the number of RPCs inside this function plus the number of iterators containing RPCs in that function. Every RPC will produce three new code fragments: two for the continuation and one for the timeout code. With the continuation we refer to the code before the RPC that sends the request message, and the response handler containing the code that continues from that point onward. Furthermore, every RPC must contain a timeout handler that will also continue after the RPC if no response was received in the timeout time.

On the other hand, iterators containing RPCs must also be considered in the cost since the complexity increases as the response handler must control the state of the iteration in every response. This means that the handler must jump back and also repeat the sending of requests if the iteration has not finished.

The continuation complexity is directly related to the Cyclomatic complexity of the method including RPCs. When the control flow of the method is very complex (high Cyclomatic Complexity) the continuation complexity is also very high. In this case, the original control flow must be rebuilt using messages and message handlers.

2.1 A Simple Example: Chord

Many distributed systems make extensive use of RPCs. Describing their algorithms using object oriented notation is straightforward, since an invocation of a method in a node implies a RPC to that node. In this line, the Chord [11] distributed routing algorithm is a suitable example of this approach.

Chord organizes nodes in a structured ring overlay where every node contains a local routing table with references to other nodes. Chord is also defined as a Distributed Hash Table (DHT) or Key Based Routing (KBR) layer, since the space of identifiers is uniformly distributed among nodes thanks to consistent hashing. In Chord, the routing algorithm is clockwise and every node is responsible of the identifiers between itself and its predecessor in the ring overlay.

Algorithm 1. Chord Routing Mechanism

---

function FIND_PREDECESSOR(id)
    $n1 \leftarrow this\_node$
    while id **is not between** (n1,n1.successor] **do**
        $n1 \leftarrow n1.closest\_preceding\_finger(id)$
    return n1
function CLOSEST_PRECEDING_FINGER(id)
    for $i \leftarrow N$ **down to** 1 **do**
        if $finger[i].node$ **is between** (n, id) **then**
            return finger[i].node
    return this_node

As we can see in the Algorithm 1, looking for a key (id) implies accessing the routing tables of nodes to find the closest node to that key. So if we invoke the *find_predecessor(id)* operation in a specific node, it will look for a node n where the identifier is in the range (n, n.successor). For example, in a Chord overlay with nodes N1, N7, N18, and N30, *find_predecessor(9)* will return the node N7.

This is a very interesting example, since closest_preceding_finger is a RPC invocation to other nodes. Indeed, it is a clear mechanism of iterative routing where the node performing the search must ask sequentially nodes that are closer to the destination.

Note that *closest_preceding_finger* is returning a reference to another Node. In a remote setting, this would imply sending a reference to the remote object.

Nevertheless, the problem arises when this code must be converted to purely asynchronous messages. This is happening in most networks and distributed simulators, but also in most Actor libraries. In this case, the developer must renounce to RPCs completely, and convert each RPC to two messages and message handlers: Message Request and Message Response.

The problem gets even worse when RPCs are invoked inside control blocks like iterators or conditionals. In these cases, the developer must also maintain the state of variables (context) between different messages. As we can see, this is happening in the *find_predecessor* method that is calling a RPC inside a *while* iterator. Even worse, in the control structure the condition can also contain RPCs (*n.successor*).

The Fig. 1 shows the control flow graph of the previous Algorithm 1, when divided in different code fragments. In this case, Actor 1 is the control flow of *find_predecessor* and Actor n is the control flow of *closest_preceding_finger*.

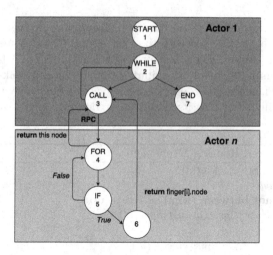

Fig. 1. Control flow Graph

The RPC call inside Actor 1 must be converted in messages to Actor n, and the return results will then resume the state of the control flow in Actor 1.

As we increase the number of RPCs, the complexity of breaking the code is even higher. Imagine now that we want to implement parallel queries to different nodes to increase the robustness of the iterative routing. If we must invoke now *closest_preceding_finger* in three nodes, the code must then handle the different messages and resume the state when necessary.

As we can see, a simple code written with RPCs must be scattered in different code fragments making more difficult its legibility and maintenance. This is a clear example of the Callback Hell in distributed systems.

3   Overcoming the Continuation Complexity Problem in Actor Models

The Continuation Complexity problem leads us to a paradox in Actor models: synchronous blocking calls are needed to correctly implement RPCs in order to avoid breaking the code into asynchronous messages and handlers. But Actor models are purely asynchronous, and using synchronous calls would block the calling Actor unique thread of control until the response arrives.

The aforementioned paradox also represents a burden for Object Oriented Actor libraries. If only asynchronous calls are allowed, the resulting code breaks with the traditional object oriented paradigm and complicates the resulting code.

To solve this problem, we present a novel method invocation abstraction called **parallel**, enabling synchronous invocations to other Actors, without stalling the current Actor's thread of control. Our parallel calls enable concurrent interleavings of method executions within a single Actor

3.1   Concurrency Control

The major challenge is to enable concurrent interleavings of method executions within a single Actor. We mainly want to allow the main Actor thread to continue processing incoming method requests while the parallel thread is blocked waiting for a response in a remote Actor due to a synchronous invocation.

We present two solutions: one based on threads and locks and another based on green threads and continuations,

Solution 1: Threads: The Actor implementation will spawn normal threads in the Scheduler and Parallel Methods threads. To achieve consistency between Scheduler and Parallel threads, we use traditional Thread Lock mechanisms that prevent multiple threads to access the same object at the same time. Similar to the Monitor Object pattern, we use a Lock in the Actor object that is only activated when parallel threads are spawned. We aim to provide here a simple solution to demonstrate that parallel threads can coexist with the Actor main thread without conflicting with the servant object shared state. Our lock mechanism is completely transparent to the developer, so that the simplicity of the message passing concurrency model is not affected.

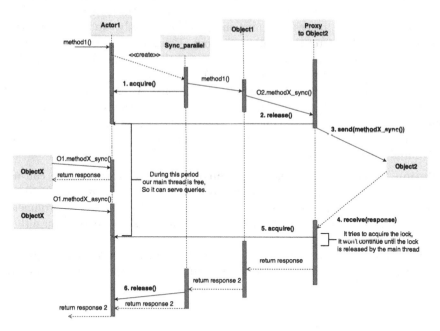

Fig. 2. Concurrency flow diagram

In Fig. 2 we can see how our solution handles the concurrency problem. In this flow diagram we can observe where it uses the Lock acquire and Lock release primitives in a call flow. In addition, it is necessary to know that a single Lock is shared between Actor and Parallel Threads wrappers for each Actor. The life cycle is the following:

1. **Acquire:** When a call is incoming, if it exists some parallel call in the object, we need to acquire the lock to be sure that only one thread at this time is using the object. In Fig. 2, we show an example with a parallel synchronous call. At this moment, a parallel thread takes the control of the object, and any other thread can not access to the object.
2. **Release:** The parallel thread sends the synchronous invocation to a remote actor. In this moment, the parallel actor releases the lock so that the main thread or other parallel threads can continue working. This is the key point where the Actor is not blocked until the response arrives, and it can process incoming messages.
3. **Acquire:** While the parallel thread is waiting the response, our main thread and other parallel threads can serve other petitions. When the response arrives to the Proxy, the Parallel thread will be able to continue executing the method. Nonetheless, it must try to acquire the Lock, because it is possible that the Lock is now in possession of another Thread.
4. **Release:** Finally, when the multicalls return object method ends, the parallel synchronous wrapper will release the Lock, and it will end its process.

As we can see, our solution ensures that only one thread access the shared state, but also that waiting for a response in a parallel thread will not preclude the main thread to process incoming messages. Obviously, we control whether the response will not return using a timeout. Using this system we guarantee that the main thread will not be blocked even if the response does not arrive.

Our solution permits to increase the Actor service time because it avoids blocking the Actor during synchronous invocations. We guarantee the correct interleavings of Actor parallel and main threads. Furthermore, we maintain the simplicity of message passing concurrency since the developer is still unaware of this concurrency control mechanisms. He must only tag the appropriate methods as *parallel* when necessary.

Solution 2: Micro Threads and Continuations: In this case, we can use Fig. 2 but removing the acquire and release invocations. In that case, we don't need to use a lock system. This is because in a single-threaded environment, two microthreads cannot modify the same state at the same time because their execution is sequential.

We assume here that the *send* and *receive* primitives in microthreads will execute a context-switch to other green thread processing the communication to other Actor. Following, we will try to explain better this process, step by step:

1. **send:** When a proxy sends a synchronous message to another Actor, it automatically releases its control to other microthread.
2. **receive:** Parallel microthread will be inactive until it will receive a message. At moment that it will receive a message it will wake up and wait for its turn to continue the method execution. The implicit continuation implies that the code continues from that point.

Since *send* and *receive* policies are executed inside the Proxy, the developer is completely unaware of context-switches and continuations. Furthermore, in this case there is no need to use locks to prevent concurrent access.

4   PyActive Abstractions

We present an Object Oriented implementation of the Actor model that is designed to support synchronous, asynchronous and parallel calls. We have implemented a prototype of this Actor library in Python that supports different remote transport protocols, and threading models: Python system threads and Stackless cooperative threads.

Our programming model for Object Actors provides explicit mechanisms for Actor creation and location, method invocation abstractions in actors, and pass by reference of Actor entities. Let us review these mechanisms in our Actor programming model.

We provide several **call abstractions** in Actors: asynchronous calls, timed synchronous calls, parallel calls and pass by reference.

An important difference in our model is that we introduce different types of method requests. The developer must explicitly establish the types of methods using annotations or meta-information that can be processed by the Actor library. As we can see in Fig. 3, we include this meta-information as properties of the class. These properties explicitly tell the Actor which methods are exposed and their different types.

Asynchronous calls are one-way invocations that do not require a response from the Actor. These are the usual calls implemented in Actor libraries since they naturally adapt to the asynchronous message passing concurrency model.

Timed Synchronous calls are two-way blocking invocations where the client waits for the response from the server during a certain time (timeout). If the timeout is reached an exception is triggered. This kind of calls are not usually recommended nor even implemented in Actor libraries since the entire calling Actor is blocked until the response arrives. This can be appropriate in state-machine protocols but it can also prevent the Actor for continuing its normal operation. But we claim that they are completely necessary to avoid the aforementioned continuation complexity.

Parallel calls imply the processing of the method invocation in a parallel thread in the Actor. As explained before they must be used to avoid stalling the current Actor when a method performs a synchronous blocking request to other Actor.

Pass by reference calls are invocations where either the parameters or the result contain a reference to another Actor. References to Actors (Proxies) must be explicitly tagged by the developer for performance but also for correctness. It is important not to confuse Objects and Actors references: where the former are restricted to a single address space, the latter can span different locations.

The best way to understand the simplicity of our approach is to implement well-known distributed algorithms.

4.1   A Complete Example: Chord

As stated before, Chord [11] is an excellent example of a distributed algorithm that makes extensive use of RPCs. We implemented a Python object oriented version of Chord (following the original pseudo-code) in 217 lines of code.

```
class Node(object):
    _sync = {'closest_preceding_finger':'2'
             , ...}
    _async = ['set_successor','fix_finger'
              ,...]
    _ref = ['closest_preceding_finger', ...]
    _parallel = [ 'fix_finger', 'stabilize']

    def find_predecessor(self, id):
        try:
            if id == int(self.id):
                return self.predecessor
            n1 = self.proxy
            while not betweenE(id,
                int(n1.get_id()),
                int(n1.successor().get_id())):
                n1 = n1.
                    closest_preceding_finger(id)
            return n1
        except(succ_err):
            raise succ_err()
        except(TimeoutError):
            raise TimeoutError()
```

```
def closest_preceding_finger(self, id):
    try:
        for i inrange(k - 1, -1, -1):
            if between(int(self.finger[i]
                .get_id()), int(self.id), id):
                return self.finger[i]
        return self.proxy
    except(TimeoutError):
        raise succ_err()

def fix_finger(self):
    if(self.currentFinger <= 0 or
       self.currentFinger >= k):
        self.currentFinger = 1
    try:
        self.finger[self.currentFinger] =
        self.find_successor(
        self.start[self.currentFinger])
    except:
        None
    finally:
        self.currentFinger += 1
```

Fig. 3. Chord implementation

We can see in Fig. 3 a fragment of the `Chord implementation` in our library. The original Chord implementation using plain Python objects only required some modifications that we detail now.

To begin with, the class must contain meta-information in four variables (*_sync, _async, _ref, _parallel*) to specify the type of methods that will be exposed remotely by the Actor.

Moreover, it is important that developers clearly distinguish when they are using object references, and when they are using Actor references. A special case is the reference to the current object (self in Python). If one Actor uses a Proxy to itself to invoke a method, it could create a deadlock. To avoid this, our Actor library sets the *self.proxy* variable to a special Proxy that avoid conflicts, and that can be passed by reference to other Actors. We can see in find_predecessor and closest_preceding_finger how they use *self.proxy* to refer to the current object and avoid conflicts. Note that in Chord, the routing table (finger table) may contain references (Proxies) to the current Actor.

Apart from these important changes, the developer just must be aware of catching the exceptions that may be produced by invoking other Actor (Timeouts). The resulting code is very simple and it can now be executed in multiple machines in a transparent way.

5   Evaluating the Expressiveness and Simplicity of Our Approach

In this experiment we are comparing the complexity of the Chord algorithm implementation in four platforms: Macedon, PlanetSim, PeerSim, and PyActive.

PlanetSim and PeerSim are P2P event simulators implemented in the Java language. They are very popular and widely used in the P2P community and they provide a simple framework for developing decentralized scalable algorithms.

Macedon is a Domain Specific Language (DSL) that generates code for the Ns-2 simulator and C++ code with sockets for experimentation. The DSL is based on event-driven finite state machines and it claims a reduction in lines of code and simplicity of the implemented distributed algorithms.

Even if we are comparing different programming languages (Java in PeerSim and Planetsim, DSL in Macedon, Python in our Actor library) the comparison is useful to understand different approaches of implementing the same Chord algorithm. PlanetSim and PeerSim are good examples of the Callback Hell since they require complex callback handlers and message programming. They had to break the elegant Chord RPCs into different code fragments clearly showing our Continuation Complexity Problem.

Macedon is a different approach that uses a DSL and state machines to simplify message handling. But again, it resulted in a complex code that is far from the simplicity of Chord sequential code using RPCs.

Before comparing the code, it is important to outline that the different versions are not implementing the Chord algorithm exactly as stated in the original article. For example, Macedon only implements a successor list of size 2, and their *fix_finger* protocol is using the simpler *update_others* variant that is not recommended for real settings.

Regarding PeerSim, it is important to outline that their implementation is not completely event-based because they also use object invocation shortcuts to simplify the code. In this line, Nodes access the *getProtocol()* method that provides a clone of the desired node.

Finally, PlanetSim provides a fully event-oriented implementation of Chord, but the implementation of the successor list does not consider all possible cases and errors in the protocol.

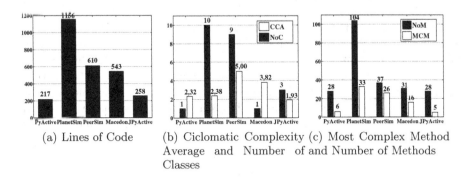

(a) Lines of Code   (b) Ciclomatic Complexity (c) Most Complex Method
Average   and   Number   of and Number of Methods
Classes

Fig. 4. Chord evaluation

As we can see in the Fig. 4 our approach (PyActive, JPyActive) is providing the simplest solution. Note that we also implemented a Java version (JPyactive) to be fair in the comparison with other Java-based solutions like PlanetSim or Peersim.

Our implementation has less LoC. Furthermore, our implementation is simpler and easier to understand that any of the presented alternatives. Our object oriented model is straightforward and it does not need additional understanding of messages, handlers and states. Macedon, PeerSim, and PlanetSim will require an understanding of messages and transitions that is more intricate that the simplicity of sequence diagrams in an object oriented design.

It is worth comparing the different approaches in code complexity (i.e., Cyclomatic Complexity). Again, our implementation is beating the other proposals in the overall complexity and in the most complex method. One important reason is that our model avoids large message handling conditionals because messages are cleanly mapped to methods. Furthermore, synchronous calls that return results are naturally mapped to method invocations, whereas event-based approaches must split these invocations in requests and responses.

As we can see, even accepting that the Python language produces less lines of code compared to Java (e.g., PeerSim or PlanetSim), we have demonstrated that our additional reduction in terms of complexity and LoC is very meaningful. There are two main reasons: continuation complexity and message handling complexity. The continuation complexity is reduced in our model thanks to synchronous calls masked by proxies. The message handling complexity is reduced by the transparent mapping of messages to method calls in the Active Object pattern.

In particular, four methods in the Chord original algorithm present Continuation Complexity: *find_predecessor*, *fix_finger*, *stabilize*, and *join*. All of them should be changed in an asynchronous programming model, and thus requiring different code fragments (request, response, and timeout) for RPCs. In our case, we implemented Chord as a slight modification of Chord's original OOP code. Just by annotating the remote abstractions in the class, we can run Chord in an Actor library that also permits remote Actors in a transparent way.

On the contrary, the rest of the implementations (Macedon, PlanetSim, PeerSim) suffer from the continuation complexity problem in different degrees. Each takes a different strategy but all of them need to break every RPC in two code fragments (request and response). Regarding Timeouts, some declare a timeout function for every method, or they can reuse the timeout handler for all methods. So for example, Macedon is breaking *find_predecessor* in three code fragments (request, reply, timeout), but they are duplicated for different states of the protocol (joined, joining). Macedon does not add another function for the iteration but the additional code is found inside the response handler. PlanetSim and PeerSim also include handlers for requests, responses and timeouts inside their code implementing implicit continuations.

6   Conclusions

We identified the Continuation Complexity Problem that occurs when synchronous invocations (RPCs) must be converted to asynchronous events, handlers and futures. The produced code is difficult to read and maintain, and it breaks with the object oriented paradigm.

To cope with the Continuation Complexity Problem, we introduced a novel invocation abstraction for Object Actors (i.e., parallel). Our parallel abstraction supports concurrent interleavings of method executions within a single Actor. We mainly allow the main Actor thread to continue processing incoming method requests while the parallel thread is blocked waiting for a response in a remote Actor due to a synchronous invocation. This approach considerably simplifies the continuation complexity problem for distributed systems requiring non-blocking synchronous invocations.

Finally, we demonstrated with well-known algorithm (e.g., Chord) that our resulting code has less lines of code, less Cyclomatic Complexity, and that it is more expressive than other event-based alternatives (i.e., PlanetSim, PeerSim, and Macedon). We believe that distributed systems can be considerably simplified using object oriented methodologies like the ones proposed in this article.

Our prototype implementation of PyActive can be downloaded from https:// github.com/cloudspaces/pyactive, under a LGPL license. This implementation includes clarifying code examples and tutorials.

Acknowledgments. Special thanks to Douglas C. Schmidt for his helpful comments about the Active Object pattern.

This work has been partially funded by the EU in the context of the project *CloudSpaces* (FP7-317555) and by the Spanish Ministerio de Ciencia e Innovación in the project *Cloud Services and Community Clouds* (TIN2013-47245-C2-2-R)

References

1. .NET platform Async and Await abstractions. http://msdn.microsoft.com/en-us/library/hh191443.aspx
2. Agha, G.: Actors: a model of concurrent computation. In: Distributed Systems. Artificial Intelligence. The MIT Press, Cambridge (1986)
3. Bainomugisha, E., Carreton, A.L., van Cutsem, T., Mostinckx, S., de Meuter, W.: A survey on reactive programming. ACM Comput. Surv. **45**(4), 52:1–52:34 (2013). http://doi.acm.org/10.1145/2501654.2501666
4. Edwards, J.: Coherent reaction. In: Proceedings of the 24th ACM SIGPLAN Conference Companion on Object Oriented Programming Systems Languages and Applications, pp. 925–932. ACM (2009)
5. García, P., Pairot, C., Mondéjar, R., Pujol, J., Tejedor, H., Rallo, R.: PlanetSim: a new overlay network simulation framework. In: Gschwind, T., Mascolo, C. (eds.) SEM 2004. LNCS, vol. 3437, pp. 123–136. Springer, Heidelberg (2005)
6. Lin, Y., Radoi, C., Dig, D.: Retrofitting concurrency for android applications through refactoring. In: Proceedings of the 22nd ACM SIGSOFT International Symposium on Foundations of Software Engineering, FSE 2014, pp. 341–352. ACM, New York (2014). http://doi.acm.org/10.1145/2635868.2635903
7. Montresor, A., Jelasity, M.: PeerSim: a scalable P2P simulator. In: Proceedings of the 9th International Conference on Peer-to-Peer (P2P 2009), Seattle, WA, pp. 99–100, September 2009

8. Okur, S., Hartveld, D.L., Dig, D., van Deursen, A.: A study and toolkit for asynchronous programming in c#. In: Proceedings of the 36th International Conference on Software Engineering, ICSE 2014, pp. 1117–1127. ACM, New York (2014). http://doi.acm.org/10.1145/2568225.2568309

9. Reynolds, J.: The discoveries of continuations. Lisp Symbolic Comput. **6**(3–4), 233248 (1993). Special Issue on Continuations, Hingham, MA, USA

10. Rodriguez, A., Killian, C., Bhat, S., Kostic, D., Vahdat, A.: Macedon: methodology for automatically creating, evaluating, and designing overlay networks. In: Proceedings of the 1st Conference on Symposium on Networked Systems Design and Implementation, vol. 1, pp. 267–280 (2004)

11. Stoica, I., Morris, R., Karger, D., Kaashoek, M.F., Balakrishnan, H.: Chord: a scalable peer-to-peer lookup service for internet applications. ACM SIGCOMM Comput. Commun. Rev. **31**, 149–160 (2001). ACM

Offloading Service Provisioning on Mobile Devices in Mobile Cloud Computing Environments

Marco Conti, Davide Mascitti$^{(\boxtimes)}$, and Andrea Passarella

IIT-CNR, Via G. Moruzzi 1, 56124 Pisa, Italy
{marco.conti,davide.mascitti,andrea.passarella}@iit.cnr.it

Abstract. Mobile cloud computing is one of the facets of cloud based systems, whereby mobile nodes obtain services from a global remote cloud platform in a more efficient way with respect to local service execution. Unfortunately, recent forecasts on cellular bandwidth (that is the key enabler for this paradigm) pose significant challenges to the practical applicability of this approach. In this paper, we explore a complementary mobile cloud computing solution, where mobile nodes can also rely on other nodes in the vicinity that could provide the sought service. These nodes are contacted via direct communication based on WiFi or Bluetooth, which therefore offloads traffic from the cellular network. In the proposed system, mobile nodes decide dynamically whether to access global or local cloud services based on the availability of the latter in their vicinity, and the load on the cellular network. Simulation results show that this solution provides lower average service provision times with respect to an alternative based exclusively on a remote cloud. As a side effect, such a system avoids cellular congestion and possible saturation, even in case of significant load.

1 Introduction

Mobile cloud computing is considered a very promising area in the cloud computing domain [5]. A popular approach to mobile cloud computing consists in moving the execution of services from mobile users' devices to the cloud. This approach is motivated by the fact that executing services on the cloud, instead of locally on users' devices, saves mobile devices resources, and service execution times can be shortened thanks to the inherent scalability of cloud service provisioning platforms. The core assumption at the basis of this approach is that mobile devices are constantly connected to the Internet through an extremely high capacity wireless network, such that it is easy to move data back and forth between the mobile devices and the remote cloud platform. In this view, the capacity leap expected from 4G cellular networks (LTE-A) [3] is supposed to fully support this mobile cloud computing paradigm.

Unfortunately, recent forecasts challenge the practical applicability of this approach. While 4G cellular networks will definitely provide much higher capacity compared to 3G, it is also expected that the data traffic generated by mobile

© Springer International Publishing Switzerland 2015
S. Hunold et al. (Eds.): Euro-Par 2015 Workshops, LNCS 9523, pp. 299–310, 2015.
DOI: 10.1007/978-3-319-27308-2_25

users will increase much faster. For example, CISCO [3] foresees that mobile traffic demand will increase by at least ten times between 2014 and 2019, while cellular capacity will grow only by a factor of 1.4 in the same time frame. This challenges the possibility to support very frequent and possibly large data transfers required by this type of mobile cloud computing solutions. In cases where the cellular network is congested, it would be too slow (or even impossible) to reach remote cloud services, thus making this approach technically unfeasible. In addition, this might also result in significant economic losses for cloud service providers, as it has been recently shown that there is a direct impact on the provider revenues of even small additional delays (in the order of hundreds of milliseconds) in accessing remote cloud services [9]. Another possible scheme for mobile cloud computing proposed in the literature consists in providing services directly at the edges of the infrastructure, i.e. on cellular base stations (eNodeB in the LTE terminology) [2]. This would not solve the aforementioned problem, as typically the bandwidth bottleneck would be in the cellular access network, and therefore even data transfer between mobile devices and eNodeBs might be problematic.

To counteract the mismatch between mobile data traffic demand and cellular capacity, a promising approach is traffic offloading [13]. In one of the typical offloading scenarios, nodes receive data through direct device-to-device (D2D) communications with other mobile nodes, instead of through the cellular network. Opportunistic networking solutions are typically used [12], whereby mobile nodes exploit direct data transfer opportunities enabled by various wireless technologies (such as WiFi or Bluetooth in ad hoc mode) when they come close enough to be in each other's direct transmission range.

In this paper, we exploit a conceptually similar approach to offload traffic related to service provisioning to mobile users. Specifically, we explore another concept for mobile cloud computing, applicable when services can also be provided locally between mobile devices, by exchanging the related data between them during opportunistic contacts. Service provisioning between mobile devices through opportunistic contacts has been investigated in the literature as the opportunistic computing paradigm [10]. In opportunistic computing, mobile nodes form *mobile clouds at the edges of the global Internet infrastructure*, through which local service provisioning is supported. While exploiting opportunistic computing, our solutions goes one step beyond. In our solution, nodes requiring a service (hereafter referred to as *seekers*) evaluate whether it is more efficient to execute the service on a remote cloud, or on a locally available mobile node (not necessarily in contact with the seeker when the service request is generated). This approach is able to exploit both remote cloud platforms, when the cellular network is not congested, and local service provisioning, otherwise. As such, it takes the best of the conventional mobile cloud computing approach and pure opportunistic computing paradigms. This approach is appealing also because of the resources already available on modern mobile personal devices. For example, high computational capability, ample storage and sensors, can be exposed to other users as services that can be accessed by other devices through direct contacts [5]. While it is clearly unreasonable to assume that any cloud service could also be provided locally, it is sensible to assume that a reduced set of services might be provided by other mobile nodes in local proximity. Note that in some cases, this might indeed even preferable. For example, when services consist in elaboration of data locally available on mobile users, it might be more appropriate for privacy reasons that data stay on the device of their owners.

Together with the specification of the algorithms to realise this mobile cloud computing approach, in this paper we also present simulation results showing that our solution is capable of offering better service provisioning time than a system where only the remote cloud is used. We show that the proposed system is able to autonomously adapt to the level of congestion of the cellular network, avoiding to contribute to its saturation, and still preserving low service provisioning times to the users, even in cases where the cellular network is highly congested.

This paper is organized as follows. Section 2 describes the main approaches in mobile cloud computing and for service provisioning through opportunistic computing. The structure and behaviour of the proposed system is presented in Sect. 3. Performance evaluation results are presented and discussed in Sect. 4. Finally, concluding remarks are reported in Sect. 5.

2 Related Work

The field of mobile cloud computing has seen multiple contributions aiming at building solutions for service provisioning with very different applications and objective [5]. Depending on the application and objectives, mobile cloud computing solutions may differ in their architectures and in how the service behaves in case of service requests. Four main types of system architecture may be individuated: remote cloud solutions, local mobile clouds, cloudlets and hybrid solutions [1].

Systems for remote cloud computing offload functionalities (computation, storage, coordination) on the remote cloud. [8] describes numerous proposals for transferring computation functionalities from mobile devices to the cloud to improve performances or with the objective of saving energy.

Local mobile clouds are systems where mobile devices collaborate in an area in order to provide functionalities to other participants, without using the infrastructure. MobiCloud [6] is a cloud framework in which mobile devices in a MANET are virtualized to service nodes or service broker, linked through a MANET routing protocol. In [10], instead, opportunistic computing is used to enable mobile users to access services on other mobile devices, with the possibility to create sequential compositions of services to extend the functionality available at individual nodes.

In cloudlets, services and resources are located dynamically on static devices connected to the wireless infrastructure in the vicinity of the mobile devices. For example [15] describes how to use cloudlets to dynamically instantiate Virtual Machines for mobile users that can be accessed through wireless LAN networks.

Hybrid solutions unite remote, local clouds and cloudlets to create systems where functionalities can be provided on different sites. Some initial proposals going into this direction have been proposed recently. For example SAMI [14] and MOCHA [16] are two examples of systems where computation activities needed by mobile devices are divided and distributed to sites of different nature. SAMI has the objective of minimizing the energy and monetary cost of computation when deciding to execute code on other mobile devices, a local cloudlet or on the remote cloud, while MOCHA uses information on latency and response times for all available remote cloud sites and the local cloudlet to decide where to execute code. However, none of these solutions exploit collaborative service provisioning among mobile devices, which is the key element of our approach.

3   Hybrid Mobile Cloud Computing Solution for Service Provisioning

In this section we present the characteristics of our solution that enables the establishment of a local mobile cloud to support the execution of services available both on the cloud and on mobile devices in the area. The main components of the system can be seen in Fig. 1: the local mobile cloud, which is made up of mobile devices that can communicate with each other through wireless interfaces and that can request and provide services (pictured in the figure as S_1, S_2, S_3, S_4) to the other nodes; the eNodeB, which grants connectivity to the infrastructure to the local mobile cloud; the remote cloud, which hosts services the mobile nodes can access through the eNodeB.

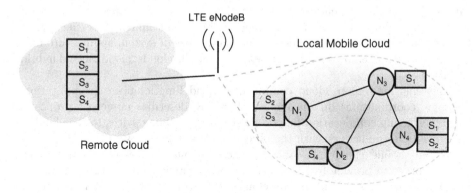

Fig. 1. Actors of the systems

At the high level, when a request for a service is generated at a mobile node (seeker), our algorithm decides whether this request should be served by the global cloud platform, or by some other mobile node nearby. We explain the details of the algorithm in the following subsections. Specifically we describe the system structure and behaviour by analysing the decision process involved in deciding how to solve a service request (Subsect. 3.1), the data that must be collected in order to take the decision (Subsect. 3.2) and the model used to determine how to resolve a request (Subsect. 3.3).

3.1   Resolution Process

The resolution process is shown in Fig. 2 and starts with the *service request generation*, when a mobile node (*seeker*) runs an application that generates a request for a service. The seeker sends a message (*eNodeB inquiry*) to the eNodeB asking for information about the state of the LTE available data rates in upload and download, and an estimate of the time needed to execute the service on the remote cloud.[1] The eNodeB, at the reception of the message, observes the bandwidth occupation and sends this data as a response (*eNodeB response*) to the seeker, including the estimate on the service execution time on the remote cloud (*remote knowledge collection*).

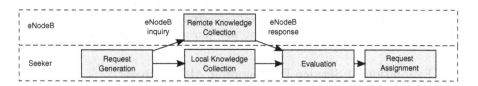

Fig. 2. Request resolution process

At the reception of the response, the seeker estimates the total service provisioning time of the request using the remote cloud service. The seeker also uses a local knowledge base containing previously collected data (*local knowledge collection*) on the other providers in the mobile cloud, like statistics on the mobility of the providers, the state of their computation queue and the offered services. The information in the local knowledge base is refreshed whenever two modes are in direct contact.

Thanks to the knowledge base, the seeker can evaluate the expected service provisioning time for all the known mobile providers that can be used to solve the request. These expected times are compared to the estimated service provisioning time of using the remote cloud service (*evaluation*).

If the seeker selects the remote cloud solution, it immediately starts sending the service request using the LTE infrastructure. Instead, if the selected provider is in the local mobile cloud and the seeker is currently not in contact with it, it waits the next contact with the selected provider in order to start sending the request. In this period of time further contacts between the seeker and other mobile providers may happen, triggering new information exchanges, a possible re-evaluation of the most suitable provider, and therefore a change in the service execution plan.

3.2   Data Collection

The information, required to decide how to serve a request, consists in the upload and download data rates in using the LTE infrastructure and the aver-

---

[1] Note that the size of this traffic is minimal, and therefore can be considered negligible from the cellular network congestion standpoint.

age execution time of the service that is requested. This data is obtained by the seeker through the *eNodeB response message* that is created by the eNodeB. The eNodeB collects the average execution times of the services requested by the nodes and stores them in a database. It estimates the upload and download data rates based on the current traffic generated by mobile users in the cell.

As will be more clear from the following section, the information required about the other mobile provider is: (i) the average duration of contact and inter-contact times with the seeker, (ii) the average data rate in the communications with the seeker, (iii) the service list of the provider, (iv) the provider queue statistics, like the average load, the average request arrival rate and the average service time, (v) the average queue of data to transfer from the provider to the seeker. This information is collected by each node by monitoring contacts with other nodes (for what concerns contact, intercontact times and average data rate), and by exchanging the other statistics during direct contacts.

3.3 Evaluation of Service Provisioning Alternatives

The seeker uses two models to evaluate respectively the expected service provisioning time for each provider in the local mobile cloud that can solve the request and the expected service provisioning time using the remote cloud.

The first model is based on the model for opportunistic computing described in [10]. For a given provider, this model gives a closed form expression for the expected value of the random variable representing the service provisioning time R_{mobile}, characterizing it as the sum of five successive periods of time that can be also formulated as random variables:

1. *Contact of the service provider* (W). The time needed by the seeker to encounter the provider after the point in time when the evaluation is performed. If the seeker is already in contact with the provider, the value is zero, otherwise it is the expected duration of the intercontact period.
2. *Data transfer* (Input time B, Output time θ). The time needed to transfer the input parameters from the seeker to the provider and the output parameters from the provider to the seeker (after the execution time is complete). These values include possible additional delays due to disconnection periods when the transfer is suspended as well as delays due to the presence of data from previous requests that need to be transferred to (or from) the same provider. The value for B is calculated as the time needed to transfer the data to the provider without disconnection, plus the expected duration of all the inter-contact phases occurring before the end of the transfer. The expected value of θ is analogous to B, but it must consider the state of the connection seeker-provider at the end of the service execution: if θ starts during in intercontact period, it must consider an added delay to begin the transfer, if it starts during a contact it considers whether there could have been disconnections before the phases to estimate its residual duration.
3. *Queue waiting time* (DQ). Once onto the provider, actual execution may be delayed due to previous pending requests. To calculate the expected time

of the phase, the model regards the provider as a $M^{[X]}/M/1$ queue and calculates the value using knowledge on the average load, service time and request arrival rate.

4. *Service execution time (DS).* The time to execute the service on the provider. It is calculated as the average previous executions on the provider of the requested service.

The formulation of the expected service provisioning time using a given mobile node becomes:

$$E[R_{mobile}] = E[W + B + DQ + DS + \theta]$$

For the remote cloud alternative, we can estimate of the service provisioning time t_{remote} using the information provided by the eNodeB in the eNodeB response and data locally available to the seeker. The service provisioning time can be estimated as the sum of the estimate of three delays: the time needed to upload data to the eNodeB t_{upl}, the time needed for the eNodeB to send data to the remote service provider and wait for the result of the computation t_{exec}, and the time needed for the seeker to download the output data of the service t_{down}. These estimates can be formulated as:

1. *LTE upload Time t_{upl}.* The time needed to transfer the service input data of size k_{input} and possibly queued data of size $k_{lte\ queue}$ from the seeker to the eNodeB, using the upload link that has a data rate of V_{upl}. k_{input} is a property of the service request generated and consequently known by the seeker. $k_{lte\ queue}$ is a value directly observable by the seeker at the moment of the evaluation. With these values, the total estimated LTE upload time can be formulated as:

$$t_{upl} = \frac{k_{input} + k_{lte\ queue}}{V_{upl}}$$

2. *Remote cloud latency and service execution time t_{exec}.* The time needed to transfer the input data from the eNodeB to the remote cloud provider, the time needed to execute the service, and the time needed to transfer the output data back to the eNodeB. Given that the amount of time spent transferring the data and executing the service is dependent on many factors that are out of the control of the system, like the actual provider location, the bandwidth available on the path to the provider, and the amount of resources dedicated to service executions, we can estimate t_{exec} using the average of previous actual values of the remote cloud latencies and service execution times for the same requested service.

3. *LTE download time t_{down}.* Similarly to the upload time, it represents the time needed to transfer the service output data, of size k_{output} which value is a property of the request, from the eNodeB back to the seeker, using the download link of data rate V_{down}, whose value is provided in the eNodeB response. t_{down} can be expressed as:

$$t_{down} = \frac{k_{output}}{V_{down}}$$

4 System Evaluation

In this section we compare the performance of the hybrid solution explained in Sect. 3 with one that only uses a global cloud platform. We show a comparison of the average service provisioning times for both approaches in a range of scenarios that differ for amount of data that are transferred as service input and output for each request, and also for the amount of requests that are generated by the devices. We also detail the behaviour of the hybrid approach by analysing the fraction of requests that are solved using mobile providers in each scenario.

Table 1. Default simulation parameters

Simulation runs per scenario	10
Number of mobile nodes	30
Simulation space	500 m × 500 m
Total simulation time	400000 s
Mobility warm-up period	10000 s
Statistics warm-up period	10000 s
Request generation phase duration	360000 s
Wi-fi connectivity range	90 m
LTE download transmission speed	300 Mbps
LTE upload transmission speed	75 Mbps
Wi-fi transmission speed	54 Mbps
Density of each service	25 %
Number of different services	15
Average mobile service execution time	10 s
Average remote cloud service execution time	5 s

Simulation were developed using TheOne, which is a reference simulation environment for opportunistic networking and computing [7]. The basic simulation parameters used in this paper are listed in Table 1. In these simulations, the mobile devices move following RandomWayPoint mobility traces as specified in [11]. We assume that mobility of nodes is confined withing a single LTE cell, served by a unique eNodeB. Each simulation run lasts 400000 s. For each request, a target service is randomly chosen and also a device is randomly chosen to act as a seeker for the request. The service and the seeker are chosen according to uniform distributions. The services that can be provided and requests are 15 in total, with each of them available on the remote cloud and on 25 % of the mobile nodes, chosen randomly following an uniform distribution. Simulated LTE data rates are 300 Mbps for download and 75 Mbps for upload based on current estimates of the maximum 4G capacity [4], opportunistic transfers are supposed to occur at the maximum capacity of 802.11g technology of 54 Mbps.

We assume that a variable number of additional mobile devices generate traffic in the same LTE cell. The number of additional devices is generated according to a standard birth/death process. The total LTE capacity is shared between the active devices (i.e., the seekers and providers, plus these additional ones), such that the bandwidth available to the seekers and the providers changes over time based on the number of other active mobile devices in the cell. The number of additional nodes can vary between 0 and 40, and the transition rate to a new state is 0.01 per second both for birth events and death events. We replicate each simulated scenario 10 times. In all runs, the events related to the transition of the process defining the additional nodes activity are exactly the same. This guarantees that the congestion on the LTE network due to the additional nodes is the same when we vary the other simulation parameters.

The tests are repeated varying the rate of request generation by the system. In "10–15" scenarios a new request is generated after a time interval in the range [10,15]s after the previous one. This value is changed in the other scenarios to "15–20" and "20–30". For each of these values the tests are repeated changing the amount of data that has to be transferred as input and output of the services, from 40 MB to 80 MB and 160 MB. In each simulation, the input and output data sizes are the same for all services and requests. All the results shown are the average results of the 10 independent simulation runs executed for each scenario, with 95 % confidence intervals.

4.1   Service Provisioning Time Comparison

Figure 3 compares the average service provisioning times for the hybrid approach and for the pure LTE approach. The x axis marks the different tested scenario, from the one generating maximum traffic (on the left) to the one generating minimum traffic (on the right).

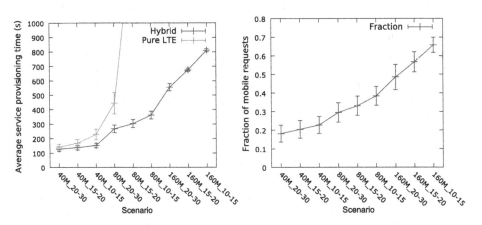

Fig. 3. Service provisioning times   **Fig. 4.** Fraction of requests

We can see that the average service provisioning times are faster for the hybrid approach in all scenarios, even when the request load is at its lowest (40 MB 20–30), the hybrid approach achieves an average that is about 10 % lower than the pure LTE approach. This difference in results grows as scenarios get heavier in load, with the 40 MB 15–20 and 40 MB 10–15 scenarios having differences respectively of about 18 % and 32 %.

This difference continues to grow as the traffic in the scenario grows, with the pure LTE approach that is unable to avoid saturation from the 80 MB scenarios and is unable to complete the service requests for any seeker. The hybrid approach, instead is able to keep service provisioning consistent without overloading the infrastructure in all the analysed scenarios.

4.2 Split of Service Executions in the Hybrid Approach

Figure 4 shows the fraction of requests served locally by mobile nodes in the different scenarios. We can see first of all that the shape of the graph resembles the one seen in Fig. 3, indicating a correlation. It is also notable that for the scenario with the lowest load the hybrid approach still assigns about 20 % of requests to the local cloud. This indicates that local service provisioning might be useful even in cases when the LTE network is not particularly congested (this is the case, for example, when the seeker and provider are already in contact when the service request is generated, and the size of the input/output parameters is not that large). In the highest load scenario the ratio rises to an average of 65 %, This indicates that our solution avoids cellular saturation, and is still able to exploit remote cloud execution when appropriate.

To further explore the behaviour of the system, we analysed the variation of the fraction of requests solved through the mobile cloud during specific simulation runs. To better understand this index, we plot it together with the fraction of additional nodes generated by the birth/death process (the fraction being computed over the maximum number of nodes, i.e. 40). In Fig. 5 we can see the results for run number 2 of the 10 total simulation runs for each scenario.

The graphs show a correlation between fraction of additional nodes generating traffic and the fraction of the requests assigned to mobile providers. Scenarios with the 40 MB requests (blue lines), corresponding to a light transfer size due to service provisioning, have long periods of time where all requests are assigned to the remote cloud, until the added traffic is heavy enough. Instead the scenario with 160 MB requests (red lines) rarely has periods with no requests assigned to mobile providers, and at the highest request generation rate ("10–15") the ratio never goes below 20 %. This last result indicate that the system consistently assign requests to mobile providers even during periods when the added traffic is negligible.

Based on the above results, we can conclude that the hybrid approach provides significant advantages in achieving better average service provisioning times. This is achieved also thanks to a dynamic detection of the status of the LTE network, that allows the proposed solution to correctly estimate whether remote or local service provisioning is more appropriate. This solution is thus able to avoid to saturate the LTE network, and to guarantee service provisioning also when the LTE network becomes congested.

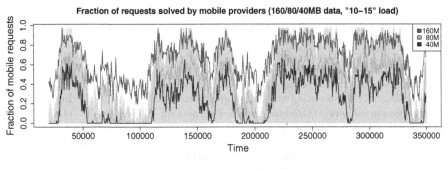

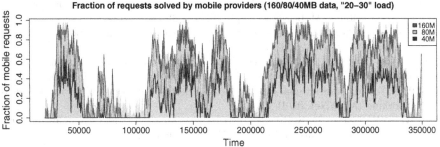

Fig. 5. Share of requests

5   Conclusions

In this paper we presented a mobile cloud computing solution that enables the creation of local mobile cloud networks to offload service provisioning from the remote cloud. We defined the behaviour of the system when a decision is to be taken whether a service should be provided from the remote platform or through some nearby mobile node, taking into account the state of the LTE network and of the surrounding devices. We presented sets of simulations to show the advantages in using this approach instead of relying exclusively on remote cloud services by showing that seekers experience better average service provisioning times and that the system is able to avoid congestion of the LTE network.

References

1. Abolfazli, S., Sanaei, Z., Ahmed, E., Gani, A., Buyya, R.: Cloud-based augmentation for mobile devices: motivation, taxonomies, and open challenges. IEEE Commun. Surv. Tutor. **16**(1), 337–368 (2014)

2. Barbarossa, S., Sardellitti, S., Di Lorenzo, P.: Communicating while computing: distributed mobile cloud computing over 5g heterogeneous networks. IEEE Sign. Process. Mag. **31**(6), 45–55 (2014)
3. Cisco: Cisco visual networking index: Global mobile data traffic forecast update, 2014–2019, February 2015
4. Dahlman, E., Parkvall, S., Sköld, J. (eds.): 4G LTE/LTE-Advanced for Mobile Broadband. Academic Press, Oxford (2011)
5. Fernando, N., Loke, S.W., Rahayu, W.: Mobile cloud computing: a survey. Future Gener. Comput. Syst. **29**(1), 84–106 (2013)
6. Huang, D., Zhang, X., Kang, M., Luo, J.: Mobicloud: building secure cloud framework for mobile computing and communication. In: 2010 Fifth IEEE International Symposium on Service Oriented System Engineering (SOSE), pp. 27–34, June 2010
7. Keränen, A., Ott, J., Kärkkäinen, T.: The one simulator for DTN protocol evaluation. In: Proceedings of the 2nd International Conference on Simulation Tools and Techniques, ICST Simutools 2009, Brussels, Belgium, pp. 55:1–55:10 (2009)
8. Kumar, K., Liu, J., Lu, Y.H., Bhargava, B.: A survey of computation offloading for mobile systems. Mob. Netw. Appl. **18**(1), 129–140 (2013)
9. Linden, G.: Marissa mayer at web 2.0. http://glinden.blogspot.it/2006/11/marissa-mayer-at-web-20.html
10. Mascitti, D., Conti, M., Passarella, A., Ricci, L.: Service provisioning through opportunistic computing in mobile clouds. Procedia Comput. Sci. **40**, 143–150 (2014). Fourth International Conference on Selected Topics in Mobile and Wireless Networking (MoWNet 2014)
11. Navidi, W., Camp, T.: Stationary distributions for the random waypoint mobility model. IEEE Trans. Mobile Comput. **3**(1), 99–108 (2004)
12. Pelusi, L., Passarella, A., Conti, M.: Opportunistic networking: data forwarding in disconnected mobile ad hoc networks. IEEE Commun. Mag. **44**(11), 134–141 (2006)
13. Rebecchi, F., de Amorim, D.M., Conan, V., Passarella, A., Bruno, R., Conti, M.: Data offloading techniques in cellular networks: a survey. IEEE Commun. Surv. Tutor. **17**(2), 580–603 (2015). Secondquarter 2015
14. Sanaei, Z., Abolfazli, S., Gani, A., Shiraz, M.: Sami: Service-based arbitrated multi-tier infrastructure for mobile cloud computing. In: 1st IEEE International Conference on Communications in China Workshops (ICCC 2012), pp. 14–19, August 2012
15. Satyanarayanan, M., Bahl, P., Caceres, R., Davies, N.: The case for VM-based cloudlets in mobile computing. IEEE Pervasive Comput. **8**(4), 14–23 (2009)
16. Soyata, T., Muraleedharan, R., Funai, C., Kwon, M., Heinzelman, W.: Cloudvision: real-time face recognition using a mobile-cloudlet-cloud acceleration architecture. In: IEEE Symposium on Computers and Communications (ISCC 2012), pp. 59–66, July 2012

A Systematic Quality Analysis of Virtual Desktop Infrastructure Technologies

Arman Sheikholeslami[1] and Kalman Graffi[2]([⊠])

[1] University of Paderborn, Paderborn, Germany
armanpts@gmail.com
[2] Technology of Social Networks Lab,
University of Düsseldorf, Düsseldorf, Germany
graffi@hhu.de

Abstract. The Virtual Desktop Infrastructure is a promising technology hosted by powerful servers or within the cloud that allows remote and potentially weak devices to run their virtualized desktop environment on a powerful machine. Mainly used in commercial environments, i.e. enterprises, also private users might be interested in this functionality. The benefits are given through customizable (virtual) hardware resources on the fly while maintaining a long lasting desktop environment. Hardware failures, resource limitations and risks due to damages to the physical hardware are omitted with desktops running upon a Virtual Desktop Infrastructure. Currently, many Virtual Desktop Infrastructure solutions are available, most important of which are XenDesktop by Citrix, Horizon View by VMware, and VDI by Microsoft. In this article, we deploy and systematically evaluate the quality of these solutions in terms of streaming quality under the workload of popular application types and under the influence of various network conditions. We conclude that Xen-Desktop by Citrix is performing best, Horizon View by VMware is close, but provides less features, while VDI by Microsoft is both limited in its quality and its functionality.

1 Introduction

Nowadays, with huge quantity of computers in the world, the administration of computers has become cost- and effort-intensive. This is due to the constant attention that computers require. Maintaining the computer hardware is both an expensive and work-intensive task. Most consumer computers are only used a few to several hours a day, but not day and night, the utilization of these devices is even not ideal. To reduce the operating costs and efforts of computers, an efficient use of computers is proposed.

In the traditional approach, software (operating system, applications, etc.) is placed on top of a dedicated hardware infrastructure, which eventually are not fully utilized, meaning that their resources, to some extents, remain idle. Hence, the costs of ownership also must cover the resources of the computers that are not actually used most of the time. A good example is a user who only

© Springer International Publishing Switzerland 2015
S. Hunold et al. (Eds.): Euro-Par 2015 Workshops, LNCS 9523, pp. 311–323, 2015.
DOI: 10.1007/978-3-319-27308-2_26

performs low-level computer tasks (online shopping, music streaming, etc.) on a high-tech laptop. While the computer is used a few hours a day, after 2–3 years, the computer might be outdated and not anymore suitable for high-end calculations. A new computer is bought. Both, from a private user's view as well as from an enterprise user's view, this is not an ideal hardware utilization.

Ideally, the computing resources made available to a desktop environment and applications in it should always meet the desired quality, even after years. For that we differentiate between the operating system and connected applications, a input/output device (such as a notebook or monitor/keyboard) as well as the computing unit with sufficient computational power, memory and storage. Basically, the concept of efficient use of computers proposes that the underlying hardware infrastructure can be separated from the input/output device and shared among multiple computer users and applications (including the operating system) such that the hardware resources can be fully exploited. In this way, users only pay for the extent of the resources that they consume. On the other hand, deploying multiple computers on one hardware infrastructure (i.e. pooling) reduces operating costs and administrative tasks. This is in particular very useful for organizations with numerous standalone computers as Converged Infrastructure [8]. This way, an administrator gets a holistic view on the status of one single hardware infrastructure and the applications deployed on it through an administration platform instead of having to deal with all standalone computers separately. This new concept of pooling hardware resources among multiple applications is known as Virtual Desktop Infrastructure (VDI) technology.

This is a technology in which a user's operating system as well as data and applications are stored in a data-center which is a shared hardware infrastructure, as displayed in Fig. 1. Then, a user can remotely connect to the data-center and access his/her operating system, applications and data as if they are on his/her own local machine. These remotely hosted virtual desktops can be both used by individual users but also in order to enable collaborative desktop sharing, with team members accessing the same desktop, and coordinating their work within this desktop environment. Virtual desktops enable teams to easily coordinate the knowledge available for them, by using one common desktop. Cloud-hosted VDIs introduces several advantages, the most important are on demand resource provision and enhancement [3], reduction of costs [2], device and location independence [3], virtualization, central maintenance and management, boost of cooperation and collaboration, and reliability and security [5,10]. An open question is with regard to the quality of the available VDI solutions.

Our contributions in this paper are the following. In Sect. 2, we introduce the three most popular VDI technologies namely: XenDesktop by Citrix, Horizon View by VMware, and VDI by Microsoft. In Sect. 3, we present our implementation of virtual desktops on top of each these three VDI technologies in a local network environment. We benchmarked these three VDI solutions in Sect. 4 using the workload of the seven dominant desktop applications identified in [9] and varying challenging network characteristics. Through the dynamics of the network conditions and the different usage patterns we are able to exactly

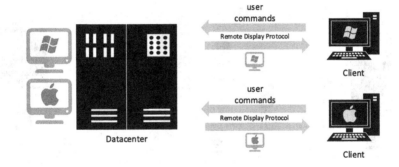

Fig. 1. Functioning mechanism of Virtual Desktop Infrastructure

identify the suitability of the three solutions for the use case of virtual desktops. In Sect. 5, we summarize the test results of each solution and we point out that both the benchmarks as well as the user test identify the XenDesktop by Citrix as best choice with Horizon View by VMware being almost on par. Microsoft's VDI on the other side falls back both in the streaming performance under any network condition but also in terms of user experience. In the following, we introduce first in the VDI as option to host virtual desktops. Besides a general overview on the requirements for such a technology, we also introduce the three most popular VDI technologies namely XenDesktop by Citrix, Horizon View by VMware, and VDI by Microsoft.

2   Considered Virtual Desktop Infrastructures

VDI is can be run by server pools, such as in Cloud environments and also on dedicated powerful servers. See Fig. 1 for this. Such an environment benefits companies as an existing infrastructure is shared and paid accordingly [2], allowing organizations to avoid huge upfront infrastructure costs. A virtual desktop is a technology that has a lot in common with VDI technology. The main differences are the type of users, user tasks and the network type over which they operate. Thus, a quality analysis of the current VDI technological solutions can provide useful insights about the current technological situation that can be used to implement the concept of VPC. Next, we introduce the three dominant VDI solutions: Citrix XenDesktop, VMware Horizon View and Microsoft VDI.

2.1   Citrix XenDesktop

Citrix, founded in 1989, is a Microsoft alliance that provides different virtualization products and services. The most famous product of Citrix is the Xen family, which consists of open-source products, mainly consisting of XenDesktop, XenServer, and XenApp. XenDesktop is a VDI by Citrix which is designed specifically for commercial environments (i.e. organizations), and delivers Windows-based Desktop and Server operating systems.

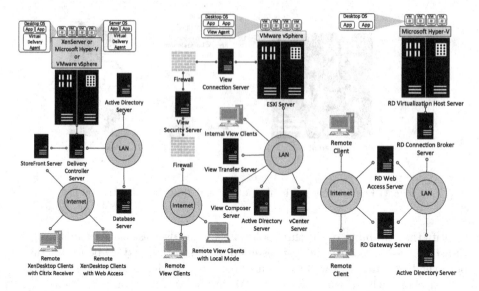

Fig. 2. Citrix Xen Desktop   **Fig. 3.** VMware Horizon View   **Fig. 4.** Microsoft VDI

Figure 2 shows standard architecture of Citrix XenDesktop, virtual desktops are installed on virtual machines in form of desktop or server operating systems. An operating system must have a Virtual Delivery Agent installed on it, and it may contain many applications. All virtual machines are hosted by a native Hypervisor, which can be of different types as mentioned before. To access a virtual desktop, a user connects to the StoreFront Server using a Citrix Receiver or a web browser. The StoreFront Server redirects the inbound connections to the Delivery Controller Server and after authentication, assigns a virtual desktop to it. The authentication is performed based on the knowledge base of Active Directory Server. Ultimately, all operations are recorded in the Database Server.

2.2 VMware Horizon View

Horizon View is a VDI solution for Windows-based desktop and application virtualization in organizations. With Horizon View, VMware claims to extend the power of data centers to devices. All virtual desktops and applications can be accessible through one single platform, making it easy for users to access the resources they need. Using automated desktop setup and provisioning, considerably less administrative effort is required for initial deployment of desktops. Additionally, the management console gives a view of the VDI mechanics and facilitates to trace and fix the problems [1]. Horizon View is constructed upon several components that work together to deliver virtual desktops. Among all, in Fig. 3, we display the most important components based on [11].

One of the most crucial components of the architecture is vSphere Server (i.e. the ESXi Server). The vSphere should be deployed on a dedicated server to store virtual desktops. More concretely, vSphere creates an individual virtual machine for each remote desktop. Then, on top of each virtual machine, the virtual desktop (guest operating system) is installed. The virtual desktop, then, can contain data and applications, like a regular desktop. Furthermore, to control the status of virtual desktops and manage resources, View Agent should be deployed on each virtual desktop. However, since the View Agent should exist in the parent image of the virtual desktop, and that virtual desktops are copies of the parent image, the View Agent will automatically be replicated among the virtual desktops. The Composer Server and vCenter Server can co-exist on one dedicated server. Furthermore, the Active Directory server can be deployed on a virtual machine. This server does not only provide Active Directory services, but also DNS and DHCP services. The other components like Connection Server, Transfer Server and Security Server should be assigned to dedicated servers each.

Figure 3 displays the architecture of a fully configured VMware Horizon View. In this architecture, clients can use virtual desktops on the premise, using LAN or through the Internet. Based on the requirements of the organizations, a variety of network architectures can be considered for implementation of Horizon View VDI. Here, we consider the most basic architecture in which one single LAN connects different servers to each other. On the premise clients can use the same LAN to access their virtual desktops. First, they access the Connection Server and then the Connection Server connects them to their virtual desktops. The same holds for clients reaching virtual desktops through the Internet, but with an additional level of security. First, they need to pass through two firewalls with the Security Server in the middle. Then, the Connection Server connects the clients to their virtual desktops.

2.3   Microsoft Virtual Desktop Infrastructure

Remote Desktop Services (RDS) is a feature of Microsoft Windows Server, which allows to access a computer remotely. In 2012, when Windows Server 2012 R2 was published, this service was extended to include Microsoft VDI. Microsoft VDI is a desktop virtualization technology, which virtualizes an operating system and allows users to remotely take control of it. Obviously, Microsoft VDI only supports provisioning of Windows-based operating systems and applications.

Microsoft VDI is comprised of many components depicted in Fig. 4, each having a responsibility in the chain of service delivery. However, some components are optional and, depending on the specification of the VDI service, may not be deployed. For example, if web access to virtual desktops is not required, Remote Desktop Web Access component will not be deployed.

Figure 4 shows an abstract architecture of Microsoft VDI. In this architecture, users accessing through a Web Browser are directed to the RD Web Access Server and users accessing through RemoteApp are forwarded to RD Gateway Server. These two servers authenticate the users using the credential storage of Active Directory Server and, then, redirect the inbound connections to the RD Connection Broker Server. RD Connection Broker Server, then, finds the appropriate virtual desktop on the RD Virtualization Host Server. Finally, the

RD Virtualization Host Server prepares the corresponding virtual machine as well as virtual desktop to be used. As soon as the virtual desktop is prepared, the access to virtual desktop is given to the connection, hence, the user can utilize it. The RD Virtualization Host Server is a service provided by Windows Server 2012 R2. As mentioned before, the RD Virtualization Host is integrated with Hyper-V, which is a virtualization service of the same operating system. As shown in Fig. 4, the Hyper-V on the RD Virtualization Host Server hosts virtual machines. On each virtual machine, a (guest) operating system is deployed, which is the virtual desktop that users connect to.

3   Technology Implementation and Evaluation Setup

In this section, we briefly discuss our VDI architecture deployment of these three technologies. First, we abstractly describe the deployment environment. To implement the three VDI technologies, based on our demand, four desktop computers were used, with following specifications: CPU - Intel Core i7-2600@3.40 Ghz, 8 GB memory, 460 GB disk space, NIC - Intel 82579LM Gigabit Ethernet Adapter. The machines are termed VDI-1, VDI-2, VDI-3 and VDI-4. Some optional components (e.g. Security Server) that have no effect on the quality of the final service delivery were not implemented. Best efforts are made to prevent these limitations to degrade the quality of service. In VDI technologies, usually a machine plays the role of a connection broker, which middles the connections oriented from LAN or the Internet requesting a virtual desktop service. For this means, one of the machines (in our case VDI-1) should have two Network Interface Cards (NICs); a LAN NIC with private IP address to connect VDI-1 to the internal LAN in which other servers reside; and an Internet NIC with a public IP address to connect to the Internet. We interconnected the four machines in a dedicated small local area network and tuned the network quality with a tool named "Clumsy". In the following, we describe, how we used these four machines to implement the VDI reference architecture of the corresponding solutions, which are presented in Figs. 2, 3 and 4.

Citrix XenDesktop. In this technology, VDI-1, which acts as the a connection broker, has two NICs since it is connected to the Internet as well as to the LAN. The four servers are used as follows: VDI-1: StoreFront Server, DNS Server, NAT Server. VDI-2: Delivery Controller Server, XenCenter, Database Server. VDI-3: Active Directory Server, DHCP Server, DNS Server. VDI-4: XenServer Server. To access a virtual desktop, a user connects to the StoreFront Server using a Citrix Receiver or a web browser. The StoreFront Server redirects the inbound connections to the Delivery Controller Server and after authentication, assigns a virtual desktop to it. The authentication is performed based on the knowledge base of Active Directory Server. Ultimately, all operations are recorded in the Database Server.

VMware Horizon View. For VMware Horizon View, each of VDI-1 to VDI-4 provides a specific service, as follows: VDI-1: View Connection Server, DNS Server, NAT Server. VDI-2: vCenter Server, View Composer, SQL Server. VDI-3: Active Directory Server, DNS Server. VDI-4: ESXi Server. Depending on the type of servers, in some cases, one machine can host one or several servers. For instance, VDI-4 is only dedicated to ESXi Server since ESXi Server stores all virtual desktops and it requires high Disk, Memory and CPU capacity. On the other hand, VDI-2 can host vCenter Server, Composer Server, and MS SQL Server at the same time since its hardware capacity allows it and that these three servers can share the same host machine with no conflict of functionality.

Microsoft VDI. We only focus on the deployment of the essential virtual desktop services and exclude the components providing non-functional services (e.g. Security Server). The hardware infrastructure used to deploy Microsoft VDI technology includes VDI-1, VDI-2, and VDI-3. The only exception is that the VDI-1, which acts as the RD Connection Broker, has two NICs since it is connected to the Internet as well as to the LAN. The role of each machine is shown in the following: VDI-1: RD Connection Broker Server, RD Web Access Server, RD Gateway Server, DNS Server, NAP Server, NAT Server. Obviously, this is not the best approach for large scale projects, for benchmarking with a limited number of virtual desktops, it does not lead to quality degradation. VDI-2: Active Directory Server, DNS Server, DHCP Server. VDI-3: RD Virtualization Host Server, Hyper-V Server, IIS Server. In our deployment, regardless of using a web browser or Remote Desktop application, a user living on the LAN or on the Internet first is connected to the VDI-1. Then, after the user is authenticated and is assigned to the right virtual desktop by VDI-1, the user connection is redirected to VDI-3 where the virtual desktops are stored. When learning about the desktop request, VDI-3 prepares the virtual desktop for service provisioning. In the following we comparatively benchmark these setups with respect to the quality of service of the desktop streaming.

4   Benchmarking of the VDI Solutions

In this section, we measure the quality of the implemented technologies. We perform a comparative measurement of the streaming quality in terms of frames per second following a benchmarking approach [6] The main metric we use are the *frames per second* (FPS) displayed to the user. While there is no hard quality limit, values below 20 are considered to lose more and more of appeal. The frames per second show how quickly and smoothly the desktop environment is presented to the user and how quickly potential input is recognized. Our test setup consists of three parts. First, the VDI solution which is tested. Second, the application use case performed in the virtual desktop, and third, the network conditions under which the solutions are tested. In Subsect. 4.1, we specify the test workload, which is defined by the task types that a user performs on a PC. To specify the test workload, we present the potential users of a VDI.

Our set of tests consists of seven computer tasks (i.e. test workload) performed on a virtual desktop. The purpose of this test set is to investigate the capability of virtual desktops in performing the typical tasks performed on a PC. In addition, task-based testing measures the Quality of Service of a virtual desktop in performing each task is also measured. To evaluate the Quality of Service of a virtual desktop, we specify nine test cases. In the first five test cases, the purpose is to find the effect of each network quality factor on the Quality of Service of a virtual desktop. For the first five test cases, we only focus on one test object, the Web Browsing test object. For this, each network quality factor is tested separately in the absence of other factors. Since VPCs may be used in different network qualities, we examine the performance of VDIs in the remaining four test cases using four network qualities.

4.1   Setup: Activities Based on Identified User Types

We categorize users into three main groups based on [9], namely Power Users, Office Users, and Home Users. Each group performs countless number of tasks on PCs, each needing a different set of requirements. However, there are some tasks that are common among users of each user type. We define in Table 1 a few task types for each user type that represent that user type. Note that, this classification does not necessarily dictate a task type to a user type since a user type may be assigned to different, and possibly all, task types in the real world. In total, we test seven computer tasks, which we introduce and explain next.

Having the tasks needed to be performed to test a virtual desktop, in the next subsections we explain the Application-Task-based Testing and User-based Testing, these two test sets we perform to assess the quality of virtual desktops.

4.2   Setup: Network Variations

The quality of the network has a large influence on the delivered quality of service. Our aim is to identify how the various network factors influence the quality individually as well as how the performance is under various levels of

Table 1. Computer tasks for home users, office users and power users

Home User Tasks		
Task 1	Web Browsing	Web surfing and flash content rendering using Google Chrome
Task 2	A/V Streaming	Playback of a 1080p HD video file in the format of MKV in this task
Office User Tasks		
Task 3	Presentation Design	Designing presentation slides using Microsoft PowerPoint 2013
Task 4	Data Analyzing	Data processing using Microsoft Excel 2013
Task 5	Word Processing	Creating textual documents using Microsoft Word 2013
Power User Tasks		
Task 6	Code compiling	Implementation, compilation and execution of an Android project using Eclipse ADT
Task 7	Image Processing	Processing graphical elements using Inkscape application

Table 2. Network types based on differing quality factors

Quality type	Delay	Drop %	Throttle %	Out of order %	Duplicate %
Type 1: Good	1 ms	0	0	0	0
Type 2: Normal	20 ms	1	5	1	3
Type 3: Average	50 ms	2	8	5	7
Type 4: Worst	200 ms	5	15	15	18

networking quality. The five network factors that we consider are the following. Delay: Latency in the packet delivery. Drop: Packet loss. Throttle: Insufficient bandwidth. Out of Order: Packets delivery in different order than they were sent. Duplicate: Receiving a packet twice since the sender thinks that the first packet is not delivered due to packet loss and retransmit the packet.

We define four categories of network quality, displayed in Table 2, namely best network quality, normal network quality, average network quality, and worst network quality. Each category is comprised of the five above mentioned network factors and each factor affects the network quality with a specific ratio. For instance, as is shown in Table 2, in a network with normal quality the delay is about 20 ms, the Drop is 1 %, the Throttle is 5 %, etc. We use an application named "Clumsy" (http://jagt.github.io/clumsy) to simulate the four network qualities listed in the table and to test the quality of Web Browsing test object with each network quality factor separately.

4.3   Video Streaming Quality: Impact of Individual Network Factors

In Table 3 we investigate the impact of each individual network factor on the resulting frame rate. Therefore we consider the use case of Web Browsing and first analyze the frame rate at a local PC. For this, the frame rate is 24.79. Next, we modify each single network factor individually and analyze the effect on the three solutions. For this, in the initial state, Delay is set to 1 ms, the drop rate to 0 %, the bandwidth throttle to 0 %, the ratio of out of order packets is 0 % and the ratio of duplicate packets is 0 % as well. In each step, only one factor is modified, while the rest stays the same, i.e. either 1 ms or 0 %. We tested the three VDI solutions under these conditions and list the results in Table 3 with the corresponding frame rates. In this context, the higher the frame rate is, the better quality will be.

The first observation is that both the selected solution as well as the network factor has an influence on the resulting frame rate. Citrix XenDesktop shows very high resilience against Delay, and very low resilience against Drop. This technology also relatively shows a good performance in case of other degraded network quality factors, such as Throttle, Out of Order, and Duplicate. VMware View Horizon is considerably resilient against Out of Order and Duplicate packets. On the other hand, Delay, Packet Loss (Drop), and Throttle have the most negative effects on the QoS of virtual desktops by reducing the frame rate of Web Browsing task from a frame rate of 24.79 to 14.56, 11.05, and 14.06, respectively. Microsoft VDI is very sensitive to low quality of any network factors. This

Table 3. Effect of network quality factors at the use case of web browsing

Quality type	Delay	Drop %	Throttle %	Out of order %	Duplicate %
Good network	1 ms	0	0	0	0
Technology	Frames per Second				
Local PC	24.79	24.79	24.79	24.79	24.79
Quality type	Delay	Drop %	Throttle %	Out of order %	Duplicate %
Normal Network	20 ms	1	5	1	3
Technology	Frames per Second				
Citrix XenDesktop	23.57	9.20	17.96	19.03	15.87
VMware Horizon	14.56	11.05	14.06	24.31	21.52
Microsoft VDI	2.44	2.55	2.39	4.71	3.92

is such that the frame rate in this task is dramatically degraded compared to 24.79 on a PC. This technology does not show any resilience to degradation of any network quality factors since in any of five network quality factors, the frame rate is dropped under 5. The largest impact of the networking factors on for the solution by Citrix and VMware is the loss of packets. Both solutions drop to a frame rate of around 10 with a drop rate of 1 %. With respect to the capabilities of a human brain, a frame rate of 10 should be still acceptable, while a frame rate of below 5 is not acceptable.

4.4 Streaming Quality of Solutions in Various Network Conditions

In this section, we performed each user task (as listed in Subsect. 4.1) on each network condition (as listed in Subsect. 4.2) with each VDI solution as well as a local PC. First, we execute the tasks on a PC and measure the resulting frame rate for each task (Table 4). In this ideal state, the frame rate is around 25 for Web browsing, audio/video streaming, presentation editing, word processing and code compiling, while the frame rate is around 12–15 for data analysis and image processing. This due to the few changes in the figure or screen lag due to calculations in the background.

Results for Citrix XenDesktop. In both best and normal network quality, Web Browsing and Video/Audio Streaming have the best performance. Surprisingly, the quality of these two tasks in best network quality is only slightly lower than the quality that a PC can deliver. However, their quality crashes in average network quality and reaches to the lowest level in worst network quality. Word processing, data analyzing, presentation designing, and image processing keep their frame rate relatively stable in best and normal network quality. Their frame rate decreases in average network quality, leading to the lowest frame rate in worst network quality. In general, XenDesktop performs these tasks with much lower frame rate than a PC. Although code compiling has the worst frame rate

Table 4. Effect of network quality on application use cases in frames per second

Network	Browse	Stream	Word	Analysis	Slides	Image Proc.	Compile
Local PC - Measure in Frames per Second							
Ideal	24.79	25.86	25.99	12.27	25.96	27.37	15.5
Citrix XenDesktop							
Type 1	22.97	24.00	5.86	12.23	4.67	11.50	3.71
Type 2	20.22	17.73	4.90	9.66	4.77	11.12	9.15
Type 3	9.56	3.97	2.01	10.61	1.60	2.89	7.38
Type 4	3.70	2.36	1.94	4.44	0.90	3.63	6.61
VMware Horizon - Measure in Frames per Second							
Type 1	20.00	23.00	12.44	7.49	18.90	24.67	13.00
Type 2	12.22	2.33	3.43	4.15	12.00	17.70	10.55
Type 3	9.36	2.18	10.57	4.08	10.05	16.15	14.08
Type 4	3.50	0.30	4.24	4.42	4.37	2.39	6.55
Microsoft VDI							
Type 1	20.87	13.17	4.30	5.69	5.48	13.51	6.32
Type 2	3.70	3.40	3.84	4.69	3.76	5.07	4.30
Type 3	3.04	2.15	5.27	2.78	1.44	2.69	1.86
Type 4	0.54	0.62	2.04	1.03	0.94	0.82	1.24

in the best network quality, compared to other tasks, it considerably improves in the normal network quality, but again slowly loses frame rate in the average and worst network quality.

Results for VMware Horizon View. In the best network quality, image processing has the best performance with 24.672 fps and data analysis has the lowest frame rate with 7.493 fps. Since the quality of the data analysis task does not deviate much in the other network qualities, we believe the cause of low frame rate is resulted from the nature of this task and the fact that the state of a user's screen is usually static and does not change very frequently. Therefore, the performance of this task is might be regardless of the network quality and can be acceptable in any network quality. Word processing, however, has a relatively erratic behavior. Starting from 12.44 fps in the best network quality, it crashes in 3.43 fps in the normal network quality, climbs up to 10.57 fps again in average network quality and, finally, crashes into 4.24 fps again. In each network quality, the same test case for each task is performed, however, the speed of executing the a task (e.g. scrolling speed) may differ in each network quality, which consequently affects the frame rate. The same behavior can also be observed for code compiling, however, with higher frame rate and less variance in each network quality comparing to word processing. Among other tasks, video/audio streaming has the highest quality degradation. Dramatically falling from 23 fps in the best network quality to, first, 2.33 fps in the normal network quality and, finally, 0.30 fps in the worst network quality, a minimum level of quality is only achievable in the best network quality with Horizon View technology. Compared to a PC, the VMware Horizon View cannot establish a similar level of quality in any of the tasks. Finally, other tasks, such as Web browsing, presentation designing (Slides), and image processing, have an expected decrease in frame rate and, consequently, the quality of services id degraded as the network quality is degraded. However, the frame rate of the image processing task crashes dramatically in the worst network quality, making it almost impossible to perform the task. The reason to this behavior is that Image Processing, as a task dealing highly with graphical features, requires high frame rate and, therefore, is more vulnerable to poor network quality.

Results for Microsoft VDI. Focusing on the results in Table 4, next we discuss the results of testing the seven tasks in four network qualities using Microsoft VI. In the best network quality, Web browsing has the best performance with 20.87 fps, image processing (13.51 fps) and video/audio streaming (13.17 fps) also has a relatively high frame rate. Word processing (4.3 fps) together with code compiling (6.32 fps), presentation designing (Slides) (5.48 fps), and data analyzing (5.69 fps) show a very poor performance. These four tasks also maintain low frame rate in normal, average, and worst network qualities. In the transition between the best network quality and the normal network quality, the quality of Web browsing, video/audio streaming and image processing dramatically falls. After that, all the tasks lose frame rate until the worst network quality, in which, with regard to their frame rates, no task can be performed. Microsoft VDI also performs the tasks with a high difference in QoS (i.e. frame rate) compared to the quality of these tasks on a PC.

Based on the benchmarking that we performed on these three VDI technologies, we can conclude that Microsoft VDI falls back compared to Citrix XenDesktop and VMware Horizon View in Quality of Service and Quality of Experience. Furthermore, compared to VMware Horizon View, Citrix XenDesktop proves to be more stable in delivery of suitable Quality of Service and Quality of Experience, as the table indicates by having more votes on normal behavior or acceptable behavior for the Citrix XenDesktop in comparison to VMware Horizon View. Additionally, the user-based testing that we performed also exposes that users are, in general, more satisfied with the quality of Citrix XenDesktop.

5   Conclusions

Introducing Virtual Desktop Infrastructure (VDI) technology as a commercial desktop virtualization approach, we believe that there should be a counterpart technology, which provides desktop virtualization for personal users, namely Virtual Personal Computer (VPC), allowing users to access their desktop environment from any place and device at any time. In this paper we chose, elaborated and implemented the architectures of three dominant VDI technologies, namely Citrix XenDesktop, VMware Horizon View, and Microsoft VDI. After a careful parameter study a setup of each technology, we defined and performed a set of test cases and which allows us to identify the impact of the network on the quality of the VPCs. We tested each technology with task-based testing. The results of the two tests gave useful insights about the QoS of each technology. Finally, we compared the three technologies from different aspects to determine a fair rating for the quality of the services that they provide. In the comparison of the feature list, Citrix XenDesktop is rated best with the other two solutions being slightly less powerful. In the comparison of the impact of the individual Network Factors VMware Horizon View proves to be robust against various single work modifications. In the combination of limited network factors, i.e. in various network conditions, Citrix XenDesktop turns out to be more able to maintain a stable frame rate. While VMware Horizon View shows also good results, Citrix XenDesktop is slightly better while Microsoft VDI is very limited and provides only a small frame rate. We conclude that Citrix XenDesktop surpasses VMware Horizon View and Microsoft VDI in terms of Quality of Service and the variety of features that it offers. Thus, we believe that Citrix XenDesktop is the most qualified VDI technology, upon which the VPC concept can be established. In future work, the type and quality of the tasks tested will be extended to match more use cases. Also we aim at conducting a user-based study measuring the quality of experience as well as at indentifying the options for peer-to-peer service provision [4, 7].

References

1. Horizon Advantages. www.vmware.com/products/horizon-view/features.html
2. Recession Is Good For Cloud Computing Microsoft Agrees. www.cloudave.com/2425/recession-is-good-for-cloud-computing-microsoft-agrees/
3. Gong, C., Liu, J., Zhang, Q., Chen, H., Gong, Z.: The characteristics of cloud computing. In: International Conference on Parallel Processing Workshops (ICPPW) (2010)
4. Graffi, K., Groß, C., Stingl, D., Nguyen, H., Kovacevic, A., Steinmetz, R.: Towards a P2P cloud: reliable resource reservations in unreliable P2P systems. In: International Conference on Parallel and Distributed Systems (ICPADS) (2010)
5. Kaufman, L.: Data security in the world of cloud computing. IEEE Secur. Priv. 7(1), 61–64 (2009)
6. Kovacevic, A., Graffi, K., Kaune, S., Leng, C., Steinmetz, R.: Towards benchmarking of structured peer-to-peer overlays for network virtual environments. In: IEEE International Conference on Parallel and Distributed Systems (ICPADS) (2008)
7. Liebau, N., Pussep, K., Graffi, K., Kaune, S., Jahn, E., Beyer, A., Steinmetz, R.: The impact of the P2P paradigm on the new media industries. In: Americas Conference on Information Systems (AMCIS) (2007)
8. Oestreich, K.: Converged infrastructure. In: CTO Forum, vol. 15, November 2010
9. Sierra, S.: The Three Types of Computer User. Digital Digressions (2006). http://stuartsierra.com/2006/07/12/the-three-types-of-computer-user
10. Simmhan, Y., Kumbhare, A.G., Cao, B., Prasanna, V.K.: An analysis of security and privacy issues in smart grid software architectures on clouds. In: IEEE International Conference on Cloud Computing, CLOUD, pp. 582–589 (2011)
11. Ventresco, J.: Implementing VMware Horizon View 5.2. Packt Publishing, Birmingham (2013)

A Trustworthy Distributed Social Carpool Method

Francisco Martín-Fernández[(✉)], Cándido Caballero-Gil,
and Pino Caballero-Gil

Department of Computer Engineering,
University of La Laguna, San Cristóbal de La Laguna, Spain
{fmartinf,ccabgil,pcaballe}@ull.edu.es

Abstract. Due to the increase in the number of vehicles over the years, roads are witnesses of frequent traffic congestions, especially in urban environments. The problem is even worse because most vehicles are occupied by a single person. Therefore, a possible solution would be to use carpooling to increase the number of people in vehicles. In this way, commuters who travel from and to nearby places will share the same vehicle. Existing carpool solutions are unpopular for most people because of the distrust generated by carpooling with strangers. Thanks to the widespread of mobile technology and social networks, it is possible to create a reliable, friendly and secure carpool system. This paper proposes the design and implementation of an integrated solution that can be used to improve existing carpool solutions. The proposal is based on a novel algorithm that rates user behaviours based on interactions and friendship degrees. In addition to this, the whole carpool system has been developed as a mobile application for Android devices, and the Open Source Project is already available on the Github platform.

1 Introduction

The number of vehicles in the world is growing at a rapid pace due to the rising of global population. This fact causes a dramatic rise in fuel prices and pollution. Therefore, governments have been forced into drastic measures to combat pollution, especially in large urban centers [15,22,25]. One of the solutions proposed by the vast majority of governments is the encouraging of use of public transport. Unfortunately, this solution is not convenient or comfortable enough for many users because of the existing constraints in time or place.

A convenient solution involves sharing cars so that empty seats can be used in most trips. This modality is known with the term carpooling and has been proposed as an effective way to reduce both pollution and spending. Another related but different proposal, known as carsharing, is based on collective fleets of cars with multiple users, but such a solution does not solve as many problems as carpooling. Ridesharing is the general term used to refer to solutions for sharing the use of a car with other people in order to travel to a given destination. Apart from carsharing and carpooling (also known as real-time or instant or dynamic or

© Springer International Publishing Switzerland 2015
S. Hunold et al. (Eds.): Euro-Par 2015 Workshops, LNCS 9523, pp. 324–335, 2015.
DOI: 10.1007/978-3-319-27308-2_27

ad-hoc ridesharing), ridesharing also includes other versions known as slugging, lift sharing and covoiturage. However, ridesharing proposals that are different from carpooling are out of the scope of this work.

The use of both types of collaborative solutions has increased since the onset of the economic crisis thanks to technology 2.0 [18]. They are applicable in almost any environment, but are especially useful in places like universities, holidays, long journeys and even urban centres. This is because in these situations both vehicle owners and passengers agree on the same motivations to consider carpooling. Usually their main goal is to share fuel cost, but there may be other reasons such as solving the parking problem, wanting to talk with others or to take care of the environment, etc.

This work proposes an improvement for existing carpooling solutions that make use of recent technological advances of smartphones and social networks. The described solution allows the establishment of trust and reputation accountability between drivers and passengers, while taking care of their privacy at the same time.

This paper is organized as follows. Section 2 mentions several related works. Section 3 introduces the general design of the proposal, which is mainly based on the reputation algorithm sketched in Sect. 4. The security of the proposal is briefly analyzed in Sect. 5. Section 6 describes the developed Android application. Finally, some conclusions and open problems can be found in Sect. 7.

2 Related Work

The first carpooling projects emerged in the late 1980s [24], but in those days, without the technology available today, many difficult obstacles such as the need to develop a user network and of a convenient communication medium had to be faced.

Gradually, the media used to organize the trips was changing from telephone to more flexible means such as the Internet, email and smartphones. Nowadays, many different carpooling platforms and services exist, but even today, they may be considered in their early stages because none has reached a critical mass of users.

Table 1 shows several features of different existing carpooling systems, including the most relevant security-related ones. In particular, we have chosen for this comparative analysis the representative systems: CarPooling [6], Blablacar [3], Amovens [1], ZimRide [28], compartir.org [9].

The main trust enforcing system in all these platforms is based on points given by users. However, bypassing this security system is quite easy because users who obtain a negative score, can create a new profile with new credentials and no points.

Apart from these practical platforms already in use, there are several papers that propose different solutions [12, 19, 23]. The work [5] shows an integrated system for the organization of carpooling service by using different technologies such as web, GIS and SMS. The authors of [21] propose a web platform to carpool.

Table 1. Comparison among several carpooling platforms

Platform	Social network	Privacy	Reputation system	Phone Cert.	Trust Alg.
Amovens [1]	yes	yes	yes	no	no
Blablacar [3]	yes	yes	yes	yes	no
CarPooling [6]	yes	no	yes	no	no
Compartir [9]	no	yes	no	no	no
ZimRide [28]	yes	yes	no	no	no
Our system	**yes**	**yes**	**yes**	**no**	**yes**

The paper [13] presents a carpooling architecture that uses a credit mechanism to encourage cooperation between users.

A more recent work is [8], where an algorithm to encourage carpooling is proposed based on assigning priority to users with positive feedbacks through a fuzzy logic scheme. Another paper, [14], defines a push service to promote carpooling through instant processing. Finally, another interesting proposal is [4], based on a secure multi-agent platform that focuses on the security services allowing both the mutual authentication between the users and the application components with the system.

The main aspect of our work is different from the aforementioned because it deals with the trust aspect of carpooling services through a combination of reputation measurement with privacy protection.

3 Carpooling Platform

The main objective of the proposed design is the increase of both usability and security. Thus, its key factors are user-friendliness and privacy.

The database schema that has been followed in this work uses the three entities mentioned below: Route, Vehicle and User. Table 2 shows all the relevant data about the Route entity that users create, and are stored in the database.

One of the main features is that users who publish their trips have their privacy fully protected. Unlike other carpooling platforms, in the described system, no user is allowed to access data such as email, phone or full name of others, unless he/she is authenticated on the platform and the algorithm for checking mutual trust returns a valid permission for him/her. In this case, the interested user can see all the data in detail. Otherwise, he/she can only send a request so that the receiver can decide whether the applicant is to be trusted or not.

The algorithm is based on trust relationships so that people who want to use the platform first need to authenticate in the platform through social networks such as Facebook, Twitter or Google+. In this way, the algorithm checks the existence of some chain of trust between the applicant and other users, based on the so-called rule of six degrees of separation [27].

Table 3 shows all the information necessary to analyze the system data and compute the degree of separation among different users in social networks, as stored in the database for each User Entity.

Table 2. Route entity details

Attribute	Description
idRoute	Unique Route identifier
idVehicle	Unique identifier of the Vehicle responsible for the Route
idUser	Unique identifier of the User responsible for the Route
From	Departure point of the Route
To	Destination point of the Route
Seats	Number of seats available in the vehicle
Price	Estimated cost of the Route
Properties	Route properties: animals allowed, smoking allowed, only women, etc
Date	Date of the Route
Repeat	If the Route is repeated, periodicity

Table 3. User entity details

Attribute	Description
idUser	Unique User identifier
idFacebook	Facebook User identifier
idTwitter	Twitter User identifier
idGooglePlus	Google Plus User identifier
idGCM	Google Cloud Messaging User identifier
Name	User real name
Phone	User phone number
Email	User email

Besides, the reputation gained through the use of the application is an influent factor, which is considered in the decision on whether carpooling with another person or not. In order to do this, at the end of every shared travel, the application asks both drivers and passengers to score the other users. Such scores are used in future trips so that seats offered by car drivers with good scores appear in better positions than others with lower scores. Also well-scored passengers have higher probability to have access to more details of drivers.

Finally, Table 4 shows the details regarding the Pairing Entity responsible for linking routes with users, as stored in the database.

Our overall system architecture used as an application model known as client-server. The client-server architecture of our system is showed in Fig. 1.

Its different elements are the following:

- **Client:** Mobile device used for the system.
- **Server:** Hosted in the cloud, and divided into two parts. On the one hand, the GCM server is the Google Cloud Messaging server that handles all the

Table 4. Pairing entity details

Attribute	Description
idRoute	Unique Route identifier
idUser	Unique User identifier
State	Current state of the Route for a passenger who has applied: accepted, pending or declined
Type	Type of Route User: passenger or driver
Rating	Rating of the route: if passenger, the driver rating; otherwise, the list of passenger ratings

notifications and is responsible for sending the notification when the receiver clients are alive. On the other hand, the DB dedicated server is the server that stores in its DataBase all the data related to the users and system. It also serves as a gateway for sending notifications between the client and the GCM server.

The life cycle of the application is shown in Fig. 2, and explained below:

– **Step 1:** The user logs on the application through any of its social networks (Facebook, Twitter, Google+). Then, its data are saved in the DB server and the device is registered in the GCM server for notifications.
– **Step 2:** Once logged in, the user has two possibilities:
   1. The user can play the role of driver, and create new routes or manage existing routes. On the one hand, if a new route is created, all related

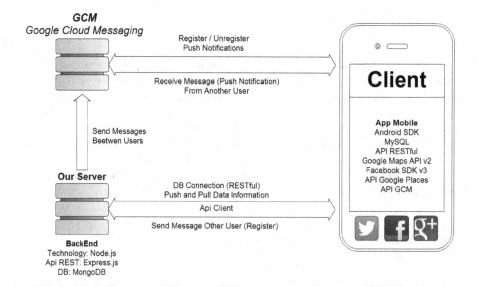

Fig. 1. Carpooling system architecture

information is stored in real time on the DB server. On the other hand, if the user is managing some old routes, first, the client informs the dedicated server to store the shares in the DB. Then, it also indicates to notify possible affected users about route changes in order to ask for acceptance/rejection to participate in the route, etc. The DB server sends the necessary information to the GCM server, so that this sends such notification to the involved clients when they are turned on and connected to the network.

2. The user can play the role of a passenger who tries to find some trip. Once a trip is found, the user sends a request to be a passenger on that route. This request must be answered positively or negatively by the creator of the route, through a notification sent within a period of time. Such a notification will go from the dedicated server to the GCM server because this is the responsible server for sending notifications to the clients.

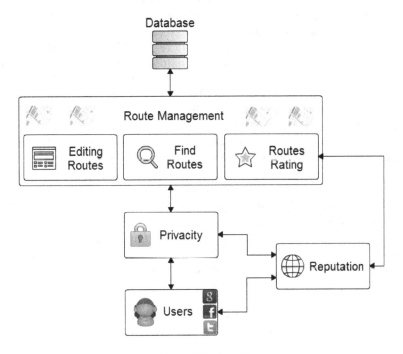

Fig. 2. Use model

The proposed scheme protects user privacy through limited and controlled access to user data, according to the trust level stated for the relationship between each pair of users. This trust level is got through the combination of direct scores and trust networks so that it provides the system with enough data to deduce whether people can trust each other or not. In this way, privacy is dealt with as one of the most important aspects of the proposed carpooling system.

A first approach to the development of a trust measurement algorithm that provides a value to each pair of users is based on the use of the PageRank algorithm to predict whether two people can rely each other . However, since this algorithm does not conform totally to the morphology of the specific problem, a second approach is also being used to complement it, based on Bayesian networks to know whether people can trust others. The refined trust measurement algorithm is available in the Android Application.

4   The Reputation Algorithm

No existing carpooling proposal offers the user a quantitative method, based on the theory of six degrees of separation, that can be used to decide whether another user is trustful to share a vehicle. Some of them even do not allow users to decide who may or may not apply your route. There are some proposed that the quantitative method based on the similarities among users [7,16,20], having to collect this information about the attributes and characteristics of each user. Our proposal aims to be simple for the user, without the user fills out some information about its attributes. With a simple click (that enables social login on the network that is previously registered) may be entered in our system and start using the platform. The main difference with our proposal is the proposed reputation algorithm. By using it, the user can use a quantitative measure to decide whether trusting another user. The algorithm is based on the theory of six degrees of separation and individual scores within our platform. Six degrees of separation is the theory that everyone is six or fewer steps away from each other in the world, so that a chain of 'a friend of a friend' statements can be made to connect any two people in a maximum of six steps. This number of steps may be reduced significantly by introducing the concept of social networks. Our application uses social networks when logging into the application to create network users to be used to interconnect with each other and provide a reliable measure of confidence. Through the use of social networks we can ensure that the six degrees of separation are reduced to only four. In particular, according to several researches on Facebook [2,10,26], the obtained average distance was 3.9 ,corresponding to intermediaries or 'degrees of separation', what shows that the world is even smaller than expected.

The reputation measurement is expressed as a number between 0 and 10, and is computed from the values given by each pair of users to inform about the reliability in each other. This measure is calculated by taking into account the two parameters mentioned above: degree of friendship and appreciation of other users on our platform. If the Facebook social network is used, the score given by the system with the degrees of friendship is broken down as follows:

- **7 points** if a user has only one degree of separation (i.e. it is direct friend).
- **6 points** if both users have a mutual friend.
- **4 points** if among those users there is a chain of friendship of more than two friends.
- **0 points** for the case that there is no chain friendliness.

Other users obtain the remaining scores from the assessments after sharing routes. When a route is completed, users who participated in it, can vote between **1 and 5** stars. Each passenger individually assesses the driver, and the driver individually assesses passengers. The weight is higher from driver to passengers than from passengers to driver, as the driver puts his/her vehicle available to the users. In order to account for the different ratings on a user, we use a simple arithmetic average. The metric taken into account for these ratings is as shown in Table 5.

Table 5. Impact of the ratings

Star rating	Driver rating impact	Passenger rating impact
1 star	−3 points	−2 points
2 stars	−1 point	0.25 points
3 stars	1.5 points	0.5 points
4 stars	2.5 points	2 points
5 stars	3 points	3 points

The maximum reputation score that a user can get is **10 points**. The system does not use a score below 0, so that 0 is the minimum score for any user. This valuation is dynamically calculated as a function of the friendship degree that a user has. It helps users to have a reliability measure about whether to trust another user of the platform. Besides, only users who have a valuation higher than **7.5 points** and/or users who have been accepted by the driver to make the route can see certain route data, such as the phone number or any other confidential data.

So the mathematical expression applied to the calculation of the reputation score in the algorithm is:

$$\left(lvFs + \frac{\sum_{i=1}^{n} rat[i]}{n} \right)$$

where:

- **lvFs:** Friendship level measured in points between 0 and 7, depending on the level of friendship each user has with other user, as explained above.
- **rat[]:** Each of the ratings a user has received both as driver and passenger, on the routes that has used. The points at which the rating of 1–5 stars are mapped.
- **n:** Total number of ratings that the user has received.

5   Security of the Scheme

Regarding the safety of the platform, Sybil attack [11] is one of notorious attacks in traditional carpooling systems. This type of attacks are hacking attacks on peer-to-peer networks where a malicious device illegitimately takes multiple identities by forging them. Due to the privacy-preserving environment of carpooling schemes, sybil vulnerability is generally hard to defend against.

In a Sybil attack the attacker subverts the reputation system of a peer-to-peer network by creating a large number of pseudonymous identities, using them to gain a disproportionately large influence. A reputation system's vulnerability to a Sybil attack depends on how cheaply identities can be generated, the degree to which the reputation system accepts inputs from entities that do not have a chain of trust linking them to a trusted entity, and whether the reputation system treats all entities identically.

A faulty node or an adversary may present multiple identities to a peer-to-peer network in order to appear and function as multiple distinct nodes. After becoming part of the peer-to-peer network, the adversary may then overhear communications or act maliciously. By masquerading and presenting multiple identities, the adversary can control the network substantially.

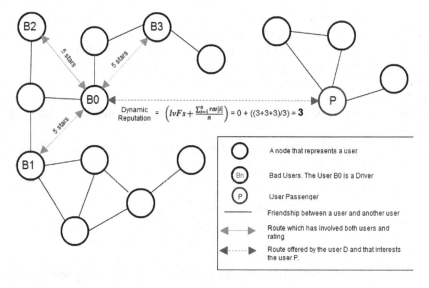

Fig. 3. Insufficient dynamic reputation rating between an bad user and a possible passenger.

In our case, for example, considering the following scenario:

A 'bad' user ($B0$, See Fig. 3) sets up several bogus accounts in social media and the proposed system ($B1$, $B2$, $B3$, etc.). He/she then advertises a possible trip from $X \mapsto Y \mapsto Z$. For the first leg ($X \mapsto Y$) he/she uses the bogus accounts to claim that his/her vehicle is full and all these 'passengers' state that they get off at Y. He/she can then get excellent scores and increase his/her reputation. At some point, this will be so high that other normal users will be able trust him/her from leg $Y \mapsto Z$.

The proposed algorithm is protected against the attack described above because most of the score of our algorithm is preceded by confidence in degrees of friendship that binds each user to another user. Thus, if a user does not know (at all) another user, very high ratings of the latter in the system are not reliable enough for the fomer. It is remarkable that in our system the minimum reliability to trust another user is 7.5 points. At most, a user can have up to 3 points in relation to ratings for the routes that has done (see Fig. 3), far from the 7.5 points that are needed at least for that user to be reliable.

6   The Android Application

The proposed design has been embodied in an Android application that is already published in the Android Play Store under the name 'Carpoolap' (See Fig. 4).

Fig. 4. Passenger and driver rating screens

The Android application is developed for the versions 3.0 or higher of the operating system. APIs like Google Maps v3.0, Google Places, Google Cloud Messaging, etc., and Facebook SDKs 3.0 and libraries like Action Bar Sherlock used to use the functionality of the new versions of Android on older versions, were used. Autocomplete in address searches, Google Maps 3D Technology, design based on the latest versions of Android, push notifications with requests or responses of passengers or drivers, etc. are among the features of the Android Application.

Each user can see the routes he/she proposes as driver, and whether potential passengers exist for those routes. Besides, with colour codes, he/she can know the routes that each user has already made and the routes that have been confirmed by users. For the assessment of users participating in a route, after finishing it, each one can give a score. The different rating screens for the passenger and driver are shown in Fig. 4.

In order to deploy the carpooling platform, a server is also needed, so we developed one using javascript technologies by frameworks like 'node.js' and 'express.js'. As a database for all the data centralized on this server, we decided to adopt a No SQL database, such as MongoDB [17]. We deployed our server on a micro instance of Amazon Web Services, specifically under Ubuntu machine with Amazon EC2 account.

7 Conclusions

By improving the confidence, security and reliability of carpooling systems it is possible to cause a greater use by the reticent society. In light of this, this paper proposes a solution to share free seats in vehicles that includes these enhancements. After the analysis of existing proposals and the review of related research works, it has not been detected any solution that uses the necessary degree of friendship to provide trust to the user. The presented proposal allows an assessment of users through their connections in social networks, based on the theory of six degrees of separations. It provides a reliable measure of confidence between users that enables the use of any carpool platform. A specific platform has been also designed and developed based on the proposed trusted algorithm. The whole code of the implementations both for the Android application and for the server are available as an Open Source Project in Github. For future work, the implementation of the solution forother mobile platforms is expected.

Acknowledgments. Research supported by the Spanish MINECO and the European FEDER Funds under projects TIN2011-25452, RTC-2014-1648-8, TEC2014-54110-R and IPT-2012-0585-370000, and the FPI scholarship BES-2012-051817.

References

1. Amovens: https://www.amovens.com
2. Backstrom, L., Boldi, P., Rosa, M., Ugander, J., Vigna, S.: Four degrees of separation. In: Proceedings of the 4th Annual ACM Web Science Conference, pp. 33–42 (2011)
3. Blablacar: https://www.blablacar.es
4. Bonhomme, C., Arnould, G., Khadraoui, D.: Dynamic carpooling mobility services based on secure multi-agent platform. In: IEEE International Conference on Global Information Infrastructure and Networking Symposium, pp. 1–6 (2012)
5. Calvo, R.W., De Luigi, F., Haastrup, P., Maniezzoi, V.: A distributed geographic system for the daily car pooling problem. Comput. Oper. Res. **31**, 2263–2278 (2004)

6. Carpooling: www.carpooling.es
7. Cho, S., Yasar, A., Knapen, L., Bellemans, T., Janssens, D., Wets, G.: A conceptual design of an agent-based interaction model for the carpooling application. In: The 1st International Workshop on Agent-based Mobility, Traffic and Transportation Models, Methodologies and Applications, pp. 801–807 (2011)
8. Collotta, M., Pau, G., Salerno, V.M., Scata, G.: A novel trust based algorithm for carpooling transportation systems. In: IEEE International Conference on Energy Conference and Exhibition, pp. 1077–1082 (2012)
9. Compartir.org: http://compartir.org/
10. Daraghmi, E.Y., Yuan, S.M.: We are so close, less than 4 degrees separating you and me! Comput. Hum. Behav. **30**, 273–285 (2014)
11. Douceur, J.R.: The Sybil attack. In: Druschel, P., Kaashoek, M.F., Rowstron, A. (eds.) IPTPS 2002. LNCS, vol. 2429, p. 251. Springer, Heidelberg (2002)
12. Fellows, N.T., Pitfield, D.E.: An economic and operational evaluation of urban car-sharing. Transp. Res. Part D: Transp. Environ. **5**, 1–10 (2000)
13. Ferreira, J., Trigo, P., Filipe, P.: Collaborative car pooling system. In: International Conference on Sustainable Urban Transport and Environment (2009)
14. Fougeres, A.J., Canalda, P., Ecarot, T., Samaali, A., Guglielmetti, L.: A push service for carpooling. In: IEEE International Conference on Green Computing and Communications, pp. 685–691 (2012)
15. Katzev, R.: Car sharing: a new approach to urban transportation problems. Anal. Soc. Iss. Pub. Policy **3**, 65–86 (2003)
16. Kuter, U., Golbeck, J.: SUNNY: a new algorithm for trust inference in social networks using probabilistic confidence models. In: Proceedings of the Conference on Artificial intelligence AAAI, pp. 1377–1382 (2007)
17. MongoDB: www.mongodb.org
18. Oram, A.: Peer-to-Peer: Harnessing the Benefits of a Disruptive Technology. O'Reilly, Sebastopol (2001)
19. Prettenthaler, F.E., Steininger, K.W.: From ownership to service use lifestyle: the potential of car sharing. Ecol. Econ. **28**, 443–453 (1999)
20. Pukhovskiy, N.V., Lepshokov, R.E.: Real-time carpooling system. In: International Conference on Collaboration Technologies and Systems, pp. 648–649 (2011)
21. Roberts, A., Pimentel, H., Karayevm, S.: CabFriendly: A Cloud-based Mobile Web App. Amazon's EC2 (2011). https://github.com/sergeyk/cabfriendly
22. Steininger, K., Vogl, C., Zettr, R.: The size of the market segment and revealed change in mobility behavior. Transp. Policy **3**, 177–185 (1996)
23. Talele, T., Pandi, G., Deshmukh, P.: Dynamic ridesharing using social media. Int. J. AdHoc Netw. Syst. **2**, 29 (2012)
24. Teal, R.: Carpooling: who, how and why. Transp. Res. Part A **21A**, 203–214 (1987)
25. Transport For London: www.tfl.gov.uk/tfl/roadusers/congestioncharge
26. Ugander, J., Karrer, B., Backstrom, L., Marlow, C.: The anatomy of the facebook social graph (2011). arXiv:1111.4503
27. Watts, D.J., Strogatz, S.H.: Collective dynamics of small-world networks. Nature **393**, 440–442 (1998)
28. Zimride: http://www.zimride.com/

OMHI - On-Chip Memory Hierarchies and Interconnects: Organization, Management and Implementation

Efficient DVFS Operation in NoCs Through a Proper Congestion Management Strategy

José V. Escamilla[1]([✉]), José Flich[1], and Pedro Javier García[2]

[1] Universitat Politècnica de València, Valencia, Spain
joseslo@gap.upv.es, jflich@disca.upv.es
[2] Universidad de Castilla-La Mancha, Albacete, Spain
pedrojavier.garcia@uclm.es

Abstract. As technology advances, applications demand more and more computing power. However, achieving the required performance is not nowadays the single target, as reducing power consumption has become a key issue. In that sense, power-control mechanisms such as Dynamic Voltage and Frequency Scaling (DVFS) are introduced in order to dynamically adapt frequency and voltage to the actual computing-power demands of applications. However, these techniques may not be as efficient as expected due to delays caused by frequency-voltage changes. Furthermore, data flows generated at high rates may cross slow voltage-frequency islands, thereby leading to congestion inside the on-chip network. To alleviate this problem, we propose a combined DVFS and congestion management strategy. Specifically, the policies to adjust DFVS levels are tuned cooperatively with the congestion management strategy, leading to power-saving achievements of up to 26 % and latency improvements for non-congested traffic of up to 43 %.

1 Introduction

Nowadays, High-Performance Computing (HPC) and multimedia-oriented applications and services demand increasing computing power. In order to satisfy this demand, manufacturers take advantage of the advances in integration-scale technology to include as many computing resources as possible into the same die. This trend has led to advanced designs in manycore chips. Regardless the specific design, these platforms require an on-chip network (NoC) [1] to support communication among all the processing and/or storage nodes. The NoC must provide high bandwidth and low latency, otherwise processing nodes will slow down as they have to wait for long to receive necessary data. Hence, the design of the NoC presents unavoidable challenges.

Among these challenges, a still open issue is how to efficiently deal with congestion situations, i.e. scenarios where any number of network paths are clogged, mainly due to oversubscribed ports (hotspots). Indeed, congestion may lead to a severe degradation in network performance if no countermeasures are taken. Another challenge is reducing power consumption. Technology has reached power and thermal limits, thus limiting clock frequency and voltage. Moreover, in

© Springer International Publishing Switzerland 2015
S. Hunold et al. (Eds.): Euro-Par 2015 Workshops, LNCS 9523, pp. 339–351, 2015.
DOI: 10.1007/978-3-319-27308-2_28

battery-powered devices, energy must be efficiently managed so as to maximize working time of the device. For these reasons, the current trend is to provide manycore chips with power-control mechanisms.

One of the most popular mechanisms is Dynamic Voltage and Frequency Scaling (DVFS) [12]. Basically, it consists in adapting the frequency and voltage based on the actual computing-power demand. Reducing the frequency and voltage leads to a significant reduction in power consumption, thus saving unneeded energy. However, DVFS must be carefully designed since reducing the working voltage and frequency may reduce also network performance. Thus, finding out the optimal conditions to increase or decrease the working voltage and frequency is critical to achieve the best trade-off between power saving and network performance. Additionally, voltage and frequency changes are usually performed in steps or levels, and those changes cause severe power and delay penalties, thus, demanding for a proper policy.

A DVFS change causes inherently the system to halt for a small period of time (due to the electronic limits) [15]. Recent proposals shadow this effect by setting different DVFS regions, called Voltage and Frequency Islands (VFIs) [11,14]. In this way, frequency and voltage for a given island become independent as they are only driven by the metrics obtained from such island. From the efficiency point of view, VFI islands achieve an undeniable enhancement [11] as applications running concurrently may have different needs, some maximizing performance while others minimizing power. Nonetheless, VFIs still pose new challenges. Data flows may cross several VFIs working at different levels. Thus, the crossing from a high-frequency VFI to a low-frequency VFI will slow down the flow, potentially leading to a congestion situation appearing on VFI boundary. Moreover, congestion may be propagated throughout the high-frequency VFI network.

Summing up, DVFS-based systems need a proper policy to perform frequency-voltage transitions and, on the other hand, need to avoid congestion when VFIs are used. To address both issues, we propose adapting a congestion-control mechanism called ICARO [4] (Internal-Congestion-Aware Hol-blocking RemOval) to DVFS-based systems with VFIs. By doing this, performance is maintained despite of the DVFS-transition delays and congestion is alleviated despite of data flows crossing VFIs with different levels. ICARO congestion metrics will be used to implement the DVFS policy to perform voltage-frequency changes. We target different possibilities to plug a congestion control mechanism with a DVFS policy. Several solutions are presented which improve different key metrics, such as power consumption or message latency. Results show that we achieve improvements on network latency of 43 % for non-congested traffic with a power overhead of approximately 8 %. For the second solution a gain of 26 % on power consumption, with an improvement on latency of 2 % at the cost of losing throughput and, finally, the last proposal achieves an improvement on latency of 19 % with a power saving gain of 20 %. As networks-on-chip consume up to the 36 % of the total chip power [17,18], the benefits of our proposal may improve substantially the overall power consumption.

The paper is organized as follows. Section 2 shows related work in DVFS and congestion-control mechanisms. Section 3 describes the ICARO-DVFS method. Section 3.6 shows analysis results for different DVFS scenarios combined with ICARO. Finally, Sect. 4 shows conclusions and future work.

2   Related Work

Related to DVFS, one key issue is the voltage-frequency regulator (VR) due to the high delays caused when changing the voltage-frequency level. DVFS regulators are designed either off-chip or on-chip. Off-chip regulators support high amounts of power, but they are slow. By contrast, on-chip regulators are very fast but expensive in terms of area and do not support much power. In [19], a hybrid scheme using both types of regulators is proposed. In systems using VFIs, the more VFIs are implemented, the more power efficiency is achieved, hence having one VFI per node would be the best case. Under this premise, in [9] authors propose a per-core VFI approach based on on-chip VRs. Despite authors state that area overhead would not be an obstacle to implement their proposal, in a newer study [19] they discard this approach due to the large area required to implement so many on-chip VRs, supporting their arguments on results obtained in [8]. An accurate DVFS model is described [15] for different real architectures, comparing with values from real systems. We use values of voltage/frequency levels (Table 2) and level change delays (Table 5) to model DVFS in our simulator.

Related to congestion, we find several solutions. Solutions for buffered NoCs are based on monitoring buffer occupancy and collecting congestion information from neighboring nodes. A congestion-free path is then used to avoid hotspot areas. In this way, RCA [5] uses multiple global metrics collected from the whole network to select at each router the output port which messages are forwarded through. However, a vicious cycle may be created since the information used to avoid the congested areas is included in the congested messages. Besides, adapting the routes to avoid hotspots may result in moving the location of such hotspots from one place to another. Moreover, avoiding hotspots may be impossible if all the flows have the same target (e.g. the memory controller).

Another solution based on adaptive routing is PARS [2], that uses a dedicated subnetwork to send congestion metrics about the buffer state at certain routers, then using these metrics to select paths that avoid hotspots. However, the problems regarding unavoidable hotspots or "hotspot reallocation" may still appear. Similarly, in [10] a token-based flow-control mechanism is proposed which uses dedicated wires to send router status information (token) used to make routing decisions and bypass router pipeline stages. However, this proposal is focused on reducing network latency but not by facing congestion harmful effects. In [16] authors collect congestion information from the whole network to make routing decisions. However, in this proposal the congestion information is collected by piggybacking the links status into the packets header. In the next section we describe ICARO [4] which attacks congestion in a more efficient manner.

Table 1. DVFS levels assumed in the ICARO-DVFS mechanism (obtained from [15])

DVFS level	$Voltage(V)$	$Freq(GHz)$	DVFS level	$Voltage(V)$	$Freq(GHz)$
Level 1	1.30	3.074	Level 4	1.15	2.281
Level 2	1.25	2.852	Level 5	1.10	1.932
Level 3	1.20	2.588	Level 6	1.05	1.540

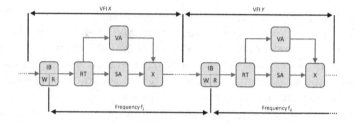

Fig. 1. Two consecutive routers belonging to different VFIs (at the boundary delimiting such VFIs).

3   ICARO-DVFS Implementation

3.1   Dynamic Voltage and Frequency Scaling

Our DVFS implementation changes voltage and frequency in levels, depending on the performance demand. Each level corresponds to a given pair of voltage-frequency fixed values (Table 1). Off-chip VRs are assumed.

DVFS levels are changed by monitoring the occupancy at router buffers. Every *poll_period* cycles across all the monitored routers sample and report their occupancy level. If any of the buffer exceeds a Q_h threshold the DVFS level is decremented (voltage and frequency are incremented). Accordingly, if all the buffers exhibit an occupancy below the Q_l threshold ($Q_h > Q_l$), the level is incremented (frequency and voltage are decremented).

3.2   Voltage and Frequency Islands

ICARO-DVFS supports VFIs, so voltage and frequency changes can be applied per VFI domain. Each VFI has its own VR which collects metrics from the routers in its domain and changes voltage-frequency accordingly. However, routers at the boundaries between VFIs must be carefully designed as data flows will cross different domains. To address this issue, we implement mixed-clock/mixed-voltage buffers [3,13] which enables to write and read at different frequencies.

Figure 1 shows the router implemented at a VFI boundary (see Sect. 3.6 for more information about routers architecture design). The *input buffer* stage is divided into two *sub-stages*, the write part belongs to the frequency domain of the upstream router while the read stage belongs to the current router frequency domain. In this way, the rest of pipeline stages (after IB) are able to work normally at its corresponding frequency. The same is performed for the flow control logic. As credit-based flow control is used, the credits buffer at the downstream router works at both frequencies, at the upstream router frequency for writing and at the current router frequency for reading.

3.3   ICARO

Our proposal merges DVFS with ICARO [4], which tackles the congestion problem in a different way as the usual one. Specifically, ICARO focuses on reducing the impact of the Head-of-Line (HoL) blocking [7] derived from congestion situations. This harmful effect happens when congested flows share buffers with non-congested flows, then the former slowing down the latter and so degrading network performance. In order to deal with HoL-blocking, ICARO separates congested flows from non-congested ones by means of the different VNs implemented as disjoint virtual channels in the network. Note that congestion situations (i.e. congested flows) are not removed but their negative impact is reduced or even eliminated. Basically, ICARO detects congestion at routers, notifies congestion to the end nodes, and they react by steering packets through different virtual networks depending whether they cross congestion spots or not.

Congestion is detected at routers. A dedicated module at each router analyzes buffers of each port and, based on the buffer utilization, computes pending requests from each input port to each output port in order to detect contention (more than one request for a given output port). If contention is detected and caused by oversubscribed input ports (and lasts for a given threshold), then the output port is declared congested. Only if one output port changes its congestion state, then a notification is triggered from the router.

A congestion notification consists of the state of all output ports of the router (one bit per output port). Notifications are sent from routers to end nodes through a dedicated network (Congestion Notification Network or CNN) implemented as a k-width segmented ring where $k = log_2(nodes) + router_{radix} + 1$. Figure 2 shows a CNN implementation for a 4×4 mesh NoC. The CNN is made of N registers, each one owned by a router and connected to the next register through a k-width link. At each clock cycle, all the registers forward their data to the next register along the ring. If a router needs to inject a congestion notification, it checks its register state and injects the notification once the register becomes free. Notifications travel along the entire ring and are removed when they reach the register where they were injected from. Notifications are delivered to all end nodes and at each node the notification is processed and stored in a notification cache as *congested point* (pairs of values made up of {congested_router, congested_port}). Registers in this network are implemented as mixed-clock/mixed-voltage buffers as well to cope with different frequency domains.

Congestion isolation is performed at end nodes. To do so, ICARO uses two VNs: one congested-VN and one regular-VN. All flows are always mapped first to regular-VNs, but a *post-processor* module checks at each cycle the flit at the head

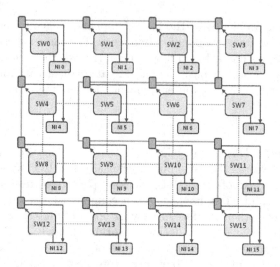

Fig. 2. CNN network example. Links in green: CNN interconnecting all CNN registers.

of the regular-VN. If the flit is a header and its path travels through a *congested point*, it is considered a congested flow so, then the flit and the remaining ones of the same message are relocated in the congested-VN relocating automatically all flits from such queue until a tail flit is found). Messages injected through a given VN never change to a different VN, thus achieving the isolation property pursued by ICARO.

3.4   Merging ICARO with DVFS

Now we show how ICARO is coupled with DVFS. Basically, ICARO notifies congestion events through the CNN network. This network is extended to send DVFS notifications as well[1]. This is easily achieved by changing the ICARO controller implemented in the router. In addition to detect congestion events, the new logic monitors all input ports queue occupancy and sends two new events through the CNN. Figure 4 shows the new notification format. Two bits are added just indicating the router requests for a level increment or decrement.

Buffer occupancy is analyzed in each router and compared against Q_h and Q_l thresholds. If any of the queues exceeds the Q_h threshold the VFI_{inc} bit is set. Once all queues occupancy are below Q_l the VFI_{dec} bit is set. Only when any of those two bits change a DVFS notification is sent through the CNN network.

At each VFI domain, the VFI module reads the notification commands from the CNN network, keeping record of all routers VFI_{inc} and VFI_{dec} bits from its domain. Two n-length bit vectors (being n the number of routers in the

---

[1] In a typical DVFS implementation, a dedicated logic collects metrics from the network and deliver them to the logic that implements the VFI policy and drives its VR to carry this out. We take advantage of the CNN network to simplify this process.

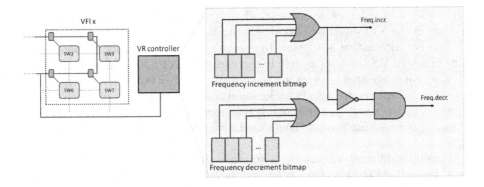

Fig. 3. Voltage Regulator controller logic

if *CNNreg.busy* && *idBelongsToVFI(CNNreg.routerID, thisVFI)* **then**
  if *CNNreg.FreqIncr* **then**
    freqIncrVector[routerID] = 1;
    if |*freqIncrVector* **then**
      increaseFrequency(thisVFI);
  else if *CNNreg.FreqDecr* **then**
    freqDecrVector[routerID] = 1;
    if |*freqDecrVector* && ∼ |*freqIncrVector* **then**
      decreaseFrequency(thisVFI);
  else
    Do nothing
  end
end

Algorithm 1: DVFS level change algorithm.

VFI domain) are implemented. VFI frequency/voltage is incremented when any of the routers request for such increment (even if a router is requesting for a decrement). Frequency decrement is performed when any router is requesting a decrement and none of the routers are requesting an increment. Figure 3 shows the logic, whereas Algorithm 1 shows the algorithm change DVFS levels.

3.5 Different ICARO-DVFS Alternatives

Besides the CNN extension, ICARO deals with different virtual networks (VNs) to decouple congested traffic from non-congested traffic. In the minimal implementation (2 VNs), just one VN is used to map congested traffic, the other one remains for non-congested traffic. As commented previously, to couple correctly ICARO and DVFS we need to sense occupancy of input ports queues. However, as we have differentiated VNs we have different options.

As a first alternative, we can sense all input ports queues, including both non-congested traffic VN and congested traffic VN. In this case, DVFS will raise frequencies and voltages whenever traffic increases to levels where congestion appears in the VFI domain. This alternative is referenced to as *ICARO-2VN*.

Another alternative is to raise frequencies and voltages only whenever the non-congested VN congests as well. In this case, the DVFS strategy will raise only when severe congestion appears in the network. In other words, when congestion caused by hotspot traffic affects background traffic in such a way in which causes regular-VNs to exceed Q_h threshold. It is supposed that this alternative will lead to more power-saving results. This alternative will be referenced to as ICARO-1VN.

Finally, a different alternative is to sense all input port's queue, but differently from *ICARO-2VN*, the DVFS strategy will be bounded to a more conservative frequency level. In this case, the maximum frequency will be set to ~2GHz (instead of ~3GHz), corresponding to *Level 5* frequency on Table 1. The reasoning behind this strategy is the effect ICARO has on performance as will decouple congested traffic from non-congested one. Therefore, increasing frequency for performance reasons will become less critical. This alternative will be referenced to as *ICARO-2GHz*. In addition, this approach allows to simplify VRs by reducing the number of voltage-frequency levels provided. Notice that area consumed by VRs depends directly on the voltage-frequency levels provided.

The three strategies will be analyzed in Sect. 3.6. All of them will be compared against three different strategies. The two first strategies will not use DFVS at all and will set the network both to minimum and maximum frequencies. They will be referenced to as *minFreq* and *maxFreq*, respectively and will allow us to set the low and up limits in terms of performance and power. The third strategy will be compounded of DVFS with the defined levels shown in Table 1 and sensing the VFI occupancy queues regardless of the congestion effects. This strategy will be referenced to as DVFS in the plots.

3.6   ICARO-DVFS Performance Analysis

Simulation Environment. We use gMemNoCsim, an in-house cycle-accurate event-driven NoC simulator. We model a 4-stage pipelined router: IB, RT, SA, X.

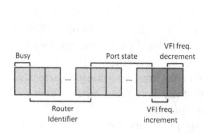

Fig. 4. CNN signal format in DVFS-based platforms

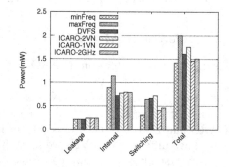

Fig. 5. Final power consumption.

Table 2. Common simulation configuration.

Topology	8×8 2D regular mesh
Routing policy	XY
Switching technique	Wormhole (flit-level)
Flow control	credits
Flit size	128 bits
Message size	5 flits
Switch queue size	16 flits

At IB flits are stored into the buffer. In the case of routers at the VFI boundary, a *coupling IB stage* (see Sect. 3.2) is implemented with two substages: *IB_W* (writing data) and *IB_R* (read data). At RT, routing computation is performed, SA performs switch allocation, and at X stage the flit crosses the crossbar and leaves the router.

Regarding traffic patterns, as ICARO is a proposal intended to deal with irregular, bursty, hotspot-prone traffic patterns, we drew up a combined traffic pattern. This traffic pattern is composed of a light uniform background traffic (at a datarate of 0.01 flits/ns) and a hotspot component. Hotspots consist in several nodes receiving each one high data rates (3 flits/ns) from 4 nodes (4-to-1 hotspots). Hotspots are active only from time 20ms to 40ms. In this way, we have a background traffic which generates no congestion, plus an aggressive traffic which causes congestion, causing HoL-blocking to the background traffic. This compound traffic pattern emulates environments where light data flows (i.e.: cores running applications with light data demand) share the NoC resources with heavy traffic generated nodes running high data demand applications or hardware accelerators which tend to generate heavy data bursts, causing congestion as well.

Simulations with DVFS are performed using real voltage, frequency and delay values shown in Table 1. For power consumption measures we use Orion 3.0 [6].

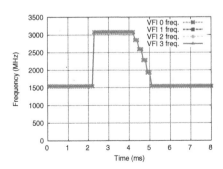

Fig. 6. VFIs frequencies for DVFS without ICARO.

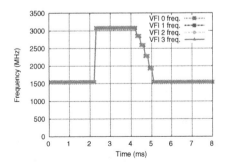

Fig. 7. VFIs frequencies for ICARO-2VN.

Results. In this section results for different configurations are shown. First, two configurations without DVFS are considered: *minFreq* for the chip running at the minimum frequency (1.540GHz) and *maxFreq* for the chip running at the maximum frequency (3.074GHz). Then, results for a DVFS scenario (without ICARO) are shown. Finally, results for the three ICARO-DVFS versions are shown. It is worth recalling that the main ICARO goal is to keep background traffic unaffected when dealing with congestion-prone traffic, such as the simulated hotspot traffic. For that reason results for background and hotspot traffic are shown separately.

Figure 10 shows average network latency results. For the DVFS cases some peaks in latency can be seen when congestion background starts and ends. These peaks clearly show the overhead derived from the VR taking some time to perform the DVFS level changes. It is worth mentioning that the first peak is higher as the VR takes more time to change from the lowest frequency to the highest. After some analysis, we decided to increase from the minimum frequency to the maximum one since this involves only one transition, incurring much less penalty with respect to a step-by-step increase. As expected, the scenario with DVFS improves in power consumption the no-DVFS scenario, but at the cost of increasing network latency (Fig. 12) and decreasing throughput (Fig. 13).

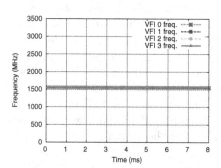

Fig. 8. VFIs frequencies for ICARO-1VN.

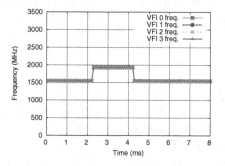

Fig. 9. VFIs frequencies for ICARO-2GHz.

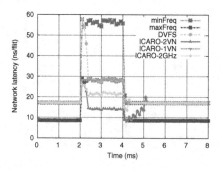

Fig. 10. Network latency for background traffic.

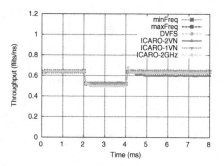

Fig. 11. Throughput for background traffic.

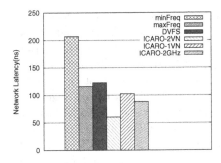

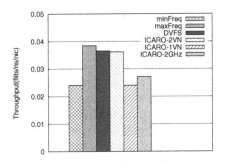

Fig. 12. Final net. latency (all traffic).   **Fig. 13.** Final throughput (all traffic).

However, according to Fig. 5, power consumption saving is more significant than performance degradation.

As can be seen in Fig. 10, ICARO proposals separate effectively background traffic from the hotspot one, preventing the HoL-blocking effect over the former. As expected, ICARO-2VN achieves the highest improvements in network latency (up to 43 %) since it takes into account all VNs to trigger the frequency-increment mechanism, and it is able to increment frequency to the maximum, but at the cost of increasing power consumption (8 %). Nevertheless, despite being the ICARO proposal with the highest power consumption, this case still keeps power consumption below "DVFS-alone" levels while improving latency.

Regarding the results for ICARO-1VN, note that only *regular-VNs* (VN 0) is taken into account to increase the VFI frequency and only background traffic is forwarded through this VN, so that this slight traffic flow is not enough to trigger the frequency-increment mechanism and all VFIs end up working at the minimum frequency. Despite running at the minimum frequency, we can see that the background network latency is kept in similar values to the DVFS case working at highest frequency. This is achieved by separating both traffic types, so preventing the HoL-blocking that the hotspot traffic could cause. In addition, as frequency is the lowest allowed, power saving is maximum, achieving an improvement of 26 %. However, as the system is working at the minimum frequency, throughput is lower than other cases that are running at higher frequencies. Nevertheless, background traffic achieves acceptable latency values.

Finally, ICARO-2GHz case could be considered as the best trade-off proposal. It takes into account all the available VNs but it is only allowed to increment frequency to the next step from the lowest frequency. This proposal does not achieve the best results in network latency and throughput, but nevertheless it improves the "DVFS-alone" case by 19 % with a significant power-saving improvement (20 %) with respect to DVFS, due to the lower frequency used.

4   Conclusions and Future Work

In this work a combination of DVFS scheme with a congestion management mechanism (ICARO) based on separating harmful traffic from non-harmful one has been presented. Using the dedicated network used by ICARO in order to also deliver DVFS metrics for triggering frequency changes has been proposed. Three different approaches have been proposed in order to combine DVFS with ICARO. The first taking into account all VNs to trigger the frequency change, achieving the best latency improvements with a slight power consumption penalty. The second one only takes into account the *regular-VNs* (VN 0) to trigger frequency changes, achieving a power consumption improvement of 26 %. Finally, the third proposal limit the frequency increase until 2GHz (instead of 3GHz), with a latency improvement of 18 % and a power-saving gain of 20 %. As future work we plan to use messages latencies as congestion metric and implement support in-order delivery support.

Acknowledgements. This work was supported by the Spanish Ministerio de Economía y Competitividad (MINECO) and by FEDER funds under Grant TIN2012-38341-C04-01 and by Ayudas para Primeros Proyectos de Investigación from Universitat Politècnica de València under grant ref. 2370.

References

1. Benini, L., De Micheli, G.: Networks on chips: a new SoC paradigm. Computer **35**(1), 70–78 (2002)
2. Chang, X., Ebrahimi, M., Daneshtalab, M., Westerlund, T., Plosila, J.: Pars an efficient congestion-aware routing method for networks-on-chip. In: 2012 16th CSI International Symposium on Computer Architecture and Digital Systems (CADS), pp. 166–171 (2012)
3. Chelcea, T., Nowick, S.: A low-latency FIFO for mixed-clock systems. In: IEEE Computer Society Workshop on VLSI, 2000. Proceedings, pp. 119–126 (2000)
4. Escamilla, J., Flich, J., Garcia, P.: ICARO: Congestion isolation in networks-on-chip. In: 8th International Symposium on Networks-on-Chip, 2014, NoCS 2014, pp. 159–166 September 2014
5. Gratz, P., Grot, B., Keckler, S.W.: Regional congestion awareness for load balance in networks-on-chip. In: HPCA, pp. 203–214. IEEE Computer Society (2008)
6. Kahng, A., Lin, B., Nath, S.: ORION3.0: a comprehensive NoC router estimation tool. IEEE Embed. Syst. Lett. **7**(2), 41–45 (2015)
7. Karol, M., Hluchyj, M., Morgan, S.: Input versus output queueing on a space-division packet switch. IEEE Trans. Commun. **35**(12), 1347–1356 (1987)
8. Kim, W., Brooks, D., Wei, G.Y.: A fully-integrated 3-level dc/dc converter for nanosecond-scale dvs with fast shunt regulation. In: 2011 IEEE International Solid-State Circuits Conference Digest of Technical Papers (ISSCC), pp. 268–270, February 2011
9. Kim, W., Gupta, M., Wei, G.Y., Brooks, D.: System level analysis of fast, per-core DVFS using on-chip switching regulators. In: IEEE 14th International Symposium on High Performance Computer Architecture, 2008, HPCA 2008, pp. 123–134, February 2008
10. Kumar, A., Peh, L.S., Jha, N.: Token flow control. In: 2008 41st IEEE/ACM International Symposium on Microarchitecture, 2008, MICRO-41, pp. 342–353, November 2008

11. Lackey, D., Zuchowski, P., Bednar, T., Stout, D., Gould, S., Cohn, J.: Managing power and performance for system-on-chip designs using voltage islands. In: IEEE/ACM International Conference on Computer Aided Design, 2002, ICCAD 2002, pp. 195–202, November 2002
12. Macken, P., Degrauwe, M., van Paemel, M., Oguey, H.: A voltage reduction technique for digital systems. In: 1990 IEEE International Solid-State Circuits Conference, 1990, 37th ISSCC. Digest of Technical Papers, pp. 238–239, February 1990
13. Marculescu, D., Choudhary, P.: Hardware based frequency/voltage control of voltage frequency island systems. In: Proceedings of the 4th International Conference on Hardware/Software Codesign and System Synthesis, 2006, CODES+ISSS 2006, pp. 34–39, October 2006
14. Ogras, U., Marculescu, R., Marculescu, D., Jung, E.G.: Design and management of voltage-frequency island partitioned networks-on-chip. IEEE Trans. Very Large Scale Integr. Syst. (VLSI) **17**(3), 330–341 (2009)
15. Park, S., Park, J., Shin, D., Wang, Y., Xie, Q., Pedram, M., Chang, N.: Accurate modeling of the delay and energy overhead of dynamic voltage and frequency scaling in modern microprocessors. IEEE Trans. Comput.-Aided Des. Integr. Circ. Syst. **32**(5), 695–708 (2013)
16. Ramakrishna, M., Gratz, P., Sprintson, A.: GCA: Global congestion awareness for load balance in networks-on-chip. In: 2013 Seventh IEEE/ACM International Symposium on Networks on Chip (NoCS), pp. 1–8, April 2013
17. Shang, L., Peh, L.S., Jha, N.: Dynamic voltage scaling with links for power optimization of interconnection networks. In: The Ninth International Symposium on High-Performance Computer Architecture, 2003, HPCA-9 2003, Proceedings, pp. 91–102, February 2003
18. Vangal, S., Howard, J., Ruhl, G., Dighe, S., Wilson, H., Tschanz, J., Finan, D., Singh, A., Jacob, T., Jain, S., Erraguntla, V., Roberts, C., Hoskote, Y., Borkar, N., Borkar, S.: An 80-tile sub-100-w teraFLOPS processor in 65-nm CMOS. IEEE J. Solid-State Circuits **43**(1), 29–41 (2008)
19. Yan, G., Li, Y., Han, Y., Li, X., Guo, M., Liang, X.: Agileregulator: a hybrid voltage regulator scheme redeeming dark silicon for power efficiency in a multicore architecture. In: 2012 IEEE 18th International Symposium on High Performance Computer Architecture (HPCA), pp. 1–12, February 2012

Superoptimizing Memory Subsystems for Multiple Objectives

Joseph G. Wingbermuehle[✉], Ron K. Cytron, and Roger D. Chamberlain

Department of Computer Science and Engineering,
Washington University in St. Louis, St. Louis, USA
{wingbej,cytron,roger}@wustl.edu

Abstract. We consider the automatic determination of application-specific memory subsystems via superoptimization, with the goals of reducing memory access time and of minimizing writes. The latter goal is of concern for memories with limited write endurance. Our subsystems out-perform general-purpose memory subsystems in terms of performance, number of writes, or both.

1 Introduction

Due to the large disparity in performance between main memory and processor cores, large cache hierarchies are a necessary feature of modern computer systems. By exploiting locality in memory references, these cache hierarchies attempt to reduce the amount of time an application spends waiting on memory accesses. Although cache hierarchies are most common, one can extend this notion to a generalized on-chip memory subsystem, which is interposed between the computation elements and off-chip main memory.

For general-purpose computers, memory subsystems are designed to have good average-case performance across a large range of applications. However, due to the general-purpose nature of these memory subsystems, they may not be optimal for a particular application. Because of the potential performance benefit with a custom memory subsystem, we propose the use of memory subsystems tailored to a particular application. Such custom memory subsystems have been used for years for applications deployed on ASICs and FPGAs [18]. Further, it is conceivable that general-purpose computer systems may one day be equipped with a more configurable memory subsystem if the configurability provides enough of a performance advantage.

Although DRAM is the most popular choice for main memory in modern computer systems today, there are several disadvantages to DRAM technology (e.g., volatility and scaling), leading researchers to seek other technologies. Because DRAM is volatile, it can be power-hungry since it requires power just to retain information. This is particularly apparent when used in a setting with infrequent main memory accesses. However, when used in a setting with frequent memory accesses, the refresh requirement for a large DRAM can greatly reduce application performance [19]. There are significant challenges to scaling down

S. Hunold et al. (Eds.): Euro-Par 2015 Workshops, LNCS 9523, pp. 352–363, 2015.
DOI: 10.1007/978-3-319-27308-2_29

DRAM cells [13] since bits are stored as charge on a capacitor, which limits energy efficiency and performance.

Several alternative main memory technologies have been proposed, including PCM [12] and STT-RAM [11]. Although there are many possible main memory technologies that could be considered, a common theme for many proposed technologies is an aversion to writes. For PCM, there is a limited write endurance, making it beneficial to avoid writes to extend the lifetime of the device. Further, on PCM devices writes are slow and energy-hungry. For STT-RAM, although writes do not limit the lifetime of the device, writes are much slower than reads and consume more energy.

Because writes are often costly with respect to energy, performance, and endurance, here we seek to determine if it is possible to modify the memory subsystem to reduce the number of writes to main memory. We are particularly interested in the possibility of reducing the number of writes beyond what a memory subsystem optimized for performance would provide.

We are pursuing this investigation using superoptimization techniques which originated in the compiler literature. The concept of superoptimization was introduced with the goal of finding the smallest instruction sequence to implement a function [14]. This differs from traditional program optimization in that superoptimization attempts to find the best sequence at the expense of a potentially long search process rather than simply improving code. In a similar vein, we are interested in finding the best memory subsystem at the expense of a potentially long search process rather than a generic memory subsystem.

Previously, we have used superoptimization techniques to improve the execution times of applications [21, 22]. In this paper, we expand the scope to include minimization of memory writes. We will show how the superoptimization technique is beneficial in terms of write minimization, and we will also show how one can use superoptimization in a multi-objective context.

To evaluate our superoptimized memory designs, we target an ASIC with an external LPDDR main memory. The ASIC assumes a 45 nm process, clocked at 1 GHz, with 1 mm^2 available for the deployment of our custom memory subsystems. The external LPDDR is a 512 Mib device clocked at 400 MHz. All on-chip memory subsystems share access to the external LPDDR memory device.

2   Related Work

Superoptimization was originally introduced in [14]. In that work, exhaustive search was used to find the smallest sequence of instructions to implement a function. This is in contrast with traditional code optimization where pre-defined transformations are used in an attempt to improve performance. Note that traditional code optimization is not truly optimization in the classical sense, but instead simply code improvement. Superoptimization, on the other hand, does produce an optimal result when applied in this manner.

Since its introduction, superoptimization has been successfully used in compilers such as GCC, peephole optimizers [1], and binary translators [2].

General design space exploration has been applied to many fields, such as system-on-chip (SoC) communication architectures and integrated circuit design. Although a single objective, such as performance or energy, is often used, design space exploration for multiple objectives is also common [17]. Of particular interest to us is design space exploration applied to memory subsystems. Design space exploration has been used extensively to find optimal cache parameters [6,7]. This line of work has been extended to consider a cache and scratchpad together [3]. However, the ability to change completely the memory subsystem for a specific application and main memory subsystem distinguishes this work from previous work.

Many non-traditional memory subsystems have been proposed. These structures are often intended to be general-purpose in nature, but to take advantage of some aspect of application behavior that is common across many applications. However, there are also many non-traditional memory subsystems designed for particular applications, usually with much effort. Such designs are a common practice for applications deployed on FPGAs and ASICs [4].

Although performance is perhaps the most common objective, non-traditional memory subsystems optimized for other objectives have also been considered. For example, the filter cache [10] was introduced to reduce energy consumption with a modest performance penalty.

The combination of multiple memory subsystem components has also been considered to various degrees. For example, the combination of a scratchpad and cache has been considered [18]. Further, the combination of multiple caching techniques including split caches has been considered [15].

3   Method

The superoptimization of a memory subsystem involves several items. First we require a memory address trace from the application. This trace allows us to simulate the performance of the application with different memory subsystems. Next, we perform the superoptimization, which involves generating proposal memory subsystems and simulating them to determine their performance.

In order to evaluate the performance of a particular memory subsystem for an application, we use address traces. To gather the address traces, we use a modified version of the Valgrind [16] *lackey* tool. This allows us to obtain concise address traces for applications that contain only data accesses (reads, writes, and modifies). We ignore instruction accesses. All of the address traces contain virtual (instead of physical) addresses and are gathered for 32-bit versions of the benchmark applications.

To evaluate the performance of the memory subsystems proposed by the superoptimizer, we use a custom memory simulator. We use a custom simulator for three reasons. First, we need to simulate complex memory subsystems beyond simple caches. Second, rather than the number of cache misses, we are interested in total memory access time. Finally, the simulator must be fast enough to simulate large traces many thousands of repetitions in a reasonable amount of time.

Table 1. Memory subsystem components

Component	Description	Parameters ($n \in \mathbb{Z}_+$)
Cache	Parameterizable cache	Line size (2^n)
		Line count (2^n)
		Associativity ($1 \ldots line\_count$)
		Replacement policy
		Write policy
FIFO	Stream buffer	Depth (2^n)
Offset	Address offset	Value ($\pm n$)
Prefetch	Stride prefetcher	Stride ($\pm n$)
Rotate	Rotate address transform	Value ($\pm n$)
Scratchpad	Scratchpad memory	Size (2^n)
Split	Split memory	Location (n)
XOR	XOR address transform	Value (n)

The memory subsystem superoptimizer is capable of simulating the memory subsystem components shown in Table 1. The CACTI tool [20] is used to determine latencies for ASIC targets.

For caches, the simulator supports four replacement policies: least-recently used (LRU), most-recently used (MRU), first-in first-out (FIFO), and pseudo-least-recently used (PLRU). The PLRU policy approximates the LRU policy by using a single *age* bit per cache way rather than $\lg n$ age bits, where n is the associativity of the cache.

The offset, rotate, and xor components in Table 1 are address transformations. The offset component adds the specified value to the address. The rotate component rotates the bits of the address that select the word left by the specified amount (the bits that select the byte within the word remain unchanged). Note that for a 32-bit address with a 4-byte word, $32 - \lg 4 = 30$ bits are used to select the word. Finally, the xor component inverts the selected bits of the address.

Other supported components include prefetch and split. The prefetch component performs an additional memory access after every memory read to do the prefetch. This additional access reads the word with the specified distance from the original word that was accessed. Finally, the split component divides memory accesses between two memory subsystems based on address: accesses with addresses above a threshold go to a separate memory subsystem from addresses below the threshold. Accesses that are not resolved within the split are sent to the next memory subsystem or main memory.

The communication between each of the memory components as well as the communication between the application and main memory is performed using 4-byte words. The bytes within the word are selected using a 4-bit mask to allow byte-addressing. The address bus is 30 bits, providing a 32-bit address space.

Table 2. Main memory parameters.

Parameter	Description	Value
Frequency	DRAM I/O frequency	400 MHz
CAS	Cycles to select a column	5
RCD	Cycles from open to access	5
RP	Cycles required for precharge	5
Page size	Size of a page in bytes	1024
Page count	Number of pages per bank	65536
Width	Channel width in bytes	8
Burst size	Number of columns per access	4
Page mode	Open or closed page mode	open
DDR	Double data rate	true

For the results presented here, the main memory is assumed to be a DRAM device. We use a DDR3-800D memory, whose properties are shown in Table 2.

To guide the optimization process, we use a variant of *threshold acceptance* [5] called *old bachelor acceptance* [9]. Old bachelor acceptance is a Markov-chain Monte-Carlo (MCMC) stochastic hill-climbing technique. Old bachelor acceptance provides a compromise between search space exploration and hill climbing.

Using stochastic hill-climbing, one typically selects an initial state, $s_t = s_0$, and then generates a *proposal* state, s^*, in the neighborhood of the current state. The state is then either accepted, becoming s_{t+1}, or rejected. With threshold acceptance, the difference in cost between the current state, s_t, and the proposal state, s^*, is compared to a threshold, T_t, to determine if the proposal state should be accepted. Thus, we get the following expression for determining the next state:

$$s_{t+1} = \begin{cases} s^* & \text{if } c(s^*) < c(s_t) + T_t \\ s_t & \text{otherwise} \end{cases}$$

For our purposes, the state is a candidate memory subsystem and the cost function, $c(\cdot)$, is described below to reflect the multiple objectives used in the optimization process.

With threshold acceptance, the threshold is initialized to some relatively high value, $T_t = T_0$. The threshold is then lowered according a cooling schedule. The recommended schedule in [5] is $T_{t+1} = T_t - \Delta T_t$ where $\Delta \in (0, 1)$. Old bachelor acceptance generalizes this, allowing the threshold to be lowered when a state is accepted and raised when a state is not accepted. This allows the algorithm to escape areas of local optimality more easily. For our experiments, we used the following schedule:

$$T_{t+1} = \begin{cases} T_t - \Delta T_t & \text{if } c(s^*) < c(s_t) + T_t \\ T_t + \Delta T_t & \text{otherwise} \end{cases}$$

To reduce the time required for superoptimization, we employ two techniques to speed up the process. First, we memoize the results of each state evaluation so that when revisiting a state we do not need to simulate the memory trace again. The second improvement is that we allow multiple superoptimization processes to run simultaneously sharing results using a database, thereby allowing us to exploit multiple processor cores.

Our memory subsystem optimizer is capable of proposing candidate memory subsystems comprised of the structures shown in Table 1. These components can be combined in arbitrary ways leading to a huge search space limited only by the constraints. For the ASIC target, the constraint is the area as reported from the CACTI tool [20].

Given a state, s_t, we compute a proposal state s^* by performing one of the following actions:

1. Insert a new memory component to a random position,
2. Remove a memory component from a random position, or
3. Change a parameter of the memory component at a random position.

We showed, in [21], that the above neighborhood generation technique is ergodic. To ensure that any discovered memory subsystem is valid, we reject any memory subsystem that exceeds the constraints. However, there are other ways a memory subsystem may be invalid. First, because we support splitting between memory components by address, any address transformation occurring in a split must be inverted before leaving the split. To handle this, we always insert (or remove) both the transform and its inverse when inserting (or removing) an address transformation.

4 Benchmarks

We use a collection of four benchmarks from the MiBench benchmark suite [8] as well as two synthetic kernels for evaluation purposes. The MiBench suite contains benchmarks for the embedded space that target a variety of application areas. For some benchmarks, the MiBench suite contains large and small versions. We chose the large version in the interest of obtaining larger memory traces.

The locally developed synthetic kernels include a kernel that inserts and then removes items from a binary heap (heap) and a kernel that sorts an array of integers using the quicksort algorithm (qsort). Rather than implement an application to perform these operations and use Valgrind to capture the address trace, the addresses traces are generated directly during a simulation run, which allows us to avoid processing large trace files for the kernels.

Because we are superoptimizing the memory subsystem, the amount of memory accessed by each benchmark is important. If a particular benchmark accesses less memory than is available to the on-chip memory subsystem, then it should be possible to have all memory accesses occur in on-chip memory, though such a design may require clever address transformations.

For the 45 nm ASIC process with an area constraint of 1 mm^2, we can store a total of 379,392 bytes in a scratchpad according to our CACTI model. This means that both the `bitcount` and `dijkstra` benchmarks are small enough to be mapped into a scratchpad, but all of the remaining benchmarks access too much memory for their footprint to fit on chip.

5 Results

5.1 Minimizing Writes

Our previous work focused on reducing total memory access time [21]. However, the superoptimization technique is generic and, therefore, can be used to optimize for other objectives. Here we investigate minimizing the number of writes. The cost function used to guide the superoptimization process is the total writes to main memory for the complete execution of the benchmark application. Thus, we are not optimizing for performance, but exclusively for a reduction in writes to main memory.

To determine if the memory subsystem superoptimized for writes is actually any better at reducing writes than a memory subsystem superoptimized for total access time, we compare each of the memory subsystems. The first column of Fig. 1(a) shows the improvement that the memory subsystems superoptimized for writes have over the memory subsystems superoptimized for total access time (that is, W_t/W_w where W_w is the total number of writes to main memory when using the memory subsystem superoptimized for writes and W_t is the total number of writes to main memory when using the memory subsystem superoptimized for access time). The second column shows the improvement that the memory subsystems superoptimized for total access time have over the memory subsystems superoptimized for writes (that is, T_w/T_t, where T_t is the total access time when using the memory subsystem superoptimized for access time and T_w is the total access time when using the memory subsystem superoptimized for writes). Thus, bars above one indicate an advantage of one superoptimized memory subsystem over another.

Here we expect all bars to be at least one, indicating that the memory subsystem superoptimized for a particular objective is at least as good for that objective as a memory subsystem superoptimized for the other objective. Indeed, all bars in Fig. 1(a) are one or greater. In some cases, there is little or no difference between the superoptimized memory subsystems. For example, for the `bitcount` benchmark, both memory subsystems reduce the number of writes to zero and the memory subsystem superoptimized for total access time provides only a slight improvement in total access time over the memory subsystem superoptimized for writes. However, in most cases, a different memory subsystem is able to provide the best results for either objective.

The memory subsystem superoptimized for writes for the `bitcount` benchmark is shown in Fig. 2(a) and the memory subsystem superoptimized for total access time for the `bitcount` benchmark is shown in Fig. 2(b). For this benchmark, the memory subsystem superoptimized for total access time provides only

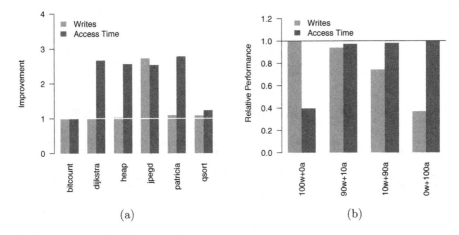

(a)   (b)

Fig. 1. (a) Write and access time improvement, relative to one another; (b) Multi-objective superoptimization (in Sect. 5.2).

a small advantage over the simpler memory subsystem that was discovered to reduce writes to main memory.

The next memory subsystems we consider are those superoptimized for the **heap** kernel. The memory subsystem superoptimized to minimize writes is shown in Fig. 2(c) and the memory subsystem superoptimized to minimize total access time is shown in Fig. 2(d). Interestingly, these memory subsystems are very similar with the only difference being the address transformation. Despite the similar appearance, the cach of the memory subsystems is able to provide a benefit over the other.

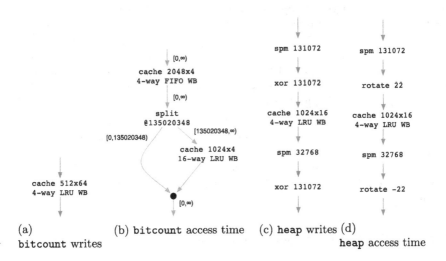

(a)   (b) **bitcount** access time   (c) **heap** writes (d)
bitcount writes   **heap** access time

Fig. 2. Superoptimized memory subsystems for **bitcount** and **heap**.

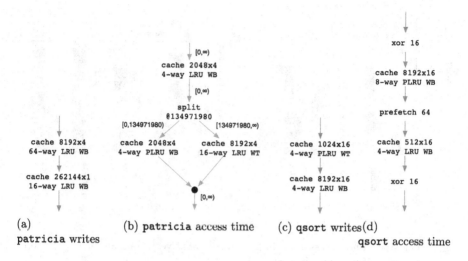

Fig. 3. Superoptimized memory subsystems for patricia and qsort.

The memory subsystem superoptimized for writes for the patricia benchmark is shown in Fig. 3(a) and the subsystem superoptimized for total access time is shown in Fig. 3(b). An interesting observation is the large and highly-associative caches that are used when minimizing writes is the objective. These caches are effective at eliminating writes, but they are quite slow.

Finally, we consider the memory subsystems for the qsort benchmark. Figure 3(c) shows the memory subsystem superoptimized for writes and Fig. 3(d) shows the memory subsystem superoptimized for total access time. One notable difference between these subsystems is the presence of the prefetch component in the memory subsystem superoptimized for total access time.

Overall, memory subsystems superoptimized to minimize total access time appear to be capable of large reductions in total access time over memory subsystems superoptimized to minimize writes. On the other hand, while a memory subsystem superoptimized for writes is often able to reduce the number of writes compared to a memory subsystem superoptimized for total access time, the improvement is usually less pronounced.

Another observation is that the memory subsystems superoptimized for writes are usually simpler than those superoptimized for total access time. Although a large cache will typically eliminate writes, the large cache will likely be slow. This implies that a large cache may be sufficient if we only care about writes, but something more exotic will likely provide better results if we want to minimize total access time.

5.2   Multi-objective Superoptimization

Here we investigate multi-objective superoptimization. From the previous section, we note that the memory subsystems that are superoptimized to minimize total access time are fairly good at reducing the number of writes to main memory, however, the memory subsystems superoptimized to minimize writes usually do better. On the other hand, the memory subsystems that are superoptimized to minimize writes often perform poorly with respect to total access time. Thus, one might wonder if it is possible to optimize for both objectives.

We use the weighted sum method to combine the objective functions to minimize writes and total access time. Figure 1(b) shows the improvement possible for various objectives for the jpegd benchmark with objective weights ranging from 100 %-writes, 0 %-access time through 0 %-writes, 100 %-access time. The graph shows uses the performance relative to the best result for writes and total access time. For the bars on the left, the graph shows W_w/W_m, where W_m is the number of writes to the main memory when using the memory subsystem superoptimized for multiple objectives and W_w is the number of writes to the main memory when using the memory subsystem superoptimized to minimize writes. For the bars on the right, the graph shows T_t/T_m, where T_m is the total access time when using the memory subsystem superoptimized for multiple objectives and T_t is the total access time when using the memory subsystem superoptimized to minimize total access time. Thus, higher values (closer to 1) indicate better results.

As can be seen in the graph, the largest differences in how good the memory subsystems perform for each objective occur when only a single objective is considered. When multiple objectives are considered, although there is some

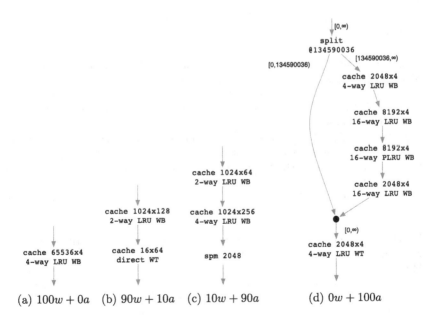

Fig. 4. Memory subsystems for jpegd.

difference in how good the memory subsystems are, the result is very close to the best for all mixtures.

Figure 4 shows the memory subsystems for each mixture. When minimizing writes is most important, we see that a simple cache suffices. However, when minimizing total access time is also important, the large cache is separated into two caches, which makes sense since smaller caches are faster. Finally, when writes are no longer considered, a very complex memory subsystem is discovered, which does little to minimize writes, but provides the lowest total access time of all the memory subsystems considered.

6   Conclusions

We have shown that it is possible to superoptimize memory subsystems for specific applications that out-perform a general-purpose memory subsystem in terms of performance, writes, or a mixture. Unlike previous work, the memory subsystems that our superoptimizer discovers can be arbitrarily complex and contain components other than simple caches. To superoptimize a memory subsystem, we use old bachelor acceptance, which is a form of threshold acceptance.

While many benchmarks do not see a substantial improvement in write optimization (relative to access time optimization), for the jpegd benchmark individually optimizing for either goal provides substantial gains when measured against that goal. In addition, it is possible to co-optimize for both objectives and realize a memory system that performs quite well for each measure.

References

1. Bansal, S., Aiken, A.: Automatic generation of peephole superoptimizers. In: ACM SIGPLAN Notices, vol. 41, pp. 394–403. ACM (2006)
2. Bansal, S., Aiken, A.: Binary translation using peephole superoptimizers. In: Proceedings of 8th USENIX Symposium on Operating Systems Design and Implementation (OSDI), vol. 8, pp. 177–192, December 2008
3. Chen, Y.T., Cong, J., Reinman, G.: HC-Sim: a fast and exact L1 cache simulator with scratchpad memory co-simulation support. In: Proceedings of 9th International Conference on Hardware/Software Codesign and System Synthesis, pp. 295–304. IEEE (2011)
4. Choi, Y.k., Cong, J., Wu, D.: FPGA implementation of EM algorithm for 3D CT reconstruction. In: Proceedings of 22nd Symposium on Field-Programmable Custom Computing Machines (FCCM), pp. 157–160. IEEE (2014)
5. Dueck, G., Scheuer, T.: Threshold accepting: a general purpose optimization algorithm appearing superior to simulated annealing. J. Comput. Phys. 90(1), 161–175 (1990)
6. Ghosh, A., Givargis, T.: Cache optimization for embedded processor cores: an analytical approach. ACM Trans. Des. Autom. Electron. Syst. 9(4), 419–440 (2004)
7. Gordon-Ross, A., Vahid, F., Dutt, N.: Automatic tuning of two-level caches to embedded applications. In: Proceedings of the Conference on Design, Automation and Test in Europe, p. 10208 (2004)

8. Guthaus, M.R., Ringenberg, J.S., Ernst, D., Austin, T.M., Mudge, T., Brown, R.B.: MiBench: A free, commercially representative embedded benchmark suite. In: Proceedings of 4th International Workshop on Workload Characterization, pp. 3–14 (2001)
9. Hu, T.C., Kahng, A.B., Tsao, C.W.A.: Old bachelor acceptance: a new class of non-monotone threshold accepting methods. ORSA J. Comput. **7**(4), 417–425 (1995)
10. Kin, J., Gupta, M., Mangione-Smith, W.H.: The filter cache: an energy efficient memory structure. In: Proceedings of 30th ACM/IEEE International Symposium on Microarchitecture, pp. 184–193. IEEE (1997)
11. Kultursay, E., Kandemir, M., Sivasubramaniam, A., Mutlu, O.: Evaluating STT-RAM as an energy-efficient main memory alternative. In: Proceedings of IEEE International Symposium on Performance Analysis of Systems and Software, pp. 256–267. IEEE (2013)
12. Lee, B.C., Ipek, E., Mutlu, O., Burger, D.: Architecting phase change memory as a scalable DRAM alternative. ACM SIGARCH Comput. Archit. News **37**(3), 2–13 (2009)
13. Mandelman, J.A., Dennard, R.H., Bronner, G.B., DeBrosse, J.K., Divakaruni, R., Li, Y., Radens, C.J.: Challenges and future directions for the scaling of dynamic random-access memory (DRAM). IBM J. Res. Dev. **46**(2.3), 187–212 (2002)
14. Massalin, H.: Superoptimizer: a look at the smallest program. In: Proceedings of 2nd International Conference on Architectural Support for Programming Languages and Operating Systems (ASPLOS), pp. 122–126 (1987)
15. Naz, A.: Split array and scalar data caches: a comprehensive study of data cache organization. Ph.D. thesis, Univ. of North Texas (2007)
16. Nethercote, N., Seward, J.: Valgrind: a framework for heavyweight dynamic binary instrumentation. In: Proceedings of ACM SIGPLAN Conference on Programming Language Design and Implementation, pp. 89–100 (2007)
17. Palermo, G., Silvano, C., Zaccaria, V.: Discrete particle swarm optimization for multi-objective design space exploration. In: Proceedings of 11th Conference on Digital System Design Architectures, Methods and Tools, pp. 641–644. IEEE (2008)
18. Panda, R.P., Dutt, N.D., Nicolau, A., Catthoor, F., Vandecappelle, A., Brockmeyer, E., Kulkarni, C., De Greef, E.: Data memory organization and optimizations in application-specific systems. IEEE Des. Test Comput. **18**(3), 56–68 (2001)
19. Stuecheli, J., Kaseridis, D., Hunter, H.C., John, L.K.: Elastic refresh: Techniques to mitigate refresh penalties in high density memory. In: Proceedings of 43rd IEEE/ACM International Symposium on Microarchitecture, pp. 375–384 (2010)
20. Thoziyoor, S., Muralimanohar, N., Ahn, J.H., Jouppi, N.P.: CACTI 5.1. HP Laboratories 2, April 2008
21. Wingbermuehle, J.G., Cytron, R.K., Chamberlain, R.D.: Superoptimization of memory subsystems. In: Proceedings of 15th Conference on Languages, Compilers, and Tools for Embedded Systems (LCTES), pp. 145–154, June 2014
22. Wingbermuehle, J.G., Cytron, R.K., Chamberlain, R.D.: Superoptimized memory subsystems for streaming applications. In: Proceedings of 23rd ACM/SIGDA International Symposium on Field-Programmable Gate Arrays (FPGA), pp. 126–135, February 2015

PADABS - Parallel and Distributed Agent-Based Simulations

On Evaluating Graph Partitioning Algorithms for Distributed Agent Based Models on Networks

Alessia Antelmi[1], Gennaro Cordasco[2], Carmine Spagnuolo[1]([✉]),
and Luca Vicidomini[1]

[1] Dipartimento di Informatica, Università degli Studi di Salerno, Fisciano, Italy
a.antelmi@studenti.unisa.it, {cspagnuolo,lvicidomini}@unisa.it
[2] Dipartimento di Psicologia, Seconda Università degli Studi di Napoli, Caserta, Italy
gennaro.cordasco@unina2.it

Abstract. Graph Partitioning is a key challenge problem with application in many scientific and technological fields. The problem is very well studied with a rich literature and is known to be NP-hard. Several heuristic solutions, which follow diverse approaches, have been proposed, they are based on different initial assumptions that make them difficult to compare. An analytical comparison was performed based on an Implementation Challenge [3], however being a multi-objective problem (two opposing goals are for instance load balancing and edge-cut size), the results are difficult to compare and it is hard to foresee what can be the impact of one solution, instead of another, in a real scenario. In this paper we analyze the problem in a real context: the development of a distributed agent-based simulation model on a network field (which for instance can model social interactions).

We present an extensive evaluation of the most efficient and effective solutions for the balanced k-way partitioning problem. We evaluate several strategies both analytically and on real distributed simulation settings (D-MASON). Results show that, a good partitioning strategy strongly influences the performances of the distributed simulation environment. Moreover, we show that there is a strong correlation between the edge-cut size and the real performances. Analyzing the results in details we were also able to discover the parameters that need to be optimized for best performances on networks in ABMs.

Keywords: Agent-Based Simulation Models · Graph partitioning · D-MASON · Parallel computing · Distributed systems · High performance computing

1 Introduction

Networks are everywhere. Complex interactions between different entities play a sensible role in modeling the behavior of both society and natural world. Such

© Springer International Publishing Switzerland 2015
S. Hunold et al. (Eds.): Euro-Par 2015 Workshops, LNCS 9523, pp. 367–378, 2015.
DOI: 10.1007/978-3-319-27308-2_30

networks – which comprises World Wide Web, metabolic networks, neural networks, communication and collaboration networks, and social networks – are the subject of a growing number of research efforts. Indeed, many interesting phenomena are structured as networks (i.e., sets of entities joined in pairs by lines representing relations or interactions).

The study of networked phenomena has experienced a particular surge of interest due to the increasing availability of massive data about the static topology of real networks as well as the dynamic behavior generated by the interactions among network entities. The analysis of real networks topologies has revealed several interesting structural features, like the small-world phenomena as well as the power-law degree distribution [10], which appear in several real network and can be extremely helpful for the design of artificial networks. On the other hand, understanding the dynamic behavior generated by complex network systems is extremely hard. Networks are often characterized by a dynamic feedback effect which is hard to predict analytically.

More generally, complex systems require innovative study methodologies. In this regard, in recent years, the two branches of the classical sciences, theoretical and experimental, have merged in the computational sciences where scientists design mathematical models and perform computational simulations of complex phenomena on real systems which are too complex to be studied analytically on theoretical grounds as well as too risky/expensive to be tested experimentally [23]. In particular, Agent-Based simulation Models (ABMs) have spread in many fields, from social sciences to the life sciences, from economics to artificial intelligence. Successes of the computational sciences have led to an increased demand for computation-intensive software implementations, in order to improve the performance of ABMs in terms of both size (number of agents) and quality (complexity of interactions). Such an amount of computing power can only be achieved by parallel computing (indeed, serial-processing speed is reaching a physical limit [22]). However, exploiting parallel systems is not an easy task; many parallel applications fail to leverage on the hardware parallelism and experience scalability limits.

The computer science community has responded to the need for tools and platforms that can help the development and testing of new models in each specific field by providing tools, libraries and frameworks that speed up and make easier the task of developing and running parallel ABMs for complex phenomena. For instance, D-MASON [5,6,26,28] is a parallel version of the MASON [4,16,17] library for running ABMs on distributed systems. D-MASON adopts a framework-level parallelization mechanism approach, which allows the harnessing of computational power of a parallel environment and, at the same time, hides the details of the architecture so that users, even with limited knowledge of parallel computer programming, can easily develop and run simulation models.

MASON like several other ABMs systems provides one or more fields to represent the space where the agents lie and interact with the other agents. A field is a specific data structure relating various objects (agents) or values together. With more details, MASON provides a number of built-in fields, such as 2D/3D geometric discrete and continuous spaces plus a network field typically used to model social interactions. Currently, D-MASON allows modellers to parallelize simulation based on geometric fields. It adopts a space partitioning approach [9] which allowed the balancing of workload among the resources involved for the computation with a limited amount of communication overhead.

The space partitioning approach described above is devoted to decomposing ABMs based on geometric fields. On the other hand, when agents lie and/or interact on a network [1] – where the network can represent social, geographical or even a semantic space – a different approach is needed. The problem is to (dynamically) partition the network into a fixed set of sub-networks in such a way that: (i) the components have roughly the same size and (ii) both the number of connections and the communication volume between vertices belonging to different components are minimized.

1.1 Our Results

In this paper we provide an extensive evaluation of the most efficient and effective solutions for the problem defined above, which is well known in literature as the graph partitioning problem. We will evaluate several algorithms both analytically and on a real distributed simulation settings. Results shows that a good partitioning strategy strongly influences the performances of the distributed simulation environment. Analyzing the results in detail we were also able to discover the parameters that need to be optimized for the best performances on networks in ABMs.

2   The Graph Partitioning Problem

Finding good network partitions is a well-studied problem in graph theory [2]. Several are the problems that motivate the study of this problem. They range from computer science problems like integrated circuit design, VLSI circuits, domain decomposition for parallel computing, image segmentation, data mining [13,15], etc. to other problems raised by physicists, biologists, and applied mathematicians, with applications to social and biological networks (community structure detection, structuring cellular networks and matrix decomposition [12,18]).

The most common formulation of the balanced graph partitioning problem is the following:

BALANCED k-WAY PARTITIONING (G, k, ϵ).

Instance: A graph $G = (V, E)$, an integer $k > 1$ (number of components) and a rational ϵ (imbalance factor).

Problem: Compute a partition Π of V into k pairwise disjoint subsets (components) $V_1, V_2, \ldots, V_k$ of size at most $(1 + \epsilon) \lceil |V|/k \rceil$, while minimizing the size of the edge-cut $\sum_{i<j} |E_{ij}|$, where $E_{ij} = \{\{u, v\} \in E : u \in V_i, v \in V_j\} \subseteq E$.

This problem has been extensively studied (see [3] for a comprehensive presentation) and is known to be NP-hard [11].

Being a hard problem, exact solutions are found in reasonable time only for small graphs. However the applications of this problem require to partition much larger graphs and so several heuristic solutions have been proposed.

The graph partitioning problem was faced using several approaches. Two version of this problem have been considered: the former takes into account the coordinate information in the space of the vertices (this is common in graphs describing a physical domain) while, in the latter problem, vertices are coordinate free. In this paper we discuss the coordinate free problem which better fits ABMs' domain.

The graph partitioning coordinate free problem requires combinatorial heuristics to partition them. For instance, considering the simplest version of the partitioning problem (2-way partitioning), that is find a bisection of the graph $G = (V, E)$ that minimize the size of the cut. A really simple solution of the problem uses the breadth first search (BFS) visit of the graph to generate a subgraph $T = (V, E' \subseteq E)$ of G also called a BFS tree. Given the subgraph T, is possible to find a cut to generate two disjoint subnetwork N_1 and N_2 such that (i) $N_1 \cup N_2 = V$ and (ii) $|N_1| \approx |N_2|$. The fact that T has been built using the BFS ensures that the size of the edge-cut is bounded.

This solution, which works well for planar graphs, is not efficient for complex graph. An additional approach is the Kernighan-Lin (KL) algorithm [15] that, starting with two sets N_1 and N_2 (describing a partition of V), greedily improves the quality of the partitioning by iteratively swapping vertices among the two sets. This solution converges to the global optimum if the initial partition is fairly good. Other approaches are the Spectral partitioning [21] and the Multilevel Approach [14]. We will focus on the most promising techniques that either use a multilevel approach or a distributed algorithm that exploits a local search approach.

METIS is a graph multilevel k-way partitioning suite developed in the Karypis lab of University of Minnesota. Shortly, METIS comprises three phases: during the coarsening phase the vertices are collapsed in order to decrease the size of the initial graph G. Consequently, starting from $G = G_0$ a sequence of graphs $G_0, G_1, \ldots, G_\ell$ is generated. Then a k-way partitioning is performed on the smallest graph G_ℓ. Then, during the uncoarsening phase the partitioning is refined, using a variant of the KL algorithm, and is projected to larger graphs on the sequence.

KaHIP (Karlsruhe High Quality Partitioning) is a suite of graph partitioning algorithms. The suite comprises two main algorithms *KaFFPa* (Karlsruhe Fast Flow Partitioner) [20], which is a multilevel graph partitioning algorithm, and *KaFFPaE* (KaFFPa Evolutionary) that uses an evolutionary algorithm approach. In this paper we analyze KaFFPa. KaFFPa, like METIS, uses the multilevel graph partitioning approach but it uses a different strategy for the uncoarsening phase of the algorithm which exploits a local search method instead of the KL approach.

Ja-be-Ja [19] exploits a distributed computing approach. It uses a local search technique (simulated annealing), to find a good partitions of the graph minimizing the edge-cut size. The energy of the system is measured by counting the number of edges that have endpoints in different components. Ja-be-Ja starts with a random balanced partitioning and then it iteratively applies the local search heuristic to obtain a configuration having a lower energy state (edge-cut size). The size of the initial components is preserved since Ja-be-Ja allows only the swapping of vertices among two components.

3 Experiment Setting

We report on simulation experiments that compare five k-way partitioning algorithms on several networks, taken from [27]. The data sets we considered include networks having different structural features (see Table 1). For each network, partitions into $k = 2, 4, 8, 16, 32$ and 64 components have been considered.

We compare the analytical results obtained (i.e., size of the edge-cut, number of communication channels required and imbalance) by each algorithm with the real performances (overall simulation time) in an ABM scenario.

Table 1. Networks.

Name	# of nodes	# of edges	Avg deg.	Max deg.	Triangles	Clust. Coeff.	Modul.
uk	4824	6837	2.83	3	1	0	0.7934
data	2851	15093	10.59	17	24442	0.485719	0.7596
4elt	15606	45878	5.88	10	30269	0.40765	0.6274
cti	16840	48232	5.73	6	362	0.004895	0.9063
t60k	60005	89440	2.98	3	0	0	0.5419
wing	62032	121544	3.92	4	6685	0.055595	0.5403
finan512	74752	261120	6.99	54	211456	0.503401	0.6469
fe_ocean	143437	409593	5.71	6	0	0	0.5947
powergrid	4941	6594	2.67	19	651	0.1065	0.6105

Simulation Environment. To evaluate real performances we developed a toy distributed SIR (Susceptible, Infected, and Removed) simulation, where, for each simulation step, each agent (a vertex of the network) has to communicate with its neighbors. The SIR simulation has been developed on top of D-MASON, exploiting the novel communication strategy which realizes a Publish/Subscribe paradigm through a layer based on the MPI standard [7,8]. Simulations have been performed on cluster of eight computer nodes, each equipped as follows:

- Hardware:
    - CPUs: 2 x Intel(R) Xeon(R) CPU E5-2680 @ 2.70GHz (#core 16, #threads 32)
    - RAM: 256 GB
    - Network: adapters Intel Corporation I350 Gigabit
- Software:
    - Ubuntu 12.04.4 LTS (GNU/Linux 3.11.0-15-generic x86_64)

- Java JDK 1.6.25
- OpenMPI 1.7.4 (feature version of Feb 5, 2014).

Simulation results, on k-way partitioning, have been obtained using k logical processors (one logical processor per component). We notice that, when the simulation is distributed, the communication between agents in the same component is much faster than the communication between agents belonging to different components. On the other hand, balancing is important because the simulation is synchronized and evolves with the speed of the slowest component.

The Competing Algorithms. We have analyzed five algorithms, briefly discussed in Sect. 2:

- Multilevel approach:
    - **METIS:** (cf. Sect. 2);
    - **METIS Relaxed:** this version of the METIS algorithm uses a relaxed version of the balancing constraint (i.e., a larger value of the parameter ϵ), in order to improve on other parameters (like the edge-cut size);
    - **KaFFPa:** (cf. Sect. 2);
- Distributed Computing Approach:
    - **Ja-be-Ja:** (cf. Sect. 2). Unfortunately, we were not able to find a real implementation of the algorithm. We used an implementation available on the public Ja-be-Ja GitHub repository [24]. This implementation is not truly distributed but is simulated through the use of the Java library GraphChi [25], that enables modellers to simulate a distributed computation on multi-cores machines. Clearly the computational efficiency of this implementation is limited and, for this reason, we could only run 100 iterations of the algorithm for each test setting. We assume that the poor results of the algorithm (cf. Sect. 4) are, at least, partially due to the small number of iteration used in our tests. In order to better evaluate the real performances of the algorithm, a real distributed implementation of the Ja-be-Ja algorithm is needed.
- **Random:** This algorithm assigns each vertex to a random component. It always provides an optimal balancing. We use this algorithm as baseline in our comparisons.

Performance Metrics. Let $G = (V, E)$ the analyzed network and let $\Pi = (V_1, V_2, \ldots, V_k)$ the partition provided by a given algorithm, we evaluate algorithms' performances using the following metrics:

- Edge-cut size (W), the total number of edges having their incident vertices in different components;
- Number of communication channels (E), two components U_1 and U_2 requires a communication channel when $\exists v_1 \in U_1$, $v_2 \in U_2$ such that $(v_1, v_2) \in E$. In other words, we are counting the number of edges in the supergraph S_G obtained by clustering the nodes of each component in a single node. We notice that this unconventional metric is motivated by our specific distributed ABMs

scenario. In our simulation environment, a communication channel, between two components U_1 and U_2, is established when at least two vertices (agents) $u_1 \in U_1$ and $u_2 \in U_2$ share an edge. Thereafter, the same communication channel is used for every communication between U_1 and U_2, consequently, these additional communications have less impact on system performances;

– Imbalance (I), the minimum value of ϵ such that each component has size at most $(1 + \epsilon)\lceil |V|/k \rceil$.

Moreover, we evaluate the real performances of each strategy by measuring the overall simulation time (T) to perform 10 simulation steps on the distributed SIR simulation.

Summarizing our experiments compares the performances (both analytically and on a real setting) of 5 k-way partitioning algorithms ($A \in \{$METIS, METIS Relaxed, KaFFPa, Ja-be-Ja and Random$\}$) with $k \in \{2, 4, 8, 16, 32, 64\}$ on 9 networks ($N \in \{$uk, data, 4elt, cti, t60k, wing, finan512, fe_ocean, powergrid$\}$). Overall we performed $5 \times 6 \times 9 = 270$ tests.

4   Results

4.1   Analytical Results

Figures 1, 2 and 3 depict the analytical results. For each plot the networks appear along the X-axis, while the values of the measured parameter appear along the Y-axis. We present the results only for $k \in \{4, 64\}$ because of space limitations; results for the other values of k exhibit similar behaviors.

Analyzing the results from Figs. 1 and 2 we notice that the performances of the multilevel approach algorithms are comparable both in terms of edge-cut size and number of communication channels. Ja-be-Ja performances are a bit worse (this is probably due to the small number of iteration used in our tests as observed in Sect. 3) but always better than the random strategy.

Results on imbalance are fluctuating (see Fig. 3). In general all the algorithms provide a quite balanced partition. Apart from the random strategy that by construction provides the optimal solution, no strategy dominates the others.

4.2   Real Setting Results

Figure 4 reports on the results obtained in the real simulation setting. The results are consistent with the analytical ones, in terms of both edge-cut size and number of communication channels, although the gaps are amplified. The results thus confirm that the choice of partitioning strategy has a significant impact on performance in a real scenario.

In order to better understand how the metrics evolves according to k, Figure 5 depicts four plots which describes, for each algorithm, the growth of the Edge-cut size (top-left), the Imbalance (top-right), the number of communication channels (bottom-left) and the Simulation time on the f_ocean network as function of the parameter k (X-axis).

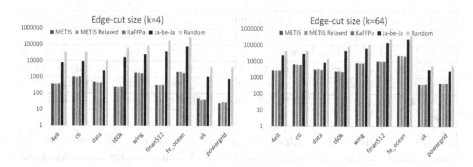

Fig. 1. Edge-cut size (W) comparison:(left) $k = 4$, (right) $k = 64$. Y-axes appear in log scale.

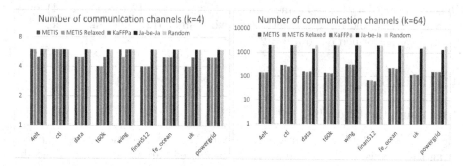

Fig. 2. Number of communication channels (E) comparison:(left) $k = 4$, (right) $k = 64$. Y-axes appear in log scale.

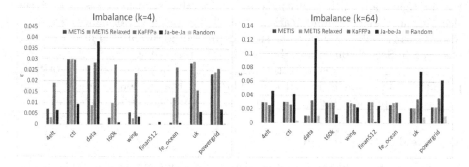

Fig. 3. Imbalance (I) comparison: (left) $k = 4$, (right) $k = 64$.

4.3   Correlation Between Analytical and Real Setting Results

Analyzing the results from Figs. 1–4, we observe that the performances of the distributed simulations are influenced by the analytical metrics. In order to better evaluate the correlation between the overall simulation times and the performances of the algorithm (measured considering the edge-cut size, the number of

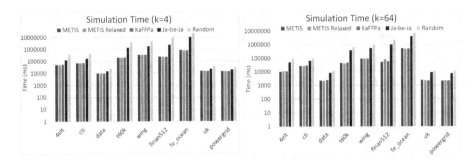

Fig. 4. Simulation time (T) comparison:(left) $k = 4$, (right) $k = 64$. Y-axes appear in log scale.

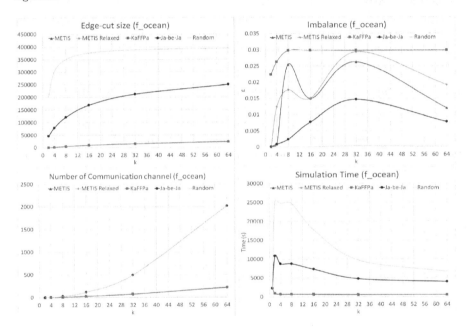

Fig. 5. Edge-cut size (top-left), Imbalance (top-right), Number of communication channels (bottom-left) and Simulation Time(bottom-right) on the f_ocean network, $k \in \{2, 4, 8, 16, 32, 64\}$.

communication channels and the imbalance), we measured the correlation using a statistical metric: the Pearson product-moment Correlation Coefficient (PCC). PCC is one of the measures of correlation which quantifies the strength as well as direction of the relationship between two variables. The correlation coefficient ranges from -1 (strong negative correlation) to 1 (strong positive correlation). A value of 0 implies that there is no correlation between the variables. We computed the correlation PCC between simulation time (T) and the three analytical metrics (W, E and I), with all the considered value of the parameter k.

In particular, we considered four variables that are parametrized by the class N of Networks ($N \in$ {uk, data, 4elt, cti, t60k, wing, finan512, fe_ocean, powergrid}), the considered algorithm ($A \in$ {METIS, METIS Relaxed, KaFFPa, Ja-be-Ja and Random}), and the parameter $k \in \{2, 4, 8, 16, 32, 64\}$. The variable $T(N, A, k)$ denotes the Simulation time; the variable $W(N, A, k)$ denotes Edge-cut size; $E(N, A, k)$ denotes the Number of communication channels; finally the variable $I(N, A, k)$ denotes the Maximum Imbalance. Table 2 presents the correlation values obtained.

We observed that:

- there is a strong positive correlation between simulation time and edge-cut size (the PCC always over 0.92);
- there is a weak/moderate positive correlation between simulation time and the number of communication channels[1] (the PCC ranges between 0.22 and 0.4). Moreover this correlation seems to be increasing in k;
- there is a weak negative correlation between simulation time and imbalance (the PCC ranges between -0.22 and -0.32).

This final result is counterintuitive: theoretically, the greater the imbalance, the larger the simulation time should be and this should lead to a positive correlation. The key observation is that a small amount of imbalance has a limited impact on the simulation time but can be extremely helpful for reducing both the edge-cut size and the number of communication channels, which seems to have a sensible payoff in terms of real performances.

Table 2. Correlation between analytical and real setting results.

	k					
	2	4	8	16	32	64
$r(T, W)$	**0.9256**	**0.9392**	**0.9431**	**0.9424**	**0.9473**	**0.9474**
$r(T, E)$	N.A.	0.2265	0.3094	0.3349	0.3509	0.3922
$r(T, I)$	-0.2244	-0.2750	-0.2903	-0.3188	-0.2971	-0.3025

5   Conclusion

We considered the problem of partitioning a network into k balanced components such that the number of edges that cross the boundaries of components is minimized. We evaluated, both analytically and on a real distributed ABM scenario, the performances of 5 heuristic approaches, which, to the best of our knowledge, are the current state-of-the-art on the problem. Experimental results show that the choice of the partitioning strategy strongly influence the performance a real distributed environment. Moreover analytical results (the edge-cut

---

[1] The correlation between $T(N, A, 2)$ and $E(N, A, 2)$ cannot be computed, since for $k = 2$ all the partitioning strategy require exactly 1 communication channel and so $E(N, A, 2)$ has standard deviation equal to 0.

size in particular) correlate with the overall simulation time in a real setting. On the other hand, according to our results, the quality of the balance among components does not relate to the real performances on the field. Likely, this result is due to the fact that we analyzed of very small imbalance range. As a future work, we plan to investigate heuristics which allow identifying more efficient partitionings, at the expense of a minor balance.

References

1. Alam, S., Geller, A.: Networks in agent-based social simulation. In: Heppenstall, A.J., Crooks, A.T., See, L.M., Batty, M. (eds.) Agent-Based Models of Geographical Systems, pp. 199–216. Springer, Netherlands (2012). http://dx.doi.org/10.1007/978-90-481-8927-4_11

2. Alpert, C.J., Kahng, A.B.: Recent directions in netlist partitioning: a survey. Integr. VLSI J. **19**, 1–81 (1995)

3. Bader, D.A., Meyerhenke, H., Sanders, P., Wagner, D. (eds.): Graph Partitioning and Graph Clustering - 10th DIMACS Implementation Challenge Workshop, Georgia Institute of Technology, Atlanta, GA, USA, February 13–14, 2012. Proceedings, Contemporary Mathematics, vol. 588, American Mathematical Society (2013). http://dx.doi.org/10.1090/conm/588

4. Balan, G.C., Cioffi-Revilla, C., Luke, S., Panait, L., Paus, S.: MASON: a java multi-agent simulation library. In: Proceedings of the Agent 2003 Conference (2003)

5. Cordasco, G., De Chiara, R., Mancuso, A., Mazzeo, D., Scarano, V., Spagnuolo, C.: A Framework for distributing Agent-based simulations. In: 9th International Workshop on Algorithms, Models and Tools for Parallel Computing on Heterogeneous Platforms (2011)

6. Cordasco, G., De Chiara, R., Mancuso, A., Mazzeo, D., Scarano, V., Spagnuolo, C.: Bringing together efficiency and effectiveness in distributed simulations: the experience with D-MASON. SIMULATION Trans. Soc. Model. Simul. Int. **89**(10), 1236–1253 (2013)

7. Cordasco, G., Mancuso, A., Milone, F., Spagnuolo, C.: Communication strategies in distributed agent-based simulations: the experience with D-Mason. In: an Mey, D., Alexander, M., Bientinesi, P., Cannataro, M., Clauss, C., Costan, A., Kecskemeti, G., Morin, C., Ricci, L., Sahuquillo, J., Schulz, M., Scarano, V., Scott, S.L., Weidendorfer, J. (eds.) Euro-Par 2013. LNCS, vol. 8374, pp. 533–543. Springer, Heidelberg (2014)

8. Cordasco, G., Milone, F., Spagnuolo, C., Vicidomini, L.: Exploiting D-Mason on parallel platforms: a novel communication strategy. In: Proceedings of the 2nd Workshop on Parallel and Distributed Agent-Based Simulations (PADABS), Euro-Par 2014 (2014)

9. Cosenza, B., Cordasco, G., De Chiara, R., Scarano, V.: Distributed load balancing for parallel agent-based simulations. In: Proceedings of the 19th International Euromicro Conference on Parallel, Distributed, and Network-Based Processing, (PDP 2011), pp. 62–69 (2011)

10. Easley, D., Kleinberg, J.: Networks, Crowds, and Markets: Reasoning About a Highly Connected World. Cambridge University Press, New York (2010)

11. Garey, M.R., Johnson, D.S.: Computers and Intractability: A Guide to the Theory of NP-Completeness. W.H. Freeman & Co, New York (1990)

12. Gupta, A.: Graph partitioning based sparse matrix orderings for interior-point algorithms. IBM Thomas J, Watson Research Division (1996)
13. Karypis, G., Aggarwal, R., Kumar, V., Shekhar, S.: Multilevel hypergraph partitioning: applications in VLSI domain. IEEE Trans. Very Large Scale Integr. (VLSI) Syst. **7**(1), 69–79 (1999)
14. Karypis, G., Kumar, V.: Multilevel k-way partitioning scheme for irregular graphs. J. Parallel Distrib. Comput. **48**(1), 96–129 (1998)
15. Kernighan, B., Lin, S.: An efficient heuristic procedure for partitioning graphs. Bell Syst. Tech. J. **49**(2), 291–307 (1970)
16. Luke, S., Cioffi-revilla, C., Panait, L., Sullivan, K.: MASON: a new multi-agent simulation toolkit. In: Proceedings of the 2004 SwarmFest Workshop (2004)
17. Luke, S., Cioffi-Revilla, C., Panait, L., Sullivan, K., Balan, G.: MASON: a multiagent simulation environment. Simulation **81**(7), 517–527 (2005). http://dx.doi.org/10.1177/0037549705058073
18. Newman, M.E.J.: Modularity and community structure in networks. Proc. Nat. Acad. Sci. (PNAS) **103**(23), 8577–8582 (2006)
19. Rahimian, F., Payberah, A.H., Girdzijauskas, S., Jelasity, M., Haridi, S.: JA-BE-JA: a distributed algorithm for balanced graph partitioning. In: 7th International Conference on Self-Adaptive and SelfOrganizing Systems. IEEE (2013)
20. Sanders, P., Schulz, C.: Think locally, act globally: highly balanced graph partitioning. In: Bonifaci, V., Demetrescu, C., Marchetti-Spaccamela, A. (eds.) SEA 2013. LNCS, vol. 7933, pp. 164–175. Springer, Heidelberg (2013)
21. Spielmat, D., Teng, S.H.: Spectral partitioning works: planar graphs and finite element meshes. In: Proceedings 37th Annual Symposium on Foundations of Computer Science, pp. 96–105, October 1996
22. Sutter, H.: The free lunch is over: a fundamental turn toward concurrency in software. Dr. Dobb's J. **30**(3), 202–210 (2005)
23. Tekin, E., Sabuncuoglu, I.: Simulation optimization: a comprehensive review on theory and applications. IIE Trans. **36**(11), 1067–1081 (2004)
24. https://github.com/fatemehr/jabeja: Ja-be-Ja GitHub repository, Accessed on May 2015
25. https://github.com/GraphChi/graphchi-java: GraphChi's Java version, Accessed on May 2015
26. https://github.com/isislab-unisa/dmason: D-MASON Official GitHub Repository, Accessed on June 2015
27. http://staffweb.cms.gre.ac.uk/~wc06/partition/: The Graph Partitioning Archive, Accessed on May 2015
28. http://www.dmason.org: D-MASON Official Website, Accessed on May 2015

Distributed Agent-Based Simulation and GIS: An Experiment with the Dynamics of Social Norms

Nicola Lettieri[1], Carmine Spagnuolo[2(✉)], and Luca Vicidomini[2]

[1] ISFOL, Università del Sannio, Benevento, Italy
n.lettieri@isfol.it, nlettieri@unisannio.it
[2] Dipartimento di Informatica, Università degli Studi di Salerno, Fisciano, Italy
{cspagnuolo,lvicidomini}@unisa.it

Abstract. In the last decade, the investigation of the social complexity has witnessed the rise of Computational Social Science, a research paradigm that heavily relies upon data and computation to foster our understanding of social phenomena. In this field, a key role is played by the explanatory and predictive power of agent-based social simulations that are showing to take advantage of GIS, higher number of agents and real data. We focus GIS based distibuted ABMs. We observed that the density distribution of agents, over the field, strongly impact on the overall performances. In order to better understand this issue, we analyzes three different scenarios ranging from real positioning, where the citizens are positioned according to a real dataset to a random positioning where the agent are positioned uniformly at random on the field. Results confirm our hypothesis and show that an irregular distribution of the agents over the field increases the communication overhead. We provide also an analytic analysis which, in a 2-dimensional uniform field partitioning, is affected by several parameters (which depend on the model), but is also influenced by the density distribution of agents over the field. According to the presented results, we have that uniform space partitioning strategy does not scale on GIS based ABM characterized by an irregular distribution of agents.

Keywords: Distributed agent-based social simulation · GIS · D-MASON · Parallel computing · Distributed systems · ABM · GIS

1 Introduction

In the last decade, the investigation of the social complexity has witnessed a deep change from both theoretical and methodological standpoint. The emerging research area of Computational Social Science (CSS) is promoting a new scientific paradigm that heavily relies upon the power of data and computation to foster the understanding of social phenomena [7,27]. The computationally inspired approach to the study of human societies is not only offering deeper

© Springer International Publishing Switzerland 2015
S. Hunold et al. (Eds.): Euro-Par 2015 Workshops, LNCS 9523, pp. 379–391, 2015.
DOI: 10.1007/978-3-319-27308-2_31

insights into social reality, but is also supporting the design of more effective and contextualized policies [34]. Indeed, many of the problems policy makers have to cope with (spanning from economic instability to the spread of epidemics) are characterised by the nonlinearity and unpredictability of complex systems and CSS tools and methodologies are showing the power of shedding new light into the core mechanics of these problems [23].

In this scenario, a key role is played by agent-based social simulation models [1, 19] that represent an innovative way to investigate how local interactions taking place at the micro level between individuals can generate emergent properties of social structures. ABM has so far allowed to study the emergence of many collective phenomena and behaviours from cooperation [3, 30], to reciprocity [24] and social norms [28] with promising results for social science and policy modeling.

More Realistic (Complex) Is Better? The design of a social simulation model is an intricate task [20]. Social dynamics are the result of complex structures of interactions that involve at different levels individual cognition and behaviour, groups, institutions and the surrounding environment. The modeling enterprise implies the operational description of factors involved in generating the macro phenomenon under investigation. Even if interesting insights into social phenomena have been yielded thanks to very simple models (see, among the others, the famous Schelling's segregation model [33]), agent-based simulation is nowadays increasingly expected to reach higher levels of realism in order to increase the explanatory and predictive power of models. This expectation implies different consequences: building agents with more complex cognitive architectures mimicking real psychological processes; explicitly representing space; reach an adequately high number of agents when simulating scale-dependent phenomena; linking simulation model to real world data.

The effects of this choice unfold at the same time on a scientific and technical level. As recently highlighted [9, 10] reaching a higher level of realism in social requires not only a strongly interdisciplinary modeling approach, but also the use of tools allowing to tackle the computational weight of more complex models. According to [29] parallelization is strictly necessary to run massive simulations *that are needed to model meaningful complex social and economic phenomena*: HPC is not simply a solution to speed-up the execution of simulation experiments, but also a way to enable completely new research questions.

In the next sections we focus on some technical issues arising when dealing with simulations with a high number of agents, real data, and GIS based environment. Our goal is twofold: analyse computational and programming issues arising when adding complexity to a relatively simple social simulation model; show how distributed computing can support advances in the investigation of social issues. We'll do it implementing a distributed simulation drawing inspiration from a well known model of norm innovation dynamic [2], a very relevant topic for many areas of social science from economics to law. We will extend the original model putting agents endowed with the cognitive architecture of social norm recognition into a simulation setting with millions individuals, explicit space and data coming from official census.

Agent-Based Model and Geographical Information Systems. The ABM community has provided several tools to build ABM simulation. Many of these tools allow the developer to use GIS data in ABM simulation.

The GIS [21] (Geographic Information Science or Geographic Information Systems) term refers to a set of theories and techniques (especially computer-based) that allows benefit geographical data and metadata in the modeling ABM. The application of GIS data in the field of ABM is relatively recent, but the interest in this field led to the creation of dedicated community [22] and as described in the chapter four of a recent book *"Geocomputation: a practical primer"* [6] the interest in this field is intended to grow.

Many ABM tools support the GIS data. Among them we have:

MASON [4] , a discrete-event simulation core and visualization library written in Java, designed to simulate a wide range of ABMs. MASON is designed and maintained by George Mason University's Evolutionary Computation Laboratory and the GMU Center for Social Complexity. MASON provides support for GIS data in an additional library named GeoMASON [35].

GeoMASON follows the same MASON design philosophy of being lightweight, modular, and efficient. GeoMASON represents the basic GIS data in a geometric shapes supported via the *JTS* (Java Topology Suite API), which allows geometries related operations. GeoMASON supports the ESRI [18] shape files providing a `GeomVectorField` Java object that represents the GIS data in the memory, and provides functionalities to access to geometries in order to read geospatial metadata and obtain geospatial positions of the objects.

Netlogo [36], a multi-agent programmable modeling environment. It is developed at the The Center for Connected Learning (CCL) and Computer-Based Modeling at Northwestern University. Netlogo provides an extension to support GIS data field. The extension allows the programmer to load vector GIS data (points, lines, and polygons), and raster GIS data (grids) into their models. Netlogo extension also supports the ESRI shapefiles.

Parallel and Distributed Multi Agent-Based Simulation. As described in [32] the scientific community have produced several tools and framework to run multi-agents system in a distributed environment:

D-MASON [11,12,17] is a distributed version of MASON library for running ABMs on distributed systems. Currently, D-MASON allows to parallelize simulation based on geometric fields and does not support the parallelization of GeoMASON. D-MASON allows to choose different communication layers: a layer based on a centralized strategy, that use the message broker Apache ActiveMQ and one based on the MPI standard; both layers adopt the Publish/Subscribe paradigm.

Flame [26] is designed to support lots of ABM. It allows parallelization by using the MPI standard to ensure the communication between the nodes. Flame is developed by the University of Sheffield and support also the GIS data.

RepastHPC [8] is the parallel version of Repast. RepastHPC is developed by the Argone institute of USA. RepastHPC uses MPI for the communications among the HPC environments. The current version RepastHPC supports GIS data.

In this paper, we perform several GIS-based ABMs on D-MASON. We use the distributed field of D-MASON in order to distribute the computation among the nodes. We notice that, we exploit GeoMason as static field that does not change during the simulation.

2   Experiment

In this section, we describe our experiment of distributed ABM GIS model implemented in D-MASON. In the following we describe the GIS data used to support the modeling of the population behaviors in the Italy region Campania. Then we provide anof our experimental ABM GIS model and the implementation of the model in D-MASON.

Model Space Representation. The environment in ABM [5] is not only a particular property of the model, but could be a relevant entity to understand the complex behavior of natural and artificial systems. Interesting features of ABM, compared to others modeling tools, concerns the interactions between the agents that do not take place in a vacuum, but happen in a structured environment that could influence and could be influenced by the agents interactions. These structured environments are named fields and can be social and physical environments (fields based on mathematical modeling like matrix), but also more complex structure like networks.

The environment representations is really crucial in order to address real-world problems (e.g., simulating the segregation in a particular area or simulating emergency strategies in natural disaster [16]). In this work we used a set of GIS "Campania dataset" data to support a model to simulate a toy experiment, inspired by a cognitive architecture model [6].

GIS Campania Dataset. The open-data platform of the *"Regione Campania"* provides the GIS dataset [31] about its region. The dataset is a ShapeFile ESRI shape on the geographical coordinate system WGS84 UTM zone 32 N and provides the subdivision of the region in geographical zones identified by a unique identifier.

Model Agents Movement Representation. A single agent in our model is a citizen living in Campania that has to travel every day to his work/study place. Agents behavior is based upon public available data released by ISTAT [25] (the Italian National Institute of Statistics), produced after the national population census made in October 2011.

The ISTAT's table contains information about 2.5 millions citizens living in Campania, which each day travel to work (or study) and then go back home.

It contains the following data: city of residence, gender, reason to travel (work or study), city of work/study, vehicle (on foot, by car, by train, etc.), time of departure, travel duration.

Model Description. The model we are going to show is a simplified version of the cognitive model designed by *Andrighetto et al.* in [2]. In our model, agents move in a representation of the Campania environment: agents' home and working places are placed on the Campania map according to real data from ISTAT.

The cognitive aspect of the model follows. There is a set of norms (graphically depicted using different colors). For each norm, agents will hold a *salience* (a value in the [0,1] interval) that represents how much that norm is important for the agent. The norm that is the most important for an agent, will characterize the agent's color (belief of the norm).

Agents continuously interact with neighbor agents trying to spread their opinion (color). When an agent meet an agent advertising a particular color, it will increase the salience for that specific norm. Agents are influenced by neighbors throughout the day, but with different weight depending on agent's state (traveling, staying at home, staying at work/study). Of course, saliences will naturally decay over time.

Campania is divided into five *provinces*: Naples, Salerno, Benevento, Avellino and Caserta. We imagined that in each province of Campania there is a norm that is prevalent (i.e. 80% of the inhabitants are of that color). For instance: Naples is mostly Red; Salerno is mostly Green; Avellino, Benevento, Caserta are mostly Blue. In the remaining 20% of the population, the 15% will be Yellow (the color not advertized by any region), while the last 5% will be of a random color that is different from the region's color. Back to our example, 80% of people in the Salerno province will be Green; 15% will be Yellow, and the remaining 5% will be a random chosen between Red and Blue.

The model simulates an entire day (24 hours) starting from midnight. When the simulation start, agents are staying at their home. Time of departure, travel duration, time of stay at work/study all depend on ISTAT data. Times and durations need to be converted into simulation steps: for instance, if travel duration for the agent is *from* 16 *to* 30 min, the simulation will assign a random duration in that interval. This duration will be converted in a number of steps, according to discretization time of the simulation (see Sect. 3.1).

The size of the simulated field and discretization time have a significant impact on the performances (in terms of efficiency) of the simulation. As we will, in Sect. 2, an agent moves at a speed that is calculated dividing the travel distance by the travel duration (simulation steps). This gives the speed of an agents, that is the maximum distance covered in a single simulation step. The largest agents' travel distance is called maximum agents ride (α) and will require a certain number of steps (maximum number of steps to perform a ride, β). So we can compute the maximum speed (α/β): this parameter has a strong impact on the distributed model performances (the smaller the better).

In order to evaluate the performances of the distributed simulation framework D-MASON we also included two further modifications to our model, concerning the way agents are placed on the map. We will refer to the model we just described as the one with **Real** positions; agents are place according the real population density. A second model, called **CRandom**, places agents uniformly at random on the entire Campania territory. The latest model, called **Random**, places agents uniformly random on a 2D continuous space. The latest model represents the best case for distribution, as it allows the model to balance the workload on multiple LPs (Logical Processors). It is, although, very unrealistic. The **CRandom** model represents a in-between case, since agents are uniformly distributed on the territory, but are still places within the Campania boundaries.

D-MASON Simulation. By noticing that most ABMs are inspired by natural models, where agents' limited visibility allow to bound the range of interaction to a fixed range named agent's Area of Interest (AOI), D-MASON adopt the so-called *space-partitioning* technique [15], where the agents' world (the *field*) is split into tiles, each assigned to a LP.

Since citizens are basically moving on a map, our agents' space consists in a rectangular area. MASON includes the Continuous2D field, where agents contained in it are located by a couple of continuous coordinates ranging from point $(0,0)$ to point $([W]idth, [H]eight))$. The distributed version embedded into D-MASON is called DContinuous2D: it retains all the features of the Continuous2D field, adding the support for two approaches to distribute the field and agents contained in it: dividing the space into vertical rectangles called *rows* (1-dimensional space partitioning or *horizontal*); or dividing it into a *rows* × *columns* matrix (2-dimensional space partitioning or *square*, see Fig. 3). With our model, the square partitioning mode provides a significant speedup over the horizontal partitioning, lowering the communication effort while distributing the computational workload of the agents to LPs.

The behavior of agents is influenced by GIS data (map, zones and cities), nevertheless GIS data is static and does not require any synchronization among LPs. Reading ISTAT data, each LP manages an area of competence, and take care of agents that live in its area of competence. This is done by reading agent's home location from the ISTAT dataset, looking for correspondent coordinates into GIS data, and converting it into 2-dimensional D-MASON coordinates.

3   Results

To evaluate the performances of the three models described above we developed the models in D-MASON. We have tested the models using two communications strategies available in D-MASON: AMQ (Apache ActiveMQ) that is the centralized communication strategy and MPI that uses the MPI standard [13,14].

Simulations have been executed on a cluster of eight nodes, each equipped as follows: *Hardware*, CPUs 2 x Intel(R) Xeon(R) CPU E5-2680 @ 2.70GHz (#core 16, #threads 32) – RAM 256 GB; *Software*, Ubuntu 12.04.4 LTS – Java JDK 1.6.25 – OpenMPI 1.7.4.

3.1   Experiments Settings

We have investigated the scalability of the simulation considering the overall simulation time needed to simulate a 5 (simulated) minutes of real world system changing both the number of LPs and the simulation workload (# of agents). As described above the model uses a discretization time to simulate the real life clock. In our tests, the discretization time is 2400 steps per hour, the field size is 3600 × 2400 and the neighbors' influence radius is 1. D-MASON allows two kinds of space partitioning: 1-dimensional and 2-dimensional. After several pilot experiments, we have chosen the 2-dimensional partitioning due to the unbalanced nature of the positioning of the agents among the fields. The unbalanced density of agents will be a crucial part of our investigation. More details will appear in Sect. 3.2. Two kinds of experiments will be presented:

Simulate 5 min of Real Life. In this test we are interested in evaluating *How much time is needed to simulate 5 min of real life?* (which corresponds to 200 simulation steps). We tested four configurations which partition the field in 4 × 4, 6 × 6, 8 × 8 and 10 × 10 tiles assigned, respectively, to 16, 36, 64 and 100 LPs. Each configuration was performed on 2.5 million agents. Figure 1 shows the results for each model (*Real, Random* and *CRandom*). For each configuration, we show the total simulation time as well as how it is partitioned into the communication overhead (that includes the management overhead introduced by D-MASON) and the computation time.

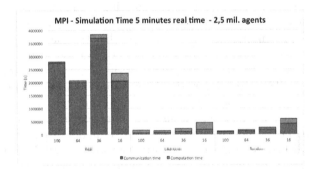

Fig. 1. Simulation performance with 4 × 4, 6×6 , 8×8, 10 × 10 partitionings - 5 min of real clock.

The performance of the simulation is strongly influenced by the positioning model. The *Random* and *CRandom* models exhibit the same unimodal trend, as the number of LPs increase and manifest a balanced ratio of communication and computation.

The *Real* test provides the worst performance and unusual trend due to an unbalanced communication overhead. We investigated this problem analyzing the simulations with different agents positioning models and we discovered that this trend is due to the non uniform positioning of the agents (see Fig. 4).

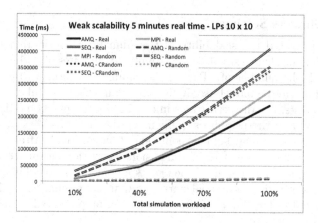

Fig. 2. Weak scalability. 10×10 partitioning, 5 min of real clock.

Weak Scalability. This experiment aims to evaluate the simulation efficiency varying the total computation workload. We tested four configurations changing the total number of agents 10 %, 40 %, 70 % and 100 % (100 % = 2.5 mil). Each configuration was performed on a 10 × 10 partitioning with 100 LPs. Figure 2 depicts the results of the three models using MPI as communication layer. Moreover we also compare the performances with the sequential version of the model implemented in MASON (we refers to this with the name SEQ). *Random* and *CRandom* tests provides a similar behavior showing good scalability. This results demonstrate the good performance of a 2-dimensional field partitioning on a uniform and quasi-uniform positioning density. On the other hand, the *Real* model manifests the worst scalability (just a bit better than the sequential version). This result is due to the communications overhead that is extremely irregular over the LPs. The Table 1 reports the speedup obtained during the weak scalability test. For each configuration, the minimum and maximum speedup are emphasized in bold. The best results are obtained by the *Random* model with 70% of computation amount and *AMQ* as communication layer; the worst performance is achieved by the *Real* positioning using the *MPI* communication layer. This confirms our hypothesis that the speedup is strongly related to agents positioning.

3.2 Analytical Analysis of ABM and GIS

Considering the results obtained in the preceding section, we decide to analytically evaluate the communication effort required by a GIS based distributed simulation that exploits a uniform 2D space partitioning approach (Fig. 3).

When a space partitioning approach is used, the amount of communication performed before each simulation step is related to: the size of the whole field ($[W]idth \times [H]eight$ in this specific analysis), the agents density distribution (d) i.e., the positioning of the agents over the field, the number of LPs (p), the

Table 1. Experiments speedup varying the workload. 10×10 partitioning, $5\,$min of real clock.

Test Name	Workload			
	10 %	40 %	70 %	100 %
AMQ - Real	**3,36**	2,49	1,97	1,74
MPI - Real	3,07	2,32	1,79	**1,46**
AMQ - Random	11,32	25,14	**35,53**	33,06
MPI - Random	**7,63**	20,01	27,29	27,78
AMQ - CRandom	7,69	21,13	29,14	**31,86**
MPI - CRandom	**5,60**	15,53	23,38	26,78

maximum agents ride distance (α), the maximum number of steps to perform a ride (β) and the agents area of interest radius (AOI) which depends on the neighbors' influence radius (NIR).

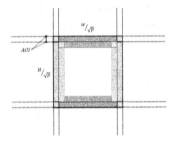

Fig. 3. D-MASON 2-dimensional uniform field partitioning on p tiles.

Recalling that using the space partitioning approach we have

$$AOI \geq \max \left(NIR, \frac{\alpha}{\beta} \right),$$ (1)

therefore the AOI should be at least equal to the ratio α/β.

Since, in euclidean space, the diameter of our field is $\alpha = \sqrt{W^2 + H^2}$, one can easily verify that

$$\frac{W + H}{2} \leq \alpha \leq W + H.$$ (2)

Hence, by using (1) and (2) we have that

$$AOI \geq \frac{\sqrt{W^2 + H^2}}{\beta} \geq \frac{W + H}{2\beta}$$ (3)

We can now evaluate the communication effort required by a GIS based distributed simulation. For each region, the communication effort δ_c is obtained by counting the number of agents which belong to the edges of the region. The edges space, as shown in Fig. 3, is composed by 16 regions of sizes $\frac{W}{\sqrt{p}} \times AOI$ (top and bottom), $\frac{H}{\sqrt{p}} \times AOI$ (left and right) and $AOI \times AOI$ (corners). The expected number of agents is obtained multiplying the size of the above described region by the density. Overall we have,

$$
\begin{aligned}
\delta_c &= p \times \left[4 \left(\frac{W}{\sqrt{p}} AOI \right) + 4 \left(\frac{H}{\sqrt{p}} AOI \right) + 8 AOI^2 \right] \times d \\
&= 4\sqrt{p} \times d \times AOI \times (W + H) + 8p \times d \times AOI^2 \\
&\leq 8\sqrt{p} \times d \times \beta \times AOI^2 + 8p \times d \times AOI^2 \\
&= 8\sqrt{p} \times d \times AOI^2 \times (\beta + \sqrt{p})
\end{aligned}
\tag{4}
$$

where the inequality is due to Eq. (3).

Consequently the communication effort is linearly influenced by the AOI (which depend on the simulation model) and the density distribution of agents (d). In details the value of δ_c varies according to the agents positioning over the field. When such value is irregular, the communication increases and affects all the regions since the whole system synchronizes before each simulation step.

This analysis motivates the poor performance of the simulation in the *Real* agents positioning experiment. Figure 4 depicts the positioning of the agents on the geographical zones in the *Campania* region. Real positioning provides a lots of zones with a small number of agents but there are also a small number of highly populated zones. Indeed, the density d over the field is non-uniform (the variance, in the number of agents per zone, is 302600129.2) and by Eq. (3) the communication effort δ_c grows proportionally with the larger value of d.

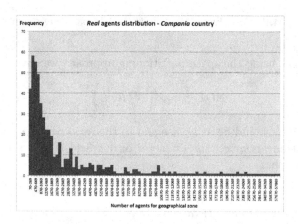

Fig. 4. Agents positioning over the region zones in *Campania*. In the figure is shown the frequency of zones in *Campania* with a certain density that ranging from 70 to 57869 people.

4 Conclusion

We considered the problem of simulation an ABM that uses GIS data. Exploiting GIS data in ABM is an important innovation in the ABM field. Several ABM examples [16] and users community [22] demonstrate the importance of this approach for improving the effectiveness of ABM model in complex systems study. Experimental results on a toy model, inspired by [2], demonstrate that the work partitioning, in a distributed GIS based ABM simulation is quite hard. According to our analysis, the main issue is the uneven positioning of the agents over the field, which jeopardize the performance of the simulation. Indeed, the speedup depends on communication effort δ_c which, in a 2-dimensional uniform field partitioning approach, is: $\delta_c \leq 8\sqrt{p} \times d \times AOI^2 \times (\beta + \sqrt{p})$.

Therefore, the performance of the simulation scale up as a quadratic function of the AOI (which depends on the model) and is linearly influenced by the density distribution (d) of the agents over the field and the discretization time (β) used in the model. As future work, we plan to study the problem of balancing the communication effort among the LPs considering the density distribution of the agents over the field according to the field partitioning strategies.

References

1. Generative social science: studies in agent-based computational modeling (2006)
2. Andrighetto, G., Campennì, M., Conte, R., Paolucci, M.: On the immergence of norms: a normative agent architecture (2014)
3. Axelrod, R.: The complexity of cooperation (1997)
4. Balan, G.C., Cioffi-Revilla, C., Luke, S., Panait, I., Paus, S.: MASON: a Java multi-agent simulation library. In: Proceedings of the Agent 2003 Conference (2003)
5. Benenson, I.: Agent-based models of geographical systems. Int. J. Geograph. Inf. Sci. **27**, 2483–2508 (2013)
6. Brunsdon, C., Singleton, A.: Geocomputation: A Practical Primer. SAGE (2015)
7. Cioffi-Revilla, C.: Computational social science. Comput. Stat. Wiley Interdisc. Rev. **2**, 259–271 (2010)
8. Collier, N., North, M.: Repast HPC: a platform for large-scale agent-based modeling. In: Dubitzky, W., Kurowski, K., Schott, B. (eds.) Large-Scale Computing Techniques for Complex System Simulations. Wiley, Hoboken (2011)
9. Conte, R., Gilbert, N., Bonelli, G., Cioffi-Revilla, C., Deffuant, G., Kertesz, J., Loreto, V., Moat, S., Nadal, J.P., Sanchez, A., et al.: Manifesto of computational social science. Eur. Phys. J. Spec. Top. **214**, 325–346 (2012)
10. Conte, R., Paolucci, M.: On agent-based modeling and computational social science. Front. Psychol. **5**, 668 (2014)
11. Cordasco, G., De Chiara, R., Mancuso, A., Mazzeo, D., Scarano, V., Spagnuolo, C.: A framework for distributing agent-based simulations. In: Alexander, M., D'Ambra, P., Belloum, A., Bosilca, G., Cannataro, M., Danelutto, M., Martino, B., Gerndt, M., Jeannot, E., Namyst, R., Roman, J., Scott, S.L., Traff, J.L., Vallée, G., Weidendorfer, J. (eds.) Euro-Par 2011, Part I. LNCS, vol. 7155, pp. 460–470. Springer, Heidelberg (2012)

12. Cordasco, G., De Chiara, R., Mancuso, M., Mazzeo, D., Scarano, V., Spagnuolo, C.: Bringing together efficiency and effectiveness in distributed simulations: the experience with D-MASON. SIMULATION Trans. Soc. Model. Simul. Int. **89**, 1236–1526 (2013)

13. Cordasco, G., Mancuso, A., Milone, F., Spagnuolo, C.: Communication strategies in distributed agent-based simulations: the experience with D-MASON. In: Mey, D., et al. (eds.) Euro-Par 2013. LNCS, vol. 8374, pp. 533–543. Springer, Heidelberg (2014)

14. Cordasco, G., Milone, F., Spagnuolo, C., Vicidomini, L.: Exploiting D-MASON on parallel platforms: a novel communication strategy. In: Lopes, L., et al. (eds.) Euro-Par 2014, Part I. LNCS, vol. 8805, pp. 407–417. Springer, Heidelberg (2014)

15. Cosenza, B., Cordasco, G., De Chiara, R., Scarano, V.: Distributed load balancing for parallel agent-based simulations. In: 2011 19th Euromicro International Conference on Parallel, Distributed and Network-Based Processing (PDP) (2011)

16. Crooks, A., Wise, S.: GIS and agent-based models for humanitarian assistance. Comput. Environ. Urban Syst. **41**, 100–111 (2013)

17. D-MASON Official GitHub Repository. https://github.com/isislab-unisa/dmason. Accessed Jun 2015

18. ESRI format. https://www.esri.com/library/whitepapers/pdfs/shapefile.pdf

19. Federico, B., Squazzoni, F.: Complexity-Friendly Policy Modelling. Routledge, London (2015)

20. Gilbert, N., Troitzsch, K.: Simulation for the Social Scientist. McGraw-Hill, New York (2005)

21. GIS. http://www.dartmouth.edu/geog58/documents/geog58syllabus.pdf

22. GIS, ABM community. http://www.gisagents.org/

23. Helbing, D., Balietti, S.: From social simulation to integrative system design. Eur. Phys. J. Spec. Top. **195**, 69–100 (2011)

24. Henrich, J., Ensminger, J., McElreath, R., Barr, A., Barrett, C., Bolyanatz, A., Cardenas, J.C., Gurven, M., Gwako, E., Henrich, N., et al.: Markets, religion, community size, and the evolution of fairness and punishment. Science **327**, 1480–1484 (2010)

25. ISTAT: Commuters 2011 dataset. http://www.istat.it/it/archivio/139381, http://www.istat.it/storage/cartografia/matrici_pendolarismo/matrici_pendolarismo_2011.zip

26. Kiran, M., Chin, L., Richmond, P., Holcombe, M., Worth, D., Greenough, C.: Flame: simulating large populations of agents on parallel hardware architectures

27. Lazer, D., Pentland, A.S., Adamic, L., Aral, S., Barabasi, A.L., Brewer, D., Christakis, N., Contractor, N., Fowler, J., Gutmann, M., et al.: Life in the network: the coming age of computational social science. Science (New York, NY) **323**, 721 (2009)

28. Neumann, M.: Homo socionicus: a case study of simulation models of norms. J. Artif. Soc. Soc. Simul. **11**, 6 (2008)

29. Paolucci, M., Kossman, D., Conte, R., Lukowicz, P., Argyrakis, P., Blandford, A., Bonelli, G., Anderson, S., de Freitas, S., Edmonds, B., et al.: Towards a living earth simulator. Eur. Phys. J. Spec. Top. **214**, 77–108 (2012)

30. Putterman, L.: Cooperation and punishment. Science **69**, 1061–1075 (2010)

31. Regione Campania: Geoportale: Geographic information system of campania. http://sit.regione.campania.it/portal/portal/default/Cartografia

32. Rousset, A., Herrmann, B., Lang, C., Philippe, L.: A survey on parallel and distributed multi-agent systems. In: Lopes, L., et al. (eds.) Euro-Par 2014, Part I. LNCS, vol. 8805, pp. 371–382. Springer, Heidelberg (2014)

33. Schelling, T.C.: Dynamic models of segregation. J. Math. Soc. **1**, 143–186 (1971)
34. Squazzoni, F., Boero, R.: Complexity-friendly policy modelling. In: Innovation in Complex Social Systems (2010)
35. Sullivan, K., Coletti, M., Luke, S.: GeoMason: geospatial support for MASON. Technical report, Department of Computer Science, George Mason University (2010)
36. Tisue, S., Wilensky, U.: Netlogo: a simple environment for modeling complexity. In: International Conference on Complex Systems (2004)

Behavioral Spherical Harmonics
for Long-Range Agents' Interaction

Biagio Cosenza[(✉)]

Embedded Systems Architecture (AES),
Department of Computer Engineering and Microelectronics (TIME),
Technische Universität Berlin, Berlin, Germany
cosenza@tu-berlin.de

Abstract. We introduce behavioral spherical harmonic (BSH), a novel approach to efficiently and compactly represent the directional-dependent behavior of agent. BSH is based on spherical harmonics to project the directional information of a group of multiple agents to a vector of few coefficients; thus, BSH drastically reduces the complexity of the directional evaluation, as it requires only few agent-group interactions instead of multiple agent-agent ones. We show how the BSH model can efficiently model intricate behaviors such as long-range collision avoidance, reaching interactive performance and avoiding agent congestion on challenging multi-groups scenarios.

Furthermore, we demonstrate how both the innate parallelism and the compact coefficient representation of the BSH model are well suited for GPU architectures, showing performance analysis of our OpenCL implementation.

Keywords: Spherical harmonics · Behavioral model · Agent-based simulation · Long-distance interaction · Collision avoidance · GPGPU

1 Introduction

Agent-Based Simulations (ABSs) include a broad range of domains. Many existing ABS frameworks offer general solutions to common problems shared between different agent domains; however, most challenging problems still stick with domain-specific solutions. An example is long-range interaction between agents, required by many real-case scenarios, but usually solved with context-specific solutions. In crowd simulation, where a crowd is modeled as a set of agents, each agent attempts to reach a target position while avoiding collisions with other agents and static obstacles in the environment. Considering the interaction of all pairs of agents becomes expensive in large crowds, and typically only neighboring agents that lie within a specified radius are take into account, limiting the possibility of look-ahead behaviors. More complex collision avoidance approaches use two algorithms: one for local collision and one for global, long-distance collision. Continuum-based approaches for collision avoidance [16] offer

© Springer International Publishing Switzerland 2015
S. Hunold et al. (Eds.): Euro-Par 2015 Workshops, LNCS 9523, pp. 392–404, 2015.
DOI: 10.1007/978-3-319-27308-2_32

an interesting solution, but they assume that agent directionality is homogenous for agents in the same cell grid; otherwise, important directional information is lost. Therefore, similar solutions are not portable between domains: they work only in contexts where directionality information can be lost without consequences or at least coarsely approximated.

In this paper, we introduce behavioral spherical harmonic (BSH), a novel behavioral model that encodes directionality information usually expressed in an agent's behavior in a compact mathematical formulation. For this purpose, we use spherical harmonics (SH): with a projection step, multiple agent directions are projected to a small set of coefficients. SH functions have useful properties and can be easily combined (e.g., multiplied). Once a new agent needs to calculate his directional-dependent behavior, the BSH can easily reconstruct the directionality information from previously projected agents.

The contribution of this paper are:

- A novel behavioral model (BSH) based on Spherical Harmonics that compactly encodes the directional information of multiple agents
- An application of BSH to support long-range interactions
- A GPU/OpenCL implementation that exploits the natural parallelism and the compact representation of BSH, as tested with several interactive agent simulations on an NVIDIA GPU.

2 Background

Researchers and practitioners of agent-based simulations and modeling have for a long time investigated the use of parallel implementations targeting a wide range of architectures, including multi-cores [15,17], GPUs [6,19], and distributed memory architectures [2–4].

Collision avoidance algorithms have been investigated by several ABS systems, where the motion of each agent is typically governed by some high-level formulation and local interaction rules (e.g., collision avoidance). ClearPath [12] presents a local collision avoidance algorithm that formulates the conditions for collision-free navigation as a quadratic optimization problem. PLEdestrians [11] introduces a bio-mechanically, energy-efficient trajectory for each individual in a multi-agent simulation. Local collision avoidance algorithms in crowd simulation often ignore agents beyond a neighborhood of a certain size. However, this cutoff can result in sharp changes in trajectory when large groups of agents enter or exit these neighborhoods. Such long-range interaction requires more computation than local collision avoidance, even for distributed and parallel simulation. HybridCrowd [7] performs approximate, long-range collision avoidance via two approaches: low-density crowds are modeled with discrete methods, while high-density crowds exploit continuum methods.

Spherical harmonics (SH) is a frequency-space basis for representing functions defined over the sphere. SH has been used in various problems, such as the heat equation, electrical fields, gravitational fields, and modeling the quantum

angular momentum of electrons. SH has also been used in computer graphics applications: Cabral et al. [1] first used SH to estimate the integral of the
BRDF by expanding the bidirectional reflection coefficient in SH. More recently,
Kaplanyan and Dachsbacher [13] used a lattice of harmonical functions to propagate indirect illumination in real-time.

Our approach is similar to a continuum approach where agents' positions
and velocities are accumulated in a background grid [16]. However, in our case,
velocities are encoded as SH, to eliminate difficulties such as the sensitivity to
the number of agent goals [22] or overcrowding in highly dense crowds [16].

3   Behavioral Spherical Harmonics

Traditional agent models such as Reynold's boid model represent an agent with
a position and a direction vector. However, cases such as those involving long-
range interaction approaches require a way to represent this information for a
group of agents (e.g., in a grid-based continuum approach, a group is represented
by all agents inside a cell). While agents' positions can be easily approximated by
exploiting their locality, directionality information is very hard to approximate:
in fact, many existing long-range approaches lose any directionality information.

Table 1. A two-dimensional example of BSH: only original agent directions (a) are
projected into SH basis (b) to calculate a vector of coefficients (c).

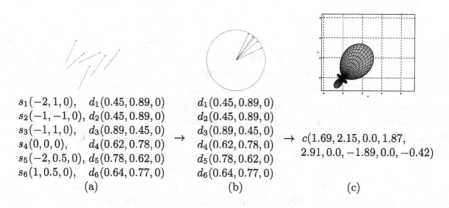

$$s_1(-2,1,0), \quad d_1(0.45,0.89,0) \qquad d_1(0.45,0.89,0)$$
$$s_2(-1,-1,0), \; d_2(0.45,0.89,0) \qquad d_2(0.45,0.89,0)$$
$$s_3(-1,1,0), \quad d_3(0.89,0.45,0) \qquad d_3(0.89,0.45,0)$$
$$s_4(0,0,0), \qquad d_4(0.62,0.78,0) \; \rightarrow \; d_4(0.62,0.78,0) \; \rightarrow \; c(1.69,2.15,0.0,1.87,$$
$$s_5(-2,0.5,0), \; d_5(0.78,0.62,0) \qquad d_5(0.78,0.62,0) \qquad 2.91,0.0,-1.89,0.0,-0.42)$$
$$s_6(1,0.5,0), \quad d_6(0.64,0.77,0) \qquad d_6(0.64,0.77,0)$$

(a)   (b)   (c)

In this work, we replace the directionality information of a group of agents
with a set of coefficients that represents a spherical function (Table 1). We introduce behavioral spherical harmonics (BSH), a novel approach to represent the
directionality information of a group of agents in a compact and efficient way.
This section introduces the mathematical background of spherical harmonics, how
directions are projected into coefficients and reconstructed from them, and the
most interesting properties of BSH. Our use of SH is similar to related work in
rendering [9,20] (e.g., we use real-value basis), therefore adopt a similar notation.

3.1   Spherical Harmonics

The spherical harmonics (SH) is a mathematical system analogous to the Fourier transform but defined across the surface of a sphere. SH is the angular portion of the solution to Laplace's equation in spherical coordinates and defines an orthonormal basis over the sphere. In general, SH functions are based on imaginary numbers, but we are only interested in approximating real functions over the sphere (i.e., agent directions). Reference to SH functions are synonymous with references to real spherical harmonic functions.

Given the standard parametrization into spherical coordinates of points on the surface of a unit sphere, the Cartesian coordinates of the point (x, y, z) can be expressed in spherical coordinates using the variables θ and φ:

$$(x, y, z) \rightarrow (\sin\theta\cos\varphi, \sin\theta\sin\varphi, \cos\theta)$$

The SH function is traditionally represented by the symbol y

$$y_l^m(\theta, \varphi) = \begin{cases} \sqrt{2}K_l^m \cos(m\varphi)P_l^m(\cos\theta), & m > 0 \\ \sqrt{2}K_l^m \sin(-m\varphi)P_l^{-m}(\cos\theta), & m < 0 \\ K_l^0 P_l^0 \cos(\theta), & m = 0 \end{cases}$$

where P is the associated Legendre polynomial and K_l^m the scaling normalization constants defined as

$$K_l^m = \sqrt{\frac{(2l+1)(l-|m|)!}{4\pi(l+|m|)!}}$$

l and m are integer constant indexes, also called the *order* or *band* (l), and the degree (m), respectively. To generate all the SH orthonormal basis functions, the parameters l and m are defined slightly differently from the Legendre polynomials: l is still a positive integer starting from 0, but m takes signed integer values from $-l$ to l. It is possible to think of the SH functions occurring in a specific order so that we can use a simpler one-dimensional vector:

$$y_l^m(\theta, \varphi) = y_i(\theta, \varphi) \text{ where } i - l(l+1) + m$$

In this paper, we use 3rd-order SH representation, therefore using only 9 basis functions as shown in Table 2; a list of the first 5 SH bands are available in [20].

3.2   Projection and Reconstruction

Let f be the spherical function we want to project to SH coefficients (we will show later how f will represent directional information of multiple agents). To calculate a single coefficient for a specific band, we integrate the product of the function $f(d)$, where d is the direction, with the SH basis function y:

$$c_l^m = \int f(d)y_l^m(s)ds$$

Table 2. Spherical harmonic basis functions for the first three bands.

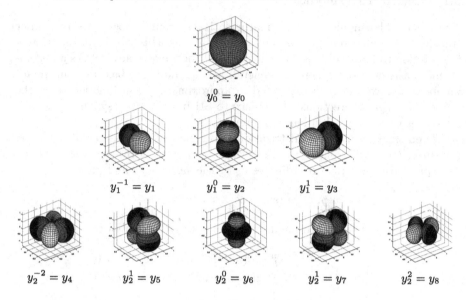

$$y_0^0 = y_0$$

$$y_1^{-1} = y_1 \qquad y_1^0 = y_2 \qquad y_1^1 = y_3$$

$$y_2^{-2} = y_4 \qquad y_2^{1} = y_5 \qquad y_2^0 = y_6 \qquad y_2^1 = y_7 \qquad y_2^2 = y_8$$

To reconstruct the function f at a given direction d, we define $\hat{f}(d)$ by performing the reverse process and summing scaled copies of the corresponding SH functions:

$$\hat{f}(d) = \sum_{l=0}^{n} \sum_{m=-l}^{l} c_l^m y_l^m(d) = \sum_{i=0}^{n^2} c_i y_i(d)$$

which is increasingly accurate as the number of bands n increases[1]. Note that the projection to nth order SH generates n^2 coefficients.

Evaluating the approximate function $\hat{f}$ at direction d simply requires the dot product between the n^2 coefficients and the vector of evaluated basis functions $y_i(d)$. The first coefficient ($i = 0$), called DC term, represents the average value of the function over the sphere.

Properties. SH functions have many interesting properties. SH bases are orthogonal, which means that the inner product of any two distinct basis functions is zero. An integration performed over the product of two SH functions is the same as a dot product of their coefficients as a result of the SH basis functions' othonormality. To project a scalar function $f(s)$ defined over a sphere S against the basis function of the SH requires a simple integration over S: $c_l^m = \int f(s) y_l^m(s) ds$. SH functions are also rotationally invariant. Other properties such as the double and triple product integral and the double product projection are covered by [20].

---

[1] We use n for the number of bands and N for the number of agents.

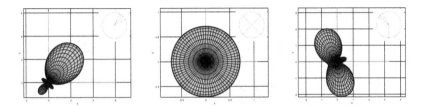

Fig. 1. Three different agent group orientations resulting in different SH functions.

3.3 Behavioral Spherical Harmonics

We apply SH functions to a group of agents whose directions will be replaced by an approximated function $\hat{f}(d)$. In a simulation using grid-based space subdivision, SH is applied for each cell, whose agent directions will be replaced by a vector of coefficients. Expressing directionality as per-cell spherical functions has different advantages. First, a single SH function replaces all agent directions contained in the cell, thus requiring far fewer interaction evaluations: once the agent directions are encoded into coefficients, successive evaluations are independent of the number of agents. Second, SH functions are more expressive than other representations, as they effectively approximate all directional information for the projected directions. For example, SH can distinguish different agent orientations, as depicted in Fig. 1:

Long-Range Collision Avoidance. Earlier agent models such as Reynolds' boid model have no long range collision avoidance: collision is local as it reacts to boids (agents) within a limited neighborhood. In this paper we introduce a behavioral model (BSH) that also uses agent's direction (i.e., velocity) to implement long-range agent interactions. BSH is calculated by summing the local collision-avoidance model plus an *avoidance* direction that expresses a long-range repulsion force. This force depends on the distance between the agent and the cell, the angle between agent's direction and the cell, and the precalculated cell's directional information. As we will show later, the directional contribution is critical to avoid congestion in long-range, multi-group scenarios (see Figs. 3, 4 and 5).

Collision Avoidance with Static Obstacles. BSH is also able to model obstacles, in the same way we express agent directionality in grid cells. This work uses a simple approach: to project obstacle information within the SH if each cell contains an obstacle. For each obstacle, depending on its shape and how agents should avoid it, a number of directional avoidance forces are projected to the SH function. For simplicity, the obstacle is placed in the center of the cell. As obstacles are static their contributions to their cells' respective SH are precalculated. Evaluating the avoidance force also takes in account of the (square of the) distance between the agent and the cell.

4   Implementation

We have implemented our agent-based simulation based on BSH in OpenCL [14] and tested on a GPU. It comprises 8 steps:

1. Calculate each agent's grid position;
2. Calculate each agent's grid hash and index;
3. Sort key-value pair (grid hash, index);
4. Reorder position and velocity vectors by sorted index and store the cell start and end indices;
5. Project velocity vectors into SH representation for each cell;
6. Simulate pairwise agent interaction;
7. Evaluate SH in the direction of agent and reconstruct velocity;
8. Draw agents (optional, requires OpenGL binding).

Steps 1–4 and 6 are common in many GPU-based agent simulations that use spatial hashing (grid) and are briefly discussed in the next section. Our approach introduces two new steps, 5 and 7, discussed in Sects. 4.2 and 4.3. Step 8 is straightforward and required only when visualization is enabled.

4.1   Spatial Subdivision with Grid

Naïve implementations compute the pairwise interaction between all agents, which has a complexity of $O(N^2)$ for N agents. A more efficient approach uses spatial subdivision such as the three-dimensional uniform grid, which divides the simulation space in uniformly sized, non-overlapping cells. Each agent is assigned to exactly one cell, depending on its position. The cell position is then hashed to give it a unique, sortable, consecutively-numbered value and stored a key-value pair with the agent's *id* as key and the cell position hash as value. This approach has been largely used in literature [5,6,8,18]. Our implementation of the spatial grid is similar to the NVIDIA particle simulation implementation [10]: steps 1–4 and 6 are essentially the same. The pairwise interaction between agents in step 6, as for related work, happens only if they are at close range: each agent looks at other agents in its own cell and the 26 surrounding cells (steps 5 and 7 take long-range interaction into account). The sorted index of the agents is used to reorder position and velocity data. To quickly locate the agents in a cell, two additional buffers containing the reordered agent's start and end indices, respectively, are needed. Additional details can be found in [10].

Agent movement is restricted to the simulation space limited by a bounding box. A negative force is used to keep agents from moving out of the box by keeping them away from the borders.

4.2   Projection of Directionality into SH Coefficients

The first additional kernel is the projection of each agent direction into a SH representation. For this purpose, we used the 3rd-order, numerical evaluation code from Sloan [21], which produces 9 coefficients. The coefficient from band 0 is a constant value and is not actually stored in the output vector. The evaluation returns an OpenCL $float8$ with the coefficients for a specific point on the sphere.

```
__kernel void SHEval3(float4* vel_in, float8* SHCoeff)
{
  float4 vel = vel_in[get_global_id(0)];
  float8 pSH;
  float fC0,fC1,fS0,fS1,fTmpA,fTmpB,fTmpC;
  float fZ2 = vel.z*vel.z;
  pSH.s1 = 0.4886025119029199f*vel.z;
  pSH.s5 = 0.9461746957575601f*fZ2 + -0.3153915652525201f;
  fC0 = vel.x;
  fS0 = vel.y;
  fTmpA = -0.48860251190292f;
  pSH.s2 = fTmpA*fC0;
  pSH.s0 = fTmpA*fS0;
  fTmpB = -1.092548430592079f*vel.z;
  pSH.s6 = fTmpB*fC0;
  pSH.s4 = fTmpB*fS0;
  fC1 = vel.x*fC0 - vel.y*fS0;
  fS1 = vel.x*fS0 + vel.y*fC0;
  fTmpC = 0.5462742152960395f;
  pSH.s7 = fTmpC*fC1;
  pSH.s3 = fTmpC*fS1;
  SHCoeff[get_global_id(0)] = pSH;
}
```

The result vector with the coefficients from the evaluation is then weighted by the scalar values of each component of an agent's direction vector. The weighted SH is summed up per cell using an optimized reduction kernel.

4.3 Reconstruction of the Avoidance Direction

BSH calculates the final avoidance force by evaluating the contribution of all cell coefficients along with those of other factors. The reconstruction kernel loads the SH coefficients for each cell; to improve performance, all agents in the same OpenCL workgroup move the coefficients into the fast local memory (i.e., loop blocking).

The avoidance force also accounts for the distance from the agent to the cell position (i.e., the center of the cell), and the direction of the agent itself. This calculation is performed on the SH coefficients and exploits some of the SH properties we have seen before. First, the contribution of c_{cell} is weighted to be inversely proportional to the distance from a to c with a scalar-vector product

$$c_d = \frac{1}{\|p_a - p_{cell}\|} c_{cell}$$

where p_a and p_c are, respectively, the position of a and c.

Successively, the resulting coefficients c_d are multiplied by a harmonical representation of the agent's direction vector (i.e., the avoidance force is stronger when the cell is in front of the agent and zero when behind it). Let c_a be the coefficients of agent directional SH functions. We recall that the product of two

SH functions is equal to the dot product of the two coefficient vectors; therefore our avoidance force for agent a and cell c is

$$R_{a \leftrightarrow c} = \hat{f}(d_{a \leftrightarrow c}) = \sum_{i=0}^{n} c_a(i) \cdot c_d(i) y_i(d_{a \leftrightarrow c})$$

For each agent a, the final long-distance avoidance force is calculated by summing up the contributions for all cells c in C:

$$R_a = \sum_{}^{c \in C} R_{a \leftrightarrow c}$$

and is added to the other agent rules (e.g., local collision avoidance).

5   Results

We tested our BSH implementation on a machine equipped with an AMD FX-6300 3.5Ghz processor and an NVIDIA GTX 960 GPU. The OpenCL code has been executed on the GPU, together with the OpenGL rendering code comprising vertex, fragment and geometry shaders. We tested different agent boid scenarios where our long-distance BSH-based model replaced the classical local-only Reynold's model. Test benchmarks focused on two aspects: performance and model evaluation. For performance, we investigated the scalability of the approach, comparing alternative bruteforce non-local approaches and analyzing the per-kernel runtime. For model evaluation, we compared BSH with a local model in known test scenarios where the lack of long-distance interaction leads to agent congestion.

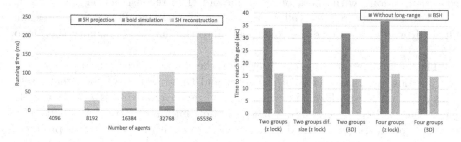

Fig. 2. Per-kernel runtime for the two-group z-lock scenario (left) and simulation runtime time for five tested scenarios (right) (Color figure online).

Per-Kernel Analysis and Agent Scalability. We first tested the per-kernel performance of our implementation on a crowd-like, two-group agent scene where agents were constrained to move only on the xy plane (z lock). Agents are initially positioned randomly in two spheres in the simulation space. Every agent has an assigned goal position at the opposite side of the simulation space and tries to move toward it. The initial directions (velocities) of all agents are set at a fixed value and aligned in the direction of the goal.

The spatial subdivision works better if the agent density is uniformly distributed over the uniform grid. In our test cases, density is higher at the position of the initial and final placement therefore performance degrades at these points. The reconstruction kernel performance is limited by the global memory access, an aspect greatly improved by our local memory cell-prefetching strategy. From this analysis, we conclude that there is still space for improvement, e.g., by changing the spatial subdivision and handling empty cells, which do not contribute to the result but are currently loaded into the memory.

Figure 2 (left) shows the time spent in SH construction and evaluation with different sizes. BSH long-range interaction complexity is $O(kN)$ instead of $O(N^2)$, where N is the number of agents and k the number of cells.

Fig. 3. Two-groups scenario without long-range interaction. $t = 3s$, $10s$ and $20s$ (Color figure online).

Behavioral Comparison with Local Models. We tried to replicate the same test benchmark of Golas et al. [7], where diametrically opposed groups try to move in opposite directions in space. Early detection of distant groups, combined with knowledge of agent direction, enable them to avoid the congestion in the center of the space. Tests were performed in both 3D and 2D (z axis locked) space, as the latter is both common in crowd simulations and more challenging for congestion because of agents' lack of freedom. We repeated the same test with two and four groups; runtimes to reach the goal (simulation times) are shown in Fig. 2 (right).

Figure 3 shows that, in the two-group scenario without long-range interaction, a congestion happens at time $t = 10s$. Figure 4, instead, shows respectively two equally sized (top) and different sized (bottom) groups that diametrically try to move in opposite directions using the BSH model. By enabling our BSH-based long-range interaction, each group reaches the target point in 15 s and no congestion happen.

In the more challenging four-group scenario, shown in Fig. 5: four groups of agents in a circular position try to reach the opposite position. Early, long-distance obstacle detection avoids the congestion so that each group *rotates* around the center instead of having a congestion there. We obtained interactive performance and reproduced the behavior modeled in [7] with a much simpler

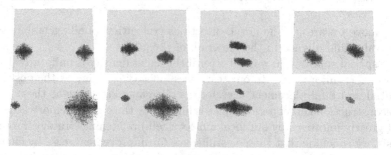

Fig. 4. BSH-based long-distance collision avoidance with two groups (z-lock). Equally sized (top) and unequal groups (bottom) are shown (Color figure online).

method than the original study's mixed approach, which used both continuum and discrete methods.

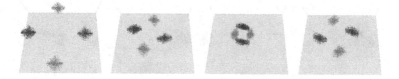

Fig. 5. BSH-based long-distance collision avoidance with four groups (z-lock) (Color figure online).

BSH is also quite flexible and can adapt to various obstacle-avoidance scenarios. We implemented two experimental scenarios where obstacle avoidance, typically based on vector fields, was replaced with few SH functions. Figure 6 illustrates the two examples discussed here. The advantages with respect of approaches based on vector fields is that they require few coefficients to describe an obstacle. For examples, the column from Fig. 6 (left) spans exactly one cell on the xz plane and 10 cells on the y axis; therefore, this scenario needs only 10 SH functions to simulate a repulsive, avoidance force for the three columns. The tunnel is modeled with directional SH repulsing only agents from one direction.

Fig. 6. Two obstacle avoidance scenarios: (left) two groups of agents avoiding three columns and (right) two one-way tunnels where agents are allowed to enter only the tunnel on their respective right side.

6   Conclusion

Behavioral spherical harmonics (BSH) is a novel approach for representing directional-dependent agent behaviors. BSH exploits the use of spherical harmonics to model the directional contribution of multiple agents with an approximated spherical function, which only requires a small coefficient vector. The approach is effective in drastically reducing the complexity of the directional evaluation, as it requires only a few agent-cell interactions instead of multiple interactions between agents.

We tested our BSH model on a long-range collision detection scenario. Our GPU parallel implementation reached interactive performance and replicated the test benchmark of state-of-the art approaches using a 3rd-order BSH that replaced all directional per-cell information with only 9 coefficients. BSH are also flexible enough to simulate more advanced obstacle collision avoidance scenarios (instead of classical vector fields-based solutions) and can be easily implemented on existing distributed and parallel simulation frameworks.

The source code is available under the BSD simplified license[2].

References

1. Cabral, B., Max, N., Springmeyer, R.: Bidirectional reflection functions from surface bump maps. In: Proceedings of the 14th Annual Conference on Computer Graphics and Interactive Techniques, SIGGRAPH 1987, pp. 273–281 (1987)
2. Cordasco, G., De Chiara, R., Mancuso, A., Mazzeo, D., Scarano, V., Spagnuolo, C.: A framework for distributing agent-based simulations. In: Alexander, M., D'Ambra, P., Belloum, A., Bosilca, G., Cannataro, M., Danelutto, M., Di Martino, B., Gerndt, M., Jeannot, E., Namyst, R., Roman, J., Scott, S.L., Traff, J.L., Vallée, G., Weidendorfer, J. (eds.) Euro-Par 2011, Part I. LNCS, vol. 7155, pp. 460–470. Springer, Heidelberg (2012)
3. Cordasco, G., Milone, F., Spagnuolo, C., Vicidomini, L.: Exploiting D-MASON on parallel platforms: a novel communication strategy. In: Lopes, L., Žilinskas, J., Costan, A., Cascella, R.G., Kecskemeti, G., Jeannot, E., Alexander, M., Hunold, S., Scott, S.L., Lankes, S., Lengauer, C., Carretero, J., Breitbart, J., Cannataro, M., Ricci, L., Benkner, S., Petit, S., Scarano, V., Gracia, J. (eds.) Euro-Par 2014, Part I. LNCS, vol. 8805, pp. 407–417. Springer, Heidelberg (2014)
4. Cosenza, B., Cordasco, G., Chiara, R.D., Scarano, V.: Distributed load balancing for parallel agent-based simulations. In: 19th International Euromicro Conference on Parallel, Distributed and Network-based Processing (PDP), pp. 62–69 (2011)
5. Erra, U., Frola, B., Scarano, V.: BehaveRT: a GPU-based library for autonomous characters. In: Boulic, R., Chrysanthou, Y., Komura, T. (eds.) MIG 2010. LNCS, vol. 6459, pp. 194–205. Springer, Heidelberg (2010)
6. Erra, U., Frola, B., Scarano, V., Couzin, I.: An efficient GPU implementation for large scale individual-based simulation of collective behavior. In: International Workshop on High Performance Computational Systems Biology (HIBI), pp. 51–58 (2009)

---

[2] http://bcosenza.github.io/bsh.

7. Golas, A., Narain, R., Curtis, S., Lin, M.C.: Hybrid long-range collision avoidance for crowd simulation. IEEE Trans. Visual. Comput. Graphics **20**(7), 1022–1034 (2014)
8. Grasso, I., Ritter, M., Cosenza, B., Benger, W., Hofstetter, G., Fahringer, T.: Point distribution tensor computation on heterogeneous systems. Procedia Comput. Sci. (ICCS) **51**, 160–169 (2015)
9. Green, R.: Spherical harmonic lighting: the gritty details. In: GDC, vol. 56 (2003)
10. Green, S.: Particle simulation using cuda. Technical report, NVIDIA (2010)
11. Guy, S.J., Chhugani, J., Curtis, S., Dubey, P., Lin, M., Manocha, D.: Pledestrians: a least-effort approach to crowd simulation. In: ACM SIGGRAPH/EG Symposium on Computer Animation, pp. 119–128 (2010)
12. Guy, S.J., Chhugani, J., Kim, C., Satish, N., Lin, M., Manocha, D., Dubey, P.: Clearpath: highly parallel collision avoidance for multi-agent simulation. In: ACM SIGGRAPH/EG Symposium on Computer Animation, pp. 177–187. SCA (2009)
13. Kaplanyan, A., Dachsbacher, C.: Cascaded light propagation volumes for real-time indirect illumination. In: ACM SIGGRAPH Symposium on Interactive 3D Graphics and Games, pp. 99–107. I3D (2010)
14. Khronos Group: Khronos Group. The OpenCL 2.0 specification (2014)
15. Luke, S., Cioffi-Revilla, C., Panait, L., Sullivan, K., Balan, G.: Mason: a multiagent simulation environment. Simulation **81**(7), 517–527 (2005)
16. Narain, R., Golas, A., Curtis, S., Lin, M.C.: Aggregate dynamics for dense crowd simulation. In: ACM SIGGRAPH Asia, pp. 122:1–122:8 (2009)
17. North, M.J., Collier, N.T., Vos, J.R.: Experiences creating three implementations of the repast agent modeling toolkit. ACM Trans. Model. Comput. Simul. **16**(1), 1–25 (2006)
18. Passos, E.B., Joselli, M., Zamith, M., Clua, E.W.G., Montenegro, A., Conci, A., Feijo, B.: A bidimensional data structure and spatial optimization for supermassive crowd simulation on GPU. Comput. Entertain. **7**(4), 60:1–60:15 (2010)
19. Richmond, P., Walker, D.C., Coakley, S., Romano, D.M.: High performance cellular level agent-based simulation with FLAME for the GPU. Briefings Bioinform. **11**(3), 334–347 (2010)
20. Sloan, P.P.: Stupid Spherical Harmonics (SH) Tricks (2008)
21. Sloan, P.P.: Efficient spherical harmonic evaluation. J. Comput. Graphics Tech. (JCGT) **2**(2), 84–90 (2013)
22. Treuille, A., Cooper, S., Popović, Z.: Continuum crowds. ACM Trans. Graph. **25**(3), 1160–1168 (2006)

Graph-Based Automatic Dynamic Load Balancing for HPC Agent-Based Simulations

Claudio Márquez[(✉)], Eduardo César, and Joan Sorribes

Computer Architecture and Operating Systems Department (CAOS),
Universitat Autònoma de Barcelona, 08193 Bellaterra, Spain
claudio.marquez@caos.uab.es, {eduardo.cesar,joan.sorribes}@uab.cat
http://caos.uab.es/

Abstract. The main problem of Agent-Based Modelling (ABM) simulations in High Performance Computing (HPC) is load imbalance due to a non-uniform distribution of the agents that may generate uneven computation and increase communication overhead, inhibiting the efficiency of the available computing resources. Moreover, the agents' behaviours can considerably modify the workload at each simulation step thereby affecting the workload progression of the simulation. In order to mitigate such problems, automatic mechanisms for dynamically adjusting the computation and/or communication workload are needed. For this reason, we introduce an Automatic Dynamic Load Balancing (ADLB) strategy to reduce imbalance problems as the simulation proceeds. The ADLB tunes the global simulation workload migrating groups of agents among the processes according to their computation workload and their message connectivity map modelled using a Hypergraph. This Hypergraph is partitioned using the Zoltan Parallel HyperGraph partitioner method (PHG). In addition, to prevent excessive all-to-all communications, the ADLB uses filtering routines to send message groups to specified recipient processes in a simple 3D grid-based structure. Our method has been tested with a biological ABM using the framework Flexible Large-scale Agent Modelling Environment (Flame), obtaining a significant impact on the application performance.

Keywords: Agent-based simulation · Graph partitioning · Message filtering · Load balancing · Performance tuning · HPC · SPMD · Flame

1 Introduction

Agent-Based Modelling (ABM) describes the system's behaviour through the interaction of a set of autonomous entities called agents in a virtual environment. The agents' behaviour is decided by sets of agent's internal operations

C. Márquez, E. César and J. Sorribes—This work has been partially supported by MICINN-Spain under contract TIN2011- 28689-C02-01 and TIN2014-53234-C2-1-R and GenCat-DIUiE(GRR) 2014-SGR-576. This research was also partially performed by a collaboration agreement with the Department of Physiology and Medical Physics at the Royal College of Surgeons in Ireland (RCSI), under the project ANGIOPREDICT: European Union FP7-funded (http://www.angiopredict.com).

© Springer International Publishing Switzerland 2015
S. Hunold et al. (Eds.): Euro-Par 2015 Workshops, LNCS 9523, pp. 405–416, 2015.
DOI: 10.1007/978-3-319-27308-2_33

and information data exchange between agents. Depending on the complexity order of these operations and exchanges, the workload of the ABM simulation may progress irregularly, producing significant variations on the workload of the entire system. All these issues negatively affect the simulation time and, in most cases, they inhibit the efficiency of the computing resources available. Consequently, when a large number of agents with complex interaction rules are simulated in a High Performance Computing (HPC) infrastructure, to be aware of these issues becomes essential.

In HPC ABM simulations, a non-uniform distribution of the agents' workload may introduce uneven CPU computing and network communication workload that delay the simulation and may propagate across all processes. This load-imbalance problem is well known in Single Process Multiple Data (SPMD) programming paradigm, which consists of a unique code replicated in all processes running on different data sets. These SPMD applications are comprised by sets of computation and synchronisation phases. In time-driven cases, these phases are repeated in each simulation step. In the same way, the communication phases of the simulation become expensive as the number of processes increases. Besides, the uneven CPU workload will also impact negatively the completion time of the simulation steps. With the purpose of mitigate such problems, automatic mechanisms for dynamically adjusting the computation and/or communication load are needed.

According to the execution of the tuning decisions, the load balancing strategies for HPC applications can be developed using centralised/hierarchical and decentralised approaches [11]. The centralised/hierarchical approaches report a high computational cost and scalability problems. On the other hand, decentralised approaches can present problems regarding the quality balance because the neighbouring processes exchange incomplete information. Whilst many load-balancing solutions can be found such as: [12–15]; these have rarely been incorporated to a multi-purpose environment. For this reason, we have been progressively developing a load balancing strategy for multi-purpose environments of ABM simulations as can be seen in [6–8].

In this paper, we present a Graph-based Automatic Dynamic Load Balancing (ADLB) strategy that allows automatic and dynamic tuning decisions in terms of computation/communication workload. The ADLB tunes the global simulation workload migrating groups of agents among the processes using a Hypergraph perspective. This Hypergraph is partitioned using the Zoltan Parallel Hyper-Graph partitioner method (PHG) [4]. In order to achieve a suitable management of the agent communications, the ADLB uses message filtering routines for sending message groups to specified recipient processes in a simple 3D grid-based structure. Our method has been tested with a biological ABM using the framework Flexible Large-scale Agent Modelling Environment (Flame), obtaining a significant impact on the application performance.

This paper is arranged in five sections. First, Sect. 2 presents the algorithm for grouping agents in a 3D grid structure and the mechanism for filtering messages based in this structure. Next, the Graph-based partitioning method is explained, and then the ADLB operation is described. The results section presents the ADLB operation for a cancer developing ABM. The final section includes the conclusions and future work.

2   3D Spatial Agent Organisation

In order to reduce the amount of agent messages in the system, a mechanism for avoiding broadcasting is needed. However, such mechanism can not rely in storing the location of each agent involved in a communication because storing this information becomes unmanageable when a large number of agents with complex interaction rules is simulated. An intermediate solution consists of grouping agents using for example a 3D grid-based structure that organises the agents' locations using a virtual division of the space to ease the message management by the simulation platform.

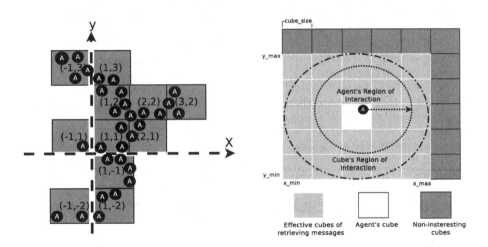

Fig. 1. Cubes covering agents' space.   **Fig. 2.** Interaction ranges.

The 3D grid-based structure divides the whole space in 3D cubic regions and builds them using a *rasterisation* approach where the objects are characterised from its shape within a 2D/3D space [10]. In the same way, the cubes of our 3D structure are only created according to the space occupied by agents. Similar approaches have been designed in 2D particle simulations [2]. Thanks to this approach, it is possible to model an indefinitely large domain. Following Fig. 2, the *cube_size* defines cubic regions of dimension *cube_size* x *cube_size* x *cube_size*. The value of *cube_size* should be estimated in accordance with the *influence range* of the agents. This influence range is usually named *halo* in the literature [9], and it is explained later.

As **Grid Construction Algorithm,** each cube is built on the fly by a function that maps each agent coordinates to its container cube (algorithm 1 shows this operation, $\lceil coordinate/cube\_size \rceil$). As a result, each cube identifier is composed of three integers that are a combination of the x-, y- and z-axis ids.

In this manner, every agent will be assigned to only one cube, and all cubes will have a positive agent counter. These cubes will be constructed along with the exploration of the existing agents across processes. The space covered by cubes is named *known space*, so new cubes will appear when an agent is located outside the known space. If an agent is located within the known space, the agent counter belonging to its agent's cube region is increased. Finally, only the agent's regions will be covered by multiple 3D cubes (Fig. 1 depicts this principle in a 2D space).

Algorithm 1. Grid Construction	**Algorithm 2.** Cube Interaction
$c\_size \leftarrow$ cube length	$c\_range \leftarrow ceil(agent\_range/c\_size)$
$c\_group_i \leftarrow$ cubes in $parallel\_process_i$	$global\_group \leftarrow$ cubes in all processes
for each $agent \in parallel\_process_i$ **do**	**for each** $agent \in parallel\_process_i$ **do**
$\quad xyz \leftarrow xyz$-coordinate of $agent$	$\quad agent\_cube \leftarrow \{cid_x, cid_y, cid_z\}$
$\quad cid_x \leftarrow ceil(x\ /\ c\_size)$	$\quad$ **for each** $cube \in global\_group$ **do**
$\quad cid_y \leftarrow ceil(y\ /\ c\_size)$	$\quad\quad c_x \leftarrow x$-component of $cube$
$\quad cid_z \leftarrow ceil(z\ /\ c\_size)$	$\quad\quad c_y \leftarrow y$-component of $cube$
$\quad agent\_cube \leftarrow \{cid_x, cid_y, cid_z\}$	$\quad\quad c_z \leftarrow z$-component of $cube$
$\quad$ **if** $agent\_cube \in c\_group_i$ **then**	$\quad\quad$ **if** $agent\_cube \in [c_{xyz} \pm c\_range]$
$\quad\quad$ ++$agent\_counter$ of $agent\_cube$	$\quad\quad$ **then**
$\quad$ **else**	$\quad\quad\quad cube \in$ the interaction region
$\quad\quad$ add $agent\_cube$ to c_group_i	$\quad\quad$ **end if**
$\quad$ **end if**	$\quad$ **end for**
end for	**end for**

Algorithm 2 shows the **Cube Interaction Algorithm.** This algorithm simplifies the access to the information of relations among the agents. Likewise, the recipient cubes of an agent message can be determined using its *halo*. Additionally, this algorithm helps to distinguish whether the recipients of an agent message are located in a cube belonging to another process or not; hence the required external network communications can be predicted. The global view of the cubes is defined gathering the cube information from every process. This global cube information contains the cube's *ternary ids* and the number of agents within each cube (the latter just for load balancing purposes). In the same way, the agent's *message connectivity map* can be built using the Cube Interaction Algorithm. The estimation of the interaction regions is performed through an Euclidean distance calculation (Algorithm 2 shows this operation). In Algorithm 2 the cube's *halo* (interval $[c_{xyz} - c\_range, c_{xyz} + c\_range]$) is obtained by dividing the agent interaction range by *cube_size* value. As explained in [8], the *halo* defines the range of the agents' messages, and hence, using this *halo*, the agents' messages can be filtered in order to avoid broadcast communications.

3 Graph-Based Agent Partitioning

The graph partitioning in HPC applications allows to represent the connectivity of different computational structures to decompose the computational domains for parallelisation. The goal is to divide the graph into equal sized sub-graphs while minimising the number of edges between different sub-graphs. In our case, these sub-graphs could represent a sub-domain of computing workload while the edges between them could represent the required communication network that need to be balanced by the ADLB. However, the communication representation offered by graph edges does not accurately represent the actual interaction of the agents as we need because agent messages may have more than one recipient. For this reason, the hypergraph partitioning approach fits better to agent interactions than graph approaches.

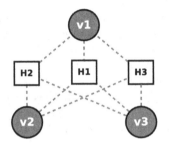

Fig. 3. Hyperedges representation.

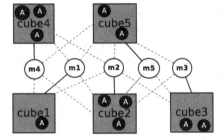

Fig. 4. Communication of cubes.

The hypergraphs contain hyperedges which connect two or more vertices as well as the agent communications having more than one recipient. Figure 3 shows an example of hyperedges denoted as H1-H2-H3 and their respective vertices are denoted as v1-v2-v3. On the other hand, hypergraph partitioning is computationally more expensive than graph partitioning, which is already NP-hard [5]. In order to reduce the excessive memory/communication requirements, we have considered the cubes as vertices and their communication connectivity as hyperedges. Additionally, the number of agents and the volume of messages per cube are added as vertices and hyperedges' weights respectively (Fig. 4 depicts this approach).

Having a proper representation of groups of agent interactions, it will help the ADLB not only to reduce the workload requirements, but also to have a proper spatial representation of the simulation as long as its workload develops variations. In ADLB, the hypergraph partitioning method has been included as the load balancing criterion.

4 Automatic Dynamic Load Balancing

As we mentioned before, agent-based applications workload can vary during the simulation due to issues related to the complexity of the model, and interaction patterns. The ADLB decides the global reconfiguration of the workload when the performance measures indicate imbalances according to an imbalance threshold value. The threshold is a value between 0.0 and 1.0 that represents the acceptable percentage of imbalance over/under the mean. Computing times and number of agents are monitored at each parallel process. This monitoring is repeated at the beginning of each iteration, then the measures are shared among the processes. Hence, each process knows the global workload situation and executes the algorithm with the same input. Consequently, all processes calculate the same reconfiguration of the workload without a central decision unit. The components of ADLB are described below.

The **automatic monitoring** component launches the load balancing procedure when the imbalance factor exceeds the given threshold. The monitoring is executed by all processes; hence each process needs to know the global load situation, thereby the processes workload measures are broadcasted along with the simulation synchronisation at the end of each iteration. In these cases, the computing time must be determined using the previous iteration results and the current number of agents because the current computing time is obtained at the end of the iteration. The predicted current computing time is described in Eq. 1. This information is broadcasted over all processes to have the global workload information and assess the imbalance degree in the activation mechanism.

$$comp\_time_{iter} = \frac{comp\_time_{iter-1} * num\_agents_{iter}}{num\_agents_{iter-1}} \tag{1}$$

In the **activation mechanism,** the process imbalance factors are calculated using the broadcasted current computing time. The imbalance factor represents the degree of imbalance according to the computing time mean. The tolerance establishes the range considered as balanced. Furthermore, depending on the tolerance range, workload imbalances can be detected (Eqs. 2 and 3 show the imbalance factor, the tolerance and the tolerance range). Consequently, as every process executes this analysis with the same inputs, the reconfiguration procedure is triggered across processes when an excessive imbalance appears.

$$ib\_factor_i = \frac{comp\_time_i}{avg\_time} \tag{2} \qquad\qquad tolerance = avg\_time * threshold \tag{3}$$
$$tolerance\_range = avg\_time \pm tolerance$$

In the **reconfiguration procedure,** ADLB decides the amount of agents and the place where the agents need to be reallocated. The reallocation is performed according to the Zoltan PHG decision [4], but at this point, the global cube connectivity map needs to be transformed into a hypergraph represented as a sparse matrix. Moreover, each hypergraph vertex id must have a unique global identifier represented as an unsigned integer. Due to the vertices depict spatial cubes which, in turn, are set of agents, ADLB must be sure that the global cube ids are unique and each parallel process has unique cubes. To accomplish this, agents belonging to external cubes need to be migrated before, then sharing the cube's location and the computing workload per cube in order to define unique global cube ids and vertex weights. Later, each parallel process stores its global cube connectivity map into a CSR sparse matrix format (CSC format is also allowed by PHG). Then, PHG performs the parallel hypergraph partitioning and returns the vertex ids that should be imported and exported. In the same way, the degree of hypergraph cutting accuracy could be set up using PHG configuration parameters. Finally, in accordance with the PHG results, ADLB will introduce *send* and *receive* agent requests across the parallel processes. After the agent migration occurs, the platform should take back the control of the simulation.

5 Experimental Results

In this section, we are focused on analysing the preliminary performance results of ADLB in a real parallel SPMD ABM platform. The experiments have been performed using the Flame platform with a biological ABM (this model is explained further on).

Flame [3] is a C/MPI-based parallel code generator that allows to run simulations on large HPC systems from an XML/C model definition (Fig. 5 shows the functional diagram). The Flame engine (xparser) parses the model definition and generates parallel code deployed under a SPMD paradigm, thereby, implies a unique code replicated among all the processes that performs a set of computing and communication phases. In Flame, the interaction between agents is handled by the message board library libmboard, which provides message memory management and message data synchronisation routines using MPI. Therefore, the agents only interact sending messages to the board library, so all messages have to be stored in a board before starting the board synchronisation

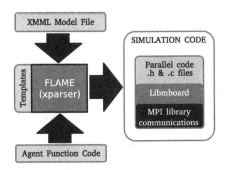

Fig. 5. Functional description of Flame.

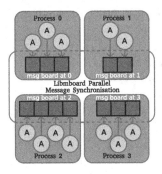

Fig. 6. Flame communication model

(see Fig. 6). Hence, libmboard organises the messages before being dispatched in such a way that the communication between processes is overlapped with computation via non-blocking MPI communications. Once the synchronisation has been completed, every parallel process will maintain a unified view of the message board. Finally, the agents should read their messages of interest from the synchronised board. However, Flame does not provide routines intended to reconfigure the computing and communication workload during the execution of the simulation. For this reason, the necessary modules to solve these requirements such as agent migration, message filtering, agent connectivity mapping and performance measurement management have been implemented in Flame. Once these functionalities are implemented, ADLB is capable of reconfiguring the global workload in accordance with the simulation workload measures.

The use case is an agent-based model that represents an expansive in-vivo tumour development behaviour [1]. This model is composed of tumour cells and tumour-associated endothelial cells which are implemented as agents. In each iteration, the agents interact computing the expansion coordinates of new cells, forces among the cells, amount of nutrients that comes from the vessels, amount of oxygen permeated through the cells as well as new coordinates using the resulting forces. Later, these procedures will determine either the growth or the death of each tumour or endothelial cell. Consequently, this model presents computing/communication workload imbalances as the simulation proceeds. Figure 7 shows a graphical representation of the model where the grey and black spheres represent tumour cell and endothelial cell agents respectively.

In terms of the initial partitioning methods, geometric and round-robin strategies are provided by Flame (FlameGeo and FlameRR respectively). The geometric approach divides the space into non-overlapping orthogonal regions depending on the spatial space simulation dimensions assigning agents according their spatial coordinates. And the round-robin approach randomly assigns agents across all processes in a way that each process stores approximately an even number of agents. Compared with the Zoltan PHG approach, the Flame partitioning methods offer worse partition quality as has been shown in [8]. Therefore, we have opted for implementing the Zoltan Hypergraph-based initial partitioning in order to ensure a better partitioning quality from the beginning

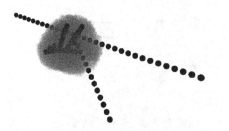

Fig. 7. Tumour development model.   **Fig. 8.** PHG grid distribution.

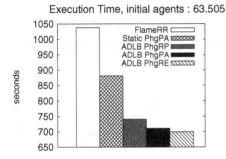

Execution Time, initial agents : 63.505

Fig. 9. Execution times.

Table 1. Flame times vs. ADLB times.

Approach	LB (sec)	Total (sec)
FlameGeo	-	26218.9
FlameRR	-	1038.1
Static PhgPA	-	881.3
ADLB PhgRP	83.3	741.3
ADLB PhgPA	63.4	710.7
ADLB PhgRE	56.9	699.7

of the simulation. In this way, we can assess the ADLB performance impacts starting from a better distribution of the agents and better message filtering.

Within the Zoltan PHG setup parameters, the hypergraph approach can be configured as *partition, repartition,* or *refine.* In the partition mode (PhgPA) the current vertices distribution is not taken into account (a partition from scratch). In the repartition mode (PhgRP) the current vertices distribution is considered to cut the hypergraph. Finally, the refine mode (PhgRE) refines the given distribution minimising the number of changes. Figure 8 shows an example of PhgPA partitioning over the resulting 3D grid of the tumour model. In addition, the PHG cut accuracy has been set up to 20 % of imbalance deemed acceptable in order to reduce the required time to find an appropriate graph cut, and all the initial graph partitions have been performed using the PhgPA mode.

The following results correspond to 20 iterations of the tumour development model executed using 128 processors. The results were obtained using Flame 0.17.0, libmboard 0.3.1 and OpenMPI 1.6.4. The experiments were executed on an IBM Cluster with the following features: 32 IBM x3550 Nodes, 2xDual-Core Intel(R) Xeon(R) CPU 5160 @ 3.00 GHz 4MB L2 (2×2), 12 GB Fully Buffered DIMM 667 MHz, Hot-swap SAS Controller 160GB SATA Disk and Integrated dual Gigabit Ethernet. In these experiments, 63.505 cells are simulated and their interaction range is 25 microns. The *cube_size* is defined as 50 microns in order to reduce the number of vertices computed by PHG.

Figure 9 shows the execution times of the ADLB versions by comparing different PHG options with two static approaches (the FlameRR default option and initial PhgPA partitioning with message filtering). Here, the ADLB versions obtain better results than the static approaches FlameRR and static PhgPA. FlameGeo has been excluded from this figure because its execution time excessively surpasses the other times, however, its execution time is contained in Table 1. As FlameGeo parts the space into orthogonal rectangles, it creates uneven or empty partitions according to the agents' spatial locations. In the same way, the FlameRR randomly distributes the agents generating a similar number of agents per process. The PHG versions gain more than 30 % over the FlameRR experiment in terms of execution time, even an initial PhgPA partitioning improves the Flame times using messages filtering. Basically, the hypergraph partitioning methods in ADLB shows similar results and the main difference relies on the total PHG overhead time as shown in the second column of Table 1.

Table 2. Details of the ADLB options.

Hypergraph method	Number ADLB calls	Average vertices per call	% Total messages internal/external	Cubes map construction (sec)	Zoltan time (sec)	Migration time (sec)	Total time (sec)
PhgRP	10	3746	95.95/4.05	10.3	70.1	2.9	83.3
PhgPA	10	3743	96.57/3.43	7.3	54.0	2.1	63.4
PhgRE	9	3745	96.53/3.47	8.8	45.1	3.0	56.9

Table 2 shows the ADLB development, its communication workload and its overhead composition summary. For all versions, the number of ADLB calls and average number of vertices is similar. The main difference is rooted in the Zoltan PHG time required for cutting the hypergraph. Furthermore, repartitioning the current partition (PhgRP) is expensive compared with partitioning from scratch (PhgPA), and refining the hypergraph (PhgRE) is the best approach for these experiments. Even so, ADLB reduces simulation time as well as the number of communications among the parallel processes. Additionally, Table 2 also shows the impact of the message filtering over the communication workload. As a matter of fact, the percentage of the amount of messages that are held in the sender process is higher than the messages dispatched to external parallel processes (internal/external respectively). In the same manner, dispatching a small amount of messages also impacts directly the performance of the recipient processes because these have to examine a smaller amount of messages and, later on, determine its significance. As a result, the ADLB strategy enhances the performance of the parallel simulation using agent migration, message filtering, agent connectivity mapping and performance measures monitoring.

6   Conclusion and Future Work

When the ABMs present irregular computing/communication patterns due to the complexity and the large number of agents, the HPC ABM simulation platforms need to be able to reallocate workload as the simulation proceeds. This is a difficult task because the platform should implement features such as agent migration, message filtering, agent connectivity mapping and performance measures monitoring. Moreover, the platform should decide the appropriate moment to launch the load balancing mechanism and decide the amount of workload to be reallocated. Therefore, to solve this need, we present the Automatic Dynamic

Load Balancing (ADLB) that implements the issues mentioned previously in order to improve the performance of the HPC ABM simulation platform.

In this paper, the ADLB is proven in a model with workload variability due to agent creation and elimination. Additionally, the ADLB decision to reconfigure the workload is tested using three methods of hypergraph partitioning. For these cases, our schema obtains good results reducing the simulation execution time up to 30 %. All in all, our approach gives better performance than the standard Flame partitioning methods, and our results confirm the importance of introducing the components of ADLB presented in this paper. The overhead of ADLB is mostly given by the execution of the Zoltan PHG method. In spite of that, its benefits directly impact the efficiency of the message filtering mechanism and the workload reconfiguration. Also, the overhead results suggest that reducing the number of vertices by increasing the *cube_size* could reduce the Zoltan overhead.

As future work, we want to find a proper cube size that minimises the Zoltan PHG overhead and keeps good performance filtering messages. In the same way, it is planned to test ADLB using other ABMs.

References

1. Angiopredict: Predictive genomic biomarkers methods for combination bevacizumab (avastin) therapy in metastatic colorectal cancer ANGIOPREDICT. EU's Framework Programme Seven (FP7) under contract 306021 (2014). http://www. angiopredict.com/
2. Bithell, M., Macmillan, W.: Escape from the cell: spatially explicit modelling with and without grids. Ecol. Model. **200**(1–2), 59–78 (2007)
3. Coakley, S., Gheorghe, M., Holcombe, M., Chin, S., Worth, D., Greenough, C.: Exploitation of high performance computing in the flame agent-based simulation framework. In: 2012 IEEE 9th International Conference on High Performance Computing and Communication, 2012 IEEE 14th International Conference on Embedded Software and Systems (HPCC-ICESS), pp. 538–545, June 2012
4. Devine, K., Boman, E., Heaphy, R., Bisseling, R., Catalyurek, U.: Parallel hypergraph partitioning for scientific computing. In: 20th International Parallel and Distributed Processing Symposium, IPDPS 2006, p. 10, April 2006
5. Lengauer, T.: Combinatorial Algorithms for Integrated Circuit Layout. Wiley, New York (1990)
6. Márquez, C., César, E., Sorribes, J.: A load balancing schema for agent-based SPMD applications. In: Parallel and Distributed Processing Techniques and Applications (2013)
7. Márquez, C., César, E., Sorribes, J.: Agent migration in HPC systems using FLAME. In: an Mey, D., Alexander, M., Bientinesi, P., Cannataro, M., Clauss, C., Costan, A., Kecskemeti, G., Morin, C., Ricci, L., Sahuquillo, J., Schulz, M., Scarano, V., Scott, S.L., Weidendorfer, J. (eds.) Euro-Par 2013. LNCS, vol. 8374, pp. 523–532. Springer, Heidelberg (2014)
8. Márquez, C., César, E., Sorribes, J.: Impact of message filtering on HPC agent-based simulations. In: Proceedings of 28th European Simulation and Modelling Conference, ESM 2014, pp. 65–72. EUROSIS (2014)

9. Parry, H.R., Bithell, M.: Large scale agent-based modelling: a review and guidelines for model scaling. In: Heppenstall, A.J., Crooks, A.T., See, L.M., Batty, M. (eds.) Agent-Based Models of Geographical Systems, pp. 271–308. Springer, Dordrecht (2012)

10. Petkovic, T., Loncaric, S.: Supercover plane rasterization - a rasterization algorithm for generating supercover plane inside a cube. In: GRAPP (GM/R 2007, pp. 327–332 (2007)

11. Plastino, A., Ribeiro, C.C., Rodriguez, N.: Developing spmd applications with load balancing. Parallel Comput. **29**(6), 743–766 (2003). http://dx.doi.org/10.1016/S0167-8191(03)00060-7

12. Solar, R., Suppi, R., Luque, E.: Proximity load balancing for distributed cluster-based individual-oriented fish school simulations. Procedia Comput. Sci. **9**, 328–337 (2012). Proceedings of the International Conference on Computational Science, ICCS 2012

13. Vigueras, G., Lozano, M., Orduña, J.M.: Workload balancing in distributed crowd simulations: the partitioning method. J. Supercomput. **58**(2), 261–269 (2011)

14. Zhang, D., Jiang, C., Li, S.: A fast adaptive load balancing method for parallel particle-based simulations. Simul. Model. Pract. Theor. **17**(6), 1032–1042 (2009)

15. Zheng, G., Meneses, E., Bhatele, A., Kale, L.V.: Hierarchical load balancing for Charm++ applications on large supercomputers. In: Proceedings of the 2010 39th International Conference on Parallel Processing Workshops, ICPPW 2010, pp. 436–444. IEEE Computer Society, Washington, DC (2010)

Preliminary Evaluation of a Parallel Trace Replay Tool for HPC Network Simulations

Bilge Acun[1][✉], Nikhil Jain[1], Abhinav Bhatele[2], Misbah Mubarak[3], Christopher D. Carothers[4], and Laxmikant V. Kale[1]

[1] Department of Computer Science,
University of Illinois at Urbana-Champaign, Urbana, USA
{acun2,nikhil,kale}@illinois.edu
[2] Center for Applied Scientific Computing,
Lawrence Livermore National Laboratory, Livermore, CA, USA
bhatele@llnl.gov
[3] Mathematics and Computer Science Division,
Argonne National Laboratory, Argonne, USA
mmubarak@anl.gov
[4] Department of Computer Science, Rensselaer Polytechnic Institute, Troy, USA
chrisc@cs.rpi.edu

Abstract. This paper presents a preliminary evaluation of TRACER, a trace replay tool built upon the ROSS-based CODES simulation framework. TRACER can be used for predicting network performance and understanding network behavior by simulating messaging on interconnection networks. It addresses two major shortcomings in current network simulators. First, it enables fast and scalable simulations of large-scale supercomputer networks. Second, it can simulate production HPC applications using BigSim's emulation framework. In addition to introducing TRACER, this paper studies the impact of input parameters on simulation performance. We also compare TRACER with other network simulators such as SST and BigSim, and demonstrate TRACER's scalability using various case studies.

1 Introduction

The design and deployment of large supercomputers with hundreds of thousands of cores is a daunting task. Both at the design stage and after the machine is installed, several decisions about the node architecture and the interconnection network need to be made. Application developers and end users are often interested in studying the effects of these decisions on their codes' performance for existing and future machines. Hence, tools that can predict these effects are important. This paper focuses on tools for predicting the impact of interconnection networks on the communication performance of parallel codes.

Prediction of communication performance on a hypothetical or actual machine requires simulating the network architecture and its components.

© Springer International Publishing Switzerland 2015
S. Hunold et al. (Eds.): Euro-Par 2015 Workshops, LNCS 9523, pp. 417–429, 2015.
DOI: 10.1007/978-3-319-27308-2_34

Discrete-event simulation (DES) based frameworks are often used to simulate interconnection networks. The usability and performance of these frameworks depend on many factors: sequential versus parallel (PDES) simulation, the level of detail at which the communication is simulated (e.g., flit-level or packet-level), whether the PDES uses conservative or optimistic parallelism methods, etc.

Existing state-of-the-art DES-based network simulators suffer from two major problems. First, sequential simulators have large memory footprints and long execution times when simulating large execution traces. Second, some simulators can only simulate synthetic communication patterns that do not accurately represent production high-performance computing applications. These shortcomings can be eliminated by using a scalable PDES engine, which improves performance and reduces the memory footprint per node, and by replaying execution traces generated from production HPC codes. To achieve this, we have developed a trace replay tool called TRACER for simulating messaging on HPC networks.

TRACER is designed as an application on top of the CODES simulation framework [6]. It uses traces generated by BigSim's emulation framework [17] to simulate an application's communication behavior by leveraging the network API exposed by CODES. Under the hood, CODES uses the Rensselaer Optimistic Simulation System (ROSS) as the PDES engine to drive the simulation [4].

The major contributions of this work are as follows:

- We present a trace-driven simulator that executes under an optimistic parallel discrete-event paradigm using reversible computing for real HPC codes.
- We show that TRACER outperforms state-of-the-art simulators like BigSim and SST in serial mode.
- We present a simulation parameter study to identify parameter values that maximize performance for simulating real HPC traffic workloads.
- We demonstrate the scalability of TRACER and show that it can simulate HPC workloads on half a million nodes in under 10 minutes using 512 cores.

2   Background and Related Work

TRACER is built upon several existing tools which are introduced briefly below.

BigSim's Emulation Framework: The first requirement of simulating a parallel execution is the ability to record the control flow and communication pattern of an application. The BigSim emulation framework [17] exploits the concept of virtualization in CHARM++ [12] to execute a large number of processes on a smaller number of physical cores and generate traces. This enables trace generation for networks of sizes that have not been built yet. Using AMPI [9], this feature enables trace generation for production MPI applications as well.

ROSS PDES Engine: ROSS [4] is a general purpose, massively parallel, discrete-event simulator. ROSS allows users to define logical processes (LPs) distributed among processors and to schedule time-stamped events either locally or remotely. ROSS provides two execution modes: conservative and optimistic. The *conservative* mode executes an event for an LP only when it is guaranteed to be the next lowest time-stamped event for it. On the other hand, the *optimistic* mode aggressively executes events that have the lowest time-stamps among the current set of events. If an event with time-stamp lower than the last executed event is encountered for an LP, *reverse handlers* are executed for the events executed out of order to undo their effects.

CODES: The CODES framework is built on top of ROSS to facilitate studies of HPC storage and network systems [6]. The network component of CODES, Model-net, provides an API to simulate the flow of messages on HPC networks using either detailed congestion models or theoretical models such as LogP. Model-net allows users to instantiate a prototype network based on one of these models. Such instantiations are controlled by parameters such as network type, dimensions, link bandwidth, link latency, packet size, buffer size, etc. CODES has been used to study the behavior of HPC networks for a few traffic patterns [6]. These traffic patterns have been implemented as one-off applications that use Model-net as a network driver. Recently, an application to replay DUMPI [1] traces has also been added to CODES.

2.1 Related Work

BigSim is one of the earliest simulators that supports packet-level network simulation [17]. It is based on the POSE PDES engine [16] which has high overheads and impacts the scaling performance of the simulator. Structural Simulation Toolkit (SST) [10] provides both online (skeleton application based) and offline (DUMPI [1] trace based) modes for simulation. However, it uses a conservative PDES engine, does not support packet-level simulation in parallel builds, and has limited scalability with flow-based models. Booksim [11] is a sequential cycle-accurate simulator that supports several topologies, but is extremely slow.

There are several network simulators that are either sequential and/or do not provide detailed packet-level (or flit-level) network simulation and/or trace-based simulation. These include the Extreme-scale Simulator (xSim) [3], DIMEMAS [7], LogGOPSim [8], MPI-Netsim [15], OMNet++ [13], and Sim-Grid [5].

3   Design and Implementation of TraceR

TRACER is designed as an application on top of the CODES simulation framework. Figure 1 (left) provides an overview of TRACER's integration with BigSim and CODES. The two primary inputs to TRACER are the traces generated by BigSim and the configuration parameters describing the interconnection network to be simulated. The meta-data in the traces is used to initialize the simulated processes. The network configuration parameters are passed to CODES to initialize the prototype network design.

We define the following terminology to describe the working of TRACER:

PE: Each simulated process (called PE) is a logical process (LP) visible to ROSS. It stores virtual time, logical state, and the status of tasks to be executed by it.

Task: The trace for a PE is a collection of tasks, each of which represents a sequential execution block (SEB). A task may have multiple backward dependencies to other tasks or to message arrivals. At startup, all tasks are marked *undone*. If a task has an *undone* backward dependency, it can not be executed.

Event: A unit entity that represents an action with a time-stamp in the PDES. We implement three types of events in TRACER:

- *Kickoff* event starts the simulation of a PE.
- *Message Recv* event is triggered when a message is received for a PE. The network message transmission and reception is performed by CODES.
- *Completion* event is generated when a task execution is completed.

Reverse Handler: Another unit entity which is responsible for reversing the effect of an event. It is needed only for the optimistic simulation mode.

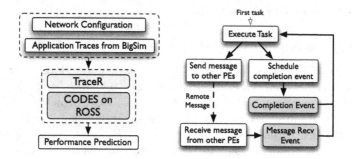

Fig. 1. Integration of TRACER with BigSim emulation and CODES (left). Forward path control flow of trace-driven simulation (right).

Let us consider an MPI application that performs an iterative 5-point stencil computation on a structured 2D grid to understand the simulation process. In each iteration, every MPI process sends boundary elements to its four neighbors and waits for ghost elements from those neighbors. When the data arrives, the MPI process performs the 5-point stencil followed by a global reduction to determine if another iteration is required. From TRACER's perspective, every MPI process is a PE. Tasks are work performed by these MPI processes locally: initial setup, sending boundary elements, the 5-point stencil computation, etc. The Kickoff event triggers the initial setup task. Whenever an MPI process receives ghost elements, a Message Recv event is generated. The dependence of the stencil computation on the receives of ghost elements is an example of a backward dependency. Similarly, posting of a receive by an MPI process is a prerequisite for TRACER to execute the Message Recv event.

Figure 1 (right) presents the forward path control flow of a typical simulation in TRACER. Application traces are initially read and stored in memory. When the system setup is complete, the Kickoff event for every PE is executed, wherein the PEs execute their first task. In the 2D stencil example, this leads to execution

Algorithm 1. Event handler implementation for PEs: code lines that begin with an asterisk (*) are required only in the optimistic mode.

---

pe_busy: A boolean; set to true if the PE is executing a task at the current virtual time.
ready_tasks: List(FIFO) of tasks that are ready to be executed on a PE if pe_busy is false.
trigger_task: Map that stores the task executed at the completion of a given task.

(a) **Execute_Task(task_id)**
1: Get the current virtual time of the PE, t_s.
2: Mark the PE busy, $pe\_busy = true$.
3: Send out messages of the task with their offsets from t_s.
4: Get the execution time of the task, t_e.
5: Schedule a Completion event for the PE at time $t_s + t_e$ for this task.

(b) **Receive_Msg_Event(msg)**
1: Find the task T that depends on the message.
2: If T does not have any undone backward dependencies, add T to *ready_tasks*.
3: **if** pe_busy == false **then**
4:     Get the next task, T', from *ready_tasks*.
5:     *Store T' and pe_busy for possible use in the reverse handler; $trigger\_task[T] = T'$, $busy\_state[T] = pe\_busy$.
6:     Call Execute_Task(T').
7: **end if**

(c) **Completion_Event(msg)**
1: Get the completed task, T, from the *msg*.
2: Mark T as *done*.
3: Set $pe\_busy = false$.
4: **for** every task, f, that depends on T **do**
5:     **if** f does not have any undone backward dependency **then**
6:         Add f to *ready_tasks*.
7:     **end if**
8: **end for**
9: Get the next task, T' from *ready_tasks*.
10: *Store T' for possible use in the reverse handler, $trigger\_task[T] = T'$.
11: Call Execute_Task(T').

---

of the initial setup task. What happens next depends on the content of the task being executed, and the virtual time, t_s, at which the task is executed.

Every task T has an execution time t_e, which represents the virtual time T takes for executing the SEB it represents. When a task is executed, TRACER marks the PE busy and schedules a Completion event for T at $t_s + t_e$ (Algorithm 1(a)). During the execution of a task, messages for other PEs may be generated. These actions are representative of what happens in real execution. When the MPI process is executing a SEB, e.g. to send boundary elements, the process is busy and no other SEB can be executed till the sending of boundary is complete. The generated messages are handed over to CODES for delivery. Note that the execution of a task in our framework only amounts to fast-forwarding of the PE's virtual time and delegation of messages to CODES; the actual computation performed by the SEB is not repeated.

When a Completion event is executed, the task T is marked done and the PE is marked available (Algorithm 1(c)). Next, some of the tasks whose backward dependencies included T may now be ready to execute. Thus, those tasks are added to a list of pending tasks, *ready_tasks*. Finally, the task at the top of *ready_tasks* list is selected and *Execute_task* function is called (Fig. 1 (right)).

As the simulation progresses, a PE may receive messages from other PEs. When a message is received, if the task dependent on the incoming message has no other undone backward dependency, it is added to the *ready_tasks* list (Algorithm 1(b)). If the PE is marked available when a message is received, the next task from the *ready_tasks* list is executed. After the initial tasks are executed, more tasks become eligible for execution. Eventually, all tasks are marked done, and simulation is terminated.

3.1   Running TraceR in Optimistic Mode

When executing in the optimistic mode, TRACER speculatively executes available events on a PE. When all the messages finally arrive, ROSS may discover that some events were executed out of order and *rolls back* the PE to rectify the error. In order to exploit the speculative event scheduling, TRACER does two things. First, during the forward execution of an event, extra information required to undo the effect of a speculatively executed event is stored. In Algorithm 1, these actions are marked with an asterisk. For both Message Recv and Completion events, the data stored includes the task whose execution is triggered by these events. For the Message Recv event, whether the PE was executing an SEB when the message was received is also stored. If this information is not stored by TRACER, it will get lost and hence the rollback will not be possible.

Second, as shown in Algorithm 2, reverse handlers for each of the events are implemented. These handlers are responsible for reversing the effect of forward execution using the information stored for them. For example, in the stencil code, reverse handler for a Message Recv event reverts the MPI process back to a state where it was still waiting for the ghost elements. In general, for a Message Recv event, the reverse handler marks the message as *not received*, while the reverse handler of a Completion event marks the task as *undone*. In addition, the tasks that were added to the *ready_tasks* list are removed from the list. Both the reverse handlers also add the task triggered by the event to the *ready_tasks* list.

Algorithm 2. Reverse handler implementations: they use extra information stored by event handlers to undo their effect.

(a) **Message_Recv_Rev_Handler(msg)**	(b) **Completion_Rev_Handler(msg)**
1: Find the task T that depends on the message.	1: Get the completed task, T, from the *msg*.
2: Recover the busy state of the PE, *pe_busy* = *busy_state*[T].	2: Mark T as undone.
3: **if** *pe_busy* == *false* **then**	3: Remove the tasks that depends on T from the bottom of *ready_tasks*.
4: Add *trigger_task*[T] to the front of the *ready_tasks*.	4: Add *trigger_task*[T] to the front of *ready_tasks*.
5: **end if**	
6: Remove T from the *ready_tasks*.	

---

4   Parameter Choices for TraceR

The complexity involved in simulating real codes over a PDES engine manifests itself in a number of design and parameter choices. The first choice is the type of PDES engine: conservative versus optimistic. While the optimistic mode provides an opportunity for exploiting parallelism by speculative scheduling of events, the benefits of speculative scheduling may be offset by the repeated rollbacks for scenarios with tight coupling of LPs. Conservative mode does not pose such a risk, but spends a large amount of time on global synchronization.

Another option that is available through the BigSim emulation is defining regions of interest in the emulation traces. TRACER can exploit this functionality to skip unimportant events such as program startup. For some applications, this can speed the simulation significantly. Next, we briefly describe some other important configuration parameters:

Event Granularity: This parameter decides the number of tasks to execute when an event is scheduled. We can either execute only the immediate task dependent on this event or all the tasks in the *ready_tasks* list. The former leads to one completion event per task, while in the latter method, a single completion event is scheduled for all the tasks executed as a set. The second option reduces the number of completion events to the minimum required.

Execution of one task per event may lead to a larger number of events and hence results in overheads related to scheduling and maintaining the event state. However, it simplifies the storage of information for reverse computation since only one task needs to be stored per event. In contrast, when we execute multiple tasks per event, a variable length array of all executed tasks needs to be stored. This leads to inefficiency in terms of memory usage and memory access. However, the number of total events is fewer thus reducing the PDES engine overheads. These modes are referred to as TRACER-single and TRACER-multi in Fig. 5.

Parameters for Optimistic Mode: There are three important parameters that are available in the optimistic mode only: batch size, global virtual time (GVT) interval and number of LPs per kernel process (KP).

- *Batch size* defines the maximum number of events executed between consecutive checks on the rollback queue to see if rollbacks are required.
- *GVT interval* is the number of batches of events executed between consecutive rounds of GVT computation and garbage collection. GVT is the minimum virtual time across all LPs and its computation leads to global synchronization.
- *Number of LPs per KP*: ROSS groups LPs into kernel processes (KPs), which is the granularity at which rollbacks are performed.

5   Experimental Setup and Configuration Parameters

Proxy Applications: We use two proxy applications for evaluating and validating TRACER. *3D Stencil* is an MPI code that performs Jacobi relaxation on a 3D process grid. In each iteration of 3D Stencil, every MPI process exchanges its boundary elements with six neighbors, two in each direction. Then, the temperature of every grid point is updated using a 7-point stencil. In our experiments, we allocate $128 \times 128 \times 128$ grid points on each MPI process, and hence have 128 KB messages. *LeanMD* is a CHARM++ proxy application for the short-range force calculations in NAMD [2]. We use a molecular system of 1.2 million atoms as input to LeanMD. We simulate three iterations in each benchmark.

Simulated Networks: We simulate a 3D torus of size 512 to 524,288 nodes to measure and compare simulator performance because 3D torus is the only topology available in all simulators used in the paper. For validation, we simulate a 5D torus because isolated allocations on IBM Blue Gene/Q (which has a

5D torus) allow us to collect valid performance data. Dimensions of the 3D tori are chosen to be as cubic as possible and those of the 5D tori mimic the real allocations on IBM Blue Gene/Q. For the 3D torus, we have experimented with two types of congestion models: a packet-level congestion model based on IBM's Blue Gene/P system (TorusNet) [14] and a topology-oblivious packet-level $\alpha - \beta$ model (SimpleNet). The simulation runs were performed on Blue Waters, a Cray XE6 at NCSA, while the emulation (trace generation) and validation were performed on Vulcan, an IBM Blue Gene/Q system at LLNL.

Evaluation Metrics: We use three metrics to compare and analyze the performance of different simulators:

- Execution time: time spent in performing the simulation (excluding startup).
- Event rate: number of committed events executed per second
- Event efficiency: represents the "rollback efficiency" and is defined as:

$$\text{Event efficiency (\%)} = \left(1 - \frac{\#rolled\ back\ events}{\#committed\ events} \right) \times 100$$

Based on the equation above, when the number of events rolled back is greater than the number of committed events (events that are not rolled back, which equals the number of events executed in a sequential simulation), the efficiency is negative. A parallel simulator may be scalable even if its event efficiency is negative. This is because while using more cores may not improve event efficiency, it may reduce the execution time due to additional parallelism.

5.1 Conservative Versus Optimistic Simulation

We begin with comparing the conservative and optimistic modes in TRACER. In these experiments, we simulate the execution of 3D Stencil on 4K nodes of a 3D Torus using 1 to 16 cores of Blue Waters. As shown in Fig. 2, the execution time for the conservative mode increases with the number of cores, but decreases for the optimistic mode (for both TorusNet and SimpleNet). Detailed profiles of these executions show that the conservative mode performs global synchronization 43 million times which accounts for 31 % of the execution time. Overall, 60 % of the total execution time is spent in communication.

In contrast, the optimistic mode synchronizes only $1,239$ times for GVT calculation with communication accounting for 10 % of the execution time. This is in part due to the overlap of communication with useful computation and in part due to the lazy nature of global synchronization in the optimistic mode. Based on these results, we conclude that the optimistic mode is suitable for performing large simulations using TRACER and we use it for the results in the rest of the paper.

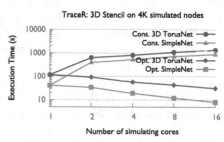

Fig. 2. Optimistic vs. conservative DES

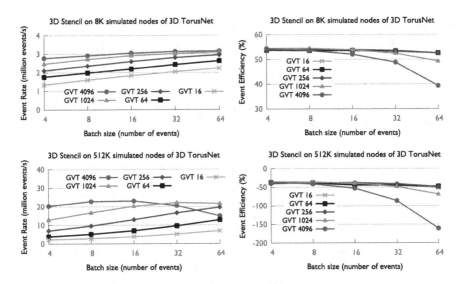

Fig. 3. Effect of batch size and GVT interval on performance: 8 K simulated nodes are simulated using 8 cores (top 2 plots), and 512 K using 256 cores (bottom 2 plots).

5.2   Effect of Batch Size and GVT Interval

Figure 3 shows the impact of batch size and GVT interval on performance when simulating 3D Stencil on a 3D torus with 8 K nodes and 512 K nodes using 8 and 256 cores, respectively. Note that the choice of the number of simulated nodes and that of simulating cores affects the results minimally except at the limits of strong scaling. These results are for the TorusNet model; similar results were obtained for SimpleNet model also. The first observation from Fig. 3 (left) is the diminishing increase in the event rate as the batch size is increased. The improvement in the event rate is because of two reasons: positive impact of spatial and temporal locality in consecutive event executions and overlap of communication with computation. However, as the batch size becomes very large, the communication engine is progressed infrequently which reduces the overlap of communication with computation. At the same time, the number of rollbacks increases due to the delay in communication and execution of pending events to be rolled back. These effects become more prominent on larger core counts as shown by the event efficiency plots in Fig. 3 (right).

Next, we observe that the event rate typically improves when a large GVT interval is used. This is because as the GVT interval is increased, the time spent in performing global synchronization is reduced. Infrequent synchronization also reduces idle time since LPs with variation in load do not need to wait for one another. These results are *in contrast* to past findings that were performed on PDES with uniform loads on the LPs [4]. When a sufficiently large GVT interval is used with a large batch size, memory limits force certain LPs to idle wait till the next garbage collection. As a result, the rollback efficiency and event rates drop as shown in the Fig. 3. Based on these findings, we use a batch size of 16 and GVT interval of 1024 for all simulations in the rest of the paper.

5.3 Impact of Number of LPs per KP

ROSS groups LPs together to form kernel processes (KPs) to optimize garbage collection. This causes all LPs in a KP to rollback if any one of the LPs has to rollback. In [4], it was shown that although smaller values of LPs per KP reduce the number of rolled back events, they do not have a significant impact on the execution time. Our findings, shown by a representative set in Fig. 4 (obtained by simulating 3D Stencil on 8 K nodes of 3D Torus with TorusNet model on 8 cores), differ – smaller values of LPs per KP *reduce* the execution time also. As we reduce the number of LPs per KP from 128 to 1, the execution time decreases by 57%.

#LPs/KP	Efficiency (%)	Time(s)
1	51	82
2	38	92
16	2	119
128	-87	189

Fig. 4. Impact of #LPs per KP.

The primary reason for the difference in impact of LPs per KP is the varying event efficiency. For synthetic benchmarks used in [4], the event efficiency is greater than 95% in all cases. As a result, any further increase caused by decreasing LPs per KP is marginal. In contrast, for real application simulations, the event efficiency is much lower. Thus, a reduction in the number of rollbacks can significantly impact the overall execution time.

6   Performance Comparison, Scaling and Validation

We now compare the performance of TRACER with other simulators and analyze its scaling performance and prediction accuracy using the packet-level model (TorusNet). Here, TRACER is executed in optimistic mode with batch size = 16, and GVT interval = 2048. The simulated network topology is 3D torus, which is the only topology available in TRACER, BigSim, and SST.

6.1 Comparison with Sequential Executions

We first compare the sequential performance of BigSim, SST (online mode), TRACER-single, and TRACER-multi for simulating 3D Stencil's execution on various node counts. Figure 5 shows that TRACER is an order of magnitude faster than BigSim. This is primarily because of the inefficiencies in BigSim's torus model and its PDES engine. Compared to SST, the execution time of TRACER-single is lower

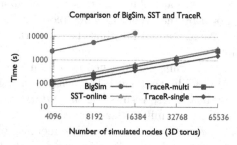

Fig. 5. Sequential simulation time

by 50 %, which we believe is due to ROSS's high performing DES engine. The performance of TRACER-single is better than TRACER-multi for these experiments. However, we found TRACER-multi to out-perform TRACER-single in other experiments for reasons that need to be explored further. In the rest of this section, we report the performance of TRACER-single as TRACER's performance.

Startup Overhead in Parallel Mode: The overhead of reading traces in TRACER for the 3D Stencil code is as low as few tens of seconds in most cases, especially on large core counts. This is because trace files can be read in parallel as the core counts increase. In general, we observe that the trace reading time is less than 5% of the total execution time.

6.2   Parallel Scaling and Validation of TraceR

Next, we present scaling results for TRACER using packet-level TorusNet and SimpleNet models. The comparison with other simulators was not possible due to the following reasons: (1) The parallel execution of BigSim, on 2–16 cores, is an order of magnitude slower than its sequential version. This is due to high overheads introduced by its PDES engine. (2) The parallel version of SST does not work with packet-level models, and hence is not available for a fair comparison.

Figure 6 presents the execution time for simulating 3D Stencil on various node counts of 3D torus. It is clear that TRACER scales well for all simulated system sizes. For the simulations with half a million (512 K) nodes, the execution time is only 95 s and 542 s using SimpleNet and TorusNet, respectively. For smaller systems, the execution time is reduced to less than 100 s, even for TorusNet.

Figure 7 (left) shows the scaling behavior of TRACER when simulating LeanMD on 32 K nodes of a 5D torus. Again, the simulation takes only 2 s and 65 s on 128 cores using SimpleNet and TorusNet, respectively. However, the speed up for simulation of LeanMD is lower in comparison to the speed up for simulating 3D Stencil. This is due to LeanMD's relatively more complicated interaction pattern and dependency graph, which causes more rollbacks on large core counts.

Validation: We simulated LeanMD on a 5D torus in order to use it for validating TRACER. IBM's Blue Gene/Q system, which has a 5D torus, provides

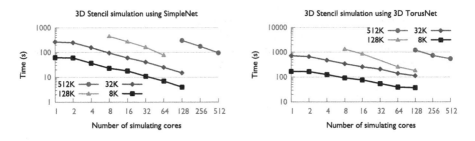

Fig. 6. Scalability of TRACER when simulating networks of various sizes.

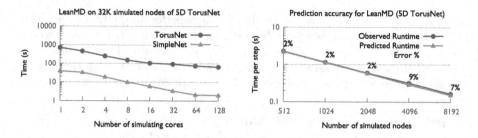

Fig. 7. Scaling and accuracy of simulating LeanMD with TRACER.

an isolated execution environment which is ideal for comparison with the performance prediction in TRACER. For the validation, LeanMD was executed on Vulcan, a Blue Gene/Q with a 5D torus network. In these experiments, we enable deterministic routing, record the execution time and the topology of the system allocated for these jobs. Next, TRACER is configured to simulate LeanMD using a 5D TorusNet model and the topology information we obtained during the real runs. Figure 7 (right) compares the prediction by TRACER with the observed performance. We observe that for all node counts (512 to 8,192 nodes) the error in the prediction is less than 9%. For most cases, the predicted time is within 2% of the observed execution time. This suggests that TRACER is able to predict the execution time of fairly complex applications with high accuracy.

7   Conclusion

We have presented a trace-driven simulator, TRACER, for studying communication performance of HPC applications on current and future interconnection networks. TRACER shows how one can leverage optimistic parallel discrete-event simulation with reversible computing to provide scalable performance. We have also shown that TRACER outperforms state-of-the-art simulators such as BigSim and SST in serial mode and significantly lowers the simulation time on large core counts. Additionally, we observed that depending on the simulated workload, the optimal set of input parameter values for a PDES-based simulator varies and needs to be identified.

Acknowledgments. This work was performed under the auspices of the U.S. Department of Energy by Lawrence Livermore National Laboratory under Contract DE-AC52-07NA27344. This work was funded by the LDRD Program at LLNL under project tracking code 13-ERD-055 (LLNL-CONF-667225).

References

1. DUMPI: The mpi trace library. http://sst.sandia.gov/about_dumpi.html
2. Bhatele, A., et al.: Overcoming scaling challenges in biomolecular simulations across multiple platforms. In: Proceedings of IEEE International Parallel and Distributed Processing Symposium 2008 (2008)
3. Bohm, S., Engelmann, C.: xSim: the extreme-scale simulator. In: HPCS (2011)
4. Carothers, C.D., Bauer, D., Pearce, S.: ROSS: a high-performance, low-memory, modular time warp system. J. Parallel Distr. Com. **62**(11), 1648–1669 (2002)
5. Casanova, H., et al.: Versatile, scalable, and accurate simulation of distributed applications and platforms. J. Parallel Distr. Comput. **74**(10), 2899–2917 (2014)
6. Cope, J., et al.: Codes: enabling co-design of multilayer exascale storage architectures. In: Proceedings of the Workshop on Emerging Supercomp. Technologies (2011)
7. Girona, S., Labarta, J.: Sensitivity of performance prediction of message passing programs. J. Supercomput. **17**, 291–298 (2000)
8. Hoefler, T., Schneider, T., Lumsdaine, A.: LogGOPSim - simulating large-scale applications in the LogGOPS model. In: Proceedings of the 19th ACM International Symposium on HPDC, pp. 597–604. ACM (2010)
9. Huang, C., Lawlor, O., Kalé, L.V.: Adaptive MPI. In: Rauchwerger, L. (ed.) LCPC 2003. LNCS, vol. 2958, pp. 306–322. Springer, Heidelberg (2004)
10. Janssen, C.L., et al.: A simulator for large-scale parallel computer architectures. IJDST **1**(2), 57–73 (2010)
11. Jiang, N., et al.: A detailed and flexible cycle-accurate network-on-chip simulator. In: IEEE Internationsl Symposium on Performance Analysis of Systems and Software (2013)
12. Kale, L.V., Bhatele, A. (eds.): Parallel Science and Engineering Applications: The Charm++ Approach. CRC Press, Taylor & Francis Group, Boca Raton, Florida, USA (2013)
13. Minkenberg, C., Rodriguez, G.: Trace-driven co-simulation of high-performance computing systems using OMNeT++. In: Proceedings of the 2nd International Conference on Simulation Tools and Techniques, p. 65 (2009)
14. Mubarak, M., Carothers, C.D., Ross, R.B., Carns, P.: A case study in using massively parallel simulation for extreme-scale torus network codesign. In: Proceedings of the 2nd ACM SIGSIM PADS, pp. 27–38. ACM (2014)
15. Penoff, B., Wagner, A., Tuxen, M., Rungeler, I.: Mpi-netsim: a network simulation module for mpi. In: Parallel and Distributed Systems (ICPADS), IEEE (2009)
16. Wilmarth, T., Kalé, L.V.: POSE: Getting over grainsize in parallel discrete event simulation. In: International Conference on Parallel Processing, pp. 12–19 (2004)
17. Zheng, G., et al.: Simulation-based performance prediction for large parallel machines. Intl. J. Parallel Program. **33**, 183–207 (2005)

Road Network Simulation Using FLAME GPU

Peter Heywood[✉], Paul Richmond, and Steve Maddock

Department of Computer Science, The University of Sheffield, Sheffield, UK
{ptheywood1,p.richmond,s.maddock}@sheffield.ac.uk

Abstract. Demand for high performance road network simulation is increasing due to the need for improved traffic management to cope with the globally increasing number of road vehicles and the poor capacity utilisation of existing infrastructure. This paper demonstrates FLAME GPU as a suitable Agent Based Simulation environment for road network simulations, capable of coping with the increasing demands on road network simulation. Gipps' car following model is implemented and used to demonstrate the performance of simulation as the problem size is scaled. The performance of message communication techniques has been evaluated to give insight into the impact of runtime generated data structures to improve agent communication performance. A custom visualisation is demonstrated for FLAME GPU simulations and the techniques used are described.

Keywords: Parallel agent based simulation · FLAME GPU · Transport network · Performance scaling · Visualisation

1 Introduction

With the increasing number of vehicles on road networks around the world and poor utilisation of existing road infrastructure capacity, there is a need for improved systems for planning and trialling proposed changes to traffic management system [16,26]. To avoid making costly or risky changes in the real world, computer modelling and simulation can be applied to evaluate proposed solutions. Transport simulation models can typically be classified into one of three categories: *macroscopic*, *mesoscopic* and *microscopic*. Macroscopic simulations (*top-down*) treat traffic as a liquid, modelling the overall system level behaviour. Mesoscopic simulations (*middle-out*) model platoons (groups of vehicles), using aggregate functions to calculate travel times and speeds [6]. Microscopic simulations (*bottom-up*) model the individual vehicles in the system and the interaction between them [23], and can be considered synonymous with Agent Based Simulations (ABS) [5]. In ABS behaviours are modelled at the individual level with agents interacting with both the local environment and other agents. Higher system level behaviours can emerge from the lower level behaviours and interactions modelled by the system.

Agent based modelling and microsimulation are being used in place of more traditional macro-level simulations as they offer a more natural method

© Springer International Publishing Switzerland 2015
S. Hunold et al. (Eds.): Euro-Par 2015 Workshops, LNCS 9523, pp. 430–441, 2015.
DOI: 10.1007/978-3-319-27308-2_35

of describing systems and allow for the emergence of more complex behaviour. Large scale and more-complex microscopic simulations are computationally expensive [3] when being processed in serial, but have been shown as suitable for acceleration through parallel methods [15,20]. Each agent in the system follows the same model, performing the same operations, as other agents of the same type, making aspects of microsimulation SIMD (Same Instruction Many Data) in nature and therefore an ideal task for General Purpose computing on Graphics Processing Units (GPGPU), which is well suited to SIMD problems. GPGPU computing has been shown to be effective for microsimulation of transport systems [24,27] and the associated tasks [7], showing that it can be used to provide computational speed-up or allow increased complexity for a similar execution time, while using low cost hardware.

This paper demonstrates the performance implications of applying the Graphics Processing Unit (GPU) to microsimulation of transport networks. It makes a unique contribution by evaluating performance scalability through the implementation of an artificial road network in which the size of the road network and the density of traffic within it can be effectively benchmarked. The Gipps car following model has been implemented using the *Flexible Large-scale Agent Modelling Environment for Graphics Processing Unit* (*FLAME GPU*) framework and the message communication techniques have been evaluated to give insight into the impact of runtime generated data structures to improve agent communication performance. A custom visualisation using GPU instancing has been developed which enables interactive simulation observation. The improved simulation performance described by this work is important in demonstrating simulations which are able to handle the increasing scale and complexity which are required to accurately model transport networks of increasing size. A coupled visualisation has the additional benefit of ensuring that traffic simulation is accessible to stakeholders involved in traffic management and infrastructure changes who are often non-modelling specialists [16].

2   Related Work

Transport microsimulation models have been used to analyse and study a broad range of driver behaviours, infrastructure layouts and the effects of traffic [4,9,12,19], showing that there are real world uses for microsimulation of transport systems for both analysis and planning without the need for costly and potentially dangerous real world experimentation.

For any study of transport systems at the microscopic level, driver behaviours such as car following [10,25], lane changing [11], interaction with road signals or traffic calming measures [13], amongst others, need to be modelled to achieve a valid, fully functional system which can be used to study other aspects of transport network behaviours.

For the purposes of this paper an example road user behaviour model is required for implementation, car following is chosen as it is arguably the most important behaviour when modelling road networks at the microscopic level.

Car following is the behaviour that on a single lane road, or within an individual lane on sections of road with multiple lanes, vehicle drivers wish to drive at their desired speed without colliding with the vehicle ahead [11].

The car following theory is that a driver reacts to the behaviour of the car(s) in front. Early models were mainly concerned with the trailing car's acceleration being proportional to the relative speeds of each car at an earlier time, or a 'history' of relative speeds [14]. Later models took into account the reaction time of the vehicle driver [10], as there is a delay between an individual receiving stimuli and performing the correct action.

The performance limits of both the driver and vehicle also affect car following behaviour, as safety concious drivers will ensure there is a gap large enough in which to stop between them and the vehicle in front (limited by an acceptable level of braking). Vehicles also have limits of acceleration performance, and so a trailing car will accelerate with no more than the vehicle's maximum acceleration until it nears the desired speed (or the speed of the vehicle in front) at which point the rate of acceleration will decrease to zero [10]. Models which are based on the principal of following at a safe distance such as Gipps' model are known as *safety distance* models.

Other models and categories of car following models have been developed, such as the *Intelligent Driver Model* proposed by Treiber et al. [25]. At it's core this model bases the acceleration of the trailing vehicle on the ratio between the "desired minimum gap" and the actual gap to the vehicle in front, with special cases for scenarios such as when traffic is in equilibrium where drivers will keep a gap to the vehicle in front which is dependant on velocity. *Psycho-physical* car following models are an alternate category in which models adjust the reactions of the driver based on the state of the vehicle [22].

3   Model

In order to demonstrate the scalable performance of Agent Based Simulations using an accelerator such as the GPU, Gipps' Car Following Model [10] was selected for implementation as it is one of the most extensively used car following models [8].

The model aims to "mimic the behaviour of real traffic", have "parameters which correspond to obvious characteristics of drivers and vehicles" to avoid elaborate calibration procedures and "should be well behaved when the interval between successive recalculations of speed and position is the same as the reaction time" [10]. The model combines limits on the performance of the driver and vehicle with the assumption that a following driver will drive in such a manner that they can safely stop if the vehicle ahead stops suddenly.

The model states that the vehicle n should not exceed its driver's target speed and the vehicle's free acceleration should increase with speed then decrease as the desired speed is approached [10]. The inequality in Eq. 1 combines these two constraints:

$$v_n(t+\tau) <= v_n(t) + 2.5a_n\tau(1 - v_n(t)/V_n)(0.025 + v_n(t)/V_n)^{\frac{1}{2}} \qquad (1)$$

Table 1. Notation for variables used by Gipps' car following model

a_n	the maximum acceleration of vehicle n
b_n	the most severe braking that the vehicle n will undertake
s_n	the effective size of vehicle n, including a margin
V_n	the target speed of vehicle n
$x_n(t)$	the location of the front of vehicle n at time t
$v_n(t)$	the speed of vehicle n at time t
τ	constant reaction time for all vehicles

The terms of Eq. 1 are explained in Table 1. The limitation of braking safely can be represented by the inequality shown in Eq. 2. This takes into consideration the following driver's reaction time, and a margin of error on the driver's behalf $\theta = \tau/2$ to avoid maximum braking and an estimate of the leading driver's most severe braking $\hat{b}$ which cannot be estimated by direct observation [10].

$$v_n(t+\tau) <= b_n\tau + \sqrt{b_n^2\tau^2 - b_n(2[x_{n-1}(t) - s_{n-1} - x_n(t)] - v_n(t)\tau - v_{n-1}(t)^2/\hat{b})} \quad (2)$$

Assuming that if the driver travels as fast as safely possible considering vehicle limitations, the new speed can be given by Eq. 3.

$$v_n(t+\tau) = \min\left\{ v_n(t) + 2.5a_n\tau(1 - v_n(t)/V_n)(0.025 + v_n(t)/V_n)^{\frac{1}{2}}, \right.$$
$$\left. b_n\tau + \sqrt{b_n^2\tau^2 - b_n[2[x_{n-1}(t) - s_{n-1} - x_n(t)] - v_n(t)\tau - v_{n-1}(t)^2/\hat{b}]} \right\} \quad (3)$$

The main restriction of Gipps' car following model is that the time-step of the simulation needs to be set to the driver reaction time τ. The model also relies on assumptions that drivers drive in a safe manner (which is often not the case) and that they are capable of estimating observable characteristics of the leading vehicle with some degree of accuracy.

4 Implementation

This section consists of four parts: the artificial road network, an overview of FLAME GPU, how Gipps' car following model is implemented using FLAME GPU & the visualisation.

4.1 Scalable Artificial Road Network

For the purposes of this paper a simple, single lane, artificial grid network is generated for agents to navigate. Road networks in the real world are designed

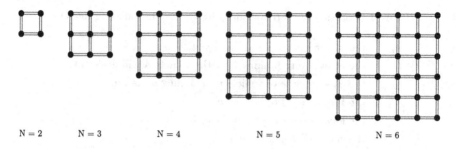

Fig. 1. Examples of the artificial road network with varying values of N. Circles represent junctions and lines represent sections of road

with real world limitations such as terrain or the location of existing roads, buildings and other spatial constraints. An artificial road network is preferable for performing controlled studies as the properties of the road network are consistent at different scales. The artificial road network is a uniform grid network, generated based on the target grid size N where $N >= 2$, as shown in Fig. 1. The grid contains N rows and N columns of junctions, with two sections of road between each adjacent node, hence the road network contains N^2 junctions and $4N(N-1)$ one-way sections of road.

4.2   FLAME GPU

FLAME GPU [21] is a "template based simulation environment" for agent based simulation on Graphics Processing Unit (GPU) architecture. Agents are represented as X-Machines which can communicate via globally accessible message lists. Messages are crucial for interaction between agents and they can be partitioned to "ensure the most optimal cycling of messages" [21].

There are currently three defined message partition schemes in FLAME GPU: non-partitioned, discrete 2D space partitioning and 2D/3D spatially partitioned space. *Non partitioned messaging* involves no filtering to reduce the number of messages each agent must iterate; it is merely a brute force approach. *Discrete partitioned messages* can be used only when sending from non mobile discrete agents, and is therefore best suited to discrete systems using Cellular Automata (CA) based approaches. *Spatially partitioned messages* originate from agents in continuous space (such as a 2D or 3D environment). The partitioning scheme requires a radius and environment bounds. The radius dictates the range to which the message iteration will extend to from its originating point, while the bounds are used to limit the area of partitioning.

Of these partitioning schemes both non partitioned messaging and spatially partitioned messaging are of interest with potential performance implications. Non partitioned messaging is computationally expensive ($O(n^2)$ message iteration loop when reading messages) but has little overhead cost with respect to dynamic construction of data structures compared to partitioned messaging schemes. Simulations using partitioned messaging generally lead to less expensive message iteration loops but an increased overhead cost as long as the partitioning system is set-up appropriately. Both non partitioned messaging and spatially partitioned messaging will be evaluated and the performance difference compared.

4.3   Implementing Gipps' Car Following Model Using FLAME GPU

Each vehicle in the system is represented by an agent. The initial values of each agent are generated by a Python script and stored in a FLAME GPU XML file for simulation state data to be parsed at runtime and copied into device memory.

The road network is stored in CUDA constant memory (via FLAME GPU's Simulation Constants) as it will not change over the course of the simulation and each agent in the simulation interacts with the same road network. This does however impose a limit on the number of nodes and roads possible within the system, due to the current limit of 64kB of constant memory being available. An alternative would be to store the road network in the CUDA Read-Only Data Cache [17] but this would restrict the GPU architectures which could be used to CUDA Compute Capability 3.0 (Kepler) and greater.

For each step in the simulation, each agent first outputs it's observable properties (location, velocity, etc.) as a message using the selected message partitioning scheme. Each vehicle then iterates through the list of relevant messages based on the partitioning scheme to find the message from the lead vehicle. Gipps' car following model (Sect. 3) is applied to the current vehicle, using the *Forward Euler Method* to calculate the vehicle's new location and velocity. Higher-order integration methods could be considered, with further related study on accuracy and performance trade-offs. Agents which have reached the end of their current segment of road randomly select a new segment from the roads connected at their current junction.

4.4   Visualisation and Graphics Techniques

A custom, cross platform visualisation is implemented to visualise the agents moving about the 3D world using OpenGL and Simple DirectMedia Layer [2], written in C++. FLAME GPU stores agent data on the GPU and it is best to avoid unnecessary and unneeded copying between device memory and host memory so CUDA *OpenGL Interoperability* [18] is used to populate *OpenGL texture buffers* with the location, length and orientation of each agent within the simulation via a CUDA kernel. *Instanced rendering* [1] allows primitives to be rendered at the correct world location for each agent, correctly orientated via custom vertex shaders. Example output of the visualisation is shown by Fig. 5.

5   Experimental Results

Two sets of benchmarking experiments are carried out to evaluate (1) the performance of the simulation as the number of agents within the system is increased,

Table 2. Suggested model parameters proposed by Gipps

a_n	sampled from the normal distribution $N(1.7, 0.3^2)\ m/sec^2$
b_n	$-2.0 a_n$
s_n	sampled from the normal distribution $N(6.5, 0.3^2)\ m$
V_n	sampled from the normal distribution $N(20.0, 3.2^2)\ m/sec$
τ	$2/3\,s$
$\hat{b}$	the minimum of -3.0 and $(b_n - 3.0)/2\ m/sec^2$

and (2) the overall scale of simulation while maintaining a fixed vehicle to road ratio. The two message partitioning schemes are compared and the performance difference highlighted for each set of experiments. Agent populations are generated using the model parameters defined in Table 2 and randomly distributed throughout the road network. The simulation has been implemented in FLAME GPU 1.4 for CUDA 7.0. Results are obtained from an Intel Core i7 4770 K machine using an NVIDIA TESLA K20c GPU with CUDA 7.0.

5.1   Vehicle Scaling for Static Road Network

The first experiment illustrates the performance scaling of the agent based simulation with respect to the number of agents in the system. A fixed grid network of size $N = 16$ and road length of $10000\,m$ is used and the number of agents varies from 2^8 up to 2^{18}, using both message partitioning techniques.

Figure 2 shows the performance against the number of agents, where performance has been measured by averaging the simulation time over 100 iterations. At very small numbers of agents, non partitioned messaging demonstrated similar performance to partitioned messaging, but with greater numbers of agents the gap in performance increases dramatically with each increase in agent population size. Spatially partitioned messaging shows a similar level of scaling with each radius, but the lower radius consistently shows higher levels of performance.

Figure 3 shows the average agent iteration performance (calculated as average iteration time/population size). With small agent counts ($<= 2^{13}$), as the population size increases the simulation performance increases as hardware utilisation increases. Larger populations ($> 2^{13}$) show a decrease in agent performance as agent population size increases due to the increased quantity of messages each agent reads. Non partitioned messaging shows significantly lower per-agent performance as the brute force approach causes each agent to read a message from each agent in the population. As the population is increased the density of agents increases on the fixed size road network. This causes agents using spatially partitioned communication to, on average, receive an increased amount of messages, but still less than would be received using the brute force approach.

The larger population sizes show a decrease in per agent performance for each increase in agent population, with a significant decrease in performance for non partitioned messaging when compared to spatially partitioned messaging.

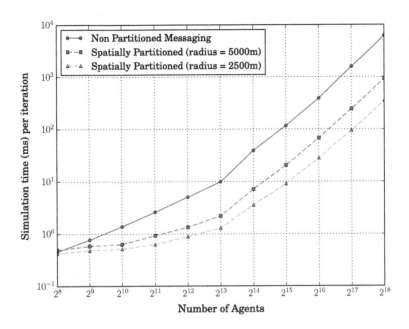

Fig. 2. Average iteration execution time for fixed grid of size $N = 16$ against agent population size, averaged over 100 iterations

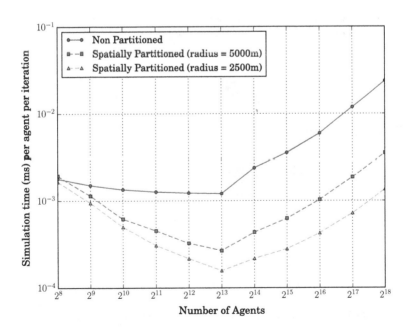

Fig. 3. Average iteration execution time per agent for fixed grid of size $N = 16$ against agent population size, averaged over 100 iterations

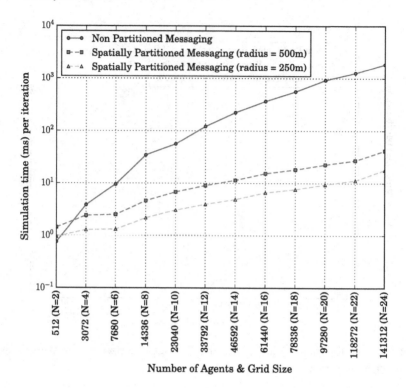

Fig. 4. Average iteration execution time for increasing Grid Size N with a fixed vehicle density of 64 agents per $1000\,m$, averaged over 100 iterations

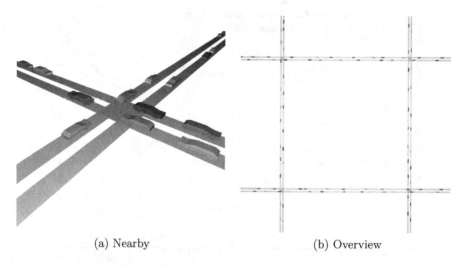

(a) Nearby   (b) Overview

Fig. 5. Screen captures of the custom visualisation running

5.2   Scaling of Vehicle and Road Network

The second experiment illustrates the performance scaling of the agent based simulation with respect to the problem size as a whole - the number of agents and size of grid generated have been scaled in unison, maintaining a constant vehicle count per section of road (64 vehicles per $1000\,m$ of road) from $N = 2$ & 512 agents to $N = 24$ & 141312 agents, with a road length of $1000\,m$. The vehicle to road ratio is kept constant to illustrate the performance difference from increasing the size of the problem as a whole, rather than just increasing the density of vehicles. Both message partitioning techniques are used and the performance difference highlighted, including using different spatial partitioning radii ($250\,m$ and $500\,m$).

Figure 4 shows the performance against the scale of simulation, where performance has been measured by averaging the simulation time over 100 iterations. This shows that as the overall size of simulation is scaled up the simulation time also increases. Non partitioned messaging shows greater performance at very small simulation sizes compared to partitioned communication. This is due to the additional computational overhead of spatial partitioning. Larger problem sizes show the benefits of using a partitioned messaging scheme to reduce the number of messages each agent must iterate through, as the performance impact of a greater problem size is significantly less for larger problem sizes. For a grid size of $N = 24$ average iteration time was approximately 44.4 & 103.4 times quicker using spatially partitioned communication with radii of $500\,m$ & $250\,m$ respectively than non partitioned messaging.

This experiment was initialised with uniform vehicle distribution. Whilst uneven distributions then occur as the simulation progresses, future work needs to consider this aspect and any associated performance implications in more detail.

5.3   Visualisation

Running the simulation with a visualisation has a negative impact on the performance of the simulation. For a simulation with grid size $N = 8$, road length $1000\,m$ and 8192 vehicles, 1000 iterations of simulation takes $15079\,ms$ without visualisation compared to $16291\,ms$ with visualisation using an *NVIDIA GeForce GTX 660*. This shows a 1.08x increase in simulation time when using the GPU for both simulation and visualisation.

6   Conclusions

Two experiments have been carried out, demonstrating that GPUs are suitable for Agent Based Simulation of road networks and are capable of scaling to handle the increasing demands of road network simulations, and the performance difference between message partitioning schemes is highlighted.

Both experiments show that FLAME GPU can successfully be used for agent based simulations of road networks and can process large amounts of agents in a reasonable time frame. The experiments also highlight the performance difference between the two message partitioning techniques. Non partitioned messaging only outperforms spatially partitioned messaging when the number of agents in the system is low enough that the additional overhead of the partitioning scheme outweighs the performance improvements and so for agent based simulations where a generally large populations of agents are used spatially partitioned messaging is more suitable, but the choice of spatial partitioning parameters need to be selected carefully. Smaller partitioning radii generally increases the performance but the radius needs to be relevant to the target simulation so that messages from relevant agents still reach each other.

Future work developing alternate message partitioning techniques specific to networked systems should allow further increase in performance compared to spatially partitioned messaging. On a road network a driver is only concerned with vehicles on the same section of roads and connected sections of roads at junctions. Developing a messaging scheme which limits the incoming agent messages to the road network structure should reduce the cost of the message iteration loop, without too large of a performance overhead. An example visualisation has also been described, demonstrating some of the techniques which can be used to create custom visualisations for FLAME GPU based simulations.

References

1. OpenGL SDK glDrawArraysInstanced manpage. https://www.opengl.org/sdk/docs/man/html/glDrawArraysInstanced.xhtml
2. Simple DirectMedia Layer (libSDL). https://www.libsdl.org/
3. Algers, S., Bernauer, E., Boero, M., Breheret, L., Di Taranto, C., Dougherty, M., Fox, K., Gabard, J.F.: Review of micro-simulation models. Institute for Transport Studies (1997)
4. Bell, M.C., Galatioto, F., Giuffrè, T., Tesoriere, G.: Novel application of red-light runner proneness theory within traffic microsimulation to an actual signal junction. Accid. Anal. Prev. **46**, 26–36 (2012)
5. Bonabeau, E.: Agent-based modeling: methods and techniques for simulating human systems. Proc. Nat. Acad. Sci. **99**(suppl 3), 7280–7287 (2002)
6. Charypar, D., Axhausen, K.W., Nagel, K.: Event-driven queue-based traffic flow microsimulation. Transp. Res. Rec. J. Transp. Res. Board **2003**(1), 35–40 (2007)
7. Charypar, D., Nagel, K.: Generating complete all-day activity plans with genetic algorithms. Transportation **32**(4), 369–397 (2005)
8. Ciuffo, B., Punzo, V., Montanino, M.: Thirty years of gipps' car-following model. Transp. Res. Rec. J. Transp. Res. Board **2315**(1), 89–99 (2012)
9. García, A., Torres, A.J., Romero, M.A., Moreno, A.T.: Traffic microsimulation study to evaluate the effect of type and spacing of traffic calming devices on capacity. Procedia-Soc. Behav. Sci. **16**, 270–281 (2011)
10. Gipps, P.G.: A behavioural car-following model for computer simulation. Transp. Res. Part B Methodological **15**(2), 105–111 (1981)
11. Gipps, P.G.: A model for the structure of lane-changing decisions. Transp. Res. Part B: Methodological **20**(5), 403–414 (1986)
12. Keenan, D.: M 62-m 1 interchange- a combined transyt/vissim micro-simulation assessment. Traffic Engi.+Control **46**(5), 178–187 (2005)

13. Kesting, A., Treiber, M., Helbing, D.: General lane-changing model mobil for car-following models. Transp. Res. Rec. J. Transp. Res. Board **1999**(1), 86–94 (2007)
14. Lee, G.: A generalization of linear car-following theory. Oper. Res. **14**(4), 595–606 (1966)
15. Nagel, K., Rickert, M.: Parallel implementation of the transims micro-simulation. Parallel Comput. **27**(12), 1611–1639 (2001)
16. Neffendorf, H., Fletcher, G., North, R., Worsley, T., Bradley, R.: Modelling for intelligent mobility (Feb 2015)
17. Nvidia, C.: CUDA kepler tuning guide - read-only data cache. http://docs.nvidia.com/cuda/kepler-tuning-guide/#read-only-data-cache
18. Nvidia, C.: Cuda c programming guide (2015). http://docs.nvidia.com/cuda/pdf/CUDA_C_Programming_Guide.pdf. Accessed 30 Mar 2015
19. Panis, L.I., Broekx, S., Liu, R.: Modelling instantaneous traffic emission and the influence of traffic speed limits. Sci. Total Environ. **371**(1), 270–285 (2006)
20. Raney, B., Cetin, N., Völlmy, A., Vrtic, M., Axhausen, K., Nagel, K.: An agent-based microsimulation model of swiss travel: first results. Netw. Spat. Econ. **3**(1), 23–41 (2003)
21. Richmond, P.: Flame gpu technical report and user guide. Technical report CS-11-03, Technical report. University of Sheffield, Department of Computer Science (2011)
22. Schulze, T., Fliess, T.: Urban traffic simulation with psycho-physical vehicle-following models. In: Proceedings of the 29th conference on Winter simulation, pp. 1222–1229. IEEE Computer Society (1997)
23. Sommer, C., Yao, Z., German, R., Dressler, F.: On the need for bidirectional coupling of road traffic microsimulation and network simulation. In: Proceedings of the 1st ACM SIGMOBILE workshop on Mobility models, pp. 41–48. ACM (2008)
24. Strippgen, D., Nagel, K.: Multi-agent traffic simulation with cuda. In: International Conference on High Performance Computing & Simulation, HPCS 2009, pp. 106–114. IEEE (2009)
25. Treiber, M., Hennecke, A., Helbing, D.: Congested traffic states in empirical observations and microscopic simulations. Phys. Rev. E **62**(2), 1805 (2000)
26. UK Department for Transport: Quarterly Road Traffic Estimates: Great Britain Quarter 4 (October - December) 2014, Februry 2015. https://www.gov.uk/government/uploads/system/uploads/attachment_data/file/402989/road-traffic-estimates-quarter-4-2014.pdf
27. Wang, K., Shen, Z.: A gpu based trafficparallel simulation module of artificial transportation systems. In: 2012 IEEE International Conference on Service Operations and Logistics, and Informatics (SOLI), pp. 160–165. IEEE (2012)

A Communication Schema for Parallel and Distributed Multi-agent Systems Based on MPI

Alban Rousset[✉], Bénédicte Herrmann, Christophe Lang,
and Laurent Philippe

Femto-ST Institute, University of Franche-Comté/CNRS, Besançon, France
{alban.rousset,benedicte.herrmann,christophe.lang,
laurent.philippe}@femto-st.fr

Abstract. The interest for Multi-Agents Systems (MAS) grows rapidly and especially in order to simulate and observe large and complex systems. Centralized machines do not however offer enough capacity to simulate the large models and parallel clusters can overcome these limits. Nevertheless, the use of parallel clusters implies constraints such as mono-threaded process of execution, reproducibility or coherency. In this paper, our contribution is a MPI based communication schema for Parallel and Distributed MAS (PDMAS) that fits High Performance Computing (HPC) on cluster requirements. Our communication schema thus integrates agent migration between processes and it guarantees message delivery in case of agent migration.

Keywords: Multi-Agent simulation · Parallelism · Communication schema

1 Introduction

The interest for Multi-Agents Systems (MAS) grows rapidly and especially in order to simulate and observe large and complex systems. Centralized machines, like desktop computer, do not however offer enough capacity to simulate the model expected: their lack of memory or their processor is not powerful enough. Parallel machines like clusters or networks of workstations can overcome these limits. Nevertheless, using a cluster or a network of workstations implies management of some constraints, such as distribution, load balancing, migration, coherency or inter-processors communications, that we do not have on a single workstation. Efficiently using these platforms, to get good performance, also requires the relay of adapted software stacks. This clearly means that the MPI interface [9] must be used as a base for parallelism and communication.

Using MPI with its mono-threaded process execution model to run MAS is however a challenge. The contribution of this paper is a MPI based communication schema for Parallel and Distributed MAS (PDMAS) that fits High Performance Computing (HPC) on cluster requirements. Our communication schema

© Springer International Publishing Switzerland 2015
S. Hunold et al. (Eds.): Euro-Par 2015 Workshops, LNCS 9523, pp. 442–453, 2015.
DOI: 10.1007/978-3-319-27308-2_36

thus integrates agent migration between processes and it guarantees message delivery in case of agent migration.

This article is organized as follows. In Sect. 2, we detail the related work on Multi-Agent Systems and parallel execution context. Then, in Sect. 3, we identify some lacks or limits in existing Parallel and Distributed Multi-Agent platforms. In Sect. 4, we give an overview of our proposition and we detail it in Sect. 5 for the communication schema and Sect. 6 for the proxy system used to follow mobile agents. We present the performance results obtained with our proposition, based on the same model used to make the survey on PDMAS [11], in Sect. 7. We finish the paper with conclusions and future work.

2 Related Work

Multi-Agent Systems are platforms which provide support to run simulations based on several autonomous agents [7]. Among the most known platforms we can cite: NetLogo [13], MadKit [8], Mason [10] and Gama [12]. For large models, these platforms are sometimes no longer sufficient to run simulations in terms of memory and computation power. This is, for example, the case in simulating individual behaviour of urban mobility [3] in a large city. In some cases increasing the size or the precision of models is however necessary to find emergent behaviours that we would never expect or never have seen otherwise. For this reason several Parallel and Distributed Multi-Agent Platforms exist such as RepastHPC [5], D-Mason [6], Pandora [1] and Flame [4] or JADE [2]. These platforms provide a native support for parallel execution of models. That is to say, support for collaboration between executions on several physical nodes, distribution of agents, communications between agents and so on. All existing PDMAS platforms propose mechanisms to communicate between agents during the simulation. But, this is done only with agents which are executed on the same process or in the buffer zone, the zone shared between two adjacent processes. For example, RepastHPC proposes mechanisms to request a copy of a remote agent from other processes, but if the copy agent is modified, modifications are never reported in the remote agent. In other words there are no synchronization mechanisms to apply modifications nor communication mechanisms to communicate directly with remote agents. Only the Flame [4] platform allows to communicate with remote agents executed on other processes. To perform the inter-process communications, Flame platform uses its own communication library based on MPI which is called Message Board Library called *libmboard*. Each process which participates in the simulation has an instance of *libmboard* in order to make synchronizations and to perform communications. One of the advantages of the *libmboard* is that sending and receiving messages is a non-blocking process. It then allows much of the communication time to be overlapped with computations. The Flame platform however offers low performances on clusters compared to others platforms (RepastHPC, D-MASON...) as shown in [11]. In addition Flame uses a proprietary programming paradigm (X-Machine) that could not be easily adopted by modellers used to standard languages as C or Java.

3   Implementing PDMAS on HPC Platforms

Targeting high performance computing implies some constraints on MAS implementation. Usually, PDMAS platforms are implemented using a Single Process Multiple Data (SPMD) programming paradigm in order to provide scalability. MAS simulations generally involve several tens of thousands of agents which potentially communicate with each other at each simulation time step. The communication bottleneck is thus a key problem as, in a parallel context, the running time is affected by the frequent communications. As the de facto standard of communication infrastructure in HPC cluster is the message passing interface (MPI) it is important to take care of the communication primitive properties in order to reduce the communication overhead. This constraint combines with another which is to have only a single mono-threaded process of execution on each allocated core. This constraint is imposed by most batch systems as SGE or SLURM. Using a single process of execution implies that we cannot use mechanisms like *listener*, *onEvent* or *onMessage* to communicate because we cannot dedicate one thread to wait for a message during the agent set execution. Messages must thus either be received by issuing non-blocking receives during the execution or at the end of the execution with a blocking receive. This illustrates the complexity of using a mono-threaded execution model to implement asynchronous communications.

Another problem set by the parallel context is the problem of message delivery in a time-driven MAS. In time-driven simulations the simulation is divided in time steps that represent the temporal discretization of the simulation. Messages between agents are thus bounded by time step. The issue is: at what time step must the message be delivered? To guarantee reproducibility, each message sent at time step n must be received before the beginning of time step $n + 1$. Indeed, as processes run asynchronously from each other, delivering messages in the same time step n cannot be guaranteed: the receiving agent can either be scheduled later or sooner in different runs, depending on the node load. For this reason delivering messages at the beginning of time step $n + 1$ is the only way to guarantee that a message will always be received at the same time step.

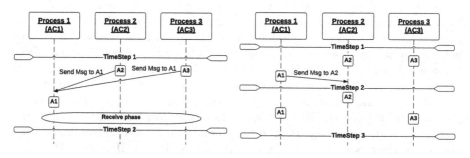

Fig. 1. Indeterminism of message order   **Fig. 2.** Indeterminism in time step

Note however that, even with delivering messages at time step $n + 1$, the stochastic nature of MAS makes it difficult to provide an absolute guarantee during the simulation as illustrated on Figs. 1 and 2. Figure 1 shows a case of indeterminism of message receive order. Let p_1, p_2 and p_3 be three processes executing a part of a simulation. If both p_2 and p_3 send a message at the same time to p_1, we cannot know in which order we need to apply them on p_1. On a centralized system these messages could be stamped with a clock value that differentiate them. In a parallel or distributed context we cannot relay on this clock value. Figure 2 illustrates the need for receive phases between time steps. Agent $A1$ is scheduled at the end of the time step and sends a message to agent $A2$ at that time. If the message is delayed on the network and agent $A2$ is scheduled at the beginning of the next time step. Then agent $A2$ may miss receiving its message at time step $n + 1$. For this reason, it is important to define receive phases at the end of each time step.

As underlined previously, the full functionality of being able to communicate with every process of the simulation, is only supported by Flame while other PDMAS limit it to the local process or neighbour processes. We advocate for inter-agent remote communications in PDMAS for two reasons. First, in models focusing on individual motions as in a city/urban mobility, agents may need to keep communicating with their contacts while moving. Due to the distribution of the simulation, agents could move anywhere on the environment, on different processes, and thus must be able to communicate with every process. Second, on graph based models, limiting agent communication to the neighbourhood leads to complex mapping constraints: non-planar graphs cannot easily be mapped on grids while keeping neighbourhood constraints.

From these reflections, we propose a communication schema for PDMAS in order to allow local and distant communications between agents without paying attention to agent location. Our communication schema allows reproducibility and guarantees that each message sent in time step n is received at the beginning of time step $n + 1$.

4   Proposition

Before presenting the communication algorithm, we give information about the Parallel and Distributed Platform that we develop. In this platform, the simulation is divided in n parts and each of these parts are distributed on p processes to perform the simulation in parallel. These processes are called *Agent Containers* (AC) and are in charge of scheduling and executing agents, of receiving messages from agents executed on other processes and of delivering these messages to its own agents. ACs also manage movement of agents between processes.

In Multi-Agent Simulations, agents must be identifiable. In PDMAS agents must be identifiable regardless of their process. For this reason we associate a *System ID*, inspired from RepastHPC and presented in Fig. 3, to each agent. This *System ID* is composed of four values: a global unique ID (GID), the ID of the process which created the agent (OwnProc), the ID of the process on which

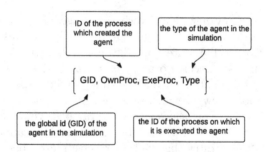

Fig. 3. Schema of the identification of an agent

the agent is currently executing (ExeProc) and the ID of the agent type (Type). With this System ID, we can know at any time where an agent has been created and where the agent is currently executed.

ACs execute four different phases at each time step to implement all the communication requirements: (1) Run agent's behaviours, (2) Receive messages, (3) Migrate agents, and (4) Update agents. In this paper we only focus on phases 2 and 4, that is to say sending and receiving messages and agent updates to perform communications even if they move on the environment. Phase 1 does not differs from other MAS and phase 3 is not necessary for understanding. The communication schema, the core of the contribution, is presented in the two next sections. Section 5 details the communication schema between agents and Sect. 6 details remote communication with mobile agents.

5   Communication Schema (Receive Message Phase)

As said previously, for coherency and reproducibility reasons, every message sent at time step n must to be received at the beginning of time step $n + 1$. Due to the stochastic nature of agents, we cannot however know how many messages must received, and from how many processes, at the end of a time step and so we cannot know when processes can proceed the next time step. For this reason we must use a termination algorithm. MPI proposes synchronization mechanisms like *barrier*, which are synchronization points, but they do not solve this problem. If we use a *barrier* to bound time steps, some faster processes will reach the synchronization point and then block until the last process reach it. Processes that did not reach the barrier could however send new messages that will not be processed by the recipient processes as they are blocked on the barrier. Thus messages are lost. This is the reason why mechanisms propose by MPI are no longer sufficient in this case.

To overcome this problem, we use a termination algorithm to reach an agreement between processes to switch to the next time step at the right time: when all processes have terminated to process the current time step. Our termination algorithm is based on a bi-directional ring with a coordinator. In our case, we use the bi-directional ring to check that all processes have terminated their messages receipt and that all processes can proceed to the next time step. We decided to use a bi-directional ring instead of a single ring, for efficiency because we divided the path in two executed in parallel.

In our proposition, agents send messages in their behaviours using method like *communicate(MSG)* but they do not directly receive messages. As said before ACs are responsible of receiving messages and to deliver these messages to agents. To proceed to the next time step, we need to be sure that each sent message is received. For this reason, an AC needs to acknowledge (*Ack*) each message of each agent in order to be sure that they are no pending messages (Fig. 4).

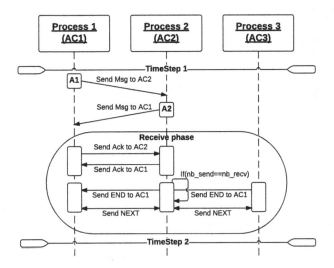

Fig. 4. An instance of receiving phase executed at each time step by each container of agent

The AC algorithm consists in waiting the *Ack* for all messages sent by its agents. Then it sends an *END* message to a coordinator, to inform that the AC has terminated the processing of its messages and wait to receive messages from the coordinator or from others processes. When the coordinator has received an *END* message from all the processes of the simulation, he sends a *NEXT* message using the bi-directional ring termination algorithm. At the end of the termination algorithm, all processes are sure that they can execute the next time step. The complete algorithm is presented in Algorithm 1.

By this way time steps are bounded by received messages phase. This algorithm works fine for agents without mobility. In case of agent mobility an AC needs to know where the target agent is run to deliver a message as agents may moves from a process to another. We explain the algorithm used to overcome this problem in the next section.

```
if (AC is coordinator) then
    while ((NbSendMessage ≠ NbAckReceived) && (nbEndReceived ≠ NbProcesses-1))
    do
        RecvMsg(Msg)
        switch Msg.TAG do
            case DATA_MSG DeliverApplyMSG(Msg) ; SendAck(Msg.Source);
            case ACK NbAckReceived++;
            case END nbEndReceived++;
        endsw
    end
    SendNextTimestep(⌈NbProcesses/2⌉);
    WaitForTermination();
else
    while ((NbSendMessage ≠ NbAckReceived) && (NextTimestep ≠ false)) do
        RecvMsg(Msg);
        switch Msg.TAG do
            case DATA_MSG DeliverApplyMSG(Msg);SendAck(Msg.Source);
            case ACK NbAckReceived++;
            case NEXT NexTimestep ← true;
        endsw
    end
    if (AC.ID = ⌈NbProcesses/2⌉) then
        SendNextTimestep(PREVIOUS_AC);
        SendNextTimestep(NEXT_AC);
    else if (AC.ID > ⌈NbProcesses/2⌉) then
        SendNextTimestep(NEXT_AC);
    else
        SendNextTimestep(PREVIOUS_AC);
    end
end
```

Algorithm 1. Receiving phase executed at each time step by each AC

6   Proxy System (Agents Update Phase)

Multi Agent Systems often use mobile agents: agent that are not fixed on the environment but rather move. This is, for instance, the case of wolves and sheep in the classical prey-predator model. In PDMAS it is necessary to distribute the environment on several processes. With agent mobility agents may move from a process (or AC) to another (process or AC) to keep the continuity of the environment and thus perform its behaviour. If we want to send a message to an agent, we need to know on which process the agent is now run. To respect the single threaded process constraint of HPC context, we use a Proxy System (PS) which consists in letting a trace of each agent on the process which creates it at the beginning of the simulation. This trace is updated during the simulation.

Algorithm 2 details how the proxy for agents is updated. We update PS when an agent move from a process (or AC) to another (process or AC). Each AC contains an hashmap of proxies for each agent that it creates at the beginning of the simulation. When an agent is going to move, the container looks if this agent have been created by itself thanks to the *System ID* of agents. If it is an agent that the process (or AC) has created, the AC changes, in its proxy hashmap, the current process of the agent where the agent is executed to the future process on which the agent will be moved. On the other cases, the AC sends a message (that contains the future process on which the agent will be moved) to the creator of this agent in order to inform the AC that one of its agent move from a process (or AC) to another (process or AC).

This phase of proxy update depends on the same termination rules as the message receipt, because we cannot know how many updates we receive and from how many processes we can receive updates. For this reason we also use the previously termination algorithm base on bi-directional ring. As this update phase is completed before we start a new time step then the proxy hashmap are always up-to-date during the agent run step.

```
while ((!End of Migration) && (nbEndReceived ≠ NbProcesses-1)) do
    if (Agent.GetOwnerProc() = AC_ID) then
        |   MapProxy[Agent.GID] ← AC_ID;
    else
        |   SendMsgMajProxy(Agent.GetOwnerProc(), Agent.FutProcess);
        |   NbSendMigration++;
    end
end
if (AC is coordinator) then
    while ((NbSendUpdates ≠ NbAckReceived) && (nbEnd ≠ NbProcesses-1)) do
        RecvMsg(Msg);
        switch Msg.TAG do
            case DATA_UPDATE_AGENT MapProxy[Msg.GID] ← Msg.FutProcess;
            SendAck(Msg.Source);
            case ACK_UPDATE NbAckReceived++;
            case END nbEndReceived++;
        endsw
    end
    SendFinishUpdating(⌈NbProcesses/2⌉);
    WaitForTermination();
else
    while ((NbSendUpdates ≠ NbAckReceived) && (FinishUpdating ≠ false)) do
        RecvMsg(Msg);
        switch Msg.TAG do
            case DATA_UPDATE_AGENT MapProxy[Msg.GID] ← Msg.FutProcess;
            SendAck(Msg.Source);
            case ACK_UPDATE NbAckReceived++;
            case NEXT FinishUpdating ← true;
        endsw
    end
    if (AC.ID = ⌈NbProcesses/2⌉) then
        SendFinishUpdating(PREVIOUS_AC);
        SendFinishUpdating(NEXT_AC);
    else if (AC.ID > ⌈NbProcesses/2⌉) then
        SendFinishUpdating(NEXT_AC);
    else
        SendFinishUpdating(PREVIOUS_AC);
    end
end
```

Algorithm 2. Updating phase executed at each time step by each AC

In this way, we always know where an agent is executed by interrogating and sending messages to the process that creates the agent at the beginning of the simulation. If the agent is not executed on this process then the process which receives the message forwards this message to the right process on which the agent is now run (Fig. 5). The message will only be acknowledged by the right container process. As a process waits until its gets all its acknowledgements

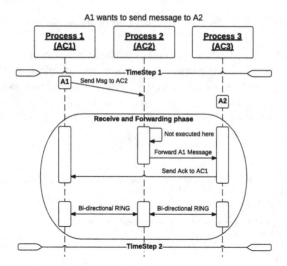

Fig. 5. An instance of updating phase executed at each time step by each AC

before sending its END message, then it guarantees that the sent message will be delivered at time step $n + 1$. In addition, for the user, this is an hidden functionality, he does not pay attention to where is the agent located, local or remote. The only mandatory information is the *System ID* of the agent you want to contact and the message will be received.

7   Experimentation

In this section we present some results using our communication schema for Parallel and Distributed Multi-Agent simulation. We have implemented the communication schema in the Parallel and Distributed Multi-Agent Platform called FractalPMAS that we develop. To assess the performance of the communication schema, we have implemented a reference model defined and already implemented in most known PDMAS platforms in [11]. This model respects the main properties that can be found in Multi-Agent Systems: perception, communication, mobility. In this model each agent is composed of 3 behaviours, performed at each time step: walk behaviour which allows agents to move in a random direction on the environment, interact behaviour which allows agents to interact and send messages to other agents and finally compute behaviour which allows agents to generate a workload.

In this reference model we also have implemented a way to evaluate the performance of our remote communication schema between agents. That is to say, instead of sending message to agents in the perception field, each agent sends messages to randomly chosen agents which are run on an other process if they are in its perception field.

About the HPC experimental settings: we have run the reference model on a 764 core cluster. Each node of the cluster is a bi-processor, with Xeon E5 (8*2 cores) processors running at 2.6 Ghz frequency and with 32 Go of memory. The nodes are connected through a non blocking DDR InfinyBand network organized in a fat tree.

Execution results on the scalability of a 10 000 agents model are given on Fig. 6, with the ideal speed-up reference. Note that the reference time used to compute the speed-up is based on a 2 cores run of the simulations as RepastHPC cannot be run on a single core. To assess scalability we vary the number of cores used to run the simulations while we fix the number of agents. We then compute the obtained speed-up. Figure 6 represents the scalability of the platform with our communication schema for local and remote communications between agents.

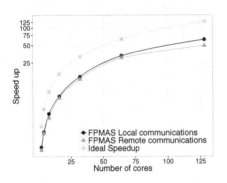

Fig. 6. Scalability of FPMAS platform running simulations using 10 000 agents, FFT 100 and 200 cycles

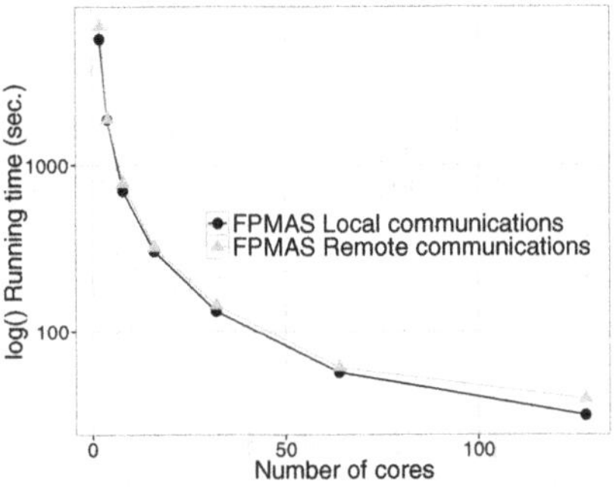

Fig. 7. Running time for FPMAS platform running simulations using 10 000 agents, FFT 100 and 200 cycles

As we can see both scale well, even if the local communications scales better. The difference between two speedup are not clearly noticeable. Obviously, remote communication offers lower performance due to the intensive exchanges between processes. Figure 7 represents the running time of simulations for 200 time steps and for local and remote communications.

Figure 8 represents the workload of our proposition on 8 cores and we vary the number of agents from 1000 to 30 000, and comparing the local communication running time and the remote communication running time.

Obviously, remote communications cannot be better than local communications, but remote communications support well the workload. For example, for 10 000 agents there is a difference of 10 % between running time for local and remote communications and for 30 000 agents there is a difference of 30 %. These values are acceptable but we need to improve mechanisms. This implementation is only a proof of concept.

To assess the viability and the performance of our communication schema, we compare in Table 1 the running time for the model defined previously [11]

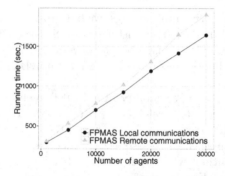

Fig. 8. Workload behaviour for FPMAS platform running simulations using 8 cores

Table 1. Comparison of running time for platforms studied in [11] with 10,000 agents

Cores	4	8	16	32	64	128
FPMAS (local com.)	2097.09	877.59	380.09	175.96	66.63	26.32
FPMAS (remote com.)	2142.68	893.6025	391.52	185.8075	67.0575	39.2125
RepastHPC	8772.93	3276.91	1277.03	724.99	497.53	367.76
Flame	17418.79	9282.20	4773.86	2428.22	1520.65	836.29

with performance obtained for other PDMAS platforms. In terms of running time FPMAS is better than other platforms. Communications (local or remote) does not impact clearly the results on this model. Compared to others platforms, better results could be explain by the way used to modelled and to structure the agents and the simulation compared to other platforms.

8   Conclusion and Perspectives

In this paper we have presented a communication schema for Parallel and Distributed Multi-Agent simulation that fit the constraints set by HPC systems. This communication schema is based on the MPI communication interface and allows communication with local and remote agents. Our contribution aims at proposing a communication schema which offers more efficiency while guaranteeing properties as reproducibility and coherency.

In our future work, we intend to better examine the efficiency of synchronization using our communication schema and also to improve the scalability of the communication schema. More improvements could be made in the implementation which is only a proof of concept. Then we will use this platform to assess load balancing in PDMAS.

Acknowledgement. Computations have been performed on the supercomputer facilities of the Mésocentre de calcul de Franche-Comté.

References

1. Angelotti, E.S., Scalabrin, E.E., Ávila, B.C.: Pandora: a multi-agent system using paraconsistent logic. In: Computational Intelligence and Multimedia Applications, ICCIMA 2001, pp. 352–356. IEEE (2001)
2. Bellifemine, F., Poggi, A., Rimassa, G.: Jade-a fipa-compliant agent framework. In: Proceedings of PAAM, vol. 99, p. 33, London (1999)
3. Chipeaux, S., Bouquet, F., Lang, C., Marilleau, N.: Modelling of complex systems with aml as realized in miro project. In: 2014 IEEE/WIC/ACM International Joint Conferences on Web Intelligence (WI) and Intelligent Agent Technologies (IAT), vol. 3, pp. 159–162 (2011)
4. Coakley, S., Gheorghe, M., Holcombe, M., Chin, S., Worth, D., Greenough, C.: Exploitation of hpc in the flame agent-based simulation framework. In: Proceedings of the 2012 IEEE 14th International Conference on HPC and Communication & 2012 IEEE 9th International Conference on Embedded Software and Systems, HPCC 2012, pp. 538–545. IEEE Computer Society, Washington, DC (2012)
5. Collier, N., North, M.: Repast HPC: A Platform for Large-Scale Agentbased Modeling. Wiley, Hoboken (2011)
6. Cordasco, G., De Chiara, R., Mancuso, A., Mazzeo, D., Scarano, V., Spagnuolo, C.: A framework for distributing agent-based simulations. In: Alexander, M., et al. (eds.) Euro-Par 2011, Part I. LNCS, vol. 7155, pp. 460–470. Springer, Heidelberg (2012)
7. Ferber, J., Gutknecht, O., Michel, F.: From agents to organizations: an organizational view of multi-agent systems. In: Giorgini, P., Müller, J.P., Odell, J.J. (eds.) AOSE 2003. LNCS, vol. 2935, pp. 214–230. Springer, Heidelberg (2004)
8. Gutknecht, O., Ferber, J.: Madkit: a generic multi-agent platform. In: Proceedings of the fourth international Conference on Autonomous agents, pp. 78–79. ACM (2000)
9. Hempel, R., Hey, A.J., McBryan, O., Walker, D.W., et al.: Message passing interfaces. Parallel Comput. 20(4), 415–416 (1994)
10. Luke, S., Cioffi-Revilla, C., Panait, L., Sullivan, K.: MASON: a new multi-agent simulation toolkit. Simulation 81(7), 517–527 (2005)
11. Rousset, A., Herrmann, B., Lang, C., Philippe, L.: A survey on parallel and distributed multi-agent systems. In: Lopes, L., et al. (eds.) Euro-Par 2014, Part I. LNCS, vol. 8805, pp. 371–382. Springer, Heidelberg (2014)
12. Taillandier, P., Vo, D.-A., Amouroux, E., Drogoul, A.: GAMA: a simulation platform that integrates geographical information data, agent-based modeling and multi-scale control. In: Desai, N., Liu, A., Winikoff, M. (eds.) PRIMA 2010. LNCS, vol. 7057, pp. 242–258. Springer, Heidelberg (2012)
13. Tisue, S., Wilensky, U.: Netlogo: design and implementation of a multi-agent modeling environment. Proc. Agent. 2004, 7–9 (2004)

Large-Scale Agent-Based Modeling with Repast HPC: A Case Study in Parallelizing an Agent-Based Model

Nicholson Collier[1,2]([⊠]), Jonathan Ozik[1,2], and Charles M. Macal[1]

[1] Global Security Sciences, Argonne National Laboratory, Argonne, IL, USA
{ncollier,jozik,macal}@anl.gov
[2] Computation Institute, University of Chicago, Chicago, IL, USA

Abstract. We present a case study for parallelizing a large-scale epidemiologic ABM developed with Repast HPC, the Chicago Social Interaction Model (chiSIM). The original serial model is a CA-MRSA model which tracks CA-MRSA transmission dynamics and infection in Chicago, and represents the spread of CA-MRSA in the population of Chicago. We utilize both within compute node parallelization using the OpenMP toolkit and distributed parallelization across multiple processes using MPI. The combined approach yields a 1350 % increase in run time performance utilizing 128 compute nodes.

Keywords: Agent-based modeling · ABMS · Repast HPC · Parallel simulation · Distributed simulation · High performance computing

1 Introduction

Agent-based models with large populations of agents can be prohibitively slow to execute. The threshold where slow becomes too slow is dependent on the types of questions that the model is intended to answer and the overall experimental design needed to provide those answers. Adequate results may be achieved within a limited period of time. However, to serve as useful *electronic laboratories*, computational models often require a battery of experimental analyses, such as adaptive parametric studies; large scale sensitivity analyses and scaling studies; optimization and meta-heuristics; inverse modeling; uncertainty quantification; and data assimilation. Sophisticated statistical techniques are increasingly being used for some of these types of analyses with ABMs [1], but due to the large number of simulations that these analyses require, efforts have been hampered by performance considerations. Some researchers have gone so far as to suggest that: "the way for ABM to become an accepted research method is not to make the models as realistic and complex as possible. An important, if not decisive, design criterion for ABMs, as well as any other simulation models, is that they must run quickly enough to be amenable to comprehensive and systematic analysis." [1] However, such comments also suggest that, if adequate performance gains can be achieved, these statistical techniques can be used for "realistic and complex" ABMs.

© Springer International Publishing Switzerland 2015
S. Hunold et al. (Eds.): Euro-Par 2015 Workshops, LNCS 9523, pp. 454–465, 2015.
DOI: 10.1007/978-3-319-27308-2_37

Given this necessity of running many simulations in a reasonable amount of time, the problem then is how to keep execution time manageable while scaling up to larger numbers of agents. The execution time of a model run, indeed its ability to run at all, is dependent on the design of the model itself, that is, on the "richness" of the agents, the computational complexity of their behavior, and the number of agents executing that behavior. A typical serial ABM iterates through all the agents at each time step and has each agent execute some behavior. The time to execute this loop is obviously dependent on the number of agents the loop has to iterate through and the complexity of the agent behavior. Consequently, as an ABM scales up to populations of increasing size and complexity, it is more susceptible to prohibitive increases in execution time as result of the time it takes to complete this behavior loop. Additionally, it is also susceptible to more mundane memory issues, ultimately limiting the number of possible agents in a model.

The solution that is utilized in this paper is to parallelize the ABM. In parallelizing the behavior loop, the agents are divided into n groups. Each group is concurrently iterated over and each agent executes its behavior. This type of parallelization can be performed both within a compute node via threading and also by distributing the agents among compute nodes, each of which has its own memory capacity. By distributing the agents among compute nodes, we also reduce any potential memory pressure as the number of agents per compute node is now lower. The remainder of this paper is a case study of how a large-scale non-parallelized ABM, a model of community associated methicillin-resistant *Staphylococcus aureus* (CA-MRSA), was parallelized and distributed to become the scalable general epidemiological Chicago Social Interaction model. Section 2 details some specifics of the CA-MRSA model. Section 3 presents the details of the parallelization process. We conclude in Sect. 4. The source code referenced in the paper is presented as a set of Github gists [2].

2   The CA-MRSA Model

The CA-MRSA Model [3] is an agent-based model of community associated methicillin-resistant *Staphylococcus aureus* (CA-MRSA) transmission. *Staphylococcus aureus* is a common cause of human bacterial infections. It is estimated that 25–40 % of the population are colonized in the nasopharynx at any given time. While colonization is asymptomatic, colonized individuals may develop an active infection [3]. Colonization may be of short or long duration, and often clears without causing an infection. Transmission is believed to be largely via skin-to-skin contact with either a colonized or infected individual. In the 1960s new antibiotic resistant isolates of *S. aureus* were identified among hospitalized patients. Called methicillin-resistant *Staphylococcus aureus* (MRSA), these isolates rapidly became an important cause of infections within healthcare settings. These are referred to as health-care associated MRSA (HA-MRSA) [4].

In the 1990s new MRSA strains that were distinct from HA-MRSA were identified in individuals who did not have healthcare exposures. These are referred to as CA-MRSA. The problem of CA-MRSA has been particular severe in the United States where incidence increased exponentially in the early 2000s [5]. By 2004, one of the

CA-MRSA strain types, USA300, became the most frequent cause of skin and soft tissue infections seen in U.S. emergency departments [6]. While uncomplicated skin infections are the most common manifestation, CA-MRSA infections may be invasive and even fatal. In 2005, the Centers for Disease Control and Prevention (CDC) estimated that there were more deaths from invasive MRSA infections than from HIV-AIDS in the U.S. [7].

Epidemiologic studies can be used to estimate the incidence and risk factors for CA-MRSA infections, but it is difficult to perform a study that examines the actual transmission dynamics within a population. The CA-MRSA model [3] was created to aid in the understanding of CA-MRSA transmission dynamics and infection in Chicago, and represents the spread of CA-MRSA in the population of Chicago based on clinical data from 2001 to 2010. The model was used to determine the types of places most important for the transmission of CA-MRSA, such as households, the County jail, hospitals and schools and the relative contributions of the colonized and infected states to transmission.

2.1   Model Structure

The full Chicago CA-MRSA model represents every person in the City of Chicago as an agent. The baseline data for this agent population is adapted from a synthetic population derived from U.S. Census files [8]. Each of the approximately 2.9 million agents resides in a household, dormitory or retirement home/long term care facility and moves among other places such as schools, workplaces, hospitals, jails and sports facilities. Each simulated hour about 2.9 million agents move to and from 1.2 million of these places, where the places are further characterized by a level of risk-of-transmission, primarily differentiated by levels of physical contact. The risk of transmission between agents is determined by the disease status (uncolonized, colonized, or infected) of other agents co-located in the same places modified by the place's level of risk.

Agents move hourly between places according to their shared activity profiles. Each agent has a profile that determines what times throughout the day he or she occupies a particular location. The profile may be overridden for two reasons: (1) an agent may seek care in a hospital for MRSA treatment, or (2) an agent may be jailed. For further information on how the agents' activity profiles, health seeking behaviors and jailing probabilities were derived from various empirical data sources, see [3].

Once in the appropriate place determined by the activity profile, the agent has contact with the other persons co-located in that place and disease transmission from one agent to another can occur. In the full Chicago model for a typical simulated 10 year run, these model dynamics yield approximately 3 trillion individual contacts.

Disease transmission consists of an uncolonized individual becoming colonized with a base probability modified by the place and activity risk as well as the co-location of colonized or infected persons. In the absence of any colonized or infected persons, transmission is not possible. More information on the CA-MRSA model disease state dynamics, estimates of population level colonization, decolonization and infection rates, and household infection rates can be found in [3].

2.2 Implementation

The CA-MRSA model was originally prototyped using Repast Simphony ReLogo [9] for a small region of Chicago and then ported to C++ using the Repast HPC [10] toolkit. The major components of the model, persons and places, are implemented as C++ classes with additional classes to represent model components such as the shared activity profiles, and activities. The base input data consists of a set of files that define persons, places and activity profiles together with a properties file that defines the model's parameters.

Model execution consists of two phases: an initialization phase and the repeated hourly time step. The initialization phase consists of reading in the various input files and creating the appropriate C++ objects (Persons, Places, etc.) from them. The hourly time step executes the code for the next simulated hour and is run repeatedly until a specified number of hours have been completed. Pseudo-code for the CA-MRSA model hourly time step is shown in Fig. 1.

```
For each person:
  Move to the place for current hour's activity
For each place:
  Run the transmission and transition algorithms
```

Fig. 1. Pseudo-code for the CA-MRSA model hourly time step.

The CA-MRSA model is a serial (non-parallelized) model. The two loops in Fig. 1 are executed serially and parallelizing them is the focus of the work described in the next section.

3 From the CA-MRSA Model to the Social Interaction Model

The CA-MRSA model was a success and yielded useful results, producing temporal and geographic trends that match the increase in CA-MRSA incidence similar to Chicago from 2001 to 2010 [3], and providing insights into the role of households, schools, and other places in the spread of the disease [3]. It was and is a useful platform for exploring alternate treatment strategies such as treating children in schools where infections or colonizations have been detected, work on which is currently on-going. However, the model is slow to execute, taking approximately 60 h to simulate 10 years with 1 h time steps, making it time consuming and difficult to do any involved computational experimentation such as the sensitivity analyses and parameter estimation methods mentioned in the introduction. The majority of the model runs were done on the Blues and Fusion clusters (310 nodes with 4960 available compute cores and 320 nodes with 2560 available compute cores, respectively) hosted at Argonne National Laboratory. As with most cluster systems, a user submits compute jobs to the cluster and then waits for the results. Given the nature of the job scheduler, the longer the job, the longer it may wait in the queue and thus the actual time to get results back is in fact longer than the 60 h of simulation run time.

Regardless of the lengthy execution time, we recognized that the model contained the core of what could become a more general epidemiological model. From the CA-MRSA model, we then derived the Chicago Social Interaction model (chiSIM). chiSIM retains the synthetic population, activity profiles and shared places of the CA-MRSA model and removes the MRSA specific disease transmission, hospitalization and treatment protocols. In this way, chiSIM simulates the hourly mixing and interactions of a population and can easily be extended to model the epidemiological consequences of such activities. Implementation-wise the hourly time step remains the two loops presented in Fig. 1, but the second loop is now a placeholder for the epidemiological consequences of co-location in a place (Fig. 2).

```
For each person:
  Move to the place for current hour's activity
For each place:
  Compute the epidemiological consequences of co-location
```

Fig. 2. Pseudo-code for the simplified chiSIM time step.

We began the parallelization work by profiling chiSIM to find the "hotspots" where the majority of the execution time was taking place. This initial profiling was performed on a desktop machine running Mac OS X using Apple's Instruments profiler [11] with a 3 zip code (post code) smaller version of the model. It indicated, not entirely unexpectedly, that the person loop in the time step consumed the majority of the execution time. This was linear with respect to the number of persons in the loop. What was unexpected was the amount of time spent in the place loop. Despite being essentially an empty placeholder for any disease specific code, the place loop did remove any person objects in each of the places as a final clean up step. This step resolved into multiple clear() calls on C++ standard library vectors that accounted for the time consumed.

3.1 OpenMP

Given the profiling data, the obvious candidates for optimization through parallelization were the person and place loops. We began by using OpenMP, a set of compiler directives, library routines, and environment variables that can be used to specify high-level parallelism in Fortran and C/C++ programs [12]. In particular, we used the OpenMP, *parallel for loop* directive to parallelize both the person and place loops. The resulting source code (Loops_OMP.cpp) can be seen in [2]. The OpenMP compiler directives begin with #pragma omp (lines 3, 7, and 14). The parallel loop directive #pragma omp for (line 14) parallelizes the loop that follows the directive (lines 15–17). Following this directive the compiler parallelizes the loop by spawning n number of threads and dividing the loop iterations among those threads, executing the iterations in parallel.

The person loop (lines 4–11) is more complicated due to the typical constraints of multi-threaded programming, concurrent access of shared memory, and so forth. In the person loop each person object selects its next activity and then moves to the place indicated by that activity. As with the place loop, the person loop is parallelized using the compiler directive (line 3). In selecting the next activity each person requires a NextAct object that can be re-used serially but not concurrently. The firstprivate (next_act) phrase in the compiler directive (line 3) directs the compiler to create one NextAct per thread, preventing concurrent access. In the loop, only the activity selection can be performed in parallel. The selection of the next activity is essentially a thread-safe read on shared activity profiles together with writes on the now thread safe NextAct object. However, the actual movement of the person to the place associated with the selected activity (line 9) is not thread safe given that the places are shared among all the persons and a concurrent write to that place would corrupt it. Consequently, the code is surrounded by a #pragma omp critical directive (lines 7–10) that insures that only a single thread executes that section at one time.

Parallelizing with OpenMP in this way did result in a faster execution, the speed increase was not linear: running with 16 threads did not result in a 16-fold speed up. Profiling, as might be expected, revealed that the presence of the critical section did tend to mitigate the speed increases provided by parallelizing the person loop. The place loop, however, did show a linear speed increase.

3.2 Parallelizing the Model with MPI

The next phase in parallelizing chiSIM was to distribute the model among multiple processes. Commodity CPUs, at the time of writing, may have up to 16 hardware threads, meaning that OpenMP parallelization could under the best conditions parallelize our loops into 16 concurrent iterations. By distributing the model across processes we can leverage the power of clusters and other high performance computing resources to parallelize the loops into thousands, and potentially 10 s of thousands, of concurrent iterations, each taking on a fraction of the required computations and, hence, running in less time. By distributing the total number of persons and places among multiple processes, each loop on each process would have a concomitantly smaller number of persons and places to iterate through, hopefully resulting in shorter run times.

chiSIM, like its CA-MRSA model precursor, is written using Repast HPC [10]. Although the original CA-MRSA model and the initial OpenMP version of chiSIM run as a single process, the ABM components provided by Repast HPC, such as the event scheduler and data collection, are designed to work in a multi-process non-shared memory environments using MPI [13]. Consequently, very little of the ABM-specific infrastructural parts of the model (e.g. event scheduling) had to be changed. The majority of the work focused on refactoring the model itself to work in the multi-process non-shared memory environment found in clusters and high performance computers. In the multi-process parallel environment, each process is responsible for agents (in this case, persons and places) *local* to that process. That process executes the code that represents the agents' behavior. Data (e.g. agents) can be shared across processes using MPI.

In parallelizing the model over multiple processes, the core concept remains the same: people move between places and contact occurs in those places. However, given that we are distributing people and places among different processes, a person's next place may not share the same process as the person. Disease transmission is dependent on the characteristics of the place in which persons are co-located, that is, on the risk associated with the place, and with the disease state of the persons in that place. Consequently, if disease transmission is to occur, then either (1) persons need to move to the process on which their next place exists, and the epidemiological consequences of the contact in that place can then be computed in that place; or (2) places need to be shared across processes such that the epidemiological consequences can be computed for any person on any process.

In refactoring the model, we chose the first option. Places are created on a process and remain there. Persons move among the processes according to their activity profiles. Implementation-wise this option was simpler than the second option, in that it was similar to the CA-MRSA model and only additional code to coordinate the movement of persons among processes was required. We also suspected and hoped that it would be possible to cluster persons around groups of places in such a way as to minimize the cross-process movement of the persons. In this chosen scheme, when a person selects its next place to move to, it may stay on its current process or it may have to move to another process if the place is not on the person's current process. The second case is the one that we hoped to minimize. The updated pseudo code for the distributed chiSIM time step incorporating cross-process person movement can be seen in Fig. 3.

```
for each person:
   place = select the place for the next hour's activity
   if place's process rank¹ == person's process rank:
      move to the place
   else:
      add person to list of persons to move place's rank

move persons to other processes
receive persons from other processes

for each person received from other processes:
   move to the current place

for each place:
   compute the epidemiological consequences of co-location
```

Fig. 3. Pseudo-code for the chiSIM time step including cross-process movement (A process rank is an integer id used to identify a process.).

In distributing the model is this way, the number of persons and places in each process is smaller and thus the number of loop iterations is smaller as well. However, cross-process movement is expensive and, in fact, a previous naïve attempt at parallelizing the CA-MRSA model ran slower than the single process serial version due to the communication cost (i.e. the time spent) of sending and receiving the persons. This inter-process communication cost has two factors: the amount of data sent and the frequency with which it is sent. To minimizing the cross-process communication we needed to send less data, and do so less frequently.

3.2.1   Minimizing the Data Cost

chiSIM is a C++ model and persons and places are implemented as C++ classes. Sending a person object from one process to another consists of sending the current state of the person object, that is, its current field values, via MPI and creating a new person object on the other end with these sent field values. When a person is moved between processes, it needs enough of its state available on the target process to execute its place selection and any disease related behavior. That required information consists of the activity profile used to select the next place and the activity risk, enough place data to select the next place from the places on the current process, and the person's current disease state.

Much of this can be cached, given sufficient memory of which we had plenty (16 to 32 GB of RAM per compute node). Rather than moving a person's entire activity profile between processes when it moves, all the shared activity profiles are read and constructed on each process during initialization. These are placed in a standard library map with a unique activity profile id as the key. When a person is moved between processes only this activity profile id needs to be transferred rather than the entire activity profile. A similar strategy was used for the required place data. All the processes read all the place data. Each place has a unique id and a process rank id where the rank id identifies the process on which the place resides. Those places that will reside on the reading process are constructed as fully functioning place objects able to compute the epidemiological consequences of contact. Those places that are not local to the reading process are constructed as only the simple *id, rank* pair. When a person is transferred between processes only the *id, rank* pair is transferred.

A person's activity profile structure does not change, although it can be overridden, and the id and rank pairs of the places used in that profile do not change. Given that the persons are essentially constituted by these data, they can also be cached. When a person arrives at a target process for the first time, the transferred data (activity profile ids, etc.) is re-assembled into a new person object. That object is then cached in a map using a unique person id as the key. The next time the same person is moved to that target process the pre-assembled person is retrieved from the map and updated with any dynamic data (i.e. the disease state) associated with the person. This pre-assembled person is then used in the person loop on the target process. This pre-assembly also avoids any overhead associated with the frequent creation of new C++ objects and the concomitant memory allocation. It also allows us to potentially eliminate the transfer of any data that can be cached within the pre-assembled person. The gist, PersonCachingExample.cpp, in [2] illustrates how persons are cached when first received from another process and subsequently retrieved from the cache.

3.2.2   Minimizing the Sending Frequency

As described earlier, persons move between processes when the place for their next activity is on a different process from the one on which they currently reside. If all of a person's possible places are on the same process, that person will never have to move between processes. To the extent that we can assign places to processes in a way that maximizes this within process movement, the frequency of cross process movement will be minimized. Fewer persons will need to be sent to other processes as part of moving to their next place.

This problem essentially maps to a *graph partitioning problem*. In this graph, each place is a vertex and each edge represents person movement between two places, that is, between two vertices. The edge weight represents the number of persons that travel between the two places. The goal, then, is to partition the graph into groups of vertices (places), such that the edge *weights* connecting these groups are minimized. That is, by putting places that are highly connected to each other on the same process, we can minimize cross-process movement.

To perform the partitioning, we created the places graph. This involved creating a vertex for each place and then, following each person's activity profile, an edge between two activities when the prior activity's place differed from the subsequent activity's place. If an edge already existed, the edge's weight count was incremented by 1. For the full Chicago scenario, the graph consisted of approximately 1.2 million vertices (places) and approximately 1.9 million edges (trips between places). To partition the graph, we used the METIS toolkit [14, 15]. METIS is a set of applications for partitioning graphs and finite element meshes. It is used in a variety of domains such as linear programming and load balancing, the latter making it a good fit for balancing our places among the distributed processes. Having partitioned the existing place graph with METIS, the places data were then updated by adding a rank attribute for each place that corresponded to the graph group as determined by METIS.

In order to establish a baseline against which the METIS partitioned places could be compared, we also created a random partitioning. The random partitioning assigned ranks to places based on their location in the input file. Given a total number of processes n, and a total number of places p, the first p/n number of places in the places file were assigned to process 0, the next p/n number of places in the file were assigned to process 1, and so on. If p is not a divisor of n, any remaining processes were assigned in round robin fashion to the n processes. When the METIS partitioning was initially benchmarked against this random partitioning, it was in fact slower. A simulated week run on 128 processes on Argonne National Laboratory's Cetus BG/Q high performance computer took 43 s for the METIS partitioning versus 41 s for the random partition. We suspected that the good performance of the so-called random partitioning had revealed a pattern in the input data that resulted in improved performance, but we were more interested in why the METIS partitioning was slower.

To investigate this further we used the TAU [16, 17] profiler, and the instrumentation API in particular. Profiling in a parallel and distributed environment can be challenging. Per-process, inter-process, and application level performance data needs to be gathered in an efficient manner, often necessitating low-level access to the underlying hardware. Thus, mature cross-platform profiling tools such as TAU are invaluable when investigating parallel distributed application performance. We used TAU to record the time spent in the person loop, the time spent in the sending and receiving persons between processes, and the amount of time to re-assemble the moved persons data into Person objects. (An example of using the TAU API can be seen in the gist, TAUProfiling.cpp, in [2].) Of these timing data sets, the first and last proved to be informative. Repast HPC, and thus chiSIM, use a conservative schedule synchronization approach where all processes execute a time step in parallel and then *wait for all processes to finish* before executing the next time step. As a consequence, the overall execution time is only as fast as the slowest process. Other processes may execute more quickly but will have to wait for the slowest process to finish. Therefore speeding up the slowest process will improve the overall run time. TAU provides per process timing data for each profiled section. The timings for the worst performing processes of a test run[1] are presented in Table 1.

Table 1. Profiling timing values for the worst performing processes using the random and METIS partitionings.

Partition type	Time in loop	Time for re-assembly
Random	28.99 s	6.95 s
METIS	32.75 s	6.09 s

We can see in Table 1 that the slowest process in the METIS partitioned case takes roughly 4 s longer than the random partitioned case to iterate over all the persons in the person loop. However, the METIS partitioned case is nearly a second faster in re-assembling cross-process person data into Persons. The latter is a good measure of how much data is being passed between processes and thus indicates that the partitioning actually works, that is, there is less inter-process communication in the METIS partitioned case. The loop timing, however, is dependent on the number of persons that have to be iterated through and indicates that there is perhaps a larger number of persons on the slowest process in the METIS partitioned case. Subsequent runs that recorded the number of persons per process at each time step and confirmed that the slowest METIS partitioned process contained more persons than the slowest random partitioned process.

The problem was that any potential speed increase gained by moving persons less frequently was being lost by unbalanced numbers of persons across processes. The METIS partitioning, while minimizing the cross-process communication, had inadvertently placed too many persons on some processes by assigning too many heavily populated places to those processes. The solution to this issue was to find a way to balance the number of persons on each process during the partitioning such that each process retained a roughly equal number of persons, while still attempting to minimize the movement of persons between processes. Fortunately, METIS can be used to achieve such a multi-objective partition by providing it with weights for the vertices in the network. We re-created the place graph but this time assigned a weight to each vertex that represented the total number of persons that visited that place. METIS was

---

[1] The test runs showed very little variation in run time between runs, with the profiling results staying constant throughout.

then rerun using both the edge and vertex weights. The model run time with this new partitioning was now faster than the baseline random partitioning. Run times for all three cases for a simulated week on 128 processes can be seen in Table 2.

Table 2. Profiling timing values for the worst performing processes using the random, METIS and METIS with vertex weights partitionings.

Partition type	Total run times
Random	41 s
METIS	43 s
METIS w/Vertex Weights	33 s

Comparing the original CA-MRSA model, which for a simulated 10 year run running on a single thread on a single process took approximately 60 h to complete, the parallelized and multi-threaded chiSIM, running over 128 processes and using 16 threads per process, took approximately 4 h. Thus, by applying multi-threading and parallelizing the model across processes, we achieved a 1350 % speed up.

4   Conclusion

If ABMs are to serve as validated and trusted electronic laboratories, they must undergo a set of experimental analyses, including adaptive parametric studies, sensitivity analyses, optimization and uncertainty quantification. For these computational experiments, which involve the execution of large numbers of simulation runs, to complete in reasonable amounts of time, the run time performance of each individual simulation needs to be improved. Here we have presented a case study for refactoring a useful, albeit slow running, model into a scalable, parallelized and distributed model whose improved run time performance opens the door for such studies. We began by parallelizing the model via multi-threading using the OpenMP toolkit and subsequently enabled it to be distributed across multiple processes over MPI. In doing the latter, the cost of cross-process communication was mitigated by moving less data and moving data less frequently. To move less data, we took advantage of a memory-rich environment by caching the required person data on each process and only moving the minimum amount necessary. To move data less frequently, we optimized the assignment of places on processes to minimize the amount of person movement between them. The realization that the movement of the persons between places could be mapped to a graph partitioning problem proved the key to the place assignment, and allowed the model to efficiently scale up to larger populations. Throughout the refactoring, we continually profiled, grounding our intuitions in hard data.

Acknowledgements. This work is supported by the U.S. Department of Energy under contract number DE-AC02-06CH11357 and National Science Foundation (NSF) RAPID Award DEB-1516428.This research used resources of the Argonne Leadership Computing Facility, which is a DOE Office of Science User Facility.The Chicago MRSA ABM was developed with support from the MIDAS Program, NIH/National Institute of General Medical Sciences, grant U01GM087729.

References

1. Thiele, J.C., Kurth, W., Grimm, V.: Facilitating parameter estimation and sensitivity analysis of agent-based models: a cookbook using NetLogo and R. J. Artif. Soc. Soc. Simul. **17**(3), 11 (2014)
2. https://gist.github.com/ncollier/8030c144c902cf803584
3. Macal, C.M., North, M.J., Collier, N.T., Dukic, V.M., Wegener, D.T., David, M.Z., Daum, R.S., Schumm, P., Evans, J.A., Wilder, J.R., Miller, L.G., Eells, S.J., Lauderdale, D.S.: Modeling the transmission of community-associated methicillin-resistant *Staphylococcus aureus*: a dynamic agent-based simulation. J. Transl. Med. **12**, 124 (2014)
4. Chambers, H.F., Deleo, F.R.: Waves of resistance: Staphylococcus aureus in the antibiotic era. Nat. Rev. Microbiol. **7**(9), 629–641 (2009)
5. Dukic, V.M., Lauderdale, D.S., Wilder, J., Daum, R.S., David, M.Z.: Epidemics of community-associated methicillin-resistant *Staphylococcus aureus* in the United States: a meta-analysis. PLoS One. **8**(1), E52722 (2013)
6. Moran, G.J., Krishnadasan, A., Gorwitz, R.J., Fosheim, G.E., McDougal, L.K., Carey, R.B., Talan, D.A.: Methicillin-resistant *S. aureus* infections among patients in the emergency department. N. Engl. J. Med. **355**(7), 666–674 (2006)
7. Klevens, R.M., Morrison, M.A., Nadle, J., Petit, S., Gershman, K., Ray, S., Harrison, L.H., Lynfield, R., Dumyati, G., Townes, J.M., Craig, A.S., Zell, E.R., Fosheim, G.E., McDougal, L.K., Carey, R.B., Fridkin, S.K.: Invasive methicillin-resistant *Staphylococcus aureus* infections in the United States. JAMA **298**(15), 1763–1771 (2007)
8. Wheaton, W.D., Cajka, J.C., Chasteen, B.M., Wagener, D.K., Cooley, P.C., Ganapathi, L., Roberts, D.J., Allpress, J.L.: Synthesized Population Databases: A US Geospatial Database for Agent-Based Models. RTI Press, Durham (2009). Publication No MR-0010-0905
9. Ozik, J., Collier, N.T., Murphy, J.T., North, M.J.: The ReLogo agent-based modeling language. In: Proceedings Of The WSC 2013, Washington, D.C. (2013
10. Collier, N., North, M.: Parallel agent-based simulation with repast for high performance computing. Simulation **89**(10), 1215–1235 (2012)
11. Instruments User Guide. https://developer.apple.com/library/mac/documentation/Developer Tools/Conceptual/InstrumentsUserGuide/Introduction/Introduction.html. Accessed 1 Jun 2015
12. OpenMP specification home page. http://openmp.org. Accessed 1 Jun 2015
13. MPI standard official website. http://www.mcs.anl.gov/research/projects/mpi/index.htm. Accessed 1 Jun 2015
14. Karypis, G., Kumar, V.: A fast and highly quality multilevel scheme for partitioning irregular graphs. SIAM J. Sci. Comput. **20**(1), 359–392 (1999)
15. METIS home page. http://glaros.dtc.umn.edu/gkhome/views/metis. Accessed 1 Jun 2015
16. Shende, S., Malony, A.D.: TAU: the TAU parallel performance system. Int. J. High Perform. Comput. Appl. **20**(2), 287–311 (2006)
17. TAU home page, https://www.cs.uoregon.edu/research/tau/home.php. Accessed 1 Jun 2015

RAMSES: Reversibility-Based Agent Modeling and Simulation Environment with Speculation-Support

Davide Cingolani, Alessandro Pellegrini$^{(\boxtimes)}$, and Francesco Quaglia

DIAG, Sapienza University of Rome, Rome, Italy
cingodvd@gmail.com, {pellegrini,quaglia}@dis.uniroma1.it

Abstract. This paper presents RAMSES, a framework for easily specifying agent-based discrete event models entailing both environment and agent entities. RAMSES offers parallel execution capabilities based on speculative event processing and an innovative software reversibility technique that copes with state restore in case the run slides along a non-consistent speculative path. Reversibility in RAMSES relies on transparent static software instrumentation, thus allowing the model developer to concentrate on the actual forward-execution logic of the simulation events occurring in the system. An experimental assessment of RAMSES is also presented, which is aimed at determining its run-time effectiveness and its potential for simplifying the development of agent-based models when compared to other (general purpose) speculative frameworks for parallel discrete event simulation.

1 Introduction

Agent-based modeling exhibits an intrinsic expressive power, making it a proven solution to study complex real-world scenarios, such as disaster rescue [1], computational sociology [2], biomedical applications [3], and economic analysis [4]. At the same time, discrete event models are mainstream formalisms for describing agent-based models, just due to the fact that agents' interactions with other entities can be abstracted as occurring at specific time instants[1].

Also, discrete event simulation techniques represent a core support for solving agent-based models relying on the discrete event paradigm. This is an important aspects, given the existence of a plethora of techniques, globally referred as Parallel Discrete Event Simulation (PDES) [5], which provides protocols and mechanisms for running complex discrete event simulation models in parallel, hence allowing for speedup in the model execution and tractability of highly complex and/or large/huge models.

However, except for a few specific cases, most of the traditional PDES platforms are general-purpose. Nevertheless, when considering agent-based simulation, the peculiarities of this kind of simulation models can be exploited in

---

[1] Interactions having a specific duration can be anyhow mapped to a couple of *begin* and *end* discrete events.

© Springer International Publishing Switzerland 2015
S. Hunold et al. (Eds.): Euro-Par 2015 Workshops, LNCS 9523, pp. 466–478, 2015.
DOI: 10.1007/978-3-319-27308-2_38

order to tailor the PDES environment API, its internal structure and run-time behavior to the actual needs of agent-based scenarios. In particular, two different types of simulation objects/entities can be considered as core building blocks: the *environment*, and the actual *agents* (both either physical or logical).

In this paper we present RAMSES—Reversibility-based Agent Modeling and Simulation Environment with Speculation-support[2]— which has been conceived by starting from the conjecture that the environment can represent the *dominant* objects' category in a wide set of agent-based simulation models. In fact, the environment can experience changes which are either independent of or dependent on the actual agents behavior, and at the same time agents interact among each other within (a portion of) the environment. We exploit this conjecture of *dominance by the environment* to set up a PDES-based execution framework in which the actual evolution of the system is driven only by discrete events which affect portions of the environment—in fact, agent/agent and agent/environment interactions can be easily mapped to events which take place within the environment only. This will be reflected, particularly, in the API offered by RAMSES to the simulation model developer.

Concerning run-time efficiency, RAMSES specifically targets parallel execution on multi/many-core environments, where the simulation's execution is partitioned among different worker-threads that share the overall simulation workload. Also, the approach to synchronize the activities of the different worker-threads to ensure a causally-consistent evolution of the simulation model (global) state, allows for *speculative event processing*, a technique that has been shown to provide high scalability in disparate execution environments (see, e.g., [6]). As for this aspect, RAMSES incorporates an innovative support for correct state restore in case of miss speculation (namely, a posteriori detection of out-order execution actually affecting causal consistency), which is based on the software reversibility approach recently presented in [7] and has been shown to have the potential to provide overhead reduction, with respect to classical (e.g. checkpoint-based [8]) state recovery. This is especially true for execution patterns of individual events entailing a reduced amount of simulation state updates, independently of the complexity of the actual logic of the events. This might be the case of agent models, since agents might inspect (read) large chunks of data from the environment, while updating the environment state with a limited number of operations (at least in the likely case).

To assess the viability of our proposal, we rely on a set of experiments carried out by using a distributed multi-robot exploration and mapping simulation model developed on the basis of the results in [9]. We compare the performance of RAMSES with an implementation of the same simulation model on top of ROOT-Sim [10], namely a highly-optimized general-purpose simulation framework offering speculative execution capabilities for PDES models. We also consider software development aspects in the comparison (e.g. required number of

---

[2] The source code of RAMSES can be found at https://github.com/HPDCS/RAMSES

code lines for the same model in the different—special vs general purpose—frameworks).

The remainder of this paper is structured as follows. In Sect. 2, related work is discussed. The internal structure of RAMSES and the exposed API are described in Sect. 3. The experimental study is presented in Sect. 4.

2 Related Work

We can find a large number of frameworks to support agent-based simulation in the literature. The MASON framework [11] pays special attention to the performance of simulation execution, addressing computing-intensive models (i.e., large scenarios with many agents), along with portability and reproducibility of the results across different hardware architectures. A parallel/distributed version (D-MASON) has been presented in [12], which relies on time-stepped synchronization and on the master/slave paradigm. We similarly address the performance of agent-based simulation execution, yet we do this for the case of speculative asynchronous (non-time-stepped) PDES, relying on the innovative generation of update undo code blocks for the reconciliation of causality errors.

Pandora [13] is a C++-based simulation framework enabling executions in parallel/distributed environments. It features several AI algorithms for supporting agents' decision making and provides python bindings (which is a benefit for inexperienced programmers). On the other hand, RAMSES provides the simulation model developer with an API that is specifically tailored for implementing simulation models in ANSI-C, which binds the interactions to the environment. This allows for a simplified implementation of simulation models, giving transparently access to highly optimized synchronization facilities to support efficient computations on multi/many-core machines.

AnyLogic [14] is a commercial multi-method general-purpose simulation modeling and execution framework, offering at the same time the possibility to support discrete-event, system dynamics, and agent-based simulation. The simulation model developer can rely on graphical modeling languages to implement the simulation models, along with Java code. Differently from this framework, we target C technology and rely on innovative synchronization protocols to carry on the simulation work. Additionally, we provide an API specifically targeting agent-based models, allowing for an easy implementation of simulation models.

FLAME [15] is a simulation framework targeting large, complex models with large agent populations to be run on HPC platforms using MPI and OpenMP. The counterpart FLAME GPU [16] targets 3D simulations of complex systems with a multi-massive number of agents on GPU devices. We keep the ability to deal with large amount of agents, yet we rely on traditional CPU-based execution of the simulation model.

RAMSES is naturally related to the literature dealing with parallel speculative processing. This paradigm is recognized as a means to achieve scalability thanks to the (partial) removal of the cost for coordinating concurrent processes and/or threads from the critical path of task processing (see, e.g., [17]).

In the PDES context, the speculative paradigm is incarnated by the well-known Time Warp synchronization protocol [18], which has been recently shown to provide scalability up to thousands or millions of CPU-cores [6]. Among the PDES platforms that have been developed by relying on Time Warp synchronization, a close one to RAMSES is ROOT-Sim [10]. This is a general-purpose speculative simulation framework for discrete-event simulation models that has been recently enhanced with the software reversibility support we exploit in RAMSES. Although ROOT-Sim has been proven [19,20] to be able to efficiently carry out the execution of agent-based models, it does not account for the requirements of developing this kind of models. Conversely, in RAMSES, we offer a specific API to let the model writer implement agent-based models more easily. Additionally, the internal runtime execution support which we propose in this paper is based on an innovative synchronization protocol different from the more traditional Time Warp-based one of ROOT-Sim.

3   RAMSES

3.1   Reference Programming Model

We target a programming model in which two different types of entities compose the overall structure of the simulated phenomenon. On the one side we have the environment, which could be of any size and shape, yet we expect it to be divided into regions. Each region has the following characteristics:

- A region has a state, which describes all the aspects of the environment. We do not place any limit on the number and kind of aspects that a region might have, thus giving the model programmer the highest degree of freedom in the definition of the environment.
- A region might host one or multiple agents at a given time instant.
- The internal state of the region might be modified either by external circumstances (e.g., an earthquake might change the shape of the terrain), or by the interaction with one or more agents (e.g., one agent might drop or collect objects into a region).
- Regions can be logically connected to each other depending on the actual model's logic, thus the environment is customizable in size and shape.

On the other side we have agents, which adhere to the following behavior:

- Agents have a state, which describes all the aspects of their current evolution within the environment. This state can describe either physical characteristics (e.g., the conditions of some parts of a mechanical agent) or logical/cognitive characteristics (e.g., the knowledge of the environment that an exploring agent has gathered so far).
- Agents are always located in a region. We note that this does not pose a limitation to the programming freedom of the model developer, as logical dummy regions can be used to host agents, in case the model requires agents to be outside of the environment, at a given point in the simulation.

- Agents can move freely in the environment, yet moving only across regions which are adjacent. Again, this does not pose a limitation to the programming freedom, as any region can be connected to any other region, depending on the model's logic.
- Agents can interact with each other. Nevertheless, this interaction can only take place when two agents are located within the same region.
- Agents can interact with the environment. In particular, they can inspect the environment to gather knowledge, or they can modify it.

We emphasize that (as already hinted) all the interactions take place within regions. Therefore, changes in the state of any entity (be it a region or an agent) which are produced by the events' execution take place according to the (simulated) time advancement of regions. We call this property *dominance by the environment*, which will be exploited by the architectural organization presented in Sect. 3.4. In particular, since our simulation framework executes according to a PDES scheme, we map only regions to the traditional notion of simulation objects. In this way, we are able to significantly reduce the amount of entities which are managed by the multi-threaded simulation infrastructure, and the associated management/synchronization costs.

3.2 Exposed API

The API exposed by RAMSES includes functions of various nature, which can be grouped into two main categories: functions to model the initial state of the simulation (in terms of description of the environment and agents) and to carry on the evolution of the system, and library functions to manipulate the topology of the environment and retrieve the simulation state of regions and agents. For the sake of space constraints, we refer to the online RAMSES documentation for a comprehensive and technical description of the whole set of API functions and supported topologies. We discuss here the basic functions, to let the reader understand the principles driving the implementation of models on top of RAMSES.

To setup and start the simulation, the model writer issues a call (possibly from `main()`) to the `Setup()` API, which allows to specify both the number of regions and agents, along with two *initialization callbacks*, say function pointers, one for the regions and one for the agents. Both pointers refer functions accepting one integer as input (which is the id number of the agent or the region, assigned by the engine) and must return a pointer to the (allocated) simulation state, which will be then managed by the simulation framework. During the initialization of an agent, a call to `void InitialPosition(unsigned int region)` must be issued, so as to specify in which region the currently being initialized agent is placed. Failing to do so results in a runtime error. After the call to `Setup()`, the simulation application can call `void StartSimulation(int n_cores)`, which creates n parallel worker-threads and carries on the simulation execution.

Concerning interactions among agents and the environment, four specific API functions allow to inject in the system new events. They are:

- void Move(uint32_t agent, uint32_t dest, simtime_t time): by issuing a call to this function, the model tells the simulation framework that at a certain time (denoted by time) the agent agent is moving from the current region which is hosting it to the region identified by dest.
- void AgentInteraction(uint32_t agent_a, uint32_t agent_b, simtime_t time, interaction_f agent_int, void *args, size_t size): this function tells the simulation framework that at time time two agents, agent_a and agent_b want to interact. The actual interaction is modeled by the function pointed by agent_int, which receives as argument the buffer pointed by args. If at time time the two agents agent_a and agent_b are not in the same region, a runtime error is issued.
- void EnvironmentInteraction(uint32_t agent, uint32_t region, simtime_t time, interaction_f environment_int, void *args, size_t size): in case one agent wants to interact with the surrounding environment, namely with a region, this function tells the simulation engine that at time time the agent agent is expected to be found in region region. If this is not the case, a runtime error is issued. On the other hand, the model code receives a call to the function pointed by environment_int, having args as the parameter.
- void EnvironmentUpdate(uint32_t region, simtime_t time, update_f environment_update, void *args, size_t size): to model updates to the environment which are not related to the interaction with agents, this API function can be used to notify that at time time an update to region should be carried out by the function pointed by environment_update.

Concerning the topology, RAMSES offers several API functions to organize the regions in common topologies. As an example, in case of random movements, by calling int FindRegion(int type) the model can receive the id of a neighbor region according to a given topology organization described by type.

3.3   Tracking Memory Updates for Reversibility

We rely on software instrumentation to transparently modify the application-level code, in order to let RAMSES engine track at runtime what are the *effects* of the forward execution of events on the simulation model's state. This information is used to build a packed version of negative instructions which only undo the effects of the forward execution, allowing for a reverse execution of events (in terms of state updates) which is independent of the actual forward event granularity (CPU requirement). The whole approach is based on the coexistence of dual executable modes (inspired to [19]), to quickly switch between two operative modes: one tracking memory updates, one which does not.

To statically instrument the application-level code, we rely on the open-source Hijacker [21] tool. By relying on Hijacker, we can specify (via a set of xml-based rules) what are the instrumentation steps to be undertaken before the final linking stage of the application is executed[3]. More specifically, we instruct Hijacker to create multiple copies of the same executable, but differently instrumented. This technique, known as *multi-coding*, creates different versions of the application which nevertheless share the same data sections within the virtual address space, but can be accessed using ad-hoc altered function names. One copy of the software is left untouched (namely, no instrumentation is applied to it). Therefore, this first version can be regarded as the original code, which therefore does not provide any possibility to undo the effects on memory (in terms of updates) by the execution of an event.

The second version, on the other hand, is managed by Hijacker so that the whole simulation model's code is scanned to find assembly instructions which have a memory address as the destination operand[4]. Before each memory-write instruction, Hijacker places a call to a specific internal trampoline, along with some instructions which generate an *invocation context* for it. This trampoline function computes the ultimate target memory address which will be accessed in write mode, and the size of the writing. The couple $\langle address, size \rangle$ is then passed as input to the internal `reverse_generator(void *address, size_t size)` module of RAMSES, which generates the reverse code instructions, just before any memory-update operation is performed.

These *negative* instructions are simply built by accessing memory at `address` and by reading `size` bytes. Since the invocation of `reverse_generator` happens right before the execution of the original memory-write instruction, this allows the module to retrieve the "old" value of the memory location belonging to the simulation model's state. Therefore, it is used to build a *negative* data movement instruction whose destination is `address`. Generally, the generation of negative instructions is not a costly operation as all the opcodes are known beforehand, allowing to use pre-compiled tables of instructions, where only the relevant parameters should be packed within, namely the old memory value and the destination address. To keep the negative instructions packed, each worker-thread operating within the RAMSES simulation engine relies on a (heap-allocated) *reverse window* structure. This structure allows to immediately determine the memory position at which a negative instruction must be stored. In particular, after having allocated at startup the reverse window, instructions are generated in a top-heading stack. This solution allows for a fast annihilation of the effects of an event, as simply jumping to the last-generated instruction (namely, the one on the top of the stack) is enough to execute the negative instructions in reverse order. This is done by issuing a `call` to the address of the top-standing instruction, thus undoing the effects until a final `ret` instruction placed at the

---

[3] Hijacker works on *relocatable object files* (specifically on the Executable and Linkable Format—ELF), therefore it must be regarded as an additional compilation step of the executable building procedure.

[4] The most significant instructions for the x86 architecture (which represents our target) are `mov`, `movs`, and `cmov` instructions, and are handled internally by Hijacker in different ways. The same is true for vectorized memory access instructions such as `movdqa`.

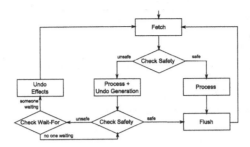

Fig. 1. Main loop flow chart

buffer end is found. Clearly, a unique reverse instruction for any different memory location that is touched by the simulation event in write mode is inserted in the reverse window (namely, the reverse instruction associated with the first update occurring on that location while processing a single event).

3.4 Runtime Execution Support

We consider a scenario where all the scheduled events (including the simulation startup events), destined to whichever simulation object, are kept within a unique pool. For efficiency reasons, we consider a classical calendar queue [22], which provides average $O(1)$ performance. The ordering of the elements into the calendar queue is based on events' timestamp. Each event also keeps information regarding which is the target simulation object (namely the region) and the actual event's type and payload. Nevertheless, the event type is not defined by the model developer. Rather, with respect to the API discussed in Sect. 3.2, the type is internally used by the engine to determine what is the type of callback to be invoked. All the events kept in the calendar queue are *schedule-committed* (hence non-retractable). In fact, in our approach the events that are scheduled during the processing of an event according to the reversibility scheme are only flushed upon the detection of the event *safety* (i.e. causal consistency).

The calendar queue data structure is coupled with an array of N entries that we name processing[]. The i-th entry is used to keep data related to the status of the i-th worker-thread, noted WT_i. This array is initialized at simulation startup with all the entries keeping the special value ∞. Each worker-thread WT_i follows through the algorithmic actions depicted in Fig. 1. It performs the FETCH operation presented in Algorithm 1, which (in case the *last_event* input parameter, indicating whether an event still to be processed is already bound to this thread, is $NULL$) atomically extracts the event e with minimum timestamp that is currently registered into the calendar queue, and records the extracted timestamp value into the entry processing[i] associated with WT_i. Atomicity ensures that an event is taken by only one thread.

Due to the multi-threaded nature and the speculative flavor of our simulation environment, no two different worker-threads can execute at the same time multiple events which entail reading/updating the same memory regions.

Algorithm 1. Fetch procedure - worker-thread WT_i

```
 1: procedure FETCH(last_event e) RETURNS: event
 2:    if e = NULL then
 3:       SPINLOCK(global_lock) //this branch is atomic via a globally shared lock
 4:       e ← GETMINIMUMTIMESTAMPEVENTFROMCALENDARQUEUE( )
 5:       processing[i] ← T(e)
 6:       SPINUNLOCK(global_lock)
 7:    end if
 8:    if ¬TRYLOCK(region_lock[e.destination]) then
 9:       repeat
10:          reupdateMin ← false
11:          minWait ← wait_time[e.destination]
12:          if T(e) < minWait then
13:             if ¬ CAS(wait_time[e.destination], minWait, T(e)) then
14:                reupdateMin ← true
15:             end if
16:          end if
17:       until reupdateMin
18:       while TRUE do
19:          SPINLOCK(region_lock[e.destination])
20:          if T(e) ≤ wait_time[e.destination] then break
21:          end if
22:          SPINUNLOCK(region_lock[e.destination])
23:       end while
24:    end if
25:    return e
26: end procedure
```

Therefore, to enforce data separation, we rely on an array of spinlocks, which we call `region_lock[]`. Whenever WT_i fetches an event e from the calendar queue, it tries to acquire the lock for the given recipient simulation object (see Algorithm 1). In case the lock cannot be taken, it means that another worker-thread is currently executing operations on the region's state. In this case, the worker-thread spins on the lock, until the other worker-thread completes its operations. We note that, due to the region dominance property defined in Sect. 3.1, this sanity check ensures as well that all worker-threads access the agents' states in data separation, as no agent can be (at the same time) in two different regions.

When an event is processed, new events possibly generated by the processing actions are temporarily buffered (hence not yet flushed to the calendar queue). However in case they eventually become schedule committed, then the FLUSH procedure is called, which atomically inserts them into the calendar queue.

To cope with consistency, and to determine event processing commitment and event schedule commitment, we exploit the values kept by the `processing[]` array. The condition that tells whether a worker-thread WT_i can safely commit the event it is handling is $\forall j \neq i : processing[i] < processing[j]$. This condition tells that the (possibly speculatively) executed event is associated with the current lower bound timestamp across all the events in the system[5]. Hence the timestamp of this event represents the commit horizon, and the event can be

---

[5] The case of simultaneous events, where $T(e)$ may be equal to $T(e')$, can be addressed using a variant of Lamport's bakery algorithm [23] either including causality information or simply thread identifiers.

safely executed or (in case of already carried out speculative execution) safely committed.

Concerning execution liveness, if the `region_lock` is taken by any worker-thread speculatively processing an event e associated with $T(e)$, and during its execution a new event e' associated with $T(e') < T(e)$ is flushed (e.g., by a worker-thread executing in non-speculative mode) into the calendar queue, we might incur in livelock. Therefore, an additional array `wait_time[]`, with one entry for each managed region, is used to notify worker-threads running in speculative mode that an event with higher priority is waiting to be processed by another worker-thread (see Algorithm 1 for the logic used to post the event timestamp value within this array entries). As depicted in Fig. 1, if a worker-thread has executed speculatively an event which is (not yet) safe, it checks whether any other worker-thread has registered within the `wait_time[]` array a timestamp which is less than that of the event currently being processed. In the positive case, the effects of the event's execution are undone (by simply jumping to the generated reverse window) and the region lock is released. In this case, the event stays bound to the worker-thread (for re-processing), and is passed in input to FETCH, which will skip extracting another event from the calendar queue. On the other hand, in case of commitment of the processed event, a $NULL$ value is passed in input (as last-event record) to the FETCH procedure.

4   Experimental Results

To assess the programmability and performance of RAMSES, we have implemented a distributed multi-robot exploration and mapping simulation model, according to the results in [9]. A group of robots is set out into an unknown space to fully explore it, while acquiring data from sensors to map the environment. Whenever a robot has to make a decision about which direction should be taken to carry on the exploration, it is done by relying on the notion of *exploration frontier*. By keeping a representation of the explored world, the robot is able to detect which is the closest unexplored area which it can reach, computes the fastest way to reach it and continues the exploration. The robots explore independently of each other until one coincidentally detects another robot. In this case, they exchange the data acquired during the exploration, thus reducing the exploration time and allowing for more accurate decisions. We have implemented this model on top of both RAMSES and ROOT-Sim[6]. The latter is an open source PDES simulation engine developed using C/POSIX technology, still targeting speculative processing. Differently from RAMSES, it is general purpose, thus offering an API based on a single application entry point, representing the event handler. ROOT-Sim transparently supports all the mechanisms associated with parallelization (e.g., mapping of simulation objects on different kernel instances) and optimistic synchronization (e.g., state recoverability). This allow us to compare the efficiency of our innovative runtime execution support

---

[6] The ROOT-Sim version is the one used as test-bed in [8].

against an already highly-optimized, but general purpose, simulation framework for PDES, targeting as well multi/many-core architectures.

We simulated an environment composed of 4096 regions, and we varied the number of agent (robot) units moving around between 100 and 1000, which allowed us assessing how the performance of RAMSES scales vs variations of the ratio between the number of regions and the number of agents.

In Fig. 2 we report data for a comparison of the performance achieved via RAMSES and ROOT-Sim with the one achieved via sequential execution of the simulation model (on top of a calendar queue scheduler)[7]. All the experiments have been carried out on an HP ProLiant server, equipped with four 2 GHz AMD Opteron 6128 processors and 64 GB of RAM. Each processor has 8 cores (for a total of 32 cores) that share a 12 MB L3 cache (6 MB per each 4-cores set), and each core has a 512 KB private L2 cache. The architecture entails 8 different NUMA nodes. The operating system is 64-bit Debian 6, with Linux Kernel version 2.6.32.5.

By the results, when the number of robots is small (namely, 100 robots), the speedup offered by RAMSES over the sequential run is low, while ROOT-Sim provides definitely better reduction of the execution time. However, for large numbers of simulated robots (namely, 1000 robots), RAMSES starts becoming competitive with respect to ROOT-Sim, by providing a speedup over the sequential run of about 15. We deduce that this performance trend is directly linked to how the simulation engine manages event concurrency. Particularly, in ROOT-Sim the robots are modeled as purely concurrent entities, which leads to the fact that if multiple robots collide within the same region, the associated events can still be processed concurrently. Instead, in RAMSES, if multiple robots temporarily reside within the same region, then all their events are sequentialized given that they are mapped to region-events at the level of the reversibility-based speculative underlying engine. However, for larger numbers of robots, we get higher likelihood that multiple regions hosting robots can be scheduled concurrently by the RAMSES engine. On the other hand, the ratio between the number of application level code lines to implement the model in RAMSES and in ROOT-Sim is of the order of 0.65, which roughly indicates 35 % reduction of the application code complexity for implementing the same model, achieved thanks to the agent-modeling suited API offered by RAMSES. Overall, RAMSES can exemplify the development of agent-based models (as compared to what allowed by a classical general purpose PDES engine) while still providing run time efficiency especially for more complex models (namely with larger ratio between active and passive objects).

---

[7] The sequential code version exactly corresponds to the one run on top of ROOT-Sim. However, a port of the version run on RAMSES on the same sequential engine provided quite similar execution times.

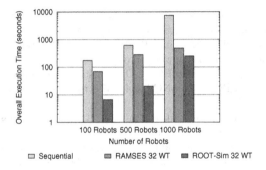

Fig. 2. Experimental results: 4096 regions, varied number of robots.

5 Conclusions

In this paper we have presented RAMSES, a framework for agent-based modeling and simulation, relying on speculative concurrent processing and an innovative synchronization (namely rollback) protocol which exploits reversibility to undo a portion of the speculative simulation which is a-posteriori detected to be inconsistent. The experimental assessment on a case study has shown that RAMSES is performance-effective especially for more complex models and, at the same time, can definitely reduce the complexity of coding agent-models when compared to what can be done on top of general-purpose parallel simulation frameworks.

References

1. Takahashi, T., Tadokoro, S., Ohta, M., Ito, N.: Agent based approach in disaster rescue simulation - from test-bed of multiagent system to practical application. In: Birk, A., Coradeschi, S., Tadokoro, S. (eds.) RoboCup 2001. LNCS (LNAI), vol. 2377, pp. 102–111. Springer, Heidelberg (2002)
2. Macy, M.W., Willer, R.: From factors to actors: computational sociology and agent-based modeling. Ann. Rev. Sociol. **28**(1), 143–166 (2002)
3. Macal, C., North, M.: Tutorial on agent-based modeling and simulation part 2: how to model with agents. In: Proceedings of the 2006 Winter Simulation Conference, WSC, pp. 73–83. Society for Computer Simulation (2006)
4. Page, S.E.: Agent-based models. In: Durlauf, S.N., Blume, L.E. (eds.) The New Palgrave Dictionary of Economics. Palgrave Macmillan (2008)
5. Fujimoto, R.M.: Parallel discrete event simulation. In: Proceedings of the 21st Conference on Winter Simulation, WSC, pp. 19–28. ACM Press (1989)
6. Barnes Jr, P.D., Carothers, C.D., Jefferson, D.R., LaPre, J.M.: Warp speed: executing time warp on 1, 966, 080 cores. In: SIGSIM Principles of Advanced Discrete Simulation, SIGSIM-PADS 2013, Montreal, QC, Canada, 19–22 May 2013, pp. 327–336 (2013)
7. Cingolani, D., Pellegrini, A., Quaglia, F.: Transparently mixing undo logs and software reversibility for state recovery in optimistic pdes. In: Proceedings of the 2015 ACM SIGSIM Conference on Principles of Advanced Discrete Simulation, SIGSIM-PADS. ACM Press, June 2015

8. Pellegrini, A., Vitali, R., Quaglia, F.: Autonomic state management for optimistic simulation platforms. IEEE Trans. Parallel Distrib. Syst. **26**(6), 1560–1569 (2015)

9. Fox, D., Ko, J., Konolige, K., Limketkai, B., Schulz, D., Stewart, B.: Distributed multirobot exploration and mapping. Proc. IEEE **94**(7), 1325–1339 (2006)

10. Pellegrini, A., Quaglia, F.: The ROme OpTimistic simulator: a tutorial. In: Mey, D., et al. (eds.) Euro-Par 2013. LNCS, vol. 8374, pp. 501–512. Springer, Heidelberg (2014)

11. Luke, S., Cioffi-Revilla, C., Panait, L., Sullivan, K., Balan, G.: Mason: a multiagent simulation environment. Simulation **81**(7), 517–527 (2005)

12. Cordasco, G., De Chiara, R., Mancuso, A., Mazzeo, D., Scarano, V., Spagnuolo, C.: A framework for distributing agent-based simulations. In: Alexander, M., et al. (eds.) Euro-Par 2011, Part I. LNCS, vol. 7155, pp. 460–470. Springer, Heidelberg (2012)

13. Wittek, P., Rubio-Campillo, X.: Scalable agent-based modelling with cloud HPC resources for social simulations. In: Proceedings of the 4th International Conference on Cloud Computing Technology and Science, CloudCom, pp. 355–362. IEEE Computer Society (2012)

14. Karpov, Y.G.: Anylogic – a new generation professional simulation tool. In: Proceedings of the 6th International Congress on Mathematical Modeling, MATH-MOD, September 2004

15. Holcombe, M., Coakley, S., Smallwood, R.: A general framework for agent-based modelling of complex systems. In: Proceedings of the 2006 European Conference on Complex Systems. European Complex Systems Society, Paris, France (2006)

16. Richmond, P., Romano, D.: Agent based GUP, a real-time 3D simulation and interactive visualisation framework for massive agent based modelling on the gpu. In: Proceedings International Workshop on Supervisualisation (2008)

17. Romano, P., Palmieri, R., Quaglia, F., Carvalho, N., Rodrigues, L.: On speculative replication of transactional systems. J. Comput. Syst. Sci. **80**(1), 257–276 (2014)

18. Jefferson, D.R.: Virtual Time. ACM Trans. Prog. Lang. Syst. **7**(3), 404–425 (1985)

19. Pellegrini, A., Quaglia, F.: Programmability and performance of parallel ECS-based simulation of multi-agent exploration models. In: Lopes, L., et al. (eds.) Euro-Par 2014, Part I. LNCS, vol. 8805, pp. 395–406. Springer, Heidelberg (2014)

20. Pellegrini, A., Quaglia, F.: A study on the parallelization of terrain-covering ant robots simulations. In: Mey, D., et al. (eds.) Euro-Par 2013. LNCS, vol. 8374, pp. 585–594. Springer, Heidelberg (2014)

21. Pellegrini, A.: Hijacker: efficient static software instrumentation with applications in high performance computing (poster paper). In: Proceedings of the 2013 International Conference on High Performance Computing & Simulation, HPCS. IEEE Computer Society, July 2013

22. Brown, R.: Calendar queues: a fast O(1) priority queue implementation for the simulation event set problem. Commun. ACM **31**, 1220–1227 (1988)

23. Lamport, L.: A new solution of Dijkstra's concurrent programming problem. Commun. ACM **17**(8), 453–455 (1974)

PELGA - Performance Engineering for Large-scale Graph Analytics

Can Embedding Solve Scalability Issues for Mixed-Data Graph Clustering?

Nadezhda Fedorova, Josep Blat, and David F. Nettleton[(✉)]

Department of Information Technology and Communications,
Universitat Pompeu Fabra, Barcelona, Spain
{nadezda.fedorova,josep.blat,david.nettleton}@upf.edu

Abstract. It is widely accepted that the field of Data Analytics has entered into the era of Big Data. In particular, it has to deal with so-called Big Graph Data, which is the focus of this paper. Graph Data is present in many fields, such as Social Networks, Biological Networks, Computer Networks, and so on. It is recognized that data analysts benefit from interactive real time data exploration techniques such as clustering and zoom capabilities on the clusters. However, although clustering is one of the key aspects of graph data analysis, there is a lack of scalable graph clustering algorithms which would support interactive techniques. This paper presents an approach based on combining graph clustering and graph coordinate system embedding, and which shows promising results through initial experiments. Our approach also incorporates both structural and attribute information, which can lead to a more meaningful clustering.

Keywords: Graphs · Embedding · Scalability · Clustering

1 Introduction

Often the data within so called Big Data is highly connected and with a complex structure. Representing it as a graph with attributes associated to nodes and relationships to edges usually provides a good model. Social Networks, Biological Networks and Telecommunications Networks are examples of areas where graph models are widely used. The representation of data as a graph allows the exploration of highly connected data through searching paths among nodes and other graph-related tasks, which are useful in different contexts of the areas exemplified [1, 2].

When the graphs become larger and their structure more complex, querying and accessing the data becomes more difficult. Interactive clustering and cluster analysis can play a key role in this case, as data-mining and statistical methods could be coupled with interactive clustering to get better solutions when handling large volumes of data [2]. Exploratory Data Analysis requires systems that are interactive for users and which incorporate commonly used techniques such as clustering, visual filtering, zooming and aggregation [3, 4], in order to process the large amount of available data in big data and graphs [5].

Our paper focuses on the issue of graph simplification techniques, and more specifically on the clustering algorithms that they rely upon [6]. These algorithms should be highly *scalable*, however, current analytical methods requiring big graph

© Springer International Publishing Switzerland 2015
S. Hunold et al. (Eds.): Euro-Par 2015 Workshops, LNCS 9523, pp. 481–492, 2015.
DOI: 10.1007/978-3-319-27308-2_39

data clustering have scalability problems and a consequent lack of interactivity, as we discuss further in the related work [5, 7]. A second important issue of graph clustering is that most solutions address either the structure of graph (its topology) or the nodes attribute information and different data types (numerical, categorical, etc.), i.e. its content information. In this paper we propose scalable graph clustering algorithms, which can incorporate both structural and contextual information of a graph.

The major contribution of this paper is to combine two existing techniques, graph embedding and clustering, in a novel way which has not being attempted previously in the literature, to solve an important problem for graph data analysts, which is interactive graph clustering.

Although parallelization is not the focus of the work presented in this paper, we have chosen an embedding and a clustering method which are highly parallelizable, and we discuss how to do this in the paper, as future work.

The paper is structured as follows: in Sect. 2 we discuss relevant related works; in Sect. 3 we outline our graph embedding and clustering approach; in Sect. 4 we present the empirical results of benchmarking the embedded graphs for different dataset sizes and numbers of clusters, discuss thresholds of interactivity for a user and discuss the parallelization of the processes. Finally, we present the conclusions and future work.

2   State of the Art and Related Work

In this Section we consider graph clustering approaches in general, mixed data type clustering approaches, k-Means clustering which we adapt for out method and graph embedding systems.

2.1   Graph Clustering Approaches

The interactive techniques, aggregation, zooming and filtering of considerable volumes of highly multidimensional data are strongly based on clustering algorithms which provide a perception of their general structure and trends, based on a good summarization [8]. Most current approaches to graph clustering can be classified as *structural* or *content-based* [8]. A purely structural approach takes into consideration only the topological information (structure) of a graph, and not the domain knowledge (attributes). Modularity, spectral or singularity based, fuzzy, Markov chain and local are some examples of the structural approach to clustering. As indicated in [9, 10], this approach leads to a random distribution of vertex properties (the meaning of this within cluster as information content is not considered). The purely content-based clustering approach takes into consideration just the domain knowledge, but not the topological information of the graph. This usually leads to clustering solutions that are domain-specific, over-specialized, and with a loose intra-cluster structure [9, 10].

2.2 Mixed Data Type Clustering Approaches

Some representative references of the number of works addressing mixed clustering in recent years are [10–13]. The most widely discussed and cited algorithm is *SA-Cluster*, described in [9]. It can be argued that it represents the state-of-the-art approach to be compared with. The algorithm aims at maintaining at the same time both homogeneous attribute values and cohesive structure within clusters. Extensive experiments over a number of real-world networks using a set of metrics, such as density, entropy, DBI (the metrics definition can be found in [14, 15]) run time, support the adequacy of the algorithm.

For the understanding of our contributions, let us describe summarily the SA-Cluster algorithm [9]. The initial graph (the "structure") is extended with additional nodes and attributes (which are associated with the nodes), thus adding new edges. In this way the attribute information is present in the structure of the new augmented heterogeneous graph. This augmented graph will be clustered on the basis of a distance combining both attribute and structural distances, which is changed iteratively in the clustering process as described next.

One starts with a (random walk) distance defined as follows: consider a transition probability matrix P over a graph which indicates the probability of transition between any two nodes, and a restart probability $c(c(1 - c)^{length(\tau)}$ which represents the probability of returning back to the initial node following a random walk of length(τ)). We note the following: τ is a path from v_i to v_j whose length is length(τ); and $c \in (0,1)$ is the restart probability. That is, before making a choice on the random walk, there is a probability c of returning to the starting node.

We note the distinction between a 'path' and a 'walk': a path can be said to link two vertices v_i and v_j, whereas a 'walk' may start at a vertex v_i and finish at another vertex v_j.

Given the definition for the random walk, the neighbourhood random walk distance between two nodes, v_i and v_j of the initial graph can be defined as:

$$d(v_i; v_j) = \sum_{length(\tau) \leq l}^{\tau: v_i \rightarrow v_j} p(\tau)c(1 - c)^{length(\tau)} \tag{1}$$

in which $p(\tau)$ is the transition probability and l is the length that a random walk can go.

The initial weights of the transition probability matrix P are 1.0 for both structural and attribute nodes, and are changed at each clustering iteration using:

$$\omega_i^{t+1} = \frac{1}{2}(\omega_i^t + \Delta\omega_i^t) \tag{2}$$

in which ω represents the weight of attribute a_i in the $(t + 1)^{th}$ iteration.

As SA-Clustering uses random walk distances it is difficult to parallelize; and, even more, not practically applicable for large graphs/networks. A range of improvements, and alternative approaches have been proposed, which we turn to next.

SI-cluster [11] is another distance-based algorithm, which is specifically focused on social networks. It is based on a heat-diffusion model of the network. It splits the initial graph into a set of influence graphs, followed by an iteration process of cluster quantification and weights update similar to that of SA-Cluster, with the difference that influence-based scores as measures are used. The SI-algorithm runtime scales better for the large datasets, and significantly outperforms all the previous algorithms. Indeed, one of the results is that SI-Cluster can handle 1 M nodes on an 8 GB machine in just over 6000 s, while the other algorithms ran out of memory. Its main limitation is that the heat diffusion model might be limited to Social Networks.

2.3   K-Means Clustering Algorithm

In the current work we have adapted the standard k-Means [16] for mixed data type clustering. We will now give a brief description of the basic algorithm. Later in Sect. 3 we will describe the adaptations made. k-Means [16] is an iterative algorithm which partitions n observations into k clusters in which each observation belongs to the cluster whose mean value is closest to the value of the observation. In each cluster, the mean value represents the 'prototype' or 'centroid' of that cluster. More specifically, consider that we given as initial input to k-Means a set of observations $(x_1, x_2,..., x_n)$, in which each observation is a d-dimensional real vector. That is a file whose rows are the observations and the columns are the attributes. The algorithm will then try to partition the n observations into k ($\leq$ n) sets S = $\{S_1, S_2,..., S_k\}$ in such as way that the within-cluster sum of squares (Eq. 3) of the distances between the centroid (mean) and the observations will be minimized. That is:

$$argmin_s \sum_{i=1}^{k} \sum_{x \in Si} \|x - \mu_i\|^2 \tag{3}$$

where μ_i is the mean of points in cluster S_i.

2.4   Graph Embedding Systems

In simple terms, graph embedding is a process in which a graph (vertices, edges) is mapped into a space in which the distance between the vertices can be read off as coordinates within that space. For example, if two nodes which are three links away in a graph are embedded in a two dimensional space, then a physical (Euclidean) distance between them would be three (units). This representation is very useful for answering distance queries, for example, in a Telecommunications Network. A more formal treatment is given in Sect. 3 of the paper.

   Two embedding systems which are commonly referenced in the literature are Orion [17], a graph coordinate embedding on Euclidean spaces and Rigel [18], which uses hyperbolic spaces. Both have a computationally expensive first step of graph embedding and coordinate computation, but then the distance between any two nodes can be quickly computed.

   Orion [17] maps the graph nodes to a low-dimensional Euclidean space coordinate system. A landmark-based approach is used: a fixed reasonably small number of nodes are selected and the distances between each pair of them are computed. Then, the remaining nodes obtain their coordinates iteratively, one by one, through a BFS (Breadth-First Search) algorithm to calculate the distances to each landmark. Landmarks are chosen according to their degree of centrality and being far apart: nodes with a higher degree of centrality and not too close to each other are preferred. Rigel [18] employs a hyperbolic coordinate system for graph embedding, making use of parallelization to reduce the computational cost, by partitioning the graph and performing the embedding in parallel. The system is also landmark based. The additional parameter for the hyperbolic space, the curvature, has to be calibrated.

According to [17], the Orion embedding of a 275 K-node graph takes about 2–3 h, with an error of 15–20 % on average, i.e., between 0.5 and 5 hops in absolute terms. Rigel, on the other hand, is in principle more time-consuming than Orion, but as the embedding can be parallelized it can serve for very large graphs. The accuracy of shortest path computation is significantly higher on average, the absolute error ranging between 0 and 0.9 hops. We will discuss the parallelization of Rigel later in Sect. 4.6.

3 Graph Coordinates Approach: Embedding + Clustering

In this Section we describe our novel approach for interactive clustering of mixed type graph data, based on embedding the graph in an appropriate coordinate system, followed by standard clustering using mixed structural and attribute distance(s).

3.1 Embedding

The embedding of a graph into a coordinate system with a distance is done by a suitable algorithm which maps every vertex to a point in this n-dimensional system (see Fig. 1). The most frequently used is the Euclidean metric space, however we have used the Hyperbolic space, employed by the Rigel [18] system, given its superior precision and performance potential. A particular type of embedding, *greedy embedding,* has been used in telecommunications. It is defined by the following property: for any two nodes p and q of the embedded graph, there is a neighbour q' of q whose (Euclidean) distance to p is less than the one between p and q ([19], p.10). Greedy embedding of telecommunication networks allows for greedy routing of messages within a network.

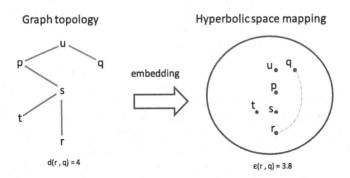

Fig. 1. Schematic representation of the process of graph coordinate embedding

We have implemented the hyperbolic distance embedding. The hyperbolic distance between two n-dimensional points x and y is defined as:

$$\delta(x, y) = \text{arccosh}\left(\sqrt{\left(1 + \sum_{i=1}^{n} x_i^2\right)\left(1 + \sum_{i=1}^{n} y_i^2\right)} - \sum_{i=1}^{n} x_i y_i\right) \cdot |c| \tag{4}$$

Where c is the curvature parameter ($c \leq 0$; $c = 0$ gives Euclidean space). Refer to [18] for specific implementation details.

More formally, to describe the general procedure of embedding, consider a graph $G = (V, E)$, where V is a set of vertices, E is a set of edges, and $s(v_i, v_j)$ is a similarity relationship between the vertex pair (v_i, v_j) in G. Then, the embedding of G into the metric space M using the hyperbolic distance function $\delta(x, y)$ as defined in Eq. 4, is a mapping $f:(G, s) \rightarrow (M, d)$, such that the function $f(s(v_i, v_j))$ in the unmapped space is equivalent to a distance function in the mapped space $d(v_i', v_j')$. We note that the objective is to minimize $s(v_i, v_j) - d(v_i', v_j')$ for each pair of vertices according to the specific choice of norm x, where v_i', v_j' are the images (in M) of the vertices v_i, v_j, respectively.

We recall that the objective of the graph-coordinate system embedding is to be able to read off the shortest paths between vertices, from the mapped (hyperbolic) space, during the clustering process. This shortest value will be used as the numerical value which represents structural information for each pair of vertices in the graph. We note that one of the vertices can be the medoid vertex for a cluster. This calculation can be done 'on the fly' as the distance is calculated between a pair of vertex points.

3.2   Clustering

From Sect. 3.1 we are now able to obtain a numerical distance value $\mathbb{D}(v_i, v_j)$ for each vertex pair in the hyperbolic space representation of the graph: the shortest path distance between them. As we have already stated that we are going to perform mixed data type clustering, we also need a categorical value. We will supply a categorical value Cv_i to each vertex i by randomly assigning categories from a set of N arbitrary category labes as alphabetic letters: A, B, C, etc.

Then, for a vertex pair $\{v_i, v_j\}$ the structural data item will be designated as value $\mathbb{D}(v_i, v_j)$ and the categorical data items will be designated as Cv_i and Cv_j. Then we will calculate the distance between two nodes v_i and v_j, as the weighted sum of the respective categorical data item and the structural data tem, thus:

$$\text{Dist} = (\sigma \times |Cv_i - Cv_{j|}|) + (\phi \times |\mathbb{D}(v_i, v_j)|) \tag{5}$$

where $\sigma + \phi = 1$, $|Cv_i - Cv_{j|}| \in \{0, 1\}$ and $\mathbb{D}(v_i, v_j) \in [0,1]$

We note that the value $\mathbb{D}(v_i, v_j)$ is calculated 'on the fly' and represents the shortest path between corresponding vertices v_i and v_j in the hyperbolic space. The weights σ and ϕ enable us to calibrate the relative weight in the overall distance of the category data item with respect to the numerical structural data item. In the experiments in Sect. 4 have used default values of $\sigma = 0.5$ and $\phi = 0.5$ to give an equal weighting.

While graph embedding is time consuming, it can be conceived as a pre-processing step before clustering. Once done, the distances between nodes and clusters can be very quickly computed, without further concern about the embedding itself.

3.3   Complete Process

Firstly we perform the transformation of the graph data G_D and structure via the Hyperbolic embedding process described in Sect. 3.1, which gives a new graph dataset G_D^M, where M is the new space into which the graph is mapped. Then we apply the adapted k-Means clustering algorithm to the G_D^M to give G_D^{MC}. The complete process is outlined in the pseudo-code embodiment shown as 'Algorithm 1'.

Algorithm 1

Inputs: Graph G_D
Outputs: Clustered graph $G_D{}^{MC}$
Process:
1. Embed graph G_D as points in space M giving $G_D{}^M$
1.1 Apply Hyperbolic embedding $G_D \rightarrow G_D{}^M$
2. Cluster points in space M
2.1 Apply k-Means adapted for mixed data types
2.1.1 $G_D{}^M \rightarrow G_D{}^{MC}$
End Process.

We note that the user could explore the most suitable clustering interactively, for instance, by modifying the weights of the mixed structural and attribute.

4   Scalability Testing

We present first the experimental setup to test the scalability of our approach, then the runtime results, followed by their comparison with other methods, and, finally we discuss interactivity, accuracy and parallelization issues.

4.1   Experimental Setup

To test the feasibility of the proposed approach, we performed hyperbolic graph-coordinate embedding followed by (mixed) clustering using an adapted version of the K-Means algorithm [16]. We considered a simple case for the distance calculation, as described in Sect. 3.2. This simplified model serves our present goal which is to evaluate the feasibility of approach. However, it could be extended to a more general set of cases. We used two different types of graphs: random-built (using R-Mat [20]), and the DBLP bibliographical data graph [21]. We tested with 10 K, 50 K, 100 K, 200 K, 500 K, and 1 M nodes. In the case of the DBLP dataset, we sampled all the available data in order to obtain the required number of nodes for each test dataset. For each dataset, we tested a number of clusters going from 10 to 100, in steps of ten (that is, 10, 20,..., 100). The hardware used was a medium/high range PC with 4 Cores, the CPU being Intel i7 960 at 3.2 GHz. Java/Netbeans were used for programming. The implementation of Rigel (source and executable of hyperbolic embedding system) was adapted from: http://sandlab.cs.ucsb.edu/rigel/. The version of k-Means was Lloyd's within the ELKI framework, adapted from: http://elki.dbs.ifi.lmu.de/.

The tests intend to check the feasibility of the following *use case*: the user starts with a coarse view of 10 clusters and requests finer resolution of the clustering up to 100 clusters. The user intends to use different weights for the mixed distance, which requires re-computing the clustering but not the embedding. Thus, we need to see whether re-computing the clustering can be interactive.

4.2   Results

The graph coordinates (sequential) hyperbolic embedding of 1 M nodes took around 6.5 h, without noticeable difference for the two datasets (Random and DLBP).. However, as it is a pre-processing step, we are not especially concerned about this time and it could be later parallelized as discussed later in Sect. 4.6. We note that the distance calculation between each node pair in the hyperbolic space and the comparison of the categorical values also for each node pair incur an overhead which makes the computational cost non-lineal for increasing graph sizes. However, we would expect a lineal performance to be obtained with parallelization, as is discussed later in Sect. 4.6.

Figure 2(a) shows the runtime in seconds for 1 M node graphs and different numbers of clusters. It confirms the linearity of the runtime with respect to the number of desired clusters, with an upper bound of approximately 83 min for 100 clusters. The run-time is approximately the same for both types of graphs. In Fig. 2(b) we see the runtime in seconds for 100 clusters and different graph sizes, which ranges from 7 s for 10 K nodes and 10 clusters up to the approximately 83 min for 1 M nodes and 100 clusters.

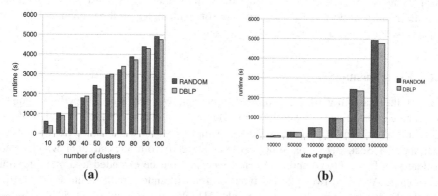

Fig. 2. (a) No of clust. vs. runtime for 1 M nodes; (b) Size of graph vs. runtime for 100 clusters.

The minimal runtime for 500 K nodes and for just 10 clusters, is around 5 min. If the graph size is 10 K or 50 K the worst-case time is 5 min. For 100 K and 200 K nodes, the runtime ranges between 1 and 15 min (see Tables 1 and 2).

Table 1. Clustering time (sec.) for random graph (number of nodes versus number of clusters)

Number of clusters	10 K	50 K	100 K	200 K	500 K	1 M
10	7	25	63	131	232	581
20	9	49	84	169	446	1013
30	18	70	162	314	623	1442
40	19	93	175	364	987	1794
50	24	121	236	497	1229	2436
60	27	144	292	566	1511	2939
70	32	162	320	662	1737	3224
80	40	193	379	719	1940	3898
90	41	217	416	858	2041	4408
100	46	239	486	972	2436	4915

Table 2. Clustering time (sec.) for DBLP graph (number of nodes versus number of clusters)

Number of clusters	10 K	50 K	100 K	200 K	500 K	1 M
10	7	22	67	72	227	394
20	11	51	106	183	386	896
30	16	71	144	310	730	1307
40	18	92	191	412	1003	1898
50	23	122	226	450	1209	2250
60	45	140	302	559	1495	3000
70	50	168	352	638	1735	3404
80	51	189	388	765	1850	3734
90	54	216	408	808	2161	4311
100	59	238	470	948	2350	4780

4.3   Comparison with Other Methods

Most of the state-of-art attribute-structural clustering algorithms mentioned previously, do not scale appropriately as they fail to work on 1 M nodes, with the exception of SI-Cluster. Furthermore, the runtime results presented show that our approach outperforms most of those algorithms, again with the exception of SI-Cluster (which had 6000 s for 1 M nodes and 4000 clusters, and so would outperform our approach on the larger number of clusters), and BAGC, which showed a higher speed. Unlike SI-Cluster, which is limited to social graphs, our approach holds for generic graphs. The approach proposed also has the advantage of potentially allowing modification of weights and only the clustering needs to be re-computed, with the runtimes indicated. Furthermore, it is not limited to categorical/discrete attributes, unlike the other approaches.

4.4   Interactivity

The results shown could be improved using a more powerful desktop computer, or a cluster, however they do provide a qualitative picture in terms of reasonable desktop interactivity for an average user, which depends as well on the context of usage. This paper is not about the parallelization of graph data processing. However, we can say that if we are able to obtain a simpler and more informative representation of a graph topology, this will make any parallelization effort easier and more effective. Furthermore, the current work can be considered a previous step to implementing a parallelized version of the hyperbolic embedding and the k-Means clustering. This is discussed in Sect. 4.6.

With reference to Tables 1 and 2 we could definitely say that 500 K and 1 M nodes currently fail to be interactive irrespective of the number of clusters, as the minimal runtime for 500 K nodes and just 10 clusters is around 5 min. If the graph size is 10 K or 50 K the worst-case time is 5 min, making full interactivity possible for the user. For 100 K and 200 K nodes the runtime ranges between 1 and 15 min, which allows some interactivity, but the number of allowed clusters would be limited. Thus, our approach scales reasonably well, supporting a reasonable interactivity up to medium size graphs and clustering. The tests show that the approach proposed makes interactivity feasible in these cases.

4.5   Accuracy

As already mentioned, we chose to use the Rigel hyperbolic embedding method because its error is much smaller than Orion's Euclidean embedding. However, its absolute error varies from 0 to 0.9 hops, which might be unacceptable in some cases. There could be ways to deal with these limitations, for example, by using overlapping clustering. Indeed, in this case we would just set the gap to $2 \times max(\phi) = 1.8$ hops, where ϕ is the absolute error. We intend to explore this in the future.

4.6   Discussion About the Parallelization of the Clustering and Embedding Processes

In [22], a parallelization of k-Means using MapReduce is presented. It is stated that for the k-Means algorithm, the main computational cost is in the distance calculations. For each iteration, nk distance computations are performed, where n is the number of objects and k is the number of clusters being formed. Within a given cluster, the distance calculation between an object and the centre is independent of the same calculation in another cluster. Hence, distance computations for different clusters can be executed in parallel. However, in each iteration, the new centres to be used in the next iteration must be updated. This obliges the iterative procedures to be executed serially. In [18] the authors implemented a parallel version of their Rigel embedding system. In Rigel, the landmark bootstrapping pre-process computes the BFS trees rooted from each landmark. This can be run independently and in parallel for each landmark on different servers. Following the bootstrapping process, each graph vertex can also be embedded independently and in parallel based on the coordinates of the global landmarks. Given the large number of nodes, their distribution across servers has to be done carefully to ensure load balancing.

5 Conclusions and Future Work

With this work we have addressed the issue of the lack of scalable algorithms for the support of interactive analytical tasks such as clustering and have opened an area for their development, focusing in particular on algorithms which incorporate both structural and contextual information of a network.

In this research we have made use of the results in the field of telecommunications and proposed applying them to solve the issues discussed for the present field of interactive clustering, related to the interactive exploration of large networks.

We have used a graph coordinate embedding approach which has shown its potential scalability as well as applicability to the mixed graph clustering techniques.

Several challenges remain ahead as future work. The first challenge is to parallelize the hyperbolic embedding process and the k-Means clustering. Secondly, we need to develop metrics which accurately measure the quality of the processing results. A third challenge is to test different distance computations and calibrate the weights.

To summarize, the idea of using constant-time methods for calculation could have a potential usage for the development of mixed graph clustering methods with application to interactive analysis techniques, as it allows for the calculation of the distance between two vertices of a graph in constant time, regardless of the graph's size.

We have identified a range in which interactive data analytics is plausible, in terms of the number of clusters and graph dataset size. We propose that the embedding pre-process followed by clustering of the mapped space within a given interactivity threshold, once parallelized, will represent a powerful and flexible environment for graph data analysts.

References

1. Bastian, M.: Visualize big graph data. Data Visualization Summit, San Francisco, 11–12 April 2013 (2013). http://www.slideshare.net/mathieu-bastian/visualize-big-graph-data
2. Batagelj, V., Brandenburg, F.J., Didimo, W., Liotta, G., Palladino, P., Patrignani, M.: Visual analysis of large graphs using (X, Y)-clustering and hybrid visualizations. IEEE Trans. Vis. Comput. Graph. **17**(11), 1587–1598 (2011)
3. Isenberg, P., Carpendale, S., Hesselmann, T., Isenberg, T., Lee, B. (eds): Research Report N0421. In: Proceedings Workshop on Data Exploration for Interactive Surfaces, DEXIS 2011, pp. 1–47 (2012)

4. Keim, D.A.: Exploring big data using visual analytics. In: Proceedings Workshops of the EDBT/ICDT 2014 Joint Conference (28 March 2014)
5. Keim, D.A., Andrienko, G., Fekete, J.-D., Görg, C., Kohlhammer, J., Melançon, G.: Visual analytics: definition, process, and challenges. In: Kerren, A., Stasko, J.T., Fekete, J.-D., North, C. (eds.) Information Visualization. LNCS, vol. 4950, pp. 154–175. Springer, Heidelberg (2008)
6. Vathy-Fogarassy, A., Abonyi, J.: Graph-Based Clustering and Data Visualization Algorithms. Springer, London (2013). ISBN 978-1-4471-5158-6
7. Cui, W., Zhou, H., Qu, H., Wong, P.C., Li, X.: Geometry-based edge clustering for graph visualization. IEEE Trans. Vis. Comput. Graph. 14(6), 1277–1284 (2008)
8. Herman, I., Melancon, G., Marshall, M.S.: Graph visualization and navigation in information visualization: a survey. IEEE Trans. Visual Comput. Graph. 6(1), 24–43 (2000)
9. Zhou, Y., Cheng, H., Yu, J.X.: Graph clustering based on structural/attribute similarities. Proc. VLDB Endowment 2(1), 718–729 (2009)
10. Xu, Z., Ke, Y., Wang, Y., Cheng, H., Cheng, J.: A model-based approach to attributed graph clustering categories and subject descriptors. In: Proceeding ACM SIGMOD International Conference on Management of Data, pp. 505–516 (2012)
11. Zhou, Y., Liu, L.: Social influence based clustering of heterogeneous information networks. In: Proceeding 19th ACM SIGKDD International Conference on Knowledge Discovery and Data Mining - KDD 2013, pp. 338–346 (2013)
12. Zhou, Y., Cheng, H., Yu, J.X.: Clustering large attributed graphs: an efficient incremental approach. In: Proceeding 2010 IEEE International Conference on Data Mining, pp. 689–698 (2010)
13. Elhadi, H.: Structure and attributes community detection: comparative analysis of composite, ensemble and selection methods. In: Proceeding 7th Workshop on Social Network Mining and Analysis SNAKDD 2013, Article no. 10 (2013)
14. Amigó, E., Gonzalo, J., Artiles, J., Verdejo, F.: A comparison of extrinsic clustering evaluation metrics based on formal constraints. Inf. Retrieval 12(4), 461–486 (2009)
15. Davies, D.L., Bouldin, D.W.: A cluster separation measure. IEEE Trans. Pattern Anal. Mach. Intell. 1(2), 224–227 (1979)
16. Hartigan, J.A., Wong, M.A.: Algorithm AS 136: a k-means clustering algorithm. J. Roy. Stat. Soc.: Ser. C (Appl. Stat.) 28(1), 100–108 (1979)
17. Zhao, X., Sala, A., Wilson, C., Zheng, H., Zhao, B.Y.: Orion: shortest path estimation for large social graphs. networks, vol. 1 (2010)
18. Zhao, X., Sala, A., Zheng, H., Zhao, B.Y.: Efficient shortest paths on massive social graphs (invited paper). In: Proceedings of 7th International Conference on Collaborative Computing: Networking, Applications and Worksharing (CollaborateCom), pp. 77–86 (2011)
19. Papadimitriou, C.H., Ratajczak, D.: On a conjecture related to geometric routing. Theoret. Comput. Sci. 344(1), 3–14 (2005)
20. Chakrabarti, D., Zhan, Y., Faloutsos, C.: R-mat: a recursive model for graph mining. In: Proceeding SIAM Data Mining Conference, SIAM, Philadelphia, PA (2004)
21. Ley, M.: DBLP — some lessons learned. Proc VLDB Endowment 2(2), 1493–1500 (2009)
22. Zhao, W., Ma, H., He, Q.: Parallel K-Means clustering based on MapReduce. In: Jaatun, M.G., Zhao, G., Rong, C. (eds.) Cloud Computing. LNCS, vol. 5931, pp. 674–679. Springer, Heidelberg (2009)

Using the Marshall-Olkin Extended Zipf Distribution in Graph Generation

Ariel Duarte-López[1]([✉]), Arnau Prat-Pérez[1], and Marta Pérez-Casany[2]

[1] DAMA-UPC, Departament d'Arquitectura de Computadors,
Universitat Politècnica de Catalunya, Barcelona, Spain
{aduarte,aprat}@ac.upc.edu
[2] DAMA-UPC, Departament Matemàtica Aplicada II,
Universitat Politècnica de Catalunya, Barcelona, Spain
marta.perez@upc.edu

Abstract. Being able to generate large synthetic graphs resembling those found in the real world, is of high importance for the design of new graph algorithms and benchmarks. In this paper, we first compare several probability models in terms of goodness-of-fit, when used to model the degree distribution of real graphs. Second, after confirming that the MOEZipf model is the one that gives better fits, we present a method to generate MOEZipf distributions. The method is shown to work well in practice when implemented in a scalable synthetic graph generator.

1 Introduction

The analysis of large real graphs has attracted the interest of the industry and academia due to its multiple applications, and as a consequence, many technologies for their analysis have emerged. In order to fairly compare the performance and features of such technologies, several benchmarking initiatives have kicked off [2,4,6]. In general, these initiatives use synthetic graph generators in seek for the flexibility not always found in real datasets.

Being able to generate credible graphs that mimic the characteristics of the real ones is of high importance, because they directly impact the performance of the systems under test. One of these characteristics is the degree distribution of the nodes in the graph. In general, it is widely accepted that in real networks the degree sequence follows a power-law, since the majority of the nodes have a small degree while just few of them are connected to many neighbours, thus having a very large degree [7].

A particular power law distribution with support the strictly positive integer numbers is the Zipf distribution. The Zipf's law shows a linear shape in the log-log scale, but in practice this is not always the case in real networks, where it is only observed for degree values large enough. For low degree nodes, the plot usually shows concavity, and less often, convexity [3]. One generalization of the Zipf's law that solves this issue is the Marshall-Olkin extended Zipf distribution (MOEZipf), which uses the Marshall-Olkin transformation to add an extra parameter that gives more flexibility to the family.

© Springer International Publishing Switzerland 2015
S. Hunold et al. (Eds.): Euro-Par 2015 Workshops, LNCS 9523, pp. 493–502, 2015.
DOI: 10.1007/978-3-319-27308-2_40

In this paper, we first prove by means of an analysis of several real graphs, the suitability of the MOEZipf model as a degree distribution. Second, we propose a method to generate degree sequences following the MOEZipf distribution, which is implemented in a scalable graph generator (The LDBC Data Generator [4]), showing that it works well in practice.

The paper is structured as follows: In Sect. 2, we introduce the MOEZipf probability distribution. In Sect. 3 we show that MOEZipf adjusts well the distributions of real graphs. In Sect. 4, we propose a method to generate random samples from a MOEZipf distribution. In Sect. 5, we show the results obtained with Datagen using the proposed approach, in Sect. 6, we conclude the paper.

2   The MOEZipf Model

A random variable (r.v.) X is said to follow a Zipf distribution with *scale* parameter $\alpha > 1$ if, and only if, its probability mass function (pmf) is equal to:

$$P(X = x) = \frac{x^{-\alpha}}{\xi(\alpha)}, \; for \; x = 1, 2, 3, \cdots, \tag{1}$$

where $\xi(\alpha) = \sum_{k=1}^{+\infty} k^{-\alpha}$ is the Riemann zeta function. The Zipf distribution is often suitable to fit data that correspond to frequencies of frequencies or to ranked data. This type of data shows a widespread pattern in their measurements with a very large probability at one and a very small probability at some very large values. Taking logarithms at (1), one obtains that the Zipf distribution shows a linear pattern in the log-log scale since

$$\log(P(X = k)) = -\alpha \log(x) - \log(\xi(\alpha)).$$

This linearity is useful to check whether the data may be well fitted or not by means of the Zipf distribution, by just plotting the empirical probabilities. However, in practice usually this linearity is just observed in the tail of the distribution, while a concavity is observed at the beginning. The MOEZipf distribution is proposed in [8], as an approximate model to adapt this behavior.

A r.v. X is said to follow a MOEZipf distribution with parameters α and β if, and only if, its survival function (SF) is equal to:

$$P(X > x) = \overline{G}(x; \alpha, \beta) = \frac{\beta \, \overline{F}(X)}{1 - \overline{\beta} \, \overline{F}(X)} = \frac{\beta \, \xi(\alpha, x + 1)}{\xi(\alpha) - \overline{\beta} \, \xi(\alpha + 1)}, \tag{2}$$

for $\beta > 0$, $\alpha > 1$ and $\overline{\beta} = 1 - \beta$. Being $\overline{F}(x)$ the SF of the Zipf(α) distribution.

The pmf of the MOEZipf may be computed by means of

$$\begin{aligned}
P(X = x) &= \overline{G}(x - 1; \alpha, \beta) - \overline{G}(x; \alpha, \beta) \\
&= \frac{x^{-\alpha} \, \beta \, \xi(\alpha)}{[\xi(\alpha) - \overline{\beta} \xi(\alpha, x)][\xi(\alpha) - \overline{\beta} \xi(\alpha, x + 1)]}, \; x = 1, 2, 3, \cdots, \tag{3}
\end{aligned}$$

Table 1. Main characteristics of the nine real networks analysed.

Network	Nodes	Edges	GCC	ACC	AD	Type
Amazon	$262K$	$1.24M$	0.2361	0.4198	0.0027	Directed
CA roads	$1.97M$	$5.53M$	0.0604	0.0464	0.1260	Undirected
DBLP	$317K$	$105M$	0.3064	0.6324	0.2665	Undirected
Livejournal	$4M$	$34.68M$	0.1253	0.2843	0.045	Undirected
NotreDame	$326K$	$1.5M$	0.0877	0.2346	-0.0617	Directed
Patents	$3.78M$	$16.52M$	0.0671	0.0757	0.1332	Directed
TX roads	$1.38M$	$3.84M$	0.0602	0.0470	0.1304	Undirected
Wikipedia	$2.39M$	$5.02M$	0.0022	0.0526	-0.0853	Directed
Youtube	$1.14M$	$2.99M$	0.0062	0.0808	-0.0369	Undirected

where $\xi(\alpha, x) = \sum_{k=x+1}^{+\infty} k^{-\alpha}$ is the Hurwitz Zeta function with parameter α. When $\beta = 1$, in (3) one obtains the pmf of the Zipf(α) distribution. An advantage of the MOEZipf distribution is that it shows a convexity or concavity behaviour at the beginning of the distribution depending on whether $0 < \beta < 1$ or $\beta > 1$ respectively, while keeping the linearity in the tail.

3 Real Graphs Analysis

This paper is motivated after the analysis of the degree distribution of nine real networks coming from diverse domains[1], using eight different probabilistic models: Geometric, Poisson, Zipf, Right-truncated Zipf, Altmann, MOEZipf, Negative Binomial and Discrete Weibull. Table 1 shows the number of nodes, number of edges, global clustering coefficient (GCC), average clustering coefficient (ACC), assortativity degree (AD) and directionality of the networks analysed. For each directed networks, both the in-degree (In) and out-degree (Out) sequences were analysed, making a total of 13 degree sequences.

The Zipf, the Right-truncated Zipf and the MOEZipf probability distributions have been considered mainly because of two reasons. On one side, because the Zipf distribution is assumed to be the node degree distribution in most scientific papers, and its Right-truncated version is a way to improve the fit in the tail of the distribution. On the other side, because we are interested in proving the suitability of the Zipf generalization: the MOEZipf distribution.

The Poisson and the Negative Binomial distributions have been included for being the first the classical distribution for counts when the events take place randomly and with the same probability, and the second its usual biparametric alternative used when the data show more dispersion than it was initially expected. However, we have observed this is not our case, since fitting the Negative Binomial oftenly results in numerical problems and when not, the fits are not satisfactory.

---

[1] Networks downloaded from http://snap.stanford.edu/datarepository.

The reason for including the Geometric and the Discrete Weibull distributions is clearly different. These distributions may be seen, respectively, as the discrete versions of the Exponential and the Weibull, which are the continuous distributions associated to *time to an event* r.v.. One advantage of the Geometric is its simplicity and that it does not require the truncation at one, because its support are the strictly positive integer numbers. The Discrete Weibull is useful when the lifetime is measured counting cycles, shocks or revolutions. In our case, it has sense think about that an individual being *active* or *alive* while he is able to create connections with the others. From this point of view, the distribution comes naturally if one thinks that the lifetime is measured counting the number of connections performed. Finally, the Altmann distribution, also known as Zipf-Alekseev distribution or Zipf with an exponential cuttoff, is used in quantitative linguistics and it is also a bi-parameter generalization of the Zipf. In this case, it is assumed that the support is finite and the tail decreases quickly since the probabilities are multiplied by $e^{-x\beta}$.

In order to fit the degree sequence for a given graph, the maximum likelihood parameter estimations were calculated by means of the *mle* function included in the R software [9]. It is known that maximum likelihood parameter estimations are good, because they are unbiased and have minimum variance. The models were compared using the *Akaike Information Criterion* (AIC) and the *Bayesian Information Criterion* (BIC) goodness of fit measures [1], which are defined as:

$$AIC = -2l(\hat{\theta}, k) + 2M\frac{N}{N - M - 1}$$

and

$$BIC = -2l(\hat{\theta}, k) + Mlog(N)$$

respectively, where $l(\hat{\theta}, k)$ is the value of the log-likelihood function evaluated at $\hat{\theta}$, the maximum likelihood estimation of θ, for a given degree sequence k. M is the number of parameters of each probabilistic model (in our case it is equal to one or two) and N is the number of nodes of the network.

Table 2 shows the ΔAIC and ΔBIC for each network and all the models. These values were computed by means of the difference between the value in the current model and the value in the best model. Therefore, for each network the best model is the one that has a zero value in ΔAIC and ΔBIC.

Our experiments reveal that the analysed degree sequences can be explained with just three out of the eight models considered, which are: the MOEZipf, the Discrete Weibull and the Altmann models. The MOEZipf model is the best in 54% of the cases, followed by the Discrete Weibull in 38% of the cases and the Altmann in 8% of the cases.

Figure 1 shows four degree sequences associated to the networks Amazon (In), DBLP, Patents (Out) and Youtube respectively; jointly with the fit of the best four models in each case. In all the cases the plots are in log-log scale. The best fit for the Amazon (In) is given by the MOEZipf model with parameter estimations $\hat{\alpha} = 3.0295$ and $\hat{\beta} = 27.1284$, the second best model in this case is the Discrete

Table 2. Values of the ΔAIC and ΔBIC for the different networks and probabilistic models.

Networks		Geometric	Poisson	Zipf	Right-trun. Zipf	Altmann	MOEZipf	Neg. Bin.	Discrete Weibull
Amazon (In)	ΔAIC	10772.3325	525546.2435	180203.9906	166775.5608	10774.3423	0	10768.3804	9774.4649
	ΔBIC	10761.856	525535.773	180193.5141	166775.5608	10774.3423	0	10768.3804	9774.4649
Amazon (Out)	ΔAIC	636386.6206	290672.7857	1060794.3393	593382.9374	636389.4636	0	–	–
	ΔBIC	636376.1615	290662.3277	1060783.8803	593382.9373	636389.4635	0	–	–
CA roads	ΔAIC	1738132.797	1118395.2451	3696976.2046	2703401.834	1738138.1355	519401.402	–	0
	ΔBIC	1738120.3059	1118382.754	3696963.7135	2703401.834	1738138.1355	519401.402	–	0
DBLP	ΔAIC	68821.822	1256991.2234	36537.236	28493.1692	2781.7322	2526.152	–	0
	ΔBIC	68811.672	1256981.0734	36527.086	28493.1692	2781.7322	2526.1521	–	0
Livejournal	ΔAIC	1472010.06	66043193.8352	744846.7078	691016.3788	59123.1575	86329.1964	58895.0102	0
	ΔBIC	1471997.4005	66043181.1758	744834.0483	691016.3787	59123.1574	86329.1964	58895.0101	0
NotreDame (In)	ΔAIC	486831.1503	5007706.9131	74.3956	34.4528	–	0	–	–
	ΔBIC	486820.4566	5007696.2193	63.7018	34.4528	–	0	–	–
NotreDame (Out)	ΔAIC	71534.3133	2643273.0597	72029.2877	66891.3556	23274.8034	0	22562.4914	10614.9758
	ΔBIC	71524.4788	2643263.2252	72019.4531	66891.3556	23274.8034	0	22562.4914	10614.9758
Patents (In)	ΔAIC	385629.9996	12328277.4843	1116962.9351	1030887.7683	32525.9313	99456.9783	28490.1532	0
	ΔBIC	385617.0027	12328264.4875	1116949.9382	1030887.7683	32525.9313	99456.9784	28490.1532	0
Patents (Out)	ΔAIC	275808.2025	7055231.2285	2608735.5631	2368252.8935	275811.9408	0	221032.981	–
	ΔBIC	275795.6501	7055218.6762	2608723.0108	2368252.8935	275811.9408	0	221032.981	–
TX roads	ΔAIC	1160225.2518	793426.0519	2497743.0319	1827262.7551	1160229.4974	394526.2436	–	0
	ΔBIC	1160213.1142	793413.9344	2497730.8943	1827262.7551	1160229.4973	394526.2436	–	0
Wikipedia (In)	ΔAIC	2205641.8423	13174755.7601	162.2935	153.6566	–	0	–	–
	ΔBIC	2205629.1642	13174743.082	149.6155	153.6567	–	0	–	–
Wikipedia (Out)	ΔAIC	651885.7283	32209782.8763	57.4127	5.3241	0	59.4128	–	–
	ΔBIC	651875.8262	32209772.9742	47.5106	5.3241	0	59.4129	–	–
Youtube	ΔAIC	581583.7338	11558597.1877	20322.1168	20032.0998	13402.6611	0	–	1939.5714
	ΔBIC	581572.8997	11558586.3536	20311.2827	20032.0998	13402.6611	0	–	1939.5714

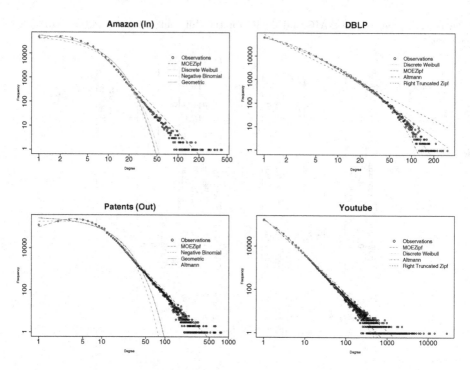

Fig. 1. Observed degree sequences in the Amazon (In), DBLP, Patents (Out) and Youtube networks jointly with the four best models in each case.

Weibull with parameters $\hat{p} = 0.7519$ and $\hat{\beta} = 0.9271$. The model that gives the best fit to the DBLP degree sequence is the Discrete Weibull with parameter estimations $\hat{p} = 0.2622$ and $\hat{\beta} = 0.3881$, followed by the MOEZipf model with parameters $\hat{\alpha} = 2.2767$ and $\hat{\beta} = 4.8613$. For the Patents (Out) degree sequence, the best model is the MOEZipf with parameters $\hat{\alpha} = 3.196$ and $\hat{\beta} = 119.264$ and, in second place, the Negative Binomial model with parameters $\hat{\gamma} = 1.4873$ and $\hat{p} = 0.8317$. The best model for the Youtube network is the MOEZipf with parameters $\hat{\alpha} = 2.089$ and $\hat{\beta} = 2.4101$, and the second best model is the Discrete Weibull with parameters $\hat{p} = 0.0044$ and $\hat{\beta} = 0.1424$. The information about how well a model behaves with respect to the others can be found in Table 2.

4   Generating MOEZipf Degree Samples

The proposed method for generating MOEZipf degree sequences is based on the well known *Inverse Principle* [5]. Given a sequence of uniformly distributed random values between 0 and 1, we obtain a sequence of values of the target distribution using its inverse cumulative probability function (cpf). Given that, the cpf is equal to one minus the SF, and that from (2) the SF of the MOEZipf is easily deduced from the SF of the Zipf, one can obtain the desired value by applying the inverse principle to the Zipf distribution after properly modifying the generated uniform random value.

Algorithm 1 shows the pseudocode associated to this procedure. Given fixed values for α and β, we first initialize variable x to be equal to the first value in the support of the MOEZipf which is one. After generating a value u uniformly from 0 and 1, it is transformed to value u' as follows:

$$u' = \frac{u\beta}{1 + u(\beta - 1)}$$

If $1 - \frac{1}{u} \leq \beta$, the final x value is equal to the first integer value such that $u' \leq F_\alpha(x)$, where $F_\alpha(x)$ is the cpf of the Zipf distribution. Otherwise, the final x is equal to the first value satisfying $u' \geq F_\alpha(x)$.

Algorithm 1. MOEZipf Generator

1: **procedure** SAMPLE_MOEZIPF(α, β)
2:     $x \leftarrow 1$
3:     $u \leftarrow$ uniform random number $[0, 1]$
4:     $u' \leftarrow \frac{u\beta}{1+u(\beta-1)}$
5:     **loop**
6:         $z_c \leftarrow F_\alpha(x)$
7:         **if** $\beta < 1$ **and** $\frac{u-1}{u} >= \beta$ **then**
8:             **if** $u' >= z_c$ **then**
9:                 **return** x
10:        **else**
11:            **if** $u' <= z_c$ **then**
12:                **return** x
13:        $x \leftarrow x + 1$

---

5 Scalable MOEZipf Generation with Datagen

Datagen is the synthetic graph generator used in the LDBC Social Network Benchmark [4]. It is designed to generate social undirected networks with different degree distributions, with correlated attributes and edges connecting people with similar characteristics in an homophylic way. Datagen is implemented using the Map-Reduce parallel programming paradigm, and therefore is able to generate large graphs by running on small commodity clusters.

We have extended Datagen with the method proposed in Sect. 4 to generate MOEZipf based graphs scalably[2]. We have generated seven synthetic graphs with a degree distributions similar to those of the seven real degree sequences analysed in Sect. 3 where the MOEZipf distribution is the best fitting model: Amazon (In),

---

[2] The implemented plugin can be found at Datagen's source code repository https://github.com/ldbc/ldbc_snb_datagen.

Table 3. Parameters of the MOEZipf distribution estimated from the original networks vs the ones estimated from the networks generated using Datagen; the generation time of each network.

Networks	Original network estimated parameters		Synthetic network estimated parameters		Generation time (s)
	$\hat{\alpha}$	$\hat{\beta}$	$\tilde{\alpha}$	$\tilde{\beta}$	
Amazon (In)	3.0295	27.1284	3.0332	27.3464	991
Amazon (Out)	9.5281	6390058.5115	9.1074	3057506.2967	1451
NotreDame (In)	2.0174	1.0657	2.0259	1.0873	1598
NotreDame (Out)	2.4215	15.6546	2.4229	15.7044	1587
Patents (Out)	3.196	119.264	3.1959	119.2742	4600
Wikipedia (In)	2.5479	1.045	2.5457	1.0431	5505
Youtube	2.089	2.4101	2.0981	2.4534	2200

Amazon (Out), NotreDame (In), NotreDame (Out), Patents (Out), Wikipedia (In) and Youtube. To generate the graphs we have used the same number of nodes, and configured the implemented MOEZipf degree sequence generation with the same parameters as those estimated from the original networks. Note that Datagen only generates undirected graphs, but for the purpose of this paper, we are only interested in being able to mimic the degree distributions and to prove that these can be generated in a scalable way.

Table 3 shows, for each one of the networks the following information. On the one hand, the parameters $\hat{\alpha}$ and $\hat{\beta}$ estimated from the original networks, which are used to generate the synthetic ones. On the other hand, the parameters $\tilde{\alpha}$ and $\tilde{\beta}$ estimated from the resulting synthetic networks. We see that, for six out of seven cases, the resulting estimated parameters from the synthetic networks are very similar to those from the original graphs. Only for the Amazon (Out) degree sequence, there is a remarkable difference in the value of the β parameter. This is because the log-likelihood function, $l(\beta, \alpha; k)$, as a function of β tends to an asymptote as β increases. More exactly:

$$l(\beta, \alpha; k) \simeq N \log(\beta) + g(\alpha; k),$$

being $g(\alpha; k)$ a function that does not involve the β parameter. Thus, there are not significant differences between the values of the log-likelihood function for two β values if both are large enough. Finally, in the last column of Table 3 we see the time taken to generate these datasets in our test machine cluster, composed by four quad-core nodes with 32 GB of RAM each and 2 TB spinning disks. In general, we see that the generation model is able to accurately generate degree sequences with the desired characteristics, in a scalable way.

Figure 2 shows two examples of degree distributions of two synthetically generated graphs. Specifically, the ones generated to mimic the characteristics of the Patents (Out) and Youtube degree sequences. We also plot the theoretical

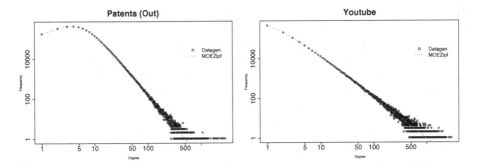

Fig. 2. Synthetically generated graphs with similar characteristics to the Patents (Out) (N = 3774767, $\hat{\alpha}$ = 3.196 and $\hat{\beta}$ = 119.264) and Youtube (N = 1134890, $\hat{\alpha}$ = 2.089 and $\hat{\beta}$ = 2.4101) graphs respectively.

MOEZipf degree distribution with the parameter estimations $(\tilde{\alpha}, \tilde{\beta})$. In both cases, we see that Datagen is able to generate a graph with a degree sequence with the same characteristics of the real ones accurately.

6   Conclusions and Future Work

We have analysed a set of degree distributions from real networks using several probability models. The (AIC) and BIC have been used to compare the different tested models. We have shown that the MOEZipf distribution is the one that better explains the degree distributions observed in real networks. Based on this result, we have presented a method to generate MOEZipf degree sequences, and implemented it as an extension to the LDBC graph generator, namely Datagen. Our experiments have shown that with the Datagen implementation, we can generate graphs with real degree distributions in a scalable way.

In this work, we have focused on generating realistic degree distributions. Future work will consist in developing techniques to reproduce other networks' structural characteristics, such as the clustering coefficient or the degree of assortativity. Moreover, currently Datagen only supports the generation of undirected graphs. In the future we will work on extending Datagen to generate directed graphs with different in-degree and out-degree distributions.

Acknowledgments. The authors, all members of DAMA-UPC, thank the Ministry of Science and Innovation of Spain, Generalitat de Catalunya, for grant numbers TIN2013-47008-R and SGR2014-890 respectively and also the EU FP7/2007-2013 for funding the LDBC project (ICT2011-8-317548). M. Pérez-Casany also thanks the Spanish Ministry of Education and Science for grant MTM2013-43992-R and Generalitat de Catalunya for grant 2014 SGR 890 (AGAUR). The authors thank Oracle Labs for the strategic support to the Graphalytics project.

References

1. Burnham, K.P., Anderson, D.R.: Model Selection and Multimodel Inference: A Practical Information-Theoretic Approach. Springer-Verlag, New York (2002)
2. Capota, M., Hegeman, T., Iosup, A., Prat-Pérez, A., Erling, O., Boncz, P.: Graphalytics: a big data benchmark for graph-processing platforms (2015)
3. Clauset, A., Shalizi, C.R., Newman, M.E.: Power-law distributions in empirical data. SIAM Rev. **51**(4), 661–703 (2009)
4. Erling, O., Averbuch, A., Larriba-Pey, J., Chafi, H., Gubichev, A., Prat, A., Pham, M.-D., Boncz, P.: The LDBC social network benchmark: interactive workload. In: Proceedings of the 2015 ACM SIGMOD International Conference on Management of Data, 619–630. ACM (2015)
5. Luc, D.: Non-uniform Random Variate Generation. Springer, New York (1986)
6. Murphy, R.C., Wheeler, K.B., Barrett, B.W., Ang, J.A.: Introducing the graph 500. Cray User's Group (CUG) (2010)
7. Newman, M.E.J.: Power laws, Pareto distributions and Zipf's law. Contemp. Phys. **46**(5), 323–351 (2005)
8. Pérez-Casany, M., Casellas, A.: Marshall-olkin extended Zipf distribution. arXiv preprint (2013). arXiv:1304.4540
9. Yee, T.W.: Maintainer Thomas Yee, and Suggests VGAMdata. Package 'vgam' (2015)

Highspeed Graph Processing Exploiting Main-Memory Column Stores

Matthias Hauck[1]([⊠]), Marcus Paradies[2], Holger Fröning[1],
Wolfgang Lehner[2], and Hannes Rauhe[3]

[1] Computer Engineering Group, Ruprecht-Karls University of Heidelberg,
Heidelberg, Germany
{matthias.hauck,holger.froening}@ziti.uni-heidelberg.de
[2] Database Systems Group, Tu Dresden, Dresden, Germany
m.paradies@sap.com, wolfgang.lehner@tu-dresden.de
[3] SAP SE, Weinheim, Germany
hannes.rauhe@sap.com

Abstract. A popular belief in the graph database community is that
relational database management systems are generally ill-suited for efficient graph processing. This might apply for analytic graph queries performing iterative computations on the graph, but does not necessarily
hold true for short-running, OLTP-style graph queries. In this paper
we argue that, instead of extending a graph database management system with traditional relational operators—predicate evaluation, sorting,
grouping, and aggregations among others—one should consider adding
a graph abstraction and graph-specific operations, such as graph traversals and pattern matching, to relational database management systems. We use an exemplary query from the interactive query workload of
the LDBC social network benchmark and run it against our enhanced in-
memory, columnar relational database system to support our claims. Our
performance measurements indicate that a columnar RDBMS—extended
by graph-specific operators and data structures—can serve as a foundation for high-speed graph processing on big memory machines with
non-uniform memory access and a large number of available cores.

1 Introduction

The proliferation of graph-shaped data in the enterprise domain and the ever-
growing need to process billion-scale graphs efficiently are the key drivers for
the evolution of a plethora of graph processing systems targeting large cluster
installations [8,11,13]. Analytic graph queries on static graphs of an immense
scale can be executed by these systems in an acceptable execution time. While
there has been a large body of work focusing on distributed, shared-nothing
graph processing frameworks and graph algorithms, transactional graph workloads comprising short-running, concurrent queries from a large number of client
applications have been largely ignored by the research community so far. Such
interactive queries usually access a small fraction of the entire graph and perform selective filter operations on vertex and edge attributes based on some

© Springer International Publishing Switzerland 2015
S. Hunold et al. (Eds.): Euro-Par 2015 Workshops, LNCS 9523, pp. 503–514, 2015.
DOI: 10.1007/978-3-319-27308-2_41

predicates, run simple graph traversals to explore the neighborhood of a vertex or a group of vertices, and aggregate attribute values.

The execution of interactive graph queries is well-supported in graph database management systems (GDBMSs), such as NEO4J [2], SPARKSEE [14] or INFINITEGRAPH [1]. GDBMSs rely on the property graph model, where a graph consists of a set of vertices and a set of edges with an arbitrary number of attributes assigned to them [17]. Additionally, they provide a clear graph abstraction, intuitive declarative or imperative graph query interfaces, and specialized storage and execution capabilities to process graph queries efficiently. Besides functional advantages over RDBMSs, GDBMSs claim to offer superior performance for graph-specific operations—graph traversals are one prominent example—by storing the graph topology in an index-free vertex adjacency structure. While they offer good performance for topology-centric queries, GDBMSs usually suffer from poor performance for attribute-centric queries that perform predicate evaluation on or aggregating of attribute values. The interactive query workload of the LDBC benchmark suite—the de-facto standard benchmark for graph processing—indicates that interactive graph queries demand a seamless integration of query processing on the graph topology and access to vertex/edge attributes in the same database system [7].

Based on an in-depth study of the LDBC interactive query workload and the *choke points* defined by the benchmark committee[1], we revisit the question whether RDBMSs are generally ill-suited for graph processing compared to native GDBMSs. Instead, we argue that large fractions of the graph queries from the interactive workload of the LDBC can benefit from an optimized handling of vertex/edge attributes and the efficient predicate evaluation of point and range queries on it. Based on these observations we identify graph-specific operations that have to be added to a RDBMS to complement the already available processing capabilities for aggregations, sorting, and predicate evaluation. We implemented one exemplary query from the LDBC interactive workload on top of a columnar RDBMS prototype, which we enhanced by graph operators and data structures. We tailor our graph operators and data structures to run on server machines with large amounts of available memory, a large number of cores, and non-uniform memory access (NUMA). Our contributions can be summarized as follows:

- Based on a detailed study of the interactive query workload of the LDBC benchmark suite, we derive functional and non-functional requirements for a columnar RDBMS with integrated graph processing capabilities and specify a set of operations that are required to process the exemplary query.
- We propose a novel architecture that extends a columnar RDBMS by adding a native graph abstraction and a graph-specific secondary index structure.
- We perform an experimental evaluation based on an exemplary query from the interactive query workload of the LDBC social network benchmark and demonstrate that our hybrid approach scales with increasing dataset sizes and also provides a NUMA-friendly graph abstraction that can leverage all available computing resources efficiently.

---

[1] http://ldbcouncil.org/sites/default/files/LDBC_D2.2.1.pdf.

2   Related Work

Although distributed, shared-nothing graph processing —inspired by Pregel [13]— recently received a considerable amount of attention in the industry and research community, there is also an increased interest to store and process large graphs on a single machine (either on disk/flash or in memory). In fact, there is evidence that even notebooks are able to outperform distributed graph processing systems in certain scenarios [10]. Graph databases, such as, NEO4J [2], TITAN [4], INFINITE-GRAPH [1], SPARKSEE [14], and ORIENTDB [3], are gaining popularity for enterprises and provide native graph storage, querying and transaction support. All of them are native graph systems with own implementations to guarantee transactionality, logging, and recovery and therefore cannot be used as a dedicated engine inside a RDBMS.

For graph analytics, where no transactions and no update support is required, there is a wide variety of single-node graph processing systems targeting multicore server machines with a large number of cores and a vast amount of memory available. SYSTEM G is a read-only graph processing system leveraging a key-value store as persistence, a set of compressed sparse row (CSR) like data structures, and is optimized towards CPU cache reuse and parallelization [21]. In comparison to our approach, they do not use a column store as primary persistence to efficiently process also vertex/edge attributes.

PGX.ISO is an in-memory graph processing system for querying graph data using graph patterns [16] and analytic queries using GREEN-MARL [9]. The focus of PGX.ISO is on read-only workloads aiming for minimizing query response time. We aim at providing an integrated solution as part of a RDBMS and design our system to also cope with transactions and concurrent write operations. Moreover, our approach can perform graph querying on the latest version of the data, without the need to replicate it into a dedicated graph system.

Recent graph processing systems, such as, LLAMA, target not only static graphs, but also allow modifications to the vertex/edge properties and the graph topology [12]. LLAMA implements a mutable CSR data structure and stores multiple snapshots of the graph, one for each update to the graph. Since the entire system is built on top of a CSR with own containers for the vertex/edge properties, it is not possible to integrate LLAMA into a RDBMS seamlessly.

Recent advances in modern hardware, including the availability of large amounts of main memory with non-uniform access (NUMA), multi-core, and SIMD instructions triggered interesting discussions in these emerging hardware technologies [5,6,22]. EMPTYHEADED is a graph pattern matching engine based on a configurable CSR data structure and compiles queries into boolean algebra expressions leveraging SIMD parallelization [5]. The focus, however, is on read-only workloads with topology-centric queries and cannot be used easily to support dynamic graphs. Cui et al. propose a set of techniques to improve the performance and scalability of breadth-first search on large NUMA machines by minimizing cross-socket communication [6]. Since we are aiming at providing general graph processing capabilities instead of specific algorithms, their results can be incorporated into our system. Zhang et al. investigate the effect of remote memory accesses for graph analytics and propose POLYMER, a NUMA-aware graph analytics system [22] with a focus on read-only workloads and a small number of attributes on vertices and edges. We believe that some of the proposed techniques concerning access to the graph topology can be also applied in our system.

Increasingly, even RDBMS provide graph support to some extent on relational tables [18–20]. Welc et al. show that a RDBMS can serve selected graph use cases (e.g., shortest path) by heavy indexing of the graph topology using B-trees and outperform native graph databases. Instead of exposing graph processing directly to SQL, Sun et al. translate GREMLIN, a traversal-oriented graph query language, into SQL statements. The deepest level of integration into a RDBMS has been proposed by providing a native graph query language, a native execution engine, and graph-aware traversal operators inside the database kernel [18].

The LDBC benchmark suite is a community effort to define a standard benchmark for graph query processing and consists of three different workloads, an *analytic*, a *business intelligence*, and an *interactive* workload [7]. While the analytic workload focuses on long-running, offline queries potentially accessing the entire graph and computing some global graph measure, the interactive queries perform transactional, short-running requests accessing only a small fraction of the graph with the focus on the selection of vertices/edges according to some predicate filter, simple aggregations, and graph traversals.

To summarize, none of the discussed graph system focuses on transactional graph workloads with interleaved read and write operations—except for native graph databases. On the other extreme, RDBMS provide transactional guarantees, but lack a high-speed graph processing layer in the form of tailored data structures for storing the graph topology. Our long-term goal is to close this gap by proposing a combination of the best of both worlds, transactional guarantees of a RDBMS combined with high-speed graph processing capabilities of a native graph processing system.

3   System Architecture

In this section we discuss the requirements and the design of GRAPHITE, a columnar RDBMS prototype with a native graph abstraction, graph operators, and graph-specific secondary index structures [15]. We designed our system with the following design goals in mind:

Native Graph Abstraction. Relational operators are not well-suited to process native graph operations, such as traversals and graph pattern matching, efficiently. Hence, GRAPHITE uses a native graph abstraction to implement graph-specific operations and redirects set-based operations, such as predicate evaluation or aggregations, to the relational operators of the RDBMS.

Query Performance. The query performance of interactive graph queries in GRAPHITE should be close or even exceed the performance of native graph databases. This requires exposing a low-level graph interface that sits on top of the graph data structures and can be used in combination with relational operators.

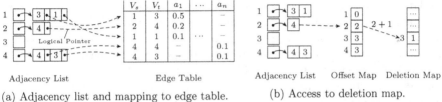

(a) Adjacency list and mapping to edge table.   (b) Access to deletion map.

Fig. 1. Usage of the adjacency list in conjunction with the relational edge table and in the presence of edge deletions.

Space Efficiency. Saving memory bandwidth is one of the keys of achieving query performance scalability on large server machines. We support lightweight compression techniques, like run-length encoding, dictionary encoding, and sparse encoding on the columns, and store only internal, dense numerical identifiers in the secondary index structures to keep the memory footprint low.

Integratability into a RDBMS. GRAPHITE is designed to be integrated as a component into a columnar RDBMS, where the primary copy of the data is kept in relational tables, accelerated by additional secondary graph index structures to store the graph topology.

Transactionality. We target interactive graph queries interleaved with concurrent updates on the graph data. Therefore a separate graph engine that operates on a snapshot of the data is not feasible. Our system inherits the transaction concept of the RDBMS and enables transactional query processing directly on the graph data. Due to space constraints, we do not discuss this aspect in detail in the course of this paper.

3.1 Columnar Graph Storage

GRAPHITE stores a graph in a columnar storage representation consisting of two column groups, one for vertices and one for edges. We describe a vertex by a unique identifier and an edge by a tuple of source and target vertex and an implicit edge direction. Both vertices and edges can have an optional type and an arbitrary set of attributes. Each column group is divided into a static, highly-compressed read partition and a dynamic, append-only write partition. To lower the overall memory consumption we can apply light-weight compression techniques on the columns, like dictionary encoding, run-length encoding, and sparse encoding.

3.2 Secondary Graph Index Structure

The in-memory representation of the graph topology is not well-suited for fast and fine-granular topological graph operations, such as the retrieval of outgoing edges for a given vertex, as it has a time complexity of $\mathcal{O}(|E|)$.

To efficiently support fine-granular topological operations, we provide a secondary index structure to store the graph topology—while the attributes remain in relational tables. We chose an adjacency list representation, since it supports fast graph operations and can handle updates of the graph topology gracefully. Our adjacency list consists of the core data structure to store the graph topology and several auxiliary data structures to support updates, deletions, and combined processing with vertex/edge attributes stored in the relational tables. Figure 1a illustrates the adjacency list and the interplay with the edge table through logical indexes that point to the corresponding entry in the table. We use a similar mechanism to address records in the vertex table. To support bi-directional topological operations, the adjacency list can be stored for both traversal directions.

We support deletion operations in GRAPHITE through an offset map and a deletion map as depicted in Fig. 1b. To avoid the cost of copying and reorganizing parts of the adjacency list when an edge deletion occurs, we use a bitmap to invalidate the corresponding entry and periodically reorganize the adjacency list data structure in a batch processing step. We address each edge in the deletion map using the relative position of the edge in the source vertex list and an offset for the source from the offset map. For example, the position of edge $e = (2, 4)$ can be computed from the summation of the offset found at position 2 in the offset map and the relative position ($p = 1$) of vertex 4 in the neighborhood list of vertex 2.

Additionally, the deletion map can be used for a reoccurring pattern in graph queries: a part of the graph is selected using predicates and subsequent operations are only executed on this subgraph. A subgraph is a lightweight materialized view requiring one bit per edge and is always connected to the complete adjacency list. It has its own deletion map, in which only vertices and edges are valid that fulfill the predicate criteria. Operations on the subgraph are performed similar to operations on the adjacency lists, except for the use of a dedicated validity map.

4   Implementation Details

We implemented our prototype in C++ and used for parallelization the INTEL TBB library[2]. Our implementation is tailored towards utilizing the available hardware resources as much as possible by using cache-friendly, concurrent data structures and parallelizable algorithms as basic building blocks, such as, duplicate detection and the retrieval of adjacent vertices. Although our focus is on improving the response time for graph operations, a careful implementation is also required for utility functions, such as predicate parsing and evaluation. For short-running queries, the parsing of a predicate can even outweigh the actual predicate evaluation and therefore should be implemented with care. In the following we provide implementation details on two important aspects of our system—the Graph API and the implementation of interactive graph queries.

4.1   Basic Graph Operations & Building Blocks

The Graph API provides a unified access to the graph topology stored in an adjacency list and vertex/edge attributes stored in the corresponding relational tables.

---

[2] https://www.threadingbuildingblocks.org.

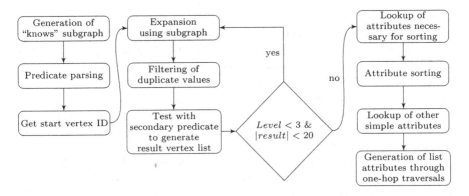

Fig. 2. Flow diagram of our implementation of Q1 from the interactive query workload of the LDBC.

We implement the Graph API such that topological operations, such as, the edge expansion for a given set of vertices, can be seamlessly combined with relational operations, specifically the retrieval of vertex/edge attributes and the evaluation of predicates on sets of vertices/edges. We represent a vertex/an edge by a unique identifier—32 bit or 64 bit—and sets of vertices/edges as dense or sparse data structures—bitsets or dynamic arrays—depending on the cardinality of the set.

We identified several building blocks that can be found in most interactive graph queries from the LDBC benchmark, such as, a conditional edge traversal with a given vertex/edge predicate and duplicate filtering on multiple vertex/edge multisets. For topological operations, we parallelize the calls to the adjacency list in the backend and use multiset semantics. For often used vertex/edge predicate combinations, we provide a lightweight subgraph concept that stores a materialized view qualified by a set of vertex/edge predicates.

Efficient duplicate filtering is crucial for achieving superior query performance, especially for traversals over multiple steps. We implemented two differences approaches for duplicate filtering: (i) a hash-based and (ii) a sort/merge-based approach. The hash-set approach is fully parallelized and uses a concurrent hash-set to probe for vertex/edge identifiers and to insert them concurrently into a new set of discovered vertices/edges. The sort/merge approach first sorts the input in parallel, followed by a merge operation with the previous discovered vertices.

4.2   Query Implementation

Our system is tailored towards the efficient execution of interactive graph queries that access only a small portion of the complete graph. We use the interactive query workload of the LDBC to verify and evaluate our system in terms of response time, scalability to larger dataset sizes, and functional completeness [7]. In the following we provide a description of the implementation of one exemplary query from the interactive workload. We chose query Q1 as representative query since it covers a large subset of the required functionality to process the entire interactive workload.

Query Q1 performs a conditional, multi-level traversal and requires efficient and interleaved access to the graph topology and the attributes. More specifically, Q1 returns up to 20 friends with a specific first name of a given person (via the 3-hop neighborhood). In addition to the set of persons, we also return summaries about their workplaces and places of study, and sort the result ascending by the friendship distance followed by the last name and the identifier.

Figure 2 depicts a flow diagram of our implementation of query Q1 and the used building blocks of the Graph API. We realized the edge expansion in the multi-hop traversal using a subgraph, so that only edges of the friendship relation are expanded. For the subsequent filtering of duplicate vertex IDs we implemented hash-based and sort/merge-based duplicate elimination routines. The retrieval of all vertices with the given name is integrated into the multi-hop traversal, allowing for an early abort of the traversal, when the anticipated number of vertices satisfying the predicate is reached. We perform the sorting of the result at the earliest possible point during the execution to minimize the number of copy operations of materialized attributes. Finally, we fetch the attribute values from the relational tables through single-hop traversals and materialize the result.

4.3   Memory Consumption

The memory consumption M of the adjacency list depends linearly on the number of edges $|E|$ and the number of vertices $|V|$, where the coefficients depend on the implementation. We implement the core adjacency list as two STL vectors of vectors using 64 bit IDs, one for the neighborhood and the other for the corresponding logical pointer to the edge attribute table.

The total memory consumption of a graph in GRAPHITE does not only depend on the adjacency list, but also on the edge and vertex attribute tables. For the LDBC data set of SF1, the adjacency list consumes $M(V, E) = 557$ MB(single direction), while the vertex and edge tables consume 1355 MB using a dictionary encoding and 32 bit IDs. These numbers are without overheads.

In general, we find that for larger scale factors of the LDBC data set, the memory footprint of the vertex and edge attributes stored in the relational tables dominates the overall memory consumption, while the space overhead of the secondary adjacency list remains small. Since GRAPHITE stores attributes in a columnar storage layout, lightweight compression techniques can be applied to reduce the memory footprint of the attributes.

5   Evaluation

In this section we evaluate our implementation with focus on how it performs on large NUMA systems. We use a four-socket Linux based system with Intel Xeon X7560 (Nehalem) CPUs. Our system is equipped with 4×8 cores @2.27 GH$_z$ with Hyperthreading enabled, 24 MB last level cache at each socket, and 512 GB DDR3 RAM. We compile GRAPHITE with INTEL TBB 4.3 update 3 and GCC 4.8 with

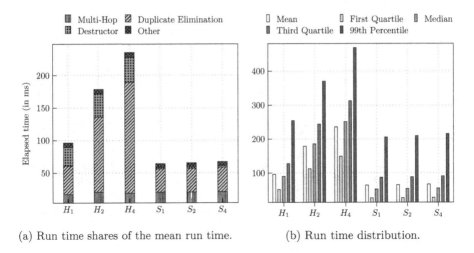

(a) Run time shares of the mean run time.   (b) Run time distribution.

Fig. 3. Elapsed time for Q1 (10k queries) using 8 cores on different number of sockets at SF100. We evaluate two different versions for duplicate elimination—hash-based H_x and sort-based S_x—where $x \in \{1, 2, 4\}$ refers to the number of utilized sockets.

the optimization flags -O3 and march=native, enabling the compiler to use the complete instruction set of the CPU.

We used the data generator of the LDBC benchmark to generate scale factors 1 to 100 and reassembled the output into a single vertex and a single edge table, respectively. We randomly generated representatives of query Q1 by using the generated parameters from the data generation process. In our experiments, we report the total elapsed time of the executed queries, including setup and destruction time of auxiliary data structures.

The only exception is the generation of subgraphs, which we exclude from the total elapsed time. Since we currently do not enforce any constraints on the graph—for example that two vertices of type *knows* can be only connected via an edge of type *knows*—we cannot easily partition the graph into isolated subgraphs. To simulate a materialized view enforcing such a constraint on vertex and edge types, we use the concept of a materialized subgraph in our experiments.

5.1 NUMA Effects

In our first experiment we analyze the NUMA behavior of GRAPHITE. We use a constant number of eight cores evenly distributed across different number of sockets and use numactl to pin threads to sockets. In Fig. 3a we report the mean run time shares using the two different duplicate filter methods. While the sort-based duplication elimination routine is not affected by the distribution across different sockets, the hash-based routine is sensitive to the thread placement policy.

The reason for this sensitivity is our global concurrent hash-set implementation that relies on atomic insertion operations. Every time a vertex ID is inserted into the concurrent hash-set, a random memory access occurs. If this memory access

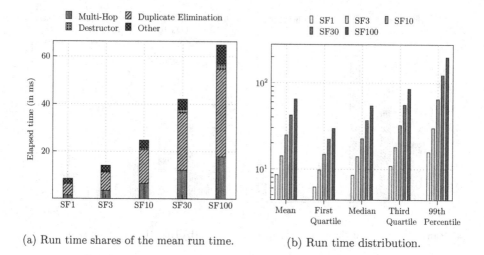

(a) Run time shares of the mean run time.   (b) Run time distribution.

Fig. 4. Run time of Q1 (10k queries) using a sorted list duplicate filter at different scale factors (SF) using 32 cores.

is redirected to different socket, the cache coherency protocol needs to be invoked. The expansion operations on the adjacency list (multi-hop) behave similarly to the sort-based duplicate elimination and are unaffected by NUMA. In Fig. 3b we depict the run time distribution of the elapsed time of Q1 for different input parameters. For both routines of duplicate elimination, the run time distribution scales to various input parameters and intermediate result sizes.

5.2   Performance

We evaluate the scalability of our approach using the sort-based duplicate filter for varying scale factors[3]—we use SF1 to SF100—and present our results in Fig. 4a.

The total elapsed time increases slower than the growth of the total data set size—for SF100 the mean run time is only 64.9 ms. For all evaluated scale factors, the largest portion of the total elapsed time is spent in the multi-hop expansion and the subsequent vertex duplicate elimination step. With increasing scale factors, we experienced an increased elapsed time for both steps.

This effect is caused by growing intermediate vertex sets after the expansion and consequently more work to be done during the duplicate elimination. Since the scale factor of the data set does not directly reflect the scaling of the graph topology—SF1 contains about 11,000 vertices of type person and about 400,000 connections between them—and the number of traversal levels is limited to three, the overall run time increase is not proportional to the total data set size.

---

[3] The numbers presented in Fig. 3a for eight core at SF100 are representative for other scale factors and core numbers: the actual run time of the hash-based approach takes longer and is more expensive to destroy.

We experienced a similar behavior when taking a closer look at the run time distribution for different input configurations of Q1 and report on the experimental results in Fig. 4b. Similar to the NUMA experimental results, we verify that the overall run time of Q1 is not directly related to the total data set size, but correlated with the size of the queried subgraph of the graph topology. Further, we experienced that the total query execution depends on the chosen input configuration and the start vertex for the traversal, resulting in significant variations for the size of the 3-hop neighborhood.

The remaining parts of the query evaluation contribute only a minor fraction to the total query execution time. For example, we apply the secondary predicate on the set of vertex IDs after the processing of the duplicate filter that already reduced the number of vertices.

The subgraph generation is not part of the querying process, but is triggered at the beginning of the query session. The elapsed time of the subgraph generation for vertex type *person* and edge type *knows* accounts with about 40.8 ms for SF1 and grows linearly to 4876.9 ms for SF100.

6   Conclusion

We presented GRAPHITE, a columnar RDBMS architecture and implementation—extended by a native graph abstraction and a graph-optimized secondary data structure—that allows seamlessly combining graph with relational operations in the same database engine. Based on a detailed study of the interactive query workload of the LDBC benchmark, we derived requirements that have to be fulfilled to support interactive queries directly on graph data stored in a RDBMS. To improve the response time of topological queries, we introduced an adjacency list as a secondary index structure that is tightly coupled with the corresponding vertex/edge attribute tables. Our prototypical implementation of Q1 from the interactive query workload of the LDBC shows a NUMA-friendly behavior, the run time scales with the dataset size of the query and shows competitive query performance compared with native GDBMS in other publications [7]. This work is currently in progress, so as next steps we plan to extend our experimental evaluation to other queries from the LDBC benchmark and to evaluate GRAPHITE in the presence of concurrent, transactional write operations.

References

1. InfiniteGraph project website. www.objectivity.com/infinitegraph
2. Neo4j project website. http://neo4j.com
3. OrientDB project website. http://www.orientdb.org/
4. Titan project website. http://thinkaurelius.github.io/titan
5. Aberger, C.R., Nötzli, A., Olukotun, K., Ré, C.: EmptyHeaded: boolean algebra based graph processing, CoRR abs/1503.02368 (2015)
6. Cui, Z., Chen, L., Chen, M., Bao, Y., Huang, Y., Lv, H.: Evaluation and optimization of breadth-first search on NUMA cluster. In: Proceedings of CLUSTER 2012, pp. 438–448 (2012). http://dx.doi.org/10.1109/CLUSTER.2012.29

7. Erling, O., Averbuch, A., Larriba-Pey, J., Chafi, H., Gubichev, A., Prat, A., Pham, M.D., Boncz, P.A.: The LDBC social network benchmark: interactive workload. In: Proceedings of SIGMOD 2015, pp. 619–630 (2015)
8. Gonzalez, J.E., Xin, R.S., Dave, A., Crankshaw, D., Franklin, M.J., Stoica, I.: GraphX: graph processing in a distributed dataflow framework. In: Proceedings of OSDI 2014, pp. 599–613 (2014)
9. Hong, S., Chafi, H., Sedlar, E., Olukotun, K.: Green-Marl: a DSL for easy and efficient graph analysis. In: Proceedings of ASPLOS 2012, pp. 349–362 (2012)
10. Kyrola, A., Blelloch, G., Guestrin, C.: Graphchi: large-scale graph computation on just a PC. In: Proceedings of the 10th USENIX Conference on Operating Systems Design and Implementation, OSDI 2012, pp. 31–46. USENIX Association, Berkeley (2012)
11. Low, Y., Bickson, D., Gonzalez, J., Guestrin, C., Kyrola, A., Hellerstein, J.M.: Distributed GraphLab: a framework for machine learning and data mining in the cloud. Proc. VLDB Endow. 5(8), 716–727 (2012)
12. Macko, P., Marathe, V.J., Margo, D.W., Seltzer, M.I.: LLAMA: efficient graph analytics using large multiversioned arrays. In: Proceedings of ICDE 2015 (2015)
13. Malewicz, G., Austern, M.H., Bik, A.J., Dehnert, J.C., Horn, I., Leiser, N., Czajkowski, G.: Pregel: a system for large-scale graph processing. In: Proceedings of SIGMOD 2010, pp. 135–146 (2010)
14. Martínez-Bazan, N., Águila Lorente, M.A., Muntés-Mulero, V., Dominguez-Sal, D., Gómez-Villamor, S., Larriba-Pey, J.L.: Efficient graph management based on bitmap indices. In: Proceedings of IDEAS 2012, pp. 110–119 (2012)
15. Paradies, M., Lehner, W., Bornhövd, C.: GRAPHITE: an extensible graph traversal framework for relational database management systems. In: Proceedings of the International Conference on Scientific and Statistical Database Management, SSDBM 2015, pp. 29:1–29:12 (2015)
16. Raman, R., van Rest, O., Hong, S., Wu, Z., Chafi, H., Banerjee, J.: PGX.ISO: parallel and efficient in-memory engine for subgraph isomorphism. In: Proceedings of GRADES 2014, pp. 5:1–5:6 (2014)
17. Rodriguez, M.A., Neubauer, P.: Constructions from dots and lines. Bull. Am. Soc. Inf. Sci. Technol. 36(6), 35–41 (2010)
18. Rudolf, M., Paradies, M., Bornhövd, C., Lehner, W.: The graph story of the SAP HANA database. In: Proceedings of BTW 2013, pp. 403–420 (2013)
19. Sun, W., Fokoue, A., Srinivas, K., Kementsietsidis, A., Hu, G., Xie, G.: SQLGraph: an efficient relational-based property graph store. In: Proceedings of SIGMOD 2015 (2015)
20. Welc, A., Raman, R., Wu, Z., Hong, S., Chafi, H., Banerjee, J.: Graph analysis: do we have to reinvent the wheel? In: Proceedings of GRADES 2013, pp. 7:1–7:6 (2013)
21. Xia, Y., Tanase, I.G., Nai, L., Tan, W., Liu, Y., Crawford, J., Lin, C.: Explore efficient data organization for large scale graph analytics and storage. In: Proceedings of BigData 2014, pp. 942–951 (2014)
22. Zhang, K., Chen, R., Chen, H.: NUMA-aware graph-structured analytics. In: Proceedings of SIGPLAN 2015, pp. 183–193 (2015)

A Multi-layer Framework for Graph Processing via Overlay Composition

Alessandro Lulli[2], Patrizio Dazzi[1(✉)], Laura Ricci[2], and Emanuele Carlini[1]

[1] Istituto di Scienza e Tecnologie dell'Informazione "A. Faedo",
Consiglio Nazionale delle Ricerche (ISTI-CNR), Pisa, Italy
{patrizio.dazzi,emanuele.carlini}@isti.cnr.it
[2] Dipartimento di Informatica, Università di Pisa, Pisa, Italy
{lulli,ricci}@di.unipi.it

Abstract. The processing of graph in a parallel and distributed fashion is a constantly rising trend, due to the size of the today's graphs. This paper proposes a multi-layer graph overlay approach to support the orchestration of distributed, vertex-centric computations targeting large graphs. Our approach takes inspiration from the overlay networks, a widely exploited approach for information dissemination, aggregation and computing orchestration in massively distributed systems. We propose Telos, an environment supporting the definition of multi-layer graph overlays which provides each vertex with a layered, vertex-centric, view of the graph. Telos is defined on the top of Apache Spark and has been evaluated by considering two well-known graph problems. We present a set of experimental results showing the effectiveness of our approach.

1 Introduction

The current production of data is far beyond what has been experienced before. For example, in 2012 was created 2.5 exabytes (2.5×10^{18}) of data every day [14]. This data comes from multiple and heterogeneous sources, ranging from scientific devices to business transactions. In many of these contexts, data is modelled as a graph, such as social network graphs, road networks and biological graphs. Clearly, data of this size makes often infeasible to process these graphs by exploiting the computational and memory capacity of a single machine. Indeed, these problems are usually faced by exploiting parallel and distributed computing architectures.

Many solutions for the parallel and distributed processing of large graphs have been designed so far. Most of the methodologies currently adopted fall in two main approaches. On the one hand, low-level techniques (such as send/receive message passing or, equivalently, unstructured shared memory mechanisms) are often complex, error-prone, hard to maintain and, usually, their tailored nature hinder their portability. On the other hand, it can be observed a wide use of the MapReduce paradigm proposed by Dean and Ghemawat [9], and inspired by the well-known map and reduce paradigms that, across the years, have been provided by a number of different frameworks [1,7,8].

© Springer International Publishing Switzerland 2015
S. Hunold et al. (Eds.): Euro-Par 2015 Workshops, LNCS 9523, pp. 515–527, 2015.
DOI: 10.1007/978-3-319-27308-2_42

The MapReduce paradigm is often used in contexts that are different from the ones for which it has been conceived. In fact, some of the most notable existing implementations of such paradigm (e.g. Apache Hadoop and Apache Spark) are often used to implement algorithms which could be more fruitfully implemented by means of different parallel programming paradigms or different ways to orchestrate their computation. This is especially true when dealing with large graphs [13]. In spite of this, some MapReduce based frameworks achieved a wide diffusion due to their ease of use, detailed documentation and very active communities of users. As a consequence, in the last years, several solutions based on the MapReduce have been adapted for performing analysis on large graphs in a native way, supporting data streams, large graphs analysis, etc. Some of these solutions have been inspired by the BSP bridging model [20], such as the Pregel framework [13], GraphX [24] and Giraph [6]. A common trait shared by these frameworks is that they provide the possibility to describe graph processing applications from the point of view of a vertex in the graph. Every vertex processes the same function independently and can only access its local context which limits its knowledge to its neighbourhood, without having a global view on the graph. In vertex-centric frameworks the complexity of the distribution and communication is cut off from the data scientist, who can only focus on the algorithmic issues.

In this paper we propose Telos, a high-level multi-layer programming environment that raises the level of abstraction of vertex-centric graph processing frameworks by supporting the composition of graph-based overlays. By means of its support to compositionality it also promotes the reuse and the combination of existing solutions and algorithms. Our approach takes inspiration by the similarities existing between large graphs and massively distributed architectures, e.g., P2P systems. In fact, an effective, efficient and interesting approach adopted in these systems to orchestrate the computation and spread the information strongly relates with (multi-level) overlay networks. An overlay can be thought as an alternative network, built upon the existing physical network, connecting nodes by means of logical links established according to a well-defined goal. It can be noticed how, by construction, the building blocks of overlays match the key elements of graphs. In fact, vertices can be seen as networked resources and the edges as links. This view gives the possibility to dynamically define graph topologies different from the original one, so enabling each vertex to choose the most promising neighbours to speed-up the convergence of the distributed algorithm.

We highlight three main aspects that can be adopted to graph processing: (i) *Local knowledge:* each node maintains a limited amount of information and a limited neighbourhood. During the computation each node relies only its own data and the information received from such neighbourhood; (ii) *Multiple views:* the definition of multi-layer overlays drives the node neighbourhood selection accordingly to specific goals, a concept successfully exploited in peer-to-peer networks [2,10]; (iii) *Approximate solutions:* algorithms running on top of overlays usually are conceived to deal with approximated data and to find approximated solutions. Telos defines a distributed framework able to support all previous strategies. Finally, the contributions of this paper can be summarized as the following:

- the definition of a high-level multi-layer programming framework targeting computations on large graphs;
- the presentation of our publicly available implementation of the framework[1] on top of Apache Spark [26] providing both a high level API to define custom layers and some built-in layers.
- a threefold evaluation of our framework to assess the scalability and two proof-of-concepts directed to exploit a multi layer evolving topology and to improve the quality of the result of a state of the art balanced k-way partitioning algorithm.

2 The Telos framework

The vertex-centric model is an approach to define computation for processing large scale graphs that have become more and more adopted in the last years, even in very different contexts. According to such model each computation is organised in a BSP-like fashion [20]. A BSP computation consists of three main pillars. *Concurrent computation* every participating computing entity (a vertex in our case) may perform local computations, i.e., computing by making use of values stored in the local memory/storage. *Barrier synchronisation* after conducting its local computation every vertex waits until all other ones have reached the same point. *Communication* vertices exchange data between themselves before they reach the barrier. Each message sent at superstep S is received at superstep $S + 1$.

During a superstep, each vertex receives messages sent in the previous iteration and executes a user-defined function that can modify its own state. Once the computation of such function is terminated, it is possible for the computing entity to send messages to other entities. The communication model is based on a barrier at the end of each superstep. Each message sent at superstep S is received at superstep $S + 1$. In other words, before the superstep $S + 1$ can begin, all vertices must have executed the superstep S.

This approach has been fruitfully exploited for computing data analysis on large graphs. Indeed, in some ways, programming according to the vertex-centric model recalls the definition of epidemic (or gossip) computing. A widely used approach in massively distributed systems that leads the nodes of a network to work independently but having a common, overall, aim. Indeed, according to a gossip protocol, nodes build network overlays by means of the information they exchange one each others, similarly to the vertices in the vertex-centric model that communicate to each other thought their graph neighbourhood.

An overlay consists of a logical communication topology, built over an underlying network, that is maintained and used by nodes. Many gossip protocols are

---

[1] https://github.com/hpclab/telos.

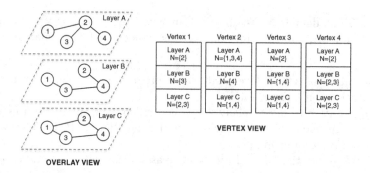

	Vertex 1	Vertex 2	Vertex 3	Vertex 4
	Layer A N={2}	Layer A N={1,3,4}	Layer A N={2}	Layer A N={2}
	Layer B N={3}	Layer B N={4}	Layer B N={1,4}	Layer B N={2,3}
	Layer C N={2,3}	Layer C N={1,4}	Layer C N={1,4}	Layer C N={2,3}

VERTEX VIEW

OVERLAY VIEW

Fig. 1. Layered architecture and interactions

combined into layers [12]. The communication can be exploited over multiple overlays with each overlay devoted to the computation of a peculiar task. As an example, Vicinity [22] is a two-layered protocol aimed at discovering similar nodes in a network in a fully distributed fashion. In Vicinity, one layer obtains a random sampling of nodes from the network, and the other layer keeps the nodes more similar with a given context.

Following the evolution of the gossip protocols, the main idea of Telos is to augment the classic vertex-centric frameworks by adding the support to a multiple layers architecture. Each vertex is associated with multiple protocols (i.e. one for each user-defined functions) which are organised into layers. In Fig. 1 is depicted a visual representation of this concept in the overlay view. For each protocol, a vertex v maintains a local context and a neighbourhood, the former represents the "state" of the vertex v considering a given protocol, whereas the latter represents the set of vertices that are exchanging messages with v in that protocol. Both the context and the neighbourhood can change during the computation and across the supersteps, given the possibility of building evolving "graph overlays".

Telos enables three different types of interactions that involve the vertices belonging to the graph: (i) *intra-vertex:* it is the access of a vertex v when executing the protocol p to the context of a protocol different from p on v; Fig. 1 represents this interaction in the vertices by showing that the context of each vertex is treated separately. (ii) *intra-protocol:* it is a message from a vertex v to a vertex u sent to the same protocol p. Intra-protocol messages sent during the super-step S will be received by the vertex u at super-step $S + 1$ (following the BSP model). (iii) *extra-protocol:* a vertex v when executing the protocol p requesting the context of protocol m on vertex u, with $p \neq m$, sends a request message to u. Upon the reception of the message, the context of vertex u at protocol m is sent back. This kind of messages are handled directly by Telos and no additional operations must be provided by the users.

Telos brings to the vertex-centric model many of the typical advantages of a layered architecture: (i) *modularity*, protocols can be composed and it is easy to improve functionality by adding layers; (ii) *isolation*, a modification of a protocol does not affect the logic of the protocols on the other layers; (iii) *reusability*, protocols can be general enough to be reused for many and possibly different computations. More in detail, Telos ease the task, for programmers, of combining different protocols. Each protocol is managed independently by Telos and all the communications and the organisation of the records are all in charge of Telos, which it manages in a fully distributed manner. Currently, the Telos framework is built on top of Spark [26]. To realise data management and distribution, the Spark framework exploits the Resilient Distributed Dataset (RDD) [25], on top of which are defined collective operations such as map, reduce and join. We developed Telos on top of the standard Spark's API, as an additional abstraction that organises the layered vertex-centric view. All the tasks for managing RDDs (including checkpointing and persistence) are transparent to the programmers and managed by our framework. The framework coordinates the protocols and masquerades the underlying support to ease the application development. The framework handles all the burden required to create the initial set of vertices and messages and provides to each vertex the context it requires for the computation. Communications are completely hidden to the programmer as well. Telos handles data dispatch to the target vertices (and the corresponding layers). In addition, the framework manages also minor activities like the control on the maximum number of steps to perform and the persistence of intermediate data in case of failures.

2.1   Protocols

Protocols are first-class entities in Telos, they drive the computation and organise the topologies in each layer of the framework. Each protocol orchestrates the context of the vertices, such as their local state and their neighbourhood, in a vertex-centric view of the graph. In fact, each protocol is in charge of (i) modifying the state of the vertices, (ii) defining a representation of the state of the vertices, which are eventually sent as messages to other vertices, and (iii) defining custom messages aimed at supporting the orchestration of the nodes.

Table 1 reports the API that a Protocol object can implement. The Protocol interface abstracts the structure of the computation running on each vertex. The core logic of a Protocol is contained in the `compute()` method. Once called, say at superstep S, the `compute()` method can access to the state of the vertex at superstep $S - 1$ and all the messages received by such vertex in step S, as well. The contract of the `compute()` method requires to return a new vertex context and a set of messages that will be dispatched to the target vertices at the superstep $S + 1$. Note that the receivers of the messages are not necessarily part of the neighbourhood of vertex v at super-step S, namely the vertex v can send messages also to vertices not belonging to its neighbourhood. The termination of a Protocol is coordinated by a "halt" vote. At the end of its computation each vertex votes to halt, and when all vertices voted to halt, the computation terminates.

The frequency at which a protocol is activated (w.r.t. the supersteps) is regulated by `getStartStep()` and `getStepDelay()` methods. These methods are

Table 1. The Protocol API

Function	Description
setStartStep()	Defines the first step on which the compute() is called
setStepDelay()	Defines the delay in terms of steps between two successive calls of compute()
beforeSuperstep()	Defines aggregators and combiners to be run before the compute()
afterSuperstep()	Defines aggregators and combiners to be run after the compute()
compute()	Defines the protocol behaviour. Receives messages sent at the previous step, modifies the state, creates new messages and eventually votes to halt
init()	To define custom initialization procedures
createContext()	Sets the initial context of a vertex
createInitMessages()	Sets the initial messages

useful when a computation involves different protocols characterised by different converge time, i.e., the amount of steps it needs to converge to a useful result. By means of these methods it is possible to regulate the activations of the protocols with respect to the amount of elapsed supersteps. Figure 2 graphically depicts the behaviour of these methods. In the figure, *Protocol A* is activated at each superstep, i.e., if invoked, its implementation of getStepDelay() method, will return 1, whereas the very same call on *Protocol B* will return 2. In a pretty similar fashion the method getStartStep() drives the *first* activation of a protocol. Going back to the aforementioned figure, when called on *Protocol A* it will return 0, whereas it will return 1 if called on *Protocol B*. Finally, beforeSuperstep() and afterSuperstep() allow to define aggregators and combiners to be executed before and after the execution of the protocol. Telos comes with two built-in protocols for building dynamic topologies or exploiting properties of graphs:

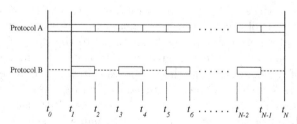

Fig. 2. The effect of getStartStep() and getStepDelay() methods

Random Protocol. The aim of this protocol is to provide to each vertex a random vertex identifier upon request. The vertex identifier must be taken uniformly and randomly in the space of identifiers of graph vertices. Telos provides two versions of this protocol, the first implementing a gossip random peer sampling protocol [21], the second implementing a distributed random number generator[2].

Ranking Protocols. These protocols are widely exploited in gossip frameworks to create and manage topology overlays [10,22]. The overlays are created and maintained according to a ranking function which measures the similarities between two vertices. In Telos we implemented a generic ranking protocol able to take as input the ranking function. It dynamically keeps in the neighbourhood of each vertex the more similar vertices according to the user defined ranking function. As an example, if every vertex is represented as a point in a two dimensional space and the similarity metrics is the euclidean distance, the ranking protocol eventually keeps in the neighbourhood of each vertex the k closest vertices.

3   Evaluation

To evaluate the effectiveness of our approach we conducted a set of three experiments. In Sect. 3.1 we validate the framework, in Sect. 3.2 we evaluate its scalability, and finally Sect. 3.3 tests our framework in a real scenario presenting a multi-layer solution for graph partitioning.

3.1   Torus Overlay

The aim of this experiment is to validate our approach. To this end we show a layered architecture built by means of our Telos framework to port concepts from the massively distributed systems to large graph processing solutions. As a proof-of-concept we built an experiment that organises the vertices and the edges of a graph according to a determined ranking function. Exploiting ranking functions to organise the overlay topology is a widely adopted approaches in highly distributed systems that we believe would be also useful in graph processing systems to drive the orchestration of the computation. In this case we a torus shaped overlay. The implementation is a two-layers approach. The bottom layer implements a random protocol, and the upper layer implements the ranking protocol. We tested the implementation on a graph made of $20K$ vertices. The results in Fig. 3 show the evolution of the graph in real time. The topology recalls the shape of a torus already at super-step 10. At super-step 20 no edges connects "distant" vertices in the torus. This experiment shows that, if properly instrumented, Telos can correctly manage multiple layers and can build the requested topology in a fewer number of super-steps.

3.2   Scalability

This experiment evaluates how the Telos framework manages larger input graphs when increasing the number of cores involved in the computation. For this experiment, we built two Erdos-Renyi random graphs (1 M vertices 5 M edges the first,

---

[2] http://www.cs.rit.edu/ark/pj2/doc/edu/rit/util/package-summary.html.

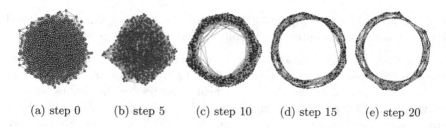

(a) step 0   (b) step 5   (c) step 10   (d) step 15   (e) step 20

Fig. 3. Evolution of Torus Computation at different Supersteps

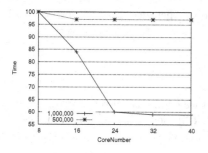 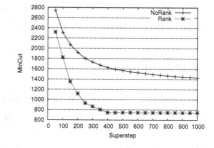

Fig. 4. Scalability as a function of the number of cores

Fig. 5. Convergence of edge-cut over supersteps

500K vertices 1.5 M edges the second) generated with the Snap library [11]. We run the torus overlay experiment described in Sect. 3.1 with both graphs varying the number of cores: $\{8, 16, 24, 32, 40\}$, and measuring of the convergence time. Results are presented in Fig. 4. Values are normalised, independently for each graph, in the range [1 ; 100], with 100 being the highest execution time. Each value is the average of 3 independent runs computed by using quad-cores workstations. Considering the 500K graph, it can be observed that using more than 16 cores does not brings any benefit. When considering the larger graph, we achieve performance benefits till 32 cores. In detail, with respect to 8 cores, 16 cores cut 15 % of the convergence time, and 24 cores cuts the 40 %.

3.3   Graph Partitioning

JA-BE-JA [16] is a distributed algorithm for resolving the balanced k-way graph partitioning problem and it works as the following. Initially, it creates k logical partitions on the graph by randomly assigning colours to each vertex, with the number of colours equals to k. Then, each vertex attempts to swap its own colour with another vertex according to the most dominant colour among its neighbours, by: (i) selecting another vertex either from its neighbourhood or from a random sample, and (ii) considering the "utility" of performing the colour swapping operation. If the colour swapping would decrease the number of edges between vertices characterised by a different colour, then the two vertices swap their colour; otherwise, they keep their own colours. In a previous work [3] we presented an implementation of JA-BE-JA in Apache Spark, outlining the adaptations that have been required in order to efficiently adapt the algorithm to match a BSP-like structure. In its original formulation, JA-BE-JA assumes that each vertex has complete access to the context of its neighbours and also their neighbourhood. To enforce this assumption, we initially introduced specific messages to retrieve the neighbourhood of any vertex. However, we noticed that forcing a strong consistency of such information slows down the performance too much. As a consequence, we provided an alternative implementation (called GP-SPARK) that introduces a degree of approximation to accelerate the computation, in which vertices piggyback their neighbourhood information in other messages. This mechanism causes the vertices to apply the local heuristics on possibly stale data, but increases the performance of the original approach providing a comparable quality of results with respect to the original version. The original GP-SPARK works with a two layered architecture composed as following: (i) the *colour swapping* protocol, that attempts the colour swapping targeting either a vertex from the local neighbourhood or from the random sampling, and (ii) the random sampling protocol that provides some random vertices to the colour swapping protocol. Here, we present GP-TELOS, an improved version of GP-SPARK that introduces a new layer with the *border ranking protocol* aimed to boost the quality of results. The objective is to give to JA-BE-JA the possibility to select from a better set of vertices when attempting colour swapping. The new layer sorts the vertices according to a *ranking function* that favours vertices to be connected with others that represent good swapping candidates. For instance, a blue vertex having 3 red neighbours would be ranked high from a red vertex having 3 blue neighbours. The ranking protocol orders the neighbourhood vertices according to a function to sort vertices being better swapping candidates. We compared the performance of GP-TELOS and GP-SPARK by means of the following metrics: (i) *edge-cut:* the number of edges that cross the boundaries of each subgraph. This metrics gives an estimation about the quality of the cut, with lower values corresponding to a better cut, and (ii) *convergence:* the number of supersteps required to achieve a substantially definitive edge-cut result. Our aim is to show that Telos does not affect the performance in term of supersteps to find a solution with respect to the GP-SPARK implementation. The experiments have been conducted on two datasets taken from the Walshaw archive [23] (3elt and vibrobox) and from the Facebook social network[3]. Figure 5 shows the convergence time in term of supersteps for the 3elt dataset with $K = 2$. Results with other datasets and different values of K are not included due to space constraints but they exhibit similar trends. The results show evidence that convergence is similar between GP-SPARK and GP-TELOS, as in both cases they achieve an almost-definitive edge-cut around the 400th superstep. In particular, after the 400th superstep GP-TELOS is stable, whereas GP-SPARK is converging but it is improving the result in every step marginally. Also, GP-TELOS yields a much better quality of results, achieving half the edge-cut of GP-SPARK. Table 2 presents the edge-cut obtained by GP-TELOS and GP-SPARK, averaging the results

---

[3] http://socialnetworks.mpi-sws.org/.

Table 2. Edge-cut value for GP-TELOS and GP-SPARK with the three datasets

K	3elt			Vibrobox			Facebook		
	GP-TELOS	GP-SPARK		GP-TELOS	GP-SPARK		GP-TELOS	GP-SPARK	
2	750	**1,433**	(**+91 %**)	14,812	22,244	(+50 %)	75,690	80,971	(+7 %)
4	1,810	2,903	(+60 %)	30,432	40,358	(+33 %)	147,991	157,282	(+6 %)
8	3,048	4,473	(+47 %)	43,728	56,954	(+30 %)	256,902	**245,682**	(**−4 %**)
16	4,191	6,344	(+51 %)	54,339	75,051	(+38 %)	348,494	353,061	(+1 %)
32	5,241	8,491	(+62 %)	67,787	95,858	(+41 %)	415,315	457,257	(+10 %)
64	6,419	10,622	(+65 %)	88,953	116,149	(+31 %)	520,391	552,714	(+6 %)

of 5 runs. We executed multiple runs by varying the number of the graph partitions with the values $K = \{2, 4, 8, 16, 32, 64\}$. It can be noticed that GP-TELOS obtains a better edge-cut in all the datasets and in all the configurations but with the Facebook dataset and 8 partitions. However also in this configuration GP-TELOS provides an edge-cut similar (just 4 % less) to the one in the GP-SPARK version. Overall, the GP-TELOS version provides a value between the 47 % and the 91 % better in the 3elt dataset and always better that the 30 % in the Vibrobox dataset. These results suggest that the new layer helps improving the results, and a layered vertex-centric approach can be used to carry out graph processing computations.

4   Related Work

A comprehensive survey of the most important currently available vertex centric programming models and of the corresponding frameworks is presented in [15]. While most of these provide a set of basic functionalities for vertex-centric computations, several related frameworks and approaches have been developed with the goal of extending and/or optimizing the basic frameworks.

Salihoglu and Widom [18] propose a set of interesting optimisations specifically targeting graph processing in Pregel-like solutions. These include performing the computation sequentially on the master node when number of nodes in the active graph is under a given threshold and merging a sets of vertices to form supervertices in order to optimize the communication cost. Both of these focus on reducing the completion time and the communication volume by instrumenting the support with automated recognition features, activated to speed-up the computation. Another interesting approach that goes beyond the Pregel-like solutions has been proposed by Tian *et al.* [19]. Their idea is to shift the reasoning from the point of view of a single vertex to the point of view of an aggregated set of vertices. By means of this change of perspective they have been able, on selected problems, to give a notable speeds-up in the computation. Both this proposal and our approach are based on the idea of pushing, by design, a shift in the paradigm that allows the implementation of more efficient solutions.

An interesting strategy to speed-up the computation is considering approaches dealing with approximated data and returning approximated solution. Zhang *et al.* [27] proposed both an approximated and an exact solution for k-nearest neighbours join developed according to the MapReduce paradigm. Their approximated solution run orders of magnitude faster than the exact one. The algorithm proposed in [4] reduces the completion time of the computation of a well known graph algorithm, the problem of finding connected components, by dynamically reducing the graph. Another algorithm, still implemented in MapReduce, is presented by Riondato *et al.* [17]. The paper proposes a randomized parallel distributed algorithm to extract approximations of the collections of frequent item-sets and association rules from large datasets. The approximate solution still guarantees, with high probability, the quality of the results.

5 Conclusions

In this paper we presented Telos, a high-level programming framework that supports vertex-centric computations based on layered overlays aimed at large graph processing, implemented on the top of Apache Spark. Telos takes inspiration from approaches that have proved to be robust and efficient in massively distributed systems that, somehow, recalls the structure of large graphs. We conducted an experimental analysis to validate the feasibility of the approach and shows its scalability with respect to the computational resources exploited. The experiments demonstrated that dynamic topologies can be effectively exploited during the computation. We believe that the ability of supporting multiple dynamic layers can be useful in many contexts, as for example to cluster users that are closer in a virtual environment [5] or for classical graph analysis problems, such as connected components and centrality measures. As a future work we plan to conduct a comprehensive analysis of the performance of the framework and a comparison with other approaches targeting large graph computation. We also plan to implement Telos on top of different parallel programming frameworks to assess the performance of our proposed approach regardless the performances provided by Apache Spark.

References

1. Aldinucci, M., Danelutto, M., Dazzi, P.: Muskel: an expandable skeleton environment. Scalable Comput. Pract. Exp. **8**(4), 325–341 (2007)
2. Carlini, E., Coppola, M., Dazzi, P., Laforenza, D., Martinelli, S., Ricci, L.: Service and resource discovery supports over p2p overlays. In: International Conference on Ultra Modern Telecommunications and Workshops, ICUMT 2009, pp. 1–8. IEEE (2009)
3. Carlini, E., Dazzi, P., Esposito, A., Lulli, A., Ricci, L.: Balanced graph partitioning with Apache Spark. In: Lopes, L., et al. (eds.) Euro-Par 2014, Part I. LNCS, vol. 8805, pp. 129–140. Springer, Heidelberg (2014)

4. Carlini, E., Dazzi, P., Lucchese, C., Lulli, A., Ricci, L.: Cracker: crumbling large graphs into connected components. In: 20th IEEE ISCC, International Symposium on Computer and Communications. IEEE (2015)
5. Carlini, E., Dazzi, P., Mordacchini, M., Ricci, L.: Toward community-driven interest management for distributed virtual environment. In: an Mey, D., et al. (eds.) Euro-Par 2013. LNCS, vol. 8374, pp. 363–373. Springer, Heidelberg (2014)
6. Ching, A.: Giraph: large-scale graph processing infrastructure on hadoop. In: Proceedings of the Hadoop Summit, Santa Clara (2011)
7. Danelutto, M., Dazzi, P.: A java/jini framework supporting stream parallel computations. In: Proceedings of the International Conference ParCo (2005)
8. Danelutto, M., Pasin, M., Vanneschi, M., Dazzi, P., Laforenza, D., Presti, L.: PAL: exploiting java annotations for parallelism. In: Gorlatch, S., Bubak, M., Priol, T. (eds.) Achievements in European Research on Grid Systems, pp. 83–96. Springer, New York (2008)
9. Dean, J., Ghemawat, S.: Mapreduce: simplified data processing on large clusters. Commun. ACM **51**(1), 107–113 (2008)
10. Jelasity, M., Montresor, A., Babaoglu, O.: T-Man: Gossip-based fast overlay topology construction. Comput. Netw. **53**(13), 2321–2339 (2009)
11. Leskovec, J., Sosič, R.: SNAP: A general purpose network analysis and graph mining library in C++, June 2014. http://snap.stanford.edu/snap
12. Lua, E.K., Crowcroft, J., Pias, M., Sharma, R., Lim, S., et al.: A survey and comparison of peer-to-peer overlay network schemes. IEEE Commun. Surv. Tutor. **7**(1–4), 72–93 (2005)
13. Malewicz, G., Austern, M.H., Bik, A.J., Dehnert, J.C., Horn, I., Leiser, N., Czajkowski, G.: Pregel: a system for large-scale graph processing. In: Proceedings of the 2010 ACM SIGMOD International Conference on Management of Data, pp. 135–146. ACM (2010)
14. McAfee, A., Brynjolfsson, E., Davenport, T.H., Patil, D., Barton, D.: Big data. The management revolution. Harvard Bus. Rev. **90**(10), 61–67 (2012)
15. McCune, R.R., Weninger, T., Madey, G.: Thinking like a vertex: a survey of vertex-centric frameworks for large-scale distributed graph processing (2015). arXiv:1507.04405
16. Rahimian, F., Payberah, A.H., Girdzijauskas, S., Jelasity, M., Haridi, S.: Ja-be-ja: a distributed algorithm for balanced graph partitioning. In: IEEE 7th International Conference on Self-Adaptive and Self-Organizing Systems (SASO 2013), pp. 51–60. IEEE (2013)
17. Riondato, M., DeBrabant, J.A., Fonseca, R., Upfal, E.: PARMA: a parallel randomized algorithm for approximate association rules mining in mapreduce. In: International Conference on Information and Knowledge Management, CIKM 2012, pp. 85–94 (2012)
18. Salihoglu, S., Widom, J.: Optimizing graph algorithms on pregel-like systems. PVLDB **7**(7), 577–588 (2014)
19. Tian, Y., Balmin, A., Corsten, S.A., Tatikonda, S., McPherson, J.: From "think like a vertex" to "think like a graph". PVLDB **7**(3), 193–204 (2013)
20. Valiant, L.G.: A bridging model for parallel computation. Commun. ACM **33**(8), 103–111 (1990)
21. Voulgaris, S., Gavidia, D., Van Steen, M.: Cyclon: inexpensive membership management for unstructured p2p overlays. J. Netw. Syst. Manag. **13**(2), 197–217 (2005)

22. Voulgaris, S., van Steen, M.: VICINITY: a pinch of randomness brings out the structure. In: Eyers, D., Schwan, K. (eds.) Middleware 2013. LNCS, vol. 8275, pp. 21–40. Springer, Heidelberg (2013)
23. Walshaw, C.: The graph partitioning archive (2002). http://staffweb.cms.gre.ac.uk/~c.walshaw/partition/
24. Xin, R.S., Gonzalez, J.E., Franklin, M.J., Stoica, I.: Graphx: a resilient distributed graph system on spark. In: First International Workshop on Graph Data Management Experiences and Systems, p. 2. ACM (2013)
25. Zaharia, M., Chowdhury, M., Das, T., Dave, A., Ma, J., McCauley, M., Franklin, M.J., Shenker, S., Stoica, I.: Resilient distributed datasets: a fault-tolerant abstraction for in-memory cluster computing. In: Proceedings of the 9th USENIX Conference on Networked Systems Design and Implementation, p. 2 (2012)
26. Zaharia, M., Chowdhury, M., Franklin, M.J., Shenker, S., Stoica, I.: Spark: cluster computing with working sets. In: Proceedings of the 2nd USENIX Conference on Hot Topics in Cloud Computing, p. 10 (2010)
27. Zhang, C., Li, F., Jestes, J.: Efficient parallel kNN joins for large data in MapReduce. In: 15th International Conference on Extending Database Technology, EDBT 2012, pp. 38–49 (2012)

Quantifying the Performance Impact of Graph Structure on Neighbour Iteration Strategies for PageRank

Merijn Verstraaten[✉], Ana Lucia Varbanescu, and Cees de Laat

University of Amsterdam, Amsterdam, The Netherlands
{m.e.verstraaten,a.l.varbanescu,delaat}@uva.nl

Abstract. Increases in graph size and analytics complexity have brought graph processing at the forefront of HPC. However, the HPC shift towards manycore accelerators (e.g., GPUs) is not favourable: traditional graph processing is hardly suitable for regular parallelism. Previous work has focused on parallel algorithms for specific graph operations, often using assumptions about the structure of the input graph. However, there has been very little systematic investigation of how strongly a graph's structure impacts the efficiency of graph operations.

With this article we make propose a step to quantify this impact, focusing on a typical operation: neighbour iteration. We design and implement four strategies for neighbour iteration and introduce a simple model to reason about the expected impact of a graph's structure on the performance of each strategy. We then use the PageRank algorithm to validate our model. We show that performance is significantly affected by the ability to effectively load-balance the work performed by these strategies across the GPU's cores.

1 Introduction

Due to its flexibility and wide applicability, graph processing is an important part of data science. With the prevalence of "big data", scaling increasingly complex analytics computations to increasingly large datasets is one of the fundamental problems in graph processing.

At the same time, hardware platforms are becoming increasingly parallel and heterogeneous, in an attempt to cope with these rapidly increasing workloads. Distributed systems and accelerator-based architectures (e.g., based on Graphical Processing Units — GPUs, or Xeon Phi) are frequently cited as solutions for handling large compute workloads, even for graph processing [1,13].

However, *both* partitioning the data and efficient execution of graph operations on parallel and distributed systems remain hard problems. The heterogeneity of the available platforms makes matters worse, because different types of platforms require different approaches to perform in their "comfort" zone.

To simplify working with graphs and to hide the complexity of the underlying platform, many different graph processing systems have been developed [5,7–9,12,17]. Most of these systems provide a clear separation between a simple-to-use front-end, where users are invited to write applications using, most often,

© Springer International Publishing Switzerland 2015
S. Hunold et al. (Eds.): Euro-Par 2015 Workshops, LNCS 9523, pp. 528–540, 2015.
DOI: 10.1007/978-3-319-27308-2_43

high-level operations, and a highly-optimized back-end, where these operations are translated to execute efficiently on a given platform (i.e., a combination of hardware and software).

Examples of high-level graph operations common in many algorithms (and thus implemented in graph processing systems) are: (a) iteration over all vertices (e.g., in graph statistics); (b) iteration over all edges (e.g., in traversals); (c) iteration over all neighbours of a vertex (e.g., in pagerank); and (d) iteration over all common neighbours of two vertices (e.g., in label propagation). Efficient mapping of such high-level graph operations to lower-level platform-specific primitives is crucial for the overall performance of the application and, consequently, for the adoption of a graph processing system.

In this work, we focus on the performance of graph operations on GPUs, seen as representative massively parallel HPC architectures. In this context, we make the following observations:

1. Speeding up graph processing by using GPUs requires efficient exploitation of the fine-grained parallelism of graph problems [6,14].
2. The efficiency in using the massive hardware parallelism (hundreds of cores) is highly-dependent on the data locality and the regularity of both operations and data access patterns [16,18].
3. The data locality and the regularity of operations and data access patterns are highly-dependent on *both* the in-memory representation of the data and the structure of the underlying graph.
4. Most high-level graph operations support different implementations, with significantly different memory representation and access patterns [3].

In summary, given a high-level graph processing operation, there are multiple ways we can choose to implement it. Which implementation is the most efficient on a given platform is highly dependent on the structure of the graph being processed [18]. While it is common knowledge that this is the case, there has not yet been a systematic study to quantify how big this effect is and to what extent it correlates with the structure of the input graph. This information has a clear impact on the performance of graph processing backends, as it would allow the system to adapt the implementation to best suit the input data.

However, to enable such adaptation, we must correlate (classes of) graphs with the performance behavior of different primitives on different platforms. To do so, we must: (1) identify possible implementations for the targeted primitive operations, (2) quantify the performance differences per (platform, dataset) pair, and (3) cluster the datasets with similar performance behavior in classes that can be easily characterized.

In this paper we show an example of how this process can be conducted, focusing on the quantification of the observed performance differences for a real application. Specifically, we present four different implementations of neighbour iteration on a GPU and use these to implement the PageRank [15] algorithm.

We measure how the performance of our implementations varies as a result of changing the input graph. Our experimental results demonstrate that the optimal implementation does not just depend on the dataset, but also on the dataset's in-memory representation. We also observe similarities between graphs of similar provenance (e.g., road networks show a different performance ranking than web-graphs), but better clustering is necessary to automate this process.

Our contribution in this paper is three-fold: (1) we design and implement four strategies to deal with neighbours iteration as a primitive graph operation, (2) we demonstrate how all these strategies can be used for PageRank, and (3) we quantify the impact these strategies have on the overall performance of PageRank when running on GPUs.

2   Background

In this section we provide a brief introduction on the PageRank algorithm, as well as a short description of the main characteristics of GPUs, the hardware platform we use for this work.

2.1   PageRank

PageRank is an algorithm that calculates rankings of vertices by estimating how important they are. Importance is quantified by the number of edges incoming from other vertices.

A generic PageRank operation works as follows. Given a graph $G = (V, E)$ the PageRank for a vertex $v \in V$ can be calculated as:

$$PR(v) = \frac{1-d}{|V|} + d \sum_{w \in N(v)} \frac{PR(w)}{\rho(w)} \tag{1}$$

Here d is the damping factor, $\rho(w)$ is the outgoing degree of vertex w, and $N(v)$ denotes the neighbourhood of vertex v, that is:

$$w \in N(v) \iff (w, v) \in E$$

This formula is usually implemented iteratively using two steps. In the first step we compute the incoming pagerank from the previous iteration. In the second step, we normalize this new pagerank using the damping factor. These operations are repeated until the difference between iterations falls below a certain threshold or the maximum number of iterations is reached.

2.2   The GPU Architecture

GPUs (Graphical Processing Units) are the most popular accelerators in High Performance Computing (HPC). GPUs are massively parallel processing units, where hundreds of cores, grouped in streaming multiprocessors (SMs), can execute thousands of software threads in parallel. Software threads are grouped into thread blocks, which are scheduled on the SMs. Threads inside the same block can easily communicate and synchronize; communication and synchronization for threads in different blocks (or for all threads on the platform) are significantly more expensive.

GPUs have a hierarchical memory model with limited, dedicated shared memory per SM and a relatively large global memory. Shared memory is only accessible by threads in the same block, while global memory is accessible to all threads. Typical sizes for global memory are between 1 and 12 GB.

For highly parallel workloads, GPUs outperform sequential units by orders of magnitude. But in cases where not enough parallelism is exposed, or in cases where there are too many dependencies between threads, or where threads diverge, the GPU performance drops significantly. Given the typical characteristics of graph processing applications — low computation-to-communication ratio, poor locality, and irregular, data-driven memory access patterns [2], the efficient use of GPUs for graph processing is not trivial. More importantly, the dataset structure and its characteristics can play a much more important role in the overall performance than in the case of the more flexible multi-core CPUs.

3 Design and Implementation

In this section we present the design and implementation of four different versions of PageRank, and discuss a simple model for estimating their performance.

3.1 Four PageRank Versions

In the iterative implementation of Eq. 1, we (1) sum the incoming pageranks for every vertex, and then (2) update the pagerank for that vertex.

To compute PageRank in parallel, a choice needs to be made on how the application is parallelized. For a massively parallel platform like the GPU, the amount of exposed parallelism should be as large as possible, so there are two simple strategies to choose from: one vertex per thread (i.e., vertex-centric parallelism), or one edge per thread (i.e., edge-centric parallelism).

Next, for the computation itself, the vertex-centric parallelisation requires a second choice, data can be either pushed or pulled from or to a vertex' neighbours. Thus, vertex-centric approaches can be further divided into *push* and *pull*. With *push*, the thread computes the outgoing pagerank of its vertex and sums that value to all the vertex' neighbours. With *pull*, the thread computes the outgoing rank of the vertex' neighbours and sums them to itself.

Algorithms 1, 2 and 3 show pseudocode implementations of the push, pull and edge-based implementations, respectively. For push and pull these kernels are executed once per vertex, for edge-based the kernel is executed once per edge. A pseudocode implementation of the rank consolidation kernel can be found in Algorithm 4.

We use the following representations. The edge based kernel uses one edge array (origin + destination vertices) and an offset array to compute degrees, resulting in $2 \cdot |E| + |V|$ ints space usage. The push and pull based kernels use Compressed Sparse Row (CSR) and reversed CSR, respectively, using $|E| + |V|$ ints of space. The pull kernel uses an additional off-set array to compute neighbour degrees, using an extra $|V|$ ints of space.

Algorithm 1. Push Vertex-based Update

```
function VERTEXPUSH(v)
    if v.degree ≠ 0 then
        outgoingRank ← v.pagerank / v.degree
    end if
    for nbr ∈ v.neighbours do
        nbr.newRank.atomicAdd(outgoingRank)
    end for
end function
```

Algorithm 2. Pull Vertex-based Update

```
function VERTEXPULL(v)
    newRank = 0
    for nbr ∈ v.neighbours do
        newRank += nbr.pagerank / nbr.degree
    end for
    v.newRank ← newRank
end function
```

Algorithm 3. Edge-based Update

```
function EDGEBASED(edge)
    origin ← edge.origin
    dest ← edge.destination
    outgoingRank ← origin.pagerank / origin.degree
    dest.newRank.atomicAdd(outgoingRank)
end function
```

Algorithm 4. Consolidate kernel

```
function CONSOLIDATERANK(v)
    newRank ← (1 - damping) / graphSize +
              (damping · v.newRank)
    diff ← abs(newRank − v.pagerank)
    globalDiff.atomicAdd(diff)
    v.pagerank ← newRank
    v.newRank ← 0
end function
```

Looking at the kernel for pull vertex-based computation, we observe that it is performing more work than strictly necessary. Computing the incoming rank from every neighbour means that vertices that share neighbours unnecessarily replicate work of dividing the rank. We could simply move this division into the consolidation kernel, performing this computation once per vertex. This requires us to use a different consolidation kernel for the last iteration to obtain the correct results, but this is not particularly difficult. Pseudocode for the modified pull kernel (entitled NoDiv) can be seen in Algorithm 5 and the corresponding consolidation kernel in Algorithm 6.

Algorithm 5. NoDiv: Pull Vertex-Based

```
function VERTEXPULLNODIV(v)
    newRank ← 0
    for nbr ∈ v.neighbors do
        newRank += nbr.pagerank
    end for
    v.newRank ← newRank
end function
```

Algorithm 6. NoDiv: Consolidate kernel

```
function CONSOLIDATERANKNODIV(v)
    newRank ← (1 - damping) / graphSize +
              (damping · v.newRank)
    diff ← abs(newRank − v.pagerank)
    globalDiff.atomicAdd(diff)
    v.pagerank ← newRank / v.degree
    v.newRank ← 0
end function
```

3.2 Estimating Performance

The above kernels show that the computational workload of pagerank is negligible. Like for many other graph algorithms, most of the workload comes from reading and writing memory. To achieve our goal of correlating algorithm performance with input data, we need a performance model for our primitives. Our performance model only considers global memory accesses and global atomic operations to reason about the relative work complexity of the different kernels.

For all models, let T_{read} be the cost of a random global read, T_{write} the cost of a random global write, and T_{atom} the cost of a global atomic add operation. For now, we ignore the variability of atomic operation contention and cache effects, in an attempt to only rank the different versions of the algorithm, and *not* predict accurate execution times.

We see in Algorithm 1 that every thread performs 3 reads (2 to compute the degree and 1 to read its pagerank), followed by d atomic addition operations, where d is the degree of that vertex. The number of operations performed by push thus boil down to:

$$T_{push} = \sum_{v \in V} (3 * T_{read} + d_v * T_{atom}) = 3 * |V| * T_{read} + |E| * T_{atom}$$

In Algorithm 2 we see that the pull kernel performs 3 reads for each neighbour of its vertex, and then performs a non-atomic write to store the new result. The total operations performed by pull thus boil down to:

$$T_{pull} = \sum_{v \in V} (3 * d_v * T_{read} + T_{write}) = 3 * |E| * T_{read} + |V| * T_{write}$$

The kernel in Algorithm 3 uses on thread per edge, and each thread performs 3 reads, 2 to compute the degree and 1 to read the pagerank, it then performs an atomic addition to store the result, resulting in:

$$T_{edge} = \sum_{e \in E} (3 * T_{read} + T_{atom}) = 3 * |E| * T_{read} + |E| * T_{atom}$$

The pagerank consolidation kernel is the same for each of the above kernels, performing 2 reads, one for the new incoming rank value and one for the old pagerank value, followed by an atomic addition and 2 writes to store the new pagerank and reset the incoming rank:

$$T_{con} = \sum v \in V (T_{read} + 2 * T_{write} + T_{atom}) = 2 * |V| * T_{read} + 2 * |V| * T_{write} + |V| * T_{atom}$$

The performance model for the optimised pull-based kernel (i.e., NoDiv, Algorithm 5) is:

$$T_{NoDiv} = \sum v \in V (d_v * T_{red} + T_{write}) = |E| * T_{read} + |V| * T_{write}$$

The corresponding consolidation needs a slight update, according to Algorithm 6:

$$T_{conNoDiv} = \sum v \in V (4 * T_{read} + 2 * T_{write} + T_{atom})$$
$$= 4 * |V| * T_{read} + 2 * |V| * T_{write} + |V| * T_{atom}$$

Summarizing, these are the performance models for a single pagerank iteration, running sequentially:

$$T_{push} = 5 * |V| * T_{read} + 2 * |V| * T_{write} + (|V| + |E|) * T_{atom}$$
$$T_{pull} = (3 * |E| + 2 * |V|) * T_{read} + 3 * |V| * T_{write} + |V| * T_{atom}$$
$$T_{NoDiv} = (|E| + 4 * |V|) * T_{read} + 3 * |V| * T_{write} + |V| * T_{atom}$$
$$T_{edge} = (3 * |E| + 2 * |V|) * T_{read} + 2 * |V| * T_{write} + (|V| + |E|) * T_{atom}$$

In most graphs, even sparse ones, we can expect $|E|$ to be at least as big as $|V|$ and usually significantly bigger. Given this assumption we can see that the edge-based implementation performs both the most reads and atomic additions. The pull-based implementation performs strictly less work than the edge-based one, as it reduces the number of reads by $3*(|E|-|V|)$. The pull-based implementation reduces the number of atomic operations required by increasing the number of write operations. The optimised NoDiv version further reduces the number of reads done by $2 * (|E| - |V|)$.

3.3 Parallel Performance

A naive reading of the performance models would conclude that the edge-based version is always slower and the only implementation worth considering are push and pull. However, in practice the comparison is not as straightforward. When running in parallel, on the GPU, the performance depends on the number of threads, chosen architecture (number of SMs), and scheduling. GPUs schedule threads in groups, usually called warps, and every thread in the warp executes the same instruction.

Divergent loops within a warp result in idle cores while executing that warp; the performance of the entire warp is thus limited to the slowest thread. This means that processing vertices of differing degrees within the same warp leads to efficiency loss due diverging loops in the push and pull kernels. The edge-based version does not suffer from divergence and all of the GPU cores are always utilised. Therefore, the choice between push/pull updates and edge-based updates is a trade-off between performing extra work for better workload balance.

The question we need to answer is: At what point does the intra-warp workload imbalance start to outweigh the extra work performed by the additional operations performed by the edge based implementation? In this work, we answer this question empirically, and demonstrate that the degree distribution plays an important role in this decision.

4 Experimental Evaluation

With the simple performance models introduced in the previous section, we expect that push and pull perform best on graphs that have a (near) constant degree, as this results in very good/perfect workload balance between all threads within a warp. Correspondingly, we expect both to perform worse for graphs that have large variation in degree.

In this section we empirically validate this hypothesis and measure the trade-off between the extra work done by the edge based version against the impact of workload imbalance for the push and pull versions. To do so, we ran all four versions of PageRank (see Sect. 3) on multiple datasets, both real world datasets from SNAP [11] and artifically generated graphs.

4.1   Experimental Setup

For running PageRank, we used a damping factor of 0.85. We ran the algorithm for 30 iterations to avoid convergence differences. The results presented here consist of the time the PageRank computation took, averaged over 30 runs, excluding data transfers to and from the GPU. We performed these measurements on an NVIDIA K20 (an HPC-oriented GPU card, with lower memory bandwidth, but larger global memory). We used version 5.5 of the CUDA toolkit.

In addition to the variations described in Sect. 3 we also implemented alternate versions of the push and pull kernels, based on the work of Hong, et al.; which showed a technique for achieving smoother load-balancing for vertex-centric programming on the GPU, leading to speed-ups up to 16x for certain graphs. [10]

For the edge-based implementation, we implemented both a struct-of-arrays and array-of-structs implementation of our edge data structure. Array-of-structs is a common optimisation technique on the CPU, but it is not clear whether the same technique is an optimisation on the GPU, and we aimed to determine this empirically.

To summarise we have 8 versions: edge-based using array-of-structs, edge-based using struct-of-arrays, push, pull, optimised pull, plus warp-optimised versions of the latter three. For the warp versions we have tried warp sizes 1, 2, 4, 8, 16, 32, and 64 with chunk sizes ranging from 1 to 10 times the warp size. All these versions are available online at https://github.com/merijn/GPU-benchmarks.

We have selected 19 datasets from several different classes of graphs from the SNAP [11] repository. These include citation, collaboration, social, computer, and road networks. The characteristics of the datasets are presented in Table 1.

4.2   Results

In Fig. 1, we show the normalised results of our experiments, meaning that the worst performing implementation of PageRank for each graph is plotted as 1, and all the others are fractions of the worst performing variant (i.e., lower is better, and the lower the bar, the higher the performance gap). For readability reasons we filtered out all the warp implementations of push and pull that did *not* perform faster than any other implementation.

Our initial hypothesis of push and pull performing best on graphs with constant degree is confirmed by the performance measured on our artificial graphs with fixed degrees. Both push and the optimised pull win on all but one of these. We also see them performing well on the road networks. This is not surprising, because the road networks have fairly little variation in terms of the degree of nodes (the highest degree is 6). On the other hand, star presents a worst-case scenario for push and pull, having a completely imbalanced workload. As confirmed by the large performance gap in the results for that graph.

Table 1. Our 7 synthetic graphs, followed by the 12 real world graphs from SNAP.

No	Graph	$|V|$	$|E|$	Description
1	chain_1000000	1,000,000	2,000,000	Bidirectional chain
2	star_1000000	1,000,000	2,000,000	Star
3	degree4_1000	999,999	4,000,000	Two dimensional mesh
4	degree6_100	999,999	6,000,000	Three dimensional mesh
5	degree_5_16	1,048,575	10,485,760	Constant out-degree 10
6	degree_10_4	1,048,575	20,971,520	Constant out-degree 20
7	degree_20_2	1,048,575	41,943,040	Constant out-degree 40
8	as-Skitter	1,696,415	22,190,596	Internet topology graph
9	cit-Patents	3,774,768	16,518,948	Citation network among US Patents
10	email-EuAll	265,214	420,045	Email from a EU research institution
11	Facebook	4,039	176,468	Social circles from Facebook
12	Gplus	107,614	13,673,453	Social circles from Google+
13	roadNet-CA	1,965,206	5,533,214	Road network CA
14	roadNet-TX	1,379,917	3,843,320	Road network TX
15	soc-LiveJournal1	4,847,571	68,993,773	LiveJournal online social network
16	Twitter	81,306	1,768,149	Social circles from Twitter
17	web-BerkStan	685,230	7,600,595	Web graph of Berkeley and Stanford
18	web-Google	875,713	5,105,039	Web graph from Google
19	wiki-Talk	2,394,385	5,021,410	Wikipedia talk comm. network

We note that even under ideal circumstances for push and pull, the edge-based implementation is not far behind in terms of performance, despite performing substantially more work than push and pull.

We also observe that there is very little difference between the two edge-based implementation. Surprisingly, these results show that the array-of-structs optimisation used to exploit cache locality on the CPU has no significant impact on the algorithm's performance on the GPU. In fact, it appears to be marginally slower on all graphs.

Another, perhaps surprising, result is that the warp versions of push and pull inspired by [10] almost never win in terms of performance. The trade-off made by the warp-optimisation is that it tries to smooth the load-balancing by performing more work than the pure vertex-centric code. As a result it is somewhere between edge-based and the push or pull based version. As a result it load-balances less well than edge-based, but has more overhead than push/pull for the ideal constant degree graphs. As such, its performance appears to combine the worst of both worlds.

4.3   Sorted Graphs

Vertices within a warp having different degrees result in workload-imbalance for the push and pull algorithms. Sorting the vertices within a graph by their

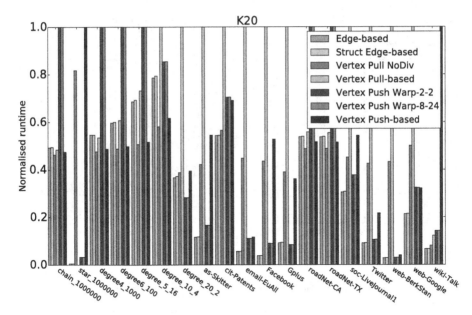

Fig. 1. Normalized performance of the PageRank implementations for our 19 graphs running on NVIDIA K20. The worst performing implementation is used for normalization - i.e., lower is better, and the lower the value, the higher the gap to the worst performing version (Color figure online).

degree would ensure that all vertices are neighboured by vertices of similar degree in the Compressed Sparse Row (CSR) representation, reducing the workload imbalance.

What we found is that sorting the vertices changes the caching and contention patterns change. The result is that in about half the cases sorting the graph vertices had no impact on the performance. In the half where it did have an impact, the results vary. For example, in Fig. 2a we see that the sorted graphs result in a substantially slower push and pull performance. On the other hand, in Fig. 2b we note an improvement for these same implementations.

Overall, our results demonstrate that different implementations of basic graph operations do depend on the structure of the input graph, as seen by the significant fluctuations in the performance of three out of four implementations on different graphs. Additionally, they illustrate that effective load-balancing is the most important feature to obtain good performance from the GPU.

Our experiments with sorting demonstrate that fixing the load-balancing for push and pull is not as straightforward as simply sorting the vertices within a graph by their degree. This due to changes in caching and contention patterns. With the exception of the cit-Patents results shown in Figure 2b, the sorting did not impact which algorithm was the best performing for a specific graph.

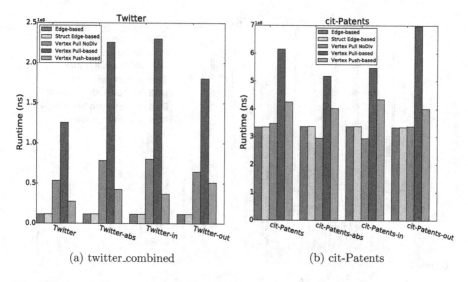

(a) twitter_combined   (b) cit-Patents

Fig. 2. Impact of sorting vertices by degree on PageRank performance (Color figure online).

What remains to be seen is whether this apparent superiority of edge-based neighbour iteration is an artifact of the PageRank algorithm we used for evaluation, or whether this holds across different algorithms.

5   Related Work

Multiple studies already demonstrate the impact of different implementations of the same graph processing algorithm on GPUs [3,10,13]. In most cases, however, such research focuses on different design, implementation, and tuning options which can be applied to *favour* the (hardware) platform, without paying attention to the datasets. In this work, we focus on the performance impact that graphs have on the *efficiency* of these optimizations, determining whether an unfriendly graph can render a given optimization useless.

Another line of research focuses on applications designed for a specific class of algorithms — e.g., efficient traversing of road networks [4] — where the properties of the graphs are taken into account when constructing the algorithm. However, this approach lacks generality, as such algorithms will simply not work for other classes of graphs. We instead aim to rank generic graph-processing solutions by their performance on different types of graphs.

Finally, several studies have observed the impact of graphs on the performance achieved by various graph processing systems [5,7–9,12,17,18], yet most of them have analyzed this dependency at the level of the full algorithm, not at the level of its basic operations. In our work, we focus on a systematic, fine-grained analysis, performed at the level of basic graph operations. We believe this bottom-up approach is key to providing a performance-aware design for new graph processing systems.

6   Conclusion

With the increased diversity of hardware architectures, different algorithms and implementations are being developed for regular graph operations. In this paper, we have studied four different strategies to implement neighbour iteration, and demonstrated their usability in PageRank. Further, focusing on the performance of PageRank on 19 different datasets, we demonstrated that different strategies have different performance behavior on different datasets.

In the near future, we will work to validate and improve our performance models. We plan to expand our experiments to other algorithms to investigate whether the apparent superiority of edge-based neighbour iteration is an artifact of PageRank, or an intrinsic property of neighbour iteration. Additionally we plan to expand this work to other graph processing primitives, such as common neighbour iteration, as found in triangle counting/listing.

References

1. Graph500. http://graph500.org
2. Lumsdaine, A., Gregor, D., Hendrickson, B., Berry, J.W.: Challenges in parallel graph processing. Parallel Process. Lett. **17**, 5–20 (2007)
3. Burtscher, M., Nasre, R., Pingali, K.: A quantitative study of irregular programs on GPUs. In: 2012 IEEE International Symposium on Workload Characterization (IISWC), pp. 141–151. IEEE (2012)
4. Delling, D., Kobitzsch, M., Werneck, R.F.: Customizing driving directions with GPUs. In: Silva, F., Dutra, I., Santos Costa, V. (eds.) Euro-Par 2014 Parallel Processing. LNCS, vol. 8632, pp. 728–739. Springer, Heidelberg (2014)
5. Elser, B., Montresor, A.: An evaluation study of bigdata frameworks for graph processing. In: Big Data (2013)
6. Gharaibeh, A., Costa, L.B., Santos-Neto, E., Ripeanu, M.: On graphs, GPUs, and blind dating: a workload to processor matchmaking quest. In: IPDPS, pp. 851–862 (2013)
7. Guo, Y., Biczak, M., Varbanescu, A.L., Iosup, A., Martella, C., Willke, T.L.: How Well do graph-processing platforms perform? an empirical performance evaluation and analysis. In: IPDPS (2014)
8. Guo, Y., Varbanescu, A.L., Iosup, A., Epema, D.: An empirical performance evaluation of GPU-enabled graph-processing systems. In: CCGrid 2015 (2015)
9. Han, M., Daudjee, K., Ammar, K., Ozsu, M.T., Wang, X., Jin, T.: An experimental comparison of pregel-like graph processing systems. Proc. VLDB Endowment **7**, 1047–1058 (2014)
10. Hong, S., Kim, S.K., Oguntebi, T., Olukotun, K.: Accelerating CUDA graph algorithms at maximum warp. In: ACM SIGPLAN Notices. vol. 46, pp. 267–276. ACM (2011)
11. Leskovec, J.: Stanford Network Analysis Platform (SNAP). Stanford University (2006)
12. Lu, Y., Cheng, J., Yan, D., Wu, H.: Large-scale distributed graph computing systems: an experimental evaluation. Proc. VLDB Endowment **8**, 281–292 (2014)
13. Merrill, D., Garland, M., Grimshaw, A.S.: Scalable GPU graph traversal. In: PPOPP 2012, New Orleans, LA, USA. pp. 117–128, February 2012

14. Nasre, R., Burtscher, M., Pingali, K.: Data-driven versus topology-driven irregular computations on gpus. In: 2013 IEEE 27th International Symposium on Parallel & Distributed Processing (IPDPS), pp. 463–474. IEEE (2013)
15. Page, L., Brin, S., Motwani, R., Winograd, T.: The pagerank citation ranking: bringing order to the web. Technical report 1999–66, Stanford InfoLab, previous number = SIDL-WP-1999-0120, November 1999. http://ilpubs.stanford.edu:8090/422/
16. Penders, A.: Accelerating graph analysis with heterogeneous systems. Master's thesis, PDS, EWI, TUDelft, December 2012
17. Satish, N., Sundaram, N., Patwary, M.A., Seo, J., Park, J., Hassaan, M.A., Sengupta, S., Yin, Z., Dubey, P.: Navigating the maze of graph analytics frameworks using massive graph datasets. In: SIGMOD (2014)
18. Varbanescu, A.L., Verstraaten, M., Penders, A., Sips, H., de Laat, C.: Can portability improve performance? an empirical study of parallel graph analytics. In: ICPE 2015 (2015)

Accelerating Minimum Spanning Forest Computations on Multicore Platforms

Guojing Cong$^{(\boxtimes)}$, Ilie Tanase, and Yinglong Xia

IBM T.J. Watson Research Center, Yorktown Heights, NY 10598, USA
{gcong,tanase,yxia}@us.ibm.com

Abstract. We propose new approaches for accelerating minimum spanning forest algorithms on shared-memory platforms. Our approaches improve cache performance and reduce synchronization overhead of the base algorithms. On our target platform these optimizations achieve up to an order of magnitude speedup over the best prior parallel *Borůvka* implementation.

Keywords: Minimum spanning forest · Locality · Synchronization

1 Introduction

Minimum spanning forest (MSF) and its special case minimum spanning tree (MST) are fundamental graph problems with practical applications (e.g., [3,10,17,18]). For MSF and MST, there exist a randomized time-work optimal algorithm and a deterministic logarithmic time algorithm on EREW PRAM [11,21], and a communication-optimal algorithm on BSP [1]. These theoretically fast algorithms have large constants in the asymptotic notation, and it is challenging to implement them for high performance. Moreover, these algorithms are not optimized for memory subsystem performance that is critical for modern architectures.

Recent experimental studies for MSF and related problems focus primarily on reducing the algorithmic overhead (e.g., see [4,6,20]). Implementations with more branches but fewer operations are shown to have performance advantages for the spanning tree (SF) and connected components (CC) problems (e.g., see [20]). Some breadth-first search (BFS) implementations optimize for the topology of specific inputs (e.g., low-diameter graphs) [5,7]. Agarwal *et al.* employ a bit-map data structure and optimize the locking mechanism for parallel BFS [2]. Hong *et al.* optimize the queues used in BFS [15] for bandwidth utilization. In general, these algorithms still exhibit random memory access behavior that results in poor memory subsystem performance. Some MSF implementations employ fine-grain synchronization with the number of locks scaling linearly with the input size. These implementations perform well on inputs of moderate sizes [12]. For large inputs they can exacerbate poor cache performance as their accesses are also random.

© Springer International Publishing Switzerland 2015
S. Hunold et al. (Eds.): Euro-Par 2015 Workshops, LNCS 9523, pp. 541–552, 2015.
DOI: 10.1007/978-3-319-27308-2_44

We consider improving locality and reducing synchronization to accelerate existing MSF implementations. Different from prior efforts that reduce the number of operations, the approaches we propose execute more instructions but with better locality. We propose three approaches that range from simple to sophisticated with different degrees of performance gain. The first approach implements graph contraction by updating the input data structure to improve locality. The second approach partitions the input edges and processes them in groups. The algorithm exhibits increasingly better locality as each group is processed. The third approach applies PRAM simulation on parallel memory accesses to remove locks and improve locality. Our optimization achieves up to an order of magnitude speedups over the base MSF implementation on our target platform.

We experiment with the most challenging types of graphs in terms of locality, that is, random graphs and scale-free graphs [14]. The input graph is represented as $G = (V, E)$, with $|V| = n$ and $|E| = m$. We create a random graph with n vertices and m edges by randomly adding m unique edges to the vertex set. Scale-free graphs are generated using the R-MAT model [9] with a = 0.45, b = 0.15, c = 0.15, d = 0.25. To complement these small diameter synthetic graphs, we also include six real-world networks from computer vision and social media. We defer their introduction to Sect. 6.

The rest of the paper is organized as follows. Section 2 introduces the base MSF algorithm that we optimize and our target platform. Section 3 presents the approach that compacts the input through edge updates. Section 4 introduces the meta algorithm that processes the edges in groups. Section 5 presents PRAM simulation that reduces synchronization and improves locality. Section 6 combines two meta approaches, and compares the performance of various implementations on both synthetic and real-world inputs. In Sect. 7 we give our conclusion and future work.

2   Base MSF Algorithm and Target Platform

For a weighted graph $G = (V, E)$, *Borůvka* start with n isolated vertices and m processors. Each processor inspects an edge $(u, v) \in E$, and if (u, v) has the minimum weight among all edges incident to u or v, (u, v) is labeled as an edge in the MSF. An edge (u, v) in the MSF causes grafting of one endpoint u to the other endpoint v or vice versa. Grafting creates $k \geq 1$ connected components in the graph, and each of the k components is then shortcut to a single super-vertex. One pass of graft and shortcut constitutes a *Borůvka* iteration. Grafting and shortcutting continue on the reduced graph $G' = (V', E')$ with V' being the set of super-vertices and E' being the set of edges among super-vertices until no grafting is possible.

Several implementations based on *Borůvka* are evaluated on symmetric multiprocessors by Bader and Cong [4]. Bor-AL employs parallel sort in *graft*, while Bor-FAL introduces a data structure that significantly reduces the cost of compacting the input. A hybrid algorithm is also proposed for MST that marries *Borůvka* with *Prim*. We choose a variant of *Borůvka* that uses locks [12] as our base MSF algorithm. It does not rely on other subroutines such as sort, and it uses roughly half of the memory consumed by Bor-AL and Bor-FAL. Its *Borůvka* iteration is shown in Algorithm 1. Due to limited space, for an edge (u, v), only grafting for vertex u is presented. In the algorithm, $I[i]$ and $Min[i]$, $1 \leq i \leq n$, represent the MSF edge (if any) incident to i and its weight, respectively. $D[i]$ is the supervertex that vertex i belongs to. At completion F contains the MSF edges found so far. Algorithm 2 shows the *Borůvka* algorithm.

Algorithm 1. *Borůvka*-iter(E, D)
1: $F \leftarrow \emptyset$
2: **for** $1 \leq i \leq n$ in parallel **do**
3: $Min[i] \leftarrow \infty$
4: **end for**
{graft}
5: **for each** $e = (u, v) \in E$ in parallel **do**
6: lock$(D[u])$
7: **if** $D[u] \neq D[v]$ and $Min[D[u]] > w(e)$ **then**
8:   $Min[D[u]] \leftarrow w(e)$
9:   $D[D[u]] \leftarrow D[v]$
10:   $I[D[u]] \leftarrow \{e\}$
11: **end if**
12: unlock$(D[u])$
13: **end for**
14: **for** $1 \leq i \leq n$ in parallel **do**
15: $F \leftarrow F \cup I[i]$
16: **end for**
{ shortcut }
17: **for** $1 \leq i \leq n$ in parallel **do**
18: **while** $D[i] \neq D[D[i]]$ **do**
19:   $D[i] \leftarrow D[D[i]]$
20: **end while**
21: **end for**
22: **return** F

Algorithm 2. *Borůvka* (E, D)
1: $F \leftarrow \emptyset$
2: **for** $1 \leq i \leq n$ in parallel **do**
3: $D[i] \leftarrow i$, $I[i] \leftarrow \emptyset$
4: **end for**
5: **repeat**
6: $F \leftarrow F \cup$ *Borůvka*-iter(E, D)
7: **until** no grafting possible
8: **return** F

Algorithm 3. *Borůvka*-updt (E, D)
1: $F \leftarrow \emptyset$
2: **for** $1 \leq i \leq n$ in parallel **do**
3: $D[i] \leftarrow i$, $I[i] \leftarrow \emptyset$
4: **end for**
5: **repeat**
6: $F \leftarrow F \cup$ *Borůvka*-iter(E, D)
7: **for** each $(u, v) \in E$ in parallel **do**
8:   $(u, v) \leftarrow (D[u], D[v])$
9: **end for**
10: **until** no grafting possible
11: **return** F

Our target platform is an IBM P755 with four Power7 chips. Each chip has 8 cores running at 3.61GHz, with each core capable of four-way simultaneous multithreading. There are 12 execution units per core shared by the 4 hardware threads. Each core has 32KB L1, 256KB L2, and 4MB L3 caches.

Our experiments show that for large random graphs and scalefree graphs between 73 % and 81 % of machine cycles are wasted on cache misses for *Borůvka*, and only less than 1 % of time is spent on shortcut. Improving locality for *graft* can potentially reduce the execution times of *Borůvka*.

3 Update Edges for Locality

Accesses to D, *min* and I at lines 6–12 in Algorithm 1 are irregular. If (u, v) is the minimum-weight edge between the two components represented by $D[u]$

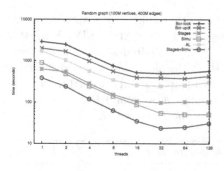

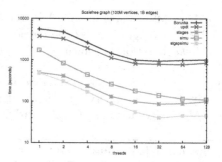

Fig. 1. Random graph   **Fig. 2.** Scalefree graph

and $D[v]$, the algorithm creates a union of the two by grafting one component to the other. While memory accesses to $D[u]$s, $D[v]$s and *etc.* determined by edges $(u,v) \in E$ are random, the D values evolve in a pattern that can be exploited for improving locality. In *Borůvka*, each iteration reduces the number of unique D values (at least by half for the largest connected component in the graph). Instead of retrieving the current components using u and v as indices, we introduce an *update* step after each *Borůvka* iteration that replaces each edge (u, v) with $(D[u], D[v])$. The revised algorithm *Borůvka-updt* is shown in Algorithm 3. The *update* step is done at lines 7–9.

The *update* step in *Borůvka-updt* increases the total number of operations and memory accesses in comparison to *Borůvka* (Algorithm 2). Indeed $2m$ extra memory accesses to D are issued at line 8 in each iteration. However, *update* makes accesses at lines 6–12 in Algorithm 1 increasingly more regular after each iteration. Indeed, the accesses at line 8 of Algorithm 3 themselves become more regular. This is because as the algorithm progresses, it becomes increasingly more likely for the two endpoints of an edge to touch on the same component (super-vertex).

We evaluate the performance improvement of *Borůvka-updt* over *Borůvka* on P755. The results with a random graph of 100 million (M) vertices and 400M edges and a scalefree graph of 100M vertices, 1 billion (B) edges are shown in Figs. 1 and 2, respectively. Speedups between 1.21 and 1.48 are achieved for the random graph, and speedups between 1.19 and 1.48 are achieved for the scalefree graph. The observed improvement is clearly due to better cache performance although more instructions are executed in *Borůvka-updt*.

4   Stages

Borůvka-updt is quite simple with modest performance gain. We propose a more sophisticated meta algorithm, *Stages*, that further improves cache performance.

Stages first partitions the edges in E into groups, $E_1, E_2, \cdots, E_g$, with $|E_i| > n/2$ $(1 \leq i \leq g - 1)$ except possibly for E_g. Then *Borůvka* is applied to the subgraph induced by E_1. All resulting connected components are contracted to super-vertices, and the endpoints of each edge in E_2 are updated. Again *Borůvka* is applied to the subgraph induced by E_2. *Stages* continues until all edge groups are processed. When Stages terminates, an MSF for graph G is computed.

Let $w_{min}(E_i)$ and $w_{max}(E_i)$ be the minimum weight and maximum weight of edges in E_i, respectively. Algorithm 4 gives the formal description of *Stages*.

Algorithm 4. Stages(E, D)

1: $F \leftarrow \emptyset$
2: **for** $1 \leq i \leq n$ **do**
3:    $D[i] \leftarrow i$
4: **end for**
5: Partition E into g groups $E_1, E_2, \cdots,$ E_g with $w_{min}(E_i) \geq w_{max}(E_{i-1}), 2 \leq i \leq g$
6: **for** $1 \leq i \leq g$ **do**

7:    $F \leftarrow F \cup Borůvka\ (E_i, D)$
8:    **if** $i < g$ **then**
9:       **for** $(u, v) \in E_{i+1}$ in parallel **do**
10:          $(u, v) \leftarrow (D[u], D[v])$
11:       **end for**
12:    **end if**
13: **end for**
14: **return** F

We prove that *Stages* indeed computes a minimum spanning forest of G. We first show that F is a spanning forest.

Lemma 1. *The edges found by* Stages *form a spanning forest.*

Proof. Algorithm 4 repeatedly invokes *Borůvka* on the groups of edges. For each group, shortcut is done on D so that all vertices in the same connected component so far will have the same D value. When *Stages* terminates, for each vertex $u \in V$, $D[u]$ represents the final connected component u belongs to. So F is a spanning graph of G. In a *Borůvka* iteration, a vertex (or super-vertex) is grafted at most once by an edge, thus F is a forest.

Theorem 1. Stages *computes a minimum spanning forest.*

Proof. We assume without loss of generality that no two edges in G have the same weight. Denote the set of edges found by *Borůvka* and *Stages* F_B and F_S, respectively. For any edge $e \in F_B$, we show $e \in F_S$. In the beginning, the D values for the two endpoints of e are different. Suppose e is processed in group E_j, $1 \leq j \leq g$. After $E_1, \cdots, E_{j-1}$ are processed, the D values for the two endpoints can not be the same. Otherwise there exists a path in F_S connecting the two endpoints, and the weights of the edges on the path are all smaller than $w(e)$. Thus $e \notin F_B$ by the cycle property, a contradiction. As *Stages* invokes *Borůvka* with E_j, it computes a minimum spanning forest of a graph with e as one of its edges. The D values of the two endpoints of e must converge. The convergence must be caused by e, otherwise by the *Borůvka* algorithm, again there exists a path in E_j connecting the two endpoints of e with the weights of the edges less than $w(e)$, thus another contradiction. So $F_B \subseteq F_S$. By lemma 1, $|F_B| = |F_S|$, so $F_B = F_S$.

For large inputs the conflicts among processors competing for the same locks are rare. With p processors $Bor\mathring{u}vka$ takes $O\left(\frac{m+n}{p}\log^2 n\right)$ time. Let the number of edges in E_i be $q \cdot n$, $1/2 < q \leq m/n$, $Stages$ takes $O\left(\frac{m}{pqn}(qn+n)\log^2 n + \frac{m}{p}\right)$ time. $Bor\mathring{u}vka$ and $Stages$ have the same asymptotic complexity when $qn = \Theta(m)$. $Stages$ degenerates into $Bor\mathring{u}vka$ when $qn = m$. In general $Stages$ has more operations than $Bor\mathring{u}vka$.

Let us consider the impact of processing the edges in groups on locality. After E_1 is processed and the MSF is computed for the induced graph, some connected components are formed and then contracted into super-vertices. Updating the endpoints of edges in E_2 with their super-vertices increases the probability that either the two endpoints of an edge are within one component or multiple edges are incident to the same components. Thus we expect E_2 be processed much faster than E_1. The components subsume even more vertices after E_2 is processed, and are again contracted into super-vertices. As $Stages$ progresses, more and more accesses to D, Min and I become regular (cache hits). The way the graph contracts is dependent on the input topology and weight distribution. Assuming all edges incident to a vertex (or super-vertex) have the same probability of being in the MSF, according to a theorem (see Theorem 2) of evolution random graph theory, a fairly large number of vertices will contract to a single super-vertex. As a result, $Stages$ is expected to have better locality than $Bor\mathring{u}vka$ for many graphs.

Theorem 2. *Under the Erdös-Rényi model there is a unique giant component of order $f(c)n$ in the graph when $m \sim cn$ with $c > 1/2$. Function $f(c) = 1 - \frac{1}{2c}\sum_{k=1}^{\infty}\frac{k^{k-1}}{k!}(2ce^{-2c})^k$ approaches 1 as c increases [19].*

A routine similar to sample sort is used in our implementation to distribute E into g buckets. Note that a full sort is not necessary for our purpose. Due to limited space we do not present the details of the partitioning algorithm.

Figures 3 and 4 show the performance improvement of $Stages$ over $Bor\mathring{u}vka$ on a random graph with 100M vertices, 400M edges and a scalefree graph with

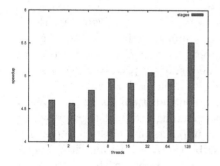
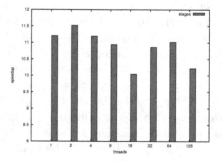

Fig. 3. Random graph   **Fig. 4.** Scalefree graph

100M vertices, 1B edges. The speedups achieved are between 4.5 to 5.5 for the random graph and between 10.2 to 11.5 for the scalefree graph.

5 PRAM Simulation

Locks in *Borůvka* (Algorithm 2) not only incur conflicts among processors but also exacerbate poor cache performance for large inputs as accesses to them are also random.

To reduce synchronization overhead, we adopt a PRAM simulation technique for simulating CRCW PRAM algorithms on EREW PRAM [13,23]. We cast *Borůvka* to the priority CRCW model where a priority function (*min*, in our case) resolves the conflict of concurrent writes. That is, when current writes to the same location occur, the one with the smallest value wins, and all others abort. The algorithm is then simulated on EREW PRAM. When implemented on multicore machines, all grafting actions on a vertex are grouped together and executed by one single processor.

ER implements concurrent reads, shown in Algorithm 5. Algorithm 5 implements indirect parallel accesses of D through R, that is, $C[i] \leftarrow D[R[i]], 1 \leq i \leq \bar{m}, |R| = \bar{m}, |D| = \bar{n}$. Lines 1–8 partition R and D into blocks (one per each processor), and group the access requests in R according to the target processor that owns the D block being accessed. At lines 9–13, each processor serves access requests to its block so that at any time there is only one processor accessing any element of D. At lines 14–19 each processor sends its retrieved D values to the requesting processors, and at lines 20–24 the D values are matched to the requests. In the algorithm, $\oplus$ is a concatenation operator.

Algorithm 5. ER $(C, D, R, \bar{n}, \bar{m}, p)$

1: divide R and D into p blocks of size $s = \bar{m}/p$ and $w = \bar{n}/p$, respectively
2: **for** $1 \leq k \leq p$ in parallel **do**
3:    sort R_k and store original location of jth element in $P_k[j], 1 \leq j \leq s$
4:    partition R_k into p blocks $R_k^j, 1 \leq j \leq p$, such that $\forall r \in R_k^j, \frac{r}{s} = j$
5: **end for**
6: **for** $1 \leq j \leq p$ in parallel **do**
7:    $R_j' \leftarrow \oplus_{k=1}^p R_k^j$
8: **end for**
9: **for** $1 \leq k \leq p$ in parallel **do**
10:    **for** $1 \leq j \leq |R_k'|$ **do**
11:      $S_k[j] \leftarrow D_k[R_k'[j]]$
12:    **end for**
13: **end for**
14: **for** $1 \leq k \leq p$ in parallel **do**
15:    partition S_k into p consecutive blocks $S_k^j, 1 \leq j \leq p$, such that $|S_k^j| = |R_k^j|$
16: **end for**
17: **for** $1 \leq k \leq p$ in parallel **do**
18:    $S_k' \leftarrow \oplus_{j=1}^p S_j^k, 1 \leq k \leq p$
19: **end for**
20: **for** $1 \leq k \leq p$ in parallel **do**
21:    **for** $1 \leq j \leq s$ **do**
22:      $C_k[P_k[j]] \leftarrow S_k'[j]$
23:    **end for**
24: **end for**
25: $C \leftarrow \oplus_{k=1}^p C_k$

Algorithm 6. $EW(W, D, R, \bar{n}, \bar{m}, p)$

1: divide R, W, and D into p blocks of size $s = \bar{m}/p$, $s = \bar{m}/p$, and $w = \bar{n}/p$, respectively
2: **for** $1 \le k \le p$ in parallel **do**
3:   sort R_k and W_k and store original location of jth element in $Pr_k[j]$ and $Pw_k[j]$, $1 \le j \le s$, respectively
4:   partition R_k and W_k into p blocks R_k^j, and W_k^j, $1 \le j \le p$, respectively, such that $\forall r \in R_k^j, \frac{r}{s} = j$, $\forall r \in W_k^j, \frac{r}{s} = j$
5: **end for**
6: **for** $1 \le j \le p$ in parallel **do**
7:   $R_j' \leftarrow \oplus_{k=1}^p R_k^j$
8:   $W_j' \leftarrow \oplus_{k=1}^p W_k^j$
9: **end for**
10: **for** $1 \le k \le p$ in parallel **do**
11:   **for** $1 \le j \le |R_k'|$ **do**
12:     $D_k[R_k'[j]] \leftarrow min(D_k[R_k'[j]], W_k'[j])$
13:   **end for**
14:   add edges for winning writes to F
15: **end for**
16: **return** F

The concurrent writes are done collectively through EW with the min priority function, shown in Algorithm 6. Similar to Algorithm 5, lines 1–9 partition the write requests (in R) and values (in D) into blocks, and group requests according to the target processor that owns the D block. At lines 10–15 a processor writes the data to the D location applying the min function. There are no concurrent writes to D at any time. With ER and EW, the *Borůvka* iteration is transformed into Algorithm 7. Note fine-grain synchronization is no longer needed.

Algorithm 7. *Simu* (E, D)

1: $F \leftarrow \emptyset$
2: **for** $1 \le i \le n$ in parallel **do**
3:   $I[i] \leftarrow \emptyset$
4: **end for**
5: **for** $1 \le i \le m$ in parallel **do**
6:   let $(u, v) = e_i \in E$
7:   $A[2*i - 1] \leftarrow u, A[2*i] \leftarrow v$
8: **end for**
9: call $ER(C, A, D, n, 2*m, p)$
10: **for** $1 \le i \le m$ in parallel **do**
11:   $d_u \leftarrow C[2*i - 1], d_v \leftarrow, C[2*i]$
12:   **if** $Min[D[d_u]] > w(e_i)$ **then**
13:     $R[i] \leftarrow d_v, W[i] \leftarrow w(e_i)$
14:   **end if**
15: **end for**
16: $F \leftarrow F \cup EW(W, D, R, min, n, m, p)$
17: **for** $1 \le i \le n$ in parallel **do**
18:   **while** $D[i] \ne D[D[i]]$ **do**
19:     $D[i] \leftarrow D[D[i]]$
20:   **end while**
21: **end for**
22: **return** F

Algorithm 7 (*Simu*) also has better locality than Algorithm 1 as random accesses to D are transformed into multiple random accesses to blocks of D. When these blocks fit in cache, performance can be improved.

The performance improvement for a random graph of 100M vertices, 400M edges and a scalefree graph of 100M vertices, 1B edges is shown in Fig. 5. The speedups are between 2.5 to 11 for the random graph and between 3 and 9 for the scalefree graph (Fig. 6).

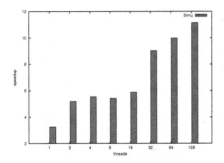

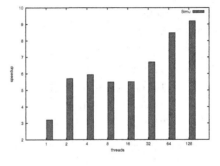

Fig. 5. Random graph

Fig. 6. Scalefree graph

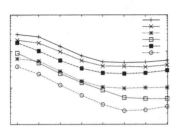

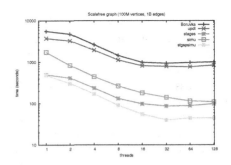

Fig. 7. In log − log plot

Fig. 8. In log − log plot

6   Combining Stages and PRAM Simulation

Both *Stages* and *Simu* are meta approaches that improve the performance of existing MSF algorithms. *Stages* exploits the properties of both the input and the *Borůvka* iteration to improve locality, while *Simu* reduces synchronization and improves cache performance through scheduling the memory accesses. *Stages* is specific to the "graft-and-shortcut" pattern, while *Simu* can be applied to many irregular algorithms. We combine the two approaches. That is, we use *Simu* as the base algorithm for *Stages*. In Algorithm 4, instead of calling Algorithm 2 at line 7, we call Algorithm 7. We call this approach *Stages+Simu*.

Figures 7 and 8 show the performance of *Borůvka*, *Borůvka-updt*, *Stages* with *Borůvka*, *Simu*, and *Stages+Simu* for a random graph with 100M vertices, 400M edges and a scalefree graph with 100M vertices, 1B edges. For both inputs, *Borůvka-updt* is faster than *Borůvka*. *Stages* and *Simu* are faster than *Borůvka-updt*. For the random graph, *Simu* is faster than *Stages*, while for the scalefree graph, *Stages* is faster than *Simu*. *Stages+Simu* is consistently the fastest among all implementations. *Stages+Simu* is more than an order of magnitude faster than the base implementation.

Table 1. networks

Network	Vertices	Edges
Bone	7798786	202895861
Adhead	12582914	327484556
Along	144441346	867447553
Journal	4846609	85702474
Phone	73037362	1248697024
Twitter	41652230	1468365181
Random	100M	400M
Scalefree	100M	1B

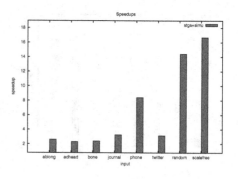

Fig. 9. Speedups

We next compare the performance of *Stages+Simu* with the best prior parallel MSF implementations on several networks. In addition to the synthetic graphs, we include two classes of real-world networks shown in Table 1. The first class contains three computer vision networks (*bone*, *adhead*, and *ablong*) constructed from the images from Siemmens Corporation Research and Robarts Research Institute [8]. A vertex is placed on a 2D or 3D grid corresponding to the pixels (or voxels). Edges connect the vertex to other vertices within the standard 8- (or 26-) neighborhood. These networks have regular structures and small weights. The second class of networks are social networks. These networks capture social relationships among entities. *journal* is a snapshot of the friendship network of the LiveJournal on-line blogging community [22]. *phone* records the phone calls whose origination or termination involve users in Cambridge, MA. *twitter* is a snap shot of the twitter networks [16]. The social networks are assigned random weights.

Figure 9 shows the speedups of *Stages+Simu* over the best prior parallel implementation (the fastest among Bor-AL, Bor-FAL, and *Borůvka*) at 32 threads. The range of speedups is between 2 to 17. The speedups are relatively modest for the vision networks (on average 2.43). This is largely due to the small weights and the regularity in the network. The speedups are larger for social networks. For *phone* the speedup is 8.4. The speedup for *twitter* is 3.1. Although *twitter* has more edges than *phone*, it has much fewer vertices. Recall that poor locality in *Borůvka* is associated with accessing D and Min with the vertices as indices. Similar networks with more vertices will likely see more performance improvement from *Stages+Simu*. Both *random* and *scalefree* have more vertices (100M), and for them the speedups are 14.4 and 16.7, respectively.

7   Conclusion and Future Work

We present accelerating minimum spanning forest computations through a series of meta algorithms. We improve locality and reduce synchronization for existing MSF implementations. The three approaches range from simple to sophisticated with different degrees of performance gain. *Stages+Simu* combines two different locality optimization approaches and can drastically improve the performance of MSF algorithms. *Stages+Simu* is up to 17 times faster than the base *Borůvka* implementation for synthetic graphs, and it is between 2 to 9 times faster for vision networks and social networks. As networks in applications become larger, locality optimization such as ours becomes even more critical to achieving high performance on current and future platforms.

In future work we will study optimization of graph algorithms on GPUs and a cluster of GPUs. We will evaluate the effectiveness of approaches presented in our study. We will also study architectural support for efficient execution of graph algorithms on current and emerging architectures.

References

1. Adler, M., Dittrich, W., Juurlink, B., Kutyłowski, M., Rieping, I.: Communication-optimal parallel minimum spanning tree algorithms (extended abstract). In: SPAA 1998: Proceedings of the Tenth Annual ACM Symposium on Parallel Algorithms and Architectures, pp. 27–36. ACM, New York (1998)
2. Agarwal, V., Petrini, F., Pasetto, D., Bader, D.: Scalable graph exploration on multicore processors. In: Proceedings of the 2010 ACM/IEEE International Conference for High Performance Computing, Networking, Storage and Analysis, SC 2010, pp. 1–11. IEEE Computer Society, Washington, DC (2010)
3. An, L., Xiang, Q., Chavez, S.: A fast implementation of the minimum spanning tree method for phase unwrapping. IEEE Trans. Med. Imaging **19**(8), 805–808 (2000)
4. Bader, D.A., Cong, G.: Fast shared-memory algorithms for computing the minimum spanning forest of sparse graphs. In: Proceedings of the 18th International Parallel and Distributed Processing Symposium, IPDPS 2004, Santa Fe, New Mexico, April 2004
5. Banerjee, D., Sharma, S., Kothapalli, K.: Work efficient parallel algorithms for large graph exploration. In: 2013 20th International Conference on High Performance Computing (HiPC), pp. 433–442, December 2013
6. Barnat, J., Bauch, P., Brim, L., Ceska, M.: Computing strongly connected components in parallel on cuda. In: 2011 IEEE International Parallel Distributed Processing Symposium (IPDPS), pp. 544–555, May 2011
7. Beamer, S., Asanović, K., Patterson, D.: Direction-optimizing breadth-first search. In: Proceedings of the International Conference on High Performance Computing, Networking, Storage and Analysis, SC 2012, pp. 12:1–12:10. IEEE Computer Society Press, Los Alamitos, CA, USA (2012)
8. Boykov, Y., Funka-Lea, G.: Graph cuts and efficient n-d image segmentation. Int. J. Comput. Vision **70**(2), 109–131 (2006). http://dx.doi.org/10.1007/s11263-006-7934-5
9. Chakrabarti, D., Zhan, Y., Faloutsos, C.: R-MAT: a recursive model for graph mining. In: Proceedings of the 4th SIAM International Conference on Data Mining, April 2004
10. Chen, C., Morris, S.: Visualizing evolving networks: minimum spanning trees versus pathfinder networks. In: IEEE Symposium on Information Visualization, Seattle, WA, October 2003
11. Chong, K.W., Han, Y., Lam, T.W.: Concurrent threads and optimal parallel minimum spanning tree algorithm. J. ACM **48**, 297–323 (2001)

12. Cong, G., Bader, D.A.: Lock-free parallel algorithms: an experimental study. In: Bougé, L., Prasanna, V.K. (eds.) HiPC 2004. LNCS, vol. 3296, pp. 516–527. Springer, Heidelberg (2004)

13. Fich, F., Ragde, P., Wigderson, A.: Simulations among concurrent-write prams. Algorithmica 3(1–4), 43–51 (1988)

14. Goh, K.I., Oh, E., Jeong, H., Kahng, B., Kim, D.: Classification of scale-free networks. Proc. Natl. Acad. Sci. 99, 12583 (2002). http://www.citebase.org/cgi-bin/citations?id=oai:arXiv.org:cond-mat/0205232

15. Hong, S., Oguntebi, T., Olukotun, K.: Efficient parallel graph exploration on multi-core CPU and GPU. In: 2011 International Conference on Parallel Architectures and Compilation Techniques (PACT), pp. 78–88, october 2011

16. Kunegis, J.: KONECT - The Koblenz network collection. In: Proceedings of the International Conference on World Wide Web Companion, pp. 1343–1350 (2013). http://userpages.uni-koblenz.de/kunegis/paper/kunegis-koblenz-network-collection.pdf

17. Meguerdichian, S., Koushanfar, F., Potkonjak, M., Srivastava, M.: Coverage problems in wireless ad-hoc sensor networks. In: Proceedings of the INFOCOM 2001, pp. 1380–1387. IEEE Press, Anchorage, April 2001

18. Olman, V., Xu, D., Xu, Y.: Identification of regulatory binding sites using minimum spanning trees. In: Proceedings of the 8th Pacific Symposium on Biocomputing (PSB 2003), pp. 327–338. World Scientific Pub., Hawaii (2003)

19. Palmer, E.: Graphical Evolution. Wiley-Interscience Series in Discrete Mathematic. Wiley, New York (1985)

20. Patwary, M., Ref, P., Manne, F.: Multi-core spanning forest algorithms using the disjoint-set data structure. In: Proceedings of the 2012 IEEE International Parallel & Distributed Processing Symposium, IPDPS 2012, pp. 827–835. IEEE Computer Society, Washington, DC (2012)

21. Pettie, S., Ramachandran, V.: A randomized time-work optimal parallel algorithm for finding a minimum spanning forest. SIAM J. Comput. 31(6), 1879–1895 (2002)

22. Stanford SNAP Large Network Dataset Collection. http://memetracker.org/data/index.html

23. Vishkin, U.: Implementation of simultaneous memory address access in models that forbid it. J. Algorithms 4(1), 45–50 (1983). http://dblp.uni-trier.de/db/journals/jal/jal4.html#Vishkin83

Importance of Runtime Considerations in Performance Engineering of Large-Scale Distributed Graph Algorithms

Jesun Sahariar Firoz$^{(\boxtimes)}$, Thejaka Amila Kanewala, Marcin Zalewski,
Martina Barnas, and Andrew Lumsdaine

Center for Research in Extreme Scale Technologies (CREST),
Indiana University, Bloomington, IN, USA
{jsfiroz,thejkane,zalewski,mbarnas,lums}@indiana.edu

Abstract. Due to the ever increasing complexity of the modern super-computers, performance analysis of irregular applications became an experimental endeavor. We show that runtime considerations are insepa-rable from algorithmic concerns in performance engineering of large-scale distributed graph algorithms, and we argue that the whole system stack, starting with the algorithm at the top down to low-level communication libraries must be considered.

1 Introduction

Large graphs are ubiquitous in fields such as social network analytics, trans-portation optimization, artificial intelligence, and power grids. The largest of graph problems can only be solved using distributed graph algorithms (DGAs), a class of algorithmic approaches in which data is distributed over multiple com-puting nodes. A distributed computation on a modern supercomputer is built on a software/hardware stack that is more complex than ever before. This com-plexity and the resulting explosion of parameters, further exacerbated by the massive irregularity and data dependency of large-scale graph problems, made performance analysis of DGAs a predominantly experimental undertaking.

We distinguish algorithm-level contributions that are often prioritized in research results from runtime-level concerns that are harder to place in the con-text of DGAs and are often hidden from application developers. We argue that in order to obtain an accurate understanding of a DGA performance, algorith-mic concerns need to be considered holistically with runtime properties. In this paper, we illustrate this inseparability of runtime and algorithmic considera-tions. Specifically, we concentrate on two graph traversal algorithms, breadth-first search (BFS) and single-source shortest paths (SSSP), which are essential building blocks for many other applications. For the sake of clarity, all exper-imental results presented here were obtained on Big Red 2 at Indiana Univer-sity [2] with 3-D torus topology and Cray's Message Passing Toolkit (MPT) 6.2.2 MPI implementation. Note that differences in hardware between different machines constitute another layer of complexity. We show that, in the extreme,

© Springer International Publishing Switzerland 2015
S. Hunold et al. (Eds.): Euro-Par 2015 Workshops, LNCS 9523, pp. 553–564, 2015.
DOI: 10.1007/978-3-319-27308-2_45

a feature of the runtime can make an algorithmic approach ostensibly not viable. This implies that the runtime is such an integral part of DGAs that experimental results are difficult to interpret and extrapolate without understanding the properties of the runtime used.

This paper is organized as follows. First, we briefly describe the relevant features of the runtime systems we used in Sect. 2. Then, we provide a brief overview of the distributed control (DC) and Δ-stepping algorithms and explain why DC is particularly suitable to expose the importance of runtime in Sect. 3. Next, in Sect. 4, we show a dramatic change in scaling behavior comparing different SSSP algorithms when implemented with two different runtimes, AM++ and HPX-5. Finally, we show that the application performance is sensitive to even smaller level changes by varying features within the same runtime system (AM++). We provide our concluding remarks in Sect. 5.

2   Runtime Systems

In this paper we use two runtime systems, HPX-5 [1] and AM++ [7]. AM++ is our legacy system centered around active messaging of the Active Pebbles [8] model. HPX-5 is being developed at the Center for Research in Extreme Scale Technologies (CREST) at Indiana University to facilitate the transition to exascale computing.

HPX-5 is intended to enable dynamic adaptive resource management and task scheduling. It creates a global name and address space structured through a hierarchy of processes, each of which serve as execution contexts and may span multiple nodes. It employs a generalization of local ephemeral tasks that permit preemption and global mutable side-effects. It is event-driven, enabling the migration of continuations and the movement of work to data, when appropriate, based on sophisticated local control synchronization objects (e.g., futures, dataflow). HPX-5 is an evolving runtime system being employed to quantify effects of latency, overhead, contention, and parallelism. These performance parameters determine a tradeoff space within which dynamic control is performed for best performance. It is an area of active research driven by complex applications and advances in HPC architecture.

HPX-5 currently has two types of network transports: isend-irecv (ISIR), and put with completion (PWC) based on the Photon [3] network library. In the experiments presented here we used the ISIR transport option. ISIR transport is based on MPI two-sided communication paradigm with asynchronous sends and receives. Currently, HPX-5 thread support level in ISIR is *funneled*.

AM++ supports fine-grained parallelism of active messages with communication optimization techniques such as object-based addressing, active routing, message coalescing, message reduction, and termination detection. While less feature-rich than HPX-5, active messages share the fine parallelism approach with HPX-5. In addition, AM++ is a relatively well-optimized implementation. For these reasons, it was our choice during the development of DC approach. Of particular relevance is its suitability to balance the competing needs of quick delivery of work vs. minimal communication overhead.

While AM++ and HPX-5 share some features and goals, there are important differences between them. AM++ is designed for bulk processing of distributed messages, while HPX-5 is a complete system providing inter and intra-node parallelism. HPX-5 provides global address space while AM++ provides only a lightweight object-based addressing layer. In HPX-5 work is divided into first-class tasks with stacks, while AM++ only executes message handler functions on the incoming message data. These features result in significant differences in scheduling.

2.1 More Details About AM++

One of the results of this paper is that performance of an application can be sensitive to the utilized nuances of runtime features. Hence, more detailed description of the runtime that we used to show this is in order.

AM++ is based on the Active Pebbles (AP) model [8]. At the core of the AP model are *pebbles*, lightweight active messages that are sent explicitly but received implicitly. The implicit receive mechanism is based on *handlers*, which are user-defined functions that are executed in response to the received pebbles. AM++ is a library interface that can be executed by many workers (threads). Each worker can execute independently, and when it calls AM++ interfaces it may execute tasks from the AM++ *task queue*, which schedules tasks such as network polling, buffer flushing, and pending handlers. At the lowest level, pebbles are sent and received using *transports* that encapsulate all low level AM++ functionality such as network communication and termination detection. Currently, the low-level network transport of AM++ is built atop of MPI, but none of the MPI interfaces are exposed to the programmer, and AM++ has supported other transports before. In order to send and handle active pebbles, individual *message types* must be registered with the transport. A transport, given the type of data being sent and the type of the message handler, can create a complete message type object. To increase bandwidth utilization, AM++ performs *message coalescing*, combining multiple pebbles sent to the same destination into a single, larger message. In the current implementation, a buffer of messages is kept by each node for each message type that uses coalescing and for each possible destination. The size of coalescing buffers is determined by the maximum number of pebbles to be coalesced and the pebble size. Messages are appended to the buffer, and the entire buffer is sent when it becomes full or it is *flushed* when there is no more activity. Message coalescing increases the rate and decreases the overhead at which small messages can be sent over a network. The transport layer costs (bookkeeping, message injection) are amortized over many messages at some cost to latency. However, this cost is expected to be offset by large problem scales that depend on throughput more than on latency.

The AM++ programming model is based on *epochs*, which are periods in which messages can be sent and during which all the resulting handlers are executed (*termination detection*). All workers must enter and exit the epoch collectively, with the exit possible only after all the handlers in the epoch are executed. AM++ only guarantees that the handlers for all the messages sent within a given epoch will have completed by the end of that epoch, but it also guarantees that calling end of an epoch test interface will progress AM++ execution. Because AM++ allows handlers to send arbitrary new messages, it relies on a *termination detection algorithm* to discover when no more handlers are left to execute and no more pebbles are in flight.

In general, AM++ workers perform two kinds of work: the worker's "private" work, and AM++ progress that can occur any time an AM++ interface is called. A thread's private work includes tasks such as local bookkeeping or preparing for an epoch. AM++ progress consists of handler execution, crucial to algorithm progress, and bookkeeping and maintenance tasks such as network polling, buffer flushing, and termination detection. In general, an AM++ program consists of general setup, including creating a transport and registering message types with the transport along with required properties such as coalescing and object-based addressing.

After all the necessary machinery is created, an AM++ program executes one or more epochs. Epochs can be executed in two significantly different ways. In *scoped epoch* execution, application work is executed first, and when the epoch ends, AM++ executes final progress including member handlers. The application can still send messages, and progress can be executed when messages are sent, but, in general, progress is only guaranteed to occur at the end of the scoped epoch resulting in a two-part work pattern. In *end-epoch test* model, application executes some work in a loop, testing for the end of the epoch. This model allows an application to interleave its own work with AM++ progress, resulting in a pattern of potentially unequal periods of time spent in each portion of the work. The end-epoch test model allows for interaction between the application and AM++, where the application generates new tasks, and the execution of handlers in AM++ progress generates more work for the application, repeating the loop until all work is exhausted.

3   Algorithms

In this section we describe the distributed graph algorithmic approaches pertinent to understanding of our results.

Graph traversal constitutes the main kernel for solving many graph theoretic problems and is a good representative of irregular applications. In this paper, we employ two graph traversal problems, namely SSSP and BFS. Let us denote an undirected graph with n vertices and m edges by $G(V, E)$. Here $V = \{v_1, v_2, \ldots, v_n\}$ and $E = \{e_1, e_2, \ldots, e_m\}$ represent vertex set and edge set respectively. Each edge e_i is a triple (v_j, v_k, w_{jk}) consisting of two endpoint vertices and the edge weight. We assume that each edge has a nonzero cost (weight) for traversal. In *single source shortest path (SSSP)* problem, given a graph G and a source vertex s, we are interested in finding the shortest distance between s and all other vertices in the graph. *Breadth First Search (BFS)* can be regarded as a special case of SSSP when the edge weights w_{ij} are set to one. In this section, we discuss two distributed graph algorithms for SSSP: Distributed Control and Δ-stepping.

3.1   Distributed Control

Unordered algorithms [6] are invariant under ordering of tasks and are therefore easier to parallelize than those algorithms in which task ordering impacts correctness of results. Nevertheless, while not necessary for correctness, task ordering can help improve performance of unordered algorithms. Our *distributed control* (DC) [9] is a work scheduling method that removes overhead of synchronization and global data structures while providing partial ordering of tasks according to a priority measure. DC uses only local knowledge to select the best work, thus obtaining an approximation of global ordering.

Specifically, global data is divided into domains. Within each domain, workers are assigned a shared memory. Processing tasks in one domain may generate work that depends on other domains. Workers put the work they generate into an unordered global task bag, and continuously try to retrieve work from there to put it into their private working sets, which are ordered according to task priority metric. For example, in the case of SSSP, the metric is the distance. The more tasks in the bag, rather than in the private working sets, the further the approximated ordering is from the ideal global ordering (Dijkstra's priority queue). DC does not use global data structures and synchronization. Ideally, the underlying runtime system delivers a task to the appropriate worker as soon as it becomes available. On the other hand, quick delivery is costly. These competing trends need to be balanced for optimal performance. For this reason, DC is particularly sensitive to the properties of runtime. In what follows, we use Δ-stepping algorithm for reference, which can be expected to be less dependent on properties of the underlying runtime system.

DC algorithm for SSSP is described in Algorithm 1. The algorithm consists of 3 parts that are executed by all threads on a distributed node: the main loop that processes tasks from the local priority queue and performs progress, the message handler that receives tasks from other workers, and the relax function that updates distances and generates new work. The main loop is preceded by initialization of the distance map, starting an epoch (Lines 1–2), and by relaxing the source vertex (Lines 3–5). In the while loop, the work on the graph is performed by removing a task from the thread-local priority queue in every iteration and then relaxing the vertex targeted by the task (Lines 8–15). Vertex relaxation checks whether the distance sent to a vertex v is better than the distance already in the distance map, and it sends a relax message (task) to all the neighbors of v with the new distance computed from v's distance d_v and the weight of the edge between v and v's neighbors v_n. Relax handler receives the messages sent from the relax function, and its only purpose is to insert the incoming tasks into the thread-local priority queue. When a handler finishes executing, it is counted as finished in *termination detection*. Because our handlers actually only postpone work, every time we insert a task into an empty queue we increment activity counter. Then, in the main loop, when the queue becomes empty, we can decrease the activity counter when all the postponed tasks are handled and the queue is empty. Note that there is no synchronization barrier in the algorithm.

Algorithm 1. Distributed Control Algorithm

Main loop

Input: Graph $G(V, E)$, source s, distances D
1: Init(D)   {set distances to ∞}
2: Epoch e {start epoch}
3: **if** thread_id $= 0$ **and** owner(s) **then**
4:      relax($s, 0$)   {relax source}
5: **end if**
6: **while not** e.end() **do**
7:        {q_t is the priority queue of the current thread}
8:      **if not** q_t.empty() **then**
9:         $(v, d) \leftarrow q_t$.pop()   {next task to process}
10:        $d_v \leftarrow D(v)$ {current distance for v}
11:        **if** $d_v < d$ **then**
12:          continue
13:        **else**
14:          relax(v, d)
15:        **end if**
16:        **if** q_t.empty() **then**
17:          activity_count$--$
18:        **end if**
19:        **if** *iterations* mod *frequency* $= 0$ **and** e.end() **then**
20:          **return**
21:        **end if**
22:     **end if**
23: **end while**

Relax handler

Input: Task (v, d)
1: **if** q_t.empty() **then**
2:      activity_count$++$
3: **end if**
4: q_t.push(v, d)   {insert task into priority queue}

Relax

Input: Task (v, d), distances D
1: **if** $d < D(v)$ **then**
2:      $D(v) \leftarrow d$
3:      $\forall v_n \in$ neighbors(G, v) : send($v_n, d_v +$ weight(v, v_n))
4: **end if**

3.2 Δ-Stepping

Δ-stepping [4] approximates the ideal priority ordering by arranging tasks into distance ranges (buckets) of size Δ and executing buckets in order. Within a bucket, tasks are not ordered, and can be executed in parallel. Processing a bucket may produce extra work for the same bucket or for the successive buckets. After processing each bucket, all processes must synchronize before processing the next bucket to maintain task ordering approximation. The more buckets (the smaller the Δ value), the more time spent on synchronization. Similarly, the fewer buckets (the larger the Δ value), the more suboptimal work the algorithm generates because larger buckets provide less ordering.

Even though Δ-stepping ordering approximates Dijkstra's global ordering, the overhead of synchronization after each bucket is significant. All workers need to wait for the last straggler to proceed. The more buckets Δ-stepping needs to process, the more computing power is wasted due to straggler effect.

Δ-stepping SSSP algorithm is described in Algorithm 2. In each epoch, vertices within the range $i\Delta - (i + 1)\Delta$ contained in a bucket B_i are processed asynchronously by worker threads(Lines 11–27). Edges are classified into two categories: light edges and heavy edges. Edges with weight less than or equal to Δ are called *light* edges and are processsed first at the beginning of the epoch (Line 13). Once processing of all light edges contained in the current bucket is done, then *heavy* edges (weight greater than Δ) are processed (Line 21). Processing vertices in the current bucket can generate new pairs for the current bucket. Worker threads cannot proceed to the next bucket unless all workers on each of the distributed node has finished processing vertices contained in the current bucket. This requires global synchronization barrier (which is implicit in the epoch). The relax function is responsible for putting a vertex in the appropriate bucket if the updated distance is better (Line 5).

DC is not equivalent to Δ-stepping with Δ set to ∞, even though in this limit, there is one unordered global task bag similar to DC. However, Δ-stepping algorithm does not impose any ordering on tasks. In contrast, DC orders the tasks retrieved by each worker (thread) from the global task bag in a thread-local priority queue. This in effect reduces the amount of redundant work to be executed. By eliminating the need for global synchronization and maintaining partial ordering of tasks based on local view, DC can achieve better runtime.

4 Application Performance Sensitivity to Runtime Features

In this section we present results which tell a cautionary tale of how changes in runtime system affect performance.

Figure 1 shows size scaling for DC and Δ-stepping with HPX-5 (Fig. 1a) and AM++ (Fig. 1b). For size scaling we keep the number of cores constant at 1024, and we increase the size of the problem, taking an average of 10 runs per point. The experiments were run on Graph 500 [5] inputs. In HPX-5 Δ-stepping clearly outperforms DC, which performs no better than chaotic execution. In AM++, DC outperforms two different versions of Δ-stepping. The Δ-stepping version, in which we sort the messages in the AM++ receive buffers as they arrive at a particular destination, is termed *delta-sort*. While at smaller scales the averages follow the same trend, they are indistinguishable within errors. For this reason, we show results at larger scales.

Algorithm 2. Δ-stepping Algorithm

Main loop

Input: Graph $G(V, E)$, source s, distances D, Δ
1: Init(D)   {set distances to ∞}
2: **for** $\forall v \in V$ **do**
3:      {group heavy and light edges}
4:      $heavy(v) \leftarrow \{(v, w) \in E \mid weight(v, w) > \Delta\}$
5:      $light(v) \leftarrow \{(v, w) \in E \mid weight(v, w) \le \Delta\}$
6: **end for**
7: $i \leftarrow 0$; $B_0.put(s)$ {put source in Bucket 0}
8: **while not** $B.empty()$ **do**
9:              {B is the array of buckets containing vertices within each Δ range}
10:     Epoch $e.start()$ {start epoch}
11:     **while not** $B_i.empty()$ **do**
12:         $M \leftarrow \emptyset$
13:         $R \leftarrow \{(w, d) \mid \forall\, v \in B_i \wedge weight(v, w) \in light \wedge d = D(v) + weight(v, w)\}$

14:         {process the neighbours in light edge set}
15:         $activity\_count - -$
16:         $M \leftarrow M \cup B_i$; $B_i = \emptyset$
17:         **for** $\forall (v, d) \in R$ **do**
18:             relax(v, d)
19:         **end for**
20:     **end while**
21:     $R \leftarrow \{(w, d) \mid \forall\, v \in M \wedge weight(v, w) \in heavy \wedge d = D(v) + weight(v, w)\}$

22:     {process the neighbours in heavy edge set}
23:     **for** $\forall (v, d) \in R$ **do**
24:         relax (v, d)
25:         $activity\_count - -$
26:     **end for**
27:     $e.end()$
28:     $i \leftarrow i + 1$
29: **end while**

Relax

Input: Task (v, d), distances D
1: **if** $d < D(v)$ **then**
2:      $oldindex \leftarrow D(v)/\Delta$
3:      $B_{oldindex} \leftarrow B_{oldindex} \setminus v$
4:      $newindex \leftarrow d/\Delta$
5:      $B_{newindex} \leftarrow B_{newindex} \cup v$
6: **end if**

This is a dramatic, qualitative change that shows how intertwined the algorithm and runtime system are. While there is an obvious difference between the two runtimes, performance can change drastically with just small changes within the same runtime system. Such changes are often outside of the application

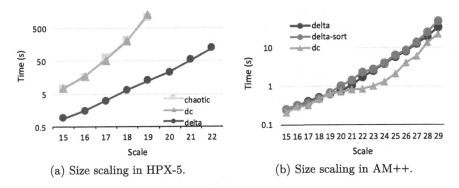

(a) Size scaling in HPX-5.   (b) Size scaling in AM++.

Fig. 1. Size scaling comparison of Δ-stepping and DC on Graph 500 input. DC is the better algorithm in AM++ but performs no better than simple chaotic version in HPX-5. Each data point is an average of 10 runs (Color figure online).

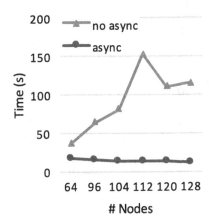

Fig. 2. Impact of asynchronous MPI progress thread on performance of distributed control in AM++.

developer's control, and can lead to misguided conclusions about algorithm performance. For example, at first, when we experimented with DC on Big Red 2, we found that DC was performing poorly (see the top line in Fig. 2), which raised concerns that DC might not be viable. The performance was decreasing with increasing number of nodes in strong scaling. Suspecting that message latencies were to blame, we experimented with transport progress despite Cray's warning at the time that thread-multiple progress required for asynchronous progress "is not considered a high-performance implementation." Fig. 2 presents strong-scaling results on Graph500 scale 31. With *asynchronous progress* (the bottom line in Fig. 2), the performance of DC has improved more than tenfold with growing node counts, entirely changing the viability of the approach.

Another example of a runtime feature that is unknown at application development time is the size of coalescing buffers. To decrease overhead at the cost

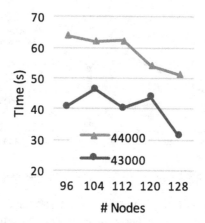

Fig. 3. Impact of coalescing buffer sizes on performance of distributed control in AM++.

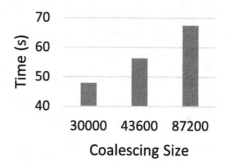

Fig. 4. Effect of coalescing size on DC BFS algorithm on a scale 31 graph in AM++.

of increased latency, AM++ performs *message coalescing*, combining multiple messages sent to the same destination into a single, larger message. Messages are appended to per-destination buffers. To handle partially filled buffers, a periodic check is performed to check for activity. In the case of DC SSSP, a single message consists of a tuple of a destination vertex and distance, 12 bytes in total. With such small messages, coalescing has great impact on the performance, but finding the optimal size is difficult.

We investigated the impact of coalescing in Graph500 scale 31 graphs when running DC SSSP with max edge weight of 100 (Figs. 3 and 4). Figure 3 shows the large impact of a small change in the coalescing size, measured by the number of SSSP messages per coalescing buffer. Changing the coalescing size by less than 2 % causes over 50 % increase in the run time. This unexpected effect is caused by the specifics of Cray MPI protocols. At the smaller coalescing size, full message buffers fit into rendezvous R0 protocol that sends messages of up to 512 K using one RDMA GET, while the larger buffers hit R1 protocol that sends chunks of 512 K using RDMA PUT operations. At the size of 44000, the bulk of the message fits into the first 512 K buffer, and the small remainder requires another RDMA PUT, causing overheads. The sizes 43000 and 86000 fill out 1 and 2 buffers, respectively, achieving similar performance. The larger size, 86000, results in better scaling properties.

Figure 4 shows the effects of coalescing on a DC BFS, which is SSSP with maximum weight of 1. Surprisingly, in this case increasing the coalescing size impacts performance negatively. We suspect that with smaller weights the probability of reward from optimistic parallelism in DC decreases, and the added latency of coalescing has a much larger effect than with larger weights. Also note that we have not actually discovered the optimal coalescing size, which would require more experiments and more resources. This shows that adjusting the coalescing size is important, and that the optimal value is not static. Rather, it depends on algorithmic concerns such as reward from optimistic parallelism.

5   Conclusions

In this paper we demonstrated that performance of DGAs strongly depends on characteristics and features of the underlying runtime. Within a particular runtime, low-level components such as bit transport can drastically impact the performance. We demonstrated this using our DC work scheduling algorithm and two examples of low-level features, namely asynchronous progress and coalescing, but the implications are of general validity. This means that for performance engineering, application developers need to design their algorithms so that they are in sync with the runtime features. Unfortunately, the interplay between different components of the stack, while acknowledged, is not well understood yet. More work is needed to explore how features such as communication paradigm, network topology, message routing and task scheduling interact with algorithmic concerns in order to determine guidelines for optimal performance.

Acknowledgments. This research used Big Red2 (Funded by Lilly Endowment, Inc. and Indiana METACyt Initiative). Support by NSF grant 1111888 gratefully acknowledged.

References

1. http://hpx.crest.iu.edu/. Accessed 25 May 2015
2. Big Red II at Indiana University. http://rt.uits.iu.edu/ci/systems/BRII.php#info. Accessed 17 Apr 2015
3. Kissel, E., Swany, M.: Session layer burst switching for high performance data movement. In: Proceedings of the 8th International Workshop on Protocols for Future, Large-Scale & Diverse Network Transports (2010)
4. Meyer, U., Sanders, P.: Δ-stepping: a parallelizable shortest path algorithm. J. Algorithms **49**(1), 114–152 (2003)
5. Murphy, R.C., Wheeler, K.B., Barrett, B.W., Ang, J.A.: Introducing the graph 500 benchmark. Cray User's Group (CUG) (2010)

6. Pingali, K., et al.: The Tao of Parallelism in Algorithms. ACM SIGPLAN Not. **46**(6), 12–25 (2011)
7. Willcock, J.J., Hoefler, T., Edmonds, N.G., Lumsdaine, A.: AM++: a generalized active message framework. In: Proceedings of the 19th International Conference on Parallel Architectures and Compilation Techniques, pp. 401–410. ACM (2010)
8. Willcock, J.J., Hoefler, T., Edmonds, N.G., Lumsdaine, A.: Active pebbles: a programming model for highly parallel fine-grained data-driven computations. In: Proceedings of the 16th ACM Symposium on Principles and Practice of Parallel Programming, pp. 305–306. ACM (2011)
9. Zalewski, M., Kanewala, T.A., Firoz, J.S., Lumsdaine, A.: Distributed control: priority scheduling for single source shortest paths without synchronization. In: Proceedings of the Fourth Workshop on Irregular Applications: Architectures and Algorithms, pp. 17–24. IEEE (2014)

Characterizing Communication Patterns of Parallel Programs Through Graph Visualization and Analysis

Denise Stringhini$^{(\boxtimes)}$ and Alvaro Fazenda

Universidade Federal de Sao Paulo, Sao Paulo, Brazil
dstringhini@unifesp.br

Abstract. Characterization of communication patterns of parallel programs has been used to better understand the behavior of such programs as well as to predict performance of large scale applications. This characterization could be performed by observing some communication attributes like volume or spatial characteristics of message passing parallel applications in different scenarios. This paper describes a methodology to characterize parallel communication patterns using a graph visualization tool in addition to a traditional monitoring tool that generates trace files. Graph visualization tools are commonly used to analyze large network connections existent in a variety of social or natural structures. Although, since it is possible to represent large scale parallel programs as graphs of communicating processes, this paper proposes a methodology that takes advantage of such kind of tool to aid in characterize communication patterns.

1 Introduction

Basically, characterization of communication patterns in message passing parallel programs resides in to explore mainly three attributes of message passing programs: spatial distribution, volume of messages and temporal distribution. The spatial behavior is characterized by the distribution of messages destinations. The volume of data transferred is characterized by the distribution of message sizes and the average number of messages. The temporal behavior is characterized by the distribution of message generation rate [12].

The importance of such characterization relies in a better understanding of communication performance which has a crucial influence on the overall performance of a parallel program. A proper understanding of communication behavior of parallel applications may support the design of better communication subsystems as well as help application developers to maximize their application performance on a target architecture [21]. Usually, the methodology to characterize communication patterns consists in to dynamically record communication events and statistically analyze and organize those data post-mortem. The characterization data are commonly presented through bar graphs or tables. An example of the characterization of communication patterns to improve the performance of MPI [17] programs could be found in [15].

© Springer International Publishing Switzerland 2015
S. Hunold et al. (Eds.): Euro-Par 2015 Workshops, LNCS 9523, pp. 565–576, 2015.
DOI: 10.1007/978-3-319-27308-2_46

This paper proposes an alternative perspective to characterize communication patterns in large scale parallel applications. The methodology consists in to analyze the data recorded in a trace file by using a graph visualization tool and some metrics based on complex networks theory. In order to do this task, we first create a communication graph from an adjacency matrix. In this work, this graph is extracted directly from the communication matrix generated by EZTrace [18], a trace file generator. Second, the generated graph is loaded into the Gephi graph visualization tool [3]. It includes several graph layout algorithms to provide different views, as well as it provides some complex networks related metrics that are also used in the characterization.

In order to construct a suitable visualization it is important to choose the best layout algorithm as well as its parameters. In addition, tools like Gephi include a variety of filters which help in highlight some specific features of communication links. Our methodology defines some applicable layout choices in order to develop a relevant communication characterization. Specifically in this work, we use a determined layout and some complex networks metrics to preliminarily characterize the spatial and volume attributes of NAS parallel benchmarks [1]. The goal is to primary explore the methodology to demonstrate its potential.

As first results, the graph visualization and analysis allowed a topology characterization that is not easily obtained by state-of-art parallel visualization tools. After some tests with several layout options, it was possible to actually visualize the toroidal stencil shape of SP-MZ NAS parallel benchmark as well as to analyze its behavior as it scales. This kind of characterization could be very useful in the development phase of parallel applications.

Besides the benefits of the characterization itself, this proposal has the advantage of using existing tools. As in [11], we also claim that this approach avoids the high costs of building totally new visualization systems. The present work preliminarily expose the potential of the technique while we develop more specific ways to apply it to parallel systems by adding new information and temporal behavior.

This paper is organized as follows. First it is presented some related work and tools used in the methodology. After, it is described the methodology and it is presented a case study along with primary conclusions.

2   Related Work

Several works on characterization of communication patterns in parallel programs have been proposed over the years that explore mainly three attributes of message passing programs: temporal, spatial and volume. Besides, there are other attributes like the communication locality, explored in [12].

In [21] both point-to-point and collective communications are considered. For point-to-point they quantify the message type, message frequency, message size, and message destinations. For collectives, they examine their type, frequency, and payload. Their results show applications studied are sensitive to changes in the system size and the problem size. Lee in [14] also measured the communication timing, sources and destinations, and message size distributions in order to characterize MPI programs. His experimental results also show such metrics could be used to predict performance.

In [19] a set of applications is characterized along four dimensions: point-to-point communication, collective communication, memory load operations, and floating point operations. Particularly for point-to-point communication, they measure distributions for number of messages, type, payload size, and size of destination clique.

This work presents a different methodology based on graph visualization and complex network theory. The first characterization provided is a topological view of the parallel application, that was not provided by any of the above mentioned related work. The first results show that is possible to easily visualize processes connections that exhibit some regularity in communication patterns and observe their behavior as the program scales. The topological view could be further explored by applying filters as the graph visualization tools are mostly interactive. Also, some common metrics from complex networks theory were used to characterize the applications. Metrics like the average degree, graph density and others were used to characterize the scalability of analyzed applications.

Besides previous work on characterization, it is also important to highlight some visualization tools as well as recent work on parallel program visualization, since in the present proposal graph visualization is key to characterization.

Vampir [13] is a parallel program visualization tool that provides a framework for program analysis, which enables developers to display program behavior at any level of detail. Performance data obtained from a parallel program execution can be analyzed with a collection of different performance views. The present work has no intention to repeat the level of detail provided by Vampir, but to present a complementary perspective.

The work in [16] presents another way to evaluate parallel programs and could be related to Vampir as another potential view. The work is related to the present effort in the sense that it allows the visualization of large parallel programs along with communication patterns. However, while their work is more focused on hardware topology, this work addresses the application topology.

Before to present the methodology, we briefly approach some basic complex network theory that are important to the characterization.

3   Complex Networks Basics

Graphs become increasingly important in modeling complicated and/or complex structures, such as circuits, images, chemical compounds, protein structures, biological networks, social networks, the Web, workflows, and even XML documents [8]. The research in graph mining and graph visualization is producing a large collection of techniques and tools that could be useful in a variety of research areas. This section explains how a large parallel message passing program can be modeled as a graph of communicating processes as well as how complex networks theory could help in characterizing communication patterns.

Recently, it can be observed a new movement of interest and research in the study of complex networks, i.e. networks whose structure is irregular, complex and dynamically evolving in time, with the main focus moving from the analysis of small networks to that of systems with thousands or millions of nodes [4]. The complex network theory is aimed mostly to analyze very large and dynamical irregular networks, but some metrics and tools could also apply to regular structures like the ones formed by processes in a parallel program.

A graph G, is a pair of sets (V, E), where V is a finite set of vertices and E is a set of edges, each edge connecting a pair of vertices. In directed graphs (digraphs), each edge has a direction and self-loops are allowed. In undirected graphs, each edge is an unordered pair of vertices, thus the adjacency is symmetric. In weighted graphs, each edge has an associated weight, which is a value assigned to the edge.

A large parallel program consists of hundreds or thousands of distributed processes. These processes could be naturally modeled as vertices of a graph. In order to execute a parallel algorithm, processes have to exchange messages, which creates connections or links between pairs of processes. These communication operations could be modeled as the edges of a graph. The number or the volume of messages exchanged could be assigned to the edges as their weight. Considering these characteristics it is straightforward to think in a parallel program as a graph whose attributes could characterize its communication patterns.

More information about complex networks theory can be found in [4, 7]. In this work we are particularly interested in metrics that are summarized below:

- **Average degree:** the degree of a node is the number of edges connected to it, or, in this context, the number of neighbors or connections of a process. In complex networks, the degree is used as one of the measures of centrality of a node, and the degree distribution is largely used to characterize a network. In this work, the average degree will be used to observe how the degree evolves along with the scalability of a parallel program.
- **Average shortest path length:** this metric measures the typical separation between two nodes in a graph and it is normally used to evaluate the transport of communication in a network. In a parallel program, this transport occurs in a regular way defined by the parallel algorithm. In the present work this metric will be used to examine how is the behaviour of the parallel program related to the distance among processes as the program scales.
- **Average clustering coefficient:** this metric is largely used, along with the degree distribution, to characterize real complex networks, like social networks, for example. It measures where two individuals with a common friend are likely to know each other [4]. In parallel programs this seems out of context, but the idea here is that it could help to understand the parallel program network if we can compare it to real networks.
- **Graph density:** this metric expresses the actual number of edges versus the number of edges that would be present if the graph was complete. In social networks, the density decreases as the network grows and our hypothesis is this is also desirable for scalable parallel programs.

3.1 Graph Visualization and Analysis

For graph visualization and analysis we chose Gephi [3], an open source network exploration and manipulation software. Developed modules can import, visualize, spatialize, filter, manipulate and export all types of networks.

Layout algorithms set the graph shape and it is the most essential operation. Graphs are usually laid out with force-based algorithms. They follow a simple principle: linked nodes attract each other and non-linked nodes are pushed apart. The Gephi tutorial, which could be found in [5], summarizes the layout choices, for example, OpenOrd (emphasis in divisions), ForceAtlas, Yifan Hu, Fruchterman-Reingold (emphasis in complementarities), and others.

The algorithms with emphasis in complementarities are used mostly to build readable graphs, which could be very convenient also to apply filters. For the representation of parallel programs our emphasis relies on the divisions or complementarities among communicating processes. The Yifan Hu layout [10], for example, has good results for large undirected graphs and could provide good visualizations for parallel programs as will be presented in this paper.

4 Case Study: Characterizing NAS Parallel Benchmarks

This section presents the methodology and the first results on characterizing parallel programs through graph visualization and complex networks metrics. The NAS parallel benchmarks [2] were chosen for its large use for testing the capabilities of parallel computers and parallelization tools. In order to present the case study, first we describe the methodology, followed by a brief description of NAS SP-MZ and BT-MZ benchmarks and finally the visualization and metrics for the characterization.

4.1 Methodology

In order to build a graph of communicating processes, it is necessary first to collect execution data: how many processes, how was the communication between them, and how was the distribution, the volume and the number of messages exchanged, for example. This task could be accomplished by using a trace file generator. Second, it is required to read the produced trace file or statistics file and generate another file with the textual representation of the graph in a specific graph format. This textual representation of the graph will be finally loaded to the graph visualization tool.

Thus, the methodology could be divided basically in two phases: graph building and graph visualization. In the graph building phase, first the communication data are collected from a trace file generator in the form of a communication adjacency matrix. Then, the graph is written in some specific textual format considering the processes as nodes and communication links as edges. The total number or volume of messages exchanged during the execution will be the weight of the edges.

In the graph visualization phase, the communication graph is loaded into a graph visualization tool that allows different layouts as well as the use of filters to visualize subgraphs. These subgraphs could be used to decrease the volume of visualized nodes if it becomes too large.

Different trace file generators could be used in order to extract information about the execution of a parallel program. Besides, there are some ways to instrument a program in order to generate data about specific events. Our approach in this work was to use EZTrace [18], a generic framework for performance analysis. In addition to provide an execution trace file, EZTrace also produces a statistic file and two communication adjacency matrix files. Since in this specific work we are interested in the communication size and in the number of messages exchanged, we used the EZTrace matrixes directly. For further works we intend to collect other events and even timestamps from the trace file.

Since EZTrace already provides the adjacency matrices, it is straightforward to build a textual representation for the graph. Several graph formats could be used for this task, like the ones supported by Gephi: GEXF, GDF, GML, GraphML, CSV, among others [5]. For simplicity, in this work we chose the GML format [9]. A script was written to read the adjacency matrices generated by EZTrace and write it in GML format. Nonetheless, in the future we intend to use GEXF format, which is a Gephi project. GEXF is XML based being more flexible and providing more features.

4.2 NAS Parallel Benchmark

The NAS Parallel Benchmarks (NPB) [2] are well-known problems for testing the capabilities of parallel computers and parallelization tools. They exhibit mostly fine-grain exploitable parallelism and are almost all iterative, requiring multiple data exchanges between processes within each iteration. The application benchmarks Lower-Upper Symmetric Gauss-Seidel (LU), Scalar Penta-diagonal (SP), and Block Tri-diagonal (BT) solve discretized versions of the unsteady, compressible Navier-Stokes equations in three spatial dimensions. Each operates on a structured discretization mesh that is a logical cube.

The NPB Multi-Zone versions of LU, BT, and SP benchmarks are LU-MZ, BT-MZ, and SP-MZ. In each, a logically rectangular discretization mesh is divided into a two-dimensional horizontal tiling of three-dimensional zones of approximately the same aggregate size as the original NPB. The major difference between the three multi-zone problems lies in the way the zones are created out of the single overall mesh [20].

The SP-MZ and BT-MZ versions are of specially interest in this work, since zones in each of the two horizontal dimensions grows as the problem size grows. The difference between the two implementations relies in the variation of zone sizes which only happens in BT-MZ implementation (in SP-MZ the zone size is fixed).

The implementation follows a stencil communication pattern with exchange of boundary values between zones taking place after each time step. Solution values at points one mesh spacing away from each vertical zone face are copied to the coincident boundary points of the neighboring zone [2]. The problem is periodic in the two horizontal directions (x and y), so donor point values at the extreme sides of the mesh system are copied to boundary points at the opposite ends of the system. This property characterizes a toroidal system and was captured by Yifan Hu [10] graph layout algorithm as demonstrated later in this paper.

4.3   Characterization Results

This subsection presents some results in characterizing NAS parallel benchmarks SP-MZ and BT-MZ implementes with MPI [17]. The characterization is presented by means of visualization and network properties: average degree, average shortest path length, average cluster coefficient and graph density.

Characterizing SP-MZ. First, a characterization is presented for class C of NAS SP-MZ, which were executed with 32, 64, 128 and 256 processes in a single node. Figure 1 presents the visualization for the four cases with Yifan Hu graph layout provided by Gephi.

Despite the reduced visualization, it is possible to observe the regularity of the shape throughout different problem sizes. Also, it is likely to identify the cylindrical aspect that characterizes a regular toroidal stencil algorithm. As the problem grows, the cylinder volume also grows instead of the cylinder diameter. It is possible to infer by this visualization that this 3D characteristic helps the algorithm to scale since it preserves a more local communication pattern.

Table 1 presents the network metrics for SP-MZ. The average degree for 32 and 256 processes are absolute values; i.e., all nodes have exactly the same degree. It is interesting to notice that the average degree does not grow significantly with the size of the problem. This means that the number of each process connections stays practically the same. This seems to be a relevant feature of a scalable parallel program, since the communication overload per process is stable as the problem size grows.

The average shortest path length has a sublinear growth. According to [4], in regular hypercubic lattices in D dimensions, the mean number of vertices one has to pass by in order to reach an arbitrarily chosen node, grows with the lattice size as $N^{1/d}$. SP-MZ has a 3D toroidal structure and the measured average path length is just a little above this expectation. This metric seems to be a good reference for scalable parallel programs, since it denotes proximity among nodes.

The average cluster coefficient presented very small values, even 0 for two cases. These two cases are the most regular cases, where all nodes had exactly the same degree. In this particular case study, a low cluster coefficient seems to be an indication of regularity or balance in the communication pattern. However, more case studies would be necessary to observe the behavior of this metric in parallel programs.

The last metric analyzed was the density which decreases as the problem size grows. As discussed before, this metric expresses the actual number of edges

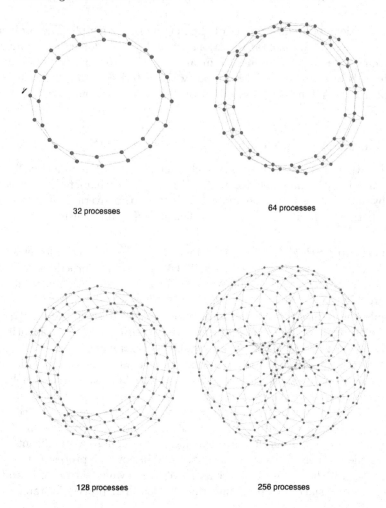

Fig. 1. Visualization of SP-MZ: (a) 32 processes, (b) 64 processes, (c) 128 processes and (d) 256 processes.

Table 1. Metrics for SP-MZ

Metric	32	64	128	256
Av. degree	*3.0*	4.5	4.25	*4.0*
Av. shortest path	4.64	4.95	5.85	8.03
Av. cluster coeff.	*0*	0.183	0.046	*0*
Density	0.097	0.071	0.033	0.016

versus the number of edges that would be present if the graph was complete. The decrease of density in this case means the relative number of connections among processes decreases with the problem size. Since an excessive number of connections usually represents communication and synchronization overload in parallel programs, this characteristic seems to be desirable in parallel programs.

Characterizing BT-MZ. The BT-MZ benchmark has a more irregular behavior. The Fig. 2 shows the graph visualization for BT-MZ using the same layout algorithm as in SP-MZ (Yifan Hu graph layout provided by Gephi). It is possible to see that the shape is undefined in BT-MZ version, except for the last case.

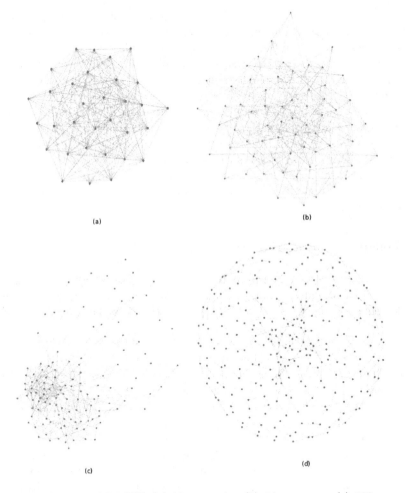

Fig. 2. Visualization of BT-MZ: (a) 32 processes, (b) 64 processes, (c) 128 processes and (d) 256 processes.

The Table 2 presents the metrics for the same problem sizes as for SP-MZ analysis. The average degree for 32 and 256 processes are absolute values; i.e., all nodes have the same presented degree.

Table 2. Metrics for BT-MZ

Metric	32	64	128	256
Av. degree	*20*	14.22	7.5	*4.0*
Av. shortest path	1.35	1.81	3.04	8.03
Av. cluster coeff.	0.64	0.21	0.06	*0*
Density	0.65	0.23	0.06	0.016

As mentioned before, BT-MZ implements variation of zone sizes which makes its structure more irregular and unbalanced than SP-MZ. This could be seen in its metrics, except for the last column, that is identical to SP-MZ for 256 processes. This means that for the last case of class C, the two versions have the same behavior related to the metrics analyzed and even considering the visualization.

The BT-MZ average degree is less stable than in SP-MZ, which is highly related to its greater irregularity. The average shortest path is inferior, except for 256 processes, while the average cluster coefficient and density are superior than in SP-MZ in most cases. As the metrics shows, it is possible to recognize characteristics that denote regularity or irregularity in the cases studied. Other studies are needed to advance in the use of these metrics for characterization and performance analysis.

5   Discussion and Future Work

The presented methodology is a preliminary work on using graph analysis tools to help in performance analysis of parallel programs. The goal is to offer a supplementary perspective of parallel applications, instead of replace any of the existent tools.

One of the main features of state-of-the-art analysis tools is the possibility to follow the events in a timeline, like for example, the traditional space-time diagram present in Vampir framework [13]. Our first approach presented here doesn't capture temporal aspects of the application. Instead, this first proposal approximates more with other traditional view, the Communication Matrix (also present in Vampir tool), but here only with final cumulative values. While the Communication Matrix is a flat 2D view, the produced graphs rather could provide topological 3D views, depending on the communication characteristics of the algorithm. Graph analysis tools, like Gephi, add different types of possible interactions for the analysis, like the generation of complex networks metrics presented here. Other suitable feature could be the use of filters, that we intend to explore in future works.

There are many possibilities yet to explore, one of them being the dynamic visualization. In order to accomplish this, we intend to capture timestamps for each communication event from the trace file and to add this information to the graph. This is possible, for example, by using the GEXF format (Graph

Exchange XML Format) [6]. This format is part of Gephi project and allows networks to be filtered with the timeline component.

6 Conclusion

This paper presents a first work on characterizing parallel applications through graph visualization and analysis. We presented a methodology where a graph of communicating processes is extracted from trace data and loaded to a graph visualization tool in order to perform the characterization. We used EZTrace to generate the trace data for NAS parallel benchmarks and Gephi graph visualization tool to analyze it.

The work was able to provide parallel program visualization and analysis for some network metrics. The characterization allowed to identify some appropriate features for parallel programs, like a stable average degree and low density. Also, it was possible to compare both implementations in terms of their structure. Even that these are preliminary results, it is possible to estimate the potential of the technique considering scalable parallel applications.

We intend to continue this work first by exploring larger versions of NAS parallel benchmarks. After that, we intend to explore different features like other layouts, filters and statistics as well as a dynamic visualization mechanism to add temporal visualization. Other possibilities like load and energy balance diagnostics will be also considered.

References

1. Bailey, D.H.: Nas parallel benchmarks. In: Padua, D.A. (ed.) Encyclopedia of Parallel Computing, pp. 1254–1259. Springer, New York (2011)
2. Baily, D., Barscz, E., Barton, J., Browning, D., Carter, R., Dagum, L., Fatoohi, R., Fineberg, S., Frederickson, P., Weeratunga, S.: The NAS parallel benchmarks. rnr-94-007.pdf (1994). http://www.nas.nasa.gov/assets/pdf/techreports/1994/
3. Bastian, M., Heymann, S., Jacomy, M.: Gephi: An open source software for exploring and manipulating networks. In: Proceedings of the International AAAI Conference on Weblogs and Social Media, San Jose (2009)
4. Boccaletti, S., Latora, V., Moreno, Y., Chavez, M., Hwang, D.: Complex networks: structure and dynamics. Phys. Rep. **424**, 175–308 (2006)
5. The Gephi website (2015). http://www.gephi.org/
6. The GEXF website (2015). http://gexf.net/
7. Ghoshal, G.: Structural and dynamical properties of complex networks. Ph.D. thesis, University of Michigan (2009)
8. Han, J., Kamber, M.: Data Mining: Concepts and Techniques. Morgan Kaufmann Publishers Inc., San Francisco (2000)
9. Himsolt, M.: GML: A portable graph file format. Technical report, Universität Passau, 94030 Passau, Germany (1999). http://www.infosun.fim.uni-passau.de/Graphlet/GML/gml-tr.html
10. Hu, Y.F.: Efficient and high quality force-directed graph drawing. Mathematica J. **10**(1), 37–71 (2005)

11. Huck, K.A., Potter, K., Jacobsen, D.W., Childs, H., Malony, A.D.: Linking perfor-
    mance data into scientific visualization tools. In: Proceedings of the First Workshop
    on Visual Performance Analysis, VPA 2014, pp. 50–57. IEEE Press, Piscataway
    (2014)
12. Kim, J.S., Lilja, D.J.: Characterization of communication patterns in message-
    passing parallel scientific application programs. In: Panda, D.K., Stunkel, C.B.
    (eds.) CANPC 1998. LNCS, vol. 1362, pp. 202–216. Springer, Heidelberg (1998)
13. Knüpfer, A., Brunst, H., Doleschal, J., Jurenz, M., Lieber, M., Mickler, H., Müller,
    M.S., Nagel, W.E.: The vampir performance analysis tool-set. In: Resch, M., Keller,
    R., Himmler, V., Krammer, B., Schulz, A. (eds.) Tools for High Performance Com-
    puting, pp. 139–155. Springer, Heidelberg (2008)
14. Lee, I.: Characterizing communication patterns of NAS-MPI benchmark programs.
    In: Proceedings of the SOUTHEASTCON, pp. 158–163. IEEE, Atlanta (2009)
15. Mercier, G., Clet-Ortega, J.: Towards an efficient process placement policy for MPI
    applications in multicore environments. In: Ropo, M., Westerholm, J., Dongarra,
    J. (eds.) PVM/MPI. LNCS, vol. 5759, pp. 104–115. Springer, Heidelberg (2009)
16. Schmitt, F., Dietrich, R., Kuß, R., Doleschal, J., Knüpfer, A.: Visualization of
    performance data for MPI applications using circular hierarchies. In: Proceedings
    of the First Workshop on Visual Performance Analysis, VPA 2014, New Orleans,
    Louisiana, USA, 16–21 November 2014, pp. 1–8 (2014). http://dx.doi.org/10.1109/
    VPA.2014.5
17. Snir, M., Otto, S., Huss-Lederman, S., Walker, D., Dongarra, J.: MPI-The Com-
    plete Reference, Volume 1: The MPI Core, 2nd edn. MIT Press, Cambridge (1998).
    (revised)
18. Trahay, F., Ru, F., Faverge, M., Ishikawa, Y., Namyst, R., Dongarra, J.: Eztrace:
    A generic framework for performance analysis. In: Proceedings of the CCGRID.
    IEEE, Newport Beach (2011)
19. Vetter, J.S., Mueller, F.: Communication characteristics of large-scale scientific
    applications for contemporary cluster architectures. In: Proceedings of the Interna-
    tional Parallel and Distributed Processing Symposium (IPDPS), Fort Lauderdale,
    Florida (2002)
20. van der Wijngaart, R., Jin, H.: NAS parallel benchmarks, multi-zone versions. rnas-
    03-010.pdf, July 2003. http://www.nas.nasa.gov/News/Techreports/2003/PDF/
21. Zamani, R., Afsahi, A.: Communication characteristics of message-passing scientific
    and engineering applications. In: Zheng, S.Q. (ed.) Proceedings of the IASTED
    PDCS, pp. 644–649. IASTED/ACTA Press, Phoenix (2005)

REPPAR - Reproducibility
in Parallel Computing

Reproducible and User-Controlled Software Environments in HPC with Guix

Ludovic Courtès[1]([⊠]) and Ricardo Wurmus[2]

[1] Inria, Bordeaux, France
ludovic.courtes@inria.fr
[2] Max Delbrück Center for Molecular Medicine, Berlin, Germany

Abstract. Support teams of high-performance computing (HPC) systems often find themselves between a rock and a hard place: on one hand, they understandably administrate these large systems in a conservative way, but on the other hand, they try to satisfy their users by deploying up-to-date tool chains as well as libraries and scientific software. HPC system users often have no guarantee that they will be able to reproduce results at a later point in time, even on the same system—software may have been upgraded, removed, or recompiled under their feet, and they have little hope of being able to reproduce the same software environment elsewhere. We present GNU Guix and the functional package management paradigm and show how it can improve reproducibility and sharing among researchers with representative use cases.

1 Introduction

HPC system administration has to satisfy two seemingly contradictory demands: on one hand administrators seek stability, which leads to a conservative approach to software management, and on the other hand users demand recent tool chains and huge scientific software stacks. In addition, users often need different versions and different variants of a given software package. To satisfy both, support teams end up playing the role of "distribution maintainers": they build and install tool chains, libraries, and scientific software packages manually—multiple variants thereof—and make them available *via* "environment modules" [4], which allows users to pick the specific packages they want.

Unfortunately, software is often built and installed in an *ad hoc* fashion, leaving users little hope of redeploying the same software environment on another system. Worse, support teams occasionally have to remove installed software or to upgrade it in place, which means that users may eventually find themselves unable to reproduce their software environment, *even on the same system*.

Recently-developed tools such as EasyBuild [7] and Spack [5] address part of the problem by automating package builds, supporting non-root users, and adding facilities to create package variants. However, these tools fall short when it comes to build reproducibility. First, build processes can trivially refer to tools or libraries already installed on the system. Second, the *ad hoc* naming

© Springer International Publishing Switzerland 2015
S. Hunold et al. (Eds.): Euro-Par 2015 Workshops, LNCS 9523, pp. 579–591, 2015.
DOI: 10.1007/978-3-319-27308-2_47

conventions they rely on to identify builds fail to capture the directed acyclic graph (DAG) of dependencies that led to this particular build.

GNU Guix is a general-purpose package manager that implements the functional package management paradigm pioneered by Nix [2,3]. Many of its properties and features make it attractive in a multi-user HPC context: per-user profiles, transactional upgrades and roll-backs, and, more importantly, a controlled build environment to maximize reproducibility.

Section 2 details our motivations. Section 3 describes the functional package management paradigm, its implementation in Guix, its impact on reproducibility, and how it can be applied to HPC systems. Section 4 gives concrete use cases where Guix empowers users while guaranteeing reproducibility and sharing, while Sect. 5 discusses limitations and remaining challenges. Finally, Sect. 6 compares to related work, and Sect. 7 concludes.

2   Rationale

Recent work on reproducible research insufficiently takes software environment reproducibility into account. For example, the approach for verifiable computational results described in [6] focuses on workflows and conventions but does not mention the difficulty of reproducing full software environments. Likewise, the new Replicated Computational Results (RCR) initiative of the ACM Transactions on Mathematical Software acknowledges the importance of reproducible results, but does not adequately address the issue of software environments, which is a prerequisite. The authors of [12] propose a methodology for reproducible research experiments in HPC. To address the software-environment reproducibility problem they propose two unsatisfying approaches: one is to write down the version numbers of the dependencies being used, which is insufficient, and the other is to save and reuse full system images, which makes verifiability impractical—peers would have to download large images and would be unable to combine them with their own software environment.

Yet, common practices on HPC systems hinder reproducibility. For understandable stability reasons, HPC systems often run old GNU/Linux distributions that are rarely updated. Thus, packages provided by the distribution are largely dismissed. Instead support teams install packages from third-party repositories—but then they clobber the global /usr prefix, which sysadmins may want to keep under control, or install them from source by themselves and make them available through environment modules [4]. Modules allow users to choose different versions or variants of the packages they use without interfering with each other. However, when installed software is updated in place or removed, users suddenly find themselves unable to reproduce the software environment they were using. Given these practices, reproducing the exact same software environment on a *different* HPC system seems out of reach. It is nonetheless a very important property: It would allow users to assess the impact of the hardware on the software's performance—something that is very valuable in particular for developers of run-time systems—and it would allow other researchers to reproduce experiments on their system.

Essentially, by deploying software and environment modules, HPC support teams find themselves duplicating the work of GNU/Linux distributions, but why is that? Historical package managers such as APT and RPM suffer from several limitations. First, package binaries that every user installs, such as .deb files, are actually built on the package maintainer's machine, and details about the host may leak into the binary that is uploaded—a shortcoming that is now being addressed (see Sect. 6.)

Second, while it is in theory possible for a user to define their own variant of a package, as is often needed in HPC, this is often difficult in practice. Users of RPM-based systems, for example, may be able to customize a .spec file to build a custom, relocatable RPM package, but only the administrator can install the package alongside its dependencies and register it in the central yumdb package database. The lower-level rpm tool can use a separate package registry, which could be useful for unprivileged users; however RPM package databases cannot be composed, so users would need to manually track down and register the complete graph of dependencies, which is impractical at best.

Third, these tools implement an *imperative* and *stateful* package management model [3]. It is imperative in the sense that it modifies the set of available packages in place. For example, switching to an alternative MPI implementation, or upgrading the OpenMP run-time library means that suddenly all the installed applications and libraries start using them. It is stateful in the sense that the system state after a package management operation depends on its previous state. Namely, the system state at a given point in time is the result of the series of installation and upgrade operations that have been made over time, and there may be no way to reproduce the exact same state elsewhere. These properties are a serious hindrance to reproducibility.

3   Functional Package Management

Functional Paradigm. Functional package management is a discipline that transcribes the functional programming paradigm to software deployment: build and installation processes are viewed as pure functions in the mathematical sense—whose result depends exclusively on the inputs—, and their result is a value—that is, an immutable directory. Since build and installation processes are pure functions, their results can effectively be "cached" on disk. Likewise, two independent runs of a given build process for a given set of inputs should return the same value—*i.e.*, bit-identical files. This approach was first described and implemented in the Nix package manager [3]. Guix reuses low-level mechanisms from Nix to implement the same paradigm, but offers a unified interface for package definitions and their implementations, all embedded in a single programming language [2].

An obvious challenge is the implementation of this paradigm: How can build and install processes be viewed as pure? To obtain that property, Nix and Guix ensure tight control over the build environment. In both cases, build processes are started by a privileged daemon, which always runs them in "containers" as implemented by the kernel Linux; that is, they run in a chroot environment, under a dedicated user ID, with a well-defined set of environment variables, with separate name spaces for PIDs, inter-process communication (IPC), networking, and so on. The chroot environment contains only the directories corresponding to the explicitly declared inputs. This ensures that the build process cannot inadvertently end up using tools or libraries that it is not supposed to use. The separate name spaces ensure that the build process cannot communicate with the outside world. Although it is not perfect as we will see in Sect. 5, this technique gives us confidence that build processes can indeed be viewed as pure functions, with reproducible results.

Each build process produces one or more files in directories stored in a common place called *the store*, typically the /gnu/store directory. Each entry in /-gnu/store has a name that includes a hash of *all the inputs* of the build process that led to it. By "all the inputs", we really mean all of them: This includes of course compilers and libraries, including the C library, but also build scripts and environment variable values. This is recursive: The compiler's own directory name is a hash of the tools and libraries used to build, and so on, up to a set of pre-built binaries used for bootstrapping purposes—which can in turn be rebuilt using Guix [2]. Thus, for each package that is built, the system has access to the *complete DAG* of dependencies used to build it.

```
 1: (define openmpi
 2:   (package
 3:     (name "openmpi")
 4:     (version "1.8.1")
 5:     (source (origin
 6:               (method url-fetch)
 7:               (uri (string-append
 8:                      "http://www.open-mpi.org/software/ompi/v"
 9:                      (version-major+minor version)
10:                      "/downloads/openmpi-" version ".tar.bz2"))
11:               (sha256
12:                (base32
13:                 "13z1q69f3qwmmhpglarfjminfy2yw4rfqr9jydjk5507q3mjf50p"))))
14:     (build-system gnu-build-system)
15:     (inputs `(("hwloc" ,hwloc)
16:               ("gfortran" ,gfortran-4.8)
17:               ("pkg-config" ,pkg-config)))
18:     (arguments '(#:configure-flags '("--enable-oshmem")))
19:     (home-page "http://www.open-mpi.org")
20:     (synopsis "MPI-2 implementation")
21:     (description "This is an MPI-2 implementation etc.")
22:     (license bsd-2)))
```

Fig. 1. Guix package recipe of Open MPI.

Package recipes in Guix are written in a domain-specific language (DSL) embedded in the Scheme programming language. Figure 1 shows, as an example,

```
;; Query the direct and indirect inputs of Open MPI.
;; Each input is represented by a label/package tuple.
(map (match-lambda
       ((label package)
        (package-full-name package)))
     (package-transitive-inputs openmpi))
                ... yields:
("hwloc-1.10.1" "gfortran-4.8.5" "pkg-config-0.28" "libpciaccess-0.13.2")
```

Fig. 2. Querying the dependencies of a package object.

the recipe to build the Open MPI library. The `package` form evaluates to a
package object, which is just a "regular" Scheme value; the `define` form defines
the `openmpi` variable to hold that value.

Line 14 specifies that the package is to be built according to the
GNU standards—*i.e.*, the well-known `./configure && make && make install`
sequence (similarly, Guix defines `cmake-build-system`, and so on.) The `inputs`
field on line 15 specifies the direct dependencies of the package. The field refers
to the `hwloc`, `gfortran-4.8`, and `pkg-config` variables, which are also bound to
package objects (their definition is not shown here.) It would be inconvenient to
specify all the standard inputs, such as Make, GCC, Binutils so these are implicit
here; as it compiles package objects to a lower-level intermediate representation,
`gnu-build-system` automatically inserts references to specific package objects
for GCC, Binutils, etc. Since we are manipulating "normal" Scheme objects, we
can use the API of Guix to query those package objects, as illustrated with the
code in Fig. 2, which queries the name and version of the direct and indirect
dependencies of our package[1].

With that definition in place, running `guix build openmpi` returns the directory name `/gnu/store/jh1a5w572mfnil8b7885n0vvy8npb31v-openmpi-1.8.1`.
If that directory did not already exist, the daemon spawns the build process in
its isolated environment with write access to this directory. Of course users never
have to type these long `/gnu/store` file names. They can install packages in their
profile using the `guix package` command, which essentially creates symbolic
links to the selected `/gnu/store` items. By default, the tree of symbolic links is
rooted at `~/.guix-profile`, but users can also create independent profiles in
arbitrary places of the file system. For instance, a user may choose to have GCC
and Open MPI in the default profile, and to populate another profile with Clang
and MPICH2.

It is then a matter of defining the search paths for the compiler, linker, and
other tools *via* environment variables. Fortunately, Guix keeps track of that and
the `guix package --search-paths` command returns all the necessary environment variable definitions in Bourne shell syntax. For example, when both

---

[1] This document is an "active paper" written in Skribilo, a Scheme-based authoring
tool, which allows us to use Guix and run this code from the document.

the GCC tool chain and Open MPI are installed, the command returns definitions for the `PATH`, `CPATH`, and `LIBRARY_PATH` environment variables, and these definitions can be passed to the `eval` shell built-in command.

4 Use Cases

We explore practical use cases where Guix improves experimentation reproducibility for a user of a given system, supports the deployment of complex software stacks, allows a software environment to be replicated on another system, and finally allows fine customization of the software environment.

4.1 Usage Patterns on an HPC Cluster

One of the key features of Guix and Nix is that they securely permit unprivileged users to install packages in the store [3]. To build a package, the `guix` commands connect to the build daemon, which then performs the build (if needed) on their behalf, in the isolated environment. When two users build the exact same package, both end up using the exact same `/gnu/store` file name, and storage is shared. If a user tries to build, say, a malicious version of the C library, then the other users on the system will not use it, simply because they cannot guess its `/gnu/store` file name—unless they themselves explicitly build the very same modified C library.

Guix is deployed at the Max Delbrück Center for Molecular Medicine (MDC), Berlin, where the store is shared among 250 cluster nodes and an increasing number of user workstations. It is now gradually replacing other methods of software distribution, such as statically linked binaries on group network shares, relocatable RPMs installed into group prefixes, one-off builds on the cluster, and user-built software installed in home directories. The researchers use tens of bioinformatics tools as well as frameworks such as Biopython, NumPy, SciPy, and SymPy. The functional packaging approach proved particularly useful in the ongoing efforts to move dozens of users and their custom software environments from an older cluster running Ubuntu to a new cluster running a version of CentOS, because software packaged with Guix does not depend on any of the host system's libraries and thus can be used on very different systems without any changes to the packages. Research groups now have a shared profile for common applications, whereas individual users can manage their own profiles for custom software, legacy versions of bioinformatics tools to reproduce published results, bleeding-edge tool chains, or even for complete workflows.

Guix supports two ways to manage a profile. The first one is to make transactions that add, upgrade, or remove packages in the profile: `guix package --install openmpi --remove mpich2` installs Open MPI and removes MPICH2 in a single transaction that can be rolled back. The second approach is to *declare* the desired contents of the profile and make that effective: the user writes in a file a code snippet that lists the requested packages (see Fig. 3) and then runs `guix package --manifest=my-packages.scm`.

```
;; This file can be passed to 'guix package --manifest'.
(use-modules (gnu packages base) (gnu packages gcc)
             (my-openmpi))

(packages->manifest
 (list glibc-utf8-locales gnu-make gcc-toolchain openmpi))
```

Fig. 3. Declaring the set of packages to be installed in a profile.

This declarative profile management makes it easy to replicate a profile, but it is symbolic: It uses whatever package objects the variables are bound to (gnu-make, gcc-toolchain, etc.), but these variables are typically defined in the (gnu packages) modules that Guix comes with. Thus the precise packages being installed depend on the version of Guix that is available. Specifying the Git commit of Guix in addition to the declaration in Fig. 3 is all it takes to reproduce the exact same /gnu/store items.

Another approach to achieve bit-identical reproduction of a user's profile is by saving the contents of its transitive closure using guix archive --export. The resulting archive can be transferred to another system and restored at any point in time using guix archive --import. This should significantly facilitate experimentation and sharing among peers.

4.2   Customizing Packages

Our colleagues at Inria in the HiePACS and Runtime teams develop a complete linear algebra software stack going from sparse solvers such as PaStiX and dense solvers such as Chameleon, to run-time support libraries and compiler extensions such as StarPU[2] and hwloc. While developers of simulations want to be able to deploy the whole stack, developers of solvers only need their project's dependencies, possibly several variants thereof. For instance, developers of Chameleon may want to test their software against several versions of StarPU, or against variants of StarPU built with different compile-time options. Finally, developers of the lower-level layers, such as StarPU, may want to test the effect of changes they make on higher-level layers.

This use case leads to two requirements: that users be able to customize and non-ambiguously specify a package DAG, and that they be able to reproduce any variant of their package DAG. Guix allows them to define variants; the code for these variants can be stored in a repository of their own and made visible to the guix commands by defining the GUIX_PACKAGE_PATH environment variable. Figure 4 shows an example of such package variants: based on the pre-existing starpu variable, the first variant defines a package for a new StarPU release candidate, simply by changing its source field, while the second variant adds the optional dependency on the SimGrid simulator—a variant useful to scheduling practitioners, but not necessarily to solver developers.

---

[2] http://starpu.gforge.inria.fr/.

```
(define starpu-1.2rc                 ;release candidate
  (package (inherit starpu)
    (version "1.2.0rc2")
    (source (origin
             (method url-fetch)
             (uri (string-append "http://starpu.gforge.inria.fr/files/"
                                 "starpu-" version ".tar.gz"))
             (sha256
              (base32
               "0qgb6yrh3k745grjj14gc2vl6a99m0ljcsisfzcwyhg89vdpx42v")))))))

(define starpu-with-simgrid
  (package (inherit starpu)
    (name "starpu-with-simgrid")    ;name shown in the user interface
    (inputs '(("simgrid" ,simgrid)
              ,@(package-inputs starpu)))))
```

Fig. 4. Defining variants of the default recipe for StarPU.

These StarPU package definitions are obviously useful to users of StarPU: They can install them with `guix package -i starpu` and similar commands. But they are also useful to StarPU developers: They can enter a "pristine" development environment corresponding to the dependencies given in the recipe by running `guix environment starpu --pure`. This command spawns a shell where the usual `PATH`, `CPATH` etc. environment variables are redefined to refer precisely to the inputs specified in the recipe. This amounts to creating a profile on the fly, containing only the tools and libraries necessary when developing StarPU. This is notably useful when dealing with build systems that support optional dependencies.

Now that we have several StarPU variants, we want to allow direct and indirect users to select the variant that they want. A simple way to do that is to write, say, a function that takes a `starpu` parameter and returns a package that uses it as its input as show in Fig. 5. To allow users to refer to one or the other variant at the command line, we use different values for the `name` field.

This approach is reasonable when there is a small number of variants, but it does not scale to more complex DAGs. As an example, StarPU can be built with MPI support, in which case Chameleon also needs to be explicitly linked against the same MPI implementation. One way to do that is by writing a function that recursively adjusts the package labeled ``mpi'' in the `inputs` field of packages in the DAG. No matter how complex the transformations are, a package object unambiguously represents a reproducible build process. In that sense, Guix allows environments to be reproduced at different sites, or by different users, while still supporting users needing complex customization.

```
(define (make-chameleon name starpu)
  (package
    (name name)
    ;; [other fields omitted]
    (inputs '(("starpu" ,starpu)
              ("blas" ,atlas) ("lapack" ,lapack)
              ("gfortran" ,gfortran-4.8)
              ("python" ,python-2)))))

(define chameleon
  (make-chameleon "chameleon" starpu))
(define chameleon/starpu-simgrid
  (make-chameleon "chameleon-simgrid" starpu-with-simgrid))
```

Fig. 5. Defining a function that returns a package object for the Chameleon solver.

5   Limitations and Challenges

Privileged Daemon. Nix and Guix address many of the reproducibility issues encountered in package deployment, and Guix provides APIs that can facilitate the development of package variants as is useful in HPC. Yet, to our knowledge, neither Guix nor Nix are widely deployed on HPC systems. An obvious reason that limits adoption is the requirement to have the build daemon run with root privileges—without which it would be unable to use the Linux kernel container facilities that allow it to isolate build processes and maximize build reproducibility. System administrators are wary of installing privileged daemons, and so HPC system users trade reproducibility for practical approaches.

Cluster Setup. All the `guix` commands are actually clients of the daemon. In a typical cluster setup, system administrators may want to run a single daemon on one specific node and to share /gnu/store among all the nodes. At the time of writing, Guix does not yet allow communication with a remote daemon. For this reason, Guix users at the MDC are required to manage their profiles from a specific node; other nodes can use the profiles, but not modify them. Allowing the `guix` commands to communicate with a remote daemon will address this issue.

Additionally, compute nodes typically lack access to the Internet. However, the daemon needs to be able to download source code tarballs or pre-built binaries from external servers. Thus, the daemon must run on a node with Internet access, which could be contrary to the policy on some clusters.

OS Kernel. By choosing not to use a full-blown VM and thus relying on the host OS kernel, our system assumes that the kernel interface is stable and that the kernel has little or no impact on program behavior. While this may sound like a broad assumption, our experience has shown that it holds for almost all the software packages provided by Guix. Indeed, while applications may be sensitive to changes in the C library, only low-level kernel-specific user-land software is really sensitive to changes in the kernel. The build daemon itself relies on features that have been available in the kernel for several years.

Non-determinism. Despite the use of isolated containers to run build processes, there are still a few sources of non-determinism that build systems of packages might use and that can impede reproducibility. In particular, details about the operating system kernel and the hardware being used can "leak" to build processes. For example, the kernel Linux provides system calls such as `uname` and interfaces such as `/proc/cpuinfo` that leak information about the host; independent builds on different hosts could lead to different results if this information is used. Likewise, the `cpuid` instruction leaks hardware details.

Fortunately, few software packages depend on this information. Yet, the proportion of packages depending on it is higher in the HPC world. A notable example is the ATLAS linear algebra system, which fine-tunes itself based on details about the CPU micro-architecture. Similarly, profile-guided optimization (PGO), where the compiler optimizes code based on a profile gathered in a previous run, undermines reproducibility. Running build processes in full-blown VMs would address some of these issues, but with a potentially significant impact on build performance, and possibly preventing important optimization techniques in the HPC context.

Proprietary Software. GNU Guix does not provide proprietary software packages. Unfortunately, proprietary software is still relatively common in HPC, be it linear algebra libraries or GPU support. Yet, we see it as a strength more than a limitation. Often, these "black boxes" inherently limit reproducibility—how is one going to reproduce a software environment without permission to run the software in the first place? What if the software depends on the ability to "call home" to function at all? More importantly, we view reproducible software environments and reproducible science as a tool towards improved and shared knowledge; developers who deny the freedom to study and modify their code work against this goal.

6   Related Work

Reproducible Builds. Reproducible software environments have only recently become an active research area. One of the earliest pieces of work in this area is the Vesta software configuration system [9]. Vesta provides a DSL that allows users to describe build operations, similar to Nix [3]. More recently, projects such as Debian's Reproducible, Fedora's Mock, or Gitian have intended to improve reproducibility and verifiability of mainstream package distributions. Google's recent Bazel build tool relies on container facilities provided by the kernel Linux and provides another DSL to describe build operations.

Reproducibility can be achieved with heavyweight approaches such as full operating system deployments, be it on hardware or in VMs or containers [1,8,10,11]. In addition to being resource-hungry, these approaches are coarse-grain and do not compose: if two different VM/container images or "software appliances" provide useful features or packages, the user has to make a binary choice and cannot combine the features or packages they offer. Furthermore, "Docker files", "Vagrant files", and Kameleon "recipes" [11] suffer from being too broad for the purposes of reproducing a software environment—they are about configuring complete operating systems—and from offering an inappropriate level of abstraction—these recipes list commands to *modify* the state of the system image to obtain the desired state, whereas Guix allows users to *declare* the desired environment in terms of software packages. Lastly, the tendency to rely on complete third-party system images is a security concern[3] Building upon third-party binary images also puts a barrier on reproducibility: Users may have recipes to rebuild their own software from source, but the rest of the system is essentially considered as a "black box", which, if it can be rebuilt from source at all, can only be rebuilt using a completely different tool set.

HPC Package Management. In the HPC community, efforts have focused primarily on the automation of software deployment and the ability for users to customize their build environment independently of each other. The latter has been achieved by "environment modules", a simple but efficient tool set that is still widely used today [4]. Build and deployment automation is more recent with the development of specialized package management tools such as EasyBuild [7] and Spack [5].

Both EasyBuild and Spack have the advantage of being installable by unprivileged users since they do not rely on privileged components, unlike Guix and Nix. The downside is that they cannot use the kernel's container facilities, which seriously hinders build reproducibility. When used in the user's home directories, each user may end up rebuilding the same compiler, libraries, etc., which can be costly in terms of CPU, bandwidth, and disk usage. Conversely, Nix and Guix support safe sharing of builds.

EasyBuild aims to support multiple package variants, such as packages built with different compilers, or linked against different MPI implementations. To achieve that, it relies on directory naming conventions; for instance, `OpenMPI/-1.7.3-GCC-4.8.2` contains packages built with the specified MPI implementation and compiler. Such conventions fail to capture the full complexity of the DAG and configuration space. For instance, the convention arbitrarily omits the C library, linker, or configuration flags being used.

EasyBuild is tightly integrated with environment modules [4], which are familiar to most users of HPC systems. While modules provide users with flexible environments, they implement an imperative, stateful paradigm: Users run a sequence of `module load` and `module unload` commands that *alter* the current environment. This can make it much harder to reason about and reproduce an environment, as opposed to the declarative approaches implemented by `guix package --manifest` and `guix environment`.

Like EasyBuild and similarly to Guix, Spack implements build recipes as first-class objects in a general-purpose language, Python, which facilitates customization and the creation of package variants. In addition, Spack provides

---

[3] "Over 30 % of Official Images in Docker Hub Contain High Priority Security Vulnerabilities", http://www.banyanops.com/blog/analyzing-docker-hub/.

a rich command-line interface that allows users to express variants similar to those discussed in Sect. 4.2. This appears to be very convenient for common cases, although there are limits to the expressivity and readability of such a compact syntax.

7   Conclusion

Functional package managers provide the foundations for reproducible software environments, while still allowing fine-grain software composition and not imposing high disk and RAM costs. Today, GNU Guix comes with 2,392 packages, including many of the common HPC tools and libraries as well as around 50 bioinformatics packages. It is deployed on the clusters of the MDC Berlin, and being discussed as one of the packaging options by the Open Bioinformatics Foundation, a non-profit for the biological research community. We hope to see more HPC deployments of Guix in the foreseeable future.

GNU Guix benefits from contributions by about 20 people each month. It is the foundation of the Guix System Distribution, a standalone, reproducible GNU/Linux distribution.

Acknowledgments. We would like to thank Florent Pruvost, Emmanuel Agullo, and Andreas Enge at Inria and Eric Bavier at Cray Inc. for insightful discussions and comments on an earlier draft. We are grateful to the Guix contributors who keep improving the system.

References

1. Boettiger, C.: An introduction to docker for reproducible research. SIGOPS Oper. Syst. Rev. **49**(1), 71–79 (2015)
2. Courtès, L.: Functional package management with guix. In: European Lisp Symposium (2013)
3. Dolstra, E., de Jonge, M., Visser, E.: Nix: a safe and policy-free system for software deployment. In: Proceedings of the 18th Large Installation System Administration Conference (LISA 2004), USENIX, pp. 79–92 (2004)
4. Furlani, J.L.: Providing a flexible user environment. In: Proceedings of the 5th Large Installation System Administration (LISA V), pp. 141–152 (1991)
5. Gamblin, T.: Spack Web Site (2015). http://scalability-llnl.github.io/spack/
6. Gavish, M., Donoho, D.: A Universal identifier for computational results. Procedia Comput. Sci. **4**, 637–647 (2011)
7. Geimer, M., Hoste, K., McLay, R.: Modern scientific software management using easybuild and Lmod. In: Proceedings of the 1st Workshop on HPC User Support Tools (HUST 2014), pp. 41–51. IEEE Press (2014)
8. Gorp, P.V., Mazanek, S.: SHARE: a web portal for creating and sharing executable research papers. Procedia Comput. Sci. **4**, 589–597 (2011)
9. Heydon, A., Levin, R., Yu, Y.: Caching function calls using precise dependencies. In: Proceedings of the ACM SIGPLAN 2000 Conference on Programming Language Design and Implementation, pp. 311–320. ACM (2000)

10. Jeanvoine, E., Sarzyniec, L., Nussbaum, L.: Kadeploy3: efficient and scalable operating system provisioning. USENIX; login **38**(1), 38–44 (2013)
11. Ruiz, C., Harrache, S., Mercier, M., Olivier, R.: Reconstructable software appliances with kameleon. SIGOPS Oper. Syst. Rev. **49**(1), 80–89 (2015)
12. Stanisic, Luka, Legrand, Arnaud: Effective reproducible research with org-mode and git. In: Lopes, L., et al. (eds.) Euro-Par 2014, Part I. LNCS, vol. 8805, pp. 475–486. Springer, Heidelberg (2014)

Reproducibility in Practice: Lessons Learned from Research and Teaching Experiments

Antonio Maffia[✉], Helmar Burkhart, and Danilo Guerrera

University of Basel, Basel, Switzerland
{antonio.maffia,helmar.burkhart,danilo.guerrera}@unibas.ch
http://www.unibas.ch

Abstract. Nowadays computer systems, with the new multi-core architectures comprising accelerators such as GPU and Intel Xeon Phi, have a high complexity and are exclusively targeting performance: it becomes more and more difficult for scientists to preserve the context of their experiments and let them be reproducible by others. In the previous years researchers mainly focused on their own work, not caring about letting it be useful for the others and for science to move forward. The majority of the experiments on parallel computers have been reported at conferences and in journals usually without the possibility to verify the results presented. While this is still the state-of-the-art, current research targets for solutions to this problem. We discuss early results regarding our workflow system based approach, implemented in order to address the reproducibility problem in the context of high performance computation. We used our framework to reproduce the results of some papers and classroom code. In order to allow an easy interface to our system and let it be accessible from everywhere we set up a web application.

1 Introduction

Reproducibility of computer experiments demonstrates scientific strength because a wider community not only can check the correctness of published results but is also able to compare different approaches. Experimental research is not time-independent: experiment parameters are changed over time with the goal of getting more precise results or better performance indices. Thus, systems that address reproducible experiments must support both present and past configuration settings in a flexible manner. In this paper, we concentrate on the reproducibility of benchmark experiments executed on high-performance computing environments.

In the last years a movement promoting reproducible research through tools and best practices is emerging. The tools mostly target the reproducibility of the data analysis [19]. High performance computing does not focus only on computational results, but also, and mostly, on the benchmarking: its latest goal is to measure performance, in terms of execution time, speedup, GFlop/s or other metrics. Still, research in HPC must target reproducibility.

S. Hunold et al. (Eds.): Euro-Par 2015 Workshops, LNCS 9523, pp. 592–603, 2015.
DOI: 10.1007/978-3-319-27308-2_48

The structure of this paper is as follows. In Sect. 2 we introduce some interesting scenarios concerning reproducibility in HPC, and a grouping of available tools for reproducible research. In Sect. 3 we summarise our reproducibility taxonomy which has been guiding the implementation of our new workflow engine: PROVA! (Italian: Convince me!). In Sect. 4, the main part of this paper, we present several case studies of reproducibility experiments, developing the scenario presented in Sect. 2. Conclusions and comments on future work are given in Sect. 5.

2   Reproducibility Scenarios and Tool Support

We first introduce three challenging scenarios which we later will explore as case studies.

Research Result Review: This is the main driving force for getting science in general to become self-correcting. Reproducible experiments require the detailed knowledge of experiment parameters and conditions. Compared to other science fields, computer science has a lot of advantages to make their research reproducible. It is the Internet that provides access not only to information but also to computing resources. It is also the possibility to set up virtual environments that are portable and can act as reproducibility platforms. But nevertheless reproducing computer science experiments is not for free.

Period of Time Observations: Software tools such as compilers evolve over time. Both code optimisation parts as well as support libraries change from release to release. Like unit testing frameworks for correctness (e.g. JUnit in a Java context) are nowadays applied by the successful software engineer, unit performance frameworks should be part of the development cycle. By this, both implementers and users of a software environment would be able to reproduce experiments and get insight into performance developments over time.

Reproducibility in the Curriculum: Strongly believing that reproducible research will be mandatory in future, it is the next generation of scientists (aka our students) that should be taught this topic as early as possible. For many years both our students and we missed reproducibility support. Assessing and grading the students' work has been hard for the examiners, while students have been suffering from redoing tedious performance experiments over and over again.

As there are many more scenarios (for example up-to-date documentation by means of executable documents; provenance support for programs and data), tools have been developed to address reproducibility issues. In a recent tool survey we have identified the following categories:

Workbench Approach: These tools concentrate on the workflow of an application, i.e. the interconnection of input, output, and computation modules. Taverna [16] and VisTrails [18] integrate data acquisition, derivation, analysis, and visualization as executable components throughout the scientific exploration process. Repeatability is facilitated by ensuring that the evolution of the software components used in the workflow is controlled by the organizations that design the workflows. This "controlled services" approach is shared by other WFMS such as Kepler [15] and Knime [1], an open-source workflow-based integration platform for data analytics.

Version Control Approach: Versioning systems such as git and gitHub are successfully applied in daily software engineering and document preparation. Sumatra is a tool for managing and tracking projects based on numerical simulation and/or analysis, with the aim of supporting reproducible research: it can be thought of as an automated electronic lab notebook for computational projects [6]. Madagascar is an open-source software package for multidimensional data analysis and reproducible computational experiments. It principally targets researchers working with digital image and data processing in geophysics and related fields: the technology developed using its project management system is transferred in the form of recorded processing histories, which become "computational recipes" to be verified, exchanged, and modified by users of the system [2].

Virtualization Approach: CDE, which stands for Code, Data, and Environment packaging, is able to automatically package the software dependencies that your code needs in order to run your experiment elsewhere [14]. Recomputation.org [10] is a repository for experiments in computational science: their goal is to follow the recomputation manifesto [11] and make computational science experiments recomputable by providing tools and a repository to store experiments in. Emulab [3] is a network emulation testbed, giving researchers a wide range of environments in which to develop, debug, and evaluate their systems, focuses on networking and distributed systems.

While these tools identify many useful features one needs, one essential element is missing: high-performance computing orientation.

Grid'5000 [5] is a large-scale and versatile testbed for experiment-driven research in all areas of computer science, with a focus on parallel and distributed computing. It is a project developed at national level in France, connecting several sites all over the territory, providing access to a large amount of resources, in a highly reconfigurable and controllable manner. Pathway is a tool for designing and executing performance engineering workflows for HPC applications. DataMill [17] is a community-based easy-to-use services-oriented open benchmarking infrastructure for performance evaluation, which facilitates producing robust, reliable, and reproducible results. It provides a platform for investigating interactions and composition of hidden factors affecting the performance measurements, such as binary link order, process environment size, compiler generated randomized symbol names, or group scheduler assignments. OnlineHPC [4] promises web-based access to HPC resources but seems to be in early stage of development.

None of these tools enable to undertake performance experiments similar to those mentioned in our scenarios above, targeting not only reproducible results, but also reproducible performance and easy access to the resources. Beside this, we would like to give the researchers the possibility to integrate their systems in our framework, which is an important feature missing in the other HPC oriented tools. As a consequence, we started our own project development one year ago.

3   PROVA!: Performance Reproducibility of Various Applications!

The aim of PROVA! is to provide an easy way to configure and run an experiment without dealing with the execution environment and then visualize the results in a meaningful way. As explained in [12], a *micro-experiment* can be thought as a triple ⟨*Problem, Method, System*⟩: our tool has been built upon such a definition. To solve a problem, a user can create a new project to which he can add methods representing his solutions to the problem. Furthermore, this tool allows the project to run on other systems configured by it.

The tool, developed for a Unix environment, is mainly composed of two entities: the framework itself, which interacts with the parallel machines, and a web interface. The framework represents the core of our system and must be installed by the system administrator. It consists of a collection of bash and python scripts, offering the possibility to install modules (method types), to create and manage projects and methods, as well as to execute experiments and visualize the output[1]. The installation part is hidden to the user, who interacts with the framework via web interface.

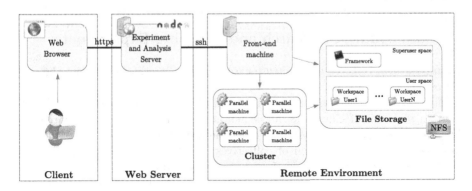

Fig. 1. Overview of PROVA!'s architecture: a user can access a web interface which interacts with the core component of the framework, placed on the parallel machine

Framework and workspace(s) must be located on a filesystem (both a local or a network one) accessible by the parallel machine on which an experiment has to be run. The clear distinction between the remote environment (composed

---

[1] A sample video showing all of the functionalities provided by our tool is available at https://youtu.be/yJqv96z8oSQ.

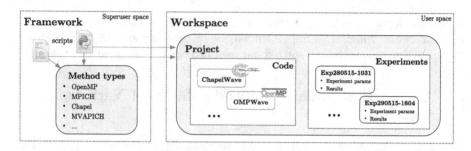

Fig. 2. Detail of the interaction between framework and workspace

of parallel machines, framework and workspaces) and the web server is shown in Fig. 1. The web server accesses the remote execution environment through an SSH connection to the front-end machine: such a connection is set up by the web interface using the URL, credentials and paths to framework and workspace.

Each *method type* consists of an installation script, which manages its dependencies, and compilation and execution script which properly handle the environment. The installation phase is carried out by the system administrator, while the other two take place when a user executes his own method. Moreover, some utilities to print performance metrics are available: when used, a script combines them into a JSON file at the end of the experiment. All of these experiments' data are organized and stored in different directories (see Fig. 2) in order to be accessed and visualized.

4   Case Studies: Research and Teaching Experiments

We used Prova! in three different use cases, which directly derive from the scenarios introduced in Sect. 2.

The first one is part of performance studies held at the University of Basel, where a sequence of Chapel [8] implementations (variants) were compared [7]. The second test case comes from a paper published in 2007 [13]. It is about a Non-Blocking Implementation of collectives in MPI. The author implemented non-blocking collectives, not existing at that time and compared them against a blocking version which was part of the MPI 1.0 specification. We tried to run his code on a different architecture and checked if we could get results comparable to his ones. The last case study concerns a replication of the performance measurements of OpenMP code written by the students attending the High Performance Computing class at the University of Basel during Spring Semester 2015.

The system used for our experiments has 4 homogeneous nodes, each equipped with 2 AMD Opteron 6274[2], running Ubuntu 12.04.4 LTS (kernel 3.8.0-38-generic), GNU gcc 4.6.3. Concerning the network, our nodes have a GbE NIC Intel Corporation 82576 Gigabit Network Connection 1 Gbit/s; the

---

[2] A full description of the microprocessor is available at the manufacturer's website.

Infiniband NIC is a Mellanox MT26428 [ConnectX VPI PCIe 2.0 5GT/s - IB QDR / 10GigE] and the Infiniband switch, also produced by Mellanox, is a IS5022 8-port Non-blocking Remotely-managed 40 Gb/s.

For all of the experiment held, each method has been run 5 times, then best and worse performance values cut off and the remaining ones averaged to get the values presented in the graphs.

4.1 Stencil Variants in Chapel

The landscape of high-performance computing is dominated by a hybrid programming model combining OpenMP and MPI in order to exploit the symmetric multiprocessor nodes and their high speed interconnections. This solution is quite complicated from a programmer's perspective and the software productivity is strongly affected by such a complexity.

For this reason, in the last couple of years, alternative approaches emerged such as problem-oriented Domain Specific Languages, libraries of high-level software patterns, and new general-purpose languages with high-level constructs for addressing the parallelism (e.g. PGAS languages). Chapel is a high-level programming language, targeting parallel computation and productivity, achieving them by implementing the PGAS model. It has been designed for running on multicore desktops and laptops, as well as clusters, cloud and high-end supercomputers.

Using our tool, we created a new project and the different methods, i.e. Chapel variants, implementing a 3-dimensional stencil computation of a wave equation (as detailed in Sect. 2 of [7]). We were thus able to reproduce that experiment getting the results shown in Fig. 3. As a performance metric, GFlop/s are used.

Visually inspecting fresh and old results, we recognize a matching behaviour: the slopes of the scaling are the same for all of the proposed variants, with a

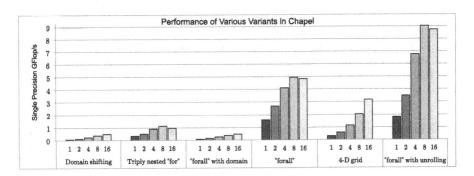

Fig. 3. Performance comparison of various Chapel implementation variants of a 3-D wave equation over a 200x200x200 grid and 100 timesteps. Once reproduced the experiment published in [7], the original graph template has been used to plot our results.

performance loss for 16 threads. The *system* where the *macro-experiment* has been run is different, whereas *problem* and *methods* used to solve it are the same. For us it was quite straightforward to carry out such a reproduction, even if the system has been changed in the meanwhile, due to the knowledge which is part of our group: code, makefiles, run scripts and graph template. Still, it was a challenge that others wouldn't have accomplished without all of the information we have.

We then went further and decided to compare different Chapel versions, using as a measure the same variants of the code. Starting from the code used in [7] we built a second *macro-experiment*: we had modules representing Chapel v1.11 (the current one) and Chapel v1.4 (the one used for the original paper).

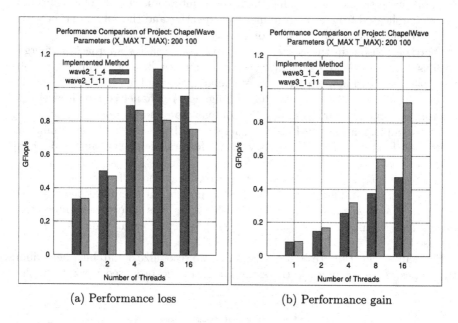

(a) Performance loss	(b) Performance gain

Fig. 4. Performance graph of a wave equation, implemented with versions 1.4 (in red) and 1.11 (in green) of Chapel: (a), obtained using the "triple nested for" variant of Fig. 3, shows a performance loss using the newer version of the compiler, whereas (b), using the "forall with domain" variant, depicts a performance gain. X_MAX represents the size of the 3-D grid, and T_MAX time-steps.

We implemented several methods using the old and newer versions of Chapel, this way benchmarking what three years of development brought to the language. When trying to compile the code with the new version of Chapel we ran into errors due to some syntax changes between the versions. Once these small issues were fixed, we were able to run the *macro-experiment*. We considered all of the variants of the original paper: we notice in Fig. 4b, referring to the variant 3 of Fig. 3, a good improvement of the performances in Chapel v1.11 (green) compared to Chapel v1.4 (in red).

At the time of the original paper, Chapel Domain Maps were not mature enough: in the meanwhile there has been a lot of work on them, as emerges clearly by the graph. The scaling curve is better in the newer version and there is significant difference for 8 and 16 threads. Interestingly, as it can be noticed in Fig. 4a, the implementation of variant 2 of Fig. 3, which uses 3 nested for loops in the compute block (with a parallelization along the z axis only), suffers a performance loss for Chapel v1.11 (in green). This variant implements an extremely basic and, in this case, inefficient parallelization scheme: it is not a surprise that the Chapel team concentrated its efforts on more advanced and helpful features. Chapel v1.11 looks better in any other variant, proving that the work of the Chapel group lead by Brad Chamberlain is useful and constantly improving the language. To design and implement such a high level language for parallel systems is a hard challenge: of course a lot must still be done for reaching a performance comparable to a state of the art approach, but usability, ease and productivity of the language are worth the effort.

4.2 Non-blocking Collectives

Our second experiment focused on reproducing an experiment published in 2007 in [13]. It presented a case study that compares the usage of non-blocking and blocking collective operations in parallel applications. Non-blocking collective operations allow, in a multi-node environment, to partially overlap communication and computation. This concept should result in a better performance compared to the blocking counterpart. The author implemented the non-blocking collectives on top of MPI-1. His tests resulted in a performance gain of up to 34 %. The NBC (Non-Blocking Collectives) library became part of MPI-3. The code for the conjugate gradient solver is available at http://htor.inf.ethz.ch/research/nbcoll/libnbc/.

The group of Prof. Schnor, at the University of Potsdam, first tried to reproduce the paper, so we could exchange opinions and get some hints on how to set the environment, sharing makefiles and run script. We set up a project and used 2 modules, MPICH2 (v3.1.4) and libNBC (v1.0.1 NBC library). After some failures, we were able to set up our environment (partially) and run the code over ethernet, distributing in a round robin manner the MPI processes across the nodes. In Fig. 5 is presented a mash-up of our results and the one of Potsdam [9]. Our curves, in blue and orange, start from a lower value and scale in a similar way to the one obtained by the Schnor group. Their machine, featuring 28 nodes of 2x Intel Xeon E5520 (quad core) behaves better when coming to higher values of cores. Our measurements, due to our system, have no concrete meaning for 12, 24 and 48 cores, since they represent an uneven distribution of the load: those values are kept for symmetry to the original graph only. Even if the architectures are different, the results show a common behaviour, with a saturation occurring from 32 cores on. Neither the experiment in Potsdam nor the one in Basel could reproduce the results presented in the original paper, where the usage of the NBC library resulted in a performance gain for practically all node counts, reaching a superlinear speedup for 96 cores (explained as

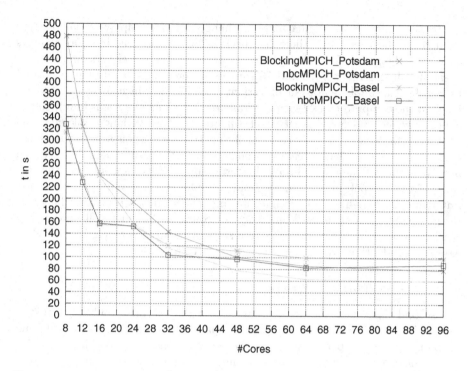

Fig. 5. Mash-up of the execution times for the non-blocking collectives reproduced experiment: in red and green are the results obtained in Potsdam, in blue and orange the ones obtained through our framework.

being due to cache effects in the inner part of the matrix vector product). In the replication attempt held in Potsdam, it was possible to run the code using Open-MPI. The original paper does not state anything about the version of OpenMPI used nor any other information about the environment. So we decided to test it using OpenMPI v1.8.2, since it is the version used in Potsdam, but we failed. When running the code which makes use of the NBC library, compiled with the previously mentioned OpenMPI version (both over ethernet and infiniband), we always get run time errors (the pure OpenMPI version of the conjugate gradient solver runs without errors). For this reason our measurements don't include execution times when using OpenMPI. In this case we faced problems, even if the code is publicly available: this clearly demonstrates how important the *system* is, considered hardware plus software configuration, as well as provenance.

4.3 Students' Work Replication

We conducted a classroom experiment, in which the students of our HPC course at the University of Basel were asked to implement the solutions to the assignments using the framework we are building: this gave to them a first glimpse of the topic of reproducibility. It is a topic of great importance and it is our duty

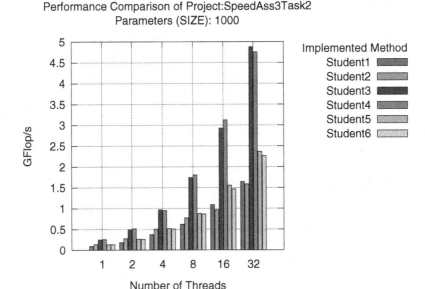

Fig. 6. Students performance results obtained through our framework: the implementation compared is a 2 dimensional matrix multiply, parallelized with OpenMP

to teach it to the next generation of scientists. Unfortunately, just a part of the research community cares about reproducibility, so it was not surprising to learn from the students that 90 % of them had no clue about what it is.

Our tool, accessed via the web interface, provided them a ready-to-use environment, where they could compile and run their source code, by simply pushing a button, thus making completely transparent to them these phases as well as intermediate output and shell commands. They could manipulate the Makefile, thus acting on the compilation phase, whereas the run phase was not customizable, being such a feature currently under development. Letting them use our prototype, allowed us to run their assignment/experiments under the exact same conditions, and get the graph they should have gotten, being sure no manipulation happened. Additionally, in this way it was not possible to wrongly run or misinterpret their results, since we had a common run and output format, as well as a common graph style for all of them. In Fig. 6 is shown a comparison of their implementation of a matrix multiply using OpenMP for the parallelization. The students who implemented a correct solution took part to this speed test experiment, where their implementations have been compared, thus getting the best performance. The code has been implemented following different strategies: optimizing the cache (data reuse), exploiting unrolling or AVX instructions.

5   Conclusions and Future Work

While HPC benchmarking over the years has evolved into a sophisticated discipline, reproducibility in such a field has been neglected. Our tool and reproduction experiments are an attempt in showing that both performance and reproducibility can be accomplished. We so far achieved replication (same system, problem, method) of students' work, re-computation of a paper of which we had complete knowledge (same method and problem, but different system). We were only partially able to recompute someone else's paper, obtaining different conclusions. Still, in this last try, we recomputed, using our tool, and got the same results another group achieved, but not relying on a replication back-end, thus verifying their outcome. Of course it is a time consuming and challenging activity: our contributions aim at making it easier, providing an environment where researchers can still target their own goals, without worrying about environment, system related and software parameters, but can still produce results which are reliable and reproducible.

In order to do so we need to address collaboration and provenance issues, which is actually where our research is focusing on now. On a technical side our goal is to build a distributed workspace system, using technologies like git or mercurial, in order for the scientists to have just a common workspace across several parallel machines and supercomputing sites, as well as a way to collaborate to a common project.

Acknowledgement. We thank the group of Prof. Schnor at University of Potsdam for a preliminary study on our second test case, and the crowd of HPC Master Students in Basel for evaluating our prototype system.

References

1. https://www.knime.org/knime
2. Madagascar (2006). http://www.ahay.org/wiki/Main_Page. Accessed 1 June 2015
3. Emulab (2010). https://www.emulab.net/. Accessed 25 July 2015
4. Onlinehpc (2012). http://www.onlinehpc.com. Accessed 30 April 2015
5. Grid5000 (2014). https://www.grid5000.fr. Accessed 27 July 2015
6. Sumatra (2014). https://pythonhosted.org/Sumatra. Accessed 1 June 2015
7. Burkhart, H., Sathe, M., Christen, M., Rietmann, M., Schenk, O.: Run, Stencil, Run!–HPC productivity studies in the classroom. In: Proceedings of the 6th Conference on Partitioned Global Address Space Programming Models (PGAS 2012) (2012). https://docs.google.com/viewer?a=v&pid=sites&srcid=bGJsLmdvdnxwZ2FzMTJ8Z3g6NWIzZTBhZTI2ZGEzZDRkZQ
8. Chamberlain, B.L. Inc, C., Chamberlain, B.L. Inc, C.: Chapel (2013)
9. Christgau, S., Puhan, D., Schnor, B.: Non-blocking collectives (2014). private communication
10. Gent, I., Kotthoff, L.: Recomputation.org (2014). http://www.recomputation.org. Accessed 1 June 2015
11. Gent, I.P.: The recomputation manifesto. CoRR abs/1304.3674 (2013). http://arxiv.org/abs/1304.3674

12. Guerrera, D., Burkhart, H., Maffia, A.: Reproducible experiments in parallel computing: concepts and stencil compiler benchmark study. In: Lopes, L., et al. (eds.) Euro-Par 2014, Part I. LNCS, vol. 8805, pp. 464–474. Springer, Heidelberg (2014). http://dx.doi.org/10.1007/978-3-319-14325-5_40

13. Hoefler, T., Gottschling, P., Lumsdaine, A., Rehm, W.: Optimizing a conjugate gradient solver with non-blocking collective operations. Elsevier J. Parallel Comput. (PARCO) **33**(9), 624–633 (2007)

14. Howe, B.: Cde: a tool for creating portable experimental software packages. Comput. Sci. Eng. **14**(4), 32–35 (2012)

15. Ludäscher, B., Altintas, I., Berkley, C., Higgins, D., Jaeger, E., Jones, M., Lee, E.A., Tao, J., Zhao, Y.: Scientific workflow management and the Kepler system. Concurr. Comput.: Pract. Exp. **18**(10), 1039–1065 (2006). http://dx.doi.org/10.1002/cpe.994

16. Missier, P., et al.: Taverna, reloaded. In: Gertz, M., Ludäscher, B. (eds.) SSDBM 2010. LNCS, vol. 6187, pp. 471–481. Springer, Heidelberg (2010). http://dx.doi.org/10.1007/978-3-642-13818-8_33

17. Oliveira, A., Petkovich, J.C., Reidemeister, T., Fischmeister, S.: Datamill: rigorous performance evaluation made easy. In: Proceedings of the 4th ACM/SPEC International Conference on Performance Engineering (ICPE), pp. 137–149, Prague, Czech Republic, April 2013

18. Scheidegger, C.E., Vo, H.T., Koop, D., Freire, J., Silva, C.T.: Querying and re-using workflows with VisTrails. In: Proceedings of the 2008 ACM SIGMOD International Conference on Management of Data, SIGMOD 2008, pp. 1251–1254. ACM, New York (2008). http://doi.acm.org/10.1145/1376616.1376747

19. Stodden, V., Leisch, F., Peng, R.D. (eds.): Implementing Reproducible Research. Chapman and Hall/CRC The R Series, Boca Raton (2014)

Towards Complete Tracking of Provenance in Experimental Distributed Systems Research

Tomasz Buchert[1,2,3](✉), Lucas Nussbaum[1,2,3], and Jens Gustedt[1,4,5]

[1] Inria, Villers-lès-Nancy, France
[2] Université de Lorraine, LORIA, Nancy, France
[3] CNRS, LORIA - UMR, Nancy 7503, France
[4] Université de Strasbourg, Strasbourg, France
[5] CNRS, Icube - UMR, Strasbourg 7357, France
{tomasz.buchert,lucas.nussbaum}@loria.fr, jens.gustedt@inria.fr

Abstract. Running experiments on modern systems like supercomputers, cloud infrastructures or P2P networks became very complex, both technically and methodologically. It is difficult to re-run an experiment or understand its results even with technical background on the technology and methods used. Storing the provenance of experimental data, i.e., storing information about how the results were produced, proved to be a powerful tool to address similar problems in computational natural sciences. In this paper, we (1) survey provenance collection in various domains of computer science, (2) introduce a new classification of provenance types, and (3) sketch a design of a provenance system inspired by this classification.

1 Introduction

Computers are becoming faster and more powerful, but our understanding is not advancing accordingly. On the contrary, since the systems become more and more complex one can argue that we know less and less about them. This discrepancy is disconcerting and calls for action in almost all domains of computer science.

Experimental research in distributed systems is especially exposed to this problem. The systems under study are complex, built from similarly complex software and hardware which interact in unexpected ways. Often the scale of experiments is large and even their execution is challenging, as is the understanding of a particular system or drawing scientifically valid conclusions. A platform may suffer from intermittent or fatal failures which should not go unnoticed. The number of relevant factors and the level of complexity has long surpassed our capacity to reason about such systems as a whole.

The complexity of the systems is not the only difficulty, however. Quite often the *description* of processes (including descriptions of scientific experiments) that run on them is complex, incomplete or even erroneous. This is another menace to *reproducibility* which is generally considered a hallmark of science.

Among the techniques that may improve both understandability and reproducibility of scientific research is *provenance*. Traditionally understood as information about origins and/or a chain of custody of a historical object, it has

S. Hunold et al. (Eds.): Euro-Par 2015 Workshops, LNCS 9523, pp. 604–616, 2015.
DOI: 10.1007/978-3-319-27308-2_49

found another meaning in computing and science as a representation of origin and transformation of a given data object during computation. In this sense it is, in fact, a form of documentation. It improves understandability and reproducibility by tracking how the processes transform data and by capturing the context where these processes take place.

However, obtaining useful provenance information is not an easy task. The problems are conceptual (e.g., what should be tracked and to which level of detail?) and technical (e.g., how to store and query provenance information efficiently?). Collection of provenance may be in conflict with performance or even correctness of the system by inadvertently changing its behavior.

This paper makes three contributions. First, we analyze provenance collection techniques in computer science with the intention to improve their use in experimental distributed system research. Second, building upon the previous observations, we classify provenance into three distinct but interrelated types. Finally, we design a provenance system that follows this distinction and can provide answers to a range of queries.

The paper is structured as follows. In Sect. 2 we make our first contribution by making a thorough analysis of provenance in various domains. In Sect. 3, as another contribution, we propose a new classification into three types of provenance. Then, in Sect. 4, we make our third and last contribution by considering implications of this classification for experimental distributed systems research and sketch a design of a provenance system. Finally, we draw final conclusions and describe our future work in Sect. 5.

2 Provenance in Computer Science

In this section, we look at provenance as an object of study on its own, and then gradually narrow the domain and discuss its use and support in general computing, scientific workflows, control-flows and, finally, in experimental research in distributed systems.

2.1 General Provenance

In this work, *provenance* is a collection of metadata associated with a run of a computational process that provides *any* kind of useful information as to how it was executed. This is a much broader term than *data provenance* which is a prevailing notion of provenance in computational life and earth sciences. Collection of data provenance is an active domain of research that meets much success in computational natural sciences [30].

Provenance can be *prospective* (i.e., obtained via static analysis) and *retrospective* (i.e., obtained postmortem) [12,13]. Additionally, one may differentiate by the level of abstraction that provenance provides [2]. Four levels of provenance can be distinguished: *L0* (abstract experiment description), *L1* (service instantiation), *L2* (data instantiation) and *L3* (run-time provenance) of increasing precision and decreasing level of abstraction. Formal approaches to the representation of provenance [9,25,27], and generic standards for interchange of provenance information[1] have been proposed.

Efficient storage and querying of provenance information (which may be voluminous) is another important aspect. Using efficient representation based on the type of provenance is a standard approach, among other techniques [4].

A common way to construct and evaluate provenance systems consists in defining *queries* that the provenance has to answer [9]. Such a use-case driven approach is common in the domain as is shown by provenance challenges evaluating capabilities of provenance systems [26].

Hierarchical logging, which is essential to our approach to track the provenance of experiments, is often used to provide a way of looking at series of events in a way that would be otherwise difficult with a linear representation. Recently, *systemd*[2] benefited from this approach to improve logging of Unix services.

From this overview we conclude that there are numerous aspects of provenance and fragmented initiatives to provide it. The lack of general provenance tracking is mainly due to different requirements imposed by different domains. In the next sections, we will observe how provenance collection is addressed in different domains of computer science. To this end, we turn to provenance in general computing, scientific workflows, control-flows and in distributed systems research.

2.2   Provenance in General Computing

In this section, we explore how provenance is provided in a general context (programming languages, scientific computing, data analysis, etc.). Provenance in general computing is rarely addressed, at least explicitly. First, provenance collection always incurs overhead that may make it unfeasible to use (e.g., in high-performance computing). Moreover, each subdomain of computing calls for a different approach and therefore can be impractical and tedious to implement in each case. We will see that provenance is, with some exceptions, often addressed in *ad hoc* manner and in a very limited sense.

Some notions of provenance in database systems has been proposed [8], the most common describing relationship between a data source, a query and the results of query execution.

Software documentation is a form of prospective provenance information that explains how the software works (or should work). *Literate programming* [22] proposes to have a verbose, natural-language description interwoven with code in a single document. Similar initiatives have been proposed in the scientific context (e.g., *literate experimentation* [31]).

A useful source of provenance is provided by *instrumentation* and *monitoring*. Deep instrumentation or monitoring may be intrusive for the execution, and change the behavior of the studied system or even cause it to malfunction.

---

[1] http://www.w3.org/TR/prov-overview/.

[2] http://freedesktop.org/wiki/Software/systemd/.

The history of how experiments evolved over time is also a form of provenance and is generally provided by version control systems (Git, Subversion, Mercurial, etc.). These systems trace the content of individual files and have no semantic knowledge about the whole system. Many systems, programming languages being a prime example, offer therefore language-specific *software archives* that host code that can be referenced (e.g., PyPI for Python or Hackage for Haskell). Studies of large, language-agnostic software repositories have been done as well, showing interesting aspects of long-term software evolution (e.g., Debsources [7]). Some retrospective studies trace authorship of modern BSD systems, as far as 40 years into the past [32].

There are solutions that build on version control systems and aim at automated capture of experiment context for easier reproducibility of research [14]. More recently, researchers propose experimental workflows based on Git branching model and literate programming with Org-mode [33].

2.3 Provenance in Scientific Workflows

Scientific workflows describe the set of tasks needed to carry out a computational experiment [16]. Their role usually consists in carrying out the computation using a given infrastructure (e.g., a computational grid or virtual machines in a cloud), but without going into details about how exactly these operations are executed. Therefore scientific workflow systems provide a high-level abstraction of computing and are used even by non-technical researchers. The efficient mapping, scheduling and execution of scientific workflows is a vivid domain of research.

The standard representation of scientific workflows uses acyclic *data-flows* to describe transformations of input data in a structured way. The acyclic graph structure implies a natural way to collect data provenance by workflow systems. The data-centric nature of scientific workflows is a well-known fact: it has been observed that the *data preparation* (i.e., initial transformation of input data to useful representation) accounts for more than 50 % of workflow structure [20].

The history of how experimental workflows evolved is rarely tracked, with some exceptions. For example VisTrails [18] enables to backtrack from a failed approach by storing historical changes in a tree.

Similarly, details of the underlying platform are also rarely collected. Since the premise of scientific workflow systems is to abstract the details of the computing platform away and still obtain qualitatively equivalent results, this is understandable. This type of provenance can be still useful, for example for debugging, but is not essential.

Examples of scientific workflow systems include Kepler, Pegasus, Taverna, and VisTrails; see [34,36] for surveys of scientific workflow systems. The details of provenance support in scientific workflow systems are explored thoroughly [19].

2.4 Provenance in Control-Flows

For the purpose of this article, we define *control-flows* as workflows consisting of a set of activities that are performed under causal, temporal and spatial constraints to achieve a specific goal, such as, in the context of this article, the collection of experimental results. This definition is closely related to the one of *business processes* in Business Process Modeling (BPM) [23]. The differences between control-flows and data-flows are studied quite extensively [3,24], including the expressiveness of both formalisms [10]. The most important distinction is that data-flows are data-centric, contrary to control-flows.

The provenance collection in BPM and control-flows does not seem to be very much explored yet. This may be due to mentioned difficulties and due to proprietary nature of many BPM systems. To our knowledge, this article may be the first to explore provenance tracking in control-flows to a larger extent.

2.5   Provenance in Experimental Distributed Systems Research

Research in distributed systems developed a wide range of methods to tame the complexity associated with experimentation. These methods can be grouped into four methodologies: simulation, benchmarking, emulation and *in-situ* experiments [21]. The *in-situ* methodology, which we focus on in this work, consists in running a real system on a real platform, and arguably requires the most extensive provenance coverage among all methodologies.

There are various solutions that control executions of *in-situ* experiments on real platforms (e.g., Plush [1], OMF [29]). The support for provenance tracking in these tools is almost nonexistent [5].

Recording and subsequently restoring the state of platform configuration is another aspect of provenance addressed to some extent by system configuration management tools like Puppet, Chef or Salt. NixOS [17] takes a more generic approach of declarative and stateless description of full system.

3   New Classification of Provenance

As has been observed above, there are many different ways to provide provenance information and methods differ between domains. In this section, we will observe that for any form of computation executed on a system like grid, cloud, or any computing platform, the general provenance can be split into 3 different types. More precisely, we will show that apart from the *provenance of data* two other types of provenance exist: the *provenance of description* and the *provenance of process*, and that all three are useful and even necessary for a complete provenance system. Although this article concentrates on the domain of experimental distributed systems research, the discussion in this section is general and applies to scientific workflow systems and even outside the scientific context.

To explain the existence of these three types of provenance, we make the following observations about *entities* that are present in an arbitrary computation on a computing platform. First, from an abstract point of view, there are two elements necessary to run it: its abstract *description* and a physical platform. The platform consists of physical *machines*, network *equipment*, installed *software* and other details. The execution of the given computation may have useful *runtime* information and may produce, receive or transform arbitrary *data*. All these objects can be separated into 3 different classes (see Table 1 for a summary).

Note that L2 provenance (data instantiation) is not covered, since experiments we focus on do not take raw data as input. However, if need be, L2 provenance can be classified under the provenance of data.

Table 1. Summary of the three proposed provenance types their position in existing classifications. L2 provenance is not present in most distributed research experiments.

Name	Entities	Moment of collection [13]	Level [2]
Data	Results, monitoring data, platform configuration	Retrospective	L3 (and L2, if present)
Description	Experiment description, platform specification	Prospective	L0 and L1
Process	Runtime information	Retrospective	L3

Provenance of data is information on how data objects were created and transformed during the execution of the given computation. This is a type of provenance that is largely synonymous with provenance itself due to its successful application in scientific workflow systems. Moreover, data provenance is *implied* by the structure of a data-flow, that is, its interpretation and representation is derived from the original structure of a data-flow.

According to the existing classifications (see [2,13]), the provenance of data is of *retrospective* and *runtime* (L3) type. It may also cover L2 provenance (data instantiation), however it is not the case in our domain.

Provenance of description is information on how the description of the computation evolved as a function of time and how its constituents came to be. This provenance type is a form of documentation, but has multiple other uses. In particular it may track dependencies of the computation, as well as authorship information, among others. We will see that in our proposed approach even more features are present (see Sect. 4.2).

This provenance is *prospective* and covers the levels L0 and L1 of provenance.

Provenance of process constitutes metadata that document details of how the execution of the computation progressed. In particular, it includes information on how it behaved in time (e.g., *when* parts of it executed) and in space (e.g., which machines were involved during execution). This kind of information is useful to understand the inner workings of the computation and the system, and resolve problems when they happen. Additionally, it documents the execution for reproducibility purposes. The provenance of process is implied by the control-flow structure, just like data provenance is implied by the structure of scientific workflows (see Sect. 4.3).

The provenance of process is *retrospective* and of *runtime* (L3) type.

One can argue, that all the mentioned supplementary types of provenance can be considered like any other data that, by definition, is tracked by the provenance of data. There are nevertheless a few reasons that warrant such a distinction.

First, the provenance of description operates at a higher level than the others. Indeed, the information it provides would not normally require the execution of the given computation, unlike the others. Second, as we will see in Sect. 4, different types of questions can be posed for each type of provenance. The presented distinction allows for more efficient storage and access, as well as more appropriate representation and visualization. Finally, provenance information is difficult to query without structured data and may be overwhelming both conceptually and in terms of resource requirements. For this reason, virtually every approach models provenance information in one way or another.

4   Design of a Provenance System

In Sect. 3 we introduced a new classification of provenance into three types. This section proposes a design of a system that takes as an assumption the control-flow structure of experiment description. Our decision is dictated by promising results obtained while running large-scale, challenging experiments represented as business processes [6]. To represent experiments, the BPM workflow patterns [35] are used, extended with *experimental patterns* that include parallel execution of commands, failure handling, etc. We have shown previously that under sensible assumptions large-scale experiments can be run robustly.

First, let us explicitly state assumptions guiding our discussion and design:

1. The experiment follows *in-situ* methodology in distributed systems research.
2. The experiment description is a control-flow based on workflow patterns.
3. The data processing does not constitute a large fraction of the experiment execution. If it is not the case then it would be reasonable to use a scientific workflow system instead.

For such an experiment, one can ask a question about requirements of a prospective provenance system. We take the following approach: (1) we find *entities* that can be distinguished in the experiment, (2) we define *questions* that can be asked about them.

The first part has been already done in the previous section. As for the second step, we start with a general principle that for a given entity X the two following pieces of information describe fully its provenance: (1) the origin of X and (2) the logical, spatial and temporal context of X.

For the objects stored as the provenance of experiment data, the prospective questions ask which activities created the given datum (logical), which physical nodes or equipment was involved (spatial) and when that datum was collected (temporal). In the case of the provenance of experiment description this leads to questions about authorship of code (logical), about the dependencies between modules (logical) and about the changes to the experiment in time (temporal; there is no spatial context, however). Finally, in the context of the provenance

Fig. 1. High-level workflow description of the exemplary experiment (modified BPMN notation). Each runtime is sequentially installed and evaluated with Linpack benchmark. Note that some parts of the workflow refer to external repositories.

Table 2. Summary of provenance types, the objects and relations they are concerned about and examples of queries that one may ask for each of them.

Type of provenance	Examples of queries
Data	*Which node produced the highest benchmark result?*
	What was the runtime system configuration of the nodes?
Description	*What are the dependencies of the experiment?*
	Are there newer versions of modules?
	Who is the author of the activity X?
Process	*What is the Gantt diagram of the experiment?*
	What is the critical path of the experiment?
	What are the failure rates of activities?
Data & Description	*Did the system specification reflect reality?*
Data & Process	*What activities executed at the node X?*
Description & Process	*Who authored a change that caused the experiment to fail?*
All types	*Who is the author of a module that produced the result X?*

of experiment process this information reduces to details on how the experiment activities executed with respect to each other and the experiment description (logical), where they executed (spatial) and when they executed (temporal).

This analysis leads to examples of questions presented in Table 2. In the following sections, a design of a provenance system is presented. It consists of three subsystems, each capturing one type of the defined provenance. We observe that the natural representation for the provenance of data, the provenance of description and the provenance of process is: by a directed graph, by a rooted acyclic graph, and by a hierarchical tree, respectively. We illustrate the discussion with an abstract example of performance evaluation of MPI runtimes with Linpack benchmark (see Fig. 1 for its workflow description).

4.1 Provenance of Experiment Data

As observed before, capturing and storing the provenance of data is a challenging task with many difficulties. However, due to our special use case (i.e., control-flow based experiments in distributed systems research) we were able to make a few assumptions. In particular, since the data transformation does not constitute a significant portion of experiments we are interested in, we can store the provenance of data (and data itself) in mostly unstructured way. As a result, we propose a simple key-value store, e.g., BerkeleyDB [28]. Distributed key stores may be preferred if high-availability or scalability is requested (e.g., Dynamo [15]). Objects stored as the provenance of data may reference each other, although we do not optimize for queries involving these relations. Abstractly, data provenance is an *arbitrary directed graph*, that presumably is sparse.

Each datum in the store has its *name*, *type*, *value* and optional *annotations*. The *name* is an identifier (not necessarily unique) of the given data artifact in the context of the current experiment run. Its *type* defines a group of objects it belongs to (e.g., nodes, results) and can be used to optimize queries by narrowing them down to a subset of elements in the store. The *value* of the datum is its raw value, it may be, for example, the result of a benchmark on a node. Finally, optional annotations are used to link the data to related entities, for example to the node that the result comes from, or a timestamp when this data object was stored. They may also link to other types of provenance.

The data stored must be explicitly marked as such. There are two reasons behind: (1) contrary to data-flows, in control-flows it is not explicitly known what *constitutes* data, (2) it narrows down the scope of what is collected and improves performance. Nevertheless, some elements of data provenance can be collected automatically, the configuration of the platform, for example.

The data provenance collected in the exemplary MPI experiment consists of benchmark results (*benchmark* type), and runtime configuration of nodes (*node* type). The benchmark results point to nodes that participated in the execution and to instances of activities that produced them (see Sect. 4.3).

4.2   Provenance of Experiment Description

In this section, we provide a design for a representation of experiments that traces the provenance of the experiment description. By *experiment description* we mean the workflow of actions executed as experiment.

Our solution to this problem is inspired by software engineering, more precisely, by (1) a version control system (Git) to track evolution and authorship of the description and (2) a module system based on programming languages (Go) to improve reproducibility, document dependencies and facilitate collaboration. Note that creative use of Git branching model is nothing new [14, 33].

However, as Git tracks content at the level of files, it does not meet all our needs. For that reason we propose a simple, yet powerful and easy to use module system that is built on top of it. It adds an additional layer that tracks dependencies of experiments. The approach is modular and ensures reproducibility and consistency of the experiment description, while remaining easy to use.

The experiment and its modules is tracked in a Git repository, and *tags* represent its evolution. Dependencies of the experiment follow the same scheme and are referenced as a pointer to a *tag* in another *repository*. It implies that a pair (*repository*, *tag*) unambiguously defines the experiment description with

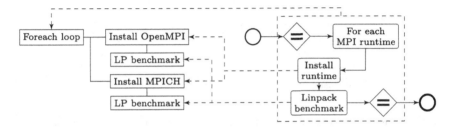

Fig. 2. Example of a mapping between the control-flow and its log. Nesting of workflows implies the hierarchical structure of the log, as is shown with dashed edges.

its all transitive dependencies. Cycles in the dependency graph are forbidden, hence the provenance of description is a *directed, acyclic graph*.

In our exemplary experiment, the main workflow references well-defined versions of modules with MPI support (module *MPI*) and Linpack support (module *Linpack*). Moreover, the latter depends on the former to launch itself.

The repositories containing the workflows can be hosted at social software repositories like GitHub, which offer useful features supporting collaboration, innovation, knowledge sharing and community building [11].

4.3   Provenance of Experiment Process

In this section we start with analysis of control-flows (based on business processes) and observe that their structure maps to a hierarchical log. We then use this structure as a representation of the process provenance.

Just like scientific workflows imply the structure of data provenance, the structure of an experiment represented as a control-flow implies a form of process provenance. From a high-level point of view, a BPM-like data-flow can be defined either as an *activity* (a basic, atomic action) or as a *pattern* (e.g., a sequence of activities). Other patterns have been defined in the literature [35].

In the example in Fig. 2, we see the same workflow that was shown in Fig. 1, and associated structure of the provenance of process. In particular, subworkflows map deeper into the log hierarchy. We see therefore that the natural representation for the provenance of process is a *hierarchical tree*.

Each log entry has some predefined data recorded: a timestamp when its execution started, timestamp when its execution finished and the node where it was executed. The log entries annotate their log with relevant information, such as data produced by this activity or a pointer to the source code. The log can be stored in the key-value store used to store the provenance of data.

5   Conclusions and Future Work

This paper made three contributions. First, we analyzed the provenance in different disciplines of computer science. Then we observed that provenance can

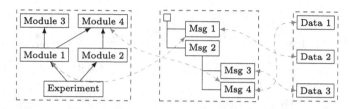

Fig. 3. Interactions between 3 types of provenance. The central role is occupied by the process provenance. It refers two-sidedly to the description provenance and to the data provenance, with no direct links between them.

be split into three different types: the provenance of data, the provenance of description and the provenance of process. Finally, we designed a provenance system for distributed systems research that can capture all of them (see Fig. 3).

Currently, we focus on the implementation. We also plan to enhance the presented design: in particular, we want to consider a formal model of provenance and verify that all useful queries can be answered within its framework.

References

1. Albrecht, J., et al.: Planetlab application management using plush. ACM SIGOPS Oper. Syst. Rev. **40**, 33–40 (2006)
2. Barga, R.S., et al.: Automatic capture and efficient storage of e-science experiment provenance. Conc. Comp. Pract. Experience **20**(5), 419–429 (2008)
3. Barker, A., van Hemert, J.: Scientific workflow: a survey and research directions. In: Wyrzykowski, R., Dongarra, J., Karczewski, K., Wasniewski, J. (eds.) PPAM 2007. LNCS, vol. 4967, pp. 746–753. Springer, Heidelberg (2008)
4. Biton, O., et al.: Querying and managing provenance through user views in scientific workflows. In: Proceedings of the 24th International Conference on Data Engineering, pp. 1072–1081, ICDE 2008, Washington, DC, USA (2008)
5. Buchert, T., et al.: A survey of general-purpose experiment management tools for distributed systems. Future Gener. Comput. Syst. **45**, 1–12 (2014)
6. Buchert, T., et al.: A workflow-inspired, modular and robust approach to experiments in distributed systems. In: The 14th International Symposium on Cluster, Cloud and Grid Computing, Chicago, Illinois, USA (2014)
7. Caneill, M., et al.: Debsources: live and historical views on macro-level software evolution. In: Proceedings of the 8th International Symposium on Empirical Software Engineering and Measurement, pp. 28:1–28:10, ESEM 2014, New York, NY, USA (2014)
8. Cheney, J., et al.: Provenance in databases: why, how, and where. Found. Trends databases **1**(4), 379–474 (2009)
9. Cohen, S., et al.: Towards a model of provenance and user views in scientific workflows. In: Proceedings of the Third Internaitonal Confernce on Data Integration in the Life Sciences, DILS 2006, pp. 264–279 (2006)
10. Curcin, V., et al.: Scientific workflow systems - can one size fit all? In: Biomedical Engineering Conference, pp. 1–9 (2008)

11. Dabbish, L., et al.: Social coding in github: transparency and collaboration in an open software repository. In: Proceedings of the ACM Conference on Computer Supported Cooperative Work, pp. 1277–1286, CSCW 2012, New York, NY, USA (2012)
12. Davidson, S.B., et al.: Provenance in scientific workflow systems. IEEE Data Eng. Bull. **30**(4), 44–50 (2007)
13. Davidson, S.B., et al.: Provenance and scientific workflows: challenges and opportunities. In: Proceedings of ACM SIGMOD, pp. 1345–1350 (2008)
14. Davison, A.: Automated capture of experiment context for easier reproducibility in computational research. Comput. Sci. Eng. **14**(4), 48–56 (2012)
15. DeCandia, G., et al.: Dynamo: amazon's highly available key-value store. SIGOPS Oper. Syst. Rev. **41**(6), 205–220 (2007)
16. Deelman, E., et al.: Workflows and e-science: an overview of workflow system features and capabilities. Future Gener. Comput. Syst. **25**(5), 528–540 (2009)
17. Dolstra, E., et al.: Nixos: a purely functional linux distribution. In: Proceedings of the 13th International Conference on Functional Programming, pp. 367–378. ICFP 2008 (2008)
18. Freire, J.-L., Silva, C.T., Callahan, S.P., Santos, E., Scheidegger, C.E., Vo, H.T.: Managing Rapidly-Evolving Scientific Workflows. In: Moreau, L., Foster, I. (eds.) IPAW 2006. LNCS, vol. 4145, pp. 10–18. Springer, Heidelberg (2006)
19. Freire, J., et al.: Provenance for computational tasks: a survey. Comput. Sci. Eng. **10**(3), 11–21 (2008)
20. Garijo, D., et al.: Common motifs in scientific workflows: an empirical analysis. Future Gener. Comput. Syst. **36**, 338–351 (2014)
21. Gustedt, J., et al.: Experimental methodologies for large-scale systems: a survey. Parallel Process. Lett. **19**(3), 399–418 (2009)
22. Knuth, D.E.: Literate programming. Comput. J. **27**(2), 97–111 (1984)
23. Ko, R.K.L.: A computer scientist's introductory guide to business process management (bpm). Crossroads **15**(4), 4:11–4:18 (2009)
24. Ludäscher, B., et al.: Scientific workflow management and the kepler system. Concurrency Comput. Pract. Experience **18**(10), 1039–1065 (2006)
25. McPhillips, T., et al.: Scientific workflow design for mere mortals. Future Gener. Comput. Syst. **25**(5), 541–551 (2009)
26. Moreau, L., et al.: Special issue: the first provenance challenge. Concurrency Comput. Pract. Experience **20**(5), 409–418 (2008)
27. Moreau, L., et al.: The open provenance model core specification (v1.1). Future Gener. Comput. Syst. **27**(6), 743–756 (2011)
28. Olson, M.A., et al.: Berkeley db. In: Proceedings of the Annual USENIX Technical Conference, pp. 43–43, ATEC 1999, Berkeley, CA, USA (1999)
29. Rakotoarivelo, T., et al.: Omf: a control and management framework for networking testbeds. ACM SIGOPS Oper. Syst. Rev. **43**(4), 54–59 (2010)
30. Simmhan, Y.L., et al.: A survey of data provenance in e-science. SIGMOD Rec. **34**(3), 31–36 (2005)
31. Singer, J.: A literate experimentation manifesto. In: Proceedings of the 10th SIGPLAN Symposium on New Ideas, New Paradigms, and Reflections on Programming and Software, pp. 91–102, ONWARD 2011, ACM, New York, NY, USA (2011)
32. Spinellis, D.: A repository with 44 years of unix evolution. In: Proceedings of the 12th Working Conference on Mining Software Repositories, pp. 13–16. IEEE (2015)
33. Stanisic, L., et al.: An effective git and org-mode based workflow for reproducible research. SIGOPS Oper. Syst. Rev. **49**(1), 61–70 (2015)

34. Talia, D.: Workflow systems for science: Concepts and tools. ISRN Soft. Eng. **2013**, 15 (2013)
35. Van Der Aalst, W.M.P., et al.: Workflow patterns. Distrib. Parallel Databases **14**(1), 5–51 (2003)
36. Yu, J., et al.: A taxonomy of scientific workflow systems for grid computing. SIGMOD Rec. **34**, 44–49 (2005)

Resilience - Resiliency in High Performance Computing with Clouds, Grids, and Clusters

A Case Study of Application Structure Aware Resilience Through Differentiated State Saving and Recovery

Anshu Dubey[1]([✉]), Hajime Fujita[2], Zachary Rubenstein[2], Brian Van Straalen[1], and Andrew A. Chien[2,3]

[1] Computational Research Division Lawrence Berkeley National Laboratory, Berkeley, CA 94720, USA
adubey@lbl.gov
[2] Computer Science Department, University of Chicago, Chicago, IL 60637, USA
[3] Argonne National Laboratory, Mathematics and Computer Science Division, Argonne, Lemont, IL, USA

Abstract. Resilience is a growing concern for large-scale simulations. As failures become more frequent, alternatives to global checkpointing that limit the extent of needed recovery become more desirable. Additionally, platforms will differ in both error rates and types, therefore, a flexible and customizable recovery strategy will be extremely helpful to the applications running on these platforms. Applications often have structures that provide logical confinement spaces that can be exploited for this purpose. We investigate a customizable recovery strategy using Chombo, a structured adaptive mesh refinement (SAMR) library, as a case study. We exploit the inherent granularities and hierarchy in SAMR to limit the impact of faults for localized recovery, and identify tunable parameters for customizing the strategy depending upon the application and platform behavior. We use Global View Resilience (GVR) library, which provides global versioning arrays for application-controlled state saving as our resiliency interface.

1 Introduction

In order to effectively utilize future large-scale, high performance computers, applications will face several challenges, including more frequent failures that manifest themselves in various ways. The usual mode of checkpoint-restart is already reaching the limit of its usefulness in large-scale simulations where a non-trivial fraction of execution time is taken up by the checkpointing process. The restarts tend to be even slower than the checkpoints and even a node failure every few hours can prove to be significantly detrimental to the applications' runtime and computational efficiency. The checkpoints and restarts are slow because they use global snapshots and parallel file system for read and write. As the number of nodes involved in a calculation increases, the mean time between node failures proportionately decreases. Node failures usually cause an abort followed by job termination in the batch queue.

© Springer International Publishing Switzerland 2015
S. Hunold et al. (Eds.): Euro-Par 2015 Workshops, LNCS 9523, pp. 619–630, 2015.
DOI: 10.1007/978-3-319-27308-2_50

To deal with frequent failures, several applications have developed the ability to avoid "abort" when there is a failure, thereby avoiding the job termination. The application is able to restart itself from a previously saved checkpoint in the same job slot and continue execution. However, there is still the cost of reading from the file system and restarting, and the cost of lost calculations since the last checkpoint. There are many efforts to provide more efficient ways of checkpointing such as: non-blocking multilevel checkpointing [12], replication-based checkpointing [15], or localized checkpointing/restart [13]. Although these, and other new technologies that will eliminate the involvement of the file system in checkpointing, are expected to reduce the costs of state saving substantially, these technologies do not adequately address the variability of error rates in different application instances. For that we need a flexible, local and customizable recovery strategy.

One option for local recovery is to carry redundant information on surrounding nodes from which a consistent global state can be reconstructed in case of a node failure. This approach was explored in an oct-tree based SAMR code, FLASH [4,5], in [6]. Another option is to exploit the structure within the application for local state saving recovery, for example [13]. Some methods combine more than one approach to achieve fault tolerance, for example [14] makes use of adaptive fault-tolerance through both checkpointing and redundancy. In this paper we take a multi-pronged approach to fault tolerance. Similar to containment domains we use the application structure to confine the extent of recovery [2]. But unlike containment domains we tailor our recovery mechanisms to specific error modes. Additionally, we make use of tuning parameters based on cost-benefit analysis to explore the available trade-offs.

We use Chombo [3], a general purpose SAMR library, augmented with the Global View Resilience (GVR) library, [7] as a case study for our approach. GVR leaves the definition of the consistent state to be saved up to the application. This allows applications to decompose their state into smaller, more localized snapshots from which recovery can be effected with minimal impact or interaction with the overall global state. Additionally, the versioning capability of GVR further reduces the cost of saving individual local snapshots as long their definition does not undergo any change. Also, the co-existence of several versions of the snapshot (the extent of versioning is also under application control) gives further flexibility in devising the recovery strategy.

The Chombo-GVR interface can recover from both resource failure and transient data corruption. Recovery from resource failure itself can be either global or local depending on circumstances. The transient data corruption errors within a node can be handled locally if they are detected immediately and their extent is known to be confined to the node. Depending upon the difficulty and/or delay in transient error detection (which is out of scope of this paper) a non-local recovery may be necessary. In future we may also include forward error correction that could use the corresponding data from coarser parts of the mesh for reconstruction similar to [6].

The focus and main contribution of this paper is devising a recovery strategy that exploits the application's structure and granularities, and provides tunable parameters for customization. We take the approach of identifying the logical confinement regions of the state spatially and temporally, and examining the error modes that can be mapped to these regions. We then devise a recovery strategy for each error mode and map it to the corresponding granularity in the application. In the final step we model the overheads for cost-benefit analysis. Though we use SAMR as our case study, our approach should be equally useful to other applications which have nested granularities or hierarchies. The paper is organized as follows, we first give a brief description of the two libraries, Chombo and GVR, in Sect. 2, followed by a discussion of the local saving and reconstruction strategy in Sect. 3. Section 4 describes preliminary cost measurements of the overheads introduced into the application by the resiliency strategy, and how they can be used as tuning parameters for specific computing platforms and/or specific instances of application use. Finally, conclusions and future work are discussed in Sect. 5.

2   The Libraries

Chombo defines patches of uniform resolution (finer) that are embedded within other patches of lower resolution (coarser) as shown in Fig. 1. Patches can be subdivided into boxes, all boxes with the same resolution constitute a level, where individual boxes may be distributed arbitrarily in physical space as long as they are fully enclosed within a region of next level of coarse resolution. Therefore a level can be viewed either as a logical entity (same resolution) (see Fig. 2) or a physical entity (union of all boxes at the same resolution), and Chombo's data structures allow either view. The solution advances with the same time-step everywhere on a given level, though it differs from other levels if subcycling is being used. With subcycling, for a refinement ratio **R** the finer level takes **R** steps for every step taken by the embedding coarse level. Most of bookkeeping in Chombo is managed on a level-by-level basis, with some cross-level management. The level meta-information includes knowledge of all boxes with their integer index space within the global mesh. This information can be harnessed to determine the adjacency of boxes for the purpose of filling the halo of ghost cells as needed. The information is also used to distribute the load among processors. The cross-level management is used for purposes such as filling the ghost cells for boxes that exist at fine-coarse boundaries, to reconcile various physical quantities such as fluxes as the fine-coarse boundaries, and synchronization of time-advancement when there is sub-cycling.

The depth of AMR hierarchy depends upon the scientific domain and the specific application. The count and shape of the patches and their boxes is not static, it changes as necessary when the solution evolves. The finer patches follow more structure in the solution space, with the finest ones existing where there is maximum structure and therefore smallest length scales in the physical domain. With subcycling the finer levels do considerably more work than the

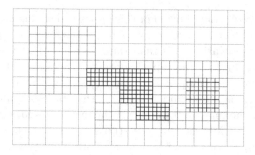

Fig. 1. SAMR mesh showing three levels of resolution.

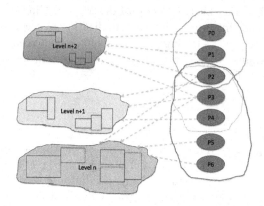

Fig. 2. A logical view of multiple levels of resolution in an AMR mesh.

coarser levels, which is why each level does its own load distribution. This way all compute resources get a mix of levels and therefore roughly equal amount of work.

GVR is a lightweight library which enables applications to run reliably on unreliable computers. It provides two main features: multi-version, multi-stream distributed arrays and a unified error handling interface. GVR provides PGAS-style distributed arrays (similar to Global Arrays [11]), but extends them with primitives to create persistent *versions* [16]. Multiple versions enable applications to perform more powerful recovery from complex errors such as *latent errors*, which cannot be detected immediately (see [8]). Different arrays can choose optimal versioning cadences depending on the array. GVR also provides a unified error handling interface for various error sources, through which application can receive error events and handle the errors. This allows application programmers to reuse an error handler for different error causes, thus reducing the cost for writing error handlers.

As mentioned in Sect. 1, GVR allows the application to define what constitutes a consistent recoverable state, and what goes into each array. In addition, GVR places no restriction on how many arrays can be defined by an application, and being PGAS-style distributed arrays, provides random access anywhere within an array. The GVR interface works by allocating arrays as requested by the application, and then letting the application store data through "put" functions. When it is safe to save the state of an array, the application can create a version through the "version_inc" function. Created versions are accessible to the application by specifying the appropriate version number. The "put" functions allow random access within the array. Similar to "put", the "get" function is used to fetch arbitrary information from a specified version of an array. There are also no restrictions on the amount of information that can be fetched in one instance of using "get". Therefore the granularity of information exchanged with an array is also under the control of the application. These flexible accessibility features of GVR, and its low overheads, make it particularly attractive for exploring containment and differentiation based recovery strategies in applications where the structure of the application can be exploited for this purpose.

GVR takes two measures to protect the contents of the array. The first measure is preserving multiple versions. GVR's API defines that old versions are read-only, which makes it easier for the library to store them in a different location or to apply coding, compression, encryption, etc. to the data. Then as a second measure, GVR stores an old version of an array in a different process' memory or a secondary storage such as node-local SSD or parallel shared file system, in order to protect the array data from resource failures such as node/process crash. When storing old versions in a secondary storage, GVR utilizes Scalable Checkpoint Restart [9] to exploit multi-level storage hierarchy and its data protection schemes for node-local storage.

3 Resilience Strategy

Our resiliency strategy is based on five simple ideas.

– Check if there is any hierarchy to be exploited in the application's structure.
– Identify granularities within the application that can be used to confine the impact of the fault and recovery from it.
– Consider the types of faults that the strategy is expected to handle, and map recovery from each fault type to the appropriate granularity of the application.
– At each granularity determine the minimum state to be saved to effect a full recovery.
– Identify tuning parameters to enable customization to specific instances of application execution.

The default checkpointing in Chombo, like many other production-grade high-performance computing (HPC) applications, saves a global snapshot of the state into a parallel file using HDF5 [10] library. Such global snapshots are saved at regular intervals, and therefore an attempt is made to minimize the amount of saved information that can be used to reconstruct the complete AMR hierarchy without any loss upon restart. For this purpose Chombo needs to save a very small amount of global state meta-information and also a moderate amount of level-specific meta-information in addition to the physical data residing on each box. Because the snapshot is global, it can only be done when all the levels are synchronized. By definition, that is the point at which the coarsest level completes its timestep.

In order to formulate a differentiated recovery strategy for AMR we consider its inherent structures. An obvious coarse granularity in AMR is a "level" which is an almost self contained unit of computation. The meta-information of a level includes complete knowledge of all existing boxes and their mapping to the processes, the evolution time and the timestep (dt), which is uniform for a level. Because the boxes in AMR are dynamically created and destroyed, a level can also do its own regridding and distribution of boxes among processors. A level interacts with the level below and the level above at the fine-coarse boundaries. The second, finer granularity exists at the "box" level. A box with its surrounding halo of ghost cells is a complete computational unit for the operators being applied to the field variables. If an error occurs in a box and can be detected before it spreads out to other boxes, it should be possible to completely confine the recovery to the affected box.

3.1   Saving Chombo State with GVR

For saving the state using GVR we view each level in the AMR hierarchy as a loosely independent component. Therefore, we construct one array for each level which includes the meta information as well as the physical data on all the boxes at that level. Figure 3 shows an example of mapping one AMR level to one array. For each box in the level, we include its index-space on the discretized mesh and the offset within the global array of the physical data belonging to the box. In order to complete a global snapshot we only need to add one more array for the global meta-information such as the number of field variables, the depth of mesh hierarchy, the refinement ratio between levels and the array version numbers for each level.

However, AMR presents an additional challenge to the GVR model. In a normal mode GVR operates by allocating resources for an array, which remain fixed throughout its existence. Versioning is used to preserve the array state as needed. This assumption is not valid for AMR where the resources used by a level change whenever there is a regridding of the mesh at that level. This limitation can be overcome in one of two ways, each with its own advantage and disadvantage. One option is to free the existing array for the level and reallocate a new one every time there is regridding. This option minimizes the space used by the array but may not be very efficient in time because there will be cost of freeing and reallocating the resources. This is more important when the cost of allocation is higher than that of incrementing the version. The other option is to allocate more space for the level's array than needed and free and reallocate only when the required space exceeds the current allocation. This option may be more efficient time-wise, but is not as efficient in space usage. We have chosen the second option with extra allocation being a tunable parameter, where setting the extra allocation to zero optimizes the space usage, and can give better performance time-wise if the size of the mesh data for the level does

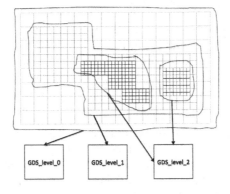

Fig. 3. Mapping AMR levels to GVR arrays

not increase with every regrid event. Such a scenario can arise, for example, where the higher refinement is following a shock. Here the part of the physical domain which is highly refined changes with time, but the amount of highly refined domain may not change very much.

Populating the Arrays. The initial state saving requires making an estimate of space to be allocated for the global meta-data and the level arrays. We populate them at the beginning of the simulation as soon as the mesh is initialized. The cadence of state-saving at each level is a tunable parameter. When it is time to save the state, the physical data of the boxes and meta-information such as "current_time" that change at every timestep are updated in the array and the version of the array is increased. A regrid event has to be treated differently. It may be necessary to reallocate an array for a level if its size has grown more than the allocation for the current array. In addition to all quantities updated at a normal timestep state save, with regrid the index-space for the boxes and their offsets also change, so they have to be updated. When no regridding is involved one can either complete a timestep computation for a level and put all the boxes data into the array at once, or one can put individual box's data as soon as it is computed within the loop. This is another tuning parameter which can be used only when state is being saved at every timestep at every level.

3.2 Failure Scenarios and Recovery Modes

We target the following failure and recovery scenarios in designing our strategy.

Permanent Resource Failure: The most common manifestation of resource degradation is node failure where recovery implies a restart on fewer nodes. Detection and notification to the application is designed be to under the control of GVR. The recovery is either global with a full restart at all levels, or it can be done at the granularity of the affected levels if situation allows. The computation will be rolled back at minimum to the beginning of the last saved timestep of the coarsest affected level. In the worst case it will have to roll back to the beginning of the last coarsest timestep saved. In the present version of Chombo resource failure recovery ends up defaulting to the global mode because all levels in the AMR hierarchy distribute their work on all processors. The instances where some levels don't have any boxes on a processor are rare. Deep AMR hierarchies with highly localized refinement patterns may benefit from non-global recovery, but those are also rare among current suite of applications using Chombo.

Temporary Resource Failure: We assume that a temporary resource failure implies that none of the data on that resource is reliable, however there is no need to reconstitute and restart. In this situation recovery at the granularity of affected levels by fetching the data from the corresponding GVR array will suffice if the snapshots were being saved at every timestep of every level. If the cadence of saving was different, consistent recovery may have to rollback further. The detection and notification to the application is again up to GVR.

Data Corruption: Data corruption is detected by the application and is a research area in its own right. In this work we are not focussing on fault detection and injection methods, except one simple detection method discussed below (also see [1] for a similar method). For many AMR applications corruption in a box can be detected by checking for $|x_n - x_{n-1}| < \epsilon$. Here x_n and x_{n-1} are the newly computed and the previous timestep's values respectively at a point in space. And ϵ is largest valid change in value at any point between two consecutive timesteps in a given operator as determined by the application expert. If data corruption is detected, we recompute x_n. There can be two possible outcomes of recomputing: the new value is the same, or it is different. If it is different from the original calculation and falls within the valid range we can either accept the value or recompute it one more time to verify correctness if more confidence is desired. However, if several errors are detected in the same box the computation for the whole box should roll back to the beginning of the timestep. The granularity of recovery is confined to a box if the last version increment was at the beginning to the current timestep. If that is not true, one has to determine the closest coarse level "m" that had a version increment at the beginning of its timestep. All finer levels including the current level and "m" have to roll back to the beginning of m's timestep. If "m = 0" it effectively becomes a global restart. If the new value is different and still outside the valid range, or if it is identical to the previously calculated one, then a more systemic problem is indicated, and the recovery may need to be abandoned. The more appropriate thing to do would be to trigger diagnostics to determine the overall state of the simulation data to see if an abort is necessary.

Meta-data Corruption: Meta-data corruption is more difficult to detect but easier to recover from. The reason why detection is difficult is because the data elements have no inherent correlation with each other. Neither is there any evolution in the values of most data elements. In current version of Chombo the meta-data is replicated on all processors, so it can simply be fetched from one of the neighbors. And if the saving is being done every timestep then it can also be fetched from GVR array. The granularity of recovery for this type of error is also at the box level. For all data corruption recoveries the random access into the GVR array is the crucial feature.

4   Tuning for a Specific Platform

Computing platforms vary in their rates and extent of failure. This will be particularly true of the future large scale platforms. Also, depending upon the specific problem being solved, the same code may run at different machine scales at different times. For some runs a local cluster is sufficient while for others a large fraction of a leadership-class machine may be necessary. Therefore, one strategy with fixed parameters is not likely to be an efficient resiliency solution everywhere. The best way to make a strategy flexible is to turn the parameters into tuning knobs wherever possible. In the current version of our strategy the tuning parameters can be: (1) the timing of various snapshots at each level, (2) whether to allocate larger array or reallocate for every regrid, (3) save as soon as every box is done or after all boxes are done, and (4) whether to trigger diagnostics upon detecting unrecoverable data error or abort.

We illustrate the cost-benefit analysis with the example of frequency of snapshots as the tuning parameter. In a state-save-recovery scenario the cost of recovery is $T_{save} + T_{lost} + T_{reconfig}$, where T_{save} is the cost of saving the snapshot, T_{lost} is the cost of lost computation which has to be redone and $T_{reconfig}$ is the cost of fetching data and reconfiguring as needed. For any level T_{save} for one snapshot is a fixed cost in between regridding steps. It includes the cost of putting necessary meta-data and the physical data from all blocks into the GVR array and incrementing the version. At regridding time it is the cost of possibly reallocating an array, putting all the meta-data and physical data into the array and incrementing its version. $T_{reconfig}$ can be as little as the cost of reading back a box's data from the last GVR array version, or it could be as large as the complete global restart. T_{lost} depends upon where the error occurred and how far back the application has to roll back.

To get an estimate of the costs involved we ran an experiment with a gas-dynamics problem where a shock hits a ramp, using built-in timers in Chombo for measurements. The quantities we measured for the AMR part of the code are the overall runtime and t_{levn}, the time to compute one timestep at level n, and $t_{reconfig}$ time for reconfiguring a level for a restart. We also measured the time to write a complete checkpoint file to the filesystem (t_{file}). For GVR we measured T_{alloc}, the time to allocate a GVR array; T_{box} time to put/get (they are very similar) one box worth of data; T_{level}, time for putting away or getting one level worth of data. The experiment was run on Edison, the Cray machine at NERSC using 128, 256, 512 and 1024 cores. For the experimental setup we used 3 levels of refinement (in all a hierarchy of 4 levels), with the problem size weak-scaling as the number of cores is increased. The parallelization model is pure MPI for the AMR, and distributed arrays for GVR. The quantities displayed in the tables are taken from measurements on rank 0 because there is very little variance in

Table 1. Measured AMR quantities in the application.

Procs	Run	t_{lev0}	t_{lev1}	t_{lev2}	t_{lev3}	$t_{reconfig}$	t_{file}
128	1581	0.82	2.65	2.91	3.13	0.63	60.33
256	1639	1.72	2.78	3.01	3.15	0.75	61.67
512	1923	1.82	2.86	3.03	3.16	1.58	125.67
1024	1841	2.19	2.83	3.01	3.18	2.9	52.67

Table 2. Measured GVR related quantities for saving state.

Procs	T_{alloc}	T_{level}	T_{box}	T_{verInc}
128	0.22	1.75	0.0048	1.02
256	0.04	1.82	0.0055	1.07
512	0.61	1.37	0.0081	0.41
1024	2.36	3.25	0.0092	1.23

timing between cores since the application operates in bulk-synchronous mode. This set of measurements are only meant to highlight the use of tuning knobs. Experimentation in many more computing environments under different fault conditions will be necessary to formulate a full cost model for AMR resiliency, and will be part of our future work.

Now let us consider a scenario where there was data corruption error in the final timestep of the finest level running on 512 cores. We can compute the cost of recovery under two contrasting snap-shot saving regimes. One where only global snapshots are being taken, and another one where every level takes its own snapshot at each one of its timesteps. Recollect that the global snapshots can only be taken when all levels are synchronized, which is the end of the coarsest time step. Here in the first scenario $T_{save} = 0.61 + 4 \times 1.37 = 6.09$ from Table 2. Assuming that we are doing subcycling $T_{lost} = 1.82 + 2 * 2.86 + 4 * 3.03 + 8 * 3.16 = 44.94$ from Table 1 and $T_{reconfig} = 1.58$ second, for the overall recovery cost of 52.61 seconds. For the second scenario the dominant cost is the saving cost because only the corrupted box will need to be read back from GVR and there is no need for reconfiguration. Again taking into account subcycling, $T_{save} = 0.61 + 1.37 + 2 * 1.37 + 4 * 1.37 + 8 * 1.37 = 20.55$, $T_{lost} = 3.16$ and $T_{reconfig} = 0.0081$, giving the cost of recovery at 23.72. The above analysis shows that different fault scenarios should consider different snap-shot saving regimes. When data corruption errors are infrequent the fixed cost of saving every timestep at every level will be an overkill. Whereas when the data corruption errors are frequent, taking the global snapshots only strategy could cause the application to repeat computations often, thereby costing much more than the fixed cost of T_{save} at higher cadence.

5   Future Work

We have presented a methodology for spatial and temporal decomposition of a complex but highly structured application in order to devise a differentiated resiliency strategy. This kind of approach is particularly important for the class of problems that do not have the option of devising fault-resistant computations. These applications have to rely on rollback-recovery, so minimizing its cost is very important to them. An important part of cost minimization is evaluation of the trade-offs between overheads and lost work with different error rates in different platforms and application instances. To facilitate this evaluation we have shown how tuning knobs can be incorporated in the strategy. One aspect of transient error recovery mode was not explored in this work: forward error correction through reconstructing from lower fidelity coarse grid data. Additionally, the cost model is preliminary, it does not take into account the possible delays, and therefore lost work, in transient error detection. Both these aspects of resiliency tend to be specific to an application instance and also domain dependent, and are not understood very well. Further out we will extend the forward-error correction work from [6] to cover more application domains that use AMR. As error detection in AMR matures, we will incorporate the error detection related costs in our model.

Acknowledgments. This work was supported by the Office of Advanced Scientific Computing Research, Office of Science, U.S. Department of Energy and completed in part with resources provided by NERSC, a DOE user facility supported by the Office of Science.

References

1. Berrocal, E., Bautista-Gomez, L., Di, S., Lan, Z., Cappello, F.: Lightweight silent data corruption detection based on runtime data analysis for HPC applications. Technical report (2014)
2. Chung, J., Lee, I., Sullivan, M., Ryoo, J.H., Kim, D.W., Yoon, D.H., Kaplan, L., Erez, M.: Containment domains: a scalable, efficient, and flexible resilience scheme for exascale systems. In: The Proceedings of SC12 (2012)
3. Colella, P., Graves, D., Keen, N., Ligocki, T., Martin, D., McCorquodale, P., Modiano, D., Schwartz, P., Sternberg, T., Van Straalen, B.: Chombo software package for AMR applications design document. Technical report, LBNL, Applied Numerical Algorithms Group, Computational Research Division (2009)
4. Dubey, A., Antypas, K., Ganapathy, M., Reid, L., Riley, K., Sheeler, D., Siegel, A., Weide, K.: Extensible component-based architecture for FLASH, a massively parallel, multiphysics simulation code. Parallel Comput. **35**(10–11), 512–522 (2009)
5. Dubey, A., Reid, L., Fisher, R.: Introduction to FLASH 3.0, with application to supersonic turbulence. In: Physica Scripta T132, : Topical Issue on Turbulent Mixing and Beyond, Results of a Conference at ICTP. Trieste, Italy, August (2008)
6. Dubey, A., Mohapatra, P., Weide, K.: Fault tolerance using lower fidelity data in adaptive mesh applications. In: Proceedings of the 3rd Workshop on Fault-tolerance for HPC at Extreme Scale, pp. 3–10. ACM (2013). http://doi.acm.org/10.1145/2465813.2465817

7. Fujita, H., Dun, N., Rubenstein, Z.A., Chien, A.A.: Log-structured global array for efficient multi-version snapshots. In: IEEE CCGrid 2015 (2015)
8. Lu, G., Zheng, Z., Chien, A.A.: When is multi-version checkpointing needed? In: Proceedings of the 3rd Workshop on Fault-tolerance for HPC at Extreme Scale, FTXS 2013. ACM (2013)
9. Moody, A., Bronevetsky, G., Mohror, K., De Supinski, B.R.: Design, modeling,and evaluation of a scalable multi-level checkpointing system. In: SC 2010 (2010)
10. NCSA: Heirarchical Data Format 5 (2008). http://hdf.ncsa.uiuc.edu/HDF5/
11. Nieplocha, J., Palmer, B., Tipparaju, V., Krishnan, M., Trease, H., Apr, E.: Advances, applications and performance of the global arrays shared memory programming toolkit. IJHPCA 20(2), 203–231 (2006)
12. Sato, K., Mohror, K., Moody, A., Gamblin, T., de Supinski, B., Maruyama, N., Matsuoka, S.: Design and modeling of a non-blocking checkpointing system. In: SC 2012 (2012)
13. Shet, A.G., Elwasif, W.R., Foley, S.S., Park, B.H., Bernholdt, D.E., Bramley, R.: Strategies for fault tolerance in multicomponent applications. Procedia Comput. Sci. 4, 2287–2296 (2011)
14. Shi, X., Pazat, J., Rodriguez, E., Jin, H., Jiang, H.: Adapting grid applications to safety using fault-tolerant methods: design, implementation and evaluations. Future Gener. Comput. Syst. 26(2), 236–244 (2010)
15. Walters, J., Chaudhary, V.: Replication-based fault tolerance for MPI applications. IEEE Trans. Parallel Distrib. Syst. 20(7), 997–1010 (2009)
16. Zheng, Z., Chien, A.A., Teranishi, K.: Fault tolerance in an inner-outer solver: a gvr-enabled case study. In: 11th International Meeting High Performance Computing for Computational Science, VECPAR 2014 (2014)

A Holistic Approach to Log Data Analysis in High-Performance Computing Systems: The Case of IBM Blue Gene/Q

Alina Sîrbu[✉] and Ozalp Babaoglu

Department of Computer Science and Engineering, University of Bologna,
Mura Anteo Zamboni 7, 40126 Bologna, Italy
{alina.sirbu,ozalp.babaoglu}@unibo.it

Abstract. The complexity and cost of managing high-performance computing infrastructures are on the rise. Automating management and repair through predictive models to minimize human interventions is an attempt to increase system availability and contain these costs. Building predictive models that are accurate enough to be useful in automatic management cannot be based on restricted log data from subsystems but requires a holistic approach to data analysis from disparate sources. Here we provide a detailed multi-scale characterization study based on four datasets reporting power consumption, temperature, workload, and hardware/software events for an IBM Blue Gene/Q installation. We show that the system runs a rich parallel workload, with low correlation among its components in terms of temperature and power, but higher correlation in terms of events. As expected, power and temperature correlate strongly, while events display negative correlations with load and power. Power and workload show moderate correlations, and only at the scale of components. The aim of the study is a systematic, integrated characterization of the computing infrastructure and discovery of correlation sources and levels to serve as basis for future predictive modeling efforts.

Keywords: Data science · Correlation analysis · HPC system monitoring · Log data integration · Predictive modeling

1 Introduction

As the size and complexity of high-performance computing (HPC) infrastructures continue to grow driven by exascale speed goals, maintaining reliability and operability levels high, while keeping management costs low, is becoming increasingly challenging. Continued reliance on human operators for management and repair is not only unsustainable, it is actually detrimental to system availability: in very large and complex settings like data centers, accidental human errors have been observed to rank second only to power system failures as the most common causes of system outages [14].

© Springer International Publishing Switzerland 2015
S. Hunold et al. (Eds.): Euro-Par 2015 Workshops, LNCS 9523, pp. 631–643, 2015.
DOI: 10.1007/978-3-319-27308-2_51

Large computing systems produce large amounts of data in the form of logs tracing resource consumption, errors, events, etc. These data can be put to use for understanding system behavior and for building predictive models to tackle the management challenges. Most studies in this direction have focused on particular subsystems rather than the system as a whole, which is a necessary condition for achieving realistic models with good predictability traits [16]. With recent progress in *Data Science* and *Big Data*, it is becoming increasingly feasible to carry out such a holistic analysis towards improving predictions by considering data from a variety of sources covering different subsystems and measures [8].

In this paper we report the results of a characterization study integrating four datasets from different subsystems in an effort to understand the behavior of a 10-rack IBM Blue Gene/Q [10] installation and quantify the correlations among power, temperature, workload, and hardware/software events as well as among different system components. In certain cases, we report the lack of correlations, which can be just as important as their presence. These results provide a first step towards identifying important features for future predictive studies.

The contributions of this paper are threefold. First, we provide a characterization of a Blue Gene/Q system from thermal, power, workload, and event log perspectives, highlighting significant features for system behavior and the presence and absence of correlations between different components. No correlation in terms of power and thermal behavior was found across components, yet events exhibit significant spatial correlations, indicating possible propagation of errors. Secondly, an integrated analysis of the four datasets searches for correlations among various metrics so as to identify further possible relations for future modeling and prediction studies. This reveals significant positive correlation between power consumption and temperature, and a weaker negative correlation between hardware/software events and power or workload. There are also indications of correlations between workload and power but only at a finer spatial granularity (at rack rather than at system scale). Thirdly, we use the preliminary indications on the importance of different features for explaining system behavior to propose a feature set to be used in future work for event prediction. An important feature of our study is its holistic nature integrating multiple datasets, to an extent not present in the literature, neither in terms of system characterization, nor in terms of correlation and predictive studies.

In the next section we describe the data, while Sect. 3 contains our analysis for individual and integrated datasets. Section 4 includes related work, and Sect. 5 discusses future predictive studies and data quality.

2   Dataset Description

Our data source is Fermi [7], an IBM Blue Gene/Q system run by CINECA, a consortium operating the largest data center in Italy. Fermi has 163,840 computing cores with a peak performance of 2.1 PFLOPS. Its workload includes large-scale models and simulations for several academic projects, including 3D models of the cell network of the heart, simulation of interaction between lasers and plasmas, neuronal network simulations, models of nano-structures and complex materials. Fermi is organized as 10 *racks*, each with 2 *mid-planes* of 16 *node-boards* with 32 16-core nodes. Each mid-plane is powered by 18 *bulk power modules* (BPM). Logging is based on standard Blue Gene/Q tools [10]. The *Mid-plane Manager Control System* performs environmental monitoring, providing power and temperature logs. The *Machine Controller* handles access to the hardware components and provides so-called *Reliability, Availability and Serviceability* (RAS) logs. Workload is extracted from the *Portable Batch System* scheduler logs, using a custom tool by CINECA. Given that all data used in our analysis originate in logs from standard Blue Gene tools, we consider the information they contain to be correct. Table 1 summarizes the four datasets.

Table 1. Four datasets that are analyzed

Dataset	Time span (2014)	Time resolution	Component	Total records
Power	28 Mar – 25 Jul	5 min	Bulk power module	9,655,298
Temperature	23 Apr – 25 Jul	15 min	Node-board	2,648,331
Workload	1 May – 27 Jul	NA	System	78,128
RAS	23 Apr – 25 Jul	NA	All	774,555

Power logs report input/output voltages and current levels for each BPM, with a 5 min resolution. By summing the input power levels over the different components, we obtained time series of power consumption for individual mid-planes, racks, and for the entire system. Power at the node-board scale cannot be reliably computed since 18 BPM power 16 node-boards (redundant system). *Temperature* logs are reported by the node-board monitor (two sensors/node-board), with a 15 min resolution. From these we computed averaged time series at node-board, mid-plane, rack, and system scales.

Workload data consist of a list of jobs with date of completion, running time, number of cores, queue time, and queue class. Fermi uses six queues, with increasing job length and core count: *serial* (on login nodes only), *debug*, *longdebug*, *smallpar*, *parallel* and *bigpar*. Two other classes — *visual* and *special* — exist, with very few jobs reserved for dedicated users. We computed the CPU time per job and time series of total daily CPU time, number of cores, and queue time. The daily CPU time per queue class was also extracted. Since only the date of job completion (not the exact time) is available in the data, totals are approximate, yet they give a very good indication of the daily load at system scale. No load information at other scales (node-board, mid-plane, rack) was available.

RAS logs consist of hardware and software events from all system components and are labeled FATAL, WARN or INFO, in decreasing order of severity. The dataset contains 163,134 FATAL, 473,982 WARN, and 137,438 INFO events. For each event, the exact time and location are included. From these data, we computed the distribution of inter-event times at system scale and also time series of the number of events in each category at various time and space resolutions.

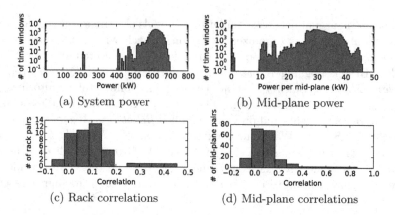

(a) System power (b) Mid-plane power

(c) Rack correlations (d) Mid-plane correlations

Fig. 1. Distribution of total power, sampled every 5 min, at system and mid-plane scale and of power correlations between racks and mid-planes.

3   Data Analysis

Each dataset alone may provide useful insight into the functioning of Fermi, while an integrated analysis has even greater potential. Hence, in this section we first study each dataset individually, identifying and comparing their features, then we integrate them to study how metrics from different subsystems correlate. Pearson correlation coefficient is used across the paper to quantify correlations.

3.1   Individual Datasets

Power Logs. The specifications for a Blue Gene/Q system declare the typical power consumption to be around 65 kW, with a maximum of 100 kW per rack [13]. However, real consumption varies depending on system load and state of components (e.g., how many nodes are up). Figure 1a–b displays the distribution of power consumption sampled at 5 min intervals, at system and mid-plane scale. Distributions are centered around the official average values: 650 kW at the system scale (10 racks) and 32.5 kW at the mid-plane scale, confirming the specifications. Moving from higher to lower scale, the distribution becomes broader. While total consumption is mostly between 50 kW and 70 kW per rack, with a bell-shaped distribution, for individual mid-planes additional peaks emerge with some showing power consumptions up to 46 kW, but also frequent values under 20 kW. Similar results were obtained at rack scale. This shows that power consumption is very heterogeneous, which needs to be taken into account for modeling. Indications are that while predicting overall system power might be easier due to greater stability in time, finer grained predictions at mid-plane scale might produce more accurate results.

It is interesting to see if power correlates across different components (racks or mid-planes). Traditional load balancing algorithms try to even out the work performed by different processing elements, and power increases with load, so we

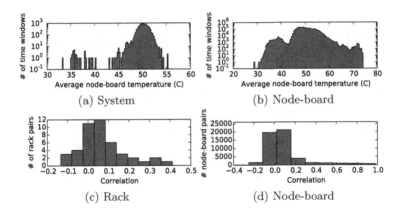

Fig. 2. Distribution of average temperatures, at system and node-board scale, and of temperature correlations among racks and node-boards.

would expect power to be correlated across different system components under heavy load. Figure 1c–d shows correlations of power consumption between rack pairs, and between mid-plane pairs. At both scales, correlations are in general very low. Only a few mid-plane pairs have correlation values above 0.5. As we will see later, the observed system load is generally high. The lack of strong correlation for power consumption among components could be interpreted as an effect of energy-aware scheduling [18], yet, this is not the case here since Fermi uses the native IBM LoadLeveler scheduler which is not optimized for power. A different explanation for the weak correlations could be poor design of the applications running on the system: if synchronization requires some program threads to wait, these will keep the nodes occupied but without using them fully. However, given the coarse resolution of the workload dataset, this hypothesis cannot be tested with the current data.

Temperature Logs. Figure. 2a–b shows histograms of average temperatures sampled every 15 min. For the overall system, with few exceptions, the distribution is again bell-shaped and narrow with one mode around 50°C. As we zoom in at node-board scale (the lowest available in the data), the distribution becomes again wider with additional peaks appearing at very high and very low temperatures. Individual node-boards can reach up to 75°C, significantly greater than the system average. Similar results were obtained at intermediate scales (rack and mid-plane). This again shows how the system appears to behave differently at different scales, with greater heterogeneity in time at the finer-grained logs. For temperature correlations among different components of the same type (Fig. 2c–d), a pattern similar to power consumption is observed. With very few exceptions, temperature exhibits low correlation across components. Results are consistent across all scales (including mid-plane not shown here). In terms of thermal isolation, this is good news, since having one hot node-board does not imply surrounding node-boards are hot as well. Yet, the fact that power

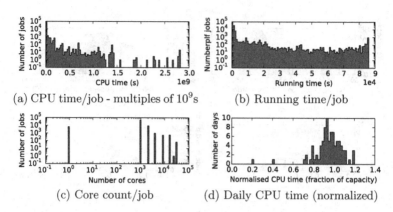

(a) CPU time/job - multiples of 10^9s   (b) Running time/job

(c) Core count/job   (d) Daily CPU time (normalized)

Fig. 3. Workload structure: distribution of CPU time, running time, number of cores per job, and CPU time consumed by jobs completed on the same day (normalized by the overall capacity of Fermi, which is 14,069,376,000 s/day).

consumption showed a similar pattern, this can be additional evidence that workload is not well balanced or applications need improvement.

Workload Logs. An important question in terms of workload regards the types of jobs submitted to the system. Figure 3a–c displays the distribution of several job attributes: CPU time, running time, and number of cores used. In terms of time requirements, jobs are very heterogeneous as evidenced by a long-tailed CPU time distribution, with a few very heavy jobs and many short jobs present. Effective running times are bimodal, with many short jobs and many long jobs (all running times under 24 h), and slightly fewer medium-length jobs. The number of cores per job is less heterogeneous, with only eight different values present, most jobs using over 100 cores and up to 32,768. So, in general, jobs are highly parallel. Out of all 78128 jobs submitted, only ~75 % were started (running times > 0) and only those will be used in the subsequent sections.

The structure of the workload data enables analysis of patterns in time only at system scale and 24 h resolution. Figure 3d shows total CPU time for all jobs *completed* each day, normalized by the overall system capacity. This does not represent the exact system load for that day, but it still is a very good indication. The data contain only the date of job completions not the exact time, making it impossible to compute how many hours each job ran in a given day — jobs completed on one day could have been started the previous day. This is why some days reach capacity exceeding 100 %. Again, roughly a bell-shaped distribution is observed, with a mean around 94 % usage, indicating very high load levels.

RAS Logs. The inter-event times at system scale, for the three event types, do not appear to follow a known distribution (Fig. 4a). FATAL events show a few very large and many very small intervals, indicating a pattern with spikes of events in short periods of time with large breaks between them. INFO and WARN events are more evenly spread in time, missing the very large inter-event times, and having a smaller fraction of very short intervals.

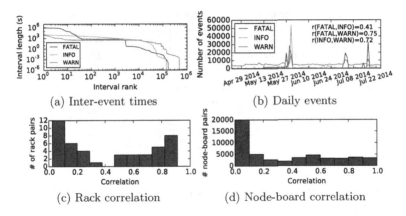

(a) Inter-event times

(b) Daily events

(c) Rack correlation

(d) Node-board correlation

Fig. 4. (a) Inter-event times for the three event categories. Intervals between events were ranked in descending order. For each interval, the x axis shows its rank and the y axis its value. (b) Total daily number of RAS events. Correlation of FATAL events for rack pairs (c) and node-board pairs (d) (Color figure online).

Figure 4b displays the time-series of daily number of events in each category and their relative correlations. WARN and INFO events are more common daily, whereas FATAL events come in spikes and appear in only a few of the monitored days. The 4 larger spikes in FATAL events correspond to issues related to the BPMs which caused shutdown of the entire system several times between 27/05 and 30/05 and shutdown of rack R30 on 04/07 and 17/07. Daily INFO and WARN events are highly correlated, and so are WARN and FATAL events. However INFO and FATAL events seem to appear together less frequently. This could mean that INFO events could be useful to predict WARN events while WARN events could predict FATAL events at this time resolution. Hence, considering both INFO and WARN events to predict FATAL events could facilitate longer prediction lead time.

A different question is whether events correlate across different components. Figure 4c–d shows the distribution of correlations between rack and node-board pairs for FATAL events. Similar results were obtained for the other events and at mid-plane scale. Unlike power and temperature, FATAL events have higher correlation across components, with a significant number of pairwise correlations larger than 0.5. This indicates that failures may propagate across components. We studied for various FATAL event types the number of different components (node-boards, power modules, etc.) affected in 5 min windows. We found that most event occurrences do involve a large number of components, sometimes up to a few hundred. So, when trying to predict component failures, one needs to take into account not only their individual behavior, but also that of the others. The way failures propagate can also give indications of the possible causes (e.g., a faulty job running on all components) and enable their automatic identification.

Fig. 5. Correlation between datasets at 24 h resolution for the overall system (Color figure online).

3.2   The Big Picture

Individual datasets have shed some light into the functioning of the Fermi system, and correlations between components. Here we integrate the four datasets to uncover further correlations between the different components and logs.

A first analysis looks at different measures for the overall system for 24 h time windows. Figure 5 shows all pairwise correlations between several time series datasets. We note strong correlation between temperature and power, confirming what has been observed in other systems as well [3]. In terms of workload, total daily CPU time, number of cores, and queue time are included. These do not appear to correlate among themselves, while CPU time is the only one among the three that does correlate with other datasets, although only moderately. Specifically, positive correlation with the temperature is present, so the system does show thermal symptoms of working harder under a high workload. A negative correlation with RAS events also exists, which is somewhat counterintuitive: one would expect more events to appear when the system works harder. However, it is quite possible for large numbers of RAS events to have resulted in system failure, which in turn resulted in fewer completed jobs for that day, explaining the negative correlation. In fact, a closer analysis of the data shows that, in general, a system shutdown (signaled by long periods of missing data in the trace) is preceded by fatal events. In some situations, events may appear also at system restore, which could be due to operator interventions made while the system was down. A negative correlation also appears between power/temperature and RAS events, again rather counterintuitively and due to the same factors as before. So, when trying to predict power consumption or FATAL events, one needs to take into consideration the negative dependence.

The data do not show any correlation between overall workload and power, however correlation could depend on the job class (queue). So we analyzed (same Fig. 5) the daily CPU Time per job class and also the coefficient of variation (CV) of the total CPU Time across the classes. A higher CV means a more unbalanced workload across the queues. The negative correlation between CPU time and

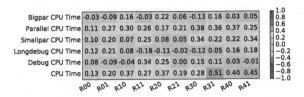

Fig. 6. Correlation between CPU time and power for the 10 racks (R00-R41) (Color figure online).

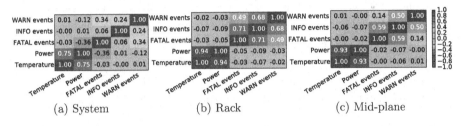

| (a) System | (b) Rack | (c) Mid-plane |

Fig. 7. Correlation between datasets at 3 different system scales (Color figure online).

RAS events is present for individual queues as well, with strongest effect for *smallpar* jobs. CPU Time CV displays some positive correlation to WARN events, which means that heterogeneity in terms of jobs per queue can be a factor leading to WARN events. However, even at this scale, no link between workload and power consumption can be found (we also explored other measures, such as job count, core count, queue time per class, with similar results). This suggests that the way workload is distributed on components is important to understand power in this system. Higher correlations might be obtained by zooming in at rack, mid-plane or node-board scales. We can do this for power, but not for workload due to the structure of our dataset. Figure 6 shows how CPU Time correlates with power consumption per rack. Indeed, higher correlations do appear, indicating structure is important, but still more detailed workload data is required. This suggests the need for changes in the structure of workload logs for Fermi and improving system logging practice, in order to see exactly at which scale correlations appear.

In a second analysis, the resolution of the data was increased to 5 min. Correlations at system, rack, and mid-plane scales are shown in Fig. 7. Due to its coarse time structure, the workload data was excluded. Power and temperature correlation grows with increased time and space resolution. This suggests that for predictions, using only one of the two features might suffice, which is good news since power logs at node-board scale are not available. However, to account for the possibility that temperatures are affected by cooling issues, power should still be monitored, even if not to be used as a modeling feature, but to check that assumed correlation is correct. A sudden decrease in correlation could also flag cooling anomalies. The negative correlation between temperature/power and RAS events is maintained, albeit at a lower value, only at system scale between power and FATAL events. This can be again explained by the existence of periods

Table 2. Possible feature set for prediction of FATAL RAS events.

Feature	Period	Scale
Temperature average and standard deviation	6 h	node-board
Correlation between temperature and power	6 h	mid-plane
Temperature correlation between node-boards	6 h	node-board
CPU time per queue	24 h	system
CPU time coefficient of variation across queues	24 h	system
Number of WARN, INFO, and FATAL events	24 h	node-board
Stdev of number of WARN, INFO, and FATAL events	24 h	node-board
Number of WARN, INFO, and FATAL events	24 h	system
Stdev of number of WARN, INFO, and FATAL	24 h	system
Correlation between temperature and event count	6 h	node-board
Correlation between power and event count	6 h	system

of system shutdown before or after events. So, correlations will be high over 24 h, but for 5 min windows, only FATAL events are correlated with power (temperatures take longer to drop, while other event types could have appeared much earlier). Between RAS events, correlations are higher within racks, indicating that propagation of errors might be strongest at the rack scale.

4   Related Work

Log analysis for characterization of large computing infrastructures has been the focus of numerous recent studies. The release of two Google workload traces has triggered a flurry of analysis activity. General statistics, descriptive analyses, and characterization studies [12,15] have revealed higher levels of heterogeneity when compared to grid systems [5]. Some modeling work has also appeared based on these data [2,17,19]. While they have provided important insight into Google clusters, focusing only on workload aspects of the system has been limiting. To be effective, it is essential to integrate data from different components and sources. Other traces have also been studied in the past [4], and tools for their analysis developed [9], but again concentrating on a single data type. Here we perform similar analyses for a Blue Gene/Q system but from several viewpoints: workload, RAS, power, and temperature, providing a more complete picture of the system under study.

RAS logs from IBM Blue Gene systems have been included in several earlier studies. In [6] prediction of FATAL events in a Blue Gene/Q machine is attempted while an earlier study of a Blue Gene/L installation is [11]. Both compare several classification tools (SVM, customized KNN, ANN, feature selection, rule-based models). These predictive studies look only at RAS events, while adding further data from other system components could improve prediction accuracy significantly, as noted by the authors themselves. In this paper we provide the first step towards such an analysis, where we perform descriptive analytics mandatory before any prediction can be attempted.

Some integration is performed in a very recent study from Google that models Power Usage Effectiveness using thermal information (temperatures, humidity, etc.) and overall system load, using an Artificial Neural Network [8]. Another recent development in this direction is a novel monitoring system [3] designed for a hybrid HPC platform. In this study, several types of data including workload, power, chiller, and machine status are recorded. In principle, these data could be used for future predictive and modeling studies, but they have not been initiated in the reported study. The OVIS project has also developed an integrated monitoring platform called the "Lightweight Distributed Metric Service" [1], recording various system metrics for optimization of application performance. The platform has been tested on several systems, but again steps towards a descriptive and predictive analytics for these data are still missing.

5 Discussion and Conclusions

Given the need for a holistic analysis of large computing infrastructures, this paper has presented a characterization study conducted with four datasets describing different subsystems of an IBM Blue Gene/Q installation. Temperature, power consumption, workload, and RAS logs were studied independently to characterize the system and then together to identify correlations between datasets.

The results obtained from correlation analysis will serve as a guideline for a future study aiming to predict in advance FATAL RAS events based on the rest of the data. One possibility would be predicting, for each node-board, the number of FATAL events in the next 24 h. Alternatively, based on the number of events, we can define discrete failure classes (e.g., NONE, FEW, MANY) to be predicted. We have compiled a set of possible features that may be suitable for this predictive task (Table 2). These cover all datasets with various time resolutions at node-board and system scale.

The first two features are suggested by the fact that power and temperatures are highly correlated. Temperatures can be used a a proxy for power, so that the higher space resolution is employed and the number of features is decreased. This only as long as correlation between temperature and power is high. A decrease in correlation will signal an anomaly, even if the proxy is no longer valid. Large temperature correlations across node-boards could also signify anomalies, since node-board temperatures were uncorrelated in our data. Workload related features are limited to daily CPU time per queue and coefficient of variation across queues, which showed highest correlation with other datasets. Features monitoring all types of RAS events at node-board level account for correlation across RAS event types, while those at system level are justified by correlations across node-boards and propagation of errors. Since prediction is aimed for 24 h periods, we use event values computed over the same time, but also deviations, to account for varying inter-event patterns. Finally, correlations between power (or temperature at node-board scale) and events should be monitored since large negative correlation could signal component failure. Even if indications are that the features listed will prove important for prediction, final evaluation of the feature set will be performed during the future predictive study itself.

Besides identifying important features, our analysis has also indicated directions for improvement in terms of data collection. Workload data in particular proved to be insufficient for our goals, so we could identify few relations to the other datasets. In the future, at least timestamps for job completion as well as job placement should be included. This additional information will enable analyzing the causes of lack of power correlation across components. Power monitoring was coarse in terms of space resolution, however more data could be extracted from the node-board power rails. Temperatures, on the other hand, could be logged at 5 min intervals rather than 15. We are aiming at prediction with long lead time, so the 15 min interval may be sufficient for applying the model, however finer granularity would allow for more refined training data. In the future we will also use data external to the computing infrastructure, such as the water and air cooling systems, together with data outside the data center, e.g. weather and seismic activity. Cross-correlations will also be investigated, resulting in further features to be added to the proposed set.

Acknowledgments. We are grateful to the HPC team at CINECA for sharing with us the log data related to the Fermi system and for helpful discussions.

References

1. Agelastos, A., et al.: The lightweight distributed metric service: a scalable infrastructure for continuous monitoring of large scale computing systems and applications. In: SC 2014, pp. 154–165 (2014)
2. Balliu, A., et al.: Bidal: big data analyzer for cluster traces. In: Informatika (BigSys workshop), vol. 232, pp. 1781–1795. GI-Edition Lecture Notes in Informatics (2014)
3. Bartolini, A., et al.: Unveiling eurora - thermal and power characterization of the most energy-efficient supercomputer in the world. In: Proceedings of the Conference on Design, Automation & Test in Europe, pp. 277:1–277:6. DATE 2014 (2014)
4. Chen, Y., Alspaugh, S., Katz, R.H.: Design insights for MapReduce from diverse production workloads. Technical report, UC Berkeley UCB/EECS-2 (2012)
5. Di, S., Kondo, D., Cirne, W.: Characterization and comparison of google cloud load versus grids. In: IEEE CLUSTER, pp. 230–238 (2012)
6. Dudko, R., Sharma, A., Tedesco, J.: Effective failure prediction in hadoop clusters. University of Idaho White Paper, pp. 1–8 (2012)
7. Falciano, F., Rossi, E.: Fermi: the most powerful computational resource for italian scientists. EMBnet J. **18**(A), 62 (2012)
8. Gao, J.: Machine learning applications for data center optimisation. Google White Paper (2014)
9. Javadi, B., et al.: The failure trace archive: enabling the comparison of failure measurements and models of distributed systems. J. Parallel Distrib. Comput. **73**(8), 1208–1223 (2013)

10. Lakner, G., et al.: IBM system blue gene solution: blue gene/Q system administration. IBM Redbooks (2013)
11. Liang, Y., et al.: Failure prediction in IBM bluegene/L event logs. IEEE ICDM, pp. 583–588 (2007)
12. Liu, Z., Cho, S.: Characterizing machines and workloads on a google cluster. In: 8th SRMPDS (2012)
13. Milano, J., et al.: IBM system blue gene solution: blue gene/Q hardware overview and installation planning. IBM Redbooks (2013)
14. Ponemon Institute Research, Emerson Network Power: Cost of Data Center Outages (2013)
15. Reiss, C., et al.: Heterogeneity and dynamicity of clouds at scale: google trace analysis. In: ACM SoCC (2012)
16. Salfner, F., Lenk, M., Malek, M.: A survey of online failure prediction methods. ACM Comput. Surv. (CSUR) 42(3), 1–68 (2010)
17. Sîrbu, A., Babaoglu, O.: Towards data-driven autonomics in data centers. In: International Conference on Cloud and Autonomic Computing (ICCAC) (2015)
18. Valentini, G.L., et al.: An overview of energy efficiency techniques in cluster computing systems. Cluster Comput. 16(1), 3–15 (2013)
19. Wang, G., et al.: Towards synthesizing realistic workload traces for studying the hadoop ecosystem. In: IEEE MASCOTS, pp. 400–408 (2011)

Addressing the Last Roadblock for Message Logging in HPC: Alleviating the Memory Requirement Using Dedicated Resources

Tatiana Martsinkevich[1]([✉]), Thomas Ropars[2], and Franck Cappello[3]

[1] Inria, University of Paris Sud, Orsay, France
tatiana.mar@inria.fr
[2] Inria, Bordeaux, France
thomas.ropars@inria.fr
[3] Argonne National Laboratory Argonne, Lemont, IL, USA
cappello@mcs.anl.gov

Abstract. Currently used global application checkpoint-restart will not be a suitable solution for HPC applications running on large scale as, given the predicted fault rates, it will impose a high load on the I/O subsystem and lead to inefficient resource usage. Combining application checkpointing with message logging is appealing as it allows restarting only the processes that actually failed. One major issue with message logging protocols is the high amount of memory required to store logs. In this work we propose to use additional dedicated resources to save the part of the logs that would not fit in the memory of a compute node. We show that, combined with a cluster-based hierarchical logging technique, only few dedicated nodes would be required to accommodate the memory requirement of message logging protocols. We additionally show that the proposed technique achieves a reasonable performance overhead.

Keywords: High-performance computing · Fault tolerance · Message logging · Hierarchical message-logging protocols · Dedicated resources

1 Introduction

As the scale and performance of newly built supercomputers grow, we are getting closer to being able to tackle extremely large problems. On the other hand, the mean time between failures (MTBF) of such systems is expected to decrease to several hours [5], making it more challenging for high-performance computing (HPC) applications to progress with computations in the presence of failures.

Today, many message-passing applications use checkpoint-restart techniques for fault tolerance. This approach may become unacceptable at large scale, however, because the decreased MTBF will require that applications take checkpoints more frequently, thus spending less time doing useful work. Some efforts have been made to lower the cost of checkpointing at scale [7,10,13]. However, the technique may still be impractical from the point of view of power consumption and time to restart the whole application every time a failure occurs.

S. Hunold et al. (Eds.): Euro-Par 2015 Workshops, LNCS 9523, pp. 644–655, 2015.
DOI: 10.1007/978-3-319-27308-2_52

Log-based fault tolerance protocols offer an alternative solution that has a better failure containment: In a message-logging protocol only the failed process has to roll back and restart in the best case. The possibility of avoiding the whole application restart makes such protocols look appealing for large-scale executions. Because processes store the message payload in their memory, however, message logging can be memory demanding, especially for communication-intensive applications [14, 16].

A basic way to limit the log size is to use periodic checkpointing followed by a garbage collection of logs. Therefore, message logging usually goes hand in hand with checkpointing. However, high checkpointing frequency would be required to avoid memory exhaustion in applications with high log rate. For instance, assuming a per-process log growth rate of 4 MB/second[1] and assuming that a process has 2 GB of memory available but can use no more than 10 % of that memory for message logging, a checkpoint would have to be taken approximately every 50 seconds.

Hierarchical message-logging protocols have proved efficient in reducing log size at an expense of weaker failure containment: These techniques apply a message-logging protocol not to individual processes but to clusters of processes. Hence, the whole cluster has to restart upon a failure. Although clustering helps reduce the average log growth rate per process, hierarchical protocols do not fully solve the log size problem because some processes may still experience a rapid growth of their logs [16].

In this work we propose to use additional dedicated resources, or logger nodes, that cooperate with the compute nodes by storing part of their message logs in the memory. They can be regarded as a memory extension for compute nodes. The purpose is to avoid being bound by memory constraints on the node when choosing the checkpointing period for an application.

The contributions of this paper can be summarized as follows:

- We provide a basic algorithm for dumping message logs to logger nodes. The algorithm uses proactive dumping in order to overlap application computations and flushing of logs.
- We evaluate the impact of different factors on the overhead of log dumping. We show that using less than 10 % of additional resources can be enough to achieve a reasonable overhead of log dumping for some applications.
- We demonstrate that using hierarchical logging protocols together with logger nodes can be the ultimate solution to the memory limitation problem in logging protocols. We use an example approximating a real-life application execution to show that one can find a balanced configuration with process clustering, logger nodes, and a memory quota that keeps the execution overhead below 10 %.

This work is structured as follows. Section 2 gives background information on message logging. Section 3 describes our algorithm for log dumping. We start

---

[1] Note that some applications have a much higher log growth rate; see [14, 16].

Sect. 4 by giving some details on the implementation of the algorithm and then we present evaluation results. Section 5 summarizes our results and discusses future work.

2   Background and Related Work

In this paper we consider MPI applications executed on an asynchronous distributed system where nodes fail by crashing. The set of processes is fixed (no dynamic process creation) and multiple concurrent failures can occur. In this context, Sect. 2.1 provides an overview of log-based fault tolerance protocols. Section 2.2 describes related work on techniques to reduce log size.

2.1   Message-Logging Protocols

Message-logging protocols save a copy of the payload of all the messages delivered by a process, as well as the corresponding delivery events (determinants), to be able to replay them in the same order upon a failure. Assuming that message delivery events are the only source of nondeterminism during the execution, this approach is enough to ensure that the process state can be restored correctly after a failure.

Implementing efficient message logging requires solving two problems: saving the message payload efficiently and saving the determinants efficiently. In both cases, data has to be stored in such a way that it can be retrieved after a failure. A simple solution to the first problem is sender-based message logging [11]. A process P_0 sending a message to a process P_1 saves a copy of the payload in its memory. If P_1 fails, P_0 is able to resend the message. If P_0 fails as well, the copy of the message is lost but it will be generated again during the re-execution of P_0. Research has shown that sender-based message logging can be implemented with almost no performance penalty on communication [16].

On the other hand, logging the determinants efficiently is more difficult because they must include the delivery order and, hence, must be logged by the receiver. Therefore, the determinants must be stored reliably in order to avoid losing them if the process fails. Techniques for determinant logging fall into three categories: optimistic, pessimistic, and causal [1]. However, they all suffer from performance issues at scale [3,17], one exception being the combination of optimistic logging with coordinated checkpointing [14].

In the context of MPI applications, a few solutions have been proposed to reduce the number of determinants to be logged, or even completely eliminate the need to log them. For example, a blocking named reception in MPI is a deterministic event and, hence, does not need to be logged [2]. The partial determinism of most MPI HPC applications can also be leveraged to fully avoid logging determinants [6,16].

Given these optimizations, the main problem that remains to be solved is related to the size of logs in message logging protocols.

2.2   Reducing the Log Size

Using checkpointing does not solve the problem of large message logs completely, because some applications have such high log rates that they would require unacceptably frequent checkpointing.

Ferreira et al. [9] studied the possibility of reducing the log size by compressing it. They showed that, while one can achieve positive results for some workloads, the method is not universally good. Additionally, the question of the impact of this technique on application performance remains open.

Hierarchical protocols that use process clustering are another approach proposed for reducing the memory footprint of message logging [4,12,16]. The amount of logged data decreases naturally because message logging is applied only to intercluster messages. Hierarchical protocols work well in many cases thanks to the low connectivity degree of the applications' communication graph: For many applications, the percentage of processes to restart in the event of a failure can be kept below 15 % while logging less than 15 % of all messages [15].

Even with hierarchical protocols, some processes might have to log a lot of data. This is the case, for instance, if a process is *at the border* of a cluster and communicates mainly with processes from other clusters. We observed this phenomenon in our tests (see Sect. 4.6) even with some optimized clustering strategy [15]. Hence, the problem of large memory footprint of message logging, along with the memory limitation of compute nodes, still remains relevant.

3   Dedicated Logger Nodes

To alleviate the problem of limited memory available to message-logging protocols, we propose to use additional dedicated resources, or logger nodes. A logger node does not participate in the computation but is used only for storing in its memory the portion of message logs that does not fit in the memory of a computation process.

Compute processes track how much memory is being used by the logging protocol during execution. Once this value reaches a predefined limit, the process has to free some memory by flushing a part of its log to a logger node.

In practice, we start flushing logs proactively to avoid the situation where the process stops progressing because it has no memory left for message logging and has to free some memory first. Specifically, we use nonblocking MPI send routines to be able to overlap log dumping with computations and thus reduce the performance penalty as much as possible.

Algorithm 1 presents a pseudo code for dumping message logs. The user specifies a memory quota M for the message-logging protocol, and we set a $DUMP\_THRESHOLD$ for the proactive dump smaller than M. Every time the process logs a message, it checks whether it has reached this threshold (lines 7–8). If yes, it tries to free some memory.

The dumping process consists of two phases. First, the process sends a memory allocation request to a logger node. If the logger accepts the request, the

Algorithm 1. Log dumping algorithm

```
1: procedure log(msg)
2:     while true do
3:         if copy(msg) then      ▷ copy() returns true if msg was copied to local logs
4:             break
5:         else
6:             dump_log(sizeof(msg))
7:     if log_sz > DUMP_TRESHOLD then
8:         proactive_dump_log()
9:
10: procedure request_logger_mem(mem_size)
11:     for each lgr in loggers do
12:         send(lgr, mem_size)
13:         resp ← receive(lgr)
14:         if resp = 1 then return lgr
15:
16: procedure dump_log(mem_size)
17:     if dump_req ≠ NULL then
18:         wait_complete(dump_req)
19:     logger ← request_logger_mem(mem_size)
20:     send(logger, log)                          ▷ log: the portion of log to dump
21:
22: procedure proactive_dump_log()
23:     if dump_req ≠ NULL then
24:         if !test_complete(dump_req) then
25:             return
26:     logger ← request_logger_mem(dump_size)
27:     dump_req ← isend(logger, log)              ▷ log: the portion of log to dump
```

process posts an asynchronous send request for the log portion it wants to free (line 26–27); otherwise, it tries another logger node. The value of $dump\_size$ is implementation-dependant. The process checks whether the request has completed when $proactive\_dump()$ is called again. No more logs are sent to loggers if the previous dump is not finished yet (lines 23–25) or if the memory usage by the protocol has gone below the $DUMP\_THRESHOLD$.

If proactive dumping of logs does not suffice and the process reaches the limit M, the process first tries to complete any pending dump request and then uses a blocking communication call to flush more memory before continuing with logging (lines 2–6).

The failure of a logger node is harmless as long as no application process, that would need messages stored by that logger for replaying, fails. If this happens, the processes that lost a portion of their logs will have to restart from the last checkpoint to generate these messages again. Careful strategies for assigning logger nodes to processes would have to be designed to limit the extend of rollbacks in unfortunate scenarios. Discussing such strategies is outside the scope of this paper. In our experiments, each process simply contacts first the logger with $id = myrank$ **mod** $nloggers$.

4   Evaluation

In this section we first describe our implementation of logger nodes. We then estimate the runtime overhead of log dumping with different numbers of logger nodes and different memory limits. We also demonstrate the benefits of combining hierarchical logging techniques with logger nodes.

4.1   Implementation

To evaluate the cost of dumping message logs to dedicated nodes we implemented a basic sender-based message-logging protocol in the PMPI profiling layer. This protocol is loosely based on our previous work [16]: We rely on the channel deterministic property of many HPC applications to avoid logging of determinants. Thus, we log only message payloads and any information necessary to be able to replay sending of messages. However, we point out that the proposed dumping algorithm could be applied to any sender-based message-logging protocol.

To facilitate memory management for the logging protocol, we allocate and free memory in blocks of fixed size. When dumping to loggers, a process sends one whole memory block at a time. After some fine-tuning tests, we chose the memory block size to be 32 KB in our evaluation tests. Logger processes are started together with the user program, and they wait for incoming requests to store message logs. A logger may accept or decline the request depending on whether it has enough memory left. If a logger declines the request, the compute process tries the next logger in round-robin fashion.

During the execution of the application, we need to decide what portion of log should be flushed during a proactive dump ($dump\_size$): if the portion is too large it may impact the application performance; if it is too small it may increase the risk of falling back to blocking mode for flushes. Hence, we think that $dump\_size$ should be computed dynamically during execution, based on the current log growth rate of the process. In our experiments, we simply use an application-specific coefficient α to compute $dump\_size = \alpha \times lograte$.

4.2   Experimental Setup

To evaluate the overhead of dumping message logs to logger nodes we conducted a set of experiments on the Graphene cluster of the Grid5000 testbed. Graphene is a 144-node cluster where each node has one 2.53 GHz Intel Xeon X3440 CPU. Each CPU has four cores and a total of 16 GB of memory per node. Nodes are connected by the high-performance InfiniBand-20G network. We use the OpenMPI-1.4.5 library.

Four applications were used in the tests: a molecular dynamics simulator LAMMPS; a numerical model CM1, used to study atmospheric phenomena;

Table 1. Application input parameters

LAMMPS	Lennard-Jones liquid benchmark, 6912000 particles, 150 steps
GTC	micell=100, mecell=100, npartdom=1, 8 steps
CM1	$1536 \times 1536 \times 40$ grid points, timax=70
MILC	nx=64, ny=64, nz=64, nt=16

and two benchmarks from the NERSC-8 benchmark suite—a 3D gyrokinetic toroidal code GTC and the MILC lattice quantum chromodynamics code. In all the experiments, each MPI process is placed on one core of a node, four MPI processes per node in total. Each logger node runs four logger processes, one process binded to each core.

For the settings of the logging protocol, α was set based on some fine-tuning tests to 0.1 for MILC, 0.2 for LAMMPS, and 1.0 for GTC and CM1. The memory threshold after which processes start proactive dumping was set to 5 MB before the memory limit used in the test (e.g., if the memory limit is 20 MB, the threshold is set to 15 MB).

We took an average runtime over four executions in all tests. We then compared the overhead[2] of an execution with message logging with the native execution time without any logging.

4.3   Dumping Overhead with Different Number of Logger Nodes

We first examine the application behavior when dumping message logs. The applications were run with 64 processes on 16 nodes; input parameters are presented in Table 1.

As we want to study the impact of logger nodes contention on performance, we set the memory limit for the logging protocol to a small value in order to force processes to start dumping logs almost immediately after they start. Each process logs all the outgoing messages. Table 2 gives information about the applications' log rate, the log size per process, and the total amount of data dumped to the loggers. To prevent memory exhaustion on loggers, we used a circular buffer of fixed size (10 MB) for incoming logs in this experiment.

Figure 1 (line labeled "*no_clu*") presents the overhead of the four applications for a number of logger nodes varying from 1 to 16. MILC has the highest overhead with 11.70 % in the test with one logger node. Such overhead is expected given the high log rate of this application and the total amount of dumped logs. The higher the log rate, the more frequently an application has to free memory for logging new messages. CM1 shows the best behavior, with only 1.76 % overhead in the test with one logger node. LAMMPS and GTC fall in between.

---

[2] The overhead computation only takes into account the execution time. Logger nodes also require using additional resources.

Table 2. Application logging statistics

	LAMMPS	GTC	CM1	MILC
Log growth rate (MB/S)	5.20	2.35	1.75	13.51
Average logged per process (MB)	300	227	232	738
Totally dumped to loggers (GB)	18.5	14.1	14.1	45.8

4.4 Combining Hierarchical Protocols with Logger Nodes

Using process clustering effectively reduces the number of messages that need to be logged, at a cost of increasing the number of processes that will have to roll back and restart should a failure occur. Combined with logger nodes, clustering can be used for finding a better trade-off between the number of logger nodes and the failure containment. We used a clustering tool [15] to generate clusters that minimize the number of messages logged. Note that in each configuration, all clusters have the same size.

Figure 1 shows how clustering 64 processes can significantly reduce the runtime overhead of dumping message logs. For example, in MILC, the overhead of the execution with no clustering (processes log all outgoing messages) can be reduced from 11.70 % to 6.70 % either by dividing the processes into 16 clusters or by increasing the number of logger nodes to two (5.75 % overhead). For LAMMPS, the configuration with one logger node and 8 clusters gives the same runtime overhead as the one with no clustering but two logger nodes. In GTC and CM1 any configuration with clustering diminishes overhead to less than 1 %.

4.5 Dumping Overhead with Different Memory Limits

Next, we investigate how varying the memory limit for logging influences the execution. In practice, the more memory the protocol has at its disposal, the longer an application can run without having to dump logs and, consequently, the smaller will be the overhead. To quantify this, we took two applications with the highest overhead—MILC and LAMMPS—and performed several runs varying the portion of the total node memory yielded to the logging protocol from 5 to 25 % (25 % of node memory counts as 4 GB, hence 1 GB for each MPI process).

Since, upon a node crash, all the MPI processes on this node would have to restart, we did not log the messages sent between the processes residing on the same physical node; instead, we considered one node as one process cluster. We also increased the number of steps for each application to make the total log size surpass the 25 % of node memory threshold and to force some log dumping in all the tests. The tests were run with 64 processes (16 nodes) and one logger node.

As seen in Fig. 2, increasing the memory limit can help further reducing the runtime overhead, but the performance gain is not always very significant.

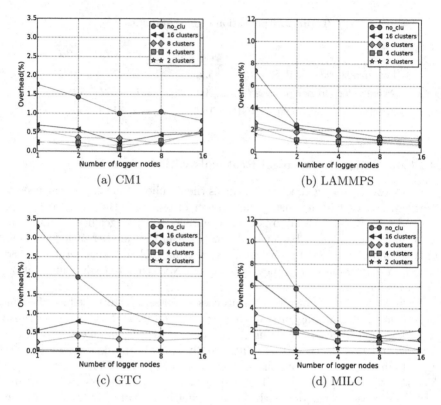

Fig. 1. Dumping overheads with different numbers of clusters and logger nodes

4.6 Use Case

Finally, we take a look at a use case that approximates a real-life application execution. We chose GTC and LAMMPS as applications that have moderate log rates and, at the same time, are relatively easy to scale. We ran them on 512 processes (128 nodes) and increased the number of steps so that they executed for 15–20 min—an optimal checkpointing period [18] for these applications considering a checkpoint cost between 30 and 60 seconds and a system with MTBF of 4 hours [8].

To find a suitable configuration of process clustering, memory quota for message logging, and number of logger nodes, we perform the following steps:

1. We run an application for several steps to record its communication pattern. We assume that the pattern stays approximately the same throughout the execution and that the log rate does not change significantly.
2. Based on the communication pattern, we get the clustering with the best balance between the log size and cluster size using a clustering tool [15], and obtain the corresponding log size.

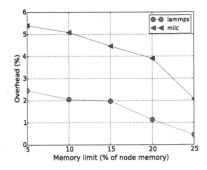

Fig. 2. Execution overhead with different memory limitations

3. Based on the predicted log size, we choose different memory quotas for the logging protocol and compute how much data in total would be flushed to loggers.
4. We choose a quota with which we would not have to use more than 10 % of additional nodes as loggers to accommodate all the flushed logs.

The resulting best configuration for LAMMPS is four clusters (128 processes per cluster), 20 % of node memory for logging protocol (3.2 GB per node), and four logger nodes to accommodate 61 GB of logs predicted to be dumped. An alternative configuration would be to limit the memory to 10 %, but in this case 16 logger nodes would be necessary. Therefore, a trade-off must be made between the memory limit and the number of logger nodes. In our case, we wanted to keep the number of loggers below 10 %, so we chose the first configuration.

The resulting configuration for GTC is four clusters, 5 % of node memory (820 MB), and three logger nodes to accommodate 47 GB of logs. Only 5 % of node memory is enough because, thanks to clustering, most of the processes do not need to log anything and only the processes at cluster border have large logs. Such clustering resulted from the specific communication pattern of GTC.

To determine the overhead, we ran tests with these configurations. The overhead is approximately 5.5 % for GTC and is 0.2 % for LAMMPS. The higher overhead for GTC is most likely due to the imbalance of log sizes between processes. As mentioned before, only the processes at cluster border had something to log, and they could have caused some desynchronization with other processes when flushing logs.

5   Conclusion

Log-based fault tolerance techniques are gaining more attention as an attractive fault tolerance solution at large scale, because such techniques allow limiting the number of processes that have to roll back and restart upon a failure. This approach is more efficient from the point of view of resource and energy usage.

The main unresolved issue of such protocols is their high memory requirement. In this work we addressed this issue and proposed using additional dedicated resources for storing part of message logs. In our tests we showed that dumping logs has a reasonable execution overhead and does not necessarily require many additional resources.

We also showed that logger nodes can be used effectively as an aid to process clustering, in order to store all the logs that exceed the available memory quota for message-logging protocol.

Future work includes evaluating the performance of recovery with logger nodes, and more generally, comparing the efficiency of the proposed approach with other state-of-the-art fault tolerant techniques.

Acknowledgements. Experiments presented in this paper were carried out using the Grid'5000 experimental testbed, being developed under the INRIA ALADDIN development action with support from CNRS, RENATER and several Universities as well as other funding bodies (see https://www.grid5000.fr).

This material is based upon work supported by the U.S. Department of Energy, Office of Science, under contract DE-AC02-06CH11357.

The submitted manuscript has been created by UChicago Argonne, LLC, Operator of Argonne National Laboratory ("Argonne"). Argonne, a U.S. Department of Energy Office of Science laboratory, is operated under Contract No. DE-AC02-06CH11357. The U.S. Government retains for itself, and others acting on its behalf, a paid-up nonexclusive, irrevocable worldwide license in said article to reproduce, prepare derivative works, distribute copies to the public, and perform publicly and display publicly, by or on behalf of the Government.

References

1. Alvisi, L., Marzullo, K.: Message logging: pessimistic, optimistic, causal, and optimal. IEEE Trans. Softw. Eng. **24**(2), 149–159 (1998)
2. Bouteiller, A., Bosilca, G., Dongarra, J.: Redesigning the message logging model for high performance. Concurrency Comput. Pract. Experience **22**, 2196–2211 (2010)
3. Bouteiller, A., Collin, B., Herault, T., Lemarinier, P., Cappello, F.: Impact of event logger on causal message logging protocols for fault tolerant MPI. In: Proceedings of the 19th IEEE International Parallel and Distributed Processing Symposium (IPDPS 2005), vol. 1, p. 97, April 2005
4. Bouteiller, A., Herault, T., Bosilca, G., Dongarra, J.J.: Correlated set coordination in fault tolerant message logging protocols. In: Jeannot, E., Namyst, R., Roman, J. (eds.) Euro-Par 2011, Part II. LNCS, vol. 6853, pp. 51–64. Springer, Heidelberg (2011)
5. Cappello, F., Geist, A., Gropp, B., Kale, L., Kramer, B., Snir, M.: Toward exascale resilience: 2014 update. Supercomput. Front. Innovations **1**(1), 1–28 (2014)
6. Cappello, F., Guermouche, A., Snir, M.: On communication determinism in parallel HPC applications. In: 19th International Conference on Computer Communications and Networks (ICCCN 2010) (2010)

7. Cores, I., Rodriguez, G., Martin, M., González, P.: Reducing application-level checkpoint file sizes: towards scalable fault tolerance solutions. In: 2012 IEEE 10th International Symposium on Parallel and Distributed Processing with Applications, pp. 371–378, July 2012

8. Di Martino, C., Kalbarczyk, Z., Iyer, R., Baccanico, F., Fullop, J., Kramer, W.: Lessons learned from the analysis of system failures at petascale: the case of Blue Waters. In: 2014 44th Annual IEEE/IFIP International Conference on Dependable Systems and Networks (DSN), pp. 610–621, June 2014

9. Ferreira, K.B., Riesen, R., Arnold, D., Ibtesham, D., Brightwell, R.: The viability of using compression to decrease message log sizes. In: Caragiannis, I., Alexander, M., Badia, R.M., Cannataro, M., Costan, A., Danelutto, M., Desprez, F., Krammer, B., Sahuquillo, J., Scott, S.L., Weidendorfer, J. (eds.) Euro-Par Workshops 2012. LNCS, vol. 7640, pp. 484–493. Springer, Heidelberg (2013)

10. Jin, H., Ke, T., Chen, Y., Sun, X.H.: Checkpointing orchestration: toward a scalable hpc fault-tolerant environment. In: Proceedings of the 2012 12th IEEE/ACM International Symposium on Cluster, Cloud and Grid Computing, CCGRID 2012, pp. 276–283 (2012)

11. Johnson, D.B., Zwaenepoel, W.: Sender-based message logging. In: Digest of Papers: The 17th Annual International Symposium on Fault-Tolerant Computing, pp. 14–19 (1987)

12. Meneses, E., Mendes, C.L., Kalé, L.V.: Team-based message logging: preliminary results. In: Proceedings of the 2010 10th IEEE/ACM International Conference on Cluster, Cloud and Grid Computing, CCGRID 2010, pp. 697–702 (2010)

13. Moody, A., Bronevetsky, G., Mohror, K., de Supinski, B.R.: Design, modeling, and evaluation of a scalable multi-level checkpointing system. In: Proceedings of the 2010 ACM/IEEE International Conference for High Performance Computing, Networking, Storage and Analysis, SC 2010, pp. 1–11 (2010)

14. Riesen, R., Ferreira, K., Da Silva, D., Lemarinier, P., Arnold, D., Bridges, P.G.: Alleviating scalability issues of checkpointing protocols. In: IEEE/ACM SuperComputing 2012, SC 2012 (2012)

15. Ropars, T., Guermouche, A., Uçar, B., Meneses, E., Kalé, L.V., Cappello, F.: On the use of cluster-based partial message logging to improve fault tolerance for MPI HPC applications. In: Proceedings of the 17th international conference on Parallel processing, Euro-Par 2011, pp. 567–578 (2011)

16. Ropars, T., Martsinkevich, T., Guermouche, A., Schiper, A., Cappello, F.: SPBC: Leveraging the characteristics of MPI HPC applications for scalable checkpointing. In: IEEE/ACM SuperComputing 2013 (SC13) (2013)

17. Ropars, T., Morin, C.: Active optimistic and distributed message logging for message-passing applications. Concurrency Comput. Pract. Experience **23**(17), 2167–2178 (2011)

18. Young, J.W.: A first order approximation to the optimum checkpoint interval. Commun. ACM **17**(9), 530–531 (1974)

Towards Understanding Post-recovery Efficiency for Shrinking and Non-shrinking Recovery

Aiman Fang[1]([⊠]), Hajime Fujita[1], and Andrew A. Chien[1,2]

[1] University of Chicago, Chicago, IL 60637, USA
{aimanf,hfujita,achien}@cs.uchicago.edu
[2] Argonne National Laboratory, Lemont, IL 60439, USA

Abstract. We explore the post-recovery efficiency of shrinking and non-shrinking recovery schemes on high performance computing systems using a synthetic benchmark. We study the impact of network topology on post-recovery communication performance. Our experiments on the IBM BG/Q System Mira show that shrinking recovery can deliver up to 7.5 % better efficiency for neighbor communication pattern, as the non-shrinking recovery can reduce communication performance. We expected a similar situation for our synthetic benchmark with collective communication, but the situation is quite different. Both shrinking and non-shrinking recovery reduce MPI performance (MPICH3.1) dramatically on collective communication; up to 14× worse, swamping any differences between the two approaches. This suggests that making MPI performance less sensitive to irregularity in performance and communicator size are critical for both recovery approaches.

Keywords: Resilience · HPC · Post-recovery · Shrinking · Non-shrinking · Network topology

1 Introduction

Future extreme scale systems are projected to experience errors regularly with MTBF (Mean Time Between Failures) less than an hour [7,8,15]. On such systems an application may experience frequent node failures [12]. To deal with this situation, researchers have proposed a number of recovery schemes, including ULFM [6] and LFLR [10] for MPI (Message Passing Interface) programs running on HPC (high performance computing) systems. A key question is how an application should cope with a node failure; should it shrink the number of nodes it uses, or should it deploy additional nodes to maintain its scale of resources and perhaps other internal application structures matched to them. In short, should it apply *shrinking* or *non-shrinking* recovery? We define these more precisely:

- **Shrinking:** an application starts with N nodes. After a node failure, it continues with the remaining $N - 1$ good nodes.

© Springer International Publishing Switzerland 2015
S. Hunold et al. (Eds.): Euro-Par 2015 Workshops, LNCS 9523, pp. 656–668, 2015.
DOI: 10.1007/978-3-319-27308-2_53

- **Non-shrinking:** an application starts with $N + n$ nodes where n are pre-allocated spares. After a node failure, the application replaces the failed node with a spare.

Shrinking recovery is attractive from a resource efficiency and management perspective. At all times, the applications are making use of all of the resources allocated to it, and there is no need to suddenly allocate resources in the middle of a run. However, the difficulty of shrinking recovery is placed on the applications, requiring it to deal with an unusual number of nodes ($N - 1$, $N - 2$, etc.) in application structure, and load balance. Of course, even in the best case, performance decreases slightly as computing power is lost with failed nodes.

In contrast, non-shrinking allocates spare nodes, but does not use them. Thus the resource efficiency of non-shrinking will be less than 100 %. Another concern is that the spare nodes used to replace the failed ones will in general be "far" away, perturbing the network locality, and reducing communication performance. This effect can be significant [4]. Because there are competing properties, which approach is most attractive for post-recovery efficiency remains unclear.

We investigate their post-recovery efficiency, that is we seek to understand under what circumstances each recovery approach gives best computing efficiency. Our approach is to develop a synthetic application that captures the three major factors that may affect post-recovery performance: communication pattern (neighbor and collective), communication fraction, and replacement node distance. We then vary each of these, studying their impact on post-recovery performance respectively. We conduct a series of 1024-node experiments on Mira [1], a Blue Gene/Q system at Argonne National Laboratory.

Our study shows that:

- For neighbor communication pattern, shrinking recovery exhibits best performance. In contrast, non-shrinking recovery performance degrades as a function of network locality nonuniformity, slowing as the replacement nodes are further away. In our experiments on BG/Q, as communication fraction increases to 40 %, this difference of efficiency can be as large as 7.5 %.

- For collective communication pattern, we observe surprisingly reversal with non-shrinking performance is best. In both shrinking and non-shrinking approaches, MPICH 3.1.4 collective performance degrades significantly, 7.8-14× worse. In the shrinking case, this is particularly dramatic, causing up to 83.9 % performance degradation for 41 % communication fraction, compared to 74.8 % loss for non-shrinking.

- Our results show that MPI collective performance is highly sensitive to physical network layout of ranks and non-power-of-two communicator size. These affects dominate the difference between our post-recovery models. Advances in algorithms or implementation of MPI collective are essential to any of these recovery approaches to be more viable. MPI is counting for at least half of shrinking performance loss in collectives.

For the rest of paper, Sect. 2 introduces our synthetic benchmark used to explore the performance of shrinking and non-shrinking recovery. Section 3

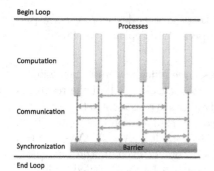

Fig. 1. Model of bulk synchronous parallel (BSP) application

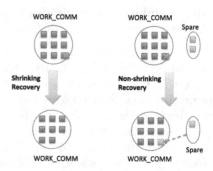

Fig. 2. Shrinking and Non-shrinking recovery

presents our experiment results on Mira. We discuss effects of multiple failures, load imbalance and load balancing cost on efficiency in Sect. 4. Related work is presented in Sect. 5. We summarize in Sect. 6, suggesting several promising directions for further research.

2   A Synthetic Bulk-Synchronous Application

We develop a synthetic application to explore the post-recovery performance of shrinking and non-shrinking recovery. Following a structure typical to numerous scientific computing applications, it has the basic structure of a bulk-synchronous parallel (BSP) model shown in Fig. 1. It iterates on alternating computation and communication phases. Within one iteration, each process first performs a number of local computations, and then communicates with other processes to exchange data. It the end, all processes reaches a barrier to synchronize. We explore several different communication structures, communication fraction, and failure locations.

Our synthetic application models the recovery behavior of shrinking and non-shrinking, illustrated in Fig. 2. After initialization, it creates a sub communicator WORK_COMM including working ranks from MPI_COMM_WORLD. In shrinking recovery, it reconstructs WORK_COMM by excluding the failed process and redistributes the data of failed one to the rest evenly. Whereas in non-shrinking recovery, it reconstructs WORK_COMM by replacing the failed rank with a spare rank and continues execution.

Our synthetic application experiments have several parameters:

1. **Communication Pattern:** we study two common communication patterns: neighbor and collective. Neighbor communication widely exists in scientific simulation. A typical neighbor communication in 3-D space is illustrated in Fig. 3. Each process has six nearest neighbors and performs point-to-point communication (we use non-blocking MPI_Isend, MPI_Irecv). In addition to

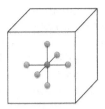

Fig. 3. Neighbor communication pattern in logical 3-D space

Table 1. Dimensions of the 5-D mesh or torus for a given partition size on Mira

#Nodes	A	B	C	D	E	Torus
1024	4	4	4	4	2	ABCE
1024	4	4	4	8	2	All
2048	4	4	4	16	2	All
4096	4	4	8	16	2	All
8192	4	4	16	16	2	All

neighbor communication, global communication is also required to gather and scatter local results. Therefore another typical communication we consider is collective, particularly MPI_Allreduce in our case as it is the dominant communication operation in many important parallel workloads [17].

2. **Communication Fraction:** we define communication fraction as the communication time divided by the total runtime. High communication fractions correspond to communication-intensive behavior. The synthetic BSP benchmark can be configured for varied amounts of computation and communication work in each iteration, and enabling control of the communication fraction. In this study, we explore communication fractions from 5 % to 40 %.

3. **Replacement Node Distance:** the replacement of failed node generally disrupts network locality, potentially reducing communication performance. For example, the replacement node is generally further away, increasing latency. We use the maximum number of hops between neighbors of failed and replacement nodes to quantify distance. The BG/Q system used has a five-dimensional torus network. A node location can be identified using five coordinates $< A, B, C, D, E >$. It is directly linked with nearest neighbors in the $\pm A, \pm B, \pm C, \pm D, \pm E$ direction. Table 1 describes the shape of given partitions on Mira [2]. For a 2048-node partition, the maximum number of hops is $2 + 2 + 2 + 8 + 1 = 15$. Users can specify which rank to fail to control the replacement node distance.

The synthetic BSP allows users to configure communication pattern, communication fraction and replacement node distance. By varying these parameters, we explore the post-recovery performance space of shrinking and non-shrinking.

3 Experiments

3.1 Experiment Setup

We use Mira [1], an IBM Blue Gene/Q system at Argonne National Laboratory for all our experiments. The MPI library we use is MPICH 3.1.4.

The synthetic BSP uses 1024 nodes in shrinking mode and 1025 nodes (one spare) in non-shrinking mode, one process per node. We run two recovery modes on the same partition allocated. Based on Mira job allocation policy, the allocation for 1025 nodes is a 2048-node partition, with torus shape $4 \times 4 \times 4 \times 16 \times 2$. For non-shrinking, rank 0 - 1023 are in WORK_COMM, while rank 1024 is the spare rank. The maximum replacement node distance is 15 and the expected value of replacement node distance is 8.

We run the program for certain number of iterations, which is divided into the first half and the second half. The recovery behavior of shrinking and non-shrinking is simulated in the middle of run. We then measure the post-recovery execution time, that is, the execution time of second half. We use that of failure free run as baseline, denoted as *base*. Each run is approximate 120 seconds. The message size per communication is 400 KB/node.

First, to compare the post-recovery performance of neighbor and collective communication, we configure the synthetic BSP to either only perform neighbor or collective communication in each run. Second, we explore the effect of failed node replacement on non-shrinking performance by setting replacement node distance to maximum 15 hops, expected 8 hops and minimum 1 hop. At last, to study the post-recovery performance across different communication fraction, we configure the number of loops for computation and communication to tune the communication fraction.

The metrics we use for comparison are post-recovery execution time and post-recovery efficiency. We define post-recovery performance as the inverse of post-recovery execution time. And the post-recovery efficiency is performance normalized to allocated resources.

$$Performance = \frac{1}{Execution\,Time} \tag{1}$$

$$Efficiency = \frac{Performance}{Resources\,Allocated} \tag{2}$$

3.2   Performance vs. Communication Pattern and Replacement Node Distance

We study the impact of replacement node distance on post-recovery performance. We first use the neighbor communication pattern, and then the collective communication pattern.

A. Neighbor Communication. Figure 4a depicts the post-recovery execution time of base (no failure), non-shrinking and shrinking cases for varied replacement node distance. The base execution time is 58.3 seconds. With non-shrinking recovery, it is 1.2 seconds slower for expected replacement node distance (i.e. 8 hops) and 2.1 seconds slower for maximum replacement node distance (i.e. 15 hops). In contrast, shrinking achieves approximate same performance as base. We observe no performance degradation. A careful look at the post-recovery

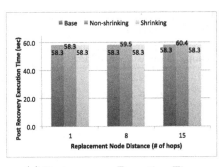

(a) Post-recovery Execution Time

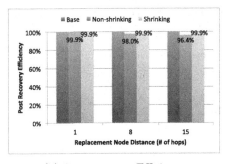

(b) Post-recovery Efficiency

Fig. 4. Impact of replacement node distance on post-recovery performance for **Neighbor** communication pattern, communication fraction = 10 %

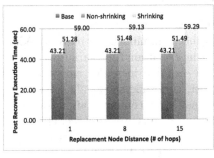

(a) Post-recovery Time

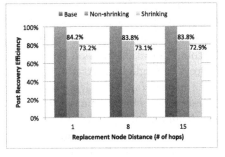

(b) Post-recovery Efficiency

Fig. 5. Impact of replacement node distance on post-recovery performance for **Collective** communication pattern, communication fraction = 2.8 %

communication time in Table 2 shows that non-shrinking has worse communication performance, 1.1 seconds slower for 8 hops and 2.1 seconds slower for 15 hops. Hence the overall performance degradation of non-shrinking comes from worse communication latency due to network topology change.

We normalize the efficiency of non-shrinking and shrinking to base in Fig. 4b. Non-shrinking suffers up to 3.5 % lower efficiency, while shrinking produces 99.9 % efficiency in all cases. The 0.1 % reduction results from node loss. Our results suggest that shrinking has better post-recovery efficiency for neighbor communication pattern.

B. Collective Communication. Fig. 5 shows the performance comparison of base, non-shrinking and shrinking for collective communication. Both non-shrinking and shrinking exhibit much worse execution time. Non-shrinking is 19 % slower and shrinking is 37 % slower. We notice that both have significantly longer collective communication time (see Table 3), which counts for most of performance degradation. Since the implementation or algorithm of collective

Table 2. Post-recovery neighbor communication time

#hops	Base	Non-shrinking	Shrinking
1	5.8	5.8	5.8
8	5.8	7.0	5.8
15	5.8	7.9	5.8

Table 3. Post-recovery collective communication time

#hops	Base	Non-shrinking	Shrinking
1	1.22	9.29	16.97
8	1.22	9.49	17.11
15	1.22	9.49	17.27

operation `MPI_Allreduce` is optimized for power-of-two number of processes, shrinking suffers more than non-shrinking.

3.3   Performance vs. Communication Fraction

We now compare the post-recovery performance across various communication fractions. Figure 6 shows the results for neighbor communication pattern. When the communication fraction is as low as 5 %, the execution time variation of both recovery is negligible. As the communication fraction increases, non-shrinking performance continues degrading. In contrast, shrinking shows almost no performance loss. For communication intensive case (40 % communication fraction), non-shrinking is 7.6 % slower compared to base and ends in 7.5 % lower efficiency. Shrinking achieves 99.9 % efficiency for varied communication fractions.

Figure 7 shows the post-recovery performance of collective communication pattern for communication fraction 4 %, 20 %, and 41 %. Non-shrinking and shrinking show the similar results as before, both suffering dramatic performance degradation. The execution time breakdown in Fig. 7a reveals that the computation time of shrinking and non-shrinking after recovery are stable, approximating base. However, the communication time are unexpectedly worse. In all cases, the communication time of shrinking is about 14× of base, compared to non-shrinking about 7.8× of base. In other word, the collective communication of non-power-of-two is about 2× worse than power-of-two cases, which counts for half of shrinking performance loss. Shrinking and non-shrinking recovery are not feasible given current low performance unless collectives are improved.

4   Discussion

While our experiments lend some insights, there are many additional parameters that must be considered for a complete solution. These include:

Number of Spare Nodes. In above experiments, we only consider one node failure and thus have one spare node. In reality, applications may experience frequent errors due to the high failure rate of system. We discuss how many spare nodes are needed in practice for non-shrinking scheme to be viable. Table 4 summarizes the notation we use.

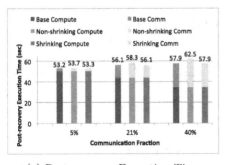
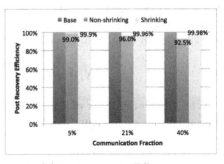

(a) Post-recovery Execution Time   (b) Post-recovery Efficiency

Fig. 6. Post-recovery performance of **Neighbor** communication pattern for varied communication fraction, replacement node distance = 8 hops

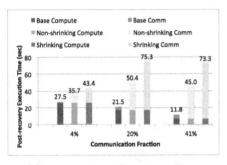
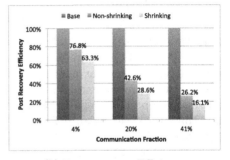

(a) Post-recovery Execution Time   (b) Post-recovery Efficiency

Fig. 7. Post-recovery performance of **Collective** communication pattern for varied communication fraction, replacement node distance = 8 hops

Table 4. Notation

Symbol	Description
N	Number of nodes used in computation
n	Number of spare nodes
λ	Node failure rate
$X(t)$	Number of failures at time t
T	Execution time in failure free case

Assume the failures occur randomly (Poisson process). The node failure rate is λ failures per hour. The interrupt rate of application is linearly proportional to number of nodes, that is, $(N + n)\lambda$. The number of failures at time t is $X(t)$. The number of failures in the interval $[0, t]$ has a Poisson distribution.

$$P\{X(t) = r\} = \frac{e^{-(N+n)\lambda t}((N + n)\lambda t)^r}{r!} \tag{3}$$

The mean of number of failures is $(N + n)\lambda t$. The probability of having less than n failures during runtime T is

$$F(n) = P(X(T) \leq n) = e^{-(N+n)\lambda T} \sum_{r=1}^{n} \frac{((N + n)\lambda T)^r}{r!} \tag{4}$$

Given probability requirements, we can derive the number of spare nodes needed by Eq. (4). To tolerate frequent failures and guarantee successful completion of run, non-shrinking recovery desires more pre-allocated resources and therefore further reduces post-recovery efficiency. In contrast, the fraction of lost computing power may be negligible for shrinking at beginning. But reaching certain number of failures, shrinking would suffer limited computing resources.

Load Imbalance. In this study, we assume the load is perfectly balanced across processes. In reality, programmers design load balance functions to distribute workload as uniformly as possible so that the overall performance constrained by the slowest process can be improved. Numerous scientific simulations essentially require periodic repartitioning of data throughout the computation and thus contain a load balance functionality. Such applications include N-Body simulation, molecular dynamics.

There are a considerable number of researchers working on mitigating load imbalance of parallel applications [3,13,14]. Recognized by these studies, it is difficult to achieve 100 % load balance. We discuss the potential influence of load imbalance on post-recovery performance.

- Non-shrinking: if there exists load imbalance and the failed node happens to be overloaded. After recovery, the replacement node inherits its data, thus being overloaded. We already observe communication performance degradation due to increased communication distance. With overloaded data, the replacement node is more likely to become the slowest process and hence harm the overall performance.
- Shrinking: efficient shrinking recovery relies on the uniform redistribution of failed node's data. The post-recovery performance is constrained by the effectiveness of load balancing functionality. In the worst cases, only one node takes the data of failed node and doubles its work. As a result, the execution time is 2×. Various load balancing algorithms has been proposed such as global algorithms [14], diffusive algorithms [9]. Data redistribution comes with a cost. In next section, we will discuss the impact of load balancing cost on recovery performance.

Table 5. Notation used in the load balancing cost model

Symbol	Description
T	Total runtime in failure free case
N	Number of nodes used in computation
n	Number of spare nodes
L	Cost of load balancing
α	Efficiency degradation fraction of non-shrinking, $(0, 1)$
Eff_{ns}	Post-recovery efficiency of non-shrinking
Eff_s	Post-recovery efficiency of shrinking

Load Balancing Cost. We now consider the efficiency given load balancing cost and multiple failures. For simplification, we ignore the cost of failure detection, recovery, and reconfiguration, assuming that these are constant among two schemes and negligible compared to total runtime. We assume that the load balancer achieves perfect load balancing by a single invocation. And the cost for each invocation is constant.

Table 5 defines the symbols. Assume the application runs on N nodes for time T in failure free environment. Suppose n failures would occur during runtime. Therefore we pre-allocated n spare nodes for non-shrinking scheme.

Non-shrinking performance degrades by α after recovery due to network topology disturbance, the value of which is constrained by the farthest replacement node distance among multiple recoveries. A coarse estimation of its runtime is $\frac{T}{1-\alpha}$ (upper bound). The efficiency is therefore given by

$$Eff_{ns} = \frac{\frac{1-\alpha}{T}}{N+n} = \frac{1-\alpha}{(N+n)T} \tag{5}$$

Shrinking performance reduces as a result of computing power loss, i.e. $\frac{1}{N}$ for one node loss. The time required to complete computation is $\frac{N}{N-n}T$ (upper bound) and the cost for each load balancing invocation is L, and therefore nL in total. The overall shrinking efficiency is

$$Eff_s = \frac{\frac{1}{\frac{NT}{N-n}+nL}}{N} = \frac{1}{(\frac{NT}{N-n}+nL)N} \tag{6}$$

Combining Eqs. (5) and (6), we derive the cost of load balancing that equalizes their efficiencies.

$$L = \frac{(\alpha N^2 - n^2)T}{(1-\alpha)(N-n)nN} \tag{7}$$

If the load balancing cost is less than the value given by Eq. (7), shrinking delivers overall better efficiency than non-shrinking.

We take the parameters used in our experiments where $N = 1024$ and $\alpha = 0.02$ (non-shrinking neighbor for 8 hops). Normalized to base runtime T, the

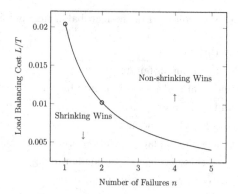

Fig. 8. Load balancing cost that equalizes efficiencies of shrinking and non-shrinking as a function of number of failures, where $N = 1024, \alpha = 0.02$

load balancing cost is depicted as a function of the number of failures in Fig. 8. The area below the curve is winning space of shrinking, while above that non-shrinking beats shrinking. For instance, with one failure, the load balancing cost needs to be less than 2 % of runtime for shrinking to win, and 1 % is required for two failures. That means for a 1-hour run, load balancing should complete within 72 seconds.

As the number of failures increases, the allowable load balancing cost drops sharply. This suggests higher quality of load balancer is desired for shrinking to be competitive under high failure rates circumstances.

5   Related Work

Teranishi et al. [16] proposed a software framework to enable Local Failure Local Recovery using ULFM which employed the non-shrinking recovery. They observed a large performance fluctuation which may come from problems of ULFM in managing new communication patterns after process loss. Our work compares both shrinking and non-shrinking and reveals performance issues due to network topology and MPI collectives.

Laguna et al. [11] discussed suitable recovery models for different application types from programmability perspective. They concluded that shrinking is easy to achieve for master-slave applications, while non-shrinking can be implemented with trivial modification for both master-slave and BSP applications. In contrast, our work studies these two schemes from efficiency perspective. Our results show that shrinking is good for neighbor communication pattern while non-shrinking is good for collective communication pattern. Analysis on additional effects indicate there are winning spaces for both schemes regarding different failure rates, communication pattern and load balancing cost.

Bhatele et al. [4,5] studied how to improve the performance of parallel applications on 5D torus network via task mapping. Their results suggest performance varies with different partitions. Careful mapping choices can significantly improve performance. Our work focus on post-recovery performance. We find that collectives are sensitive to network topology change due to node failures. In addition, non-shrinking communication performance degrades as a function of replacement node distance. Our results suggest 5D network topology affect choices of recovery model.

6   Summary and Future Work

We develop a synthetic BSP application to explore the post-recovery performance of shrinking and non-shrinking approaches. Exploring three factors – communication pattern, communication fraction and replacement node distance, we found that shrinking performs best for neighbor communication pattern, while non-shrinking performance degrades as it disrupts network locality. However with collective communication structure, both recovery schemes degrade badly. Advances of MPI collective implementations or algorithms are needed before this comparison is revisited.

Interesting future directions include experiments of investigating the impact of load balancing cost, load imbalance, use of non-blocking collectives. Further study on real applications is also desirable.

Acknowledgments. This work was supported by the Office of Advanced Scientific Computing Research, Office of Science, U.S. Department of Energy, under Award DE-SC0008603 and completed in part with resources provided by ALCF under Contract DE-AC02-06CH11357. We thank Ignacio Laguna and David Richards of LLNL for discussion and suggestion that assisted our work.

References

1. Mira. https://www.alcf.anl.gov/mira
2. Running jobs. https://www.alcf.anl.gov/user-guides/running-jobs
3. Bhandarkar, M.A., et al.: Adaptive load balancing for mpi programs. In: International Conference on Computational Science, ICCS 2001 (2001)
4. Bhatele, A., et al.: Mapping applications with collectives over sub-communicators on torus networks. In: Proceedings of the International Conference on High Performance Computing, Networking, Storage and Analysis, SC 2012 (2012)
5. Bhatele, A., et al.: Optimizing the performance of parallel applications on a 5d torus via task mapping. In: IEEE International Conference on High Performance Computing. IEEE Computer Society (2014)
6. Bland, W., et al.: An evaluation of user-level failure mitigation support in MPI. In: Proceedings of the 19th European Conference on Recent Advances in the Message Passing Interface, EuroMPI 2012 (2012)
7. Cappello, F.: Fault tolerance in petascale/exascale systems: current knowledge, challenges and research opportunities. Int. J. High Perform. Comput. Appl. **23**(3), 212–226 (2009)
8. Cappello, F., Geist, A., Gropp, W., Kale, S., Kramer, B., Snir, M.: Toward exascale resilience: 2014 update. Supercomput. Front. Innovations **1**(1), 5–28 (2014)

9. Cybenko, G.: Dynamic load balancing for distributed memory multiprocessors. J. Parallel Distrib. Comput. **7**, 279–301 (1989)

10. Heroux, M.A.: Toward resilient algorithms and applications. In: Proceedings of the 3rd Workshop on Fault-tolerance for HPC at extreme scale, FTXS 2013 (2013)

11. Laguna, I., et al.: Evaluating user-level fault tolerance for MPI applications. In: Proceedings of the 21st European MPI Users' Group Meeting, EuroMPI/ASIA 2014 (2014)

12. Moody, A., Bronevetsky, G., Mohror, K., Supinski, B.R.d.: Design, modeling, and evaluation of a scalable multi-level checkpointing system. In: Proceedings of the 2010 ACM/IEEE International Conference for High Performance Computing, Networking, Storage and Analysis, SC 2010 (2010)

13. Pearce, O., et al.: Load balancing n-body simulations with highly non-uniform density. In: Proceedings of the 28th ACM International Conference on Supercomputing, ICS 2014 (2014)

14. Schloegel, K., et al.: A unified algorithm for load-balancing adaptive scientific simulations. In: Proceedings of the 2000 ACM/IEEE Conference on Supercomputing, SC 2000 (2000)

15. Snir, M., et al.: Addressing failures in exascale computing*. Int. J. High Perform. Comput. IJHPC **28**(2), 129–173 (2013)

16. Teranishi, K., Heroux, M.A.: Toward local failure local recovery resilience model using MPI-ULFM. In: Proceedings of the 21st European MPI Users' Group Meeting, EuroMPI/ASIA 2014 (2014)

17. Widener, P., Ferreira, K.B., Levy, S., Hoefler, T.: Exploring the effect of noise on the performance benefit of nonblocking allreduce. In: Proceedings of the 21st European MPI Users' Group Meeting, EuroMPI/ASIA 2014 (2014)

Canaries in a Coal Mine:
Using Application-Level Checkpoints
to Detect Memory Failures

Patrick M. Widener[1]([⊠]), Kurt B. Ferreira[1], Scott Levy[2],
and Nathan Fabian[1]

[1] Center for Computing Research, Sandia National Laboratories,
Albuquerque, NM, USA
{patrick.widener,kbferre,ndfabia}@sandia.gov
[2] University of New Mexico, Albuquerque, NM, USA
slevy@cs.unm.edu

Abstract. Memory failures in future extreme scale applications are a
significant concern in the high-performance computing community and
have attracted much research attention. We contend in this paper that
using application checkpoint data to detect memory failures has potential benefits and is preferable to examining application memory. To
support this contention, we describe the application of machine learning techniques to evaluate the veracity of checkpoint data. Our preliminary results indicate that supervised decision tree machine learning
approaches can effectively detect corruption in restart files, suggesting
that future extreme-scale applications and systems may benefit from
incorporating such approaches in order to cope with memory failures.

1 Introduction

Fault-tolerance has been identified as a major challenge for exascale-class systems. As systems grow in scale and complexity, failures become increasingly
likely. Due to the plateauing of CPU clock rates, a system $1,000x$ more powerful than today's petascale systems will likely need $1,000x$ more components
to deliver this increased performance [5]. This increase in component count
will likely lead to a commensurate increase in the system's failure rate. This
is compounded by the fact that shrinking transistor feature sizes and near-
threshold voltage logic needed to address energy concerns may further increase
the hardware failure rates. Given these dire predictions and the dynamics of
fault-tolerance techniques, significant effort has been and is being devoted to
improving system resilience.

P. M. Widener, K. B. Ferreira, N. Fabian—Sandia National Laboratories is a multiprogram laboratory managed and operated by Sandia Corporation, a wholly-owned
subsidiary of Lockheed MartinCorporation, for the U.S. Department of Energy's
National Nuclear Security Administration under contract DE-AC04-94AL85000.

© Springer International Publishing Switzerland 2015
S. Hunold et al. (Eds.): Euro-Par 2015 Workshops, LNCS 9523, pp. 669–681, 2015.
DOI: 10.1007/978-3-319-27308-2_54

The current *de facto* standard for fault-tolerance on high-performance computing (HPC) systems is coordinated checkpoint/restart. The success of checkpoint/restart on current systems depends on two assumptions: (1) failures are not commonplace; and (2) systems receive notification of failures, i.e., silent data corruption is rare. While these assumptions hold on today's systems, whether they will continue to hold on next-generation extreme-scale systems is unclear.

Silent data corruption (i.e., undetected bit flips) is of particular concern for future systems, and is not mitigated by checkpoint/restart. These undetected bit flips are such a concern that *application-* and *algorithmic-based* fault tolerance methods has become an active research area [7,8,11,15]. These methods, which are tailored to the computational characteristics of specific applications, are designed to ensure a correct answer even in the presence of failures in application memory. These methods typically work by (1) encoding redundant data into the problem such that data from failed nodes can be recomputed [7,8,15]; or (2) exploiting an algorithm-specific relationship between the parallel application and its individual data chunks. Data lost due to a failure affects the result by possibly increasing the error of the solution or by forcing surviving nodes to run longer until the problem has converged. Therefore, the number of nodes lost determines the application time-to-solution or the error associated with the solution [11]. A key feature of these methods is that they typically must protect the entire memory footprint for the application, which can be substantial.

In contrast to current algorithmic methods, we propose to detect errors by analyzing checkpoint files written by the application instead of examining the application's entire memory footprint. In particular, we propose using checkpoint files to detect silent data corruption in HPC applications. This position has a number of advantages over more traditional application-based methods. For example:

- Current extreme-scale algorithms already use checkpointing for fault-tolerance, and will therefore require little modification to take advantage of this method.
- By definition checkpoints represent the critical state of the application. The entire memory footprint can be regenerated from this critical state.
- Checkpoints are typically much smaller than the application's memory footprint and therefore will likely require lower overheads to protect.
- Errors that occur but do not eventually impact checkpoint data are ignored as they do not impact an application's critical state.
- Error detection methods may have lower overheads than the detection and correction mechanisms found in algorithmic approaches.
- Checkpoint verification can run in parallel with application computation, not interfering with application progress.
- Checkpoint data is widely used as input for downstream tasks such as analytics and visualization. Making checkpoints a basis of fault-detection efforts also protects the operation of such downstream computations.

We make the following contributions in this paper:

- We introduce an application-independent strategy of verifying application checkpoints as proxies for application memory corruption.

- We describe the application of particular unsupervised and supervised machine learning (ML) methods to the problem of verifying checkpoint data.
- Using checkpoints from an execution of a well-known simulation, we examine the clustering and prediction accuracy of our chosen methods. While unsupervised clustering does not appear to distinguish corrupted data well, we found that a supervised learning method trained on bit-level errors can classify corrupted checkpoints with reasonable accuracy.

2   Checkpointing on Current Systems

Checkpoint/restart is the most widely studied and deployed set of techniques for mitigating the cost of failure recovery in large-scale high-performance computing (HPC) systems. Applications periodically save their critical state, a *checkpoint*, to some form of storage that is likely to survive the failure. Upon failure, a *restart* is performed: the last known good checkpoint is retrieved from stable storage, loaded into memory, and computation resumes.

Checkpoints contain the critical data of an HPC application – the data needed to fully recreate the state of the application after a failure. They are typically highly optimized and considerably smaller than the runtime memory footprint of the application. For example, Table 1 shows the per-process memory footprint for two key production applications from Sandia National Laboratories: LAMMPS [21] (a well-known molecular dynamics code) and CTH [9] (a shock physics code). These key US Department of Energy applications run for long periods of time in production modes and exhibit a range of different communication structures. From this table, we see that their application-based checkpoints are significantly smaller than their entire memory footprint. The CTH checkpoints are roughly 5 % of the application's memory footprint. The LAMMPS checkpoints are approximately 19 % of the memory footprint for this LAMMPS problem, EAM[1].

Because application checkpoints capture the critical state of an application but are a small fraction of the size of the application's entire memory footprint, we contend that checkpoints can be effectively and efficiently exploited to protect against silent data corruption in the memory of HPC applications. Since they contain the critical state of the application, we can identify any errors that would corrupt the solution produced by the application. Because checkpoints are so much smaller than the application's memory footprint, the overhead of examining them to identify the effects of data corruption will likely be much lower than that of considering all of application memory directly.

3   Approach: Using Checkpoints as Failure Detectors

We identify two types of checkpoint corruption, *indirect* and *direct*. Indirect corruption occurs when a silent error in application memory is captured and

---

[1] This is the largest checkpoint over tested LAMMPS inputs (EAM, LJ, SNAP, CHAIN, RHODO). The average checkpoint size is considerably smaller – 7 %.

Table 1. Per-process memory footprint and application-based checkpoint sizes for CTH and LAMMPS. *Memory Footprint* is averaged across the lifetime of the application. *APP Checkpoint Size* is averaged across all checkpoints and nodes. The final column is the relationship of these averages, checkpoint size to the memory footprint size, expressed as percentage.

Application	Memory Footprint (MB)	APP Checkpoint Size (MB)	CKPT % of Footprint
CTH	583	26.1	4.5%
LAMMPS (EAM)	3,256	608.0	18.7%

preserved in a checkpoint. In this case, detection of a corrupted checkpoint is an indication that the application has been corrupted and may produce an untrustworthy result. Recovery in this case requires restarting the application either from a known-good checkpoint or from the beginning. Direct corruption occurs when the checkpoint itself is corrupted without affecting the state of the application. Although the application is unaffected, if a failure occurs before the next checkpoint is taken, restoring the state of the application from the checkpoint would allow the corruption to propagate into the application's memory. Recovery in this case could be accomplished by either re-checkpointing the application or rolling back to an earlier known-good checkpoint.

Automatic classification using selected machine learning techniques can help us determine whether a checkpoint contains one or more errors. By training a supervised learning classifier using known-good checkpoints along with ones that include known errors, newly-generated checkpoints can be identified as valid or not. This identification carries a degree of certainty which will vary according to the learning method chosen, the semantics of the checkpoints themselves (necessarily an application-dependent factor), and the amount and variety of checkpoints used for training data.

Choice of features for training data is an interesting issue in this case. Checkpoint metadata or provenance information can contribute meaningfully. For example, a checkpoint size which differs from expectations might be a sign of a truncation. Also, a particular node with known memory issues or other significant maintenance history might be represented as additional features in a potential model. Determining features based on the checkpoint data itself will likely prove more complicated. Assigning features based on checkpoint data semantics is most straightforward but is necessarily application-specific; however, this would allow for considerable reduction of feature dimensionality by eliminating highly-correlated data. More generic approaches such as considering raw bit patterns in the output are possible, but present undifferentiated feature ranges and will likely pose scalability issues; consider that checkpoint files with sizes measured in hundreds of megabytes are not uncommon. Also, the choice of learning method is dependent on how checkpoint data and metadata are mapped into a feature space: decision trees or Bayesian methods may work better with heterogeneous data while support vector machines are more appropriate for data which can be scaled into a common numeric range.

Ideally, such a classification step would be performed immediately upon checkpoint generation. However, it may not be feasible for an application to perform classification itself at each checkpoint without seriously degrading solve time. If *in situ* classification is not possible, it may be possible to maintain in-band detection by providing a communication channel whereby an application can be notified when a previous checkpoint has been determined invalid. It may be possible to accomplish classification within an acceptable checkpoint interval through the use of co-processors such as GPGPUs or reserved processor cores or machine nodes. This is similar to how analytics are performed in so-called "in-transit" solutions; in this approach classification tasks would be treated as another type of data analysis. This would provide feasibility advantages in that perturbation effects are typically already addressed to varying degrees in these environments, and also in that such approaches are already using checkpoint data as input to visualization and analysis tasks. If classification cannot be performed in a checkpoint interval, an out-of-band method, potentially requiring the retention of checkpoint data for lengths of time greater than a checkpoint interval, will be required.

4   Using Learning Approaches to Classify Checkpoints

To explore the possible application of ML approaches to checkpoint error detection, we conducted a series of experiments which we detail in this section.

4.1   Application Checkpoint Description

For this work, we consider errors in the aforementioned LAMMPS production molecular dynamics application. From LAMMPS, we consider the SNAP potential. SNAP is a computationally intensive, quantum accurate potential that uses the same kernel as GAP [1]. This potential was chosen for a number of reasons: (1) this represents an important scalable workload used at extreme-scale, and (2) due to the small number of atoms, checkpoints are exceedingly small – 92 bytes per MPI process. These 92 byte checkpoints allow us to investigate the efficacy of our position while not having to worry about performance overheads.

4.2   Modeling Checkpoint Data

We chose for our investigation to treat the 128,000 92-byte restart files from LAMMPS as samples of 92 one-byte features. This choice disregards potentially useful information that might be derived from the files. For example, an examination of the logical structure of the restart files would result in fewer features per sample, as each restart file is a serialization of a C++ application object using data types which are multiple bytes in length. Using the logical structure of the restart file could also give an indication of how features should be weighted when applying different ML methods.

Despite these considerations, we believe our approach still provides useful insight. We are most concerned with the detection of single-bit errors, which should be better isolated using a larger number of single-byte features. Also, as different applications write different information in their checkpoints, exploiting the structure of the restart files is necessarily an application-dependent modeling approach that would need to be repeated for other applications. This information can also be difficult to acquire if access to the source code for the application in question is unavailable. Our approach is a proof-of-concept, but it does provide for examining checkpoints with arbitrary structure.

We synthesized corrupted restart files with different scales of errors. To represent silent data corruption or "bit-flips", we introduced errors by flipping one, two, or three bits in a single restart file. This was done by choosing a byte at random in the restart file, and then choosing a random bit within that byte to invert; multiple bit flips were done by repeating this process. We synthesized larger-scale errors by choosing either one byte or three bytes at random and substituting a random bit pattern. These patterns are consistent with error patterns found on current systems [26].

We use the `scikit-learn` [20] Python toolkit for our experiments. `scikit-learn` contains implementations of many different ML algorithms, allowing implementation changes with relatively little overhead. Several other toolkits of this kind exist, most notably the Weka class library [14]. While performance of the classification algorithms was not a primary concern in this work, attempting online or near-line classification might require parallelized or more performant approaches for applications with larger restart files.

4.3   Choosing an ML Technique

Although we expect correlations between files written out as part of a group checkpoint, they may not necessarily relate to whether errors occur within any single file. For simplicity we consider each checkpoint file as an independent and identically distributed sample of potential error. Because each byte is a feature, the space we are considering here is not contiguous; in fact, certain byte values for certain features will probably never arise for a checkpoint value, and should be construed as erroneous. This implies a high dimensional solution space where regions of the space which consist of plausible values are separated by large "voids", regions where the contained observations are not plausible in our context. Our expectation here is very much a non-linear relationship among the features, observations into the solution space, and the likelihoods of a bit error occurring in any given file. Based on this, we consider both a k-means clustering [18] and CART, a tree classifier as appropriate first passes to capture those regions and the relationship between them and detected errors, the results of which are discussed later in this section.

Moving beyond these initial attempts to capture the space, several possibilities exist for exploration in future work. Unsupervised approaches, self-

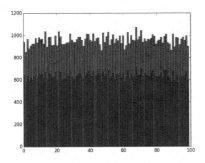   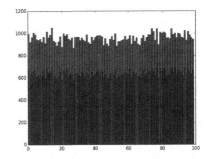

(a) Clustering with 100 clusters, 1-bit errors   (b) Clustering with 100 clusters, 3-byte errors

Fig. 1. K-means clustering results. The X-axis is cluster index, and the Y-axis is the number of samples in each cluster.

organizing maps or growing neural gas [13], may provide better information about the layout or structure of the file space, especially to understand whether and where these void regions lay between the good. In particular k-means clustering provides an opportunity to explore proximity measures beyond Euclidean distance and determine if there is a better comparison between points in the high dimensional space. With exploration of the features themselves, including imposing structure from the definition of the file, we may find additional correlations in the features allowing some reduction from raw byte counts, such as bag-of-words or Latent Dirichlet Allocation [2] used in text. Following Rennie et al. [22], we may find good results using Naive Bayes with more information rich features.

4.4   Unsupervised Learning: Clustering with K-Means

We first investigated an unsupervised learning method, k-means clustering. Our goal here was to explore whether explicit labeling is a necessity for this set of data. We used the `scikit-learn` *KMeans* module to perform clustering. The input samples were the set of uncorrupted restart files combined with a set of corrupted restart files with a specific error type as described above, and we used 100 as K. We conducted three separate clustering tests, with the results displayed in Fig. 1. These figures stack the histogram of the uncorrupted clusters on the bottom with the corrupted clusters histogram on top.

If clustering is to be effective at distinguishing restart file corruption, we would expect to see a majority of the samples corresponding to corrupted restart files collected in a subset of the clusters, and similarly for those samples corresponding to uncorrupted restart files. The figure shows that, instead, both sets of samples are relatively uniformly distributed across the set of clusters. Note also that the general uniform shape does not change as the scale of error changes across the subfigures. Similar results hold for $K = 10, 50, 200, 300$, not presented here due to space constraints. Our approach here is straightforward, without

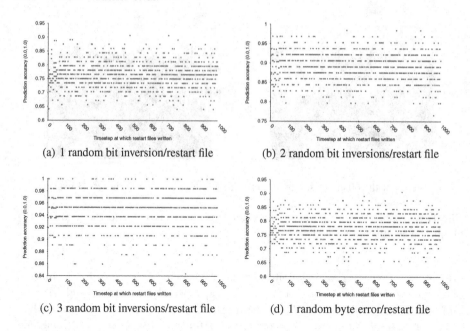

(a) 1 random bit inversion/restart file   (b) 2 random bit inversions/restart file

(c) 3 random bit inversions/restart file   (d) 1 random byte error/restart file

Fig. 2. Prediction accuracy of each classifier on the same type of error, across all ranks and timesteps of the set of restart files.

any significant tuning of the clustering algorithm. However, for the purposes of our exploration, an unsupervised learning approach does not seem to be effective in distinguishing restart files with errors. We therefore turn our attention to explicitly labeled samples and a supervised method.

4.5   Supervised Learning with Decision Tree Methods

As detailed above, we chose a decision tree-based method as a test case for supervised learning (comparing a training set of files against collections of files known to be corrupted or not) on our checkpoint data. As with the unsupervised K-means experiments, we treat each 92-byte restart file as a sample with 92 features, namely the constituent bytes of the file. We first trained a separate decision-tree classifier on each type of our synthetically corrupted data (1,2,3-bit and 1,3-byte). For this experiment, we trained each classifier on the entire set of uncorrupted restart files (labeled as good inputs) and on the type-specific set of corrupted files (labeled as bad inputs). We then evaluated the prediction accuracy on the entire set of bad files. Since the classifier had already built a model using the bad samples, we expected high accuracy as this experiment served as a best-case trial of the decision tree method on these inputs.

These results are presented in Fig. 2. Each point on each plot is the prediction accuracy for the restart files, across all nodes at each timestep for which corrupted data was synthesized (if a restart file was written by a node at a timestep in the uncorrupted data, we synthesized a file with each type of data

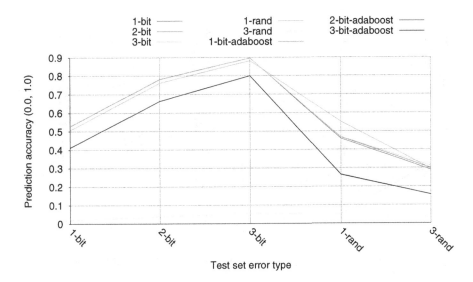

Fig. 3. Prediction accuracy of each classifier against the test set of each type of random errors (1-3 bit, 1 and 3 byte)

corruption). The data indicates that the bit-scale-trained classifiers have better accuracy detecting bit-scale errors than do the byte-scale classifiers on byte-scale errors. The 2-bit and 3-bit classifiers in particular are able to correctly classify the corrupted files with high accuracy.

In order to get a more general idea of the ability of the different classifiers to correctly identify multiple types of corrupted data, we then conducted an MxN comparison where we measured the prediction accuracy of each classifier on each type of our synthetic corrupted data. In this trial we also included classifiers trained using the AdaBoost ensemble method [12] for an example of an additional supervised learning method. Additionally, for this experiment we separated the corrupted data into training and testing sets, only running the prediction on the testing set of error data. Figure 3 displays the results of this experiment. All save one of the classifiers performed best at identifying restart files with at most 3 inverted bits. The notable exception in this case was the classifier trained on 3 random bytes, which exhibited poor prediction performance on every type of corrupted data tested. In addition, the prediction accuracy of all the classifiers suffered when tested against the higher scale (1-byte and 3-byte) errors. While our experiments were not intended to conclusively explain all behaviors of the set of classifiers, we hypothesize that increasing the scale of errors essentially introduces noise into the feature set, complicating accurate prediction.

Finally, although our experiments were not designed to comprehensively measure performance, we measured relative execution time of the different classifiers for the MxN comparison. Presented in Fig. 4, our results show that the AdaBoost ensemble classifiers took considerably longer than the single decision tree classifiers for each type of data corruption we examined. When considered

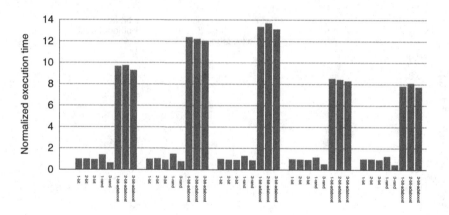

Fig. 4. Classifier execution time normalized to the performance of the 1-bit classifier.

against the results of Fig. 3, it seems clear that a large cost in prediction execution time for the AdaBoost classifiers produces no advantage in predictive accuracy. It is dangerous to generalize from this result, as it reflects dependencies on our test data as well as a lack of tuning of the training methods for the classifiers. However, for future applications of these types of learning methods for automatic classification of restart files, these types of investigations may prove useful.

5   Related Work

To the best of our knowledge, no existing work addresses silent data corruption in HPC applications by ensuring the veracity of checkpoints. That said, resilience methods which ensure progress in the face of both detected and undetected failures are diverse and popular. In this section, we briefly outline some of the more closely related studies and contrast them with our work.

Checkpointing: The prevalent method of defensive fault-tolerance mitigation in modern applications, coordinated checkpointing periodically writes global application or system state to stable storage [10]. Consistent application state snapshots are enforced through global barrier synchronization. When a process fails, all application processes can then be restarted from a known-good, globally consistent state. Algorithmic approaches borrowed from the distributed computing domain [6] allow applications to generate consistent checkpoints without using barriers, avoiding increasingly expensive global synchronization.

Issues of coordination and limited bandwidth to stable storage have given rise to uncoordinated or asynchronous checkpointing [3,10,16,24]. In these systems, nodes do not synchronize or coordinate in any way when they checkpoint, but they also keep a log of their sent messages on stable storage. Nodes restarting from local asynchronous checkpoints can then reconstruct a local state consistent with the application global state by replaying from their log stored messages received from other nodes.

These checkpointing methods provide no facilities for dealing with SDC in the application, requiring algorithmic- or application-based mechanisms to ensure these failures are detected and/or properly dealt with.

Algorithmic-Based Fault Tolerance: Algorithmic-based fault tolerance mechanisms are based on algorithms designed to be capable of ignoring errors while delivering a correct answer, or which are able to correct errors using techniques such as redundant data or computation. Algorithmic-specific data redundancy methods work by encoding additional data into the problem such that data from failed nodes can be recomputed; the algorithm is modified to update the encoding as computation progresses [7,8,15]. In contrast, computational redundancy relies on algorithm-specific relationships between the parallel application and its individual data chunks. Data loss due to failure can affect the result by increasing the margin of error or by extending the time for which surviving nodes must run in order for the problem to converge [4,11].

Machine Learning for Anomaly Detection: Machine learning techniques have been widely used to detect and classify different types of anomalies. Li *et al.* used 1-gram and naive Bayes methods to identify different file types [17]. Other anomaly detection contexts include malware behavior analysis [23], network intrusion detection [25], and internet traffic classification [19]. To our knowledge, these techniques have not yet been applied to checkpoint/restart artifacts.

6 Conclusion

Preserving the reliability of future extreme scale applications will require new approaches for ensuring the veracity of their computations. We contend that validating checkpoint data is a more feasible approach than examining application memory footprints. In this initial study, we described how checkpoint data can be used to detect errors in application memory that are captured in a checkpoint. As a proof of concept, we investigated the usefulness of machine learning methods for automatically detecting checkpoint corruption.

Our initial results indicate that supervised learning approaches may be preferable to clustering for detection of checkpoint corruption. In particular, we determined that decision trees show promise for detecting small errors (as many as 3 inverted bits out of a 92-byte checkpoint) with reasonable accuracy. Based on these results, we are refining our machine learning techniques to improve their performance and to account for a broader range of failure modalities. More generally, we hope that our investigation helps to generate more interest in using machine learning techniques for fault-tolerance. Many machine learning alternatives exist, with different abilities to tune for accuracy and different performance characteristics, and much of the promise of this approach is yet unexplored.

References

1. Bartók, A., Payne, M., Kondor, R., Csányi, G.: Gaussian approximation potentials: the accuracy of quantum mechanics, without the electrons. Phys. Rev. Lett. 104(13), 136403 (2010)
2. Blei, D., Ng, A.Y., Jordan, M.I.: Latent dirichlet allocation. JMLR 3, 993–1022 (2003)
3. Bosilca, G., Bouteiller, A., Cappello, F., Djilali, S., Fedak, G., Germain, C., Herault, T., Lemarinier, P., Lodygensky, O., Magniette, F., Neri, V., Selikhov, A.: MPICH-V: Toward a scalable fault tolerant MPI for volatile nodes. In: Conference on High Performance Networking and Computing (SC2002), pp. 1–18. Baltimore, MD, November 2002
4. Bridges, P.G., Hoemmen, M., Ferreira, K.B., Heroux, M.A., Soltero, P., Brightwell, R.: Cooperative application/OS DRAM fault recovery. In: Alexander, M., D'Ambra, P., Belloum, A., Bosilca, G., Cannataro, M., Danelutto, M., Traff, J.L., Vallée, G., Weidendorfer, J., Martino, B., Gerndt, M., Jeannot, E., Namyst, R., Roman, J., Scott, S.L. (eds.) Euro-Par 2011, Part II. LNCS, vol. 7156, pp. 241–250. Springer, Heidelberg (2012)
5. Cappello, F., Geist, A., Gropp, W., Kale, S., Kramer, B., Snir, M.: Toward exascale resilience: 2014 update. Supercomput.Front. Innovations 1(1) (2014). http://superfri.org/superfri/article/view/14
6. Chandy, K.M., Lamport, L.: Distributed snapshots: determining global states of distributed systems. ACM Trans. Comput. Syst. 3(1), 63–75 (1985)
7. Chen, Z.: Extending algorithm-based fault tolerance to tolerate fail-stop failures in high performance distributed environments. In: IPDPS, pp. 1–8. IEEE (2008)
8. Chen, Z., Dongarra, J.: Algorithm-based checkpoint-free fault tolerance for parallel matrix computations on volatile resources. In: 20th International Parallel and Distributed Processing Symposium, 2006. IPDPS 2006, April 2006
9. Hertel, E.S.J., Bell, R.L., Elrick, M.G., Farnsworth, A.V., Kerley, G.I., McGlaun, J.M., Petney, S.V., Silling, S.A., Taylor, P.A., Yarrington, L.: CTH: A software family for multi-dimensional shock physics analysis. In: Proceedings of the 19th International Symposium on Shock Waves, pp. 377–382, July 1993
10. Elnozahy, E.N.M., Alvisi, L., Wang, Y.M., Johnson, D.B.: A survey of rollback-recovery protocols in message-passing systems. ACM Comput. Surv. 34(3), 375–408 (2002)
11. Engelmann, C., Geist, G.A.: Super-scalable algorithms for computing on 100,000 processors. In: Sunderam, V.S., van Albada, G.D., Sloot, P.M.A., Dongarra, J. (eds.) ICCS 2005. LNCS, vol. 3514, pp. 313–321. Springer, Heidelberg (2005)
12. Freund, Y., Schapire, R.E.: A decision-theoretic generalization of on-line learning and an application to boosting. J. Comput. Syst. Sci. 55(1), 119–139 (1997)
13. Fritzke, B., et al.: A growing neural gas network learns topologies. Adv. Neural Inf. Process. Syst. 7, 625–632 (1995)
14. Hall, M., et al.: The WEKA data mining software: an update. SIGKDD Explorations 11(1) (2009). http://www.cs.waikato.ac.nz/ml/weka/
15. Kuang-Hua, H., Abraham, J.A.: Algorithm-based fault tolerance for matrix operations. IEEE Trans. Comput. 33, 518–528 (1984). http://dx.doi.org/10.1109/TC.1984.1676475
16. Lemarinier, P., Bouteiller, A., Herault, T., Krawezik, G., Cappello, F.: Improved message logging versus improved coordinated checkpointing for fault tolerant MPI. In: IEEE International Conference on Cluster Computing, pp. 115–124 (2004)

17. Li, W.J., Wang, K., Stolfo, S.J., Herzog, B.: Fileprints: Identifying file types by n-gram analysis. In: Information Assurance Workshop, 2005, IAW 2005. In: Proceedings from the Sixth Annual IEEE SMC, pp. 64–71. IEEE (2005)
18. Lloyd, S.: Least squares quantization in PCM. IEEE Trans. Inf. Theor. **28**(2), 129–137 (1982)
19. Nguyen, T.T., Armitage, G.: A survey of techniques for internet traffic classification using machine learning. IEEE Commun. Surv. Tutorials **10**(4), 56–76 (2008)
20. Pedregosa, F., et al.: Scikit-learn: Machine learning in Python. J. Mach. Learn. Res. 12, 2825–2830 (2011). http://scikit-learn.org/
21. Plimpton, S.J.: Fast parallel algorithms for short-range molecular dynamics. J. Comput. Phys. **117**, 1–19 (1995)
22. Rennie, J.D., Shih, L., Teevan, J., Karger, D.R., et al.: Tackling the poor assumptions of naive bayes text classifiers. In: ICML, vol. 3, pp. 616–623. Washington DC (2003)
23. Rieck, K., Trinius, P., Willems, C., Holz, T.: Automatic analysis of malware behavior using machine learning. J. Comput. Secur. **19**(4), 639–668 (2011)
24. Saito, Y., Shapiro, M.: Optimistic replication. ACM Comput. Surv. **37**(1), 42–81 (2005)
25. Sommer, R., Paxson, V.: Outside the closed world: on using machine learning for network intrusion detection. In: 2010 IEEE Symposium on Security and Privacy (SP), pp. 305–316. IEEE (2010)
26. Sridharan, V., DeBardeleben, N., Blanchard, S., Ferreira, K., Stearley, J., Shalf, J., Gurumurthi, S.: Memory errors in modern systems: the good, the bad, and the ugly. In: Proceedings of the Twentieth International Conference on Architectural Support for Programming Languages and Operating Systems, ASPLOS 2015, pp. 297–310. ACM, New York (2015). http://doi.acm.org/10.1145/2694344.2694348

ROME - Runtime and Operating Systems for the Many-Core Era

Energy Characterization and Optimization of Parallel Prefix-Sums Kernels

Angelos Papatriantafyllou[✉]

Faculty of Informatics, Institute of Information Systems, Research Group Parallel
Computing, Vienna University of Technology (TU Wien), Vienna, Austria
papatriantafyllou@par.tuwien.ac.at

Abstract. Prefix-sums appear frequently in numerous computational
tasks, and many performance efficient parallel prefix-sums algorithms
have been introduced for shared and distributed memory architectures.
However, as far as we know, the energy consumption behavior of these
algorithms is unknown, as well as the energy-performance trade-offs.

This paper is a first attempt to address the energy aspects of CPPS
(cache-aware parallel prefix-sums), a high performance parallel prefix-
sums kernel specific for x86 shared memory architectures. We provide
implementation details for CPPS and various sequential prefix-sums
algorithms that are used as building blocks. We measure performance
and energy consumption of CPPS with different configurations (sequential prefix-sums kernel, CPU frequency, number of threads and thread
placement policy). The results show significant energy savings, from 24 %
to 55 %, when configuring CPPS with an optimized rather than a non-
optimized sequential prefix-sums kernel for various different CPU frequency levels and number of threads.

1 Introduction

Energy consumption has become an important concern in large scale computer
systems, such as, servers and clusters for grid, cloud and high performance computing (HPC). Thus, designing energy efficient applications in the context of
large scale HPC is an unavoidable challenge. In this paper, we investigate the
energy footprint of a fundamental and memory bound kernel, the parallel prefix-
sums. The parallel prefix-sums, or parallel scan, is a key building block in the
implementation of many parallel algorithms.

Due to its low arithmetic intensity, prefix-sums exhibits a great amount of
CPU stalls, rendering it a prime candidate for investigating and optimizing its
energy behavior. Thus, we introduce CPPS algorithm, as well as a variety of
optimized sequential prefix-sums kernels and thread placement policies, used
as CPPS's building blocks to optimize for performance and energy efficiency.
Thanks to its better memory bandwidth utilization, CPPS outperforms other
publically available implementations [1,10,12,16].

To characterize the energy and performance behavior of CPPS, we investigate
several configurations, i.e., sequential prefix-sums kernels, CPU frequency levels,

© Springer International Publishing Switzerland 2015
S. Hunold et al. (Eds.): Euro-Par 2015 Workshops, LNCS 9523, pp. 685–696, 2015.
DOI: 10.1007/978-3-319-27308-2_55

number of threads and thread placement policies. The most important results of our experiments are: (1) significant energy savings, from 24 % to 55 %, and better energy reduction rate while descending to lower CPU frequencies when CPPS is configured with an optimized rather than a non-optimized sequential prefix-sums kernel in various different CPU frequencies and number of threads; (2) the optimized sequential prefix-sums kernels can improve CPPS's performance from 24 % to 54 %, compared to a non-optimized sequential kernel when running on the maximum CPU frequency; (3) thread placement across NUMA nodes plays a significant role resulting in energy reductions of CPPS up to 47.5 % when placing threads under the same socket with almost negligible performance degradation, and up to 56.73 % when considering both sequential kernel and thread placement policy.

Notation. Henceforth, we refer to sequential prefix-sums kernel as SPK, to optimized sequential prefix-sums kernel as OSPK, and to thread placement policy as TPP.

The rest of this paper is organized as follows. Section 2 introduces CPPS and presents different implementations for its building blocks. Section 3 describes assumptions and issues concerning energy and performance. Section 4 shows the experimental results. Section 5 concludes the paper.

2   Implementation

The operation of computing all prefix-sums (partial sums) for an array, also called a *scan*, is a fundamental parallel algorithm's building block [2,9,13]. Given an input array x of n elements, the problem is to compute the *(inclusive) prefix-sums* $\oplus_{j=0}^{i} x[j]$, for all indices i, $0 \leq i < n$, for a given, associative operation $\oplus$. In the following, the prefix-sums will be computed *in-place* with the ith prefix-sum stored in $x[i]$. The parallel prefix-sums problem is a well-studied problem and many theoretical (PRAM) and practical ideas have been proposed and presented over the past 30 years. Many implementations for x86 systems and GPUs are publically available [1,6,8,10–12,15,16], but none of them address energy aspects.

2.1   CPPS Algorithm

We introduce CPPS (cache-aware parallel prefix-sums) algorithm, as shown in Algorithm 1. It has been built on Pthreads for x86 shared memory systems. We chose Pthreads over other parallel frameworks, like OpenMP, mostly due to the flexibility of thread manipulation. The algorithm runs over an array x of n elements with a predetermined associative operator OP. CPPS consists of three phases in which the array x is divided in chunks of size Achunk*p+Bchunk and processed in parallel by p threads, where Achunk corresponds to a segment of elements assigned to every thread (first phase) and Bchunk corresponds to an additional segment assigned only to thread $t = 0$ (third phase). The size of Achunk is architecture specific since it is mostly based on LLC's (last level

---

Algorithm 1. CPPS: a cache-aware parallel prefix-sums algorithm

```
 1 cpps(x[], n, Achunk, Bchunk, t) //t: thread-id
 2   offset = getoffset(t); //Start for each thread (cell-id)
 3   for(i = offset; i < n; i = getoffsetnextchunk(t))
 4     y = x+i;
 5 //phase 1: SPK on y[s,...,nelems-1]
 6     s = 0; nelems = Achunk;
 7     seq_kernel(y+s, nelems);
 8 //phase 2: collect y[nelems-1], sum last_elems[0,...,t]
 9     last_elems[t] = y[nelems-1];
10     barrier(); sum=0;
11     for(th=0; th<((t!=0)?t:p); th++)
12       sum OP=last_elems[th];
13 //phase 3: t 0: SPK on y[s,...,nelems-1]
14 //t [1,(p-1)]: propagation on y[s,...,nelems-1]
15     if (t==0)
16       y[p*Achunk] OP= sum;
17       s = p*Achunk; nelems = Bchunk;
18       seq_kernel(y+s, nelems);
19     else
20       for (i=s; i<nelems; i++)
21         y[i] = sum OP y[i];
```

---

cache) size, main memory latency and number of active cores per socket. The Achunk must be lower than the system's LLC size and be bigger than the size of the next cache level (ex. L2). Otherwise, fetching chunk-sizes of L2- or L1-size entails faster computation of a CPPS's cycle (all phases) and more frequently being affected by the main memory latency. In addition, the size of Bchunk is dependent on the size of Achunk. In this paper, we do not cover how to find the best values for these parameters.

Both the first (lines 6–7) and the second phase (lines 9–12) are common for all the threads working on a distinct Achunk. In the last phase (lines 15–21), thread $t = 0$ runs prefix-sums sequentially (line 17) on a Bchunk segment while the other threads still work on their own segment. Intuitively, CPPS improves the parallelism of the last phase by assigning to thread $t = 0$ another segment.

In more details, in the first phase, each thread is assigned a Achunk segment on which it invokes a sequential prefix-sums, called seq_kernel, from s, corresponding to the begin of the Achunk, and for number of elements *nelems*. In a next section, we discuss different SPKs that we can apply. In the second phase, each thread passes to the shared array, last_elems, the last computed element of its own Achunk and synchronizes with the others at the barrier point. Subsequently, after exiting the barrier each thread performs a partial reduction on the last_elems from 0 to t. Only thread $t = 0$ reduces the entire array. At the last phase, thread $t = 0$ is assigned a Bchunk and runs the seq_kernel. The other threads propagate the result from phase 2 to their elements.

Algorithm 2. Trivial SPK

```
1 trivial_seq(x[], n)
2   for(i=1; i<n; i++) x[i] = x[i] OP x[i-1];
```

2.2   Sequential Prefix-Sums Kernels

One of the building blocks of CPPS and of the other publically available algorithms is a SPK. As far as we know, the other public implementations use the trivial SPK (Algorithm 2). The one used in Intel's SHOC benchmark suite [8] is an exception since it has been designed to exploit the wide vector registers of Intel's Xeon Phi accelerator. We show empirically later that trivial_seq is not the most performance/energy efficient SPK, mostly due to its data dependencies. For that reason, we have identified and implemented different categories of SPKs, based on the ideas of Chatterjee et al. [4] applied on register-based vector computers, leveraging several architectural features, such as, vectorization and hardware prefetching. Their main goals are: (1) maximizing instruction parallelism by vectorization and (2) improving pipelining by breaking data dependencies. The following categories consists of algorithms working on x, an array of n elements, and an associative operator OP.

The first category is comprised of two template algorithms, the vectorized seq1 (Algorithm 3) and the non-vectorized seq2 (Algorithm 4); both reuse data by chunking. In order to break the data dependencies we exploit the associativity property of prefix-sums operation. We execute independent prefix-sums operations by accessing different parts of x. To this end, x is split in chunks of size seg (line 2). The seg is determined at compile time by setting values for V, $V2$, $A2$ and A, where V corresponds to a vector register size (ex. SSE-width, AVX-width, etc.) and A to a multiple of V. $V2$ and $A2$ are not linked to vector features but to an alternative way of segmenting and chunking x. Many different versions can be produced by these templates by changing the above parameters; different configurations yield different performance.

Both algorithms unfolds in three phases. The first and third phase eliminate the data dependency. In the first phase (lines 5–9 and 5–8, respectively), an intermediate buffer, called sum, is used for storing the reduction (sum, multiplication, etc.) of the elements of each processed chunk; the reduction of the ith chunk is stored in sum$[i]$. The algorithms, in every iteration, update different sum's cell. In the second phase (lines 11 and 10–11, respectively), they run an inclusive prefix-sums on sum. In the final phase (lines 13–14 and 13–16, respectively), they use the sum$[i]$ to update the elements of the $i + 1$ chunk. There are many differences between the two templates. For instance, seq1 performs extra copies (buffer temp) in order to vectorize. seq2 runs inclusive prefix-sums on the last phase, contrast to seq1 which propagates sum elements to the chunks.

The vectorized instructions of seq1 exhibits no performance gain over the other OSPKs due to the limited amount of computational operations over the loaded data but it is expected to dissipate less energy due to single instruction

---

Algorithm 3. seq1: a vectorized SPK with data reusability

```
1 seq1(x[], n)  //V and A are defined at compile time
2   sum[V]; temp[V]; seg = A/V; new_n = (n/A)*A-A;
3   for (k=0; k<new_n; k=k+A)
4 //phase 1: collecting the reductions of V segments into sum
5     for (i=0; i<V; i++) sum[i] = x[k+i*seg];
6     for (j=1; j<seg; j++)
7       for (i=0; i<V; i++) temp[i] = x[k+i*seg+j];
8       sum = vectorize(sum,temp);
9       for (i=0; i<V; i++) x[k+i*seg+j] = sum[i];
10 //phase 2: inclusive prefix-sums on sum
11    for(i=1; i<V-1; i++) sum[i] = sum[i] OP sum[i-1];
12 //phase 3: propagation on x[k+seg,...,k+seg*V]
13    for(j=seg; j<seg*V; j++)
14      x[k+j] = sum[(j-seg)/seg] OP x[k+j];
15      x[k+A] = x[k+A] OP x[k+A-1];
16    trivial_seq(x,rest_of_array);
```

---

multiple data (SIMD) usage. SIMD is capable to increase the performance per Watt in many applications because less instructions need to be decoded, fetched, issued, etc., resulting in less instruction cache misses and pipeline pressure.

The second category, seq3, is comprised of algorithms based on the template described by Algorithm 5. seq3 is an alteration of the trivial_seq algorithm by transforming its loop to a two level nested loop with different loop unrolling depth for the inner loop. The outer loop uses $k \times V$ as a stride which is defined at compile time. The k corresponds to the number of iterations of the inner loop and V corresponds to the size of each loop. We do not provide results about which is the best k and V. However, they are architecture specific parameters, assisting compiler to provide better code optimizations (loop unrolling). We annotate as seq3_k:d the algorithms with loop unrolling depth d equal to 1,2,...,k.

2.3 Thread Placement Policies

The memory bandwidth of modern processors is saturated after a certain number of cores fetch data in parallel; their number varies across different processors. Since CPPS is a memory bandwidth intensive algorithm, crossing the saturation point explains its poor scalability. More bandwidth can be acquired when running over NUMA architectures while these systems demonstrate linear memory bandwidth scalability by adding NUMA nodes. Avoiding the bandwidth saturation is crucial, and a common tactic for algorithms having regular memory accesses, such as CPPS, is to place threads across the NUMA nodes (memory-affinity). Subsequently, we would expect increase in CPPS's performance by spreading threads across NUMA nodes. Therefore, we focus on two policies, usually called Scatter and Compact, to investigate the performance-energy trade-off. The Scatter corresponds to evenly distributed threads across NUMA nodes

Algorithm 4. seq2: a non-vectorized SPK with data reusability

```
1 seq2(x[], n) //V2 and A2 are defined at compile time
2   sum[V2]; seg = A2/V2; new_n = (n/A2)*A2-A2;
3   for (k=0; k<new_n; k=k+A2)
4 //phase 1: collecting reductions of V2 segments into sum
5     for (i=0; i<V2; i++) sum[i] = x[k+i*seg];
6     for (j=1; j<seg; j++)
7       for (i=0; i<V2; i++)
8         sum[i] OP= x[k+(i*seg)+j];
9 //phase 2: inclusive prefix-sums on sum
10    for (i=1; i<V2; i++)
11      x[k+i*seg] OP= sum[i-1];sum[i] OP= sum[i-1];
12 //phase 3: segment-oriented propagation of x
13    for (i=0; i<V2; i++) sum[i] = x[k+i*seg];
14    for (j=1; j<seg; j++)
15      for (i=0; i<V2; i++)
16        sum[i] OP= x[k+(i*seg)+j]; x[k+i*seg+j] = sum[i];
17    x[k+A2] = x[k+A2] OP x[k+A2-1];
18    trivial_seq(x,rest_of_array);
```

Algorithm 5. seq3: two-level-nested-loop SPK

```
1 seq3(x[], n) //k and V are defined at compile time
2   len = (n/(k*V))*k*V;
3   for(i=1; i < len; i+=k*V)
4     trivial_seq(x+i, V);
5     ...
6     trivial_seq(x+i+(k-1)V, V);
7   trivial_seq(x,rest_of_array)
```

and the Compact corresponds to consecutive core allocation starting from physical core 0.

3 Discussion

Current compilers, such as, gcc and Intel's icc are unable to optimize trivial_seq mostly because of the data dependencies. That leads to inefficient hardware pipelining and many wasted CPU cycles running on maximum frequency, penalizing performance and energy consumption. Eventually, algorithms, such as CPPS, perform poorly and consume more energy. We assume that this behavior could change by configuring CPPS with one of the proposed OSPKs.

Manipulating frequency and analyzing its impact to performance and energy is of major importance. We are interested in DVFS (Dynamic Voltage and Frequency Scaling) exploration of the sequential and parallel side of prefix-sums and the correlation between them. We assume that CPPS's performance-loss while descending to lower frequency levels does not increase with the same rate when it is configured with an OSPK rather than trivial_seq. In the same manner, we expect greater energy savings in lower frequencies with OSPKs.

Thread placement can also influence CPPS's performance when running on NUMA architectures, independently of number of threads and SPK. We could assume that by placing less threads per NUMA node the memory bandwidth per thread could be increased and eventually its overall performance be improved. However, the energy cost increases, when applying different TPP, such as Scatter, proportionally to the number of activated nodes. In general, it is unclear how much the performance improves and which are the factors suggesting to choose a different TPP other than Compact. Therefore, investigating the energy-performance trade-off is significant for different TPPs.

4 Experiments

We validate our assumptions through physical energy/time measurements on a system called Pluto. This system consists of two 8-cores Intel Xeon E5-2650 processors, giving a total of 16 cores, clocked at 2.6 GHz. Each 8-core processor has its own NUMA partition. This gives a total of 2 NUMA partitions across the system. The memory hierarchy consists of 3 levels of caches (L1(private), L2(private), L3(shared)) where the LLC is shared among 8 cores. All the benchmarks have been compiled with GCC 4.8.3-9 with -O3 optimization level and executed 30 times. The following results depict median values over the 30 runs.

The experiments show performance and energy behavior of the CPPS algorithm and its building blocks (TPP, SPK) when the associative operator addition (+) is used. The underlying mechanism of TPP is assisted by hwloc [3], a useful tool knowing the mapping between physical-cores and OS-cores. We capture the energy in a socket-based level and the total energy consumption is given by $t\_energy = \sum_{s=1}^{ns} E_s$, where E_s denotes the energy consumption of socket s and ns the number of occupied sockets. The energy measurements, reported in Joules, are derived by RAPL (Run Average Power Limit). For all the experiments we use only arrays of size 10^9 32-bit integers. Experiments on floats or doubles are omitted due to space constraints. However, the results are quantitatively similar. We chose very big problem sizes mostly because of the granularity that RAPL estimates energy (every 1 ms). For the CPPS's testbeds in-parallel first-touch page placement has been applied. All the threads initialize their assigned memory addresses prior to the computational phase.

RAPL. Since the advent of Intel's Sandy Bridge architecture a new feature has been integrated in Intel's processors for accurately estimating energy consumption, called RAPL [7]. It provides an interface which interacts with the MSRs (Model Specific Registers), specific hardware registers delivering information about energy and power consumption. The RAPL interface is divided into four different domains. The domains are: PKG (whole CPU Package), Two power planes: PP0 (processor cores only) and PP1 (a specific device in the uncore),

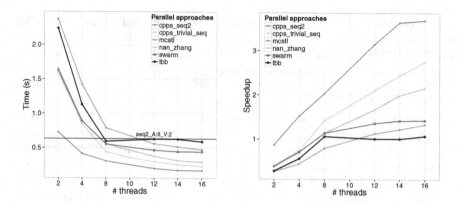

Fig. 1. Performance and absolute speedup comparison between two instances of CPPS (seq2, trivial_seq) and other public approaches for problem size of 10^9 32-bit integers. The sequential kernel seq2_A:8_V:2 has been used as a baseline for the speedup

and DRAM (memory controller). PP1 and DRAM are available on desktop and server CPUs, respectively. A more detailed documentation is located in [5].

DVFS Configuration. Intel's processors, excluding Haswell, regulate their cores under the same power state, implying that all cores must operate on the same frequency. For that reason, in every case, we fix the same frequency for the whole system (all cores) in order to preempt OS to choose different frequency.

CPPS Against Others. Comparing CPPS's performance against publically available implementations is essential before reasoning about CPPS's energy and performance capabilities. Thus, in Fig. 1, we demonstrate results of CPPS's performance and absolute speedup against other public implementations (MCSTL [12], TBB [10], Nan Zhang [16], SWARM [1]). In this experiment, seq2_A:8_ V:2 has been used to get a baseline comparison for the speedup values. CPPS has also been configured with this OSPK and trivial_seq. The other implementations work by default with trivial_seq. As can be seen, CPPS outperforms all the other approaches and exhibits better scalability. The improvement in performance and scalability is due to better cache reusability, better load balancing along the 3 phases of CPPS, and the selection of an OSPK.

Thread Placement. As discussed, CPPS's performance can benefit from Scatter over NUMA architectures. However, in Pluto, there are three factors implying why Scatter slightly improves performance ($< 4\%$). First, the memory bandwidth is saturated only with 4 cores (half socket). Second, the memory bandwidth scalability is low 2.4 over 8. Third, two NUMA nodes are not enough to compensate the memory bandwidth saturation. For instance, by spreading 12 threads in two sockets, we still operate on the maximum memory bandwidth per socket, CPPS performance does not improve and energy consumption doubles.

In this experiment, CPPS is configured with Compact and Scatter thread placement, for both trivial_seq and seq2_A:128_V:16. The results are depicted

Table 1. Performance/energy comparison between 4 different CPPS's configuration sets for problem size of 10^9 32-bit integers by combining members of a SPK set: seq2_A:128_V:16 and trivial_seq with those from TPP set: Scatter and Compact

SPK	# threads	Time (ms)		Energy (J)		Gain (%) Scatter/Compact	
		Scatter	Compact	Scatter	Compact	Energy	Time
seq2_A:128_V:16	2	1229.4	1230.4	86.0	45.73	46.86	−0.08
trivial_seq	2	1592.1	1585.8	105.69	55.48	47.50	0.39
seq2 gain over trivial_seq (%)	2	22.78	22.40	18.55	17.56		
seq2_A:128_V:16	4	653.0	655.4	57.65	31.38	45.56	−0.36
trivial_seq	4	848.4	847.1	68.48	37.14	45.75	0.15
seq2 gain over trivial_seq (%)	4	23.02	22.63	15.80	15.51		
seq2_A:128_V:16	8	339.6	352.5	43.06	24.88	42.21	−3.80
trivial_seq	8	439.1	441.7	49.52	27.91	43.62	−0.59
seq2 gain over trivial_seq (%)	8	22.67	20.20	13.03	10.86		
seq2_A:128_V:16	12	232.4	233.5	39.11	39.44	−0.85	−0.48
trivial_seq	12	298.7	298.3	44.15	43.35	1.81	0.12
seq2 gain over trivial_seq (%)	12	22.18	21.70	11.40	9.43		
seq2_A:128_V:16	16	184.4	183.9	39.63	39.70	0	0
trivial_seq	16	227.4	227.3	43.02	42.76	0	0
seq2 gain over trivial_seq (%)	16	18.94	19.38	7.88	7.15		

in Table 1; all configurations run on the maximum frequency (2.6 GHz). The energy has been monitored with RAPL's package domain (PKG). The performance penalization is negligible, as expected, under both TPPs. However, Compact policy demonstrates high energy savings for both instances, −0.86 %– 46 % and 1.81 %–47.50 % respectively. This is mostly due to the number of activated sockets. The Scatter mode always activates two sockets, in contrast to Compact which activates only one (< 8 threads). In addition, the Table shows that choosing an OSPK yields even more energy gains, 9 %–17.56 %.

SPK. The SPK is a dominant performance/energy factor of CPPS. We have shown, in Table 1, that an OSPK can significantly increase performance of CPPS. Likewise, the energy consumption of CPPS can be reduced even further by using DVFS and other OSPKs. Intuitively, choosing a lower frequency is not performance-loss-free. However, the information provided in this paper can be useful when maximizing the performance under power caps. Thus, we investigate the energy consumption of several OSPKs on different frequencies before plugging them into CPPS. In the next step, we show the energy consumption of CPPS when applied the energy efficient SPKs derived from the current results.

In Fig. 2 depicts (1) left figure, the energy consumption of different SPKs across all the frequency levels of Pluto (1.2–2.6 GHz) and (2) right figure, the energy gain for each SPK separately when shifting from the highest (2.6 GHz) to lower frequency levels. We monitor energy based on the reports of RAPL's core domain (PP0). We choose PP0 over PKG and DRAM mainly because PP0's behavior is highly dependent on the CPU frequency, according to [14], and PKG/ DRAM frequency control is not supported in the current architecture. From both figures, it derives that other SPKs (seq1, seq2, seq3) with several configurations

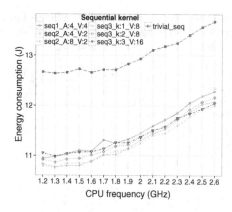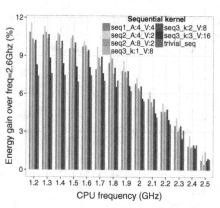

Fig. 2. Energy consumption comparison between `trivial_seq` and various OSPKs (`seq2`, `seq3`) on different frequency levels for problem size of 10^9 32-bit integers

(i.e. `seq1_A:4_V:4`, `seq3_k:2_V:8`, etc.) exist, outperforming and consuming less energy than `trivial_seq`. The right figure points out the percentage energy gain for the same SPKs of left figure. Here, some OSPKs, such as, `seq3_k:2_V:8` scale in terms of energy by lowering the frequency while `trivial_seq` shows no energy scalability lower than 1.6 GHz. In general, these results enhance the investigation of CPPS's energy behavior in different P-states by plugging in different OSPKs.

CPPS+SPK+DVFS. In the previous experiments we showed that `trivial_seq` is not an energy efficient SPK and we have introduced OSPKs which can obtain better performance and significant energy savings. It is also depicted that the OSPKs exhibit energy scalability under DVFS. These are strong indications that CPPS can consume less energy by choosing the best SPK-frequency configuration. Subsequently, the last experiment has been built to show the impact of several different of these configurations to CPPS's energy, captured by using RAPL's PP0 domain, and performance for different number of threads.

Figure 3 shows CPPS's energy consumption (left figure) and performance (right figure) for different setups (number of threads, SPKs and DVFS). For the sake of readability, only 6 distinct frequencies are reported. The results show strong correlations with the previous results and unveil that the number of threads contributes to which SPK-frequency configuration should be selected. All the SPKs give better energy consumption in lower frequencies independent of the number of threads. The energy consumption increases when deploying more than 8 threads, due to the activation of the second socket and the memory bandwidth saturation on the first socket. The memory bandwidth saturation can cause severe performance loss to CPPS and eventually leads to energy increase.

In addition, Fig. 3 shows great energy reductions and performance improvements when using OSPKs against the `trivial_seq`, independent of the number of threads and the CPU frequency. By choosing an OSPK over `trivial_seq`, CPPS can achieve great energy gains (24 %–55 %). For instance, by using two threads, frequency 2.4 GHz and `seq2_A:8_V:2`, CPPS achieves 35 % less energy compared

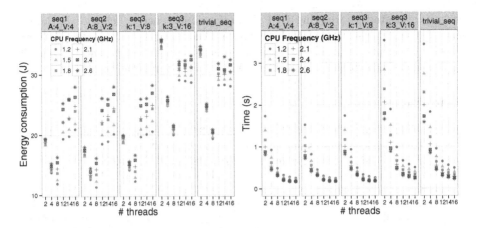

Fig. 3. CPPS's energy and performance behavior when configured with different SPKs and executed under different frequencies for problem size of 10^9 32-bit integers

to `trivial_seq`. At the same time, it is noticeable that lower the frequency we choose, higher is the performance reduction penalty (right figure). However, CPPS's performance penalization rate varies across SPKs and number of threads. For instance, by using an OSPK, such as, `seq1_A:4_V:4` or `seq2_A:8_V:2` or `seq3_k:1_V:8`, and two threads, CPPS's performance penalization rate increases (3.7 %–8.2 %) while descending to lower frequency levels but improves with more threads (16 threads: 1.3 %–5.2 %). In contrast, by activating `trivial_seq` the rate range is 4 %–8.4 % and stays constant in more threads.

5   Conclusion

This paper has presented CPPS (cache-aware parallel prefix-sums) and a variety of OSPKs (optimized sequential prefix-sums kernel). We have provided performance/energy results of CPPS running with different configurations (SPK (sequential prefix-sums kernel), TPP (thread placement policy), CPU frequency and number of threads), as well as for various SPKs. Overall, through experiments we demonstrate that the OSPKs can improve CPPS's performance from 24 % to 54 % compared to `trivial_seq` when running on the maximum frequency. We demonstrate that choosing OSPK over `trivial_seq` delivers more energy savings (24 %–55 %) to CPPS in lower frequencies. Our results indicate better energy reduction rate while descending to lower frequency levels when OSPKs are plugged into CPPS rather than `trivial_seq`. In addition, we show the impact of thread placement across NUMA nodes to the energy consumption. Our results indicate significant energy reductions up to 47.5 % when placing threads in fewer NUMA nodes with almost negligible performance degradation and up to 56.73 % when considering both OSPK and TPP.

In general, finding the most energy efficient CPPS is a multivariable optimization problem and the necessity of developing an auto-tuning mechanism generating performance/energy optimized CPPS code is crucial. In the future, we are interested in studying CPPS's performance/energy behavior on larger shared memory systems and on Intel's Xeon Phi coprocessor. Exploiting latter's wide register vectors could lead to more energy savings and potentially benefit applications like summed-area table (SAT) which extensively use SPK.

References

1. Bader, D.A., Kanade, V., Madduri, K.: SWARM: a parallel programming framework for multicore processors. In: Proceedings of the 21th International Parallel and Distributed Processing Symposium (IPDPS), pp. 1–8, (2007)
2. Blelloch, G.E.: Vector Models for Data-Parallel Computing. MIT Press, Cambridge (1990)
3. Broquedis, F., Clet-Ortega, J., Moreaud, S., Furmento, N., Goglin, B., Mercier, G., Thibault, S., Namyst, R.: hwloc: a generic framework for managing hardware affinities in HPC applications. In: Proceedings of the 18th Euromicro Conference on Parallel, Distributed and Network-based Processing (PDP), pp. 180–186 (2010)
4. Chatterjee, S., Blelloch, G.E., Zagha, M.: Scan primitives for vector computers. In: Proceedings Supercomputing 1990, pp. 666–675 (1990)
5. Corporation, I.: Intel 64 and IA-32 Architectures Software Developer's Manual vol. 3 (3A, 3B & 3C): System Programming Guide, April 2015
6. Dotsenko, Y., Govindaraju, N.K., Sloan, P., Boyd, C., Manferdelli, J.: Fast scan algorithms on graphics processors. In: Proceedings of the 22nd Annual International Conference on Supercomputing (ICS), pp. 205–213, June 2008
7. Hähnel, M., Döbel, B., Völp, M., Härtig, H.: Measuring energy consumption for short code paths using RAPL. SIGMETRICS Perform. Eval. Rev. **40**(3), 13–17 (2012)
8. Rahman, R.: The scalable heterogeneous computing benchmark suite SHOC for Intel Xeon Phi^{TM}. http://software.intel.com/en-us/blogs/2013/03/20/the-scalable-heterogeneous-computing-benchmark-suite-shoc-for-intelr-xeon-phitm
9. Reif, J.H. (ed.): Synthesis of Parallel Algorithms. Morgan Kaufmann Publishers, San Francisco (1993)
10. Reinders, J. (ed.): Intel Threading Building Blocks: Outfitting C++ for Multi-core Processor Parallelism. OReilly Media, Sebastopol (2007)
11. Sengupta, S., Harris, M., Garland, M.: Efficient parallel scan algorithms for GPUs. NVIDIA Corporation, Technical Report (2008)
12. Singler, J., Sanders, P., Putze, F.: MCSTL: The multi-core standard template library. In: Kermarrec, A.-M., Bougé, L., Priol, T. (eds.) Euro-Par 2007. LNCS, vol. 4641, pp. 682–694. Springer, Heidelberg (2007)
13. Snir, M.: Reduce and scan. In: Padua, D., (ed.) Encyclopedia of Parallel Computing, pp. 1728–1736. Springer, US (2011)
14. Subramaniam, B., Feng, W.: Towards energy-proportional computing for enterprise class server workloads. In: Proceedings of the 4th ACM/SPEC International Conference on Performance Engineering (ICPE), pp. 15–26, April 2013
15. Yan, S., Long, G., Zhang, Y.: StreamScan: fast scan algorithms for GPUs without global barrier synchronization. In: Proceedings of the 18th ACM SIGPLAN Symposium on Principles and Practice of Parallel Programming (PPoPP), pp. 229–238, February 2013
16. Zhang, N.: A novel parallel scan for multicore processors and its application in sparse matrix-vector multiplication. IEEE Trans. Parallel Distrib. Syst. (TPDS) **23**(3), 397–404 (2012)

An OS-Oriented Performance Monitoring Tool for Multicore Systems

Juan Carlos Saez[✉], Jorge Casas, Abel Serrano,
Roberto Rodríguez-Rodríguez, Fernando Castro, Daniel Chaver,
and Manuel Prieto-Matias

Facultad de Informática, Complutense University of Madrid, Madrid, Spain
{jcsaezal,jorcasas,abeserra,rrodriguezr,fcastror,dani02,mpmatias}@ucm.es

Abstract. Hardware performance monitoring counters (PMCs) have proven effective in characterizing application performance. Because PMCs can be only accessed directly at the OS privilege level, kernel-level tools must be developed to enable the end user and userspace programs to access PMCs. A large body of work has demonstrated that the OS scheduler can perform effective runtime optimizations in multicore systems by leveraging per-thread performance-counter data. Notably, while existing tools greatly simplify collecting PMC application data from user space, they do not provide a simple mechanism making it possible for the thread scheduler to use performance counters for its own purpose.

To address this shortcoming we present *PMCTrack*, a novel tool for the Linux kernel that provides a simple architecture-independent mechanism making it possible for the OS scheduler to access per-thread PMC data. Despite being an OS-oriented tool, PMCTrack still allows gathering PMC values from user space, enabling kernel developers to carry out the necessary offline analysis and debugging to assist them during the scheduler design process. In addition, the tool provides both the scheduler and the userspace PMCTrack components with other insightful metrics available in modern processors that are not directly exposed as PMCs, such as cache occupancy or energy consumption. In this paper, we analyze different case studies that demonstrate the potential benefits of PMCTrack.

Keywords: Performance monitoring counters · PMCTrack · OS scheduler · Linux kernel · Asymmetric multicore · Cache monitoring · Intel CMT

1 Introduction

Most modern complex computing systems are equipped with hardware Performance Monitoring Counters (PMCs) that enable users to collect application's performance metrics, such as the number of instructions per cycle (IPC) or the Last-Level Cache (LLC) miss rate. These PMC-related metrics aid in identifying possible performance bottlenecks, thus providing valuable hints to programmers

© Springer International Publishing Switzerland 2015
S. Hunold et al. (Eds.): Euro-Par 2015 Workshops, LNCS 9523, pp. 697–709, 2015.
DOI: 10.1007/978-3-319-27308-2_56

and computer architects. Notably, direct access to PMCs is typically restricted to code running at the OS privilege level. As such, a kernel-level tool, implemented in the OS itself or as a driver, is usually in charge of providing userspace tools with a high-level interface enabling to access performance counters [4,7,16].

Previous work has demonstrated that the OS can also benefit from PMC data making it possible to perform sophisticated and effective runtime optimizations on multicore systems [8,9,13,19,20,25]. While public-domain tools to access PMCs make it possible to monitor application performance from user space, they do not provide an architecture-independent API empowering the OS itself to leverage PMC information in different subsystems, such as the thread scheduler. As a result, many researchers turned to architecture-specific *ad-hoc* code to access performance counters when implementing different scheduling schemes [8,9,13]. This approach, however, leads the scheduler implementation to be tied to certain processor models, and at the same time, forces developers to deal with (or even write themselves) the associated low-level routines to access PMCs on each architecture targeted by the scheduler.

To overcome these limitations, we propose *PMCTrack*, an OS-oriented PMC tool for the Linux kernel. PMCTrack's novelty lies in the *monitoring module* abstraction, an architecture-specific extension responsible for providing any OS scheduling algorithm that leverages PMC data with the performance metrics it requires to function. This abstraction makes it possible to implement architecture-independent OS scheduling algorithms. Notably, in doing so, the developer does not have to deal with the platform-specific low-level code to access PMCs on a given architecture, which greatly simplifies the implementation.

PMCTrack is also equipped with a set of command-line tools and user space components. These userland tools assist OS-scheduler designers during the entire development life cycle by complementing the existing kernel-level debugging tools with PMC-related offline analysis and tracing support. Moreover, due to the flexibility of PMCTrack's monitoring modules, any kind of metric provided by modern hardware but not exposed directly via performance counters, such as power consumption or an application's cache footprint, can also be exposed to the OS scheduler or to user applications as PMCTrack's *virtual counters*.

To demonstrate the effectiveness and flexibility of our proposal, we analyze three case studies on real multicore hardware. The first case study showcases the ability of PMCTrack's monitoring modules to aid in the implementation of state-of-the art thread schedulers for asymmetric single-ISA multicore systems [9,11, 19,20,24] in the Linux kernel. The second one focuses on cache-usage monitoring via PMCTrack's support for Intel Cache Monitoring Technology [14]. Leveraging this technology, we propose a technique to build applications' Miss-Rate Curves (MRCs) on a real system. The third case study illustrates PMCTrack's ability to carry out energy and power consumption measurements on different processor models. The rest of the paper is organized as follows. Section 2 discusses related work. Section 3 outlines the design of PMCTrack. Section 4 focuses on the case studies to evaluate our design and finally Sect. 5 concludes.

2   Related Work

Hardware performance monitoring counters are usually exposed to the software as a set of privileged registers. For example, in x86 processors, PMCs can be accessed from the system software via Model-Specific Registers (MSRs) [6]. Other processor architectures, such as ARM, give more freedom to the processor implementer on how these counters are ultimately exposed to the OS [1].

Several tools [4,7,15,16,23] have been created for the Linux kernel over the last few years, enabling to hide the diversity of the various hardware interfaces and providing users with convenient access to PMCs from user space. Overall, these tools can be divided into two broad categories. The first group encompasses tools such as OProfile [4], perfmon2 [7] or perf [16], which expose PMCs to the user via a reduced set of command-line tools. These tools do not require to modify the source code of the application being monitored; instead they act as external processes with the ability to receive PMC data of another application. The second group of tools provides the user with libraries to access counters from an application's source code, thus constituting a fine-grained interface to PMCs. The libpfm [7] and PAPI [15] libraries follow this approach.

The perf [16] tool, which relies on the Linux kernel's *Perf Events* subsystem, is possibly the most comprehensive tool in the first category currently available. Not only does perf support a wide range of processor architectures, but also empowers users with striking software tracing capabilities enabling them to keep track of a process' system calls or scheduler-related activity, or various network/file-related operations executed on behalf of an application. Despite the potential of perf and the other aforementioned tools, neither of them implement a kernel-level architecture-agnostic mechanism enabling the OS scheduler to leverage PMC data for its internal decisions. PMCTrack has been specifically designed to fill this gap. As PMCTrack, perf has also the capability to expose non-PMC hardware-related data exposed by modern hardware to the user, such as the LLC occupancy. However, we found that the complexity of Linux Perf Events subsystem, on which perf is based, makes it difficult to add the necessary support. We elaborate on this issue in Sect. 4.2. Instead, PMCTrack's monitoring modules constitute a more straightforward vehicle to expose this kind of metrics to users and to the OS scheduler.

3   Design

Figure 1 depicts PMCTrack internal architecture. The tool consists of a set of user and kernel space components. At a high level, end users and applications interact with PMCTrack using the available command-line tools or via *libpmctrack*. These components communicate with PMCTrack's kernel module by means of a set of Linux /proc entries exported by the module.

The kernel module implements the vast majority of PMCTrack's functionality. To gather per-thread performance counter data, the module needs to be fully-aware of thread scheduling events (e.g., context switches, thread creation).

In addition to exposing application's performance counter data to the userland tools, the module implements a simple API to feed with per-thread monitoring data to any scheduling policy (class) that requires performance-counter information to function. Because both the core Linux Scheduler and scheduling classes are implemented entirely in the kernel, making PMCTrack's kernel module aware of these events and requests requires some minor modifications to the Linux kernel itself. (Augmenting a recent version of the Linux kernel – 2.6.38 and above – to support PMCTrack entails including two new source files to the kernel tree, and adding less than 20 extra lines of code.) These modifications, referred to as PMCTrack kernel API in Fig. 1, comprise a set of notifications issued from the core scheduler to the module. To receive key notifications PMCTrack's kernel module implements the pmc_ops_t interface shown in Listing 1. Most of these notifications get engaged only when PMCTrack's kernel module is loaded and the user (or the scheduler itself) is using the tool to monitor the performance of specific applications.

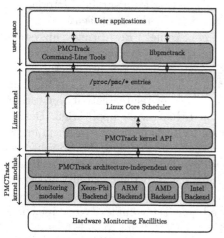

```
typedef struct pmc_ops{
/* invoked when a new thread is created */
  void* (*pmcs_alloc_per_thread_data)
          (unsigned long,struct task_struct*);
/* invoked when thread leaves the CPU */
  void (*pmcs_save_callback)(void*, int);
/* invoked when thread enters the CPU */
  void (*pmcs_restore_callback)(void*, int);
/* invoked every tick on a per-thread basis */
  void (*pmcs_tbs_tick)(void*, int);
 /* invoked when a process invokes exec() */
  void (*pmcs_exec_thread)
          (struct task_struct*);
/* invoked when thread exists the system */
  void (*pmcs_exit_thread)
          (struct task_struct*);
/* invoked when thread descriptor is freed up */
  void(*pmcs_free_per_thread_data)
          (struct task_struct*);
/* invoked when the scheduler requests
   per-thread monitoring information */
  int (*pmcs_get_current_metric_value)
          (struct task_struct*, int, uint64_t*);
} pmc_ops_t;
```

Fig. 1. PMCTrack architecture

Listing 1. pmc_ops_t interface

PMCTrack's kernel module consists of various components. The architecture-independent core layer implements pmc_ops_t interface and interacts with PMCTrack userland components. This layer relies on a Performance Monitoring Unit (PMU) backend to carry out low-level access to performance counters, as well as for translating user-provided counter configuration strings into internal data structures for the platform in question. At the time of this writing, PMCTrack includes four backends providing the necessary support for most modern Intel and AMD processors, for some ARM Cortex processor models and for the Intel Xeon Phi Coprocessor. PMCTrack's kernel module also includes a set of platform-specific *monitoring modules*. The primary purpose of a monitoring module is to provide the end user or a scheduling algorithm implemented in the kernel with high-level performance metrics or other insightful runtime information potentially exposed by the hardware (via PMCs or by other means), such as power consumption or a process's last-level cache occupancy.

3.1 Usage Models

PMCTrack can be used to gather performance counter data from the OS scheduler (using an in-kernel interface) and from user space.

(A) Accessing PMC data from the OS scheduler. This feature enables any scheduling algorithm in the kernel (i.e., scheduling class) to collect per-thread monitoring data, thus making it possible to drive scheduling decisions based on tasks' memory behavior or other microarchitectural properties. Turning on this feature for any thread from the scheduler's code boils down to activating a flag in the thread's descriptor. A scheduling algorithm relying on PMCTrack typically enables in-kernel monitoring for all threads belonging to its scheduling class.

To ensure that the implementation of the scheduling algorithm that leverages this feature remains architecture independent, the scheduler does not configure nor deals with performance counters directly. Instead, one of PMCTrack's *monitoring modules* is in charge of feeding the scheduling policy with the necessary high-level performance monitoring metrics, such as a task's instruction per cycle ratio or its last-level cache miss rate.

PMCTrack may include several monitoring modules compatible with a given platform. However, only one can be enabled at a time: the one that provides the scheduler with the PMC-related information it requires to function. In the event several compatible monitoring modules are available, the system administrator may tell the system which one to use by writing in a special /proc file. The scheduler can communicate with the *active* monitoring module to obtain per-thread data via the following function from PMCTrack's kernel API:

```
int pmcs_get_current_metric_value(struct task_struct* task,
     int metric_id, uint64_t* value);
```

For simplicity, each metric is assigned a numerical ID, known by the scheduler and the monitoring module. To obtain up-to-date metrics, the aforementioned function may be invoked from the tick processing function in the scheduler.

Monitoring modules make it possible for a scheduling policy relying on performance counters to be seamlessly extended to new architectures or processor models as long as the hardware enables to collect necessary performance data. All that needs to be done is to build a monitoring module or adapt an existing one to the platform in question. From the programmer's standpoint, creating a monitoring module entails implementing an interface very similar to pmc_ops_t. Specifically, it consists of several callback functions enabling to notify the module on activations/deactivations requested by the system administrator, on threads' context switches, every time a thread enters/exits the system, whenever the scheduler requests the value of a per-thread PMC-related metric, etc. The programmer typically implements only the subset of callbacks required to carry out the necessary internal processing. Notably, in doing so, the developer does not have to deal with performance-counter registers directly. Specifically, the programmer indicates the desired counter configuration (encoded in a string) to the PMCTrack architecture-independent core. Whenever new PMC samples are collected for a thread, a callback function of the monitoring module gets invoked, passing the samples as a parameter. Due to this feature, a monitoring module will only access low-level registers to provide the scheduler or the end user with other hardware monitoring information not modeled as PMCs, such as energy consumption.[1] This information is exposed to the user via *virtual counters*.

(B) Using PMCTrack from userspace. In addition to the in-kernel API presented above, PMCTrack also enables to gather PMC data from user space by using the `pmctrack` command line tool or `libpmctrack`.

The `pmctrack` command allows the user to gather an applications's performance data at regular time intervals (a.k.a., time-based sampling - TBS) or by using the interrupt-on-counter-overflow feature available on most modern performance monitoring units (a.k.a., event-based sampling - EBS). This command enables to specify counter and event configurations using mnemonics in much the same way as existing user-oriented tools [4,7,16]. In addition, the program supports monitoring both multithreaded and single-threaded applications and has event-multiplexing capabilities (several event sets can be monitored in a round-robin fashion). To complement this command-line tool with real-time visualization of high-level performance metrics (such as the IPC or the LLC miss rate) we also created PMCTrack-GUI, a Python front-end for `pmctrack`. Figure 2 shows a screenshot of PMCTrack-GUI. This application extends the capabilities of the PMCTrack stack with other relevant features, such as an SSH-based remote monitoring mode or the ability to plot user-defined performance metrics.

`Libpmctrack` enables to characterize performance of code fragments via PMCs in sequential and multithreaded programs. Libpmctrack's API makes it possible to indicate the desired PMC configuration to the PMCTrack's kernel module at any point in the application's code or within a runtime system. The programmer may then retrieve the associated event counts for any code snippet (via TBS or EBS) simply by enclosing the code between invocations to the `pmctrack_start_count()` and `pmctrack_stop_count()` functions.

Not only do libpmctrack and the pmctrack command enable the user to gather PMC application data but also have the ability to provide users with any other relevant information exported by the active monitoring module as a *virtual counter*. In Sects. 4.2 and 4.3 we leverage this capability. To feed libpmctrack and the pmctrack program with PMC and virtual-counter data, the PMCTrack's kernel module stores this information in kernel-space ring buffers.

Despite the fact that some features of the `pmctrack` command and libpmctrack are also available in existing tools [15,16], the design of PMCTrack coupled with the virtual counter abstraction makes it simpler to expose any new insightful information provided by the hardware to userland tools. Specifically, in tools

---

[1] Most modern Intel processors and many ARM development boards provide energy consumption readings via separate registers or sensors (see Sect. 4.3).

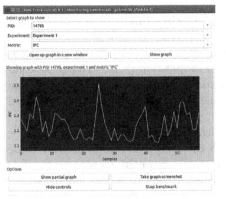

Fig. 2. PMCTrack-GUI

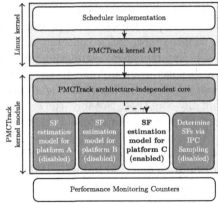

Fig. 3. PMCTrack monitoring modules

such as perf [16] or PAPI-C [15], the Linux kernel and the associated userspace components must be typically modified to benefit from new hardware monitoring facilities. In PMCTrack, by contrast, this extra support can be provided by creating a new monitoring module (modifying PMCTrack's kernel loadable module), which can be done even without rebooting the system.

4   Case Studies

4.1   Scheduling on Asymmetric Single-ISA Multicore Systems

Previous research has highlighted that asymmetric single-ISA multicore (AMP) processors, which couple same-ISA complex high-performance *big* cores with power-efficient *small* cores on the same chip, have been shown to significantly improve energy and power efficiency over their symmetric counterparts [10]. The ARM big.LITTLE processor [2] and the Intel Quick-IA prototype [3] demonstrate that AMP designs have drawn the attention of major hardware players.

Despite their benefits, AMPs pose significant challenges to the OS scheduler. One of the main challenges is how to effectively distribute big-core cycles among the various applications running on the system. Previous work has proposed thread scheduling algorithms to optimize throughput and fairness on AMPs [9,11,19,20,24]. Notably, the key to optimizing both metrics is to factor in the big-to-small speedup (aka, *speedup factor*) of the various threads when making thread-to-core mappings. A thread's speedup factor is defined as $\frac{IPS_{big}}{IPS_{small}}$, where IPS_{big} and IPS_{small} are the thread's instructions per second ratios achieved on big and small cores respectively.

Three different schemes have been explored to determine per-thread speedup factors (SFs) online. The first approach boils down to measure SFs directly [10,24], which entails running each thread on big and small cores to track the IPC (instructions per cycle) on both core types. Previous work has demonstrated that this approach, known as *IPC sampling*, is subject to inaccuracies in SF estimation associated with program-phase changes [21]. The second approach relies on *estimating a thread's SF* using its runtime properties collected on any core type at runtime using PMCs [9,19]. Unfortunately, estimating SFs via PMCs requires to derive predictions models specifically tailored to the platform in question [9,19]. The third technique is PIE [24], a hardware-aided mechanism enabling accurate SF estimation from any core type. Notably, the required hardware support for PIE has not yet been adopted in commercial systems.

To leverage the first two approaches, which can be used in off-the-shelf AMPs, the OS scheduler needs to access PMCs in the platform in question. By using the approach depicted in Fig. 3, PMCTrack monitoring modules make it possible to aid in creating an architecture-independent implementation of the scheduler. Overall, the various schemes to obtain threads' SFs can be implemented as separate PMCTrack monitoring modules: one that leverages IPC sampling and several others that provide SF-estimation on the various platforms supported by the scheduler. Apart from the architecture-agnostic scheduler implementation, this design approach provides three additional benefits. First, the scheduler implementation is completely decoupled from the underlying scheme to determine the SF; the kernel developer or the system administrator can decide which scheme to use by activating the corresponding monitoring module. Second, existing SF-enabled modules can be modified and new ones can be created for a particular scheduler even without rebooting the system. Third, since the SF can be seamless exposed as a virtual counter to PMCTrack's command-line tools, per-thread SF and PMC traces can be gathered from user space for debugging purposes. Notably, in previous work [20] we leveraged this potential of PMCTrack monitoring modules to implement state-of-the-art asymmetry-aware scheduling algorithms [9,11,19,24] in the Linux kernel.

4.2   Cache Monitoring

Intel's Cache Monitoring Technology (CMT) [6] is a new feature, introduced in the Intel Xeon E5 2600 v3 product family, that allows an operating system or a Hypervisor/Virtual Machine Monitor (VMM) to determine the current last-level cache (LLC) usage of the various applications running on the platform. At a high level, CMT works as follows. The OS or VMM assigns a certain ID, referred to as the Resource Monitoring ID (RMID)[2], to each application/VM. Cache occupancy is monitored by CMT-enabled hardware on a per-RMID basis, so the OS or the VMM can read LLC occupancy for a given application/VM at any time. To make this possible, the processor needs to be aware of the RMID of every thread (or virtual CPU) currently running on the system. To this end, the hardware exposes a per-core privileged register that stores the RMID associated with the thread currently running on it. The OS is in charge of updating per-core RMID registers when threads' context-switches take place.

---

[2] Because the amount of RMIDs available is limited by the hardware implementation, the OS must be equipped with a carefully crafted RMID allocation policy.

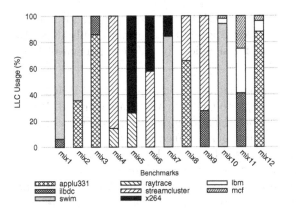

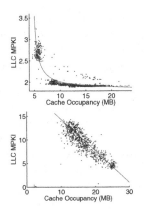

Fig. 4. Breakdown of LLC occupancy for different mixes.

Fig. 5. MRCs for the *lbm* (top) and *omnetpp* (bottom) applications.

A patch [5] has been recently created to augment perf [16] with Intel-CMT capabilities. This support is expected to be included in future Linux kernel releases. We found that PMCTrack's implementation is simpler and exhibits some important advantages over perf's implementation. First, our implementation is done in a loadable kernel module rather than on the kernel itself, which greatly simplified the development. Second, it uses less than 500 lines of code against the 1500 lines used by the perf patch for the Linux kernel [5]. Moreover, perf's implementation entails making changes to 7 different source files from the Linux kernel, whereas our implementation requires adding a new file to PMC-Track's sources, and changing another source file to register the new monitoring module. Third, because Intel-CMT support is encapsulated in a monitoring module, any shared-resource contention-aware scheduling policy implemented in the Linux kernel could easily retrieve an application's LLC usage (via PMCTrack's API) and perform effective thread-to-core mappings [14]. At the same time, the monitoring module exposes the LLC usage to the userspace tools as a virtual counter.

(A) LLC occupancy analysis. We first performed an analysis on the LLC occupancy of 12 multiprogram workloads consisting of sequential programs (lbm and mcf from the SPEC CPU 2006 suite) and parallel applications (from SPEC OMP 2012 and PARSEC). All multithreaded applications run with 4 threads. To carry out the experiment, we employed a 14-core "Haswell-EP" Xeon E5-2695 v3 processor operating at 2.3 GHz, which features a 35 MB last-level (L3) cache.

Figure 4 shows the average per-application LLC occupancy for the entire execution of the various workloads. Our experiment reveals that some applications, like the *swim* SPEC OMP parallel program, use a great portion of the LLC (65–95 %) when running concurrently with sequential applications or with other multithreaded SPEC OMP or PARSEC programs. Conversely, other parallel programs, like *ilbdc* from the SPEC OMP suite, typically occupy a much more reduced portion of the L3 cache regardless of the co-runner application. As expected, other applications account for significantly different portion of LLC depending on the co-runner.

(B) MRCs online generation. As a more sophisticated application of PMCTrack and CMT, we now introduce a technique to generate Miss Rate Curves (MRCs) online. The MRC reports an application's cache occupancy on a given cache level (usually the LLC) vs. a certain related performance metric, like the number of Misses Per Kilo Instructions (MPKI). MRCs can be employed for different purposes, such as to efficiently distribute a shared cache among threads [18,22]. Several mechanisms have been proposed [18,22] for building these curves, but they all pose different limitations, such as requiring hardware support or relying on code instrumentation.

We now describe an online technique that leverages Intel's CMT to generate the MRCs of co-running applications. Overall, the proposed technique works as follows. Using PMCTrack we gather the MPKI and the LLC occupancy of the co-running applications periodically, thus obtaining different discrete MRC points. Then, when enough points have been collected, we apply regression analysis to obtain the whole MRCs for the applications. Note, however, that when several applications share a cache, they usually reach an equilibrium state in the distribution of the cache. To obtain points in the whole range of cache sizes, we slow down co-runner applications by applying duty-cycle modulation techniques to the cores where they run. This allows other applications to increase their occupancy, which in turn, makes it possible for us to explore different MPKI values for the whole cache size range. Figure 5 illustrates two examples of curves obtained with this technique. The MRC for the *lbm* application shows a steep MPKI fall for small cache occupancy values and then saturates from a certain cache size point on. Conversely, the MRC for the *omnetpp* program, shows a linear MPKI drop for the whole range of cache sizes.

4.3 Measuring Power and Energy Consumption

PMCTrack also has the ability to interact with power and energy measurement facilities of modern high-performance Intel processors [6] and low-power ARM big.LITTLE systems [2]. The necessary support is provided by a set of PMCTrack monitoring modules. As such, energy-related information is readily available at runtime to both the OS scheduler and to the end users via virtual counters.

On Intel systems we turned to the Running Average Power Limit (RAPL) feature [6], which employs a software power model based on hardware monitoring to approximate energy usage. Specifically, energy consumption can be gathered independently for different power domains (core-level, processor package/un-core and DRAM). Figure 6(a) and (b) show power consumption measurements reported by PMCTrack on the Intel Xeon E5 v3 processor described in the previous section. Specifically, the data illustrate both package-level and DRAM power

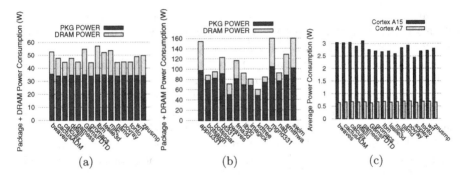

Fig. 6. Average power consumption gathered via Intel RAPL for (a) FP SPEC CPU2006 (b) and SPEC OMP 2012 benchmarks. (c) Average per-cluster power consumption for FP SPEC CPU 2006 benchmarks on an ARM big.LITTLE processor.

measurements for several floating-point sequential programs (SPEC CPU2006) and parallel applications (SPEC OMP 2012). As evident, sequential programs exhibit almost constant package consumption across the board, since the application is using only one core in the processor package.

PMCTrack also provides support for 32-bit ARM big.LITTLE processors featuring one cluster of Cortex A15 *big* cores and another cluster of Cortex A7 *small* cores. In our evaluation, we used the ARM CoreTile Express development platform, which is equipped with a set of sensors enabling to measure power and energy consumption on a per-cluster basis. Figure 6(c) shows the observed average cluster power consumption of floating-point SPEC CPU 2006 benchmarks when running alone on the various core types. Information retrieved via the aforementioned sensors reveals that big A15 cores yield up to 4.9x the power consumption of small A7 cores. Still, both ARM cores exhibit significantly lower package-level power consumption for the same benchmarks compared to that of the high-performance Intel processor we used (Fig. 6(a)).

To validate the results shown in Fig. 6, we measured power consumption using perf [16] and lm-sensors [12] on the Intel and the ARM systems respectively. (Unlike PMCTrack, neither of these tools enables to monitor energy consumption on both platforms.) The results, omitted due to space constraints, reveal similar measurements to those reported by PMCTrack (deviations no greater than 1 %).

5   Conclusions and Future Work

In this paper we have proposed PMCTrack, a tool enabling the OS scheduler to leverage performance monitoring counter (PMC) information in decision making. By using PMCTrack's monitoring module abstraction, the implementation of any scheduling policy that relies on per-thread PMC data to function remains fully platform independent. Not only do monitoring modules provide the OS scheduler with PMC-related metrics but also have the ability to feed it with virtually any insightful information exposed by modern hardware and not necessarily provided via PMCs, such as the LLC occupancy or the energy/power consumption. Despite being an OS-oriented tool, PMCTrack is also equipped with a set of userland tools that allow to gather hardware-performance monitoring information from user space in various ways.

In an earlier work [20], we leveraged the potential of PMCTrack's monitoring modules in assisting scheduling algorithms for asymmetric single-ISA multicore systems implemented in the Linux kernel. By using PMCTrack's in-kernel API and libpmctrack, we plan to evaluate OS and runtime-level scheduling schemes that leverage information on cache occupancy and power consumption.

PMCTrack's source code has been released[3] under the GPLv2. Additional information on PMCTrack will be available at PMCTrack's official website [17].

Acknowledgements. This work has been supported by the Spanish government through the research contract TIN2012-32180 and the HIPEAC3 (see footnote 3) European Network of Excellence.

References

1. ARM: Arm Architecture Reference Manual. http://infocenter.arm.com/
2. ARM: Benefits of the big.LITTLE Architecture. http://www.arm.com/files/downloads/Benefits_of_the_big.LITTLE_architecture.pdf
3. Chitlur, N., et al.: QuickIA: exploring heterogeneous architectures on real prototypes. In: Proceedings of HPCA 2012, pp. 1–8 (2012)
4. Cohen, W.: Tuning programs with oprofile. Wide Open Mag. **1**, 53–62 (2004)
5. Flemming, M.: perf: Intel cache QoS monitoring support (2014). https://lkml.org/lkml/2015/1/23/590
6. Intel: Intel 64 and IA-32 Architectures Software Developer's Manual Volumes 3A and 3B. http://www.intel.com/products/processor/manuals
7. Jarp, S., Jurga, R., Nowak, A.: Perfmon2: a leap forward in performance monitoring. J. Phys. Conf. Ser. **119**, 042017 (2008)
8. Knauerhase, R., et al.: Using OS observations to improve performance in multicore systems. IEEE Micro **28**(3), 54–66 (2008)
9. Koufaty, D., Reddy, D., Hahn, S.: Bias scheduling in heterogeneous multi-core architectures. In: Proceedings of Eurosys 2010, pp. 125–138 (2010)
10. Kumar, R., et al.: Single-ISA heterogeneous multi-core architectures for multi-threaded workload performance. In: Proceedings of ISCA 2004, pp. 64–75 (2004)
11. Li, T., et al.: Operating system support for overlapping-ISA heterogeneous multi-core architectures. In: Proceedings of HPCA 2010, pp. 1–12 (2010)
12. Lm-sensors: HW monitoring by lm-sensors (2015). http://www.lm-sensors.org/
13. Merkel, A., et al.: Resource-conscious scheduling for energy efficiency on multicore processors. In: Proceedings of EuroSys, pp. 153–166 (2010)
14. Nguyen, K.: Benefits of intel(r) cache monitoring technology in the intel(r) xeon(tm) processor e5 v3 family (2014). https://software.intel.com/en-us/blogs/2014/06/18/benefit-of-cache-monitoring
15. Papi: Overview. http://icl.cs.utk.edu/projects/papi/wiki/PAPIC:Overview
16. Perf: Wiki tutorial on perf (2015). https://perf.wiki.kernel.org/index.php
17. PMCTrack: project official website. http://pmctrack.dacya.ucm.es/

---

[3] https://github.com/jcsaezal/pmctrack.

18. Qureshi, M., et al.: Utility-based cache partitioning: a low-overhead, high-performance, runtime mechanism to partition shared caches. In: MICRO (2006)
19. Saez, J.C., et al.: Leveraging core specialization via OS scheduling to improve performance on asymmetric multicore systems. ACM Trans. Comput. Syst. **30**(2), 38 (2012). Article 6
20. Saez, J.C., et al.: ACFS: a completely fair scheduler for asymmetric single-ISA multicore systems. In: Proceedings of ACM SAC 2015 (2015)
21. Shelepov, D., et al.: HASS: a scheduler for heterogeneous multicore systems. ACM OSR **43**(2), 66–75 (2009)
22. Tam, D.K., et al.: RapidMRC: approximating L2 miss rate curves on commodity systems for online optimizations. In: Proceedings of ASPLOS 2009, pp. 121–132 (2009)
23. Taniça, L., Ilic, A., Tomás, P., Sousa, L.: SchedMon: a performance and energy monitoring tool for modern multi-cores. In: Lopes, L., et al. (eds.) Euro-Par 2014, Part II. LNCS, vol. 8806, pp. 230–241. Springer, Heidelberg (2014)
24. Van Craeynest, K., et al.: Fairness-aware scheduling on single-ISA heterogeneous multi-cores. In: Proceedings of PACT 2013, pp. 177–187 (2013)
25. Zhuravlev, S., Blagodurov, S., Fedorova, A.: Addressing cache contention in multicore processors via scheduling. In: Proceedings of ASPLOS 2010, pp. 129–142 (2010)

A Topology-Aware Performance Monitoring Tool for Shared Resource Management in Multicore Systems

Nicolas Denoyelle[(✉)], Brice Goglin, and Emmanuel Jeannot

Inria Bordeaux - Sud-Ouest – LaBRI, Université de Bordeaux, Talence, France
{Nicolas.Denoyelle,Brice.Goglin,Emmanuel.Jeannot}@inria.fr

Abstract. Nowadays, performance optimization involves careful data and task placement to deal with parallel application needs with respect to the underlying hardware topology. Monitoring the application behavior provides useful information that still needs to be matched with the actual placement, for instance to understand whether bottlenecks are caused by the sequential code itself or by shared resources in parallel programs.

We propose an insightful monitoring tool based on two cornerstones of hardware performance counters monitoring and hardware locality modeling, respectively named PAPI and hwloc. It enables a dynamic visual analysis of parallel applications' phases at runtime, revealing their possibly variable and heterogeneous behaviors and needs. A purpose designed application shows that the topology-aware visual representation of hardware counters can help figuring out shared resource bottlenecks and ease the task placement decision process in runtime systems.

1 Introduction

The memory wall makes data locality increasingly important on the road to exascale. Data and computing tasks have to be colocated to better exploit the performance of parallel platforms. Many research projects focus on locality-aware data and/or task placement, for parallel programing models ranging from MPI and OpenMP to graphs of tasks. However finding out which placement is the best remains a difficult exercise that depends on the topology and characteristics of the hardware and on the application needs. Indeed, the hardware is increasingly complex, and software affinities can be of different kinds. For instance memory-bound tasks may prefer being scattered all across the machine, while, on the contrary, communication and synchronization may want to keep them close. Runtime systems require help identifying these needs and bottlenecks before they can place tasks accordingly.

Performance monitoring is a very active software area that offers many tools to gather information about the execution of tasks, the bottlenecks, *etc.* We introduce, in this paper, a new way to analyze performance by crossing the roads of performance monitoring and topology-aware placement. We propose an

© Springer International Publishing Switzerland 2015
S. Hunold et al. (Eds.): Euro-Par 2015 Workshops, LNCS 9523, pp. 710–721, 2015.
DOI: 10.1007/978-3-319-27308-2_57

extension of the Hardware Locality software (hwloc [2]) that enhances its graphical representation of the topology with performance monitoring information. This new tool enables optimization of the placement of parallel tasks based on visual monitoring.

The remaining of the paper is organized as follows. Section 2 presents the context of our work before the state of the art is described in Sect. 3. Section 4 details the goals, features and implementation of the proposed tool while an in-depth use case is studied in Sect. 5.

2 Context

The domain of parallel computing has undergone a shift in the way applications are executed with the advent of multicore systems. Nowadays, systems with more than 10 cores and a deep memory hierarchy (multiple levels of caches) are common place. Moreover, deeper data paths (flash, non-volatile memory, RAM, caches) and larger systems (the next Intel Knight Landing processor will provide more than 60 cores with 4 threads each) are expected in a near future. Such architectures feature many characteristics that make the execution highly sensitive to the way the computations are mapped. Indeed, threads exhibit different kinds of affinities as they do not use the same amount of memory or exchange the same amount of data.

Several works [6,7,10] showed that the way the affinity is managed has an important impact on the application performance: memory accesses depend on the mapping of the threads and the data location. Therefore, it is crucial to understand how this mapping impacts the performance. Moreover, it is the case for every steps of the application: the data allocation, the I/O (network, storage, etc.) or the computation. This is even more intricate when computation is composed of phases where the affinity between tasks changes. For instance a computation phase may be compute intensive, *e.g.* heavily use floating-point units, before another phase is memory intensively. To cope with this phase heterogeneity, some systems feature co-scheduling where compute-intensive applications are mixed with memory-bound ones expecting that the different application bottlenecks (here memory/cache vs. compute units/cores) will not interfere with each other.

In any case, whether the system executes one application or co-schedules several, it is very important to be able to efficiently map the processes and the threads on the different cores. To understand the impact of such mapping and analyze the performance of the running application(s), in the light of the mapping, applications and system developers need tools to monitor the application behavior. Such monitoring tool need not only to be able to display the performance of the application but also need to link the performance with the topology where the application is running. We believe that this last part is very important as the performance can only be understood if it is matched with the memory hierarchy and the used cores.

3   State of the Art

Performance analysis can be performed at different levels of granularity, from individual instructions up to the entire program. Analyzing the performance at the instruction level with tools such as MAQAO [1], PIN [9] or Intel VTune Amplifier is a part of the development and optimization process. We rather focus on optimizing through better placement during the execution. Moreover we target parallel applications with a regular execution pattern (for instance applications programmed with MPI, PGAS and/or threads) without dynamic scheduling of many tasks that would require a finer grain. Our coarse grain approach targets the entire application or different phases during its execution by observing its behavior from a higher level as the Unix top tool would.

Coarse-grain performance analysis still requires dynamic monitoring over time. It may involve real time tools such as numatop or tiptop [12], or offline temporal analysis with one of the existing tracing tools such as VampirTrace [8]. We base our work on these existing approaches while focussing on topology-aware performance study both in real-time or for post-mortem analysis.

Multiple metrics may be used to diagnose topology-related performance issues, including memory link contention, cache conflicts, or computing unit shared accesses. Performance counters are the main solution for analyzing the behavior of codes and numerous tools are available such as PAPI [3] or the Linux perf utility. We focus on intra-node performance in this paper while other metrics exist for entire cluster-wide, such as congestion in network switches or links, which may be studied with tools such as SCALASCA [4] or Paraver [11].

Analyzing performance based on the topology of the architecture is not a very active research topic yet. Indeed, discovering all the computing and memory resources in computing platform has only been recently mastered with tools such as hwloc [2]. Former approaches were often less portable or do not expose as many details about cache sharing *etc.* MemAxes [5] offers fine-grained memory performance analysis with a graphical radial hierarchy display. However, it only focuses on static post-mortem analysis of memory accesses while our approach is dynamic and works for all performance metrics and more kinds of resource sharing. LIKWID [13] is a set of performance analysis tools that use advanced knowledge of the hardware topology. This knowledge is used for task placement while we also propose to combine it with performance monitoring for better analysis. LIKWID is actually complementary to our work, it will soon use hwloc for better topology discovery, while we may use LIKWID performance monitoring abilities when they will be exported as a C programming interface.

4   Topology-Aware Performance Monitoring

Here, we describe the proposed extension of lstopo utility : design, usage and implementation.

4.1   Objectives and Features

lstopo is a utility from hwloc which function is to display machines topologies. The main goal of the new lstopo extension is to provide a fast and simple way to analyze the architecture behaviour during a program execution. Such a hardware based outlook can be used just to get a quick glance on the machine state as well as for more complex studies such as task placement optimization. It fits especially well multi-phase applications such as code coupling or complex structure traversal.

The original lstopo displays the hierarchy of computing resources (processors, NUMA nodes, cores, threads, caches, *etc.*) as nested boxes (see Fig. 1(a)). Inner boxes represents smaller resources (*e.g.* cores within processors or even hyperthreads).

The extension aims to stay as simple as the original tool. From the user perspective, the new graphical output keeps the existing boxes organization intact but changes their inner text and colors to report performance information. Box names are replaced with performance monitored values, whose variation (with respect to the maxima reached across the execution) is also represented by a horizontal line and the background color. At a given rate, the bar moves vertically and the color changes according to the monitored value (see Fig. 1(b)): from green to red (with different intermediate shades of yellow and orange). This implementation keeps the original technologies used in hwloc: The Cairo library is still used to draw the graphical output but it now periodically refreshes the display to update counters.

As explained in the next section, a few lines of input configuration enable the displaying of live, derived performance counters.

Because you cannot always get a graphical display on HPC platforms, performance counters may also be recorded with low overhead for later offline display. Indeed, just like hwloc lets you manipulate topologies of remote machines, the new lstopo may also load performance counters for more convenient displaying on another host. Moreover, performance counters may also be exported in a trace file in PAJÉ format[1] for later post-mortem analysis with any paje trace analyzer.

Several options can be set such as sampling rate, replay speed, accumulating values or not. Moreover, we provide two monitoring modes: *per node* where performance counters are displayed for all the process running on the NUMA node and *per process* where performance counters are displayed for a given process.

Finally, for those whom want to record specific part of an application, a library interface is provided to record parts of a whole application and set markers to delimit phases into the trace.

4.2   Usage and Configuration

Figure 1(a) shows the original lstopo output on a dual-core Intel i7-4600U processor. Figure 1(b) shows the same display with --perf option appended. Coloured boxes represent the monitors.

---

[1] http://paje.sourceforge.net/index.html.

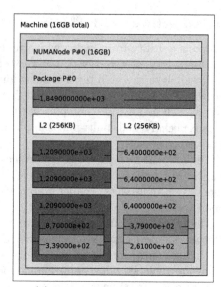

(a) lstopo classic output   (b) lstopo performance output

Fig. 1. Graphical lstopo output (Color figure online)

The topology structure is a hierarchy of resources. For each hierarchy level (cores, caches, threads (PU), *etc.*), the user may set an arithmetic expression of counters meant to represent a metric associated with that level. A file containing such a description is specified to lstopo with the option --perf-input and is written with the following syntax:

```
name {hwloc_obj_type_t where to accumulate,
      algebraic formula using PAPI counters}
```

An example of such syntax is:

```
CYC_per_INS {PU, PAPI_TOT_CYC/PAPI_TOT_INS}
PER_CORE_L3_MISS {Core, PAPI_L3_TCM}
PER_NUMA_L3_MISS {NUMANode, PAPI_L3_TCM}
```

In this example, the program would count on each processor hyperthread the number of cycles (PAPI_TOT_CYC), the number of instruction (PAPI_TOT_INS) and the number of cache misses in the L3 (PAPI_L3_TCM). The latter is summed by Core (2nd line) and by NUMA node (3rd): in this case all the cache misses are displayed at the node level. The formers are used to compute the ratio of cycles per instruction on each hyperthread (1st line).

More complex expressions could be used to translate raw counter values into higher-level criterias such as the memory bandwidth, or another performance monitoring library could be used instead of PAPI to directly gather such information.

4.3   Implementation

The tool uses hwloc to build the topology and store counters' values into its nodes. The lstopo utility (which shows the machine topology) was updated to add a hook plugin, periodically sampling hardware counters, and changing nodes rendering as the monitors' hierarchy is updated.

Data: map(hwloc object type, counters), hwloc topology, process ID
Result: trace(timestamp, topology object, monitor value)
1 Spawn a thread per leaf waiting in a barrier;
    /* The main thread triggers counter's collect periodically   */
2 **repeat**
3   **forall the** *topology's leaves* **do**
4 | **if** *isRunning(leaf,pid's thread)* **then** activate(sampling(leaf));
5   **end**
6   wait(barrier);
7 **until** *wait(timer)*;
    /* The others gather samples   */
8 **forall the** *thread* **do**
9   **repeat**
10   wait(barrier);
11   **if** *thread's leaf is not activated* **then** continue ;
12   read(counters);
13   **forall the** *node in leaf's parents into the monitor hierarchy* **do**
14   **forall the** *counters* **do**
15   **if** *counter physical location is under node* **then**
16   sum counters into node;
17   **if** *Current leaf is the last to update node* **then**
18   compute the user input arithmetic expression of counters ;
19   **else**
20   **if** *Current leaf is the first to update node* **then**
21   Set the node and sibling counters value to the read counter ;
22   **end**
23   **end**
24   **end**
25   **until** *isAlive(pid)*;
26 **end**

Algorithm 1. Dynamic counter aggregation algorithm.

When performance monitoring is enabled, the topology is redrawn periodically after gathering counters.

The new `lstopo` can also attach to a process to track and record a single process placement and performance values.

Performance counters are usually collected for each processing unit leaf of the topology (hyperthreads in the above example) but `lstopo` may accumulate them in parents. For counters that are not per-core, they are usually displayed higher in the hierarchy, for instance in the system or NUMA node box.

As an example, displaying the last level cache (LLC) miss count on the LLC itself would sum the total number of LLC miss performed on all cores, whereas displaying it on each Core would show the miss count performed by each Core. Algorithm 1 describes this behavior synthetically.

The aggregation currently only implements the addition of counters from all children resources, but we plan to support average, min and max operations as an optional flag in the language in the near future.

5   Analyzing Tasks Concurrency Gives a Room for Thread Placement

Here, we will illustrate a situation where a visual hint can be useful to choose thread placement. In this example the monitoring mode is the *per node* one: we monitor all the processes of the node.

5.1   Spreading or Packing Threads?

Tasks affinity is a widely studied problem in HPC because it can suit several optimizations such as, MPI-process placement, node allocation, co-scheduling, *etc.* At the node granularity, the efficiency of scheduling threads under a shared cache depends both on the pressure they put on the cache and the reuse distance of their shared data. Two solutions often discussed are: either spread threads to balance the pressure on caches, or pack them to optimize shared data access [10]. These two placement policies are widely used and implemented in most OpenMP Runtime. But whether you should use one or the other is left to the user responsibility.

5.2   A Use Case of Threads' Interference Balancing, Using the Cache Miss Ratio

Some works use the cache miss ratio as a metric to measure pressure on cache [14] and decide on thread's placement policy.

Based on this observation we build a small application able to put arbitrary pressure on the last level cache, and thanks to hardware counter information we will be able to see where are the threads pinned on the Cores, and the amount of pressure they put on the last level cache.

The application we monitor is a walk into a linked list. It basically consists in loading data and therefore should be sensitive to memory stress. Each item in the list is sized to fit into a cache line and the list is randomly linked to avoid successful prefetching by the processor.

Before doing any measure, we walk the whole list so that each attempt to resolve the next pointer will trigger a cache miss if the list size is greater than the cache size as shown in Fig. 2.

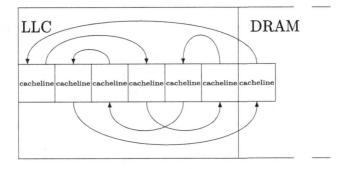

Fig. 2. Randomly linked list.

5.3   Experimental Conditions

Figure 3 shows the LLC miss count evolution when changing the list size and running n threads walking each a cloned list.

The vertical line at 2^{20} shows that walking simultaneously 4 lists of size 2^{20}KiB, results in a reasonable amount of LLC misses even if the 4 lists should fit into the last level cache.

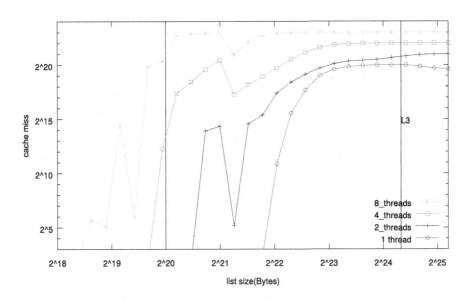

Fig. 3. Evolution of cache miss count of the node when increasing pressure on cache.

Hence we build two lists *list1* and *list2* of respective memory size $s1 = 2^{20}$KiB and $s2 = 2^{24}$KiB. The 4 threads of the former one may have their whole data set fit simultaneously in the last level cache, whereas 2 threads of the latter

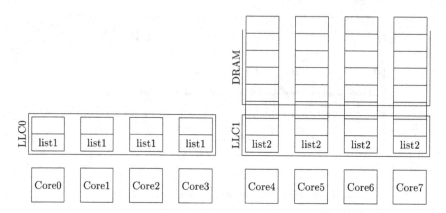

Fig. 4. Co-scheduling low-pressure threads, then high pressure threads.

would already overflow the cache. Using a topology with two 8-core processors, we co-schedule 4 threads, each one walking a clone of *list1* and 4 threads, each one walking a clone of *list2* spread across the processors so each processors hosts 4 threads. In the first scenario we schedule 2 threads of *list1* and 2 threads of *list2* on each processor whereas in the second scenario Fig. 4, 4 *list1* are walked on a processor and 4 *list2* are walked on the other.

5.4   How Lstopo Shows the Situation

In this context, co-scheduling walks of *list1* with walks of *list2* would grow the number of miss for *list1* walks and slow the miss count for *list2* walks, whereas doing the opposite strategy would reverse the tendency. What about the total number of cache misses?

Figure 5 illustrates both scenarios from lstopo view. The topology has been restricted to only 4 cores per processors and cache boxes are hidden for clarity. The input configuration files used was the one described before in subsection implementation.

The upper most red and green boxes represent the machine NUMA nodes and we display on them the total amount of LLC miss for each node. The red, yellow and green outer boxes represent the machine cores 3,4,8,9 in logical numbering. Each single core LLC miss count is displayed on it. The red, yellow and inner boxes represent the machine hyperthreads on which is displayed the hyperthread cycles per instruction ratio.

In the first scenario Fig. 5(a), we use the scatter placement strategy, and see distinctly the pressure being balanced across the nodes. Whereas the second scenario Fig. 5(b) exhibits the packed strategy lowering considerably the pressure on the LLC for *list1* walk threads. However, the latter increases the number of cache misses on the most pressured cache by more than twice, suggesting that the first scenario is better than the second one to optimize total LLC miss count.

Actually, the execution walltime of the first scenario is 8.32 s while the second one is 11.08 s.

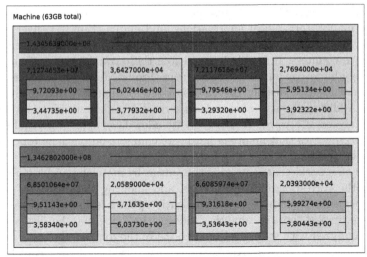

(a) Linked list walk, scattered threads

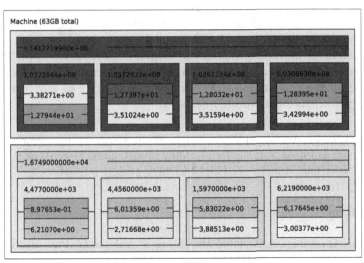

(b) Linked list walk, packed threads

Fig. 5. Two scenarios' comparison with lstopo (Color figure online).

6   Conclusion and Future Work

The road to exascale requires careful design of parallel runtime systems with respect to software affinities and hardware locality so that task and data can be properly colocated. Analyzing hardware performances values and matching them with topology information is crucial to understand and optimize resources utilization. In this article, we presented a tool based on hwloc[2], able to collect performance, topological informations, and match them to deliver valuable hints. This tool extends the lstopo utility to display *per node* or *per process* performance counters. It is able to aggregate these counters at a given level of the topology hierarchy and to combine them through algebraic formulas. Colors and bars are used to display the values of these counters dynamically on the topology. Additionally, it is able to keep a trace of an execution to be replayed later or analyzed afterward. We showed with a low-level application and relevant performance metrics that mapping hardware counters on machine topology can bring out locality issues.

We are now working at improving the output by matching performance counters with the corresponding source code, and allowing the display of multiple counters per box. Then detection of application phases is also being investigated in the case of post-mortem analysis. Indeed, the trace may be displayed as a graph or analyzed with statistical tools to study the dynamic behavior of applications during the execution. Applications with varying heterogeneous behavior may indeed benefit from dynamic re-placement between phases.

Finally, our performance monitoring currently relies on PAPI high level abstraction and consequently inherits its strength such as simplicity of use, but also its weaknesses. For instance, PAPI does not expose advanced memory access counters (available in recent processors with Intel PEBS or AMD IBS). This limits our current abilities contrary to MemAxes which manually supports them. Depending on the support for most relevant technologies we envision support for other performance monitoring interfaces.

Acknowledgment. We would like to thanks Erwen Rohou for insightful discussion, Heike McCraw and Asim Yarkhan for providing us with useful hints about PAPI. This work is partially funded under the ITEA3 COLOC project #13024.

References

1. Barthou, D., Rubial, A.C., Jalby, W., Koliai, S., Valensi, C.: Performance Tuning of x86 OpenMP codes with MAQAO. In: Müller, M.S., Resch, M.M., Schulz, A., Nagel, E. (eds.) Tools for High Performance Computing 2009, pp. 95–113. Springer, Heidelberg (2010)
2. Broquedis, F., Clet-Ortega, J., Moreaud, S., Furmento, N., Goglin, B., Mercier, G., Thibault, S., Namyst, R.: hwloc: a generic framework for managing hardware affinities in HPC applications. In: The 18th Euromicro International Conference on Parallel, Distributed and Network-Based Computing, PDP 2010, Pisa, Italy. IEEE, February 2010
3. Browne, S., Dongarra, J., Garner, N., London, K., Mucci, P.: A scalable cross-platform infrastructure for application performance tuning using hardware counters. In: Proceedings of the 2000 ACM/IEEE Conference on Supercomputing, SC 2000, IEEE Computer Society, Washington (2000)

---

[2] Available from https://github.com/NicolasDenoyelle/dynamic_lstopo.

4. Geimer, M., Wolf, F., Wylie, B.J.N., Ábrahám, E., Becker, D., Mohr, B.: The SCALASCA performance toolset architecture. In: Proceedings of the International Workshop on Scalable Tools for High-End Computing (STHEC), Kos, Greece, pp. 51–65, June 2008

5. Gimenez, A., Gamblin, T., Rountree, B., Bhatele, A., Jusufi, I., Bremer, P.T., Hamann, B.: Dissecting on-node memory access performance: a semantic approach. In: Proceedings of the 2000 ACM/IEEE Conference on Supercomputing, pp. 166–176. IEEE Press, New Orleans, LA, November 2014

6. Hursey, J., Squyres, J.M., Dontje, T.: Locality-aware parallel process mapping for multi-core HPC systems. In: 2011 IEEE International Conference on Cluster Computing (CLUSTER), pp. 527–531. IEEE (2011)

7. Jeannot, E., Mercier, G., Tessier, F.: Process placement in multicore clusters: algorithmic issues and practical techniques. IEEE Trans. Parallel Distrib. Syst. **25**(4), 993–1002 (2014)

8. Knüpfer, A., Brunst, H., Doleschal, J., Jurenz, M., Lieber, M., Mickler, H., Müller, M.S., Nagel, W.E.: The vampir performance analysis tool-set. In: Proceedings of the 2nd International Workshop on Parallel Tools for High Performance Computing, July 2008, HLRS, Stuttgart, pp. 139–155 (2008)

9. Luk, C.K., Cohn, R., Muth, R., Patil, H., Klauser, A., Lowney, G., Wallace, S., Reddi, V.J., Hazelwood, K.: Pin: building customized program analysis tools with dynamic instrumentation. In: Proceedings of the 2005 ACM SIGPLAN Conference on Programming Language Design and Implementation, PLDI 2005, pp. 190–200. ACM, New York (2005)

10. Majo, Z., Gross, T.R.: Memory management in NUMA multicore systems: trapped between cache contention and interconnect overhead. SIGPLAN Not. **46**(11), 11–20 (2011)

11. Pillet, V., Labarta, J., Cortes, T., Girona, S.: PARAVER: a tool to visualize and analyze parallel code. In: Nixon, P. (ed.) Proceedings of WoTUG-18: Transputer and Occam Developments, pp. 17–31, March 1995

12. Rohou, E.: Tiptop: Hardware Performance Counters for the Masses. Research Report RR-7789, November 2011

13. Treibig, J., Hager, G., Wellein, G.: Likwid: a lightweight performance-oriented tool suite for x86 multicore environments. In: Lee, W.C., Yuan, X. (eds.) ICPP Workshops, pp. 207–216. IEEE Computer Society (2010)

14. Zhuravlev, S., Blagodurov, S., Fedorova, A.: Addressing shared resource contention in multicore processors via scheduling. SIGPLAN Not. **45**(3), 129–142 (2010)

Diamond Rings: Acknowledged Event Propagation in Many-Core Processors

Stefan Nürnberger[1], Randolf Rotta[1]([✉]), Gabor Drescher[2], Daniel Danner[2], and Jörg Nolte[1]

[1] Brandenburg University of Technology, Cottbus-Senftenberg, Cottbus, Germany
{snuernbe,rrotta,jon}@informatik.tu-cottbus.de
[2] Friedrich-Alexander University Erlangen-Nuremberg, Erlangen, Germany
{drescher,danner}@cs.fau.de

Abstract. Hardware and software consistency protocols rely on global observability of consistency events. Acknowledged broadcast is an obvious choice to propagate these events. This paper presents a generalized ring topology for parallel event propagation with acknowledged delivery. Implementations for various many-core architectures show increased performance over conventional approaches. Therefore, diamond rings are a prime candidate for implementations of distributed memory models.

1 Introduction

A central component of consistency protocols are low-latency, high-throughput notification mechanisms that guarantee global observability to the initiator [1]. For this purpose, we propose a new broadcast topology called *diamond rings*. Its design targets broadcasting of events that are rather small while the final acknowledgement of their propagation is crucial. The event processing may be postponed locally as long as the propagation goes on. Usually, larger data is just referenced by the events instead of being transmitted directly. It is the nodes' task to copy or update any additional data as necessary.

A prime example for such mechanisms are coherence protocols that provide multiple reader single writer (MRSW) access on memory locations. Before writing to a location, exclusive access has to be obtained for the writer by sending a request for ownership. Every node that has a valid copy must be informed of this request in order to invalidate their outdated copy and revoke any previous write access. The writer can proceed only after all other nodes have been notified and acknowledging the successful broadcast is therefore essential. A similar scenario are update protocols. A central node sequences the atomic data modification requests and then broadcasts the updates. The individual requests are complete once their update has reached all replica.

Low latency is clearly desirable for such broadcasts in order to reduce the stall time of writers [2]. Just as much desirable is high throughput in order to reduce the congestion when pipelining updates and independent ownership requests.

Broadcast topologies provide a trade-off between latency and throughput. The latency is caused by overheads along the longest path. Keeping it short

© Springer International Publishing Switzerland 2015
S. Hunold et al. (Eds.): Euro-Par 2015 Workshops, LNCS 9523, pp. 722–733, 2015.
DOI: 10.1007/978-3-319-27308-2_58

requires asymmetric topologies with a large number of communication partners per node [2], which introduces imbalanced overhead among the nodes.

The throughput is increased by pipelining multiple broadcasts and is limited by the single node with the highest processing overhead. Thus, topologies with balanced overhead and few communication partners per node are required. The highest throughput is achieved by rings with a single successor per node [3].

Ignoring the delivery acknowledgement, conventional balanced trees present a sensible trade-off between latency and throughput. However, the acknowledgements require additional reductions from the leaves to the tree root. In this scenario, the proposed diamond rings provide better throughput and latency than conventional balanced trees. In comparison to asymmetric topologies, they provide better throughput in exchange for slightly worse latency.

Section 2 reviews related work. The new diamond rings are introduced in Sect. 3 and compared qualitatively against conventional topologies. The broadcast mechanism was implemented for a variety of many-core architectures as discussed in Sects. 4 and 5 compares them quantitatively.

2   Related Work

Efficient broadcasts received a lot of research, which can be divided into three categories: theoretical foundations, software-, and hardware-implementations.

The theoretical work focuses on finding optimal broadcasting trees for specific models of computation and communication networks. [4] summarises early work for very simple models of communication that ignore, for example, the message latency The most prominent enhanced models are POSTAL [5] and LogP [6]. The POSTAL model considers communication latency and simultaneous send/receive operations. The LogP model extends this by incorporating processor overhead, communication bandwidth, finite network capacity and multi-port I/O. Optimal broadcast algorithms in the LogP model were presented by [2].

Implementations face additional challenges like varying network latency and the efficient computation of optimal topologies at runtime [7]. Minimal-height lopsided trees can be constructed to cope with mixed-latency networks [8]. Other works focus on specific network architectures. For instance, [9] evaluates different broadcast algorithms on the Intel SCC [10] processor. They show that exploiting the SCC's 2D mesh with flat trees performs better than naive balanced trees. Finally, [3] points out that rings provide even better throughput.

Hardware-based approaches [1,11,12] optimise broadcast operations by dedicated support on the router and switch level. In practice, they apply the same ideas and topologies as software-based algorithms but have to cope with stricter resource constraints. Likewise, our proposed diamond ring topology can be applied in soft- or hardware and requires just point-to-point communication.

To the best of our knowledge, none of the previous research considered broadcasts with acknowledgement as a combined operation and the trade-off between latency versus throughput is often neglected. Research focused on the broadcast latency alone or, as in [13], only on the acknowledgement path.

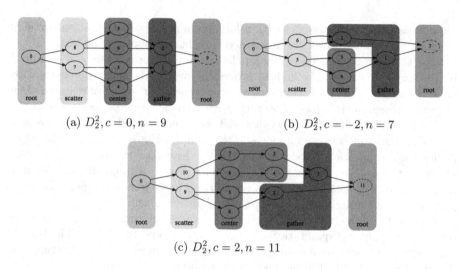

(a) $D_2^2, c = 0, n = 9$ (b) $D_2^2, c = -2, n = 7$

(c) $D_2^2, c = 2, n = 11$

Fig. 1. Diamond Rings of arity 2 with different values of contamination. The two root nodes are conceptually the same but are drawn separately for clarity.

3   The Diamond Ring Structure

Based on the observation that the ring topology provides the best throughput but worst latency [3], we propose a generalisation towards parallel rings. This should trade loosing some of the throughput for a significantly reduced latency.

The *diamond ring* is a directed graph D_k^l with $|V(D_k^l)| = n$ nodes. The overall shape is a k-ary balanced tree of high l with the leaves merged to a mirrored tree as shown in Fig. 1a. It consists of four classes of nodes, called *root*, *scatter*, *center*, and *gather* nodes. The roots the two trees are merged into one root node. Each of the k^l center nodes is part of exactly one ring and the root is the only node that lies on all k^l rings.

This topology has a couple of advantages for the implementation of low overhead broadcasts. The path length is bounded by $O(\log n)$ due to the construction based on trees. The per-node memory requirement is $O(k)$ because memory is needed for each of the maximal k neighbours.

3.1   Extending to Arbitrary Node Counts

In practice, the desired node count does not match the size of a pure D_k^l. In such cases, c additional nodes must be introduced or removed beyond its regular topology, turning the graph into what we call a *contaminated* diamond ring.

The number of surplus nodes never exceeds the breadth of the ring center. Therefore, all potential modifications can be accomplished by inserting or removing up to k^l center nodes. With the center being the part exhibiting the highest degree of parallelism, this also implies that the ring's length is never increased by more than 1.

When deciding for the proper l for a given node count n, if $n > |V(D_k^l)| + k^l$ (i.e., more than k^l nodes have to be added), just choose D_k^{l+1} and remove some of the k^{l+1} nodes from the center. This always suffices, since the larger topology D_k^{l+1} features additional k^l nodes as counterpart to the old center nodes, as well as k^{l+1} new center nodes, i.e.

$$|V(D_k^{l+1})| = |V(D_k^l)| + k^l + k^{l+1} .$$

There are alternative ways to handle contamination. For example, one can only add further center nodes. This is beneficial since the removal of nodes in the larger graph leads to multiple connections between the last level scatter and first gather node. However, the length of the longest path is also increased in this scheme. Figure 1 shows some examples for D_2^2 with different values of contamination.

3.2   Numbering and Addressing Scheme

A node is able to determine its neighbours solely by using its own node ID, the graph arity, and number of nodes in the topology. Beyond that knowledge, no further communication between the participating nodes is needed for topology setup. The parameters l (level, or depth) and c (contamination) are determined as $min\{l \mid -k^l < c \le k^l\}$, where $c = n - |V(D_k^l)|$.

The node class (scatter, gather, etc.) is then determined by (1). The neighbours of a node are determined by (2) for a D_k^l with $c = 0$. The equations derive directly from the number of nodes in a balanced tree. Considering contamination requires some special cases, which are not shown here for brevity. Also omitted is the computation of offsets for root and gather nodes that receive messages from multiple predecessors, which requires basically a residue check. This is needed when disjoint message buffers or queues are used for the k predecessors.

$$type(id) = \begin{cases} \text{root node,} & \text{if } id = 0 \\ \text{scatter node,} & \text{if } \frac{n+k^l+1+c}{2} \le id \\ \text{center node,} & \text{if } \frac{n-k^l-1}{2} < id < \frac{n+k^l+1+c}{2} \\ \text{gather node,} & \text{otherwise} \end{cases} \tag{1}$$

$$neighbours(id) = \begin{cases} \{n - i \mid i = 1..k\}, & \text{if } type(id) = \text{root} \\ \{n - (k(n-id)+i) \mid i = 1..k\}, & \text{if } type(id) = \text{scatter} \\ \{(id-1)/k\}, & \text{if } type(id) = \text{center} \\ \{(id-1)/k\}, & \text{if } type(id) = \text{gather} \end{cases} \tag{2}$$

3.3   Comparison to Tree-Based Broadcast with Reduction

One advantage of diamond rings over broadcast trees is the significantly reduced number of messages sent. Considering the center of a diamond ring with k^l nodes, the balanced tree requires exactly one more level to reach all nodes in the graph before beginning the reduction. Together with the first reduction step to get back to the diamond ring's center, it adds up to $2k^l$ additional messages sent for the tree based reduction. The total number of nodes in a broadcast tree is $k^{l+1} - 1$. That means twice the number of messages for binary trees ($k = 2$). The factor decreases with larger k. With the same reasoning, it becomes clear that the longest path from the root, through all nodes, and back to the root is exactly two hops shorter for diamond rings.

The most important property is the reduced workload on inner nodes. Each node is an active part of the diamond ring broadcast exactly once. In contrast, balanced trees require the inner nodes to forward the messages *and* the acknowl- edgements. Hence, they are active twice for a single broadcast. In the diamond ring this is the case only for the root node, sending out a request and later receiv- ing the acknowledgement. Inner nodes in the balanced tree engage in $2(k + 1)$ active communications either sending or receiving a message.

However, there is also a drawback for diamond rings in comparison to bal- anced trees regarding latency. In the tree broadcast the first thing a receiving node does is forward the message. Then it will continue with the required work before handling the acknowledgement. In a diamond ring, all work that needs to be acknowledged must be performed before the message is forwarded to the neighbours. Depending on the amount of work that is required for each mes- sage, latency may be worse for the diamond rings despite the marginally shorter hop count. If message reception (i.e., observability) is the only criterion that needs acknowledgement, forwarding may take place immediately. In a pipelined scenario, this increased latency does not affect overall throughput.

3.4   Root Node Overhead

In the proposed diamond ring, the root node sends messages to k different neigh- bours and receives k messages. In comparison, all other nodes communicate with at most $k + 1$ neighbours. This constitutes a throughput bottleneck, which can be alleviated quite easily.

An additional gather node can be introduced as companion to the root. It takes the position of node n in Fig. 1 and forwards the acknowledgement as a single message to the root. The path length thereby increases by one, which increases the latency slightly. Both, root and helper node, can issue acknowledged broadcasts. All nodes would have at most $k + 1$ communication neighbours, thus eliminating throughput bottleneck.

4   Implementation Notes and Benchmark Variants

The diamond ring topology as introduced in the previous section defines the basic communication scheme. It can be implemented in very different communication models ranging from shared memory to hardware-based message passing. As a first step we implemented a simple task-based framework targeting Tilera, Xeon, and XeonPhi processors. The next section details this framework. Then, the three evaluated broadcast variants *diamond rings* (DR), *sequenced diamond rings* (SDR), and *balanced trees* (BT) are presented.

4.1 Communication and Task Scheduling

The three target many-core architectures provide a Linux environment. To simplify porting, we implemented the framework as multi-threaded C++ application. The POSIX threads API is used to create one application thread per hardware thread (or core) and bind them via thread affinity. All threads operate in the same cache-coherent shared memory, which is used for communication.

In order to be able to compare throughput effects, a large number of concurrent broadcasts needs to be pipelined. Thus, each thread has to manage several overlapping activities. These are represented by task objects akin to active messages and contain a function pointer and additional payload for this function. Each thread has a thread-local LIFO task scheduler based on a double-ended queue from the C++ STL. For asynchronous inter-thread communication, each thread owns a multi-producer singe-consumer FIFO queue. The scheduler polls this queue when no local tasks are available or when send operations are stalled due to congestion. Received tasks are enqueued to the back of the local dequeue.

On the Xeon and XeonPhi processors, the communication queues were implemented as fixed-size ring buffers. Just pointers to statically allocated tasks residing in shared memory are communicated in order to avoid dynamic memory management. The Tilera architecture has a low-latency point-to-point network called UDN. It can be used to send small messages directly from one core to another and the intermediate network behaves as a FIFO queue. Our implementation uses the UDN for inter-thread communication by sending task pointers.

This is a quite general framework providing more than the simple broadcasts might require. However, actual applications usually need more than just broadcasts. In our experience, over-simplified broadcast communication channels tend to not cooperate well with the higher-level communication and scheduling.

4.2 Benchmark Variants

The following three benchmark variants were implemented for the evaluation as presented in the next section.

Balanced Trees (BT). The reference implementation is based on a balanced n-ary tree topology. Upon receiving a broadcast message, each node sends the broadcast message to its children and, then, processes the broadcast event locally. An acknowledgement message is sent back to the parent node after the local processing is completed and acknowledgement messages were received from all children. A separate node-local acknowledgement counter is used for each broadcast to track the outstanding acknowledgements at each node.

Diamond Rings (DR). The nodes operate differently depending on their position in the diamond ring. All scatter, center, and gather nodes begin processing the broadcast event on the first message received. They propagate the broadcast message to their successors after the local processing is complete and the broadcast message was received from each predecessor. Scatter and center nodes have just a single predecessor. The root node first sends the broadcast to its successors and, then, processes the event itself. The broadcast is completed at the root node after the local event processing completed and the broadcast message was received from each of the root's predecessors. Again, a node-local counter is used by gather nodes and the root to track outstanding messages.

Sequenced Diamond Rings (SDR). Tree and diamond ring topologies do not mandate any ordering of concurrently propagated events. The communication layer and the node-local task scheduling can reorder their messages and tasks. However, many application scenarios like, for example, request for ownership and distributed atomic updates require a strict ordering according to the event sequence at the root node.

The sequenced diamond ring implementation enforces in-order processing of pipelined broadcasts at each node. For this purpose, the root node assigns a sequence number to each event. A node-local sequence counter is used to delay broadcast tasks that are out of sequence. The sequencing can be implemented orthogonal to the broadcasts but a combined implementation was chosen to exploit cross-cutting optimisation opportunities.

5   Evaluation

This section compares the latency and throughput of acknowledged event broadcasts based on diamond rings against balanced trees. Trees are commonly used to propagate events and collect acknowledgements. Balanced trees were chosen because they achieve better throughput than skewed/asymmetric trees.

Based on the analysis in Sect. 3.3, following hypotheses are examined: (1) The longest path is shorter in diamond rings than in balanced trees. Hence, diamond rings should have a slightly lower latency as long as processing the broadcast event itself costs no time. (2) The balanced tree nodes have to process more messages than diamond ring nodes. Hence, the latter should provide higher throughput. In consequence, diamond rings would provide a better trade-off between throughput and latency than balanced trees and tree in general.

In order to evaluate these hypotheses, latency and throughput were measured in micro-benchmarks without actual application-level event payload. The latency is the time needed to complete individual broadcasts on otherwise idle cores. The throughput is measured with bursts of up to 128 pipelined broadcasts. In contrast to application benchmarks, this approach allows to study the performance differences in isolation.

The next subsection presents individual results for the three evaluation architectures and the last subsection discusses the overall results.

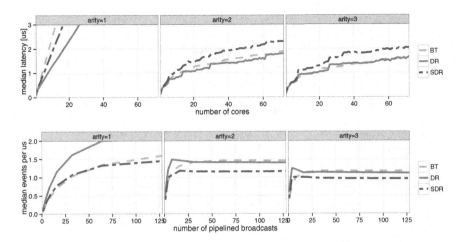

Fig. 2. Median latency and throughput on Tilera TILE-Gx72.

5.1   Benchmark Results

The measurements are carried out on the Tilera TILE-Gx72 and Intel Xeon-Phi 5110P many-core processors. For comparison, a large multi-core Intel Xeon machine is included. Both many-core architectures are based on in-order execution cores whereas the multi-core utilises out-of-order execution.

72-Core Tilera TILE-Gx72. This many-core processor contains 72 three-issue in-order VLIW cores running at 1 GHz. The cores are interconnected through several 2D mesh networks. The benchmark implementation uses Tilera's low-latency user-dynamic network (UDN) to communicate the pointers to messages and shared memory to access the message contents.

Figure 2 shows the latency and throughput results for arity 1, 2, and 3. All measurements were repeated 100 times. The mapping of topology nodes to cores was not specifically optimised. The highest throughput was achieved with arity 1 and diamond rings. With arity 2, the throughput is similar for diamond rings and balanced trees and diamond rings have a slightly better latency.

On this processor, processing overheads seem to dominate the communication overhead and latency significantly. The additional processing needed to order pipelined broadcasts in the sequenced diamond rings increases the latency compared to un-ordered balanced trees while the throughput is similar.

4x10-Core Intel Xeon E5 4640v2. This machine consists of 4 processors with 10 out-of-order cores per processor and two hardware-threads per core running at 2.2 GHz. The processors are connected through a cache-coherent QPI network. The communication is implemented via shared memory using a multiple-producer/single-consumer ring-buffer.

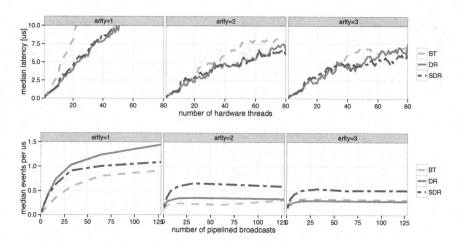

Fig. 3. Median latency and throughput on Intel Xeon E5 4640v2.

Figure 3 shows the results for this machine. Again, the highest throughput was achieved with arity 1 and diamond rings. With arity 2 and 3, the throughput of sequenced diamond rings the best while the latency is similar for all three.

Surprisingly, the sequenced diamond rings perform best, which could benefit from two characteristics of the architecture: The cores are designed for good single-thread performance, which compensates the additional processing overhead; And the enforced ordering might reduce the pressure on the limited bandwidth of inter-processor QPI links.

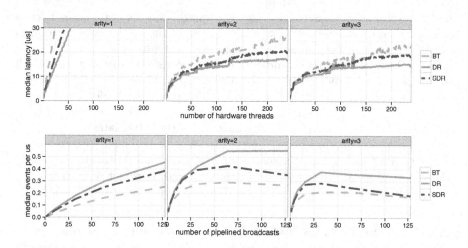

Fig. 4. Median latency and throughput on Intel XeonPhi 5110P.

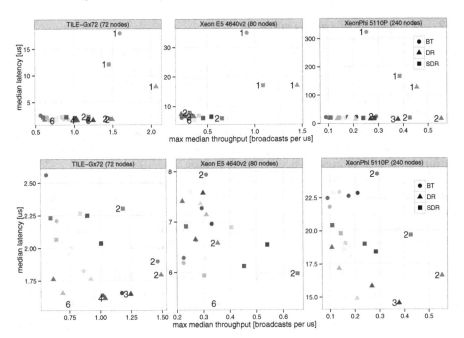

Fig. 5. Comparison of the single-broadcast latency against the largest observed throughput with pipelined broadcasts. Both figures show the same dataset but the lower figure excludes arity 1 for better readability. The arity is encoded by color and is, in addition, written left to interesting points. The better variants are to the lower right corner. Please note the different scales.

60-Core Intel XeonPhi 5110P. This many-core processor contains 60 in-order cores with 4 hardware-threads per core running at around 1 GHz. The cores are connected through two bi-directional rings. The benchmark uses the same ring-buffer implementation as above.

Figure 4 shows the results for this machine. The best throughput was achieved with arity 2 instead of 1. This is probably due to the arity 1 pipeline being much longer (240 stages) than the number of pipelined broadcasts. Diamond rings achieved better throughput and latency than balanced trees.

Ramos and Hoefler [14] presented an optimal design for small broadcasts and reductions on the XeonPhi processor using dedicated communication structures. For 60 cores, they report 10 μs latency for broadcasts plus 10 μs latency for reductions, i.e. acknowledgements. In comparison, the balanced 2-ary tree (24 μs) and 2-ary diamond ring (15 μs) presented here perform quite well while reaching all 240 threads and using a more general task-based model.

5.2   Discussion of the Results

Figure 5 compares the trade-off between latency and throughput directly for a larger selection of tree arities. The x-axis shows the peak median throughput and the y-axis the median latency for each benchmark variant.

The first column shows the TILE-Gx72. The Pareto optimal variants, beginning with lowest latency, are diamond rings with arity 6 (1.6 µs, 0.7 per µs), 4, 3, 2 (1.8 µs, 1.5 per µs), and finally diamond rings with arity 1 (8 µs, 2 per µs). For most arities, diamond rings performed better than balanced trees, which performed better than sequenced diamond rings.

The second column shows the results for the multi-core Xeon. The Pareto optimal variants, beginning with lowest latency, are sequenced diamond rings with arity 6 (5.4 µs, 0.35 per µs), then arity 2(6 µs, 0.65 per µs), and finally diamond rings with arity 1(17 µs, 1.45 per µs). For most arities, sequenced diamond rings performed better than diamond rings, which performed better than balanced trees.

Finally, the third column represents the many-core XeonPhi. The Pareto optimal variants, beginning with lowest latency, are diamond rings with arity 3 (15 µs, 0.37 per µs) and finally arity 2 (17 µs, 0.55 per µs). For most arities, the diamond rings performed better than sequenced diamond rings, which performed better than balanced trees.

On all three architectures, diamond rings achieved a higher throughput than balanced trees. The latency can be reduced by using larger arities. However, the latency does not decrease much beyond arity 2 while the throughput degrades quickly. In conclusion, diamond rings and sequenced diamond rings with arity 2 are a good choice for acknowledged event delivery.

6   Conclusions

We have presented a novel topology for efficient acknowledged broadcast to be used in memory consistency protocols. By combining the advantages of low latency in tree-based topologies and the high throughput achieved in ring-shaped communication, our diamond ring topology balances the overall utilization of the network and resource requirements on the participating nodes. We have implemented diamond rings on a multitude of platforms and compared their performance to existing approaches. Referring to the hypotheses made in Sect. 5, our evaluation results show that (1) the shorter path lengths in diamond rings result in lower latencies on all measured platforms, (2) the reduced computational load per node gives rise to higher overall throughput performance in diamond rings when compared to balanced trees. The choice of arity offers a trade-off decision between both those performance indicators, with higher arity reducing the latency at the cost of throughput. This shows that diamond rings constitute a prime candidate for use as an underlying communication layer in software memory consistency protocols.

Acknowledgments. This work was supported by the German Research Foundation (DFG) under grant no. NO 625/7-1 and SCHR 603/10-1. The evaluation on the Intel XeonPhi was supported by the German Federal Ministry of Education and Research (BMBF) grant no. 01IH13003C.

References

1. Jerger, N.E., Peh, L.S., Lipasti, M.: Virtual circuit tree multicasting: a case for on-chip hardware multicast support. In: ISCA 2008, pp. 229–240. IEEE (2008)
2. Karp, R.M., Sahay, A., Santos, E.E., Schauser, K.E.: Optimal broadcast and summation in the logp model. In: Fifth Annual ACM Symposium on Parallel Algorithms and Architectures, SPAA 1993, pp. 142–153. ACM (1993)
3. Al-Khalissi, H., Bucty, R., Berekovic, M.: Efficient barrier synchronization for OpenMP-like parallelism on the intel SCC. In: Proceedings of the International Conference on Parallel and Distributed Systems - ICPADS, pp. 10–17, December 2013
4. Hedetniemi, S.M., Hedetniemi, S.T., Liestman, A.L.: A survey of gossiping and broadcasting in communication networks. Networks **18**(4), 319–349 (1988)
5. Bar-Noy, A., Kipnis, S.: Designing broadcasting algorithms in the postal model for message-passing systems. In: SPAA 1992, pp. 13–22. ACM (1992)
6. Culler, D., Karp, R., Patterson, D., Sahay, A., Schauser, K.E., Santos, E., Subramonian, R., Von Eicken, T.: LogP: towards a realistic model of parallel computation. In: Proceedings of the Fourth ACM SIGPLAN Symposium on Principles and Practice of Parallel Programming, PPOPP 1993, vol. 28, pp. 1–12. ACM, San Diego (1993)
7. Bruck, J., De Coster, L., Dewulf, N., Ho, C.T., Lauwereins, R.: On the design and implementation of broadcast and global combine operations using the postal model. IEEE Trans. Parallel Distrib. Syst. **7**(3), 256–265 (1996)
8. Golin, M., Schuster, A.: Optimal point-to-point broadcast algorithms via lopsided trees. Discrete Appl. Math. **93**(2), 233–263 (1999)
9. Matienzo, J., Jerger, N.E.: Performance analysis of broadcasting algorithms on the intel single-chip cloud computer. In: IEEE International Symposium on Performance Analysis of Systems and Software (ISPASS 2013), pp. 163–172. IEEE (2013)
10. Howard, J., et al.: A 48-core ia-32 message-passing processor with DVFS in 45nm CMOS. In: IEEE International Solid-State Circuits Conference Digest of Technical Papers (ISSCC 2010), pp. 108–109. IEEE (2010)
11. Malumbres, M.P., Duato, J.: An efficient implementation of tree-based multicast routing for distributed shared-memory multiprocessors. J. Syst. Archit. **46**(11), 1019–1032 (2000)
12. Turner, J.S.: An optimal nonblocking multicast virtual circuit switch. In: 13th Proceedings IEEE of Networking for Global Communications, pp. 298–305. IEEE (1994)
13. Rothermel, K., Maihofer, C.: A robust and efficient mechanism for constructing multicast acknowledgement trees. In: Proceedings of Eight International Conference on Computer Communications and Networks, 1999, pp. 139–145. IEEE (1999)
14. Ramos, S., Hoefler, T.: Modeling communication in cache-coherent SMP systems - a case-study with Xeon Phi. In: Proceedings of the 22nd International Symposium on High-Performance Parallel and Distributed Computing, pp. 97–108. ACM (2013)

UCHPC - UnConventional High Performance Computing

Energy-Performance Tradeoffs for HPC Applications on Low Power Processors

Enrico Calore[1]([⊠]), Sebastiano Fabio Schifano[2], and Raffaele Tripiccione[1]

[1] Dipartimento di Fisica e Scienze Della Terra, Università di Ferrara and INFN,
Ferrara, Italy
enrico.calore@fe.infn.it
[2] Dipartimento di Matematica e Informatica, Università di Ferrara and INFN,
Ferrara, Italy

Abstract. Energy efficiency is becoming more and more important in the HPC field; high-end processors are quickly evolving towards more advanced power-saving and power-monitoring technologies. On the other hand, low-power processors, designed for the mobile market, attract interest in the HPC area for their increasing computing capabilities, competitive pricing and low power consumption. In this work we study energy and computing performances of a Tegra K1 mobile processor using an HPC Lattice Boltzmann application as a benchmark. We run this application on the ARM Cortex-A15 CPU and on the GK20A GPU, both available in this processor. Our analysis uses time-accurate measurements, obtained by a simple custom-developed current monitor. We discuss several energy and performance metrics, interesting *per se* and also in view of a prospective use of these processors in a HPC context.

1 Introduction

The computational performances of current HPC systems are increasingly bounded by their power consumption, and this is only expected to become worse in the foreseeable future. This is also relevant from the point of view of operating costs; indeed, large computing facilities are considering the option to charge not only running time but also energy dissipation.

In response to these problems, high-end processors are quickly introducing more advanced power-saving and power-monitoring technologies [7]. On the other hand, low-power processors, designed for the mobile market, are gaining interest as it appears that they may eventually fill (or at least reduce) their performance gap with high-end processors and still keep a competitive edge on costs, thanks to the economies of scale associated to large production volumes of mobile devices [4,13]. The power consumption problem is starting to be approached also from the software point of view, with developers focusing not only on performance, but also learning to optimize codes to achieve the most acceptable trade-off between performance and energy efficiency [5,17].

In this paper we address one facet of these issues. We analyze in details, using accurate measurements, the role played by hardware factors and by some software aspects in the energy-performance landscape of real-life HPC applications.

© Springer International Publishing Switzerland 2015
S. Hunold et al. (Eds.): Euro-Par 2015 Workshops, LNCS 9523, pp. 737–748, 2015.
DOI: 10.1007/978-3-319-27308-2_59

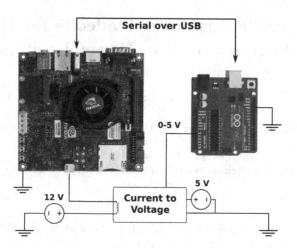

Fig. 1. Power monitoring setup. A benchtop power supply provides a constant 12 V voltage; the supply current passes through a current-to-voltage converter, whose analog output depends linearly on the current value. An Arduino UNO board digitizes and store these values and –at the end of the test– downloads them to the Jetson TK1 through a serial over USB connection.

Our application benchmark is a code based on Lattice Boltzmann methods, widely used in CFD, while our hardware testbed is a low-power Tegra K1 SoC (System on a Chip), embedding a multi-core CPU and a GPU. We use two versions of our code, optimized respectively for CPU and GPU, with different configurations and compilation options. We then measure energy consumption and performance of the computationally intensive kernels, using several clock frequency combinations, and building a large database of measured data. We then analyze these results, also guided by a simple but effective model of the energy behavior of our test system.

2   The Hardware Testbed

The hardware setup that we use is based on a NVIDIA Jetson TK1 development board, embedding a Tegra K1 SoC, and a custom current monitoring system, able to acquire and store current values and – at the end of the test – download them to the Jetson TK1. Our setup is shown in Fig. 1.

The Tegra K1 SoC, hosted on the Jetson TK1 board, has a CPU and a GPU on a single chip; the CPU is a NVIDIA "4-Plus-1", a 2.32 GHz ARM quad-core Cortex-A15 and a low-power shadow core; the GPU is a NVIDIA Kepler GK20a with 192 CUDA cores (with 3.2 compute capability). Both units access a shared DDR3L 2 GB memory bank on a 64-bit bus running at up to 933 MHz.

This system has several energy-saving features: cores in the CPU can be independently activated and the frequency of the CPU, GPU and memory system can be individually selected in a wide range (CPU: $204 \cdots 2320.5$ MHz in

20 steps; GPU: $72 \cdots 852$ MHz in 15 steps; Memory: $12.75 \cdots 924$ MHz in 12 steps). The system includes a *performance governor* that by default keeps only the low-power shadow core of the CPU active at low frequency when the processor is idle, and activates the other cores and increases their clock frequencies, as activity is detected within the system. The GPU clock frequency is also scaled in a similar fashion. For our tests, we find it more useful to disable this system and explicitly control all units and their frequency, in order to obtain accurate power consumption data for known values of frequencies and active cores.

We selected this board as our testbed for several reasons: (i) this SoC contains a multi-core CPU as well as a GPU, so we may test both architectures; (ii) this chip allows fine and independent control of the clock frequencies of CPU, GPU and memory interface; (iii) low-power systems are constantly improving their performance, so these systems may quickly become interesting building blocks for HPC platforms; (iv) the low power requirements of this system make it easy to develop an accurate power monitoring system.

```
int fd;
struct termios newtio, oldtio;

// Initialize Arduino Serial conn.
fd = init_serial(&oldtio, &newtio);

// Start arduino data acquisition
start_arduino_acq(fd);

run_my_function();

// Start arduino data read-out
start_arduino_readout(fd, filename, 900);

// Close serial connection
close_serial(fd, &oldtio);
```

Code 1.1: Example of code run on the Jetson board to trigger data acquisition and readout.

```
// This is called every ms by
// an hardware timer
ISR(TIMER0_COMPA_vect) {
  if (acquireData) {
    byte i;
    unsigned int sensorValue = 0;
    // Average over avgSamples readings
    // one read costs about 0.11ms
    for (i = 0; i < avgSamples; i++) {
      // read the input on analog pin0
      sensorValue += analogRead(A0);
    }
    isendBuffer[idx] = sensorValue;
    idx++;
  }
}
```

Code 1.2: Function executed every 1 ms on Arduino UNO board to acquire current samples.

The Jetson TK1 is powered by a single 12 V source, so its overall power consumption can be easily derived by current measurements. We have developed a simple system able to measure the current flowing into the Jetson TK1 board with very good accuracy and time resolution (≈ 1 msec) and able to correlate measurements with the execution of specific software kernels. The setup uses an analog current to voltage converter (using a LTS 25-NP current transducer) and an Arduino UNO board; the latter uses its embedded 10-bit ADC to digitize current readings and stores them in its memory. We synchronize the Arduino UNO and the Jetson TK1 through a simple serial protocol built over an USB connection. With this setup, a generic application running on the Jetson TK1 only needs to trigger the Arduino UNO to start acquisition immediately before launching the kernel function to be profiled. After the function under test completes, acquired data is downloaded from the Arduino UNO memory, so it can be stored and analyzed offline. The monitor acquires current samples with 1 ms granularity; for increased accuracy, multiple consecutive readings (e.g. 5 in our case) are performed and averaged. This setup is able to correlate current measurements with specific application events with an accuracy of a few milliseconds, minimally disrupting the execution of the kernel function to profile.

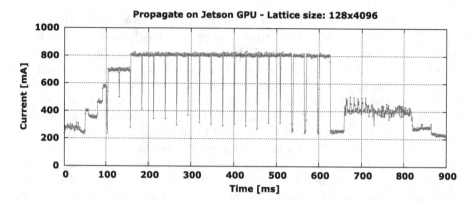

Fig. 2. Raw data collected by the current monitoring system as the Jetson GPU runs 20 iterations of a CUDA kernel. Current increases during the first iterations as the performance governor (in default mode) increases the clock frequency.

Code. 1.1 shows how to instrument a test program, while Code 1.2 shows the routine running on Arduino UNO every millisecond to acquire a current sample. Figure 2 shows a snapshot of raw current measurements; the plot refers to a CUDA kernel running 20 times consecutively on the Jetson's GPU, highlighting the good time resolution and accuracy. In this case, the configuration of the performance governor was the default one, so power consumption changes during the first iterations, reflecting automatic frequency scaling.

Once N current samples $i[n]$ are available for the time interval T_S corresponding to the execution of a given kernel, different power metrics can be computed. The instantaneous power can be computed as $p[n] = V \times i[n]$ and the average power as $P_{avg} = \frac{1}{N} \sum_{n=0}^{N-1} p[n]$. Another popular metric, the so-called *energy-to-solution* is defined as $E_S = T_S \times P_{avg}$.

3   The Application Benchmark

Lattice Boltzmann methods (LB) are widely used in computational fluid dynamics, to describe flows in two and three dimensions. LB methods [16] – discrete in position and momentum spaces – are based on the synthetic dynamics of *populations* sitting at the sites of a discrete lattice. At each time step, populations hop from lattice-site to lattice-site and then incoming populations *collide* among one another, that is, they mix and their values change accordingly. LB models in n dimensions with p populations are labeled as $DnQp$; we consider a state-of-the-art $D2Q37$ model that correctly reproduces the thermo-hydrodynamical evolution of a fluid in two dimensions, and enforces the equation of state of a perfect gas ($p = \rho T$) [14,15]; this model has been extensively used for large scale simulations of convective turbulence (see e.g., [1,2]). In the algorithm, a set of populations ($f_l(x,t)$ $l = 1 \cdots 37$), defined at the points of a discrete and regular lattice and each having a given lattice velocity c_l, evolve in (discrete) time according to the following equation:

$$f_l(\boldsymbol{x}, t + \Delta t) = f_l(\boldsymbol{x} - \boldsymbol{c}_l \Delta t, t) - \frac{\Delta t}{\tau} \left(f_l(\boldsymbol{x} - \boldsymbol{c}_l \Delta t, t) - f_l^{(eq)} \right) \tag{1}$$

The macroscopic variables, density ρ, velocity $\boldsymbol{u}$ and temperature T are defined in terms of the $f_l(x, t)$ and of the $\boldsymbol{c}_l$s (D is the number of space dimensions):

$$\rho = \sum_l f_l, \qquad \rho \boldsymbol{u} = \sum_l \boldsymbol{c}_l f_l, \qquad D\rho T = \sum_l |\boldsymbol{c}_l - \boldsymbol{u}|^2 f_l, \tag{2}$$

the equilibrium distributions ($f_l^{(eq)}$) are themselves a function of these macroscopic quantities [16]. In words, populations drift from different lattice sites (*propagation*), according to the value of their velocities and, on arrival at point $\boldsymbol{x}$, they change their values according to Eq. 1 (*collision*). One can show that, in suitable limiting cases, the evolution of the macroscopic variables obeys the thermo-hydrodynamical equations of motion of the fluid. Close inspection of Eq. 1 also shows that the algorithm offers a huge degree of easily identifiable parallelism; this makes LB algorithms popular HPC massively-parallel applications.

An LB simulation starts with an initial assignment of the populations, in accordance with a given initial condition at $t = 0$ on some spatial domain, and iterates Eq. 1 for each point in the domain and for as many time-steps as needed. At each iteration two critical kernel functions are executed: (i) propagate moves populations across lattice sites collecting at each site all populations that will interact at the next phase (collide). Consequently, propagate moves blocks of memory locations allocated at sparse addresses, corresponding to populations of neighbor cells; (ii) collide performs all the mathematical steps associated to Eq. 1 and needed to compute the population values at each lattice site at the new time step. Input data for this phase are the populations gathered by the previous propagate phase. This step is the floating point intensive step of the code.

These two kernels are the most time consuming parts of any LB simulation. It is very helpful for our purposes that propagate involves a large number of sparse memory accesses, so it is strongly memory-bound. collide, on the other hand, is strongly compute-bound, heavily using the floating-point unit of either processor, and the performance of the floating-point unit is the ultimate bottleneck.

4   Measurements

Our benchmark is based on codes implementing the LB algorithm described in the previous section and exploiting to a large extent the available parallelism. On the GPU we run an optimized CUDA code, developed for large scale CFD simulations on large HPC systems [3,9]. On the CPU we run a plain C version [6,11] using NEON SIMD *intrinsics* exploiting the vector unit of the ARM Cortex-A15 cores. We also use OpenMP for multi-threading within the 4 cores and OpenMPI for future testing purposes on multiple boards.

We have instrumented both kernels as described in Sec. 2, and performed a large number of test runs, monitoring the current profile at all times during the

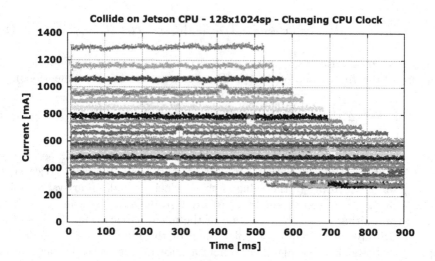

Fig. 3. Current measurements while running the collide kernel on the CPU with 4 OpenMP threads for a 128 × 1024 points lattice. Each run (plot line) is performed at a different CPU clock frequency, spanning between 204MHz (lowest green line) and 2.3GHz (highest red line). The Memory clock is set at its maximum value (Color figure online).

tests, accumulating a large data-base of measured data. On the software side, we have included runs with different numbers of OpenMP threads (for CPU) and CUDA block sizes (for the GPU); on the hardware side we have logged data for most combinations of the adjustable clock frequencies, disabling automatic frequency scaling. The C code using NEON *intrinsics*, was run on the CPU manually forcing the use of the G cluster (i.e. the high performance quad-core). When running on the GPU, the CPU was forced to use the LP cluster (i.e. the low performance shadow core). For the sake of a fair comparison, all tests adopt single precision for floating point data, since the Cortex-A15 is a 32-bit CPU and double precision vector instructions are not available.

Figure 3 shows current data for collide given different settings of the CPU clock (GPU and memory clocks are fixed); similar results are available for the propagate kernel, for most of the clock combinations and for both GPU and CPU.

5   Results and Discussion

We consider *energy-to-solution* (E_S) and *time-to-solution* (T_S) – and the correlations thereof – as relevant and interesting parameters when looking for tradeoffs between time and energy conflicting requirements. Figure 4 shows measured values of T_S (vertical axis) and E_S (coded by colors) for propagate and collide kernels and for several clock frequency settings, when running on both CPU and GPU processors. From these plot, we see, for instance, that energy consumption is dominated by the collide kernel (notice the different color scales). propagate

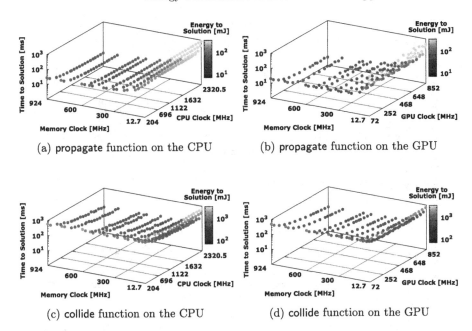

(a) propagate function on the CPU

(b) propagate function on the GPU

(c) collide function on the CPU

(d) collide function on the GPU

Fig. 4. Time- and energy-to-solution of the profiled kernels while running on the CPU and GPU with different CPU, GPU and memory clock frequencies. Lattice size is 128x1024 points.

is equally performing and power-greedy on both processors; this was expected, since on this system the CPU and GPU share the same memory.

To better highlight the time/energy tradeoff, we plot E_S as a function of T_S, on either processors and for both kernels, see Fig. 5. Interestingly enough, E_S scales approximately linearly with T_S, but large fluctuations are present. A crude way to understand this behavior is as follows: as the processor executes a kernel, it consumes power in two ways: (i) the power associated to the (constant in time) background current (including the leakage current of the processor and the current drawn by ancillary circuits on the board) and (ii) the power associated to the switching activity of all gates of the processor as it transitions across different states while executing the program. The first term implies, in our crude model, a constant power rate (P_0), while the second term implies an average energy dissipation CV^2 every time a bit in the state of the processor toggles during execution (V is the processor power supply, while C is an average value of the capacitance associated to the output of each gate); this model derives directly from early power analyses found in classic books in VLSI design [12], and recently discussed in [8]. While we are fully aware that the actual situation is more complex, we let this simple model guide our further analysis. We fit E_S as a function of T_S as follows:

$$E_S = E_0 + P_0 \times T_S \tag{3}$$

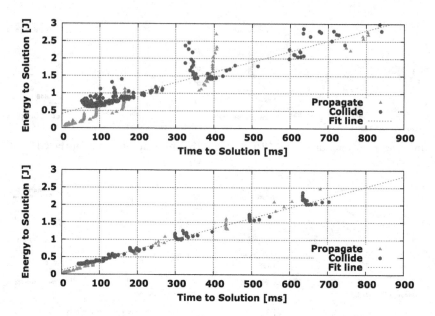

Fig. 5. Measured values of E_S vs. T_S on the CPU (top) and GPU (bottom), for the collide (blu) and propagate (red) kernels corresponding to several values of the clock frequencies. Results of a fit of collide data to Eq. 3 of is also shown (Color figure online).

P_0 should be independent of the program under test, while E_0 should depend on the kernel and the processor executing it, as – to first approximation – it counts the number of state transitions that the processor has to go to execute the code, *irrespective* of the frequency at which they happen.

Possible sanity checks for our models are: (i) P_0 is the same for all measured kernels and processors, and (ii) its value is close to the one derived from current measurements as the system rests in the idle state.

We fitted the two parameters from data for the collide kernel, obtaining $E_0^{CPU} = 410$ mJ, $P_0^{CPU} = 2.99$ W, $E_0^{GPU} = 120$ mJ, $P_0^{GPU} = 3.00$ W; as expected the two values for P_0 are almost equal and consistent with the value, ≈ 3 W, obtained from current readings (≈ 250 mA) when the system is idle.

It is interesting to subtract from E_S the contribution associated to the background current, as computed from Eq. 3, and define $E_0^K = E_S - P_0 \times T_S$, that should depend only on the profiled kernel (labelled by superscript K) and on the processing unit. Figure 6 plots E_0^K as function of T_S; this shows a clean lower-bound constant envelope of all data points – as expected from our model – with large fluctuations, clustering around some values of T_S. The insets in Fig. 6 provide a closer look at two such clusters, showing for each point a label with GPU (left) and memory (right) frequency. This clarifies the origin of these clusters: their points correspond to cases in which one of the two subsystems (either memory or compute-unit) [10] has become the performance bottleneck;

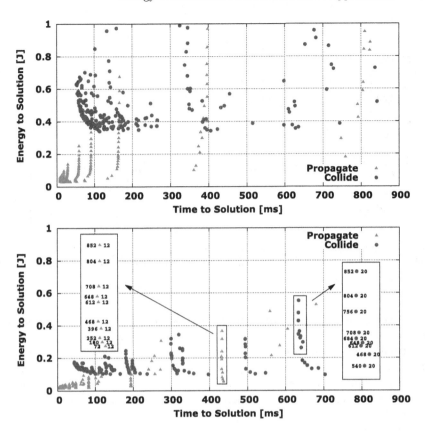

Fig. 6. Measured values of E_0^K, defined in the text, as a function of T_S, for the collide (blue) and propagate (red) kernels on CPU (top) and GPU (bottom). The insets zoom onto two data clusters, showing for each point the GPU (left) and memory (right) clock frequency in MHz (Color figure online).

increasing the frequency of the other subsystem means that the latter has to go through system states (stalled states) that do not advance the computation, so performance remains approximately constant, while energy dissipation increases.

This analysis helps identify best values of processor/memory clock pairs for each kernel, given a target T_S or an assigned energy budget. This is particularly relevant of course when T_S is close to its lower possible value: indeed, this is the only area (enlarged in Fig. 7 for the collide kernel on GPU) where one can look for an optimal energy/time trade-off; in fact, the plots make it evident that an accurate matching of clock frequencies is an effective way to reduce E_0^K; on the other hand, accepting lower performance – that is settling for T_S significantly longer than the best possible value – does not reduce E_0^K but rather increases the energy burden associated to the $P_0 \times T_S$ contribution, and consequently total energy dissipation. We also note that different kernels may have different ideal clocks pairs, so, after finding a satisfactory tradeoff for each of them, it helps if

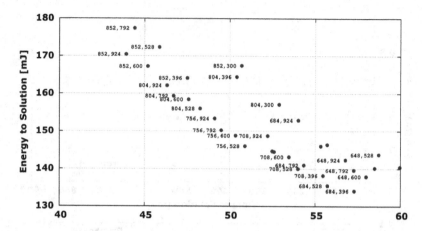

Fig. 7. Close-in view of the E_0^K vs. T_S graph, in a region corresponding to the best possible values for T_S. For each data point, we list the GPU (left) and memory (right) clock frequencies (MHz).

they can be dynamically adjusted before each kernel starts. Clock adjustments, in our test case, may improve E_0^K by large factors; however what is really relevant is the total energy dissipation, E_S, for which the background contribution is not small and linearly dependent on time; so the bottom line is that: (i) careful energy optimization may reduce E_S by $\approx 10 \cdots 20\%$ at best, and (ii) contrary to intuition, using very low clock frequencies is an ineffective way to reduce dissipation.

6 Conclusions and Future Works

The analysis of the previous section suggests the following remarks:

- to first approximation, the best energy saving option for this class of processors, correspond to running the system at a frequency close to the highest possible value, as determined from data shown in Figs. 5, 6 and 7, and then (if possible) remove power from the (sub-)system.
- as a corollary, options to run codes at very low frequencies are almost useless; it is probably more useful to add more flexible (and fast) options to remove power from parts of the processor; efficient ways to save the state of the subsystem before shut down would be most welcome.
- limited but not negligible power optimization is possible by adjusting clocks on a kernel-by-kernel basis; this is best done via direct energy profiling of the actual codes; it is then important that low-power system are able to measure their consumption with minimal disruption to the running code and make results easily available.
- reducing the latency time associated to clock changes is also important to make the selection of the best clock values possible even for short kernels, without significant performance loss.

– a more radical way to address the problem is to reduce V, as one reduces clock frequencies; in fact, to first approximation, V scales linearly with frequency, while power is proportional to V^2. We are not sure to which extent this strategy is already carried out for the Jetson TK1; we stress that this should be done consistently across the whole system.

In this paper, we have described a number of power benchmarks of a Jetson TK1 processor, made possible by a power monitoring system with good time resolution and accurate time correlation with the execution of the kernels under test. We have been able to disentangle the energy dissipation associated to the actual computation and the one associated to background currents. We have shown that – at least for this low power system – background dissipation has a significant impact on overall energy dissipation; in spite of that, limited but not negligible optimization is possible by carefully matching the values of all clock frequencies on the system; we have finally discussed possible new features that low-power systems should have to improve energy tuning.

We plan to continue along this line of analysis in several ways: (i) improving the current monitoring system, to have more information available and to measure how the various parts of the system contribute to energy dissipation; (ii) extend the analysis to more advanced low-power systems supporting double precision floating point maths, such as the forthcoming Jetson X1 board, and to high-end HPC accelerators, such as NVIDIA K40 or K80 GPUs; (iii) consider not only hardware-based tuning, but also software options toward energy saving: work is in progress along these directions.

Acknowledgements. This work has been done in the framework of the COSA, COKA and Suma projects, supported by INFN. The Jetson TK1 development board used as a testbed was awarded to E.C. for the best paper at UCHPC 2014.

References

1. Biferale, L., Mantovani, F., Sbragaglia, M., Scagliarini, A., Toschi, F., Tripiccione, R.: Reactive Rayleigh-Taylor systems: front propagation and non-stationarity. EPL **94**(5), 54004 (2011). doi:10.1209/0295-5075/94/54004
2. Biferale, L., Mantovani, F., Sbragaglia, M., Scagliarini, A., Toschi, F., Tripiccione, R.: Second-order closure in stratified turbulence: simulations and modeling of bulk and entrainment regions. Phys. Rev. E **84**(1), 016305 (2011). doi:10.1103/PhysRevE.84.016305
3. Calore, E., Schifano, S.F., Tripiccione, R.: On portability, performance and scalability of an MPI OpenCL lattice boltzmann code. In: Lopes, L., et al. (eds.) Euro-Par 2014, Part II. LNCS, vol. 8806, pp. 438–449. Springer, Heidelberg (2014)
4. Choi, J., Dukhan, M., Liu, X., Vuduc, R.: Algorithmic time, energy, and power on candidate HPC compute building blocks. In: IEEE 28th International Parallel and Distributed Processing Symposium, pp. 447–457 (2014). doi:10.1109/IPDPS.2014.54

5. Coplin, J., Burtscher, M.: Effects of source-code optimizations on GPU performance and energy consumption. In: Proceedings of the 8th Workshop on General Purpose Processing Using GPUs, GPGPU 2015, pp. 48–58 (2015). doi:10.1145/2716282.2716292

6. Crimi, G., Mantovani, F., Pivanti, M., Schifano, S.F., Tripiccione, R.: Early experience on porting and running a lattice boltzmann code on the xeon-phi co-processor. Procedia Comput. Sci. **18**, 551–560 (2013). doi:10.1016/j.procs.2013.05.219

7. Hackenberg, D., Ilsche, T., Schone, R., Molka, D., Schmidt, M., Nagel, W.: Power measurement techniques on standard compute nodes: a quantitative comparison. In: 2013 IEEE International Symposium on Performance Analysis of Systems and Software (ISPASS), pp. 194–204 (2013). doi:10.1109/ISPASS.2013.6557170

8. Kim, N., Austin, T., Baauw, D., Mudge, T., Flautner, K., Hu, J., Irwin, M., Kandemir, M., Narayanan, V.: Leakage current: moore's law meets static power. Computer **36**(12), 68–75 (2003). doi:10.1109/MC.2003.1250885

9. Kraus, J., Pivanti, M., Schifano, S.F., Tripiccione, R., Zanella, M.: Benchmarking GPUs with a parallel lattice-boltzmann code. In: 25th Int. Symposiumon Computer Architecture and High Performance Computing (SBAC-PAD), pp. 160–167. IEEE (2013). doi:10.1109/SBAC-PAD.2013.37

10. Laurenzano, M.A., Tiwari, A., Jundt, A., Peraza, J., Ward Jr, W.A., Campbell, R., Carrington, L.: Characterizing the performance-energy tradeoff of small ARM cores in HPC computation. In: Silva, F., Dutra, I., Santos Costa, V. (eds.) Euro-Par 2014 Parallel Processing. LNCS, vol. 8632, pp. 124–137. Springer, Heidelberg (2014)

11. Mantovani, F., Pivanti, M., Schifano, S.F., Tripiccione, R.: Performance issues on many-core processors: a D2Q37 lattice boltzmann scheme as a test-case. Comput. Fluids **88**, 743–752 (2013). doi:10.1016/j.compfluid.2013.05.014

12. Mead, C., Conway, L.: Introduction to VLSI systems, vol. 802. Addison-Wesley, Reading (1980)

13. Rajovic, N., Rico, A., Puzovic, N., Adeniyi-Jones, C., Ramirez, A.: Tibidabo: making the case for an ARM-based HPC system. Future Generation Computer Systems **36**, 322–334 (2014)

14. Sbragaglia, M., Benzi, R., Biferale, L., Chen, H., Shan, X., Succi, S.: Lattice boltzmann method with self-consistent thermo-hydrodynamic equilibria. J. Fluid Mech. **628**, 299–309 (2009). doi:10.1017/S002211200900665X

15. Scagliarini, A., Biferale, L., Sbragaglia, M., Sugiyama, K., Toschi, F.: Lattice boltzmann methods for thermal flows: continuum limit and applications to compressible Rayleigh-Taylor systems. Phys. Fluids (1994-present) **22**(5), 055101 (2010). doi:10.1063/1.3392774

16. Succi, S.: The Lattice-Boltzmann Equation. Oxford University Press, Oxford (2001)

17. Wittmann, M., Hager, G., Zeiser, T., Treibig, J., Wellein, G.: Chip-level and multinode analysis of energy-optimized lattice Boltzmann CFD simulations. Concurr. Comput. Pract. Exp. (2015). doi:10.1002/cpe.3489. ISSN: 1532-0634

A Cache-Aware Performance Prediction Framework for GPGPU Computations

Alexander Pöppl[(✉)] and Alexander Herz

Institut für Informatik, Technische Universität München,
Boltzmannstraße 3, 85748 Garching Bei München, Germany
{poeppl,herz}@in.tum.de

Abstract. We present a model for the automated prediction of average execution times for OpenCL-based computations on GPUs. The model encompasses the whole execution of the computation, including the transfer to and from the GPU, and the kernel execution itself. In contrast to existing static prediction frameworks, we incorporate the caches available on modern GPUs into our model. Using our benchmark suite, we show that memory access patterns can be grouped into five patterns that exhibit significantly different memory access performance. By extending our static analysis framework to differentiate the performance behavior of these memory access patterns, we improve on predictions made by existing GPU performance models. In order to evaluate the quality of our model, we compare cache-aware and cache-unaware predictions for a large set of randomly generated OpenCL kernels with their actual execution time.

1 Introduction

OpenCL is a powerful platform to express data parallel computations on a wide range of accelerator devices which are commonly used in HPC applications [2]. It has been recognized that task-allocation, i.e. the distribution of computations onto the different available computing resources, on heterogeneous systems is an important problem [5,11].

To address this problem, schedulers for heterogeneous platforms, such as Qilin [11] or StarPU [5] have been proposed. The quality of their schedules is highly dependent on a realistic execution time prediction for the individual computations on each specific device. Measuring the execution time for all computations on all possible devices is very time and energy consuming. Therefore, static execution time prediction models have been established [3,8,10].

These models enable high quality predictions on early generation GPGPUs. However, the caches introduced into the memory hierarchy of later GPGPU generations are neglected. We have benchmarked a large set of randomly generated memory accesses on a range of current GPGPUs. Our measurements show that the accesses can be categorized into five patterns with distinct performance characteristics. Using these measurements, we extract a performance characteristic for each pattern and incorporate it into our performance prediction model.

© Springer International Publishing Switzerland 2015
S. Hunold et al. (Eds.): Euro-Par 2015 Workshops, LNCS 9523, pp. 749–760, 2015.
DOI: 10.1007/978-3-319-27308-2_60

Finally, we evaluate the quality of our improved model on a large set of randomly generated OpenCL kernels. The contributions of this paper are as follows:

- We show that memory accesses can be categorized into patterns with distinct performance characteristics.
- We present a fully static OpenCL computation performance prediction model.
- We evaluate a large set of randomly generated kernels to show that our cache-aware model enables improved predictions on GPGPUs with cached memory hierarchies.

1.1   Example

A frequent application for OpenCL computations are stencil operations on two-dimensional arrays. A simple example of such a stencil computation is given in Eq. 1 which we will apply on an array of size $n * m$. The example is chosen to illustrate the effects of different access patterns on the execution time.

$$b(i,j) = a(i,j)^2 - a(1,j) \tag{1}$$

The equation uses a stencil on the input array a to compute all elements of the output array b. The complete computation is performed in the following steps.

1: $n_{\mathrm{WI}} = m * n$
2: $mem_{GPU}^{input} \leftarrow device.alloc(n_{\mathrm{WI}} * s_{\mathrm{WI}})$
3: $mem_{GPU}^{output} \leftarrow device.alloc(n_{\mathrm{WI}} * s_{\mathrm{WI}})$
4: copyDataToGPU($\rightarrow mem_{GPU}^{input}$)
5: $device.kernel(n_{\mathrm{WI}}, n_{\mathrm{WG}}, m, n)$
   $\Rightarrow \forall id \in \{0, .., n_{\mathrm{WI}}\}.\ sq\_mod(mem_{GPU}^{input}, mem_{GPU}^{output}, m, n)$
6: copyDataFromGPU($\rightarrow mem_{GPU}^{output}$)

First, memory segments for the input array and the output array, both with data type size, s_{WI}, need to be allocated on the GPU (line 2 and 3). Next, we have to transfer the data from the host system to the GPU (line 4). In line 5, we execute the kernel which applies Eq. 1 for each element of the output array. The kernel code for sq_mod is shown below. In order to execute the kernel, we have to specify the number of work-items (i.e. output array elements), n_{WI}, and the number of work-items per work-group, n_{WG}, which will be executed in parallel. The parameter id, shown in the result of the kernel execution above, represents the index of the work-item the kernel is currently applied on. It is not explicitly given as a parameter, but can be obtained during the execution of the kernel using the function get_global_id(0). Finally, the results of the computation need to be copied back to the host system for further processing (line 6).

```
kernel void sq_mod(global float *matrix, global float *res,
                   unsigned int m, unsigned int n) {
    size_t current_pos = get_global_id(0);
    unsigned int current_row = current_pos / n;
    unsigned int current_col = current_pos % n;
    res[current_pos] = matrix[current_row * n + current_col]
            * matrix[current_row * n + current_col]
            - matrix[current_col];
}
```

1.2 Prediction of Kernel Execution Times

We will develop our performance prediction model by subdividing the complete computation into several steps analogous to the example in the previous section. Hence, the overall execution time of an OpenCL computation is given by Eq. 2 which adds up the time required to copy data to the device (step 4), executing the kernel (step 5) and copying the result back (step 6). Here n_{WG} holds the number of work-items in a single work-group, and n_{XU} the number of execution units, i.e. the degree of parallelism on the device. The execution time of the actual kernel (step 5) is calculated using Eq. 3. The average execution time of each of the elementary operations $W_{Op}(n_{Op}) * t_{Op}(n_{WI})$ is added to the base overhead $t_{Base}(n_{WI})$ and divided by the utilization of the GPU $U(n_{WG}, n_{XU})$. W_{Op} are functions determining how the execution time scales with the number of operations n_{Op} of the same type occurring in the same kernel. We found that for the basic operations, the execution time does not scale linearly with the number of operations of the same type (see Subsect. 2.4). The family of functions t_{Op} assigns an execution time based on the elementary expression and the number of work-items n_{WI}. The utilization function $U(n_{WG}, n_{XU})$ describes the degree of parallelization achieved by the GPU based on the number of execution units and the size of the work-group. We will discuss each cost component in the following sections.

$$t(n_{WI}, s_{WI}, n_{WG}) = t_{Transfer}(n_{WI}, s_{WI}) + t_{Kernel}(n_{WI}, n_{WG}) \tag{2}$$

$$t_{Kernel}(n_{WI}, n_{WG}) = \frac{t_{Base}(n_{WI}) + \sum_{Op \in \text{Expr.-Types}} W_{Op}(n_{Op}) t_{Op}(n_{WI})}{U(n_{WG}, n_{XU})} \tag{3}$$

2 Runtime Model

In this section, we describe the individual components of our model for the prediction of OpenCL kernels executed on a specific GPU. We will first model the costs of the data transfer, followed by the costs for the individual kernel components. Loops, conditional statements and intrinsic functions for operations such as the square root or the sine are not yet regarded in the model. For most of the measurements, we ran microkernels with the operation that was to be classified and compared its performance with another microkernel that lacked the operation but was otherwise identical. We took multiple samples for each data point, in order to ensure a standard error ratio of 0.02.

2.1 Transfer of Data to and from the Device

Most modern GPUs have a dedicated portion of memory separate from the system's main memory, to be used exclusively by them. As mentioned above, data needs to be transferred to and from that memory. In order to predict the time spent on data transfer, one has to consider two components. The first one is the bandwidth bw, which is determined by the underlying bus system, typically

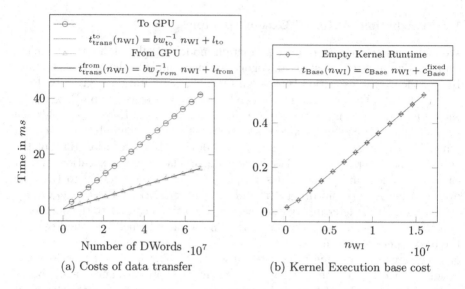

(a) Costs of data transfer   (b) Kernel Execution base cost

Fig. 1. On the diagram to the left, the time spent on transferring memory from and to the GPU is shown. The diagram on the right shows the base cost for kernel execution.

PCI Express, and the second one the signal propagation and access latency l_{prop}, which is determined by all the effected components, i.e. the bus systems and the memory modules [1, 4, 7].

We measured the time it took to transfer an array with n_{WI} work-items between system and device memory. These measurements, with their results displayed in Fig. 1a, show a linear dependency between the amount of data transferred and the transfer time. It can be seen that there is significantly more time spent copying data to the GPU than on copying the results back again, although the size of the data remains the same. This effect is also mentioned by Fuji et al. [7], who state driver optimizations as a reason for the different costs. Our model reflects this effect with separate assignments for the bandwidth bw and latency l being required for each direction [7].

2.2 Base Cost of Kernel Execution

Computations on GPUs are performed in a highly parallel fashion, with each work-item being computed in its own thread. These need to be started, coordinated and put into blocks, which causes a non-negligible amount of overhead, that, as shown in Fig. 1b, scales linearly in regards to the number of computed work-items.

2.3 Influence of the Work-Group Size

Each work-item belongs to a work-group. Work-items within a work-group are executed concurrently, and only once all work-items belonging to one work-group

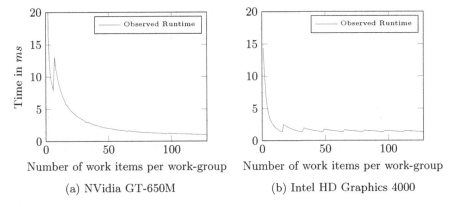

Fig. 2. Execution time for different work-group sizes. We only show the results of work-groups with less than 100 work-items in order to highlight the performance penalties of using work-group sizes that are slightly bigger than multiples of the number of execution units. The kernel we used to evaluate this behavior performs one read from and write to the global memory, and one floating point division.

are finished may work-items from another start their calculations. It follows that the work-group needs to be sufficiently large in order to fully utilize all available processing elements of the GPU. Additionally, all work-groups need to have the same size, hence the total number of work-items needs to be evenly divisible by the work-group size. However, using the biggest possible work-group size is not always optimal for maximizing GPU utilization.

We can observe the effects of improper resource utilization in Fig. 2, especially on the HD 4000. There is a clear performance degradation whenever the utilization of the execution units is less than optimal. We model the utilization as $U(w, n_{\mathrm{XU}})$, defined in Eq. 4. Term A denotes the portion of the computation that can be performed using all available execution units, while B is the remainder of the execution which does not fully utilize the available resources. Note that the size of the work-group is not determined automatically, but set by the programmer when the kernel execution is started.

$$U(n_{\mathrm{WG}}, n_{\mathrm{XU}}) = \underbrace{\frac{\left\lfloor \frac{n_{\mathrm{WG}}}{n_{\mathrm{XU}}} \right\rfloor}{\left\lceil \frac{n_{\mathrm{WG}}}{n_{\mathrm{XU}}} \right\rceil}}_{A} + \underbrace{\frac{n_{\mathrm{WG}} \bmod n_{\mathrm{XU}}}{n_{\mathrm{XU}}} \frac{\left\lceil \frac{n_{\mathrm{WG}}}{n_{\mathrm{XU}}} \right\rceil - \left\lfloor \frac{n_{\mathrm{WG}}}{n_{\mathrm{XU}}} \right\rfloor}{\left\lceil \frac{n_{\mathrm{WG}}}{n_{\mathrm{XU}}} \right\rceil}}_{B} \tag{4}$$

2.4   Basic Operations

Generally, GPU kernels consist of memory accesses and arithmetic expressions. We evaluate the behavior of arithmetic expressions, signified by the four basic operations $+$, $-$, $*$ and $/$. In order to model the execution time of basic operations, the number of work-items n_{WI} and the accumulated number of each type

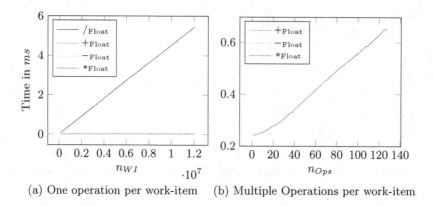

(a) One operation per work-item   (b) Multiple Operations per work-item

Fig. 3. The diagrams above display the progression of the execution time for basic operations, based on the number of work-items on the left and based on the number of operations in a single kernel on the right.

of basic operations n_{Ops} performed within the kernel must be taken into account. Our measurements (results depicted in Fig. 3a) show that there is a linear relation between the number of work-items and the execution time. For the number of operations within a work-item, we found the execution time to increase linearly as well, but only after a certain number of operations, as shown in Fig. 3b. We modeled this behavior with Eq. 5.

$$W_{\mathrm{op}}^{\mathrm{type}}(n_{\mathrm{Ops}}) = \begin{cases} a\ n_{\mathrm{Ops}}^{b} + c & : n_{\mathrm{Ops}} \leq n_{\mathrm{Ops}}^{\mathrm{sat}} \\ a'n_{\mathrm{Ops}} + c' & : n_{\mathrm{Ops}} > n_{\mathrm{Ops}}^{\mathrm{sat}} \end{cases}$$
$$t_{\mathrm{op}}^{\mathrm{type}}(n_{\mathrm{WI}}) = c_{\mathrm{op}}^{\mathrm{type}} n_{\mathrm{WI}} \tag{5}$$

The GPU dependent constants a, a', b, c, c' are obtained by fitting $W_{\mathrm{op}}^{\mathrm{type}}$ (n_{Ops}) to Fig. 3b, the constant $c_{\mathrm{op}}^{\mathrm{type}}$ is obtained by fitting $t_{\mathrm{op}}^{\mathrm{type}}(n_{\mathrm{WI}})$ to Fig. 3a.

2.5   Memory Accesses

Memory accesses scale, similarly to basic operations, linearly in regards to the number of work-items and to the number of the same access in the kernel. As expected from the three-tier memory model (with *private*, *local* and *global* memory) of OpenCL, we observed a large spread in execution time for accesses to different types of memory. In the kernel introduced in Subsect. 1.1, we see two of the different memory types in use. Private memory is implicitly used for all the parameter values and local variables. The pointers given as a parameter to the kernel point to segments of the global memory. There is one write access to the global memory, and three read accesses, with two of them accessing the same address in the same kernel execution. The third only accesses items from the first row. While local memory is not featured in the example it could be used by declaring a variable outside the kernel, e.g. `local float mem[4]`.

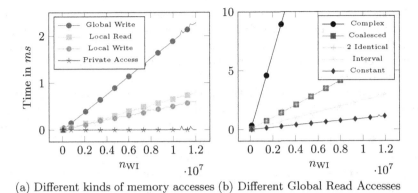

(a) Different kinds of memory accesses (b) Different Global Read Accesses

Fig. 4. The diagrams above display the results of our measurements for the cost of different memory accesses. In the left picture, the different kinds of memory accesses are compared to each other. On the right side, read accesses to the global memory with different access patterns are displayed. The memory accesses used for these measurements are the ones given in the text.

These are usually implemented using different memory types, which, as we concluded from the result of our measurements, depicted in Fig. 4a, differ significantly in terms of access time. Private memory accesses are practically cost-free. Local accesses, while more expensive, are still significantly faster than global accesses.

However, only distinguishing between different memory types has proven insufficient for obtaining precise estimations the execution time of kernels. In the following, we discuss groups of memory access patterns identified by our measurements which are shown in Fig. 4b. Each pattern is associated with a characteristic memory access latency, induced by the caches utilized by the respective pattern. In the patterns, x denotes the index of the current work-item which can be computed using $get\_global\_id(0)$ inside the kernel.

Some memory accesses always read from the same address, e.g. `matrix [0x2a]`. The content of this address only needs to be cached once. Further reads, including those made from other work-items that are able to access the same cache, do not need to fetch from the off-chip memory a second time. We refer to these as *constant accesses*.

If all of the addresses that are reached by an access are in a range that fits into the cache – the size of which may be queried from the OpenCL runtime – of that device (e.g. `matrix[x&0xFF]`), the values can still be held in the cache, and expensive off-chip accesses may be avoided. While this kind of read is more expensive than the constant one, the costs of the *interval access* are still below the costs of other global accesses.

The most common memory access ranges over a memory area that is significantly greater than the typical cache (e.g. `matrix[x]`). However, as this is the default case, the GPU vendors implemented optimizations [12], and typically several addresses will be loaded at once, reducing the number of accesses to the off-chip memory significantly. This kind of access is called a *coalesced access*.

In some kernels, there are *multiple identical accesses* to the same address (e.g. `matrix[x] * matrix[x]`). We found subsequent accesses to the same address within the same kernel to be cheaper compared to accesses to a different address. On the GT-650M, we observed subsequent reads to the same address to be without any extra cost, while for other GPUs the overhead was comparable to constant accesses. The reason for the speedups may be compiler optimizations. These values may be stored in a cache, or the compiler may store them in a register file. This eliminates or severely reduces the cost of subsequent accesses.

Accesses that do not fall into those categories, are referred to as *uncoalesced accesses*. With those, caches cannot hide the latency, and the off-chip memory needs to be accessed frequently. In consequence, these kinds of accesses are at least one order of magnitude slower than the others.

Note that for some access patterns, our analysis needs to compute the size of the input arrays statically which is not always possible.

3   Empirical Evaluation

With the model described in the previous section, we built an analysis that iterates over the syntax tree of the OpenCL kernel and collects the number of occurrences of each elementary expression. Given the kernel, the experimentally gathered constants for the GPU operations, the number of work-items n_{WI} and the desired work-group size n_{WG}, we can predict the total execution time for the computation. Figure 5a displays the analysis result for a computation using the kernel from the example in Subsect. 1.1 with an array size $m * n = n_{WI}$ of 4096×4096.

In Fig. 5b, the time spent executing the example from Subsect. 1.1 with different input array sizes is compared to predictions that were made during its compilation. For arrays with more than 128×128 entries, the observed result is very close to the predicted one. Only for smaller arrays does the model slightly over-estimate the approximation. This may be caused by the larger uncertainty in the measurements for very small arrays.

4   Quantitative Evaluation

To evaluate the quality of the predictions made with the model, we generated random valid OpenCL kernels that perform stencil computations. We created execution time predictions for each kernel, and compared them to the arithmetic mean of the run time of five different runs of the same kernel. This was done for array sizes ranging from 32×32 to 8192×8192 elements. We performed this evaluation on two thousand generated kernels, separated into two categories with one thousand samples each. Kernels in the first category have a small number of expressions and the complexity of memory access patterns is limited to simple patterns as well. Such kernels may conceivably be used in productive environments, and will henceforth be referred to as realistic samples. In the other category, the complexity of the kernels is not restricted. In order to avoid stack

Cost Type # in	Kernel	Time in μs
$-_{\text{float}}$	1	74.16
$*_{\text{float}}$	1	74.54
$+_{\text{int}}$	1	55.13
$*_{\text{int}}$	7	81.04
$/_{\text{int}}$	4	1506
private access	1	0.0
interval global read access	1	770.9
continuous global read access	1	2335
base cost	1	3191
work-group size	1024	-
final prediction		8089

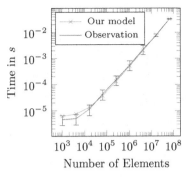

(a) Prediction table for 2^{24} work-items (Array of size 4096×4096)

(b) Comparison between predicted and actual execution time

Fig. 5. This table shows the predictions for the example kernel presented in Subsect. 1.1. On the left, the individual elementary expressions are listed for a fixed work-item size on the test system, and on the right the overall predictions are compared to the actual execution time of the kernel. The prediction for this kernel may be computed as follows: $t_{\text{Kernel}}(n_{\text{WI}}, n_{\text{WG}}) = M_{\text{WG}}(n_{\text{WG}})((c_{\text{Base}} + c_-^{float} + c_*^{float} + c_+^{int} + \frac{7}{7}c_*^{int} + \frac{4}{4}c_/^{int} + c_{\text{global}}^{ivl} + c_{\text{global}}^{cont})n_{\text{WI}} + c_{\text{Base}}^{fixed})$. Both examples were measured on a NVidia GT-650M.

overflows during the generation, we limited the number of subexpressions to at most 50 elementary expressions for the calculation. Each generated memory access may have up to fifty subexpressions in its index expression.

The histograms in Fig. 6 display the result of this evaluation. We used the quotient $\frac{\text{prediction}}{\text{result}}$ as a measure of the quality for the result. A perfect prediction yields 1.0, values smaller than that indicate an underestimation, and larger values an overestimation. In the histograms, one may see that the prediction performed poorly in some cases. A possible reason may be an incorrect classification of memory accesses, where the actual runtime was lower than the predicted one. Nevertheless, on the Quadro K4000, we observed deviations of less than 30 % from the perfect result in realistic sample set for 71 % of the samples. For the unrestricted sample set 43 % were in that interval. The GT-650M has a slightly different behavior. Here, 63 % of the predictions for the realistic set deviate less than 30 % from the perfect result. For the unrestricted sample set, 50 % deviate less than 30 %. We also compared our model to a version that does not use our memory access patterns (see Fig. 6e). In contrast to the run that used our model, only 61 % instead of 71 % of all samples deviate by less than 30 %. This shows that the quality of the prediction can be improved by taking GPU caches into account.

5   Related Work

In the eight years since GPGPU programming emerged, there have been several approaches to modeling the execution time of programs running on the GPU. They can be grouped into two major groups, static and dynamic approaches.

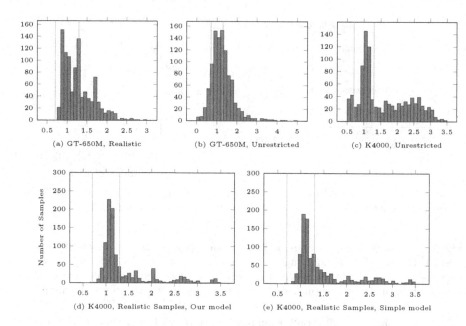

Fig. 6. The diagrams show distributions of benchmark results for both the test with an unrestricted as well as with a restricted set of OpenCL kernels. We performed the evaluations on a NVidia GT-650M notebook GPU and a Quadro K4000 workstation GPU. The X axis denotes the quotient $\frac{t_{prediction}}{t_{result}}$. The closer this quotient is to 1, the better the prediction. Using the diagrams in the second row, one can compare the quality of predictions made using our model with the quality of the predictions made using a simple model that does not model cache behavior.

C. Luk et al. [11] and G. Diamos and S.Yalamanchili [6] propose dynamic approaches in order to make scheduling decisions for their respective heterogeneous environments. They do this by observing run times of kernels executed on the GPU and using the gathered information to extrapolate information about future kernel executions. One big disadvantage with dynamic approaches is the fact that they do not possess information before the kernel is executed for the first time. Without any static metric, this has a negative impact on the quality of schedules involving computations on unknown kernels. One possible alleviation of this problem to use a static approach such as ours for the initial estimation, and then use the dynamically gathered data to improve on the initial value [5,6,8,11].

D. Grewe and M. O'Boyle [8] propose a static, machine-learning based approach. They consider OpenCL kernels, and split them into components. They take a wider range of basic operations, e.g. *sqrt* or *sin* into account. However, the paper does not model different global memory accesses and their possible caching [8].

K.Kothapalli et al. [10] contribute a static performance model based on NVidia's CUDA framework. They analyze the program based on specifications provided by NVidia. Their model is more closely tied to the architecture of the NVidia hardware. They distinguish between the different kinds of memories, e.g. local and global, but do not incorporate caches into their model [10].

C. Martel et al. [3] propose a performance model that splits the execution time of a kernel into three components: computation time, time spent on transferring from global to local memory, and time spent on transfers from local to private memory. The described model is more detailed in regards to the effects of the size of the work-group, but also neglects caches.

6   Conclusion

In this paper, we presented an approach for the prediction of OpenCL kernel execution times. The model we presented takes the different subcomponents of the computation into account, and also distinguishes between the transfer of data to and from the GPU, and the computation itself. Memory accesses, which are a significant factor for the determination of the overall kernel execution time, are classified according to their cache-behavior.

For smaller OpenCL kernels, which conceivably occur in productive environments, our model is able to deliver predictions that are sufficiently accurate for use in productive applications that require estimation about the duration of tasks in heterogeneous environments. These systems may utilize the model in order to get an initial estimation of the duration of a task without the need to execute it, and enable them, in concert with other models, e.g. for CPUs or Accelerator platforms, to find a schedule that optimizes the overall utilization and performance of the system.

In future work, we plan on including language features that are currently not considered into the model, e.g. for loops, and the intrinsic functions defined by the OpenCL standard. Another topic of interest is the *Standard Portable Intermediate Representation*, which will be incorporated in the OpenCL standard in version 2.1 and may enable us to gain a more fine-granular view of the operations performed on the hardware and hence provide more elementary predictions [9].

Acknowledgments. This work was partly supported by the German Research Foundation (DFG) as part of the Transregional Collaborative Research Centre "Invasive Computing" (SFB/TR 89).

References

1. Intel X79 express chipset block diagram. http://www.intel.de/content/www/de/de/chipsets/performance-chipsets/x79-express-chipset-diagram.html
2. Top 500 list, November 2014. http://www.top500.org/lists/2014/11/
3. Alberto, C.M.M., Sato, H.: Linear performance-breakdown model: a framework for GPU kernel programs performance analysis. Int. J. Netw. Comput. 5(1), 86–104 (2015)

4. Weiler, A., Pakosta, A.: High-speed layout guidelines. Technical report, Texas Instruments, November 2006
5. Augonnet, C., Thibault, S., Namyst, R., Wacrenier, P.-A.: STARPU: a unified platform for task scheduling on heterogeneous multicore architectures. In: Sips, H., Epema, D., Lin, H.-X. (eds.) Euro-Par 2009. LNCS, vol. 5704, pp. 863–874. Springer, Heidelberg (2009)
6. Diamos, G.F., Yalamanchili, S.: Harmony: an execution model and runtime for heterogeneous many core systems. In: Proceedings of the 17th International Symposium on High Performance Distributed Computing, HPDC 2008, pp. 197–200. ACM, New York (2008). http://doi.acm.org/10.1145/1383422.1383447
7. Fujii, Y., Azumi, T., Nishio, N., Kato, S., Edahiro, M.: Data transfer matters for GPU computing. In: 2013 International Conference on Parallel and Distributed Systems (ICPADS), pp. 275–282, December 2013
8. Grewe, D., O'Boyle, M.F.P.: A static task partitioning approach for heterogeneous systems using OpenCL. In: Knoop, J. (ed.) CC 2011. LNCS, vol. 6601, pp. 286–305. Springer, Heidelberg (2011)
9. The Khronos Group: The OpenCL specification (provisional), version 2.1, January 2015. https://www.khronos.org/registry/cl/specs/opencl-2.1.pdf
10. Kothapalli, K., Mukherjee, R., Rehman, M., Patidar, S., Narayanan, P., Srinathan, K.: A performance prediction model for the CUDA GPGPU platform. In: 2009 International Conference on High Performance Computing (HiPC), pp. 463–472, December 2009
11. Luk, C.K., Hong, S., Kim, H.: Qilin: exploiting parallelism on heterogeneous multiprocessors with adaptive mapping. In: 42nd Annual IEEE/ACM International Symposium on Microarchitecture. MICRO-42, pp. 45–55, December 2009
12. NVidia: OpenCL programming guide for the CUDA architecture. Programming Guide, September 2012. http://hpc.oit.uci.edu/nvidia-doc/sdk-cuda-doc/OpenCL/doc/OpenCL_Programming_Guide.pdf

Towards Application Variability Handling with Component Models: 3D-FFT Use Case Study

Vincent Lanore[1]([✉]), Christian Perez[2]([✉]), and Jérôme Richard[1]([✉])

[1] École Normale Supérieure de Lyon, Lyon, France
vincent.lanore@ens-lyon.fr, jerome.richard@inria.fr
[2] Inria Avalon Research Team, LIP, Lyon, France
christian.perez@inria.fr

Abstract. To harness the computing power of supercomputers, HPC application algorithms have to be adapted to the underlying hardware. This is a costly and complex process which requires handling many algorithm variants. This paper studies the ability of the component model L^2C to express and handle the variability of HPC applications. The goal is to ease application adaptation. Analysis and experiments are done on a 3D-FFT use case. Results show that L^2C, and components in general, offer a generic and simple handling of 3D-FFT variants while obtaining performance close to well-known libraries.

Keywords: Application adaptation · Component models · High-performance computing

1 Introduction

To harness the computing power of supercomputers, high-performance computing (HPC) applications must have their algorithms adapted to the underlying hardware. Adaptation to a new hardware can involve in-depth transformations or even algorithm substitutions because of different scales, features, or communication/computation ratios. Since hardware evolves continuously, new optimizations are regularly devised. As a consequence, application codes must often be tweaked to adapt to new architectures so as to maximize performance; maintainability is rarely taken into account.

Adapting an application code to a specific use has a cost in terms of development time and requires very good knowledge of both the target platform and the application itself. It might also prove difficult for someone other than the original code developer(s). Moreover, unless automated, adapting the code for a specific run is, in many cases, too costly.

A promising solution to simplify application adaptation is to use component-based software engineering techniques [14]. This approach proposes to build applications by assembling software units with well-defined interfaces; these units are called *components*. Components are connected to form an *assembly*. Syntax

© Springer International Publishing Switzerland 2015
S. Hunold et al. (Eds.): Euro-Par 2015 Workshops, LNCS 9523, pp. 761–773, 2015.
DOI: 10.1007/978-3-319-27308-2_61

762   V. Lanore et al.

and semantics of interfaces and assemblies are given by a *component model*. Such an approach enables easy reuse of (potentially third-party) components and simplifies adaptation thanks to assembly modifications. Also, some component models and tools enable automatic assembly generation and/or optimization [5,8]. Component models bring many software engineering benefits but very few provide enough performance for high-performance scientific applications. Among them is L²C [4], a low-level general purpose high-performance component model built on top of C++ and MPI.

This paper studies the ability of L²C to handle HPC application variability on a 3-dimensional Fast Fourier Transform (3D-FFT) use case: a challenging numerical operation widely used in several scientific domains to convert signals from a spatial (or time) domain to a frequency domain or the other way round. Our experiments and adaptation analysis show that it is possible to easily specialize 3D-FFT assemblies (hand-written, with high reuse, without delving into low-level code and with as little work as possible) while having performance comparable to that of well-known 3D-FFT libraries.

The paper is structured as follows. Section 2 gives an overview of related work. Then, Sect. 3 deals with component models and introduces L²C. Section 4 describes the assemblies that we have designed and implemented with L²C for various flavors of 3D-FFTs. Section 5 compares the 3D-FFT L²C assemblies with existing FFT libraries both in terms of performance and in terms of reuse/ease of adaptation. Section 6 concludes the paper and gives some perspectives.

2 Related Work

This section briefly discusses related works in HPC application adaptation. For space reasons, only selected relevant publications are presented.

To efficiently run applications on several hardware architectures, it is usually required to have algorithm variants that specifically target each architecture. An efficient variant can then be chosen and executed according to hardware and software characteristics. Variants and choices can be directly implemented in the application code using conditional compilation or using conditional constructs. But, it leads to a code difficult to maintain and to reuse due to the multiplication of concerns in a same code (*e.g.*, functional and non-functional concerns).

Other approaches rely on compilation techniques to handle variants or choices. Many domain-specific languages (*e.g.*, Spiral [7]) allow the generation of efficient FFT codes but do not allow the application developers to easily handle variants since they are implemented inside compilers or associated frameworks. Some approaches like PetaBricks [1] aim to describe an FFT algorithm in a high-level language and provide multiple implementations for a given piece of functionality. This enables the expression of algorithms and their variations. However variants can be complex to reuse through multiple applications as it is the responsibility of the developer to support compatibility by providing portable interfaces.

Other approaches such as the FFTW codelet framework [10] and the Open-MPI MCA framework [13] build efficient algorithm implementations by composing units such as pieces of code or components for a specific purpose. These approaches solve a problem by decomposing it into smaller problems and use a set of specialized units to solve each one. These approaches provide some forms of adaptation framework but, to our knowledge, it is not possible to easily integrate new and/or unique optimizations.

Also, both these examples are specialized frameworks whose top-level algorithms are difficult to change.

This paper studies whether components can be used to adapt HPC applications in a simpler and more generic manner than commonly used approaches.

3 Component Models

3.1 Overview

Component-based software engineering [11] is a programming paradigm that proposes to compose software units called components to form a program. A component model defines components and component composition. A classical definition has been proposed by Clemens Szyperski [14]: *A software component is a unit of composition with contractually specified interfaces and explicit context dependencies only. A software component can be deployed independently and is subject to third-party composition.* In many component models, interfaces are called ports and have a name. To produce a complete application, components must be instantiated and then assembled together by connecting interfaces. The result of this process is called an assembly. The actual nature of connections is defined by the component model and may vary from one model to another.

Component models help to separate concerns and to increase reuse of third-party software. Separation of concerns is achieved by separating the role of component programming (low-level, implementation details) from component assembly (high-level, application structure). Reuse of third-party components is possible because component interfaces are all that is needed to use a component; it is thus not necessary to be familiar with low-level details of the implementation of a component to use it. Component models also allow different pieces of code to use different implementation of the same service as opposed to libraries.

Separation of concerns and reuse would allow to easily mix pieces of codes from different sources to make specialized assemblies. Thus, adaptation would no longer require in-depth understanding of existing implementations (separation of concerns) or re-development of existing optimizations (reuse).

Many component models have been proposed. The CORBA Component Model [6] (CCM) and the Grid Component Model (GCM) [2] are notable examples of distributed models. However, they generate runtime overheads [15] that are acceptable for distributed application but not for HPC. The Common Component Architecture [3] (CCA) aims to enhance composability in HPC. CCA is mainly a process-local standard that relies on external models such as MPI for inter-process communication. As a consequence, such interactions do not appear in component interfaces. The Low Level Components [4] (L^2C) is a minimalist HPC component model built on top of C++ with a negligible overhead at run-time. It provides amongst other things primitive components, local connections (process local *uses/provides* ports), MPI connections (MPI communicator sharing), and optionnally remote connections (CORBA based *uses/provides* ports).

As this paper studies the use of L^2C to ease HPC applications, the next section presents L^2C in more detail.

3.2 L^2C Model

The L^2C model is a low level component model that does not hide system issues. Indeed, each component is compiled as a dynamic shared object file. At launch time, components are instantiated and connected together according to an assembly description file or to an API.

L^2C supports features like C++ method invocation, message passing with MPI, and remote method invocation with CORBA. L^2C components can provide services thanks to *provides* ports and use services with *uses* ports. Component dependencies are inferred from connections between interfaces. Multiple *uses* ports can be connected to a unique *provides* port. A port is associated with an object interface and a name. Communication between component instances is done by member function invocations on ports. L^2C also provides MPI ports as a way to share MPI communicators between components. Components can expose attributes used to configure component instances. The C++ mapping defines components as plain C++ classes with a few annotations (to declare ports and attributes). Thus library codes can easily be wrapped into components.

A L^2C assembly can be described using a L^2C assembly descriptor file (LAD). This file contains a description of all component instances, their attributes values, and the connections between instances. Each component is part of a process and each process has an entry point (an interface called when the application starts). It also contains the configuration of MPI ports.

As described in [4], L^2C has been successfully used to describe a stencil-like application with performance similar to native implementations.

4   Designing 3D-FFT Algorithms with L^2C

This section analyses how L^2C, as an example of a HPC component model, can be used to implement distributed 3D-FFT assemblies. To that end, we have first designed a basic 3D-FFT assembly. Then, we have modified it to incorporate several optimizations. All the assemblies presented here have been implemented in C++/L^2C, and relevant assemblies are evaluated in Sect. 5. Let us first focus on the methods used to compute a 3D-FFT.

4.1   3D-FFT Parallel Computation Methods

3D-FFT parallel computation can be done using 1D or 2D domain decomposition [12]. The whole computation can be achieved by interleaving data computation steps and data transposition steps. Computation steps involve applying

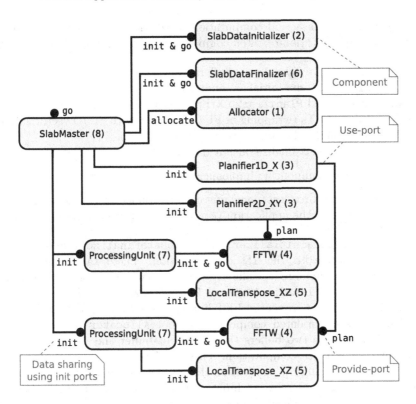

Fig. 1. Local (one process) basic 3D-FFT assembly using 1D decomposition.

multiple sequential 1D/2D FFTs. Data transposition can be achieved by using all-to-all global exchanges. Transposition performance is the major bottleneck.

1D decomposition involves 2 local computation steps, and 1 or 2 transpositions depending on the final data layout. For a given cube of data of size $N \times N \times N$, this approach is scalable up to N processing elements (PEs) at which point each PE has a slab of height 1.

2D decomposition involves 3 local computation steps, and between 2 and 4 transpositions depending on the final data layout. It scales up to $N \times N$ PEs.

To increase 3D-FFT computation performance and to enable a better adaptation to hardware, a sequential 3D-FFT algorithm variant can be selected at initialization using a planning step. Information about the algorithm selection is stored in a plan that is then executed at runtime.

4.2 Basic Sequential Assembly

Figure 1 displays a single node sequential assembly that implements the 1D-decomposition algorithm presented above. It will be the base for parallel assemblies. It is based on the identification of 8 tasks that are then mapped to components: 6 for the actual computation, and 2 for the control of the computation. The computation-oriented components implement the following tasks:

1. `Allocator`: allocate 3D memory buffers.
2. `SlabDataInitializer`: initialize input data.
3. `Planifier1D_X` and `Planifier2D_XY`: plan fast sequential FFTs.
4. `FFTW`: compute FFTs (wrapping of FFTW library, with SIMD vectorization).
5. `LocalTranspose_XZ`: locally transpose data.
6. `SlabDataFinalizer`: finalize output data by storing or reusing it.

The two control components implement the following tasks:

7. `ProcessingUnit`: broadcast incoming calls to connected components.
8. `SlabMaster`: drive the application (*e.g.*, initialize/run FFT computations).

Task 2 (`SlabDataInitializer`), 6 (`SlabDataFinalizer`) and 8 (`Slab Master`) are specific to the 1D decomposition. These tasks and Task 5 (`LocalTranspose _XZ`) are specific to a given parallelization strategy, here sequential. Task 3 (`Planifier1D_X` and `Planifier2D_XY`) and Task 4 (`FFTW`) are specific to a chosen sequential FFT library (to compute 1D/2D FFT).

All computation-oriented components except `Allocator` rely on memory buffers. They can use two buffers (*i.e.*, an input buffer and an output buffer) or just one for in-place computation. These buffers are initialized by passing memory pointers during the application startup. For this purpose, these components provide an `init` port to set input and output memory pointers, but also to initialize or release memory resources.

All computation-oriented components except `Allocator` provide a **go** port which is used to start their computation.

As FFT plans depend on the chosen sequential FFT library, Component `FFTW` (Task 4) exposes a specific `Plan` interface that is used by `Planifier1D_X` and `Planifier2D_XY` (Task 3). This connection is used to configure the FFT components after the planning phase.

The application works in three stages. The first stage consists in initializing the whole application by allocating buffers, planning FFTs and broadcasting pointers and plans to component instances. In the second stage, the actual computation happens, driven by calls on the **go** ports of component instances in such a manner as to interleave computations and communications.

The last stage consists in releasing resources such as memory buffers. The whole process is started using the **go** port of the `SlabMaster` component.

The assembly has been designed to be configured for a specific computation of a 3D-FFT. Buffer sizes and offsets are described as components attributes; they are not computed at runtime.

4.3   Parallel Assembly for Distributed Architectures

The distributed version of the assembly is obtained by deriving an MPI version of `SlabDataInitializer` (Task 2), `SlabDataFinalizer` (Task 6), `SlabMaster`

(Task 8). Basically, it consists in adding a MPI port to them. LocalTranspose_XZ components are replaced by MpiTransposeSync_XZ which also exhibit MPI ports used for distributed matrix transpositions. Furthermore, this assembly is duplicated on each MPI process (with different attributes). MpiTransposeSync_XZ instances of a same computation phase are interconnected through their MPI ports, so that they share an MPI communicator. It is also the case for SlabMaster, SlabInitializer, and SlabFinalizer instances. Data distribution depends on the chosen decomposition (1D or 2D).

4.4   Assembly Adaptation

This section presents three possible adaptations of the parallel assembly presented above: load balancing for an heterogeneous distributed system, adjustments of the number of transpositions, and use of a 2D decomposition.

Heterogeneous Assembly. A first example of adaptation is taking into account heterogeneous hardware architectures, such as for example the thin and large nodes of the Curie supercomputer. When all nodes do not compute at the same speed and data is evenly distributed between nodes, the slower nodes limit the whole computation speed due to load imbalance. To deal with this problem, load balancing is needed and thus data must be unevenly distributed between nodes. Since load balancing of 3D-FFTs depends on data distribution, a solution is to control data distribution through component attributes. A new transposition component must be implemented to handle uneven data distribution. Thus, handling heterogeneous systems can be easily done by reusing components from the previous section with small modifications.

Reducing the Number of Transpositions. Optimizing the transposition phase is important as it is often the main bottleneck. As explained in Sect. 4.1, the final transposition can possibly be removed with 1D decomposition (and up to two transpositions using a 2D decomposition) depending on the desired orientation of the output matrix. This can be done by adding an attribute to the Master component: in each process, the second ProcessingUnit component instance connected to the SlabMaster via init and go ports is removed, and the transposition component is connected to it via the same port type; the go and init *uses* ports of the SlabMaster component are directly connected to the associated *provides* ports of components implementing the Task 4 of the last phase. As the SlabMaster behavior during the initialization depends on whether a final transposition is used or not (the final buffer differs), a boolean attribute is added to the SlabMaster to configure it. So, the number of transpositions can be easily adjusted using assembly adaptation and component replacement.

2D Decomposition Assembly. 2D decomposition assemblies are needed to scale beyond the limitation of the 1D decomposition described in Sect. 4.1. This

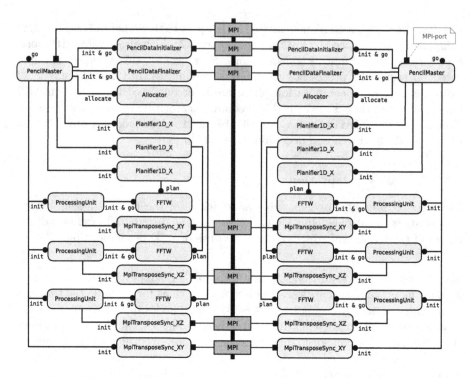

Fig. 2. Distributed 3D-FFT for 2 MPI processes using 2D decomposition.

can be done by adapting the assembly as displayed in Fig. 2. A new transposition component is introduced as well as

PencilMaster, PencilInitializer, and PencilFinalizer components which replace SlabMaster, SlabInitializer, and SlabFinalizer. These new components provide two MPI ports to communicate with instances, that handle the block of the 2D decomposition of the same processor row, or on the same processor column. In this new assembly (not well optimized), two computing phases are also added and are managed by the PencilMaster. Because the 2D decomposition introduces a XY transposition of distributed data not needed in the 1D decomposition, a new transpose component was needed. However, the XZ transposition component can be reused from the 1D decomposition. Although 2D decomposition requires writing multiple new components (with a code similar to those into 1D decomposition assemblies), most optimizations from 1D decomposition assemblies can be applied.

Discussion. Studied 3D-FFT assembly variants are derived from other assemblies with local transformations such as adding, removing, or replacing components, or just tuning component parameters. Usually, these transformations are simple to apply, enabling easy generation of many 3D-FFT variants.

Global transformations are modifications that impact the whole assembly (components and connections). They usually correspond to a major algorithmic variation. As such, they are more difficult to apply.

5   Performance and Adaptability Evaluation

This section evaluates the component-based approach in terms of performance and adaptability of some assemblies described in the previous section. Performance and scalability are evaluated on up to 8,192 cores on homogeneous architectures and up to 256 cores on heterogeneous architectures. Adaptability is defined as the ease to implement various optimizations, and how much code has been reused from other assemblies.

Variability experiments were done on 5 clusters of the Grid'5000 experimental platform [9]: Griffon[1], Graphene[2], Edel[3], Genepi[4] and Sol[5]. Performance and scalability experiments were done on thin nodes of the Curie supercomputer[6]. Each experiment has been done 100 times and the median is displayed. Error bars on plots correspond to the first and last quartile.

All experiments involve complex-to-complex 3D-FFTs and use a minimum number of transpositions (*i.e.*, 1 with 1D decomposition, 2 with 2D decomposition). The FFT libraries used as reference are FFTW 3.3.4 and 2DECOMP 1.5.

All libraries are configured to use a synchronous complex-to-complex 3D-FFT using FFTW sequential implementation (with FFTW_MEASURE planning) and double precision floating point.

5.1   Performance and Scalability Evaluation

Figure 3 displays the completion time obtained for matrices of size 1024^3 on the Curie thin nodes for a 1D decomposition (Fig. 3a) and 2D decomposition (Fig. 3b). Overall, the performance of L^2C assemblies, FFTW and 2DECOMP are close with both 1D and 2D decomposition. With 1D decomposition, we note that L^2C is slightly slower than 2DECOMP and the FFTW (up to 17 %). This gap is due to the local transposition not being optimized enough in the 3D-FFT L^2C implementation (*e.g.*, cache-use optimization). Due to the lack of 2D decomposition support of the FFTW, this library does not appear on Fig. 3b. With 2D decomposition, the gap between 2DECOMP and L^2C is lower (less than 8 %). This is a very good result as 3D-FFT L^2C implementations have been done in some weeks, and therefore they are not highly optimized. The results also show that L^2C scales well up to 8,192 cores on 2D decomposition. Beyond this limit, the L^2C deployment phase has yet to be optimized to support it.

---

[1] 92 nodes, 2 CPU/node, 4 cores/CPU, Xeon L5420 (2.5 GHz), 20G InfiniBand.

[2] 144 nodes, 1 CPU/node, 4 cores/CPU, Xeon X3440 (2.53 GHz), 20G InfiniBand.

[3] 34 nodes, 2 CPU/node, 4 cores/CPU, Xeon E5520 (2.27 GHz), 40G InfiniBand.

[4] 72 nodes, 2 CPU/node, 4 cores/CPU, Xeon E5420 QC (2.5 GHz), 40G InfiniBand.

[5] 50 nodes, 2 CPU/node, 2 cores/CPU, AMD Opteron 2218 (2.6 GHz), 1G Ethernet.

[6] 5040 nodes, 2 CPU/node, 8 cores/CPU, Xeon E5-2680 (2.7 GHz), 40G InfiniBand.

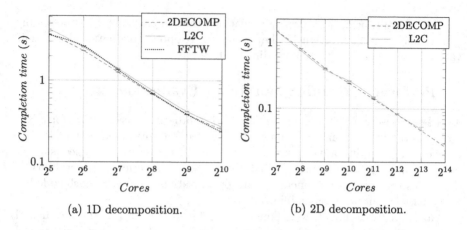

(a) 1D decomposition.   (b) 2D decomposition.

Fig. 3. Completion time of 1024^3 complex-to-complex homogeneous 3D-FFT on Curie using both 1D (a) and 2D decompositions (b).

5.2   Adaptation and Reuse Evaluation

Heterogeneous Experiments. Figure 4 shows the completion times obtained for matrices of size 256^3 on the clusters Edel and Genepi up to 256 cores for a 2D decomposition (Fig. 4). Orange area corresponds to the homogeneous case because only one Edel 8-core node is used. From 16 cores and up, half the cores are from Edel nodes and the other half from Genepi nodes. The Edel cluster is overall faster than the Genepi cluster.

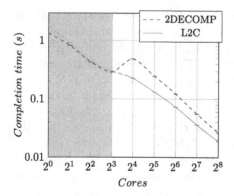

Version	C++ LOC	Reused code
1D-hm-2t-naive	944	-
1D-hm-2t-opt	1041	69%
1D-hm-1t	932	77%
1D-ht-2t	1101	71%
1D-ht-1t	985	80%
2D-hm-2t	1100	86%
2D-ht-2t	1150	68%
2D-ht-4t	1150	100%

Fig. 4. Completion time of 256^3 complex-to-complex heterogeneous 3D-FFT on Edel and Genepi using 2D decomposition.

Fig. 5. Number of lines of code (LOC) for several versions of the 3D-FFT application. hm: homogeneous; ht: heterogeneous; nt: n transpositions.

We observe that from 8 to 16 nodes 2DECOMP performance decreases and L^2C performance improves. That is because 2DECOMP does not balance its load and is thus limited by the speed of the slowest cluster. It means the heterogeneous L^2C assembly successfully takes advantage of both clusters and is not limited by the speed of the slowest one.

Reuse. Table 5 displays code reuse (in terms of number of C++ lines) between some of the L^2C assemblies. Reuse is the amount of code that is reused from the assemblies listed higher in the table. Version code names are decomposition type (1D or 2D), followed by hm for homogeneous assemblies or ht for heterogeneous assemblies, and end with nt where n is the number of transpositions used.

We observe a high code reuse between specialized assemblies: from 68 % to 100 % without any low-level modification. Also note that our L^2C implementations are much smaller than 2DECOMP (11,570 lines of FORTRAN code); that is also because 2DECOMP implements more features.

Since our components are medium-grained and they have simple interfaces (see Sect. 4), modifying an assembly for one processing element is only a matter of changing a few parameters, connections and adding/removing instances. This process involves no low-level code modification. It is done at architecture level and is independent of possible changes in the component implementations. Thus, components ease the integration of new or unique optimizations.

Discussion. Performance results show that L^2C assemblies scale up to 8,192 cores with performance comparable to the reference libraries on Curie using 1D/2D decompositions. Adaptation results show that components help to ease implementation of new optimizations and help to combine them. Several specialized assemblies have been written with high code reuse (from 68 % to 100 % reused code without any low-level modification). Specialization (*e.g.*, heterogeneous case) is often achieved using simple assembly transformations.

6   Conclusion and Future Work

To achieve adaptability of high-performance computing applications on various hardware architectures, this paper has evaluated the use of component models to handle HPC application variability. A 3D-FFT use case has been evaluated. 3D-FFT algorithms have been modelled and specialized using component models features (component replacement, attribute tuning, and assemblies). The same work could be applied on other HPC applications to ease their adaptations.

The experimental results obtained on Grid'5000 clusters and on the Curie supercomputer show that 3D-FFT L^2C assemblies can be competitive with existing libraries in multiple cases using 1D and 2D decompositions. It is consistent with previous results obtained on a simpler use case [4]. So, using an HPC-oriented component model adds a negligible overhead while providing better software engineering features. Adaptation results show that performance of libraries can be increased in some special cases (*e.g.*, heterogeneous cases) by adapting assemblies. Re-usability results show that components enable the writing of specialized applications by reusing parts of other versions.

Results are encouraging even though more work on the L^2C implementation is needed to let it scale to at least tens of thousands of nodes. Moreover, assembly descriptions need to be rewritten for each specific hardware. As this process is fastidious and error-prone, such descriptions should be automatically generated.

Future works include working on automating assembly generation to ease maintenance and development of assemblies by using a higher level component model, such as HLCM [5]. Automatic parameter tuning will of course be needed.

References

1. Ansel, J., Chan, C., Wong, Y.L., Olszewski, M., Zhao, Q., Edelman, A., Amarasinghe, S.: PetaBricks: a language and compiler for algorithmic choice, vol. 44. ACM (2009)

2. Baude, F., Caromel, D., Dalmasso, C., Danelutto, M., Getov, V., Henrio, L., Pérez, C.: GCM: a grid extension to fractal for autonomous distributed components. Ann. Telecommun. **64**(1–2), 5–24 (2009)

3. Bernholdt, D.E., Allan, B.A., Armstrong, R., Bertrand, F., Chiu, K., Dahlgren, T.L., Damevski, K., Elwasif, W.R., Epperly, T.G., Govindaraju, M., et al.: A component architecture for high performance scientific computing. Int. J. High Perform. Comput. Appl. **20**(2), 163–202 (2006)

4. Bigot, J., Hou, Z., Pérez, C., Pichon, V.: A low level component model easing performance portability of HPC applications. Computing **96**(12), 1115–1130 (2013). http://hal.inria.fr/hal-00911231

5. Bigot, J., Pérez, C.: High performance composition operators in component models. In: High Performance Computing: From Grids and Clouds to Exascale, Advances in Parallel Computing, vol. 20, pp. 182–201. IOS Press (2011). http://hal.inria.fr/hal-00692584

6. Boldt, J.: The Common Object Request Broker: Architecture and Specification (1995). http://www.omg.org/cgi-bin/doc?formal/97-02-25

7. Bonelli, A., Franchetti, F., Lorenz, J., Püschel, M., Überhuber, C.W.: Automatic performance optimization of the discrete fourier transform on distributed memory computers. In: Guo, M., Yang, L.T., Di Martino, B., Zima, H.P., Dongarra, J., Tang, F. (eds.) ISPA 2006. LNCS, vol. 4330, pp. 818–832. Springer, Heidelberg (2006)

8. Bozga, M., Jaber, M., Sifakis, J.: Source-to-source architecture transformation for performance optimization in BIP. IEEE Trans. Indus. Inform. **6**(4), 708–718 (2010)

9. Desprez, F., Fox, G., Jeannot, E., Keahey, K., Kozuch, M., Margery, D., Neyron, P., Nussbaum, L., Pérez, C., Richard, O., Smith, W., Von Laszewski, G., Vöckler, J.: Supporting experimental computer science. In: Rapport de recherche RR-8035, INRIA (2012). http://hal.inria.fr/hal-00722605

10. Frigo, M., Johnson, S.: The design and implementation of FFTW3. Proc. IEEE **93**(2), 216–231 (2005)

11. McIlroy, M.D.: Mass-produced software components. In: Proceedings NATO Conference on Software Engineering, Garmisch, Germany (1968)

12. Pekurovsky, D.: P3DFFT: a framework for parallel computations of fourier transforms in three dimensions. SIAM J. Sci. Comput. **34**(4), C411–C437 (2012). http://dblp.uni-trier.de/db/journals/siamsc/siamsc34.html
13. Squyres, J.M., Lumsdaine, A.: The component architecture of open MPI enabling third-party collective algorithms. In: Getov, V., Kielmann, T. (eds.) Component Models and Systems for Grid Applications, pp. 167–185. Springer, Heidelberg (2005)
14. Szyperski, C.: Component Software: Beyond Object-Oriented Programming, 2nd edn. Addison-Wesley Longman Publishing Co. Inc., Boston (2002)
15. Wang, N., Parameswaran, K., Kircher, M., Schmidt, D.C.: Applying reflective middleware techniques to optimize a QoS-enabled CORBA component model implementation. In: COMPSAC, pp. 492–499. IEEE Computer Society (2000). http://dblp.uni-trier.de/db/conf/compsac/compsac2000.html

Optimized Force Calculation in Molecular Dynamics Simulations for the Intel Xeon Phi

Nikola Tchipev[1], Amer Wafai[2], Colin W. Glass[2], Wolfgang Eckhardt[1],
Alexander Heinecke[3], Hans-Joachim Bungartz[1], and Philipp Neumann[1(✉)]

[1] Department for Informatics, Technische Universität München,
Boltzmannstr. 3, 85748 Garching, Germany
philipp.neumann@tum.de
[2] High Performance Computing Center Stuttgart,
Nobelstr. 19, 70569 Stuttgart, Germany
[3] Intel Corporation, Santa Clara, CA, USA

Abstract. We provide details on the shared-memory parallelization for manycore architectures of the molecular dynamics framework ls1-mardyn, including an optimization of the SIMD vectorization for multi-centered molecules. The novel shared-memory parallelization scheme allows to retain Newton's third law optimization and exhibits very good scaling on many-core devices such as a full Xeon Phi card running 240 threads. The Xeon Phi can thus be exploited and delivers comparable performance as IvyBridge nodes in our experiments.

1 Introduction

Molecular Dynamics (MD) simulations are an established tool in life sciences [5] and, more recently, in chemical and process engineering [8]. The latter requires the simulation of a large number of particles, reaching the order of millions, or even more. In particular, the software framework ls1-mardyn[11] has specialized on this field, providing efficient treatment for short-range, non-bonded, 12-6 Lennard-Jones interactions of rigid multi-centered molecules via the linked-cell method.

Due to the compute intensive nature of MD, much research has been and currently is conducted to exploit modern HPC architectures such as GPUs [1] or the Xeon Phi [6,12].

This paper presents enhancements and extensions of an original shared-memory parallelized Xeon Phi implementation of ls1-mardyn[7]. In [6,7], it has been shown that a gather-scatter-based implementation is a promising approach to efficiently run MD simulations on Xeon Phi and potentially on the upcoming AVX-512 standard to Xeon. This is due to the standard "masking" SIMD approach becoming less efficient than the gather-scatter one for the vector width of eight (double-precision) elements [6]. We introduce an improvement in the gather-scatter SIMD vectorization, which renders the implementation efficient for bigger numbers of interaction sites per molecule.

© Springer International Publishing Switzerland 2015
S. Hunold et al. (Eds.): Euro-Par 2015 Workshops, LNCS 9523, pp. 774–785, 2015.
DOI: 10.1007/978-3-319-27308-2_62

We particularly focus on a new shared-memory implementation, which scales up to 240 threads on 60 Xeon Phi cores, thereby retaining Newton's third law optimization. It is based on linked-cell coloring with eight synchronization stages, independent of the number of threads and linked-cells. It avoids the pitfalls of load-balancing and halo-layer overhead compared to domain decomposition variants using OpenMP [9,12]. Tuned for scalability on the Xeon Phi, the shared-memory implementation also exhibits excellent performance on Xeon. We further investigate hyperthreading performance, as it plays a crucial role on Xeon Phi.

The optimized sequential and parallel performance allow us to draw significant comparisons between the performance on Xeon and Xeon Phi. It is demonstrated that Xeon Phi has the potential to keep up with or even outperform Xeon, and thus allows to double the performance of the complete host-accelerator system. As all presented improvements concern the force calculation kernel, we restrict this discussion to it. It represents the most time consuming part of MD simulations (60% to $\geq 90\%$ of total simulation time) as it *locally* exhibits a $\mathcal{O}(N^2)$ behavior, while remaining operations are handled in $\mathcal{O}(N)$.

We introduce the short-range MD problem in Sect. 2. The sequential and parallel algorithms and respective implementations are detailed in Sect. 3. Performance evaluations are provided in Sect. 4, including detailed single-core and full-node analysis for both Xeon Phi (MIC) and IVB nodes. We conclude and give an outlook to future work in Sect. 5.

2   Short-Range Molecular Dynamics

In ls1-mardyn, Newton's equations of motion are solved for all molecules. Each molecule is modeled as rigid body and consists of $N \geq 1$ interaction sites, cf. Fig. 1(a). The computationally most expensive part is given by the force accumulation: each interaction site of molecule i interacts with the interaction sites of all other molecules $j \neq i$, $i,j \in \{1, ..., N\}$. For many target applications of ls1-mardyn, it is sufficient to only consider short-range interactions: molecules are sorted into linked-cells with mesh size $\geq r_c$ and only molecules within a cut-off distance r_c—that is molecules inside a certain linked-cell, or its neighbored cells—interact with molecule i, cf. Fig. 1(b). Due to Newton's third law (N3), each site-site interaction force acts identically (but with opposed signs) on each site. Each site-site pair thus needs to be evaluated only once [5]. This N3 optimization allows a reduction of computation time by a factor of 2. It, however, introduces race conditions if neighbored linked-cells are processed concurrently by differing threads, which represents a major obstacle to shared-memory parallelization [2]. For further details on the simulation core, we refer to [11].

3   Implementation

3.1   SIMD Vectorization

ls1-mardyn features a hand-written intrinsics kernel for the force calculation [3,7]. Prior to the force calculation, the molecule data necessary for the

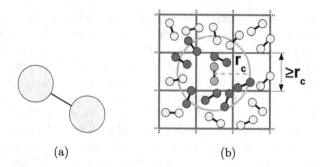

(a)   (b)

Fig. 1. (a) Molecule with two interaction sites. (b) Short-range interaction: only the molecules within the red circle with cut-off radius r_c interact with the red-colored molecule. All molecule sites colored in blue (and no other) interact with the sites colored in red in the employed cutoff-scheme.

force calculation is converted from an Array-of-Structures (AoS) layout to a Structure-of-Arrays (SoA) layout to enforce data contiguity and alignment. If no shared-memory parallelization is employed, only a "sliding window" of approx. three linked-cell layers is temporarily converted to SoA format [4]. We include a comparison to the sliding window non-OpenMP version, which we will refer to as win.

If shared-memory parallelization is employed, all cells need to be available in SoA format simultaneously, in order to enable their parallel processing. Moreover, it was observed, that freeing the SoAs after the force calculation and allocating them anew prior to the next force calculation can present a bottleneck in some cases. Thus, in the presented implementation, SoAs are not freed until the very end of the simulation. Reusing the allocated SoAs between iterations does not remove the necessity of "AoS-to-SoA" and "SoA-to-AoS" pre- and postprocessing steps, however: molecules may move between linked-cells and, thus, may need to be moved from one SoA to another, all the while maintaining the necessary contiguity and alignment.

Cutoff Mode. In ls1-mardyn, a center-of-mass (CoM) cutoff mode is employed. The cut-off condition needs therefore to be evaluated only between the centers-of-mass of the molecules (see Fig. 1(b)). Besides, all sites of a molecule always interact with full molecules and share the same interaction partners w.r.t. the cut-off condition.

Intrinsics Kernel. Listing 1.1 shows a schematic of the (already optimized) gather-scatter kernel for MIC. For every molecule m1 of soa1, first, the cutoff-condition between m1 and all molecules from soa2 is evaluated (line 4). The indices of the sites of the molecules from soa2, with which m1 will interact, are stored within the iV vector via the **packstore** intrinsic function. We proceed to compute the forces between the sites of m1 and the needed sites from soa2 (lines 6–12). If m1 has only one interaction center (line 6), we "broadcast-load" the site data of m1 into _mm512d registers, "gather-load" site-data from soa2 via iV and compute the first set of LJ-forces. The forces are then accumulated in an _mm512d register for m1 and scattered to soa2 via the Newton's third law optimization (if applied). When the iteration is complete, the accumulated forces for the site of m1 are horizontally added to the respective SoA entry. If m1 has more than one interaction center, the else-clause is entered, where the current optimization takes place. The optimization consists of a loop-interchange of the for-loops over the entries of iV and the sites of m1 in lines 8 and 10, respectively. Due to the CoM condition, all sites see identical interaction partners and, hence, we can first gather data via the index vector and *then* loop over the sites of the molecule. Thus, we have traded expensive gather-loads and scatter-stores for cheaper broadcast-loads.

Listing 1.1. Gather-scatter kernel schematic

```
1   Indexvector iV;  // indices of interaction-partner sites
2   for m1 in soa1 { iV.clear();
3       // evaluate CoM cutoff-condition
4       for m2 in soa2 { ... mask_packstore(iV, m2.sites...) }
5       // compute LJ-Kernel forces
6       if (m1 is single-centered) {for i in iV {...}}
7       else {
8           for i in iV {
9               r2 = gather_load(i[0:7], soa2.R, ...) // get partner pos.
10              for site in m1 { r1 = bcast_load(m1.r); f = LJ(r2-r1)...}
11              scatter_store(i[0:7], soa2.F,...)
12   } } }
```

On IVB, due to the absence of gather- and scatter operations, the entire soa2 is traversed and unnecessary force-entries are masked away [6,7]. The introduced loop-interchange does not improve performance there, as it trades in normal loads for broadcast-loads, which have similar costs.

In [6] a theoretical upper bound of 20 % of peak performance is given for IVB. On scenarios comparable to the ones presented here, values of 11 % – 16 % are observed [3,6]. The MIC implementation further suffers from the costly packstore in line 4, and the expensive gather- and scatter operations, further reducing the attainable percentage of peak performance.

3.2   Shared-Memory Parallelization

Mode no3: The first mode consists of simply not using the N3 optimization between linked-cells. It stems from other accelerator architectures, where resolving the race-condition was observed to be more costly than recomputing the respective forces [3]. Processing the cells, thus, becomes an embarrassingly parallel operation, cf. Fig. 2(a). In the present no3 implementation, the N3 optimization *is* employed when computing interactions *within* a single cell.

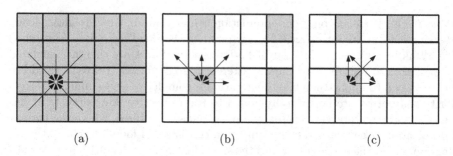

(a)   (b)   (c)

Fig. 2. Approaches for shared memory parallelization of pairwise force evaluations (simplified illustration for 2D case). The yellow-colored cells can be processed in parallel. Red squares indicate "write-regions" for the lower-left yellow-colored cell, arrows indicate pairwise cell handlings for the yellow-color traversal. (a) `no3`: All cells can be processed in parallel, but force contributions need to be computed twice, that is once for each molecule of a pairwise interaction. (b) `c18`, corresponding to 6 colors in 2D case. (c) `c08`, corresponding to 4 colors in 2D case.

Colored Modes `c18` and `c08`: Both of these approaches retain the N3 optimization by introducing a suitable coloring. The first one, `c18`, is based on the "standard" cell traversal order found in many implementations, including `ls1-mardyn`. After molecule interactions within a certain linked-cell have been computed, one iterates over the neighboring linked-cells, which have an index greater than the index of the current cell in a lexicographic ordering, and computes the pairwise forces. Coloring this traversal requires a stride of 2 in the "last" dimension and strides of 3 in all previous dimensions. For 3D simulations, this results in $2 \cdot 3^{3-1} = 18$ colors and, respectively, synchronization stages, see Fig. 2(b).

In this work, we introduce the more compact cell-pair traversal mode, which was originally developed for strictly local operations on grids cells in a Lattice Boltzmann context `c08` [10]. Instead of only computing force contributions for pairwise interactions with the yellow-colored cells, molecule pairs are also handled for certain diagonally neighbored linked-cell pairs, see Fig. 2(b). Strides of 2 in all dimensions suffice for this scheme, resulting in only $2^3 = 8$ colors/sync. stages. This reduction further implies larger amount of work *per color* and, hence, allows the use of a larger number of threads.

In the current implementation, the indices of the individual colors have been precomputed at startup and are processed via a dynamic scheduling, to allow for potential load-balancing. We point out that both the `c18` and `c08` approaches exhibit a reduced computational intensity as compared to `win`: after a thread has processed a "patch" of cells (of size 18 for `c18` or 8 for `c08`), it needs to load another patch, which almost always will be a fully disjoint set of SoAs. On the other hand, the `win` mode reuses SoAs already residing in cache for up to three consecutive "patch" processings.

3.3   MPI Parallelization

The win approach employs standard domain decomposition employing a Cartesian grid topology [2,3]. Each process is extended by halo linked-cells which are filled by respective molecular information from the neighbored processes. Forces between molecules belonging to the process-local linked-cells and halo regions are computed on each respective process. As we consider only time spent in the force calculation, the MPI implementation used for reference has a somewhat unfair advantage, as we disregard time for communication in our analysis.

4   Results and Evaluation

4.1   Test Setup

We consider combinations of the following configurations: two system sizes with 0.16 million and 1.32 million molecules (0.16M and 1.32M denoted hereafter), two cutoff radii ($r_c = 3\sigma$ and $r_c = 5\sigma$), and different numbers of Lennard-Jones interaction sites ("1CLJ" and "4CLJ" consisting of one and four centers, respectively), corresponding to the potential $U_{LJ}(x_j - x_i) := 4\epsilon((\frac{\sigma}{\|x_j - x_i\|})^{12} - (\frac{\sigma}{\|x_j - x_i\|})^{6})$ and force contributions $F_{ij} = -F_{ji} = -\nabla U_{LJ}(x_j - x_i)$ with parameters σ, ϵ and positions x_i, x_j of the interaction sites. The simulations were executed for 51 timesteps, each starting from a configuration of molecules initially arranged on a regular grid. The presented values are the mean values collected over four repetitions. A density of $\rho\sigma^3 = 0.3$ was used. The Super-MIC partition of the SuperMUC cluster[1], was used. The cluster nodes consist of a dual-socket eight-core Intel® IvyBridge host processor Xeon® E5-2650@2.6 GHz (IVB) with enabled hyperthreading and two Intel® Xeon Phi™ 5110p coprocessors with 60 cores@1.1GHz.

4.2   Single Core Performance

In order to set appropriate expectations for performance on both MIC and IVB, we first analyze single-core performance for the system size of 0.16M molecules. Since at least two threads per core are needed to fill the instruction pipeline [13], hyperthreading is expected to play a crucial role on the Xeon Phi. To enable a fair comparison, we also evaluate the hyperthreading performance on IVB.

In the hyperthreading analysis, we pin threads/processes to the same core and disregard any "classical" overhead of parallelization: threads running on the same core can be cheaply synchronized via the L1 cache, and, as they share physical resources, any load-imbalance among them automatically implies more physical resources for the thread with the higher computational load.

We also investigate the performance penalty of the "patched" access to the SoAs by considering a variant of the c08 mode, which accesses data in "colored" mode even when only a single thread is running ("col 1 thread" as opposed to "noncol 1 thread").

---

[1] https://www.lrz.de/services/compute/supermuc/supermic/.

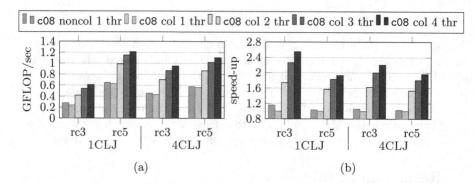

Fig. 3. Single core performance on Xeon Phi for one to four threads pinned on the same core. (a) Absolute performance in GFLOP/sec. (b) Speed-up due to hyperthreading, relative to the "c08 col 1 thread" version.

Hyperthreading on Xeon Phi. The penalty of the colored access is deduced from measurements "noncol 1 thread" and "col 1 thread", cf. Fig. 3. It is highest for 1CLJ rc3 and amounts up to 16 %, since this interaction is the least compute intensive and, hence, most memory intensive. As all other scenarios are more compute intensive, the impact is lower (3–5 %).

Next, we compare the measurements "1 thread" and "2 threads" in Fig. 3(b). The observed speed-ups range between 1.5 and 1.75, with the best speed-up obtained in the 1CLJ rc3 case and smaller speed-ups in the other scenarios. This behavior is due to bad pipelining properties of the LJ kernel and is in agreement with previous work [3]. Using 3 and 4 threads, further speed-ups are obtained. This is due to overlapping gather-scatter operations with FLOPs, and probably also the fact that the Xeon Phi cores feature an in-order execution mode. Consistent performance improvements are obtained and the 4-thread variant always delivers the highest FLOP-rate. This suggests that an optimal Xeon Phi implementation will employ the full 240 threads per MIC card. Oversubscription with 5 threads was also investigated, but led to degraded performance.

Hyperthreading on IvyBridge. Fig. 4 shows the respective analysis on IVB for c08 and win. Comparing "noncol 1 thread" and "col 1 thread" variants, we observe the same trend as on MIC, only this time it is weaker −7 % for 1CLJ rc3, 0–3 % for the remaining interactions. This shows, that the colored scheme is also a good solution for hyperthreading on the IVB architecture. Next, we compare "col 1 thread" and "win 1 process", and "col 2 threads" and "win 2 processes" in Fig. 4(a). A visible difference is observed for 1CLJ (35 % for 1CLJ rc3, 14 % for 1CLJ rc5) likely due to differing memory management. The 4CLJ scenarios are sufficiently computationally intensive to hide the differences in memory management (1.6 % and 0.4 % for 4CLJ with rc3 and rc5). Speed-ups due to hyperthreading in Fig. 4 arise as expected [4]. In our experiments, 40 % for 1CLJ rc3 and ca. 20 % in the other scenarios are obtained.

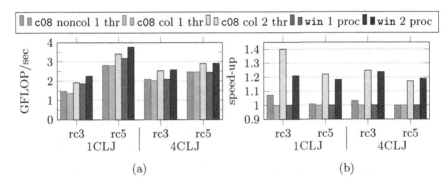

Fig. 4. Single core performance on IvyBridge for one to two threads/processes pinned on the same core. (a) Absolute performance in GFLOP/sec (b) Speed-up due to hyper-threading, relative to "c08 col 1 thread" and to "win 1 process".

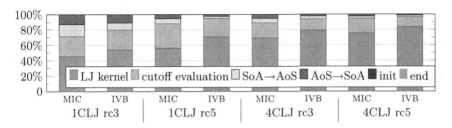

Fig. 5. Percentage of time spent in the force calculation on MIC (c08 col 1 thread) and IVB (win 1 process).

Absolute Performance. The dependence of the absolute performance from the number of interaction sites is shown in Fig. 6(a). On both MIC and IVB, 1CLJ is an exception from the trends. This is due to the fact, that the 1CLJ case spends the least amount of time inside the LJ Kernel, and, hence, runs closer to the higher FLOP-rate of the cutoff-evaluation, see Fig. 5. On MIC, the difference between 1CLJ and the other cases is also emphasized by the special treatment of the single-centered molecules in the if-statement of Listing 1.1.

On IVB, the performance is saturated at around 4–5 CLJ, as the performance of the LJ-Kernel is attained. This is around 14 % of the theoretical single-core peak performance, which is in agreement with previous results. Overall the values lie in the range of 9–14%.

The MIC implementation has become *scalable in the number of interaction sites*. The performance continually rises, reaching 9.3 % of single-core peak for 16CLJ, as the floating point performance becomes more and more saturated. Overall, the values range between 4 % and 8 %. In contrast, the version without the loop-interchange stagnates at around 5 % of peak-efficiency, which is likely the limit of the gather-scatter performance. In the 2–10 CLJ range, the gain continually increases from 1.1 to 1.7 with both implementations exhibiting a

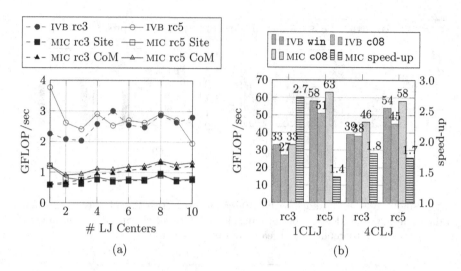

Fig. 6. (a) Single core performance as a function of the number of interaction sites. On MIC the "c08 col 4 threads" variant was used, while on IVB "win 2 processes". "Site" denotes the version before the loop-interchange, "CoM" - afterwards. (b) Final GFLOP/sec for 240/32 threads/processes, 1.32M molecules. Hatched bar indicates total speed-up of the c08 mode against reference version [7].

boost at 8CLJ and 4CLJ, as in those cases the gather- and scatter operations collect only contiguous data from one and two cache-lines, respectively. The gains at 4CLJ are 1.24 and 1.32 for the rc3 and rc5 cases, respectively. The gains for the no3 mode (not shown) were observed to be roughly half of those presented for c08, as the no3mode does not need to scatter forces to the second SoA. Another factor, affecting the Xeon Phi performance, is the lack of addition and multiplication operations, which can be fused - only a total of 7 operations out of 43 can be fused: 2 in the cutoff-evaluation and 5 in the LJ-Kernel. This means that most of the time, the FPU is executing non-fused (i.e., either add *or* multiply) operations, which halves floating point performance. This effect is not as limiting on the IVB, due to the employed hyperthreading.

Assuming "perfect upscaling" by a factor of 60 (MIC) and 16 (IVB), we see that MIC has the potential to outperform IVB by a factor of up to 1.4–1.5.

4.3   Shared-Memory Parallelization

Figure 7 presents the performed strong scaling experiments. The non-colored versions of the c08 and c18 variants were used for the timings on 1 thread.

Comparing the c08, c18 and no3 schemes using 1 thread on MIC shows that restoring N3 gives a speed-up of 1.3 to 1.55. The scheme c08 performs around 5%–10% faster than c18, except in the 1.32M rc3 4CLJ case, where both schemes show similar performance. At 60 cores we observe a parallel efficiency of around 85% for all rc3 scenarios except 0.16M rc3 1CLJ (75%). For

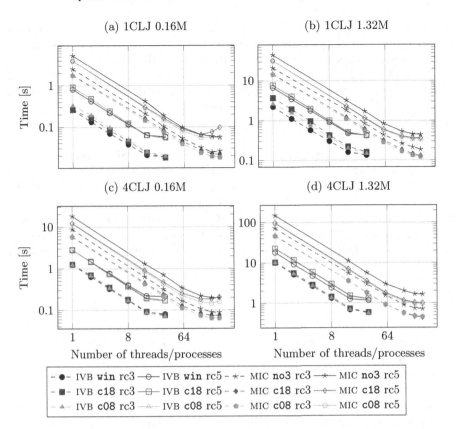

Fig. 7. Strong scaling on MIC and IVB. Threads were pinned with the "scatter" option.

the rc5 scenarios, the values are between 90 and 94 % for all cases except 0.16M rc5 1CLJ (82 %). This demonstrates that our implementation and approach are very well suited for manycore architectures such as MIC. The speed-ups in the hyperthreading range are almost 2 for the 1.32M and 0.16M rc3 configurations which is in agreement with the results from Sect. 4.2. The 0.16M rc5 case, however, does not exhibit a sufficient level of parallelism due to the small number of linked-cells in the strong scaling limit.

Considering IVB performance we also see that the adapted "Flops are free" approach is indeed reasonable and the MPI implementation is hard to beat, despite its redundant calculations, and in agreement with [2]. Analyzing in more detail, we see that the source of the good win performance does not lie in scalability, but in superior sequential performance. The obtained speed-ups, relative to the base version of the same parallelization mode, are in all cases higher for the c08 variant, ranging between 16.9 and 18.4 versus values between 13.5 and 17.5 for win. Comparing the start of the curves in detail, the win can, however, be up to 10–20% faster than the colored variant, likely due to the better cache performance. Parallel efficiency on 16 cores is between 81 % in the 1CLJ 160k rc3 case and ≥89 % in the other cases for the c08 variant.

In the 1.32M scenarios (and even in some 0.16M scenarios), we attain speed-ups of comparable magnitude to the ones predicted in Sect. 4.2. Comparing IVB win and MIC c08 at full thread utilization, MIC is faster than IVB by factors 1.09 (1CLJ rc3), 1.23 (1CLJ rc5), 1.27 (4CLJ rc3), and 1.22 (4CLJ rc5). This is close to our simple upper bound (1.4–1.5) assuming perfect upscaling, cf. Sect. 4.2. These speed-ups are not consistently attained in the 0.16M case as this configuration exhibits around 8 times fewer linked-cells and, respectively, parallelism.

Figure 6(b) shows the final attained FLOP-rates and total speed-up compared to the reference ls1-mardyn version used in [7]. The 4CLJ scenarios benefit from both the gather-scatter and the N3 optimization, which multiplied together, give the observed speed-ups of 1.7–1.8. The 1CLJ scenarios experience only the N3 speed-up, explaining the factor of 1.4 for 1CLJ rc5. The 1CLJ rc3 scenario, being least computationally intensive, experienced a (considerably) larger speed-up than 1.4 due to the addressed bottleneck of the SoA reallocation, as mentioned in Sect. 3.

5   Summary

We presented an improvement to the gather-scatter-based molecular dynamics implementation and a shared-memory parallelization approach operating on the linked-cell structure of the molecular dynamics simulation.

As seen in Sect. 4.2, the number of expensive gather- and scatter-operations could be reduced by simple swapping of loops. This allowed to speed-up simulations of multi-centered molecules. The presented c08 scheme efficiently parallelizes the linked-cell algorithm in shared-memory environments with minimal synchronization steps and satisfying the N3 optimization. In particular, the Xeon Phi architecture could be exploited and delivered slightly more performance than the Ivy Bridge host. The accelerator card thus builds a valuable hardware extension for molecular dynamics. Hybrid MPI-OpenMP simulations using this scheme and extending the analysis to the whole simulation, as opposed to the presented calculation, are part of future work.

Optimization Notice: Software and workloads used in performance tests may have been optimized for performance only on Intel microprocessors. Performance tests, such as SYSmark and MobileMark, are measured using specific computer systems, components, software, operations and functions. Any change to any of those factors may cause the results to vary. You should consult other information and performance tests to assist you in fully evaluating your contemplated purchases, including the performance of that product when combined with other products. For more information go to http://www.intel.com/performance.

Intel, Xeon, and Intel Xeon Phi are trademarks of Intel Corporation in the U.S. and/or other countries.

Acknowledgements. This work was partially supported by the Intel Parallel Computing Center ExScaMIC, and the Bundesministerium für Bildung in Forschung (Germany) in the scope of the project "SkaSim - Skalierbare HPC-Software für molekulare

Simulationen in der chemischen Industrie", Förderkennzeichen 01IH13005F. We further thank Wolfgang Hölzl for productive discussions.

References

1. Brown, W.M., Wang, P., Plimpton, S.J., Tharrington, A.N.: Implementing molecular dynamics on hybrid high performance computers short range forces. Comput. Phys. Commun. **182**(4), 898–911 (2011)
2. Buchholz, M.: Framework zur Parallelisierung von Molekulardynamiksimulationen in verfahrenstechnischen Anwendungen. Dissertation, Institut für Informatik, Technische Universität München, München, August 2010
3. Eckhardt, W.: Efficient HPC implementations for large-scale molecular simulation in process engineering. Dissertation, Institut für Informatik, Technische Universität München, München, June 2014
4. Eckhardt, W., Heinecke, A., Bader, R., Brehm, M., Hammer, N., Huber, H., Kleinhenz, H.-G., Vrabec, J., Hasse, H., Horsch, M., Bernreuther, M., Glass, C.W., Niethammer, C., Bode, A., Bungartz, H.-J.: 591 TFLOPS multi-trillion particles simulation on SuperMUC. In: Kunkel, J.M., Ludwig, T., Meuer, H.W. (eds.) ISC 2013. LNCS, vol. 7905, pp. 1–12. Springer, Heidelberg (2013)
5. Griebel, M., Knapek, S., Zumbusch, G.: Numerical Simulation in Molecular Dynamics: Numerics, Algorithms, Parallelization, Applications, vol. 5, Springer, Heidelberg (2007)
6. Heinecke, A.: Boosting scientific computing applications through leveraging data parallel architectures. Dissertation, Institut für Informatik, Technische Universität München, München, January 2014
7. Heinecke, A., Eckhardt, W., Horsch, M., Bungartz, H.J.: Supercomputing for molecular-dynamics simulations: handling multi-trillion particles in nanofluidics. Springer Briefs in Computer Science, Springer, June 2015
8. Horsch, M., Niethammer, C., Vrabec, J., Hasse, H.: Computational molecular engineering as an emerging technology in process engineering. it-Information Technology Methoden und innovative Anwendungen der Informatik und Informationstechnik, 55(3), 97–101 (2013)
9. Kunaseth, M., Richards, D.F., et al.: Scalable data-privatization threading for hybrid MPI/OpenMP parallelization of molecular dynamics. In: International Conference on Parallel and Distributed Processing Techniques and Applications (2011)
10. Neumann, P., Bungartz, H.J., Mehl, M., Neckel, T., Weinzierl, T.: A coupled approach for fluid dynamic problems using the pde framework peano. Commun. Comput. Phys. **12**, 65–84 (2012)
11. Niethammer, C., Becker, S., Bernreuther, M., Buchholz, M., Eckhardt, W., Heinecke, A., Werth, S., Bungartz, H.J., Glass, C.W., Hasse, H., Vrabec, J., Horsch, M.: ls1 mardyn: the massively parallel molecular dynamics code for large systems. J. Chem. Theor. Comput. **10**(10), 4455–4464 (2014)
12. Pennycook, S., Hughes, C., Smelyanskiy, M., Jarvis, S.: Exploring SIMD for molecular dynamics, using intel xeon; processors and intel xeon phi coprocessors. In: 2013 IEEE 27th International Symposium on Parallel Distributed Processing (IPDPS), pp. 1085–1097, May 2013
13. Ranman, R.: Intel Xeon Phi Coprocessor Architecture and Tools. Apress open, New York (2013)

VHPC - Virtualization in High-Performance Cloud Computing

A Simplified TDP with Large Tables

Yu Zhang[✉]

Rechnerarchitektur, Fakultät Für Informatik,
Technische Universität Chemnitz, 09126 Chemnitz, Germany
`zhayu@hrz.tu-chemnitz.de`

Abstract. Among the performance bottlenecks for the virtual machine, memory comes next to the I/O as the second major source of overhead to be addressed. While the SPT and TDP have proved to be quite effective and mature solutions in memory virtualization, it is not yet guaranteed that they perform equally well for arbitrary kind of workloads, especially considering that the performance of HPC workloads is more sensitive to the virtual than to the native execution environment. We propose that based on the current TDP design, modification could be made to reduce the 2D page table walk with the help of large page table. By doing this, not only the guest and host context switching due to guest page fault could be avoided, but also the second dimension of paging could be potentially simplified, which will lead to better performance.

1 Introduction

In the context of system virtualization, SPT (shadow page table) and TDP (two-dimensional paging)[1] are the two mature solutions for memory virtualization in the current hypervisors. Both of them perform address translation transparently from the guest to the host. In dealing with the translation chain from GVA (guest virtual address) to HPA (host physical address), the SPT combines the three intermediate steps for each GVA→HPA into a single entry, which contains the wanted address and saves further efforts to walk through both of the guest and host page tables as long as the cached entry is not invalidated in any form. However, as SPT is a part of the hypervisor and must be kept as consistent as possible with the guest page table, the processor had to exit from the guest to host mode to update the SPT and make it accessible, during which a considerable number of CPU cycles could have been wasted. TDP comes as a remedy by keeping GVA→GPA translation in the guest, while shifting GPA→HPA translation from the hypervisor to the processor. The expensive `vmexit` and `vmentry` due to guest page fault are avoided by TDP. Unfortunately in case of TLB-miss (translation look-aside block) the multi-level page table must still be walked through to fetch the missing data from the memory. Because of this nature, the TLB is not quite helpful in preventing page table from being walked when running workloads with poor temporal locality or cache access behavior. As a result,

---

[1] TDP it is known as the AMD NPT and Intel EPT. For technical neutrality reason TDP is used to refer to the paging mechanism with hardware assistance.

© Springer International Publishing Switzerland 2015
S. Hunold et al. (Eds.): Euro-Par 2015 Workshops, LNCS 9523, pp. 789–801, 2015.
DOI: 10.1007/978-3-319-27308-2_63

the performance gain could be more or less offset by the overhead. We attempt to combine the merits of the two methods and meanwhile avoid the downsides of them by adapting the mmu code in the hypervisor.

For TLB contains a number of the most recently accessed GPA→HPA mappings, the more likely these entries will be needed in future, the more time could be saved from the page table walk in subsequent operations. To the nature of the paging methods themselves, the efficiency of both SPT and TDP rely on to what extent the cached results of the previous page table walks could be reused. Since the SPT cannot be maintained without interrupting the guest execution and exit to the host kernel mode, there will be little chance other than reducing the occurrence of the page fault in the guest to improve the performance of SPT. This, however, largely depends on the memory access behavior of the individual workload and remains beyond the control of the hypervisor. TDP, on the hand, bears the hope for performance improvement. Currently the TDP is adopting the same paging mode as the host does, known as "multi-level page table walk-through". It is an N-ary tree structure [1], where N could be 1024 in 32-bit mode, or 512 in 64-bit or 32-bit PAE modes. In the 32-bit mode only 2 level page table are involved for walking through, which poses minor overhead. However, the overhead grows quickly non-negligible as the paging level increases. In spite of the various paging modes adopted in the guest, only two modes - the 64-bit and the 32-bit PAE modes are available for the TDP. In the worst case if all TLB large missed, up to 24 memory accesses are possible for a single address translation.

Though undesirable, this has presumably been done for two reasons: 1. compatibility between the host and guest paging modes, and more importantly, 2. efficiency in memory utilization. However, as the TDP table is in the hypervisor and invisible to the guest, it is actually up to the hypervisor to adopt the paging mode without having to maintain this kind of compatibility [2]. For the tree structure forms a hierarchy of the 1-to-many mappings, mappings could be built in a "lazy" way only on demand, significant amount of memory space for entries could be saved compared with the 1-to-1 mapping based structure, say, an array. On the other hand, this structure also means more memory access and time cost while looking up an element within it. As performance rather than memory saving comes as the top concern, paging methods more efficient than the current one may exist. One candidate is naturally a 1-to-1 mapping based structure, such as an array, or a hash list. With more memory being invested to save all the possible GPPFN (guest physical page frame number) to HPPFN (host physical page frame number) mappings, fewer memory accesses suffice[2] in the second dimension of the TDP. By doing this, the whole translation from GVA to HPA is expected to be effectively simplified and accelerated due to a reduced paging structure in TDP table. In addition, a simplified TDP method combines the merits of both TDP and SPT - to avoid the vmexit as well as to maintain the relatively short mapping chains from GVA to HPA. Until signif-

---

[2] This is the case only if a single large table is used. In our design, however, due to the limitation of memory chunk size in the kernel, multiple tables could be used.

icant change is made available to the paging mode of the current processor, it could be a better practice merely by modifying the current hypervisor software.

2   Related Work

Major work focusing on improving the memory virtualization could be summarized as the following. To work around the unfavorable sides and combine the best qualities of SPT and TDP, one attempt is to enable the hypervisor to reconfigure its paging method at run-time as a response to the ever changing behavior of the workloads in memory accessing, which were implemented in the past in a few hypervisors such as Xen and Palacios according to [3,4]. Although not all workloads could be benefited from this, overall performance gain have been observed for the selected benchmarks. The downside, however, is that it adds further complexity to the hypervisor with the methods of performance metric sampling, paging method decision making, as well as the dynamic switching logic. Furthermore, such activities in the kernel could also do harm to the performance.

To reduce the overhead for walking through the multi-level page tables in TDP, a hashed list is applied to provide direct address mapping for GPA [2]. In contrast with the $O(n^2)$ complexity of the conventional multi-level forward page tables for both GVA→GPA and GPA→HPA translations, the hashed page table has only one paging level and achieves a complexity of $O(n)$ in theory. The performance is at least not worse due to the reduced page table walk and cache pressure, showed by the benchmark. Since the hash table is a data structure more capable in searching, inserting and deleting etc., and relatively easier to be implemented within the existing framework of the hardware and software, current TDP design could be simplified by applying it for better performance. As more reflections were cast on the current multi-level paging modes, a variety of changes have been prompted for a simplified paging work. Theoretically, a "flat nested page table" could be formed by combining the intermediate page levels from 4 to 1, which results in an 8 memory access for the translation from GVA to HPA, and a reduced overhead for 2D TDP walk [5]. By extending the processor and hypervisor with the "direct segment" function, the memory access for the GVA to HPA translation could even be further reduced to 4 or 0 [6].

For the TLB plays a critical role in reducing the address translation overhead [7] and justifies the use of TDP, it becomes another concern besides the paging level. Specific to the AMD processor, a way is suggested in [8] to accelerate the TDP walk for guest by extending the existing page walk cache also to include the nested dimension of the 2D page walk, caching the nested page table translations, as well as skipping multiple page entry references. This technique has already gained its application in some AMD processors. Not limited to virtual cases, attention is paid in [9] to compare the effectiveness of five MMU cache organizations, which shows that two of the newly introduced structures - the variants of the translation outperform the existing structures in many situations.

3   Structures and Operation of the TDP

As a potential technical breakthrough, TDP is different from SPT in many aspects. However, for compatibility reason, the main structure of SPT is still reused by TDP. This, though at first may seem quite misleading, enables the TDP to fit seamlessly into the current framework previously created for SPT. As far as TDP feature is available in the hardware, it is preferred to SPT for general better performance. While in the absence of TDP hardware feature, SPT may serve as a fall-back way and the only choice for the hypervisor to perform the guest-to-host address translation.

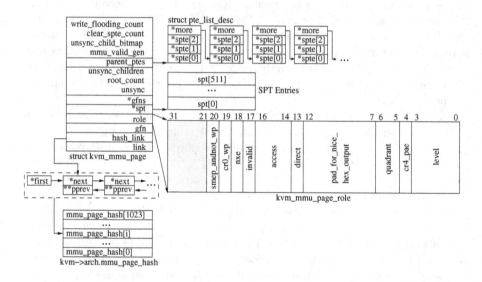

Fig. 1. Data Structure for SPT reused by TDP in KVM

In KVM, SPT and TDP share the same data structure of the virtual MMU and page tables (surprisingly, both are named as shadow page table). The shadow page table is organized as shown by Fig. 1, of which kvm_mmu_page is the basic unit gluing all information about the shadow pages together. For each level of the shadow page table, a pageful of 64-bit sptes containing the translations for this page are pointed to by *spt, whose role regarding the paging mode, dirty and access bits, level etc. are defined by the corresponding bits in role. The page pointed to by spt will have its page->private pointing back at the shadow page structure. The sptes in spt point either at guest pages, or at lower-level shadow pages [10]. As the sptes contained in a shadow page may be either one level of the PML4, PDP, PD and PT, the pte_parents provides the reverse mapping for the pte/ptes pointing at the current page's spt. The bit 0 of parent_ptes is used to differentiate this number from one to many. If bit 0 is zero, only one spte points at this pages and parent_ptes points at this single spte, otherwise,

```
1    static void set_tdp_cr3(struct kvm_vcpu *vcpu, unsigned long root)
2    {
3            struct vcpu_svm *svm = to_svm(vcpu);
4            svm->vmcb->control.nested_cr3 = root;
5            mark_dirty(svm->vmcb, VMCB_TDP);
6            ...
7            svm_flush_tlb(vcpu);
8    }
9
10   static void init_kvm_tdp_mmu(struct kvm_vcpu *vcpu)
11   {
12           struct kvm_mmu *context = vcpu->arch.walk_mmu;
13           ...
14           context->page_fault = tdp_page_fault;
15           ...
16           context->root_hpa = INVALID_PAGE;
17           context->direct_map = true;
18           context->set_cr3 = kvm_x86_ops->set_tdp_cr3;
19           ...
20           context->inject_page_fault = kvm_inject_page_fault;
21           ...
22   }
23
24   static void init_vmcb(struct vcpu_svm *svm)
25   {
26           struct vmcb_control_area *control = &svm->vmcb->control;
27           struct vmcb_save_area *save = &svm->vmcb->save;
28           ...
29           if (npt_enabled) {
30                   /* Setup VMCB for Nested Paging */
31                   control->nested_ctl = 1;
32                   clr_intercept(svm, INTERCEPT_INVLPG);
33                   clr_exception_intercept(svm, PF_VECTOR);
34                   clr_cr_intercept(svm, INTERCEPT_CR3_READ);
35                   clr_cr_intercept(svm, INTERCEPT_CR3_WRITE);
36                   save->g_pat = 0x0007040600070406ULL;
37                   save->cr3 = 0;
38                   save->cr4 = 0;
39           }
40           ...
41   }
```

Fig. 2. VMCB configuration for TDP

multiple sptes are pointing at this page and the parent_ptes & 0x1 points at a data structure with a list of parent_ptes. spt array forms a directed acyclic graph structure, with the shadow page as a node, and guest pages as leaves [10].

KVM MMU also maintains the minimal pieces of information to mark the current state and keep the sptes up to date. unsync indicates if the translations in the current page are still consistent with the guest's translation. Inconsistence arises when the translation has been modified before the TLB is flushed, which has been read by the guest. unsync_children counts the sptes in the page pointing at pages that are unsync or have unsynchronized children. unsync_child_bitmap is a bitmap indicating which sptes in spt point (directly or indirectly) at pages that may be unsynchronized. For more detailed description, the related Linux kernel documentation [10] is available for reference.

Multiple `kvm_mmu_page` instances are linked by an `hlist_node` structure headed by `hlist_head`, which form the elements in the hash list - `mmu_page_hash` pointed to by `kvm->arch`. Meanwhile it's also linked to either the lists `active_mmu_pages` or `zapped_obsolete_pages` in the `kvm->arch`, depending on the current state of the entries contained by this page. Both SPT and TDP keep their "shadow page table" entries and other related information in the same structure. The major difference lies in the hypervisor configuration of the run-time behaviors upon paging-fault-related events in the guest. While the SPT relies on the mechanism of "guest page write-protecting" and "host kernel mode trapping" upon guest page fault for keeping the SPT synchronized with the guest page table, the TDP achieves the same result by a hardware mechanism. As VMCB (virtual machine control block) by AMD or VMCS (virtual machine control structure) by Intel is the basic hardware facility the TDP makes use of, it's the key thing making difference. Code snippet in Fig. 2 shows the configuration of VMCB for TDP, and that the root address of the TDP page table is kept in the VMCB structure. Meanwhile the guest is configured as exitless for paging-fault exception, which means that the page fault events is handled by the processor. With this configuration, guest is left running undisturbed when the guest page fault occurs.

Besides, as SPT maps GVA to HPA, the `spt` entries are created and maintained in a per-process way, which leads to poor reusability hence higher memory consumption. These are obvious downsides especially when multiple processes are running in parallel. In contrast, the TDP maintains only the mappings from GPA to HPA, which effectively eliminated such problems associated with SPT. Guest page table is also accessed by the physical processor and forms the first dimension of the entire page table walk. In this way the TDP can not only eliminate the cost for frequent switching between the host and guest modes due to SPT synchronization, but also simplify the mappings and maintenance efforts the "shadow page tables" needs.

Two stages are involved in the buildup of the TDP table, namely, the creation of the virtual mmu, and the filling of TDP page tables upon guest page fault during the execution of the guest. As Fig. 3 depicts, in the context of the function `kvm_vm_ioctl`, the virtual mmu is created for the first time along with the guest VCPU. It is also when the VMCB is configured. One thing to be noticed is that, as the root address of the TDP page table, the `root_hpa` of the `kvm_mmu` is left without to be allocated a page table, which is deferred to the second stage.

Figure 4 depicts the context function `vcpu_enter_guest`, in which operations related to the second stage take place. This function serves as an interface for the inner loop[3] in the internal architecture of the QEMU-KVM, dealing with host-guest mode switching. Before the guest mode is entered by the processor, much preparation work needs to be done in this context, including the checking and handling of many events, exceptions, requests as well as mmu reloading or I/O emulation. The only thing needed for mmu reloading is to allocate a page

---

[3] The outer loop is formed by `ioctl` commands issued by QEMU from the user-space, dealing with user-space and host kernel-space switching.

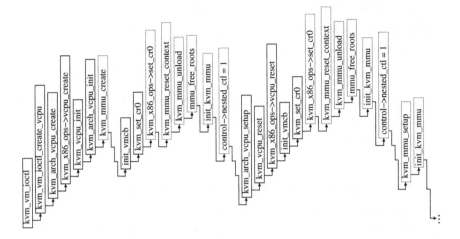

Fig. 3. Framework for virtual MMU creation in KVM

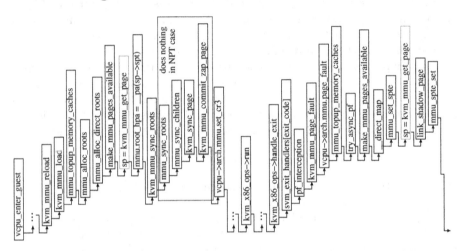

Fig. 4. Framework for page fault handling in KVM

for the TDP table and make the starting address of it known to the root_hpa of the kvm_mmu and the CR3 of the VCPU, which is performed by kvm_mmu_load.

Guest begins to execute until it can't proceed any further due to some faulty conditions. More often than not, control flow had to be returned to the hypervisor or the host OS kernel to handle the events the guest encountered. Obviously too much vmexit are an interference and grave source of overhead for the guest. With TDP, however, guest is free from vmexit upon guest paging faults. As the guest enters for the first time into execution, the paging mode is enabled and the guest page tables are initialized, however, the TDP tables are still empty. Any fresh access to a page by the guest will first trigger a guest page fault. After

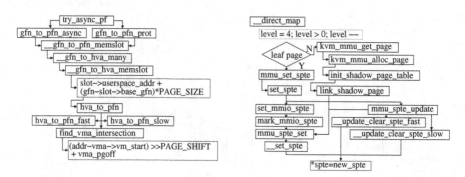

Fig. 5. pfn calculation for faulting address and the mapping into TDP tables

the fault is fixed by the guest, another page fault in the second dimension of the TDP is triggered due to the missing entry in TDP table.

tdp_page_fault is the page fault handler in this case. As illustrated by Fig. 5, first the host page frame number - pfn is calculated for the faulting address through a chain of functions in try_async_pf. The pfn is then mapped one level after another into the corresponding positions of the TDP tables by the function __direct_map. In a predefined format, the entry for a faulting address is split into pieces of PML4E, PDPE, PDE, PTE as well as offset in a page. During the loop, iterator - an instance of the structure kvm_shadow_walk_iterator is used to retrieve the latest physical, virtual addresses and position in the TDP tables for a given address, of which iterator.level determines the number of times for the mapping process.

4   Design and Implementation of the Simplified TDP

Although the conventional TDP shown in Fig. 6 is mature and the default configuration for better performance, for a certain kind of workloads the limitation is still obvious. They may suffer large overhead due to walking into the second dimension of multi-level page table upon heavy TLB-miss. It is ideal to have a "flat" TDP table by which the wanted pfn can be obtained with a single lookup. Unfortunately, there has long been a problem to allocate large chunk of physically continuous memory in the kernel space. Three functions, namely vmalloc(), kmalloc() and __get_free_pages are used to allocate memory in the current Linux Kernel. The first allocates memory continuous only in virtual address, which is easier to perform but not desired dealing with performance. The second and the third allocate memory chunk continuous in both virtual and physical addresses, however, the maximum memory size allocated is quite limited, thus tends to fall short of the expectation for this purpose. In addition, kmalloc() is very likely to fail allocating large amount of memory, especially in low-memory situations [11]. The amount of memory __get_free_pages can allocate is also limited within $2^{MAX\_ORDER-1}$, where MAX_ORDER in the current Linux Kernel for x86 is 11, which means that each time at most 4MB memory

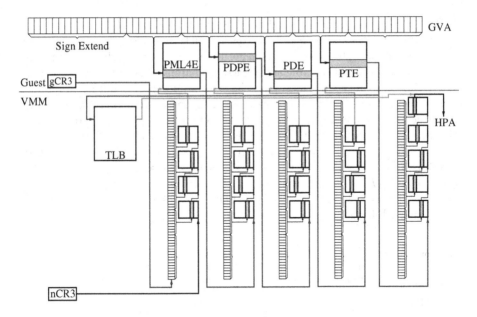

Fig. 6. The conventional TDP with 4 paging levels

can be obtained in the hypervisor. In this condition what we could do is to make the TDP table as "flat" as possible, and to reduce the number of paging with it. Here "flat" means large and physically continuous memory chunk for TDP table. Instead of having thousands of TDP tables managed by their own kvm_mmu_page instances, we want to merge as many TDP tables as possible into a larger table managed by fewer kvm_mmu_page instances.

There could be various ways to implement this, depending on how the indices of a page table entry are split. Two things are to be noticed for this: 1. to leave the indices for paging as long as possible, and 2. to reuse the current source code for KVM as much as we can.

Consequently, we come up with a quite straightforward design by merging the bits for currently used indices within a guest page table entry. As Figs. 7 and 8 depict, the former PML4, PDP (higher 18 bits) could be combined as a single index to the root of a TDP table segment, and similarly PD and PT (lower 18 bits) as the index for a physical page. By filling the TDP table entries in a linear ascend order for the GPPFN, the HPPFN could be obtained conveniently by a single lookup into the table. As a result, for the currently used maximal address space of a the 64-bit(48 bits effectively in use) guest, we may have $2^{18} = 256K$ segments for the TDP tables, with the index of each segment ranging from 0 to $2^{18} - 1$ to the host physical pages. The TDP table size is enlarged by 2^9 times, while the number of the table segments could be reduced to $\frac{1}{2^9}$ of the former.

This is actually a fundamental change to the current mmu implementation. Several data structures and functions oriented to the operations upon $4KB*2^9 =$

$2MB$ TDP page table must be adopted to the type upon $4KB * 2^{18} = 1GB$. For example, as depicted by Fig. 9, the data structure of kvm_mmu_page could be modified as following to reflect the change: 1. since in a "flat" table, there is only two levels and a single root table as parents, the parents-children relation is quite obvious. Besides, all the first level pages have a common parent but no children at all. Members such as unsync_children, parent_ptes and unsync_child_bitmap are not necessary; 2. members as gfn, role, unsync etc. are multiplied by 512 to hold the informations previously owned by an individual $4KB * 2^9 = 2MB$ page table; 3. spt points to a table segment covering an area of $4KB * 2^{18} = 1GB$; 4. link is moved to a newly introduced structure - page_entity to identify the $4KB * 2^9 = 2MB$ pages that are either in the active or zapped_obselete list. By modifying it this way, the depth of the TDP table hierarchy could be reduced from 4 to 2, while the width expanded from 2^9 to 2^{18}.

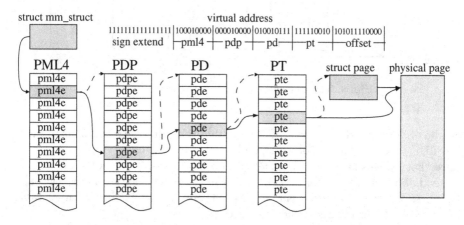

Fig. 7. Paging mode in the second dimension of conventional TDP [12].

Since each kvm_mmu_page instance contains 2^{18} table entries now, there will be less kvm_mmu_page instances in use, which means that 2^{18} rather than 2^9 sptes need to be mapped to a single kvm_mmu_page instance. This could be achieved by masking out the lower 30 bits of an address and setting the obtained page descriptor's private field to this kvm_mmu_page instance, as shown in Fig. 10. Other major affected functions include 1. shadow_walk_init, 2. kvm_mmu_get_page, 3. _direct_map, 4. kvm_mmu_prepare_zap_page, 5. kvm_mmu_commit_zap_page and 6. mmu_alloc_direct_roots.

Taken a guest commonly with 4GB memory as an example. A page contains $4KB/8B = 512$ entries, and for the 4GB, $4GB/4KB = 2^{20}$ entries are needed, so $2^{20}/512 = 2048$ pages of 4KB size should be used to save all the table entries. All together it makes a space of about $4KB * 2048 = 8MB$ size. Although this may be far more than in the conventional TDP case, it is a modest demand and acceptable compared with a host machine configured with dozens of GB RAM.

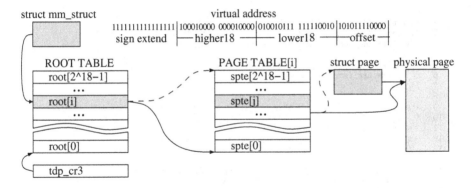

Fig. 8. Paging mode in the second dimension of simplified TDP.

```
 1   struct kvm_mmu_page {              1   struct page_entity {
 2   //struct list_head link;          2       struct list_head link;
 3       struct hlist_node hash_link;  3       gfn_t gfn;
 4       gfn_t gfn[512];               4       union kvm_mmu_page_role role;
 5       union kvm_mmu_page_role role[512];  5   bool unsync;
 6       u64 *spt;                     6       u64 spte;
 7       gfn_t *gfns;                  7       int root_count;
 8       bool unsync[512];             8   };
 9       int root_count[512];
10   //unsigned int unsync_children;
11   //unsigned long parent_ptes;
12       unsigned long mmu_valid_gen[512];
13   //DECLARE_BITMAP(unsync_child_bitmap, 512);
14   #ifdef CONFIG_X86_32
15       int clear_spte_count[512];
16   #endif
17       int write_flooding_count[512];
18   };
```

Fig. 9. (a) modified `kvm_mmu_page`. (b) newly defined `page_entity` as the new entity for hash lists, as a replacement of the former `kvm_mmu_page`.

On the other hand, with the 2MB TDP large pages, only 4 `kvm_mmu_page` instances are sufficient to cover the entire 4GB address space. Only 4 entries are filled in the root table, which poses no pressure at all to the TLB. For an arbitrary guest virtual address, at most $2*5+4 = 14$ (10 in hypervisor, 4 in guest) memory accesses are enough to get the host physical address - far less than that of the current translation scheme (20 in hypervisor, 4 in guest). With a flatter TDP page table and reduced number of memory access, the KVM guest is expected to be less sensitive to workloads and yield higher performance.

5   Conclusion and Further Work

We studied the current implementation of the SPT and TDP for the KVM, and attempted to simplify the second dimension paging of the TDP based on a change of the table structure and the related functions in the hypervisor. With

```
1    #define BASE_INDEX_MASK ~(u64)((1ULL << 30) - 1)
2    #define BASE_INDEX(addr) ((u64)(addr) & BASE_INDEX_MASK)
3    static inline struct kvm_mmu_page *page_header(hpa_t shadow_page)
4    {
5          struct page *page = pfn_to_page(shadow_page >> PAGE_SHIFT);
6          return (struct kvm_mmu_page *)page_private(page);
7    }
8
9    static struct kvm_mmu_page *kvm_mmu_alloc_page(struct kvm_vcpu *vcpu, int direct)
10   {
11       struct kvm_mmu_page *sp;
12       sp = mmu_memory_cache_alloc(&vcpu->arch.mmu_page_header_cache);
13       sp->spt = mmu_memory_cache_alloc(&vcpu->arch.mmu_page_cache);
14       if (!direct)
15         sp->gfns = mmu_memory_cache_alloc(&vcpu->arch.mmu_page_cache);
16       set_page_private(virt_to_page(BASE_INDEX(sp->spt)), (unsigned long)sp);
17       return sp;
18   }
```

Fig. 10. Way to map 2^{30} addresses to a single kvm_mmu_page instance

this change on software, the current TDP paging level could be reduced and the overall guest performance will be improved. We have implemented a part of this design and found that, the large TDP page table could be allocated without problem as long as the amount is less than 4MB. However, as it is a relative radical change to the traditional mainstream KVM source code, many functions within the mmu code are affected, an executable implementation as well as a benchmark result are unfortunately not yet available. In future we will keep on engaging with this task and work out a concrete solution based on this design.

References

1. Preiss, B.R., Eng, P.: Data Structures and Algorithms with Object-Oriented Design Patterns in Java. Wiley, Chichester (1999)
2. Hoang, G., Bae, C., Lange, J., Zhang, L., Dinda, P., Joseph, R.: A case for alternative nested paging models for virtualized systems. Comput. Archit. Lett. **9**, 17–20, University of Michigan (2010)
3. Wang, X., Zang, J., Wang, Z., Luo, Y., Li, X.: Selective hardware/software memory virtualization, VEE 2011, Department of Computer Science and Technology, Beijing University, March 2011
4. Bae, C.S., Lange, J.R., Dinda, P.A.: Enhancing virtualized application performance through dynamic adaptive paging mode selection, Northwestern University and University of Pittsburgh, ICAC 2011, June 2011
5. Ahn, J., Jin, S., Huh, J.: Revisiting hardware-assisted page walks for virtualized systems. Computer Science Department, KAIST, ISCA 2012, April 2012
6. Gandhi, J., Basu, A., Hill, M.D., Swift, M.M.: Efficient memory virtualization. University of Wisconsin-Madison and AMD Research, October 2014
7. Adavanced Micro Devices Inc, AMD-V Nested Paging White Paper. Adavanced Micro Devices, July 2008

8. Bhargave, R., Serebin, B., Spadini, F., Manne, S.: Accelerating two-dimensional page walks for virtualized systems. Computing Solutions Group and Advanced Architecture & Technology Lab, March 2008

9. Barr, T.W., Cox, A.L., Rixner, S.: Translation Caching: Skip, Don't Walk (the Page Table), Rice University, June 2010

10. Linux kernel Documentation about MMU in KVM. https://www.kernel.org/doc/Documentation/virtual/kvm/mmu.txt

11. Johnson, M.K.: Memory allocation. Linux Journal, issue 16, August 1995. http://www.linuxjournal.com/article/1133

12. Rubini, A., Corbet, J.: Linux Device Drivers, 2nd edn, June 2014. http://www.xml.com/ldd/chapter/book/ch13.html

GPGPU Virtualisation with Multi-API Support Using Containers

John Walsh[✉] and Jonathan Dukes

School of Computer Science and Statistics, Trinity College Dublin,
The University of Dublin, College Green, Dublin 2, Ireland
{John.Walsh,Jonathan.Dukes}@scss.tcd.ie
http://www.scss.tcd.ie/

Abstract. Virtualisation of GPGPUs using PCI-Passthrough is limited to costly specialised hardware. API-Interception provides an alternative software-based approach to GPGPU virtualisation that has been shown to provide good performance and increased utilisation on High Performance and High Throughput Computing systems. Furthermore, user applications can transparently access many non-local GPGPU resources. However, current API-Interception implementations have either limited batch system support or none at all. This paper introduces a new multi-component system that supports multiple API-Interception implementations on several batch systems. The system consists of: (a) a factory component that produces lightweight Linux Containers using Docker, where each Container supports one or more API-Interception implementations and controls a single GPGPU; (b) a registry service that manages the Container resources; and, (c) a set of plugin scripts that bridge between the batch system and the registry. This paper also evaluates the performance of benchmarks on the prototype.

Keywords: Linux Container · Docker · Virtual GPGPU · API-Interception · Registry batch systems · Utilisation

1 Introduction

Over the last decade High Performance Computing (HPC) and High Throughput Computing (HTC) have seen a shift towards massively parallel computation using many-core accelerators, such as General Purpose Graphics Processing Units (GPGPUs) and Intel's Xeon Phi, as a way to boost application performance [6]. At the same time, Machine Virtualisation and Cloud Computing have led to a growth in loosely-coupled and highly-scalable parallel computing models such as Map/Reduce. Indeed other benefits of Cloud Computing include user-customisable execution environments and improved resource isolation. Although these features could be beneficial to HPC/HTC systems, HPC and Machine Virtualisation/Cloud Computing would appear to be somewhat juxtaposed – full Machine Virtualisation can decrease application performance [18]. Furthermore,

© Springer International Publishing Switzerland 2015
S. Hunold et al. (Eds.): Euro-Par 2015 Workshops, LNCS 9523, pp. 802–812, 2015.
DOI: 10.1007/978-3-319-27308-2_64

despite the benefits that Cloud can offer, it is not always practical or desirable to integrate cloud solutions (e.g. OpenStack) into existing HPC/HTC environments. However, an alternative approach using Containers (isolated process namespaces) looks promising [9,10,21].

This paper introduces a new lightweight system that adds a GPGPU virtualisation management layer on top of existing HPC infrastructures. This system virtualises GPGPUs (vGPGPU) and allows them be treated as *floating generic consumable resources* (FGCR), i.e. vGPGPU's are no longer logically bound to a machine. The extent to which a Local Resource Management System (LRMS), such as Torque [7]/MAUI [2], SLURM [5], can manage and schedule FGCR-based jobs is dependent on the choice of LRMS, so a new registry service has been developed to aide vGPGPU management. Two forms of GPGPU virtualisation are used in conjunction to create the vGPGPUs: lightweight machine virtualisation using Containers; and API-Interception. The former provides resource isolation whilst maintaining performance, and the latter allows one or more physical GPGPUs on remote machines to be seamlessly accessed as if they were local. Indeed, this form of combined GPGPU virtualisation may also help application developers avoid the need to use multiple APIs such as MPI. The proposed approach builds on existing virtualisation software to provide access to vGPGPUs. The contributions of this work are encapsulated in a system model consisting of: (a) a new vGPGPU Factory service to orchestrate the creation of vGPGPU VMs; (b) an external vGPGPU resource management service that enhances the existing LRMS and provides vGPGPU resource allocation where no such support exists in the LRMS; and (c) support for multiple API-Interception implementations and GPGPU hardware types within the one LRMS.

Section 2 looks at HPC and resource management, Cloud Computing for HPC, Virtualisation and GPGPU Virtualisation, and related work. This describes the influences and motivating factors behind the proposed model. The design and implementation is presented in Sect. 3, and two LRMS case-studies are discussed. Section 4 uses several benchmarks to examine the performance of the combined GPGPU vitualisation. Finally Sect. 5 summarises the objectives, how these have been achieved and the experimental findings before suggesting potential future work to improve and further evaluate the prototype.

2   Background and Related Work

HPC focuses on delivering the optimal computational power and capability possible, thereby allowing user jobs to execute as quickly as possible. HPC systems may be shared among hundreds or thousands of users from different scientific backgrounds and with different application needs. Such sharing requires management tools to optimise utilisation without overcommiting resources, and this is typically the responsibility of an LRMS (or *batch system*). The LRMS will queue user jobs until it determines that the specified job resources are available for it to execute. Typical resources include CPUs, but may also include network cards and GPGPUs that are implicitly bound to a machine called a worker-node (WN). A second type of resource, which can be accessed from any WN, is called a *floating* resource. An example of a floating resource is a software licence. Non-floating resources can be configured either as a property of a WN, or they can be declared as a *generic consumable resource*. Properties are used to define the nature of a resource, whereas generic consumables are used to declare that the resource can be used concurrently on its associated WN a finite number of times. Floating Generic Consumable Resources (FGCR's) are used to declare that a set of resources can be used from any WN, but can only be used concurrently at most by the configured amount. FGCRs are often used to maintain a global count of how many times a finite resource is concurrently used. Support for micro-managing FGCRs may need to be provided by some system external to the LRMS. The level of support for integrating external resource management systems with an LRMS is not uniform.

Cloud Computing is geared towards loosely-coupled and on-demand computing tasks. It attempts to optimise utilisation of physical machine resources by allowing CPU, disk and other resources to be assigned to one or more Virtual Machines (VMs). VMs have their own independent machine environment, and they can be highly customised to execute specific user applications or services. Some Cloud Computing providers, such as Amazon, cater for HPC provisioning of hardware, including GPGPUs. Economic models have also shown the cost of running some HPC applications in a Cloud environment may be significantly cheaper than in a dedicated HPC environment [11]. However, the performance of HPC in Cloud is still an issue: namely, machine virtualisation has an impact on application performance.

These concerns can be alleviated by allowing the cloud management system to provision the physical machine (bare-metal provisioning), however this does not optimise resource utilisation. An alternative method using Containers avoids full virtualisation of the machine in software. Containers are restricted process namespaces executing on top of an existing operating system. They can have their own network address, and are used to allow processes to run as isolated micro-services. Executing processes in a Container has negligible impact on its performance. Furthermore, Containers can be configured to directly access individual hardware devices such as GPGPUs. Multiple solutions exist to build and deploy Containers [1,3]. Docker has received much attention because it allows container images to be layered upon one another, and it supports machine image templates. These facilitate rapid Container deployment.

GPGPU Virtualisation models can be classified into four categories: API-Interception, Kernel Device Passthrough, PCI-Passthrough, and PCI-Switching.

API-Interception is a software method for virtualising GPGPU resources. GPGPU hardware is normally accessed through calls to an API such as CUDA or OpenCL. These calls may be *intercepted* (or *hooked*) before being directed to a physical GPGPU. This technique is used to provide transparent access to remotely installed GPGPUs as if they were local. Remote virtual GPGPUs use a *frontend/backend* model in which the *frontend* intercepts all API calls (and their data) and transfers them over the network to a selected *backend* for execution. Several API-Interception implementations have been developed for both CUDA (e.g. rCUDA [17], GridCUDA [15]) and OpenCL (VCL [8], dOpenCL [13], SnuCL [14]) runtime libraries. However, some not been actively developed in recent years and do not implement recent changes to their respective APIs.

Kernel Device Passthrough allows a GPGPU device (e.g. /dev/nvidia0) to be passed into a VM, and has the advantage of working with all GPGPUs. Impact on performance is negligible – 0 % for Containers [20] and 3 % for gVirtus [19].

PCI-Passthrough allows physical hosts to cede control of PCI-devices to a VM. This requires hardware support on the CPU, GPGPU, motherboard, and VM hypervisor. Relatively few GPGPUs can exploit this method. A recent study concluded that PCI-Passthrough has negligible performance impact [20].

PCI-Switching is a low-level technology that allows a physical machine equipped with additional specialist hardware to be assigned external PCI devices attached to the switch. Although this technology allows very flexible hardware (re)configurations, equipment cost is a significant disadvantage.

Some GPGPU virtualisation methods may be layered on top of each other, for example, a VM-encapsulated GPGPU using Kernel Device Passthrough, PCI-Passthrough or PCI-Switching can provide the first layer, with the API-Interception backend services providing the second layer. This combination allows the VM's GPGPU to be accessed remotely from a frontend node.

The prototype model presented in Sect. 3 is related to prior work that integrates rCUDA and VCL into SLURM. The weaknesses of these implementations are that: (i) they are SLURM specific; and (ii) if both systems are integrated with SLURM, both solutions attempt to manage the same vGPGPUs independently, so there are potential resource management conflicts. The prototype is designed to support several LRMSs and API-Interceptions technologies by using a single external vGPGPU management system. The use of LRMS prolog and epilogue scripts to extend the capabilities of the LRMS is inspired by ViBatch [16].

3   vGPGPUs as LRMS Resources

This paper proposes combining Kernel Device Passthrough (using Containers) with API-Interception, i.e. the Containers are assigned to a unique GPGPU, and one or more API-Interception software installed – these are *backend VMs*. Worker-nodes are configured at runtime as API-Interception *frontends*. The backend VMs are treated as a set of FGCRs, and are independent of the WNs. This section describes a model that facilitates API-Interception based vGPGPU resources usage on a range of different LRMSs. It consists of three new component parts: (a) the *vGPGPU Factory* subsystem creates backend VMs; (b) the Registry, which is used to aide both the installation and management of the backend VMs; and (c) a set of LRMS-specific script-based plugins that act as a bridge between the user's vGPGPU job, the LRMS, and the Registry.

These vGPGPUs should be easy to use, with much of the complexity hidden from the user. To aid this, a simple set of new key/value job attributes are supported, namely: the number of nodes (CPU cores), the number of vGPGPUs per node, and the type of API-Interception used in the job.

3.1   The vGPGPU Factory

The vGPGPU Factory is a service that either creates new backend VMs or restarts existing ones. The service executes on nodes with physical GPGPU hardware, and starts by examining the hardware profile. Several properties (e.g. the GPGPU OS device name/number, the device vendor) are evaluated when a GPGPU is found. If a backend VM does not already exist, then a new one is constructed and labeled with a *Universally Unique Identifier* (UUID). The UUIDs are derived either directly from the GPGPU hardware (Nvidia), or constructed from a combination of the physical machine's hostname and the GPGPU's OS device name (AMD). The Nvidia and AMD hardware dependent variables (CUDA_VISIBLE_DEVICES or GPU_DEVICE_ORDINAL respectively) are set to the GPGPU's device number. Variables and GPGPU devices are passed into the VM at build time, helping to restrict access to the specified device. This construction method provides logical isolation of the VM's GPGPU. Finally, the GPGPU vendor value is used to determine which API-Interception software is installed and started on the VM. This is VCL for all Nvidia- and AMD-based VMs, and rCUDA for Nvidia-based VMs. The construction also ensures that multiple API-Interception virtualisation stacks are supported according to the hardware type. Docker [12] is used to build the VM and to install the rCUDA/VCL software. In addition, network bridging using Pipework [4] is used in preference to Docker's native Network Address Translation (NAT) solution because rCUDA did not function correctly under NAT, and because Pipework allows IP address assignment to the VM. In this way the VM's IP address can be managed through the Registry and assigned to the VM when it is initially created or instantiated.

3.2   vGPGPU Registry Service

The set of backend VMs form a pool of unmanaged resources. To add management capabilities, a new web-based service, the *vGPGPU Registry Service* (or *Registry*), has been developed. This helps manage two aspects of backend VMs: their life-cycle and their allocation to jobs. The Registry augments the resource management provided by the LRMS. The service implements a simple interface (Fig. 1), and the state of the backend VMs are maintained in a persistent database. The protocol and database schema are designed to be independent of LRMS implementations. The assignment of the individual backend VMs to a job is managed at runtime by requesting resources from the Registry. The request returns a list of backend VM IP addresses. In this prototype implementation the Registry interface is implemented using the HTTP protocol.

Method	Description
register	Registers a new vGPGPU container that is being added to the pool. **Input**: Container UUID, GPU Vendor, GPU Device Number; **Output**: IP address of Container
unregister	Unregisters a vGPGPU container that is being removed from the pool. **Input**:Container UUID; **Output**: None.
request	Request a vGPGPU allocation for a job. The Registry returns the information needed to construct the vGPGPU front-end. **Input**: JobID, Number of vGPGPUs, Node Number, API-Interception Method; **Output**: List of vGPGPU Container IP addresses.
release	Release a vGPGPU allocation when it is no longer required by a job. The released vGPGPUs become available for allocation to another job. **Input**: JobID; **Output**: None.
query	Return information such as the number of free vGPGPUs and the number of vGPGPUs supporting a specified API (e.g. CUDA, OpenCL). **Input**: QueryName, API-Interception Method; **Output**: Integer.

Fig. 1. vGPGPU Registry Service Interface

3.3 LRMS Integration

The LRMS plugin component is the only subsystem that requires specific customisation. Two LRMS use-cases demonstrate this integration: (i) SLURM; and (ii) Torque/MAUI. The key differences between the LRMSs affect how vGPGPU jobs are handled and scheduled – these include support for non-CPU resources (e.g. FGCRs), and how arbitrary job parameters are propagated into the job's execution environment. However, despite these differences, vGPGPU jobs depend upon three LRMS-independent factors: (i) the number of frontend nodes; (ii) the number of backend VMs required by each frontend; and, (iii) the API-Interception to be used. The prototype assumes a natural mapping between an LRMS node – which in practice is a CPU core – and a vGPGPU frontend node. This implies that the number of frontend nodes is specified by declaring the number of nodes (or cores) required. LRMS environment variables are used to define the number of backend VMs (*VirtualGPGPUPerNode*) and the API-Interception required (*VirtualGPGPUType*). These can be passed from the LRMS to the frontend WN, where they are used by job prolog/epilogue scripts. The scripts transparently hide the complexity of configuring the vGPGPU job environment and interact with the Registry to allocate backend VMs.

Use-case 1: SLURM

The flow of a SLURM-based vGPGPU job is illustrated in Fig. 2. In Step (1) the number of frontend nodes is specified by requesting normal SLURM nodes; backend VMs are specified by requesting one or more *vgpgpu* licences; and the VirtualGPGPUPerNode and VirtualGPGPUType variables are also *exported* to the WN environment. The job will remain in a waiting state until the specified number of nodes and vgpgpu licences are available – this is managed entirely by

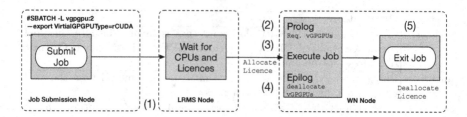

Fig. 2. The flow of a vGPGPU job through the SLURM LRMS

SLURM. During Step (2) a SLURM task prolog script will transparently execute. This checks that both VirtualGPGPUPerNode and VirtualGPGPUType are defined. If they are defined, then the prolog script requests a list of backend VMs from the Registry and then sets up the API-Interception execution environment. In Step (3) the GPGPU job will execute as normal; Finally, in Step (4), a SLURM task epilogue is transparently invoked to signal to the Registry that the backend VMs be made available for another job. However, the licence counter will not be incremented until the job exits in Step (5).

Use-case 2: Torque/MAUI

Torque/MAUI is a more complex use-case because it has limited support for generic consumable resources (implemented as a MAUI software patch), and limited support for FGCRs – it can only decrement a consumed resource by 1 at a time. To bypass these limitations, a new job pre-processing service and monitoring service have been developed. The flow of a Toruqe/MAUI vGPGPU job is illustrated in Fig. 3. In Step (1) the number of frontend nodes is defined to be the number of nodes; the VirtualGPGPUPerNode and VirtualGPGPUType are declared as variables, and these will be *exported* to the WN environment. In Step (2) a pre-processing filter examines the job definition; if the Virtual-GPGPUPerNode and VirtualGPGPUType variables are set, an additional job directive is inserted to instruct Torque to place the job into a *holding* state; furthermore, the filter injects an additional call to a prolog script. The held job can only be released by an external *Monitor*. Once the job is released, Step (3), the prolog requests a list of backend VMs from the Registry and configures the job environment. Finally, in Step (4) the job is executed and the job exits. The Torque/MAUI implementation does not execute an epilogue script – backend VM recovery is left to the Monitor service.

The Monitor service continuously executes on the node where the LRMS runs. It has LRMS operator privileges, allowing it to unhold jobs. During each iteration, the Monitor implements garbage collection of completed vGPGPU job backend VMs and releases them for further use. The Monitor queries the number of free resources, and then iterates over the list of held jobs; if there are sufficient free backend VMs, then the Monitor requests that the required backend VMs are allocated to that job on its behalf, and the job is then released from its hold

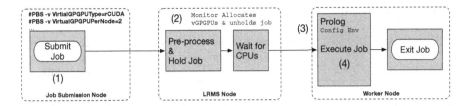

Fig. 3. The flow of a vGPGPU job through the Torque/MAUI LRMS

state. Unheld jobs must wait for available CPU cores. Only one job is released at a time, and this ensures there requests are free of race conditions.

4 Evaluation

To investigate whether the extra virtualisation layers (Docker and rCUDA/VCL) impact the performance and viability of the prototype, it is necessary to examine how applications behave. Two simple experiments were selected. The first examines the performance of a compute-intensive GPGPU application with minimal communication, while the second is a bandwidth intensive application that moves data from the WN to the GPGPU and back. Five scenarios were studied to help compare how each layer impacts performance, namely: (i) Native performance with direct access to the GPGPU (Local); (ii) WN access with rCUDA running locally on the WN (Local-rCUDA); (iii) WN access to a local GPGPU through rCUDA and a Docker container (Local-rCUDA/Docker); (iv) WN access to remote GPGPU using rCUDA only (Remote-rCUDA); and (v) WN access to a remote GPGPU using rCUDA and Docker (Remote-rCUDA/Docker). The network fabric uses 1-Gbit/Sec Cat5e Ethernet. The GPGPUs were Nvidia GTS 450s. The compute intensive application was executed 1,000 times for each scenario, while the bandwidth intensive application was executed 100 times.

Experiment 1:
The Black-Scholes application is provided by Nvidia to demonstrate how GPG-PUs can be used to calculate the price of European financial market options. This application is distributed with the Nvidia CUDA Software Development Kit. Input values and initial conditions are hard-coded into the application, and a total of 8,000,000 options are calculated. There is minimal data transfer between the CPU and the GPGPU, so this application is a good indicator of how well an application will perform when it is not dependent on network I/O. The results in Table 1 show the total time taken to run each GPGPU scenario. The ratio between the time taken to run and the corresponding time taken on the local GPGPU is shown. The results consistently indicate that in both Local and Remote GPGPU cases, the combination of rCUDA and Docker has a negligible impact on the overall runtime in comparison to just using rCUDA alone.

Table 1. Execution data for Nvidia Black-Scholes application (1,000 invocations)

Access method	Total time (1000 jobs)	Relative performance	average per-job GPUTime (msec)	Average per-job memory bandwidth
Local	2773.52s	1.0	3.59	22.26 GB/s
Local-rCUDA	2810.99s	1.014	3.60	22.25 GB/s
Local-rCUDA/Docker	2831.12s	1.021	3.60	22.24 GB/s
Remote-rCUDA	3524.73s	1.271	3.60	22.24 GB/s
Remote-rCUDA/Docker	3524.69s	1.271	3.60	22.25 GB/s

Experiment 2:

The BandwidthTest application also comes from the Nvidia Software Development Kit. Its purpose is to measure the memcopy bandwidth of the GPGPU and memcpy bandwidth across the PCI-e bus. In the case of rCUDA and Docker, the application should generate significant network I/O that will have an impact on its performance. The results for these application runs are tabulated in Table 2.

Table 2. Execution data for Nvidia BandwidthTest application (100 invocations)

Access method	Total time (100 jobs)	Relative performance	Host to device bandwidth	Device to host bandwidth
Local	55.10s	1.0	3224.27 MB/s	3268.48 MB/s
Local-rCUDA	72.96s	1.32	2924.77 MB/s	1701.18 MB/s
Local-rCUDA/Docker	92.90s	1.69	1227.15 MB/s	1632.54 MB/s
Remote-rCUDA	665.05s	12.07	114.89 MB/s	120.61 MB/s
Remote-rCUDA/Docker	665.10s	12.07	114.87 MB/s	122.52 MB/s

The results show that even locally, rCUDA and Docker will have a noticeable impact on the application performance. The performance of remote GPGPUs under is very poor under 1-Gbit/Sec Cat5e Ethernet, with the bandwidth test taking over twelve times longer than running the same application locally.

5 Conclusions and Future Work

The prototype meets its core-objective to provide a lightweight model that integrates multiple API-Interception technologies into several batch systems. The experimental data shows that: (i) when local (i.e. contained to the same physical hardware) vGPGPU jobs execute computationally intensive applications, neither rCUDA nor Docker have an impact. There is a performance impact of circa 25 % in both remote cases (where the frontend node is on separate hardware to the backend VM); and (ii) the bandwidth experiment results show that the performance degradation due to rCUDA and Docker is compounded at a local level, but Docker's impact is masked in the remote case.

Both results imply that the 1-Gbit/Sec Cat5e network infrastructure is problematic, and further tests are needed to see if any improvements can be made to the TCP/IP performance under both rCUDA and Docker. Further experiments also need to be carried out at a larger scale, and with low-latency networking such as Infiniband. The GPGPU locality results (Tables 1 and 2) indicate that if allocation preference were given to such local backends, then the job throughput may increase. This hypothesis has yet to be tested. Finally, the relationship between Nodes, CPU Cores and Cores per Node is more complex than that handled by the prototype, so further work is needed to accomodate a broader range of vGPGPU computing environment scenarios.

Acknowledgments. This work carried out on behalf of the Telecommunications Graduate Initiative (TGI) project. TGI is funded by the Higher Education Authority (HEA) of Ireland under the Programme for Research in Third-Level Institutions (PRTLI) Cycle 5 and co-funded under the European Regional Development Fund (ERDF).

References

1. LXC. https://linuxcontainers.org/
2. Maui. http://www.adaptivecomputing.com/resources/docs/maui/index.php
3. OpenVZ. http://openvz.org
4. Pipework. https://github.com/jpetazzo/pipework
5. SLURM. http://www.schedmd.com/slurmdocs/
6. Top 500 Supercomputers. http://www.top500.org/
7. Torque. http://www.adaptivecomputing.com/products/open-source/torque/
8. Barak, A., Shiloh, A.: The Virtual OpenCL (VCL) cluster platform. In: Proceedings of Intel European Research & Innovation Conference, p. 196 (2011)
9. Duran-Limon, H.A., Silva-Banuelos, L.A., Tellez-Valdez, V.II., Parlavantzas, N., Zhao, M.: Using lightweight virtual machines to run high performance computing applications: the case of the weather research and forecasting model. In: IEEE 4th International Conference on Utility and Cloud Computing, 2011, pp. 146–153 (2011). http://doi.ieeecomputersociety.org/10.1109/UCC.2011.29
10. Felter, W., Ferreira, A., Rajamony, R., Rubio, J.: An updated performance comparison of virtual machines and linux containers. In: 2015 IEEE International Symposium on Performance Analysis of Systems and Software, ISPASS 2015, Philadelphia, PA, USA, March 29–31, 2015, pp. 171–172 (2015). http://dx.doi.org/10.1109/ISPASS.2015.7095802
11. Gupta, A., Kalé, L.V., Gioachin, F., March, V., Suen, C.H., Lee, B., Faraboschi, P., Kaufmann, R., Milojicic, D.S.: The who, what, why, and how of high performance computing in the cloud. In: IEEE 5th International Conference on Cloud Computing Technology and Science, CloudCom 2013, pp. 306–314 (2013). http://dx.doi.org/10.1109/CloudCom.2013.47

12. Holla, S.: Orchestrating Docker. Packt Publishing, Birmingham (2015)
13. Kegel, P., Steuwer, M., Gorlatch, S.: dOpenCL: Towards uniform programming of distributed heterogeneous multi-/many-core systems. J. Parallel Distrib. Comput. **73**(12), 1639–1648 (2013). http://dblp.uni-trier.de/db/journals/jpdc/jpdc73. html#KegelSG13
14. Ganesalingam, M.: Type. In: Ganesalingam, M. (ed.) The Language of Mathematics: A Linguistic and Philosophical Investigation. LNCS, vol. 7805, pp. 113–156. Springer, Heidelberg (2013)
15. Liang, T., Chang, Y.: Gridcuda: A grid-enabled CUDA programming toolkit. In: 25th IEEE International Conference on Advanced Information Networking and Applications Workshops, WAINA 2011, pp. 141–146 (2011). http://dx.doi.org/10. 1109/WAINA.2011.82
16. Oberst, O., Hauth, T., Kernert, D., Riedel, S., Quast, G.: Dynamic extension of a virtualized cluster by using cloud resources. J. Phys. Conf. Ser. **396**(3), 032081 (2012). http://stacks.iop.org/1742-6596/396/i=3/a=032081
17. Peña, A.J., Reaño, C., Silla, F., Mayo, R., Quintana-Ortí, E.S., Duato, J.: A complete and efficient CUDA-sharing solution for HPC clusters. Parallel Comput. **40**(10), 574–588 (2014). http://dx.doi.org/10.1016/j.parco.2014.09.011
18. Regola, N., Ducom, J.C.: Recommendations for virtualization technologies in high performance computing. In: Proceedings of the 2010 IEEE Second International Conference on Cloud Computing Technology and Science, pp. 409–416. CLOUD-COM 2010 (2010). http://dx.doi.org/10.1109/CloudCom.2010.71
19. Vella, F., Cefala, R., Costantini, A., Gervasi, O., Tanci, C.: GPU computing in EGI environment using a cloud approach. In: International Conference on Computational Science and Its Applications (ICCSA) 2011, pp. 150–155 (2011)
20. Walters, J., Younge, A., Kang, D.I., Yao, K.T., Kang, M., Crago, S., Fox, G.: GPU passthrough performance: a comparison of KVM, Xen, VMWare ESXi, and LXC for CUDA and OpenCL applications. In: IEEE International Conference on Cloud Computing, IEEE (2014)
21. Xavier, M.G., Neves, M.V., Rose, C.A.F.D.: A performance comparison of container-based virtualization systems for mapreduce clusters. In: 22nd Euromicro International Conference on Parallel, Distributed, and Network-Based Processing, PDP 2014, pp. 299–306 (2014). http://dx.doi.org/10.1109/PDP.2014.78

Performance Evaluation of Containers for HPC

Cristian Ruiz[1,2,3(✉)], Emmanuel Jeanvoine[1,2,3], and Lucas Nussbaum[1,2,3]

[1] Inria, 54600 Villers-lés-Nancy, France
[2] LORIA, Université de Lorraine, 54600 Nancy, France
[3] CNRS, LORIA- UMR 7503, 54600 Nancy, France
cristian.ruiz@inria.fr

Abstract. Container-based virtualization technologies such as LXC or Docker have gained a lot of interest recently, especially in the HPC context where they could help to address a number of long-running issues. Even if they have proven to perform better than full-fledged, hypervisor-based, virtualization solutions, there are still a lot of questions about the use of container solutions in the HPC context. This paper evaluates the performance of Linux-based container solutions that rely on *cgroups* and *namespaces* using the NAS parallel benchmarks, in various configurations. We show that containers technology has matured over the years, and that performance issues are being solved.

Keywords: HPC · Virtualization · Containers · NAS parallel benchmarks

1 Introduction

The use of containers has been popularized during the last years as a lightweight virtualization solution. Briefly, this approach brings several benefits. First, using containers allows one to embed a full software stack in order to run an application in various contexts to enforce portability. Like classical virtualization, running applications inside containers enables isolation from the host system and from other containers. Administrator rights can therefore be assigned to users inside a container without impact on the host. On the top of these advantages, several projects surf on this trend, like the popular Docker project. Typically, containers are commonly used by software developers so that all members of a project can test the code within the same software environment. Containers are also used for demonstration purposes when applications need the deployment of a complex ecosystem, and more recently, for production purposes since it is a keystone for a clean deployment of several services.

Beyond classical uses of containers, we have investigated the interest of such an approach for experimental purposes. In a nutshell, and in addition of the benefits mentioned before, using containers to achieve experiments has other advantages. Embedding the full software stack required by an application allows to perform repeatable and reproducible experiments. Indeed, assuming that the source code of the application is available, as well as the software stack shipped

© Springer International Publishing Switzerland 2015
S. Hunold et al. (Eds.): Euro-Par 2015 Workshops, LNCS 9523, pp. 813–824, 2015.
DOI: 10.1007/978-3-319-27308-2_65

in a container, anyone is able to reproduce an old experiment in conditions that are similar to the original ones (provided that it is possible to run it on the same, or on similar hardware). In the field of distributed systems, using containers also has the advantage to oversubscribe resources with a minor overhead, compared to classical virtualization solutions. Thus, running dozens of virtual nodes on physical nodes is an easy task that allows to emulate platforms with an higher scale than they physically have.

If containers ease the way to perform experiments on distributed systems, we wanted to study the impact of using containers on the realism of experiments. Indeed, we will see in this paper that containers use several low level features of the system that might induce some modifications of code execution compared to an execution on real hardware. More specifically, we focus on a particular class of applications: the HPC applications. Such applications would really benefit from running inside containers since the software stack required is usually complex, involving a communication middleware and several solver libraries. They are likely to be influenced by the versions of their dependencies and by their compiler. Running different HPC applications on the same platform, with a single software stack is tricky and in some cases might not be possible. As far as they use very strict communication patterns and precise memory exchanges, the behavior of HPC applications is likely to be affected, and possibly in a bad way.

There are two important aspects that should be evaluated: isolation and performance as discussed in [18]. However, in this paper we focus on performance evaluation. The goal is to study the impact of using containers when running HPC applications, and more precisely to bring an answer to the following question: *does it make sense to use containers in the context of HPC?*

The rest of the paper is organized as follows. Section 2 briefly presents the various virtualization solutions and details the internals of container-based solutions. Then, Sect. 3 explores the related work that aim at evaluating virtualization solutions in the context of HPC. Section 4 presents an experimental evaluation of using containers for various HPC applications using NAS benchmarks [1]. Finally, Sect. 5 concludes the paper and presents the future work.

2   Context: Virtualization and Containers

Virtualization can trace its roots back to the mainframes of the 1960's and 1970's, but the idea has evolved a lot over time. The general purpose is to simulate the execution of several computers on a single one. The computer where the virtualization takes place is called *host* and the simulated computers are called *guests*. Basically, two families of virtualization can be distinguished: hardware-level virtualization and OS-level virtualization.

Hardware-level virtualization is what is usually meant when speaking about virtualization. An hypervisor, running either in the host operating system or in the hardware, is dedicated to executing and managing the guest virtual machines. Various ways to achieve virtualization, providing various trade-offs between performance and flexibility, have been designed over the years [2]. One important point is the interface offered to guests: in some cases, the virtualization solution will simulate real existing hardware, enabling guests running an unmodified operating system; in others (with e.g. paravirtualization in Xen or KVM's *virtio* devices), the virtualization solution exposes abstract devices that can provide better performance thanks to a reduced overhead, but require the guest operating system to be aware of the virtualization solution.

OS-level virtualization is usually called container-based virtualization. Here, the host kernel allows the execution of several isolated userspace instances that share the same kernel but possibly run a different software stack (system libraries, services, applications). Linux-VServer and OpenVZ are two early attempts to provide such containers in Linux. Both are out-of-tree patches (not included in the *vanilla* Linux kernel). More recently, several efforts have been carried out to provide the required features in the standard Linux kernel. First, *cgroups* (control groups), introduced in 2006 (Linux 2.6.24) can be used to group processes and limit their resources usage. Second, *namespace isolation* can be used to isolate a group of processes at various levels: networking (*network namespace*, to allocate a specific network interface to a container), filesystem (*mount namespace*, similar to chroot), users (*user namespace*), process identifiers (*PID namespace*), etc.

Several containers solutions have been developed on top of *cgroups* and namespaces: LXC, Google's lmctfy, Docker, *systemd-nspawn*. It is worth noting that those solutions differentiate on how containers and images are managed (downloaded, created, etc.) but that they all use the same underlying kernel interfaces. Their efficiency and their interest in the context of HPC, which are the focus of the present paper, are thus independent of the management solution used. As will be explained in Sect. 4, the experiments described in this paper were performed using Distem [12], our own emulation solution that leverages LXC. However, it was mainly used to facilitate the management of containers on hosts, and emulation features were disabled.

3   Related Work

There has been a large number of attempts at evaluating the interest and the usability of all virtualization solutions for HPC. For example, In [19], Youssef et al. evaluated Xen using HPC Challenge benchmarks and LLNL ASC Purple benchmarks, with up to four nodes. In [9], Xen and KVM are compared in both paravirtualized and full virtualization modes using micro-benchmarks and the HPC Challenge benchmarks. Another study [10] focuses on the I/O performance of Xen, KVM and OpenVZ. Part of the evaluation is done using the NAS parallel benchmarks.

Public Cloud platforms have also been evaluated. Amazon EC2 has been evaluated [7] using Intel MPI benchmarks using clusters of up to 16 nodes, and Microsoft Azure has been evaluated for scientific applications [15].

The performance of container solutions have been the focus of less work. An early work [8] compared the performance of VMWare, Xen, Solaris containers and OpenVZ using custom benchmarks. In [5], the I/O performance of Docker is evaluated using MySQL. The extended version of that work [6] includes evaluations using Linpack, Stream, RandomAccess, nuttcp, netperf, fio, Redis and MySQL, and shows that Docker exceeds KVM performance in every tested case. However, all the tests were performed on a single machine. In [17], VMWare Server, Xen and OpenVZ are compared using NetPerf, IOZone, and the NAS Parallel Benchmarks. OpenVZ is shown to be the solution with performance close to the native one. A last study [18] includes evaluations with LXC. Linux VServer, OpenVZ, LXC and Xen are compared using the HPC Challenge benchmarks and the NAS Parallel Benchmarks on up to four nodes. That work outlines similar performance between all containers-based solutions, consistently better than Xen. This paper differentiates from the previous one in that we evaluated the following points: performance gains with different version of Linux kernel, overhead in the presence of oversubscription for executing HPC workloads and overhead of containers under a high HPC workload. Our experimental setup included up to 64 machines which aims at evaluating loads and configurations expected to be found in HPC environments.

4   Experimental Evaluation of Containers

In this section, we want to answer the following question: *what is the impact of using container-based virtualization to execute HPC workloads?* We split this question into three more specific ones:

- Q1. What is the overhead of oversubscription using different versions of Linux kernel?
- Q2. What is the performance of inter-container communication?
- Q3. What is the impact of moving an HPC workload with several MPI processes per machine, to containers?

It has already been demonstrated that in terms of computation time, OS-level virtualization techniques have almost zero overhead [18]. However, the use of virtual network device will certainly introduce an overhead into the computation time and network performance, due to the additional processing required by the Linux kernel. Therefore, the goal is to measure this overhead when executing HPC workloads. The overhead was measured performing three different experiments:

- The first experiment shows factors that affect the overhead introduced to the execution of HPC workloads: Linux kernel version, virtual network device and number of containers run on the machine (oversubscription).
- The second experiment measures the overhead caused by inter-container communication.
- The third experiment measures the overhead caused by the virtual network interconnection.

4.1   Experimental Setup

Experiments were conducted using the Grid'5000 Testbed [3], on the *paravance* cluster located in the *rennes* site. Each node of this cluster is equipped with two Intel Xeon E5-2630v3 processors (with 8 cores each), 128 GB of RAM and a 10 Gigabit Ethernet adapter. Regarding the software stack, we used: Debian Jessie, Linux kernel versions: 3.2, 3.16 and 4.0, TAU version 2.23.1, OpenMPI version 1.6.5 and NPB version 3.3. We wrote recipes[1] to install the necessary software using Kameleon [11], which automates and ensures the installation of the same software stack on the containers and on the real machines.

We instrumented the benchmarks: LU, EP, CG, MG, FT, IS from NPB benchmark suite [1] using TAU [13] in order to carry out the evaluation. Each benchmark exhibits different communication patterns: EP communicates few times using `MPI_Reduce`, IS and FT use all-to-all communication, CG uses a one dimensional chain pattern, LU and MG a ring pattern. These behaviors were characterized in [14]. Table 1 shows the percentage of CPU and communication time observed for all the benchmarks used. In all the experiments, resources are not over-provisioned which means that the number of containers deployed are less or equal to the number of cores present on the physical machines where containers are deployed on. Each experiment is run 20 times and mean values are plotted together with a 95 % confidence interval.

Linux provides many different ways to bring networking to containers. First, physical interfaces can be dedicated to a specific container (with LXC's *phys* mode). But there are also several ways to share a physical network interface between several containers. A single NIC can emulate several different NICs using either Linux's *macvlan* support, or hardware SR-IOV support in the NIC. Or the single NIC can be connected to a software bridge, to which containers will be connected using Linux *veth* devices pairs. In this paper we only use this latter configuration, as it is both the default and the most flexible way to achieve networking with containers solutions such as LXC and Docker. However, we plan to compare this *veth + bridge* setup with other options in our future work.

4.2   Linux Kernel Version and Oversubscription

In this section, we show the impact of the three following factors: oversubscription using containers, virtual network interface and Linux kernel version. The performance of the virtual network interface is evaluated under a mix of communication that takes place between containers hosted on the same machine (*inter-container communication*) and containers hosted in different machines. Research question *Q1* is addressed in this section.

Setup: We used 8, 16, 32 and 64 physical machines where we deploy from 1 to 8 containers per physical machine. We run the chosen benchmarks both inside the containers and natively on the machines using several versions of Linux kernel: 3.2, 3.16 and 4.0. Here, an under-provisioned HPC workload is used

---

[1] https://github.com/camilo1729/distem-recipes.

which means that the machines are not fully used, just one MPI process per machine or container (depending on the experiment).

Results: Figure 1a and b show the execution time of the benchmarks executed on: (a) *native* using 32 physical machines and (b) 32 containers. The 32 containers were hosted using different number of physical machines (from 8 to 32). Figure 1a shows the behavior observed with the CG benchmark, which is representative of what happens with almost all benchmarks; the kernel 3.2 introduced a prohibitive performance degradation in the execution time of the benchmarks which appears when more than two containers are deployed per physical machine. Figure 1b shows an unexpected result for the benchmark EP where the Linux kernel 3.2 shows a better behavior. Deep kernel inspection has to be performed here to understand exactly what happens. Overall, we observed a maximum performance gain of around 1577 % when passing from 3.2 to 3.16 and 22 % when passing form 3.16 to 4.0. These values were calculated after removing the performance gains observed running the benchmarks natively.

The overhead of changing the number of physical machines (from 8 to 64) that host the containers is shown in Fig. 1c for Linux kernel 4.0. The most affected benchmarks are MG, LU and FT. Regarding the benchmark FT the overhead comes from the fact that it uses blocking all to all communication which generates a lot of traffic. The other two benchmarks are affected because their memory access pattern provokes cache misses when several processes are allocated on the same physical machine. The highest overhead observed ranges from 15 % to 67 % and corresponds when 8 containers are deployed per physical machine.

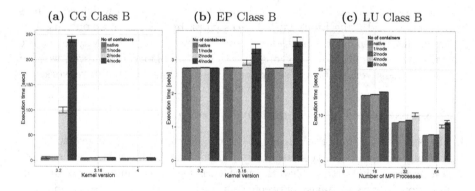

Fig. 1. Kernel version overhead using up to 64 nodes.

Conclusions: Despite the remaining overhead in network, considerable improvements have been made in the Linux kernel over the versions[2] for the execution of intensive network application in large setups. The way containers are maped

---

[2] See commit 8093315a91340bca52549044975d8c7f673b28a1 introduced in Linux 3.11.

Table 1. Profiles of the different NAS benchmarks obtained when executed with 16 MPI processes. Time is given in milliseconds. For the case *multinode* 8 physical machines were used

		CG.B		EP.B		FT.B		IS.C		LU.B		MG.C	
		%	Time	%	Time	%	Time	%	Time	%	Time	%	Time
Multinode	cpu	47	3285.85	79	4342	58	4276	60	3161	78	11221.429	70	4822.81
	comm	39	2721.28	3	142	28	2019	21	1097	15	2106.848	15	1024.00
	init	15	1044.65	19	1044	14	1044	20	1044	7	1049.755	15	1044.55
Container	cpu	71	4831.80	80	4682	75	5415	67	3313	83	14621.023	84	6451.96
	comm	14	934.52	2	141	10	722	11	560	11	2014.924	3	206.01
	init	15	1052.53	18	1051	15	1052	21	1053	6	1056.211	14	1057.48
SM	cpu	70	4714.92	78	4595	76	5440	66	3311	81	14989.101	80	6456.2
	comm	14	937.96	4	258	10	725	13	640	13	2349.951	7	601.9
	init	16	1039.72	18	1038	14	1039	21	1040	6	1039.657	13	1038.3

into the infrastructure have an important impact on performance. Two factors should be taken into account: (a) the memory access pattern of applications and (b) the fact that there is a considerable difference in communication time between containers located in the same physical machine and containers located in different physical machines.

4.3   Inter-Container Communication

The goal of this test is to measure specifically the performance of inter-container communication by comparing it against communication among physical machines and communication among MPI processes hosted in the same physical machine. This section addresses the research question *Q2*.

Setup: We run the chosen benchmarks from NPB using 4, 8 and 16 MPI processes in different configurations: (a) *container:* using 2, 4 and 8 containers configured with two cores and deployed on 1 physical machine, (b) *SM:* using just one physical machine (processes communicating via shared memory) but running the equivalent number of MPI processes, (c) *multinode:* using 2, 4 and 8 physical machines.

Results: Figure 2 shows the impact on the execution time for the different benchmarks. Inter-container communication through the virtual network device is compared against communication between real machines and communication between MPI processes that use the shared memory module *sm* provided by OpenMPI.

We can observe that for some benchmarks (MG, LU, and EP) the execution time is lower in the configuration *multinode* (using different physical machines) than in the configuration *SM* (execution within the same machine). This seems counterintuitive as MPI processes over different machines use the network, however, it could be due to cache misses and memory bandwidth saturation. Under these conditions, we observe that *containers* have a behavior similar to *SM* with a maximum overhead of 13.04 % for MG.C. This overhead gets smaller as more MPI processes are used, making containers slightly better regarding communication time as it is shown in Table 1. The table also shows that the communication time in most of the cases is always better using the virtual network device than using the real network. Additionally, we can observe that the time spent in the MPI_Init method given by *init* in the table is roughly the same. This reduces the possibility that the run of the benchmarks were impacted by some network issue. The presence of variability in the configuration *SM* is due to the fact that the MPI processes are distributed differently each run. The version of MPI used does not bind automatically MPI processes to cores in the machine.

Conclusions: Although inter-container communication is faster than communication among physical machines, there is an important degradation of the CPU performance for applications that are memory bound. However, it should be remarked that MPI shared memory communication suffer from the same limitation. In this scenario communicating over the virtual network device does not add an extra cost.

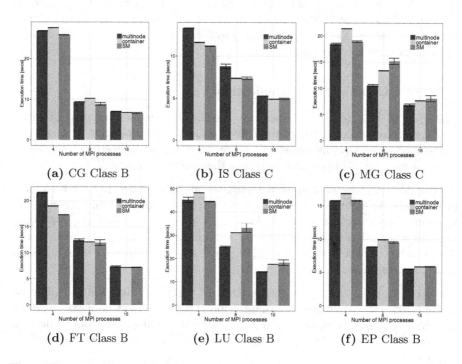

Fig. 2. Execution time using different NAS benchmarks. In the experiment a single MPI process is run per core. Containers were deployed on a single physical machine. In the multinode case up to 8 real physical machines were used.

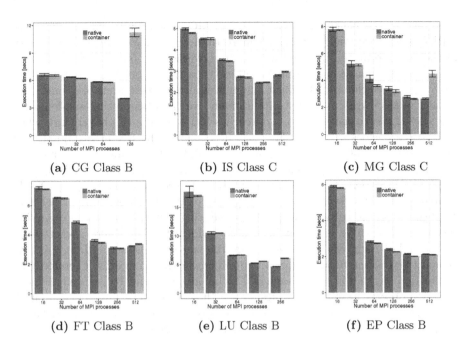

Fig. 3. Evaluating `veth` overhead using a single container per machine. The container was configured with all cores available (16) on the host. The applications were executed inside the containers and natively on the physical machine using one MPI process per core.

4.4   Multinode Inter-Container Communication

We performed a similar experiment as the one shown in the previous section. However, in this section the goal is to measure the overhead of communicating containers located in different physical machines where several MPI processes are run per container. This experiment illustrates the use of containers as a mechanism to improve the portability of complex software stacks and addresses the research question $Q3$.

Setup: We deployed a single container per physical machine. We run the different benchmarks natively and using containers for an increasing number of physical machines (1, 2, 4, 8, 16 and 32). Each container is configured with all cores available (16 cores). We run 16 MPI processes per physical machine or container (depending on the experiment) which makes a total of 512 MPI processes (32 physical machines).

Results: Figure 3 shows the execution time of the applications running inside containers and running directly on the machine. The figure show the results just before the speed up starts to drop down. We can classify the results into two groups: (1) a group composed of the benchmarks FT, EP and IS which send a few number of MPI messages (around 20 messages per execution), (2) a group composed of the benchmarks LU, CG and MG which send a large number of MPI messages (around a 100 times more than the first group of benchmarks). In the first group, we observed a maximum overhead of 5.97 % (with 512 MPI processes). In the second group, we observed a higher overhead starting from 30 % for the benchmark LU. Such a high overhead is due to network congestion present in the virtual interface. Additionally, we can observe that suddenly the overhead obtained using containers reaches 180 % for the CG benchmark when 128 MPI processes are used. This can be explained by the highly number of MPI messages sent by this benchmark, around a 1000 times more than the first group of benchmarks which increase network congestion and leads to TCP timeouts. This behavior has been already observed in [4] and it is probably related to the TCP *incast problem* [16]. We could only observe the presence of TCP timeouts and retransmissions by monitoring network traffic and observing execution traces. We have not been able to identify if or where packets were dropped. The high overhead comes from the fact that the kernel Linux sets by default the *TCP minimum retransmission timeout* (RTO) to 0.2 s. Therefore, the application has to wait a minimum of 0.2 s before continuing to receive messages. This was observed around 20 times during the execution of the CG benchmark which added 4 s to its execution time. We were able to tweak the RTO value, setting it to $2ms$ which reduced the overhead from 180 % to 24.7 %.

Conclusions: This section showed how network bound applications can be severely affected by the default container network interconnection. We found a way to alleviate the overhead by tweaking parameters of the Linux network stack. The overhead observed could be diminished by integrating more advance network interconnection such as Linux's *macvlan*, SR-IOV or OpenvSwitch[3].

5   Conclusions and Future Work

In this paper, we study the impact of using containers in the context of HPC research. To this end, we conduct different sets of experiments to evaluate two interesting uses of containers in the context of HPC research: portability of complex software stacks and oversubscription. The evaluation was carried out using several benchmarks with different profiles of execution and a significant number of machines which is a configuration expected to be found in an HPC context. The evaluation shows the limits of using containers, the type of application that suffer the most and until which level of oversubscription containers can deal with without impacting considerably the application performance. While considerable overhead using containers were obtained, it was shown that the technology is getting mature and performance issues are being solved with each new release of the Linux kernel. Future work will be dedicated to complete this study by measuring the impact of using containers on disk I/O and other containers features like memory limitation.

---

[3] http://openvswitch.org/.

Acknowledgments. Experiments presented in this paper were carried out using the Grid'5000 testbed, supported by a scientific interest group hosted by Inria and including CNRS, RENATER and several Universities as well as other organizations (see https://www.grid5000.fr).

References

1. NAS Parallel Benchmarks. http://www.nas.nasa.gov/publications/npb.html
2. Agesen, O., Garthwaite, A., Sheldon, J., Subrahmanya, P.: The evolution of an x86 virtual machine monitor. SIGOPS Oper. Syst. Rev. **44**(4), 3–18 (2010). http://doi.acm.org/10.1145/1899928.1899930
3. Balouek, D., et al.: Adding virtualization capabilities to the grid'5000 testbed. In: Ivanov, I.I., van Sinderen, M., Leymann, F., Shan, T. (eds.) CLOSER 2012. CCIS, vol. 367, pp. 3–20. Springer, Heidelberg (2013)
4. Bédaride, P., et al.: Toward better simulation of MPI applications on Ethernet/TCP networks. In: Jarvis, S.A., Wright, S.A., Hammond, S.D. (eds.) PMBS 2013. LNCS, vol. 8551, pp. 157–180. Springer, Heidelberg (2014). https://hal.inria.fr/hal-00919507
5. Felter, W., et al.: An updated performance comparison of virtual machines and linux containers. In: ISPASS 2015, pp. 171–172, March 2015
6. Felter, W., et al.: An updated performance comparison of virtual machines and linux containers. Tech. report, IBM (2015)
7. Hill, Z., Humphrey, M.: A quantitative analysis of high performance computing with amazon's ec2 infrastructure: the death of the local cluster? In: Grid 2009, pp. 26–33, October 2009
8. Matthews, J.N., et al.: Quantifying the performance isolation properties of virtualization systems. In: Experimental Computer Science, p. 6 (2007)
9. Nussbaum, L., Anhalt, F., Mornard, O., Gelas, J.P.: Linux-based virtualization for HPC clusters. In: Linux Symposium, Montreal, Canada (2009)
10. Regola, N., Ducom, J.C.: Recommendations for virtualization technologies in high performance computing. In: CloudCom 2010, pp. 409–416 (2010)
11. Ruiz, C., Harrache, S., Mercier, M., Richard, O.: Reconstructable software appliances with kameleon. SIGOPS Oper. Syst. Rev. **49**(1), 80–89 (2015)
12. Sarzyniec, L., et al.: Design and evaluation of a virtual experimental environment for distributed systems. In: PDP 2013, pp. 172–179, Belfast, February 2013
13. Shende, S.S., Malony, A.D.: The tau parallel performance system. Int. J. High Perform. Comput. Appl. **20**, 287–331 (2006)
14. Subhlok, J., et al.: Characterizing NAS benchmark performance on shared heterogeneous networks. In: HCW 2002, Washington, D.C., USA, p. 91 (2002)
15. Tudoran, R., et al.: A performance evaluation of azure and nimbus clouds for scientific applications. In: CloudCP 2012, New York, NY, USA, pp. 4:1–4:6 (2012)
16. Vasudevan, V., Phanishayee, A., Shah, H., Krevat, E., Andersen, D.G., Ganger, G.R., Gibson, G.A., Mueller, B.: Safe and effective fine-grained TCP retransmissions for datacenter communication. In: Proceedings of the ACM SIGCOMM 2009 Conference on Data Communication, SIGCOMM 2009, pp. 303–314. ACM, New York (2009). http://doi.acm.org/10.1145/1592568.1592604
17. Walter, J., Chaudhary, V., Cha, M., Guercio, S., Gallo, S.: A comparison of virtualization technologies for HPC. In: AINA 2008, pp. 861–868, March 2008

18. Xavier, M., et al.: Performance evaluation of container-based virtualization for high performance computing environments. In: PDP 2013, pp. 233–240, Belfast, February 2013

19. Youseff, L., et al.: Evaluating the performance impact of xen on mpi and process execution for hpc systems. In: VTDC 2006, p. 1, Washington (2006)

The Virtual Puppet Master: Adaptive Streaming on Top of an SDN-Enabled Virtual Infrastructure

Roberto Canonico, Enrico De Maio, Pasquale Di Rienzo,
and Simon Pietro Romano[⊠]

Università degli Studi di Napoli Federico II, Napoli, Italy
{roberto.canonico,spromano}@unina.it,
{enr.demaio,p.dirienzo}@studenti.unina.it

Abstract. In this paper we present the Virtual Puppet Master, an orchestration framework for the dynamic deployment of real-time services. We show how to leverage both virtualization and Software Defined Networking in order to seamlessly implement a scalable live streaming architecture supporting effective, on demand deployment of a hierarchical distribution tree, as well as live migration of network nodes. The architecture is illustrated both from the design and from the implementation perspective. A first qualitative assessment of the overall functionality of the framework is also introduced.

1 Introduction

This paper aims to demonstrate how the combined use of virtualization and Software Defined Networking (SDN) can significantly ease the deployment of advanced network services in cloud-based scenarios. We will focus on live streaming over the Internet, which is by no doubt one of the killer applications for today's OTT (Over The Top) operators, due to its stringent requirements in terms of both scalability and dynamic deployment of the delivery infrastructure.

The framework we present has been called *Virtual Puppet Master* (VPM) to indicate its capability to dynamically create, configure, monitor and modify a hierarchical distribution tree made of a number of nodes, each playing a specific role in the overall streaming chain connecting a single source to a distributed set of clients. The architecture is entirely built around the concept of virtualization and naturally lends itself to a cloud-based deployment. The SDN paradigm comes into play for all functions associated with the creation and dynamic management of an overlay network of content delivery nodes. It also proves fundamental when implementing support for the so-called 'live migration' of a subset (i.e., both nodes and links) of the overall distribution tree.

The paper is organized as follows. In Sect. 2 the SDN paradigm will be briefly introduced. In Sect. 3 we will discuss the design of our framework, called *Virtual Puppet Master*, from a design perspective. Section 4 will dig into our implementation choices. Section 5 will present some qualitative results obtained

© Springer International Publishing Switzerland 2015
S. Hunold et al. (Eds.): Euro-Par 2015 Workshops, LNCS 9523, pp. 825–836, 2015.
DOI: 10.1007/978-3-319-27308-2_66

after deploying a real-world test scenario through the VPM approach. Finally, Sect. 6 will conclude the paper, by also discussing directions of our future work.

2 Software Defined Networking

The acronym SDN stands for "Software Defined Networks" and it represents an innovative networking approach aimed to give network administrators methodologies to design, build and manage networks within dynamic and fast-paced environments. The basic trait of SDN consists in decoupling the part of a switch that handles decisions, called control plane, from the part that just refers to the forwarding table, named data plane. In an SDN-compliant switch the forwarding table is updated by obeying to directives coming from external entities. The entity in charge of instructing an SDN-based switch is named controller, and it is basically a software component that, on a side, interacts directly with one or more switches through a well-defined protocol (at the time of this writing, the *OpenFlow* protocol [4]) and, on the other side, checks requests from business applications. In other words, an SDN controller has two interfaces: (i) a southbound API, used by OpenFlow to communicate with SDN switches; (ii) a northbound API, used for interactions with business applications. Most controllers typically implement this last API as a REST service.

SDN offers an abstraction of the underlying network. By using a controller, its northbound API in particular, the real network is abstracted from the business application. This feature makes programmers' job easier as well, because they just have to learn one API for all switches.

OpenFlow is, at the moment, the SDN-defined controller-switch protocol and is implemented by all known SDN switches implementations.

3 The Virtual Puppet Master: Design Considerations

In this section we will examine the design of the VPM infrastructure. We will introduce the technologies used, motivating their choice and showing the final architecture. The code name we chose for the research project is *Virtual Puppet Master* because of its ability to alter, from behind the scenes, the network in which an application is deployed. Hosts belonging to the network are, in fact, just like puppets in a show: they think they have total control over their actions and choices, while in reality they are manipulated by an orchestrating external entity taking decisions on their behalf.

Adaptive streaming is such an exhaustive example that we decided to build our architecture with this type of scenario in mind. The defined architecture had to comply to a number of both functional and non-functional requirements. Among such requirements, we herein cite scalability, reconfiguration, fault tolerance, application agnosticism, user friendliness, customization and monitoring.

Given the agility and scalability requirements, we opted for a hierarchical design, in particular a tree. Due to the absence of loops, this topology allows for simpler routing and management algorithms, as just one path connecting two nodes will always exist. However, the availability of just one path also means that, in case of failures, some nodes will not be reachable, which conflicts with the fault tolerance requirement. For this reason, we chose to give the user the opportunity to specify redundancy links among switches, so that in case a switch crashes, an alternative path will be found.

We opted for an overlay network architecture. As hosts are virtual, it seems just appropriate to make the network they are plugged in virtual as well. Virtual machines have the illusion of belonging to the same network, while host nodes reside on different local networks. The fact that VMs belong to the same network means that, for any application running on them, there is no need to worry about network details like addresses translations and port forwarding. This makes guest cooperation immediate, a very desirable requirement on a cloud computing infrastructure.

When an SDN controller is present into the network, the traffic has to be explicitly allowed by flow rules. This means that just creating connections between switches does not automatically make a stream flow. We decided to build our network logic around this concept: in order to make a stream flow from the root to a leaf, the user has to explicitly ask for it. In our logic, we will define a path as a sequence of switches and links starting from the root and terminating in a leaf. Each switch has flow rules installed allowing a packet to jump to the next hop. In other words, a path can be defined as such only if the flow rules allow packets to travel across it. About the tree, we will distinguish among three types of nodes: (i) Root node (unique); (ii) Relay node(s); (iii) Leaf node(s). A VM present on one of these nodes will become respectively a root, a relay or a leaf VM. The user will thus be asked to mark a node with one of these types. This approach leads to the creation of what in the literature is called a *role-based tree*. According to the node type and depending on whether a VM belonging to the installed application is present or not, the flow installation procedure will slightly change. If a node is marked as root or lies along the path but does not host any VM, an application packet will have to cross it and go directly to the next hop. On the contrary, if a VM is present and the node is not a root, application packets will have to be forwarded first to the VM and eventually from the VM to the next hop.

Migrating a VM from a hypervisor to another can be a very difficult operation in this kind of infrastructure. This is due to the fact that a guest might be in the middle of a communication with an external client or another VM and, by migrating it, this communication might be lost. So, a full 'network' migration is needed. Based on the above considerations, for what concerns the migration algorithm, we took inspiration form a recent work about the live migration of ensembles (shortened in LIME) whose details are explained in [2]. The referenced paper illustrates in detail how to effectively perform this operation by preliminarily cloning the network instead of just moving it right away. This approach leads to the best performance as the VM, once migrated, can immediately start its services, since packets are already flowing to its new location. So, when a migration request is received, we first check if there is any flow from the root to the leaf where that VM is currently hosted. If the answer is yes, we check if there is already a flow towards the new switch that this VM will be attached to (this is done because another VM might be already running there). If the answer is yes also in this case, we do nothing as there is already a path towards that leaf. On the contrary, if there is no path, we first compute it like if the VM were already there and install flow rules on switches to enforce it. After this operation, we start the migration process. Note that, during migration, packets will be replicated on the two paths (or cloned, in the original LIME terminology). Once migration is successfully completed, the old path is removed. The migrated VM will receive data right away because packets will be already flowing: in this way, latency is minimized.

4   VPM Implementation

The VPM has been designed as a management application capable to provide the network administrator with means to: (i) alter the state of the network by creating topologies and redundancy links, or by issuing specific flow rules; (ii) monitor hypervisors, VMs and network state; (iii) migrate a VM from a hypervisor to another; (iv) add/remove resources (like hypervisors) on demand.

We decided to adopt a Model-View-Controller design pattern, implemented as a web application. The fact that the application is accessible by a common browser makes it portable across different operating systems, with no particular installation or technology, besides standard JavaScript and HTML5.

In the following of this section we will briefly introduce the most important choices we took when dealing with the implementation of the VPM.

For the virtualization part of our architecture, we chose KVM (Kernel-based Virtual Machine) [5], mainly because of its robustness to hardware heterogeneity when it comes to VM migration, as well as for the support of full hardware virtualization. KVM is also supported by *OpenStack* [6], our first-choice cloud platform. As KVM is just for the virtualization part, we have used *Qemu*[1] to emulate network and storage. Qemu was chosen as it is the de facto user-level application for KVM. In particular, network emulation is needed to implement the overlay network we talked about in the previous section. Storage emulation is done as well, to make a shared ISCSI disk available to VMs as a local disk. We also relied on *libvirt*[2], a universal API developed by the RedHat Corporation that allows applications to interface with a lot of different virtualization solutions, by also providing monitoring tools to check both guests and hosts status.

In order to migrate a VM, a disk sharing technology is needed. Here we opted for ISCSI, a particular type of Storage Area Network (SAN) and block-level disk-sharing technique.

Openvswitch is the OpenFlow switch implementation of our choice. It is a software implementation of an OpenFlow switch, released under the Apache 2.0 license and available for all Linux distributions as a kernel module. Openvswitch

---

[1] http://www.qemu.org.

[2] http://www.libvirt.org.

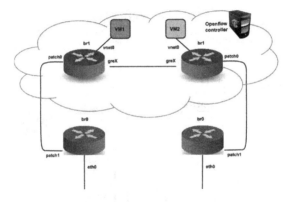

Fig. 1. Openvswitch setup

obviously supports OpenFlow. Though, it implements its own management protocol as well. By management protocol we mean that Openvswitch offers the user a way to interact with its internal structure, thus allowing to create switches, ports and links between switches. This feature has nothing to do with OpenFlow, but it is needed as, according to our requirements, we need to provide the user with a way to create networks by connecting switches.

In order to properly isolate the overlay from the physical network, we opted for the design illustrated in Fig. 1, making use of the Openvswitch capability of creating multiple bridges. Our implementation specifies 'br0' as default gateway so that the Linux network stack can implement GRE (Generic Routing Encapsulation) tunneling by making use of the 'eth0' interface, inaccessible without this workaround.

As the figure indicates, each node has two local bridges, br0 and br1, connected with patch ports. While br0 has a working NIC attached (eth0) and can exchange packets with the external network, br1 is isolated, with GRE tunnels as its only way to communicate. We opted for this setup because it is a very convenient and clear way to separate business traffic from VMs traffic. Bridges br1 are the only ones belonging to the overlay network and, because of that, they are also the only ones connected to the OpenFlow controller. In this way we make sure to examine and handle just the packets addressed to our application, hence saving a lot of overhead. Patch ports will be used on leaf nodes of the distribution tree, when a packet will need to 'jump' from the overlay network to the physical network. Just in this specific case, a special flow rule will be issued, allowing that packet to flow across the patch port, thus arriving at the bridge br0 (and eventually at eth0). This setup, commonly known as *isolated bridge*, is widely used in production environments.

Fro what concerns the control layer, we opted for Floodlight, an Apache licensed Java-based OpenFlow controller. It is fully extensible, based on a plugin system. This means that if there is some unavailable feature, it is possible to create it. We extensively used this system for VPM as we needed custom

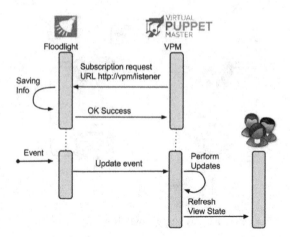

Fig. 2. VPM-Floodlight Notification service

behavior for some features. We implemented our own Floodlight module to perform some management operations. Our communication protocol makes use of the Observer design pattern (see Fig. 2): at start, the management application asks the controller to be notified of events and communicates a callback URL. Each time a significant event happens, the plugin makes a POST request to the specified URL containing data about that particular event. This solution decouples the management application from the plugin as the latter does not need to contain any static reference to the former.

In order for our management application to create links between OpenFlow switches, we needed a Java implementation of OVSDB, the *Open vSwitch Database Management Protocol*. Instead of creating it, we took the implementation done by the 'opendaylight-ovsdb' group and modified it. Opendaylight [1] is a collaborative SDN project which includes a Java-based OpenFlow controller with a rich set of plugins. One of them, in particular, interacts with a remote OVSDB database. We decided to make a stand-alone library version of the plugin by removing all the dependencies from the controller and taking just the protocol implementation part.

The management application is the core of the whole system. The user interface, as already anticipated, is a mix of HTML and JavaScript controls, while the backend is implemented in Java, through servlets. Exchanged messages are instead formatted as JSON objects.

The *Dashboard* tab, as the name suggests, is aimed to give the user an overview of the network nodes, here represented just for what concerns the hypervisor part (for the whole network there is in fact a dedicated tab). A list of registered hypervisors is shown (see Fig. 3). Offline ones are marked gray while online ones can be marked with different colors according to their current CPU utilization percentage (depending on two dynamically configurable threshold values).

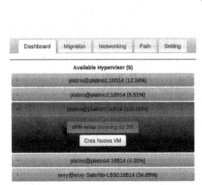

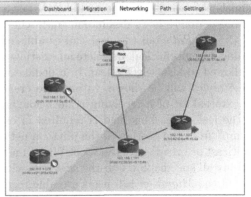

Fig. 3. The VPM dashboard tab   **Fig. 4.** The VPM network tab

Inside the *Network* tab, the user can create connections between switches in order to build a tree network topology with some redundancy links. To allow users to draw topologies, we made use of a JavaScript library called *mxGraph*, coupled to a server component capable to receive and process graphs sent by the client. This tab will show every switch currently attached to the controller (see Fig. 4), which are candidates for the final topology. Note that, being a VPM node both a hypervisor and a switch, these switches represent hypervisors as well and in fact, by hovering the mouse on a generic device, a list of installed VMs will appear. In order to create a connection, the user has only to drag the mouse from one switch to the other, while to set the role a right click on a switch will open a context menu on which it is possible to choose if that switch is a root, a relay or a leaf. We decided to let the user draw a generic topology, be it a tree or not; anyhow, when the "send tree" button is pressed a server side algorithm will compute the topology to actually make a tree. Spare links will be identified as redundancy connections.

With reference to tree creation, we used Kruskal's Minimum Spanning Tree algorithm [3] combined with some application logic. In fact, this algorithm is unaware of a node type and, by just giving it a generic topology, we would have no guarantees that the role of a certain node is respected. Moreover, the user could have made errors in the topology creation, like relays not connected to any leaf, which would inevitably bring to an erroneous topology. So, before giving the topology to the algorithm we first remove any dangling branches, which are branches ending with a relay or a node whose role was not set. Then, to make sure that the computed tree is the one the user wanted, we appropriately set link weights according to the type of its endpoints. In particular, each type is associated with a value, as follows: (i) Root: 0; (ii) Relay: 1; (iii) Leaf: 2. A link weight is set to the sum of its edge values. Finally, we provide such a topology as an input to the actual Kruskal's algorithm. This process will compute the correct tree. Only links which belong to the tree will be actually translated into GRE tunnels (by using our custom library), because they are the only links needed for our traffic to flow. Redundant links will be stored and used upon necessity.

On the *Path* tab the user can establish a path starting from the root and ending in a specific leaf, or delete an existing path. After selecting a root, the user is allowed to also select a leaf. In a dedicated panel, any existing path between these nodes will be shown. In order to create a path it is also required to set an external IP of a receiving node belonging to the physical network relative to the leaf node. This field is required in order to make the packets of a flow "jump" from the overlay to the physical network. Any kind of IP, be it unicast, multicast or broadcast, is allowed. When a new path is defined, a backend servlet will install specific flows on the selected switches along the path.

On the *Migration* tab users are able to migrate a virtual machine from one host to another. Since only guests, situated on leaves, are allowed to be migrated, they will be the only ones to be shown. In order to perform such an operation, the user has to simply drag and drop the desired VM from the source to the destination hypervisors. In the backend, the `Libvirt` API is leveraged to perform the migration process, while calls to a dedicated path manager component implement the LIME-inspired migration algorithm we explained in Sect. 3. A further servlet can be periodically polled by the client to retrieve information about the progress status of a specific migration.

5 Qualitative Tests

In this section we will first present the testing environment and then describe the streaming demo application. Finally, by using screenshots, we will give an overview of the final result. As VPM is still in a beta release state, please note that testing is just functional. Quantitative evaluations, involving throughput and latency measurements, are the subject of our future work.

We wanted our testing platform to be portable, so we simulated a 5 host virtual environment inside of an HP Proliant N54L 708245-425 micro server. This server is equipped with an AMD Turion II Neo N54L dual core processor, with 8 GB RAM, 2 network interface cards, and 2 Hard Disks (80 and 150 GB respectively). In order to achieve the best performance, we installed a bare metal hypervisor, VMWare vSphere ESXi 5.5, to simulate "physical hosts" through VMs. Due to the absence of any local user interface, this hypervisor can only be remote-controlled by its dedicated client software. This client-server architecture, which is common to most type I hypervisors, is necessary to make the virtualization as more efficient as possible. In Fig. 5 you can see an overview of our testbed.

HDs are organized this way: 160 GB are shared across VMs and used to simulate their virtual hard disks, while 80 GB are allocated to a specific VM with a raw device mapping technique (as this VM will represent our ISCSI target, it needs dedicated storage). Hosts are divided in 5 VMs, numbered from platino0 to platino5, having 1 GB RAM and 20 GB HD each. Among them, platino0 is designed to be an ISCSI target as well, and it mounts a dedicated

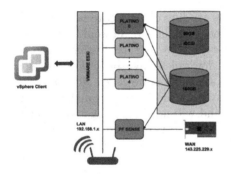

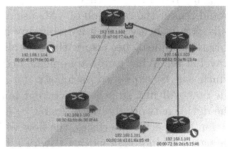

Fig. 5. The VPM Testbedb   **Fig. 6.** Streaming demo topology

80 GB HD as an external peripheral. There is an additional VM mounting an open source firewall called *pfSense*[3], which provides NAT and DHCP functions as well. This VM creates a 192.168.1.x/24 LAN while providing external access through its physical WAN interface. A second NIC, not displayed in the figure, is also allocated to pfSense. This NIC is attached to an external router so that it becomes part of the virtualized LAN as well, along with any physical host currently attached to it. With this setup we allow for more complex scenarios, where any number of devices can become part of our testbed.

Each virtualized node is an Ubuntu server 13.10 (Saucy Salamander). We have chosen this distribution because of its low minimum requirements and also due to the fact that almost all needed software is already present in its default repositories, making the setup process significantly faster. Two bridges, br0 and br1, are set up like we saw in Sect. 3. In order to create the overlay network inside a Qemu instance, a proper XML file is processed through the libvirt API. By using the software open-iscsi, each node mounts the ISCSI target located at platino0, so 5 LUNs (Logical Unit Numbers), each one representing an already configured VM, are available.

Guest VMs come with an Ubuntu server 13.10 OS installed as well. The streaming technology supported is GStreamer[4], an Open Source multimedia framework already present in the Ubuntu default repositories. In particular, the gst-launch utility was used to create a live stream of a sample video file. Two bash scripts have been created, the former of which is used on the root VM, while the latter works for both relay and leaf nodes.

By using our web GUI, we created the topology shown in Fig. 6. Figure 6 shows that the created topology presents some redundant links, colored in black. Two leaves are specified, one with a direct connection to the root node (platino2) and another one using an additional node as relay.

The demo streaming application works as follows: the root VM will just broadcast the live stream to the network broadcast address, 10.0.0.255. Under

---

[3] http://www.pfsense.org.
[4] http://gstreamer.freedesktop.org.

normal circumstances, this would imply the flooding of the entire network and would render the relay job of VMs useless, because the stream would just naturally flow to every switch ignoring any halfway entity. For our testing purposes this is just ideal, because without explicit flow rules these packets would not travel at all. What we have implemented is a logic that we called *sink or swim*, which can be expressed as follows: (i) if no flow rule is issued on the switch, the flow will just stop at the current hop, and will not be propagated through the device network interfaces ('sink'); (ii) if a flow rule is issued with an output action for specific interfaces, the flow will travel just across said interfaces even though it should be broadcast ('swim'). Figure 7 shows an example. Even though the root guest specified the network broadcast as destination, you can note how the stream just flows towards the leftmost leaf, like it would do in a unicast scenario. This is also a very good demonstration of VPMs ability to 'fool' virtual hosts.

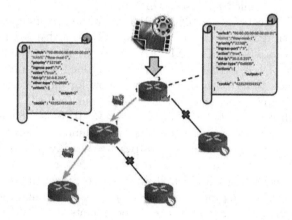

Fig. 7. "Sink or Swim" paradigm

As a preliminary test, we decided to boot only the VMs on the root and leaf nodes. This means that relay nodes will act as a "pass-through" nodes, by just sending packets to the next hop along the path. We hence started a stream and, after verifying that no external user could receive it, we activated a path to the rightmost leaf, specifying 192.168.1.181 as external destination IP address (Fig. 8).

On a leaf node, which contains a VM, we instead find two rules: one to forward packets to the VM and another to relay them from the VM to the next hop. The "action" field in the last flow rule enforces the rewriting of the destination IP to 192.168.1.181 before relaying the packet to the external network. After this operation, we can verify that the stream correctly arrives at destination, as illustrated in Fig. 9.

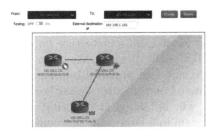

Fig. 8. Creating a path   **Fig. 9.** Stream correctly received

As a further test, we booted up the relay VM on the relay node, to verify the correct operation of the Notification System. This action triggered the "add VM" event, with a subsequent alert message destined to the VPM.

We also made sure that the VPM had successfully changed flows belonging to the switch on which the new VM was booted. This test was a success, also leading to the same flow configuration we described for the leaf switch (except for the recipient address translation rule).

Fig. 10. VPM migration testing   **Fig. 11.** Video degradation effects

We finally forced the migration of the VM situated on the rightmost leaf to the leftmost one, while the user on the external node was watching the live stream (see Fig. 10).

Migration was successful and, looking at each involved switch, we noticed that flows were not present anymore on the right path and a new path, towards the new leaf, had been automatically created. About downtime, it was estimated, over a mean on 10 migration attempts with the same video source, to be about 2 s, which is perfectly reasonable for a live streaming application. During these 2 s, the user just experienced some frame losses (as it can be appreciated in Fig. 11), but continuity of service was preserved and the overall impact was acceptable.

6   Conclusion

In this paper we presented the Virtual Puppet Master, an architecture for the orchestration of advanced services on top of SDN-enabled clouds. We discussed both design and implementation of the architecture and provided information about the results of preliminary tests we conducted on a small-scale testbed.

Our future work on the VPM framework will be aimed at quantitatively assessing the performance attainable by the system in a large-scale deployment.

Acknowledgments. This work was partially funded by the Italian Ministry of Education, University and Research (MIUR) within the framework of projects PON01 01007 "PLATform for INnOative services in future internet" (PLATINO) and PON04a2_C (SMART HEALTH).

References

1. Feamster, N., Rexford, J., Zegura, E.: The road to sdn. Queue **11**(12), 20:20–20:40 (2013)
2. Keller, E., Ghorbani, S., Caesar, M., Rexford, J.: Live migration of an entire network (and its hosts). In: Proceedings of the 11th ACM Workshop on Hot Topics in Networks, pp. 109–114. HotNets-XI, ACM, New York (2012)
3. Kruskal, J.B.: On the shortest spanning subtree of a graph and the traveling salesman problem. Proc. Am. Math. Soc. **7**, 48–50 (1956)
4. McKeown, N., Anderson, T., Balakrishnan, H., Parulkar, G., Peterson, L., Rexford, J., Shenker, S., Turner, J.: Openflow: enabling innovation in campus networks. SIGCOMM Comput. Commun. Rev. **38**(2), 69–74 (2008)
5. Medina, V., García, J.M.: A survey of migration mechanisms of virtual machines. ACM Comput. Surv. **46**(3), 30:1–30:33 (2014)
6. Sefraoui, O., Aissaoui, M., Eleuldj, M.: Openstack: toward an open-source solution for cloud computing. Int. J. Comput. Appl. **55**(3), 38–42 (2012)

Author Index

Printed in the United States
By Bookmasters